T0333788

AUSTRIAN BANKS IN THE PERIOD OF NATIONAL SOCIALISM

Austrian Banks in the Period of National Socialism focuses on the activities of two major financial institutions, the Creditanstalt-Wiener Bankverein and the Länderbank Wien. It details the ways the two banks served the Nazi regime and how they used the opportunities presented by Nazi rule to expand their business activities. Particular attention is given to the role that the Creditanstalt and Länderbank played in the "Aryanization" of Jewish-owned businesses. The author also examines the two banks' relations with their industrial clients and considers the question of whether bank officials had any knowledge of their client firms' use of concentration camp prisoners and other forced laborers during World War II. *Austrian Banks in the Period of National Socialism* is Gerald D. Feldman's contribution to the multiauthor, two-volume study *Österreichische Banken und Sparkassen im Nationalsozialismus und in der Nachkriegszeit,* which was originally published in German by C. H. Beck in 2006.

Gerald D. Feldman (1937–2007) was one of the preeminent historians of Germany of his generation. He joined the history department at the University of California, Berkeley, in 1963 and spent his entire career there. His numerous publications include the seminal study *The Great Disorder: Politics, Economics, and Society in the German Inflation, 1914–1924* (1993). In the later years of his career, Feldman focused on the activities of private companies during the Nazi era and their involvement in the regime's economic policies. He served as an advisor to the Presidential Commission on Holocaust Assets in the United States. An active supporter of European-American scholarly dialogue, Feldman participated in the founding of the Friends of the German Historical Institute, Washington, DC, and was the group's president at the time of his death.

PUBLICATIONS OF THE GERMAN HISTORICAL INSTITUTE

Edited by
HARTMUT BERGHOFF
with the assistance of David Lazar

The German Historical Institute is a center for advanced study and research whose purpose is to provide a permanent basis for scholarly cooperation among historians from the Federal Republic of Germany and the United States. The Institute conducts, promotes, and supports research into both American and German political, social, economic, and cultural history; into transatlantic migration, especially during the nineteenth and twentieth centuries; and into the history of international relations, with special emphasis on the roles played by the United States and Germany.

Recent Books in the Series:

Eric C. Steinhart, *The Holocaust and the Germanization of Ukraine*

Hartmut Berghoff and Uta Andrea Balbier, *The East German Economy, 1945–2010: Falling Behind or Catching Up?*

Thomas W. Maulucci, Jr., and Detlef Junker, editors, *GIs in Germany: The Social, Economic, Cultural, and Political History of the American Military Presence*

Alison Efford, *German Immigrants, Race, and Citizenship in the Civil War Era*

Lars Maischak, *German Merchants in the Nineteenth-Century Atlantic*

Ingo Köhler, *The Aryanization of Private Banks in the Third Reich*

Hartmut Berghoff, Jürgen Kocka, and Dieter Ziegler, editors, *Business in the Age of Extremes*

Yair Mintzker, *The Defortification of the German City, 1689–1866*

Astrid M. Eckert, *The Struggle for the Files: The Western Allies and the Return of German Archives after the Second World War*

Winson Chu, *The German Minority in Interwar Poland*

Christof Mauch and Kiran Klaus Patel, *The United States and Germany during the Twentieth Century*

Monica Black, *Death in Berlin: From Weimar to Divided Germany*

John R. McNeill and Corinna R. Unger, editors, *Environmental Histories of the Cold War*

Roger Chickering and Stig Förster, editors, *War in an Age of Revolution, 1775–1815*

Cathryn Carson, *Heisenberg in the Atomic Age: Science and the Public Sphere*

Michaela Hoenicke Moore, *Know Your Enemy: The American Debate on Nazism, 1933–1945*

Matthias Schulz and Thomas A. Schwartz, editors, *The Strained Alliance: U.S.-European Relations from Nixon to Carter*

Austrian Banks in the Period of National Socialism

GERALD D. FELDMAN

INTRODUCTION BY PETER HAYES
Northwestern University

GERMAN HISTORICAL INSTITUTE
Washington, DC
and

CAMBRIDGE
UNIVERSITY PRESS

CAMBRIDGE
UNIVERSITY PRESS

32 Avenue of the Americas, New York, NY 10013-2473, USA

Cambridge University Press is part of the University of Cambridge.

It furthers the University's mission by disseminating knowledge in the pursuit of
education, learning, and research at the highest international levels of excellence.

www.cambridge.org
Information on this title: www.cambridge.org/9781107001657

GERMAN HISTORICAL INSTITUTE
1607 New Hampshire Avenue, N.W., Washington, DC 20009, USA

First published 2015

Printed in the United States of America

A catalog record for this publication is available from the British Library.

Library of Congress Cataloging in Publication Data
Feldman, Gerald D.
Austrian banks in the period of National Socialism / Gerald D. Feldman, Peter Hayes.
pages   cm. – (Publications of the German Historical Institute)
Includes bibliographical references and index.
ISBN 978-1-107-00165-7 (hardback)
1. Banks and banking – Austria – History – 20th century.   2. Banks and banking – Corrupt
practices – Austria – History – 20th century.   3. Finance – Government policy – Austria – History –
20th century.   4. World War, 1939–1945 – Finance – Austria.   5. Austria – History – 1938–1945.
I. Hayes, Peter, 1946 September 7–   II. Title.
HG3008.F45   2014
332.109436'09044–dc23   2014043399

ISBN 978-1-107-00165-7 Hardback

Contents

Foreword

Austrian Banks in the Period of National Socialism is the last book Gerald D. Feldman completed before his death in 2007. As Peter Hayes explains in his introduction, this book has its origins in a larger multiauthor project that came about as a result of a class action against the Bank Austria Creditanstalt. That work, *Österreichische Banken und Sparkassen im Nationalsozialismus und in der Nachkriegszeit*, was published in German in 2006. It was decided after Feldman's death to publish his sections as a stand-alone work in English.

The German Historical Institute is honored to be able to include *Austrian Banks in the Period of National Socialism* in its series with Cambridge University Press. This series is conceived as a forum for international scholarly dialogue, and few scholars of his generation did more to promote dialogue between German and American historians than Gerald Feldman. Toward that end, Feldman helped establish the Friends of the German Historical Institute. He was a longtime member of the board of the Friends and served as president from 2002 until his death. With the publication of *Austrian Banks in the Period of National Socialism* in its book series, the German Historical Institute pays tribute to a preeminent scholar and sorely missed supporter.

The publication of *Austrian Banks in the Period of National Socialism* would not have been possible without the tireless efforts of Gerald Feldman's widow, Norma von Ragenfeld-Feldman. She was assisted in preparing the manuscript for publication by Stephen Gross, Jennifer Zahrt, and Heidrun Homburg. In close collaboration with the author, Dr. Homburg translated Feldman's English manuscript for the German publication, and in the process she suggested many revisions and refinements that he gratefully adopted for the English publication as well. Frank Smith, formerly senior editor at Cambridge University Press, provided invaluable guidance and assistance in the early stages of the publication process.

I would like to thank Frank Smith's successors at Cambridge University Press, Eric Crahan and Deborah Gerschenowitz, for their support in including *Austrian Banks in the Period of National Socialism* in the German Historical Institute's series. I am grateful to Peter Hayes for agreeing to write an introduction to this work. David Lazar handled the German Historical Institute's share of the editorial labors in bringing *Austrian Banks in the Period of National Socialism* to print.

Finally, I want to call the reader's attention to the acknowledgments included in *Österreichische Banken und Sparkassen im Nationalsozialismus und in der Nachkriegszeit*. Gerald Feldman and his three coauthors – Oliver Rathkolb, Theodor Venus, and

Ulrike Zimmerl – voiced their gratitude to a long list of colleagues, archivists, translators, bank employees, and assistants who helped them in compiling the documentation they used in writing their respective sections of *Österreichische Banken und Sparkassen im Nationalsozialismus und in der Nachkriegszeit*. Had he lived to oversee the publication of *Austrian Banks in the Period of National Socialism*, Gerald Feldman would no doubt have taken the opportunity to thank his coauthors and the many individuals who provided assistance or advice.

Hartmut Berghoff, Director
German Historical Institute

Introduction

Peter Hayes

This book consists of chapters that Gerald Feldman wrote as a member of the Independent Historical Commission of Bank Austria Creditanstalt. That entity came into being as a result of a judicial settlement "*in re* Austrian and German Bank Holocaust Litigation" agreed to by plaintiffs and defendants and codified in the order of Judge Shirley Wohl Kram of the Federal District Court of the Southern District of New York on January 6, 2000. She directed Bank Austria Creditanstalt, as the legal successor of the two Nazi-era banks discussed in this volume, the Creditanstalt-Wiener Bankverein and the Länderbank Wien AG, to assemble and support a team of historians charged with "among other things, investigating the activities of Austrian banks during the National Socialist era, publishing the results, and attempting to identify by name those who were harmed." The heading "activities" referred not only to the general banking business, but also to the banks' roles in discriminating against and dispossessing Jews inside and outside of Austria, in helping to incorporate Austria into the German Reich, and in seeking to benefit from German expansionism. Feldman and the three Austrian members

of the commission – Oliver Rathkolb, Theodor Venus, and Ulrike Zimmerl – met to lay the foundations for the project on June 30, 2000, and the group presented its findings to Judge Kram in English almost exactly six years later, on June 15, 2006. A German version appeared later that year under the title *Österreichische Banken und Sparkassen im Nationalsozialismus und in der Nachkriegszeit.*[1] The book before you is the English text of Feldman's contributions to the German volume.

When Feldman and his Austrian colleagues agreed to serve on the Commission, they took up a daunting challenge. The Bank had neither an organized archive, nor finding aids to the documents it possessed. Its predecessor firms' extensive former ties to both the German entities that acquired controlling interests in them in 1938 and to firms in the Nazi empire that they sought to control entailed a wide-ranging search for source material in multiple corporate and state archives in several countries. Identifying, pulling together, and assimilating all this material was the sort of task on which Gerry Feldman thrived, but even with assistance and considerable institutional support, it took time. Fortunately, no one will have to do the job again, as the documents cited in this book are now collected in the Historical

Peter Hayes is the Theodore Zev Weiss Holocaust Educational Foundation Professor in the department of history at Northwestern University. He has written widely on German industry during the Nazi era. His books include *Industry and Ideology: IG Farben in the Nazi Era* (2000) and *From Cooperation to Complicity: Degussa in the Third Reich* (2007).

[1] Gerald D. Feldman, Oliver Rathkolb, Theodor Venus, and Ulrike Zimmerl, *Österreichische Banken und Sparkassen im Nationalsozialismus und in der Nachkriegszeit*, 2 vols. (Munich 2006).

Archive of Bank Austria Creditanstalt, where they are accessible to interested researchers.

A second dimension of the challenge Feldman and his colleagues faced was the highly charged context in which they worked. Not only did the Commission emerge from adversarial legal proceedings, but its mission was defined, only in part yet explicitly, as laying the basis for compensation and restitution to identifiable victims. But assessing guilt is neither the only, nor even the primary activity of historians. Moreover, in Austria doing so has an awkward history, bound up with the nation's exculpatory self-image after 1945 as "Hitler's first victim." Finally, there was the residue in many minds of the exaggerated image of corporate power in Nazi Germany bequeathed by the 1940s, notably by Franz Neumann's *Behemoth* and the reports on the Deutsche and Dresdner Banks produced by the Office of the Military Government of the United States (OMGUS) in Germany.[2] All of these circumstances created preconceptions or expectations that a dispassionate historical analysis was bound to disappoint.

Of course, Feldman was no stranger to these challenges, which overlapped with those he encountered while producing his monumental study of *Allianz and the German Insurance Business, 1933–1945*.[3] Neither was he unfamiliar

with the history of banks in the Third Reich, having participated in the historical commission that delivered *The Deutsche Bank 1870–1995*.[4] This background, along with the mastery of narrative and analysis demonstrated in his first path-breaking book, *Army, Industry, and Labor in Germany 1914–1918*, and in his three brilliant and prodigious studies of the German economy after World War I, *Iron and Steel in the German Inflation 1916–1923*, *The Great Disorder*, and *Hugo Stinnes*, explain why Bank Austria Creditanstalt sought out his expertise in 2000 and accepted without question the conclusions he presents in this book.[5] It represents the culmination of an extraordinary body of work by a scholar who was indefatigable, irrepressible, fair-minded, sharp-eyed, fearless, and, especially in person but also occasionally to devastating effect in print, mordantly funny.

Gerry Feldman was a master of the long form: few of his books weigh in at less than the substantial size of this one. He loved to show the intricacy of human action and the manifold nature of causation. He reveled in unraveling corporate maneuvers and financial legerdemain, and he delighted in revealing what his protagonists were really up to. He believed with all his heart that, contrary to the oft-quoted artistic dictum, more is more. These passions and convictions, along with the personal qualities and intellectual skills mentioned in the preceding paragraph, are all on display in this book.

Above all, Feldman is determined here to help readers see the past whole, in all its complexity, without recourse to simplifying shortcuts. Neither Austrians nor banks were

---

[2] See my introduction to Franz Neumann, *Behemoth* (Chicago 2009), especially pp. xv–xvi; and my review of Christopher Simpson (ed.), *War Crimes of the Deutsche Bank and the Dresdner Bank* (New York 2002), in *German Studies Review* 26 (2003), pp. 65–66.

[3] (New York 2001). He was not alone in facing these challenges. Other individual historians and historical commissions given privileged access to long withheld corporate archives encountered considerable mistrust and criticism in the 1990s and the first decade of this century and then, like Feldman, produced works that stood up to close analysis. A few prominent examples are Johannes Bähr, Ralf Banken, and Thomas Flemming, *MAN: The History of a German Industrial Enterprise* (Munich 2009); Saul Friedländer, Norbert Frei, Trutz Rendtorff, and Reinhard Wittmann, *Bertelsmann im Dritten Reich* (Munich 2002); Lothar Gall (ed.), *Krupp im 20. Jahrhundert* (Berlin 2002); Peter Hayes, *From Cooperation to Complicity: Degussa in the Third Reich* (New York 2004); Stephan H. Lindner, *Inside IG Farben: Hoechst during the Third*

Reich (New York 2008); Joachim Scholtyseck, *Der Aufstieg der Quandts* (Munich 2011); and Henry Ashby Turner Jr., *General Motors and the Nazis* (New Haven 2005). Feldman spoke and wrote eloquently about the difficulties of practicing responsible history in a highly politicized and litigious context; see his "The Business History of the 'Third Reich' and the Responsibilities of the Historian," Occasional Paper, Center for German and European Studies, University of California, Berkeley, January 1999.

[4] (London 1995).

[5] Respectively (Princeton 1966), (Princeton 1977), (New York 1997), and (Munich 1998).

mere victims or cowed agents of the Nazi regime; they were instead active participants in it, seeking advantage within the prevailing parameters of policy, sometimes succeeding and sometimes not. Hermann Göring's desire to mobilize the Austrian economy for the Four Year Plan and thus to acquire important industrial assets, sometimes from the Viennese banks under examination, did not prove incompatible with the desires of the Ostmark's Nazi leaders to improve the local economy, protect its business from being bought up by Germans, and thus to gain popularity. In fact, the dispossession of the Jews could and did serve as the point at which the two programs intersected. Similarly, integration with the Reich and an expanded economic role for Vienna could go hand in hand, as Berlin fostered leading and semiautonomous roles for the Creditanstalt and the Länderbank in binding the economies of Southeastern Europe to Germany's.

All of this Feldman traces with characteristic grace and clarity. His deft pen portraits convey the characters and aspirations of the protagonists; his accounts of business deals lay bare the stakes and negotiating strategies of the parties; and his sure grasp of the direction of political and economic policy at any given moment makes his depiction of the links between developments at the micro and macro levels authoritative. There is much here to admire, and each reader will come away with personal-favorite apercus, anecdotes, and aha moments. To read Feldman's work is always to be struck by his phenomenal command of the sources and his fluency in weaving them together.

Chapter 1 is particularly instructive on the interaction of publicly traded and state-owned banks in the Third Reich and on the importance of an enterprise's political patrons in navigating the competitive minefield that the regime planted. Chapter 2 tells in dispiriting detail how readily the Creditanstalt took advantage of Nazi racism while throwing Jewish clients to the wolves. Although many aspects of corporate complicity in discrimination against Jews have become familiar through recent research, one still winces upon reading that the Creditanstalt directed all its Jewish

customers in October 1941 to do their bank business henceforth in the basement of the main office and only between 2 and 3 P.M. at the branches, so that their presence would not offend the senses of "Aryan" clients.[6]

Chapter 3 shows how seductive the temptations of Nazi expansionism proved, especially to bankers nostalgic for Vienna's former economic importance to Southeastern Europe. More specifically, the chapter documents the Creditanstalt's zeal in (a) persuading companies doing business with its subsidiaries in Germany's Eastern European client states to dismiss Jewish managers, even before the respective governments so required, and (b) serving the banking needs of Nazi agencies that plundered occupied Poland and of companies that exploited slave labor. Chapter 4 tallies the Creditanstalt's enormous financial services to the buildup of German armaments production in Austria, especially in providing loans to the Steyr-Daimler-Puchwerke AG (SDPAG) and other firms associated after 1938 with the Reichswerke Hermann Göring. Here, as in the activities of the construction companies the bank owned, its pronounced implication in the Nazi regime's murderous slave labor program becomes unmistakable.[7]

Part II of this volume tells an even more distasteful tale because it deals with the Austrian involvements of the Dresdner Bank, an institution less scrupulous about enabling Nazi crimes than the Deutsche Bank that figured more prominently in Part I as the principal shareholder in the Creditanstalt.[8] The Dresdner

---

[6] Notable other works on banks' involvement in the persecution of the Jews are Harold James, *The Deutsche Bank and the Nazi Economic War against the Jews* (New York 2001); Ludolf Herbst and Thomas Weihe (eds.), *Die Commerzbank und die Juden 1933–1945* (Munich 2004); and Dieter Ziegler, *Die Dresdner Bank und die deutschen Juden* (Munich 2006).

[7] The fundamental works on some of the installations financed are Bertrand Perz, *Projekt Quarz: Steyr-Daimler-Puch und das Konzentrationslager Melk* (Vienna 1991), and Florian Freund, *Arbeitslager Zement: Das Konzentrationslager Ebensee und die Raketenrüstung* (Vienna 1989).

[8] The Dresdner Bank also has been the subject of an extraordinarily thorough four-volume study by

had acquired the Mercurbank of Vienna in 1931 as part of the takeover of the German Darmstädter und Nationalbank. One learns in Chapter 5 that the Mercurbank, with the support of its new parent, began "Aryanizing" its senior management in 1932, even before Hitler came to power in Berlin, but that it nonetheless was reproached constantly by National Socialists in Austria during the 1930s for insufficient support of their cause. The result, after the Anschluss, the acquisition of the formerly French-owned Länderbank Wien, and the taking of its name, was a policy on the part of the now expanded bank of bending over backward to serve the Third Reich's wishes, especially in expediting the "dejewification" (*Entjudung*) of the Austrian economy. The climactic Chapter 6 details the continuous efforts of Nazi leaders in Vienna to dictate the Länderbank's leading personnel during the war; the bank's attempts to expand its presence in Eastern Europe, both in partnership with the Dresdner and on its own; the bank's functioning as the "repository for the liquidation of Jewish assets" via the accounts of the emigration agencies for Austria and the Protectorate of Bohemia and Moravia and as the nexus for the Dresdner's sale of plundered gold to Turkish buyers in 1942–1944; and, finally, the bank's role in consortia that financed increased

aircraft production in the Ostmark and in handling the account of the *Sonderkommando Eichmann*, into which payments flowed for the concentration camp inmates who labored at many of the new factories.[9]

Gerald Feldman was a profoundly serious scholar. He never lost sight of the fact that he was investigating and trying to account for one of the great tragedies in world history, Germany's *Amoklauf* in the first half of the twentieth century. To write long stretches of this and others of his books, he had to sift through heartbreakingly poignant accounts of chicanery and callousness. Yet he was also always the happiest of intellectual warriors, a man truly thrilled to be involved in the process of discovery, utterly engaged in it, ever ready to challenge the "terrible simplifiers" sometimes drawn to it, and yet consistently capable of finding moments of wry amusement in the sorrowful actions and thoughts of some of his historical subjects and, yes, some of his contemporaries, too. *Austrian Banks in the Period of National Socialism* is a fitting capstone to an extraordinarily fruitful and luminous career. In it, one of the great historians of Germany of this or any other era displays all his remarkable gifts and performs his final nonpareil service to knowledge.

---

a historical commission; see Klaus-Dietmar Henke et al., *Die Dresdner Bank im Dritten Reich* (Munich 2006).

[9] On the gold trade, see Johannes Bähr, *Der Goldhandel der Dresdner Bank im Zweiten Weltkrieg* (Leipzig 1999), and Jonathan Steinberg, *Die Deutsche Bank und ihre Goldtransaktionen während des Zweiten Weltkrieges* (Munich 1999).

PART I

THE CREDITANSTALT-WIENER BANKVEREIN

CHAPTER ONE

Ownership, Organization, and Personnel of the Creditanstalt-Wiener Bankverein, 1938–1945

I. INTRODUCTION: THE CREDITANSTALT-WIENER BANKVEREIN AS A UNIVERSAL BANK AND INDUSTRIAL HOLDING COMPANY

When the Germans marched into Austria on March 12, 1938, the Creditanstalt-Wiener Bankverein (CA), Austria's largest and most important bank, was recovering from a crisis that had earned it the embarrassing appellation of "Debit Anstalt" in international banking circles.[1] Its fall had been both tortuous and sensational. Founded in 1855 as the k.k.privilegierte österreichische Credit-Anstalt für Handel und Gewerbe under the leadership of the Rothschilds, the CA was indispensable to Vienna's role as the financial center of the Austro-Hungarian empire and also to its position as a major financial center for Central and Southeast Europe. It had been founded on the model of the Crédit Mobilier, the Rothschilds adopting the banking methods of the rival Pereires to secure their position in railroad construction and reestablish their somewhat shaken position in Vienna in the process. The Rothschilds remained a strong force in the bank, although the Viennese branch's engagement

with the Creditanstalt was a source of tension with the family's other European branches.[2] In the decades before the war, however, what distinguished the Creditanstalt was its industrial engagement that took the form not only of granting operating credits and floating shares and bond issues for major industrial enterprises but also of acquiring extensive holdings in industrial enterprises. It certainly was appropriate that it was an Austro-Marxist, Rudolf Hilferding, who coined the term "Finanzkapital." But if his famous book of the same name had ideological and predictive analytical intentions that went well beyond the description of the interpenetration of banking and industry and the dominant influence of the banks, the description itself was probably even more relevant to the Austrian banks and especially the Creditanstalt than it was to the German universal banks with which it has become associated. The Creditanstalt was not only a universal bank but also a giant concern that, in 1913, encompassed 102 enterprises, including five banks and four insurance companies but also no fewer than

---

[1] Kennedy Library, Boston. James Warburg Papers, Box 2, James Warburg to Max Warburg, Aug. 13, 1931. The name of the bank was changed at the general shareholders' meeting of June 16, 1939, to Creditanstalt-Bankverein. For purposes of convenience, it will generally be referred to here as the "Creditanstalt" or "CA."

[2] Niall Ferguson, *The World's Banker. The History of the House of Rothschild* (London 1998), pp. 597–598. A useful survey of the history of the bank is to be found in the history it published to celebrate its centenary, *Ein Jahrhundert Creditanstalt-Bankverein* (Vienna 1957). This has now been significantly supplemented by Oliver Rathkolb/Theodor Venus/Ulrike Zimmerl (eds.), *Bank Austria Creditanstalt. 150 Jahreösterreichische Bankengeschichteim Zentrum Europas* (Vienna 2005).

twenty machine construction and metalworking companies and six timber and woodworking enterprises. It was significantly involved
in mining and smelting, in the sugar industry,
and in the wholesale business of sugar, paper,
and coal. Directors of the CA sat on no fewer
than 121 administrative boards of various enterprises. At the same time, a complex system of
networks developed in which industrialists sat
on the administrative board of the CA, and the
leading personalities of banking and industry
were personally, socially, and financially inter-
connected. The CA was particularly engaged in
providing current account credits to the companies with which it was associated and acted as
a center of intelligence and information for the
enterprises with which it worked. The special
quality of the CA, therefore, was that it was at
once a universal bank and also a concern with
stakes in major industrial enterprises and holding companies, a significant number of which
were located outside of what was to become
the post-1918 Austrian state.[3]

The breakup of the empire and the creation
of the First Austrian Republic was to have catastrophic consequences for the Creditanstalt,
and most historians agree that the bank failed
to adjust appropriately to the new and much
more difficult circumstances. On the one hand,
the bank refused to accept the implications of
the loss of empire and continued to pursue a
"Danubian" international strategy and become
genuinely multinational despite the "nostrification" policies of the successor states and the
dramatic loss of business due to the shrinkage
of available capital and reduction of regional
trade and commerce. Encouraged by both
the domestic political and economic elite and
international interests to play a role for which
it was no longer suited, the CA and other
Austrian banks proved inefficient intermediaries in the granting of credits, increased the
costs of industrial financing, and even became
dependent on foreign shareholders. This was
especially the case under the indifferent presidency (1920–1933) of Louis de Rothschild,
whose name, until the crisis of 1931, earned
the CA international confidence that it in no
way deserved. In 1931, foreign creditors owned
one-third of the shares of the CA. On the other
hand, the vulnerability of the Creditanstalt was
increased by inflation and hyperinflation in the
early years of the Republic, the high costs and
interest rates of the subsequent period, and the
growing dependence on short-term foreign
capital. Most importantly, it took over increasing amounts of industrial shares and financed
more and more unprofitable industrial enterprises. The endemic bank failures of the 1920s
led to major amalgamations in the banking
sector, and the CA became the repository for
banks that either sold out or failed. Indeed, it
went so far as to take over not only these banks
but also their industrial holdings, as was the
case with the Anglo-Austrian bank in 1926 and,
most disastrously, the Boden-Credit-Anstalt in
1929, which the CA acquired to satisfy political
pressures.[4]

---

[3] Rudolf Hilferding, *Das Finanzkapital*, 2 vols.
(Frankfurt a.M. 1974). For an excellent discussion of the problem of "Finanzkapital," see Dieter
Stiefel, *Finanzdiplomatie und Weltwirtschaftskrise.
Die Krise der Credit-Anstalt für Handel und Gewerbe*
(= Schriftenreihe des Instituts für bankhistorische Forschung e.V., Frankfurt a.M. 1989), pp.
87–105. See also the seminal work of Eduard März,
*Österreichische Bankpolitik in der Zeit der Wende
1913–1923* (Munich 1981), p. 537. Hilferding, the
son of a Viennese Jewish businessman, became
a German citizen in 1919 and had an important
political career in Germany during the Weimar
Republic, serving as the spokesman for the SPD
on financial matters and as finance minister in the
Stresemann Cabinet in 1923 and the Hermann
Müller government in 1928–1929. He fled the
National Socialist regime in 1933 but was delivered
over to the Gestapo in 1941 by the Vichy regime
and died under undetermined circumstances in
a Paris prison. See William Smaldone/Rudolf
Hilferding, *The Tragedy of a German Social Democrat*
(Illinois 1998).

[4] In addition to the works of Stiefel and
März cited earlier, there is a substantial lit-
erature on the origins and outcome of the
Creditanstalt Crisis of 1931; see Peter Eigner, *Die
Konzentration der Entscheidungsmacht. Die personellen
Verflechtungen zwischen den Wiener Großbanken und
Industriegesellschaften, 1895–1940*, Diss. (Vienna 1997);
Fritz Weber, *Vor dem großen Krach*, unpublished
Habilitation (Salzburg 1991); Hans Rutkowski, *Der*

The losses of the CA were hidden from the public view by accounting techniques involving the systematic overestimation of the industrial shares in its portfolio, thus making the payment of dividends possible as well as the underestimation of holdings that were of questionable value. Such practices could not, of course, continue forever, and in May 1931 the CA announced a loss of 140 million Schilling. This rapidly proved to be an underestimation. In the end, the total losses amounted to 1 billion Schilling, the equivalent of half the Austrian budget and 10 percent of Austria's national income in 1930.[5] The protracted revelation of the bank's problems, which were in part a legacy of the Boden-Credit-Anstalt but also of depreciated assets and bad loans that had been given to a limited group of very large companies, required a piecemeal process of reconstruction that fundamentally transformed the Austrian banking system and the CA with it. The first reconstruction plan of May 1931 was motivated, on the one hand, by the belief, propagated by the bank and basically untrue, that Austrian industry depended on the CA, and, on the other hand, by the desire to preserve the Austrian government's liberal economic policy

Zusammenbruch der Oesterreichischen Credit-Anstalt für Handel und Gewerbe und ihre Rekonstruktion. Ein Beitragzurösterreichischen Bankenkrise (Bottrop 1934); Eduard März/Fritz Weber, "The Antecedents of the Austrian Financial Crash of 1931," in: *Zeitschrift für Wirtschafts- und Sozialwissenschaften* 103/5 (1983), pp. 497–519; Aurel Schubert, *The Creditanstalt Crisis of 1931* (Cambridge 1991). See also Monika Ebner, *Der Bankenzusammenbruch des Jahres 1931 in Österreich*, Diss. (Vienna 1969); Peter Eybl, *Die Wirtschafts- und Bankenkrise des Jahres 1931 unterbesonderer Berücksichtigung der Sanierung der Credit Anstalt*, D.A. (Linz 1993); Walther Federn, *Der Zusammenbruch der österreichischen Kreditanstalt* (Tübingen 1932); Carl H. Geng, *Der Zusammenbruch der Kreditanstalt und die Sanierungsmaßnahmen der Bundesregierung*, D.A. (Vienna 1970); Andreas Lackner, *Der Zusammenbruch der Credit-Anstalt 1931. Eine Literaturübersicht*, D.A. (Vienna 1993).

5 Unpublished paper by Fritz Weber, "The Failure of the Austrian Creditanstalt and Its Consequences," delivered at the conference "Krise und Erneuerung des Bankwesensim 20.Jh." (Crisis and Renewal in 20th Century Banking), European Association for Banking History (Ljubljana, May 2001).

by limiting state intervention to the rescue of the bank itself. The reality was that while 68.75 percent of Austrian corporations did business with the bank, 13.75 percent actually would have gone under if the bank had been allowed to collapse. The government, however, did not want to permanently invest and thus intervene in industrial activity and therefore opted for what it hoped would be a temporary intervention to aid the CA in collaboration with the National Bank, the Rothschilds, and the other shareholders. It anticipated that the international committee of 130 banks set up to deal with the CA crisis would be a source of new capital, whereas the actual intention of the committee members was to withdraw with as little loss as possible. The international committee compelled the economically weak Austrian government to guarantee the CA's liabilities and, in the process, had to make a large loan to the Austrian government to shore up its currency. At the same time, French pressure forced the Austrians to abandon participation in a projected Austro-German customs union proposed by the Brüning government in Germany.

The result was a second reorganization plan of January 1933 that was mandated by the League of Nations–mediated loan to Austria of July 1932. Under its terms, the CA's shares were devalued, the Austrian government assumed 51 percent ownership of the bank, and half the foreign debts were turned over for sale by a new company in Monaco, the Société Continentale de Gestion (Gesco), while the other half were reduced and to be paid off over seven years. A special nine-person reorganization committee composed of six Austrians and three representatives of foreign creditors had been set up in September 1931. It operated between September and late December 1931 and was then succeeded by an eleven-man executive committee to oversee the completion of the bank's reorganization. This executive committee was composed of nine prominent Austrians and representatives of two of the CA's principal creditors. A new general director had been designated in the summer of 1931 in the person of Adrianus van Hengel, a

Dutch banker who had the confidence of the international committee. A parallel appointment of great significance was that of Viktor Kienböck, a former finance minister who became president of the Austrian National Bank in February 1932 and who, like van Hengel, favored a restrictive and deflationary policy. Kienböck was especially anxious to rationalize what remained of the Viennese banks, especially the Niederösterreichische Escompte-Gesellschaft, which had been even more derelict in its accounting duties than the CA, and the Wiener Bankverein, the behavior of which had been much better but which also had difficulties standing on its own feet. In March 1933, he developed a reconstruction plan that resulted, at the end of the year, in an arrangement whereby the banking business of the Escompte-Gesellschaft was turned over to the CA, which raised its capital by 25 million Schilling to 167 million Schilling, while the Escompte-Gesellschaft itself was transformed into an industrial holding company under the sole ownership of the Nationalbank and with the name Industriekredit Aktiengesellschaft. The concentration process that made the CA the only Austrian Major bank left in Vienna was completed in May 1934 when the Wiener Bankverein was merged with the CA, effective December 31, 1933, under the name Oesterreichische Credit-Anstalt-Wiener Bankverein. Finally, in January 1936, the Austrian government, claiming inability to cover its obligations with respect to the CA's international debts, reached an agreement with the Creditanstalt International Committee under which the debts were reduced from 140 million Schilling to 77.8 million Schilling.[6]

But if the CA had now emerged as Austria's super bank, it was a far cry from the pretensions of 1919. First, it had been "Austrified," that is, with the exception of some banking interests in Yugoslavia, Poland, and Hungary, it was a purely Austrian bank servicing the Austrian economy and Austrian industry.

[6] Stiefel, *Finanzdiplomatie und Weltwirtschaftskrise*, pp. 214–233.

Second, majority ownership was now in the hands of the Austrian state, and while the government avoided interference in the day-to-day activities of the bank, the CA was very much in tune with the economic policies of Kienböck and the corporatist *Ständestaat* presided over by Chancellor Kurt Schuschnigg. It was a measure of the "Austrification" that had taken place that van Hengel, who was killed in a plane crash in 1936, was replaced by Josef Joham (1889–1959), a native Austrian banker from Carinthia who had distinguished himself in the Tyrol. Joham became general director on June 15, 1936, thus beginning a tenure as leading director of the CA that was, despite varying titles and the briefest of interruptions, to last through four political regimes until his death.

The streamlining and a significant "Austrification" of the administrative council of the CA became especially evident in the course of 1933–1934. In 1933, thirty-six of the old members of the council, thirteen of them non-Austrians, departed, two of them having passed away. Seven of the nine new members were non-Austrians, but the old leadership of the council changed. Former finance minister Emanuel Weidenhoffer replaced Louis Rothschild as president; timber industrialist Franz Hasslacher replaced Hans Mauthner as first vice-president; Dutch banker C. E. ter Meulen replaced Siegmund Brosche as second vice-president. In 1934, the administrative council had twenty-one members, eight of whom were non-Austrians, while by 1937 the number of members stood at nineteen, eight of whom were non-Austrians. There were no non-Austrian executives on the administrative council; however, ter Meulen left in 1936, and Alexander Weiner, who came on the Council in 1934, served as vice-president along with Hasslacher. The executive committee increased slightly in size but also was dominated by its prominent Austrian members. In 1934, it was composed of fifteen members, four of whom were non-Austrian. In 1937, it had thirteen members, three of whom were non-Austrian. Hasslacher had been a member since 1933 and acted as a link between the administrative council and the executive committee.[7]

The "Austrification" of the management of the CA actually began during the crisis in 1931 with new appointments in July when Alexander Spitzmüller was named general director and the management board was reconstituted with the appointments of Joham, Erich Heller, and Franz Rottenberg. The only holdover from the past board was fifty-four-year-old Oskar Pollak, who had joined the management board in 1930. He was an internationally active, highly respected, and very experienced banker previously connected with the Wiener Bankverein and untainted by the crash. Pollak was a Jew, as was Rottenberg, a matter of some importance already in 1931 when the major role of Jews in Austrian banking was being demagogically blamed for the crisis by Chancellor Karl Buresch. He thought it impossible for a Jew to be appointed to the leading position in the CA, and the first person asked was the only available non-Jewish manager, Baron Viktor von der Lippe, who refused the job. Apparently unaware that Rottenberg was Jewish and thinking him a blue blood who might have qualified for a chamberlain at the Habsburg court, Buresch then suggested Rottenberg, only to be told by Finance Minister Josef Redlich, himself a Jew, that Rottenberg qualified only for King David's court. It was at this point that the seventy-year-old Spitzmüller took the job, while Rottenberg, who was and remained general director of the Austrian Kontrollbank and had held important positions in industrial organizations, was appointed to the management

board as a regular member.[8] The last new member of the management board appointed in July 1931 was Erich Heller (1886–1958), an engineer with substantial experience in Austrian industry. He had worked at the AEG-Union until 1924, when he took over as head director of the Tiroler Wasserkraftwerke AG, and subsequently became a director of the federal railways. His industrial experience in Austria enabled him to play a key role in the industrial affairs of the CA and to resume a connection with the CA after the war.

In the period just prior to the Anschluss, Joham had already become the key figure at the CA. He had been on excellent terms with both Spitzmüller and van Hengel before assuming the general director position upon the latter's death. Born in Bad Kleinkirchheim in Carinthia, Joham came from peasant stock and was the son of a finance official. He was apparently a very successful student, pursuing his studies in Klagenfurt, Graz, and then at the Neue Wiener Handelsakademie, where he attained a doctor of law degree. He briefly worked at the Vienna Commercial Court before assuming a position in the Allgemeine Verkehrsbank in Vienna in 1913. This gave him an opportunity to gain not only experience in an institution that had an extensive range of commercial and industrial clients and in every technical aspect of banking but also, as he later noted, to afford him "through constant contact with Austrian economic life an insight into the entire economy and its organization."[9] In 1914, while remaining on the staff of the Verkehrsbank until 1922, Joham was sent to Innsbruck to deal with the reorganization of the Bank für Tirol und Vorarlberg, which had suffered heavy losses in the crisis of 1912–1913.

---

[7] See *Compass* for the years 1930–1937. Peter Eigner and Peter Melichar are in error when they indicate that Hasslacher replaced Joham on the executive committee in 1939. Hasslacher served continuously beginning in 1933. Joham ceased to be a member after the Anschluss and Hasslacher replaced him as chairman. The management board, including Joham, regularly attended the meetings of the executive committee. See Archiv der Bank Austria Creditanstalt (= BA-CA), in Vorstandsarchiv der Creditanstalt (= CA-V), the protocols of the executive committee for 1938–1939.

[8] See Carvel de Bussy (ed.), *Memoirs of Alexander Spitzmüller Freiherr von Harmersbach (1862–1953)* (New York 1987), pp. 274–275. On Buresch's anti-Semitic campaign, see Karl Ausch, *Als die Bankenfielen. Zur Soziologie der politischen Korruption* (Vienna, Frankfurt, Zürich 1968), p. 379.

[9] Deutsche Bank (= DB), B 57, Curriculum vitae prepared for Hermann J. Abs, Dec. 30, 1938. Needless to say, this vita omitted reforms and public functions of the "system" period.

While maintaining his Vienna connections, he was also able to develop further his skills and contacts at a major provincial bank. In addition, he lectured at the University of Innsbruck and traveled to other commercial centers of Europe.

Apparently, Joham's services were deemed vital enough to earn him an exemption from military service, so that he continued his banking activities throughout the war and played an important role in negotiating the complex problems that the loss of South Tyrol entailed for the bank. He gained considerable experience in dealing with the salary and pension problems arising from the unionization of the banks and the expensive concessions made in Vienna. Most importantly for his career, the Bank für Tirol und Vorarlberg not only weathered the inflation but also, as the Hauptbank für Tirol und Vorarlberg, took the lead in a series of mergers between 1926 and 1930 that both consolidated its leadership in the region and established Joham's reputation. His career was further enhanced by his role in the development of the hydroelectric companies in the region. He became the director of the bank in 1921 and held this position for the next decade until he was summoned to the management board of the Creditanstalt.

Undoubtedly, Joham's experience with reorganizations, personnel problems, and rationalization efforts in the Tyrol had qualified him to play a key role in the Creditanstalt mess. He worked closely with van Hengel in determining how much the CA had actually lost and in reconstructing the bank's balance sheets, but he also dealt with the bank's personnel and organization problems and represented it in business and governmental circles. He was personally in charge of the acquisition of the Niederösterreichische Escomptebank's business and the merger with the Wiener Bankverein, handling the organizational consolidation as well as the move to the Schottengasse headquarters. Joham also dealt with the extraordinarily difficult problem of reducing personnel and personnel costs. Pensions were an especially thorny issue made more complicated by the acquisition of the Bankverein, but Joham

succeeded in his negotiations with the Foreign Creditors Committee to provide a capital coverage for pensioners that reduced the number to be provided for by the bank from 4,052 in 1934 to 383 in 1937, thereby cutting the cost per year from 10.1 million Schilling to 470,000 Schilling. He also worked at reducing active personnel, which stood at 2,079 at the end of 1930 and went down to 1,087 at the end of 1933. Apparently, a great many Wiener Bankverein personnel were almost immediately let go; the number of employees reached a new high of 2,113 in 1934 but was reduced to 1,722 by the end of the year, to 1,688 at the end of 1935, and then rose slightly to 1,703 at the end of 1936, and stood at 1,738 at the end of 1937. Obviously, there had been a substantial reduction of personnel since 1930 but only a very limited one since the end of 1934. It is quite revealing, however, as to who had been targeted for some of the staff reductions. As Joham reported in late 1938, "In the course of these necessary staff reductions, despite repeated resistance and threats from Jewish customers at home and abroad, I carried out a step-by-step Aryanization of the personnel insofar as it was compatible with business requirements at that time. The number of Jewish employees was 506 at the end of May 1931, to which were added 47 through the takeover of the Wiener Bankverein, whereas it was only 190 shortly before the transformation."[10]

While it is important to recognize that Joham wrote these lines in a curriculum vitae addressed to Hermann Josef Abs of the Deutsche Bank in late 1938 with the intent of making himself appear more palatable to Austria's new rulers, it is also clear that Joham made no bones about the fact that he pursued a dual policy of keeping Jews when it was necessary for operations but otherwise reducing their number even despite opposition from the CA's clients. This was fully in keeping with the aforementioned tendency to make the Jews scapegoats for the CA collapse in 1931, a tendency intensified by the failure of the insurer Phönix in 1936 and, of course, by the influence exerted by National Socialist

[10] Ibid.

Germany and its Austrian supporters. Joham, however, was not a National Socialist and did not claim to be one, but he was to prove a quintessential survivor. If he sailed with the wind, he steered with great competence, and he made sure that others were aware of his achievements.

He boasted a long list of accomplishments since joining the management board in 1931. Not only did he develop the credit business of the CA branches, but he also cultivated and integrated the provincial banks under CA control, the Hauptbank for Tirol and Vorarlberg-Tiroler Landesbank and the Bank für Oberösterreich und Salzburg, by making appropriate personnel changes and improving their business practices. Joham was concerned about the vitality of provincial banking and thus pushed with ultimate success for a merger of the Bank für Steiermark and the Steiermärkischen Escompte Bank. At the same time, he exercised his influence as president of the Banking Association in 1937 to reduce and simplify credit conditions, represented the interests of the banks in the general council of the Austrian National Bank, and, of course, represented the CA in the international banking community.[11] "Austrification" had not meant a total abandonment of foreign interests where they were still viable, and the taking over of the Wiener Bankverein provided an opportunity to benefit from its branch in Budapest and to strengthen banking ties in Italy, Poland, and Yugoslavia.

A far more delicate issue prior to the Anschluss was, of course, the relationship with Germany, and Joham was in no position to deny his ties to Kienböck and to the *Ständestaat* and its opposition to proponents of Anschluss. Certainly it was true that Joham maintained his connections to German banking circles, and this became all the more necessary after the acquisition of the Wiener Bankverein in which the Deutsche Bank held shares and on whose administrative council it was represented. Indeed, the relationship dated back to the Deutsche Bank's assistance to the Wiener Bankverein during the crisis of 1873. Quite independently of this historical relationship,

however, the Deutsche Bank had also come to the aid of the Creditanstalt in 1931 by participating in a consortial credit to the Creditanstalt of 4 million dollars. Additionally, because of its special interest in Yugoslavia, the Deutsche Bank had also engaged in discussions with the CA about gaining joint control of the Allgemeine Jugoslawische Bankverein, a bank in which the CA had almost half the shares in 1937 before gaining a majority in the course of 1938. Thanks to the takeover of the Wiener Bankverein, the Deutsche Bank became a very minor shareholder in the CA in 1936. Deutsche Bank director Gustav Schlieper was coopted into the CA administrative council thereby. After he passed away in the fall of 1937, his successor on the council was Hermann Josef Abs, who was coopted into the administrative board in late November 1937. Neither Schlieper nor Abs served as representatives of the Deutsche Bank but rather *ad personam*. Obviously, this was a convenient fiction. The reality was that Germany's most important private bank was represented by major figures on the CA administrative council even though the number of shares it held was tiny. Joham seemed anxious to get to know Abs once he had been appointed, and a meeting was arranged on March 3–4, 1938, at the invitation of the Creditanstalt where, as Abs later asserted, "further close collaboration between both institutions and especially about an increased activity in common in the Southeast were negotiated and agreed upon."[12] While there is no record of these actual meetings, it is hard to escape the conclusion that both men were not only cementing relations in the present but also positioning themselves to work together should there be a dramatic change in German-Austrian relations and possible Anschluss. Furthermore, they undoubtedly expected a strengthening of the German position and were thus anticipating the future constellation of forces.[13]

---

[11] Ibid.

[12] See DB, B 51, exposé of the Deutsche Bank of May 31, 1938, and in DB, P 6502, Bl. 2–40, the correspondence between the Deutsche Bank and Abs between Nov. 1937 and the beginning of March 1938.

[13] For a reliable and well-researched examination of the CA and Deutsche Bank relations, see

Joham himself had no personal interest in a political change and indeed was riding high prior to the Anschluss. In later years, he looked back on the management of the bank by van Hengel and then by himself as a time when the bank was put on a solid basis again and when the Austrian economy began to show genuine signs of recovery.[14] At the meeting of the administrative board on June 30, 1937, Joham announced the reduction of the CA's capital from 167 million to 101 million Schilling, while successfully requesting the council's approval for the transactions that led to the capital coverage of the pension fund. Joham was thus not only able to produce a credible balance but also a credible net profit of 4.6 million Schilling. In reality, the profit was understated and was later admitted to be close to 12 million. The general director was even more upbeat at the November 26 meeting, when Abs was elected to the council, and Joham reported at length on the industrial recovery that was taking place. Similarly, on March 4, 1938, only days before the Anschluss, Joham reported a net profit of 11.5 million Schilling, again an understatement of the real profit, and received the commendation of the council, not only for the bank's success but also for the general public confidence this created in the economy.[15]

What made the CA significant, however, was not its comparatively modest balance but rather its influence and role in Austrian industrial life, as evidenced by its ability to report in 1937 that it was engaged with 142 financial, industrial, and commercial enterprises either as a creditor or as a shareholder. The CA was especially prominent in the machine and metals, the electrical, and the textile industries, and it was also prominent in the chemical and construction materials industries. Members of the management board held major positions in these industrial enterprises. Rottenberg served on the administrative boards of thirty-six enterprises and was president of eighteen of them. Heller served on the administrative boards of twenty-eight industrial enterprises and was president of eleven of them. The former was especially prominent in textiles, while the latter was particularly involved in the machine and metals industry but also in the rubber industry companies taken over from the Bankverein, for example, Semperit. Pollak and Joham also served on the administrative boards of major enterprises.[16]

Joham was deeply committed to the role of the CA as an industrial concern and stoutly defended it against critics. Manifestly, these combined functions created an ambiguous relationship between the bank's functions as a lender and as a holding company for a significant portion of Austrian industry. The bank was accused by its critics of over-capitalizing the enterprises it owned and neglecting the needs of other segments of Austrian industry. In a major article on "Banks and Industry" of November 1937, Joham authored a strong defense of the CA's practices. Historically, he pointed out, the Austrian public had failed to provide the capital needed for industrial development and the role of promoting industry had fallen to the banks. The situation had become worse after the lost war

---

Christopher Kopper, *Zwischen Marktwirtschaft und Dirigismus. Bankenpolitikim "Dritten Reich" 1933–1939* (Bonn 1995), pp. 292–307. There is no direct evidence that Joham invited Abs to discussions "in the expectation of an imminent unification of Austria and Germany" ("in Erwartungeinerbaldigen Vereinigung Österreichsmit Deutschland"), as Kopper suggests on p. 293. Certainly such expectations were widespread, but it is important to remember that Hitler did not decide on the Anschluss until after his troops crossed the border and neither Joham nor Abs could calculate how political developments might determine their freedom of action. A solution that fell short of an Anschluss would create different possibilities than would otherwise have been the case.

[14] Josef Joham, "Rede von Generaldirektor Dr. Josef Joham zur Hundertjahrfeier der Creditanstalt-Bankverein" (Vienna 1955), esp. pp. 1–12.

[15] See BA-CA, CA-V, the administrative council minutes and appended reports of June 30 and Nov. 26,

1937, and March 4, 1938. On the actual profits, see the report of the political archive of the Foreign Office, Berlin (= PA Berlin), R 11097, Bericht der Deutschen Botschaft, Nov. 24, 1937.

[16] See Peter Eigner, *Die Konzentration der Entscheidungsmacht. Die personellen Verflechtungenzwischen den Wiener Großbanken und Industriegesellschaften, 1895–1940*, Diss. (Vienna 1997), pp. 517–519.

and especially during the economic crisis, and Joham insisted that it was false to argue that the banks, and above all the Creditanstalt, had done too much for industry under these circumstances: "The Creditanstalt believes itself to have a good conscience from the total economic perspective insofar as it has succeeded in leading a large number of enterprises important to the German economy out of the crisis by means suitable to each individual case."[17] In Joham's view, charges of overcapitalization of such enterprises on the part of the Creditanstalt failed to recognize that the strengthening of the enterprises in question helped to ensure that, in the long run, they would be healthy enough to make real credit requests rather than seek further veiled capital participations by the banks. He rejected contentions that the bank was slowing down the process of industrial independence by arguing that general economic considerations rather than theoretically desirable banking practices were the top priority in the case of the industries in the Creditanstalt portfolio. Joham praised the close relationship between banking and industry in Austria, especially the role bankers played in advising and guiding industrial enterprises, and he saw the existing system as a guarantee of maintaining and strengthening the private sector against all those who would undermine it.

While publicly less open about the matter, he also no doubt felt that the Creditanstalt had a great stake in maintaining its industrial holdings, viewing them as valuable investments to be retained wherever possible. This policy was the source of tension between the Creditanstalt and some large German enterprises, the most prominent examples being Krupp and IG Farben. In the case of Krupp, the issue was the Krupp family's interest in the reacquisition of the Lower Austrian Berndorfer Metallwarenfabrik Arthur Krupp AG, which dated back to 1843, and had been taken over by Bertha Krupp's uncle, Arthur Krupp, in 1917. It was an important producer of metal products, but it also possessed the large Markenstein estate in the vicinity of the plant. Because of its postwar unprofitability, Berndorf was the subject of various reorganization efforts in the course of which it became a public corporation. Its chief creditors were the Creditanstalt and a Swiss banking group, and when the latter insisted on repayment of its credits in 1928, and the Creditanstalt did not have the necessary funds to finance a full reorganization, the Krupps agreed to contribute 5 million Schilling to help fund a temporary reorganization with the understanding that the Krupp contribution would receive recognition when a full reorganization became possible. The Krupps thus retained a standing interest in the reacquisition of Berndorf and viewed the 5 million Schilling investment as a "preliminary contribution" to the ultimate reorganization of Berndorf at some future time and as something to be taken into account should the Krupps seek to purchase back their controlling interest. When the economic situation demanded a new reorganization in 1932, however, the Krupps were no longer able to participate financially or restore their control because of the foreign exchange regulations, and the Creditanstalt assumed majority control over the company, owning 86.90 percent of the shares by 1937, and investing some 40 million Schilling of what was, to be sure, government money in its reorganization. The aging Arthur Krupp served on as president of the administrative council in what was an increasingly representative function. The manner in which the reorganization was carried out caused some bad feeling toward the Creditanstalt on the part of the Krupps, who felt that they had been inadequately consulted and were victims of "Viennese bank practices."[18] Because Arthur Krupp was childless, both he and the Krupp family hoped to bring the enterprise back into family possession and also expected that Krupp von Bohlen und Halbach's second son, Claus von Bohlen, would take over its management. Discussions with the Creditanstalt toward this

---

[17] Bundesarchiv Berlin-Lichterfelde (= BAB), R 25.01, Vol. 4363, Bl. 62–64; Josef Joham, "Banken und Industrie," in: Wiener Wirtschaftswoche (Nov. 3, 1937).

[18] See Historisches Archiv Krupp, Essen (= HAK), Werksarchiv (= WA), 4/2873, memorandum by Johannes Schröder, May 30, 1938.

end had taken place at various times and were then pursued more seriously in 1936–1937 with Austrian authorities.

These efforts took place at a time when the Creditanstalt's investment in Berndorf was beginning to pay off. The company employed 2,000 workers, had been modernized, and was benefiting from the economic upturn. There was not much incentive to sell, and perhaps this was why the Krupp interests made an effort to circumvent direct negotiations with the CA and Joham. Johann Joeden of the Krupp-Gruson Works conducted the negotiations in close collaboration with Claus von Bohlen; both had retained a lawyer in the person of the Austrian finance minister in 1935–1936, Ludwig Draxler, who had also served on the administrative council of the CA since 1934. Draxler was authorized to approach Austrian National Bank President Kienböck, who had already spoken to Claus von Bohlen but not to Joham. The latter would only be involved in negotiations if Kienböck signaled that there was something about which to negotiate. Kienböck, who had a reputation for being very amiable in his encounters with the Germans while systematically blocking German economic penetration of Austria at every turn,[19] showed no principled opposition to the reacquisition of Berndorf by the Krupp interests but made clear that the foreign exchange and clearing situation was such as to make the costs prohibitive. The Krupps decided to terminate the negotiations and wait for more favorable circumstances. Underlying the entire situation, of course, were the political circumstances involved.[20] As Director Robert Glatzl of the Creditanstalt later explained, "[A]s a functionary of the Creditanstalt, I can confirm here that at no time, either before 1938 or after 1938, was there any intention of selling their shares in Berndorf-Krupp, especially because the relationship of the German Reich to the Federal State of Austria, as is well known, was a very disagreeable one and the Austrian State, as the largest shareholder of the Creditanstalt strenuously resisted the

foreignization [*Überfremdung*] of Austrian corporations through German capital participation."[21] The Creditanstalt was thus spared further confrontation with the Krupps in 1937, and there is no reason to think that Joham and his colleagues were unhappy about escaping the problem, even if the escape was to be short lived.

Prior to the Anschluss, the interest of IG Farben in the Pulverfabrik Skodawerke Wetzler AG (SWW), the largest chemical enterprise in Austria primarily located in Moosbierbaum, was less pressing and more ambivalent than that of Krupp in Berndorf, but it nevertheless became increasingly active prior to the Anschluss. The CA had an 88.83 percent stake in the company, which was managed by Isadore Pollak, who was internationally regarded as a great talent in the industry, and by Otto Engländer. CA management board director Franz Rottenberg served as president of the administrative board of the SWW. IG Farben had shown an interest in at least partial ownership of the firm since 1931, although it considered the enterprise insufficiently developed and rationalized to make a purchase effort at that time. After being unsuccessful in its efforts to dissuade the SWW from building a nitrogen plant, IG Farben provided technical and financial assistance in return for a payment as compensation for its market loss. It might have remained content with this arrangement and its other chemical industry holdings in Austria, the Carbidwerk Deutsch Matrei AG and Dynamit Nobel AG in Vienna. It owned the latter through Dynamit Nobel of Bratislava, which was owned through the IG-owned Dynamit AG of Troisdorf. But the IG felt threatened in Austria and Central Europe by the Aussig Verein of Czechoslovakia and sought to gain a majority of the SWW in 1936. Pollak and Rottenberg refused to part with majority control, however, and played off various other chemical companies in Central Europe and Italy against IG Farben, so that ultimately IG Farben was prepared in September 1937 to settle for less. Initially, the idea was to integrate the SWW into IG Farben's sales organization,

[19] See PA Berlin, R 110996, the report on Kienböck of Feb. 17, 1937, for the German Foreign Office.
[20] See HAK, WA, 4/2874, Joeden's correspondence with Claus von Bohlen and others.

[21] Staatsarchiv Nürnberg (= StA Nürnberg), Rep. 502, A-40, 3599, Glatzl testimony.

represented in Austria by the Anilinchemie AG, with the SWW holding shares along with the two IG-controlled companies in Austria. In December, there was discussion of establishing a production company combining all four of the companies, but IG Farben insisted on protecting its patents and controlling the new enterprise. This was vetoed by the Austrian government and opposed by Pollak, Rottenberg, and Joham. As Joham stated after the war, "Such a surrender of share holdings, especially majority holdings, in Austrian enterprises contradicted what was at that time a firm principle of the Austrian Creditanstalt. For us it was an axiom to hold on with an iron fist to holdings of this kind, which we considered to be large reserves. There was no reason for us to exchange the real value involved along with the reserves for Austrian Schilling that would then more or less lie idle. If this was true in general for all our participations, then it was especially the case for our block of shares in Skoda-Wetzler, which was the greatest chemical company in Austria. Under no circumstances did we want it to fall into foreign hands."[22] Finally, just prior to the Anschluss, both sides settled on a compromise under which the SWW and the Carbidwerk Deutsch-Matrei agreed to merge in what was to be called the Ostmark Chemie AG. IG Farben was to act as a sponsor and possible participant, but the CA would retain its majority of the SWW shares.[23]

Given this resistance to German pressures, there was no reason for the Germans to feel that Joham was a friend and every reason to believe that, like Kienböck, he was pleasant enough when one met him but more or less an obstacle to the efforts of the Germans to penetrate the Austrian economy. This was true with respect to banks as well as industrial acquisitions, and Joham, who had been very active in provincial

Austrian banking, was anxious to strengthen the CA's grip on these banks wherever they existed and to keep German influence to a minimum. He did not like sharing control with the Bayerische Hypotheken- und Wechselbank over the Bank für Kärnten in Klagenfurt. The CA owned 49.6 percent of the shares, but 47.5 percent was tied by a 1927 agreement with the Bavarian bank requiring that important matters pertaining to the Bank für Kärnten be settled through negotiation and mutual agreement. If Joham found this burdensome, as he apparently did, the Bavarian bank found its holdings in the Bank für Kärnten and in the Salzburger Kredit- und Wechselbank rather unprofitable. Indeed, it probably would have sold them off except for the fact that this would have run against the German policy of giving up no asset in Austria no matter what the cost. In late 1936 the German Foreign Office strongly intervened with the Foreign Exchange Office of the Reich Economics Ministry (RWM) on behalf of the Bayerische Hypotheken- und Wechselbank in Munich to reverse a refusal to grant a special request by the bank to credit Reichsmark debts of the Salzburger Kredit- und Wechselbank in Salzburg and the Bank für Kärnten in Klagenfurt against the blocked mark securities accounts of the two Austrian banks. If the decision were reversed, then the Bayerische Hypotheken- und Wechselbank would retain its existing holdings in the two Austrian banks even though they were bringing it financial loss and thus conform to the aforementioned Reich policy. The Foreign Office pointed out that it was urgent for the Foreign Exchange Office to allow this expensive breach of the foreign exchange regulations, which it finally did despite the cost of 1.6 million RM. The German Foreign Office noted that Joham had been heard to say that he intended to use the unclarified status of the shares as an opportunity to try, as he had in the past, to drive the Bayerische Hypotheken- und Wechselbank out of the Bank für Kärnten.[24]

[22] StA Nürnberg, Rep. 502, Nl 10998, Affidavit of Joham, Sept. 13, 1947.

[23] Ibid., Nl 7368, Affidavit of Joham, May 10, 1947; ibid. Nl 7389, Pollak to Rottenberg, Jan. 5, 1938, and Pollak to Bernhard Buhl of IG Farben, Jan. 5, 1938. This account parallels that of Peter Hayes, *Industry and Ideology. IG Farben in the Nazi Era*, 2nd ed. (Cambridge 2001), pp. 219–223.

[24] See note by Clodius of the Foreign Office to the Reich Bureau for Foreign Exchange Management, Nov. 6, 1936; Clodius to the Bayerische Hypotheken- und Wechselbank, Nov. 6, 1936;

Joham does not appear to have been a similar threat with respect to the Bayerische Vereinsbank's permanent holdings in three Austrian provincial banks, the Hauptbank für Tirol und Vorarlberg–Tiroler Landesbank, Innsbruck; the Bank für Oberösterreich und Salzburg, Linz; and the Steiermärkische Escompte Bank, Graz. It had held these shares since 1920, and in 1934, the German Foreign Office had asked the banks not to surrender any of these shares without first asking for Foreign Office approval. When the opportunity arose in 1937 to increase the Bayerische Vereinsbank's stake in the Steiermärkische Escompte Bank, Graz, due to a capital share increase reflecting the improvement of business conditions, the Bayerische Vereinsbank turned to the Foreign Office, and the latter asked and secured approval from the Foreign Exchange Office for the purchase of the additional shares on the grounds that everything possible should be done to increase German engagement in the Austrian economy. A selling point in this case, however, was the fact that the Creditanstalt itself was planning to participate in the capital increase. By participating, the Bayerische Vereinsbank was afforded the opportunity at once to maintain its engagement without destroying the balance of ownership and to profit from the improved conditions.[25]

On the eve of the Anschluss, the Creditanstalt was a formidable major bank. It had suffered severe setbacks during the economic troubles since 1918 and, in particular, the crisis of 1931, but, having been reorganized, it became a major instrument of the Austrian government, which controlled a majority of its shares. Having by and large shed its "Danubian" ambitions, the Creditanstalt was in a position to make the most of its "Austrification." Its leadership, like the leadership of Austria, was conservative in

its economic policies but committed to operating as a great concern and dominant force in Austrian economic life, and the Anschluss occurred at a time when economic recovery was taking place. The "Austrification" of the Austrian economy did not, to be sure, please the Germans, who viewed Austrian economic policy as incompatible with German interests and shortsighted with respect to Austrian interests. The German leadership was very unimpressed with Austrian economic development and had a different view of how economic recovery should be promoted. Hitler's chief economic advisor and point man for the infiltration of Austria, Wilhelm Keppler, was especially critical of Kienböck for pursuing a "deflationary policy à la Brüning" that prohibited Austria from utilizing its resources and ending its unemployment. Prior to the Anschluss, when Germany was pursuing "evolutionary paths" in its penetration of Austria, Keppler was convinced that a monetary and customs union with Germany and an intensification of trade relations would make it possible for Austria to enjoy an economic recovery analogous to that of Germany. Field Marshall Göring, anxious to mobilize Austrian resources for the Four Year Plan, suggested to Keppler in mid-February 1938 that Kienböck might be ousted and replaced by Hans Fischböck, a prominent National Socialist. Fischböck was then heading the successor life insurance company to Phönix Life, the Österreichische Versicherungs AG (ÖVAG), and was to become commerce minister and then economics, labor, and finance minister after the Anschluss.[26] If not as hostile to Joham as to Kienböck, the German leaders by no means thought that Joham's reductions and simplifications of credit conditions as head of the Banking Association were adequate to the needs of Austrian industry. In Ambassador Franz von Papen's view, the entire effort reflected an attempt by Austrian banking and industry to cover up their meager accomplishments.[27]

PA Berlin, R 110996, Reich Bureau for Foreign Exchange Management, Der Leiter, March 8, 1937.

25 PA Berlin, R 110997, Clodius to Bayerische Vereinsbank, Aug. 21, 1937; Bayerische Vereinsbank to Foreign Office, Sept. 3, 1937, and to the Reich Bureau for Foreign Exchange Management, Sept. 3, 1937; Kalisch to the Reich Bureau for Foreign Exchange Management, Sept. 22, 1937.

26 PA Berlin, R 27509, Keppler to Ribbentrop, Feb. 10 and Feb. 7, 1938, and memo for Veesenmayer, Feb. 14, 1938.
27 Ibid., R 110997, Von Papen to the Foreign Office, Sept. 23, 1937.

Insofar as the Austrian banking system was concerned, the German political leadership placed its bet on the Mercurbank, which was owned by the Dresdner Bank but which had proven extremely difficult either to Aryanize or to effectively "Germanize" prior to 1938.[28] Nevertheless, the great prize in Austrian banking was and remained the Creditanstalt. The improved economic situation made it more attractive than it had been for many years, and the Germans worried that the British were showing a dangerous influence in a reengagement with its fortunes. It was, therefore, quite natural for Director Hans Pilder of the Dresdner Bank to contemplate and to suggest to the German Foreign Office how much more effective it would be to take control of the Creditanstalt rather than rely on the Mercurbank to secure German influence in Austrian finance and industry. In February 1938, he did indeed propose an alternative to the Mercurbank card, namely, the bringing of the Mercurbank, the Eisenstädter Elektrizitätswerke, and the Veitscher Magnesitwerke – all owned by the Dresdner Bank – into the Creditanstalt in return for the Creditanstalt's purchase of the Austrian government shares, which would then go to the Dresdner Bank. The latter could in this way maintain its hold over the Austrian enterprises it already controlled and gain a third of the shares of the CA along with the vast influence over the Austrian economy that came with it. The precondition for such an operation, as Pilder noted, was the consent of the Austrian government as well as of the foreign creditors and shareholders of the CA, and the willingness of the CA to concede to the Dresdner Bank the influence such a holding would deserve.[29] Retrospectively, these appear as impossible hurdles under existing conditions. Nevertheless, they show that the CA had once again become a formidable institution by the time of the Anschluss, in no small measure because of its "Austrification," and that, in the event of a drastic change in political conditions,

"Germanization" might not only constitute a threat but also an opportunity.

2. THE PURGE OF THE CREDITANSTALT AND THE BATTLE FOR ITS CONTROL, 1938–1939

Purging the CA

The Austrian National Socialist "illegals" had waited long and impatiently for the day when they could crawl out of the woodwork, and they moved rapidly once the German troops invaded Austria on March 11–12, 1938.[30] Much of the initial effort to "cleanse" enterprises of Jews and supporters of the old order came from "below." In the case of the Creditanstalt, the first initiatives to purge and coordinate the bank were taken by a subaltern official, Rudolf Pfeiffer, who had been a Party activist since 1933. Pfeiffer was involved with the economic agencies of the Party and in the supplying of economic intelligence to Berlin. In the days before the Anschluss, he became quite open in his activities, urging military officers to support an Anschluss. On March 11, he led 200 members of the Deutsche Klub to the Chancellery, where they broke through a police cordon, and then proceeded to greet the new chancellor, Seyß-Inquart, with the collective singing of the appropriate hymns. Pfeiffer turned to more serious business in the next days, setting out enthusiastically to work on March 12–13 to bring the New Order to the Creditanstalt.[31] On Saturday, March 13, he paid an early morning visit to Joham accompanied

---

[28] See Chapter 5 in this volume.

[29] PA Berlin, R 110997, Foreign Office report on British interest in the CA, Nov. 24, 1937, and Pilder to Clodius and Aktennotiz, Feb. 1938.

[30] Although available quantitative evidence is inadequate, there is considerable evidence of other kinds pointing to a Nazification of the Austrian business community during the economic crisis of the early 1930s so that businesspeople ranked prominently among the illegals but also revealed themselves to be strong supporters of the Anschluss once the Germans marched in. See the valuable study of Stefan Eminger/Karl Haas, "Wirtschaftstreibende und Nationalsozialismus in Österreich. Die Nazifizierung von Handel, Gewerbe und Industrie in den 1930er Jahren," in: *Zeitgeschichte* 29/4 (July, Aug. 2002), pp. 153–176.

[31] This discussion is based on Pfeiffer's own description in Österreichisches Staatsarchiv (= ÖStA), Archiv der Republik (= AdR), Bundesministerium

by the National Socialist cell leader (*Zellenleiter*) Josef Dienst. Pfeiffer instructed Joham not to make any economic decisions without the approval of Pfeiffer in his capacity as an economic aide to the Party, and Joham was also instructed to recognize Dienst as the official representative of the employees. Pfeiffer continued his busy morning by instructing all the important sections of the bank to clear all their actions with designated representatives of the Party, and he also issued a ban on payments by the bank. Pfeiffer's actions were a classic illustration of the National Socialist "revolution" as it had occurred in Germany and was now occurring in Austria. The National Socialist Cell Organization (Nationalsozialistische Betiebszellenorganisation, or NSBO) had obviously infiltrated the leading sections of the bank, which explains why Pfeiffer was in a position to designate his representatives. Later in the day on March 13, he summoned a meeting of the "illegal Bank Association" to openly gather his forces now that they no longer needed to bide their time in the Trojan horse that Pfeiffer and his compatriots had constructed within the bank. The role he claimed as the Party's representative in economic matters was only officially confirmed when he was formally appointed "Special Representative of the NSDAP in Economic Questions for the Creditanstalt-Bankverein assigned by the Land Leadership of the NSDAP." Similarly, his ban on bank payments was retroactively approved from above by the commerce minister, with the proclaimed goal of the measure to prevent a run on the bank by Jews and those hostile to the new regime. Pfeiffer did not devote his attentions exclusively to the CA; he also took a half hour to visit the head offices of the Länderbank, still French owned, to instruct that bank that all important decisions taken were subject to the approval of Party representatives. Nevertheless, his attention was devoted mainly to the CA, to which he returned to instruct the removal of Jewish bank directors and to promote personnel changes in enterprises that were in the control of the bank or to which it had given large credits with the object of preventing "the dragging away of assets or sabotage."

Because the elimination of Jewish and other politically undesirable bank officials developed in stages and the individual circumstances surrounding their departure varied and is usually inadequately recorded, it is difficult to pin down how much Pfeiffer had "accomplished" on March 12 and 13. In any event, Franz Rottenberg submitted his letter of resignation to the bank on Monday, March 15, although placing himself at the disposal of the bank should he be needed.[32] He reported after the war that the actual conditions of his departure were extremely demeaning, which probably meant that he was told in no uncertain terms to resign over the weekend, and were ultimately life threatening. He was seized by the SA at his home in Baden bei Wien during the week of March 15, placed on a truck, and then tossed out of the moving vehicle, resulting in a compound fracture of his right arm. He was subsequently taken to the Party headquarters, the "Brown House" (Braunes Haus), in Vienna but allowed to leave. He attributed his release and the saving of his life to having met someone there whose life he had once saved and who now returned the favor.[33]

---

für Inneres (= BMI), Gauakt Rudolf Pfeiffer, Nr. 50957. See also Eigner/Melichar, "Enteignungen und Säuberungen" in: Ziegler (ed.), *Banken und "Arisierungen,"* pp. 45–46.

[32] BA-CA, Archiv der Creditanstalt Personalabteilung (= CA-PA), Personalakt Franz Rottenberg, Franz Rottenberg to the CA, March 15, 1938.

[33] StA Nürnberg, Rep. 502, Nl 10997; for Rottenberg's account of his experiences, see his statement of Sept. 15, 1947. Unfortunately, Saul Friedländer in his pathbreaking study, *Nazi Germany and the Jews, vol. 1: The Years of Persecution, 1933–1939* (New York 1997), p. 243, speaks of Franz Rottenberg as "Franz Rothenberg" and incorrectly claims that Rottenberg was killed when thrown from the truck. In fact, he survived the war and worked for the Creditanstalt again. Friedländer also claims that the "Deutsche Bank confiscated the Rothschild-controlled Kreditanstalt." The Rothschilds did not have control of the CA and, as will be shown, it was not until 1942 that the Deutsche Bank had a majority of the CA shares, and these were not confiscated. Raul Hilberg, *Die Vernichtung der europäischen Juden*, Vol. 1 (Frankfurt a.M. 1990), p. 99.

Rottenberg was a proud man who was not easily cowed, and he put up a fight for the financial rights due to him for his forced retirement. He had been paid his salary up to March 31, 1938, and his honoraria for supervisory board memberships amounting to 28,375.86 RM. As was the case with other Jewish pensioners, he received his pension through September 30, 1938, which in his case amounted to a payment of 800 RM in May 1938 and then 2,933.33 RM on January 24, 1939 for a total of 3,733.33 RM. Under his contract and under the Austrian law dealing with bank employees, however, he was entitled to a yearly pension of 10,000 RM a month and a settlement of 67,000 RM based on his thirty-two years of service and his age (58). On June 16, 1939, he wrote to the bank asking that his pension and royalties to which he was entitled under his contract be sent directly to his home because he did not have a legal representative, and he asked that this be done rapidly "since my situation is extremely precarious."[34] The head of the personnel office, Jörg Unterreiner – an "illegal" and NSBO activist who had received high marks for the infiltration of the banking sector prior to the Anschluss and who came to work at the CA under Pfeiffer in June 1939[35] – took the matter up with Hans Fischböck, at this time the chairman of the CA management board. Fischböck proposed that Unterreiner negotiate an agreement with Rottenberg under which the pension would be paid as of July 1 provided Rottenberg agreed to give up all other claims against the CA. Perhaps this, under the circumstances, "generous" offer from a genuinely evil individual reflected a residual respect on Fischböck's part for so distinguished a banker, but when Unterreiner consulted with local authorities about the proposal, he was told that the government would not consider authorizing a pension for Rottenberg because he was not a social hardship case. The most that would be considered was a lump sum in the form of a one-time cash settlement that was no more than one and a half times Rottenberg's yearly pension. Rottenberg was outraged by the negative response he received from Unterreiner, and he wrote once again on July 7 to the CA asking that his contractual rights be realized: "It is extraordinarily distressing that I, who will be 60 years old in a few months – my wife (a full Aryan) is 76 years old – must bother you, while the gentlemen at the Industrie-Kreditbank, an institution that is in *liquidation*, are receiving their contractual payments *without regard to their age*; should it be just me who is to be punished for having had the honor of being a member of the management board of your institution."[36]

But it was not a battle that Rottenberg was going to win. When Unterreiner sent Rottenberg a letter inviting him to discuss the matter, Rottenberg called about an appointment but pointed out that actually such a discussion was not necessary because all they had to do was mail the pension payments. Unterreiner responded by making it clear that there could be no discussion of a pension but only of a lump sum settlement, whereupon Rottenberg responded that there was nothing to talk about, that his age and service entitled him to his rights and that he would continue to petition the CA until he received his pension.[37] The matter was now turned over to lawyers, and Rottenberg was offered a settlement of 10,000 RM, which he refused. In the meantime, the deadline for taking such civil claims to the authorities for arbitration ran out on November 15, 1939, a "right" that Rottenberg did not exercise and that undoubtedly would have brought him no relief.[38] Happily, however, Rottenberg lived to collect his money. On April 29, 1945, he was awarded a total of 133,666.40 RM, 67,000 RM owed him for having been dismissed from the bank, and 66,666.40 RM for eighty months of back pension payments between October 1, 1938 and May 31, 1945.

34 BA-CA, CA-PA, Personalakte Franz Rottenberg, Rottenberg to the CA, June 16, 1939.
35 ÖStA/AdR, BMI, Gauakt Jörg Unterreiner, Nr. 118098.
36 BA-CA, CA-PA, Personalakt Franz Rottenberg, Rottenberg to the CA, July 8, 1939.
37 Ibid., Report of Unterreiner, July 11, 1939.
38 Ibid., see letter from the CA attorney to Dr. Hans Lowenfeld-Russ, Dec. 5, 1939.

Furthermore, he was reemployed by the CA. If he survived the war and was not deported, it probably was because his wife was an Aryan, but he may also have benefited from the kind of protection that rescued him from the clutches of the SA thugs who had imprisoned him in March 1938.[39] There is no evidence that anyone else put up this kind of fight for their pension rights.

Oskar Pollak was much less fortunate, although he kept his position longer than Rottenberg at the insistence of Franz Hasslacher. He continued on into late March without formally stepping down, and his resignation was announced by the administrative council on April 7, 1938. His resignation from the administrative council of the Allgemeine Jugoslawische Bankverein, where he represented the CA as the bank's major shareholder, was not tendered until June 22, 1938, although Joham had joined the council as vice-president in his stead on April 30. Little more is known about his personal fate. Some information may be garnered from a letter he wrote to a colleague at the Jugoslawische Bankverein in February 1940, where he had served as head of the administrative council and chief representative of the CA until September 1938. In this letter, he asked for assistance in aiding a stateless Jewish engineer of his acquaintance to find refuge with family members in Belgrade, and then wrote in conclusion: "Things are unchanged with me. My children have already left the country; I am thus somewhat lonely along with my wife."[40] He apparently continued to live in Vienna at

Nusswaldgasse 19, from where, at the age of sixty-four, he was deported on May 20, 1942, to Maly Trostinec near Minsk and murdered six days later – one of the almost 9,000 Jews who met their end at that particular place.[41] Pollak was not alone among the high-ranking Creditanstalt personnel in suffering such a fate. Ernst Ornstein, a vice-director, was deprived of his promised pension and was deported on June 10, 1942, in his case from Prague to Ujadov, Estonia, which often served as a way station to the extermination camp at Majdanek in Poland.[42] There may have been others, and at least one high official at the CA, Vice-director Otto Russo, is reported to have committed suicide right after the Anschluss.[43]

The "Jewish problem" in Vienna was viewed as especially severe by Austria's new masters. The stock exchange, for example, was shut down on March 12, and the RWM was uncertain as to when to reopen it and how to staff it. As Abs reported to the Deutsche Bank advisory council in Cologne at the end of March, "a great problem in Austria is the non-Aryan question. Of 125 members of the Vienna stock exchange, 103 are non-Aryans. Of the lawyers, only 4% are Aryans, and it is similar in various other professions."[44] As noted earlier, the CA had gradually reduced the number of Jews in its ranks even before the Anschluss. At the time of the Anschluss, two members of the management board, thirty-six of the fifty-four leading functionaries, and 148 of the officials of the bank were Jews or of mixed heritage. But already by the beginning of November 1938, State

---

[39] Ibid., memorandum of May 29, 1945. It is curious that the CA dated his resignation as having taken place on April 7, 1938, when rehiring him in 1946; see the letter of the bank of Feb. 26, 1946. April 7 was the date that the administrative council reported that Rottenberg and Pollak had resigned, and the CA, when acknowledging his resignation on that date, referred to a verbal notification from Rottenberg of his resignation and not the letter of March 15.

[40] Jugoslawisches Staatsarchiv (= AJ), Allgemeiner Jugoslawischer Bankverein (= AJB) 151, 90/115, Pollak to Hochner, Feb. 1, 1940; ibid., 2/2; Pollak's resignation was read to the council on Oct. 24, 1938.

[41] See the database of Austrian Jews murdered in the Holocaust http://www.doew.at.

[42] Ibid.; see ÖStA/AdR, BMF, Allgem. Reihe 1938, 32864/1938, on the pension case of Ornstein, as well as that of another CA vice director, Marcell Goldarbeiter.

[43] See HAK, FAH 23/512, the interesting remarks on conditions at the CA in a letter written by Tilo Freiherr von Wilmowsky, March 19, 1938.

[44] DB, P 41, Bl. 111, Meeting of the Rhenish-Westphalian Advisory Council, March 31, 1938, and RGVA Moscow, 1458/2/305, Bl. 14, memorandum by Koehler of the RWM on a visit made by himself, Lange, and Riehle to Vienna on March 25/26 on the Austrian banking situation.

Commissar for the Private Economy Walter Rafelsberger was able to report that every single one of them had been let go thanks, in large part, to what he described as "a methodical application of the Law for the Protection of the Austrian Economy of April 14, 1938," which provided the authorities with the discretion they needed to enforce this purge. It is reasonable to assume that most of the Jews had been dismissed in the spring.[45]

The purge was not limited to Jews, however, and it was a precarious time for supporters of the old regime. Rumors were circulating in Berlin and elsewhere that Joham would be thrown out. Such rumors, however, were false, at least for the moment, and the better informed knew that Joham was still serving and believed that he would continue to do so because "he cannot be done without due to his overwhelming command of the Austrian and Southeast European business."[46] This certainly seemed to be confirmed by his presence and role at the regular CA shareholders' meeting held in Vienna on March 25, 1938, where he presented the report of the management board as the bank's general director.

It was an important meeting that openly signaled the major changes taking place at the top echelons of the bank since the German takeover of Austria. The chairman of the administrative council, Emanuel Weidenhoffer, had already stepped down. Normally, Hasslacher would have presided, but he had been summoned to Linz to meet with Göring. His position seemed reasonably safe, however, because he was viewed in powerful Berlin circles as "an enthusiastic supporter of the new Greater Germany."[47] A major industrialist who was highly regarded

as a self-made man with considerable acumen, Hasslacher had distinguished himself politically by being rather forthright about his Greater German position without getting into an excessive amount of trouble. He had never been an "illegal" and managed to keep on good terms both with important German political and economic leaders and with the authoritarian Austrian regime. Dollfuß had actually offered Hasslacher a position in his cabinet a number of times, but Hasslacher refused and, after the 1934 Putsch, tried to persuade the Schuschnigg regime to take a softer line toward the National Socialists, especially in his native Carinthia. In an account of his pre-Anschluss activities for the National Socialist regime, he claimed to have been extremely frustrated in these efforts and that he had become estranged from the corporatist regime. He claimed that he had worked closely with German business and political leaders, had reported regularly to von Papen and the German authorities on the Austrian economic situation, and had advised the Germans on the measures he deemed necessary. He claimed that he became increasingly outspoken in support of the Anschluss and was becoming the victim of economic and political reprisals. At his postwar trial, Hasslacher took a different tack for obvious reasons, but his account of his actions was not inconsistent with his earlier one. He admitted to his Greater German sentiments and desire to reconcile the corporatist regime with the National Socialists, spoke openly about his relationship with von Papen, who had attended hunting parties at his estate, but stressed that he had not seen von Papen after the Anschluss, and generally emphasized his promotion of Austrian economic interests both before and after the Anschluss. He was clearly a very successful trimmer, and he did not suffer much politically either after 1934 or after 1938 because he was a highly respected businessman with great professional authority in Carinthia, Vienna, and Berlin thanks to his command of the timber business. In addition to his relationship with von Papen, he also seems to have befriended Ernst Kaltenbrunner, who headed the police and SD in Vienna. Hasslacher did not apply for membership in the Party until 1938 and was formally

[45] RGVA Moscow, 1458/2/101, short report on the Activity of the Reich Commissariat for the Private Economy in the Area of Finance, Nov. 3, 1938. This report contained a rundown on the firing of Jews at all the banks.

[46] Ibid., 1458/2/305, Bl. 14–15, Koehler memorandum on visit to Vienna on March 25/26. On the rumors concerning Joham's dismissal, see HAK, FAH 23/512, the letter of Tilo Freiherr von Wilmowsky, March 19, 1938.

[47] See RGVA Moscow, 1458/2/305, Bl. 14, Koehler memorandum.

admitted in 1940. Both the Gestapo and the Security Service of the SS kept an eye on him but seem to have come to the conclusion that he was a reliable person politically and above all dedicated to Austrian business interests. While more radical and committed National Socialists claimed he had done little or nothing for the cause prior to 1938 and distrusted him for his concentration on business capability rather than political conviction in his personnel policies – his futile efforts to prolong Oskar Pollak's position on the management board were taken particularly ill – it proved impossible to displace him or even criticize him openly. It was Weidenhoffer who, when forced to step down from his position on March 16, pleaded with Hasslacher to step into the post of president of the administrative council. Hasslacher did not think he would be acceptable, but Joham also put pressure on Hasslacher and went to Finance Minister Fischböck to urge the appointment. Hasslacher, however, would only accept the job if Joham was retained as head manager of the CA. Hasslacher's supporters hoped he would be formally appointed president on March 25, but this was temporarily albeit unsuccessfully blocked by die-hard National Socialists in the bank.[48]

The great novelty at the March 25 shareholders' meeting, however, was that the very recently appointed Hermann Josef Abs assumed the chairmanship of the meeting at Hasslacher's request and thus unmistakably signaled a new and important role for the Deutsche Bank. Normally, the chair would have been taken by Alexander Weiner, the second vice-president, but Weiner was a Jew and had resigned.[49] It cannot be said that Abs distinguished himself by much more than his physical presence at this event. The report to the assembly was provided by Joham and was duly accepted. Abs made a point of noting how great a privilege it was to preside over the first meeting following the Anschluss and then proceeded to read verbatim from the opening of the annual report containing the standard appreciation of the allegedly great achievement of Adolf Hitler's joining of Austria to Germany and glowing assertions about the economic and social benefits this would bring in its wake. This was conventional fare in all company reports penned after the Anschluss, and it cannot be said that the Creditanstalt version was any more or less fawning and sycophantic than what its counterparts were producing or going to produce. All this said little more about Abs other than that he could read and lead the assembly in a rousing Hitler salute. As shall be shown, he had more important things on his mind and other ways to express his talents.

The meeting did, however, produce a first wave of changes in the administrative council, which was to be followed by a second wave in the summer. These are summarized in the chart below.

[48] A Gauakt has not been found for Hasslacher, and a brief but detailed report on his activities prior to 1938 and written by himself in the summer of 1938 is reprinted in: Ludwig Jedlicka/Rudolf Neck (eds.), *Vom Justizpalast zum Heldenplatz. Studien und Dokumente* (Vienna 1975), pp. 479–480. The original document cannot be located in the AdR. Much more revealing and important is the documentary material and his own testimony at his postwar denazification trial to be found in the Steiermärkisches Landesarchiv (= StmkLA), Vr 734/1946, Landesgericht für Strafsachen Graz, Franz und Jakob Hasslacher. Especially important, in addition to Hasslacher's own testimony, is a report of April 11, 1947, by police official Karl Ebner who had access to both the Gestapo and SD records (Bl. 447–449). On his appointment as president and on his efforts to retain Pollak, see his testimony (Bl. 83–84). On the resistance to Hasslacher's appointment as president of the administrative council and the delay, see the testimony of Joham, Sept. 23, 1946, (Bl. 330) and the report of the Banking Section of the BMF on the shareholders' meeting, ÖStA/AdR, BMF, Allgem. Reihe 1938, 27027/1938.

[49] Weiner was a partner in the private banking house of Ephrussi & Co., was able to emigrate in 1938, was a banker in New York City at the end of the war, and received restitution in Austria in 1954. See Peter Melichar, *Neuordnung im Bankwesen. Die NS-Maßnahmen und die Problematik der Restitution.* Veröffentlichungen der Österreichischen Historikerkommission. Vermögensentzug während der NS-Zeit sowie Rückstellungen und Entschädigungen seit 1945 in Österreich, vol. 11 (Vienna, Munich 2004), p. 228. On Abs's role in Austria, see Lothar Gall, *Der Bankier Hermann Josef Abs. Eine Biographie* (Munich 2004), esp. pp. 51–58.

The Administrative Council of the CA in 1938

Dr. Emanuel Weidenhoffer, Vienna, President (resigned, March 25)

Franz Hasslacher, Spitala.d. Drau, Vice-president, President (as of January 27, 1939)

Karl von Hinke, Vienna, Vice-president (as of March 25)

Alexander Weiner, Vienna (resigned, March 25)

Herman J. Abs, Berlin

Roberto Adler, Milan (resigned, March 25)

Alberto D'Agostino, Milan (March 25–December 21)

Dr. Herbert Auer von Welsbach, Vienna (as of March 25)

Werner Axt, Vienna (as of July 23)

Jacques Bizot, Paris (resigned, November 11)

Dr. Heinrich Bleckmann, Vienna (as of July 23)

Claus von Bohlen und Halbach, Berndorf (as of July 23)

Dr. Rudolf Buchinger, Staasdorfbei Tulln (resigned, March 4)

Auguste Callens, Brussels

Dr. Ing. Armin Dadieu, Graz (as of November 25)

Dr. Ludwig Draxler, Vienna (resigned, March 5)

Ing. Theo Groß, Berlin (as of November 25)

Dr. Max Ilgner, Berlin (as of July 23)

Dr. h.c. Ing. Karl Innerebner, Innsbruck (as of July 23)

Karl Klinger, Gumpoldskirchen

Dr. Ing. Ernst Kraus, Vienna

Franz Langoth, Linz (as of March 23)

P. Lindenberg, London (resigned, March 25)

Dr. A. J. Mayer, Zurich (resigned, late 1938 or early 1939)

Dr. Alfred Olscher, Berlin (as of June 22)

Friedrich Reinhart, Berlin (as of July 23)

Hermann Rhomberg, Dornbirn (as of July 23)

August Rohdewald, Berlin (as of July 23)

Gottfried Schenker-Angerer, Vienna (as of March 25)

Philipp von Schoeller, Vienna (as of March 25)

F.V. Schuster, London (resigned, March 25)

Dr. Hans Stigleitner, Vienna (resigned, March 4)

Michael Teretschenko, Monaco (resigned, July 15)

Friedrich Tinti, Pöchl (resigned, April 8)

Abs announced the departure of eight administrative council members: Emanuel Weidenhoffer, Alexander Weiner, Roberto Adler, Rudolf Buchinger, P. Lindenberg, Sir Victor Schuster, Hans Stigleitner, and Ludwig Draxler. They were all either Jews and/or foreigners, as was the case with Weiner, Adler, Lindenberg, and Schuster, or persons prominently associated with the old regime like Weidenhoffer, Buchinger, Stigleitner, and Draxler. The new members presented no such difficulties. Alberto D'Agostino succeeded Adler as a representative of the Banca Commerciale. The others, Herbert Auer Freiherr von Welsbach, Karl von Hinke, Franz Langoth, Gottfried Schenker-Angerer, and Philipp von Schoeller, were all Party members and, in some cases, very active ones. Auer von Welsbach had been a Party member since 1935. A prominent Carinthian chemical industrialist, he had joined his company's illegal NSBO cell and was active in organizing industry for the Party in Carinthia.[50] Karl von Hinke, director of the Steirische Gußstahlwerke and a leading heavy industrialist, was known to have given money to the Brown House in Munich as early as 1933 and had protected and employed "persecuted" National Socialists. His appointment was the result of a direct recommendation by the NSDAP.[51] In contrast to the other newly appointed council members,

[50] See ÖStA/AdR, BMI, Gauakt Auer Freiherr von Welsbach, Nr. 87779.
[51] Ibid., Gauakt Karl von Hinke, Nr. 17662; ÖStA/AdR, BMF, Allgem. Reihe 1938, 27027/1938; on the NSDAP choice of Hinke, see the report of the Banking Section on the shareholders' meeting.

Franz Langoth was a genuine political activist and political appointment. He had gained prominence by organizing the economic support of the families of National Socialists who had been imprisoned and was made head of the National Socialist People's Welfare Organization for Upper Austria after the Anschluss. He joined the SS in 1938 and was later to serve as mayor of Linz.[52] Gottfried Schenker-Angerer was also an activist of sorts despite his business engagements. A director of the Schenker & Co. transportation company, he had been a member of the Party since 1933 and led an SA group that had a somewhat violent reputation.[53] Despite such "qualities," he was suspect in some Party circles for having been a Rotarian. The appointment of Philipp von Schoeller to the council made perfectly good business sense because the association between the Bankhaus Schoeller and the CA was a close one, cemented above all by their ownership, along with the Heinrich Bleckmann family, of 80 percent of the shares of the important Schoeller-Bleckmann steel company. Bleckmann also joined the council in July. Most importantly, however, Schoeller had cast his lot with the National Socialists in 1936, whether out of opportunism or conviction or some mixture of the two, and was a member of an SA group of which Schenker was one of the leaders. The new regime made the most of his prestige, appointing him president of the Vienna Fair and a member of the Vienna Town Council.[54]

One of the striking aspects of the appointments to the council at the end of March was their strong Austrian character. This was reinforced by the fact that two Austrian industrial figures were retained, Karl Klinger, the president of Richard Klinger AG, a gasket and automobile parts manufacturer, and Ernst Kraus of the Austrian Siemens-Schuckertwerke AG, both of whom had joined the council as result of the merger of the Wiener Bankverein. Klinger was known to have given a considerable amount of money to the Party and to have provided jobs and aid to "illegals."[55] As for Kraus, he certainly must have had the right credentials, but his most important quality was that he represented the Siemens concern with which the CA did a great deal of business. He remained on the council and then the supervisory board until the end of the war.[56] More Austrians were added in the course of the year in addition to Bleckmann: Werner Axt, who came from the Industriekredit and was director of the Alpen-Elektrowerke AG; Karl Innerebner, a prominent Innsbruck engineer whose construction firm specialized in railroad and power plant construction; textile manufacturer Hermann Rhomberg from Dornbirn, who was the most influential business leader in Vorarlberg and had supported the National Socialists; Armin Dadieu, a Graz chemistry professor who was the governor and Gau economic advisor of Styria and had played a major role in the National Socialist takeover of Graz, thus helping it earn the title of the "City of the People's Uprising." Dadieu was obviously a purely political and undoubtedly very useful appointment.

The most telling new appointments in the remainder of 1938, however, were those of Reich Germans Claus von Bohlen und Halbach, Max Ilgner, Alfred Olscher, Friedrich Reinhart, August Rohdewald, and Theo Gross.

[52] ÖStA/AdR, BMI, Gauakt Franz Langoth, Nr. 20947.

[53] See ibid., Gauakt Gottfried Schenker-Angerer, Nr. 81044.

[54] See ibid., Gauakt Philipp von Schoeller, Nr. 55521. On the ownership of Schoeller-Bleckmann, see BAB, R8 135/9255 the report of the Deutschen Revisions- und Treuhand-Aktiengesellschaft of Jan. 20, 1939. See also Gerhard Botz, *Nationalsozialismus in Wien. Machtübernahme und Herrschaftssicherung 1938/39* (Buchloe 1988), p. 446. A member of the family, Elisabeth von Schoeller, who refused to collaborate and spent the National Socialist years in Turkey, claimed to American intelligence authorities that Schoeller decided to collaborate in order to save his assets. See NARA, RG 226, 190/3/30/6, Box 949. Nr. 81040 the report of June 10, 1944.

[55] Klinger was not, however, a member of the Party at the time and only applied later. After the war, he contested being a sympathizer and claimed to have sought to do good for those in need whatever their politics. See ÖStA/AdR, BMI, Gauakt Karl Klinger, Nr. 58597.

[56] DB, P 6502, Bl. 190–191, Joham to Abs, Dec. 30, 1938.

While the address given for Claus von Bohlen und Halbach read Berndorf, he was manifestly a representative of the Krupp interests in Essen as well and, of course, of their interest in the works at Berndorf. Max Ilgner was a member of the IG Farben management board and thus represented the interests as well as the influence of the German chemical giant. Alfred Olscher, a Party member whose key role will be discussed later in this chapter, had been head of the Finance Policy Section of the Reich Finance Ministry (RFM) until he was appointed a member of the management board of the Vereinigte Industrie Unternehmungen AG (VIAG) in April 1937 to replace the Jewish director Edgar Landauer. The VIAG, on whose supervisory board Olscher had been serving while still in the ministry, was the holding company for the industrial enterprises owned by the Reich, and Olscher was also appointed to the management board of the Reichs-Kredit-Gesellschaft (RKG), Germany's fourth largest bank at the time, which was entirely owned by the Reich through the VIAG.[57] There were two other persons associated with Olscher who were also put on the CA council, Werner Axt and August Rohdewald, the latter coming from the RKG. Finally, Friedrich Reinhart, the head of the management board of the Commerzbank, also joined the CA council in the summer, while Theo Gross, a state commissar and deputy minister for agriculture and forestry, was placed on the council in November. A powerful group of Reich Germans had joined the council, while the persons who had represented the international committee and were non-German and non-Austrian resigned their posts because new arrangements, to be discussed later, rendered their presence superfluous. The total disappearance of international members on the council was not entirely welcome, however. The resignation of Alberto D'Agostino soon after his appointment was regretted despite his mandate from the international committee

because he was an important person in Italian financial life and was associated with the Banca Commerciale Italiana. Auguste Callens was not associated with the international committee but was rather a director of the Société Générale de Belgique, a partner of the Creditanstalt in the control of the Jugoslawische Bankverein. His continued presence on the board was deemed very desirable.[58]

The changes on the administrative council described earlier also led to substantial changes in the executive committee, which had been created as a watchdog in the wake of the Creditanstalt crisis and which inevitably faced a loss of its functions as new arrangements were established with the international committee. At the time of its April 29 meeting, most of the foreign and previous Austrian members had left, while Gottfried Schenker-Angerer joined the group. Olscher entered the Council in June. By September, the last remaining foreigners, Jacques Bizot and Alberto D'Agostino, were no longer attending, and they finally resigned in the last months of the year. Victor Brauneis, the former secretary-general of the Austrian National Bank, died in the spring. For all intents and purposes, therefore, during the second half of the year, the executive committee was composed of Hasslacher, Olscher, Schenker-Angerer, and a government section head from the Austrian Finance Ministry, Johann Rizzi.[59]

At the April 29 executive committee meeting, its members were also presented with a new management board. Joham was still there, but he was not riding quite as high as he had been during the previous month. His continued presence on the management board was being sharply criticized in National Socialist circles. Friedrich Ottel, a Privatdozent in economics employed in 1938 in the Secretariat of the Österreichische Industrie-Credit AG and subsequently to serve as a director with power of attorney at the CA from 1940 to 1945, seemed to have access to Ministerial Director Lange of the RWM and

[57] Manfred Pohl, *VIAG Aktiengesellschaft 1923–1998. Vom Staatsunternehmen zum internationalen Konzern* (Munich 2001), pp. 129–132. See also StA Nürnberg, Rep. 502, A-52.

[58] DB, P 6502, Bl. 190–191, Joham to Abs, Dec. 30, 1938.

[59] See BA-CA, CA-V, the protocols of the executive committee.

produced a memorandum on April 7 arguing, among other things, that Joham should be dismissed because "a real change to a National Socialist economic policy cannot be expected from Dr. Joham, an unconditional supporter of the previous system."[60] This was not to happen, but at the beginning of April Joham was on the list of those scheduled for arrest and incarceration in a concentration camp by the Gestapo, and his house was searched. His membership in a Catholic fraternity seemed to have been of particular importance in his placement on the Gestapo list, but his relations with the previous government were undoubtedly the chief reason for his suspect status. It was only through Hasslacher's intervention with Fischböck, who was unaware of the situation, that Joham was spared arrest at the last minute and allowed to stay on the management board of the CA, albeit now only in the capacity of a director rather than as general director. As was later reported, "Hasslacher invariably took the position that these accusations were unjust and were always made to the State Police out of jealousy and resentment."[61] His survival in this status was yet another tribute to his recognized capacities as a banker, but he later complained that the departure of Rottenberg and Pollak and the Aryanization of the bank personnel as well as the dismissals and new appointments made it difficult to function on a daily basis. Joham undoubtedly did not enjoy such disruption, but his complaints about the firing of Jews would surely have been more credible had he not claimed credit for reducing their number in an orderly fashion during his service as general director.[62]

Aside from Joham, the only holdover from the pre-Anschluss period was Erich Heller, who was made chairman of the management board and was sometimes referred to as general director without having Joham's status and authority or even an increase in pay. This was viewed as a temporary arrangement. Heller's chief focus was on industrial matters, as had been the case before, and the decision to elevate him was made in order to avoid the cost and trouble of having to find a new general director at a time when the introduction of the German corporation law was anticipated in the very near future. Heller had not been politically active under the old regime, and the most that could be said about him politically is that he consorted in Greater German and National Socialist circles.[63]

The three new management board directors who came onto the scene in April were much more politically involved.[64] This was especially the case, of course, with Rudolf Pfeiffer, who was appointed at the express wish of the Party, and Arthur Seyß-Inquart, the National Socialist successor to Schusschnig and subsequent Statthalter of Austria. Pfeiffer had begun his banking career at the Wiener Bankverein in 1920 and was made an official of the legal section, where he worked until his promotion. Pfeiffer's chief qualification obviously was his politics, and it turned out to be more or less his only qualification. In addition to the activities during the Anschluss described earlier, Göring had charged him on March 27 with oversight of the Aryanization of the banking business, a task he continued under Rafelsberger, the commissar for the private economy. He was to play the role of the leading Party man in the bank in 1938–1939.[65]

[60] See RGVA Moscow, 1458/2/77, Bl. 34 and 84–90, Ottel to Lange, March 29, 1938, and his memorandum on the transformation of the Austrian banking system of April 7. See also ÖStA/AdR, BMI, Gauakt Friedrich Ottel, Nr. 122521.

[61] See StmkLA, Vr 734/1946, Bl. 364, 448, 83, 17–18, the testimony and reports by Karl Ebner, Oct. 3, 1946, and April 11, 1947, Hasslacher's own testimony, and Joham's letter to Hasslacher of Aug. 27, 1946, Landesgericht für Strafsachen Graz, Franz und Jakob Hasslacher.

[62] See StA Nürnberg, Rep. 502, Nl 10998, Joham's affidavit of Sept. 13, 1947.

[63] See his very thin Gauakt ÖStA/AdR, BMI, Gauakt Erich Heller, Nr. 17861. On the legal considerations moving his appointment, see ibid., BMF, Allgem. Reihe 1938, 38031/1938.

[64] For the contracts with the new board members, all negotiated at the end of March, and reports on their careers, see ibid., 55128/1938.

[65] ÖStA/AdR, BMI, Gauakt Rudolf Pfeiffer, Nr. 50957. See also, Eigner/Melichar, "Enteignungen und Säuberungen" in: Ziegler (ed.), Banken und "Arisierungen," pp. 45–46.

Hans Friedl had served in the Vienna headquarters since 1927 as a vice-director and head of the Industrial Inspectorate, and since 1931 as head of the Secretariat as well. He had long been a National Socialist sympathizer and was praised in SA and SS circles for taking risks to help "illegals."[66] He appears to have been reasonably competent.

Ludwig Fritscher, like Pfeiffer a subordinate official in the bank who did not even hold the power of attorney, was also appointed to the board. Once a Catholic pastor in Melk, Fritscher had left the Church and was a member of the NSDAP in 1931 and also joined the SS. He does not seem to have had any banking experience, having worked for the Wechselseitige Brandschaden und Janus Allgemeine Versicherungs-Anstalt between 1928 and 1936 and then, following the Phönix scandal, having been transferred to the Österreichische Versicherungs AG (ÖVAG), where he worked until his appointment to the CA. He was befriended with Fischböck, who had headed the ÖVAG between 1936 and was appointed commerce minister in March 1938, as well as with other leading Austrian National Socialists – the chancellor and then Statthalter of Austria, Seyß-Inquart; Gauleiter Hugo Jury of the Lower Danube; and the mayor of Vienna, Hermann Neubacher – and both his work for the Party and connections undoubtedly explain his appointment to the CA management as well as his later appointment to the presidency of the Viennese Stock Exchange, where his name was quite useful.[67] Manifestly, therefore, the expanded management board had been reconstituted with political considerations in mind. As would be demonstrated in the period ahead, it certainly suffered in experience and quality when compared to the days of Rottenberg and Pollak.

Banking Ambitions and National Socialist Politics: The Struggle for the CA

Matters were not helped by the fact that Joham himself was under a cloud, especially because

he was Abs's chief partner in the plans the Deutsche Bank had been developing in connection with the Creditanstalt and the projected expansion into Southeast Europe. This relationship was undoubtedly founded on the discussions that had taken place on March 3–4, that is, before the Anschluss, but conditions changed once that event had taken place, and it was Joham who took the initiative to invite Abs to come to Vienna to examine the questions now facing the two banks. Abs was accompanied by Helmuth Pollems, deputy director in the Foreign Section of the Deutsche Bank; Walter Pohle, who worked in the Berlin Secretariat and was to play a major role in the expansion of the Deutsche Bank; and Director Erhard Ulbricht from the accounting office. It was an extended stay that lasted from March 17 to 31, the major negotiations between the bank leaders taking place between March 17 and 26 and thus being in a very advanced stage at the time when the shareholders' meeting was taking place on March 25.[68] Joham was very clear about the purpose of his initiative and what he had in mind. Given the presence of the Deutsche Bank on the administrative council and the long friendship between the two banks, the CA would welcome the "support" of the Deutsche Bank "so that in this way, it would be in the position to also meet the requirements of the Austrian economy in the future as an independent institution operating according to economic principles."[69] The CA then proceeded to open up its books in full detail, providing in some cases the reports sent by the various sections of the bank to the management board at the end of the year. There were also verbal reports by high officials of the CA. Vice Director Friedrich Kinscher discussed changes in the balance sheet, explained the way the bank conducted its business, and provided information on the balances of the most important companies belonging to the CA concern.

66 ÖStA/AdR, BMI, Gauakt Hans Friedl, Nr. 7726.
67 Ibid., Gauakt Ludwig Fritscher, Nr. 124407.
68 DB, B 51, on March 21, the Deutsche Bank petitioned the Foreign Exchange Office to allocate enough foreign exchange to permit extension of the stay of the four men for another ten days.
69 Ibid., memorandum of March 31, 1938.

Director Marcell Goldarbeiter – a Jewish director shortly to be let go and to be denied the pension in April that he had been promised in February[70] – then proceeded to report in detail on all credits given by the bank involving more than 100,000 Schilling. The discussions involved consideration of the "new circumstances" and their significance for the bank, and among these was the "Jewish question." In considering the value of outstanding credits and financial engagements – because of its peculiar character as an industrial holding company, not only current account credits but also industrial investment credits and mortgage credits were involved – notice had now to be taken of "special dangers because of the political transformation."[71] It was estimated that between 20 and 30 million Schilling of the 56.3 million Schilling in accounts receivable over 100,000 Schilling were "Jewish." The value of these credits and the problem of securing their value therefore, were significant questions. There were, of course, other issues involved in assessing the bank's position in the future, the effect of the currency reform – the conversion rate from Schilling to Reichsmark had been pegged at 3:2 on March 17 – and the introduction of German foreign exchange regulations.

Needless to say, much of the discussion must have been quite speculative because it was very difficult in the early days of the annexation to predict the adjustment of the Austrian to the German economy, and what concerned Joham most of all was the best possible adjustment to the new situation, and the answer was that "a strong capital participation of the Deutsche Bank in the CA was viewed as the best economic solution."[72] Fundamentally, what Joham then proposed was that the Deutsche Bank purchase the shares in the bank previously controlled by the Austrian government and the Austrian National Bank as well as shares held by the pension fund and by a subsidiary company of the CA controlling its real estate holdings, the Realitäten AG, and thus become the largest shareholder of the CA. Basically, this was a program for the "privatization" of the CA, and it could not be undertaken without the permission of Austrian Finance Minister Rudolf Neumayer, head of the National Bank Viktor Brauneis, and Commerce Minister Hans Fischböck. The initiative had not come from Abs but rather from Joham, although the two men were in complete agreement, and Joham conducted the initial negotiations "because the CA had the interest in the transaction."[73] These negotiations probably took place on March 20 or 21, and both Neumayer and Brauneis were prepared to support the proposal. Fischböck, however, developed reservations after consulting with Wilhelm Keppler, who had been installed by Göring as the Four Year Plan "Reich Plenipotentiary for Austria" and who had responded negatively.[74] For the time being, the Deutsche Bank was advised that the acquisition of the shares "did not appear advisable in the present moment."[75] Certainly disappointed, but obviously undaunted, Joham then proposed that the two banks sign a "friendship pact" to confirm their alliance and intentions.

This rather remarkable document went through a number of iterations before being signed in Vienna on March 26, 1938, by Abs and Pollems for the Deutsche Bank and Joham and Heller for the CA.[76] The preamble stressed the decade-long friendship of the two banks and the membership of the Deutsche Bank on the CA administrative council, somewhat an exaggeration because the long-term relationship had been with the Wiener Bankverein. The agreement itself was attributed to the discussions on March 4–5 and then, at the invitation of the CA, to those between March 17 and 26. According to the first section of the pact, the Deutsche Bank, "in pursuance of a proposal by the Creditanstalt," and subject to the

---

70 ÖStA/AdR, BMF, Allgem. Reihe 1938, 32864/1938.
71 See DB, B 51, the remarks on the balance sheet of the CA.
72 Ibid., memorandum of March 31, 1938.

73 Ibid.
74 See also the secret internal report at the Deutsche Bank by Director Eduard Mosler for Director Hans Rummel, March 22, 1938, ibid.
75 Ibid., memorandum of March 31, 1938.
76 The final signed version, on which the following discussion is based, is in ibid.

approval of the Reich Economics Ministry, declared itself ready to purchase up to the following number of common and preferred shares: 120,000 CA common shares owned by the Land of Austria; 20,000 CA common shares in the possession of the Austrian National Bank; 50,000 common shares of the CA in the possession of the Österreichische Industriekredit-Aktiengesellschaft; 43,032 preferred shares of the CA from the CA's pension fund. Taken together, these shares amounted to 51 percent of the capital of the CA, and the two sides therefore hastened to declare that "in the interest of the economy of the Land of Austria, it is viewed as necessary that the Creditanstalt remains as an independent private bank run by the management board according to commercial and economic principles."[77]

The second section of the pact detailed the services the Deutsche Bank was prepared to provide to assist the CA in adjusting to the economic and legal conditions created by the Anschluss. This included the sending of personnel from the Deutsche Bank to assist the CA in foreign exchange matters, legal and tax issues, accounting problems, and other areas where help could be given. At the same time, the bank was prepared to bring personnel from the CA to the Deutsche Bank and its branches to become acquainted with German conditions and how to function under them. The Deutsche Bank also declared itself willing to promote the liquidity of the CA by offering to set aside 20 million RM to participate in credits of 1 million RM or more already granted by the CA; additionally, it was willing to offer up to 10 million RM to cover temporary cash needs at the best bank terms, to share its credit lines with the CA with its foreign corresponding banks for the purchase of raw materials needed by the Austrian economy, and to invite the CA to participate in Deutsche Bank credit and financing projects in Austria of 1 million RM or more. Reciprocally, the third section of the pact stipulated that the CA was to favor the Deutsche Bank for all credit and financing

projects in Austria where it was seeking a partner and to welcome the participation of the Deutsche Bank in all such ventures amounting to more than 1 million RM. In general, the pact provided that the two banks favor one another in all relevant business matters and cooperate in the launching of issues on the stock exchanges and in representations to the authorities. Finally, and of exceptional importance given past history and present intentions, "both concluding parties believe that Vienna should have a special place for the carrying out of Greater German industrial and commercial business. In this sense, providing the existence of an appropriate material basis in its relations to the Creditanstalt, the Deutsche Bank, while considering the special traditional bonds to Berlin, will wherever possible pursue its business in Southeast Europe via Vienna."[78]

This was an extraordinarily important provision because it meant that the Deutsche Bank recognized the traditional connections between the CA and its southern neighbors, was prepared to use the CA as its proxy wherever appropriate, and thus offered the CA a chance to recapture some of the position lost by Austria in 1918 under the protective wings of Germany's largest bank. It should not be thought, however, that this was some kind of charitable exercise on the part of the Deutsche Bank, whose representatives made clear that "an appropriate material basis" for such an arrangement was "a participation of at least 75 percent" because "the Deutsche Bank must also be in the position to be able to decide on changes in the statutes without having to be dependent on the agreement of the other shareholders."[79] Obviously, therefore, more was at stake than a simple takeover of the 51 percent of the shares discussed in Section 1 of the pact because, if these plans for cooperation in Southeast Europe were realized, then the Deutsche Bank expected to own three-quarters of the shares. Naturally this was left unstated in the pact, but Joham and his colleagues were aware of the long-term intentions of their partner. That said, Joham could hardly

77 Ibid.

78 Ibid.
79 Ibid., memorandum of March 31, 1938.

be accused of "selling out" to the Deutsche Bank because he would be gaining protection and support in a dangerous environment, and his operation radius would also be increased. Joham made clear that asking the Deutsche Bank to join in credit and finance transactions amounting to more than 1 million RM[80] was a decision that the CA had to make, but he hastened to add that, in principle, such requests would be made. The reality was that the CA needed the capital and needed a powerful protector, and Joham was quite ready to seek the support of the authorities for the friendship pact and to join with the Deutsche Bank in announcing their strengthened relationship. When informed of the agreement, Neumayer and Brauneis hastily gave their approval, and Fischböck did likewise by telephone on March 26 after consulting with Hasslacher and Heller. Not only Joham, therefore, but also the leading persons at the CA stood behind the projected arrangement as did leading persons in what was left of the Austrian National Socialist government.[81]

At the same time, those involved in the formulation and signing of the friendship pact were becoming aware that they were facing both competition and hostility as they undertook what also had been intended to be a preemptive measure. Vienna was filled with German bankers after the Anschluss, and they observed one another but were also being observed with concern from on high. On March 19, Abs's colleagues at the Deutsche Bank sent him an urgent telegram reporting that, as it was sarcastically put, "two neighbors" had already laid claim on CA shares and urging Abs to place an option on the shares in the pension fund held by the Creditanstalt as well as the shares held by the Creditanstalt on its own account.[82] The "neighbors" in question were Carl Goetz of the Dresdner Bank and Otto Christian Fischer, head of the Reichs-Kredit-Gesellschaft (RKG) and also head of the Reich Group for Banking.

There is no evidence that the Dresdner Bank had its eyes on these shares, its exclusive concentration appearing to be on the Mercurbank and its intended merger with the Länderbank. Otto Christian Fischer, however, showed considerable interest in what all his colleagues were doing, suggesting for example that special commissars be appointed to watch over the still French-owned Central European Länderbank to prevent the shifting of capital resources.[83] Fischer's interlocutors at the RWM could not quite figure out what he wanted, an expansion of the RKG or a bigger role for the Reich Group. In any case, in a memorandum of March 24, the RWM took the position that the appointment of special commissars or the engagement of the Reich Group was unnecessary. The integration of the Austrian banking system seemed to offer few problems: the Mercurbank was already in the hands of the Dresdner Bank; the Länderbank was under surveillance; the Creditanstalt appeared under control, the writer of the memorandum correctly noting that the Jewish management board directors had departed and erroneously believing that Joham had departed as well. To be sure, the RWM was aware that representatives of the major Berlin banks had been actively negotiating in Vienna for the previous ten days, that Abs and Rummel had been seen there, and that Karl Rasche and Hans Pilder had also been there for some time. In any case, the RWM official had the impression that "Herr Fischer fears that he will be presented with a fait accompli through the results of the negotiations going on among the great banks and that he is now trying, through his position as head of the Reich Group for Banking, to gain influence."[84]

It was not only in that capacity, however, that Fischer was interested in asserting his position. On March 12, 1938, that is, one day after the

---

[80] The memorandum of March 31 refers to Schilling, and this is in error because the pact refers to RM, ibid.

[81] Ibid.

[82] Ibid., Deutsche Bank to Abs, March 19, 1938.

[83] RGVA Moscow, 1458/2/104, Bl. 3, Fischer to Funk, March 19, 1938.

[84] Ibid., 1458/2/77, Bl. 19–21, memorandum, March 24, 1938. On Fischer, see Harold James, *Verbandspolitik im Nationalsozialismus. Von der Interessenvertretung zur Wirtschaftsgruppe. Der Centralverband des Deutschen Bank- und Bankiergewerbes 1932–1945* (Munich 2001), pp. 53–57, 199–208.

entry of German troops into Austria, Alfred Olscher of the VIAG, which owned the RKG, sent a letter to Keppler congratulating him on his role in the Anschluss. They had already in the past discussed various business issues connected with Austria, but Olscher pointed out that the Austrian banking situation deserved special attention. The Creditanstalt, the majority of whose shares belonged to the Austrian state, still presented difficulties, and there were also "difficulties" in the personnel of the management board. If Keppler had any intention of doing anything about these problems, Olscher wanted to assure Keppler that the VIAG and the RKG were prepared to offer their services in every possible way. Not only did the RKG have expert personnel for currency questions, but Directors Fischer and Rohdewald of the RKG, according to Olscher, also possessed expertise in foreign economic and business matters. Thus, from the very beginning, the VIAG and RKG had made themselves available for the solution of the CA's "difficulties."[85]

This personal engagement duly noted, Fischer certainly was correct in suspecting that both the Deutsche Bank and the Dresdner Bank were intent on preempting the situation. Thus, when the Dresdner Bank sent out a circular announcing its relations to the Mercurbank and urging its business friends to use its services, Abs's colleagues sent him a copy in Vienna on March 25 and urged him to consult with the CA about sending out a similar announcement on the Deutsche Bank–CA connection. This was promptly done and, on March 28, the branches of the Deutsche Bank announced the relationship, urging its friends and customers to use the services of the CA, the largest private bank in Austria, and stressing the CA's connections in the Balkans. Director Mosler made a point of mentioning the close relationship of the two banks publicly at the general shareholders' meeting of the Deutsche Bank on April 6.[86] At the end of March,

therefore, things appeared to be going swimmingly with the plans of the Deutsche Bank and the CA. This was reflected in an exchange of letters between Abs and Joham that simply oozed with satisfaction and mutual admiration. Joham wrote on March 28, thanking Abs for his role in making their pact a reality and for chairing the shareholders' meeting, and asserted that their pact would serve the economy in the Greater German realm. He especially hoped that they would realize their plans in Southeast Europe. Abs responded on April 1, thanking Joham and his colleagues for their hospitality, agreeing with him fully on the economic benefits their pact would bring, expressing the hope that it would soon receive the necessary official proposal, and stating the belief that the CA would be able to expand its role with great success in Southeast Europe "when the preconditions that were discussed for our support in your Southeast Europe business are created in the foreseeable future."[87]

Nevertheless, Abs had certainly been aware from the outset that the intimate connection he was trying to forge with the CA could call forth opposition and needed legitimation. For this reason, he asked Ernst W. Schmidt, the head of the Economic Analysis Section of the Deutsche Bank, to draft a position paper dealing with the question. Schmidt began with a paean to the German banking system, which, in his view, had developed "in lively interchange with the development of the state and the economy."[88] The major banks, with their system of branches, had ensured an equitable distribution of credit and capital across the Reich. The spreading of this system to Austria thus required a special connection between these large banks and the banks of Austria that had, in Schmidt's view, to be close and personal and thus direct and based on the relationship between the large banks and individual Austrian banks. This meant that the responsibility for general business and credit

[85] PA Berlin, R 27506, Olscher to Keppler, March 12, 1938.

[86] See DB, B 11, for Mosler's remarks on April 6, 1938; see Deutsche Bank to Abs, March 25, 1938, and

ibid., B 51, circular of the Cologne branch of the Deutsche Bank, March 28, 1938.

[87] Ibid., Joham to Abs, March 28, 1938 and Abs to Joham, April 1, 1938.

[88] Ibid., P 6502, Bl. 49–53, Exposé, April 1, 1938.

policy "cannot be carried out in the framework of two completely independent institutions, but requires of necessity in one form or the other the placing of the smaller Austrian institution in the tow of the larger." Such dependence would be particularly beneficial for the Austrian side, according to Schmidt, because of Austria's shortage of capital. Through its subordination to a major German bank, the Austrian bank would automatically have access to the capital resources of its German ally, and the two sides could also work together in the banking business in general, in foreign trade, and in the support of industrial enterprise. Schmidt insisted this in no way constituted "an expansion in the usual sense," that it was the Reich, not the Deutsche Bank, that could be said to have expanded, and that the two banks were similar structures because they both were major banks even if one was substantially smaller than the other. It was thus "a consolidation of two similar structures ... caused by the political Anschluss." The Creditanstalt, therefore, was not a regional bank, as some had argued, but rather a major bank, although this did not mean that the projected alliance meant an expansion of the major banks at the expense of other types of banks. There was no reason, argued Schmidt, that Austria should be excluded from having a major bank, although this certainly was not, in his opinion, incompatible with the regional bank concept.

It goes without saying that there was much special pleading and slippery argumentation in all this, and Abs, while basically accepting Schmidt's concept, nevertheless urged that he add some more concrete points of argument. He suggested, for example, that special mention be made of the need for effective representation in Berlin because of the strong centralization of economic policy under existing conditions. It was important, in Abs's view, to detail the business that the two banks had in common and to provide concrete evidence of their previous cooperation. Abs placed special emphasis on the importance of the foreign trade common to both banks; the representation of German interests by the Deutsche Bank in Bulgaria, Turkey, Holland, and Poland; and the CA's

strong presence in Hungary and Yugoslavia. He thought it important to note that the Deutsche Bank could offer the CA commercial credits through its corresponding banks abroad. Abs believed the prospects for personnel exchanges to be worthy of mention, but he was especially interested in something being said about the role of the Deutsche Bank in military contracting, above all with respect to credits for armaments and the air force. He clearly considered it crucial to be more specific about the preservation of the independence of the CA despite its integration with the Deutsche Bank, especially with respect to its special tasks arising from its individual structure resulting from Austrian conditions, this being an oblique reference to its role as an industrial concern, and about the special tasks of Vienna in the Balkans. Finally, Abs viewed it as essential to make reference to the fact that the privatization of the CA was in accordance with the general policy of banking sector reprivatization, but that one could not expect the privatization of the Austrian capital market in the foreseeable future. The CA would face great competition if it did not attach itself to a major German bank, and it followed that "the independence of Austrian industry would also be better served by means of an Austrian banking institution that depended on a German major bank."[89]

While the Deutsche Bank fortified itself with such arguments at the beginning of April without specifying to whom they were actually addressed, things began to go sour. Joham was arrested, then released but demoted, while Heller took over the general director position. On April 3, he had a long interview with Fischböck, who informed him that the political authorities had "serious reservations" about the friendship pact. Heller came away with the impression that one would now have to deal with the authorities directly and also informed Abs and the Deutsche Bank leaders in Berlin on the following day that the activities of the Mercurbank and the Dresdner Bank were now becoming a matter of great concern.[90]

89 Ibid., Comments by Abs for Schmidt, April 6, 1938.
90 Ibid., B 51, memorandum by Pohle of April 6, 1938.

It is difficult to tell how much Heller or those at the Deutsche Bank and the CA knew about the moves being made by Karl Rasche of the Dresdner Bank and the close connection between Rasche and Hans Kehrl, an ambitious and brutal technocrat who had headed the Textiles Section of the RWM and had been assigned to work with Keppler in the organization of the Austrian economy for the Four Year Plan. Mosler was aware of the plans for the Dresdner Bank–owned Mercurbank to take over the Viennese branch of the Central European Länderbank by March 30 at the latest, and Joham knew about them as well; he had told Baron von der Lippe on March 31 that there was little point in trying to discuss a possible arrangement with the CA.[91] Whether Heller or the others were aware that Rasche was seeking to acquire the big Austrian provincial banks and to gain the shares in certain public enterprises and that he was working hand in hand with Kehrl is less clear,[92] but the CA and the Deutsche Bank leadership were developing a strong sense that the Mercurbank was being especially favored by Keppler and the other relevant authorities in Austria.

No less disturbing, however, was the clear evidence of Keppler's hostility toward the Deutsche Bank and its goals in Austria. This came from Hans Steinbrink of the Flick concern, who was close to Keppler, being a member of his so-called circle and who also served as a contact man for the Deutsche Bank in its effort to find out what Keppler was thinking. Steinbrink saw Keppler on April 12 and spoke to Abs by phone on the following day, reporting, according to Abs's notes, that Keppler was "in a *very* miserable mood toward the Deutsche Bank. He – Steinbrink – does not know from where this mood comes. Keppler had literally said: 'D.B. wants to steal. Abs came with 20 men to Vienna in order to take over the CA.' Dr. Steinbrink then asked whether he knew Abs. K. denied knowing him. Steinbrink: But Abs is very new and unburdened by things for

which he, Keppler, might have had reason to reproach the D.B. in the past. Keppler said: Abs is actually the best of them all."[93] Steinbrink concluded by urging Abs to make personal contact with Keppler but also to consult with RWM State Secretary Rudolf Brinkmann about the situation.

It is not entirely easy to figure out exactly why Keppler had taken such a hard stance toward the Deutsche Bank and Abs. Part of it undoubtedly was the general hostility toward the big Berlin banks he already exhibited during the hearings on the banking system, the *Bank-Enquete*, in the fall of 1933, where Keppler sought to promote National Socialist banking principles.[94] More immediately, however, the favoritism toward the Dresdner Bank and Mercurbank and hostility toward the Deutsche Bank may at least in part have stemmed from the close cooperation between Keppler, the Austrian National Socialist leadership, and the Dresdner Bank prior to the Anschluss, when they sought to Aryanize the Mercurbank and use it as an instrument to penetrate Austria. The Deutsche Bank had not been very helpful in this penetration program and, indeed, had been criticized for failing to make its weight felt in Austria and abdicating potential influence there.[95] Even more pertinent perhaps was an incident involving Deutsche Bank director Hans Rummel, which he reported to Abs in connection with the Keppler problem. In October 1937, Rummel had a conversation with Edmund Veesenmayer, Keppler's adjutant, who asked that the Deutsche Bank do as much business with the Mercurbank as possible because it was German owned. Rummel responded that this would be difficult because

---

[91] See ibid., Mosler to Abs, March 30 and Chap. 5 in this volume, p. 419.

[92] See Chap. 5, pp. 422–423.

[93] DB, B 51, Abs's handwritten notes on conversations of April 11 and 13 with Steinbrink. Harold James confuses Steinbrink with Kienböck in "Banks and Business Politics in Germany," in: Francis R. Nicosia/Jonathan Heuner (eds.), *Business and Industry in Nazi Germany* (New York 2004), p. 58.

[94] See Kopper, *Bankenpolitik*, p. 93.

[95] *Documents on German Foreign Policy 1918–1945* (= DGFP), series C, vol. 2 (Washington, DC 1959), Nr. 451, memorandum by Habicht, May 14, 1934.

the Deutsche Bank had worked very closely with the Creditanstalt. Veesenmayer then suggested that they discuss the problem further, but nothing came of the matter. Manifestly, however, Rummel thought that this event was important in understanding the differences that were now arising.[96]

Nevertheless, it would be a mistake to overstress the significance of these experiences. The enthusiasm for the Dresdner Bank and the Mercurbank plans to take over the Länderbank, an institution in foreign ownership, was hardly surprising. While it would be absurd to take seriously the charge by Keppler, one of the regime's master plunderers, that Abs was a thief, there was a political goal at stake, namely, the desire of Keppler and Kehrl to prevent Germans from the "old Reich" from taking advantage of the new situation to buy up and take over Austrian assets, above all Austrian industrial firms, for a song. They were anxious also to win the support of the Austrian population by showing respect and concern for their interests, or at least so far as the situation would allow. As Kehrl later noted in his incredibly unapologetic postwar autobiography, they were bent on preventing German business interests, which were descending on Austria like "locusts," from carrying out the "colonization" of Austria.[97]

As Abs discovered, these motives were very much in play when he had a chance to talk matters over with Kehrl, who had been seeking an interview with Abs since April 4 and finally succeeded in having a meeting at the RWM on April 11. Kehrl began the conversation by saying that he wanted to talk to Abs about the "unfortunate negotiations in Vienna" and went on to declare, as Abs reported, "that it will not do that we purchase the shares of the Austrian

Creditanstalt from the holdings of the state [Bund] and in that way achieve full control over almost all of Austrian industry."[98] In the view of Kehrl and his associates, the government should hold on to the shares, especially because they were undervalued and it would be unbearable if a private purchaser were to pocket the profit. Kehrl also could not understand how the pact with the CA could have been made without prior consultation with the relevant authorities. When Abs interjected that he found these reproaches incomprehensible, Kehrl insisted he was not being reproachful but rather simply making it clear that an agreement could not be signed with the CA determining the disposition of the shares.

It is hard to see how Abs could not have viewed these remarks as anything but a reproach, but he nevertheless defended himself by pointing out that the pact explicitly stated that its provisions were subject to the review of the authorities and that the Deutsche Bank was simply responding to a proposal by the CA by declaring its willingness to take over the shares. No provision had been made with respect to price, and there had been consultations with the ministries in Vienna, the National Bank, and authorities in Berlin. Kehrl claimed that he did not know about this but nevertheless insisted that they should also have consulted with the most important persons in Berlin, to which Abs replied that they would have been happy to do so if they knew whom to contact and where. Kehrl urged a meeting with Keppler, although he admitted that this could not take place until after the Easter holiday, thus giving Abs an opportunity to remind Kehrl that he had been trying to see Keppler for some time but that he knew Keppler was dealing with much more important tasks and did not think he should be disturbed by questions of lesser import.

This seems quite disingenuous because the record shows consultations with Neumayer, Brauneis, and Fischböck, with Fischböck being

96 DB, B 51, memorandum by Pohle for Abs, April 13, 1938.
97 See Hans Kehrl, *Krisenmanager im Dritten Reich. 6 Jahre Frieden– 6 Jahre Krieg. Erinnerungen* (Düsseldorf 1973), pp. 118–138, esp. pp. 129–132. It is impossible not to agree with Kopper, *Bankenpolitik*, p. 299, N 1083, that the authors of the postwar report on the Deutsche Bank for OMGUS made the error of identifying themselves with Keppler's charge.
98 DB, B 51, Abs sent his report on the meeting to Director Karl Kimmich on April 12. The quotations and discussion included later in this passage are from these documents.

the bearer of negative reactions to the pact. In any case, Kehrl told Abs that there had been much discussion of the Deutsche Bank–CA negotiations in Berlin and that he, Kehrl, "had to make considerable effort to stand up for me [Abs], since he knows me and my negotiating style for years." Nevertheless, Kehrl felt that Abs simply had to understand that gaining control of the CA meant gaining influence over Austrian industry. Abs categorically denied any such ambition, pointing out "that we do not have the slightest ambition with respect to the industrial holdings. What is of greatest importance for us is only to engage in pure banking business in Austria, and it is impossible that this be rightfully denied to us over the long run.… If we should attain influence over the Creditanstalt through the takeover of shares, then our goal would only be to lead the Creditanstalt according to the kind of sound banking principles that are the rule with us. What interests us is not any influence over industry but rather simple everyday banking business." Kehrl readily conceded that one could not deny the Deutsche Bank the right to do banking business in Austria but pointed out that the friendship pact had placed the taking over of shares very much in the foreground, and that Joham had been made somewhat "laughable" by having his signature on the document.

Abs claimed that the negotiations were conducted with the "entire" CA management board and not just Joham, although this certainly was stretching things a bit because Heller was the only other member of the board left at the time and the other board members involved were providers of information and not negotiators. He also claimed that the pact had been made so detailed in order to prevent any objections and pointed to all the provisions made for the improvement of the CA's liquidity. Kehrl did not contest this anymore than he did the traditional friendship between the banks, but he insisted that the detailed discussion of the share takeover preceding the list of benefits the Deutsche Bank would provide effectively meant that the latter depended on the Creditanstalt. Abs claimed, however, that these services were in no way linked to the

taking over of shares, and that such a linkage only existed in the section dealing on business in Southeast Europe, where Abs argued, it was perfectly sensible for the Deutsche Bank to want to have an influence over the CA if it were to turn over some of its active business to that bank. This made some sense to Kehrl who, however, pointed out that he did not have a copy of the pact before him. If he did, however, then he might have found Abs rather disingenuous on this point too; it is hard to see how the Deutsche Bank was supposed to acquire a larger interest in the CA without first gaining control of the shares mentioned in the first part of the pact and then building on those holdings.

In the last analysis, however, Abs thought that the key issue for Kehrl was the industrial holdings of the CA. Kehrl did indeed charge that the Deutsche Bank negotiators had actually discussed the taking over of CA holdings, while Abs claimed that they had not discussed a single holding or packet of shares. Kehrl expressed astonishment about this, mentioning the Steyr-Daimler-Puch works in particular, to which Abs retorted that there had been no such discussion. The discussion ended with Abs asking that Kehrl relay their conversation to Keppler and to express the desire to meet with Keppler personally.

It is rather obvious that Abs was trying to present the friendship pact in the best possible and most innocent light, claiming nothing but goodwill toward the CA and emphasizing the fact that the CA had taken the initiative and that the Deutsche Bank had no ulterior motives. The fact that the initiative came from Joham and the CA certainly was convenient, and there was no good reason for Abs not to follow up on what was a promising opportunity. Both Abs and Joham were conscious of the fact that the details of their agreement were subject to review, but no one can accuse them of seeking out those authorities who might have been most critical or concerned about the effort to achieve Deutsche Bank majority control over the CA, which is to be found both at the beginning and at the end of the friendship pact. At the same time, the use of Fischböck, who was known to Joham, as an intermediary with

Keppler and Kehrl, and Abs's similar employment of Steinbrink suggests that they were at a disadvantage in dealing with Keppler and Kehrl. Rasche of the Dresdner Bank did not have such problems in taking his initiatives because he had direct access to Keppler and Kehrl. The suspicions of the Deutsche Bank were very great, however, and the pact was bound to call forth the worst possible construction on what Abs and Joham were about.

Furthermore, despite Abs's claims to the contrary, the industrial holdings of the CA were of immense significance. While Abs may be credited with telling the truth when he said that he was primarily interested in doing normal banking business in Austria, he was hardly innocent about the fact that such banking business, insofar as the CA was involved, inevitably meant engagement with the CA's industrial holdings. An important part of the information provided by the CA to the Deutsche Bank in the negotiations pertained to very specific industrial holdings. Everyone knew that German companies were showing great interest in buying up Austrian industrial enterprises and that German banks would profit from acting as intermediaries in such arrangements. There is no evidence that this was a subject of discussion in the negotiations, but such matters certainly were discussed in the natural course of business. Director Rummel, for example, reported that the Bayerische Motoren-Werke were showing interest in Steyr-Daimler-Puch, as did Joham. Neither Rummel nor Joham thought the idea discussable at the moment, but Rummel, who was on the supervisory board of BMW, did not like the idea, feeling that the company had enough to do as is, while Joham made clear that he would take no initiative in the matter.[99] Even more revealing, however, was a conversation between Abs and Heller in Berlin on April 6, where Abs inquired about the availability of a large Austrian coal company in which a German coal company might invest. Heller pointed out that the Kohlenhandelsgesellschaft in Vienna was owned jointly by the CA and

the Montana AG, but that the Montana was non-Aryan and would have to sell its shares. The German Klöckner concern had already expressed interest, but Heller considered that solution undesirable because the company would lose its freedom of action at a time when it was making very high profits. Heller promised to look around, however, to see if he could find something for the Deutsche Erdöl AG, which was a customer of the Deutsche Bank, and also promised to perform similar services in connection with Fanto, an oil refiner, and look for German oil and gasoline companies that might be interested in acquiring it.[100] The issue of the CA's industrial holdings, therefore, could hardly be dismissed as easily as Abs pretended.

While Abs was hoping and waiting for an interview with Keppler, however, Heller and Friedl had a very discouraging interview with Fischböck on April 14. Heller reported to Abs by phone that Fischböck had officially informed him that Keppler had turned down the friendship pact. Keppler's letter claimed that after consulting with the Reichsbank, the Reich Finance Ministry, and the Reich Economics Ministry, it had been decided that the majority of the shares held by the Land of Austria would remain in its possession. There was some thought of giving minority blocks of shares to the Reichsbank, the Deutsche Bank, and the RKG and/or the VIAG. Abs had already heard much of this from Joham the previous evening, and in Joham's report, the Deutsche Bank had not even been mentioned as a potential holder of shares. The bad news did not stop here, however; Fischböck, having finished reporting on Keppler's letter, went on to inform Heller and Friedl confidentially that he had himself spoken to various persons in the ministries as well as to Bank Commissar Friedrich Ernst and Reichsbank President Schacht and discovered that they too were opposed to a close connection between the Deutsche Bank and the CA. Furthermore, Fischböck claimed that the Deutsche Bank management had also been informed and that Schacht had told Abs this personally. Abs found

99 Ibid., Note by Pohle on a conversation with Rummel, April 13, 1938.

100 Ibid., Note by Pohle on meeting between Abs and Heller, April 6, 1938.

this aspect of the report rather odd because he had not spoken to Schacht since the beginning of the year. Whatever the case, Fischböck stressed that no one opposed a continuing friendship between the CA and the Deutsche Bank and that everyone insisted on maintaining the CA's independence.[101]

Fischböck had by no means finished providing bad news, however; he then went on to urge the CA management to be ready to participate in discussions about giving up at least two of the CA's affiliated banks, which were to go over to the Mercurbank, then in the process of acquiring the Länderbank. There were to be only two big banks in Austria, the chief bank being the CA, but the Mercurbank was intended to play a major role as well and was to develop its network of branches by taking over the affiliates of the CA. The other banks would more or less disappear, and the CA would take over the banking business of the Österreichische Industriekredit AG. The CA was to begin working closely with the RKG and the VIAG. Fischböck apparently paid no attention whatever to business in Southeast Europe, which Abs had repeatedly emphasized, but he did stress that the big Berlin banks were not going to be allowed to set up their own branches in Austria.

Heller had been anxious to report this information right away to Abs because he and his colleagues were "*very* troubled and confused" by what they had heard, and took the opportunity to express their gratitude to the Deutsche Bank for its friendship and support. Abs reciprocated by making clear he intended to act in the spirit of their friendship, especially because he was the only representative of a large Berlin bank on the administrative board, and he told Heller that he was planning meetings with the authorities in Berlin as well as with Keppler, and he also urged Heller and his colleagues to come to Berlin for discussions.

Abs himself was a bit confused at this point because there were contradictions between what Joham and Heller had told him about

the conversation with Fischböck along with the question as to where all the claimants to CA shares suddenly had come from. Some of the answers came on April 19, when Abs and Mosler had an interview with Schacht, whom they informed about their dealings with the CA. Schacht told them that the Gold Discount Bank, a subsidiary of the Reichsbank created in 1924 at the end of the inflation that had held the shares of the Dresdner Bank for the Reich until 1937 and was heavily engaged in handling monetary and financial "arrangements" for emigrating Jews, had wished to acquire the CA shares but was no longer under consideration. Then the Reichs-Kredit-Anstalt and the VIAG had applied to take over the shares held by the Austrian National Bank and the pension fund. In any case, the Austrian National Bank was to be liquidated, and its assets, including the CA shares, were to become the property of the Reich.[102]

Obviously a great deal had been transpiring without the knowledge of Abs and his colleagues, and Abs was anxious to know from whence the initiatives were coming and what role, if any, the CA was playing in the new situation. When Joham called to find out if Abs had seen Schacht, Abs replied affirmatively but did not provide any information about what Schacht had actually said. He told Joham that a meeting with Heller to discuss the Deutsche Bank–CA relationship would be necessary, but he first wanted to see others at the Reichsbank and in the ministries and to talk to Keppler. He asked Joham to keep this in strictest confidence and, at the same time, tried to clear up the contradictions between the reports of Heller and Joham on the meeting with Fischböck. Joham confirmed that Fischböck actually claimed that there was opposition to a deepening of the Deutsche Bank–CA relationship, that Fischböck had negotiated directly with the ministries and the Reichsbank, including with Schacht, and that there was some willingness to have the Deutsche Bank get a minority share in the CA along with the Reichsbank, the RKG, and/or

---

[101] Ibid., Abs's notes on a telephone call from Heller on April 15, 1938.

[102] Ibid., memo by Mosler, April 20, 1938.

the VIAG.[103] The negative position of Keppler and Fischböck was confirmed even more forcefully on April 23, when the CA informed Abs that the rejection of the friendship pact had been sent in writing by Fischböck's office, which also instructed the CA not to engage in any further negotiations with respect to it.[104]

At the end of April, the Deutsche Bank seems to have lost the initiative completely and was even being pushed aside, a situation made all the more evident by the news that the CA had offered preferred shares to the VIAG. When Abs expressed astonishment over this to Joham on May 4 and pointed out that the VIAG was simply serving the interests of the RKG, Joham inquired whether the Deutsche Bank might not get into contact with the VIAG about the entire matter. Abs, however, made clear that it had no reason to do so and that "the RKG must get into contact with us if it places any value on the friendship of the Deutsche Bank."[105] At the same time, the Deutsche Bank telegraphed the CA that the offer of the shares was incompatible with the friendship pact, to which the CA replied that the offer was made because of the "wish from on high" and expressed the hope that the Deutsche Bank would maintain its friendship with the CA.[106]

The reality was that the CA did not have freedom of action, and this was made plain when Mosler paid a visit to Ministerial Director Hugo Berger of the Finance Ministry, with whom Mosler had originally consulted on March 19 while the friendship pact was being negotiated in Vienna. Mosler expressed disappointment that 42,000 CA shares from the pension fund and another 18,000 shares held by the CA itself were being offered to the VIAG. He reminded Berger of the traditional relationship between the Deutsche Bank and Disconto-Gesellschaft and the CA and of the fact that the Deutsche Bank had, on the invitation of the CA itself, offered to purchase the shares and thus had a

prior option. He added that the friendship pact had the approval of "all the Austrian authorities," which was to say the least something of an exaggeration. Berger responded by informing Mosler that the decision about the shares had been made very shortly after their last conversation on March 19, and the Deutsche Bank was just going to have to accept this reality. In addition, it was going to have to swallow some other new developments, namely, that the VIAG and the RKG, and yet "another bank" – the Commerzbank – were going to get seats on the administrative board of the CA. Mosler was understandably furious and pointed out that the CA had been unfairly cut out of the acquisition of the shares. He insisted that the Deutsche Bank would have to be given permission to set up branches in Vienna and elsewhere in Austria under these circumstances because, as a bank with branches throughout the Reich, it could not be excluded from the newly acquired Austria. Berger did not respond to this except to say that the Deutsche Bank did not need such branches because it had a seat on the CA administrative board. Thus, the friendship pact on which the Deutsche Bank had counted for establishing its position in Austria had been rejected; the Deutsche Bank had been denied the right to bid for the CA shares it had hoped to acquire; and now it was being denied the right to seek an alternative in establishing its own branches in Austria. And finally, to add insult to injury, the Deutsche Bank was going to lose its exclusive position as the only major Berlin bank on the CA administrative council and also to have to swallow a strong VIAG presence on the council as well.[107]

It was not simple for the Deutsche Bank leadership to know just how and where to counterattack under these circumstances. It faced opponents with different agendas who had successfully mounted initiatives behind its back. The Austrian National Socialists certainly were not of one mind. On May 12, Director Heinz Osterwind, who was looking after Deutsche Bank interests in Vienna, met with the National Socialist mayor of Vienna, Hermann

[103] Ibid., memorandum on telephone discussion between Abs and Joham, April 19, 1938.
[104] Ibid., CA to Abs, April 23, 1938.
[105] Ibid., memo by Abs, May 4, 1938.
[106] Ibid., Exchange of telegrams, May 4/5, 1938.

[107] Ibid., memorandum by Mosler, May 7, 1938.

Neubacher, an old Austrian National Socialist who had been in the wood business and had also been involved with urban communal housing. The primary subject was meant to be the program in Southeast Europe, an area where the Deutsche Bank was designated to play a major role and where Neubacher was soon to become heavily involved as well. When the discussion turned to the Deutsche Bank–CA relationship, Neubacher stated that he found recent developments incomprehensible. He did not think anything more could be done about the VIAG taking over the CA shares, but in his view this meant that the Deutsche Bank would have to look after its own interests by setting up its own Vienna branch. He promised to support this with Fischböck, and he thought it fit in well with the program of leaving "Austria to the Austrians."[108]

The problem was, however, that the Germans were ruling the roost in Austria despite all the protestations to the contrary, and for Joham the problem was to which Germans he was supposed to turn. He had heard that negotiations were taking place over Yugoslavia and especially over the Allgemeine Jugoslawische Bankverein in Berlin, a subject of obvious interest to him because the CA held a majority of the shares. This was one of the things that had brought him and Abs together in the first place, and his preference for working with the Deutsche Bank was clear. As Pohle reported on May 13, however, Joham had called to inform the Deutsche Bank that "the agency with which they are forced to work more closely, is extraordinarily interested in the Yugoslav business."[109] Obviously this was a reference to the VIAG and the RKG.

By this time, however, Abs had become aware that the competition in the Southeast European business was coming from the RKG and especially from Director August Rohdewald, who had transferred from the Dresdner Bank to the RKG in March 1938 and had developed a program for the RKG's expansion. Abs now sought both to undo the

blockage created by the ban on the friendship pact and to minimize the damage produced by the share transfer to the VIAG. The Deutsche Bank's Legal Section helped in the first effort by coming up with a finding on May 11, 1938, that the friendship pact did not require formal approval and could also therefore not be rejected by government authorities because no money or shares had changed hands. It was not a contract but rather a statement of intentions.[110] At the same time, Abs used his connections with the RWM to meet on May 14 with State Secretary Rudolf Brinkmann, who had recently been appointed second in command at the ministry, from where Abs returned loaded with support and ammunition. Brinkmann absolutely agreed that the friendship pact did not require governmental assent in its existing form and also insisted that Fischböck's contention that the Berlin authorities were opposed to a deepening of the Deutsche Bank–CA relationship was false, at least insofar as he was concerned. Furthermore, he was of one mind with Abs that the Deutsche Bank could not accept "that the Reichs-Kredit-Gesellschaft has lately sought, on the basis of the VIAG's holding of CA shares, to inject itself into the business of the CA, in particular, as a result of the ambition of Herr Rohdewald, to enter into the Southeast European business."[111] Brinkmann stated repeatedly that the function of the VIAG was to act as a trustee for the shares, and agreed that the Deutsche Bank had no reason to bring the RKG into its collaboration with the CA in Southeast Europe. Abs thus found it possible to press the point that the Deutsche Bank viewed Vienna as its bridge to Southeast Europe and that its collaboration with the CA toward this end depended on a financial foundation because it could not work with a bank over which it had no influence. He noted that this view was held by all those who understood the economic circumstances in Vienna, and that the measures so far taken and current tendencies would lead to "the impossible situation that the Deutsche Bank would be compelled

---

108 Ibid., report by Pollems on a conversation with Osterwind, May 12, 1938.
109 Ibid., Note by Pohle, May 13, 1938.

110 Ibid., Note by Legal Section, May 11, 1938.
111 Ibid., memorandum by Pollems, May 14, 1938.

in the future pursuit of its South East European interests to constantly go around or jump over the Ostmark and the Vienna center."[112]

The conversation with Brinkmann gave Abs considerable leverage with Joham, who was in the middle of the tug-of-war between the Deutsche Bank and its supporters and the RKG. This became evident when Joham called on May 14 to report that Rohdewald had inquired as to whether any agreement had been made with respect to the CA's stake in the Jugoslawischer Bankverein and had expressed distress that the Deutsche Bank and the Dresdner Bank had been carrying on discussions about the Yugoslav bank as if it was their business. Abs disregarded this news and instead turned to the information he had received from Joham and Heller concerning Fischböck's claims that the authorities in Berlin were opposed to the development of the Deutsche Bank–CA friendship. When Joham tried to retreat a bit and point out that the objection that had been raised was to "too close a friendship" based on capital participation, Abs told Joham that he would be interested to learn that they had made inquiries with Schacht, the RFM, and the RWM, and they all claimed that they were totally ignorant of ever having taken such a position. What this meant is that Fischböck had either lied about or exaggerated what he had heard in Berlin. Whatever the case, the Deutsche Bank was now on the offensive. It had told the VIAG that the time had come for an understanding about the CA, but the VIAG had not responded thus far. Despite the recent difficulties, the Deutsche Bank was prepared to pursue an "intimate friendship" with the Creditanstalt, but it did not intend to ask favors from others in the process. Abs had been told that the VIAG was acting as a trustee for the Reich in its holding of CA shares, and this did not entitle it to thrust the RKG upon the CA. The VIAG had to respect the friendship between the Deutsche Bank and the CA, and Abs hastened to note that the friendship pact did not require official permission. Abs asked, therefore,

that Joham be very cautious in entering into agreements and to make no concessions to the RKG, and pointed out that Keppler had gone too far in rejecting the friendship pact and presenting the RKG to the CA as a partner. When Joham indicated that they were suffering under the situation and that it was hardly feasible to put up resistance, Abs declared that "it is out of the question for us that we share with others. One can certainly discuss setting up spheres of interest and common business. Otherwise we must go our own way."[113] The message was quite clear. Either Joham would pursue a dilatory policy with respect to RKG demands and work with the Deutsche Bank under the assumption that the VIAG was not an owner of the CA but rather a trustee, or the Deutsche Bank would go it alone.

This by no means settled matters for the other side, however, because the RKG had a rather different interpretation of the taking over of the shares by the VIAG. Thus, on May 21, Director Otto Neubaur of the RKG, in a telephone conversation with Deutsche Bank director Hans-Alfons Simon, then in Vienna, claimed that the taking over of the CA shares meant that the shares could be transferred to the RKG, the Commerzbank, and the Deutsche Bank, so that these three banks could then form a condominium in Austria, Southeast Europe, and, in particular, Hungary, and use the CA as their instrument for this common purpose. Rohdewald had a "comprehensive program" for creating a systematic regulation of the division of these areas among the three banks, a matter that was to be discussed in Berlin after Whitsuntide. Neubaur also informed Simon that the branches of the Steiermärkische Escompte Bank and the entire Bank für Oberösterreich und Salzburg were to be separated from the CA and turned over to the Mercurbank in order to strengthen it.[114]

Despite such disturbing news, the Byzantine character of the political situation in Vienna

[113] Ibid., notes on the conversation May 14 by Pollems, dated May 17, 1938.
[114] NARA, RG 407, Box 1030, 270/69/23/01, memorandum by Mosler on report by Simon about the conversation, May 21, 1938.
[112] Ibid.

was beginning to alter its configuration and this was having some favorable repercussions for the Deutsche Bank. Of particular importance was the appointment of the former Gauleiter of the Saar, Josef Bürckel, as Reich Commissar for the Reunification of Austria and the Reich on April 23, 1938, a post granted him as a reward for his services in organizing the plebiscite of April 10. Bürckel did not take well to competition and had his own band of officials. The most prominent were Karl Barth, who served as a political advisor, and Rudolf Kratz, who dealt with administrative and economic affairs. The more Bürckel took control of affairs in Vienna, the more Keppler was pushed to the sidelines. Initially, he counted on Göring in the hope of retaining his position in economic matters, but at the turn of the year he learned that Hitler had decided to relieve him of his position as Reich Plenipotentiary for Austria and dissolve his office. Shortly afterward, he left Vienna to perform other functions for Göring and the Four Year Plan.[115]

A complementary process was taking place in Berlin, where the RWM was turning its back on Keppler's plans, while those evinced in the Deutsche Bank–CA combination were viewed as being more in tune with those of the ministry. This had already been evident in the discussion between State Secretary Brinkmann and Abs, and the former conveyed this message to Party and local officials in Vienna. According to Brinkmann, Keppler had been behind the idea of turning the CA over to the RKG, and Brinkmann took a dim view of the proposal: "This project is completely impossible because the Austrian Creditanstalt is the only institution that could drive forward the German economic expansion into the Southeast. There are great plans in motion, in particular the plan to strive for a customs union and also as far as

possible a currency alignment with Yugoslavia. For this one needs an institution that is not only established in the Southeast already but also offers the necessary practical and personnel qualifications. That is the Deutsche Bank; no other comes into question."[116]

This shift to the Deutsche Bank side was already evident in a report of May 30 by Joachim Riehle of the Banking Section of the RWM on negotiations and interviews in Vienna. In an interview with Kratz the latter pointed out that there was much irritation in Vienna at the favor shown the Mercurbank and incomprehension over the treatment of the Deutsche Bank, whose interests in the Balkans required either an arrangement with the CA or a branch of its own. When Riehle asked who was in charge of economic matters in Austria, Kratz told him it was Bürckel. When Riehle talked to Joham, however, the latter claimed the key person was Keppler, who had already forced the CA to give up important industrial holdings – a matter to be discussed later in this study – and who had told the CA that it would have to give up branches and subsidiary banks to the Mercurbank. Another angle was provided by Fischböck – since May 30 minister for economics and labor and for finance in an evaporating Austrian government – who wanted to strengthen the CA by giving it the entire mortgage bank sector, a proposition that Riehle rejected on the grounds that other plans had been made for these institutions. Last, Riehle spoke to Kehrl, who advocated setting up two large regional banks in Austria and thought that the Mercurbank needed to be strengthened by taking over regional banks and their branches. Riehle then informed Kehrl, however, that the RWM and the banking commissar opposed any changes until they had surveyed the situation. Riehle shared this view and felt it important to take the banking needs of the Land of Austria into account, but also to ensure that the major German banks had satisfactory representation in Vienna. Kehrl seemed to think that the Deutsche Bank's administrative board seat

---

[115] See Radomir V. Ludža, "Die Strukturen der Nationalsozialistischen Herrschaft in Österreich," in: Gerald Stourz/Birgitta Zaar (eds.), *Österreich, Deutschland und die Mächte. Internationale und Österreichische Aspekte des "Anschlusses" vom März 1938* (Vienna 1990), pp. 471–492. See also, PA Berlin, R 27506, Keppler to Eberhardt, May 19, 1938, and Keppler to Ermert, June 2, 1938.

[116] ÖStA/AdR, Bürckel-Materie, Box 92, 2165/0, Vol. 1, Kratz memorandum, May 16, 1938.

on the VIAG was "sufficient representation," an attitude that was questioned by those who read Riehle's report in Berlin. Insofar as the VIAG shares were concerned, Fischböck pointed out that the choice had been between having the Land of Austria take them over or placing them with the VIAG. The VIAG was chosen for the simple reason that the Land of Austria was going to be dissolved. Apparently, Fischböck's chief goal with respect to these shares was to have them sold to the public, and this was why the VIAG's role was defined as a trustee for the shares rather than as their owner.[117]

Be that as it may, Joham and the CA had been forced in April and May to negotiate with the VIAG and its representatives as well as authorities in Vienna and Berlin about the transfers of the various CA shares and assets held by the former government and its institutions. By the end of May, matters had been settled, and, as Abs had been complaining, the VIAG takeover of CA shares was substantially greater than was initially anticipated. The legal basis for the take-over of the shares held by the Land of Austria and the National Bank was the law of March 13, 1938, incorporating Austria into the Reich and the law of March 17, 1938, under which the Austrian National Bank was liquidated and its assets turned over to the Reichsbank. This meant that the VIAG now became the trustee for 142,852 common shares and 1,632 preferred shares of the CA, approximately 35 percent of its stock.[118]

Additionally, however, the VIAG took over other blocks of shares that were intended for its own account and not to be held in trust that, when combined, were of almost equal value to the government holdings just described. The acquisition of these holdings was connected with the intended liquidation of the Industriekredit AG, which had belonged to the National Bank since the restructuring of the Niederösterreichische Escompte-Gesellschaft.[119] The liquidation was ordered on April 23, 1938, by the Reich Finance Ministry, which took over all the assets of the Industriekredit, and was conducted in cooperation with the VIAG acting as trustee for the ministry. The shares of the CA were to be transferred to the VIAG as part of its capital share increase scheduled for May 1938. Additionally, there was to be an exchange of shares between those held by the Industriekredit and those held by the CA, with the exchanged CA shares also included as assets in the VIAG capital share increase. The remaining shares of the Industriekredit were to be sold off with the assistance of the CA.[120]

This became the basis for an agreement between the VIAG and the CA at the end of April 1938, whereby the CA was made its partner and trustee in the liquidation of the Industriekredit and received accounts due from and shares held in various industrial enterprises of no interest to the VIAG. The bulk of the industrial shares held by the Industriekredit, however, were sold off, by and large to German enterprises. In return for those assets, however, that the CA received and for the business services from which the CA would profit, the VIAG retained 49,014 CA shares previously left with the Industriekredit in order to boost its status along with CA shareholdings in important power companies of interest to the VIAG – 45,900 shares in the Österreichische Kraftwerke AG, 18,700 shares in the Tiroler

---

117 See RGVA Moscow, 1458/2/305, Bl. 21–23, Riehle's report of May 30, 1938. There is a second copy in 1458/2/61, where Kehrl's assertions are questioned in the margins. For Fischböck's motives and the trustee role of the VIAG, see NARA, RG 4–7, Roll 1030, 270/69/23/01, testimony by Otto Neubaur, Jan. 12, 1945.

118 This discussion is based on a variety of documents dealing with the transactions described. See ÖStA/AdR, BMF, Allgem. Reihe 1938, 39275/1938, the drafts of the various syndicate agreements involved and correspondence with Fischböck. BA-CA, CA-V, Joham reported on the transaction to the CA executive committee meeting of May 27, 1938. See also BA-CA, CA-TZ, Sekretariat grün, Box 25/CA 20a, b, c1, File 20c, the CA report on these transactions of Oct. 23, 1946.

119 See ibid., Box 28/CA 20 d-m, File 20h, the Report on the Österreichische Industriekredit Aktiengesellschaft of Oct. 24, 1946.

120 PA Berlin, R 27506, Agreement between the RFM (Schwerin von Krosigk) and the VIAG (Olscher and Schirner), April 23, 1938.

Wasserkraftwerke AG, and 102,500 shares in the Steirische Wasserkraft- und Elektrizitäts-AG. Most distressing to the CA – and the Deutsche Bank – however, was that the VIAG also demanded and received 43,032 preferred shares from the CA pension fund along with 18,000 preferred shares held in the CA-owned real estate enterprise, the Realitäten AG.[121]

Olscher had suddenly informed the CA in the middle of April that the RFM and RWM had asked that these assets be turned over to the VIAG. When the CA objected, Olscher pointed out that provisions of German corporate law that had already been introduced into Austria banned a corporation from owning its own shares or owning its own shares through a company it controlled. Violation of these regulations was punishable by law, and resistance on the part of the CA could also lead to difficulties with the government. At the same time, Olscher not only used his leverage as a "large shareholder" through the VIAG's control over the former shares of the Austrian government in the CA to declare that the VIAG wished to acquire the two blocks of shares, but he also informed the CA that the ministries in Berlin were opposed to disposing of the shares in any other way.[122] The CA leadership was also irritated that the compensation for these blocks of shares was calculated at their nominal value and thus below their market value. Whatever the case, the shares acquired by the VIAG on its own account, as noted earlier, were almost the equivalent of what it held in trust and gave it what was tantamount to a 70 percent stake in the CA. The only qualification to this, and it was to prove an important one, was that the Land of Austria retained a three-year option to take back its shares and to recover a majority holding in the CA. The CA leadership undoubtedly felt that they had not received sufficient compensation in the form of accounts receivables and industrial shares to

make up for what it had surrendered, although certain financial burdens in connection with the liquidation of the Industriekredit were eliminated.

Agreement of April 30, 1938 between the VIAG and the CA

I. TO BE TRANSFERRED TO THE VIAG

43,032 syndicated preferred CA shares in the possession of the pension fund 16,137,000 S

18,000 preferred CA shares in the possession of the Realitäten AG 6,750,000S

38,103 syndicated shares of the Österreichische Kraftwerke AG 3,810,300 S

7,797 blocked shares of the Österreichische Kraftwerke AG 779,700 S

18,700 syndicated shares of the Tiroler Wasserkraftwerke AG 1,870,000 S

90,000 syndicated shares of the Steirische Wasserkraft u. Elektrizitäts AG 2,925,000 S

12,500 such bonus shares valued at öS 32,50 per share 406,250 S

Total 32,678,250 S= 21,785,500 RM

II. TO BE TRANSFERRED TO THE CA FOR THE INDUSTRIEKREDIT PORTFOLIO

a) Shareholdings

11,190 shares of "Semperit" Österreichisch Amerikanische Gummiwerke AG 1,119,000 S

6,873 shares of Brüder Reininghaus AG für Brauerei und Spiritusindustrie 1,375,000 S

4,200 shares of the Kärntnerische Eisen- und Stahlwerks-Gesellschaft 420,000 S

3,710 shares of the Zellulose- und Papierfabriken Brigl & Bergmeister AG 556,000 S

3,360 shares of the Leykam-Josefsthal AG für Papier- und Druckindustrie 201,000 S

---

[121] BA-CA, CA-V, CA executive committee meeting of May 27, 1938.

[122] See BA-CA, CA-TZ, Sekretariat grün, Box 25/CA 20a, b, c1, File 20c, the memo on Olscher's telephone call to Heller of April 14, 1938.

(continued)

2,080 shares of the Erste Österreichische
Glanzstoff-Fabrik AG 208,000 S
150,000 S holding in the Stärke-
Vertriebs-G.m.b.H. 150,000 S
Total 4,029,000 S= 2,686,000 RM

b) Accounts Receivable

	Debit Balance	Credit Balance
18 companies	19,325,482.11 RM	1,445,215.59 RM
Other balances from current bank business	1,686,621.17 RM	8,238,599.13 RM
Totals	21,012,103.28 RM	9,683,814.72 RM
Balance = 11,328,288.56 RM		

III. TO BE PAID: 850,000 RM TO THE
CA FOR TAKING OVER 112 INDUSTRIEKREDIT
EMPLOYEES

Sources: CA Executive Committee meeting
of May 27, 1938, BA-CA, BA-V; Report on
the Österreichische Industriekredit AG, Oct.
24, 1946, BA-CA, BA-TZ, Sekretariat Grün,
Kt. 28, 20h.

Finally, the CA agreed to take over 112 active
employees of the Industriekredit with the
exception of Jews or persons "involved with
Jews," for which it was to be compensated
850,000 RM. At this time, 4 of the 18 leading
functionaries and 22 of the 133 employees were
Jews; all the Jews were dismissed, thus affording
some reduction in the number of those to be
reemployed. Of the eight directors, three were
Jewish, but they had been fired already.[123]

It is important to bear in mind and worth
reiterating that this transaction between the
CA and the VIAG gave the VIAG ownership of
approximately 35 percent of the CA's stock and
had been cobbled together from the CA shares
of the National Bank already in its possession,
the Industriekredit, the pension fund, and the
Realitäten AG. In reality, however, the VIAG
controlled 70 percent of the shares because
the shares formerly held by the now defunct
Austrian government were held by the Land of
Austria, soon also to disappear, and were placed
by Fischböck under the effective control of the
VIAG. The VIAG, Industriekredit, and Land of
Austria signed a syndicate agreement in May
1938 agreeing to administer the shares in common and according one another first option
if there was an intention to sell the shares but
placing the responsibility for this administration
with the VIAG. Because the Industriekredit was
going into liquidation and the Land of Austria
was slated to disappear, the VIAG was left owning 35 percent of the shares but acting as trustee
for 35 percent on behalf of entities soon to be
nonexistent.[124]

Manifestly, the situation of the relationship
between the CA and the Deutsche Bank in
Vienna had changed greatly since the heady
negotiation of the friendship pact back in
March. The CA leadership felt victimized, having been forced to surrender not only valuable
shares from its affiliates but also shares in electric power companies. Furthermore, as will be
shown later, it was confronted with demands
to sell off substantial industrial holdings to
German enterprises. It was also threatened with
the forced surrender of its provincial banks. As
for the Deutsche Bank, it faced well-entrenched
rivals in the VIAG and worried about the position of the RKG, while its own holdings in the
CA remained minimal. Abs's position on the
administrative council was important, but it
was not backed to significant material leverage
in the form of shares. While the contacts with
the RWM and the eclipse of Keppler augured
well for the future, the time had come for the

123 RGVA Moscow, 1458/2/101, short report on the
Activity of the Reich Commissariat for the Private
Economy in the Area of Finance, Nov. 3, 1938.
See also, Hans Kernbauer, *Währungspolitik in der
Zwischenkriegszeit. Geschichte der Oesterreichischen
Nationalbank von 1923 bis 1938* (Vienna 1991), p. 421.

124 See ÖStA/AdR, BMF, Allgem. Reihe 1938,
39275/1938, the syndicate agreements.

Deutsche Bank to launch a major offensive to assert its interests.

This was done in the form of an exposé on the relationship of the Deutsche Bank and the CA, which was sent to State Secretary Brinkmann and Ministerial Director Kurt Lange of the RWM on May 31, but then also circulated to Reichsbank President Schacht and to Kratz and others in mid-June.[125] The document was a much expanded and revised version of the document composed by Ernst Schmidt of the Deutsche Bank's Economic Analysis Section that now took into account the points and emphases urged by Abs. The opening pages dealing with the Deutsche Bank–CA collaboration dating back to the 1870s, and much detail was provided about the various types of business they conducted together and stress was placed on the role of the Deutsche Bank in the banking crisis of 1931. The friendship pact was in this way placed in the context of a long and continuous development and viewed as its logical culmination. Without specifically saying so, the rejection of the friendship pact by the authorities, leaving aside whether that rejection had a legal basis, and the transfer of shares to the VIAG was thereby portrayed as a violation of a long-standing historical relationship. The resulting situation for the Deutsche Bank was presented as intolerable. On the one hand, it was denied an intimate relationship with the CA. On the other hand, despite its size and huge network of branches, the bank had no branch in Vienna and would have to get special permission to establish one.

The situation had significant implications for business in Southeast Europe, where the CA and the Deutsche Bank had important connections, but where the CA did not have the capital to meet the needs of its international business without help. Despite the developments described, the Deutsche Bank declared itself willing to work with the CA to promote German economic interests in Southeast Europe, thereby capitalizing on the unique position of the Deutsche Bank in those areas

in order to benefit the economy of Austria. It did not mince words about its unwillingness to bring in third parties: "Consequently one must reject as inappropriate further plans under which the Reichs-Kredit-Gesellschaft, the Commerzbank, and the Deutsche Bank should conclude a mutual friendship with the Creditanstalt, without one or the other institution receiving special prior rights or a significant voice in personnel questions, etc. In such a combination, the Deutsche Bank would be the sole giving member, while the other partners would limit themselves to enjoying a one-sided benefit, especially in Southeast Europe."[126] In the view of the Deutsche Bank, experience had shown that three competing banks seeking to make common cause in this manner could never develop a united policy but rather would constantly be vying with one another for advantage.

The question now, from the standpoint of the CA, was whether it would still be possible, despite the VIAG's possession of what was formally a minority block of shares in the CA, to develop the friendship pact "to bring about a close relationship between the two institutions in which there was the prospect to found a truly intimate friendship not extendable to other partners, on whose basis alone a fruitful common effort in the Southeast European region can be achieved."[127] Once again, the authors of the exposé emphasized that Austria did not have the capital to undertake the necessary tasks of its own reconstruction and the expansion into Southeast Europe alone, and that just as it needed capital from the Reich, so the CA had to depend on a major bank with a wide network of branches. At the same time, the CA, because of its special characteristics as well as the peculiarities of the Vienna banking situation, would maintain its independence even as it was integrated into the Deutsche Bank network. The alternative was that the Deutsche Bank would have to set up its own branch in Vienna in order to fulfill its tasks in the Balkans and also to contribute to the Austrian economy in matters of trade and the defense economy.

---

125 The cover letters and the exposé are to be found in DB, B 51.

126 Ibid.
127 Ibid.

This exposé was a skillful piece of work, and it was timed perfectly to deal with the favorable turn in the bureaucratic situation. No doubt, Rohdewald was still pushing his plans, Joham reporting that Rohdewald's scheme for banking activity in Yugoslavia was intended to include IG Farben as well as the banks involved there. It must have been a relief, therefore, when Abs and his colleague, Director Karl Kimmich, met with Olscher of the VIAG and learned that he did not support Rohdewald. Indeed, Olscher claimed that the taking over of the VIAG shares was mandated by the government and was not a VIAG initiative or decision. He admitted that consideration was being given to the acquisition of shares on its own account, which was why the VIAG had increased its capital. He maintained, however, that the VIAG respected the Deutsche Bank friendship with the CA and opposed the RKG disturbing it in any way. He knew that there were those in the RKG who thought otherwise, but he considered their demands "unjustified and destructive."[128] Undoubtedly less agreeable was Olscher's remark that a division of banking interests in the Balkans had to be possible and that the RKG and the Commerzbank would now be represented on the administrative council of the CA. Olscher also insisted, however, that the Deutsche Bank continue to maintain its presence there in the person of Abs. Olscher, of course, was less innocent than he claimed because, as has been shown earlier, he had offered the VIAG's and the RKG's services to Keppler as early as March 12, but he does seem to have decided to significantly diminish the role the RKG might play and was less intent on bringing Rohdewald and his plans into play.

In any case, Olscher was moving in a more favorable direction from the standpoint of the Deutsche Bank, which did not, however, eliminate the more general opposition to the Deutsche Bank–Creditanstalt connection in other quarters. These tensions had much to do with the sense that the CA was too big and that its industrial holdings presented special difficulties. The RWM leadership did not care much about this issue – Brinkmann telling Kratz that the RWM was powerful enough to prevent abuse[129] – but some of the leading National Socialists in Vienna continued to feel that the alliance of the largest banks in Germany and Austria constituted a danger and that the CA needed to be cut down to size by giving the Mercurbank/Länderbank some of the CA's provincial banks.

The incipient creation of the Länderbank Wien AG out of the Mercurbank, the Austrian holdings of the Zentral-Europäische Länderbank, and the Austrian holdings of the Živnostenská Banka was something of a sore point with the RWM, however, because it had been created by the collaboration of the Dresdner Bank, Keppler's office, and Kehrl. The RWM was willing to approve the new bank retroactively, but it was not prepared to sanction its further expansion by the takeover of the CA's provincial banks and branches, and it made a special point of calling Kratz's office in early June and specifically warned against any further expansion of the Mercurbank group at the expense of the CA.[130] Kehrl himself seems to have beat a retreat on this subject, claiming to the RWM that there never had been an intention to have the CA give up branches to the Mercurbank, but it had only initially appeared sensible to sell provincial banks to the Mercurbank where the latter did not have branches rather than have new branches opened up in the same place. Since the Mercurbank had taken over the Länderbank, according to Kehrl, the problem of sufficient Mercurbank branches had been solved. This was, to say the least, a disingenuous interpretation of what Rasche had in mind.[131]

Furthermore, all this did not end the animus against the Deutsche Bank in Viennese government circles. At a meeting attended by Bürckel and Fischböck, the claim was made that the

[128]   Ibid., memorandum by Pollems, June 6, 1938.

[129]   ÖStA/AdR, Bürckel-Materie, Box 92, 2165/0, Vol. I, Kratz memorandum, May 16, 1938.

[130]   Ibid., Kratz to Barth, June 14, 1938.

[131]   RGVA Moscow, 1458/2/61, Bl. 314–315, Kehrl to RWM, June 30, 1938.

Deutsche Bank had asked for a list of CA industrial holdings so that the Deutsche Bank might find purchasers in Germany. This, of course, was a repetition of the old charge of Keppler and Kehrl that the Deutsche Bank intended to "rob" the CA of its industrial holdings. It also suggested that the Deutsche Bank was prepared to violate the ban on the acquisition of Austrian assets without government permission. The CA denied that any such thing had occurred and asked the Deutsche Bank to confirm this. In its confirmation, the Deutsche Bank pointed out that the list of CA holdings was published in the bank's business report and could be read by anyone and that, with the exception of the Krupp Berndorf works where, as will be discussed later, the Deutsche Bank was approached by Krupp, the Deutsche Bank had not been involved in any such engagements.[132]

At this point, however, the Deutsche Bank was less interested in mollifying its enemies than cultivating the RWM, whose interest in promoting foreign trade and exports at this time fit in quite well with the Deutsche Bank arguments.[133] At a meeting on June 29, Ministerial Director Lange expressed gratitude for the Deutsche Bank exposé, reported that he had discussed it with Brinkmann, and stated their appreciation of the Deutsche Bank position. He virtually apologized for the difficulties experienced by the Deutsche Bank by pointing out that during periods of transition, such as the one they were now experiencing, there were bound to be more difficulties than usual. He pointedly remarked, however, that the situation was stabilizing and that the RWM was in charge: "Now that Herr Keppler has received other functions, nothing can happen, by order of the Reich Economics Ministry and General Field Marshall Göring, in Austria, especially in banking matters, without the agreement of the Reich Economics Ministry."[134] In any case, the RWM was seeking the opinion of the

authorities in Vienna on the Deutsche Bank exposé, and Lange asked Abs to provide more information and a concrete proposal. This obviously could not be provided on the spot, but Abs took advantage of the opportunity to reiterate that the Deutsche Bank could not be shut out of Austria, to emphasize the significance of foreign trade, and to point out that the Deutsche Bank and the Dresdner Bank had agreed that it was not feasible to divide up their business in the Balkans and Turkey, although they did think it might be possible to cooperate in various instances with the CA. It was not possible, however, to cooperate with banks that had not been engaged in these areas, and it would be incomprehensible to their business partners in the Balkans if they were not represented in Vienna, which was the "bridge" to Southeast Europe. Lange agreed to this in principle but asked Abs for a proposal that would state what was involved in an "intimate friendship" with the CA. Abs responded that this involved, in the short run, an influence on CA personnel policies and, in the long run, "a certain material attachment." Abs stressed, however, that they were not interested in dominating Austrian industry. All in all, Lange was encouraging, and the discussion also afforded an opportunity to discuss personnel matters at the CA, especially what Abs viewed as the unsatisfactory staffing of the second level of management.

Indeed, the Deutsche Bank was not without its suspicions of the CA and its dealings, especially after learning about its contacts with the VIAG and RKG and especially with Rohdewald. Note was taken by Directors Rösler and Pohle, for example, of a visit of management board director Fritscher to Berlin on June 30–July 1 when they sought in vain for a meeting and then hunted Fritscher down to find him accompanied by another person who was not introduced to them and stood off to the side. They then discovered that the person in question was slated to become the CA representative in Berlin and that Fritscher had been in Berlin to meet with Banking Commissar Ernst about the establishment of such an office. The only conclusion one could draw was that Fritscher had deliberately avoided informing

[132] DB, B 51, CA to Deutsche Bank, June 17, 1938, and Deutsche Bank to CA, June 20, 1938.

[133] See Willi A. Boelcke, *Die Deutsche Wirtschaft 1930–1945. Interna des Reichswirtschaftsministeriums* (Düsseldorf 1983), pp. 193–200.

[134] DB, B 51, Abs memorandum, June 29, 1938.

the CA or discussing the matter with them. The CA had, in fact, already hired Captain Robert Nemling, who was to begin work at the rather high salary of 15,600 RM a year, with additional payment for office and staff costs, to represent the interests of the CA in Berlin in dealing with Party, government, and economic agencies. Furthermore, there were good grounds for the Deutsche Bank's suspicions. The appointment of Nemling, who had been a lobbyist for many years and was head of the Berlin office of the Austrian Export Promotion Institute, had been discussed with Olscher of the VIAG and Rohdewald of the RKG and received their approval sometime before mid-May. At that time, Rohdewald's approval was also sought, and Nemling was asked to come by Rohdewald's office for an interview before a final decision was made. Nemling, therefore, had also taken the job with Rohdewald's blessing, and it was not long before Rohdewald, who was obviously quite tenacious when it came to Southeast Europe, summoned him to a discussion to express the hope that there would be close cooperation between the RKG and the CA in Yugoslavia and Romania.[135] These measures by the CA should not be viewed as some kind of "betrayal" of the friendship pact with the Deutsche Bank, but the CA leadership had obviously decided that they also needed to look after their own business independently in Berlin, a not unreasonable conclusion given the rival groups and chaotic manner in which decisions were being made.

It is also useful to remember that the Deutsche Bank had continuously indicated that setting up its own branch in Vienna was an alternative to conducting its business, as it preferred, via the CA. This alternative was reiterated by Director Karl Sippell of the Deutsche Bank management board to State Secretary

Erich Neumann of Göring's staff, another high official provided with the bank's exposé. Apparently, the banking issue had not been discussed with Göring in a recent meeting with Bürckel, but Neumann assured Sippell that the Reich Marshall was strongly supportive of efforts to advance German interests in Southeast Europe. He wondered about the politics behind the treatment of the Deutsche Bank, but Sippell indicated that recent discussions between Abs and Kratz and Bürckel had produced more understanding for the Deutsche Bank position. In any case, Neumann offered his support and expressed understanding for Sippell's insistence that, if the Deutsche Bank could not enter into any kind of condominium with other banks in Vienna, it would prefer to go it alone. As the "strongest bank," the Deutsche Bank could not be denied its proper place.[136]

Most importantly, on July 9, the Deutsche Bank responded to Lange's request for a concrete proposal stating its views and wishes with respect to the CA.[137] Although this latest exposé repeated the old arguments, it was now couched in terms of the Deutsche Bank's responsibility to service the economic needs and participate in the economic responsibilities of the "Ostmark," as Austria was now called, with special emphasis on foreign trade and military expenditure but also on reconstructing the Austrian economy. The choice between an "intimate relationship" with the CA and the setting up of a branch of its own was stated very starkly. The Deutsche Bank viewed itself as a "friend, adviser, and supporter" of the CA, while the CA was to function as an *"independently directed regional bank."* Insofar as foreign trade in Southeast Europe was concerned, there were obvious advantages in combining resources and contacts of the two banks, and making available Deutsche Bank credit facilities, but their collaboration was a major factor in Vienna's role as a bridge to the Southeast and would also open up new possibilities, "for example, the development of the stake in the

135   Ibid., memo by Pohle, July 5, 1938. See ÖStA/AdR, BMF, Allgem. Reihe 1938, 51951/1938, the contract and its approval. BA-CA, CA-TZ, Sekretariat rot, Box 53/ÖCA-WBV, 1838/9,10,11, File 9b/4, Nemling and Rohdewald, see CA to Rohdewald, May 19, 1938 and memorandum by Nemling on a meeting with Rohdewald, July 21, 1938.

136   DB, B 51, memo by Sippell, July 5, 1938.
137   Ibid.; for the discussion that follows, see the memorandum dated July 9, 1938.

Allgemeine Jugoslawische Bankverein AG so as to turn it into a purely German bank, which has until now not been capable of realization despite repeated efforts." Deliberately or not, the Deutsche Bank also challenged the adequacy of the CA as its own representative in Berlin and Germany by emphasizing that the Deutsche Bank could provide trained personnel to deal with demands and complexities of doing business in the old Reich as well as abroad and provide advice and assistance in dealing with both customers and government agencies.

Just as the Deutsche Bank had a network of branches throughout Germany, so the CA had a network in Austria, and the integration of the banks in the Ostmark into the banking system of the Reich would best be served by collaboration with German banks that had representation in all the places where stock exchanges existed. Pointedly, the exposé made note of the fact that the Länderbank now enjoyed such an advantage by being tied into the branch system of the Dresdner Bank. The Deutsche Bank and the CA could now also benefit from one another's banking services, as could their customers.

The Deutsche Bank took the position that the great tasks of the Ostmark – elimination of unemployment, defense, Aryanization, and exports – required a "complete break with the previous economic policy of Austria." The Austrian banks had to be relieved of their liquidity problems if they were to be ready to deal with these issues, and here the CA could receive substantial cash advances if and when they were needed. This was an advantage already enjoyed by the Mercurbank because of its ownership by the Dresdner Bank. Similarly, the two banks could join forces in granting large credits for some of the big projects being launched in Austria, which was not to say that either of them were inhibited from credit operations of their own and the CA from fulfilling its functions as a regional bank.

Once again, however, the Deutsche Bank stressed the importance of basing its services to the CA on a material foundation and repeated the usual incantation that it was "unreasonable" to ask the Deutsche Bank to let other

banks, which were neither willing to participate properly nor able to contribute anything, come to the table. This time, however, the Deutsche Bank was quite concrete about what it expected. In view of the changed situation resulting from the fact that 50,000 CA shares of the Österreichische Industriekredit had gone over to the Reich and another 61,032 preferred shares were being held in trust by the VIAG, an "intimate relationship" with the CA would only be possible if the CA were afforded certain possibilities that would realize the intentions of the friendship pact. The first of these was that the Deutsche Bank be allowed to step into the position of the Land of Austria with respect to its option to acquire the shares held in trust by the VIAG, specifically, the 120,000 shares previously belonging to the Land of Austria, the 20,000 shares previously belonging to the Austrian National Bank, and the 61,032 preferred shares acquired by the VIAG from the pension fund. These were to be offered to the Deutsche Bank at a fair price. Over and above this, the Deutsche Bank wished to have the rights of the Land of Austria with respect to the VIAG holdings. Second, insofar as the valuation of the shares under existing circumstances could not be clearly determined, the Deutsche Bank was to get a multiyear option on the purchase of the 140,000 shares and the 61,032 preferred shares with a fixed agreement as to how the price was to be determined. Again, it was to exercise the rights enjoyed by the Land of Austria with respect to its trustee, the VIAG.

The demands of the Deutsche Bank did not stop here, however, because the capacity of the CA to operate as an independent regional bank depended, in its view, on having leadership that had the confidence of the Deutsche Bank and that was sufficiently acquainted with conditions in the Greater German Reich to work with their German colleagues. In addition, the Deutsche Bank was to have first call on all business conducted by the CA with other partners, and the CA was gradually to adjust its internal structure to that of the Deutsche Bank. Although this meant that, in the long run, the CA would become a German-style universal credit bank, the Deutsche Bank nevertheless thought it essential that the CA hold on to its industrial holdings and "that an *alienation* of these holdings should only be undertaken after the most careful examination of all the circumstances and be without damage to the Creditanstalt or the interests of the Deutsche Bank." This was a most extraordinary provision and certainly must have been the product of consultations with Joham and his colleagues; as will be shown later, the CA was being subjected to considerable loss of holdings at this time.

Apparently, the Deutsche Bank now also felt its hand strengthened enough to insist that the RWM declare that it had no reservations about an intimate relationship between the two banks, thus nullifying the Austrian Finance Ministry's refusal to accept the friendship pact. The latter had led the Deutsche Bank to consider setting up its own branch in Vienna, and now that Austria had become a part of the Reich, there were no grounds to exclude the Deutsche Bank from doing business there. It would continue to pursue this path if the friendship pact and the possibility of acquiring the shares in question were rejected. The Deutsche Bank exposé concluded by pointing out that a decision was pressing because the demands for credits were mounting, resulting in a rising flood of potential business transactions.

The reality was, however, that the Deutsche Bank had set forth a maximum program that was anything but easy to realize despite the support it had from important quarters in the RWM. The wheels set in motion by the VIAG acquisitions continued to turn. The administrative council was scheduled to meet on July 15, and the shareholders' meeting was scheduled for July 23. The role of the VIAG as a shareholder was to be approved at the early assembly and to be announced at the later one. The Deutsche Bank would find itself very much on the sidelines at these events. Olscher was already on the board as well as on the executive committee, and the position of the Deutsche Bank was bound to be relativized by the scheduled election of Rohdewald from the RKG and Reinhard from the Commerzbank to the administrative council. A meeting between Abs and Olscher was scheduled for the beginning

of August. It was believed but not actually known that at this meeting Olscher would propose some slight reduction of the VIAG shares in favor of the Deutsche Bank and also offer Abs a seat on the executive committee, which would have signaled a special position for the Deutsche Bank. Abs had discussed this possibility with Joham, who had confirmed that there were no barriers to Abs joining the committee. If there was thus some hope that the Deutsche Bank might climb its way back up toward realizing the goals of the friendship pact, the alternative of opening a branch in Vienna was by no means certain to gain approval. The Commerzbank was also toying with the idea of setting up a branch in Vienna, but Fritscher told Abs that Fischböck was taking the position that no major bank was going to set up a branch in Vienna under any circumstances. That, of course, included the Deutsche Bank as well.[138]

In any case, Abs was spending a good deal of time running about seeing authorities in Vienna and Berlin in his efforts to realize Deutsche Bank goals, but not everyone at the Deutsche Bank was convinced that the effort was worthwhile. Karl Kimmich thought they were wasting precious time and energy, writing to his junior colleague on July 20 that when he had a chance encounter with Olscher, he asked Olscher what he had in mind for the meeting in early August, only to learn that Olscher had no plans except to bring Rohdewald to the meeting to discuss collaboration in Yugoslavia. Such collaboration certainly was of no interest to the Deutsche Bank. Another irritation was the information that their Viennese "friends" had set up a CA office in Berlin but that Captain Nemling "still has not found his way to us." The Deutsche Bank had, however, received a letter produced by the CA asking the companies close to the Deutsche Bank like the Vereinigte Stahlwerke, the Deutsche Gesellschaft für elektrische Unternehmungen (Gesfürel), and Siemens use the services of the CA in making payments in

---

138 Ibid., Report by Pohle for Rösler, July 18, 1938. The administrative council meeting of July 15, 1938, and the shareholders' meeting of July 23, 1938, are to be found in BA-CA, CA-V.

Austria. The Deutsche Bank response was very lukewarm. So long as the situation had not been clarified, in Kimmich's view, there was the danger that the Deutsche Bank would finally end up establishing a branch in Vienna only to find that it had turned some of its chief clients over to the CA. At the same time, the CA was being notably reticent in responding to questions about Aryanization, a matter that engaged the Deutsche Bank at the moment, and this attitude "also clearly shows once again the extent of the friendly cast of mind of the other side."[139]

Kimmich obviously did not trust the Austrians at the CA and now wondered if Abs was on the right path, and while he well understood the reasons for not tearing down the bridges that had been built before one knew what was possible, there was the very real danger that the highly aggressive Länderbank would take all the business: "We thus give up our valuable connections in the old Reich and thereby suffer a truly marked loss of clients and prestige."[140] The time was fast coming, in Kimmich's view, when decisions had to be made, and he thought that Abs should no longer accept Kratz's practice of making vague promises and putting him off. If Kratz did not offer any more, in Kimmich's view, then one should go directly to Bürckel and push matters forward.

Kimmich admitted that he was speaking for himself at the moment, but it is useful to remember that, unlike the recently arrived Abs, he had been on the Deutsche Bank managing board since 1933 and was to become its spokesman in 1940. Nevertheless, Abs stuck tenaciously to his course, trying to dismantle the obstacles in Vienna and asking for and receiving

an interview with Fischböck in August. Here he reiterated all the arguments contained in his bank's memoranda to the RWM and other authorities and insisted that a bank with 273 branches in the old Reich could not now be excluded from the Ostmark. The one new note he struck was to argue that the Deutsche Bank, if it were allowed proper participation in the ownership of the CA, would help "in the reorganization of the CA from a very active industrial holding bank it had been into a regional great bank with branches according to the German conception of a bank."[141]

Nevertheless, events were to show that Fischböck remained hostile to Deutsche Bank's investment in the CA as well as to the major banks setting up branches in Vienna. Kehrl also remained an obstacle to Deutsche Bank ambitions, something he made clear in a letter of August 26 to the Deutsche Bank by setting forth his disagreement with the exposé of May 31 in no uncertain terms. He did not see any incompatibility between the VIAG share takeover and the friendship between the CA and the Deutsche Bank, and he insisted that the two most important Austrian regional banks, the CA and the Länderbank, were sufficiently liquid to attend to the credit needs of the area and did not need further support. There was thus, in his opinion, no need for the dependence of the CA on a major bank, and also no need for the establishment of branches of the major Berlin banks in the Ostmark. Kehrl thought this would lead to overbanking and reduce the effectiveness of the banks already available. While welcoming the collaboration of the CA and the Deutsche Bank in Southeast Europe, he had discussed the matter with Olscher and was certain that fruitful collaboration was possible and desirable and that the existing situation did not stand in the way of underscoring the very special position of the Deutsche Bank in the Balkans.[142]

---

[139] DB, B 51, Kimmich to Abs, July 20, 1938. On July 23, 1938, the Deutsche Bank had inquired about reports concerning the establishment of a new institute to deal with Aryanizations, and wondered if this was going to have consequences in the old Reich as well. The CA replied on July 26 that it was not a new institute that was being founded but rather an organization for the transfer of Jewish-owned real estate and that the technical leadership was to be given to the CA-owned Österreichische Realitäten, ibid.

[140] Ibid., Kimmich to Abs, July 27, 1938.

[141] Ibid., Notes on the meeting with Fischböck of Aug. 24, 1938. Abs had asked for the meeting on Aug. 9, and the report of the meeting was sent by Pohle to Gottschick of the RWM on Aug. 26.

[142] Ibid., Kehrl to Deutsche Bank, Aug. 26, 1938.

It was a measure of the frustration of the Deutsche Bank at this point that, while continuing to cultivate friendly authorities in Berlin, it also moderated its program substantially. It informed Banking Commissar Ernst, to whom the Deutsche Bank now also appealed, that in the long run one could not deny the Deutsche Bank a place in the Ostmark. In answer to Ernst's query as to whether it was prepared to acquire a majority of the CA, the Deutsche Bank responded affirmatively, assuming the condition of the bank was satisfactory and the price was acceptable. It was, however, also prepared to settle for a 25 percent minority, provided that the Gold Discount Bank acquired another 25 percent and then made a binding agreement with the Deutsche Bank with respect to the voting of these shares as well as a first option on their purchase should their sale be considered.[143]

The reaction to such ideas, however, was mixed and confusing. At a meeting between Hasslacher and the RWM officials Riehle and Lange, held on September 21 at the CA itself, there was strong sentiment in the RWM that the Deutsche Bank had good reason to complain about its treatment but also a firm decision not to allow the Deutsche Bank to set up its own branch. Lange and Brinkmann were especially enthusiastic about the role that could be played by collaboration of the two banks in Southeast Europe, where they complemented one another, the one bank being present in places where the other was not and vice versa. Also, given the sacrifices the Creditanstalt was being forced to make, it was necessary to provide compensation, and the financing of foreign trade operations was most promising in this respect. The Deutsche Bank would also be able to help in dealing with the heavy pension burdens of the CA. Finally, in the view of the RWM, the CA lacked "experienced and reliable personnel who are also capable of managing banks in the manner of the Third Reich."[144] Here, too, the Deutsche Bank could help out. Manifestly, the RWM leaders

were identifying themselves with the Deutsche Bank arguments, and this went so far as being prepared to accept the idea that the Deutsche Bank acquire the shares belonging to the Land of Austria if the VIAG were willing to agree as well. The reaction of the Austrian authorities, however, was mixed. Georg Schumetz, representing Rafelsberger's Commissariat for the Private Economy, which was playing an increasing role, and who had arrived late at the meeting, took a relatively positive view but felt that the Deutsche Bank's stake should be limited to 20 percent. At a meeting on the next day at Bürckel's office, Kehrl and Fischböck firmly opposed any capital share participation in the CA by the Deutsche Bank. Bürckel, however, was not similarly opposed. There was nevertheless general approval for closer collaboration between the Deutsche Bank and the CA if for no other reason than to prevent the establishment of a Deutsche Bank branch in Austria. This, of course, was a virtual agreement that something would have to be done to satisfy the Deutsche Bank ambitions in Austria. From the side of Bürckel's office, therefore, there were no further reservations about the position of Lange and Brinkmann.[145]

An important new dimension of the situation at this point was Olscher's view of the situation and his willingness to come to terms with the Deutsche Bank. It is worth noting that the enthusiasm of the VIAG, or at least of Olscher, for the CA shares had never been connected to an expansion of its interests in the banking business but rather to the opportunities offered by acquisitions in the Austrian electric power business and the big power projects being launched by Göring. Because the Deutsche Bank was not being allowed to acquire the shares, it was convenient to use the VIAG as a trustee, but, as Olscher told the VIAG supervisory board on September 23, there was thus "in no way a permanent situation being created. Moreover, we have taken the position from the outset that the holding is

143 Ibid., Deutsche Bank to Ernst, Sept. 15, 1938.
144 ÖStA/AdR, Bürckel-Materie, Box 92, 2165/0, Vol. I, Kratz to Ernst, Sept. 21, 1938.

145 Ibid., Kratz to Riehle, Sept. 29, 1938, and DB, B 51, unsigned minutes of meetings of Sept. 21/22, dated Sept. 30, 1938.

an indirect VIAG holding and will not in the end be passed on to the bank belonging to us, the Reichs-Kredit-Gesellschaft." This was also, he explained, why the two major banks, the Deutsche Bank and the Commerzbank, which were not represented in Austria – the Dresdner Bank being represented in its ownership of the Länderbank – were in the administrative council of the CA.[146]

For Olscher, the situation in the fall of 1938 was too unstable to allow for an immediate decision about changes in the level of control of the CA. The Austrian political authorities were extraordinarily sensitive about everything connected with such matters, and a decision about allowing the large German banks to have branches had not really been made. He did not anticipate such a decision until the Austrian government was formally dissolved and the Finance Ministry ceased to exist, probably in March 1939. Furthermore, when this happened the CA shares belonging to the Land of Austria would also change hands. In a meeting with Abs on September 30, Olscher was rather critical of the Deutsche Bank's ceaseless negotiations when everything was in such flux. Indeed, even the corporation law under which the CA had been operating was going to change in the coming year with the full introduction of German corporation law. The administrative council was going to be transformed into a supervisory board and adjustments would have to be made. Olscher suggested that the chairman of the supervisory board could be an Austrian, possibly Hasslacher, and there would be deputy chairmen, one of whom might be Abs. Supervisory committees might also be set up to handle business in the Balkans, the Deutsche Bank probably chairing the committee for Turkey and Bulgaria. At the moment, however, Olscher could not foresee the Deutsche Bank taking a significant stake in the CA. But this was precisely what

the Deutsche Bank expected, as Abs made clear, and Abs also told Olscher that Bank Commissar Ernst had likewise been informed that the Deutsche Bank found it unacceptable to administer the CA in collaboration with a group of other banks. For Olscher, there was no point in remaining involved with the CA if the Deutsche Bank and Commerzbank were allowed to set up branches in Vienna and decided to do so because this would have left the VIAG with indirect control over the CA as it would now be facing such competition. Under such circumstances, he was prepared to surrender his shares to the Reich.

At this point, however, Olscher began to spin out another option under which the VIAG would acquire the Land of Austria's shares, thus combining the 39 percent it held with the 36 percent held by the Land of Austria to produce a 75 percent majority and then to give a third of this holding, that is 25 percent of the shares, to the Deutsche Bank. At the same time, the VIAG and Deutsche Bank would sign a contract to work in common in dealing with the issues involving the CA, with the understanding that the role of the Deutsche Bank would be dominant with respect to all banking questions. Both parties would be granted first option on purchase of their respective shares. In this connection, Olscher mentioned that a time could well arrive when the VIAG, because of its many stronger interests, would lose interest in holding on to the CA shares. He stressed that such a solution could not be implemented immediately because of resistance in Austria and, in particular, because the dissolution of the Austrian Finance Ministry was a prerequisite. In any case, Olscher promised to present these ideas in discussions with the RWM and to broach them very cautiously in Vienna. Olscher also asked if the Deutsche Bank might be willing to take a 75 percent stake in the CA, to which Abs replied that "this was a problem that certainly could be solved, but that we however would only examine it when it became acute."[147]

---

[146] Vereinigte Industrieunternehmen AG (= VIAG), VIAG Archiv München, Supervisory Board meeting, Sept. 23, 1938, VIAG Archiv, Munich. I am grateful to Andrea Schneider for placing this material at my disposal. See also Pohl, VIAG, pp. 132–137.

[147] DB, B 51, memo by Abs, Sept. 30, 1938.

Olscher had thus become an ally of the Deutsche Bank, and this dramatically changed the situation despite the difficulties yet to be faced. Those difficulties were very much in evidence when Abs met with Olscher and Rohdewald on November 1, 1938. Olscher had already met with Fischböck, Bürckel, Kehrl, Rafelsberger, and Schumetz, and the upshot of the discussions was a generally negative attitude toward Deutsche Bank participation in the ownership of the CA. Olscher personally was prepared to give the Deutsche Bank a 37.5 percent stake, but even talk of a 25 percent stake met with resistance from Kehrl and the Viennese. When Olscher asked Abs, however, if the Deutsche Bank could accept a participation of between 15 percent and 20 percent Abs categorically refused and declared that they would rather have nothing and a free hand than anything under 25 percent. Abs also would not accept the notion of taking something less with the idea of later increasing it and rounding it out, and he was prepared to go back to the Viennese authorities and take this position. Olscher pointed out that at the moment the Deutsche Bank had less than a 1 percent stake in the CA, so it did not have much leverage to take the position it did. Of course, this was also an argument that favored the Deutsche Bank's demand for a substantial stake if it were to do serious business with the CA. Insofar as the question of the role of the Deutsche Bank in the CA was concerned, Olscher thought that the first chairman of the supervisory board that was to be established in the new year should be an Austrian, perhaps Fischböck or Neubacher, with Hasslacher as first deputy chair, and the VIAG and the Deutsche Bank holding the other two deputy chairs. Olscher also intended to draw up the projected contract between the VIAG and the Deutsche Bank.

Olscher and Rohdewald then brought up the issue of setting up special banking committees for business in Southeast Europe, each committee to be chaired by the bank that traditionally held a leading position in the country in question. Thus, the CA would chair the committees on Hungary and Yugoslavia, the Deutsche Bank would chair the committees for Bulgaria and Turkey, and the Dresdner Bank would play the chairmanship role for Romania and Greece. Abs, who undoubtedly would just as soon as not have discussed this program at all, asked what the committees were actually supposed to do in practical terms and then promised to discuss this question with his colleagues.[148]

By this time, of course, the Sudeten crisis had run its course, and the German leadership was preoccupied with the digestion of recent conquests and the preparation of future ones. This undoubtedly intensified the weariness over the endless negotiations connected with the CA, where there were also pressing personnel concerns, and this pushed matters forward toward a denouement by the end of 1938. Some of the decision making, especially with regard to personnel, was now affected by conflicts among the Austrian National Socialists. As Olscher reported in a meeting on November 5 to which he had invited Abs, Neubaur, and Heller, a battle had broken out between Fischböck and Bürckel over Aryanization; major industrial and commercial Aryanizations had been taken out of the hands of the Property Transfer Bureau and transferred to the newly established Section C of the Kontrollbank. Fischböck was anxious to have major Aryanizations handled with economic rather than political considerations receiving top priority and had appointed Hermann Leitich, who had been at the CA and was considered highly competent. Leitich's disregard of political considerations when choosing Aryanizers, however, offended those anxious to reward Party loyalists, among them Bürckel, who wanted Leitich removed. A compromise was then worked out. Josef von Paić, a protégé of Bürckel and a National Socialist, who, however, was highly regarded for his competence and had previously served at the Österreichische Industriekredit AG and then at the Länderbank, would be appointed as a second director at the Kontrollbank. But in order to provide Paić with the necessary prestige, he was first to be appointed to the management board of the CA and then put on leave to work at the

---

[148]   Ibid., memo by Abs, Nov. 1, 1938.

Kontrollbank. Underlying this plan to give Paić a position at the CA was, as Abs noted, a stratagem "on the part of certain circles to further shake the position of Dr. Joham, upon whose retention Herr Heller and Herr Olscher as well as myself place the greatest value in the interest of the bank."[149] As it turned out, however, there was a long-standing animosity between Paić and Pfeiffer, so that the former could not serve at the CA with the latter. It was decided, therefore, to put Paić in the Kontrollbank immediately, but with the prospect of joining the CA board in a year or two when other employment would have been found for Pfeiffer, "who shows himself not to be up to the tasks of a management board member of the Creditanstalt."[150] All this was very revealing about the politics surrounding the personnel situation at the CA and the delicate position of Joham. Also significant, however, was the fact that Olscher had asked Abs to discuss these problems, "because he no longer wants to discuss personnel matters with us, and views us rather as a partner in the joint administering majority of the Creditanstalt."[151]

The cementing of the VIAG–Deutsche Bank relationship was made easier by the retreat of Fischböck, which was undoubtedly greatly promoted by the fact that he was losing his job. Fischböck's position had been very much influenced by an ideological predisposition against private credit banks, and he took the view that credit banks should be state banks, a view he knew was not held in Berlin. He was not happy to hear from Hasslacher in early November that 20 percent to 25 percent of the CA's preferred shares were being bought up by a group of investors led by the private banking house of Pinschof & Co., but he seems not to have objected. He transferred the CA shares held by the Land of Austria to the Reich Finance Ministry and expected them to be held by the VIAG, but he made clear that he was no longer interested in what the government in Berlin did with them. He was willing to have the Deutsche Bank take 10 percent

to 15 percent, but the bank wanted more. He himself preferred to see as many of the shares taken by small shareholders as possible. The eclipse of Fischböck was confirmed by Bank Commissar Ernst, who in effect told Abs to pay no attention to Fischböck's wishes and to stand by the demand for 25 percent. He also made clear that Rafelsberger and Schumetz had nothing to say in the matter. Bürckel's office had already agreed to a 25 percent Deutsche Bank stake. Schumetz, however, was also supportive, reporting to Director Karl Ritter von Halt of the Deutsche Bank that the Party in Vienna welcomed a 25 percent stake for the Deutsche Bank and that "by now there have been enough preliminary negotiations, and it was finally time for deeds."[152]

The deeds were done in December, when Lange assured Abs that everyone was now agreed on the Deutsche Bank getting 25 percent and that Olscher, who may have been holding back because of concern over opposition, now also agreed. Lange was happy to see the matter initially settled at this level, and he was also in full accord with Olscher's proposal that Hasslacher become chairman of the future supervisory board, with Olscher and Abs serving as vice-chairmen. Indeed, he found this an "ideal" solution. Within the Deutsche Bank itself, there was considerable satisfaction with the contract in the making between the Deutsche Bank and the VIAG drawn up by Olscher, which gave the Deutsche Bank responsibility for advising and taking care of the CA in all business and organizational matters as well as the right to propose a member of the management board but required regular contact and consultation with the VIAG on all matters of importance, especially those involving the exercise of the majority voting rights enjoyed by the VIAG.[153]

[149] Ibid., memo by Abs, Nov. 7, 1938.
[150] Ibid.
[151] Ibid.

[152] Ibid., Abs report on telephone call from Joham on Nov. 5, 1938, dated Nov. 7, 1938; memo by Abs on discussion with Ernst, Nov. 8, 1938; Hall to Abs, Nov. 22, 1928.
[153] Ibid., memo by Pohle of Dec. 2, 1938 on conversation between Abs and Lange on Dec. 1, and memo by Kimmich of Dec. 10, 1938.

On December 30, 1938, the Deutsche Bank and the VIAG signed a consortial contract to which was attached a letter from the VIAG to the Deutsche Bank concerning the advising and care for the Creditanstalt in organizational questions by the Deutsche Bank.[154] Under the agreement, the VIAG sold 48,500 common shares and 35,000 preferred shares to the Deutsche Bank at 100 percent but excluding 1938 dividends. The two concerns entered into a consortium to administer jointly their holdings in the CA and to collaborate in all organizational and business affairs, and to do all their basic business in the Ostmark through the CA. The VIAG would make sure that the RKG pursued the same policy. The two concerns would vote together, after agreeing on how they would vote before all shareholders' meetings and all supervisory board meetings, especially with respect to the presentation of the CA's balance sheets, dividends and their distribution, changes in statutes, election of supervisory board members, and appointment of management board members. In order to preserve the indigenous character of the CA, appointments to the organs of the CA were to be wherever possible persons from the Ostmark. The VIAG was to have the right to appoint three members of the supervisory board, while the Deutsche Bank was to make two appointments. The two concerns, including the RKG, would seek to do as much of their business in the Ostmark using the services of the CA as possible, and they were agreed that the business in Southeast Europe would be organized by the German banks with an appropriate employment of the CA in such business. The consortium would work to maintain the profitability of the CA. They were to give each other first option on the sale of CA shares in their possession, but they were not to hold shares in common. The Deutsche Bank renounced the right to set up its own organization or branch in the Ostmark, while the VIAG promised not to transfer or sell any of its shares to a bank or bank-like organization. The contract was to have an initial life of ten years, provided that

neither party's shareholdings in the CA were to drop below 10 percent, and it was automatically renewable for two-year periods unless notice of nonrenewal were given six months before it was scheduled to run out. In the VIAG letter to the Deutsche Bank appended to the agreement, the Deutsche Bank was assigned the task of advising and caring for the CA with respect to "all business and organizational questions" to ensure its profitability while consulting with the VIAG on all "important" questions.

The wording of the letter had been worked out rather carefully and reflected the Deutsche Bank's insistence on having its powers and authority defined as broadly as possible. Where Olscher thought it enough to charge the Deutsche Bank with handling "organizational" issues because such questions covered everything, Abs and Kimmich argued that it was precisely because organizational issues so easily spilled over into personnel and banking business itself that it was important to mention these areas as well. At the same time, where Olscher had originally wished that the Deutsche Bank be obligated to consult with the VIAG on all "basic" questions, the Deutsche Bank asked that this be changed to "important questions," and thereby narrowed the scope of consultation. As everyone recognized, both terms were rather vague, but the Deutsche Bank felt it crucial that the consultations take place over weighty matters. Also, it argued that the basic responsibility would ultimately lie with the management board, and it would be up to the board to take issues it deemed important to the presidium of the supervisory board once German corporation law was introduced. This would be composed of the chairman of the supervisory board and a representative of the VIAG and the Deutsche Bank, that is, Hasslacher, Olscher, and Abs, who would form a "working committee" in place of the current executive committee. The chief concern of the Deutsche Bank at this point, and certainly one in which the VIAG concurred, was that organizational improvements take place at the CA to improve profitability, and it intended to send Hans Rummel and some of the "specialists" at the Deutsche Bank to shape things up in Vienna. It was a

---

154   Both documents are to be found in DB, B 52.

measure of the dissatisfaction with operations in Vienna that while there was general agreement on the preference to be shown for the appointment of Austrians to the CA management board, the issue of competence was foremost and the way was left open for the appointment of non-Austrians.[155] The tenacity of the Deutsche Bank and Abs had thus paid off. It was an extraordinary achievement given the fact that the Deutsche Bank had been a totally insignificant shareholder in the CA, and Otto Neubaur of the RKG was shocked to learn this after the war. In his view, "they had bluffed in an extraordinarily skillful manner."[156]

Whether one interprets the role now being played by the Deutsche Bank as that of friend, missionary, or colonizer, or some mixture of the three, the intention to reform and improve the CA was very serious. On January 11, the Deutsche Bank wrote to the CA management board to notify it formally of its acquisition of 25 percent of the shares from the VIAG. This would make possible the kind of closer relationship envisaged in the friendship pact of the previous year and place the Deutsche Bank in a position to give the CA the benefit of its experience: "It will always be a pleasant obligation to support you in the future in every conceivable way with advice and assistance." According to the Deutsche Bank, recent discussions and consultations had demonstrated that the CA lacked the capability of attaining a sufficient "soundly based profitability" in the changed economic and business situation, but the investigations also revealed that there were numerous possibilities with respect to both expenditures and receipts where improved profitability was possible. Toward this end, the Deutsche Bank had worked out a program, which was being presented in the form of an exposé for the CA management, pulling together what had already been discussed by way of reforms. Additionally, it was assigning section director Georg Steinmann to assist on the expenditure side and Director Hermann Kübel of the Nürnberg branch to introduce them to new methods of dealing with the earnings side of the bank's operations. At the same time, CA officials were to be sent to Deutsche Bank branches to study firsthand the ways of doing things in the old Reich. Abs himself planned to introduce the Deutsche Bank advisors and discuss the implementation of the program when attending the executive committee meeting on January 20, at which time he also proposed to discuss problems of credit granting and the cash flow of the bank.[157]

Not surprisingly, the management board welcomed the assistance Abs and his colleagues offered, agreed to implement the proposals, and put Joham and Pfeiffer in charge of the project. It is quite clear from the correspondence and the exposé that the Deutsche Bank had done a considerable amount of interviewing and of investigating the affairs of the CA prior to concluding the actual agreement with the VIAG. The seven-page exposé was highly technical in nature, and this is no place to discuss its details, but it was fundamentally a program for the modernization and rationalization of what was viewed as an excessively complicated and expensive set of procedures employed by the CA. It was intended to educate not only the personnel of the bank but also its customers, with an eye toward reducing costs. Additionally, the CA was also urged to carry out the reform program in one of its branches that might then serve as an example for the other branches.[158]

While by no means pushing the CA to sell off its holdings in companies, the Deutsche Bank was now much less inhibited about offering its services in such eventualities, pointing out that its extensive contacts to large and medium-sized industrial firms made it possible to provide the CA with suitable purchasers who

[155] Ibid., memo by Abs on discussion between Olscher and Schirner of the VIAG and Kimmich and himself, Dec. 30, 1938.

[156] NARA, RG 260, Office of Military Government for Germany, United States (= OMGUS), Finance Division (= FINAD), 2/191/7, Neubaur Affidavit, July 22, 1947.

[157] DB, B 5, Deutsche Bank to CA, Jan. 11, 1939.

[158] See the meeting of the CA management board on Jan. 18, 1939, with the appended letters from the Deutsche Bank and the exposé by Steinmann dated Dec. 1938, in: BA-CA, CA-V, Vorstandssitzungen 1939.

had the capital that was necessary to develop the enterprises up for sale and who would also turn to the CA for banking services. Here again, the German banking model was being held up to the CA as an alternative or at least a supplement to the industrial holding model with which it was accustomed.[159]

Such generous offers, however, were combined with considerable criticism about major matters of organization. The division of labor and administration of regular operations in the management board was viewed as incorrect and dysfunctional, and a considerable number of suggestions were made for changes. But apparently the distribution of duties on the management board remained a problem; Kimmich viewed the way tasks were divided as an "impossibility," which he thought had "obviously been dictated by impossible considerations" from a banking point of view.[160] The details are of no immediate concern here, but the "impossible considerations" were of course the political ones, especially in that they pushed Joham, clearly the most competent banker of the lot, formally into the background even though his manifest authority and expertise are constantly apparent in the surviving correspondence and documentation. Joham was well aware that he remained a political problem, and he had prepared a lengthy curriculum vita for Abs in case Abs needed to intervene on his behalf – an eventuality that did not arise. On December 30, 1938, however, he decided to send it anyway because of the changes that were taking place and the possibility that Abs might find it useful with respect to the situation on the management board.[161]

Joham may have continued to be the logical chairman of the management board, but this was politically impossible, while the continuation of Heller, who was held in high regard, was nevertheless inappropriate given that he had more experience in industry than in banking. Thus, Olscher and Abs faced the problem of finding a suitable chairman of the management board, but the solution in the end revealed the kinds of problems about which Kimmich was complaining. The "solution" was none other than Hans Fischböck. The impending dissolution of the Austrian government and its ministries, including his own, meant that he needed a job, and Olscher already had him in mind in December. Fischböck signaled his interest by failing to approve the appointment of Hasslacher as chairman of the CA administrative council at the end of December 1938, which led Abs to suspect that Fischböck was thinking of himself for the position.[162] Ultimately, however, it was the position of chairman of the management board that was under consideration. The case for giving him this position was clear. He had worked at the CA years before and had headed the ÖVAG, and he was a major figure in the Party in Austria. The case against it, however, was also obvious. As Director Rummel of the Deutsche Bank noted in February 1939, the major problem of the CA was cost containment. Improved business conditions were leading to a reduction of demand for credits, so that profitability depended on a reduction of costs. What was needed, therefore, was leadership that would work hard at reducing costs and especially personnel, but Fischböck did not seem the right person for this because he would obviously be expected to act as the Party's company leader (*Betriebsführer*) and represent the CA in its dealings with the government and the Party. The appointment would also place more burdens on Fritscher and Joham. Both Rummel of the Deutsche Bank and Neubaur of the VIAG felt that Fischböck's appointment would reduce the value of their CA shares because Fischböck would not look after shareholders' interests.[163] Nevertheless, Fischböck's need for a prestigious job and political considerations finally won out, and Kehrl helped in the negotiations by working through the terms of the appointment. Fischböck would become chairman of the management board, but he agreed that decisions would be arrived at according to collegial principles, and personnel decisions at the higher

[159] DB, B 52, Deutsche Bank to CA, Feb. 6, 1939.
[160] Ibid., Kimmich to Abs, July 1, 1939.
[161] Ibid., B 57, Joham to Abs, Dec. 30, 1938.

[162] Ibid., B 52, memo by Abs, Dec. 30, 1938.
[163] Ibid., B 57, Rummel to Abs, Feb. 14, 1939.

level would be determined by the supervisory board so that Fischböck's role in personnel matters would be restricted to salaried personnel. In effect, Fischböck's role as chairman of the management board was intended to be quite limited in reality, and there appeared to be some hope that his appointment as company leader would make Pfeiffer superfluous. This was more easily said than done.[164]

The way was thus prepared for the first meeting of the supervisory board of the CA under the newly introduced German corporation law on May 2, 1939. Hasslacher was elected chairman and was to preside at meetings, and Olscher and Abs were elected deputy chairmen. Hasslacher then moved the appointment of the existing management board with Hans Fischböck as a new member and chairman of the board, and Heller stepped down from this position. Fischböck was also named company leader, and Pfeiffer yielded this position. As for Fischböck, he expressed his gratitude for the confidence placed in himself, and declared that he "considers it his leading major duty to lead the institution according to private economic principles in accordance with the interests of the State and the Party."[165]

Fischböck's appointment marked a plateau in the struggle for the control of the CA and the management of its internal affairs that had begun with the friendship pact of March 26, 1938. The period is instructive as an illustration of the relationship between banking and politics in the Third Reich and is testimony not only to the extraordinary ambition of Abs and the Deutsche Bank but also to the tenacity with which they pursued their interests and the compromises they had to make. The Creditanstalt was now owned by a powerful consortium of the Deutsche Bank and the VIAG and was managed by a managerial group strongly influenced by Party members. The Creditanstalt had little to say about the restructuring of its ownership, and Joham and, in particular, Heller

had survived only because of their competence. Joham's initiatives and Heller's backing, however, were important in shaping the outcome. Under the circumstances, time would tell whether the CA was a victim or a beneficiary of the transformation of its situation that had begun with the Anschluss.

3. INDUSTRIAL HOLDINGS AND PROVINCIAL BANK ALLIANCES

Lost Holdings

After the Second World War, the Creditanstalt, led by Joham, was to portray itself as a victim of German plundering of its holdings, although it was to give the Deutsche Bank credit for having saved it from some of the imprecations of the regime. There can be no question that the CA suffered extremely heavy and painful losses following the Anschluss, and its postwar claims that it had been compelled to sell off and surrender some of its most important and valuable industrial assets to German interests were unquestionably true.[166] The list was formidable; it is partially represented here with the percentage of CA ownership shown in parentheses: The Berndorfer Metallwarenfabrik Arthur Krupp AG (86.90%) was sold to Krupp-Essen. The Donau-Chemie AG (Pulverfabrik Skodawerke Wetzler AG) (88.83%) was sold to IG Farben. The Teudloff-Vamag Vereinigte Armaturen- und Maschinenfabriken AG (51%) shares were sold to Vereinigte Armaturen GmbH, Mannheim, and the Creditanstalt's holding in the Wiener Lokomotivfabrik (13%) was sold off to Firma Henschel & Sohn, Kassel. The Reichswerke Hermann Göring acquired the Continentale Motorschifffahrts AG (Comos) (57.34%), the Erste Donau-Dampfschifffahrtsgesellschaft (25.50%), the

[164] Ibid., Minutes by Kimmich, March 14 and March 22, 1939.

[165] BA-CA, CA-V, Meeting of the CA Supervisory Board, May 2, 1939.

[166] See NARA, Microcopy T-83, Roll 101, the memorandum of the Creditanstalt-Bankverein of November 1945 on the Repatriation of the Shares of the Bank and Its Concern Enterprises (Denkschrift der Creditanstalt-Bankverein hinsichtlich Repatriierung von Aktien der Bank und deren Konzernunternehmungen).

Kärntnerische Eisen- und Stahlwerks AG (66.80%), the Steirische Gussstahlwerke AG (100%), the Steyr-Daimler-Puch AG (78.20%), the Feinstahlwerke Traison AG (84.4%), and 7,059 shares of the Simmeringer Maschinen- und Waggonbau AG. Most of the aforementioned sales were made in 1938–1939. A few took place later; for example, the VIAG asked the CA to sell its shares in the Vereinigte Wiener Metallwerke AG (98.89%) to the Vereinigte Aluminiumwerke in Berlin in 1940. The CA was unable to continue its efforts to maintain its interest in the Elin AG für elektrische Industrie (25.48%) and sold its shares to the Deutsche Continental Gas Gesellschaft Dessau in March 1940. There were further losses in 1942, which will be discussed later in this study.[167]

Some of these lost holdings, as in the cases of Berndorfer Metallwarenfabrik and Donau-Chemie, had been of interest to their German purchasers even before the Anschluss. Others, especially those acquired by the Reichswerke Hermann Göring, were acquisitions sought and acquired after March 1938. In all cases, however, they appeared to run counter to the alleged goal of Keppler, Kehrl, Fischböck, and other National Socialist leaders as well as the RWM to prevent Germans and German enterprises from the old Reich from coming in and buying up Austrian assets. The RWM had formally banned the unauthorized acquisition of Austrian enterprises by Germans by law on March 19, 1938.[168] On March 29, Fischböck and Keppler instructed the CA that there were to be no sales of blocks of shares or holdings without permission.[169] Consistency, however, was not one of the hallmarks of National Socialist economic policy, and those

who spoke most loudly about maintaining the integrity of Austrian assets were often those most engaged in violating it, especially Kehrl and Keppler. Also, the "protection" of the Austrian economy did not necessarily mean its protection against all acquisitive Germans and was often a means of ensuring that such assets came into desired German hands. In any case, there was no single policy that explains how and why the CA lost twenty-one of its major industrial holdings, and it is important to examine some of the cases before drawing any conclusions about what the motives and the results were.

The Berndorfer Metallwarenfabrik

The Berndorfer Metallwarenfabrik Arthur Krupp AG, as noted earlier in this study, had been the subject of negotiations between the Krupp firm in Essen and the CA before the Anschluss. Krupp wanted to reacquire the company and had contributed to its refinancing in 1928, but the CA had provided the lion's share of the money for the refinancing, which finally began to pay off in 1936–1937. Polite negotiations continued, but the CA had no real interest in selling Berndorf back to the Krupps, and Krupps could not seriously think of a repurchase prior to the Anschluss because of the foreign exchange regulation barriers. Nevertheless, Gustav Krupp von Bohlen und Halbach remained bent on recovering the enterprise that had borne the family name for a century. The family's reasons to take action became even more compelling around the time of the Anschluss. Arthur Krupp, who always viewed Berndorf as his property even though he had been forced to surrender his shares for financial reasons, was aging and ailing, and he passed away on April 21, 1938. In addition, suitable employment had to be found for the sole Krupp heir, Claus von Krupp, Gustav's second son.[170] Moreover, there were also important business considerations. The Krupps were well aware that other German enterprises were interested in Berndorf, a factor that opened up the dread prospect that Berndorf might be snatched away and

---

[167] See ibid., and Liselotte Wittek-Saltzberg, *Die wirtschaftspolitischen Auswirkungen der Okkupation Österreichs*, Diss. (Vienna 1970), pp. 168–204. Full lists compiled after the war are to be found in BA-CA, CA-TZ, Sekretariat grün, Box 28/CA 20 d-m.

[168] Reichsgesetzblatt (= RGBl) I (1938), p. 264 and Kehrl, *Krisenmanager*, pp. 128–129.

[169] BA-CA, CA-TZ, Sekretariat rot, Box 1/AVA, BfK, Wiener BV, Fischböck to CA management board, March 29, 1938.

[170] HAK, WA 40/308, E 1276, Affidavit at Nürnberg of Johann Joeden, June 30, 1947.

that some other corporation might have use of the Krupp name. It was generally known that the Luftwaffe was keen on Berndorf taking up the production of aluminum. At the end of March, Director Werning of the Dürener Metallwerke had a discussion with Director Paul Goerens of Krupp in which the former stated that the Dürener could provide technical assistance to Berndorf and suggested that it might participate in the purchase of the Berndorf shares. Additionally, the Württembergische Metallwarenfabrik, whose production program complemented that of Berndorf, was also expressing interest. Finally, the firm of Basse & Selve, which was based in the Westphalian town of Altena, had a long-standing involvement with Berndorf, and while claiming less interest than before, nevertheless expected Krupp to give it priority if it were to seek a partner. There was always also the danger that the military would establish a plant of its own. In any case, on April 12, 1938, Krupp's syndic, Johann Joeden, informed Gustav Krupp von Bohlen und Halbach that there were at least three potential German contenders for Berndorf and that Werning had given them the friendly advice to move speedily before other German firms or state agencies entered the field.[171]

The only protection against such a development was the law of March 19 prohibiting German purchases of Austrian assets, but this was a formal barrier to Krupp as well. The CA also knew that German companies were interested in Berndorf. A revealing piece of internal correspondence at the CA at once confirmed the reality of the Krupps' fears of competitors as well as the CA's hopes that the law would act as a shield for its interests. On April 27, one of Heller's aides, Robert Glatzl, an official at the CA since 1922, reported a conversation with an intermediary for "a respectable large enterprise in the old Reich" that was interested in Berndorf. Glatzl told him that "there is no tendency at this time in our institution to alienate

concern enterprises, and this all the less so as the acquisition of Austrian enterprises by capitalists from the old Reich is at present barred by decrees or at least made more difficult." Glatzl did promise to let his colleague know if there was any intention to sell Berndorf, to which Heller remarked in the margins: "does not come into question."[172]

For Krupp, therefore, the tasks were manifold. It had to gain permission to negotiate with the CA, to prevent other old Reich interests from getting into the act, and to persuade it to sell Berndorf back to Krupp. Needless to say, Krupp was one of the mightiest concerns in the Reich, and the family enjoyed excellent business and political contacts. One of its most valuable personal assets was Gustav Krupp von Bohlen und Halbach's brother-in-law, Tilo Freiherr von Wilmowsky, a member of the Krupp supervisory board since 1910 who had a special interest in Central European economic affairs, was a leading figure in the Central European Economic Congress, and had also been a member of the supervisory board of the Mercurbank/Länderbank since 1935. He was highly respected and enjoyed a wealth of contacts. Wilmowsky worked hand in hand with the Krupp family in Essen as well as with Claus von Bohlen in the effort to bring Berndorf back into the Krupp fold. As early as March 20, he was able to inform Claus von Bohlen that he had spoken with Seyß-Inquart, whom he knew well, about their intentions and was told that the shares could not be bought without Keppler's permission. Even earlier, however, he was arranging for Gustav Krupp von Bohlen und Halbach to see Keppler about Berndorf, "an old Krupp family enterprise whose future has been and still is the object of numerous considerations."[173] Whether the meeting took place

---

[171] Joeden affidavit, June 30, 1947, ibid., 1277; note on a discussion between Director Goerens of Krupp and Director Werning of the Dürener Metallwerke, March 30, 1938, and HAK, WA 4/2874, memo by Joeden, April 28, 1938.

[172] BA-CA. Industriebeteiligungsarchiv der Creditanstalt (= CA-IB), Krupp, 41/01, Report by Glatzl to Heller, April 27, 1938.

[173] PA Berlin, R 27506, Wilmowsky to Keppler, March 15, 1938. Wilmowsky took the opportunity to wax nostalgic about their first conversation back in 1933 and the pride Keppler must feel at his contribution to German unity.

is uncertain, but Wilmowsky's letters to Keppler succeeded in their purpose, although Keppler's final approval was limited and reserved. On April 2, Keppler informed Wilmowsky that he had consulted with Göring, who had no objections to Krupp acquiring a majority of the shares, and that he was prepared to inform the Viennese ministries accordingly. He cautioned, however, that the ultimate approval would have to come from the RWM, which had banned share sales, and that the RWM would not tolerate being confronted with undesired decisions. Krupp, therefore, would have to negotiate with the CA. Keppler also pointedly indicated that Krupp could not only consider the interests of Krupp in taking over Berndorf: "I presume it to be self-understood that in the taking over of this enterprise you will do everything necessary in order to bring the Austrian economy into a condition that is now desirable in the general German interest and not only in the Austrian interest alone."[174]

Exactly what was expected remained rather unclear at this moment. Krupp was in any case in no position to deal with demands concerning an enterprise that was not in its hands, so that the real problem at this stage was convincing the CA to negotiate. An attempt by Director Hans Pilder of the Dresdner Bank on March 21 to get Joham to agree to negotiate met with rather negative results. The Dresdner Bank had close connections with Krupp, and both Wilmowsky and Pilder served on the administrative council of the Mercurbank. Wilmowsky apparently had asked Pilder to see Joham. Pilder had considerable negotiating experience and undoubtedly hoped to get some of the Berndorf business for the Mercurbank. Whatever the case, Joham was very resistant. He claimed that he could undertake no negotiations until the effects and implications of the currency reform became clear, but he also felt that the CA could not renounce

negotiating with other parties. Personally, he expressed his predilection for dealing with Krupp but without binding himself. In reporting on the conversation to Wilmowsky, Pilder admitted that Joham had a point in refusing to negotiate immediately, not because of the RWM ban on share sales to Germans that could easily be overcome in Pilder's view, but rather because of the currency situation. It was hard to assess the real value of accounts receivable and stocks of goods under the newly introduced 3:2 exchange rate and much depended on the official setting of prices and wages. What Pilder did find odd was Joham's refusal to bind the CA to deal with Krupp alone, insisting that he had no reason to give up an option without immediately getting something for it. When Pilder told Joham that he found this attitude "neither comprehensible nor friendly," Joham very cautiously stated he would be happy if Krupp in the end secured the enterprise. Pilder seems not to have hid his frustration, purposely leaving Joham with the impression "that his attitude seemed to me to be less than generous and accommodating."[175]

Pilder not only reported on his conversation with Joham to Wilmowsky but also to Abs, speaking as one German banker involved in Austrian affairs to another. He told Abs that he thought Joham's position was "wrong," pointing out, as Abs reported, that "he would consider it unfortunate if such negotiations, as is often usual today, are initiated through political agencies, and he would further consider it unfortunate if others were able to get ahead of the Krupp family by means of political support."[176] In Pilder's view, he and Abs should at least make sure that there was some discussion with the Krupp family so that one could make reference to such prior contacts should other contenders for Berndorf come on the scene. Abs responded that they were instructed by the authorities not to engage in negotiations pertaining to the sale of participations, and he also felt that negotiations were premature under

174 Ibid., Keppler to Wilmowsky, April 2, 1938. It and other relevant correspondence is also to be found in the Krupp Archive, see Wilmowsky to Claus von Bohlen, March 20, 1938; HAK, WA 4/2874, Keppler to Wilmowsky, April 2, 1938, and Wilmowsky to Claus von Bohlen, April 13, 1938.

175 Ibid., FAH4C192, Pilder to Wilmowksy, March 21, 1938.
176 DB, B 51, memo by Abs, April 12, 1938.

the circumstances. Abs, however, did indicate his willingness to talk to the leadership at the CA about the issue; he basically agreed "that one should try to solve these problems as well as all other problems through the private sector, and it would not be appropriate to introduce political agencies in support of one's own negotiations." When Pilder went on to say that if Berndorf were sold to Krupp, the CA could be promised a seat on the Berndorf supervisory board and half of Berndorf's business, Abs was careful to say nothing. It was not hard to guess, after all, who wanted to get the other half of the business, which, under existing conditions, was fully in the hands of the CA.

While Pilder was trying to mobilize Abs, Wilmowsky was discovering that Abs was on the CA administrative council, and immediately concluded that Abs, whom he and Claus von Bohlen knew, would be the "best intermediary." Abs promised Wilmowsky that he would speak to the CA leaders, and Wilmowsky began to feel confident that things were moving forward.[177] Pilder had not made matters easier for Abs, who found Joham and his colleagues extremely irritated by Pilder's undiplomatic and demanding attitude. Abs, in contrast to Pilder, felt that "one must handle the gentlemen of the Austrian Creditanstalt somewhat more cautiously." He intended, however, to keep his promise to promote negotiations with Krupp and also to urge that the price be arbitrated by calling on the services of auditors from the government-controlled Deutsche Revisions- und Treuhand AG.[178]

While obviously relying very heavily on Abs, those involved at Krupp were well aware that the Deutsche Bank was a long way from owning or controlling the CA and made sure they had more than one arrow in its quiver. Joeden also went to the Finance Ministry in late April 1938 to test the waters there. In his meeting with Ministerial Director Berger, who was very involved in the question of the government-owned CA shares, Berger pointed out that the ministry was anxious to keep things stable in Austria and would not intervene for or against negotiations with the CA over Berndorf and that the decision lay with the bank. He also would not promise that the ministry would intervene if the CA resisted Krupp. At the same time, however, he urged Joeden to contact Olscher without telling anyone who made the suggestion, indicating that Olscher and the VIAG would have a voice in CA decisions. Needless to say, Joeden did not communicate his conversation to Abs.[179]

On May 4, Gustav Krupp von Bohlen und Halbach and Claus von Bohlen paid a call on Abs to thank him for intervening on their behalf in connection with Berndorf. They also intended to thank Hasslacher for the "friendly disposition of the Creditanstalt." Abs informed them that he had talked to Joham and that, in contrast to its previous position, the CA was now ready to sell. Nevertheless, Abs was also cautious about how things might turn out, pointing out that the CA was offering Krupp "a first chance," and remarking that "now the most important thing is the price question."[180] In short, he was making no promise that the negotiations would be successful.

Olscher, who was by this time also involved, took a similar position and so informed the CA management board on May 4. On the one hand, he reported on recent conversations with Keppler, who had made clear that Göring had not only sanctioned the sale of the shares but also ordered that only Krupp came into question as a purchaser. Olscher had the feeling, however, that both Keppler and Göring may have thought that the shares were not in the hands of the CA but rather of the Industriekredit, and he had clarified the matter with Keppler. This did not change Krupp's position as the sole potential purchaser, but it did change the negotiating position of the CA because Olscher made clear to Keppler that the price would have to be based on economic considerations and would need to take into account the anticipated improvement of conditions in Austria.

[177] HAK, WA 4/2874, Wilmowsky to Claus von Bohlen, April 13, 1938.
[178] Ibid., memorandum by Joeden, April 28, 1938.
[179] Ibid.
[180] DB, B 51, memo by Abs, May 5, 1938.

Olscher also informed the CA of a conversation with Director Ewald Löser of Krupp, in which Olscher reported that Krupp would be the only candidate for the purchase of the shares but that the firm would have to negotiate directly with the CA. He disabused Löser of any notion that might have been entertained with respect to a sale based on the stock market quotation of March 11, which was 111.20 percent, and Löser seemed to understand this. In Olscher's view, Krupp could afford to pay a good price, but he offered his services as a mediator if an agreement could not be reached.[181]

Abs and Olscher, therefore, were pushing the CA to negotiate, but they were also leaving the CA with a free hand in settling on a price. The preliminary negotiations began on May 9, when Claus von Bohlen and Heller met in Vienna. The former reported in great detail on the discussions.[182] Claus von Bohlen began by expressing his appreciation for the opportunity to discuss Berndorf, reminding Heller of a conversation they had the previous year during a visit of German industrialists to Vienna when Heller had assented to his remark that "in the last analysis it is not the task of banks to direct industrial enterprises on their own," and had also stated that the CA was not in principle opposed to selling blocks of shares. Heller confirmed that these views continued to pertain, although this was somewhat odd because Heller was the dominant figure in the CA's industrial holdings. Whatever the case, he placed particular emphasis on the special significance of negotiating with and selling to the Krupps. But when it came to the actual issues in negotiation, there were substantial differences. Claus von Bohlen stressed the CA's moral obligation to Krupp for its large contribution to the 1928 reconstruction, while Heller remarked that the CA lawyers could find neither a legal nor a moral obligation to take this into account. The result was to table this issue for a later date.

The Krupps, apparently, were prepared to discuss buying only a majority of the shares and leaving a minority with the CA, but Heller pointed out that experience had shown the CA that minority stakes did not work: "A bank is accustomed to view and to direct an industrial enterprise in some respects differently than a private businessman. This has often produced differences of opinion. H[eller] would regret if for this reason differences showed up precisely with respect to our firm. It would be important to the CA, therefore, to sell the block of shares as an entirety." At the same time, Heller did insist that Berndorf continue to use the CA as its bank. Claus von Bohlen agreed to buy the entire block of shares if the price were satisfactory and also to use the CA as Berndorf's bank under normal circumstances.

Both sides agreed that expert help was necessary to properly assess the value of Berndorf, and while Heller promised to furnish materials, the Krupps were to send expert members of their staff to make an on-the-spot determination. There was considerable disagreement, however, about the basic principles on which the price should be determined. Heller took the view that consideration had to be given both to the heavy CA investment in the modernization of the company and to its future earning power given the anticipated upswing in the Austrian economy resulting from recent events. Claus von Bohlen agreed that the condition of Berndorf was quite satisfactory at the moment but that it would soon face stiff competition from the more modern works in the old Reich and might also face higher raw materials and labor costs. Furthermore, there was also some difference over the estate at Markenstein, which belonged to Berndorf. Heller believed its timber to be of value and hoped to sell it along with Berndorf, while Claus von Bohlen expressed reservations about taking it. A final problem was who would be obligated to bear the costs of liquidating the unprofitable brass sheet plant at Achenrain and the job losses that its closure would entail.

Needless to say, it would be absurd for a historian writing more than sixty years after the event to try to determine in any detail whether the

[181] HAK, WA 40/308, E 1286, Olscher to CA management board, May 4, 1938.
[182] For the discussion and quotations that follow, see ibid., WA 4/2874, Claus von Bohlen memorandum of May 9, 1938.

CA actually received a "just price" for Berndorf in the end. There were plenty of blatantly unjust prices that were paid for Austrian assets in the Austria of 1938, but they were hardly big business deals among large Aryan enterprises like Krupp and the CA. The CA claimed after the war that it was cheated, and at the Nürnberg trials the purchase was treated as another illustration of Krupp acting as a "plunderer." The charge, at least in this instance, was absurd. Political pressures certainly played a role in forcing the CA to sell what it would not have sold otherwise, but there were also political counter-pressures that influenced the outcome. What is of enduring historical interest is not whether, for example, the metal stocks at Berndorf were properly valuated but rather the constellation of persons, mentalities, and motives involved in the sale of Berndorf to Krupp.

Claus von Bohlen thought his first meeting with Heller went well, and he and the expert team sent by Krupp were satisfied and even impressed by their subsequent visit to Berndorf. The works made a fine impression and showed all the signs of the investment and modernization that had taken place in recent years. To be sure, this process had not been completed and substantial investments would be necessary, especially in view of the changes in production that would be required by the new political circumstances. There was general agreement on the Krupp side, however, that Berndorf was "definitely viable and through its favorable situation as a unique work in the new 'Ostmark' even has quite fine future prospects."[183] There was no evidence that they were troubled by their negotiations on May 16 with the CA.

The same cannot be said for Robert Glatzl, who negotiated on behalf of the CA with Claus von Bohlen, Finance Director Johannes Schroeder, and an engineer from the Krupp-Gruson-Werk in Magdeburg. In a lengthy report to the management board, Glatzl began by emphasizing that he tried to make the negotiations as friendly as possible and to deal with the numerous points of contention

with the Krupp delegation in an objective manner. All this was a long way of saying that he controlled his temper. He did not do so in his report. Quite early in the document he remarked: "I want to note already at this point that I gained the impression that the sale of our Berndorf shares to the Krupp firm in Essen can hardly be considered since in the course of the almost ten-hour discussion I became increasingly convinced that these gentlemen imagine they will able to secure this engagement at an especially low price; but they also appear not to want to pay this low price in cash since they only negotiated about bank credits here, and when I named the present rate for concern credits of about 8 percent, the gentlemen declared that for them the highest rate to come in question would be 5 percent. I then answered that to my knowledge the credit in the Reich at the present costs about 6½."[184] Although there was agreement on how to deal with Achenrain, the Markenstein estate presented particular problems because Krupp wanted the CA to hold on to it with an option to buy after a few years, whereas Glatzl took the position that Markenstein was a composite part of Berndorf and an asset integral to the value of its shares. If the CA sold Berndorf then, in his view, it sold Markenstein. Glatzl was also irritated by Krupp's desire to claim that Berndorf had bad accounts receivable where none could be identified and to undervalue the stocks of metals at the plants. He also thought, as had been argued by Heller and himself in the preliminary negotiations, that the price should include something for goodwill in view of all that had been done to increase the value of Berndorf by the CA and should also reflect the fact that the CA was selling on the cusp of an economic boom. The Krupp negotiators, however, argued that the value should be calculated on the basis of the condition of the company before the Anschluss. It was a measure of how put upon Glatzl felt that he asked the Krupp negotiators to consider that "Herr Baurat Heller and I bear a significant responsibility in these negotiations and that we,

---

[183] Ibid., Claus von Bohlen to Wilmowsky, May 19, 1938.

[184] HAK, WA 40/308, E 1288, Report on the discussions in Berndorf on May 16, 1938.

being conscious of this responsibility, are also not in a position to make concessions that are lacking in any plausible basis."[185] While Krupp was prepared to use the CA as its bank, there was some hesitation at making this arrangement binding for a decade and paying the going rate for credits. There was also quibbling about who was to pay the Berndorf pensions and cover past foreign exchange losses, and the Krupp negotiators were particularly hard-nosed about the machinery and equipment at the company and, in Glatzl's view, remarkably insensitive to the amount of investment that had gone into Berndorf in recent years. Indeed, insofar as they were willing to take over the machinery, the Krupp negotiators calculated the amortization and book value at 21 percent of their cost. Glatzl considered "negotiations on this basis completely out of the question because the Creditanstalt has no reason to sell the mark to the respected house of Friedrich Krupp in Essen for 10 or 20 Groschen." While Glatzl did not contest that Krupp would have to invest around 9 million RM in Berndorf, he pointed out that 7 million RM of this would be for a new production program and that the economic situation was such that it would rapidly pay its way. He was totally unsympathetic to complaints about the high cost of employee and worker housing that had been built in Berndorf, Glatzl argued, in order to lure the many technicians and skilled workers to Berndorf from Vienna, a policy pursued much earlier by the Krupps themselves. Both sides agreed that the valuation of various other facilities at Berndorf would have to wait on the technical investigation under way, but Glatzl was very dissatisfied with the Krupp attitude, noting that Claus von Bohlen had made a passing remark suggesting that they hoped to get Berndorf for its nominal worth with a small premium. He claimed that companies paying a 9 percent to 10 percent dividend in the old Reich were purchased at nominal worth because social welfare contributions and taxes ate up the profit. In this connection, Claus von Bohlen complained effusively

about the setting up of large weapons plants by the Gustloff-Stiftung in nearby Hirtenberg, which in his view would significantly reduce the value of Berndorf because such weapons factories paid very high wages and benefits and this would inevitably affect conditions at Berndorf. Glatzl's conclusion was bitter and grim: "In view of the course of the discussions described, I saw no reason to make any binding statement about any of the points in question, because I have the feeling that the House of Krupp in Essen would like to acquire the enterprise for a nominal amount, but not for its actual worth."[186]

Krupp's technical report, which arrived a few days later, simply added to the sense of anger directed at Krupp at Berndorf and at the CA. The chief manager at Berndorf, Fritz Hamburger, considered the report "disloyal in the highest degree." He was horrified by the way the report "sought to understate the enormous values available at Berndorf." Given the situation in the Reich, they were convinced that both the productive and the social investments needed in the coming years would pay for themselves. Indeed, Glatzl considered the entire report "unworthy" of a concern with Krupp's reputation, and he would just as soon have stopped negotiating.[187] The issue, of course, was not dignity but also money. Krupp offered to buy the shares at 135 percent, while the CA asked for 270 percent. The difference, therefore, was very substantial, as Heller reported to the executive committee on May 27, where he was nevertheless instructed to continue negotiating.[188]

Krupp's low offer, aside from the desire to use its position to pay as little as possible, reflected both family interests and its reading of the recent history of Berndorf. The purchase of Berndorf was not to be undertaken by Friedrich Krupp

185 Ibid.

186 Ibid.
187 BA-CA, CA-IB, Krupp, 41/01, Glatzl, report for Heller, May 24, 1938. See also StA Nürnberg, Aug. 5, 1947, Nl 11177, Glatzl's affidavit at Nürnberg.
188 BA-CA, CA-V, executive committee, May 27, 1938. For the negotiating positions, see HAK, FAH4C192, report on a discussion with Olscher, June 15, 1938.

AG but rather by the Krupp family, and it was intended as a capital investment for the family. The high price reduced the incentive because Gustav Krupp von Bohlen und Halbach had five sons and, as was reported to Heller, he did not appear willing to give Claus such an "expensive dowry" because he had four other sons to take care of.[189] The other reason for the low Krupp offer undoubtedly was the strong feeling that it had been disloyally treated by the CA, both with respect to Krupp's investment in 1928 and with respect to the CA's promise to treat Krupp as a partner during the period of Austro-German tension. In a memorandum of June 9, Joeden recounted the entire history in great detail and came to the conclusion that Krupp had at the very least "a moral right to preferential treatment."[190]

If Krupp had counted on Abs to smooth the way for negotiations, it now counted on Olscher to bring down the CA's price. When Claus von Bohlen initially asked for Olscher's help at the end of May, Olscher pointed out that it was not the VIAG's or the RKG's policy to interfere directly in the affairs of enterprises over which they had influence. Furthermore, the VIAG did not have an absolute majority and would find it difficult in any case to tell the CA to sell a block of shares for a definite price. Shortly thereafter, Olscher did talk to Joham, who simply found the price offered by Krupp too low without responding to Olscher's query as to whether the price demanded by the CA might not be too high. Joham did indicate he might come down if the CA could sell the Markenstein estate but that the CA could not accept responsibility for accepting the low price Krupp offered. Indeed, Olscher found himself in something of a quandary in trying to mediate because Krupp had set its offer as the top limit, and he could not take it upon himself to push this limit with the CA. Olscher also did not push Gustav Krupp von Bohlen und Halbach's proposal that the matter be sent to arbitration by the Deutsche Revisions- und Treuhand AG because Krupp was a member of its administrative council, but he appeared more willing to suggest this when he was reminded that the VIAG and Fischböck were also members.[191]

Nevertheless, at a meeting with Claus von Bohlen on June 15, Olscher continued to feel that negotiation was preferable to arbitration, and he thought some of the demands of the CA could be reduced, for example, for the stocks of metal at Berndorf, which would probably be replaced by the Reich in any case, and for Markenstein. Olscher felt the price could be brought down to 168 percent, perhaps even to 160 percent, while the Krupp director, Ewald Löser, thought 120 percent was enough but was willing to contemplate 145 percent. Where Löser stressed the uncertainties with respect to materials and wages, Olscher obviously felt there was a limit on what he could try to get the CA to accept.[192] The reality, no longer expressed by anyone, was that the CA never wanted to sell in the first place, and its constant reiteration of its own investments in Berndorf was the only way left to make its case and resist the low offers from Krupp.

The Austrian resistance was significant, however, and it surprised − and irritated − the Germans. As Löser reported concerning a conversation with a board member of the RKG: "According to him, all the Austrian negotiations are made difficult presently because the Austrians, and especially the Viennese, are aggravated by the strong patronization or pressure from Berlin or from the old Reich, and because of this irritation they are reserved and even negative with respect to many questions, especially economic and business ones. To a certain extent, the slogan 'Austria for the Austrians,' or, otherwise expressed, 'more independence for the Austrians,' has been successful. That has shown itself in the case of Keppler and also shows itself now in many economic negotiations. They also

[189] BA-CA, CA-IB, Krupp, 41/01, Glatzl to Hamburger, June 10, 1938.
[190] HAK, WA 4/2874, memorandum by Joeden for Bohlen and Löser, June 9, 1938.

[191] Ibid., Claus von Bohlen to Gustav Krupp von Bohlen und Halbach, May 28, 1938 and memo by Claus von Bohlen on telephone conversation with Olscher, June 2, 1938.
[192] Ibid., Discussion with Olscher, June 15, 1938.

noticed it at the Reichs-Kredit-Gesellschaft regarding questions on which they had to work with the Creditanstalt. In this way, the influence that could have been exercised by the VIAG (Olscher) in the Berndorf question was being reduced. Dr. Schaeffer then added that he was telling me this so that we should not be surprised if the influence one could exercise from here for a speedy settlement of the Berndorf business was diminishing. Here in Berlin itself, they probably have – in any case judging by recent developments – overestimated the possibilities of influencing Austrian business enterprises."[193]

Nevertheless, the Berndorf issue was coming to a conclusion. On June 19, Gustav Krupp von Bohlen und Halbach authorized Claus von Bohlen to offer a maximum of 150 percent, to remove Markenstein from the transaction, and to make a number of other concessions, but then to make clear that the price was far too high, that they did not think there was a chance of much profit, and that the offer would be cancelled if it were not accepted soon. While Löser and Olscher did not think the Deutsche Revisions- und Treuhand AG would welcome the task of arbitration, Gustav Krupp von Bohlen und Halbach had heard otherwise from one of its chief managers, Wilhelm Voss, who pointed out that it had set up an office in Vienna for precisely such purposes.[194] This did not, however, prove necessary because a final agreement was worked out by June 24 and accepted by the executive committee of the CA and by Krupp. Under this arrangement, the 65,195 shares were to be sold at a rate of 148.85 percent, with Markenstein being taken over by the CA, Achenrain by Krupp, and Krupp agreeing to use the CA as Berndorf's bank under standard conditions. The CA also agreed to take responsibility for accounts receivable uncovered by reserves. The offer was in fact at 155 percent, but the exclusion of Markenstein and other CA concessions had reduced the actual

price to 148.85 percent. Subsequently, various adjustments were made to the agreement, so that the sale price in July was set at 161.5 percent, or about 8,400,000 RM, while the calculation of all the complicated arrangements produced an estimated actual share sales rate of 216 percent.[195]

Several differences between the two sides were ironed out in the summer and early fall, but the transaction still needed the sanction of the Party authorities. On the one hand, Neubacher and other Party leaders seemed to feel that it was important that the CA sell some of its industrial holdings, and the sale of Berndorf seemed to fit in with this idea.[196] On the other hand, Party leaders wanted assurances that Krupp would satisfy Party expectations. The Gau economic advisor for the Lower Danube, Heinz Birthelmer, for example, was rather irritated that he had not been consulted about the purchase, especially because he feared that Krupp would scale back the facilities at Berndorf. He had to be reassured that the reverse would be the case and that the commissar for the private economy, Rafelsberger, had approved the sale.[197] Actually, Rafelsberger had not made matters easy, giving his temporary approval in July provided that Berndorf would produce aluminum in sufficient quantities with the assistance of an experienced German aluminum company. In a further discussion, Rafelsberger indicated that Krupp should collaborate with the Dürener Metallwarenfabrik, which the Krupp representatives found quite astonishing because they thought they had a free hand in choosing their partner. They pointed out to Rafelsberger that they had put off a decision until they had actually purchased the shares, whereupon Rafelsberger declared that it did not matter to him with whom they worked just as long as they produced aluminum and received approval from the military authorities for their

193 Ibid., FAH 4C192, Löser to Gustav Krupp von Bohlen und Halbach, June 24, 1938.
194 Ibid., WA 4/2873, Gustav Krupp von Bohlen und Halbach to Claus von Bohlen, June 19, 1938.

195 BA-CA, CA-IB, Krupp 41/01, discussion of June 24, 1938, between Claus von Bohlen, Heller, and Glatzl, and BA-CA, CA-V, executive committee meeting, June 24, 1938, and July 15, 1938.
196 HAK, WA 40/59, Testimony by Wilmowsky at Nürnberg, March 31, 1947.
197 Ibid., WA 4/2874, Wilmowsky to Claus von Bohlen, June 30, 1938.

plans. It was only after this approval was secured that Krupp could proceed with its plans at Berndorf.[198] Thus, even after the Anschluss and despite its successful reacquisition of Berndorf, Krupp found doing business in Austria more of a problem than had been imagined. At this point, however, the CA had every interest in promoting Krupp's investments in Berndorf, having been transformed now from the owner to the house bank of the enterprise.

The Pulverfabrik Skodawerke Wetzler AG (SWW)

In some contrast to the pre-Anschluss stalemate over Berndorf, IG Farben and the CA were on the verge of working out a compromise concerning the SWW when the Germans marched into Austria. This transformed the negotiating situation of the IG and the CA in a most decisive way. For one thing, the chief SWW negotiators were no longer on the scene. Rottenberg, as has been shown, was thrown out of the CA, arrested, mistreated, but then released. General Director Isidor Pollak was also arrested almost immediately but then freed. This was followed, however, by a Gestapo house search on April 30, during which he was trampled on in front of his sister, suffered a stroke or heart attack, and died before reaching the hospital. The Gestapo men involved complained about ruining their heels.[199]

Not only had the negotiators on the CA side changed, however, but the negotiating situation had also been radically transformed. Günther Schiller, an aide to Director Max Ilgner of IG Farben, who had served as the chief negotiator with Pollak and Rottenberg, emphasized this in a report to Ilgner after the Anschluss and pointed out that there were going to be heavy investments in Austria and warned that

there were now competitors for the SWW in the form not only of other chemical companies but also of the Reichswerke. Ilgner, a driving force in the IG's expansion into Austria and a strong proponent of a Southeast Europe orientation as well, felt it essential that the IG protect its interests in Austria and reopen its bid for a majority control of the SWW. Ten days after the Anschluss, the IG's commercial committee decided that it would resume negotiations on such a basis and sent Paul Haefliger, a member of the committee, a Swiss citizen, and one of the more internationalist figures in the concern, to negotiate with Joham.[200]

On March 29, Haefliger met with Joham and with Isidor Pollak, who had not yet been murdered. Haefliger knew that Pollak was there for formal reasons, and he was also quite conscious of the fact that Joham's position was shaken. Nevertheless, he realized at the same time that anyone leading the CA would have to look after its obvious interests. Thus he proposed, and Joham readily accepted, the idea that the IG would take a 70 percent stake, leaving the CA with a solid minority holding. In response to Joham's remarks that he could not sell the shares for an inadequate price and that the CA should benefit from the anticipated future development of the firm, Haefliger proposed that the Deutsche Revisions- und Treuhand AG be called in to assess the present value of the shares but that they also negotiate an arrangement whereby the CA receive an interest-bearing payment for a number of years so as to benefit from the subsequent development of the business. Nonetheless, because of the removal of Jews from the management and administrative council of the company one could not wait on the sale of the shares before the IG took control. Pollak thus officially proposed that Günther Schiller be delegated to the management of the SWW and that IG personnel be appointed to replace the Jews on the administrative council so that it could be a functioning body and also approve Schiller's

[198] Ibid., Rafelsberger to Krupp, July 11, 1938, and negotiations with Rafelsberger of July 8/9, 1938.

[199] StA Nürnberg, NI 435, Affidavit by Franz Rottenberg, Sept. 13, 1947. The situation was described to Rottenberg by Pollak's sister. A slightly different version of Pollak's death was provided by his maid Elisabeth Kindler in an affidavit of Sept. 14, 1947, who only mentions his having a stroke or heart attack resulting from the shock of the Gestapo visit. StA Nürnberg, K 61.

[200] Hayes, *Industry and Ideology*, pp. 104–105, 200, 221–225; see also StA Nürnberg, J 3, Ilgner's testimony at Nürnberg.

appointment. Haefliger also told Joham that the IG was prepared to send technical and commercial experts and administrative assistance to fill the gaps that had been created because of the Anschluss. At the same time, Haefliger revealed that IG Farben's basic program for Austria remained the same as it had been before the Anschluss. The SWW was to be joined with the Austrian plants of Dynamit Nobel to form a new Ostmark Chemie AG. The Anilinchemie AG was to be dissolved and replaced by a new sales organization bearing the name Ostmark Chemikalien-Handelsgesellschaft, which would then handle the sales of the IG's products in Austria.[201]

Needless to say, all these arrangements required the approval of the political authorities in Vienna, and immediately after his discussion with Joham, Haefliger began a round of visits to those on whose blessing their realization would ultimately depend. Fischböck was first on the list, and Haefliger emphasized "that we are not here to exploit the situation but rather to perform constructive work." Fischböck seemed open enough to the proposals, asking that Joham present them in writing directly to him, and indicating that he was in constant contact with Keppler about such matters. Haefliger was well aware how much depended on Keppler's attitude, and because he could not see Keppler immediately, he visited Keppler's aide Edmund Veesenmayer on March 31 instead. The latter thought the proposed new company made sense, but he warned Haefliger that IG Farben would not receive a "carte blanche." While prepared to see IG representatives come temporarily into the management bodies of the SWW because of the situation, they were not to receive honoraria and were to be replaced by Austrians wherever possible in the final arrangement. This solicitude for the Austrians was repeated when Haefliger finally got to see Keppler on April 2, the latter noting that it is not wished "that the IG buys up all the small chemical enterprises

in Austria."[202] Manifestly, it was important to lay the groundwork by making such visits, and Haefliger also took advantage of the opportunity to test the waters with respect to IG plans in the Sudetenland and in Czechoslovakia. What also becomes apparent from Haefliger's activities at this time, however, was that the dismissal of Jews and other political undesirables was not only a problem at the SWW but also at IG Farben's Anilinchemie, Dynamit Nobel, and Deutsch-Carbid Matrei, so that a host of IG people had to be brought in and close attention had to be paid to satisfying the local authorities and the Party.

By April 10 all the necessary steps appear to have been taken to gain permission for the IG Farben plan. Joham had dutifully written to Fischböck on March 31 outlining the projected agreement and his understanding with Haefliger, while the IG had given its approval to Haefliger's negotiations, and the latter sent Keppler a report on April 9 of IG Farben's plans for the organization of its chemical enterprises in Austria and on its negotiations with the CA. Haefliger stressed the urgency of bringing the negotiations to a conclusion, not only because of the personnel issues involved but also because of the need to integrate the Austrian chemical industry into the Four Year Plan.[203]

Fischböck, however, was not in quite as much of a rush as IG Farben. It was not until April 20 that he sent Joham's petition for permission to sell the shares to Keppler and advised that they first get an auditor's report from the Deutsche Revisions- und Treuhand AG before making a final decision as to whether to approve the sale.[204] A further problem developed when

---

[201] Ibid., Nl 3981–3982; Haefliger provided a detailed report on his visit to Vienna on March 29/April 2, 1938, and he also sent a letter to Joham on March 29, summarizing their discussion.

[202] Ibid., Haefliger report of April 6, 1938.
[203] Copies of Joham's letter to Fischböck of March 31, 1938 are to be found in ibid., and in PA Berlin, R 27507. For Haefliger's report and its approval by the Chemicals Committee, see StA Nürnberg, Nl 14743, and for IG Farben's proposal to Keppler of April 9, 1938, see ibid., Nl 4024. There is a very useful account of the course of the negotiations prepared for the IG Farben management board meeting of Oct. 21, 1938, in BAB, R 8121, A 4000.
[204] PA Berlin, R 27507, Fischböck to Keppler, April 20, 1938.

Rafelsberger decided to install state commissars not simply for the SWW but for all the IG plants in Austria. In part, this was a reaction to disagreements with Schiller, but it was also an expression of reservations about IG Farben more generally and a potential threat to its arrangement with the CA. The commissars had the power to override any decisions made by the management or the administrative councils installed by the IG.[205] This occurred on May 5, and two days later leading IG officials showed up at the RWM in Berlin to complain to the leading officials there, among them Kehrl and State Secretary Brinkmann. For the moment, however, these were problems that had to be solved in Vienna, and Ilgner was empowered by the IG to negotiate with Rafelsberger, whose star was rising as Keppler's in Austria was fading.[206]

On May 9, Ilgner headed for Vienna, where he met up with Heinrich Gattineau of his staff, who had already been sent to lobby with his National Socialist connections in Vienna. Other negotiators for the IG were Haefliger, Hans Kügler, and Karl Meyer from Ilgner's staff. They negotiated with an array of the high and mighty in Vienna, especially Bürckel; Fischböck; Neubacher, who had worked for IG Farben when in exile and knew Gattineau; Kehrl and Veesenmayer, who now served as Kehrl's aide; Rafelsberger and his aide Georg Bilgeri; and last, a ranking German Labor Front official in Austria, Nemec. The reason for the appointment of the commissars, it turned out, was the dissatisfaction of the employees at Deutsch-Matrei and Dynamit Nobel about personnel and business policies of IG Farben, especially prior to the Anschluss, when Jews had supposedly been favored over Aryans and the IG had supposedly given in to too many Czech demands. These complaints, when combined with the difficulties surrounding the SWW negotiations, seemed to have convinced Rafelsberger that the IG was operating counter to the general lines of policy

that had been laid out and that it was also planning to subordinate its Austrian plants completely to its operations in the old Reich instead of expanding its Austrian operations and hiring Austrians for the leading positions. Keppler, who met with Ilgner, also complained about the IG's failure to fire its Jewish representatives in Southeast Europe and its allegedly soft policy in dealing with Jews in general.[207]

Given this array of problems, it took considerable string-pulling and effort to achieve a compromise and to get rid of the commissars, but on May 13 an agreement was reached under which IG Farben promised to consult with Rafelsberger on all significant appointments and to appoint a special person for Austria who would keep regular contact with Rafelsberger. In return for a basic approval of the negotiations with the CA over the SWW, the IG pledged to modernize and expand its facilities in Austria and, where possible, to build new plants and increase product lines. Furthermore, it promised to hire the chief commissar Rafelsberger had appointed, place him in charge of what was now being called the Donau-Chemie once it was created, and also to make him the head of the Austrian section of the economic policy division of IG Farben. The obstreperous Schiller was temporarily replaced by Gattineau, who could continue to cultivate his Party contacts in Vienna, but the long-term personnel problems were solved on May 24 when Ilgner was placed in charge of Austria and Southeast Europe for the IG, while another IG director, Ernst R. Fischer, was assigned to Vienna as IG Farben's chief representative in Vienna as well as chief negotiator in dealing with the CA.[208]

By this time, Pfeiffer had replaced Joham as chief negotiator for the CA, and there was no further talk of even a minority CA stake in the SWW because the acquisition of the SWW was now part of a larger IG program for the reorganization of the entire chemical industry

[205] See ÖStA/AdR, BMF, Allgem. Reihe 1938, 48933/1938, on the state commissar at the SWW, Richard Pelz.

[206] See BAB, R 8121, A 4000, the report to the IG Farben management board meeting of Oct. 21, 1938.

[207] Ibid., and StA Nürnberg, J 3 and Nl 13026, Interrogation of Ilgner and affidavits of April 29, 1947.

[208] See BAB, R 8121, A 4000, the report to the IG Farben management board meeting of Oct. 21, 1938.

in Austria and of various arrangements made in Czechoslovakia and Hungary. On June 17, the IG Farben management board formally approved the purchase of the SWW on the basis of the auditor's report. The projected purchase was viewed with limited enthusiasm. On the one hand, IG officials was reasonably confident that the plants at Moosbierbaum could be made profitable, but costs would have to be reduced and unprofitable production lines shut down. This would not be easy because wages would have to be raised and housing provided to meet government and Party standards, and one had therefore to hope that the costs would be made bearable by the anticipated economic pickup. These mixed feelings were reflected in the IG response to the auditor's report, which recommended a price of 210 percent. In view of the recently imposed reduction of chemical prices by the government and the anticipated investment costs, however, a decision was made to offer only 180 percent.[209]

  Both the CA and the IG now assumed that they could move ahead quickly, and Pfeiffer made an unscheduled announcement of the conclusion of the negotiations at the meeting of the CA executive committee on July 15. To everyone's surprise, however, the government representative at the meeting, Johann Rizzi, declared that he had reservations about the agreement and that it was subject to further discussion. The executive committee thus accepted the agreement subject to government approval. The source of the difficulty was that the SWW had in its portfolio a block of shares amounting to 50 percent of the Sprengstoffwerke Blumau AG that actually belonged to the Land of Austria. Another 25 percent belonged to the SWW, and the remaining 25 percent to the former or present directors of the SWW. The military authorities in Berlin considered this a very important military producer and were absolutely insistent that IG Farben not be allowed to have any influence on it, a condition that obviously would arise if the IG bought the SWW with the Blumau shares still in its portfolio.

Indeed, they wanted all the shares in the hands of the Reich. The Army Weapons Office had warned the Austrian authorities that they would be held responsible if the shares were sold without its approval. As a consequence, the Austrian Ministry of Commerce informed Heller that it had to refuse approval of the sale of the SWW shares to IG Farben until the Blumau shares were separated out and returned to the Land of Austria or transferred to the Reich.[210]

  This created a very untoward situation that delayed the sale of the SWW shares until October. The Blumau shares had been purchased in 1926 for a very low price as a consequence of the difficulties of the Bayerische Sprengstoffwerke. It had been a surprisingly good investment, earning double the invested capital during each of the eleven and a half years since the purchase. The IG was particularly put off by the situation. In his negotiations at the Austrian Finance Ministry, Fischer pointed out that the decision of the IG to offer 180 percent for what was now 90 percent of the SWW shares reflected a conscious decision to pay too high a price for the shares, namely, 7,560,000 RM. Blumau had been included in the shares and had an estimated value of 800,000 RM. The army was proposing that the IG buy the SWW with Blumau and then sell Blumau at cost, which the IG rejected as adding to the loss it was taking in the purchase.

  Given the pressures from the Party and the government to conclude an agreement with the CA rapidly, there could be no talk of resuming the already concluded negotiations. Finally, an arrangement was worked out between the IG and the authorities under which the SWW would sell its shares and those of its directors for 200,000 RM, thus enabling the Reich to control 100 percent of Blumau. At the same time, the IG would take over the nonmilitary production of Blumau, which it estimated to be worth 400,000 RM, but would also promise to supply raw materials to the Blumau plant

---

[209] Ibid.

[210] Ibid., BA-CA, CA-V, CA executive committee meeting of July 15, 1938; see ÖStA/AdR, BMF, Allgem. Reihe 1938, 50623/1938, for the position of the Finance Ministry and its reasons.

that would be used solely for military purposes. These arrangements were concluded on September 21, and the agreement with the government was signed in early October, whereupon the government authorized the CA sale of the SWW shares to IG Farben. The shares were sold for 7,424,130 RM, to be paid in five installments bearing 5 percent interest.[211]

The CA had thus been driven out of the chemical business in Austria and, in contrast to the sale of Berndorf, was not even given the status of the SWW's house bank. The efforts to save the SWW for the CA on the part of Rottenberg and Isidor Pollak had come to naught because of the Anschluss. The IG leadership was probably sincere in thinking that it had paid too much for the SWW, and its primary motive had been protection against competition in Austria and government intervention. The creation of the Donauchemie AG in 1939, however, did not spare IG Farben irritating demands by Rafelsberger for Party appointments to the company's boards, and it turned out to be of little value in Ilgner's plans for IG expansion into Southeast Europe.[212]

Feeding at the Creditanstalt Trough: The Reichswerke and Others

In contrast to the sales of the shares of Berndorf and the SWW, where there had been negotiations prior to the Anschluss and a long-standing interest in the acquisition of shares by, respectively, Krupp and IG Farben, the CA endured the loss of key holdings in which there were no negotiations or discussions prior to the Anschluss. They resulted from the empire building of major political figures in the Reich, above all Field Marshall Hermann Göring, and the string-pulling and lobbying of major German enterprises and industrialists who had

the ear of Göring, Keppler, and other National Socialist bigwigs. Göring, of course, took great pains to propagate the notion that Austria was to be showered with blessings under the new dispensation, and much was made of his scenic business trip down the Danube from Linz on March 25. As part of the grand design for Austria, Tulln near Linz was to be the site of gigantic new Reichswerke plants that were originally to be built in Fulda. While on this voyage, he held court with various German and Austrian business leaders and discussed Austria's integration into the German economy and its projected contributions to the Four Year Plan. His voyage was then followed by a triumphant entry into Vienna on March 26, where he held a speech in the hall of the Northwest Train Station before 20,000 people in which he derided the old regime, presented an extensive seventeen-point economic program that would end unemployment and bring prosperity to Austria, and declared his intention to remove the Jews from Austrian economic life and, indeed, from Austria. The program called for the termination of financial and trade barriers with Germany; measures for indirect rearmament in the form of airfields and barracks and building up the armaments industry; harnessing of Austria's water power and mineral and oil resources; development of the chemical and cellulose industries, better exploitation of timber resources; modernization of Austrian agriculture; and Autobahn, bridge, railroad, and canal construction.[213]

Göring was in fact quite intent on showing the Austrians that a new day was dawning and, as he wrote to Keppler on April 7, he was anxious to actually begin some of the big projects he had mentioned in his Vienna speech and thus demonstrate "that unique National Socialist energy."[214] He had already laid plans for the creation of the aforementioned giant industrial complex for the Hermann Göring Werke in

---

[211] Ibid., 53816/1938, report to Ministerial Councilor Zeidelhack, July 10, 1938, and Zeidelhack to Ministerial Councilor Schönberger, July 19, 1938; negotiations between Commerce Ministry and IG representatives, Aug. 6–8, 1938; BAB, R 8121, A 4000, report to the IG Farben management board meeting of Oct. 21, 1938.

[212] See Hayes, *Industry and Ideology*, pp. 228–232.

[213] See Norbert Schausberger, *Rüstung in Österreich 1938–1945* (Vienna 1970), pp. 27–29; the program is presented in full on pp. 186–187.

[214] PA Berlin, R 27506, Göring to Keppler, April 7, 1938.

Linz, the building of seven airfields and barracks north of the Alps, but he was above all interested in building a giant dam and power plant in the Tauern and demonstrating that the project was underway. In his view, this would silence doubters, astound the outside world, and give a psychic lift to the Austrians. He counted on the VIAG to take general direction of the project and, indeed, of all the projected Austrian power plant projects. It was this that gave the VIAG so great an interest in taking control of the electric power works shares that had belonged to the Industriekredit.[215]

Göring's megalomanic ambitions, however, also meant that attention had to be paid to the heavy industrial production facilities in Austria that might be useful for the vertical structure of the Reichswerke with their center in Linz. Keppler and Kehrl, who had set themselves up in a huge office in Vienna, began to draw up a list of shares of enterprises to be taken over in regular consultation with Olscher and Director Otto Neubaur of the RKG. The latter had been sent to Vienna in March 1938 to examine the holdings of the Industriekredit and sort out what was to be kept and what was to be sold. The shares of the Alpine Montangesellschaft in the hands of the Industriekredit, for example, fell into the category of assets to be kept even though the company was owned by the Vereinigte Stahlwerke (Vestag). The Vestag was shortly forced to surrender the Alpine to the Reichswerke because the ore deposits were deemed vital to the Reichswerke. The VIAG acquisition of CA shares and designation as a trustee for what had been previously owned by the Austrian government were part of this process of looking after Göring's interests by Keppler and Kehrl, as was the joint liquidation of the Industriekredit and total acquisition of the power industry shares by the VIAG. Neubaur was put in charge of dealing with the personnel and financial problems of the various enterprises involved, and the initial idea was for Keppler, Kehrl, and Fischböck to form a kind of committee to make final decisions on purchases

and prices, although this never really functioned effectively because they had no interest in dealing with what they did not want to take over or have taken over. Furthermore, it was exceptionally convenient to use the influence and services of the VIAG and RKG in dealing with these matters, especially when CA holdings were involved.[216]

The heavy industrial holdings of the CA were an important target for the Hermann Göring Werke.[217] The takeover of the shares of Steyr-Daimler-Puch clearly illustrate the procedures typically used to at once purge and appropriate enterprises that fell into this category. The Steyr firm had been a major manufacturer of weapons during the First World War, after which it turned to airplane motors, automobiles, and bicycles. It was taken over by the CA in 1931, and in 1934 it merged with the Austro-Daimler-Puch Werke and became an important producer of motorcars. The CA had installed its own management in 1931, and in 1938 the company was headed by an engineer, Generalrat Paul Götzl, and Heller served as president of the administrative council. Götzl, a Jew, was high on Fischböck and Pfeiffer's list of those to be dismissed, and he was removed by Heller on March 15 and replaced by General Director Georg Meindl of the Alpine Montan. An SS man well connected to Göring, Meindl was fanatical, ambitious, and talented, and he knew exactly what was expected of him. He rapidly came to an agreement with Heller to dismiss the entire administrative council and replace its members with such worthies as the former head of the Alpine and early Party loyalist, Anton Apold, who was a leading Austrian industrialist, and Fritz Falkensammer, another Austrian Party man who was being given special assignments in connection with Autobahn construction. Meindl was especially anxious to

---

[215] See Pohl, *VIAG*, pp. 133–134.

[216] NARA, OMGUS, FINAD 2/191/7, Neubaur Affidavit, July 22, 1947.

[217] On the expansion of the Reichswerke in Austria, see Richard Overy, "The Reichswerke 'Hermann Göring': A Study in German Economic Imperialism," in: R. J. Overy, *War and Economy in the Third Reich* (Oxford 1994), pp. 144–174, esp. pp. 149–150.

put high Austrian Party functionaries on the Council who were held in esteem in Germany and favored by Seyß-Inquart and Fischböck. As Meindl put the matter: "I consider the replacements in the manner proposed, especially if they are undertaken immediately, to be exceptionally valuable, since in that way the largely Jewish character of the previous administrative council disappears in one fell swoop."[218]

When the new and still rump administrative council met on March 30, Heller formally presided but Meindl was clearly in charge. Heller accepted his reelection to the presidency by stating that he would give it up if this was required by the restructuring of the firm or a change of chief shareholder, an obvious indication that the CA would not be in charge much longer. Meindl, however, was anxious to demonstrate that much better days were ahead for Steyr-Daimler-Puch under his leadership and to win over its workers, who had a reputation for radicalism and dissatisfaction. There had been considerable concern that Austria would give up motorcar production and that even more workers would be let go than had been the case already. Meindl had already taken personal charge of labor relations, and he now reported that "he had also had the distinction of being able to participate in the memorable steamship journey of General Field Marshall Göring and also along with President Heller in the extremely important economic discussions,"[219] and that he had used the opportunity to gain support for the continued production of various types of automobiles. He had also contacted the Supreme Command of the Army and the RWM and had immediately received contracts that would enable them to take up weapons production again, while Göring and General Ernst Udet held out the prospect of a contract

for 50,000 machine guns. Needless to say, the administrative council welcomed these happy prospects, and Heller chimed in to say that he had observed how it was above all Meindl's persuasive powers that had led to the decision to continue vehicle production and "save automobile production at Steyr." Meindl could ask for little more by way of support, except for authorization to fire seven Jews at the company's head offices, to undertake further personnel changes as he deemed fit, and to introduce the Führer Principle in the management of Steyr.

This principle was also at work in the Austrian economy, where the CA was instructed to sell its shares of Steyr-Daimler-Puch, the Steirische Gußstahlwerke, and the Maschinen- und Waggonfabriken in Simmering to the Reichswerke. The instructions were probably given in late March or early April, and auditor reports were solicited from the Deutsche Revisons- und Treuhand AG and used as the basis for negotiation with the Reichswerke. At the executive committee meeting on June 24, Heller requested permission to accept an offer of 160 percent for the Steyr-Daimler-Puch shares. In principle, it also accepted an offer of 225 percent for the Steirische Gußstahlwerke shares, but appointed a committee composed of Hasslacher, Olscher, and Heller to see if a better price could be negotiated. The committee seemed content to get 65 percent for the Simmering shares. It is important to note that while the CA was preparing to sell these shares, its engagement as a bank in funding the development programs of some of these companies remained substantial. In May, the committee had authorized the raising of an 11.6 million RM cash credit for Steyr-Daimler-Puch that was granted in April to 15 million RM. At the June 24 meeting, the committee agreed to a 5.5 million RM investment credit for the Steirische Gußstahlwerke in addition to a 4.4 million RM credit granted previously. These were, of course, credits to be repaid with interest, but the CA was rather sensitive to Steyr-Daimler-Puch starting up huge and expensive projects with materials and cash it had provided as the owner of the company, and Heller was not shy about

[218] BA-CA, CA-IB, Steyr-Daimler-Puch, 35/12, note by Heller, March 15, 1938, and Meindl to Heller, March 21, 1938. There is a very useful discussion of the history of the firm and discussion of Meindl in NARA, RG 338, Box 110, 290/56/03/02.

[219] BA-CA, CA-IB, Steyr-Daimler-Puch 35/10, meeting of the administrative council, March 30, 1938.

telling Meindl to wait until the sale had been concluded before beginning work on them.[220]

On July 15, the executive committee and the administrative council approved the sales to the Reichswerke of 68,792 shares of the Steyr-Daimler-Puch at 160 percent; 50,000 shares of the Steirische Gußstahlwerke at 225 percent, the CA committee having been unable to get a better price; and 6,089 shares of the Maschinen- und Waggonbau-Fabriks AG, Simmering at 65 percent. Insofar as the Reichswerke needed to make its ownership of these enterprises 100 percent of the shares, the missing shares had already been taken over from the portfolio of the Industriekredit or, as was the case with the Simmering company, from the Bankhaus Schoeller.[221] What added to the bleakness of July 15 for the CA, however, was not only these sales to the Reichswerke, and the loss of Berndorf and Skoda-Wetzler, which also received the sanction of the CA's governing bodies on this occasion, but also the sale of 25,303 shares of the Wiener Lokomotiv-Fabriks-AG (13%) to Henschel & Sohn in Kassel at 107 percent and 2,897 shares (16.56%) of the insurer Phönix to the German insurance giant, Allianz und Stuttgarter Verein Versicherungs-AG in Berlin.

The sale of the Wiener Lokomotiv shares is an especially interesting case, less for the size of the holding than for the manner in which it came to pass, which is highly revealing of the forces at work after the Anschluss, and for the manner in which the CA found itself at once a participant and victim in the Henschel take-over. The initiative for the transfer came from Wilhelm Tengelmann, an economic advisor to Göring, personal friend of Keppler, chairman of the supervisory board of the coal-producing Hibernia AG, and general director of the Oberbayerische Kohlen-Bergbau AG. He was also a member of the supervisory board of Henschel. On a visit to Vienna on March 25, he and other managers of Henschel visited the Wiener Lokomotivfabrik. The two companies had a long-standing business relationship, and Henschel offered the latter a large contract with the object of combatting the danger of further unemployment in Vienna. While contemplating these presumably good works, it came to their attention that the majority of the shareholders of the Wiener Lokomotivfabrik were non-Germans and Jews: a Belgian group, the Bankhaus S.M. Rothschild, and the Bankhaus Gebr. Gutmann. The last two were Jewish-owned. This was yet a further incentive for the Henschel group to decide to try to gain control of the Austrian firm, especially in view of the company's need for large investments and also because of Henschel's "own expansionist needs." Tengelmann asked Keppler that the acquisition of these shares by Henschel be exempted from the ban on acquisitions in Austria because Henschel had productive and not speculative intentions and also asked that Henschel be given a prior option over other possible competitors. Keppler, Göring, Kehrl, and State Secretary Brinkmann of the RWM all gave their approval quite rapidly, so that Keppler was able to inform Tengelmann in April that the acquisition had been approved and to apprise Henschel shortly thereafter. It was self-understood that the CA would also sell its shares, but additionally the CA also acted as a go-between for the acquisition and transfer of the shares held by the Belgian group. Apparently, it was not involved in the Aryanization of the Rothschild and Gutmann shares.[222]

As in the case of Henschel, so too in the case of its minority holding in the Phönix

---

[220] BA-CA, CA-V, executive committee meetings of April 29, May 27, June 24, 1938; see BAB, R 8135, Nr. 9368, the audit of Steyr-Daimler-Puch requested by the CA on April 21, 1938; see also BA-CA, CA-IB, Steyr-Daimler-Puch, 35/13, Heller to Meindl, June 3, 1938.

[221] BA-CA, CA-V, executive committee and administrative council meetings on July 15, 1938. See also the discussion in Wittek-Saltzberg, *Die wirtschafts-politischen Auswirkungen*, pp. 173–175.

[222] Tengelmann to Keppler, March 26, 1938; Keppler to Tengelmann, April 2, 1938; PA Berlin, R 27506, Henschel to RWM, April 21, 1938; ÖStA/AdR, Ministerium f. Wirtschaft u. Arbeit (= MfWuA), Vermögensverkehrsstelle (= VVSt), Box 713, Statistik, Zl. 7857, CA to Reichsstatthalter, May 5, 1938; BA-CA, CA-IB, Wiener Lokomotivfabrik 46/1, Keppler to Henschel & Sohn, April 13, 1938.

Elementar Versicherungsgesellschaft, the Creditanstalt found itself effectively forced to surrender its participation in order to satisfy the desire of Allianz to take over Phönix Elementar. Following its scandalous collapse in 1936, Phönix Leben had been separated from its parent company and established as the Österreichische Versicherungs-AG (ÖVAG). Fischböck had been its head until his elevation to higher and more political functions after the Anschluss. As part of the 1936 settlement, the Italian insurance giant Assicurazioni Generali, the Munich Reinsurance Company (Munich Re), and the Creditanstalt joined in a syndicate to guarantee Phönix Elementar for at least three years. By the time of the Anschluss, the company was recovering, although still not in satisfactory shape. Munich Re had been contemplating bringing its sister company Allianz into the arrangement for some time, especially in order to improve Phönix Elementar's management, but a lack of enthusiasm on the part of the Allianz leadership and foreign exchange problems stood in the way. Here, once again, the Anschluss changed the situation. It is noteworthy that Kurt Schmitt, who had been general director of Allianz between 1921 and 1934 and Reich economics minister in 1933–1935, and subsequently became general director of Munich Re, not only telegraphed his congratulations to Keppler on his appointment as Reich Plenipotentiary for Austria, but also arranged for a visit during the last days of March.[223] It reasonable to assume that Schmitt used the occasion to discuss German insurance interests in Austria and to pave the way for new arrangements involving Munich Re and Allianz.

In any case, the time had now come to bring about a change in Phönix Elementar's leadership, first, because the present general director, Eberhard von Reininghaus, had been closely tied to the old regime and also had some Jewish ancestry, and second, because at this point the plan of having Allianz effectively take over the company could be carried out. Schmitt's candidate for the new leader was Hans-Schmidt Polex, who came from the Allianz-owned Bayerische Versicherungsbank. The real issue was what role the Italians would now play, and Schmitt left the door open for them to have a minority holding and even to keep the Creditanstalt involved because he was aware that the Italians welcomed some Austrian participation. Ultimately, however, the Generali leadership, after a meeting with the Germans in Venice in May 1938, came to the conclusion that it was best to sell out. It is noteworthy that the Creditanstalt was not even present and, indeed, had no real voice in the matter either with respect to the future organization of the company or with respect to its own shares. Allianz and Munich Re then decided to each buy half the CA shares, which were sold for 80 percent. This was higher than their notation on the market at the time, and the Reich Supervisory Board for Insurance actually considered the price paid somewhat too high. The name Phönix Elementar, which had too many past Jewish associations to make it palatable, was soon changed to Wiener Allianz and was indeed fully integrated into the Allianz concern.[224]

This was probably the least irritating of the holdings lost to Allianz at the time because the CA had considered selling the shares earlier. But it was not its only surrender of insurance assets, however; it also owned 11.14 percent of the shares of the ÖVAG. In the summer of 1938, the German Labor Front took over the ÖVAG, having long sought to gain entry into the Austrian market for its Volksfürsorge insurance organization and having been frustrated by the Austrian government, and the company was subsequently renamed the Ostmärkische Volksfürsorge. The acquisition of the ÖVAG had been much eased by the fact that the City of Vienna owned 37.14 percent of the shares and

---

223   PA Berlin, R 27506, Keppler to Schmitt, March 22, 1938. The following discussion is based on the account in Gerald D. Feldman, *Allianz and the German Insurance Business, 1938–1945* (New York 2001), pp. 289–304 and Marita Roloff/Alois Mosser, *Wiener Allianz. Gegründet 1860* (Vienna 1991), pp. 240–247.

224   The sale was only formally approved at the turn of 1938/1939. See Bundesarchiv Koblenz, B 280, Nr. 25125, the official correspondence with the government agencies.

both Mayor Neubacher and Göring approved it. The CA sold the shares at original cost, which its management board deemed inadequate although the other shareholders were given a price lower than the price they had paid.[225]

As this example shows, the CA's loss of holdings by no means ended with the sales approved on July 15. While those sales added up to 30 million RM and thus, as Abs noted apparently with some satisfaction, greatly increased the CA's liquidity, the CA's managers were certainly less happy with the situation, and they also knew more was coming. In fact, Heller noted that there was interest in the purchase of the Feinstahlwerke Traisen AG vorm. Fischer, without specifying from where it came. The company was an important producer of quality steel products that had done quite well in recent years, had its own waterpower resources, and employed more than 800 workers. Since 1927, it had been run by a Czech Jew, Erwin Subak, and its administrative council included a number of Jews as well. They resigned in early April and were replaced by Aryans, among them the general director of the Alpine Montanwerke, Hans Malzacher; Dr. Arthur von Lenz; and Eduard Prinz von und zu Liechtenstein. CA Director Heller served as president of the administrative council and Robert Glatzl also served on the council. Subak became the object of savage attacks by the National Socialist company cell, which accused him of being a "ruthless exploiter of our national comrades," attacked him as a supporter of the old political order, demanded his immediate dismissal, and declared that his continuation as an employee had caused

such outrage among the workers that "the personal safety of Herr Subak can no longer be guaranteed."[226] Heller had a much more positive view of Subak and even contemplated keeping him on for a time as a consultant, but this proved impossible under the circumstances. On June 23, as required by the state commissar for the private economy, they were able to send SS Brigadeführer Ernst Kaltenbrunner a copy of Subak's dismissal. This does not appear to have been done with any enthusiasm on the part of Heller, as is suggested by the declaration at the supervisory council on May 7 that "in view of the fact that Herr Erwin Subak has always acted with special loyalty, it is the intention of the chairman to also dissolve the employment of Herr Subak in a similarly loyal manner."[227]

Heller seems to have entertained hopes that the CA could hold on to the company, and although he was aware of interest in purchasing the company and duly reported this to the CA executive committee on July 15, he urged that they exercise restraint in dealing with further offers for CA holdings.[228] Indeed, the CA also begged for a measure of restraint on the part of the Reichswerke. When Hans Malzacher, the general director of the Alpine and recently appointed member of the administrative board of Traisen, asked Heller if the CA were prepared to sell its shares, Heller replied that the CA was indeed reducing its industrial holdings, but that nevertheless a "pause" was deemed necessary

---

[225] See Dieter Stiefel, *Die Österreichischen Lebensversicherungen und die NS-Zeit. Wirtschaftliche Entwicklung. Politischer Einfluß. Jüdische Polizzen* (Vienna 2001), pp. 75–98. See also Ingo Böhle, "Die Expansion der Volksfürsorge Lebensversicherung in den mitteleuropäischen Raum 1938–1945," in: Harald Wixforth (ed.), *Finanzinstitutionen in Mitteleuropa während des Nationalsozialismus (= Geld und Kapital. Jahrbuch der Gesellschaft für mitteleuropäische Banken- und Sparkassengeschichte 2000)*, pp. 181–211, esp. pp. 181–189. For the dissatisfaction of the CA, see BA-CA, CA-V, the Treuhand Report on the CA for 1938, pp. 78–79.

[226] BA-CA, CA-IB, Feinstahlwerke, 38/03–04, National Socialist Factory Cell Organization to the management board, April 13, 1938.

[227] Ibid., Feinstahlwerke, 38/01–02, administrative council meeting, May 7, 1938. Letter to Kaltenbrunner, June 23, 1938. On July 20, 1938, Heller and Glatzl also signed a strong letter of reference for Subak, both praising his skills and expressing regret over his departure. Subak went abroad to find new employment and Heller, pursuant to his request, had the settlement of RM 11,105 paid to his aging mother, who lived in Vienna. See ibid., Feinstahlwerke, 38/03–04, letter to Foreign Exchange Bureau, Vienna, July 25, 1938.

[228] BA-CA, CA-V, executive committee meeting of July 15, 1938; and DB, P 6502, Bl. 88–89, notes by Abs, transcribed by Pohle, July 20, 1938.

by the executive committee at the moment. As Heller explained, "the crucial considerations for this decision above all ... have been the strong increase of liquidity, which is the result of the numerous recent sales of large blocks of shares by my institution, and the false view developed by the public as well as in our concern that a rapid liquidation of the industrial holdings of the Österreichische Creditanstalt-Wiener Bankverein is in progress."[229] At the same time, Heller expressed a willingness to take up the matter again once things quieted down. Perhaps Heller hoped that Malzacher might provide this CA holding with a measure of protection, but the Reichswerke had big plans for the Feinstahlwerke Traisen. This became clear in October 1938 when the company was visited by officials from Berlin, who announced that plans were afoot to make the company the largest processed steel foundry in the Ostmark. Capacity was to be increased not to 300 tons per month, as was then planned, but rather to 1,000 tons per month. This was to be accomplished very rapidly.[230] The Reichswerke was very much on the move. It did not take long, therefore, for the Reichswerke to announce, not only that it was interested in Traisen but also in a number of other important CA holdings. It clearly demonstrated that there were limits to the "restraint" the CA could exercise, although one notes an increasing effort on the part of the CA to get a better price and even to resist some demands.

There were times when it was possible to reach a quick and acceptable settlement with the Reichswerke, as was demonstrated by the sale of the CA shares in the Kärntnerische Eisen- und Stahlwerks-Gesellschaft, Ferlach. In this instance, the Reichswerke offered a price and an arrangement covering the firm's losses that the CA was prepared to accept without further discussion. Subsequently, the Reichswerke offered a high price in place of debt coverage, and this was accepted by the CA. In the case of assets deemed more valuable, however, the CA chose to hold out for a better price.

When Heller announced at the September 16 meeting of the executive committee that the Reichswerke was after Traisen, of which the CA owned 84.4 percent, Heller proposed that the CA await a renewed expert valuation, decide on a price, and then tell the Reichswerke that it could not accept the offer before January 1, 1939, but had to accept it at the end of that month. The Deutsche Revisions- und Treuhand AG had concluded that the shares were worth 300 percent or more, but the CA had asked that the accuracy of the valuation be checked, and Heller felt that the price would lie somewhere between 300 percent and 400 percent. Actually, it ended up being even higher after further valuations that took new facilities and 1938 profits into account justified a price of 500 percent of the nominal worth price for the 7,596 shares or 2.5 million RM. The Reichswerke, after checking this valuation, agreed to 500 percent, and it also agreed to continue using the banking services of the CA.[231]

Certainly the most painful and contentious of the Reichswerke's acquisitions from the CA were its shipping interests, and none reveals more blatantly the manner in which Göring, Keppler, and Kehrl could ride roughshod over CA and, indeed, Austrian interests when it suited them. The origins of the Reichswerke's interest in the Erste Donau Dampfschifffahrts-Gesellschaft (DDSG) and the Continentale Motorschifffahrts AG (Comos) were plainly evident in May 1938, when Keppler noted a meeting involving State Secretaries Friedrich Landfried of the RWM and Paul Körner of the Four Year Plan Office in which the issue of Danube shipping was taken up in the context of collaboration between the Reichswerke and Hibernia in the field of shipping. They proposed the creation of new companies that would "swallow up the old Danube companies" and build a fleet from Salzgitter. Consequently, an immediate ban was placed on founding new companies or selling shares related to Danube shipping.[232] It cannot be said that the DDSG, which in addition to its

[229] BA-CA, CA-IB, Feinstahlwerke, 38/04, Heller to Malzacher, July 16, 1938.
[230] Ibid., report for Heller, Oct. 26, 1938.
[231] BA-CA, CA-V, executive committee meetings of Sept. 16 and Dec. 9, 1938.
[232] PA Berlin, R 27506, note by Keppler, May 18, 1938.

fleet owned two dockyards, one in Budapest, and a mine and railroad yard, was in good shape. It appears to have been poorly managed, was overstaffed, had a high pension burden, was in need of modernization, and suffered from an unprofitable passenger service.[233] It needed government subsidies before the Anschluss, but evidently Keppler and the Reichswerke leaders planned to change all that.

In early August, General Director Wilhelm Voss of the Reichswerke and Max Waldeck of the Reich Transportation Ministry discussed what they considered to be a dire need to put some order into the DDSG situation with Heller, and this was followed on August 12 by a letter from Keppler announcing that "it is the wish of the Führer that a consolidation of Danube shipping take place, and General Field Marshall Göring has charged me with getting this reorganization started." After discussing various desired personnel changes, he also announced that the Reichswerke intended to take over the shares in the DDSG held by the Land of Austria, and he asked Heller to negotiate with the Italian shareholders in the company. Given the fact that the Führer and Göring personally wished to have the shares taken over, Keppler could not imagine that the Italians would present "serious difficulties." Heller apparently had made some difficulties of his own, and Keppler reminded him that it was the wish of the "higher authorities" that the Comos also be included in the intended consolidation. While understanding Heller's reservations, he nevertheless asked Heller to present an offer for the sale of the shares either to himself or to the Reichswerke because "higher considerations are decisive here." Finally, Keppler considered the matter extremely urgent and asked that it be taken up by the administrative council as soon as possible.[234]

This letter was a classic demonstration of what the National Socialists meant by a "steered economy," and it goes without saying that Heller was not in a position to do much about it. Insofar as the DDSG was concerned, he offered the CA shares at 50 percent of their nominal value, that is, 66.67 RM per share, with the proviso that the CA would receive the added difference if Fischböck sold the Land of Austria's shares for more. The CA took the position that the affairs of the DDSG might improve to the point of justifying such a price. Apparently, the Reichswerke thought this price too high, and the negotiations dragged on through 1938 and led to an extraordinary arrangement at the end of the year under which the CA placed its shares in trust for the Reichswerke because the latter claimed it had to have the voting majority at the next shareholders' meeting to undertake the reorganization measures it wished. This arrangement was to last until the end of March 1939, and if an agreement still had not been reached on price, then the matter was to be submitted to arbitration. In addition to this concession, the CA also surrendered its claim to the interest payments due it on its outstanding credit to the DDSG so that it would only receive such interest after the projected issuance of new shares for DDSG reconstruction showed a return larger than 5 percent. In the end, however, the pressure from Berlin was such that the CA accepted 30 percent of the nominal value for the shares, that is, 40 RM per share, and thus took a 2.2 million RM loss.[235]

In the context of the pressures being applied, the resistance of the CA leadership in the case of the Comos could almost be termed heroic. After learning of the Reichswerke's interest in August, Heller initially tried to persuade the Reichswerke that the company was important to the business of the CA. Thus, the CA

[233] See BA-CA, CA-V, the Treuhand report on the CA for 1938, pp. 127–128, and ÖStA/AdR, BMF, Allgem. Reihe 1939, 11862/1939, the comments by Voss at the DDSG supervisory board meeting of June 26, 1939.

[234] StA Nürnberg, Nl 13031, Keppler to Heller, Aug. 12, 1938.

[235] BA-CA, CA-V, executive committee meetings of Sept. 16 and Dec. 9, 1938; see NARA, T-83, Roll 101, the memorandum of the Creditanstalt-Bankverein of November 1945 on the Repatriation of the Shares of the Bank and Its Concern Enterprises (Denkschrift der Creditanstalt-Bankverein hinsichtlich Repatriierung von Aktien der Bank und deren Konzernunternehmungen).

was prepared to make a variety of administrative arrangements to satisfy the purposes the Reichswerke had in seeking the shares. The matter was then dropped for the time being until the DDSG matter could be settled, but it was clearly going to be taken up again. General Director Voss then renewed the discussions in the fall, asking for the CA shares, not only in Comos but also in the Climax Motoren-Werke und Schiffswerft Linz AG. The CA had invested heavily in the latter company, whose work was now also of interest to the navy and whose activity was picking up. The central issue for the CA, however, was the Comos, which it seems to have viewed as a very special asset. At the end of January 1939, not only the management board but also the executive committee were of one mind in rejecting the sale of the shares.[236] It was not long, however, before Göring's office thundered back, informing the CA on April 29, that "it is with the express approval of the Führer and Reich Chancellor that the block of shares of Comos in your hands shall go to the Reichswerke and that especially the Herr General Field Marshall takes this position as he has before."[237] The CA was instructed to begin negotiations with General Director Voss immediately and, not surprisingly, this was done albeit with a notable lack of enthusiasm and as much resistance on the price question as possible. Indeed, it was not until October 1940 that an agreement was finally reached under which the CA shares were sold for 4,420,000 RM, but also an agreement that if the Reichswerke were to consider selling the shares at a later time, the CA was to have first option. As for the Climax shares, here the pressure exercised by Kehrl and Bürckel put an end to the discussion of alternative arrangements, and the ownership of what was now called the Schiffswerft Linz was sold to the Reichswerke and the DDSG.[238]

Happily for the CA, not all its losses of holdings were quite so total, involuntary, and protracted as those described and they sometimes allowed for a continued engagement with the enterprises involved and even retention of share participation. This was probably the case with the Teudloff-Vamag Vereinigte Armaturen- und Maschinenfabriken AG, where the CA found itself pressured to give up its majority position to the Vereinigte Armaturengesellschaft, Mannheim. The latter was a syndicate of the six largest instrument panel producers in Germany and had large contracts from the RWM, and it used this situation to argue that it needed to have a majority influence on the leading Austrian producer and also maintained that the Teudloff-Vamag, whose prices were 60 percent above German levels, would not be competitive once customs barriers were eliminated. Although the CA did put up some resistance, especially because of its heavy investment in the reorganization of the firm during the Depression, the Mannheim company apparently had the ear of Bürckel, and the CA gave in to the pressure after his personal intervention. The CA maintained 19 percent of the shares, and part of the arrangement was for the CA to provide the credits and funding for Teudloff-Vamag so that the investments and the character of the company remained "Austrian."[239]

When all is said and done, however, the CA had surrendered a great deal in 1938–1939, and, as will be shown later, there was more to come after the war broke out. Most important certainly were the sales of its electrical power shares to the VIAG and its most important industrial holdings to the Reichswerke, but its stakes in Berndorf and Skoda-Wetzler were also major industrial holdings. The leadership of the CA fought either to prevent these losses or to get better prices, but it was an exaggeration for the CA to claim, as it would after 1945, that it was "plundered" or "blackmailed." Certainly, the CA had little freedom of action in dealing with these demands, and it tried to put as good

[236] Ibid., and BA-CA, CA-V, executive committee meeting, Sept. 16, 1938, Jan. 20, 1939.
[237] NARA, T-83, Roll 101, Creditanstalt memorandum of November 1945.
[238] Ibid., BA-CA, CA-V, executive committee meetings, May 17, 1939, Oct. 22, 1940; management board meeting, Nov. 1, 1940; Wittek-Saltzberg, *Die wirtschaftspolitischen Auswirkungen*, p. 176.
[239] NARA, T-83, Roll 101, Creditanstalt memorandum of November 1945, and BA-CA, CA-V, executive committee meeting, Jan. 20, 1939.

a face as possible on what had been surrendered. Thus, on July 23, 1938, Hasslacher held a speech before the general shareholders' meeting in which he explicitly listed some of the blocks of shares surrendered to the Reichswerke and then went on to say: "I want to emphasize this because I believe that I am able to assert in this connection that the Creditanstalt has in every respect made the best possible effort to embrace faithfully the spirit and the trajectory of the present time and also to do its best to bear it in mind."[240] He went on to point out how difficult it had been to deal with the "withdrawal" of some 200 employees and with all the changes that had taken place. Mixing apologia, pathos, and pandering, Hasslacher declared: "We want only, without intending to expand on this, to wish and to hope that the Creditanstalt, too, can perform its modest tasks in the great reconstruction that we have to undertake, in close agreement with all the significant state and Party agencies, an agreement which we have sought to achieve and have been able to establish for the benefit of our narrower homeland, for the benefit of our economy, which, as is generally known, has been all too strongly stressed in the System Period, and for the benefit too of our national comrades, who, if one is allowed to say so, even though morally and spiritually strengthened during this time, are economically somewhat weakened."

What all this really suggested was that the CA was, if anything, itself a product of the "System Period" and as such was fair game for the new persons and forces that had moved into Austria in March 1938. It had, indeed, been brought down more than a peg or two and, because of its central place in the old Austrian economy, was subject to the tender mercies of the more voracious elements of the new regime. At the same time, the CA was the embodiment of the role of Austrian banks as holding companies, so that the very legitimacy of its style of banking was called into question.

That said, what kind of balance can one draw from this account of the Creditanstalt's surrender of equity stakes after the Anschluss? To what extent might it have been the consequence of a clear policy involving both the Germanization of specific industrial holdings and a sharp turn in the direction of more German as opposed to Austrian banking practices? The leadership of the Creditanstalt drew up its own balance in its report to the shareholders of June 1939: "Concerning the question of the separation of the tasks of regular banking business from the management of industrial interests, the principle informing our position is that the separation of banks from permanent industrial capital stakes is desirable, whereby majority blocks of shares in essential enterprises in the interest of a strong development of the Greater German national economy must be placed into the hands of those who bring about in a planned manner a better organization of production and sale of the said enterprises. Thus a number of holdings have been transferred into other hands, whereby the continuation of friendly connections with these enterprises and the maintenance of ongoing banking business have not been interrupted. The credit business with some of these enterprises has even experienced an expansion."[241]

As has been shown, however, the sale of CA holdings in 1938–1939 had in origin and result nothing significantly to do with adapting to German banking methods, even if Fischböck would have liked to place CA holdings into a holding company, and Abs was most interested in what Germans considered traditional banking practices. In reality, the alienation of important industrial assets had everything to do with fulfilling the desires of certain large enterprises in Germany and satisfying the programs connected with the Four Year Plan and the Reichswerke. They in no way represented some principled and desired move in the direction of more traditional German banking methods. Fundamentally, what transpired was a Germanization of Austria's power industry and heavy industry, and although the notion of ridding the Creditanstalt of its industrial holdings

---

[240] Ibid., meeting of the Exceptional General Shareholders' Assembly, July 23, 1938.

[241] BA-CA, CA-V, Report to the 82nd General Assembly of the Shareholders, June 16, 1939.

may have been employed as part of the rationale for what had occurred, it most certainly was not a serious driving force. Certainly, it was true that the CA became a major provider of credits to the companies in the Reichswerke, Berndorf, and other former holdings, although it must have been hard to swallow having to share its role as a credit provider to Steyr-Daimler-Puch and other Reichswerke acquisitions with the Länderbank on a 75 percent to 25 percent basis.[242] As will be shown, the CA was integrated into the consortial banking arrangements that supported the industrial expansion required by the Four Year Plan. This, however, had nothing to do with a genuine change in banking practice.

Indeed, shortly after the misleading statement in the June 1939 business report that the CA was distancing itself from its previous engagement in industrial investment, it was belied by another passage noting that "in the course of the new ordering of economic relations in the Ostmark, there also followed the acquisition of some new holdings by us, such as, among others, enterprises in the paper and pulp industry, the stone products industry, a bridge-building company, and a foreign trade company."[243] As this statement indicates, the Creditanstalt was actually acquiring new industrial and commercial holdings at the very time it was being forced to sell off the holdings discussed earlier in this chapter. One source of these acquisitions was the rapid and brutal Aryanization policy conducted in Austria that led to an increase in the equity holdings in cases where the Creditanstalt was already invested as well in the acquisition of new assets, some of which it sold and some of which it kept. Furthermore, the size of these holdings even grew as Germany expanded and the Creditanstalt became involved in the holdings of banks and companies in Southeast and Eastern Europe. As will be shown in the third chapter of this study, the CA was to be well "compensated" for the losses it had suffered since the Anschluss, at least so long as the Third Reich

existed, and its story under that regime must and will inevitably turn from the CA as "victim" to the CA as participant and perpetrator in the National Socialist economy.

Rescuing the Provincial Banks for the CA

While the CA lost some of its important industrial holdings prior to the outbreak of the war, it did manage to hold on to its branch network and its very important provincial banking holdings and even to expand them. In June 1939, the CA had thirty-two branches in Vienna and fifteen branches in Austria, three of them in recently annexed territories. It also had a branch in Hungary and controlled the Allgemeine Jugoslawische Bankverein AG Belgrade-Zagreb, which itself had branches in Ljubljana and Novi-Sad. In July 1938, the CA decided to take over the Steiermärkische Escompte Bank, Graz, an old holding in which it held 92 percent of the shares. This was primarily a rationalization measure aimed at ending the competition between the bank and the CA branch in Graz and also at making the expanded branch more competitive. It easily won the approval of the authorities. The capacity of the CA to hold on to its control of Austria's major provincial banks, however, was rather more of an accomplishment. In the end, it held on to its 49.6 percent holding in the Bank für Kärnten in Klagenfurt, which had branches in Spittala.d.D., Villach, and Wolfsberg, although 47.5 percent of the CA shares were locked into an arrangement made in 1927 with the other major shareholder, the Bayerische Hypotheken- und Wechselbank under which no important decisions could be made without the agreement of the two large shareholders. It also owned and retained its 79.2 percent stake in the Bank für Oberösterreich und Salzburg in Linz, which had twelve branches, and the same held true of its 83 percent holding in the Hauptbankfür Tirol und Vorarlberg-Tiroler Landesbank in Innsbruck, which had six branches.[244]

---

[242] Ibid., executive committee meeting, May 17, 1939.
[243] BA-CA, CA-V, Report to the 82nd General Assembly of the Shareholders, June 16, 1939.

[244] Only a bare-bones account of the regional banks in the CA concern and the CA branches as they relate to the relations between the banks

The threats to CA control over its provincial banks were varied and very much dependent on political and personal constellations that ended up working in the CA's favor but also tested both the mettle and the luck of the bank's leadership. One of these threats has been dealt with earlier in this chapter, namely, the tendency of Keppler and Kehrl to favor Karl Rasche's proposal that the CA's holdings in the provincial banks be sold to the Länderbank. This danger ended in the late spring of 1938 with the departure of Keppler and the RWM's insistence that the special favor being shown to the Mercurbank/Länderbank at the expense of the CA be terminated.[245]

At the same time, however, the RWM had created some difficulties for the CA that threatened to take it out of the mortgage business and also to divest it of its holdings in the Bank für Kärnten. The connection between these two issues arose from the privatization and then the sale of the Österreichische Creditinstitut für öffentliche Unternehmungen und Arbeiten (ÖCI) to the Bayerische Hypotheken- und Wechselbank (Bayernbank) shortly after the Anschluss. The ÖCI, having belonged almost entirely to the Austrian government, had been used to hide losses that might have otherwise appeared in the budget and to assist in the liquidation of defunct banks. The idea of selling it to the Bayernbank apparently came from the ÖCI director, Karl Weninger, who hoped to turn the bank into a mortgage bank.[246] This fit in with a scheme of

Joachim Riehle of the Banking Section of the RWM to concentrate mortgage banking in Austria by establishing one large mortgage bank in the publicly chartered banking sector and another in the private sector. He had made this proposal as early as April 4 to Bank Commissar Ernst, who was interested enough to ask to be kept informed.[247] The Deutsche Bank got wind of the scheme in mid-May through Hans Oesterlink, the head of the Centralbodenbank, Germany's leading mortgage bank, and a member of the working committee of the Deutsche Bank supervisory board. Oesterlink confidentially informed Pollems of Riehle's plan to have the CA give up its mortgage portfolio to the ÖCI, which would initially function as a mixed bank and eventually become a pure mortgage bank once it built up its own portfolio. The CA would not only have to leave the mortgage business but would also receive nothing for its portfolio until such time as the bank developed and the Bayerische Hypothekenbank might be inclined to sell its portfolio. Oesterlink manifestly had a low opinion of this plan and did not think it in the interest of either the Deutsche Bank or the CA. He urged that the CA be informed of this and be told to reject the establishment of what was being named the Hypotheken- and Credit-Institut (CI) and which was to be headquartered in Vienna and to function as a mixed bank. Furthermore, the CA also was to insist that it would only collaborate if there was some guarantee that the bank would function in an orderly manner and that other private Austrian and German credit banks be brought into the picture. When Pollems informed Heller of what he had learned from Oesterlink, Heller took the signal and pointed out that the CA had the right to do mortgage business according to its charter, and it could not legally be forced to give this asset away "on the basis of vague promises." Although willing to participate in a mortgage bank, the CA would only do so if "we also have an influence on its leadership."[248]

and the political authorities will be presented here. For a fuller discussion, see Ulrike Zimmerl, "Regionalbanken im Nationalsozialismus: Die Instrumentalisierung österreichischer Geldinstitute in den Bundesländern," in Gerald D. Feldman, Oliver Rathkolb, Theordor Venus, and Ulrike Zimmerl, Österreichische Banken und Sparkasen im Nationalsozialismu and in der Nachkriegszeit, vol. 2 (Munich, 2006), pp. 13–258. For the list of branches and holdings, see BA-CA, CA-V, the CA Business Report for 1938 of June 15, 1939. On the takeover of the Steirische Escompte Bank, Graz, see ibid., S.P. Akten, Nr. 1164/1, the executive committee meeting, July 15, 1938, and the administrative council minutes of July 23, 1938, as well as the rather unenlightening file therein.

[245] See p. 35 in this chapter.

[246] Melichar, *Neuordnung im Bankwesen*, pp. 23, 27–28.
[247] RGVA Moscow, 1458/2/84, Bl. 55, memo by Ernst on Austrian Banking Reorganization, July 19, 1938.
[248] DB, B 51, memo by Pollems, May 19, 1938.

Indeed, the wily Joham sought to negotiate precisely such an arrangement. In early July 1938, he entered into negotiations with Weninger of the CI and officials of the Bayernbank about a plan to enable the CA to take a stake in the CI. The notion was to turn the CI into an independent mortgage bank, that is, independent of the Bayernbank as well, once it had attained a mortgage portfolio of at least 50 million RM. The CA was then to have a 2:1 participation ratio, but the CI was to handle all the mortgage and mortgage bond business of the CA. No other bank was to be allowed to invest in the CI. Until the CI became independent, a matter to be determined by the RWM, the CA was to receive a commission on the mortgages it had placed in the CI portfolio. A representative of the CA was to serve as chairman of the CI supervisory board. As should be clear from this arrangement, the CA was indeed offering to give up its mortgage business, but in return it was becoming a major participant in the CI, thus remaining in the mortgage business by proxy and getting a return on the mortgage and mortgage bond business.[249]

Nothing came of this shrewd scheme, and the CA was extremely resistant to all plans to take it out of the mortgage business, which it viewed as profitable and important to its business. It constantly played upon the fact that the ÖCI, now the CI, was already a credit bank and in combining the functions of a credit bank and a mortgage bank, would be in constant competition with the CA. Some thought had actually been given to creating another pure mortgage bank, but Olscher had argued successfully against it on the grounds that a certain amount of credit business was always tied up with mortgage business. Also, this would have left the CI as a pure credit bank, and this would have produced more competition for the CA. Although the authorities in Vienna and Berlin tried to argue that the CI was not in the business of giving large credits in the style of the CA, the

CA rejected all such arguments. Also, the CA dealt in mortgage bonds, as did the branches of the Bavarian banks, and it was hard to see why it should not continue to do so or even, as it was threatening, to create an organization through its branches for marketing such bonds. Clearly, therefore, the CA could not be wrenched loose from its mortgage activity without compensation, and while the RWM was arguing that the CA should concentrate more on foreign business and had to surrender some of its old activities, there were limits to which one could pressure the CA when it was giving up so much already.[250]

Happily for the CA, the Riehle plan, which seems to have been something of an *idée fixe*, ran into difficulties with Riehle's colleagues in Berlin. Bank Commissar Ernst found it very unconvincing, as he debated with Riehle over the matter in mid-September. He could see no reason to favor the CI, which had a totally insignificant mortgage business, over the CA, which had a larger portfolio. Riehle claimed in response that the CA had shown an inclination to give up its mortgage portfolio and only subsequently took a more negative line, that it was too involved in business with the Bayerische Vereinsbank to collaborate with the Bayerische Hypotheken- und Wechselbank and, most importantly, that there was an incompatibility between the CA's credit business and its mortgage business and that the combination violated current German practice. He also thought for legal reasons it would be hard to obligate the CA to move its portfolio later. Ernst remained quite unpersuaded, pointing out that the end result of the Riehle plan would be to have two mixed mortgage banks, the CI and the CA. He saw no reason to add to the burdens of the CA, which was hard pressed to give up holdings anyway, and thought it best to wait on further

---

[249] ÖStA/AdR, BMF, Allgem. Reihe 1938, 49735/1938, Joham to Fischböck, July 8, 1938 with minutes of the meeting of July 1, 1938 in Munich.

[250] These problems are reiterated in a variety of documents of the Austrian authorities and in their meetings in the RWM; see ÖStA/AdR, Bürckel-Materie, 2165/0, Vol. 1, Box 92, especially, memorandum on the organization of the credit apparatus, May 9, 1938; Kratz to Ernst, Sept. 21, 1938, Kratz memorandum of Aug. 30, 1938, and Kratz to Ernst, Sept. 21, 1938.

developments.[251] By the end of September, Riehle began to back down a bit. On the one hand, the larger issue of the relationship between the CA and the Deutsche Bank was at center stage, and he recognized that the CA was under excessive pressure. On the other hand, everything connected with the mortgage business in Austria had become a bit confused because the capital market was strained and the government was refusing to permit mortgage banks to float new emissions. Riehle thus concluded that he had to wait on events. His hope was that the CA might be inclined to give up its portfolio rather than subject itself to the kind of regulation required for banks doing mortgage business in Germany.[252]

The question now was whether the matter might not be solved through direct negotiations between the CA and the CI, but the results at the end of December 1938 were very negative indeed. In negotiations with Joham and his colleagues, Weninger proposed that his bank take over the CA mortgage portfolio and buy up the mortgage bonds issued in connection with them for a price yet to be determined. The Bayerische Hypothekenbank (Bayernbank) would also take over the CA shares in the Bank für Kärnten, thus gaining virtually 100 percent of the shares for the Bayernbank, which was the proprietary bank of the CI. Also, Weninger wanted to have his bank granted a stake in the Kontrollbank, an institution owned by a consortium of banks that included the CA whose chief activities had become the management of Reich-guaranteed loans in Austria and the sale of large Jewish assets. In return for these concessions, Weninger offered a stake in a Salzburg iron merchant firm, Carl Steiner & Co. As Joham reported to Olscher, he and his colleagues rejected the proposition out of hand, viewing the proposal that the CA accept participation in a single firm in return for these concessions as totally inadequate. The CA expected an offer equivalent in value to what

was being given, perhaps the commercial business of the CI and similar concessions.[253]

The tone of Joham's letter suggests that he actually found Weninger's offer insulting but also that he felt confident that he had some protection from Olscher and Abs, who, it will be remembered, were working out their participation in the CA at this time. However, Riehle and his plan continued to loom over the situation, and the CA apparently was prepared at least to discuss some arrangement regarding the mortgage issue and the Bank für Kärnten. In February 1939, Fischböck reported that the CI and the CA had come to an agreement under which the former would take over the mortgages and mortgage loans by which the CA mortgage bonds were secured. This would require the agreement of the RWM to a substantial new emission and, at Fischböck's behest, the Hypotheken- und Kreditinstitut duly applied for the right to issue a 25 million RM emission of mortgage and communal bonds, 20 million to cover the CA mortgages and 5 million to cover municipal bonds. This request of the RWM was in addition to a prior request for 25 million to cover other mortgage business.[254]

At the same time, the Bank für Kärnten issue was put back on the table, when the Bayernbank wrote to the CA on April 13, 1939, in a letter that was more interesting for Heller's and Joham's marginalia than for its actual content. The Bayernbank claimed that there was a "basic agreement" between the two banks that the CA's stake should be given up as part of "the simplification of banking in the Ostmark." Apparently, given the question mark in the margin, Heller was unable to remember agreeing to anything or to understand why giving up the shares would simplify anything. The Bavarians went on to declare that they had tried to fulfill the CA's wish to have payment for the shares made in kind rather than in money, but

[251] RGVA Moscow, 1458/2/84, Bl. 364, memo by Ernst, Sept. 17, 1938, on a discussion with Riehle on Sept. 14.

[252] DB, B 51, memo, probably by Abs, Sept. 30, 1938.

[253] DB, P 6502, Bl. 175–176, Joham to Olscher, Dec. 23, 1938.

[254] ÖStA/AdR, BMF, Allgem. Reihe 1939, 32130/1939, Klucki to Riehle, Feb. 18, 1939 and CI to RWM, Feb. 15, 1939.

that this had proven impossible. They therefore offered cash payment instead at 100 percent for the shares, plus the 1938 dividends. What made Heller and Joham balk in particular, however, was the suggestion that the CA was responsible for holding up the settlement "of one of the few questions in the banking organization of the Ostmark that was still open." In Heller's view, the reason for the CA's turning down the offer lay, "to put it mildly," in the "proposal presented." To this, Joham added a hearty "Yes."[255]

Such niceties notwithstanding, the political situation did not permit a cessation of negotiations and an agreement was reached between the Bayernbank, the CI, and the CA covering all the relevant issues on May 22, 1939. The CA agreed to sell its shares in the Bank für Kärnten for cash effective June 30, 1939, but that sale was to be kept a secret until at least June 30, 1940. The CA was to continue its position in the Bank für Kärnten as before while the management of the bank was to be informed that it now had to report to the Bayernbank on all questions. The secrecy was to be maintained at the request of the CA, which was apparently concerned about the effect of such knowledge on its other subsidiary banks. The agreement further called for the CA to provide the CI with 9 million RM from its mortgage loan portfolio. In return, the CI would exchange 4 million of its own mortgage bonds for an equivalent number of CA mortgage bonds. The remaining 5 million RM owing to the CA was to be paid in three equal installments in cash on December 31, 1939, and June 30 and December 31, 1940, along with 4.4 percent interest owing from June 30, 1939. The CI was also to take over the CA loans – totaling approximately 8.5 million RM – that had been made to the cities of Klagenfurt and Villach. The CA would be liable for the nullification of the bonds but not for their collectability. In return, the CI would issue 4.4 percent municipal bonds in an almost equivalent amount to the account of the CA and the remainder in cash. The agreement also provided complicated arrangements for the

issuance of short-term loans to the municipalities by the two banks should they be necessary. The entire contract was made contingent on government approval of its terms and of the projected CI emissions of municipal bonds that would be necessitated by the agreement.[256]

In the end, however, nothing came of either part of this agreement, both of which got lost in the shuffle of the economic "steering" of the RWM, regional political interests, and the remarkable ability of Joham and his colleagues to let things drift when it was to their interest. At the end of 1939 matters were held up by differences between the CA and the city of Klagenfurt. Then, the RWM auditors wished to examine the books of the CI before making a proposal as to the date when the CA was supposed to turn over its mortgage portfolio.[257] There was, after all, a war going on, and the status of these questions was not what it had been back in May. In fact, the agreement of May seemed very defunct by January 1940. In a telephone conversation with Joham, therefore, Director Carl Kraemer of the Bayernbank told Joham that according to notes of his bank they had agreed back in May that the Bayernbank would temporarily assume chief administrative responsibility for the Bank für Kärnten in 1940. He himself could not remember this, and all he could recall was that Joham wanted the giving over of the CA shares to the Bayernbank to be kept secret, and Kraemer urged Joham to stay on the supervisory board until the issue of the shares was settled. Joham, however, remembered quite well that the administrative arrangement had been contingent on the negotiated agreement that had not yet come to pass, and he took advantage of the situation to help Kraemer not to think about what he had so conveniently forgotten. He thus pointed out that things had

[255] BA-CA, CA-TZ, Sekretariat grün, Box 7/BfK I, II, V-X, Bayernbank to the CA, April 13, 1939.

[256] BA-CA, CA-TZ, Sekretariat rot, Box 1/AVA, BfK, Wiener B, File 1/12, Agreement of May 22, 1939; on the secrecy issue, see ibid., Sekretariat grün, Box 9/BfK XXII–XXIX, XXXI, 1/1, discussion between Director Kraemer of the Bayernbank and Joham, Jan. 2, 1940.

[257] ÖStA/AdR, BMF, Allgem. Reihe 1939, 35100/1939, Minute by Güttl, Nov. 14, 1939, and Knackes of RWM to Güttl, Nov. 1, 1939.

changed considerably since their discussion and that the negotiations had been linked to the mortgage portfolio question. This, like the negotiations over the Bank für Kärnten, now appeared to have become dormant so that the entire matter was likely to be delayed for a long time. For this reason, the CA had assumed that it would continue to rotate the administrative responsibility for the bank because the idea of not doing so appeared to have been overtaken by events.[258]

This is not to say that the interests of the CA in Carinthia were completely safe and sound. Riehle could interfere in the situation at any time because the RWM had a supervisory function over the banks. The war was leading to growing pressure for the rationalization of the banking sector, and while this would become particularly intense in 1942–1943, rationalization was a general goal of the RWM before then and involved the RWM in any changes that might be contemplated. The RWM fought against overbanking and the duplication of branches by any single bank. In Carinthia, the CA was particularly vulnerable to becoming a rationalization target because it was one of the large shareholders in the Bank für Kärnten and also had its own branches in the area. Neither the RWM nor the banks, however, could fail to take the Gauleiter into account. The Gauleiter and the Gau economic advisors had very decisive voices in dealing with the disposition of regional financial institutions, and their conceptions of the economic interests of their region and their economic, political, and personal ambitions for the present and future required constant cultivation. In the case of Carinthia, the key figures were Gauleiter Friedrich Rainer and Gau Economic Advisor Alois Winkler. From this perspective, the CA was especially lucky in its relationship to Franz Hasslacher, who came from the region, was president of the CA supervisory board, and was also on the Bank für Kärnten supervisory board. As a major figure in Carinthia, he had the ear of Rainer

and therefore was an especially important political asset despite the fact that he had turned down Rainer's request to serve as president of the Gau Chamber of Commerce.[259]

It seemed impossible to prevent new initiatives from Berlin in the Bank für Kärnten question. In May of 1941, Riehle brought it up yet once again in a conversation with Fritscher, now suggesting that the CA sell its shares to the CI, which would then be asked to turn the Bank für Kärnten into a branch of the CI. Riehle's reason was that he felt the CA was overrepresented in Lower Styria. This, however, could only happen if the Gauleiter agreed. It did not take long for the CA to mobilize its forces against this, however, and Hasslacher, Abs, Rafelsberger, at this time on the CA supervisory board for reasons to be explained later, and the entire CA management board showed up in Berlin and argued that it was improper to solve the problems of Lower Styria at the expense of the CA, that an "objective" solution had to be found, and that the Gauleiter's voice had to be heard. They suggested that a solution might be found in dissolving the Bank für Kärnten, with the CI possibly getting the Klagenfurt bank, while the CA would receive the other branches and perhaps further compensation.

Under the circumstances, one could not of course totally refuse to discuss Riehle's proposal that the CA give up its holding in the Bank für Kärnten, and Fritscher, Joham, and Pfeiffer duly did so with the Bayernbank and CI leadership on July 13, 1941. The CA directors were blunt about their preference for waiting until the end of the war, but they were also prepared to give up their holding in return for an appropriate equivalent. They proposed that the Bank für Kärnten be dissolved and that its branches be divided by the RWM as was deemed appropriate with the CA getting additional cash compensation should this be necessary. The Bayernbank and CI negotiators, however, turned down the

---

[258] BA-CA, CA-TZ, Sekretariat grün, Box 9/BfK XXII–XXIX, XXXI, File 22/1, Telephone conversation between Kraemer and Joham, Jan. 2, 1940.

[259] See StmkLA, Vr 734/1946, Bl. 100 and 376b, Landesgericht für Strafsachen Graz, Franz und Jakob Hasslacher, Hasslacher's postwar testimony of May 17, 1946.

liquidation of the Bank für Kärnten, proposing instead that it be merged with the CI, the CA selling its shares for 120 percent and dividing such business as was not being handled by the Bank für Kärnten branches. While the CA representatives felt that the dissolution of the Bank für Kärnten, whether by liquidation or merger, first had to have the approval of the Gauleiter, the Bayernbank and the CI took the position that approval had to be given first by the RWM, whose task it would then be to get the agreement of the Gauleiter. The Bayernbank and CI leaders probably were aware that Rainer and Winkler had already agreed to Riehle's plan involving the dissolution of the Bank für Kärnten, and if so, they must have been as surprised as Riehle to learn some weeks later that the Gau authorities had changed their mind, were now concerned that it would bring too much competition into the mortgage field, and were also contemplating turning the Bank für Kärnten into a Gau bank. As will be shown shortly, the notion of setting up Gau banks was something of a rage among the Gauleiter at this time. In any case, Riehle needed to get back to the Gau authorities and, because the waters had been muddied once again, further action had to be suspended.[260]

Nevertheless, Riehle felt emboldened to return to the charge in the spring of 1942, when he was demanding once again that the Bank für Kärnten matter be cleared up, now saying that the CA should either take over the bank entirely and give up its CA branches in the region or keep its branches and let the CI take over the Bank für Kärnten. When Hasslacher received this news, he was greatly irritated, commenting, "Well, still the old standpoint, although Gauleiter Rainer does not want to change anything!"[261] While Riehle continued to wonder when the CA would finally stop talking about

giving up the Bank für Kärnten and actually do it, the working committee of the CA remained undisturbed by Riehle's impatience, advising a wait-and-see attitude "because it would be desirable not to change anything while the war still continued."[262]

This stonewalling, however, could no longer be sustained in the fall of 1942 for the pressure for banking rationalization was becoming very intense, and so Gau Economic Advisor Winkler summoned the bank leaders for a meeting on October 6 with Riehle and the president of the Supervisory Office for Banking, Konrad Gottschick. Hasslacher represented the CA, Kraemer the Bayernbank, and Director Wilhelm Rauber the Bank für Kärnten.[263] Winkler began the discussion by setting forth the goals of Gauleiter Rainer, which were to have strong banks in the Gau, a united structure for the Bank für Kärnten, but a single and not a double sphere of influence for the CA. Riehle then presented his plan. Like Rainer, he wished that the CA be strongly represented in the area but not be doubly present. The CA's presence, he thought, should be made through its branches rather than through the Bank für Kärnten. Because of the Bayernbank's services during the Depression, when it had come to the rescue of the Bank für Kärnten, its presence should remain in that bank. Then, however, Riehle went on to propose that the Länderbank take over the CA's holding in the Bank für Kärnten and thus satisfy its repeated request that it be properly represented in Carinthia. In this way, Riehle argued, two other major banks would be in the province along with the CA, and the Vienna-Munich connection would be maintained in the changed ownership of the Bank für Kärnten.

---

260 BA-CA, CA-V, Fritscher to Hasslacher, May 26, 1941; meeting of June 13, 1941; report on meeting with Riehle, July 17, 1941, ibid.; working committee meeting, May 23, 1941.

261 BA-CA, CA-TZ, Sekretariat grün, Box 9/BfK XXII–XXIX, XXXI, File 22/1, Heinisch (Gau Economic Adviser's Office, Vienna) to Hasslacher, March 25, 1942.

262 RGVA Moscow, 1458/2/91, Bl. 169–170, Meeting with Riehle, April 22, 1942, and BA-CA, CA-V, working committee meeting, June 10, 1942.

263 BA-CA, CA-TZ, Sekretariat grün, Box 9/BfK XXII–XXIX, XXXI, File 22/3, Winkler to CA, Sept. 22, 1942. See DB, P 6508, Bl. 46–50, the discussion and quotations that follow are from the meeting held on Oct. 6, 1942. Hasslacher himself composed the lengthy report on the meeting.

The great surprise in this proposal was the sudden introduction of the Länderbank into the picture, and it proved extremely unpopular among the bankers present. Kraemer declared that he was "extraordinarily disappointed and that he had expected something else." Hasslacher, by contrast, made no bones about his outrage at the proposal. In his view, it had nothing do with bank rationalization and displayed an obliviousness to the past history of the relationship between the parties involved, which, he claimed, had been one of loyal cooperation as well as conformity to the interests and desires of the Gau leadership. When Winkler tried to suggest that the relationship had been less rosy than described, both Kraemer and Rauber seconded Hasslacher's remarks. Hasslacher pointed out that he had no negotiating powers but that he could well imagine the CA either leaving the Bank für Kärnten or taking it over completely while giving up the branches if it were certain that other banks would not be allowed to come in by other means.

What he rejected most angrily and firmly was the Riehle plan: "The idea of excluding the CA and bringing the Länderbank in its place means not only doing damage to the CA but also a severe insult.... The CA was the first to make the necessary readjustments and created all the necessary preconditions for the correct conduct of business at home and abroad, and, in addition, was strongly represented in its leadership by Carinthians since two of its management board members and the chairman of the supervisory board are Carinthians. It is not the fault of the CA that the Länderbank has entered upon another inheritance and for this reason has not been active in Carinthia until now. It would be more than odd to simply put a bank that has previously contributed nothing to the province in the place of one that has until now made an effort to do its best in every way, and then to justify this solely on the grounds that other banks should come into the Gau."

Hasslacher pointed out that similar arguments could be used to bring in other banks, such as the Bank für Deutsche Arbeit, and also insisted that a question of principle was involved because there were comparable efforts to weaken the CA position elsewhere. While Riehle defended his office by claiming that the decisions in other areas had been very favorable to the CA and explained in response to a complaint by Hasslacher that the meeting had to be held without prior consultation because the Gauleiter was going on a trip, Kraemer now decided to join the fray and form a "fighting partnership" with the CA by characterizing the Riehle solution as "unjust and inexplicable." It was not simply a matter of the role both his bank and the CA had played in 1931, but also the tendency reflected in the preference shown the major Berlin banks over regional banks. In his view, the Länderbank was simply another version of the Dresdner Bank, and he did not think that anything could change that. This produced an argument with Gottschick, who came to the defense of the Länderbank and its capacity for independence, but Rauber, like Kraemer, insisted that collaboration with the CA had been without friction.

Clearly, the discussion had become quite heated, and Winkler sought to calm things down by stressing the substantial role of the CA in the Southeast and also noted that the old scheme of having the CI take over the CA share had been dropped because the provincial mortgage banks had been functioning well and competition from the CI was undesirable. Hasslacher too now sought to play the statesman by stressing that things were not going to be decided on the spot, but that it was important not to hold out any expectations to the Länderbank. Kraemer also argued that if the CA gave up its shares in the Bank für Kärnten, there was no reason why they could not be sold to the general public, implying thereby that the Bayernbank would remain the sole large shareholder and the CA would keep its branches. The most important result of the meeting was that what Riehle had initially presented as more or less a decision by the RWM and the Gauleiter was now treated as a "proposal" that would remain on the table until a better one could be found. He did insist, however, that a solution be found quickly and that the CA have a single and not a double role in the province. Another important result, however, was that Hasslacher and Kraemer agreed to act in common and not deal with third parties until they were agreed between themselves. Riehle's unexpected and undesired achievement had been to turn the two major shareholders in the Bank für Kärnten into what Hasslacher had rightly described as a "fighting partnership."

The "partners," to be sure, continued to spar with one another. When the CA invited Kraemer to negotiate in late October 1942, Kraemer once again proposed that the CA sell its shares to the CI, and when this was rejected he suggested that the CA sell some of its shares to the Bayernbank, giving it a clear majority, and thereby disarm those who charged the CA with being in competition with the Bank für Kärnten. The Bank für Kärnten would then pursue policies independent of any consideration for the CA, but they would all agree to keep the Länderbank out. The CA, however, thought it a mistake to raise the question of ownership stakes again, preferring, rather, to stand united against the Länderbank coming in, except with its own branch if the authorities so insisted, and thought it advisable to seek a solution through Gauleiter Rainer.[264] The initiative now fell to the CA and especially to Hasslacher's contacts with Rainer. The Gauleiter was persuaded to drop the idea of bringing in the Länderbank and now welcomed an arrangement under which the CA would come to an agreement with the Bayernbank that would maintain their joint engagement in the Bank für Kärnten but would also bring the CA branches into the bank. Rainer liked the idea, not only because it kept the two banks engaged in Carinthia, but also because it produced the desired concentration and rationalization in the banking field.[265]

But what kind of agreement were the CA and Bayernbank supposed to make after so many failed efforts? The basic outlines of what constituted the settlement seem to have owed their existence to Hans Rummel of the Deutsche Bank, who had met with Joham about other matters in Agram (Zagreb) in January 1943. Rummel's point of departure was a skepticism about the chances of keeping the Länderbank out of Carinthia for any length of time because he was convinced that Rainer had promised Anton Apold, the president of the Länderbank supervisory board, to let the Länderbank gain a foothold in the foreseeable future. Once the Länderbank set up a branch in Carinthia, it would do its business at the expense of the CA and the Bank für Kärnten through the "usual methods" of offering better bank conditions and the like. Consolidation, therefore, made sense for competitive reasons as well, and Rummel suggested, first, that the CA sell its participation in the Bank für Kärnten, second, that the CA branches then be brought into the Bank für Kärnten, third, that the capital of the Bank für Kärnten then be increased and that the ratio of CA to Bayernbank ownership be determined by the actual value of what they had contributed to the total value of the bank plus an additional amount of participation for the Bayernbank in recognition of its long-standing relationship with the Bank für Kärnten and its prestige requirements. As Rummel recognized, if one literally took the value of the assets provided by the two sides, the ratio could be 75 percent for the CA and 25 percent for the Bayernbank. Nonetheless, he also felt that the Bayernbank was entitled to a "stake plus."[266]

It was this proposal that Joham brought to the table in his negotiations with Kraemer in Munich on February 16, 1943. The two men agreed that they had to act quickly and do what was bearable for both sides, and Kraemer was aware that the Gauleiter was friendly to the solution proposed and also that no one, including himself, had produced a better option. It was hard to accept a minority position because the relative status of the Bayernbank and the CA in general did not justify it, but Kraemer also knew that it was justified when it came to their holdings in Carinthia. The discussion was not without haggling about the participation

[264] BA-CA, CA-TZ, Sekretariat grün, Box 9/BfK XXII–XXIX, XXXI, File 22/1, Meeting of Joham, Buzzi, and Kraemer, Oct. 28, 1942.

[265] Ibid., Joham to Kraemer, Jan. 23, 1943.

[266] Ibid., memorandum by Rummel, Jan. 1943.

quota, Joham initially offering 20 percent to 30 percent, Kraemer asking for 30 percent to 40 percent. He was especially concerned about a stake that recognized the prestige needs of the Bayernbank, that assured it a prominent position on the supervisory board, favor to be shown for its mortgage and mortgage bond business, and that the CA conduct the business involved in Carinthia.[267]

In the final agreement hammered out in late March 1943 and effectuated during the coming months, the two sides settled on a 70 percent to 30 percent participation ratio, with the CA to take over the actual administration of the bank. The CA tried to extract some concessions from Rainer with mixed success. It argued that the actual participation ratio in monetary terms would have been 85 percent to 15 percent so that the CA had made a great sacrifice and thus requested that it be allowed to keep at least a branch in Klagenfurt to satisfy the needs of its old customers. Rainer, however, flatly turned this down, pointing out that it ran counter to his concentration efforts. He did, however, accept the CA demand that no other bank be allowed to set up branches in Carinthia even if that would be "painful" for the Länderbank. He also promised full support for the activities of the bank and promised not to allow the shutting down of certain branches as was originally planned because the branches were now part of the larger bank.

Rainer was indeed pleased to have so promising a provincial bank under his jurisdiction, and shortly before the founding of the bank on a new basis in late May became rather aggravated when the CA tried to push through a renaming of the bank the "Kreditanstalt für Kärnten." Joham apparently believed that Rainer had no objections to this and the CA was anxious to provide its old customers with a more familiar name. In the end, however, they decided that Rainer's favor was more important than the name, and the Bank für Kärnten retained its name. On June 29, 1943, the general shareholders' meeting approved the capital share increase

of 1 to 3 million RM. The actual transfer of CA branches to the bank took place on July 1, while the actual integration of the branches into the bank was to take place at the end of August. The Bayernbank was accorded a voice in all basic affairs of the bank and in the granting of credits more than 500,000 RM. Negotiating these terms had taken some time, but the Bank für Kärnten was now 70 percent owned by the CA and managed by it. Given the fact that the original plan of the RWM was for the CA to sell its mortgage business and its holdings in the Bank für Kärnten, the outcome can reasonably be viewed as an unanticipated but very solid achievement for Joham, Hasslacher, and the CA and a telling illustration of the kind of politics that characterized the political economy of the Third Reich in Austria.[268]

By comparison with the Bank für Kärnten, the CA had a much easier time protecting its interests in the Hauptbank für Tirol und Vorarlberg and the Bank für Oberösterreich und Salzburg. This was largely thanks to the support it received from the RWM, which, in contrast to the grief Riehle had caused in connection with the Bank für Kärnten, acted as a protective shield against the ambitions, first of the newly formed Länderbank Wien, as has been shown elsewhere, and subsequently of regional Gauleiter.

The first effort to abscond with a CA affiliate from this quarter came from the office of the Gauleiter of the Tyrol and Vorarlberg, Franz Hofer, the head of whose financial office, SS Hauptsturmführer Gustav Linert, had begun discussions with Bürckel's office in the fall of 1938 about the Gau taking over the Hauptbank für Tirol und Vorarlberg. The bank was 82 percent in the hands of the CA, 13 percent in the possession of the Bayerische Vereinsbank, and the remainder in private hands. In a letter to Kratz of November 24, 1938, Linert pointed out that the bank had

---

[267] Ibid., memorandum by Joham on the discussions with Kraemer, Feb. 16, 1943.

[268] Ibid., Discussion with Rainer, March 12, 1943; Joham to Rainer, April 12, 1943; Rainer to the CA, April 13, 1943; memorandum on discussion with Rainer, May 25, 1943. See also BA-CA, CA-V, the reports to the working committee of Jan. 27, March 23, July 28, 1943.

weathered the Depression very well and was in excellent shape. The fact that this owed much to the leadership of Joham before he went to the CA was not mentioned, but note was taken of the fact that 80 percent of its employees were National Socialists before the Anschluss and that its personnel were of high quality. There would be no risk for the Gau in taking the Hauptbank shares over from the CA and investing in a bank that could easily provide the lion's share of the credit business in the Gau. This would enable the Gau leadership to steer available capital in the right economic direction.[269] From the perspective of Bürckel and Kratz, this was a policy issue that had to be decided by the RWM. On the one hand, they had the sense that government policy favored regional banks, and this fit in with the desires of the Gau leadership in the Tyrol. On the other, they wanted to avoid precipitous action by Hofer and Linert but also to have the question settled quickly. The situation seemed especially pressing at the end of 1938 because the desire to create independent Gau banks was not limited to the Tyrol because the CA takeover of the Steirische Escompte Bank led to fears on the part of Gauleiter August Eigruber in Linz and Rainer in Klagenfurt that the CA would pursue its rationalization policy by fusing the Oberbank and the Bank für Kärnten. Hans Stigleitner, one of the officials dealing with banks and savings banks in Austria, felt that the desire of the Gauleiter to have their own regional banks was "understandable and justified," although he was puzzled as to where they were supposed to find the capital needed to take over these banks. In his view, the CA could well accept losing these provincial banks because it had its own branches in the areas involved to handle local business while all big business was handled from Vienna.[270] Under the circumstances, Kratz felt that the RWM had to take a position with alacrity "if one is to avoid

that through the independent actions of local authorities developments take place that later must be viewed as undesirable."[271]

The RWM responses came in early 1939 and were strongly opposed to the Gauleiter taking over any of the CA provincial banks. They were also quite revealing of the general policies of the RWM in Austria. The RWM viewed the question from the perspective of the capital requirements of Austria. Austria was largely dependent on its own banking resources for capital because the great Berlin banks were not being allowed to set up their own branches in Austria. The demand for credit, however, was likely to increase greatly in the near future, and it was difficult to see how this demand could be met on the provincial level where the capital base was so weak. The RWM suspected that the idea in the Tyrol and elsewhere was to consolidate the provincial banks owned by the CA with the Land mortgage banks, but this ran counter to the RWM's goal of trying to consolidate the Land mortgage banks throughout Austria. It was in fact uncertain as to whether this would prove sufficient to enable the mortgage banks to stand on their own feet. A mixing of the two types of banks was deemed undesirable. The RWM also believed that the Gauleiter were too much influenced by Vienna's tendency in the past not to supply sufficient capital to the provinces, but now that Austria was part of the Reich, and banks in the Reich, and especially in Bavaria, were in a position to offer credits if Vienna did not, one could expect that the Vienna banks would react properly to the danger of a loss of business. Smaller credits could be supplied by local savings banks and cooperatives. Furthermore, the RWM was in a position to apply pressure on the Viennese banks insofar as they failed to provide needed capital. A most important consideration for the RWM, however, was that the CA be given a chance to recover from the blows it had been experiencing, and this could hardly happen if it lost its subsidiary banks. Indeed, this would only encourage it to increase the role of its branch network, and this would run counter to the efforts to avoid

269 ÖStA/AdR, Bürckel-Materie, Box 93, 2165/6, Linert to Kratz, Nov. 24, 1938.

270 Ibid., memo by Ernst on discussion with Stigleitner, Dec. 21, 1938.

271 Ibid., Kratz to Riehle, Dec. 21, 1938.

redundancies on the branch level. While the RWM was willing to leave open the idea of creating a regional bank in the Tyrol if the other Gauleiter were not making similar demands, it felt that the entire Hauptbank question needed to be left open for the time being.[272]

Subsequently, Kratz's office came forth with a compromise idea under which the influence of the Gauleiter might be increased through participation in the CA's provincial banks. Riehle himself discussed the issue with Gauleiter Hofer, where the latter seemed to be opposed to mixing the Hauptbank with the semi-public mortgage banks and thus to have no idea of how to take over the Hauptbank even if he still wanted to do so. He wondered whether a large German bank like the Deutsche Bank might not buy up some of the shares so as to give the Hauptbank more independence from the CA, whereupon Riehle pointed out that the RWM could not influence such decisions. If the connection of the Hauptbank to the CA were loosened, then the CA would have to increase the number of its branches, and because there was a general consensus that the Hauptbank was functioning well, such problems as there were could be settled in the course of time.[273]

The RWM continued to pursue this policy of letting sleeping dogs lie, but this also meant that it expected the CA not to bestir matters either. When the bank commissar learned that Hofer was petitioning to acquire the Hauptbank and turn it into a Gau bank, he advised the CA through Rummel of the Deutsche Bank "to do nothing that could give cause to promote these efforts, especially not to allow any changes at the moment in the other affiliations."[274] Hofer's fear that the CA would follow the Steirische Escompte Bank model and fuse the big provincial banks with the CA was well founded, and Fischböck, who became general director at the CA in May 1939, seems to have been particularly keen on

this idea. Hofer, however, wanted to prevent strengthening the influence of Vienna still further. While Fischböck was even prepared to contemplate offering the Gauleiter a 50 percent stake in the provincial banks, Riehle and his colleagues did not see any pressing need to deal with these problems and preferred to take no initiatives.[275]

The trouble was that while Hofer seems to have been reassured for the time being and had accepted the RWM position, pressures were mounting from the side of Gauleiter Eigruber in Linz, who had taken up the idea of using the Bank für Oberösterreich und Salzburg, shortly to be renamed the Bank für Oberdonau und Salzburg, and commonly known as the Oberbank, as the basis for creating a Gau bank of his own or at least of greatly increasing the participation of the Gau in the Oberbank. At the time of the Anschluss, the CA had owned 79.2 percent, of the shares, the Land of Upper Austria, 16.2 percent of the shares, the Bayerische Vereinsbank 0.025 percent of the shares, and the remainder was in the hands of individual shareholders. If the CA was able to keep Eigruber at bay, it was because of the RWM's reservations about a large Gau stake in the bank. Indeed, the negotiations dragged on through the first half of 1940, and Riehle met repeatedly with Eigruber and his staff in efforts to persuade the Gauleiter to give up the idea of setting up a Gau bank and possibly using the Oberbank for this purpose.[276]

The decisive meetings on these issues were held at the end of August and beginning of September 1940 when Riehle met Eigruber and his staff in Linz to discuss the credit and banking situation in the Upper Danubian Gau, that is, not only the Oberbank and Gau bank issues but also the mortgage banks and credit cooperatives, the role of the nearby Bavarian banks, and other such matters. In their private conversation, Eigruber initially and rather

[272] Ibid., Gottschick to Kratz, Jan. 3, 1939.
[273] Ibid., Kratz to RWM, Feb. 1, 1939 and RWM to Kratz, Feb. 28, 1939.
[274] DB, P 6502, Bl. 209, memo by Rummel for Abs, Jan. 16, 1939.
[275] RGVA Moscow, 1458/2/91, Bl. 82, 85, Landfried to Koehler and Martini, June 30, 1939 and Riehle to Martini, July 27, 1939.
[276] See BA-CA, CA-V, p. 223, the report by Fischböck to the CA management board of March 2, 1940, and ibid., p. 525, report by Joham of June 1, 1940.

peremptorily demanded the establishment of a Gau bank and made another series of demands, only then to back down in the face of Riehle's arguments that the creation of a Gau bank was a bad idea. This, however, apparently took considerable persuasion and, in return, Eigruber made a series of demands connected with the reorganization of the savings and cooperative banks and the publicly chartered mortgage banks. Riehle sought to persuade Eigruber that the setting up of mortgage bank branches in the region would lead to competition for capital with the existing small banks and suggested an arrangement whereby the branches of the Oberbank would finance some of the long-term mortgage business of the public chartered mortgage bank. Most importantly, however, Eigruber demanded more influence over the Oberbank, and there had apparently been negotiations between Fischböck and the Gau in which the possibility of giving the Gau a majority or close to majority holding had been discussed. Riehle pointed out that the RWM guidelines on banking prohibited the government from gaining influence over bank activity by means of direct participations and urged instead that this be done indirectly by having members of the business community placed on the supervisory board who would act in the manner desired by the Gau. Riehle also promised to at least consider the Gau request that the CA branch in Linz be dissolved provided one could be confident that the CA influence in Linz through the Oberbank was sufficiently strong.[277]

This was followed by a series of negotiations between Joham and SS Oberführer Franz Langoth, who was president of the Oberbank supervisory board as well as a member of the CA supervisory board and also one of the major National Socialist leaders in Linz. At a meeting on September 4, Langoth told Joham that Eigruber and his staff were very satisfied with their negotiations with Riehle, for while the Gau agreed not to expand its holding in

the Oberbank, the desire of Eigruber to have the Oberbank as an independent regional bank was recognized as justified. Joham had been empowered to follow up on a phone conversation that Eigruber had already had with Fischböck dealing with the Oberbank. One of the issues discussed was the possible appointment of Josef Paić, who was finishing his stint at the Kontrollbank, as director on the management board of the Oberbank. The problem of the poor relations between Paić and Pfeiffer continued to act as a barrier to Paić's appointment to the CA board, so his appointment to the Oberbank was seen as a temporary solution. The appointment was touchy because the proposed salary was very high, and Paić did not come from the region. Another personnel issue, this time raised by Eigruber, was the demand that Oberbank supervisory board member and Gau financial officer Franz Danzer receive a 6,000 RM pension although the legal basis for such a pension was nonexistent. Eigruber and Fischböck had also discussed the possible sale of the Gau shares in the Oberbank, although no date had been set.

Langoth, however, now announced to Joham that such a sale and the regulation of other questions could not take place until a more systematic approach was taken to ensure the independence of the Oberbank as a regional bank. He believed this could be done through the signing of a contract between the Gau and the CA that would not only state this in black and white but that would also give the Gau a corresponding voice in appointments to both the management board and the Supervisory Board. In Joham's view, this stood in contradiction to what Eigruber and Fischböck had agreed upon and also presented legal problems. He proposed instead that the CA offer a "loyalty statement" to the Gau that it would consult with the Gau on all important questions relevant to the Oberbank. There were other points of difference between the CA and Eigruber that emerged from the Langoth-Joham negotiation. The Gau was demanding that the CA let its branch in Linz be absorbed into the Oberbank, a proposition Joham rejected on the grounds that the CA continued to have a vital interest

277 RGVA Moscow, 1458/2/80, Bl. 299–302, memorandum of Sept. 9 on the meetings in Linz, Aug. 31–Sept. 2, 1938.

in maintaining its branch. While Langoth did not withdraw Eigruber's stated intention to sell the Gau shares in the Oberbank sometime, he now suggested that one condition, from which he distanced himself personally, might be that the CA sell off its own Oberbank shares insofar as they exceeded 50 percent. When Langoth also proposed that the bank increase its capital, Joham rejected this on the grounds that the bank was so liquid at the moment that a capital share increase would be an "embarrassment."[278]

In dealing with Eigruber, Joham and his colleagues were not, of course, dealing with a normal government official in a normal government but rather with a National Socialist satrap close to the "Führer" who had no hesitations about using his powers. Langoth had feared that the CA's resistance would put Eigruber out of sorts, and he was right. The Gauleiter was especially angry over the interpretation given to his telephone call with Fischböck, which Eigruber viewed as a nonbinding conversation and, as Langoth reported to the CA management board on September 14, Eigruber "felt taken by surprise and is considering ideas of a complete separation from the Oberbank and the withdrawal of the supervisory board members delegated to it with his agreement."[279] This would have been tantamount to a kiss of death because doing business in the area depended on the good will and support of the Gauleiter, but Langoth assured Joham and his colleagues that Eigruber's bad mood could be dispelled by "clever action" on the part of the CA.

Langoth suggested that the CA drop the issue of Paić and also the question of the Gau disposing of its shares and come to an agreement on the other issues. Insofar as the Gau sale of the shares was concerned, the CA indicated that what was important was not the sale itself but to whom the shares might be sold, and they could settle for a guarantee that the shares would not be sold to the competition. The CA was prepared to delay the Paić issue until the new year, when he would need a job, and suggested that a first-rate banker was needed as chairman of the board at the Oberbank, and Paić was the right person. The Danzer pension was not something the CA was prepared to fight about, although it did suggest that accepting such a pension might be politically damaging to Danzer, a fear Langoth did not share or did not care about. The CA also gave in on the issue of a capital share increase.

With these matters settled, Langoth and Joham then worked together on the draft of a letter to Eigruber assuring him that the CA would not undertake any measures connected with the Oberbank that were not in conformity with the interests of the Gau, expounding on the importance of the Gau's support and leadership, and assuring that the Oberbank would be managed as an independent regional bank so long as the Gau remained interested in the existence of the Oberbank. In return, the Gau was to pledge not to increase its participation in the bank and also to give the CA first option on any shares it might sell. The CA also agreed to raise the Oberbank's capital from 2.8 to 5 million RM so as to recognize its rank as a bank and its developmental possibilities. Further, the CA would not make any appointments to the management board or supervisory board except in consultation with the Gau. While abstaining from a promise to dissolve the Linz branch of the CA, it did promise to make a demarcation of functions between the branch and the Oberbank that would prevent the former from being detrimental to the development of the latter.

This was obviously a compromise arrangement designed to assert the political power of the Gau over the Oberbank without having the Gau assume a majority position through shares. The CA kept the latter, but was obviously constrained in exercising what were its legal rights. It was all a good illustration of the powers of the Gauleiter at the regional level, and the agreement enabled the CA to have a respite from Eigruber's demands. As it turned out, Paić went off to work for the Länderbank, so that this issue solved itself. Also, wartime demands

---

[278] A copy of Joham's report on this meeting is to be found in DB, P 6504; it was also presented to the CA management board on Sept. 7, 1940, BA-CA, CA-V, p. 877.

[279] Ibid., p. 904ff., management board meeting of Sept. 14, 1940.

made an increase in the capital of the Oberbank much more justifiable than it had been in 1940, and it was raised from 2.8 million RM to 6 million in October 1941.[280]

It was not until the late spring of 1942 that Eigruber returned to the charge again, now asking that the Gau be allowed to increase its share to 25 percent. The context of this demand was undoubtedly the general mobilization of the Gauleiter to increase their economic power and the incipient creation of the so-called Bormann Committee of Gau Economic Advisors that was to attempt to increase the control over the major banks by the Party. Whatever the case, when Langoth presented this to the CA, Joham advised that the CA offer 500,000 RM in shares from its own holdings at 125 percent, which was the price at the time of the capital share increase of the previous year. In return, the CA was to ask that it receive first option on repurchase, that the Gau agree that its stake was to be viewed as finally regulated at this level and continue to give support to the Oberbank, and last, that the Gau support the continued existence of the CA branch in Linz. Danzer formally accepted these terms for the Gau on July 13, 1942.[281]

Nevertheless, despite the agreement of both sides, it was to take yet another year for the agreement to go into effect because of the reservations of the RWM, in this case from both Riehle and Reich Economics Minister Funk, who objected to the idea of the public hand having such a large participation in a private enterprise because this would in effect make the government responsible for the fate of a private bank. By the summer of 1943, however, a scheme had been worked out that had the approval of the RWM under which Eigruber could have the shares sold to companies and persons named by himself who would in effect represent the Gau's interests. The

500,000 RM in CA shares were then sold to the Kraftwerke Oberdonau AG (150,000 RM), the Wolfsegg-Traunthaler Kohlenwerks-AG (50,000 RM), and the Trustee for the Fürstlich Schwarzenberg'schen Vermögens (300,000 RM). The CA retained a first option on the repurchase of these shares as well as of the 1.5 million RM in shares that continued to be held by the regional government. At war's end, it held 4,287,900 RM worth of the 6 million RM in shares, or 71.4 percent. Its branch in Linz had also escaped the "bank rationalization." Indeed, it even escaped the bombers.[282]

More generally, the CA had emerged from years of National Socialist rule with its provincial banks still in its possession and had thus weathered both the gang of Gauleiter who were seeking other solutions and the peculiarities of RWM economic leadership. Given what had happened and was going to happen to some of its industrial holdings, the dangers were obviously very real, and good negotiating and political skills had proven essential. Certainly, the control exercised by the CA over these banks was not the same as it had been before 1938 or afterward, and adjustment had to be made in the ways of the dictatorship. This was an area, however, in which the CA had become quite adept.

4. THE DEUTSCHE BANK TAKES CONTROL AND THE WARTIME ORGANIZATION OF THE CA

The Deutsche Bank Becomes the CA's Majority Shareholder

The stabilization of the CA's ownership and leadership, marked by the agreement between the VIAG and the CA at the end of 1938 and the appointment of Fischböck as titular general director of the management board shortly thereafter, was only a hiatus in the Deutsche Bank's struggle to gain actual control of the CA. As will be shown in the second part of

---

[280] Ibid., p. 859, management board meeting, Oct. 16, 1941.

[281] BA-CA, CA-V, working committee meeting, June 10, 1942. On the Bormann Committee, see Kopper, *Bankenpolitik*, pp. 349–353. For the acceptance of the terms, see BA-CA, CA-TZ, Sekretariat grün, Box 3/BOS I–X, Box 4/BOS XI–XVII, Danzer to CA, July 13, 1942.

[282] Ibid., Eigruber to Funk, July 15, 1943, and other relevant correspondence. See also BA-CA, CA-V, the working committee meetings of Jan. 27 and March 23, 1943.

this study, despite its loss of holdings and other difficulties described earlier in this chapter, the business of the CA increased very substantially after the Anschluss, when it became active in Aryanizations, consortial and other credit business, and, in particular, in expansion abroad. It worked quite closely with the Deutsche Bank in the Czech lands, Poland, and Southeast Europe, sometimes acting as the Deutsche Bank's partner, sometimes as its proxy. Under these circumstances, the Deutsche Bank remained as anxious as ever to increase its holding in the CA.

This holding had been very small, indeed amounting to not much more than was required to qualify for admission to the administrative council in 1937. Prior to the deal with the VIAG at the end of 1938, when the Deutsche Bank acquired 25 percent of the shares of the CA, the Deutsche Bank's actual holding in the CA amounted to less than 1 percent of the shares, and most of this small holding was actually acquired in late 1938. At the beginning of 1938, the Deutsche Bank had only 260,600 Schilling in shares, and these were increased by the purchase of 1,700 shares denominated at 637,500 Schilling in September 1938 from the Bankhaus Steinhäusser for which the Deutsche Bank paid 361,590 RM as per October 14, 1938. This private bank had formerly been the Viennese Bankhaus Ephrussi & Co., the leading figure of which had been the former Jewish vice-chairman of the CA in Vienna, Alexander Weiner. In late April 1938, after being raided by the Gestapo, the bank was largely taken over by the Aryan Carl August Steinhäusser, who had come to the bank from the Disconto-Gesellschaft years before and held 20 percent of the shares. The bank was renamed the Bankhaus C.A. Steinhäusser, vorm. Bankhaus Ephrussi. The Deutsche Bank had held some shares in the Bankhaus Ephrussi until 1933, when it sold them off, but friendly relations continued. A few days after the Anschluss, and thus prior to its Aryanization, Ephrussi sought to renew its close connections with the Deutsche Bank and offered to send Alexander Weiner to Berlin to discuss possible joint business under the changed circumstances. Probably sensing that Weiner's days as a banker

were numbered but desiring to maintain an old banking connection, Director Mosler urged Abs to discuss the offer verbally when he was in Vienna but to put off further pursuit of the matter for the time being.[283] Subsequently, however, Steinhäusser received a standing order to purchase CA shares for the Deutsche Bank, and this led to the aforementioned acquisitions in September–October. The Deutsche Bank also picked up a small block of shares from its branch in Mannheim in December 1938, so that just prior to the contract with the VIAG, it had 1 percent of the shares. This was, indeed, Abs's great bluff in his dealings with Olscher. Whereas Olscher thought the Deutsche Bank held 6 percent of the shares prior to the contract, it in fact owned only 26 percent of the shares at the end of 1938, the 25 percent sold to it by the VIAG, and the 1 percent it owned already.[284]

Nevertheless, it planned to own more. In mid-December, Abs had asked Steinhäusser to refrain from any more purchases on the stock market until further notice, undoubtedly because of the impending settlement with the VIAG, which cost the Deutsche Bank 16,833,333 RM. On January 3, 1939, however, Abs instructed Steinhäusser to resume "purchasing material at the conditions agreed upon by us."[285] While Steinhäusser seems to have been the chief source of CA "material" during the coming two years, the Deutsche Bank also acquired CA shares from the banking house of H. Albert de Bary in Amsterdam and, after the conquest of Belgium in 1940, from the Brussels-based Société Générale de Belgique and Compagnie Belge de l'Étranger.

[283] On the Aryanization of the Bankhaus Ephrussi, see Melichar, *Neuordnung im Bankwesen*, pp. 116–132. On Ephrussi's overtures to the Deutsche Bank, see DB, B 51, Mosler to Abs, March 21, 1938.

[284] For an accounting of the share ownership by the Deutsche Bank, see DB, V2/166, Ulrich to Tron, Sept. 25, 1952. See DB, P 6530, Bl. 8–12, the correspondence with Ephrussi dealing with the purchase of 1,700 shares in Oct. 1938.

[285] See ibid., Bl. 16, 22, 37, Deutsche Bank to Steinhäusser, Dec. 14, 1938; Deutsche Bank to VIAG, Dec. 30, 1938; Deutsche Bank to Steinhäusser, Jan. 3, 1939, all signed by Abs and Pollems.

The Belgian purchases required RWM permission because they involved use of the German-Belgian clearing arrangement. The fact that the Deutsche Bank was increasing its CA holdings through purchases on the open market was thus known to and approved by the RWM. In any case, by the beginning of 1942 the Deutsche Bank controlled 36 percent of the CA shares. It is worth noting that Abs paid close attention to the disposition of these shares, instructing in July 1941 that they not be sold and that the account not be accessed by anyone without his personal permission.[286]

The acquisition of these shares was a part of a broader program for the future relationship of the Deutsche Bank and the CA in which Director Joham and some of his colleagues at the CA played important roles and worked closely with Abs. The development of this program was triggered by a conversation between Joham and Director Walter Pohle of the Deutsche Bank, who had become the dominant figure in the takeover of the Böhmische Union Bank (BUB) at the time of the German occupation of the rest of Czechoslovakia in March 1939. As will be shown in the third chapter of this study, the CA was actively expanding its interests as Germany expanded its territory, was seeking "compensation" for its losses after 1919, and was in fact eager, in alliance with the Deutsche Bank, to become the dominant bank in Southeast Europe. Joham stood at the forefront of this effort, and he took the opportunity of Pohle's presence in Vienna in late June 1940 to have a "friendly and confidential" discussion of common problems, the content of which he reported to Abs a few days later. In Joham's view, their activities in the former Czechoslovakia were going to be a source of "disturbances for the future." The best solution, in Joham's view, was for the CA to take over the BUB, a proposition that Pohle considered to be "not a bad idea." Joham also pointed out that such

an arrangement would help the Deutsche Bank to increase its holdings in the CA. Joham recognized that there was opposition in Berlin to any close economic link between the Ostmark and Bohemia, and he also knew that the idea might not please everyone on the CA management board. Nevertheless, Joham wanted to put the idea and discussion with Pohle down on paper for Abs, "since I assume that the Deutsche Bank will be concerned in the near future with great world economic questions, and it would perhaps view the Creditanstalt as the suitable vehicle for the banking business in the South East sector, something which you are considering in any case."[287]

While Abs had repeatedly stressed such a role for the CA beginning with the friendship pact, the issue had taken on a much greater topicality by the summer of 1940 because of the war and German conquests. The RWM was consulting with Director Fritscher about the reorganization of the banking system in Southeast Europe, and this triggered a meeting in Bad Gastein on August 10, 1940, attended by Abs, Hasslacher, Fritscher, and Joham. Abs took a position that must certainly have pleased Joham, namely, "that the Creditanstalt should be the institution to handle the Southeast as a whole, whether through its own branches or through subsidiary institutes is a question of the political preconditions." He argued that the most important of these was that a greater role be given to Vienna by Berlin. Abs was in fact even more ambitious for the CA than Hasslacher and Fritscher, who both suggested that the Dresdner Bank might be included along with the CA in the Southeast. Abs advised against any such combination and urged "that the Creditanstalt – assuming certain preconditions that relate to the Deutsche Bank as given – claim this sector for itself." Having been persistently hostile to sharing Southeast Europe with uninvited competition, for example, the Reichs-Kredit-Gesellschaft and Commerzbank in 1938, Abs obviously hoped to cut out the Deutsche Bank's chief rival in private sector banking. But he also made clear that the promotion of the CA's role was not to constitute a self-denying ordinance

286 Ibid., Bl. 1, memo by Adams, July 11, 1941; for the Belgian purchases, see Deutsche Bank to Riehle, Nov. 11, 1940, ibid., Bl. 217. This volume also contains correspondence bearing on the other purchases, particularly from Steinhäusser. See DB, V2/166, the general accounting, Tron to Ulrich, Sept. 25, 1952.

287 DB, P 24158, Joham to Abs, July 3, 1940.

for the Deutsche Bank. When Hasslacher, his appetite now whetted, proposed that the CA set up a bank in each country of the region, Abs reminded him that the CA did not have the personnel needed to staff banks in Athens, Bucharest, and Sofia and that the Deutsche Bank already had a foothold in these places and could represent the interests of the CA once the Deutsche Bank had established its own position more firmly. Fritscher stressed that the RWM would only agree to a special role for the CA if it were as independent as possible while at the same time recognizing that the CA could only assume such a position in alliance with the Deutsche Bank. This was a difficult circle to square, but Abs intended to square it, and he pointed out that while the Deutsche Bank "in principle wants to be represented in the entire world," it would only renounce engagement in a sector if the conditions were consistent with its ambitions. What emerged from this discussion was a very clear program:

There is unanimous agreement that in the future the Creditanstalt should establish itself as the sole German bank in the lands of the Southeast, for which, however, the Deutsche Bank demands as a precondition that Vienna also obtain a corresponding political position with respect to the Southeast and that the Deutsche Bank receive a yet stronger participation in the Creditanstalt. To attain this, an agreement between the Creditanstalt, Deutsche Bank, and VIAG is necessary. One must explore how this effort of the Deutsche Bank can be brought into agreement with the view of the RWM, whereby the Creditanstalt should be presented as a strong independent and self-determining Viennese institution. What is to be avoided at all costs is that the Dresdner Bank, because of the situation in which the Deutsche Bank attains a stronger position in Southeast Europe through the Creditanstalt, should similarly receive a corresponding expansion of its sphere of interest in the Southeast.[288]

Things were not to move as quickly as the tone of this program suggests, but Abs tended both to think for the long run, while bowing to political necessities in the short run, and to pursue a wide-ranging set of interests and activities that he indeed hoped would encompass the world.

Nevertheless, the basic intention was clear enough, namely, to use the CA as the Deutsche Bank's instrument to establish a dominant banking position in Southeast Europe, provided one could attain a majority of the shares and have a propitious political situation.

There certainly were many signs that the VIAG would not stand in the way because Olscher and his colleagues were losing interest in the CA. In large part, this was because the VIAG was not primarily concerned with banking but rather with electric power and related industrial operations, and it found the CA an expensive distraction. In May 1941, Hans Kehrl began to intrude more directly in VIAG affairs, becoming a member of the board of supervisors in early 1942, and he pushed the VIAG in the direction of expanding its industrial interests in power and aluminum. Added to this was the continued dissatisfaction with the management of the CA, a worry shared by the Deutsche Bank whose considerable efforts to improve the situation still had not resulted in a stable management or organization. To some extent, the VIAG was itself responsible for the problems in the CA management board because it had absconded with Erich Heller and placed him on the VIAG management board in the spring of 1940. He then was elected to the CA supervisory board as a representative of the VIAG. It was a serious loss because Heller was the member of the management board most versed in industrial affairs.[289] Whether Fischböck's services to the bank were of similar value is doubtful, and his appointment as economics minister in the occupation regime in the Netherlands after May 1940, where he employed the Aryanization skills developed in Austria under Syeß-Inquart, kept him quite busy. Beginning in June, he ceased to attend management board meetings, although he continued to attend meetings of the supervisory board working committee and the supervisory board as a member of the management board through April 1941. He had formally resigned at the end of 1941, and he withdrew from all his official

288 Ibid., meeting in Bad Gastein, Aug. 10, 1940.

289 See BA-CA, CA-V, Hasslacher's speech at the general shareholders' meeting on April 29, 1940.

positions in Vienna at the beginning of 1942 when he was appointed Reich price commissar. Because a replacement could not immediately be found, Otto Neubaur of the RKG and VIAG was asked to step in as temporary chairman of the CA management board.[290] By the end of 1941, therefore, the personnel situation on the management board – and indeed at the bank more generally – was anything but satisfactory. The great barrier to giving the Deutsche Bank a majority came from divisions between the economic policy makers, where Riehle stood on the side of letting the Deutsche Bank take over the majority while Kehrl and Keppler, on the other side, were opposed to expanding the strength of the Deutsche Bank. At the end of 1941, however, Olscher succeeded in getting Kehrl to relent and agree to a Deutsche Bank majority control in return for a guarantee that there would be no merger between the Deutsche Bank and the CA and that the CA would be granted a large role in the banking business of Southeast Europe.[291]

At the same time, Olscher now actively pursued an arrangement with the Deutsche Bank. Quite aside from the fact that the Deutsche Bank was overseeing the Creditanstalt's banking business anyway, Olscher was aware that the Deutsche Bank was quietly acquiring CA shares in anticipation of eventually gaining a majority. On December 18, 1941, Olscher paid a visit to Deutsche Bank director Karl Kimmich to discuss a transfer of the CA shares. He guessed that the Deutsche Bank already had about 40 percent of the shares, a subject on which Kimmich chose to remain silent. Apparently, Olscher had already spoken to Abs and Rummel, to whom he indicated that the VIAG did not want cash for the shares needed to establish a Deutsche Bank majority but rather shares in industrial assets. Initially, Olscher had considered acquiring CA

industrial holdings, but he had come to the conclusion that this was a "Mischmasch" of limited interest and that such acquisitions might call forth political opposition. Of far greater interest at this point was Deutsche Bank assistance in acquiring shares connected with holdings in the possession of the Reichswerke Hermann Göring, which were being sold off at this time for the purposes of trimming down that industrial monstrosity.[292] The VIAG was anxious to gain shares held by the AEG in the Schlesische Elektrizitäts- & Gas AG as well as other shares controlled by General Director Paul Pleiger of the Reichswerke as part of its efforts to round off its electric and gas power empire in the east. The Deutsche Bank had already promised to assist the VIAG in gaining the AEG holdings, but Kimmich was unable to guarantee that the request could be satisfied immediately or accept a fixed date for doing so. Olscher, in fact, was also more than ready to come to a settlement on the sale of the CA shares because of the personnel problems involved. He pointed out that Neubaur did not want to stay in Vienna forever and that someone had to take responsibility for improving the quality of the management. Either the Deutsche Bank would provide first-rate people or the VIAG would have to do so at the expense of the RKG, something he clearly did not want to do. Kimmich, however, was not overly forthcoming in responding to Olscher's proposals. Olscher suggested that things would be made easier by approaching Statthalter Baldur von Schirach and trying to sell the arrangement with the argument that it would serve the business in Southeast Europe. He also argued that the VIAG would have to hold on to 25 percent of the shares as a guarantee that the Deutsche Bank would not set up a branch in the Ostmark, but that these shares could be distributed among its electric power companies. He further urged that the VIAG shares be valued at 150 percent plus a bonus because the transfer would involve giving the Deutsche Bank a majority. Kimmich suggested, however, that the price seemed too

[290] See DB, P 6507, Bl. 186, 189. For Fischböck's resignation as head of the Viennese Economic Chamber (Wirtschaftskammer) and president of the Chamber of Industry and Commerce in Vienna, see ibid., B 53, his letter to Reichsstatthalter Baldur von Schirach, Jan. 13, 1942.

[291] See NARA, RG 260, 2/191/7, the testimony by Neubaur, May 7, 1946.

[292] See Overy, "Reichswerke," in *War and Economy*, pp. 161–166.

high, especially in view of Olscher's complaints about the bank's management.[293]

A few days later, Kimmich discussed these issues with Neubaur and found him taking a somewhat different line than Olscher. Neubaur felt that the shares could be paid for either with the Silesian power works shares or with CA holdings. Where he did agree with Olscher, however, was on the personnel question, Neubaur pointing out that not only the management board but also the lower levels of the management were in great need of improvement. In his view, the bank was "badly led." It did not even have a section for foreign business, and while the CA was claiming that it should get more foreign business, it was not properly organized to deal with it.[294]

The question of how to pay off the VIAG for majority control of the CA thus remained rather confused at the beginning of 1942. The time did not appear quite ripe for paying with the Silesian power works shares. The Deutsche Bank was indeed committed to gaining some of these shares for the VIAG through the AEG, and the latter's general director, Hermann Bücher, was committed to helping the Deutsche Bank in this regard in gratitude for business favors he had received. Nevertheless, it was all part of a more complicated set of business arrangements that would take time.[295] The other option of paying for the shares with CA holdings left open the question of which holdings were to be used and how much of its stake in the CA the VIAG was going to sell.

At this point, however, the complications were multiplied thanks to Fischböck, who used the moment of his resignation from his various Viennese offices to challenge the entire structure of the CA in a letter to the Gau economic advisor, Walther Rafelsberger, whose power and influence in all matters pertaining to the Austrian economy remained very substantial. He seems to have periodically discussed the structure of the CA, and he now returned to the issue in a formal epistle setting down his views. Fischböck conceded that the future of the CA now depended on the intensification of its relationship with the Deutsche Bank. But he did not think that the CA's future rested with its industrial holdings, which in his view did not belong in the bank. He also thought that the Deutsche Bank was not terribly interested in these holdings. The VIAG, by contrast, was in the business of operating as an industrial holding company, and no one knew and could organize the selling of the CA's industrial holdings better than Erich Heller. Fischböck therefore suggested that the CA's industrial holdings and the credits granted in connection with them be placed in a new holding company that would be sold to the VIAG. The VIAG would pay for these largely with its CA shares, which would flow back to the CA and could then be destroyed. This would automatically leave the Deutsche Bank with a majority holding in the CA. The result would be the coexistence of two enterprises. The first would be a CA "cleansed" of its industrial holdings under the control of the Deutsche Bank. The Deutsche Bank would have to pledge to maintain the CA's independence and promise it more business in the Southeast and in the Protectorate. The other would be an industrial holding company controlled by the VIAG that would administer the old CA holdings or, where appropriate, sell them off. The banking business of this holding company could be dealt with through an agreement between the VIAG and the Deutsche Bank. Obviously intending to make the entire plan appealing to Rafelsberger, Fischböck proposed that Rafelsberger assume the chairmanship of the management board of the industrial holding company, which he deemed more compatible with the role of a Gau economic advisor than assuming a counterpart position in the CA, but he also suggested that Rafelsberger be given a position on the supervisory board of the CA and be made a member of its credit committee. Fischböck felt reasonably certain that Hasslacher would be asked by the Deutsche Bank to stay on as president of the supervisory board and that the VIAG would be agreeable to his presidency of

---

[293] DB, B 53, report by Kimmich, Dec. 18, 1941.
[294] Ibid., report by Kimmich, Dec. 22, 1941.
[295] Ibid., report by Kimmich on meeting with Bücher, Dec. 23, 1941.

the industrial hold supervisory board as well. Fischböck admitted that Hasslacher would probably object to the CA's surrender of its industrial participations because this had been a difference on their views for some time, but he was convinced that the two big shareholders, the Deutsche Bank and the VIAG, would find their interests protected by the plan and would support it. The real advantage, in Fischböck's view, was that "this proposal lies to a high degree in the interests of Vienna because, once appropriate agreements are made with the Deutsche Bank, it creates the precondition for enabling the Central European interests of the Deutsche Bank to be cared for through the Creditanstalt and thus via Vienna."[296]

Fischböck's intervention was shrewdly directed because Rafelsberger was quite eager to boost the role of Vienna as a financial and economic center for dealing with Southeast Europe, and he watched closely over the possibilities for pushing this program with both the Creditanstalt and the Länderbank Wien. At the same time, it gave Fischböck an opportunity to promote his old program of detaching the CA's industrial holdings from the bank. His plan immediately provoked a good deal of anxiety among those involved because Abs was away from Berlin and Hasslacher, whose opposition had been predicted by Fischböck, was very afraid that something might be decided before he could meet with Abs. Hasslacher apparently did not mince words on the subject, reporting after the war that, when learning of the plan to detach the CA holdings, "I became so wild that I was told from Berlin that one had never seen me so furious before."[297] Hasslacher hurriedly called Rummel at the Deutsche Bank to plead that the takeover of the CA shares be held up until Abs's return and pointed out that "the gentlemen in Vienna are of the view that even

though the holdings have to be given up sometime, but not now since this would weaken the position of the Creditanstalt-Bankverein too much."[298] At the same time, Olscher was not particularly happy with Fischböck's intervention either, complaining that through his "testament-like remarks" to Rafelsberger, the outgoing Fischböck was exercising too great an influence on events. Olscher was also concerned about remarks made by Riehle that the RWM would block a transfer of a majority in the CA to the Deutsche Bank.

Whatever the case, the situation was extremely fluid and uncertain, and it was to take almost another three months before the terms under which the Deutsche Bank was to gain its majority were set. This was accompanied by an effort to deal with the very unsatisfactory personnel situation at the CA. While these two issues were entangled with one another in the ongoing discussions, they will be separated in this presentation for purposes of analysis and to prevent the tale from being even more confusing.

In a meeting on January 27, 1942, between Olscher and Kimmich, there appeared to be a consensus that the Deutsche Bank was going to get majority control of the CA and also that the latter was going to lose its industrial holdings to a newly created holding company. According to Olscher, the Party leadership in Austria – Rafelsberger; Reichsstatthalter Baldur von Schirach; and Gauleiter Hugo Jury of the Lower Danube – was behind this arrangement, and the RWM was now also supporting it. The one very significant holdout was Hasslacher, who had spoken to Olscher and who believed that the projected transfer of shares in the Silesian power works with the assistance of the Deutsche Bank to the VIAG would obviate the need for the CA to give up its industrial holdings. Hasslacher also told Olscher that Abs was agreeable to this arrangement. Here, as in the 1938 negotiations, Kimmich was of a different opinion and took a more traditional approach, telling Olscher that "banks should not operate any industries and that it is therefore in principle

[296] Ibid., Fischböck to Rafelsberger, Jan. 13, 1942.

[297] StmkLA,Vr 734/1946, Landesgericht für Strafsachen Graz, Bl. 85, Hasslacher testimony at his trial, Franz und Jakob Hasslacher. This may have been slightly exaggerated because Hasslacher was trying to take credit for saving Austrian industrial assets from the Germans and enabling the Austrians to make postwar claims against Germany.

[298] DB, B 53, Rummel note to Abs, Feb. 2, 1942.

more correct to separate the holdings, subject to the consideration of individual cases."[299] Kimmich reiterated this position to Hasslacher, who followed Olscher's visit with a visit of his own. Hasslacher expressed surprise that the Deutsche Bank seemed to support the divestment of the CA holdings because he understood that Abs opposed such an action. While agreeing in principle to the idea that the holdings should ultimately be divested, Hasslacher emphasized that certain holdings were essential to the bank's business, the Semperit company, for example, and that the bank could not afford to give up its holdings in any generalized way. He was prepared, however, to have some holdings sold so as to increase the capital of the CA by 10 million RM. What emerges from this conversation with Hasslacher is that Kimmich really opposed industrial investments in principle, arguing that gains from some holdings were offset by losses in others so that the bank was distracted from fundamental banking business and was not employing its capital properly. Hasslacher, by contrast, was obviously stalling on the surrender of holdings and remained wedded to retaining the role of the CA as an industrial holding company, his claims that he agreed with Kimmich in principle notwithstanding. While Hasslacher clung to the notion that the CA shares to be acquired by the Deutsche Bank might be paid for with the electric power company shares VIAG was trying to acquire, Kimmich came to the conclusion that this idea was not practicable at the moment and that the shares should be paid for in CA industrial shares that the CA could afford to give up and urged Hasslacher to negotiate with Olscher along such lines.[300]

At this point, however, there was considerable confusion about where Abs stood on these questions because apparently both Olscher and Hasslacher had the impression that he was prepared to let the CA retain its holdings.[301] This feeling was in fact correct and reflected Abs's basic willingness to make concessions to

Austrian banking practice in order to win the CA's support for longer-term goals. The result was a more limited approach that concentrated attention on the sale of VIAG shares and the attainment of a 51 percent majority for the Deutsche Bank in return for a limited alienation of the CA's industrial holdings. Thus, Abs and his colleague Rummel entered into a series of meetings with the VIAG leadership and Hasslacher in the first weeks of February that shifted the discussion along the lines described. Where the VIAG leadership had originally thought it was to sell 25 percent of its CA shareholdings to the Deutsche Bank in return for CA industrial holdings, Abs and Rummel made clear that they only wished to have 15 percent of the shares so as to gain a 51 percent majority, while the additional 10 percent was to be marketed to the public in the Ostmark for cash. The VIAG was basically agreeable to this, and it also declared that it was not interested in the Fischböck plan to take over a holding company with the CA's industrial holdings. Olscher had never wanted this, and Abs and Rummel suspected that Heller and Neubaur had been pushing the scheme until it was vetoed. Furthermore, the CA was to be brought into the anticipated agreement on the sale of the CA shares, which was not to be conducted at the CA's expense.[302]

The form of this engagement of the CA was developed in a discussion with Hasslacher on February 12, where Abs and Rummel spoke about setting up a long-term consortium to handle the CA shares to be sold to the public that would include the CA itself along with Schoeller & Co. and Steinhäusser. Additionally, the Deutsche Bank intended to affirm that it would maintain the independence of the CA and never turn it into a branch of the Deutsche Bank. It would also affirm its intention to build up the CA's Southeast European business, leaving the CA the major role it already had in Budapest, Belgrade, and Zagreb, while the Deutsche Bank would play the chief role in Sofia and Bucharest. However, the Deutsche Bank was prepared to bring the CA into this business on a small scale as well, while remaining insistent

299 Ibid., report by Kimmich, Jan. 27, 1942.
300 Ibid.
301 Ibid., note by Director Ulrich for Abs, Jan. 27, 1942.

302 Ibid., file memorandum by Abs, Feb. 17, 1942.

that its own direct business in Southeast Europe had to be maintained because it could not send all its old customers to Vienna. The Deutsche Bank declared that it stood ready to help the CA to expand its business in Southeast Europe, but much depended on the loosening up of centralization from Berlin, a process difficult to promote in wartime. These were, of course, measures designed to please Rafelsberger and other Party elements in Vienna who wanted the new arrangement to promote Vienna's role, but they were also intended to satisfy the considerable ambitions of the CA without giving it the absolutely central position in Southeast Europe that had been discussed back in the summer of 1940. The CA's appetite, to be sure, had not been sated. Hasslacher, for example, wanted the support of the Deutsche Bank for the entry of the CA into the Turkish market, a request that Abs flatly turned down on the grounds that this was not in Southeast Europe and was a region where the Deutsche Bank had been active for decades. Even more significant, however, was Hasslacher's proposal that the Deutsche Bank agree to transfer the Böhmische Union Bank (BUB), its most important holding in the Protectorate, over to the CA should the government decide to dissolve the Protectorate and thus make the region more dependent on Vienna and the Lower Danube region. This was a return to Joham's idea expressed to Pohle in July 1940, but it no longer seemed feasible in that form in 1942. Thus, Abs and Rummel also turned this proposal down, but did express a willingness to have the CA increase its holdings in the BUB when the latter's projected capital share increase took place and also arrange for the CA and the BUB to have active management board members placed on their respective supervisory boards.[303]

To a great extent, the basic lines of a rearrangement of the ownership of the CA were now settled, but the two principal shareholders still had to iron out the details. Abs, Rummel, Neubaur, Heller, and Olscher sought to move the process forward at a meeting on

February 17. One important change had taken place in that the VIAG no longer wished to hold on to any of its CA shares. It not only wanted to sell 25 percent, of which 15 percent was to give the Deutsche Bank a majority and the remainder was to be sold to the public, but it also wished to sell the 25 percent that still remained in its possession. It preferred to be paid not in cash but rather in industrial holdings that it considered useful for its purposes, and it wanted to exclude tax considerations by coming to an agreement with the government on a settled sum that would be divided between the two parties. The Deutsche Bank agreed to this last point and was also willing to take over the entire 50.92 percent holding of the VIAG, but it continued to insist that all it wished to retain was 51 percent and to have a bank consortium hold and sell the remainder. The VIAG refused an invitation to join the consortium but thought that its subsidiary electric power companies in the Ostmark might temporarily acquire some of the shares. Insofar as the payment in shares was concerned, the Deutsche Bank was prepared to see some CA industrial holdings used for this purpose and pointed out that even Hasslacher was agreeable to this, but insisted that it was impossible to have all the CA shares paid for in this manner. In fact, however, Olscher remained basically uninterested in the CA industrial holdings, none of which he saw as permanent investments for the VIAG, although he did note that a few of them might be of interest to VIAG subsidiary firms in the electric power industry. Insofar as the VIAG did acquire such holdings, it planned to lodge them in the old Industriekredit, which belonged to the Reich and was presently in liquidation, and to sell them off to suitable buyers and thereby acquire capital for the VIAG's own expansion. In any case, both sides agreed that the holdings should be acquired in consultation with the CA and that the latter should be promised options on their reacquisition and a voice about their prospective purchasers. At the same time, however, Abs was able to hold out the prospect of supplying Olscher with something Abs thought really interested him, namely, holdings from what was now being called the "G"

[303] Ibid., file memorandum by Abs on meeting of Feb. 12, 1942/Feb. 17, 1942.

business, that is, holdings being sold off from the Reichswerke Hermann Göring, even though this would take some time. While Olscher was no longer certain how the state-controlled sector of the economy was going to be organized, Abs and Olscher were able to agree that various prospects would be investigated and that the acquisition of "G" holdings would be used by the VIAG as compensation for the CA shares while the remainder would be covered by CA industrial holdings. The calculation was that the entire package of CA shares would be sold for 54 million RM, 40 million RM of which would be paid in "G" shares and the remaining 14 million RM in CA industrial holdings.[304]

The details of these arrangements were further hammered out by Abs, Heller, Olscher, and Rummel on a train ride to Vienna on February 26, and then discussed with Hasslacher and Rafelsberger on the next day, and finally with the CA management board members Joham, Friedl, Fritscher, and Pfeiffer on February 28. As usual, political considerations played a significant role in determining important details. Rafelsberger and Fischböck had wanted to sell the shares not needed for the Deutsche Bank majority to the City of Vienna. The VIAG and Deutsche Bank sought to block this effort by placing these shares in a consortium that would sell the shares at an attractive price to reliable persons in the Ostmark who would not speculate with the shares but hold on to them as a long-term investment. In this way, the shares would not be in the hands of an entity subject to political pressures, a possibility particularly alarming to the Deutsche Bank should it at some time try to acquire a 75 percent majority in the CA. This public marketing of the shares might take some time, however, because there was little enthusiasm in the public at this time for long-term investments. There were political issues involved in creating a consortium. Rafelsberger vetoed inviting the Bankhaus Nicolai to join because he viewed it as too speculative, while he reportedly objected to giving the Bankhaus Schoeller the leadership or co-leadership of the consortium because he and

Philipp von Schoeller were in competition for the position of president of the Vienna Chamber of Commerce and Industry recently vacated by Fischböck. The most important political factor, however, was that the Deutsche Bank continuously had to guarantee that it would maintain the independence of the CA and that it would show good faith and be concrete in its claims to wishing to assist the expansion of the CA's business in Southeast Europe. It was important that both the Deutsche Bank and the Creditanstalt make every effort to avoid the impression of trying to eviscerate the CA when taking over CA holdings as part of the deal.

In the negotiations on February 28, Olscher made much of the alleged difficulties the VIAG had in separating itself from the CA and insisted that it was only doing so because of the opportunities being offered the CA in the Southeast by the Deutsche Bank. Abs responded to this by increasing the list of concessions to be made to the CA, promising to work to give the CA a one-third stake in the BUB, concessions in Romania and Greece, exchanges of information on regional prospects and developments, and personnel and technical assistance. Insofar as the takeover of holdings was concerned, there was an agreement in principle to work with the CA on this, and while a list of potential candidates was drawn up, the goal was not to attain a certain sum but rather to keep the needs and interests of the CA in mind. Rafelsberger and Hasslacher both approved of this approach, and while Gauleiter Jury continued to feel that the CA should ultimately give up its industrial holdings, he did not think this should be done in a hasty manner and certainly not in wartime. By the beginning of March, the political and governmental authorities supported the Deutsche Bank–VIAG plan, and one could begin to work out the details and draft the necessary agreements.[305]

In contrast to the high degree of compulsion employed in the takeover of the CA's holdings

---

[304] Ibid., meeting of Feb. 17, 1942.

[305] See the memorandum drawn up by Abs on March 2, 1942, summarizing the arrangements made on Feb. 26, and the memorandum of March 3, 1942, summarizing the previous discussions and especially the meeting of Feb. 28, 1942, ibid. The CA industrial

in 1938–1939, the sale of industrial assets in 1942 in connection with the takeover of a majority of the CA shares was done in consultation with the CA leadership. This would most certainly had been otherwise if the Fischböck scheme to create a holding company of CA holdings under VIAG control had succeeded, but the abandonment of that plan meant that the CA was to be treated with greater solicitude despite the fact that Olscher and Kimmich favored having the CA function in the style of a German bank and dispense with its industrial holdings. The assumption of majority control by the Deutsche Bank, after all, also meant the privatization of the CA, and the style of this operation contrasted sharply with the VIAG takeover in 1938, when majority ownership simply transferred control by one government to another with the VIAG serving as a trustee for the German government. The endlessly repeated pledge by the Deutsche Bank that it would honor the independence of the CA and not turn it into a branch of the Deutsche Bank, as well as the capacity of the CA – to be sure, with the support of Rafelsberger and Olscher – to extract a greater role in the Southeast European business of the Deutsche Bank than the latter had initially been prepared to grant, all pointed to greater autonomy for the CA. After the war, the CA was to claim that the holdings it surrendered in 1942 were part and parcel of its exploitation by the Germans and that the banking holdings it received "were never sought on the part of the Creditanstalt and were forced upon it."[306] This was rubbish.

As has been shown already and will be shown in greater detail later, the CA was mightily interested in such holdings and welcomed them.

When Heller, Neubaur, and Olscher of the VIAG met with Friedl and Hasslacher of the CA to discuss which CA industrial holdings might be given up, Friedl laid down certain ground rules for the discussion. First, the value of what was to be surrendered was to be based on the value of the CA shares to be acquired by the Deutsche Bank to attain its majority and not the total value of the CA shares owned by the VIAG. The shares to be acquired by the Deutsche Bank were estimated at 11 million RM. Second, the CA expected to retain the banking business of the industrial enterprises involved. Finally, the choice of the holdings had to be compatible with the economic interests of the bank and the industrial enterprises involved.[307]

The first holding that Friedl offered was 100 percent of the shares of the Mürztaler Holzstoff- und Papierfabrik. The estimated value of the company was 1.8 million RM; its value lay primarily in the three power plants it owned, which were worth 1.25 million RM. The CA negotiators were well aware that subsidiary power works belonging to the VIAG were interested in acquiring the power works, just as they knew that the company itself was a candidate for being shut down. The VIAG was willing to acquire the power plants, but was unwilling to take the entire company. The VIAG representatives showed no interest in a second holding mentioned by Friedl, the Wienerberger Ziegel AG, but they were much more amenable to acquiring a majority interest in a major Austrian construction firm, the Universale Bau-AG. The CA owned 87 percent of Universale, which had a total capital of 10 million RM and was selling on the exchange at 190 percent. The CA did not want to sell its holding in its entirety, but rather to retain 26 percent so that it could also have a significant construction company serve its own purposes as well as those of the VIAG. Furthermore, Friedl

holdings listed as possible payment for the shares were: Universale Hoch- und Tiefbau-AG, Vienna; Ostmark-Keramik AG, Vienna; Eisenwarenfabriken Lapp-Finze AG, Graz; Hutter & Schrantz AG, Siebwaren- und Filztuchfabriken, Vienna; Kassen-, Aufzugs- u. Maschinenbau AG F. Wertheim & Co., Vienna; Maschinenfabrik Heid AG, Vienna; Wiener Brückenbau- und Eisenkonstruktions-AG, Vienna; Semperit Gummiwerke AG, Vienna.

[306] NARA, T-83, Roll 101, memorandum of the Creditanstalt-Bankverein of Nov. 1945 on the Repatriation of the Shares of the Bank and Its Concern Enterprises (Denkschrift der Creditanstalt-Bankverein hinsichtlich Repatriierung von Aktien der Bank und deren Konzernunternehmungen).

[307] For this discussion, see DB, B 53, the memorandum by Friedl of March 26, 1942.

also set as a condition that the VIAG would be obligated to offer the majority stake it would receive back to the CA or else to sell its shares on the stock exchange to the general public. Heller declared the VIAG to be basically in agreement with this proposal. If these shares were sold at the going price of 190 percent, then the Mürztaler shares and the Universale shares would amount to the 11 million RM needed to cover the CA shares needed for a Deutsche Bank majority. Because the VIAG showed interest in purchasing other CA holdings, however, the discussion continued. When the VIAG named four companies – Ostmark Keramik, Hutter & Schranz, Maschinenbau Heid, and Wiener Brückenbau – Friedl rejected the sale of these companies as contrary to the financial interests of the CA. He, in turn, suggested the sale of three other holdings – Schöller-Bleckmann AG, Eisenwerke Lapp Finze, and Schember – and also mentioned its stake in the Aryanized conglomerate Kontropa (Bunzl & Biach). VIAG, however, had no interest in any of these companies. The upshot of the meeting was that both sides settled on the Mürztaler power plants and Universale as the holdings to be used in payment for the CA shares to go to the Deutsche Bank.[308]

The way was thus paved for a comprehensive agreement between the CA's two major shareholders, and this was developed at a meeting in Vienna on April 8, 1942, between Abs and Rummel for the Deutsche Bank and Neubaur and Olscher for the VIAG.[309] The agreement is worth describing in detail so that its logic can be clear and intelligible.

The distribution of the CA's capital at the outset was the following:

VIAG	RM 36,000,000	50.92%
Deutsche Bank	RM 25,492,000	36.00%
Other Shareholders	RM 9,248,000	13.08%
Totals	RM 70,700,000	100%

The plan now was for the VIAG to sell 17,675,000 RM in shares, that is, 25 percent, to the Deutsche Bank, while retaining 18,325,000 RM, or 25.92 percent, of the CA shares. The Deutsche Bank would thus own 43,127,000 RM, or 61 percent, of the CA shares. The Deutsche Bank, however, would only hold 36,057,000 RM, or 51 percent, of the shares as a permanent holding, and the extra 10 percent, that is, 7,070,000 RM in shares, would be sold in small blocks to "Alpine" investors by the Deutsche Bank and the CA.

In return for the 17,675,000 RM in shares it was selling to the Deutsche Bank, the VIAG would receive the CA holdings acquired by the Deutsche Bank as had been agreed between the VIAG and the CA on March 26, namely, the three hydroelectric works of the Murztaler Holzstoff- und Papierfabriks AG, worth 1,250,000 RM, and 5,814,700 RM in shares of Universale Hoch- und Tiefbau AG. These shares would be valued at 190 percent, that is, 11,047,930 RM, but the Deutsche Bank would acquire them from the CA for 8,047,930 RM. In short, the CA would receive 9,297,930 RM from the Deutsche Bank for the holdings given to the VIAG whose total value (Mürztaler + Universale) was determined to be 12,297,930 RM. The CA, therefore, appears to have come out at the short end of this part of the arrangement by 3 million RM. Exactly how the discrepancy between the nominal value of the holdings and their price on the stock exchange was calculated is unclear, but the VIAG seems to have asked and received a bonus for providing the shares required to give the Deutsche Bank its majority stake as well as a price that took into account the increased value of CA shares between 1939 and 1942.[310]

It is important to recognize, however, that the Deutsche Bank itself was making a very heavy investment in the CA shares it was purchasing from the VIAG over and above the amount it needed to gain a majority control of the CA. The VIAG asked as a total price for the 25 percent in CA shares it was selling of 26,512,500 RM. This left 17,214,570 RM to be paid by the Deutsche Bank from

---

308 Ibid. On the plans to shut down the actual Mürztaler plants, see BA-CA, CA-IB Mürztaler, 11/01, Heller to Karl Augustin, March 26, 1941.

309 This discussion follows the memorandum dated April 9, 1942, in DB, B 53.

310 Ibid., see Heller to Abs, March 31, 1942.

its own portfolio. In the agreement made on April 8, the Deutsche Bank agreed to provide 14,530,625 RM in shares of major German enterprises, primarily, but not exclusively from power and electric companies, for example, 2 million RM in Rheinisch-Westfälische Elektrizitätswerke shares and 1 million RM in Gesellschaft für Elektrische Unternehmungen shares. However, this still left a balance owing to the VIAG of 2,683,945 RM, which the VIAG hoped to have paid in RWE or Schlesische Elektrizitäts- und Gaswerke shares insofar as the Deutsche Bank could make these available.[311]

Obviously, the VIAG continued to be a major shareholder in the CA under this arrangement, although the participation quota between the Deutsche Bank and the CA was now reversed. The VIAG now was to hold 25.92 percent, that is 18,325,000 RM, in CA shares, while the Deutsche Bank was to hold 51 percent. Under these circumstances, the two sides agreed to maintain their pooling agreement made at the end of 1938, which gave each party a first option on future sales of their respective shares. Because of the new situation, the VIAG was to have two instead of three representatives on the supervisory board, while the Deutsche Bank was to have three representatives instead of the previous two. The agreement was to last until 1952. At the same time, the VIAG expressed its basic preparedness to sell its holdings at a suitable time in small blocks of shares to "Alpine" investors. Finally, the Deutsche Bank agreed to fulfill its obligations to maintain the CA's independence and to promote its activities in Southeast Europe.

Both the independence of the CA and its projected increased role in Southeast Europe would require a substantial improvement in the staffing of the bank, and this was a theme that accompanied and even preceded the negotiations that have been described. The appointment of Neubaur as bank spokesman was never meant to be more than provisional, and the loss of Heller and then of Fischböck made a permanent solution imperative. This was all the more the case because there was general agreement that the only truly satisfactory members of the

management board were Friedl and Joham. The former was quite adept at dealing with industrial holdings, a skill all the more important with Heller's departure. Joham was obviously the most talented banker of the lot. It was he who reported on the condition of the bank at supervisory board meetings and who seems to have been Abbs's chief interlocutor when it came to international business, but he was and remained under a political cloud because of his connection with the deplored "System Period." Pfeiffer was considered unsuitable as a managing director, while Fritscher suffered from a severe hearing loss that led to all kinds of misunderstandings and problems. The former's personal animosity to Josef von Paić, who was regarded as competent and a coming man for the CA, had blocked Paić's appointment in 1938, and while Paić had been promised a position on the CA management board after the conclusion of his work at the Kontrollbank, when the time came in late 1940, the conditions were viewed as unpropitious by all sides, and Paić took up an offer from the Länderbank Wien at no cost to his good relationship with the CA leadership.[312]

Abs was probably relieved because he viewed Paić as a potential rival to Joham, but he was also desperate to find a suitable person for the CA management board, and in late 1940, he began to push for Ferdinand Bausback, who had been a director at the Württembergische Vereinsbank and then, after its takeover by the Deutsche Bank, the director of its Stuttgart branch from 1920 to 1927. During this period, he collaborated closely with Deutsche Bank Director Emil Georg von Stauss, playing an important role in the merger of Daimler-Benz in 1926. In 1927–1928, he was a director at the Deutsche Bank branch in Frankfurt a.M. before going to Berlin to join the management board of UFA Film, another enterprise that fell under the sway of Stauss and was suffering from serious financial problems. At this time, he also became a part owner of the Bankhaus Hugo Oppenheim & Sohn in Berlin. In 1933, he joined the supervisory board of the

[311] Ibid., memorandum of April 9, 1942.

[312] DB, B 57, Paić to Fischböck, Sept. 20, 1939.

publishing house of Ullstein, and subsequently he collaborated with Reichsbank President Schacht in Aryanizing the publishing house. In 1938, he became a part owner of the successor to Ullstein, the Deutsche Verlags KG. Bausback was thus a banker with considerable experience in the media, apparently was highly regarded, and certainly had good connections.[313]

These qualifications notwithstanding, Abs came up against formidable resistance when he sought to push for Bausback's appointment by inviting him to meet the CA management board in the fall of 1940. When Rafelsberger got wind of the visit, he immediately wrote to Abs and pointed out that they had already discussed the need for a new management board member but had also agreed that such a person should be sought out, preferably, from the ranks of the CA itself and from Vienna or at the very least from Austria. Only in the most exceptional circumstances, that is, when a great talent was available or no one else could be found could the candidate be a non-Austrian. Abs replied by arguing that this was in fact the situation and that both the VIAG and the Deutsche Bank felt that Bausback was the best candidate because they needed someone who could deal with business in the old Reich and also in Southeast Europe and, in their view, no such person was at hand either in the CA or in Austria.[314]

Apparently, Rafelsberger thought himself to be such a person, and Abs, Olscher, Heller, and Hasslacher found themselves confronted with the candidacy of Rafelsberger, who had nominated himself, at the turn of 1940–1941. As in the case of Fischböck, Rafelsberger was another prominent Austrian Nazi looking for an important and lucrative job. He actually seems to have presented himself at an earlier stage of the game, but was vetoed by the chief shareholders, that is, the VIAG and the Deutsche Bank. In any case,

the renewed candidacy was discussed at a meeting in Berlin on January 23, where Hasslacher was instructed to negotiate with Rafelsberger on a substantial set of conditions. First, Joham was to be "politically rehabilitated" and made speaker of the management board by unanimous agreement. Second, Pfeiffer was to be sent off to some other enterprise and thus leave the management board. Third, "a new, hundred-percent banker was to enter the board." Bausback was deemed the primary candidate. Fourth, Rafelsberger either had to agree to or be neutral concerning the Deutsche Bank's achieving majority control of the CA. His opposition to this had led to his rejection as a management board member when he had last presented himself. Fifth, Fritscher was to become the new party company leader. Sixth, Rafelsberger could maintain his position as head of Vienna's city-owned utilities, but he could only do so if no conflict of interest was involved, for example, in the capacity of an honorary councilman of the city government. Finally, Rafelsberger had to recognize that there would inevitably be a conflict of interest between his position as a CA management board director and his position as Gau economic advisor.[315]

Rafelsberger apparently lost interest when he heard these conditions, which were probably intended to produce that result. He would not give up his Gau economic advisor position, and he remained undecided on the rehabilitation of Joham. In the end, he declared that he would be satisfied with a position on the supervisory board and its working committee, a situation that would also satisfy his financial requirements. Insofar as the Bausback candidacy was concerned, Fischböck had discussed the matter with Reich Economics Minister Funk, who vetoed Bausback and, indeed, any candidate who did not come from Austria. Some, but not much, thought was given to the appointment of Wilhelm Rauber of the Bank für Kärnten, and nothing came of this either.[316]

[313] On Bausback, see DB, P 3/B 861, his personnel file; Harold James, *The Deutsche Bank and the Nazi Economic War against the Jews* (Cambridge 2001), pp. 47–48, and Manfred Pohl/Angelika Raab-Rebentisch, *Die Deutsche Bank in Stuttgart 1924–1999* (Munich 1999), pp. 69–71.
[314] DB, B 57, Rafelsberger to Abs, Nov. 3, 1940, and Abs to Rafelsberger, Nov. 13, 1940.

[315] Ibid., memorandum on discussion of Jan. 23, 1941.
[316] Ibid., Hasslacher to Abs, Jan. 27 and Feb. 7, 1941; Olscher to Hasslacher, Feb. 12, 1941; memo by Abs, Feb. 17, 1941; Hasslacher to Abs, Feb. 26, 1941; Heller to Abs, Feb. 27, 1941.

The question of finding a new director and replacing Neubaur on a permanent basis was only taken up seriously again at the beginning of 1942 in the context of the plan to give the Deutsche Bank a majority stake in the CA. If the Deutsche Bank was to take charge now, the fishing expedition had to come to an end and a viable solution had to be found. Once again, proposals were made to ask Rafelsberger; Riehle of the RWM was mentioned; there was talk of appointing the former section head of the Austrian Finance Ministry, Ministerial Director Ludwig Klucki, who was about to leave the RWM. Abs vetoed them all and instead strongly supported the appointment of Richard Buzzi, who had served as the manager of foreign exchange operations for the Bodencreditanstalt and then as a director at the Austrian National Bank before being appointed head of the Vienna branch of the Reichsbank. While Hasslacher was concerned that Buzzi was sixty years old and thus seemed to be another provisional candidate, Abs had known Buzzi for some time and respected his capacities. Buzzi was a Party member and was liked in both Party and government circles. It thus appeared that the right man had been found, assuming he would accept the job, which he was initially reluctant to do.[317]

An effort was also made to deal with the problems of Pfeiffer and Fritscher, both of whom were political friends of Gauleiter Jury and Gau Economic Advisor Rafelsberger. Neubaur took upon himself the task of persuading them that political virtues were not enough and that the bank could not be run by persons who were either incompetent or deaf. Apparently, the message came across and the Party leadership agreed that they could be let go if appropriate positions could be found for them. Who might replace them was less clear. There was some talk of asking Walter Schmidt of the Wiener Zentralsparkasse and also of appointing a Deutsche Bank official soon to leave the military service to head

the credit business of the bank or another person from the Deutsche Bank who was a South German and seemed suitable. In any case, settling the personnel issues was part and parcel of the transfer of the majority to the Deutsche Bank, and when Abs laid down the terms of the forthcoming agreement on March 2, the personnel issues were dealt with forthrightly. Fischböck was to formally resign now that he had become price commissar and, by implication, cease to interfere in CA affairs. Joham was to stay without restrictions, and Abs made clear that "political reservations are not to be employed. I have demanded unified handling of the foreign business and set forth the reasons why Joham is especially suitable for this position." Friedl was to stay on and handle the bank's industrial holdings. A job was to be found for Pfeiffer elsewhere. Abs insisted that Fritscher had to go but agreed to Rafelsberger's demand that there would be a decent interval between Pfeiffer's disappearance and Fritscher's. A position was to be found for the latter, although Abs admitted this would not be easy. Last, a new director was to be appointed from the ranks of the Deutsche Bank, but he was to have Rafelsberger's approval.[318]

There can be no question that Abs was quite serious about giving the CA a large and important role in Southeast Europe and that his interest in boosting Joham's position and in improving the staffing of the CA was motivated by such intentions. He intended to give the CA's minority stakes in the BUB, the Banca Comerciale Romana (Comro) in Bucharest, and the Deutsch-Bulgarische Kreditbank as compensation for the loss of the Universale Bau shares. The position of the CA in the BUB was to be strengthened, a CA management board member was to join the supervisory board of the Comro, while Joham was already representing the CA in Sofia. The CA was also to become involved in the Deutsche Bank's activities in Greece. The CA was thus to work with the Deutsche Bank in

---

[317] For Hasslacher's reservations, see the Kimmich memo of Feb. 2, 1942; for Abs's strong support of Buzzi, see the Abs minute of Feb. 17, 1942; for Buzzi's personal history and qualifications, see DB, B 53, the Abs memorandum of March 2, 1942.

[318] For these developments, see the Kimmich memo of Jan. 27, 1942, and the meeting of the VIAG and Deutsche Bank leadership on Feb. 17, 1942; Abs memorandum of March 2, 1942, ibid.

areas where the CA had not previously been active, but the Deutsche Bank, while acknowledging the position of the CA in Budapest, Belgrade, and Zagreb, also anticipated collaboration in those areas. Furthermore, the Deutsche Bank intended to provide technical and personnel assistance in this business. While claiming that the Deutsche Bank was prepared to support the CA even at its own expense, Abs stressed that the CA had lagged behind in getting all that could be gotten in the areas where it was already engaged. As usual, Rafelsberger remained a bit dissatisfied, feeling that the CA's position in the BUB could be yet stronger and suggesting that the CA take over the BUB if the Protectorate was dissolved. Indeed, in a private conversation back in March, Rafelsberger went so far as to argue that the CA should get 51 percent, perhaps even two-thirds of the shares of the BUB, the Comro, and the Bulgarian Kreditbank.[319] Abs declined to answer either affirmatively or negatively and referred Rafelsberger to Deutsche Bank director Rösler, who was charged with the BUB. At the same time, he also refused to speculate about future developments, reporting that he told Rafelsberger that "I lack the imagination for such developments and am not in the position to study the possibilities. I can only tell him one thing: we will always do that which is politically determined and economically smart."[320] This was indeed the leitmotif of Abs's career and helps to explain the remarkable success now within his grasp.

The Deutsche Bank's takeover of the majority of the CA at the beginning of May 1942 was the culmination of efforts that began with the friendship pact of March 1938 and illustrated Abs's remarkable skills as a negotiator and banker and his incredible ability to combine tenacity with flexibility. The subsequent development of the CA's business in Southeast Europe and the collaboration of the two banks in various parts of German-dominated Europe will be taken up in detail later in this study.

Here, however, something more needs to be said in conclusion about the personnel changes Abs and his colleagues hoped to effectuate. They did manage to procure the services of Buzzi, who agreed to serve as spokesman for the CA and as a primus inter pares on the management board. Joham and Friedl were firmly rooted in the new board, and Riehle went so far as to praise Joham's work. Getting rid of Fritscher and Pfeiffer proved difficult and was only partially successful. Fritscher, who was an SS Sturmbahnführer, was worried that he would lose his position and seems to have pulled as many strings as he could to retain it. Rafelsberger thought Fritscher quite able but did not feel he could be kept on very long because, as he pointed out to an SS colleague, "the situation is actually such that Fritscher can catch remarks only at a distance of two meters and that he is not able to act in debates."[321] Riehle, however, insisted that Fritscher be kept on because he had apparently done a very satisfactory job of organizing credits for the Ethnic German Liaison Office, an SS organization that promoted racial settlement policies in occupied Europe. Riehle felt that recognition needed to be given for such successful activity, and the CA leadership was constrained to keep Fritscher while urging him to take time off to look after his health. In November 1944, Fritscher suffered a fatal accident. He was not replaced on the board.[322]

The solution found for Pfeiffer was to place him on leave from the CA on "special assignment" to the Protectorate "for the purpose

[319] BAB, Nr. 7073, Bl. 53–54, Report by SS Hauptsturmführer Kapiller on conversation with Rafelsberger, March 9, 1942.
[320] DB, B 53, Abs memorandum, April 11, 1942.
[321] BAB, Nr. 7073, Bl. 55–56, report by SS Hauptsturmführer Kapiller on a conversation with Rafelsberger, March 9, 1942.
[322] On the Liaison Office, see Valids O. Lumans, *Himmlers Auxiliaries. The Volksdeutsche Mittelstelle and the German National Minorities of Europe, 1933–1945* (Chapel Hill 1993). For Riehle's decision on Fritscher and praise of Joham, see RGVA Moscow, 1458/2/91, Bl. 169–170, the meeting with Olscher, Abs, Rummel, and Riehle at the RWM on April 22, 1942, and DB, B 57, the minute of June 19, 1942. On Fritscher's demise, see Hasslacher to Abs, Nov. 30, 1944, ibid.

of taking charge of matters pertaining to the Mährische Bank," one of the banks picked up by the CA in the partition of Czechoslovakia.[323] Pfeiffer tried to resist this solution, and had the bizarre notion that he could stand on his "record," a notion of which even Fischböck sought to disabuse him.[324] At this point, even the support of Gauleiter Jury was insufficient to keep Pfeiffer on the management board. Rafelsberger also decided that Pfeiffer was a liability and "had to reject the behavior of Pfeiffer as unmanly, because it made an extraordinarily bad impression on him when Pfeiffer ran from one member to the other at the beginning of the supervisory board meeting in order to beg each of them for a vote. He [Rafelsberger] considers it extremely unclever on the part of Pfeiffer that he himself belittles his position in Moravia that will be presented to him as a springboard and to describe it as a position aimed at pushing him aside." Rafelsberger thought Jury was acting "clumsily" in planning to go with Pfeiffer to Prague to personally present him to his future colleagues and staff at the Prague branch of the Mährische Bank because "Pfeiffer does not make so good an impression that Prague will immediately embrace him with open arms."[325] Obviously, Pfeiffer's sudden rise to glory in March 1938 had been followed by a precipitous decline.

Abs did succeed in bringing a new member into the management board of the CA who came from the Deutsche Bank in the person of Walter Tron. Trained as an economist, Tron began his banking career in 1923 in a branch of the Disconto-Gesellschaft. After the merger with the Deutsche Bank, he served in various posts, becoming director of the Mannheim branch in 1937 and then becoming director at the important Leipzig branch in 1939. A Party member since 1937, Tron demonstrated considerable skill in dealing with Party leaders and protecting the interests of the important

Leipzig branch. He was very well suited to the tasks in Vienna, and Abs not only recommended him but also secured the easy support of the Viennese Party leadership.[326]

By this time, Abs was thus able to sell a CA director from the old Reich to the Austrians. In taking over the majority of the CA shares for the Deutsche Bank, Abs made a point of being as solicitous as possible of Austrian sensibilities. At a press conference on May 5, 1942, he placed great stress on the desire to fend off suggestions that the CA might be forced to assume the character of a German bank and give up its industrial holdings and emphasized that the views of the Ostmark business community had to be respected. Similarly, he explained the problems of Austria in terms of its late entry into the Reich and its failure to experience the reconstruction Germany had enjoyed between 1934 and 1938. In addition, he pointed out, "the non-Aryan element there, which had a special significance, was liquidated in a very short time, indeed in so short a time that without the introduction of old Reich entrepreneurs and old Reich personalities in the Ostmark it could not be solved in a normal way."[327]

The appointment of Tron undoubtedly illustrated this very well, and certainly no one spoke about what had been lost in the persons of Rottenberg and Pollak, although one wonders if anyone thought about them when hunting about for an "old Reich personality" for the CA management board. Be that as it may, it should not be thought that relations were very rosy despite all the good will Abs tried to show toward his Austrian colleagues. It is hard to imagine that the Austrians at the CA did not suffer from the condescension with which they were treated, and they appear to have made their own resentment felt. Tron did not have an easy time of it in his new assignment, as is exhibited by letters he wrote after beginning his work in Vienna: "The task in Vienna is to be sure very interesting, but extraordinarily difficult. I have

---

[323] BA-CA, CA-V, CA supervisory board meeting, June 10, 1942.

[324] DB, B 57, Heller to Hasslacher, June 13, 1942.

[325] BAB, Nr. 7073, Bl. 47–48, report by SS Hauptsturmführer Kapiller on conversation with Rafelsberger, June 16, 1942.

[326] Manfred Pohl/Angelika Raab-Rebentisch, *Die Deutsche Bank in Leipzig 1901–2001* (Munich 2001), p. 100.

[327] DB, B 53, press conference, May 5, 1942.

not been greeted ... with open arms, and one would rather have me sitting there as a quasi minister without portfolio. I am, after all, from the old Reich, and what's more, the 'smell' of the Deutsche Bank clings to me.... This situation was known to exist from the outset, and Berlin too had no illusions about it. On the contrary, one is already satisfied if for the time being I just get into the swing of things in Vienna. But the task will not be easy to fulfill."[328] Months before his appointment to the CA management board, Tron found himself lacking in enthusiasm for Vienna and the Viennese. Vienna and its surroundings remained attractive, but the city and its people seemed to have lost charm and luster: "Very little is left of the pretty, agreeable Vienna. The people are too preoccupied with themselves and beyond this eternally unsatisfied. They miss their goulash, their whipped cream, etc., and they cannot get used to the new tempo at all. In addition to this, prices have risen very substantially. In the evenings, Vienna – aside from the theatres – is a dump. What is offered in the cabarets is below the level of a German small town."[329] Apparently, it did not occur to Tron that the Vienna he was describing might have had something to do with almost

four years of being part of the Third Reich. In another letter, written after his transfer to Vienna, Tron commented that "the mentality of the people is so basically different from ours that one stands before virgin territory in every respect. The job is ... fraught with extraordinary difficulties that probably, if at all, can be solved only gradually after a victorious end to the war. One is not welcomed down there as an 'old Reich German,' and the recent marriage with the Deutsche Bank is judged as an absolutely one-sided matter, naturally in favor of the marriage partner from the Ostmark."[330] What is interesting about these letters is not simply that they show the sense of German superiority over the Austrians and a rather colonial attitude, but also the extent to which the colonized were seeking to reap as much advantage as possible from the colonizers. One had to get something back, after all, for surrendering one's goulash and whipped cream. Manifestly, the Austrians had ambitions of their own and had sought, from the outset, to maximize them through their suspect German partners. This should be kept in mind when considering the business they conducted together between 1938 and 1945.

---

[328] DB, V 2/58, Tron to Alfred Rosewick, Aug. 17, 1942.
[329] Ibid., B 57, Tron to Fritz Bode, Jan. 17, 1942.

[330] Ibid., B 58, Tron to Gerhard Polters, Aug. 18, 1942. I am grateful to Martin Müller of the DB for bringing these documents to my attention.

CHAPTER TWO

The Creditanstalt, Its Jewish Customers, and Aryanization

The long-neglected history of the despolia-tion of Austrian Jewry has become the subject of extensive study and examination in recent years thanks to the monumental labors of the Austrian Historical Commission, and some of the research and findings have made substan-tial use of the archival materials in the Bank Austria-Creditanstalt.[1] There would be no point in repeating certain case studies in detail here, especially because they often involve dis-cussions that bear less on the role of the banks than on the actual roles of the government and Party in Aryanization and also pay con-siderable attention to problems of restitution. Nevertheless, it is important to look at issues of Aryanization and such case studies from the perspective of the bank, its leaders, and their policies, and that is the essential purpose of what follows.

In considering the role of the CA in the vari-ous aspects of Aryanization both in the Ostmark and in other parts of Europe, two general points need to be made in providing the context for this discussion. First, while there were undoubt-edly many anti-Semites in the CA before March 1938, the Anschluss made it possible for the CA to become an overtly anti-Semitic enterprise. Not only were Jews rapidly eliminated from its staff and often replaced by Party members, but National Socialists and committed anti-Semites were also appointed to key positions in its management, most notably Rudolf Pfeiffer, who became managing director, and Ludwig Fritscher. Not only were the employees of the CA treated to a steady diet of National Socialist views and ideas in the staff assemblies and the company newspaper, but a specific vision of the role of the Jews in the pre-Anschluss economy was also propagated by the bank leadership. Thus, at the assembly on November 11, 1938, Pfeiffer not only extolled the new ethos, val-ues, and prospects represented by Hitler's "peo-ple's state" and his hopes that the CA would become a National Socialist "model enterprise" but also insisted that a change in the company spirit would be needed to achieve that goal. The disappearance of Jewish persons and influence had a particular role: "The previously extant contradictory conceptions concerning the rela-tionship of working persons with one another and concerning the nature and functions of a bank inculcated by the alien spiritual tenden-cies of the Jewish-international capitalist and Bolshevist types have disappeared thanks to the eradication of alien elements from our enter-prise. The times and economic conceptions

[1] The studies of greatest relevance here are Ulrike Felber/Peter Melichar/Markus Priller/Berthold Unfried/Fritz Weber, *Ökonomie der Arisierung. Part 1: Grundzüge, Akteure und Institutionen,* and *Part 2: Wirtschaftssektoren, Branchen, Falldarstellungen.* Veröffentlichungen der Österreichischen Histro-kerkommission, Vols. 10/1 and 10/2 (Vienna 2004). See also, Hans Safrian/Hans Witek, *Und Keiner war Dabei. Dokumente des altäglichen Antisemitismus in Wien 1938* (Vienna 1988).

of liberalism in the banks linked to the names of Bosel, Castiglione, Popper, Ehrenfest, Rothschild are finally and forever over. (Cries: Heil - strong applause.).''[2] The historical interpretation of the Jews being responsible for Austria's economic woes was regularly reiterated by the CA leadership. In a speech in 1943, for example, supervisory board Chairman Franz Hasslacher attributed Austria's troubles to the "corrosive influence of the Jews."[3] Similarly, in a February 1944 speech on Austria's economic collapse after 1918, Director Fritscher attributed much of the disaster between 1918 and 1938 – blissfully indifferent to the evidence of the disaster in the offing – to the Jewish influence throughout Central and Southeastern Europe in every aspect of life and especially to the role of Eastern European Jews, who "like a swarm of locusts" infested and manipulated the stock market.[4]

The second general point to be made about the role of the CA in Aryanization is that it, along with the other banks in the Third Reich, had been assigned an important role as an administrator of Jewish blocked accounts. When the authorities ordered the blocking of Jewish accounts – and eventually all Jewish accounts

were blocked – it became the task of the banks to set up and administer the accounts that were designed to ensure that Jews had only limited access to their funds. These funds were blocked as security that Jews would pay the taxes and levies imposed on them and would not emigrate without having done so. Subsequently, the banks also served as a depot for other blocked Jewish assets in their vaults, such as jewelry and securities. Needless to say, the banks could not refuse to obey government orders in connection with these pauperizing and humiliating restrictions on Jews' access to their own property, but these responsibilities were eventually to bring the banks into direct engagement with the measures taken with respect to the deportation of Jews and the disposal of Jewish assets. One also needs to consider the manner in which the responsibilities of the banks were implemented. Finally, as will be shown, the blocked accounts were often very useful to the CA when conducting Aryanization activities of direct benefit to itself.[5]

The management of blocked accounts and deposits was reflected in a series of general instructions of the bank management that relayed instructions from various government authorities or passed on through the Reich Group for Private Banks but that also dealt with specific operating instructions for the CA itself. It is important to note that the blocking of accounts was by no means limited to Jews. On March 17, 1938, the CA management ordered the blocking of the accounts and deposits belonging to political or semipolitical organizations on the right – those on the left had been blocked since February 12, 1934 – as well as those belonging to the Habsburg and Bourbon-Parma families.[6] The major concern, however, was with the accounts of persons wishing to leave the country. The bank became a watchdog for the authorities with respect to emigrating customers. A directive

[2] BA-CA, CA-TZ, Sekretariat rot, Box 53/ÖCA-WBV, 1838/9,10,11, File 11, assembly of the entire staff of the CA, Nov. 11, 1938. See also Ulrike Zimmerl, '"Kameradschaft, Abreitsfreude und Leistungskampf." Die Betriebszeitschrift 'Gemeinschaft' der Creditanstalt-Bankverein, Wien, 1939–1943,"in Gerald D. Feldman/Oliver Rathkolb/Theodor Venus/Ulrike Zimmerl, *Österreichische Banken und Sparkassen im Nationalsozialismus und in der Nachkriegszeit*, vol. 1 (Munich 2006), pp. 189–218. The importance of social egalitarianism and social benefits emphasized at these events and in the company newspaper has recently and very correctly been emphasized by Götz Aly in his groundbreaking *Hitlers Volksstaat. Raub, Rassenkrieg und nationaler Sozialismus* (Frankfurt a.M. 2005). There was a link between the elimination of Jewish employees and the employment of Party members at the CA as well as everywhere else in the economy.

[3] Zimmerl, '"Kameradschaft, Abreitsfreude und Leistungskamp,"' p. 191.

[4] BAB, R63, Vol. 33, Bl. 104–116, lecture held by Fritscher on Feb. 17, 1944 and sent to Augenthaler, the business manager of the Südosteuropa-Gesellschaft, March 1944.

[5] See the study on the expropriation of the Jews by Martin Dean, *Robbing the Jews: The Confiscation of Jewish Property in the Holocaust, 1933–1945* (New York 2008), ch. 3.

[6] BA-CA, CA-V, General Management Instruction, Nr. 17, March 17, 1938.

of April 12 declared that a customer planning to move abroad had to declare whether he or she already had a domicile abroad or whether he or she was a resident planning to emigrate. In the first case, the bank had to be provided proof that the customer was in fact a foreign resident before the account's address could be changed. In the second instance, the account or deposit in question was immediately to be designated a "blocked emigrant account," and the Reichsbank was to be informed. A subsequent instruction required that customers planning to emigrate be urged to provide the bank with a document indicating that there were no tax claims against the customer so that the bank could avoid "time-consuming inquiries" when dealing with the account in the future.[7] Not only did the CA work hand in hand with the tax authorities in administering these accounts, but it also collaborated closely with the Property Transfer Bureau (Vermögensverkehrsstelle, VVSt), which was engaged in selling off Jewish enterprises and property. The monies paid to Jews for these assets were put into blocked accounts, and deposits into these accounts were to be recorded by the bank and reported to the VVSt, which had disposition of the accounts as long as the individuals in question resided in the Reich. If the seller had also been a customer of the CA or one of its branches, then the various accounts were to be combined into one blocked account. Once the customer left the Reich, further reporting on the account to the VVSt was no longer required and the bank had to report only to the foreign exchange offices about the account. While the account blockage through the VVSt was suspended so long as the customer remained abroad, the bank was accountable to the foreign exchange authorities with respect to the still blocked

account.[8] Whatever the case, by the summer of 1938, the CA had become the administrator of the accounts of its Jewish customers for the benefit of regime agencies and had sought to streamline its handling of those accounts so as to be as effective as possible in this capacity.

Needless to say, this was a perversion of the generally accepted relationship between banks and their Jewish customers, and matters became much worse after the pogrom of November 9–10, 1938. The pogrom was followed by the "Decree for the Exclusion of Jews from German Economic Life" of November 12, and the "Decree for the Mobilization of Jewish Assets" of December 3, 1938, the most important steps in the legalized expropriation of the Jews.[9] These measures significantly affected the handling of Jewish accounts at the CA and other banks. On November 14, 1938, instructions were given that Jews were not to withdraw more than 400 RM from their accounts without special permission from the foreign exchange authorities and that this was to include equivalent value in items in safety deposit boxes and securities. Safety deposit boxes, previously unregulated, could now only be opened in the presence of a bank official, and transfers to the tax authorities were permitted but had to be undertaken by the bank.[10] Apparently, the implementation of this order proved problematic for the banks because of the need to identify their Jewish clients, and on November 22 Jews were again allowed to freely dispose of the money in their accounts insofar as these were not formally blocked.[11] At the same time, except in pressing cases, Jews were barred from selling securities in the value of more than 1,000 RM without permission of the Economic Group for Private Banking, and they were required to deposit all their securities in a bank.[12] On December 9, 1938, the CA ordered that all such deposits be identified

[7] Ibid., General Management Instruction, Nr. 51, April 12, 1938, and General Management Instruction Nr. 101 of May 30, 1938. Interestingly, safety deposit boxes were excluded from this requirement at the time; see General Management Instruction, Nr. 91, May 17, 1938, ibid.

[8] Ibid., General Management Instruction, Nr. 124 of July 9, 1938 and Nr. 137 of Aug. 29, 1938.

[9] Reichsgesetzblatt (= RGBl) I, pp. 1580 and 1709.

[10] Ibid., General Management Instruction, Nr. 182, Nov. 14, 1938.

[11] Ibid., General Management Instruction, Nr. 190, Nov. 22, 1938.

[12] Ibid., General Management Instruction, Nr. 194, Nov. 26, 1938.

with a "J."[13] The role of the banks as enforcers increased yet further in connection with
the payments for the so-called Atonement
Tax (also known as the Jewish Wealth Tax
[Judenvermögenabgabe]) of 1 billion RM
imposed on the Jews in the November pogrom.
Jews were not initially permitted to use securities to pay the first installment of this tax unless
they could demonstrate that they no longer
had cash, jewelry, or other valuables on hand to
cover it. If this was the case, they had to provide
the bank with a declaration to this effect that
was to be filed with their deposit records. Only
under such circumstances could they then pay
the Atonement Tax with securities that were
to be reported as payment to the revenue
offices and to be deposited to the account of
the Prussian State Bank (Seehandlung), which
acted as the depository for such securities for
the Finance Ministry. The CA charged Jews
fees for these transactions according to a fixed
schedule.[14] There were yet more fees to be
charged in 1939 as the regime permitted the
increasingly impoverished Jews to pay their
various taxes with securities. In April, for example, the Economic Group for Private Banking
charged 3 RM for processing inquiries connected with granting permission for the transfer of securities from one Jewish account to
another, and the CA charged an additional 3
RM for the same "service," so that the Jewish
account holder had to pay 6 RM each time he
or she requested permission to transfer securities in order to deal with their problems.[15] It is
worth noting that there is evidence that the CA
itself was directly interested in the marketing
of Jewish-owned securities that had fallen into
the clutches of the Seehandlung in connection with the payment of the Atonement Tax.
Chairman Fischböck of the CA management
board had discussed the issue with Riehle in
May 1939, and the CA then sent a list of bonds

issued by the CA and various Austrian states
and municipalities adding up to more than 7
million RM, pointing out that the CA had an
interest in marketing some of these, was already
in contact with the Seehandlung about them,
and had in fact sold some to customers.[16]

Under a secret decree of August 16, 1939,
Jews rapidly lost control over the disposition of
their accounts as the authorities began issuing
security orders that compelled Jews to establish accounts, designated "limited disposition
security accounts," with a bank authorized to
deal in foreign exchange. Withdrawals were
limited to 300 RM per month to cover normal
living expenses, but additional amounts could
be taken out to pay taxes, contributions to the
Jewish community, legal and medical fees, and
for emigration purposes.[17] For purposes of the
internal management of Jewish accounts and
the collection of fees, the CA decided in late
September 1939 to set up a special series of
current accounts with the designation "N A 7"
(Non-Aryan) and to make the proper changes
in its booking machinery.[18] Although some of
the administrative problems connected with
the management of these accounts were eased
by the government policy of letting Jews use
their accounts and securities without restriction
for purposes of demonstrated emigration plans,
the implication of the complex regulations was
that the bank had to check on whether monies taken out by Jews from their accounts for
special purposes were removed legitimately and
to contact the currency agencies in cases of
doubt. Here again, the banks were turned into
enforcers who administered Jewish accounts
in accordance with the security orders of the
regime and the manifold regulations governing accounts.[19] As might be expected, these
regulations grew in complexity as the Reich

---

[13] Ibid., General Management Instruction, Nr. 201,
     Dec. 9, 1938.

[14] Ibid., General Management Instruction, Nr. 208,
     Dec. 15, 1938, and Nr. 213, Dec. 21, 1938.

[15] Ibid., correspondence pertaining to the General
     Management Instruction, Nr. 67, April 17, 1939,
     with the Reich Group, April 21, 1939.

[16] RGVA Moscow, 1458/2/91, Bl. 70–71, CA to
     Riehle, May 24, 1939.

[17] BA-CA, CA-V, see Dean, *Robbing the Jews*, ch. 4, and
     the very detailed General Management Instruction
     of Oct. 2, 1939.

[18] Ibid., General Management Instruction, Nr. 156,
     Sept. 30, 1939.

[19] See the remarkably complex procedures set out
     in the General Management Instruction, Nr. 181

expanded and banks had to deal with Jewish accounts connected with the former Czech lands and other German-controlled areas.

The culmination of the expropriation of Jewish accounts was the infamous Eleventh Implementing Decree of the Reich Citizenship Law of November 25, 1941, under which all German Jews and stateless Jews living abroad lost their citizenship and their assets were made forfeit to the Reich. Banks had to identify and then surrender the monies in such accounts when called upon to do so by the Gestapo or the Finance Ministry. This measure was undertaken in connection with the deportation of Jews to the East, which was initiated on a large scale beginning in the fall of 1941. In many cases, Jews who were deported were sent to Litzmannstadt (Lodz) and other places, including Auschwitz, located in the territory of the Reich and were thus not "living abroad" in the sense of the Eleventh Implementing Decree, but Jews were required to sign away all their assets to the Reich before deportation so that the proceeds of their accounts and deposits could be confiscated by Gestapo or Finance Ministry order. All this did not prove quite as simple as it sounded, however, and carrying out the decree presented extraordinary difficulties for banks and insurance companies because they had many accounts whose owners could not clearly be identified as Jewish or who had left Austria and the Reich at an earlier date and whose current citizenship was uncertain. Banks that blocked and turned over the proceeds of such accounts could be liable to lawsuits abroad. The banks were thus very concerned about the extent to which they were obligated to conduct investigations into such accounts and also wished to limit their liability by having the Gestapo or the Finance Ministry cover their

actions. Given the personnel shortages at the banks and the limited resources of the Gestapo and other government agencies, the deadlines for reporting accounts were regularly extended, and there was considerable confusion. Matters were particularly difficult in Vienna, where many accounts, particularly at the CA, dated back to the old empire and the nationality or race of the owners could not be determined. CA director Pfeiffer, who acted as the representative of the Economic Group for Private Banking in Vienna, had to regularly importune the authorities for clarification about the contradictory instructions issued by various authorities and the obligations of the banks. A special complication in Vienna was whether Gestapo orders for the surrender of assets took precedence over the authority of the Central Agency for Jewish Emigration, which was unique to Vienna and Prague. The Eleventh Implementing Decree produced a host of abstruse problems that exercised both the banks and the authorities. These were of course usually of little moment to most of the Jews involved, who were being murdered, but there is no evidence whatever that the CA or other banks had any qualms about having to play a more active role as enforcers under the decree. The flood of bank queries and complaints had to do with the lack of clarity surrounding the decree and the manpower problems it created.[20]

Indeed, what seemed most troublesome to the CA and other banks was that the handling of Jewish accounts and business in connection with the regulations often required Jews to enter bank premises, a situation that seemed to disturb non-Jewish customers and led to complaints that they had to rub elbows with Jews.

---

of Nov. 7, 1939. All these suggest that officials at the banks could play a very intrusive role in the lives of the Jews seeking to take money from their accounts. For evidence on this score with respect to another bank, see Hannah Ahlheim, "Die Commerzbank und die Einziehung jüdischen Vermögens," in: Ludolf Herbst/Thomas Weihe (eds.), *Die Commerzbank und die Juden 1933–1945* (Munich 2004), pp. 138–172.

[20] See the excellent discussion in: Harold James, *Verbandspolitik im Nationalsozialismus. Von der Interessenvertretung zur Wirtschaftsgruppe. Der Centralverband des Deutschen Bank- und Bankiergewerbes 1932–1945* (Munich 2001), ch. 6. There is a large collection of queries and complaints in NARA, T83/96. For such documents dealing with the CA and Pfeiffer, see especially his correspondence with the Economic Group for Private Banking of March 1942.

The CA solution to the "problem" was stated in a management directive of October 20, 1941:

The entire customer business with Jews will therefore be shifted to the basement. Thereby one has the possibility, except in a few exceptional cases, of keeping Jews from the main hall. The porter has the responsibility of having Jews entering the bank make use of the side entrance. The non-Aryan series of the current account section and customer counter 4 will be consolidated, and customer counter 4 is responsible for all affairs of the Jewish customers. Insofar as other places in the bank are involved, they can get the necessary information from counter 4 either by telephone, or the Jews are to be sent through entryways in the back to the relevant officials. All business with Jews in the central headquarters will be limited to the period from 9 a.m. to 1 p.m. In order to also avoid contact between Aryan and non-Aryan customers in the Vienna branches, the handling of Jewish customers at the counters is to be scheduled for the period 2–3 p.m.[21]

One can only imagine what a nightmare banking must have been for Jews remaining in Vienna under these cruel conditions.

All this, however, was part and parcel of the elimination of Austria's Jews from the economy through the forcible takeover of their assets, the sale of those assets to Aryans under various forms of duress, and the outright expropriation of Jewish property and belongings. These actions were undertaken with a unique combination of viciousness and brutality, on the one hand, and state-organized and controlled expropriation and forced sale, on the other. The Jews played such a significant role in the Austrian economy and the financial issues and logistics seemed so serious that Göring thought it would take four years to complete their elimination.[22] The "task" was basically accomplished by the end of 1939, although the disappearance of the Jews from their enterprises often left some complicated and messy problems. One of the outstanding characteristics of the Aryanization process in Austria was the

high degree of organization and surveillance by government and Party authorities. There was, to be sure, an initial phase of "wild Aryanization" in the spring of 1938 characterized by plunder, the taking over of Jewish enterprises by "commissars" and "administrators," some of them self-appointed, and the forcing of Jews to sell their possessions and enterprises at very low prices. Some Jews simply left everything behind and fled the country. The government and Party leadership in both Berlin and Vienna, however, were anxious to put an end to "wild Aryanizations," which were viewed as wasteful and which often resulted in the expropriation of businesses by incompetent Party loyalists and illegals seeking compensation and restitution (*Wiedergutmachung*) for their alleged sufferings at the hands of the old regime and the Jews. A first step toward a more organized approach was taken in April, when Jews were forced to report their assets. It was followed by the establishment of the Property Transfer Bureau on May 18, 1938, by the Austrian Ministry of Economics and Labor. The agency was headed by State Commissar for the Private Economy Walter Rafelsberger. This was a large and complex organization with the function of organizing, coordinating, and deciding upon the sale of Jewish enterprises and property in every branch of the economy. This did not entirely stop the abuses of the "commissars" and "administrators," and Rafelsberger's office made an effort to weed out some of the corrupt, incompetent, and superfluous officials in the summer of 1938 by requiring that they could only continue their activities if their appointments were confirmed.[23] In November 1939, with the transfer of authority in the Ostmark to the Reich Statthalter's (governor's) office, authority over Aryanizations was transferred there as well and the VVSt went into liquidation except for

---

[21] BA-CA, CA-V, General Management Instruction, Nr. 102, Oct. 20, 1941.
[22] BAB, R2/15612, Bl. 2, 4–5, Ministerial Director Schwandt of the RWM, April 9, 1938 and the interior minister note to the RWM, April 5, 1938.

[23] On the VVSt, see the valuable study by Gertraud Fuchs, *Die Vermögensverkehrsstelle als Arisierungsbehörde*, D.A. (Vienna 1989). The commissars and administrators are discussed in Chapter 4. There is an excellent general account of the Austrian Aryanization administration and measures in Felber et al., *Ökonomie der Arisierung*, pt. 1, ch. 3.

cases that remained to be cleared up. It continued to function, however, in revised form in the
Ostmark Statthalter's administration, although
its caseload diminished considerably because of
the disappearance of most of the Jews.

Although the VVSt remained the chief
authority in dealing with Aryanizations in
1938–1939 and then in its subsequent bureaucratic incarnations in the Statthalter's office, it
had been found unsuitable for dealing with large
enterprises, where the process of Aryanization
was often quite complex and where the authorities were anxious to ensure that such enterprises were placed in the right hands and also
that Aryanization profits, that is, the difference
between what was paid to Jews and the market
value of the assets sold, went to the Treasury. In
October 1938, at the behest of Fischböck, the
Österreichische Kontrollbank für Industrie und
Handel, which earlier had been used for various
commercial operations, was assigned the task of
handling large-scale industrial Aryanizations.
Previously owned by the Creditanstalt, the
Mercurbank, and the Bankhaus Rothschild, the
Kontrollbank was formally in the hands of their
successor banks, the Creditanstalt (65.8 percent),
Länderbank Wien (20.2 percent), and E. von
Nicolai & Co (14 percent), after the Anschluss.
The actual work of Kontrollbank Aryanization,
however, was done by a new Section C man-
aged by a lawyer and official appointed by
Fischböck, Walther Kastner.[24]

As shall be shown, the CA did a great
deal of business with the VVSt and the
Kontrollbank connected with its participation
in Aryanizations, but it also serviced or sought
to service them in a variety of other ways.
One was holding their accounts. In the case of
the VVSt, the CA held the lion's share of the
accounts taken over by the Statthalter's office
from the VVSt dealing with Aryanization, so
that in August 1945, 3,988,390 RM remained
after the account had taken in a total of
16,758,457 RM and expended 12,770,067

RM. The Länderbank Wien and the Gewerbe
und Handelsbank, which also held the VVSt
accounts for the Statthalter's office, had balances
of 297,515 RM and 1,524,962 RM respectively,
the former taking 694,919 RM into its account
and giving out 397,404 RM, the latter taking in
2,003,758 RM and giving out 478,796 RM.[25]
In the case of the Kontrollbank, the CA held an
account of 2,348,506 RM for Section C, while
the Länderbank Wien held 585,844 RM and
E. von Nicolai held 510,927 RM on account
for Section C.[26]

There was yet another area in which the CA
almost became deeply involved in the servicing
of the VVSt's Aryanization activities. As might
be expected, the VVSt was very interested in
the takeover and sale of Jewish properties, but
this proved to be one of the most confusing and
unclear of its efforts. Quite aside from the fact
that the Gestapo and other agencies had seized
Jewish properties since the Anschluss, Jews had
also transferred or sold their properties and
had also taken out mortgages on them. While
the head of the relevant section of the VVSt,
Müller, was anxious to gain control of the situation, he had been frustrated because the regime
was concerned about negative foreign policy consequences in the event that ownership
had been transferred abroad or foreigners held
mortgages on the properties. In October 1938,
however, Müller presented a report in which he
argued that the Reich's foreign policy situation
was extraordinarily favorable at the moment
and it was vital to protect the "national property," which he apparently considered Jewish
real property to be, by placing stringent controls on its use and sale. He also suggested that
the Österreichische Realitäten AG (ORAG),
the CA's holding company for its real estate, be
called upon to handle the takeover and marketing of Jewish real property for which suitable
Aryan buyers had not yet been found. This was
to proceed in the manner by which Section C

[24] On the activities of the Kontrollbank, see
ibid., pp. 105–119, and the business reports and
audits of the Kontrollbank in BA-CA, CA-IB,
Kontrollbank, 34/01.

[25] See ÖStA/AdR, MfWuA, VVST, Box 1369, Zl.
604/46, III-E1, accounts.

[26] BA-CA, CA-IB, Kontrollbank, 34/01, 1939 Audit of
the Kontrollbank.

of the Kontrollbank had been created to deal with the sale of large Jewish enterprises.[27]

The idea of using the ORAG for such purposes was not new. Back in July 1938, the CA confidentially informed the Deutsche Bank that plans were afoot to have the ORAG assigned the task of acting as a trustee for dealing with the technical problems of transferring Jewish real estate into Aryan hands, and Joham had also discussed the matter with Abs.[28] Real estate, however, had not been given high priority by the authorities and was only placed under control by the decree of December 3, 1938. Even then, however, the authorities issued guidelines on December 9 instructing that no effort be made to sell off Jewish real properties except in certain instances, limiting the personnel in the section dealing with real property, and declaring that purchasers had to be politically acceptable and that the amount paid to Jews be limited to 70 percent of the purchase price with the remainder paid to the VVSt Aryanization account. Insofar as the Realitäten AG was to be brought into the picture, it was to be in the service of Section C of the Kontrollbank, and the proceeds of the sale were to go to the Treasury. Furthermore, other real estate organizations could be called in outside Vienna. By June 1939, when the VVSt was being liquidated and its offices transferred to the Statthalter's office, the situation in its understaffed real estate office had become much worse because the demand for Jewish real property had grown. A proposal by the Dorotheum, which had acted as the pawn house for the collection and auctioning of Jewish goods, of October 1940, suggested that the handling of Jewish real property remained in disarray, and this ultimately was the fruit of various arbitrary seizures of property after the Anschluss, the interest of government agencies in taking over Jewish buildings for their own purposes, and ideas of turning such properties over to returning veterans after the war. In any case, there is no evidence that the Realitäten

AG was ever involved to the extent Müller once proposed.[29]

This is not to say the ORAG was not seriously involved in the management and sale of Jewish real estate assets. Founded in 1932, the ORAG had been assigned the task of administering and, where deemed advisable, selling real estate acquired by the CA through the former Wiener Bankverein as well as from enterprises in the CA concern and debtors to the CA. In 1939, the ORAG was merged with the Universale-Redlich & Berger Bau AG, which had been founded in 1921, in such a way that the ORAG acquired the assets of Universale but the new entity was then renamed the Universale Hoch und Tiefbau AG. The company, in which the CA held a majority stake until that stake was surrendered in the takeover by the Deutsche Bank in the spring of 1942, was the major construction company in the Ostmark, and the CA continued to hold a 26 percent interest. Although its real estate operations remained important, they became subsidiary to the large construction projects in which Universale was engaged.[30]

Nevertheless, the section of Universale that had once been the ORAG was engaged in the purchase, sale, and administration of Jewish properties that had been taken over by the authorities, and it sought more such business because it produced lucrative honoraria. In February 1941, it was very concerned when the properties of Alice "Sara" Klinger,[31] which

---

[27] ÖStA/AdR, Bürckel Materie, 2160/00, Vol. 3, Report by Müller to Bürckel, Oct. 5, 1938.

[28] See DB, B 51, CA to Deutsche Bank, July 26, 1938, and handwritten notes of Abs dated July 1938.

[29] ÖStA/AdR, Bürckel Materie, 2160/00, Vol. 3, guidelines of Dec. 9, 1938, Wagner to Bürckel, June 29, 1939. Dorotheum proposal, Oct. 1940, ibid., VVAt, Box 1376, D44. Historikerkommission (ed.), *Vermögensentzug während der NS-Zeit sowie Rückstellungen und Entschädigungen seit 1945 in Österreich: Schlussbericht der Historikerkommission der Republik Österreich.* (Vienna 2003), pp. 92–95.

[30] BA-CA, CA-IB, Universale, 16/03-04, report for the working committee, probably by Lanz, Dec. 3, 1941. On the Dorotheum, see the study of Stefan August Lütgenau/Alexander Schröck/Sonja Niederacher, *Zwischen Staat und Wirtschaft. Das Dorotheum im Nationalsozialismus* (Vienna, Munich 2006).

[31] Jews had been required to take on middle names of "Israel" or "Sara" in order to make them more

it had been administering since June 1939, were suddenly turned over to the administration of a lawyer named Georg Kurzbauer by the Reich commissar for the management of enemy property. This was apparently done because she had been reported living in France, although she had in fact died and her heirs lived in Switzerland and the United States. The property had been heavily indebted because of tax and other obligations, and Universale was on the brink of finally making it profitable. Universale was therefore quite confused as to what its relationship was supposed to be to the new administrator and objected to the prospect of having its authority and possibly its honorarium removed just as its efforts were about to come to fruition. Consequently, it appealed to the CA for support, which it received, and also asked the CA lobbyist in Berlin, Captain Robert Nemling, to intervene with the commissar. As it turned out, there were numerous such cases, and Nemling reported that the commissar's office was not in a position to negotiate with every property administrator falling within its purview. While Universale would have to accept Kurzbauer as the major administrator of the properties in question, the honorarium of Universale would remain at its existing level even though Kurzbauer would now also get an honorarium. The matter continued to concern Universale, however, which asked that the CA intervene in Berlin so that its administration of such properties could be safeguarded in the future.[32]

At the same time, it was anxious to expand these activities after it learned from Nemling in April 1941 that rumors were already circulating in Berlin that the property of Jews who were abroad would be confiscated by the government. Nemling also informed Universale that the commissar for the management of enemy property, former banking commissar Friedrich Ernst, was thinking of placing Universale in charge of the Vienna properties involved.[33] Universale was indeed interested in gaining the administration of the properties of Jewish émigrés seized by the Gestapo, and in August 1941 wrote to Fritscher of the CA to ask for his support and sent along a copy of its letter to the office charged with winding up the affairs of the VVSt. The letter pointed out that Universale already administered property of Jew émigrés and had great experience in administering such properties, while it expressed concern that some of these properties were being turned over to lawyers and other such persons to administer. As it argued: "We are of the view that our corporation should be considered first when it comes to the supervision of Jewish property in Vienna and in the 'Ostmark' in general in view of our well-known seriousness and capital resources, our substantial well-practiced administrative apparatus, as well as our extensive many years of practice in this region, but above all in view of our political reliability that is known to you. We believe therefore with good reason to be able to claim for ourselves not only that we should retain the administration of the previously administered houses of Jewish emigrants but also that our company above all should be assigned the temporary administration of further properties of this type."[34] Unfortunately, there is no record as to how successful Universale was in its pleas to maintain its position and get a larger share of this business, but it manifestly worked hand in hand with the CA in this effort.

It is important to recognize that the CA did not welcome every opportunity that came along to engage in the Aryanization business. This is illustrated by its handling of Aryanization credit requests presented to the credit committee of

identifiable. There is one recorded instance where a customer of the CA, eighty-eight-year-old Julla Oppenheimer, informed that she did not find correspondence and money transfers under the name "Sara" "agreeable" (*angenehm*). See Sophie Lillie, *Was einmal war. Handbuch der enteigneten Kunstsammlungen Wiens* (Vienna 2003), p. 801.

32 BA-CA, CA-IB, Universale, 16/01-02, Universale to the Reich Commissar, Feb. 26, 1941; Universale to Nemling, Feb. 27, 1941; Lanz to the Reich Commissar, Feb. 27, 1941; CA to Universale, March 11, 1941; CA memorandum, March 10, 1941.

33 Ibid., Universale, 16/01-02, Nemling to Universale, April 6, 1941.

34 Ibid., Universale to Fritscher, and to Fritz Dubowsky, Aug. 19, 1941.

the Economic Aid Program for Austria that had been set up under the auspices of the RWM in April 1938. Funded by a consortium of banks led by the CA and Länderbank Wien, the technical management of the Economic Aid Program was lodged in the Kontrollbank. Initially funded with 50 million RM, 25 million RM were reserved for individual and smaller credits to be handled by individual banks while another 25 million RM were to be given as consortial credits. In the case of the former, the loans were guaranteed by the Reich up to 85 percent, while the latter were guaranteed by the Reich at 100 percent. The loans were attractive to the banks, at least from the perspective of their balance sheets, because of the Reich guarantees. Applicants had to be vetted for political reliability and economic viability by the Gau economic advisor, the Chamber of Commerce, and other Party and economic agencies, and a bank had to express willingness to act as banker for the project involved. The purpose of the entire program, which was strongly supported and supervised by Hans Kehrl, was to help the economic recovery of Austria, support small and medium-sized businesses, and make the Austrian economy competitive with the rest of the Reich. The applications to assist Aryanizers were particularly tricky because many of the applicants lacked experience or capital or both while usually having good political credentials. Needless to say, as certain cases show, the economic qualifications weighed very heavily for the CA and other banks.[35]

A particularly telling case was that of Hermine Johne, who requested a credit of 15,000 RM in order to take over and operate the sock and ladies' stocking firm of Ludwig Landauer in Vienna. She needed 6,000 RM to buy the Landauer firm and had been approved by the VVSt, while she needed 9,000 RM to buy raw materials. Johne seemed particularly worthy from a political point of view because

both she and her husband had been Party supporters. He had to flee Austria in 1934, and she found herself unable to maintain their knitwear factory. Subsequently, her husband had an accident in the course of his Party activities that left him disabled. The Chamber of Commerce and the Guild of Knitwear and Hosiery Producers supported the application on the grounds that there was a need for such businesses in Vienna and that she had the necessary experience as well as the good character required. This would enable her to be gainfully employed and to maintain the workers employed at the plant. Both the Gau economic advisor and other Party agencies emphasized the political sacrifices the pair had made. It was also noted, however, that Johne had not provided a plan for the further development of the enterprise or information about the duration of the credit. The couple was basically impecunious and offered the machines at the company as security. In any case, the CA, to its regret, found it impossible to give the credit, even with an 85 percent Reich guarantee. Manifestly, it found the risk too great.[36]

The CA also turned a cold shoulder to the application for a 50,000 RM credit by the Schottwiener Gipswerke F.X. Wellspacher in Schottwien, Vienna. In this instance, the applicant, Josef Deisinger, claimed he needed the money to rationalize his enterprise, which had suffered heavily from the competition of the largest gypsum producer in Austria, the Schottwien-Semmering AG. The latter had been in Jewish hands, and Deisinger, in addition to this credit for his own factory was also seeking a Reich-guaranteed credit of 200,000 RM to Aryanize it and then merge it with his factory. The rationalization was thus to proceed by undertaking the necessary work of repair and modernization at Deisinger's company and by joining the Aryanized firm to his own work. In contrast to Johne, the Gau economic advisor did not think much of Deisinger, who had been quite apolitical until his recent decision to apply for Party membership and whom he

---

35 See Gerald D. Feldman, "German Banks and National Socialist Efforts to Supply Capital and Support Industrialization in Newly Annexed Territories: The 'Austrian Model,'" in: *Zeitschrift für Unternehmensgeschichte* 50/1 (2005), pp. 5–16.

36 BAB, R2/15539, Bl. 87–92, 13th and 16th meetings of the credit committee, Nov. 9 and Dec. 20, 1938.

characterized as a "materialist ... who slyly looks after his own advantage." Of greater moment, however, was the long-standing unprofitability of the gypsum market due to overcapacity, excess competition, and low prices, so that the Chamber of Commerce believed that profitability could only be achieved if the Aryanization of Schottwien-Semmering was approved and if higher prices could be attained. The application was given conditional support, both from the Chamber and from the Association of the Stone Industry. As for the CA, it was uninterested in running the risks involved alone and suggested that both the credit for Aryanization and for Deisinger's company be applied for under the rubric of consortial credits with 100 percent Reich guarantee. There is no evidence that such a credit was granted.[37]

In contrast to this case, there was substantial enthusiasm on the part of Franz Carl Schlossmacher, who asked for credits of 170,000 RM for the operation of the Ido Schuhfabrik Berl & Co. Schlossmacher had paid 750,000 RM for this Jewish-owned company by selling shares he owned and the shoe factory he had been operating in Poland. He was thus a Reich German who had decided to return and settle in Vienna. His Aryanization of Ido had the approval of the VVSt, and the large sum he had paid was meant to cover the various taxes and costs of the Berl family, which exceeded the 650,000 RM the factory was worth. Schlossmacher thus needed money to fall back on should the firm have liquidity problems. He believed that the company would have substantial success because there was great demand for the shoes it produced, which were not luxury or stylish ones but rather shoes needed for practical purposes. He noted that he was quite experienced in the business and that his decision to give up his Polish enterprise and come to Vienna bespoke his seriousness of purpose. He offered to take a mortgage on the plant as security for the loan. The application was strongly supported by the Gau economic advisor, the Chamber of Commerce, and the branch trade

association. The first noted that Schlossmacher was "nationally" minded – in short, he was not a Party member but still politically reliable – and a person of good character and experience. There was general agreement that it was important to keep the company operating because it employed 160 workers and was likely to employ more as the economy picked up. Further, there was a general admission that the firm had been very well run by its former owners and was likely to function well in good hands. As for the CA, it not only was prepared to support the credit but also to refrain from asking Schlossmacher to pay his private debts to the bank for as long as the credit to the company was in force. Ultimately, a decision was made not to give Schlossmacher a Reich-guaranteed credit because his assets were too great, but the CA decided to give him the 170,000 RM as a personal credit.[38]

Another example of a substantial CA credit being approved for the Aryanizers of a well-run Jewish enterprise was the 150,000 RM credit approved for Wilhelm Speil and Franz Hudler of Gmünd for their takeover of the food wholesaler E. Löwy & Sohn in Gmünd. The company was sold with VVSt approval for 226,667 RM and the sum was placed in a blocked account at the CA. The loan was to cover part of the purchase price. The company, founded in 1887, did substantial business in the upper Waldvierte, and had a good distribution organization. The two purchasers were Party members with business experience who had worked hard for the movement, and the continuation of the firm was viewed to be in the general economic interest of the region. The CA was prepared, therefore, to provide a credit guaranteed by the Reich at the level of 70 percent.[39]

In another instance, the CA approved giving a 30,000 RM credit to the small chemical products company of Egon Wildschek, which

[37] Ibid., Bl. 195–200, 16th meeting of the credit committee, Dec. 20, 1938.

[38] Ibid., R2/15533, Bl. 286–289, 9th meeting of the credit committee, Sept. 15, 1938. ÖStA/AdR, 02/RWH/Kg 232, Deutsche Revisions- und Treuhand AG to the CA, Sept. 19, 1938 and to the RWM, Oct. 26, 1938.

[39] Ibid., Bl. 536–539, 10th meeting of the credit committee, Sept. 29, 1938.

was Aryanizing the firm of Dr. Wilhelm Stadler in Liesing. The Gau considered Wildschek an "especially urgent case" because the applicant had been a "fighter for the movement" and needed the support to reestablish himself. The Chamber of Commerce did not consider the firm economically vital but did point out that it produced sought-after specialty products that it sold at a lower price than in the old Reich. It could also expect a restoration of its contracts with the city government once it was Aryanized. In general, the granting of the credit was supported as a reasonable investment, and the CA was willing to grant the credit if it was 85 percent guaranteed by the Reich. As it turned out, Wildschek decided not to take the credit because he was able to pay the purchase price with other means. In response to a CA offer to provide the credit for other expenses, Wildschek asked that the matter be delayed until the end of the war because he was about to be drafted. He did not want the company to operate in his absence and was also concerned that it might be shut down to save raw materials.[40]

Even more solicitude was shown to the application for an 18,000 RM credit for Karl Pichler, a major of the reserve, and a dental technician, Josef Leiter, whom the VVSt had permitted to buy out the Jewish-owned café and restaurant Schab and Pichler. Pichler had a 20 percent interest in the establishment and had been business manager since 1920, while Leiter had run a coffeehouse in the Josefstadt. They had renamed the enterprise, which was located on the Ringstrasse and had been renovated in 1935, the Kaffeerestaurant Kyffhäuser. Leiter had been a Party member since 1931 and was very active; Pichler had only joined in July 1938, but both were viewed as politically reliable. The Chamber of Commerce strongly supported the credit on the grounds that "the Aryanization of Jewish coffee houses is certainly in the general interest," and that the applicants were experienced in the business.

The CA, which had already advanced a credit of 10,000 RM, was willing to grant the credit provided that the applicants paid back the advance. This investment was not without its difficulties for the CA. The war was not propitious for the business, and Leiter and Pichler found it difficult to meet their payments in 1940. By 1942, the debts had increased, and the CA was complaining that, while debts and interest were being promptly paid, too much money was being spent on personal needs. Nevertheless, the credit was repaid in August 1944.[41]

The CA was also willing to support a Reich-guaranteed credit of 35,000 RM to Franz Unger, who for forty-two years had been an employee of Jewish book dealer M. Kuppitsch Witwe. The bookshop, which was located in the vicinity of the university, had existed since 1789, making it the oldest one in Vienna, and had specialized in law and political science. Because all the other Jewish book dealers in the vicinity of the university were to be shut down, it could anticipate increased business. Unger was viewed as politically reliable and highly competent, and although he had little money himself, his son was a doctor and could also guarantee the loan. The loan was repaid in January 1942.[42]

As these examples show, there was a great range in the Aryanization, and the ugly cases described, both large and small, show that the CA took a cautious but positive approach in providing credits in many instances. It tended to give credits where the future prospects seemed most promising, and they were often most promising when the Aryanizers were taking over enterprises that were already established and successful thanks to the investment of business skill and talent by their former Jewish owners. Because Aryanization involved a massive transfer of assets within Austria and Germany, the CA, as Austria's largest bank and

---

40 Ibid., R2/15540, Bl. 131–134, CA to Treuhand, Feb. 5, 1940, ÖStA/AdR, 02/RWH/Kg 1014. 17th meeting of the credit committee, Jan. 12, 1939.

41 Ibid., Bl. 231–233, 17th credit committee meeting of Jan. 12, 1939. See also correspondence in ÖStA/AdR, 02/RWH/Kg 923.

42 Ibid., R2/15540, Bl. 234–235. 17th credit committee meeting of Jan. 12, 1939, and ÖStA/AdR, R 02/RWH, Kg 953, CA to Treuhand, Jan. 30, 1942.

a major industrial holding company, could hardly escape involvement in Aryanizations, be they small or large, and there is no evidence that it wanted to do so. This did not mean, however, that it had broad opportunity to act on its own initiative, as did some of the major German banks in the old Reich, not least because the authorities in Vienna played so large a role in Aryanization and had their own agenda. This was all the more the case because, as has been shown, the CA was viewed with some suspicion by the National Socialist authorities and was being forced to sell off important assets at the height of the Aryanization process in 1938–1939. Aryanization might have afforded some opportunities for the CA to seek "compensation" by acquiring Aryanized enterprises, but these proved quite limited. Aryanization was an integral part of the business of the CA during this period but hardly a major part of it. This is not to argue that the bank should in any way be exonerated for its role in a very dirty business that became "business as usual," but rather to place Aryanization in the context of the CA's more general activities during the National Socialist period, many of which were quite problematic for other reasons.

To understand the CA's role in Aryanizations, it is necessary to consider certain policies and practices of the Viennese authorities. The German banks obviously had a head start over the Austrians in this area, but they too had to adapt to the peculiarities of the Austrian situation, and a May 4, 1938, conversation between Heinz Osterwind of the Deutsche Bank and Rafelsberger, along with George Schumetz, his aide in the implementation of Aryanization measures, is quite instructive about the Aryanization situation. Osterwind was well aware of the policy of favoring Austrians in the buying up of Jewish enterprises, and his special interest in the interview was to determine the extent to which business interests from the old Reich might gain entry into the Ostmark. Rafelsberger informed Osterwind that they did not have any fixed guidelines in this area, but he also stressed that they did indeed seek to prevent "weak Austrian economic positions from

being overrun from the old Reich."[43] When it came to larger Aryanizations, however, they encountered situations in which financial and other considerations made it necessary to call on help from the old Reich. Osterwind had the impression that the authorities were very anxious to speed up the Aryanization process and were willing to make concessions on letting in Germans if no compelling Austrian interest stood in the way. While advice from the economic organizations was sometimes sought, the ultimate decision lay with the government authority, which was open to concrete proposals. Also, Osterwind felt that old Reich firms seeking to Aryanize an enterprise were best advised to negotiate directly with the Austrians in charge of the former Jewish enterprise so that such a proposal could be submitted.

What the conversation with Rafelsberger and Schumetz revealed was that a built-in mechanism had been created that forced rapid Aryanizations to take place. Under a decree of April 30, 1938, every Jewish-owned enterprise employing a significant number of workers or employees was to be taken over by a commissar or administrator with the right to take all measures necessary to keep the business operating. The non-Aryan owner was deprived of all control over the enterprise. At the same time, however, the enterprise was not Aryan but also could not be closed down and its employees had to be kept on the payroll. For example, if the enterprise was a coffeehouse, then it had to keep its lights on and, if it employed a band, then the band had to play. Because under existing conditions such enterprises scarcely had any customers, as Osterwind explained, "this naturally meant a daily loss for the non-Aryan owner and a gradual eating up of his resources. One thereby gradually forces the non-Aryan owner to sell his enterprise as soon as possible." If the owner was unable to find a buyer, then the authorities set a price and decided

---

43 Sächsisches Staatsarchiv Leipzig, Deutsche Bank, 623, Heinz Osterwind to the Deutsche Bank, May 4, 1938. I am grateful to Harold James for placing this document at my disposal.

how much time the owner would have to sell the business. In cases where former employees wished to take over the business or where someone with the necessary skills was found, as in the case of the book dealer Unger, for example, the purchase price did not have to be paid immediately for the Aryanization to take place. In the case of larger enterprises, a trustee was put in charge and given the responsibility for assessing the value of the business and setting the price either by himself or with the aid of an accounting firm. In either case, the assumption was that the non-Aryan business would under no circumstances benefit from the anticipated economic upswing and that it would take time for it to recover from its non-Aryan reputation. The price would also take into account any deficits failings of the firm with respect to working and social provisions that would have to be remedied by the new Aryan owner. Obviously, there would be no accounting for good will because a Jewish enterprise could only have "bad will." In short, the owner of a Jewish enterprise would be forced to sell because he or she would be without customers and would then be forced to accept a price that penalized the owner for the disadvantages incurred by the very fact of being Jewish. Finally, as Osterwind noted, the Creditanstalt was very much engaged in this business through the taking over of shares and stakes in Jewish enterprises in the function of a trustee and could either conduct assessments and valuations itself or turn them over to auditors. As the large cases described later in this chapter will show, it was an active participant in the measures of economic sadism constructed by the regime to force Jews to sell their enterprises for prices artificially depressed by the discrimination exercised against them.

I. GERNGROSS AG

A significant example of the CA's involvement in the aforementioned practices connected with Aryanization was the case of Gerngross AG, one of Vienna and Austria's largest and most famous department stores.[44] Founded in 1911, it was primarily a family enterprise. Family members, all Jewish, owned some 62.5 percent of the 200,000 shares, which were priced in March 1938 at 30 Schilling a share. The CA owned between 20.5 percent and 22.5 percent of the shares. The remaining shares were distributed among shareholders, some of whom were Jewish and some of whom were "racially unidentifiable." In any case, the prominence of the firm made it an immediate target for Aryanization. It was placed under an administrator, Josef Hermann. The family members were told they would have to sell their shares, and the pressure on was intensified by the arrest of Robert Gerngross. This may have influenced his brother Albert, a Swiss citizen, to sell his shares.[45] Robert and his wife were later murdered in the deportations of 1942, but the other Austrian members of the family were able to go into exile in 1939 after they had sold their shares and paid the Jewish Assets Tax and Reich Flight Tax. It is worth noting that there was a considerable amount of wealth involved, both in Austria and in Switzerland. On April 14, 1938, a custody account in the amount of 47,000 Swiss Francs was transferred to the CA, which in turn paid the balance to the authorities and closed the account on April 29. Two similar accounts totaling 18,400 Swiss Francs were transferred to an account at the Länderbank Wien on August 16, 1938. This account was closed on September 6, and the monies paid to the authorities. The Gerngross family owned substantial amounts of cash, stocks and bonds, real estate, jewelry, and other assets in Vienna. Paul and Martha Gerngross had to pay a Jewish Assets Tax assessment of 740,999 RM, of which 152,875 RM was for the Reich Flight Tax. The exact disposition of their various assets is unclear, and their

44 For accounts that employ some of the documents used here on the Gerngross Aryanization and restitution, see Felber et al., *Ökonomie der Arisierung*, pt. 1, pp. 126–128; pt. 2, pp. 84–92.

45 See Gregor Spuhler/Ursina Jud/Peter Melichar/ Daniel Wildmann, *"Arisierungen" in Österreich und ihre Bezüge zur Schweiz*. Veröffentlichungen der Unabhängigen Expertenkommission Schweiz (= UEK) – Zweiter Weltkrieg, Vol. 20 (Zurich 2002), pp. 55, 68, 71–73, 118.

art collections must be taken into account, but it should be obvious that the Gerngrosses lost more than their department store.[46]

The big problem really was not forcing the Gerngross family members to sell their shares but rather finding willing purchasers because of the "Jewish character"[47] of the enterprise. Commerce Minister Hans Fischböck, who had taken a special interest in the matter, solved this problem by assigning the CA the task of Aryanizing the company. The CA bought out the Gerngross family members, assumed trusteeship over their shares and other non-Aryan shares, and then sold the shares to Aryans approved by the Property Transfer Bureau. On April 27, 1938, the CA reported that it had taken over the 122,487 Gerngross family shares on the previous day and, with those shares and those it owned, now controlled 79.91 percent of the company. The family had also agreed to let the CA retain 2,422 shares belonging to Otto Gerngross, who was living in Ankara, Turkey, in a blocked account. In all, the Gerngross family owned 124,909 shares. It was also negotiating with the Bankhaus Friedenstein & Co. to surrender another 4,000 shares that were also in a blocked CA account. Additionally, the CA had identified another 10,480 shares, largely in its customer deposit boxes, and apparently expected that the owners would sell. Another 6,886 shares remained, the owners of which could not be identified by "race" and another 4,079 shares belonging to Aryans. The CA suggested that no immediate effort be made to identify the owners of these scattered shares because the matter could be cleared up at the next general shareholders' meeting, when their owners had to identify themselves. This appeared all the more prudent because the

CA could shortly expect to control 90 percent of the shares once the already identified Jewish shareholders sold out. Fischböck was also notified by the CA that the old administrative council had been completely changed and that the nominees of Rafelsberger and the commissarial head of the Industrial Association, August Schmid-Schmidsfelden, had been appointed. Also, all non-Aryan employees had been "eliminated."[48]

Manifestly, the CA was proving itself a reliable trustee for Fischböck in dealing with Gerngross and, in the process, acting as an enforcer of the measures to force Jews to give up their assets and their jobs. Apparently, however, the CA negotiators were not yet fully attuned to the swindling practices of Fischböck and his ilk and may also have hoped to deal as honorably as possible with the Gerngross family, with whom it had been doing business for some years. Whatever the case, the CA had drawn up a document under which the Gerngrosses turned over their shares to the CA with the understanding that the CA was obliged to use a 25 Schilling price per share as a guideline in the selling of the shares to Aryan purchasers approved by the authorities and to pay the amount received to the account of the Gerngross family members originally owning the shares. The 25 Schilling price was intended as a temporary price subject to modification upward or downward depending on the findings of a valuation by the Deutsche Revisions- und Treuhand AG. After the currency conversion to Reichsmark, the temporary price stood at 16.67 RM per share. However, Fischböck, now minister for economics and labor, gave a verbal order that the Gerngross group was to get no more than 12 RM a share. Because the Gerngross family also had certain contractual obligations to the firm's senior personnel, it apparently negotiated as hard as possible with the CA to increase the price per share. In any case, the CA reported to Fischböck that the negotiations had been "tough." Finally, at the end of 1938, the two sides settled on 11.5 RM per share, that is, 50

---

46 Much can be learned from the Claims Resolution Tribunal decision of April 4, 2003 that awarded the Gerngross heirs 858,895.32 Swiss Francs. See http://www.crit-ii.org/_awards/_/apdfas/Goldmann_David.pdf. Holocaust Victim Assets Litigation, Case Nr. CV96-4849, March 5, 2003, Claims Nr. 22432/PY, 22434/PY, 22435/PY. On the art collections, see Lillie, *Was einmal war*, pp. 395–402.

47 BA-CA, CA-V, CA executive committee, and management board, April 29, 1938.

48 ÖStA/AdR, MfWuA, VVST, Box 636, Statistik, Zl. 3801, CA to Fischböck, April 27, 1938.

pfennig below Fischböck's upper limit. At the same time, all other Jewish shareholders were also to receive no more than 11.5 RM per share.[49]

While a number of candidates for the take-over of Gerngross appeared on the scene, those finally accepted by the Property Transfer Bureau belonged to a German group from the Hannover area, all Party members and all Aryans married to Aryans, as was stated in their application to State Commissar Rafelsberger. None of them had been in the department store business. Wilhelm Ackmann was a whole-sale radio dealer in Hannover; Alfred Ludwig was a seed merchant in Osnabrück; Egon Koch was an accountant and tax advisor in Hannover. Leaving aside any behind-the-scenes political string-pulling that may have taken place, their chief nonpolitical qualification seems to have been their readiness to pay 20 RM per share for the "Jewish" shares and 30 RM per share for the CA holding in Gerngross that the purchasers insisted on acquiring as well. Fischböck urged the CA to sell its stake, thus adding it to the list of holdings sold off under German pressure. The three Aryanizers agreed to pay two-thirds of the purchase price from their own resources, and to borrow the rest from the CA, which they also pledged to use for their banking business. The CA thus lost its stake in Gerngross but retained the retailer as a customer. The purchasers also agreed to pay an "Aryanization fee" of 8.50 RM per share for each of the shares previously owned by Jews and promised that they would run the business in a manner that would be "Austrian" in style, and that they would make due provision to comply with the Labor Front's "beauty of labor" standards for their employees. From a financial point of view, the terms of the sale were bound to be satisfactory to Fischböck and the CA. The government received the dif-ference between the 11.50 RM the CA paid out for each share and the 20 RM the pur-chasers paid to the CA for those shares. The CA, however, also made a profit of 8.50 RM on each of these shares because it was paid 20 RM

per share in addition to its earnings on its own Gerngross shares that it sold at a higher price. This amounted to a profit of somewhat more than a million RM for its "services" as a trustee for Fischböck and an intermediary in the sale of the shares Gerngross, renamed by its new owners as the "Kaufhaus der Wiener."[50] The CA could also look forward to doing consid-erable credit business with the new owners. In assessing the CA's role, it is very important not to do so on the basis of later developments, the fact for example that the new owners did not manage the company well and that it was badly run down at the end of the war, after which the Gerngrosses returned and received restitu-tion. No one in 1938 knew what Austria would look like in 1945, and the important point is that in 1938 the CA made a handsome profit for its services, sold off its shares for a good price, and could entertain expectations that doing business with the new owners would be lucrative. In this context, it was rather disingen-uous of the CA to specify the 42,574 Gerngross shares it held and sold off in February 1939 at Fischböck's urging to the consortium of pur-chasers as yet another holding forcibly sold to German interests in its postwar memorandum calling for the repatriation of holdings sold off to Germans during this period.[51]

2. TILLER BEKLEIDUNGS- LIEFERUNGS- UND UNIFORMIERUNGS-AG

The Aryanization of the Austrian uniform pro-ducer Tiller was also accomplished with CA involvement, but a takeover by old Reich inter-ests was avoided and the CA ended up with a

---

49 Ibid., Weber of the VVST to Friedl of the CA, Dec. 15, 1938.

50 Ibid., Weber to Rafelsberger, Jan. 3, 1939 and Rafelsberger to CA, Feb. 10, 1939. See also BA-CA, CA-V, CA management board meeting, March 16, 1939.

51 See NARA, Microcopy T-83, Roll 101, the memorandum of the Creditanstalt-Bankverein of November 1945 on the Repatriation of the Shares of the Bank and Its Concern Enterprises (Denkschrift der Creditanstalt-Bankverein hinsi-chtlich Repatriierung von Aktien der Bank und deren Konzernunternehmungen).

participation in the company. Founded in 1865 and turned into a corporation in 1916, Tiller was a leading producer of uniforms. At the time of the Anschluss, its chief shareholders were Emil and Josef Toffler and Otto Ziemer, three Jews who together owned 10,869 of its 12,500 shares. Emil Toffler was largely responsible for running the company. Toffler and Ziemer were far-sighted enough to move a significant portion of their assets to England before the Anschluss, in violation of Austrian foreign exchange laws, and then to flee Austria immediately upon the German invasion. An administrator was appointed to run the company in the person of Rudolf Demus, a Party member who was possibly being rewarded for having denounced the Toffler family. This did not, however, make Tiller Aryan, and it was threatened with ruin unless it was so designated. Minister Fischböck asked the CA to take over the non-Aryan shares as a trustee, and this made it possible for Tiller to be declared Aryan by Rafelsberger. Tiller had an account with the CA's Mariahilferstrasse branch, and the CA hoped to continue the relationship as compensation for its role as trustee. It did not initially seem interested in acquiring shares itself. The CA also did not have the right to sell the shares to potential buyers because it was acting as a trustee for the VVSt. At the turn of 1939–1940, the responsibility for Aryanizing Tiller was turned over to the Kontrollbank, which now assumed the trusteeship position previously held by the CA. The Kontrollbank intended to determine the financial status of Tiller and the value of the shares, but it ran into considerable difficulty dealing with Tiller's only foreign branch, in Sarajevo, whose Jewish director refused to cooperate with the Kontrollbank-appointed directors of Tiller in any way and employed every available legal recourse to block an examination of the branch's books. As a result, the Kontrollbank could not price the shares even though no fewer than eight interested parties had contacted the bank. Among these were some old Reich firms – Josef Dykhoff & Wilhelm Bührer in Berlin, Boecker G.m.b.H. in Essen, and the Bayerische Uniformlieferungs AG (Bulag). The last-mentioned company described itself

as the most important uniform manufacturer in Germany. It had received recognition from the Gau for its performance and was the first such company to be proposed as a "National Socialist Model Plant."[52]

The problems connected with Sarajevo were "solved" in early 1941 by the German invasion of Yugoslavia, which permitted the elimination of the Jewish personnel and their replacement by local persons. In fact, Tiller's leadership hoped to engage in further Aryanization in the region by buying up available firms and warehouses, but these intentions were frustrated because the authorities took them over. This led to a decision to set up yet another branch in Agram/Zagreb.[53]

Most importantly, however, the new circumstances also made it possible to complete the Aryanization of the mother company, and the Kontrollbank, which held 12,086, that is, 96.7 percent of the shares, invited potential purchasers to step forward by April 7, 1941. By this time, however, an Ostmark solution was in the making in the form of a syndicate comprised of the CA, which was to take over 31.3 percent of the shares; Hans Frohn, who was to act as chief shareholder and buy 58.3 percent of the shares; and Rudolf Demus, who was to take 10.4 percent of the shares. Frohn, a former director of the rubber producer Semperit who had been standing in for General Director Franz Messner, purchased the Tiller shares with the proceeds of his sale of his Semperit shares and assumed the leadership of Tiller. The CA apparently wished to compensate Frohn for the loss of his position at Semperit. Demus was probably brought into the syndicate because of his role as earlier administrator of the company and his relations with Rafelsberger. He required a CA loan of 90,000 RM to purchase his shares, and he put up the shares as security for the loan. His

---

[52] ÖStA/AdR, MfWuA, VVST, Box 1408, Kontrollbank to the VVSt, Jan. 31, 1940 and Bulag to the Kontrollbank, Jan. 24, 1940. BA–CA, CA–IB, Tiller, 22/04. For a good general account, see the memorandum of Dec. 17, 1946.

[53] Ibid., Tiller, 22/01-03, Meeting of the Tiller supervisory board, Sept. 19, 1941.

function appears to have been largely political, and he showed little interest in becoming a serious shareholder in the company. Although Frohn was the chief shareholder, the CA was given a particularly important role in the affairs of Tiller because it was designated the leader of the syndicate and all shares were to be deposited at the CA.[54]

Under the agreement signed on June 26, 1941, that served as the culmination of the "company dejewification (*Entjudung*)," the Kontrollbank received 824,000 RM. The shares were bought for 72 RM a piece, after an initial offer of 60 RM – and the distribution of shares and their value was as follows:

Creditanstalt	3,750 shares	270,000 RM
Hans Frohn	6,445 shares	464,040 RM
Rudolf Demus	1,250 shares	90,000 RM

The Kontrollbank had to pay the Reich Treasury 268,776 RM for Ziemer's 3,733 shares, which were held in a blocked account because of his violation of the foreign exchange laws of the pre-Anschluss regime. Strictly speaking, therefore, this was not an Aryanization, and the same held true for a small block of shares bought by the Kontrollbank on the open market. The remaining 64.87 percent belonging to the Toffler family and other Jewish shareholders did fall under the Aryanization rubric.

The Kontrollbank thus made a return of 426,141 RM. The syndicate did pay a high price for the shares, which were selling for 15–19 RM on the market, although one should note that the CA was a shareholder in the Kontrollbank and thus indirectly profited from the arrangement. Of more consequence, undoubtedly, were the good prospects of the company, which had substantial military contracts. The Jewish shareholders, now living in New York and Palestine, received nothing, of course, and they were not expected to receive anything.[55]

As might be expected, Tiller was increasingly engaged in production for the war effort and was able to pay a 6 percent dividend in 1943. At the beginning of that year, it received permission to produce orders and military decorations, but it was then ordered not to do so on the grounds that the company name was Jewish and would have to be changed before permission could be granted. Tiller protested and, as it turned out, the discovery was made that the name was not Jewish and the company had only come into Jewish hands after World War I. Its main business, of course, remained uniforms. In 1944, 31 percent of its production, which was valued at 2.8 million RM, was for the military. Nineteen forty-five was a much less successful year for obvious reasons, and it culminated in considerable damage to the company and plundering. After the war, the CA and Frohn continued to maintain an interest in the company once the Tofflers and other Jewish owners received compensation for their shares.[56]

3. ÖSTERREICHISCHE KERAMIK AG

An Aryanization could, in fact, lead to a significant enhancement of the CA's industrial concern, as was the case with the Wilhelmsburger Steingut- und Porzellanfabrik AG in Wilhelmsburg a.d. Traisen, the Steingut-Union Lichtenstern & Co. in Vienna, and the Elektriztätswerk Richard u. Oskar Lichtenstern in Wilhelmsburg a.d. Traisen. The Wilhelmsburger was Austria's major producer of sanitary and household ceramic and porcelain wares, sharing the domestic market only with the 100 percent CA–owned Steingut-Industrie AG. Gmunden-Engelhof. Sixty-seven percent of the firm belonged to Kurt Lichtenstern, a Jew living in Switzerland, while 23 percent belonged to Paul Mocsari, an Austrian Jew. The remaining 10 percent was held by Berlin banker Hans Arnhold. The Steingut-Union was 75 percent owned by Lichtenstern and 25 percent owned by Mocsari. It was devoted to the

---

[54] Ibid., Tiller, 22/04, memorandum by Fiala, June 27, 1941, ibid., 22/09, and memorandum for Joham, March 15, 1946.

[55] The documentation is to be found in ibid., Tiller, 22/01.

[56] See the documentation in ibid., Tiller, 22/01 and 09.

marketing and distribution of Wilhelmsburger production, and the legal separation of the two firms had as its primary purpose tax savings. The electrical power plant in Wilhelmsburg belonged to Kurt Lichtenstern, who had inherited it from his father, Richard, and to his brother Oskar, who lived in Czechoslovakia. The three companies were thus 100 percent Jewish owned. When the Germans took over Austria, Mocsari and Oskar Lichtenstern, who were Austrian citizens, fled, the former ending up in the United States. State Commissar Rafelsberger appointed Walther Salvenmoser as commissarial administrator with instructions to prepare a plan for the rapid Aryanization of the three companies. Salvenmoser had been an inspector in the CA's industrial concern and had excellent Party credentials, although he had a terrible relationship with Director Pfeiffer, who had once accused him of being a "spy" for the CA management board.[57]

The urgency in Aryanizing the Wilhelmsburg firm arose from the fact that if it maintained its Jewish character for too long it would lose its customers and its employees would lose their jobs. The Hermann-Göring Werke in Linz, the Luftwaffe offices in Vienna, and various government agencies and private firms were refusing to buy its products, and there was a danger that firms from the old Reich would invade the Austrian market, which, until this time, had been amply supplied by Wilhelmsburg and the CA-owned factory in Gmunden. In fact, the latter was being used to rescue the former by buying Wilhelmsburg's production and selling it as if it were produced in Gmunden. In suggesting a prospective Aryanizer, Salvenmoser was in a somewhat embarrassing situation because the logical candidate was the CA, that is, his employer. Initially, he proposed that independent auditors value the assets in question, but

then everyone, including the Jewish "sellers," accepted his services. Salvenmoser negotiated with the CA and with the Jewish owners through their lawyers, and by late June the Aryanization plan could be presented to the Property Transfer Bureau for approval.

The basic plan was to bring together the Wilhelmsburger and Gmunden plants into one corporation, terminate the separate corporate existence of the Steingut-Union because the basis for its existence was considered "unjustified from the standpoint of tax morality," and bring the five electric power plants and the land on which they were located into the corporation with the object of selling off some of the former to St. Polten and using the land for worker housing. The CA would thus have 100 percent ownership of the entire new corporation that would include both that which was being Aryanized and its own plant in Gmunden. Salvenmoser, however, was intent on having the CA acquire these assets on very favorable terms, and his guidelines for determining the sales price is a good illustration of the way Jews were treated in such Aryanizations. A "static determination of the value of the assets and obligations on the basis of an actual book balance sheet" was to be undertaken. In addition, there was to be a "dynamic determination of the intrinsic value on the basis of the last business period taking into consideration all the factors conditioned by the present new circumstances. One must especially keep in mind that Jews ought have no part in the upswing of the nation, that National Socialist economic leadership has to take account of caring for the welfare of the employees and that the attainment of the greatest profitable profit must be pushed into the background. No consequence in the valuation of the enterprise is to be drawn from the fact that Jewish property is from the outset entailed by bad will."

Although it was typical in cases of Aryanization to valuate compensation by refusing to take goodwill into account, in this instance Salvenmoser proposed to give with one hand what he intended to take with the other in a stunning example of National Socialist ideas of equity and social policy. He not only argued

---

57 The hostility was so great that Salvenmoser refused to accept a letter of recommendation from the CA because it was signed by Pfeiffer. See the correspondence of November 1938 on this rather abstruse quarrel in the CA Personalakte for Pfeiffer. This discussion of the Aryanization is based on the report of Salvenmoser of June 28, 1938, in BA-CA, CA-IB, ÖSPAG, 09/03-04.

that the condition of the Wilhelmsburger plants was problematic and would require investment but also that the housing and living conditions of the workers there were substandard and that "the necessary means would logically be demanded of the present owners since, in view of the large profits they made over the years, they would have without difficulty been in a position to redress these grievances. Here they certainly should not be imposed upon to suddenly pay all the costs that are necessary to provide for a healthy and appropriate provision of housing for all the workers and employees in Wilhelmsburg that would be adapted to the National Socialist view of the *Volksgemeinschaft* ["people's community"]. For reasons of fairness they should only be called upon to care for the reconstruction of the existing 150 housing units that were built during their era of ownership, while the necessary housing expenses for the remainder of the employees (250) including the related constructions will be carried by the A.G. from its own means. In this way the A.G. takes upon itself the greater sacrifice since they have to care for the numerically larger part of the workforce."

On the basis of these "principles," Salvenmoser then calculated that the "social construction program" costs to be paid by the previous owners amounted to 760,000 RM and then threw in another 115,000 RM for upkeep requirements that had not been met. He deducted this 785,000 RM from the estimated potential earnings of Wilhelmsburg, which he placed at 1.4 million RM, leaving a balance of 525,000 RM. He then added 1,191,000 RM for other assets, above all the land owned by the company, subtracted 199,000 RM for other creditors, and ended up with 992,000 RM, which he rounded off to a sales price of one million RM for the Jewish owners to be paid by the CA along with its own investment in the social program for the workforce. In the event that it subsequently be determined that Salvenmoser had underestimated the worth of the company, the difference was to go to the Property Transfer Bureau. At the same time, Salvenmoser pointed out that the Jewish owners claimed that because they were already abroad, they were not subject to

the Reich Flight Tax because they were "foreigners" insofar as the exchange laws were concerned. It is hard to tell, however, whether he was once again being disingenuous because this status did not mean that Reichsmark could be transferred to their accounts abroad. In any case, after the war, the lawyer representing the Jewish owners declared that his clients had received nothing.[58] One thing was very clear, however, which is that there was great pressure to settle so that the Wilhelmsburger plant could function again. The economic reasons certainly were very important: the competitive situation of the Austrian plants would change greatly to their disfavor once they were no longer protected from German competition at the end of 1938. No less important, however, was the pressure from the Party leaders in the Lower Danube and in Vienna, undoubtedly because they also did not want a "dragged out Aryanization" to disadvantage the Austrian plants that had previously supplied the region. In July 1938, the CA bought out the Jewish-owned shares for 1 million RM, and the enterprise was subsequently called the "Ostmark Keramik."[59] Director Friedl was named president of the supervisory board, while Salvenmoser became general director.

The Ostmark Keramik subsequently enjoyed modest growth, acquiring the Znaim/Znojmo branch of the firm of Ditmar-Urbach in Prague in 1939. This was also an Aryanization, and the acquisition resulted in an increase of the company's capital from 800,000 RM to 4.1 million RM.[60] In general, as might be expected, the company was adversely affected by the war, its workforce being reduced from 803 in 1944 to 688 and then 115. Salvenmoser, a very ambitious man, may have been somewhat frustrated by the modest situation of Ostmark Keramik and, in the winter of 1944, accepted an invitation from the CA to serve on the management board of

---

[58] Ibid., ÖSPAG, 09/06/02, G. Payer to Kurt Grimm, May 16, 1946.
[59] BA-CA, CA-V, CA working committee meeting, July 15, 1938.
[60] See BA-CA, CA-IB, ÖSPAG, 09/06/02, report of Jan. 28, 1946, and ibid., ÖSPAG, 09/09, supervisory board meeting of Dec. 8, 1939.

Stölzle Glas AG and almost immediately proposed a merger of Ostmark Keramik and Stölzle
under his management.[61] Nothing came of this
proposal, and Salvenmoser's months at Stölzle
and at Ostmark Keramik were numbered in any
case. Obviously he was not the right person to
undo the Aryanization he had devised and preside over the restitution to the former owners,
now American citizens. This was subsequently
hammered out in the early postwar years with
the CA retaining an interest in what became
Österreichische Keramik.

4. ÖSTERREICHISCHE BETTFEDERNFABRIKS-AG

Yet another firm was added to the CA
industrial concern in the race to Aryanize
in 1938, and this was the Österreichische
Bettfedernfabriks-AG, to be renamed the
Östmarkische Bettfedernfabriks-AG in 1939.
The company had been founded in 1921, the
chief shareholder being Fritz Jokl, who was
Jewish, and who had teamed up with Heinrich
and Gisela Gans, also Jews. The Anglo-Austrian
Bank also became a shareholder at the founding and served as a supplier of credit until its
place was taken by the CA after the CA takeover of the Anglo-Austrian Bank. At the time
of the Anschluss, Jokl held 3,050 shares (20.3
percent) and the Gans family 2,806 shares (19
percent), and the CA held 3,494 (23 percent)
of the 15,000 shares.[62] The remaining shares
were held either by relations of the chief Jewish
shareholders or scattered small investors. It is
worth noting that the CA was not only the
house bank of Bettfedern, which processed
feathers for bedding and furniture, but had also
served as a 28.6 percent shareholder and creditor of the Bettwarenfabrik Adolf Gans AG, 70
percent of whose shares were held by Heinrich

and Karl Gans. In this case, however, the Gans
brothers took care of their own Aryanization,
so to speak, by offering to sell their shares to
Walter Hiedler of the Mercurbank, and Hiedler
asked the CA for an option on its shares in the
Bettwarenfabrik Adolf Gans. Because the latter
had not been at all profitable to the CA and
Hiedler, an influential Party man supported by
Rafelsberger, would control a large majority,
the CA decided against taking any interest in
this Aryanization and sold its shares to Hiedler
in April 1939 after he had settled with the Gans
brothers.[63]

Bettfedern, however, was another matter
because Jokl was the largest shareholder and
also served as general director. He immediately went on leave in late March 1938 and was
to end up in the United States. His second in
command for many years, Rudolf Hörandner,
took over as administrator of the company and
presided over the Aryanization of its personnel,
including the termination of Jokl's contract.
He subsequently formally replaced Jokl.[64] The
most important development, however, was the
Aryanization of the ownership of the company so that it could do business effectively. On
June 1, the CA received permission from the
Property Transfer Bureau to buy the Jewish
shares, and on June 15, it informed Hörandner
that the CA now controlled 80 percent of
the shares. Further purchases were to increase
the bank's stake to 92 percent. In any case,
Bettfedern could now stamp "Aryan Firm"
between two Swastikas just below its letterhead
and identify itself where useful as belonging to
the CA concern.[65]

Needless to say, it was very rare for Jews to
retain the monies they received from the sale of
their shares to Aryanizers. In this case, there is a
very precise record of what happened to Jokl's
liquid assets before he departed Germany in
1939. His blocked account at the CA was transformed into an emigrant blocked account. He

---

[61] See ibid., Universale, 16/09, Salvenmoser to Friedl,
Feb. 22, 1944.
[62] BA-CA, CA-IB, Gans, 02/02, report to Heller of
April 5, 1938 places the distribution of shares at
50.2 percent for Jokl and Gans and 23.3 percent
for the CA, which differs only slightly from the
Columbus Project Report on Aryanizations.

[63] See Columbus Project Report on Aryanizations.
[64] See BA-CA, CA-IB, Gans, 02/02, Hörandner to
Fiala of the CA, Sept. 26, 1938, and Hörandner to
Jokl, Sept. 1 and Sept. 19, 1938.
[65] Ibid., CA to Bettfedern, June 15, 1938, and
Bettfedern to Fiala, Aug. 3, 1938.

received 40,650.43 RM for the sale of his 3,050 shares to the CA and received another 13,452.48 RM from other sources, bringing the total to 54,340.03 RM. Before his departure, he was forced to pay 15,987 RM in Reich Flight Tax, 11,609.70 RM for the Jewish Assets Tax, 7,752.77 RM for tax arrears, and 4,806 RM for the emigration fee. Thus, 40,155.47 RM, or 73.9 percent of his account, went into government coffers. From what was left, he paid 5,544.56 RM for moving and transport of his goods, 4,188 RM for train and ship expenses, and 4,806 RM for living and other expenses. His total expenditures thus amounted to 54,340.03 RM. He had also spent 40 RM in bank charges, 1 RM for each cash withdrawal, 10 RM for transforming his blocked account into an emigrant blocked account, and 1.50 RM for the reporting of his bank assets. If it was something of a miracle that he ended up with a positive bank balance of 277.12 RM, the explanation was the 1.25 percent[66] per annum interest he received on his account. Aryanization in such a case, therefore, was not simply the forced sale of assets but also a prelude to the despoliation of the seller.

The successful Aryanization of Bettfedern, thus conducted at the ultimate expense of its chief shareholder, meant not only that the company could do business safely and with the powerful backing of the CA but also that it could turn its attention to the elimination of its Austrian Jewish competition. A notable case was the Jewish firm of Leo Schotten in Mattersburg. The firm was in ill repute for acting as a front for the illegal sale of feathers by itinerant peddlers, but it would have been placed under the control of a commissarial administrator in any case. The person in question, a Herr Reisinger, had approached Bettfedern with an offer to sell its machinery and inventory in June 1938. When Bettfedern took up the offer after its Aryanization, however, Reisinger withdrew his offer and, very much to Hörnander's distress, announced that he was hoping to take over Schotten himself with the help of an interested party from the old Reich. To the objection

that Austrian rather than German firms were to be favored in such Aryanizations, Reisinger responded that the takeover would be done under his name. In effect, he would be acting as a front for German interests. Hörnander found this in every way objectionable, as he explained to Heinrich Fiala, the CA manager and member of the Bettfedern administrative council who looked after Bettfedern affairs for the CA. The trade association of which Bettfedern was a member had inquired with the Property Transfer Bureau about what was to be done with the smaller firms making feather bedding and was told that the small ones would be shut down except in such cases as Bettfedern had an interest in taking over them or their equipment. Bettfedern called upon the trade association to complain to the Property Transfer Bureau and insist that Reisinger be barred from taking over Schotten. It appears no sale took place, nor was the machinery and inventory sold to Bettfedern. The problem dragged on into the fall of 1939, at which time Reisinger was arrested, probably in connection with corrupt practices, and another Party member, Gustav Franzl, took charge at Schotten. At the same time, the trade association recommended shutting down Schotten, while Bettfedern again appealed to the Property Transfer Bureau to approve the sale of the plant and its equipment and inventory to Bettfedern. The appeal was successful; Schotten returned after the war to claim his machinery.[67]

The development of Bettfedern between 1938 and 1945 owed much to its ownership by and association with the CA. This was most evident in the acquisition of the land and facilities of the Gebr. Schiel AG Seidenfabrik in Ober-Waltersdorf in the spring of 1939. Prior to this time, Bettfedern had been renting its factory facilities, and its expansion depended on getting facilities of its own as well as acquiring the machinery it needed. The availability of the shut-down plant of Gebr. Schiel in Ober-Waltersdorf appeared to answer this problem because the company, whose headquarters

---

[66] Figures presented in the Columbus Project Report on "Aryanizations."

[67] BA-CA, CA-IB, Gans, 02/02, Bettfedern to Fiala, Aug. 8, 1938; Bettfedern to Property Transfer Bureau, Oct. 18, 1939.

were in Prague, was in the Deutsche Bank's sphere of interest, and the bank was anxious to sell the property and buildings to increase Schiel's liquidity. The major obstacle was that the Reich Wheat Bureau and the Ministry for Food and Agriculture in Berlin had sequestered the buildings to store wheat, and while Bettfedern was prepared to buy the facilities, the sequester would have to be lifted before it could do so. Director Pohle of the Deutsche Bank asked the CA to use its influence to remedy this situation. The CA's efforts to accomplish this from Vienna, however, proved a failure, and ultimately Fiala and Hörandner traveled to Berlin and, with the help of the Deutsche Bank, gained direct access to the authorities. Hörandner argued that the existing facilities in St. Marx were too small and insufficient and that it would be impossible to procure the construction materials needed to build a new plant. The Schiel facilities at Ober-Waltersdorf were thus the only feasible solution to the Bettfedern situation; Fiala and Hörandner succeeded in convincing the Berlin authorities to lift their sequester and permit purchase of the Schiel facilities.[68]

The other major difficulty for the firm that only became worse in the course of the war was the procurement of raw materials, that is, feathers. The chief sources of supply were Poland and Hungary, although there were some imports from Yugoslavia and Bulgaria as well. The CA began to use its branch in Budapest to make contact with Hungarian suppliers as early as August 1938, and this source became more important after June 1940 when the supply of feathers, with the exception of those from Hungary, was handled from a central agency in Berlin. Nevertheless, Hörandner, who was a very aggressive representative of his company's interests, continuously complained that the Austrian firms, especially his own, were disadvantaged by their treatment from Berlin in both the quantity and quality of what they received. Despite labor and raw materials shortages,

however, Bettfedern emerged as one of the five most important companies of its type in the Reich, largely thanks to the Ober-Waltersdorf plant, which was financed primarily with CA credits. In March 1943, Fiala was able to report that the company had been declared important for the war effort because it worked exclusively for vital domestic consumer requirements, especially in areas hit by air raids and despite the fact that it was working at only one-third capacity because of raw materials shortages.[69] It is worth remarking, however, that some of the raw material used came from what today must be viewed as disturbing sources. In 1944, Fiala noted that the company was processing war spoils from the east.[70] It is likely that some of the feathers from Poland came from depots of Jewish goods or the products of Jewish labor. Even more telling was the demand of the Russian occupation authorities in September 1946 for deliveries as reparations because feathers bought in 1942 from the Berlin central agency had been plundered in Russia.[71] The major restitution issues after 1945, however, involved the former Jewish owners who claimed compensation for what, since 1938, was more than 90 percent owned by the CA.

5. ARYANIZATIONS AND THE CA WOOD AND PAPIER INTERESTS: JAC. SCHNABEL & CO.

The CA had been heavily engaged in the wood and paper business, and this continued to be the case after the Anschluss. It became involved in a number of very significant Aryanizations, sometimes directly, sometimes indirectly. Its most important direct and complete takeover of a Jewish company in this field was Jac. Schnabel & Co., where the CA ended up acquiring a

---

68 Ibid., Gans, 02/04-05, Pohle to the CA, April 17, 1939, and Bettfedern to Schiel, April 5, 1939, and memorandum by Fiala, May 11, 1939.

69 Ibid., Gans, 02/02, CA Vienna to CA Budapest, Aug. 31, 1938, and ibid., Gans, 02/04-05, meeting of Nov. 4, 1940 and related documents. See also BA-CA, CA-V, report of Fiala of March 23, 1943 to the CA working committee.

70 See Columbus Project Report on "Aryanizations."

71 BA-CA, CA-IB, Gans, 02/06, Österreichische Bettfedernfabriks-AG to the Judicial Section of the Russian Section for Reparations, Sept. 12, 1946.

formerly Jewish-owned company despite its initial reluctance to do more than sell the shares in its possession. Of less significance was the role of the CA in the Aryanization of the factories connected with Adolf Leitner & Brüder, which were finally sold off to an interested party by the CA.[72]

The Schnabl firm had been founded in 1859 and produced a wide range of paper products, including colored paper, cigarette paper, and playing cards. Jacob Schnabl had died in 1937; his heir and his wife, Margarete Schnabl, served as chief partner in the company, which also had four other non-Aryan partners. At the time of the Anschluss, Schnabl employed 244 workers and owed the CA about 1.5 million RM in legitimate debts. The company was placed under an administrator, Pg. Hermann Aldenhoven, but the CA found the situation "insupportable because the firm cannot work as non-Aryan and the Creditanstalt is threatened with losing its money."[73] For all intents and purposes, Schnabl was so indebted to the CA that it belonged to the bank anyway. The CA, therefore, proposed to buy out the owner with a payment of 30,000 RM so that she could pay her inheritance taxes. It could have pressed its claim in court on the grounds that the company had no capital at all, but that would have taken too much time and the delay could have destroyed the company because it would still be Jewish. The CA, therefore, asked the Property Transfer Bureau to let the CA replace its commissar and create a situation in which the company ceased to be Jewish.

It was successful in this effort, and on August 4, 1938, the CA and its subsidiary company, the Vereinigte Papier-Industrie AG (VPI), which acted as a sales organization for the CA paper concern, became a partner in the cigarette paper division of Schnabl with an investment of 20,000 RM, while the CA itself put up 300,000 RM so as to become a partner. Margarete Schnabl was to receive 32,119 RM to pay the inheritance tax on Jacob Schnabel's estate, and what remained was to be divided between herself and the silent Jewish partners. In return, she was to surrender her partnership.[74]

Rather more difficult was the question of what to do with the company. Initially, the CA appeared quite ready to sell at a loss. Potential purchasers turned up with projects to dismantle the company and pay for the parts they appropriated. The Association for the Paper and Pulp Processing Industry was anxious to shut down the company altogether so as to make way for smaller competitors.[75] By the fall of 1938, however, Schnabl was becoming increasingly attractive as an investment for the CA, especially because it was doing good business despite the lowering of prices imposed by the government. Not only were there promising results, but Aldenhoven, who was now managing the company for the CA and others connected with the company, seems to have taken the initiative in promoting its development under CA auspices. In a letter to the Vienna NSDAP of October 19, 1938, he pointed out that Friedl and he had agreed on the need to oppose any plan to shut down the company, and Aldenhoven noted that the CA had increased its grants of credits in order to ensure its undisturbed progress despite the fact that one could not expect it to meet expectations of normal private sector profitability. He was infuriated when an official of the Paper and Pulp Industry Association pointed out that a German competitor might buy out Schnabl and close it down and suggested that "German industrialists have many Reichsmark and flee from the Reichsmark and are therefore willing to invest significantly more in objects than they are worth." As Aldenhoven indignantly remarked in a very denunciatory tone, "Is it compatible with National Socialist basic

---

[72] The paper and wood industries and the Aryanizations in this branch are discussed in detail by Peter Melichar, in: Felber et al., Ökonomie der Arisierung 2, ch. 4. Other aspects of the CA wood and paper holdings will be discussed in the next section in connection with the Leykam-Josefsthal AG für Papier- und Druckindustrie.

[73] BA-CA, CA-IB, Samum Schnabl, 22/01-02, Heller and Friedl to the VVSt, May 25, 1938. The actual amount paid to Margarete Schnabl for taxes was 32,119 RM.

[74] Ibid., Protocol of Aug. 4, 1938.

[75] Ibid., memorandum for Friedl, June 30, 1938.

principles to shut down the economic assets of a plant with a retinue of 250 which can be very greatly built up in order to protect weaker enterprises?" He concluded by strongly recommending that Schnabl be made part of the CA concern.[76]

In a revealing memorandum of January 31, 1939, almost certainly composed by Aldenhoven, he not only claimed Schnabl was overcoming the difficulties of the past but also proposed that it improve its situation by taking over the assets of the Viennese firm of Dr.R. Pollak, which was scheduled to be Aryanized. He pointed out that the company had a modern plant that, however, was not fully exploited. This was partially blamed on the bad economic conditions of the previous years, but primarily on the insufficient funds of the previous Jewish owner, which was the precondition for full use of the facilities and also "on a measure of profitability that was to some extent secured through the methods of the Jewish liberalist economic period (cartels, price conventions and the like)."[77] Manifestly, this was a rather odd notion of liberal economics, but the real point the author was trying to make was that Schnabl had succeeded in bringing down prices and making itself competitive but that it remained endangered as the only high-quality paper producer in the Ostmark. The competition in the old Reich was anxious to shut Schnabl down, and this would damage both the economy and labor market of the Ostmark. Rationalization, therefore, was essential, "but this cannot only be carried out from the perspective of the profitability of the businessman, but it also is a necessity which lies completely along the lines of the national economic and social principles and strivings of the Four Year Plan."[78] Although it was important to increase productivity, Schnabl was not seeking to buy a new factory but rather to have its plant in Heligenstadt

take over the machines and workers of the soon-to-be-liquidated Pollak firm. This would permit the creation of a large Ostmark plant "while, on the other hand, factory buildings and locations that were previously used by small plants could not survive in the long-run would become available and, given the shortage of such objects, would become freed for more useful purposes."[79] Schnabl, therefore, had expressed its interest in taking over the machinery and workers at Pollak to the VVSt, and was doing so by skillfully using the rubbery language of National Socialist economics along with anti-Semitic barbs, all of which combined with a strong appeal to Ostmark economic interests against the rapacious firms from the old Reich. Thus, the Aryanized had been transformed into Aryanizer in this incredible display of Darwinian business practice.

The actual takeover of Schnabl by the CA came to full fruition only in August 1941, when the Statthalter's office approved the agreement with Margarete Schnabl and was willing to spare the CA payment of an Aryanization fee and certain other charges. A change of name was required, however, and the company was renamed "Samum Vereinigte Papierindustrie K.G., Wien." At the same time, it expanded further by buying up the Breitenau plant of the Leykam-Josefsthal AG für Papier- und Druckindustrie, which needed cash for its investments in Poland. Whether Leykam actually took over the Breitenau facilities is unclear, however, because Samum subsequently provided the facilities to the Wiener Neustädter Flugzeugwerke at the behest of the Reich Ministry for Armaments and War Production.

Aldenhoven and the CA continued to struggle for Samum against more formidable odds during the war. In late 1943, it was put on a list of plants to be shut down after Speer's Central Planning Office had requested such a list from the Reich Bureau for Paper. Aldenhoven pulled as many strings as he could in Berlin to get Samum off the list, using his contacts to gain contracts for cigarette paper from one bureau and gaining support from another

---

[76] Ibid., Aldenhoven to the NSDAP Vienna, Oct. 19, 1938, Samum Schnabl, 22/03-04. See also Felber, et. al, *Ökonomie der Arisierung*, Pt. 2, p. 351, n143.

[77] BA-CA, CA-IB, Samum Schnabl, 22/01-02, memorandum, probably for the CA, Jan. 31, 1939.

[78] Ibid.

[79] Ibid.

bureau to declare that Samum was essential for a special kind of paper.[80] The struggle continued into 1944, when efforts by old Reich industrial interests to close down Samum foundered on the gratitude felt for its surrender of the Breitenau plants mentioned earlier as well as on Samum's continued stress on its indispensability.[81]

Protecting Samum's plants against Allied bombers, however, proved much more difficult, and it suffered severe damage before the war came to an end and Margarete Schnabl and the other Jewish partners could claim restitution. She was to own 25.5 percent of the shares of what now was known as Samum AG, vormals Schnabl & Co. The CA and Vereinigte-Papier Industrie held 51 percent, and the remaining silent Jewish partners received the rest.[82]

When it came to the Aryanization of the Leitner family interests, the CA played the kind of intermediary role it had originally wished to assume with respect to Jac. Schnabl & Co. The Leitners, who had long taken loans from the CA and had used the marketing services of the CA-owned Vereinigte Papier Industrie, originally owned five factories: the Ybbsthaler Pappenfabriken Adolf Leitner & Bruder, which had plants in Lunz am See and Hollenstein; the Timmersdorfer Holzstoff- und Pappenfabrik Emerich Kren & Co. with plants in Timmersdorf and Möderbrugg; and the Mürzzuschlager Holzstoff- und Pappenfabriks-GmbH, which operated a cardboard factory in Mürzzuschlag. These factories sold to wholesalers in Austria and also did considerable export business. In December 1938, the CA placed them in a holding company, the Pappen- und Holzstofferzeugungs-GmbH. The VVSt had sold the factories to the CA for 400,000 RM – the book value was 844,449 RM – in August 1938. The CA was to act as trustee for the factories with the right to lease them to the Pappen- und

Holzstofferzeugung-GmbH for production purposes. The CA had taken over the plants in order to collect on the debts owed the CA for the Leitner family and to prevent the plants from being put out of business as Jewish enterprises. At the time of the sale, the state commissar for the private economy had made it a condition that the CA sell only to a buyer or buyers approved by the VVSt and that every effort be made to sell the factories to a single buyer. The CA would also be obligated to pay an Aryanization fee. While the VVSt retained jurisdiction over the ultimate sale, the Leitner enterprises were among the cases taken over by the Kontrollbank, which thus played some role in the effort to sell off these assets.[83]

Finding a buyer proved difficult. A Berlin businessman, Robert Martin, was prepared to purchase the Lunz am See and Hollenstein plants, which were the best of the factories, but he did not really have the necessary means. Things began to look up when two potential Austrian purchasers, von Behr, who was already active in the business, and an immigrant from the Tyrol named Josef Zuegg, appeared on the scene. The VVSt wanted the two to join together in taking over all the plants, but both balked at the Aryanization fee. Ultimately, Zuegg was prepared to purchase all the factories if he was relieved of the fee. At the same time, the CA, which had considerable losses because of poor export prices, felt it had paid too much for the plants and wanted some consideration from the RWM. Kastner of the Kontrollbank was very friendly to a solution that eliminated the Aryanization fee as well.[84] The end result was that the CA came out of the arrangement with a 60,000 RM profit in addition to the elimination of the old debts successfully achieved through its trusteeship. No Aryanization fee was paid, and the Leitners had monies on their blocked accounts from the initial sale to the CA that could be used to pay their various taxes and impositions.

[80] Ibid., memorandum by Lanz of the CA, Oct. 2, 1943.
[81] Ibid., Samum to Friedl, Jan. 11, 1944.
[82] Felber et al., *Ökonomie der Arisierung*, pt. 2, p. 356.

[83] BA-CA, CA-IB, Pappe- und Holzstoff, 41/01, memorandum by Fiala, Aug. 16, 1940.
[84] Ibid., CA to VVSt, Oct. 6, 1939, and memorandum of Feb. 9, 1940.

6. BUNZL & BIACH, BOSSI HUTFABRIKS-
AKTIENGESELLSCHAFT, AND EBREICHSDORFER
FILZHUTFABRIK S. & J FRAENKEL AG

Of all the Aryanizations carried out by the National Socialist regime in Austria and in particular by the Kontrollbank, that of the concern of Bunzl & Biach was undoubtedly the most complicated and, for the CA, certainly a rather frustrating experience. The full story, which certainly deserves telling, is beyond the scope of this study.[85] This discussion will concentrate on two issues: first, the general course of the Aryanization and the role of the CA in its development and outcome, and second, the development of the CA concern's hat industry, which was related to the Bunzl holdings.

Founded in 1854 in Pressburg/Bratislava, the firm moved to Vienna in 1881 and made its headquarters there in 1883. Having withstood the war, inflation, and depression, the concern was run at the time of the Anschluss by the six Bunzl brothers: Martin, Robert, Hugo, Emil, Felix, and George. Its finances were handled by two holding companies in Zug Switzerland, Raccolta AG and Tafag AG. It had become a large, multinational concern that dealt with wood, paper, pulp, rag, and textile products. In Austria, it had major works in Ortmann (Lower Austria), where it produced paper, wool, and cotton products and also had hat manufacturing facilities; it ran a major paper factory in Wattens (Tyrol); its Viennese plants sorted rags. Yet another important holding in Austria was the Papierfabrik Lenzing, which had been part of the CA concern until it was acquired by Bunzl & Biach in 1935–1936 with the purpose of making it a major cellulose producer. In London, Bunzl & Biach marketed cotton and wool, while in Czechoslovakia and Hungary it sorted, processed, and marketed rag products. It also had facilities in Yugoslavia and Italy.[86]

As will be shown, there was great interest in Aryanizing Bunzl & Biach intact, but it did not prove possible to prevent the Papierfabrik Lenzing from being taken over by the Thuringian National Socialists running the Thüringische Zellwolle AG. This created some complications for the CA because it had provided large long-term credit to Bunzl & Biach of 5.5 million Schilling in February 1937, to which was added a 6 million Schilling credit in September.[87] It also, however, created complications for the Aryanizers of Lenzing, who "bought" Lenzing from the CA in May 1938. The financing of Lenzing was then taken over by a consortium whose chief members were the Dresdner Bank and the Länderbank Wien, which not only financed the expansion originally planned by Bunzl & Biach but also the refunding of expended credits to the CA.[88]

The CA certainly was interested in seeing its loans repaid, and it was later to have good reason to be glad to be relieved of its engagement in Lenzing. Nonetheless, the question of what role, if any, the CA would play in the Aryanization of Bunzl & Biach was of no small interest to the bank. This was clearly demonstrated in a letter from General Director Heller to Rafelsberger of June 3, 1938, in which he informed Rafelsberger that, following the takeover of Lenzing, the leadership of Bunzl & Biach had approached the management of the Leykam-Josefsthal Actiengesellschaft für Papier- und Druck-Industrie, which belonged to the CA concern, and proposed that Leykam join forces in making a proposal for the Aryanization of the Ortmann plants. Leykam had agreed to collaborate in investigating whether such a takeover by the Leykam firm might be desirable through an examination of the situation at Ortmann. Because the Deutsche Revisions- und Treuhand AG had undertaken an assessment of the entire Bunzl & Biach concern,

---

85 The Bunzl & Biach case, insofar as the Länderbank Wien was involved, is dealt with in detail in Chapter 6, pp. 533–541. See also, Felber et al., *Ökonomie der Arisierung*, pt. 2, pp. 311–335.

86 See ÖStA/AdR, Bürckel Materie, Box 12, File 25, the organization chart. Lenzing already appears as belonging to Bunzl & Biach in the 1936 issue of *Compass*.

87 BA-CA, CA-V, Board of Management meetings of Feb. 13, Sept. 2, and Sept. 17, 1937.

88 On the arrangements between the CA and Bunzl & Biach to terminate the former's credits, see management board meeting, June 1, 1938, ibid. On the role of the Dresdner and Länderbank banks, see Chapter 5, p. 464.

including Ortmann, in connection with the takeover of Lenzing, Heller was hoping that Rafelsberger would place this report at the disposal of Leykam.[89]

Rafelsberger and those charged with the Aryanization of Bunzl & Biach, however, had other plans in mind, and what would be tantamount to a CA-Leykam takeover of the jewels in the concern's crown in cooperation with Bunzl & Biach did not number among them. From the viewpoint of Rafelsberger in Vienna and the authorities in Berlin, three considerations were paramount. First, Bunzl & Biach employed a substantial number of workers and employees, and their livelihood depended on the successful Aryanization of the Austrian concern. Ortmann, for example, employed between 1,100 and 1,200 persons and was responsible for turning an otherwise industrially backward region into a prosperous one. Second, the concern was simply too big for any single purchaser to have the 300–400 million RM that would be required to purchase it as a single entity. Third, the concern was a major exporter, most of the production going to England and abroad but a great deal also to other European countries. The foreign exchange thus gained was of vital interest to the Reich, while the international connections of the Bunzl family were essential for the retention of this international business. To break up Bunzl & Biach in the manner envisaged by the Leykam-CA group was possibly to tear asunder this valuable international complex and open the way for a Jewish anti-German coalition of Bunzl & Biach branches and friends. In short, one had to Aryanize Bunzl & Biach while keeping its operations going and securing the flow of foreign exchange. In order to attain this goal, one had to work with the Bunzl brothers while forcing them to come to acceptable terms.

These considerations played a substantial role in the special mix of brutality and solicitude with which the family and some of the higher-ranking personnel were treated. On the one hand, as in so many Aryanization cases,

incarceration of family members in Dachau was important in "persuading" Jewish owners to cooperate. Two family members were sent to Dachau, Max Bunzl and Hans Bunzl, the son of Emil Bunzl. Max Bunzl was released at the behest of Rafelsberger on the advice of those he had appointed to handle the Aryanization; Hans was murdered in the camp. Max had been twice arrested. The first time he was let go, much to the irritation of the National Socialist activists at Ortmann, but then he was arrested again and sent to Dachau, only to be released again. At the end of 1938, Rafelsberger's office was struggling to get other officials of Bunzl & Biach released by the Gestapo, which was refusing to do anything about the situation. There was in fact much activist resentment at Ortmann by the manner in which the Bunzls continued to run the concern along with Central Director Hans Schoenberg, while the commissarial administrators looked the other way or actually approved. Indeed, the Party commissars appointed by Rafelsberger's office appeared to be friendly to the Jews.[90]

Especially suspect was Privatdozent Dr. Ernst Hatheyer, a young economist appointed to negotiate with the Bunzl brothers, Schoenberg, and their lawyer. At a meeting on July 4, 1938, they developed a complicated program for the Aryanization of Bunzl & Biach.[91] Under the very convoluted arrangement Hatheyer concocted in this initially nonbinding discussion with his Jewish interlocutors, the Bunzl brothers were to give up 76 percent of the shares of Bunzl & Biach in Vienna, and 50 percent of their two holding companies in Zug. The Tafag Holding Co., which had been connected to the Lenzing

---

[89] ÖStA/AdR, MfWuA, VVSt, Industrie, Box 336, Zl. 288, Vol. I, Heller to Rafelsberger, June 3, 1938.

[90] See ÖStA/AdR, Bürckel Materie, Box 12, File 25, the various critical reports sent to Rafelsberger, May 24, 1938, and June 7, 1938; complaint by Rafelsberger's office to Bürckel, Dec. 12, 1938. See also Felber et al., *Ökonomie der Arisierung*, pt. 2, p. 323. See also Gregor Spuhler et al., *"Arisierungen" in Österreich und ihre Bezüge zur Schweiz. Beitrag zur Forschung*. Veröffentlichungen der Unabhängigen Expertenkommission Schweiz (= UEK) – Zweiter Weltkrieg. Vol. 20 (Zurich 2002), pp. 120–126.

[91] ÖStA/AdR, Bürckel Materie, Box 12, File 25, memorandum on meeting of July 4, 1938.

company, was to be liquidated, and the funds in the two holding companies consolidated into the Raccolta AG. The Bunzls were also to give up their villas and private property at Ortmann. The Bunzl brothers were to be allowed to have a 3 million RM fund at their disposition in the Reich to cover legal and other expenses as well as half their funds in Switzerland. The Vienna Group, as the Aryanized concern in Vienna was now called, was to pay the Reich Flight Tax and the various other costs and fees involved in the Aryanization as well as income and corporation taxes. At the same time, the Bunzl brothers were to retain 24 percent of the Vienna Bunzl & Biach shares, and 50 percent of the shares of the two Swiss holding companies. They were to be entitled to at least a 4 percent dividend on the Vienna shares, plus additional dividends should they issued.

The essential purposes of these terms, which were obviously not typical for Aryanizations, were made quite explicit in the protocol of the discussion. They were "the maintenance of the Bunzl & Biach concern as a single unit and to maintain it as a large source of foreign exchange for the German Reich. This goal that is being sought through this arrangement is only to be attained with the collaboration of the Bunzl brothers. It is above all necessary that the four Bunzl brothers and Central Director Schoenberg, who wish to emigrate abroad, make this possible in that they can work in the interest of exports to England or to Switzerland. In order to successfully organize this task, the additional advisory collaboration of these persons in confines of the new independent Vienna AG is also unconditionally necessary. In order to carry this out, the State and Party agencies will have to give the named persons the possibility of repeated travelling into and out of the German Reich."[92]

In addition to this cooperation, the Bunzl brothers were also to give the Vienna Group a four-year option to buy out the 24 percent shareholding of the Bunzl brothers as well as the 50 percent Swiss holding, and also to agree not to have stakes in the branches of the

concern for at least five years. Furthermore, the Bunzl family and Schoenberg were to draw salaries for their services abroad, and to have their moving costs and various other expenses paid by the Vienna Group. Thus, the Bunzl brothers and their chief executive officer were now turned into reasonably well-paid employees of the Aryanized concern.

Although the actual terms of these discussions were probably unknown to the Party district leadership, the Party officials nevertheless had the feeling that the interests of the Party were being neglected and that no effort was made to get rid of the Jews who continued to be employed by the concern. Hatheyer showed understanding for this position, which he considered to be justified, but went on to point out "that the firm of Bunzl & Biach AG is a widely spread international enterprise and that he must view it as his task to lay down the broad line to be followed, so that an Aryanization can take place bit by bit without the existence of the enterprise and especially its foreign connections being disturbed."[93]

The basic structure of the agreement developed by Hatheyer was maintained when the Kontrollbank was created in August 1938 and took over the Bunzl & Biach Aryanization.[94] Maintaining the special character of these arrangements was no easy task. When the RWM, for example, ordered that no further payments in foreign currency be made to Jewish employees who either went as firm representatives abroad or worked for foreign firms, Hatheyer immediately complained and warned that most of the raw materials used by the concern were in Jewish hands and that the concern would be paralyzed under the conditions mandated by the RWM. He feared that the "already existing bad mood and irritation of our Jewish foreign representatives, upon whose good will we are still often dependent, will increase further."[95] Hatheyer also appealed to Bürckel and Rafelsberger, proudly vaunting his achievements, above all the recovery of the concern's

92 Ibid.

93 Ibid., memorandum on meeting of July 11, 1938.
94 Ibid., memorandum, Aug. 24, 1938.
95 Ibid., Hayether to RWM, Nov. 25, 1938.

exports in the second half of 1938 and the accompanying elimination of Jewish employees in the Ostmark plants and offices. He received strong support from both men.[96] An even thornier issue developed after the November pogrom and the initiation of the Atonement Tax on Jewish assets. Here again Hatheyer, with the support of all the major Party and state offices in Vienna, successfully appealed to the Finance Ministry not to sacrifice the incentives that had been given to the Bunzls to cooperate in using their name and associations to promote German exports for foreign exchange. He warned that the contract made with the Bunzls would thus be violated and found unacceptable, and that employing the arbitration provisions provided for in the contract would most likely backfire. Furthermore, he felt compelled to remark "on the loyal manner in which the Bunzl brothers as Jews in the critical period (September until November 1938) and even after the proclamation of the Jewish laws and decrees did not allow themselves even once to be pulled away from the active position in favour of German exports to which they had obligated themselves contractually."[97]

These various concessions to the Bunzls, whatever their benefits in terms of sales for foreign exchange, had turned the sale of the shares held by the Kontrollbank into a very difficult proposition. The shares could not be and were not intended to be in the permanent possession of the Kontrollbank, whose obligation it was to sell the shares of the concern to an Aryan purchaser. The Kontrollbank had bought the shares for 3 million RM but had also had to pay 9.5 million RM in Reich Flight taxes, so that the shares could not be sold off for less than 12.5–13 million RM. Furthermore, a prospective buyer was bound to insist that the Aryanization fee along with other forgiven taxes and fees remain forgiven by the Ministries of Economics and Finance. Finally, the approval

of any sale would have to come from Berlin, where Kehrl would play the decisive role. He was, however, likely to follow the advice of Ministerial Councilor Friedrich Bauer, who was charged with overseeing the spun products and paper industries.[98]

This set of circumstances was fatal to the ambitions of the CA. While the attempt to take over Ortmann via Leykam had obviously failed, the Kontrollbank holding was viewed by the CA as a compensation for the losses of its shipping interests – Comos and the DDSG – to the Hermann Göring-Werke. At a meeting of Olscher, Hasslacher, and Heller in June 1940, the shares were viewed as "a valuable supplementation of the present engagement of the Creditanstalt in the paper industry." There was also talk of appointing Kastner, who would be in need of a job once the Kontrollbank was liquidated, to the Bunzl & Biach management board.[99] In the late fall of 1940, the CA again pressed its claims, proposing that it take over the trusteeship of the concern once the Kontrollbank was formally liquidated at the end of the year. Kehrl initially appeared friendly to the idea, which he had negotiated with Fischböck, although Bauer favored a consortium of the CA and Länderbank Wien.[100] In the meantime, a number of firms and concerns had expressed interest in Bunzl & Biach, but they shied away from taking over so variegated a firm and wanted to slice away the parts that interested them. Kehrl, however, was quite insistent that the enterprise not be carved up, but he had fewer objections to turning the concern over to a consortium. At the turn of 1940–1941, the initiative seemed to lie with the Dresdner Bank, which was pushing one of its clients, the Berlin automobile dealer Eduard Winter, for the position of chief shareholder.[101] The Länderbank and the CA were to be equal

96 Ibid., Hayether to Bürckel and to Rafelsberger, Nov. 30, 1938.
97 Ibid., Hayether petition to Finance Ministry, Dec. 14, 1938, and Finance Ministry to Bürckel, March 13, 1939.
98 BA-CA, CA-IB, Bunzl & Biach, 33/01, unsigned memorandum of Sept. 19, 1940.
99 DB, P 6503, Meeting of June 15, 1940; BA-CA, CA-IB, Climax, 34/02, memorandum for Joham, May 26, 1940.
100 Dresdner Bank (= DrB), Nr. 30316–2001, Minutes of Oct. 7 and Dec. 6, 1940.
101 The Winter candidacy is discussed in detail in Chapter 6, pp. 534–541.

minority members of a consortium headed by Winter. The CA made clear that it would have no part of such an arrangement, and it apparently persuaded Rafelsberger to tell the RWM as much as well as to argue the case that the CA had been the old bank connection of Bunzl & Biach, that it was the first to present itself as a potential purchaser, and that it was now prepared to accept a 60 percent share of the capital while leaving the rest to whomever wished to acquire it. Rafelsberger made clear that he viewed the CA position as "not unjustified" and as a matter of great significance for the future of Vienna.[102]

At the same time, the CA persisted in its own efforts to get a substantial piece of the enterprise, and in its negotiations with the RWM for the sale of its shipping interests, the RWM seems to have expressed willingness for the CA to receive at least a 30 percent share of Bunzl & Biach as part of its compensation.[103] While Kehrl and others blocked the claim on 60 percent, the "Viennese" interests expressed by Rafelsberger ultimately blocked the Dresdner Bank's attempt to push the Winter candidacy. Kastner seems to have turned against Winter, and the arrangement with Winter was also rejected by the Ostmark Statthalter, Baldur von Schirach. There could be no question about the fact that the CA had engaged in a considerable amount of political string-pulling to undermine the Dresdner Bank project. In early July 1941, Länderbank director Leonard Wolzt reported to Karl Rasche of the Dresdner Bank that he had a "friendly discussion with the Creditanstalt" in which he inquired whether they were willing to divide the Bunzl & Biach shares if Winter withdrew his proposals. The CA officials responded with "visible relief," and assured Wolzt that the difficulties in Vienna would be solved under such conditions.[104] Both banks intended to give some of their business clients parts of these holdings, assuming Kehrl approved the arrangement. While some consideration was given to

other candidates once Winter dropped out, by April 1942, the decision was taken to return to what had been the original plan and to divide the shares among the Vienna banks, the CA and Länderbank receiving 36 percent each, with E. von Nicolai and Scholler getting the rest. Bunzl & Biach was at this point renamed "Kontropa" and it bought the shares and options from the Kontrollbank, the latter thus concluding its last large-scale Aryanization. Because of the loss of the Russian market and lumber supply problems, the RWM decided that the shares should be bought at 115 percent instead of 120 percent. They were to be obligated to sell their shares within three years. Insofar as the 50 percent in shares (nominally valued at 4.5 million Swiss francs) of the Bunzl & Biach holding were concerned, the Reich Finance Ministry regarded them as extremely risky and asked the banks and Kontropa to purchase the shares and options for 800,000 RM. The Reich was really in no position to do much with the international holdings and connections of the Bunzls at this stage of the game. Half the holdings were in England or the United States; the Croatian company had been confiscated by the Ustasha government because it was viewed as Jewish; the Slovak holdings were subject to the severe restrictions of that state's anti-Semitic laws; the Hungarian holdings had been reduced to a seventh of their operations because the concern was half Jewish; the Serbian holdings had been severely bombed and then subjected to a war profits tax. Manifestly, the Bunzl & Biach holdings and the German expectations connected with them had become victims of German military victories and the world war.[105]

The CA had failed to realize its great ambitions with respect to the development of its wood and paper concern through the acquisition of Bunzl & Biach factories at Orthmann and Wattens, but it did have better luck in the expansion of its engagement in the hat

---

[102] RGVA Moscow, 1458/2/91, Bl. 165–166, Rafelsberger to RWM, Dec. 23, 1940.

[103] BA-CA, CA-V, CA management board meeting, Feb. 4, 1941.

[104] DrB, Nr. 30316–2001, Wolzt to Rasche, July 5, 1941.

[105] See ÖStA/AdR, MfWuA, VVSt, Box 1374, the unsigned memorandum on the reprivatization of the Bunzl concern, April 2, 1942. BA-CA, CA-IB, Bunzl & Biach, 33/01, the contract between Kontropa and the Kontrollbank, dated June 26, 1942, and related arrangements.

production business. This came through its 100 percent holding in the Bossi Hutfabrik AG and its 78 percent share in the Ebreichsdorfer Filzhutfabrik S & J. Frankel AG. The Bossi firm, which had already undergone a restructuring in the early 1930s, was still losing money before the Anschluss, and a decision was taken in 1937 to close down its facilities in Vienna and move to Ebereichsdorf in the hope of reducing costs and increasing efficiency. The facilities at Ebereichsdorf turned out to be unsatisfactory as well. The Eberichsdorfer company was also doing poorly, and the CA distrusted its accounts, which it suspected of being designed to justify excessively high executive salaries. Following the Anschluss, the Reich Group for the Clothing Industry and the RWM decided to force a rationalization of the Austrian hat industry in the hope of reducing price competition and improving exports. This inevitably drew in the hat manufacturing plant of Bunzl & Biach at Ortmann as well. Those charged with this task recommended that Bossi cease to engage in basic manufacture, that the Bunzl & Biach plant stop producing hats made of hair and take over Bossi's wool hat production, and that Ebreichsdorfer close its wool hat manufacturing and produce only hats made out of hair. At the same time, it urged that Bunzl & Biach, as the owner of the Ortmann hat factory, and the CA, as the majority shareholder in Bossi and Ebreichsdorfer, set up a plant for producing wool and hair hats in a factory to be acquired by the VVSt belonging to the Jew Emerich Fischer. The entire restructuring project required the paying off of old debts, the modernization of plants, and the reorganization of the companies. Bunzl & Biach would thus not only provide plant facilities but also become half owner of Bossi. In March 1941, a further decision was taken for the CA to sell its holding in Bossi to Ebreichsdorfer. In any case, Bossi, Ebreichsdorfer, and Bunzl & Biach thus established a hat syndicate with a clear division of labor.[106]

The multifaceted nature of Aryanization was very evident throughout and beyond these arrangements. The arrangement between Bunzl & Biach, which was represented by Hatheyer, was one between a concern that still was not formally Aryanized with the CA and Ebreichsdorfer. The leading director of Ebreichsdorfer until the German takeover was a Hungarian citizen and Jew, Geza Aczel, who was immediately removed from his position by the Gestapo, along with the head of the men's hat division, Rudolf Szpira, and of the women's hat division, Hans Freund, along with two other Jewish employees. An especially important aspect of these plans, however, was the acquisition by Bossi, with CA support, of the property of Emerich Fischer, who had bought a property in Vienna with the intention of setting up a felt hat factory called Kagran, which he then closed down, presumably in response to the political situation. The VVSt approved the sale of the property for 150,000 RM with the provision that the money be put in a blocked account and that Bossi pay the mortgage owing to the Böhmische Union-Bank.[107] Subsequently, the CA argued that Bossi should be relieved of any Aryanization fee because what was being purchased was a property and not a business. This seems to have been stretching matters quite a bit because after the war Fischer asked for restitution in the form of return of the machines that had been in the building or their monetary value.[108]

It is worth noting that the Aryanization interests of Ebreichsdorfer and the CA did not stop at the borders of the Reich. Thus, in November 1940, the CA (Glatzl and Friedl) turned to Fischböck, at the time general commissar for economics and finances in the Netherlands, to ask his assistance in the possible acquisition by Ebreichsdorfer of the N.V.

106 ÖStA/AdR, MfWuA, VVSt, Box 336, Zl. 288, Vol. I., Glatzl report of Dec. 30, 1938; BA-CA, CA-IB,

Bossi, 33/02, Agreement of Oct. 28, 1938, signed by Hatheyer, Geitner, and Friedl; BA-CA, CA-V, CA management board meetings, Jan. 19, 1939, March 20, 1941.

107 BA-CA, CA-IB, Ebreichsdorfer, 04/03-04, CA to Otto Koch, Dec. 21, 1938.

108 See ibid., Ebreichsdorfer, 04/09, the correspondence between 1947 and 1951.

Tweede Mij. Hoedhaar firm in Rotterdam, which was a major source of raw materials and a firm of considerable reputation. It was a "Jewish firm," and the owner was resisting visits by potential Aryan buyers. Fortunately, this effort was frustrated by the fact that 90 percent of the shares had been sold to a consortium in the United States and the money for which it was sold could not be found because Dutch Jews, in contrast to their Austrian counterparts, were not required to report cash held abroad.[109]

While the Bossi-Ebreichsdorfer companies pursued plans to establish themselves in Turkey, Rumania, and Hungary, the war stood in the way of their export plans and the companies became increasingly involved in production for the Wehrmacht, especially as the demand for headgear increased as a consequence of the Russian campaign.[110] It reflected in miniature the fate of the entire effort to mobilize the resources of Bunzl & Biach for the cause of German exports. At the same time, it also reflected the expansive goals of the CA and their close connection to Aryanization outside the Reich, which will be dealt with in greater detail later on in this study.

7. DAVID GOLDMANN, THE WOLLWARENVERKAUFS AG, AND THE UJPESTER AG

Bunzl & Biach was an unusual Aryanization case in that the authorities sought to keep Jews engaged in their own enterprise as minority shareholders. More typical, however, was the goal of eliminating all Jewish shareholding. This, however, could also involve difficult negotiations and even produce self-interested solicitude on the part of the CA for its victims, as was demonstrated in the case of David Goldmann (1887–1967). Born in Atzelsdorf, Goldmann and his wife, Juliane, lived in Vienna at Freiheitsplatz 10–12. For reasons that are not entirely clear,

he was a Czech citizen. He was in any case a very active businessman in Vienna, and he also had business interests in Switzerland. In 1934, Franz Rottenberg, a CA director and president of the administrative council of the CA–owned Guntramsdorfer Druckfabrik AG, concluded a contract with Goldmann, who was already a member of the administrative council, under which Goldmann was to serve additionally as leading director of Guntramsdorfer. He held this position at the time of the German invasion, but he and his family fled Austria on March 11. He did not show up for work again and was dismissed for violation of his contract on March 25.[111]

Obviously, he would not have lasted long in his positions at Guntramsdorfer in any case. Of greater moment, however, were his shareholdings in CA enterprises. He owned minority stakes in two textile firms, one in Vienna, the other in Budapest, in which the CA held a majority of the shares. Both firms had been held by a CA-controlled holding company in Rotterdam, the Vereeinigde Textiel-Maatschappijen NV. The Goldmann interests were lodged in a holding company, the Real Commerce SA in Chur. In the case of Wollwaren, Rotterdam owned 68.14 percent of the shares; Goldman owned 31.86 percent. The CA had the right to name three of the administrative council members; Goldmann was allowed to name two (Goldmann himself and Emil Ornstein). Goldmann was entitled to 15 percent of the net profit of Wollwaren and Ujpester, and he also had a contract for his administrative services that paid him a yearly salary. Rotterdam owned 68 percent of Ujpester, and Goldmann's Chur holding

---

[109] Ibid., Ebreichsdorfer, 04/02, CA to Fischböck, Nov. 15, 1940 and report by Glatzl, April 24, 1941.

[110] See ibid., Ebreichsdorfer, 04/09, the report of the management board of May 3, 1944.

[111] Information on his family and background can be found in the Claims Resolution Tribunal connected with the restitution of his Swiss bank account by his daughter. The Goldmanns lived in England and then went to New York City in 1940. See http://www.crit-ii.org/_awards/_/apdfas/Goldmann_David.pdf. Holocaust Victim Assets Litigation, Case Nr. CV96-4849, March 5, 2003, Claim Nr. 213626/SH. For his appointment at the Guntramsdorfer see BA-CA, CA-IB, Guntramsdorfer, 06/04, his letter of appointment of Feb. 20, 1934, and his letter of dismissal of March 25, 1938.

company held 32 percent of the shares. Here, too, Goldmann could name two of the supervisory board members, in this case himself and his brother Siegfried, but Emil Orenstein was also a member of the board. And here, too, David Goldmann drew a salary for his services. The CA in Vienna and Budapest acted as the house bank for the companies in their respective cities. Until March 1938, Rottenberg acted as the chief CA representative for both firms. Since 1936, the Ujpester held a gold reserve acquired from past profits outside Hungary that was to be proportionally divided between Rotterdam and Chur. The gold was in the possession of Goldmann, and he had proposed dispersing it in January 1938, but the matter had not been settled before the German march into Austria. While Goldmann held the gold, the CA held Goldmann's shares in the two firms. The companies had been doing quite well before 1938, Ujpester in particular making respectable profits. At the end of 1936, a share of Wollwaren stood at 148 percent of par, and a share of Ujpester stood at 280 percent of par. Wollwaren performed various collecting services for Ujpester for which the latter paid the former, but the money was not transferred because of the exchange controls, so that Ujpester was indebted to Wollwaren.[112]

Following the Anschluss, one of Wollwaren's directors, Otto Lenk, took over as commissarial administrator. This was deemed necessary in view of both Goldmann's managerial role and of his minority stake in the company. In resigning from this position in December 1939, Lenk claimed that he managed the company in such a way as to prepare for its Aryanization by dismissing all Jewish personnel and replacing them with Aryans. At the same time, the administrative council was placed under the leadership of CA Director Friedl, and Jews were eliminated from the council. He also reported that the CA in September had acquired the minority shares from the Vereenigden Textiel-Maatschappijen N.V., which was soon to be liquidated, and thus owned 100 percent of Wollwaren. Consequently,

the firm was fully Aryanized and his services as an administrator were no longer necessary.[113]

Actually, the Aryanization was rather more dramatic and complicated than Lenk's somewhat bland account suggested. David's brother Siegfried Goldmann had been arrested and incarcerated in March 1938, whereupon David sent a message through his Prague lawyer Rudolf Monter to CA General Director Heller. The letter informed Heller that the situation had caused him to have a nervous breakdown and that he was in a Prague sanatorium. He assured Heller that he had left matters in order at the factories, and advised Heller that his condition required that he turn his affairs over to his lawyer. He hoped that the CA would be forthcoming in view of his past services to the CA. Monter, who met with CA manager Josef Patzak, represented Goldmann as indicating that "it would still be possible for him to do a great deal for the Creditanstalt."[114] Monter's major reason for coming personally, however, was to express David Goldmann's hope that the CA would help bring about the release of his brother. According to Monter, Siegfried had been arrested in place of David, for whom the Gestapo was looking. Patzak replied negatively to this request, pointing out that the CA had no idea what the charges were and that David Goldmann could solve the problem only by showing up in Vienna and proving himself innocent.

Fortunately, this advice was not followed, and by the end of April the CA was doing some threatening of its own in connection with the gold in Goldmann's possession that belonged to Wollwaren. It refused to go to Prague or Budapest to negotiate with Goldmann's lawyers. It made clear that it were well aware that the Real Commerce belonged to Goldmann and was a cloak for his interests. The CA warned that it would bring criminal charges against Goldmann if he did not give

---

[112] Ibid., Wollwaren, 18/04, report by Glatzl, April 9, 1938.

[113] Ibid., Wollwaren, 18/06-07, Lenk to State Commissar for the Private Economy, Dec. 21, 1938, which also contains his final report to the administrative council of Feb. 6, 1939.

[114] Ibid., Wollwaren, 18/04, memo by Patzak, March 29, 1938. The actual letter from Goldmann to Heller is in ibid., Wollwaren, 18/02.

up the key to the safe deposit box containing the gold.[115]

In reality, however, both sides wished to negotiate, Goldmann undoubtedly because of the vulnerability of his brother and various other private interests he was trying to protect, the CA because Goldmann still held some important cards. He was a foreign citizen, and the arrangements connected with the two companies had been made through a holding company in Chur that he controlled and the holding company in Rotterdam. A syndicate had been formed between Wollwaren and Ujpester, and Goldmann was in a position to seek arbitration or go to court if it were not terminated by mutual agreement. He also held the gold to be divided between the shareholders in proportion to their holdings, although the CA held his shares in Wollwaren. Negotiations were conducted in Vienna between Goldmann's lawyer and the CA. Goldmann apparently reduced some of his initial demands, and an agreement was finally hammered out in late June 1938 that then took the form of a contract dated July 23, 1938, between the holding companies in Rotterdam and Chur representing, respectively, the CA and Goldmann. The purpose of the CA was to "eliminate the Jewish minority" and thereby achieve the "complete Aryanization of both corporations." Under the agreement, Goldmann gave up all managerial rights and the salaries that came with them with respect to both companies. He agreed to surrender 45.99778 kilograms of gold to the CA, which would in turn place the gold at the disposal of the Reichsbank and also agreed to compensate the CA for half the gold exchange rate losses incurred through the delay in delivering the gold. At the same time, Goldmann would retain his portion of the gold, that is, 21.64602 kilograms. Goldmann agreed to sell both blocks of shares for 600,000 Hungarian pengö. The logic behind this odd arrangement was that the CA would not have to pay Goldmann in a highly valued currency, while the CA could thus

dispense with the debt owed by the Ujpester to Wollwaren that had been and remained uncollectable because of the Hungarian exchange controls. Goldmann would receive the pengö in his account in Budapest and could use it there as he wished. In return, Goldmann would surrender his shares in Wollwaren to the CA and also place his shares in the Ujpester at the disposal of the CA. Finally, assuming the German authorities would agree to this settlement, the CA would report favorably on Goldmann's handling of the matter and ask the German authorities to look with favor upon Goldmann's desire to maintain the private property of himself and his brother in Vienna, to avoid any reprisals against family members, and to allow them to leave the Reich.[116]

From the perspective of the CA, these arrangements were very advantageous for a number of reasons. Quite aside from having a binding agreement that would not be contested by Goldmann, the financial aspects were extremely favorable. The CA thought the shares were worth 900,000 pengö, not 600,000 pengö, which was quite a saving in addition to the advantage of having the payment made in Hungary with pengö that could not otherwise be transferred. Additionally, Goldmann's service contracts were ended effective March 1938, so that he bore the full personal loss involved. In making its argument requesting support for this contract from the Reichsbank Main Office in Vienna and to the VVSt, the CA was in a position to use these arguments, especially the gold delivery to the Reichsbank, to argue that the economic interests of the Reich were well served by the agreement. The VVSt approved the agreement on September 28, 1938.[117]

If Goldmann accepted a loss of money and assets through this arrangement, he also lost out on one of his chief efforts in the

---

[115] Ibid., Wollwaren, 18/04, telephone conversation between Glatzl and Goldmann's Prague lawyer, Monter, April 30, 1938.

[116] For the contract of July 23, 1938, see ibid. See also the report for the CA management board on the agreement, June 22, 1938, and the undated draft of the CA's petition for the acceptance of the agreement to the Reichsbank Main Office in Vienna, see ibid.

[117] Ibid., VVSt to CA, Sept. 28, 1938, and CA attorney Erich Führer to Friedl, Oct. 5, 1938.

negotiations, namely, to include a binding agreement under which the CA holding company in Rotterdam would legally obligate itself and the CA to protect the private properties and possessions of David and Siegfried Goldmann, as well as guarantee the personal safety of the family members remaining in Austria. The CA refused to take on such a legal obligation, which would have made it vulnerable to legal action abroad, and only agreed to speak favorably on behalf of Goldmann in recognition of his not standing in the way of the Aryanization and the material losses he incurred as a result.[118]

Given what the future months would bring, it is doubtful that Goldmann could have maintained such leverage as he was seeking for very long in any case, but it is worth noting that he had very good reason to at least try to secure these assets. His very substantial art collection included oil paintings by Rubens and Parmigiaino that were either seized for the Vienna museums or for the projected "Führer Museum" in Linz or auctioned off by the Dorotheum in his house.[119] He was not spared human loss either. His brother Siegfried, possibly released after his initial arrest, was in the Nisko deportation of October 10, 1939, and did not return.[120] David Goldmann did return, at least through his lawyers, to angrily claim restitution of his shares in 1946,[121] and the claims of his family continued over half a century. There was, to be sure, one fly in the ointment for the CA. In October 1940, the Ujpester Tuchfabrik was taken over by the Soproner Haas AG to form the "Soproner und Ujpester Tuch- und Teppich-Fabriken AG, Budapest." The Gestapo confiscated the 10.18 percent of the shares that previously belonged to the Realcommerce S.A., and thus presumably belonged to David Goldmann, as Jewish property. The CA persistently sought to purchase the shares back, but

because it was still trying in 1944, this suggests that it had no success.[122]

8. OTTO STRAUSS AND THE LAMPEN-UND METALLWARENFABRIKEN R. DITMAR GEBRÜDER BRUNNER AG

A somewhat less self-interested instance of the CA's effort to eliminate a major Jewish shareholder in an important industrial enterprise is to be found in the case of Otto Strauss, the general director of the major Austrian producer of lamps and heating apparatuses, condensers, enamel products, porcelain and glass products, and home movie cameras and projectors. It did a very important export business. Until the Anschluss, the Lampen-und Metallwarenfabriken AG was headed by Strauss, a highly respected and talented businessman and vice-president of the Vienna Industrialist Association who had successfully taken over the majority of the shares in a struggle with the Niederösterreichische Escompte-Gesellschaft in 1932. The bank wanted to install a second general director and to change the production program. Strauss opposed both measures as harmful to the interests of the company, and there was general consensus that Strauss was correct. The manner in which Strauss financed his success was less laudable. He borrowed the money to buy the shares from Dietmar-Brunner itself and turned the title to the shares over to a holding company he set up in Zug, Switzerland, the Lohan AG, and he also assigned his debt to Dietmar-Brunner to the Lohan AG. At the same time, he placed the actual shares with a number of Viennese banks and then borrowed against them. Furthermore, because Dietmar-Brunner was doing excellent export business before the Anschluss, Strauss was able to raise substantial loans and the actual situation of the company was unknown to anyone on the administrative council. Indeed, the financial straits of the company only became

---

[118] Ibid., report to the management board, June 22, 1938.

[119] Lillie, *Was einmal war*, pp. 408–415.

[120] http://www.doew.at.

[121] BA-CA, CA-IB, Wollwaren, 18/04, Goldmann to CA, Dec. 13, 1946.

[122] See memorandum by Patzak of Jan. 15, 1944, 3.Vol., 07/07. On the further development of the firm, see Chapter 3, pp. 283–286.

clear following the Anschluss. Strauss simply disappeared – he seems to have ended up in Paris – and the administration of the company was taken over by one of its officials, Anton Biro, who then discovered that the claims against the Lohan AG were worth nothing and that the company was effectively bankrupt although its actual status was veiled by the liquidity arising from its export operations.[123]

Biro's first solution to the mess was to invite the Berlin-based Auergesellschaft, which had worked closely with Ditmar-Brunner and produced similar products, to take it over, but the existing regulations barring German firms from taking over Austrian enterprises unless there were no Austrian bidders required him to turn first to a potential Austrian buyer. He therefore initially turned to the CA, but the cost involved led Heller to turn him down. He then could turn to the Auergesellschaft, whose management board would have liked to take over Ditmar-Brunner but was heavily engaged elsewhere. The Auergesellschaft, however, did refer Biro to the Deutsche Bank, which declared itself willing to reorganize Ditmar-Brunner, but only in collaboration with the CA. The incentive, as reported by Biro, was Ditmar-Brunner's large export business, and it led to an agreement that the Deutsche Bank and the CA would each undertake 50 percent of the costs.

Nevertheless, the matter was complicated by the fact that Strauss had title to the shares but had also committed fraud. When the Gestapo got wind of the situation, it seized some of the shares and also contemplated issuing an international warrant for Strauss's arrest. Prosecuting Strauss, however, presented great problems that led both Ditmar's administrative council and the Deutsche Bank and the CA to oppose such a measure. Seventy percent of Ditmar's business was exports to some sixty-five countries, and Strauss, whatever his financial deficiencies,

had done a splendid job of cultivating this business. There was good reason to fear that the issuance of a warrant would lead his large circle of friends abroad to rally behind him and would result only in turning his international customers against Ditmar and potentially lead to a blocking of Ditmar's very substantial currency holdings abroad. Ultimately, therefore, the most desirable solution was for Strauss to abandon his title to the shares in return for a forgiveness of its encumbrance on them and also to renounce all claims to payment for his services as general director. Once Aryanized by the CA-Deutsche Bank takeover of Ditmar's ownership and settlement of its debts, Ditmar would be free to continue its exports without complication and also to pursue the military contracts that were to be its mainstay in the coming years.

Thus, as in the cases of Bunzl & Biach and David Goldmann, export considerations and holdings abroad enabled Jews to exercise some leverage over the Aryanizers. While this did not eliminate tedious negotiations with Strauss's lawyer, and ultimately had to be settled with the Kontrollbank, which was given formal control of the shares, the CA and Deutsche Bank were able to take over the ownership of Ditmar in November 1938 after paying off the Gestapo for the shares it held and paying the Kontrollbank a fee of 50,000 RM.[124] Insofar as one can tell, the Deutsche Bank and the CA had stepped into the breach in order to assist in keeping Ditmar's business afloat, and the evidence suggests that they had no interest in holding on to the company, which they sold in early 1940 to the Staatseisenbahngesellschaft (STEG) for 2.9 million RM.

9. THE MONTANA KOHLENHANDELSGESELLSCHAFT

In contrast to Ditmar-Brunner, where the CA divested itself of Aryanized assets after settling for a modest profit, the Aryanization of the Montana Kohlenhandelsgesellschaft provides

[123] The basic account was provided by Biro to Fischböck, Oct. 28, 1938, BA-CA, CA-IB, Ditmar, 36/01-03. See also, Gregor Spuhler et al., *"Arisierungen" in Österreich und ihre Bezüge zur Schweiz*. Veröffentlichungen der Unabhängigen Expertenkommission Schweiz (= UEK) – Zweiter Weltkrieg, Vol. 20 (Zurich 2002), pp. 131–136.

[124] ÖStA/AdR, MfWuA, VVSt, Statistik, Box 698, Zl 7750, Vol. 1.

yet another illustration of the CA's augmentation of its concern at the expense of Jewish owners or, perhaps better said, partners. As in the case of David Goldmann, the CA was dealing not only with a major Jewish shareholder in its dealings with Emil Kahane but also with a person on whom it had relied in a managerial role. The Montana Kohlenhandelsgesellschaft was founded in 1928, and its origins were in the Coal Division of the CA, the primary function of which was to supply coal to the CA concern. It was half owned by the Gebrüder Guttmann, which sold off its shares in 1932. Subsequently, the CA owned the Kohlenhandelsgesellschaft, while the Montana Aktiengesellchaft für Bergbau, Industrie und Handel functioned as a holding company. It shares belonged primarily to three Jews: Emil Kahane, Friedric Weill, and Rudolf Steiner. The Montana AG controlled or held shares in the bitumimous coal mines of the Steirische Kohlenbergwerke AG, the Niederösterreichische Kaolin- und Steinwerke AG in Zöbern, the Steirischen Magnesit AG, and the Continentale Gesellschaft für angewandte Elektrizität in Basel.[125]

The CA moved with considerable brutality in dealing with the Jewish ownership of Montana. Thus, in reports of early May, the CA announced that it had been quite successful in getting rid of the Jewish business management, putting Hans Friedl and a Party member since 1933 and illegal since 1934, Adolf Bauer, in their place. The remaining Jewish employees were fired and replaced with non-Jews where necessary. The CA stressed the importance of the coal marketing company to the bank because it functioned as its coal supplier for the CA concern and "is severely hampered in its activity since the continuing 50 percent participation of a non-Aryan corporation is damaging and endangers its business activity. It is therefore

urgently necessary to bring this situation to an end as soon as possible." The CA proposed buying out the Montana AG stake in the Montana Kohlenhandelsgesellschaft for the nominal value of the holding (50,000 Schilling) plus half of the inventory (30,000 Schilling). At the same time, the CA pointed out that the Montana AG was under a commissarial administrator, Bauer, who had been appointed on April 8, 1938, and that the "the payment of this purchase price does not entail any benefit for the Jewish shareholders of the Montana AG." It was to be nothing more than a shifting of money from company to company, while the commissarial administrator was there to ensure that the Jewish shareholders could not lay their hands on the money and to address the question of what those shareholders would get for the Montana AG. The two companies could now theoretically go their own way, and the Aryanization of the Montana AG would, the CA cynically noted, be simplified by the separation of the two companies in this manner.[126]

This account veiled certain unpleasant aspects of the aforementioned transaction. One of them was that Friedl and Bauer had threatened Kahane and the other Jewish persons at Montana with the Gestapo if they did not agree to the proposal and that Kahane felt compelled to sign a notarized document transferring the coal trading company from the Montana AG to the CA in April 1938. At the same time, Friedl became concerned that a Jew might not be legally qualified to undertake such an action anymore if his company was under commissarial control. Consequently, a new contract was drawn up and signed by Bauer on May 19, 1938, for the Montana AG undertaking the same transfer for the same 80,000 Schilling (53,333.33 RM). Originally, the CA planned to sell this holding to another purchaser, but then decided to reward Bauer, who was to function as general director of the Montana AG throughout

[125] There is a good discussion in Theo Venus, "Geschichte der Bankhaus Gutmann," unpublished MS, pp. 126–130, but see the published account in: "Abgebrochene Rückkehr – Der Fall des Bankhauses Gebrüder Gutmann," in: Verena Pawlowsky/Harald Wendelin (eds.), *Die Republik und das NS-Erbe*, vol. 2 (Vienna 2005), pp. 152–170, 216–217f.

[126] See BA-CA, CA-IB, Montana, 21/01, 21/05, the report of the CA to President Robert Hammer of the Wiener Giro- und Kassenverein, May 3, 1938 and Hans Gürtler to the Restitution Commission, Feb. 28, 1948.

the war and had strong Party support, by selling the Montana AG its holding in the Montana Kohlenhandelsgesellschaft in April 1939. The price, however, was now 128,141.89 RM, that is, two and a half times what the CA had paid a year earlier. It was a measure of how much the CA had underpaid for this asset in 1938 that it was charged an Aryanization fee of 28,886 RM by the VVSt. This obviously did not take away its profit.[127]

This did not, of course, solve the problem of Aryanizing the Montana AG, which had its own special issues but did not involve the CA as directly. At the end of September 1938, the Kontrollbank was assigned the task of Aryanizing the concern. Of the 30,000 shares, 9,180 were owned by the concern itself. The remaining shares were divided between Kahane, Weill, Steiner, and the Steierische Magnesitwerke AG in Vienna. While the details are unclear, Kahane seems to have been forced to sell his 7,560 shares to the Kontrollbank, and he fled Austria at the end of the year. The Kontrollbank was able to acquire the shares held by the Steierische Magnesit and other shares held in Austria. By mid-May 1939, the Kontrollbank held 19,440 shares of Montana and was prepared to liquidate it on the grounds that such a holding company was no longer needed under the new political and economic order. Weill and Steiner proved much more of a problem because they had fled to Switzerland and would not come to terms. Unfortunately, they were unable to prevent the 9,985 shares they held in Switzerland from being auctioned off by court order, while the 575 shares they held in Vienna were seized by the authorities, held for payment of taxes, and then sold to the Kontrollbank. The Swiss shares were purchased by Willy Bühler, who eventually sold them to the Bankhaus Krentschker

& Co., which did a great deal of Aryanization business, and the same bank also bought the shares held by the Kontrollbank at the end of 1939 and thereby completed the Aryanization of the Montana AG.[128] It was not liquidated and Bauer remained at its head for the duration.[129] At the same time, the CA continued to operate its coal sales organization, which was to present other kinds of problems to be discussed later in this study.

This discussion of the role of the CA in Aryanizations in Austria hardly exhausts the subject or its complexity. An important set of illustrations, based on deep research and a much fuller presentation than the examples discussed earlier in this chapter, is to be found in Ulrike Zimmerl's study of the CA and the Aryanization of the Vienna hotels.[130] What should be clear, however, is that the CA was an active and engaged player in the Aryanization of enterprises in Austria, both large and small. Beginning in late 1938, however, the borders of the Reich began to expand significantly and, as shall be shown in the next section, the role of the CA in Aryanization took on new and larger dimensions.

---

[127] Ibid.

[128] Undated postwar report, probably of May 1947, on the development of the Montana concern in the period 1938–1939 by Director Karl Josef Tambornino, ibid. Important information is also contained in the files of the Steierische Mangnesit-Industrie AG, especially in a memorandum of May 30, 1939, ibid., BA-CA, CA-IB, Magnesit, 41/01.

[129] On the important restitution issues raised by this case, see Oliver Rathkolb, "Die ungeschriebene Geschichte. Creditanstalt-Bankverein und Österreichische Länderbank und die Entschädigung bzw. Restitution von Vermögenswerten jüdischer Kunden und Kundinnen nach 1945," in Feldman/Rathkolb/Venus/Zimmerl, Österreichische Banken und Sparkassen im Nationalsozialismus und in der Nachkriegszeit, vol. 1., pp. 741–748.

[130] Ulrike Zimmrl, "Die Wiener Ringstrassenhotels Bristol und Imperial während der NS-Zeit. Die Creditanstalt-Bankverein und ihre Beteiligung an den Hotel Bristol AG, Hotel Imperial AG und 'Imperial' Weinhandels AG," in Feldman/Rathkolb/Venus/Zimmerl, Österreichische Banken und Sparkassen im Nationalsozialismus und in der Nachkriegszeit, vol. 1, pp. 279–323.

CHAPTER THREE

An Expanding Creditanstalt in an Expanding German Empire

Some years were to pass before the leadership of the CA discovered the "victimhood" of Austria and its leading bank, and although Joham, Hasslacher, and other holdovers from the old regime chafed under various aspects of German domination, they not only settled in reasonably well under the new order but actively sought to benefit from it. Joham had successfully sought safeguards for the CA and found them under the protective wing of the Deutsche Bank and its ascending star, Hermann Josef Abs. Thanks to Abs, the CA was able to retain its status as a major, if diminished, industrial holding company and become a proxy for the Deutsche Bank or its actual partner as the Deutsche Bank followed the National Socialist flag across Europe. As will be shown, this frequently meant becoming a partner in crime as well, but it is of central importance to recognize that the CA leadership actively sought to gain as powerful and as autonomous a position for itself as possible. Germans like Director Tron may have complained about Austrian *Schlamperei* (sloppiness) and the Austrians' lackadaisical attitude toward the "great tasks" the Germans were incessantly talking about, but the record shows that the CA was quite effective in fulfilling its self-assigned task of looking after its own interests and expanding its business as much as political conditions would allow. It is important to bear in mind that the CA's behavior was not dissimilar to that of other Austrian institutions and of persons, and it had a long history of engagement

in Southeast Europe and Poland. Furthermore, Austrians were prominent in the political, economic, police, and military organizations in the occupied territories and in the Reich's satellite states and often were key players in networks to which the CA could turn. In any case, if one is to understand the business activities and actions of the CA between 1938 and 1945 and its role in Aryanization, it is essential to place them in the context not only of its role in Austria, as has been done in the previous chapter, but also of its expanded role in the financial and economic structures of conquered Europe. This chapter, therefore, gives an account of the CA's development and expansion as a bank and concern outside the boundaries of the former Austria and considers the extent to which this expansion came to be viewed in the context of an integrated Deutsche Bank-Creditanstalt program for its future activities in Europe.

I. THE EXPANSION OF THE CA'S BANKING BUSINESS

Limited Expansion in the Sudetenland

The annexation of the Sudetenland in the fall of 1938 came at a somewhat unpropitious time for the leaders of the CA. On the one hand, the CA was still under the control of the VIAG and was dealing with the demands being made for the surrender or sale of its holdings. On the other hand, the Deutsche Bank had not yet attained the 25 percent stake in the CA it was to acquire at the end of the year, and the CA was basically to be a bystander in the negotiations conducted between the Reich Economics Ministry (RWM) and the major German banks aimed at dividing up the branches of the Czech banks in the Sudetenland among the competing German banks. The CA had to be both cautious in its pretensions and modest in its ambitions. This did not mean that it was shy about stating its wishes and laying its claims. On October 4, it sent a note to the RWM asking that the CA be included in the distribution of Sudetenland branches, pointing out that the CA "appears predestined to take over such branches, since they and the banks acquired in the period of mergers previously had their own branches in these territories which were taken over in the postwar period by Czech institutions, so that the reacquisition of these branches should be considered as their repatriation."[1] Joham was careful to keep Abs informed about the CA's claims and intentions. He told Abs on October 5 that the CA wished to acquire three branches bordering on Austria and was planning to undertake negotiations with the Böhmische Escompte-Bank toward this end. The CA had in fact contacted the Böhmische Escompte-Bank (Bebca) along with other Czech banks inviting them to discuss the sale of their Sudeten branches. Abs informed Joham that the Deutsche Bank also intended to be active in the "new territories," and wanted not only to come to an understanding with the CA but also to represent the CA's interests in dealing with the RWM and other relevant agencies. He urged Joham to get into contact with Riehle and also to keep the Deutsche Bank abreast of developments.[2]

The RWM was anxious to control the situation and at a meeting with the banks on October 8 Ministerial Director Kurt Lange told them that further direct negotiations between the German and Czech banks were not desired and invited them instead to present their wishes to the RWM. The CA hastened to do so, informing Riehle on October 10 that it had made contact with the Anglo-tschechoslowakische und Prager Creditbank, the Bebca, the Böhmische Industrialbank in Prague, and the Mährische Bank in Brünn/Brno about selling off branches but had not yet received an answer. Specifically, the CA was now interested in setting up four branches that might be available in Böhmisch Krumau/Czesky Krumlov, where there were branches of the Böhmische Industrialbank and the Deutsche Agrar- und Industriebank; in Nikolsburg/Mikulov, where there were branches of the Bebca and Kreditanstalt der Deutschen; in Znaim/Znojmo, where there were branches of the Bebca, the Anglo-tschechoslowakische und Prager Creditbank, the Böhmische Industrialbank, and the Kreditanstalt der Deutschen; and in Lundenburg/Breclav, where there were branches of the Bebca, the Böhmische Industrialbank, and the Mährische Bank. The CA promised to follow Lange's injunction and refrain from further negotiations but hoped "that our wishes will receive extensive consideration in the systematic allocation of bank assignments by the Reich Economics Ministry."[3]

To justify its right to participate in the spoils, the CA's Economic Policy Section cooked up a self-serving historical exposé, the basic thrust of which had already been pronounced in its note to the RWM of October 4. In this lengthier presentation sent to the RWM on October 11, the CA argued that the sale of its branches in Southern Moravia to the Böhmische Escompte-Bank in 1919, the majority of whose shares had once been owned by the Živnostenská banka and consequently by the Viennese banks that controlled the Czech banks, was made under duress as a consequence of the Czech "nostrification" policies. They were branded as violations of the Treaty of St. Germain and nothing less than an effort to drive the Vienna

---

[1] RGVA Moscow, 1458/10/232, Bl. 280, CA to RWM (Riehle), Oct. 4, 1938. A copy of this was sent to Reich Banking Commissar Ernst on Oct. 10, 1938, ibid., 1458/10/227, Bl. 152.

[2] DB, P 6502, Bl. 119, memo by Abs, Oct. 5, 1938. See also RGVA Moscow, 1458/10/232, Bl. 152, letter of CA to Reich Bank Commissar Ernst, Oct. 17, 1938.

[3] RGVA Moscow, 1458/10/232, Bl. 55–56, CA to Riehle, Oct. 10, 1938.

banks and the entire "German" credit business out of the Czech lands.[4] Indeed, the CA argued that the Czechs had taken over 101 branches of banks now part of the CA along with the best accounts in their portfolios. Furthermore, the CA insisted that there were economic and social arguments for its position because "a very large part of Viennese interests then lay and now lie again in the annexed Sudetenland, whose sphere of connection to the Danubian capital is in no way exclusively a matter of sentiment. The natural export direction of Sudeten industry points to a high degree to the South East. Along with the necessity of compensation [*Wiedergutmachung*] for the economic misery of Vienna which was not least of all brought about by Czech measures, there is also the economic advantage which this international city through its location, connections, and experiences offers in the Sudetenland as well as in the Southeast states."[5] On the basis of these arguments and pretensions, the CA sought to establish "a moral claim to far-reaching consideration in the new territories."[6]

These arguments were, to say the least, problematic. While one may agree with historian Harald Wixforth, who has studied the German bank takeovers in the Sudetenland, that the CA presented no concrete evidence of Czech intentions, it is probably going too far to argue that the CA, along with the other Austrian banks, sold its branches in the Sudetenland immediately after World War I on the basis of free negotiations with the Czech banks. Czech "nostrification" and "nationalization" policies left little choice for the Austrian banks under the economic and political conditions existing after the war. Conditions in 1938 simply reversed the situation, and now it was the Czech banks that had to give way. Wixforth is on firmer ground, however, in arguing that there was nothing peculiarly "German" about these branches because they, like the prewar Viennese banks that had owned them, were

intended to service a multinational empire. Holding on to them under post-1919 conditions made little sense, and claiming that the Vienna of the Greater German Reich deserved compensation for the losses of the Vienna of the Austro-Hungarian Empire was nothing more than a variation on National Socialist revisionism. Furthermore, the CA in its argumentation studiously avoided the effects of its own collapse and of the sustained crisis of the Austrian banks after 1931, which weakened what had still been a significant engagement of Austrian banks in the Czech economy.[7]

On October 13, Joham duly sent Abs the aforementioned memorandum, which had been sent to Riehle two days earlier, justifying the CA's claims to acquire Sudetenland bank branches from the Czech banks.[8] At the same time, the CA sought to press the issue by lobbying with the banking commissar's office, the Reichsbank, and the RWM to ensure that its wishes were not overlooked. The CA lobbyist in Berlin, Captain Robert Nemling, was instructed to make the case with the relevant authorities. As he reported back to Vienna: "I remarked by

4 RGVA Moscow, 1458/10/232, Bl. 106–111, CA to RWM (Riehle), Oct. 11, 1938.
5 Ibid.
6 DB, P 6502, Pohle to Abs, Oct. 17, 1938.

7 Harald Wixforth, "'Die Wiedererwerbung der Filialen ist als Repatriierung anzusprechen'– Die Expansionsbestrebungen der Österreichischen Creditanstalt-Wiener Bankverein in das Sudetenland 1938/39," in: *Zeitschrift für Bankgeschichte* (1/2001), pp. 62–77, and Harald Wixforth, *Auftakt zur Ostexpansion. Die Dresdner Bank und die Umgestaltung des Bankwesens im Sudetenland 1938/39* (= Hannnah-Arendt-Institut. Berichte und Studien Nr. 31, Dresden 2001), esp. pp. 81–84. For a good discussion of the situation of the Austrian banks in the Czech Republic in 1919, see Eduard März, *Österreichische Bankpolitik in der Zeit der großen Wende 1913–1923 am Beispiel der Creditanstalt für Handel und Gewerbe* (Munich 1981), pp. 346–347 and, more generally, Fritz Weber, *Vor dem großen Krach. Die Krise des österreichischen Bankwesens in den zwanziger Jahren* (Habilitationsschrift, Universität Salzburg, Vienna 1991), pp. 87–144, 330–367. On the effects of the Creditanstalt collapse, see Vlastislav Lacina, "Tschechische Banken und ihre Verbindungen zum österreichischen Bankwesen bis 1945," in Oliver Rathkolb/Theo Venus/Ulrike Zimmerl (eds.), *Bank Austria Creditanstalt. 150 Jahre Bankengeschichte im Zentrum Europas*(Vienna 2005), pp. 239–252.
8 DB, P 6502, Bl. 129, Joham to Abs, Oct. 13, 1938; ibid., Bl. 137, memo by Pohle, Oct. 17, 1938.

way of introduction that the interests of the CA correspond to the interests of the state since it is owned by the state. Aside from this, the [bank] leadership tries to act in complete accord with the state economic policy, in order to pursue its functional tasks along these lines."[9] By this time, however, the CA's chief Viennese competitor, the Länderbank Wien, had been mobilized, and while the CA hoped to make a joint effort to secure branches in cooperation with its competitor,[10] the basic decisions were determined not in terms of the CA's preoccupation with serving as the portal to Southeast Europe; rather, what counted were the industrial usefulness of the Czech lands to the Reich and the political influence and string-pulling that underlay so much of the regime's decision making. In this instance, the authorities were primarily interested in divvying up the Czech bank branches among the major German banks. In the case of the Sudetenland and later the Protectorate, the Dresdner Bank had the upper hand because of Director Karl Rasche's close connections with, among others, Göring and Hans Kehrl. It was a measure of the dangers presented by the Dresdner Bank-Länderbank combination that the Mährische Bank, which had branches in Znaim/Znojmo and Lundenberg, reported to the CA on October 24 in response to CA solicitations that a representative of the Länderbank had visited the Mährische Bank and pointed out that the Dresdner Bank was not only prepared to buy up the branches in Znaim/Znojmo and Lundenberg but also the five Mährische branches in the northern area. In this way, the Mährische Bank might be in a position to sell off all seven of its Sudetenland branches in one fell swoop. It decided, therefore, to pursue its negotiations with the Dresdner Bank/Länderbank and suspend its discussions with the CA.[11]

The Mährische Bank, however, was not to be in a position to play the Deutsche Bank-CA group against the Dresdner Bank-Länderbank Wien group. The crucial decisions in the question of the division of the Sudeten banks were being made by Riehle and Bank Commissar Ernst. On October 5, they had already agreed that Ernst was to draw up a plan for the division of the branches, to discuss it with Riehle, and then to decide the matter jointly. The government obviously was anxious to control the competition among the German banks, and it did.[12] The bank commissar decided on October 14 to assign the Dresdner Bank all of the Bebca branches in the Sudetenland along with another four belonging to the Živnostenská banka. The Deutsche Bank was to acquire the branch networks of the Böhmische Union Bank (BUB) and the Deutsche Agrar- und Industriebank (DAIB). Abs and Director Oswald Rösler of the Deutsche Bank had been negotiating with the Bebca and viewed it as being able to offer better business than the BUB. It was a disappointed Abs who, after discussions with Ernst, informed the CA on October 25 that the Länderbank was being offered the Bebca branches coveted by the CA but that the CA was being offered the opportunity to acquire branches in Znaim/Znojmo, Lundenburg/Breclav, and Krumau/Czesky Krumlov from other Czech banks. Abs urged the CA to negotiate directly with the Czech banks whose branches were to be offered for sale: the Czech Agrarbank, which had a branch in Lundenburg/Breclav; the Mährische Bank in Brünn/Brno, which had branches in Znaim/Znojmo and Lundenburg/Breclav; and the DAIB, which had branches in Znaim/Znojmo, Lundenburg/Breclav, and Böhmisch-Krumau/Czesky Krumlov.[13]

The CA must also have been quite disappointed. It had kept the RWM abreast of its contacts with various Czech banks and the responses it had received to its inquiries of

9   BA-CA, CA-TZ, Sekretariat rot, Box 53/ÖCA-WBV, 1838/9,10,11, File 9b/4, report by Nemling, Oct. 20, 1938.

10 See BA-CA, CA-V, the remarks of Heller at the CA executive committee meeting, Oct. 21, 1938.

11 BA-CA, CA-TZ, Rechtsabteilung rot, Box 2/CA-BV 15b/38/1,2, File 2a, Mährische Bank to CA, Oct. 24, 1938.

12 See RGVA Moscow, 1458/10/232, Bl. 111, the memorandum of Oct. 11, 1938 on the decision of Oct. 5.

13 DB, P 6502, Bl. 142, Abs to CA, Oct. 25, 1938.

October 5. As late as October 19, Joham and Heller seemed to think that they could purchase branches from the Bebca and assured the banking commissar that they intended to consolidate branches in any city where they were permitted to set up their own branch.[14] The Gau economic advisor of the Lower Danube, Heinz Birthelmer, who also happened to be a member of the supervisory board of the Länderbank Wien, now stepped in to force the CA and the Länderbank to come to a settlement under his auspices.

As a result, the CA would get branches only in Znaim/Znojmo and Lundenburg/Breclav, while its affiliate, the Bank für Oberösterreich und Salzburg, would acquire branches in Böhmisch-Krumau/Czesky Krumlov. On October 25, the CA soberly reported to Ernst on its negotiations with the Länderbank Wien and their agreement on the CA receiving the branches of the Böhmische Industrialbank and of the Mährische Bank in Lundenburg/Breclav and Znaim/Znojmo. The Länderbank was to get the Bebca branch in Nikolsburg, where the CA would have no presence at all. Furthermore, the Bebca branches in Lundenburg/Breclav and Znaim/Znojmo, the branches of the Anglo-tzechoslowakischische und Prager Kreditbank in Znaim/Znojmo, and the branch of the Czechische Agrarbank in Lundenburg/Breclav would also go to the Länderbank. The Oberbank would take over the branches of the Böhmische Industrialbank and the Deutsche Agrar- und Industriebank in Böhmisch-Krumau/Czesky Krumlov. Birthelmer made a point of informing Ernst that these arrangements had his blessing.[15] It is worth noting that the Länderbank Wien also had its eye on potential branches in Böhmisch-Krumau/Czesky Krumlov, but this was blocked by Gauleiter Oscar Hinterleitner. He told Bank Commissar Ernst that he supported the plan of the Oberbank to take over

the branches of the DAIB and the Böhmische Industrialbank in Krumau/Czesky Krumlov and thus consolidate at least two banks in a town that already had six banks and only 9,000 inhabitants. While willing, therefore, to see the Oberbank establish itself in Krumau/Czesky Krumlov because of the anticipated increase in business in the area, he did not think any more banks, especially a branch of the Länderbank Wien, at all desirable.[16]

The Sudetenland acquisitions, as noted earlier, were modest gains for the CA. These branches, however, like all the branches bought up by the German banks at this time, were purchased on terms that enabled the German banks to exclude accounts receivable – often from Jews or Czechs living in what remained of Czechoslovakia – that were viewed as not collectable or dubious, and to refuse the obligation to hold and accept the Czech bonds and loans in the bank portfolios. While the latter conditions were modified after the takeover of the remainder of the Czech state and the conversion of Czech bonds into German bonds, the conditions laid down for the purchase of Czech bank branches in the Sudetenland meant paying a price well below the value of the assets acquired, stripping the Czech banks that had owned them of valuable assets, and burdening those banks with accounts the Germans would not accept.[17]

The CA took a very triumphant tone in describing to its employees its new acquisitions in Lundenburg/Breclav and Znaim/Znojmo. The bank newspaper made, for example, a point of reminding everyone that the Germans

---

14 RGVA Moscow, 1458/10/227, Bl. 261–262, CA to Ernst, Oct. 17, 1938, and ibid., Bl. 274, CA to Ernst, Oct. 19, 1938.

15 Ibid., Bl. 328–329, 339, CA to Ernst, Oct. 24, 1938, and Oct. 25, 1938.

16 BA-CA, CA-TZ, Sekretariat grün, Box 5/BOS XVIII–XXIV, File 1, Hinterleitner to Ernst, Nov. 15, 1938. It is not impossible that he may also have scotched the plan to give the CA the branch because some Austrian agency had called the Reichsbank in Berlin to say that it was improper for the CA to establish itself in Krumau and that the appropriate bank was the Oberbank. See RGVA Moscow, 1458/10/227, Bl. 236, minute of Oct. 18, 1938.

17 See the contracts with the Czech banks in BA-CA, CA-TZ, Rechtsabteilung rot, Box 2/CA-BV 15b/38/1,2, File 2a; CA-TZ, Sekretariat grün, Box 5/BOS XVIII–XXIV, File 2; RGVA Moscow, 1458/10/28, Bl. 2–13.

constituted 82 percent of the population of Lundenburg/Breclav in 1918 but only 11 percent in 1938 because of the allegedly systematic Czech policy of discriminating against Germans. Now, however, the sugar factory was once again in German hands and local industry was growing because, as the paper remarked, "the Jews left the city on October 8, 1938, and many Beneš supporters went elsewhere, as the many empty places of business bear witness. The German population is once again increasing rapidly." Znaim/Znojmo was famous for its cucumbers and pickles. According to the bank's newspaper, the city's "largest and most productive pickle factories were in Jewish hands" and had been charging outrageous prices, but the situation had totally changed and demand for Znaim/Znojmo cucumbers and pickles and other farm products soared as a result.[18] All this boded well for the new CA branches. The Lundenberg branch on Hermann-Göring-Strasse was formally opened on April 17, 1939, with Pfeiffer delivering a glorifying speech before the assembled bank officials from Vienna and local Party and government figures. The Znaim branch on Konrad Henlein-Platz was opened on August 7 in a newly refurbished building that reflected the bank's commitment to the "Beauty of Labor."[19]

Carving Up the Czech Banks in the "Protectorate"

The entry of German troops into Prague on March 15, 1939, which followed the establishment of Slovak "independence," and the creation of the Protectorate of Bohemia and Moravia found the CA leadership in a much less modest mood than had been the case after the seizure of the Sudetenland. The Deutsche Bank meanwhile had become a major shareholder in the CA and the CA was anxious to benefit from its patronage under the new circumstances. On March 18 Hasslacher sent a letter to Abs informing him that "the Creditanstalt naturally has the greatest interest in substantially widening its field of activity in connection with the surprising political solutions of recent days. This is justified not only by the earlier close relationships with the newly integrated territories but also by all the other economic connections along with the advantage of the geographical location. Unfortunately, thus far we have no knowledge of the plans of the RWM and the intentions of the major banks in Berlin, but we believe that our principal shareholders too will consider a significant involvement of the Creditanstalt of importance. In any case, the management board and I came to the mutual decision today to pursue this matter straightaway with sustained effort in Prague and Brünn/Brno as well."[20]

It rapidly became clear, however, that managing the banking situation in the former Czechoslovakia was an immensely complicated task. On April 1 Joham reported to the CA executive committee that the management's efforts to gain influence through an ownership stake in a Prague bank were ongoing and that it was also seeking an influence in Moravia through a "friendship pact" with the Mährische Bank.[21] There were good reasons for the "Prague bank" to remain unspecified at this point. Much of the CA's future in these areas, of course, depended on the success of the Deutsche Bank in establishing a substantial foothold for itself in the region. The takeover of the Sudeten branches of the Czech banks was viewed by the Deutsche Bank – as it was by the Dresdner Bank – as a prelude to the attainment of a larger position in Czech banking for the service of German interests well before the destruction of Czechoslovakia in March 1939. In November 1938, the Deutsche Bank proposed to Bank Commissar Ernst that it take over the Deutsche Agrar- und Industriebank (DAIB) as soon as its planned reorganization was completed. The Deutsche Bank would thus acquire

[18] BA-CA, CA-TZ, Sekretariat rot, Box 11/CA-BV XV, XVI/1–3, "Unsere neueröffneten Filialen," in: *Gemeinschaft* 1/4 (Nov.–Dec. 1939), pp. 3–4.
[19] "Feierliche Eröffnung unserer Filiale in Lundenburg/Breclav," in: ibid., *Gemeinschaft* 1/3 (Sept.–Oct. 1939), pp. 4–5.

[20] DB, P 6502, Bl. 279, Hasslacher to Abs, March 18, 1939.
[21] BA-CA, CA-V, CA executive committee meeting, April 1, 1939.

the DAIB in Prague and Brünn/Brno and perhaps set up a branch in Pressburg/Bratislava as well. In their proposal, Rösler and Abs stressed the desirability of creating a purely German firm in rump Czechoslovakia to service, promote, and protect German interests remaining there as well as to expand them and to assist in the repatriation of the shares of Sudeten companies. They also stated their intention of giving the CA a stake in the bank "in order to emphasize the position of the City of Vienna and employ the knowledge and experience of the Creditanstalt-Wiener Bankverein."[22] The Reich Economics Ministry, however, refused to approve this plan, first because it viewed it as premature and second, and probably more importantly, because Hans Kehrl opposed it. In his view, the leading bank in promoting German interests had to be the Bebca, which had large industrial holdings, interests, and connections, and he wanted it under the control of the Dresdner Bank or possibly under the control of both the Dresdner Bank, and the Deutsche Bank. Whatever the case, his preoccupation was with putting the Bebca in German hands and using it to promote German industrial interests, especially those of the Reichswerke. The plans for using the DAIB for such purposes were thus suspended and repeatedly sabotaged by Kehrl. After the German takeover in March 1939, the Deutsche Bank was virtually forced to refinance the DAIB, in part by acquiring securities of emigrating Jews, but the DAIB ceased to be a factor in its calculations for attaining a strong position in the former Czech economy. At the same time, Kehrl ceased to show interest in having the Deutsche Bank participate with the Dresdner Bank in taking over the Bebca.

Ultimately, the division of labor in the Protectorate, and eventually in Slovakia, was a repetition of what had occurred in the Sudetenland: the Dresdner Bank based its expansion on a takeover of the Bebca, and the Deutsche Bank had to accept second best and settle for the BUB. Both banks distinguished themselves by exercising extraordinary brutality in dealing with the Czech banks. The Dresdner Bank's man in the region, Freiherr von Lüdinghausen, arrived in uniform to take over the Bebca, behaving abominably in this process. Thirty-one-year-old Walther Pohle outdid him by coming to the BUB the day *before* the military occupation, allegedly to discuss the Sudeten accounts. He then took charge with a maximum degree of arrogance and cruelty, declaring the bank to be a "Jewish enterprise," ruthlessly dismissing as many Jews as the situation would allow, and working hand in hand with the Gestapo to achieve his purposes. Turning the BUB into an Aryan enterprise necessarily made the condition of the bank worse because it had a substantial Jewish leadership and clientele, and the Deutsche Bank was far from happy about being virtually forced to acquire it, finding itself stuck with what it considered to be second best. Solving the managerial problem required the Deutsche Bank not only to rely on Pohle but also to take a second banker from its own ranks, namely, Max Rohde of the Saarbrücken branch of the Deutsche Bank, who acted as second in command. In dealing with the BUB's finances, the Deutsche Bank presented the condition of the bank as far worse than it actually was, forced a draconian capital reduction in December 1939, sought and eventually received government subsidization for the reorganization of the BUB, and employed a variety of dubious tactics to take it over. In June 1940, the DAIB, upon which the Deutsche Bank had placed some of its hopes, was taken over via the BUB.[23]

---

[22] RGVA Moscow, 1458/10/82, Bl. 122–126, CA to Ernst, Nov. 28, 1938. There is an excellent discussion of the DAIB and these issues in Harald Wixforth, "Im Visier deutscher Finanzinteressen. Die Deutsche Agrar- und Industriebank in Prag und ihr Schicksal 1938–1940," in: Harald Wixforth (ed.), *Finanzinstitutionen in Mitteleuropa während des Nationalsozialismus (= Geld und Kapital. Jahrbuch der Gesellschaft für mitteleuropäische Banken- und Sparkassengeschichte (* Stuttgart 2000), pp. 127–164.

[23] There is a good discussion of the takeover of the BUB in Harold James, *The Deutsche Bank and the Nazi Economic War against the Jews* (München 2001), pp. 152–162. See also the correspondence dealing with appointments to the administrative council; see the Archiv des Finanzministeriums Kladno, 1479.

The outcome of the struggle between the Deutsche Bank and the Dresdner Bank clouded the CA's hope to secure a significant place in Prague, at least for the moment. The Deutsche Bank had offered the CA a capital stake in the BUB and had reserved the position of second deputy chairman on the administrative council for the CA. An actual agreement on CA participation, however, was put off, apparently somewhat to the irritation of the CA. At the beginning of January 1940, Fischböck took up the issue with Rösler and inquired whether the time had not come to make an agreement, but Rösler urged that they wait a few months until the capital of the BUB could be increased. The practical problem obviously was that the Deutsche Bank's reorganization program, which entailed a capital reduction and other financial measures, made it very difficult to determine the size of a CA stake. A further complication at this time was that Riehle had informed the Deutsche Bank that he found a CA minority stake in the BUB "less attractive" than other options. In order to show good faith, the Deutsche Bank successfully pushed to have Director Fritscher of the CA receive a position on the BUB administrative council. As Rösler pointed out to Abs, the appointment of Fritscher was an important gesture to the CA given the Deutsche Bank's stake in the CA: "We have an interest in further deepening our relationship with the Creditanstalt and view the entry of a representative of the Creditanstalt into the administrative council of a bank that is close to us and also active in the eastern region as a means toward that end. Similar considerations have led us in other cases to ask our friends to enter into the supervisory boards of companies that are close to us. The Union Bank would only have business advantages from a closer relationship with the Creditanstalt...."[24] There can be no question, therefore, that the Deutsche Bank wanted to

cultivate and use the CA, hence holding out prospects for the future. But for the time being the CA would have to accept smaller pickings in the Czech lands. Interest in controlling the BUB did not wane, and Joham began to scheme for a CA takeover of the BUB in 1940. It was only in 1942, however, at the time the Deutsche Bank assumed a majority at the CA, that the CA was given a one-third share in the BUB in the context of expansionist plans to be discussed later in this study.

In contrast to the CA involvement in the BUB, Riehle found the CA engagement with the Mährische Bank in Brünn/Brno quite attractive. On April 6, 1939, the two banks concluded a "friendship pact" undertaken "in view of the change in the political and economic situation that has taken place through the creation of the Protectorate of Bohemia and Moravia within the framework of the Greater German Reich."[25] They agreed to work more closely together so as to meet the requirements of the anticipated upturn in Austrian-Moravian economic relations, to employ one another's services insofar as binding commitments to work with another bank did not exist, and to offer one another stakes in large business operations. They would also keep one another informed about "changes in industrial enterprises in Bohemia and Moravia" and seek to participate in such business. They agreed to represent the interests of one another in dealing with other banks, enterprises, and the authorities, and to collaborate in floating emissions on the Vienna stock exchange and other stock exchanges in the Reich. The CA goal in this agreement was to strengthen and expand its influence in Moravia. It also intended to buy up shares in the Mährische Bank wherever possible, having already purchased the bank's branches in Znaim/Znojmo and Lundenburg/Breclav, and it also planned to acquire the BUB branches in Moravia. In general, the Mährische Bank was viewed as a solid institution that had not been affected very negatively by the German takeover, and it had only a few industrial losses in

---

[24] DB, B 176, Rösler to Abs, Dec. 8, 1939; Deutsche Bank to BUB, Nov. 27, 1939; Rösler to Abs, Jan. 8, 1940. On Riehle's views, see ibid., P 6502, Bl. 317, the telegram by Rohdewald to Heller, April 5, 1939.

[25] Copies are to be found in ibid., Bl. 319–327, and BA-CA, CA-V, S.P. Akten, Nr. 1037.

Slovakia. As noted earlier, Riehle encouraged the CA to expand its influence in Moravia in every way possible, and the Mährische Bank was viewed as the most important instrument toward this end.[26]

Nevertheless, the authorities in Berlin did not encourage the wider ambitions and schemes of the CA in Moravia as much as the CA leadership would have liked. In September 1939, the CA tried to justify its bid for a stronger position in Upper Silesia by pointing to its interests in Moravia. As Fischböck told Bank Commissar Ernst, "the Creditanstalt has a plan in mind whereby the Böhmische Unionbank in Prague would be divided regionally between the Deutsche Bank and the Creditanstalt, so that the Bohemian branches would go to the Deutsche Bank and the Mährische Bank to the Creditanstalt."[27] When Fischböck asked whether such a plan might be worth pursuing, Ernst said he did not think so because a decision had been made to keep the Protectorate independent and not let the German banks penetrate there any further. Whatever the case, neither the government nor the CA's ally, the Deutsche Bank, was prepared to divide the BUB in this manner.

CA Ambitions in Slovakia and the Union-Bank Pressburg

The most important and most complicated of CA acquisitions in the Czech lands in 1938–1940 involved those in Slovakia. While certainly interested in establishing a foothold in an area adjacent to the Ostmark, notwithstanding the largely agrarian character of the country and the predominance of small enterprises, the CA actually had its eye on the very important German companies and business opportunities, especially in Pressburg/Bratislava. From the outset, however, there was considerable uncertainty about what the CA should seek

and what it would get. The discussion about a German banking presence in Slovakia began months before Slovakia became a separate fascist state. In late November 1938, the German consulate in Bratislava strongly urged that the German banks make their presence felt, and the Deutsche Bank swiftly responded with a memorandum to the RWM announcing its interest in establishing itself throughout Southeast Europe, and it then proposed in February 1939 that it be allowed to join with the CA in purchasing 90 percent of the Escompte- und Volkswirtschaftliche Bank, which was owned by the Tatra banka. The Dresdner Bank was to get the Pressburger Handels- und Kreditbank, which belonged to the Bebca. Joham duly reported this plan to the CA executive committee on February 21, cautioning, however, that everything was "in flux."[28] It was indeed, and when Joham next turned to the question at the April 1 meeting, he announced that they no longer intended to acquire the Escompte- und Volkswirtschaftliche Bank and were considering instead a participation in the Pressburger Handels- und Kreditbank AG, although this too had not been finally decided. The executive committee authorized him to open a branch in Pressburg/Bratislava, to take a stake in a bank, or to take over an existing bank branch in that city.[29]

This authorization to do anything that could be done made a great deal of sense under circumstances, given that was not the bankers but rather Hans Kehrl who was calling the tune. He seems to have thought that the two banks projected for takeover were too small in themselves, that what was needed in Slovakia was a major German bank, and that the best solution was for the Dresdner Bank/ Länderbank Wien to take over the Pressburger Handels- und Kreditbank AG in collaboration

[26] See ibid., S.P. Akten, Nr. 446, the CA report to Riehle, Oct. 18, 1939. Fischböck also emphasized Riehle's position in a report to the board of management on Dec. 9, 1939, BA-CA, CA-V.

[27] RGVA Moscow, 1458/15/125, Bl. 143–144, memo by Ernst, Sept. 27, 1939.

[28] Ibid., executive committee meeting, Feb. 21, 1939. A useful account of the Slovak financial system is to be found in Roman Holec, "Das Bank und Kreditgenossenschaftswesen in der Slowakei 1939–1945," in: Wixforth (ed.), Finanzinstitutionen in Mitteleuropa, pp. 165–179.

[29] BA-CA, CA-V, executive committee meeting of April 1, 1939.

with the Deutsche Bank/CA and then buy up the Escompte- und Volkswirtschaftliche Bank. Typically, the Dresdner Bank took the lead and negotiated with the Bebca in Berlin and Basel for the purchase of all the shares of the Pressburger Handels- und Kreditbank AG by the Länderbank Wien. The outcome of these negotiations and the sales arrangements were duly presented to the Bebca on February 4, 1939, thus placing the Bebca branch in the hands of the Länderbank Wien before the establishment of the fascist Slovak state.[30] It was understood, however, that the Deutsche Bank/CA would then take over half the shares. Apparently, the Länderbank wanted to determine who the head of the supervisory board would be, but Fischböck worked out an arrangement with Kehrl under which the person would be neutral and thereby assure parity between the two parties. Things were not as smooth as they looked, however, because the CA decided that it deserved and wanted a more independent position in Slovakia and lost interest in sharing a bank with the Länderbank. On March 27, the CA wrote to Commissar Bürckel asking for support in its efforts to stake out an independent claim in Pressburg/Bratislava. The CA argued that it was interested in resurrecting Vienna's position as the leading center for trade with Slovakia and that it was the ideal place to deepen and develop relations with the new Slovakia in the interest of the Reich as a whole. As was now its custom, the CA sought to give its position historical legitimacy and be compensated for alleged post-1918 wrongs by arguing that it had always had a branch in Pressburg/Bratislava until "the forceful measures of the Czechoslovak government made further direct activity there impossible."[31] The indirect relationships had continued, however, and the CA agreed to share a bank in Pressburg/Bratislava with the Länderbank. Because of the changed political circumstances in mid-March, the CA now wished to take a stake in another Slovak bank or take it over in its entirety, thereby

possibly giving up the 50 percent stake with the Länderbank and having its bank devote itself almost entirely to the promotion of Slovak agricultural and timber products in order to supply the raw materials needs of the Reich. The CA also informed Bürckel that it was in the process of establishing a "Gesellschaft für Außenhandel mbH," that is, a company that would have the special purpose of promoting economic relations with the Southeast European countries and that could give special attention to trade with Slovakia.

Underlying this approach was a report of March 27 from Director Fritscher of the CA, who had managed to see the confidential economic treaty between Germany and Slovakia. He noted that, as in the case of Romania, economic relations, especially in the agrarian and forestry sectors, were concentrated on Berlin, creating the danger that Vienna would be left out in the cold. One had to show that Vienna had both the financial wherewithal and the technical skills to handle the entire import and export trade with Slovakia. The bank plan as well as the establishment of a trade corporation were viewed by Fritscher and his allies as mechanisms whereby Vienna could successfully challenge Berlin.[32] It is doubtful that the CA was ever terribly enthusiastic about the partnership with the Länderbank in any case, especially because the Dresdner Bank was likely to play a very dominating role and had been assigned the Bebca in Prague. The CA withdrew from the arrangement in mid-May, which coincided with the formal establishment of the Gesellschaft für Außenhandel (Corporation for Foreign Trade) in which the CA had a 75 percent share and the Bankhaus Schoeller a 25 percent share.[33]

It also coincided with a new possibility resulting from negotiations with the Prague-based Legio Bank,[34] which had substantial holdings

30 BA-CA, CA-V, S.P. Akten, Nr. 426, Dresdner Bank to Bebca, Feb. 4, 1939.
31 Ibid., CA to Bürckel, March 27, 1939.

32 Ibid., Fritscher memorandum of March 27, 1939.
33 See ibid., the correspondence with the Dresdner Bank terminating the collaboration. See BA-CA, CA-V, CA executive committee meeting, May 17, 1939, the Gesellschaft für Außenhandel.
34 The Legio Bank was founded after the war with the back pay and possibly also some Russian gold

in Slovakia and offered the CA an option on 50 percent of the shares of the Slovakische Allgemeine Creditbank, Bratislava (SVUBCA). The idea in May 1939 was for the CA to reconstruct the SVUBCA and then to integrate it into the Pressburg/Bratislava branch of the BUB.[35] The problem was that the new Slovak state, while certainly a German satellite, was by no means so much of a puppet that it was prepared to accept dictates from Berlin with respect to the organization of its banking system. On the one hand, the Bratislava regime was highly suspicious of Prague and its banks and anxious to shed Prague influences. On the other hand, it was also anxious to look after its own national interests and the concerns of its native businessmen, and while willing to give German interests their due was not prepared to do so at excessive expense to its native institutions. German authorities and the German bankers, therefore, had to rein in their ambitions and engage in complicated arrangements in order to deal with Slovak interests and sensibilities.[36]

Developments in Prague had shown that the Deutsche Bank was forced to concentrate its attentions on the BUB because the Bebca was completely controlled by the Dresdner Bank. This meant that the CA had to center its plans in Slovakia to a considerable extent on the BUB branch in Pressburg/Bratislava. By late fall 1939, however, the position of the BUB branch in Pressburg/Bratislava had become untenable because the Slovak authorities wished to drive as many Prague banks as possible, including the BUB, out of Slovakia and were blocking the development of the Pressburg/Bratislava

branch. The only solution seemed to be the creation of a Pressburg/Bratislava branch as an independent bank in Slovakia in the context of the Deutsche Bank concern, of which the BUB and the CA were important parts. BUB director Pohle was anxious to bring in the CA as a partner and had discussed the problem with the CA official charged with Slovak affairs, Dr. Franz Deschka, but the CA had delayed taking action because of its desire to acquire shares of the SVUBCA. By October 1939, however, Pohle told Abs that action had to be taken and that the modalities of the CA's participation could wait until after the Pressburg/Bratislava branch was established as an independent entity. All he now wanted was for Abs to persuade Fischböck and Deschka that the "new" bank in Pressburg/Bratislava be launched.

This seemed all the more sensible because the situation of the SVUBCA had become more and more intransparent. Pohle and Fritscher had met with Legio Bank representatives and found that the bank's financial status had been affected because it had been constrained to give up so many of its branches and subsidiaries to the Hungarians. In subsequent discussions with SS Obersturmbannführer Eilers, who acted as German trustee for the Legio Bank, Fritscher and Deschka encountered resistance to the idea of giving up the Slovak branches because they were much of what now remained of the Legio Bank. At the same time, it was unclear how long it would be before the Slovak government forced a separation of these branches from the Legio Bank. In short, something could be done about the BUB branch in Pressburg/Bratislava, but the question of how to deal with the SVUBCA and the Legio Bank branches in Slovakia remained unresolved. For the time being, therefore, the CA took an option on the purchase of the Legio Bank assets and concentrated its attention elsewhere.[37]

The CA, therefore, decided in November 1939 to take the path urged by the BUB and concentrate on the reestablishment of the BUB branch in Pressburg/Bratislava as an independent bank

---

of the famous Czech Legion that marched home through Russia. It was apparently a very successful bank, and its art deco building was a famous landmark in Prague.

35 For these intentions, see BA-CA, CA-TZ, Rechtsabteilung rot, Box 9/Union-Bank, Preßburg XII, File 11, the Promemoria of Nov. 9, 1939.

36 For an excellent discussion of the peculiarities of German-Slovak relations, see Tatjana Tönsmeyer, *Das Dritte Reich und die Slowakei 1939–1945. Politischer Alltag zwischen Kooperation und Eigensinn* (Paderborn 2003).

37 DB, B 174, BUB to Abs, Oct. 13, 1939, and Fritscher memorandum of Dec. 22, 1939.

with CA participation. The new bank would have share capital of 50 million Ks, 45 million Ks in share capital and 5 million Ks in reserves. The CA was to provide somewhat more than half the capital, that is, 28 million Ks, while the BUB was to provide 22 million Ks. A substantial portion of the capital base of the bank given by the BUB was composed of accounts receivable from the Chemische Industrie Dr. Blasberg & Co. and the very large timber firm of J. Ph. Glesinger. The CA also put in some accounts receivable from Glesinger, but 26 million Ks was to be gradually provided by means of the German-Slovak clearing arrangement. The two participating banks were to form a syndicate in which the leadership lay with the CA.[38] An important underlying consideration in these plans was that the new institution might benefit from Slovak government plans to strengthen the country's banking sector through consolidation. The CA and BUB anticipated that it might participate in the liquidation of some branches of the Prague banks and add branches and capital to the newly created bank. This indeed had been and remained the intention of the CA option on the Legio Bank holdings in Slovakia.

There was, however, a good deal of tension and mistrust between the German and Slovak sides. Hence the RWM, especially in the person of Ministerial Director Riehle, paid close attention to the developments in Pressburg/Bratislava, both to make sure that the two German banks that were being set up were accorded normal facilities and opportunities by the Slovak government and to safeguard that they did not compete in ways that were counterproductive. In mid-December Riehle met with Max Ludwig Rohde of the BUB and with Franz Stephan, the director of the BUB branch in Pressburg/Bratislava, soon to be made independent under CA-BUB leadership and later to be named the Union-Bank Pressburg. Stephan informed them that the Slovak Finance Ministry appreciated the amount of capital being put in by the two German banks and was prepared to support the creation of new branches "where German-speaking islands are involved." Riehle

also had the sense that the Slovak authorities might sanction a merger of the new bank with the Slovakische Allgemeine Creditbank. He was adamant, however, that the two German banks not compete but collaborate with one another in dealing with the Slovak authorities.[39] Riehle undoubtedly found it difficult not to be able to rule the roost in Pressburg/Bratislava the way he did in Prague. He thus insisted in a discussion with Fischböck that the banks in Slovakia not have any participations in Prague banks. Director Rösler of the Deutsche Bank found this attitude more than acceptable because it meant that the bank in Pressburg/Bratislava would not make any claims on the BUB. Indeed, Rösler told Fischböck that "if the Creditanstalt would consider it worthwhile to acquire the entire capital of the Pressburger Bank, then this is something one could discuss."[40] At the same time, however, he considered it important that a BUB representative sit on the supervisory board of the Pressburg bank because of the continued business between Slovakia and the Czech area and because of the experience a person from the BUB would have to offer.

At the turn of 1939–1940, therefore, the "new" bank appeared to be on the brink of establishing itself, but it was not formally created until late in the year and was well behind its competitor, the Deutsche Handels- und Kreditbank (DHKA).[41] This was partly due to advantages enjoyed by the Dresdner Bank/ Länderbank in the Czech lands and the slowness with which the CA came to a decision about what it wanted to do in Slovakia, as well as the issues involving the BUB; but it was also due to the difficulties German-Slovak disagreements created for the construction of the new bank. Despite the injunctions of both Riehle and the extremely active commercial attaché in

---

[38] Ibid., BUB to CA, Nov. 16, 1939.

[39] Ibid., memorandum by Stephan, Dec. 16, 1939.
[40] Ibid., Rösler to Abs, Jan. 8, 1940.
[41] The DHKA is dealt with in Chapter 6, pp. 507–518, which parallels and supplements the discussion here, and it is also discussed by Harald Wixforth in *"Die Expansion der Dresdner Bank in Europa,"* in: *Klaus-Dietmar Henke (ed.), Die Dresdner Bank im Dritten Reich,* 4 vols. (Munich 2006), vol. 3, ch. IV.

Slovakia, Erich Gebert, who was also Gau economic advisor in Salzburg, that the two German banks work together, they were often competitors. This was particularly the case with respect to the Zipser Bank AG in Käsmark/Kezmarok and the Zipser Kreditbank AG, Leutschau/Levoča, which serviced a German and Hungarian clientele in the Carpathian region, and the Cereháter Bank, which had a German clientele in Unter-Metzenseifen/Medzev. The Deutsche Partei of Slovakia played an important role in the regions, and the DHKA had apparently approached these banks first. But in discussions with Director Stephan on December 28, 1939, the Käsmark bank had also shown an interest in teaming up with what was to be the future Union-Bank. Stephan had the sense that their interest stemmed from the perception that the DHKA was excessively German in character, and that the CA-BUB bank would be more sympathetic to the Hungarian clientele. This attitude was understandable given the CA's background in the old Austro-Hungarian empire. The dilemma for Stephan was how to keep his bank in the running for the Zipser Bank without encouraging the latter, which was being courted by the DHKA, to increase its demands in negotiations with the CA-BUB bank.[42] Nevertheless, the possibility of taking over the three banks in question increased at the beginning of 1940, when Gebert invited Stephan to discuss whether the bank would be interested in these banks and how the acquisitions might be organized. The CA responded very rapidly, assuring Gebert that it would be willing to take over the three banks.[43]

Despite such prospects, the reality was that the CA-BUB had picked up nothing at the beginning of 1940. The bank had an option on the shares of the Slovakische Allgemeine Creditbank held by the Legio Bank, with whom it had made a friendship pact in May 1939, but the previously mentioned difficulties of the Legio Bank made it difficult to implement the arrangement. The CA prolonged its option for a full year at the beginning of 1940, but there was considerable concern that Slovak circles wanted to block such a takeover. What the CA-BUB would get after the much-discussed Slovak bank concentration process took place was also up in the air. On February 10, 1940, therefore, the CA wrote to the German embassy in Pressburg/Bratislava to ask that it not only support its ambitions with respect to the Zipser Bank but also stand behind its plan to acquire the Slovakische Allgemeine Creditbank from the Legio Bank. In this way, the new German bank would have a network of branches that would be effective and, more important, would have branches in the German areas of Slovakia. The CA was concerned that the Slovak government bank concentration policies would denude the Legio Bank of important branches.[44]

From the standpoint of the German authorities in Pressburg/Bratislava, the first issue was to regulate the relationship between the two German banks before their competition got out of hand and to determine who was going to get the Zipser Bank. Gebert decided to act as mediator and in March 1940 he proposed a settlement in collaboration with Eugen Reisinger, head of the Economic Office of the Deutsche Partei. This proposal is interesting both for the intentions and principles outlined with respect to the German banking presence in Slovakia and the reasons for the decision on how to divide the various banking assets available to the two German banks.[45] Gebert gave as his primary concern the promotion of German interests by making his decisions from the perspective of what was best from a "national-political" perspective. Because the Slovak government

---

42   See BA-CA, CA-TZ, Rechtsabteilung rot, Box 9/Union-Bank, Preßburg XII, the minute by Stephan, Dec. 28, 1939, and the memo by Fritscher, Dec. 30, 1939.

43   Ibid., memo by Stephan, Feb. 7, 1940, and CA to Gebert, Feb. 10, 1940.

44   Ibid., Minutes by Fritscher, Dec. 30, 1939 and Jan. 5, 1940, and CA to German Embassy, Feb. 10, 1940.

45   The discussion that follows is based on the memorandum sent by Gebert to Stephan on March 5, 1940, to be found in ibid. Fischböck reported the decision to Riehle on March 9, 1940, ibid. There is also a copy sent by the BUB to Rösler on March 11, 1940 in DB, B 174.

had agreed to allow two German banks in the country, it was essential they be constructed in a functional manner that bespoke the "justified prestige claims of their patron banks," that there not be a great difference in their respective capabilities, that neither be so advantaged that the other would be reduced to insignificance, and that they each reflect the "standing" of a German institution. While it was essential that the two banks cooperate and maintain Germany's reputation, it was also important that they not cooperate so much as to create the impression of being one bank because the goal was to have two effective German banks in existence. For this reason, each bank had to have a network of branches and make sure that the larger Germanic areas in Slovakia were properly serviced while avoiding an excess of local competition. In the case of the Zips, the dominant considerations were "ethnic-political" ones and the banks had to be "a significant instrument of the ethnic-political work in the Zips." For this reason, these banks had to be in the hands of the particular bank that was so oriented as well as dedicated.

On the basis of these principles, Gebert decided that the Zipser Bank and its branches as well as three small banks in the region serving German and/or Hungarian clientele, the Zipserkreditbank, the Cerehàter Bank, and the Georgenberger katholische Volksbank, would be assigned to the DHKA, that is, to the Dresdner Bank-Länderbank group, while the Slovakische Allgemeine Creditbank (SVUBCA) and Bratislavaer Allgemeine Bank AG and their branches and affiliates would go to the Deutsche Bank-CA-BUB group. Gebert defended this decision by arguing that the Dresdner Bank had taken the lead in concerning itself with the "economic opening up" of Slovakia from a banking standpoint and had been the first to approach representatives of the Zipser Bank. More importantly, it had done this work of economic development in close contact with the Deutsche Partei in Pressburg/ Bratislava and had been most diligent in following certain guidelines of the Party in economic matters. At the same time, the Deutsche Partei had been crucial in developing the DHKA's

role as a savings bank, a function vital to the Zips region. In a somewhat left-handed compliment, the report did admit the BUB had played a significant role in promoting German economic interests in the Zips and in breaking the hold exercised previously by the Živno banking network, "but all of this occurred primarily with concern for its own economic interests and not in close collaboration with the respective dominant, politically important institutions in the Zips."

Turning to more practical considerations, Gebert argued that giving the Zips banks to the DHKA would provide it with a sufficiently large balance so that it would not appear miniature in size compared to its competitor if such a competitor absorbed the SVUBCA. It also would be easier to get the support of the Slovak government if the new CA-BUB bank would not be assigned two banking complexes but only one, thus creating a better balance between the two German banks. Because the DHKA was more attuned to savings bank functions, it was also more appropriate that it took over the similarly oriented Zips banks, while the SVUBCA complex had maintained a more commercial and industrial orientation. Gebert considered it essential, however, that the two German banks rapidly take over and integrate their respective holdings. He was very critical of the DHKA tendency to show excessive respect for the local and independent character of the Zips banks because this would allow them to retain too Hungarian a character. Gebert called on both the DHKA and the CA-BUB to take over their respectively assigned assets as rapidly and effectively as possible because the primary concern was to establish two strong German banking groups in the Slovak economy.

This was an unpleasant surprise for both the CA, which had apparently anticipated being asked to negotiate with the Zipser banks, and for Gebert, whose reasoning the BUB considered dubious and rather insulting. The BUB did not think the DHKA had some monopoly in serving German interests, especially because its Pressburg/Bratislava branch had played a big role in the financing of mining timber deliveries. The Deutsche Bank was no less annoyed, pointing out that the Dresdner Bank had no priority in serving German business and that the original idea had been for the Deutsche Bank and the Dresdner Bank to found a bank in Slovakia together by using the Bebca branch, and that it was only the creation of the Protectorate that led the two banks to go their separate ways. At the same time, the economic logic of the mediation proposal was not without its advantages for the CA-BUB. The Zipser banks were primarily in the mortgage and savings business, and the Legio branches were more attractive from a commercial and industrial perspective, but one had to be concerned that the Legio Bank would be in a position to honor the option it had given to the CA. There were reports that it had offered the branches to a Slovak business group if the CA did not take the option, and this was bound to increase resistance to a CA-BUB takeover of the SVUBCA branches. It was quite possible, the BUB leadership feared, that Gebert was somewhat premature in his belief that the SVUBCA branches were at the CA-BUB's disposal.[46]

But even if the representatives of these banks complained about the historical interpretation grounding Gebert's proposal, they knew that they needed Gebert's help and wished to clear the air without engaging in counterproductive polemics. In a meeting attended by Fischböck, Rohde, and a representative of Gebert's, the CA-BUB made clear that it accepted the proposal but not the way it had been justified and asked that the invidious comparison between the CA-BUB and the Dresdner Bank group be corrected. On March 18, the CA invited a host of leading Pressburg/Bratislava personalities to a dinner for the obvious purpose of cultivating both Slovak and German officialdom and economic leadership. Riehle, who came with his staff and members of the business community, was also in attendance. He used the occasion to negotiate further with the Slovak authorities on the division of Slovak branches among the two German banking groups. The next day, Fischböck, Fritscher, Pfeiffer, Deschka, Stephan,

and Rohde attended a meeting with Riehle. Fischböck reported on his negotiations with a Reichsbank representative and the Legio Bank leaders in which an agreement was reached that the CA would get the SVUBCA and the other Legio Bank branches. The price, however, would be determined in a year or two, once the CA had the opportunity to do an audit and decide what should be paid. Riehle emphasized that he had discussed the matter with the Slovak authorities and made clear to them that the Legio branches and the SVUBCA were "an area belonging to German interests." Not mentioned here but also of relevance was the proposal that the branches of certain other Czech banks scheduled to be liquidated in the concentration process could be acquired by the two German banks. In any case, the upshot of this meeting was an agreement in principle on a merger of the BUB branch and the SVUBCA in what was to be called the "Union-Bank," which would be under CA control.[47]

Although the allotment of banks and banking branches between the two German banks in Slovakia was now settled as far as the German authorities were concerned, the actual acquisition of these assets would not be without problems. The DHKA had difficulties bringing the Zipser banks to terms, especially because of Hungarian resistance and rivalries between the Germans and Hungarians.[48] Nonetheless, the problems connected with the acquisition of the SVUBCA and the Legio Bank branches were far more serious because they led to acute altercations with the Slovak Finance Ministry, clearly revealing the tensions between Germany and the newly created Slovak state.

Riehle and Gebert may have thought that matters were settled with respect to the acquisitions of what was to be the Union-Bank, but the Slovak Finance Ministry had an unpleasant surprise in store for the Germans. The divergent views became quite evident, ironically, on April 1, 1940.

---

[46] Ibid., Rohde to Rösler, March 11, 1940, and Deutsche Bank to BUB, March 16, 1940.

[47] Ibid., Deutsche Bank to BUB, March 20, 1940, and memorandum by Rohde, March 19, 1940, and RGVA Moscow, 1458/10/235, Bl. 292–293, memo by Riehle, April 6, 1940.

[48] See Chapter 6, pp. 507–513.

On that date, representatives of the CA and the Legio Bank met in Prague to negotiate the terms of the latter's sale of its Slovak assets. The Legio Bank agreed to sell its shares in the SVUBCA that were deposited at the Slovak National Bank and to sell the Legio Bank's own Slovak business by lodging it in the SVUBCA. This involved the sale of its own branches, its share holdings currently held at the Legio Bank headquarters in Prague, and nearly all its real property in Slovakia. The CA accepted this offer along with the various arrangements for determining the price and organizing the disposition of assets connected with the offer.[49] But during the conclusion of this negotiation, the Slovak Finance Ministry issued a decree dated April 1 under which the entire SVUBCA was to be absorbed by the Tatra Bank. This bank was particularly favored by the Slovak government because it ranked as one of the two leading banks in Slovakia after the war and served local Slovak needs from the outset. On the same day the CA was buying the SVUBCA, the Slovak Finance Ministry was assigning it to the Tatra Bank!

The Germans were not amused. The German embassy in Pressburg/Bratislava issued a verbal protest against this action on April 2, and the Slovak Foreign Office responded with a lengthy memorandum on April 6.[50] The memorandum suggested that Germans often misunderstood the natural tendency of the Slovak state to defend its political freedom by securing its economic independence after years of domination by Jewish capital, Hungarian capital, and Czech capital. The Slovaks denied that they had violated the March 18 agreement between Riehle and Director Alexander Hrnčár of the Finance Ministry by arguing that it was a mistake to think that the Slovak government had already agreed to the CA taking over the SVUBCA. The Finance Ministry felt compelled to act when it learned of the agreement between the Legio Bank and the CA and when it noted that the SVUBCA officers were instructed to follow CA instructions. Indeed, the authors of the memorandum concluded that it was the CA that had shown bad faith in giving such instructions that virtually turned the SVUBCA into a branch of the CA. While the Slovak authorities were prepared to allow the liquidation of various bank branches in Slovakia, they claimed that they wanted to do this on a commercial basis with government approval and not by fiat. They also charged that the Legio Bank was selling off branches to the Hungarians without consulting with the Slovak government. In any case, the CA was charged with bypassing the Slovak authorities, turning the new bank into a branch of the CA, and confronting the Slovak authorities with the worst kind of "economic liberalism" in which the strong were allowed to overpower the weak. The issue, however, was not one of principle only, but of real economic concern because the SVUBCA had a capital base of 58 million Ks, which was 28 percent of the banking capital in Slovakia and, in addition, had a balance of 745 million Ks or 21 percent of the bank balances in the country. The ministry argued that Slovak economic circles were hardly in a position to just give up this "economic instrument," all the less so because most of the investors in the SVUBCA were Slovaks. From this perspective, the Germans in the present case were simply replacing the Czechs in controlling Slovak capital, of which there was precious little available. The goal, according to the ministry, was to get rid of not only the political legacy of 1919 but also its economic legacy, and the Legio Bank was viewed as a prime embodiment of this foreign economic domination over Slovakia. The Slovak Foreign Office insisted that the actions of the Finance Ministry would ultimately benefit Slovak-German relations by improving Slovakia's position in their clearing arrangements, while also arguing that Slovakia could hardly be expected to treat German citizens better than its own. The memorandum's author suggested that opponents of Slovak measures were really out to undermine Slovak-German relations and were acting out of "private egotistical interests." Above all, the Slovak government felt it essential to improve its situation in the clearing arrangements, and it

49   DB, B 174, Gedächtnisprotokoll, April 1, 1940.
50   The discussion that follows is based on the memorandum of April 6, 1940, in RGVA Moscow, 1458/10/235, Bl. 300–312.

could not do so by transferring yet more capital abroad.

Needless to say, this memorandum reflected Slovakia's difficult situation. It had achieved "independence" from the Czechs but at the cost of subordination to Germany, and it was chafing under German domination. Nonetheless, as far as the German embassy was concerned, the memorandum did not deal with the "core problem" raised in its note of April 2, namely, that the directive from the Finance Committee was not a departure from the agreements of March 18 but rather a complete rejection of them. Indeed, the memorandum suggested that the Slovak government never had any intention of achieving agreement on the German standpoint on March 18 as a real basis for settlement. The charge that the Germans had shown bad faith through the CA-Legio Bank negotiations was rejected, first because the government was unaware of the negotiations, and second because they were subject to Slovak government approval in any case. Most important, however, was the fact that the Germans understood the Slovak government to have committed itself to a solution to the bank question that it then turned upside down by turning the SVUBCA over to the Tatra Bank. Last, the German embassy insisted that there was no reason to suggest that Germany was neglectful of Slovak interests and pointed out, with remarkable disingenuousness given the role Germany was playing in Europe as well as Slovakia, "that there will be no agency of the Reich that would represent in the least any private, capitalist aggregates of interests manifested by German economic groups against the natural and justified claims as well as the vital rights of another state and its economy." On a less elevated level, not only Gebert and the German diplomats in Pressburg/Bratislava felt double-crossed by the Slovak Finance Ministry, but Riehle did too. He had done much of the negotiating and had intended to use the occasion of a visit of Slovak officials to Berlin to try to force a reversal of the decree of April 1.[51]

The Slovak authorities, however, clung fast to their position. On May 3, Gebert reported to Fritscher that they, but especially Slovak National Bank President Imrich Karvaš, were taking the position that the decree could not be changed because the Legio Bank and the SVUBCA had been restructured with government subsidies and that the arrangement with the CA was unacceptable. The mystery of why the Slovak Finance Ministry had waited until April 1 to issue its decree when the CA option had existed for six months remained unanswered. Gebert thought that the Slovak officials had not been open in their dealings, and Riehle's feathers were completely ruffled. At a meeting attended by Keppler, Riehle, Karvaš, and Hrinčar, the two German negotiators took the position that the decree undermined their negotiations and had to be set aside. At this point, Karvaš agreed with Keppler that the decree should not be allowed to stand in the way of a "reasonable settlement." When Riehle then met with Hrinčar on April 26, he set as a minimal demand that the Tatra Bank not exercise its rights under the decree and demanded that the Slovak government confirm this within a week and also come forward with some proposals as to how the liquidation of the Czech banks in Slovakia was to take place in the context of the protection of German interests. What made the situation particularly alarming were reports that the Tatra Bank was already undertaking an examination of the Legio Bank books with the support of the Slovak government. Riehle now demanded two things: first, that the Slovak government agree to give the two German banks an appropriate foundation for their subsequent work; second, to make it possible for them to have the necessary capital to function. At this point, he viewed these as "prestige questions" for German banking and threatened that the German banks would withdraw from Slovakia if these questions were not answered positively with all the consequences this would entail for German economic activity in Slovakia.[52]

---

[51] Ibid., Bl. 202–203 and 303–305, German Embassy to Slovak Foreign Office, April 8, 1940, and memorandum by Riehle, April 6, 1940.

[52] BA-CA, CA-TZ, Rechtsabteilung rot, Box 9/ Union-Bank, Preßburg XII, Gebert to Fritscher, May 3, 1940 with memorandum of Riehle, April 26, 1940.

The result of the negotiations that followed produced a series of face-saving arrangements in which the Finance Ministry decree was upheld but the German side got more or less what it wanted anyway. On June 17, 1940, the CA made an agreement with the Tatra Bank in Pressburg/Bratislava under which the Tatra Bank was to replace the CA as the second party to the agreement negotiated between the CA and the Legio Bank on April 1. Accordingly, the Tatra Bank would take over the SVUBCA and the other Slovak assets that had been sold to the CA, allowing for some changes in the arrangements to be negotiated directly between the Tatra Bank and the Legio Bank. On the terms that had been agreed upon on April 1, the Tatra Bank would then sell to the CA various Legio Bank branches as well as the branches of the SVUBCA along with their accounts, including those in Pressburg/Bratislava. The CA was to take over a specified number of employees, excepting, as usual, Jews. The Tatra Bank planned to liquidate the SVUBCA and to take over its remaining branches. In this way, the Slovak government's desire to have the Tatra Bank take over the Legio Bank in Slovakia and thus strengthen the Tatra Bank was realized, while the nascent Union-Bank was to take over some of the branches it wished to have.[53]

An examination of the arrangements agreed to in the late spring of 1940 makes evident that the Germans had been forced to reduce their claims considerably. The basic principle of the compromise required the two German banks to limit themselves to branches where ethnic German interests were dominant or where the economic interests of the Reich justified a German banking presence. In the case of the DHKA, the Germans proposed that this bank take over various banks and branches – all of them legitimized by "ethnic German interests" – in thirteen locations, primarily in the Zips. As for the Union-Bank, instead of the anticipated twenty-six branches of the Legio Bank, the German side suggested that it have a presence in only nine places: Sillein/Žilina, where there

were important German economic interests and connections, especially with Upper Silesia; Tyrnau/Travna, and Neutra/Nitra, where there were German settlements; Bystrica/Banská and Trentsen/Trenčin, where Germans had economic engagements; Preschau/Prešov and Vranov, where German timber interests were located; Krickerhau/Handlova, where there was an ethnic German presence; and Rosenberg/Ruýomberok, where Germans had industrial interests.[54] In the final agreement on May 31, however, the number of DHKA branches was reduced to nine, and the Union-Bank was limited to Sillein/Žilina, Neusohl/Banská Bystrica, Preschau/Prešov, and Krickerhau/Handlova. At the same time, the Slovak government did promise to assist in various ways to make the gathering of the necessary capital easier, especially by repatriating participations in Slovak enterprises abroad, thereby easing the clearing situation.[55]

The way was now finally open for the founding of the Union-Bank Pressburg. A decision was made to raise the capital of the new bank to 55 million Ks, because the reserves were increased from 10 percent to 20 percent, or 7.5 million Ks. This was done at the request of the Slovak Finance Ministry, which had originally asked that the reserves be held at a Slovak bank in the form of Slovak government bonds, but then dropped this requirement in return for a raising of the reserves. The participation of the CA was to be five-ninths of the capital, that of the BUB four-ninths. The payment of the capital sums was made by the Deutsche Bank on the account of the CA and the BUB, and the Reichsmark equivalent was deposited into the German-Slovak clearing account so that the Slovak National Bank could credit the nascent Union-Bank with the 55 million Ks

---

53 The agreement of June 17, 1940 is to be found in DB, B 174.

54 Ibid.; this information is provided in a protocol containing the German proposal for a settlement dated May 22, 1940.

55 Ibid., Gedächtnisprotokoll, May 31, 1940. Subsequently, the Union-Bank also opened branches in Deutsch Proben (Pravno) and Pressburg, Dürre Maut. See BA-CA, CA-TZ, Rechtsabteilung rot, Box 9/Union-Bank, Preßburg XII, the circular instruction of the CA, July 7, 1941.

according to the proportions established for the two banks.[56]

The Union-Bank Pressburg was formally founded on October 29, 1940, at the Carleton Hotel in Pressburg/Bratislava. The administrative council was headed by Ludwig Fritscher of the CA with Rohde as deputy chairman. Of the seven other members, two were Germans, Rohdewald of the RKG, and Hermann Kaiser of the Deutsche Bank, representing the chief shareholders in the CA. The others were prominent businessmen representing the German element in Slovak industry: Gabriel Dutcho of the Fa. Chemische Industrie Dr. Blasberg & Co., Martin Haidmann of the Slovak railroads, landowner August Haupt-Stummer from Chalmova, Rudolf Pollet of the Aktiengesellschaft vorm. Coburg Berg- und Hüttenwerk, and Fritz Sobotka, director of Siemens, Pressburg/Bratislava. Franz Stephan was confirmed in his position as director of the bank, while two new directors from the BUB, Ernst Friedrich and Theodor Krenek, who had been deputy directors there were appointed to Pressburg/Bratislava.[57]

In his remarks for the occasion, Fritscher, as might be expected, thanked the two governments for their help and cooperation in making the founding of the Union-Bank possible. He assured one and all that the new bank was not of the individualistic-capitalistic type that concentrated on profits but one that worked for the common good. It worked with German capital but also with Slovak deposits, and its task was to serve both economies. He assured one and all that the bank "does not come into Slovakia in order to be exploitative here but to take over the necessary intermediation role in Slovak-German economic dealings."[58]

One of the Union-Bank's key tasks, nevertheless, was to promote German ideology and interests, and it was a highly politicized institution. Even before the formal establishment of the bank, for example, the CA kept an eye out for the employment of Jews in enterprises with which the bank was associated. On May 3, 1940, it inquired of the BUB in Pressburg/Bratislava as to whether Jews were employed in Slovak firms and what positions they held. The source of this inquiry was a meeting between Deschka of the CA and Gebert where the question was raised whether it was true that non-Aryans were being employed at the Chem. Industrie Dr. Blasberg & Co. It turned out that this company employed two Jews and that the AG für Asphaltierungen und Straßenbau, another company that dealt with the BUB in Pressburg/Bratislava, employed a Jew. While the CA had nothing to do with either of these firms directly, the fact that it was now working with the BUB meant that it had to be concerned about how the employment of such persons might affect the relationship between the BUB and the Deutsche Partei. It hoped that the BUB would see to it that the persons in question were let go and replaced, if at all possible, with ethnic Germans.[59]

The engagement of the German embassy in Pressburg/Bratislava and its involvement with the creation of the Union-Bank has already been demonstrated in the case of Gebert, but the activist character of the embassy was most evident in the appointment of an especially radical National Socialist, Manfred von Killinger, as ambassador to Pressburg/Bratislava in August 1940. He announced almost immediately after his arrival that he expected the German enterprises in Slovakia to show a high level of performance, and he was very happy with the role being played by the two German banks in promoting industrial and economic progress. Nevertheless, he felt it important that in the future this activity would be more reflective of "National Socialist and German economic

56 DB, B 174, BUB to Rösler, Aug. 19 and 22, 1940, and Deutsche Bank to the Foreign Exchange Office of the Finance President Berlin, Sept. 9, 1940.
57 The details are to be found in BA-CA, CA-TZ, Rechtsabteilung rot, Box 7/Union-Bank, Pressburg I–X.
58 The speech was reprinted verbatim in the CA newspaper, Gemeinschaft 2/4 (Oct.–Dec. 1940), pp. 59–60, BA-CA, CA-TZ, Sekretariat rot, Box 11/CA-BV XV, XVI/1–3.

59 BA-CA, CA-TZ, Rechtsabteilung rot, Kt. 9/ Union-Bank, Preßburg XII, CA to BUB Pressburg and Prag, May 3, 1940.

principles," above all in lending and interest rate policies. He asked the banks to provide him with at least rough balances every half year as well as lists of the groups to which they had given credits. Shortly thereafter, Killinger wrote to the Union-Bank pointing out that great efforts had been made to increase the liquidity of the banks and "without wanting to anticipate their dispositions in individual cases or to influence them individually," he hoped that they would engage in a measure of planning so as to provide more funds to medium-sized and small enterprises. He wished them to be ready to take advantage of Reich-guaranteed investment and Aryanization credits. Stephan wrote back almost immediately to express gratitude for the help the bank had received and to assure Killinger that it was using the money to support German interests and would certainly want to help out the groups Killinger mentioned. He also proudly and probably with some exaggeration declared that "among the German banks we have managed most of the transfers of Jewish enterprises into Aryan, German hands and continue to be active in this direction in the interest of the German people. We will not lack in business enthusiasm and we want to do everything in order to ease the constructive work for the German population here."[60]

Whether the Union-Bank was as enthusiastic as it sounded in its pandering to Killinger, who was to leave Pressburg/Bratislava for Bucharest in 1941, is hard to determine, and the business that really interested the bank was certainly its bigger business. The BUB branch in Pressburg/Bratislava had a considerable number of industrial customers of interest to the CA, and the Union-Bank was anxious to benefit from the connections the CA and the Deutsche Bank. It asked the CA to turn over its voting rights at shareholder meetings of firms in Slovakia with which the Union-Bank did business, specifically the Dynamit Nobel, the Apollo Mineralölraffinerie, and the AG vorm. Coburg Berg- u. Hüttenwerke AG, but also

others the CA might think of.[61] Needless to say, the Union-Bank operated in keen competition with its German rival, but there was plenty of business to do in Slovakia and, more important, the Union-Bank was becoming part of a larger complex of banks in East Central and Southern Europe that were linked to the CA and, of course, the Deutsche Bank.

Hungary

There are obvious parallels as well as differences between the situations of Hungary and Slovakia. Both were satellite states that had economic interests of their own and a considerable measure of autonomy in operating their economies that they sought to protect in dealing with the Germans. Slovakia was a new state, having been part of Hungary until 1919 and then having been joined to the Czech lands until 1939. Hungary, by contrast, was certainly the larger and more important of the two and had a long history and strong national self-consciousness. As a revisionist state, it was linked to Germany in seeking to recover territories lost under the Treaty of Trianon in 1919 while maintaining its independence. In contrast to Slovakia, where the CA had to "recover" an allegedly "lost" position, the CA had maintained a presence in Hungary throughout the interwar period so that its task was not to create something new but to build upon what it already had.

The Hungarian branch of the CA was founded in 1903 to represent the interests of the CA in Budapest. It cannot be said to have played a particularly significant role in either Austrian or Hungarian economic life between 1918 and 1938, although it was headed for many years by highly regarded Hungarian banker Ignatz Fischl, who retired in August 1938. He had certainly passed retirement age, may have been Jewish, and undoubtedly was not the right person to address the new situation of the branch created by the Anschluss. He was replaced in August 1938 by another established Budapest banker, Erwin Bokor, who had been a director at the Ungarische Allgemeine Kreditbank

---

[60] Ibid., Killinger to BUB Pressburg, Aug. 8, 1940 and Sept. 23, 1940; BUB Pressburg to Killinger, Sept. 26, 1940.

[61] Ibid., Box 7/Union-Bank Pressburg I–X, memo, Oct. 13, 1941.

and had then become managing director of the Association of Hungarian Cooperative Banks. In the latter capacity, he had extensive dealings with the Germans in matters of wheat exports to Germany.[62] It was politically necessary to have a Hungarian as head of the bank. Bokor's second in command at the bank, however, was a German citizen and NSDAP member, Johann Böhm, who was a chief manager with power of attorney in 1938 and was appointed deputy manager in 1941. Whatever his Party affiliation, he was most certainly an Austrian sent to Budapest by the CA; he returned to Vienna and the CA after the war where he lived as a pensioned director until his death in 1971.[63] The appointments of Bokor and Böhm were part of a larger personnel transformation at the bank in which a total of twelve directors, bank officials with power of attorney, and higher officials of the bank were retired, while some former officials in the bank were recalled from retirement.[64] Obviously, these personnel changes reflected the desire to remove as many Jews as possible and to promote leading personnel more suitable to the pursuit of German interests.

The Anschluss turned the Hungarian branch of the CA from the small branch of the most important bank in a small country into the small branch of an ambitious bank of the Third Reich. On March 30, the Budapest branch received the guidelines from Vienna under which it "was to devote itself to the service of German-Hungarian economic relations as the branch of a bank of the German Reich."[65]

Needless to say, this entailed an Aryanization of the branch. But Hungary was neither Germany nor Austria, and although the Hungarian governments certainly were anti-Semitic, some were more so than others. Leaving the most extreme fanatics and fascists aside, they were all committed to anti-Semitism in theory but were not prepared to destroy the Hungarian economy in its name. Jews played an exceptional role in Hungarian economic life, and all sectors of the economy were heavily dependent on Jews. In 1930, for example, 59.4 percent of Hungary's bank employees and officials were Jews. The full reality of Hungarian dependence on Jews, the series of anti-Semitic measures enacted beginning in 1938 notwithstanding, would be brought home to Hungary after the German takeover in the spring of 1944 and the establishment of a Hungarian regime committed to the complete expulsion of the Jews from Hungarian economic life. The result was sheer chaos and the breakdown of business operations as well as the subsequent murder of Hungarian Jewry by the Germans with the help of their Hungarian supporters.[66]

Prior to 1944, however, the Germans doing business in Hungary dutifully complained about the lack of teeth in and failures of implementation of the Hungarian anti-Semitic measures, but they agreed in practice that Jews had to be kept on until personnel could be found to replace them. In November 1938, Bokor and Böhm were able to report to Edmund Veesenmayer of the Economic Policy Organization of the NSDAP, who later was to play a devastating role in the Holocaust in Hungary, about the progress of the Aryanization of their bank. All the leading positions were in Aryan hands, and

[62] See the translated newspaper reports of 1938 in BA-CA, CA-TZ, Sekretariat rot, Box 34/CA-BV Filiale A-B'pest 1934–1938.

[63] On his nationality and Party membership, see Hungarian National Archives (= UStA, Magyar Országos Levéltár), Z 162/13, CA branch Budapest to the Military Attaché at the German Embassy in Budapest, June 24, 1941. See BA-CA, CA-P, Personalakt Böhm's retirement and death. See BA-CA, CA-V, rank, the board of management meeting of April 5, 1941.

[64] Report in UStA, Z 1561/2, the Pester Börse, Sept. 8, 1938.

[65] BA-CA, CA-TZ, Sekretariat rot, Box 34/CA-BV Filiale A-B'pest 1934–1938, Budapest CA to CA Vienna, March 31, 1938.

[66] There is an important literature dealing with this problem. A succinct summary is to be found in Ronald W. Zweig, The Gold Train: The Destruction of the Jews and the Second World War's Most Terrible Robbery (London 2002), ch. I. There is an extremely valuable account in Raul Hilberg, Die Vernichtung der europäischen Juden, 3 vols. (Frankfurt a.M. 1994), II, pp. 859–926. The most detailed and important study is Randolph L. Braham, The Politics of Genocide: The Holocaust in Hungary, 2 vols. (New York 1994). See ibid., vol. I, p. 80, on the number of Jewish bank employees.

before long only a quarter of the staff would be Jewish. They hoped that Budapest would soon carry out a·thorough Aryanization, and they were making a point of consulting with the political authorities before filling vacant positions.[67] Because the staff was to grow substantially in 1939–1940, and 120 persons were employed in September 1940, it is hardly surprising that Aryanization did not meet the standards of Berlin and Vienna.[68] Aryanization of the staff was in fact one of the major programs of the bank, and there were indeed substantial results by mid-1940. In March 1938, the bank had on its staff forty-eight male Jews, including nine directors and managers with power of attorney, and nine female Jewish employees. It employed six male and three female Aryans on its staff. In addition to these sixty-six employees, it also employed twenty-six helpers and messengers. In May 1940, as Pfeiffer reported to the CA management board after a visit to Budapest, the Budapest branch had forty-seven male and thirty-two female Aryans, but it still had fourteen non-Aryans, of whom two were managers with the power of attorney. The staff had increased to ninety-three, to which were added twenty-six helpers and messengers. Pfeiffer noted that the power of attorney had been withdrawn from the two Jews who had it previously, so that there were no Jews in the leadership of the bank. Nevertheless, the "achievement" involved was not without its problems. The business of the bank had increased by 30 percent, but the staff was almost entirely new. Eighty-six new employees had been hired since 1938, but fourteen had soon left because they were incompetent, or had been drafted into the army, or because they found another position. Needless to say, the leadership both in Vienna and in Budapest was intent on eliminating Jewish employees, but it was proving to be a difficult task.[69]

In September 1941, the number of Jews was reduced to fewer than ten, but the management admitted that its recruitment efforts to meet its needs were not as successful as desired. As it explained, "in Hungary it is in and of itself very hard to hire an Aryan staff, since the Hungarian middle class has always striven to put their sons into the civil service or the officer corps. Our task is also made difficult because we have to require a command of the German language, which need not be perfect but must at least show a knowledge of the spoken word."[70] Bokor and Böhme seemed to have less to complain about when it came to the loss of Jewish business. While they admitted that Jews were taking their business elsewhere, these losses were allegedly compensated for by new customers who turned to the branch because of its solid reputation.[71] It is significant, however, that the guidelines sent to Budapest after the Anschluss did not ban making loans to Jewish clientele but rather urged "special caution" in doing so.[72]

Furthermore, there is some evidence that Jews could make matters difficult for the CA branch in Budapest at times. An interesting case in this connection was the effort by the Vereinigte Aluminium-Werke AG (VAW), Berlin, which was a branch of the VIAG, to have the Aluminiumerz Bergbau und Industrie AG Budapest use the CA branch in Budapest to finance its bauxite deliveries to the VAW. The majority of the shares of the Budapest firm were in the hands of the VAW and the Otavi company, which belonged to the Deutsche Bank. The Budapest firm, however, insisted on using the Ungarische Allgemeine Creditbank for this business, arguing that its 8 percent interest rate was most favorable. This irritated the CA leadership in Vienna, Heller noting that the other shareholders in the Aluminiumerz Bergbau und Industrie AG were in the hands of non-Aryan Hungarians and that General

---

[67] BA-CA, CA-TZ, Sekretariat rot, Box 34/CA-BV Filiale A-B´pest 1934–1938, CA Budapest to Veesenmayer, Nov. 26, 1938.

[68] See ibid., Nr. 35, Fritscher to Riehle, Sept. 21, 1940.

[69] BA-CA, CA-V, CA management board meeting, May 24, 1940.

[70] UStA, Z 162/15, Report on 1940, Feb. 4, 1941.

[71] BA-CA, CA-TZ, Sekretariat rot, Box 34/CA-BV Filiale A-B´pest 1934–1938, CA Budapest to Veesenmayer, Nov. 26, 1938.

[72] BA-CA, CA-V, CA executive committee, April 5, 1938.

Director Hiller was also a non-Aryan. In short, Heller suggested that the unwillingness to use the Creditanstalt-Budapest was a consequence of Jewish influences and an effort to drive the CA Budapest out of the business. He instructed the CA Budapest to lower its interest rate to 7.5 percent or even to 7 percent so that the VAW's general director, Ludger Westrick, could instruct the Aluminiumerz Bergbau und Industrie AG to use the CA Budapest insofar as the latter felt capable of granting the credits and to use the Ungarische Allgemeine Creditbank only as a last resort.[73] Obviously, one would have preferred to be rid of Hiller and the Jewish shareholders, but what was most important was transferring their business to the CA Budapest.

Manifestly, the situation was a very different in Hungary than in Germany and Austria, where Jewish shareholders and directors had disappeared from the scene. Indeed, the unpredictability and complexity of Hungarian anti-Semitic legislation affected Jews and Germans alike. This is well illustrated by the CA Vienna's interest in acquiring the shares of the Szegediner Hanfspinnerei for its Hanf-, Jute und Textilit AG. Early in 1939, Glatzl asked Bokor to try to find out who owned the shares; through his contacts, he discovered that two Jewish families owned a substantial portion of them. He learned through discreet inquiries that the Jewish shareholders were apparently inclined to sell because of impending anti-Semitic legislation. As Bokor reported in May, however, his efforts had not produced results because "in connection with the new law concerning Jews, every shareholder who before had shown a certain inclination to give up his property has apparently come into a better situation so that he has given up his intention to sell."[74] The situation was to become worse with the passage of time, but this instance is revealing of the uncertainties for all concerned.

The vagaries of Hungarian anti-Semitism, however, were not the most important complications of doing business in Hungary. That country's alliance with Germany was highly opportunistic and was primarily motivated by the desire to regain and acquire territory, first from the late Czechoslovakia, then from the Romanians, and finally from the division of Yugoslavia. Hungary expanded greatly between 1938 and 1941, which added complexities to the reorganization of the banking system in the region. Be that as it may, the end result of the Hungarian "success" was that Hungary found itself politically and economically dominated by Germany and constantly struggling to assert itself wherever possible, which served to irritate the Germans without placating domestic critics who worried that Hungary was irrevocably surrendering its autonomy.[75]

Not surprisingly, Germans tended to view their Hungarian ally with more than a little cynicism. Director Fritscher of the CA gave a particularly jaundiced appraisal to Bank Commissar Ernst at the beginning of 1939: "Hungary has until now gone along with the German Reich because it thus has had the prospect of reacquiring the lost territories in Czechoslovakia. For similar reasons, the Hungarian high nobility is prepared at this time too to make a military alliance with Germany. One should take note in this regard, however, that the Hungarian high nobility has always been closely connected with the Catholic Church, on the one hand, and with Jewry, on the other. To this must be added that thanks to its feudal views, it has always undermined any social improvement for the agricultural workers. Because of the big shortage of labor in Greater Germany, already last summer numerous Hungarian agricultural workers

---

[73] BA-CA, CA-TZ, Sekretariat rot, Box 35/CA-BV Filiale B'pest 1939–1945 – Bz, Heller to CA Budapest, Nov. 14, 1939.

[74] Ibid., Bokor to the Hanf-, Jute- und Textil-Industrie AG, Vienna, May 20, 1939, and other relevant correspondence.

[75] See Holger Fischer, "Das ungarisch-deutsche Verhähltnis in der Zwischenkriegszeit: Freira um-Partnerschaft-Abhängigkeit," in: Roland Schönfeld (ed.), *Germany and Southeastern Europe – Aspects of Relations in the Twentieth Century* (Südosteuropa-Studien 58, Munich 1997), pp. 59–70 and Michael Riemenschneider, *Die deutsche Wirtschaftspolitik gegenüber Ungarn 1933–1944. Ein Beitrag zur Interdependenz von Wirtschaft und Politik unter dem Nationalsozialismus* (Frankfurt a.M. 1987).

went to Austria and beyond that to Germany. They have become aware of the significantly better social conditions in Germany and have taken their experiences back home. This has led to an extraordinary increase in the tensions within Hungary itself, which, in turn, results in certain differences between the Hungarian Government and Greater Germany."[76]

Germans doing business in Hungary, therefore, had to step warily and avoid giving offense to their Hungarian hosts. In August 1938, for example, the Budapest branch planned to contact all the Germans living in Hungary, make them aware of the services of the bank, and try to win customers. It not only wanted them to open savings accounts and do other banking transactions, but especially to use the bank to procure currency when going on vacation and to the Congress of Germans Living Abroad shortly to be held in Stuttgart. At the same time, however, it wanted the Vienna Central Office to send out the 4,000 advertisements to these Germans in Hungary because "the branch cannot … for reasons of Hungarian domestic politics begin the advertisement either with 'Dear National Comrade' or close it with 'Heil Hitler.'"[77] Such difficulties would not arise if the advertisement came from Vienna.

The most serious problems for the CA Budapest, however, were the nationalist economic and financial policies of the Hungarians and the clearing and compensation arrangements between Germany and Hungary into which the CA Budapest had to be plugged after the Anschluss. The basic arrangement was that Hungarian exports to Germany were paid for in Reichsmark in an account of the Hungarian National Bank at the Reichsbank, while the Hungarian seller or the creditor was paid in pengö. The amounts paid by the German purchaser were booked either on a compensation account or on a special export account. The former was for goods that received an export subsidy, while the latter was for unsubsidized

goods. The function of the arrangement was to create a balance in the goods needed by both parties. The reality was that Hungary was increasingly dependent on Germany for both its imports and its exports while the role of Hungary in Germany's foreign trade was quite small. In 1938, 30.1 percent of Hungary's imports came from Germany while 27.4 percent of its exports went to Germany. In 1941, these percentages were, respectively, 58.1 percent and 59.9 percent. Hungary provided 2.1 percent and 2.09 percent of Germany's imports and exports respectively in 1938. The corresponding figures were 5.07 percent and 5.70 percent in 1941. Hungarian dependence is obvious from these figures, but the most serious problem came to be the imbalance in the clearing account. Germany's debt mounted steadily after 1938 and astronomically after 1942 when the Hungarian National Bank was forced to give interest-free advances on German purchases and swallow a massive distortion of the imbalances in the clearing arrangements.[78]

Naturally, the CA Budapest was very interested in becoming part of the network of banks involved in these compensation and clearing arrangements because there were substantial provisions and commissions involved as well as the granting of credits to fund exports and imports. It had handled about 8 percent of the trade between Austria and Hungary before the Anschluss, but Germany was of course much bigger business and the CA Budapest had not previously been one of the banks engaged in the direct compensation trade with Germany. Under the circumstances after the Anschluss, the CA Budapest would have had to do all its business with Germany, including the business with the CA Vienna, indirectly. It was thus extremely anxious to be recognized both by the Hungarian National Bank and by the German authorities as one of the banks licensed to work directly in this field.[79]

---

[76] RGVA Moscow, 1458/2/83, Bl. 130, Minute by Ernst, Jan. 23, 1939.

[77] BA-CA, CA-TZ, Sekretariat rot, Box 34/CA-BV Filiale A-B´pest 1934–1938, CA Budapest to CA Vienna, Aug. 12, 1938.

[78] Riemenschneider, *Wirtschaftspolitik*, pp. 82–83, 388–390.

[79] BA-CA, CA-TZ, Sekretariat rot, Box 34/CA-BV Filiale A-B´pest 1934–1938, CA Budapest to CA Vienna, March 31, 1938.

When the CA Budapest representatives went to plead their case with Director Robert Quandt, the head of the Banking Section of the Hungarian National Bank, on April 5, 1938, they were treated to a remarkable display of Hungarian obstinacy. Quandt pointed out that the Viennese branches of the Hermes AG and the Zentral Wechselstuben AG lacked the foreign exchange privileges that the Austrian branches had in Hungary, something about which he had continually complained without any results. If this situation were not changed in the ongoing discussions with Germany, he warned, he would have to consider seriously whether the CA Budapest should retain its authorization to deal in foreign exchange. When his interlocutors rather tactlessly responded, as was reported, "that our branch has a far greater economic significance in Hungary than the Viennese branches of the small Hungarian branches in your [i.e., Quandt's] country," Quandt is said to have replied that "given his nationalist position the smallest Hungarian provincial savings bank meant more to him than an international big bank, even if it also were one of the 'big five' banks."[80] When asked if the Budapest branch would get the authorization it wanted if similar rights were given to the Hungarian branches in Vienna, Quandt, perhaps to bring home the point, replied that there were other factors involved as well and that he would have to consult with his superiors.

At this point, the CA Budapest asked the Vienna headquarters to appeal to Berlin and use pressure from that quarter to bring the Hungarians to terms. The tactics of the CA Budapest leadership had been anything but brilliant. Originally they had asked their colleagues in Vienna to hold off asking the Reichsbank Clearing Office to authorize the CA Budapest to act as a clearing and compensation bank until permission was obtained from the Hungarian National Bank. After the encounter with Quandt, however, the CA Budapest asked the Vienna office to turn to the Reichsbank Clearing Office and secure approval from that

quarter and then use that approval to put pressure on the Hungarians. The problem was that the Reichsbank Clearing Office was trying to keep the number of such banks limited, and by turning directly to the Hungarian National Bank, the CA Budapest had opened the way for the Hungarians to make claims of their own.

The ongoing discussion with Quandt that had begun in early April, therefore, continued into late November, while the Hungarian National Bank petitioned the Reichsbank Clearing Office to allow three new Hungarian banks to do clearing business in Germany in addition to the eight already authorized to do so. As Bokor reported to Captain Robert Nemling, the CA lobbyist in Berlin, Quandt repeatedly said that there was "no question" that the CA Budapest would be authorized. This was in some contradiction to the position taken by Hungarian National Bank president Lipôt Baranyai, who assured Bokor there was no link between the CA Budapest request and the requested German authorization for more Hungarian banks. Matters were not helped by the fact that the position of the authorities in Berlin was also contradictory, the relevant Reichsbank director Jost at once assuring the CA that it stood "100%" behind the authorization for the CA Budapest but then declaring that it would have to consult with higher authorities because of the Hungarian banks. In the end, Nemling proposed that the CA management board in Vienna take the best news it received from both sides and combine the positive view of the Reichsbank Clearing Office with the statement of Baranyai to declare that its Budapest branch was authorized to participate in the clearing operations between Germany and Hungary.[81] This did not, however, move Quandt, who told Bokor that he needed a decision about the authorization for the Hungarian banks "since he has to fight to the last for the interests of the banks here."[82] Finally, Jost decided that it was best for himself to go straightaway to Budapest and settle the question in direct dialogue with the officials there.

[80] Ibid., CA Budapest to CA Vienna, April 5, 1938.

[81] Ibid., Nemling to CA Vienna, Nov. 15, 1938.
[82] Ibid., Bokor to Nemling, Nov. 22, 1938.

Apparently this worked, and the CA Budapest entered the charmed circle of those engaged in the clearing operations between Hungary and Germany on January 1, 1939. It was reported to have handled 20 percent of Hungary's foreign exchange operations in 1941.[83]

If it had been up to the CA Vienna, its Budapest branch would have handled all the foreign exchange operations with Germany, and while this was clearly impossible it hoped to keep serious German competition out and to beef up the capabilities of the branch by infusing it with more capital. On February 21, 1939, the CA executive committee stated its intention to raise the equity base of the Budapest branch from 1 million to 4 or 5 million pengö, and informed Bokor of this decision while urging him to cultivate the German colony in Hungary and getting as much of its business as possible so as to satisfy the increased demand for credit that was anticipated. The CA Vienna, however, seems to have been rather slow in actually allocating the new capital to Budapest, deciding to do so only in late November 1939, albeit in the amount of 5 million pengö. The Vienna headquarters itself made a massive effort to mobilize its industrial and other contacts, for example, the Deutsche Bank and Abs, to increase the business of the Budapest branch.[84]

There were obstacles, however, to increasing business in Budapest as much as the CA would have liked. One, for example, was the requirement that the bank participate in the Hungarian Investment Loan. In 1939, this amounted to 761,600 pengö for the bank itself, but in addition the bank was expected to finance or actually pay for the loan obligations of the firms with which it dealt. This came to an additional 2,422,100 pengö for the twenty-two firms in question. The banks could borrow the money from the Hungarian National Bank at 5.8 percent and were forced to pay it back over eight years. A speedy repayment was impossible, so that the money was effectively tied up. As Joham pointed out in response to this news, "it is clear that the cash flow position of the bank thus suffers a further reduction, which, however, we have to regret from the standpoint of the building up of regular banking business."[85] But the impositions did not end here; in May the Budapest branch reported that it also had to contribute 120,000 pengö to the City of Budapest loan. Furthermore, it pointed out that it was not a good idea to complain or ask for a reduction because the last time the bank did so it was threatened with sanctions by the authorities. Finally, there was the mandatory purchase of Hungarian national bonds, which the banks agreed to divide among themselves in proportion to their capital. In the case of the CA Budapest, this amounted to 1.5 percent of its deposits.[86]

Despite these experiences, in the spring and summer of 1939 some serious thought was given to increasing the German presence in Hungary in the form of a condominium of banks whereby the CA would have a 33 percent stake through its branch, the Dresdner Bank would take a 25 percent stake through its Merkurbank, and then the Deutsche Bank and the Reichs-Kredit-Gesellschaft would each take a 21 percent stake. The intention was to establish a new bank in the form of a pool that, if it functioned successfully, might lead to further steps. Hasslacher had apparently discussed the idea with Olscher, and he then floated it with Abs in a letter of July 11, 1939. Abs, however, was not enthusiastic. He told Hasslacher: "I do not believe that such a bank would be suitable to vigorously enter into the Hungarian business, since it is known how

[83] Ibid., Nemling to CA, Nov. 24, 1938 and Bokor to Veesenmayer, Nov. 26, 1938. How the Hungarian banks fared is unclear from the available record. See also Josef Koliander, *Die Beteiligung und Kreditverflechtung der deutschen Banken in Südeuropa*, Diss. (Vienna 1944), pp. 189–190. See also UStA, Z 162/15, the Balance Report as of Dec. 31, 1940.

[84] BA-CA, CA-V, CA executive committee, Feb. 21, 1939; ibid., CA board of management meeting, Nov. 27, 1939, and BA-CA, CA-TZ, Sekretariat rot, Box 35/CA-BV Filiale B'pest 1939–1945 – Bz, CA to Bokor, Feb. 22, 1939. Ibid., Boxes 34–35 are filled with correspondence aimed at promoting the Budapest branch.

[85] Ibid., Joham to Bokor, March 21, 1939, and CA Budapest to CA Vienna, April 17, 1939.

[86] Ibid., CA Budapest to CA Vienna, May 15, 1939.

much the Hungarian economic circles favor their own national banks. I consider it to be a privilege that the Creditanstalt has its own branch in Hungary and do not believe that a common institution has more favorable business prospects than a branch, although I do not mean to imply that everything is being done to staff this branch correctly. Past experiences of condominiums in the area of banking do not boost one's courage to begin anew with such institutions, and the German banking situation in Hungary, I believe, also does not at all make such a step necessary."[87] Given Abs's attitude, it is hard to imagine that the discussion was pursued in any serious way for the rest of 1939.

Nevertheless, the business of the Budapest branch did indeed increase, while the efforts to increase the equity capital of the branch and to improve its liquidity regularly ran afoul of the strictures of the Hungarian National Bank. A year after Vienna had approved increasing its capital equity, the Budapest branch reported that the National Bank had no objection to an increase of the equity, but it did object to using the CA Vienna's blocked pengö account in Budapest for this purpose. It changed its position in July 1940, so that the way was theoretically free for the use of these monies.[88] For the time being, however, the increase in nominal capital remained in limbo, but the capital requirements of the bank increased with the increased Hungarian trade, so that in September 1940 Joham announced to the CA executive committee that they were going to advance 3 million RM to the Budapest branch for German exports to Hungary that would then be recovered in the clearing account. At the same time, the German Clearing Office was advancing a credit of 15 million RM to the ten Hungarian banks dealing in foreign exchange, including 1.1 million RM to the CA Budapest, to help fund German exports to Hungary.[89]

The liquidity needs of the CA Budapest were known by the RWM and viewed with sympathy. This enabled the CA in the fall of 1940 to sell off the CA's holdings in the Ungarische Asphalt AG, Budapest, of which 40 percent was owned by the CA Vienna and the CA Budapest. The company was presenting increasing problems in 1940 of both a personnel and financial nature. On the one hand, the CA was anxious to fire as many of the company's Jewish employees as possible in accordance with recent Hungarian legislation because the Ungarische Asphalt was not getting Hungarian government contracts because of the number of Jews it employed. At the same time, however, the CA Budapest had an extraordinarily difficult time replacing Jewish personnel and was thus in something of a quandary as to what to do. On the other hand, the company was engaged in projects in Romania and Yugoslavia with partners that were becoming ever more expensive and it was beginning to be financially threatened. Hence, the CA was increasingly interested in selling its shares. The Pester Ungarische Commercialbank, which had a long-standing minority interest in the Ungarische Asphalt, would have been a logical purchaser of the CA Budapest's shares of the company. But because the RWM was reluctant to have Germans surrender any holdings in the Balkans, the CA first looked for a German purchaser. It approached Universale Bau AG, which, however, did not want to enter the asphalt industry in Hungary. Another possibility was the Munich firm of Sager-Woerner, which had large contracts and good connections with the Organisation Todt. It was engaged in building roads in the Balkans to connect Romania and Germany, thereby facilitating oil deliveries, and could conceivably have used Budapest to direct its operations. In the end, however, Sager-Woerner found Ungarische Asphalt unattractive for the same reasons the CA did and declined to acquire the company, preferring to go it alone in Hungary. At this point, the CA asked for and received permission to sell its holding to the Pester Ungarische Commercialbank on the grounds that, for the CA, a 40 percent share "did not make it possible to exercise the kind of influence on the

[87] DB, P 5603, Bl. 77, 80–82, Abs to Hasslacher, July 11, 1939 in response to a letter to Abs of July 7, 1939.

[88] BA-CA, CA-TZ, Sekretariat rot, Box 35/CA-BV Filiale B'pest 1939–1945 – Bz, CA Budapest to CA Vienna, Feb. 28, 1940, and Bokor to Joham, July 29, 1940.

[89] BA-CA, CA-V, CA executive committee meeting, Sept. 3, 1940.

company that was needed to conduct its business in an orderly manner and in conformity with the interests of the Reich."[90] The Pester Ungarische Commercialbank agreed to pay off the company's credit from the CA Budapest and to guarantee the obligations of the company in Yugoslavia and Romania.[91] The RWM consented to the transfer of the shares held in Vienna to Budapest as well as to the arrangement that the CA retained the pengö it had received for its own use, that is, for the benefit of the CA Budapest.

As previously noted, the money was especially needed to fund Hungarian exports to Germany, an economic activity in which the Budapest branch was increasingly engaged, and in October Joham announced an effort to make a 5–10 million pengö transfer for such purposes.[92] Here, as in every other such matter, the approval of the Hungarian National Bank had to be secured, and Joham traveled to Budapest where, joined by Bokor, he negotiated on November 13 and 21, 1940, with Baranyai and Quandt. Joham's initial request was for permission to make a 10 million RM transfer, but to be allowed to make it in stages as need arose. Additionally, however, he asked that the CA be allowed to transfer money back as well if it were not all needed and requested further that reasonable interest be transferred back on the capital. Joham justified the request by the increased commerce between Hungary and Germany and also noted that the CA Budapest had invested 11 million pengö in the Hungarian National Loan, which constituted 50 percent of its deposits. Apparently, Baranyai was only moderately impressed. He was willing to look with favor on a capital transfer "within a limited range," but he would not even discuss the idea of transferring capital back or having interest paid on it. He pointed out that

the Hungarian economy did not need foreign capital that was short-term and purely intended to finance commercial operations. It was only interested in long-term investment that would be available for decades. Furthermore, if the CA Budapest increased its business, then it would have to increase its participation in the National Loan. Otherwise, the other banks would complain about the CA branch's having an unfair advantage through the infusion of the new capital. When Joham objected that the CA Budapest was paying quite a bit already and did not have branches that would enable it to gain more depositors and money for the loan, Baranyai made clear that he could not support the establishment of branches and that he did not think there was enough business to justify a 10 million RM transfer and would only support between a third and half that sum.[93]

This preliminary discussion had been somewhat rushed to take advantage of the presence of Karl Clodius, the deputy head of the Economic Policy Division of the German Foreign Office, who was regularly involved in negotiations with the Hungarians. Subsequently, Joham consulted with Clodius and returned with Bokor to resume the negotiations at the Hungarian National Bank on November 21. He now reduced the requested capital transfer to 5 million RM (8 million pengö) and dropped his request to be allowed to transfer money back. At the same time, he asked for a more generous treatment of CA Budapest rediscount rights at the National Bank. These had been limited to 1 million pengö based on the official equity of the bank in the same amount, while the actual working capital of the bank was 22 million pengö and, after the transfer, would be 30 million pengö. Joham declared that the primary purpose of the capital transfer was to fund cattle and wheat exports to Germany. Baranyai was willing to accept the reduced capital transfer, while continuing to emphasize that Hungary

---

[90] BA-CA, CA-IB, Asphalt, 45/01, CA to Foreign Exchange Office, Oct. 9, 1940. See this source for the account given here.

[91] BA-CA, CA-V, CA board of management meeting, Sept. 30, 1940.

[92] Ibid., CA executive committee meeting, Oct. 20, 1940.

[93] There are two protocols of the Nov. 13, 1940 meeting at the Hungarian National Bank, but there are no significant differences between them. They are to be found in BA-CA, CA-TZ, Sekretariat rot, Box 35/CA-BV Filiale B'pest 1939–1945 – Bz.

had a controlled money market and that large transfers were potentially destabilizing. He was noncommittal on the amount of the rediscounting he would allow and recognized that the stated equity of the bank was purely formal. He now urged that, if for no other than "prestige reasons," it be substantially increased. This would also mean that more equity would be locked into Hungary, which would create a more favorable attitude toward the bank. This, of course, was something for which the CA had been asking for some time, and Joham and Baranyai now agreed that the nominal capital of the bank should be raised from 1 million to 5 million pengö. At this point, Baranyai hastened to remind Joham and Bokor that the other banks would see in this agreement, which raised the working capital of the bank by a sixth, a reason to ask for a larger contribution to the National Loan by a sixth, that is, from 1.5 percent to 1.8 percent of deposits. Joham and Bokor thought this fair and accepted it.[94]

As the new money came in, it was rapidly expended on projects that provide a useful snapshot of the activities of the CA branch in Budapest. Accordingly, 800,000 pengö were spent on prepayment of goods to be delivered to Germany, while 1 million pengö were advanced for the prepayment of coal deliveries to Hungary from Germany. Another 2.3 million pengö were provided as operating credits for German firms that had subsidiary companies in Hungary, that is, Ford Motor Company, Robert Bosch, and the Oldwerke AG.

Finally, 4 million pengö were provided for the investments of the subsidiary companies of German firms in Hungary. Julius Meinl AG received 3 million pengö to build a new plant, and Persil GmbH. received 1 million pengö to buy a new plant. The Verein der Reichsdeutschen in Ungarn got 300,000

pengö to renovate a building, and Karlheinz Rindermann received 75,000 pengö to Aryanize the bottling plant of the 4711 Eau de Cologne company.[95]

Nevertheless, the resources of the CA Budapest remained limited in rather frustrating ways. In May 1941, for example, Abs asked if the CA might be interested in taking over the $238,723 credit it had given to the Königliche Ungarische Eisen-, Stahl- und Maschinenfabriken Budapest. An almost equal credit of $228,723 had been given by the Ungarische Allgemeine Creditbank. The Budapest branch had to turn down the offer because it was too high an engagement for the bank, which felt it was already reduced in its freedom to maneuver because of other long-term engagements.[96]

Obviously, the Ungarische Allgemeine Creditbank was in a better position to deal with such business, and there was considerable frustration at the CA in Vienna about the limitations on its branch in Budapest – all the more so as its expectation of having a monopoly on German banking interests in Hungary was being disappointed. The Länderbank Wien owned a small banking outlet in Budapest, the Mercurbank, but aside from dismissing its Jewish personnel in the summer of 1938, the future of the Dresdner Bank and Länderbank Wien in Hungary was uncertain. Some thought was given to the subject at the end of 1938 thanks to the prodding of Veesenmayer, who was on the Länderbank Wien supervisory board as well as a member of the Economic Policy Organization of the NSDAP. His initial inclination seems to have been for the CA and the Länderbank to team up to promote German interests in Hungary, a proposition that Dresdner Bank director Karl Rasche objected to because he felt that they had to maintain their independent position in Hungary. The Dresdner Bank decided to

---

94 Here, too, there are two protocols of the meeting of Nov. 21, 1940, that do not differ significantly and are to be found in ibid. It is worth noting that Baranyai was unfriendly to anti-Semitic measures aimed at driving the Jews from the economy and was also critical of the German alliance; he was arrested in the coup of 1944. See Braham, *Politics of Genocide*, I, pp. 238–239, 510, 537, II, p. 1132.

95 BA-CA, CA-TZ, Sekretariat rot, Box 35/CA-BV Filiale B'pest 1939–1945 – Bz, CA Budapest to Klenz in Vienna, May 20, 1941, and CA Vienna to RWM, May 27, 1941.

96 See ibid., the correspondence of May–June 1941.

pursue its interests in Hungary but was not at all certain as to what exactly it wanted.[97]

It was not long before the CA Budapest got wind of the Dresdner Bank's activities. On December 10, 1938, it reported to Vienna that there were rumors that the Dresdner Bank did not think Mercurbank was capable of much growth and that it wanted to take advantage of the Hungarian government's plans to consolidate and concentrate banks and acquire influence in some medium-sized bank anxious to retain its independence. When Bokor reported this to Vienna, Directors Joham and Fritscher were somewhat surprised because they thought there had been an informal agreement concerning the division of banking activity in Southeast Europe. During their last visit to Berlin, they had the impression from Veesenmayer and other ranking persons in Berlin that the Dresdner Bank and the Länderbank had no interest in establishing a strong position in Budapest and that there was a general desire to avoid the presence of too many German banks and too much competition among them. They therefore asked Nemling to look into the matter and see if there was anything to the rumors.[98]

In the meantime, Bokor began to get more solid information from the managing director of the German-Hungarian Chamber of Commerce, H. Rolf Fritzsche, who reported that he had met some time before with Carl Lüer, the chairman of the Dresdner Bank supervisory board, and Director Hans Pilder. They were negotiating for an expansion of the Dresdner's position in Budapest and also asked Fritzsche for information. Fritzsche took the position that there was no need for the presence of another major bank in Budapest because it could lead to a sharp competition between the Dresdner Bank and the CA. He went on to point out to Bokor, however, that the decision would ultimately lie with the RWM and whether one or two banks were going to be

given the Hungarian market in Southeastern Europe. Either the Dresdner Bank would be allowed to develop a base in Budapest, or the Mercurbank would be offered to the CA. Fritzsche asked that his comments be kept confidential but that the CA keep Fritzsche informed about its wishes at the upcoming discussions in Berlin. Understandably, Bokor considered the matter of vital concern to the CA Budapest.[99]

Despite the alarms at the end of 1938, however, very little seems to have happened or been decided until late 1940, probably because the carving up of the Czech banks, the war, and the expansion of Hungary created a rather uncertain situation in the banking sector there. It was only when the great need for more capital to deal with German-Hungarian trade developed in the course of 1940 that the expansion of the German banking presence in Hungary came to the forefront. The RWM reached the conclusion that the Mercurbank in Budapest was too small to deal with the needs of the Dresdner Bank, a view that was shared by the Dresdner Bank. Nonetheless, the RWM had not drawn up any concrete plans beyond the general idea that the Dresdner Bank should gain a stake in one of the medium-sized Hungarian banks. Thanks to Hans Pilder and his French connections, this intention took on concrete form in the summer of 1940 when Pilder learned that Schneider-Creusot (Union Industrie Financière) wished to sell its shares in the Ungarische Allgemeine Creditbank (UAC) and that there were other French-held shares belonging to the Rothschilds and the Union Parisienne that might be available for purchase. Clodius was very favorable to the idea of the Dresdner Bank taking a strong minority stake in the bank by this means, as was the RWM, while Veesenmayer and Keppler took a very positive attitude as well. Negotiations were launched and the Dresdner Bank acquired 17 percent of the UAC shares in the course of 1941.[100]

[97] See Chap. 5, pp. 447–449.

[98] BA-CA, CA-TZ, Sekretariat rot, Box 34/CA-BV Filiale A-B´pest 1934–1938, Joham and Fritscher to Nemling, Dec. 10, 1938.

[99] Ibid., Bokor to Pfeiffer, Dec. 23, 1938.

[100] See memo by Pilder, Aug. 16, 1940; Pilder to Augenthaler, RWM, Sept. 16, 1940; memo by Pilder, Sept. 17, 1940; NARA, T83/182–183, correspondence on the takeover of the French shares,

The green light given to the Dresdner Bank was an open secret. At the CA working committee meeting of October 22, 1940, Joham stated that the CA would also make a claim to acquire a participation in the UAC, but that it was meanwhile looking into the possibility of acquiring a stake in the Pester Ungarische Commercialbank. At the same time, Fritscher was negotiating with Riehle at the RWM, where he announced that the CA wanted a stake in the UAC "because the branch of the CA in Budapest is too weak and is also not very capable of being developed." Fritscher bluntly stated that he did not want to use its money in Hungary to strengthen the branch but rather "to purchase a stake in an established Hungarian institution."[101]

Joham pursued this possibility in discussions with Ferenc Chorin, who was one of the most influential men at the Pester Ungarische Commercialbank and a leading figure in Hungarian business and political circles. Apparently, Joham was quite open in his discussion as was Chorin and stressed above all the interest the PUC might have in German investors given the fact that the Dresdner Bank was planning to have a substantial holding in the UAC. Chorin admitted that he had given the idea of German shareholders some thought but pointed out that the PUC was going to celebrate its hundredth anniversary in 1941 and had never had foreign shareholders. At the same time, the situation at the UAC was causing him to think again, and Joham did his best to inform him about the CA and its program for Southeast Europe. Chorin pointed out that the PUC also had such a program and planned to expand it, promising to discuss Joham's idea with his colleagues. He pointed out, however, that such an investment by the CA would mean that the branch in Budapest would have to be closed. In addition, the CA stake could not

go beyond 25 percent, the shares of the bank presently owned by his family and the Dreher family. He also expressed the wish that the Deutsche Bank be at least indirectly involved because the PUC considered this of particular importance. Whatever the case, the entire idea was contingent on Dresdner Bank taking a stake in the UAC, and he stressed that "the entire plan must be kept strictly secret and its implementation must be justified and handled with especial intelligence." Chorin and Joham agreed to discuss the idea further.[102]

These discussions produced no results, however, and the precondition of having the Dresdner Bank invest in the UAC did not become official until the end of 1941. Whatever the case, by the summer of 1941 Joham concluded that acquiring a stake in a Hungarian bank was not really possible and came up with a new idea that he confidentially communicated to Abs on August 4. He had just returned from Budapest, where the low liquidity of the CA branch posed more of a problem than ever, especially because its refinancing possibilities remained extremely limited. Because acquisition of a stake in a Hungarian bank was unlikely in the near future, Joham wondered if one might not consider setting up a new bank, with the majority of the capital coming from the German side and a minority from some Hungarian bank. One could create a "Bankverein für Ungarn" with a capital of 25 million pengö. The Germans would take 15 million pengö in shares and the Pester Ungarische Commercialbank 10 million pengö in shares. Because the CA Vienna had placed 30 million pengö at its Budapest branch, it could draw on this money to provide its portion of the capital without difficulty. They would be in a position to solve the liquidity problems with the inflow of cash and resulting discounting privileges. Moreover, they could

---

and announcement of the Dresdner Bank participation, Dec. 12, 1941.
[101] RGVA Moscow, 1458/9/158, Bl. 127–130, executive committee meeting, Oct. 22, 1940, BA-CA, CA-V and RWM meeting, Oct. 14, 1940.

[102] DB, P 24158, Joham sent this report to Abs on Oct. 31, 1940. Chorin was a converted Jew and one of a small group of prominent Jews given safe passage in 1944 after buying off the SS. See Braham, *Politics of Genocide*, I, pp. 260, 546, 557–558, 560. On Joham's continued negotiations with the Pester Ungarische Commerzialbank, see BA-CA, CA-V, the executive committee meeting of Dec. 4, 1940.

get the personnel they wanted from the start rather than have to deal with existing personnel problems. Joham had sounded out Chorin about this idea, who found it very promising and believed it would have general support.[103]

Joham also received positive feedback from Abs, who was undoubtedly influenced by Chorin as well as by the competition from the Dresdner Bank and the increased business in Hungary to take a more positive attitude than he had in 1939. Joham now decided to present his idea to the executive committee on August 12, where he received very strong backing from Abs. The German branch of the CA could never attract the kind of deposits that a Hungarian bank could, nor could it enjoy such advantages. Abs also thought that the Pester Ungarische Commercialbank was a first-rate bank and the right kind to have as a partner.[104] When Joham and Hasslacher discussed the plan with Clodius in Berlin, the latter was initially agreeable although he preferred another Hungarian bank as partner, namely, the Pester erste vaterländische Sparcassa-Verein, which had been very accommodating in its dealings with the Reich. Subsequently, however, after consultation with the RWM and the Reichsbank, Clodius informed the CA that there were "political reservations" about restructuring the Budapest branch as a new bank with strong Hungarian minority stake. The CA was asked to drop the plan for the time being, and there is no evidence that it was ever taken up again.[105]

In the end, the expansion of the CA Budapest turned out to be very modest and was largely geared to servicing the ethnic German community. It was also sometimes the beneficiary of Hungary's expansion into the partitioned neighboring states of Czechoslovakia, Yugoslavia, and Romania. In June 1941, Joham contacted Riehle to inform him that a new transfer of 5 million RM would be necessary, thereby asking, in effect, that the 5 million it had given up in its initial request for 10 million RM now be requested. Joham did note,

however, that the Hungarian National Bank had indicated it would consider further requests and pointed out that the expansion of Hungary would give the CA Budapest "expanded tasks." Because new negotiations with the Hungarians were in the offing, Joham asked Riehle to represent the CA's request in "the interest of the ethnic German groups in the newly acquired territories."[106]

Certainly the most important acquisition, which took place in the fall of 1941, was the Apakiner Bank- und Sparkasse AG. It was one of a number of small banks that served a largely ethnic German clientele. It had a good reputation and had worked well despite alleged mistreatment by the Serbian authorities and the National Bank. Apparently, the fact that it had been taken over by the CA Budapest attracted an increased number of customers and produced positive results.[107] The other acquisition of the Budapest branch was also in what had become southern Hungary, namely, the branches of the Allgemeine Jugoslawische Bank-Verein and the Kroatische Landesbank in what the Germans called Neusatz, the Hungarians called Ujvidek, and the Yugoslavs called Novi-Sad. Because the Jugoslawische Bank-Verein was controlled by the CA, this was effectively a transfer within the CA banking concern, although it required the permission of the Hungarian and German authorities. A city of 64,000 with a considerable number of Germans, Neusatz was an important Danube port and commercial center, and the CA decided to maintain a branch there. Because it had become Hungarian, however, it was logical to make it a branch of the CA Budapest, a move the Hungarian authorities approved. They did insist, however, that the new branch also take the holdings of the Kroatische Landesbank AG, which was controlled by the Dresdner Bank. This was finally worked out at the end of 1942.[108]

---

[103] DB, P 6504, Bl. 247, Joham to Abs, Aug. 4, 1941.

[104] BA-CA, CA-V, CA executive committee meeting, Aug. 12, 1941.

[105] DB, P 6504, Bl. 310, Joham to Abs, Oct. 27, 1941.

[106] BA-CA, CA-TZ, Sekretariat rot, Box 35/CA-BV Filiale B'pest 1939–1945 – Bz, Joham, telegram to Riehle, June 24, 1941.

[107] The details and newspaper reports are to be found in UStA, Z 1560/10/10; see also ibid., Z 1561/2/3, the CA Budapest business report for 1941.

[108] See BA-CA, CA-TZ, Sekretariat rot, Box 35/CA-BV Filiale B'pest 1939–1945 – Bz, CA to

The CA Budapest did not seek to open branches in the Carpatho-Ukraine region taken from the Czechs or the Transylvanian areas taken from the Romanians, although it did seek – and did succeed in getting – some of the industrial accounts of the BUB in the Carpatho-Ukraine region, the "Cservenka" Zuckerfabriks AG, the "Clotilde" AG für chemische Industrie, and the "Szolyva" AG für Holzverkohlung, and to cultivate the ethnic Germans in Transylvania.[109] As examples to be discussed later in connection with Aryanizations will show, the CA Budapest did have very important holdings and engagements that paralleled those of its proprietary institution in Vienna – Del-Ka Schuh-Handels: AG, Stefan Felmayer & Söhne AG, Hanf- Jute- u. Textilit-Industrie AG, Philipp Haas & Söhne'sche AG, Stölzle's Söhne AG – but it constantly suffered from a shortage of capital and from Hungarian interference. The war led to a substantial increase in Hungarian resistance to German economic penetration: the more Hungary became Germany's creditor, the more the Hungarians could use the clearing arrangements to be selective about German investment. The grotesque situation of the Jews and the ambivalent relationship with Germany were described, if not analyzed, by Director Tron of the CA in September 1942. Russian air raids on Hungary alarmed the population and some had noted that in the wake of these attacks, "the Jews in Hungary have again become very presumptuous." At the same time, the Hungarians were also very obstreperous because "concerning economic matters, the expressly Hungarian position toward German interests has intensified significantly and is

apparently also being strongly promoted officially."[110] In response to an inquiry about purchasing a textile plant in Hungary, Tron referred the interested party to the CA Budapest but warned that there would be no credits in Hungary for such purposes and that efforts to transfer money would be met with a negative response because "the acquisition of Hungarian enterprises by Germans was frowned upon at this time."[111] As a well-informed German source, probably Director Böhme of the CA Budapest, reported, "one apparently fears that with the progress of Aryanization, there will be, if one does not set up any dam, an exchange of foreign (primarily German) capital for Jewish capital."[112] Little wonder that Clodius did not want the CA to set up its own bank in Hungary for political reasons.

The tight capital situation of the CA Budapest also affected its own credit practices. It frequently demanded a guarantee for German credit seekers from the Deutsche Bank even when one would normally not demand it. One German firm actually turned to a Hungarian bank, which made no such demand. Such practices by German banks angered political observers like Rafelsberger and his aide in Berlin, Kratz, who felt that the CA Budapest was slowing down business, making it expensive, and setting a bad example. In his view, it should have behaved in the manner of German banks and not demanded guarantees for customers with established reputations. It was time, in his view, for the German banks in the Balkans to be called to account, and "in any case it would be very good to let these gentlemen know that they are being observed in the way they conduct business."[113]

While the CA Budapest never lived up to Vienna's expectations, it probably served German interests as well as it could under the circumstances. It was undoubtedly was in

Supervisory Board for Banking, Nov. 11, 1941 and the lengthy correspondence dealing with this. UStA, Z 1561/2, the settlement with the Kroatische Landesbank of Dec. 28, 1942.

[109] See BA-CA, CA-TZ, Sekretariat rot, Box 35/ CA-BV Filiale B'pest 1939–1945 – Bz, CA to Deutsche Bank, April 5, 1939 and related correspondence on the chemical works, and CA Budapest to CA Vienna, Sept. 7, 1940; on the ethnic German banks in Kronstadt/Brasov and Hermannstadt/ Sibiu, see UStA, Z 1561/2/3, the participations of the CA Budapest, the Status Report of Feb. 9, 1942, p. 6.

[110] DB, V2/2, Tron to Uhlig, Sept. 30, 1942.
[111] Ibid., Tron to Joachim Veith, Jan. 21, 1942.
[112] DB, P 25005, Report on Hungary at the CA conference on South-East Europe, July 15–17, 1942, p. 3.
[113] BAB, R 63/83, Bl. 70–71, Kratz to Rafelsberger, June 30, 1942.

more "orderly" condition than its competitors in the spring of 1944 when the Germans entered Budapest and SS troops surrounded the Ungarische Allgemeine Creditbank because it was "teeming" with Jews. As one Austrian observer from the Länderbank Wien complained, there was total chaos at the bank.[114] This "problem" had been "solved" at the CA Budapest. The Budapest branch had been free of Jews for some time. Indeed, Joham gave an optimistic report in late April 1944 about the Budapest branch, "which, in contrast to the other Hungarian banks, has been completely untouched by the recent events and has shown a significant improvement of its liquidity because of a growth of deposits and larger receipts for clearing business."[115] In late September, Joham found the Budapest branch to be basically stable, and its liquidity actually somewhat improved because "as the branch has had only few Jewish customers, its business has remained completely unaffected by the Aryanization measures in progress."[116] This happy state of affairs, however, was being disturbed by the advance of the Russians, and in late November Joham described the various measures being taken to get rid of pengö holdings, the effort to collect on as many accounts receivable as possible, and the preparations to evacuate the branch to Sopron.[117]

Poland: Competition between the CA and the Deutsche Bank

Unlike Slovakia and Hungary, where the Germans had to pay some attention to the authoritarian regimes with which they were allied, the Polish regime was simply toppled in the invasion that began World War II. Poland itself was divided between areas annexed to Germany – Danzig, West Prussia, Poznan, and Upper Silesia – and large portions of the former Congress Poland, including Warsaw, and Austrian Poland (Galicia), including Cracow, which were

placed under the control of German administration, the Generalgouvernement (GG). Until the German invasion of Russia in 1941, the so-called Curzon Line was used to demarcate the areas of German and Russian occupation. Following the invasion of Russia, some of the newly conquered territory, especially around Lemberg/ Lviv, was incorporated into the GG, while the remainder was placed under the administration of Ukraine. The annexed areas of what had been Poland contained the country's most important industrial and agricultural assets, but there was significant industry and agriculture in the GG as well. The German occupiers intended to eliminate Poland as a state, exploit its resources, and engage in large-scale transfers of Poles and Jews to the East and provide "living space" for German settlers. A special agency, the Head Trusteeship Office East (Haupttreuhandstelle Ost= HTO) was established as part of the Four Year Plan organization to administer the transfer of Polish and Jewish property and assets into Aryan hands and was placed under the leadership of Max Winkler. He was a former mayor of Graudenz and had worked for the German Foreign Office before the Anschluss in organizations promoting the economic penetration of Austria and assisting the "illegals." By and large, the HTO concentrated its activities in the annexed areas, but it did have a section that dealt with Polish assets in the old Reich, which included Austria and Upper Silesia. One of its "achievements" was the liquidation of every Polish and Jewish bank in the annexed territories. The GG had its own banking section and a complicated administrative structure, and it pursued a somewhat different policy toward banks under its control. It was the HTO and the GG that also pursued the policies of expropriating Polish and Jewish assets and, to the disappointment of the German banks, limited although by no means excluded the role of the banks as intermediaries in the "Germanization" and "Aryanization" processes.[118] This did not mean that the German

---

[114] See NARA, RG 407, Box 1030, the report by Felix Graf Czernin of May 24, 1944.

[115] BA-CA, CA-V, CA Working Committee meeting, April 26–27, 1944.

[116] Ibid., Sept. 26, 1944.

[117] Ibid., Nov. 22, 1944.

[118] There is a useful short summary of German economic policies in Poland by Werner Röhr, "Zur Wirtschaftspolitik der deutschen Okkupanten in Polen 1939–1945," in: Dietrich Eichholtz (ed.), *Krieg und Wirtschaft. (= Studien zur deutschen Wirtschaftsgeschichte 1939–1945* (Berlin 1999),

banks had nothing to do. The financing of industrial and agricultural activity in Poland required large amounts of capital, and from the very outset the German banks sought to establish themselves in both the annexed areas and the GG and entertained substantial expectations.

This was very much in evidence in the case of the CA, which was to prove remarkably aggressive in its ambitions and even stepped on the toes of the Deutsche Bank in its rush to assume a position in Poland. The background to this development, however, is a very complicated one. Doing business in Poland had not been very popular after 1919. Although the Deutsche Bank had hung on to its Breslau and Kattowitz branches, the Dresdner Bank found dealing with the Polish government too difficult and the profitability too low because of Polish "nostrification" tendencies, and it had pulled out. The Länderbank Wien was in the process of liquidating its Kommerzialbank in Cracow when the war broke out. The CA showed very little interest in the Kattowitz branch of the Deutsche Bank, whose director, Richard Gdynia, complained in May 1939 to Johannes Kiehl, the Deutsche Bank management board director charged with overseeing

these branches, that the CA scarcely gave it any business and failed to put its blocked Zloty at the branch's disposal when they were badly needed.[119] The situation in the spring and summer of 1939 was particularly serious because the crisis in German-Polish relations was leading to large-scale withdrawals. These difficulties evaporated as Germany's advancing armies created banking opportunities. Kiehl came into rapid contact with both Riehle and the office of the supervisory board for banking and supplied them with detailed information on the Polish banking situation as it had developed since 1919. In the meantime, the Economic Policy Section of the Deutsche Bank produced a memorandum on September 7 defining the principles and goals of policy in Poland. It began by noting that "however the final solution of the Polish question will be determined, it appears certain that Germany will want to secure priority in these territories. Unquestionably, the present territory of Poland belongs in the German 'living space' both because of the significant but often not at all utilized agricultural reserves which this land contains and the available industrial areas here and there, which surely represent a valuable addition to the industrial potency of Germany." Insofar as the banking field was concerned, the British and the French had lost control of their interests, which had significant, and the Germans could fill the vacuum. From the perspective of the Deutsche Bank, it was important to have an appropriate base in Poland and to use the institutes already available to build up the bank's position. While other German banks undoubtedly would be asked to play a role, it was essential that the Deutsche Bank make use of its advantages. The Deutsche Bank Economic Policy Section proposed taking over and merging the Allgemeine Kreditbank AG, which had an important branch in Kattowitz, and the Banque Franco-Polonaise, both of which were in French hands, and also taking over the Schlesische Kredit-Anstalt in Bielitz, which also had a branch in Kattowitz and Teschen. A strong position would be created in Silesia, although the majority of the

pp. 221–252. On the policies of despoliation and expropriation, see Zbigniew Landau, "Polish and Jewish Entrepreneurs during the German Occupation," in: Harold James/Jakob Tanner (eds.), *Enterprise in the Period of Fascism in Europe* (Aldershot, Burlington 2002), pp. 178–188. More generally, see Zbigniew Landau and Jerzy Tomaszewski, *Wirtschaftsgeschichte Polens im 19. und 20. Jahrhundert* (Berlin 1986), ch. 7. A valuable account of policies and conditions in the GG is to be found in Jan Tomasz Gross, *Polish Society under German Occupation: The Generalgouvernement 1939–1944* (Princeton 1970). On the HTO, see Jeanne Dingell, *Zur Tätigkeit der Haupttreuhandstelle Ost, Treuhandstelle Posen 1939 bis 1945* (Frankfurt a.M. 2003), esp. pp. 195–200 and Bernhard Rosenkötter, *Treuhandpolitik. Die "Haupttreuhandstelle Ost" und der Raub polnischer Vermögen 1939–1945* (Essen 2003), pp. 47–252. For an excellent discussion of the banks and the roles of the HTO and GG, see Ingo Loose, "Die Beteiligung deutscher Kreditinstitute an der Vernichtung der ökonomischen Existenz der Juden in Polen 1939–1945," in: Ludolf Herbst and Thomas Weihe (eds.), *Die Commerzbank und die Juden 1933–1945* (Munich 2004), pp. 223–271.

[119] DB, P 24222, Kiehl to Abs, May 4, 1939.

shares of the Schlesische Kredit-Anstalt were in the hands of the Warschauer Disconto-Bank. The latter was also of interest to the Germans because of its prosperous branch in Lodz. The congruence between the goals of the Deutsche Bank and the Germanization intentions of the National Socialist regime could hardly have been more clearly demonstrated.[120]

But what the Deutsche Bank was contemplating in theory was also to be implemented in reality, albeit with variations. Because it had never left Poland, the Deutsche Bank had a great advantage over its competition, and the Dresdner Bank, in contrast to the situation in the Czech lands, was often forced to play second fiddle in dealing with the authorities in both Berlin and Poland.[121] A few days after the aforementioned memorandum was written, Kiehl informed Felix Theusner, who directed the Deutsch Bank's Breslau branch, that the military occupation authorities wanted the Deutsche Bank to open up branches in Bielitz, Teschen, and Oderberg and also to go to Cracow. This whetted Theusner's appetite, and he urged Kiehl also to consider opening a branch in Posen because much of Posen's prewar commercial business was done via Breslau. It was important to act before another big bank took the initiative.[122]

These Deutsche Bank officials, however, were racing ahead of Germany's armies, which had not yet taken Warsaw, and also ahead of the authorities in Berlin, who were trying to gain control of the situation. On September 19, Kiehl informed Theusner that setting up branches in Bielitz, Teschen, and Oderberg had been approved, although the Dresdner Bank was also laying claim to Teschen. The RWM, however, refused to approve setting up a branch in Cracow, where conditions were considered unsatisfactory. Kiehl saw few advantages to pushing for a branch in Posen because the agricultural and sugar business involved could be

done via Danzig, but he thought it very important for the Deutsche Bank to establish itself in Warsaw. He asked Theusner to use his personal political contacts to push the idea, cynically remarking that "as a bank we must be cautious lest we are suspected of pursuing egoistical interests; you, as an individual, are acting as a patriot."[123]

Kiehl could boast greater success when it came to Cracow. Various business interests, eager to exploit its geographic advantages and to profit from the role it would presumably play in reviving the economy, had been successfully lobbying Riehle in Berlin. As a result, the RWM agreed to the establishment of a banking branch in the city, and this inevitably led Kiehl to think about other places in Galicia – Tarnow, Rzesow, Pržemysl, and Lemberg/Lviv. He confessed, however, to running ahead of circumstances and that "initially we will … bridle our entrepreneurial spirit" because it was not yet clear if the Russians would get Lemberg/Lviv and Pržemysl. In fact, they got both.[124]

Meanwhile, and to the discomfort of Abs and Kiehl, the CA was unbridling its own entrepreneurial spirit, and all such show of the modesty and self-restraint as had existed in the previous year when the Czech lands were being carved up was now being cast to the winds. Both Fischböck and Hasslacher had paid visits to Berlin in September. They had spoken with Rösler and discussed the Upper Silesian and Teschen areas, and this was followed by a conversation between Hasslacher and Abs. Obviously, Fischböck and Hasslacher were interested in finding a place for the CA in the forthcoming settlement of banking arrangements in these regions. Abs told Hasslacher – or

[120] Ibid., Vorschlag zur Frage einer allfälligen Interessennahme am polnischen Bankwesen, Sept. 7, 1939.
[121] This is very convincingly demonstrated by Harald Wixforth, *Expansion der Dresdner Bank*, ch. V.
[122] DB, P 24222, Theusner to Kiehl, Sept. 16, 1939.
[123] Ibid., Kiehl to Theusner, Sept. 19, 1939. Theusner subsequently reported that the local Gauleiter was of little help. He seems to have been well connected because he also wrote to his personal friend Hans Lammers, the secretary of the Reich Chancellery, who came from Silesia but who proved not to be of much help either. See ibid., Theusner to Kiehl, Sept. 22, 1939.
[124] Ibid., Kiehl to M.L. Rohde of the BUB branch in Mährisch-Ostrau, Sept. 22, 1939.

at least he thought he had told Hasslacher – that any arrangement between the Deutsche Bank and the CA would have to wait on the establishment of political order in these areas and also pointed out that Kiehl's views were important because he was in charge of the Deutsche Bank interests in the Silesian industrial area. Abs noted that he and Hasslacher had discussed the possibility of CA activity in Cracow and other cities in the region and also a potential joint participation in the BUB branch in Moravia. There had, however, been no concrete agreements. It was thus with some surprise that Abs learned from Kiehl that Fischböck had called up and, making reference to the Abs conversation with Hasslacher, wanted to discuss the CA taking over the newly established Deutsche Bank branches in Teschen, Bielitz, and Oderberg.[125]

Abs hastened to inform Hasslacher that there had been a misunderstanding about their conversation with Kiehl, who certainly must have been irritated by Fischböck's presumptions and who was also pursuing an agenda of his own in collaboration with Director Gdynia in Kattowitz. This centered on the Schlesische Kredit-Anstalt that, as noted earlier, had its headquarters in Bielitz with branches in Teschen and Kattowitz while the majority of its shares were in the hands of the Warschauer Disconto-Bank. The Schlesische Kredit-Anstalt was a very solid bank with a good reputation, and it was seeking permission to reopen and, using its old connection with the CA, of which it once had been a subsidiary, was counting on the latter to assist it in this endeavor. Indeed, the bank had gone very far in this direction, writing on September 20 to the CA with the question of whether "in view of our good relations over many years, you have an interest in our institute and would want to pave the way for collaboration in the future."[126] On the one hand, the bank painted a dire picture of its immediate situation because only some twenty officials and a director had remained in Bielitz

while the Poles and Jews had fled. The bank had no money, and it was not being permitted to operate. On the other hand, it stressed the attractions of the bank with respect to its past history and its ownership. Only 17 percent of its shares were in Jewish hands, and the majority was in Aryan possession. A major shareholder was the general director of the Warschauer Disconto-Bank, Viktor Mikulecki, who had served for many years as an official of the Finance Ministry in Vienna. The administrative council was composed of 8 Aryans and 4 Jews, and its staff members in the three branches of Bielitz, Kattowitz, and Teschen were primarily Aryan, specifically, 112 Aryans and 28 Jews. The Schlesische Kredit-Anstalt also provided a very detailed account of the bank's balances and accounts. Its biggest selling point, however, was that the authorities were discussing the possibility of setting up a regional bank alongside the Deutsche Bank, which had recently established its own branch in Bielitz. If this were to be the case, then the Schlesische Kredit-Anstalt, because of its soundness, was the ideal vehicle for such an institute. The CA responded to this appeal on September 25, stating that "we are engaged in the examination of a possible strengthening and expansion of our business connections in Silesia and hope to soon have the opportunity to engage in a discussion about possible collaboration."[127]

This was not the program Kiehl and Gdynia had in mind. Gdynia knew the leading directors of the Schlesische Kredit-Anstalt quite well and apparently persuaded them to get their books in order and make contact with him and the Deutsche Bank before taking any further steps. Gdynia urged Kiehl to look into the question of acquiring the bank because it would fit in well with what it had already accomplished by way of expansion in Reichenberg, Prague, and Vienna. Manifestly, Gdynia did not view the CA as the Deutsche Bank's partner in Poland and did not want to let the Poles play the CA against the Deutsche Bank. Kiehl could not have agreed more. He told Gdynia

[125] DB, P 6503, Bl. 126, Abs to Hasslacher, Sept. 28, 1939.
[126] BA-CA, CA-V, S.P. Akten, Nr. 441, Schlesische Kredit-Anstalt, Bielitz to CA, Sept. 20, 1938.

[127] Ibid., CA to Schlesische Kredit-Anstalt, Sept. 25, 1939.

that the Deutsche Bank already had its eye on the Schlesische Kredit-Anstalt, for which there was high regard, and that the Deutsche Bank branch in Kattowitz had actually moved into the Schlesische Kredit-Anstalt branch building there. Kiehl informed Gdynia that he had contact with a key figure he knew at the bank in Bielitz, Vice-president Weinschenck, who had been one of the signatories of the letter to the CA, and also with persons connected with the Warsaw bank to make sure that they did not make any arrangement with the CA.[128]

As if these machinations were not complex enough, a somewhat comic element was added to the situation when two representatives of the Commerzbank suddenly showed up in Bielitz and claimed that they had been appointed trustees for the Schlesische Kredit-Anstalt with the task of selling it. This was news to everyone, including the Berlin banking authorities, but the conversations with Ministerial Director Gerhard Wolf demonstrated how unsettled matters really were. The Schlesische Kredit-Anstalt, like all Polish banks, was to have its trustee, a man named Hecht, but he did not come from the Commerzbank. Of even more moment, however, was Wolf's declaration that all the German bank branches set up in the Olsa, Polish Silesian, and Galician areas had to be viewed as provisional until it was decided which banks would be allowed to stay permanently and where they could do so. For the banks involved, it was going to be very important to be able to demonstrate either prior presence in the places in question or substantial business connections. As matters were being made much more complicated by the claims put forth by the CA, Wolf feared that there would be quite a struggle for Bielitz. Kiehl sought to emphasize that Weinschenck and the other administrators of the Schlesische Kredit-Anstalt who had not fled the Germans were all solidly behind dealing with the Deutsche Bank. As Kiehl later

pointed out to Gdynia, Weinschenck's firm, G. Josephys Erben, had a close relationship with the Deutsche Bank that went back many years. This conversion from the CA to the Deutsche Bank was undoubtedly inspired by the presence of the Deutsche Bank officials in the area; still, one consequence of the newly found preference for the Deutsche Bank on the part of Weinschenck and his allies was that negotiations with the CA were broken off.[129]

Nevertheless, CA General Director Fischböck fought on. He was undeterred by information he might have received from Hasslacher, Kiehl, Abs, or anyone else suggesting that the CA should hold back in staking its claims. At the meeting of the working committee of the CA supervisory board on October 12, therefore, Fischböck declared that the CA should set up branches in the area of Bielitz-Teschen in the eastern area of Upper Silesia as well as branches in Cracow, Tarnov, Rzeszow, and Przemysl. Because the Deutsche Bank had already set up branches in Bielitz and Cracow, he proposed that the Deutsche Bank cede these to the CA. While Abs reserved his decision until he could consult with the Deutsche Bank management board, the CA committee approved an effort to set up branches in Cracow, Tarnow, Rzeszow, and Przemysl.[130]

The behavior of Fischböck and his colleagues in this matter has to be understood both in terms of the mentality the CA leadership had developed since the Anschluss and the strategy it was evolving as a consequence of German expansion, as well as the CA connection with the Deutsche Bank. As was the case in the Czech lands and Slovakia, so too in Poland; the CA legitimized its claims by pointing to the past. This also turned out to be a relevant strategy, quite aside from the CA's method of constantly seeking "compensation" for past losses, because the authorities tended to favor claims – Kiehl had discovered this in his own efforts to justify Deutsche Bank ambitions – that were based on evidence of prior presence or of ongoing business relationships. Accordingly, when the CA representatives discussed their claims in Poland

[128] DB, P 24222, Gdynia to Kiehl, Sept. 28, 1939, and Kiehl to Gdynia, Oct. 3, 1939.

[129] Ibid., Kiehl to Gdynia, Oct. 13, 1939, ibid.; on the termination of Schlesische Kreditbank-CA negotiations, see Weinschenck to Kiehl, Nov. 8, 1939.

[130] BA-CA, CA-V, CA working committee meeting, Oct. 12, 1939.

with Riehle on October 13, the latter asked for specific details, which the CA provided a few days later. The CA pointed out that until 1918 it had branches in Bielitz, Cracow, Novozielitza, Tarnow, and Teschen. Indeed, the Austrians had a substantial presence in the Polish territories before the war, the Viennese major banks having no fewer than twenty branches and offices there as well as interests in Polish banks and enterprises.[131] Prior to 1931, the CA was forced to give up its holdings in four banks in Galicia and in some industrial enterprises because of the political and economic circumstances. But, contrary to the impression the CA sought to create, the situation in Poland actually favored Austrian banking engagement because of the underdevelopment of the Polish banking system.[132] Whatever the fate of some of its branches, the CA retained interests in five Polish banks and a dozen oil and heavy industrial companies. These were not lost because of Polish pressure but rather because of the economic crisis and the bankruptcy of the CA. As a result, a substantial number of shares were placed with the Société Continentale de Gestion, including 27 percent of the shares of the Schlesische Kredit-Anstalt. The only Polish holding left to the CA was 10.4 percent of shares in the Allgemeine Bank-Verein in Warsaw that had been in the portfolio of the Wiener Bankverein, the rest being in the hands of the Société Générale de Belgique in Brussels. The CA now felt that the time had come to regain these losses. Having legitimized its claims on the basis of the past, the CA went on to declare its present intentions: "It is the aim of the Creditanstalt to establish itself again in the former West Galician territories, that is, in those territories that stretch from the Protectorate eastward to the borders of the U.S.S.R. running North to include those places that lie on the main railroad line Mährisch-Ostrau-Cracow, Premysl."[133]

The CA, however, as this description implied, was not only seeking to regain something akin to the position it had held in the old Austro-Hungarian empire; it was also striving to establish a network of banking positions for itself in Central Europe with the ultimate goal of being the dominant bank in the Southeast European business of the German banking system. One must remember that the CA was still trying to make advances in both Slovakia and Moravia at this time, and it went on from its ambitions in Poland to discuss its goals in both those places. In the case of Slovakia, it was still trying to take over the 80 percent stake of the Legio Bank Prague in the Slovakische Allgemeine Creditbank, Pressburg and then to bring the BUB branch in Pressburg into that bank. It was being frustrated in this effort by the fact that the Legio Bank was under an administrator appointed by the Gestapo, by the Hungarians taking over branches of the Slovakische Allgemeine Creditbank in their newly acquired Slovak territory, which was making it difficult to calculate the value of the bank shares, and, in the end, by transfer problems. As has been shown, the CA would ultimately have to settle for the BUB branch in Slovakia that became the Union-Bank Pressburg. Finally, there were the CA interests in Moravia, which were also being frustrated despite the friendship pact the CA and the Mährische Bank Brünn/ Brno had signed back in April 1939. The shares were in the hands of the state and the town of Znaim, which were not inclined to sell them to the CA. While the CA had managed to get branches for itself in Znaim/Znojmo and Lundenburg/Breclav, it continued to be thwarted in its efforts to gain control of the BUB branches in Moravia. Similarly, the desire of the CA to gain the Moravian branches of the Böhmische Industrialbank in the Protectorate also remained unfulfilled. In sum, the upshot of the memorandum presented to Riehle was that the CA had a plan to establish a network for itself running from the borders of the USSR through Galicia and part of Silesia to Slovakia and Moravia but that it was only partially attaining its goals. To some extent, this was because of the claims of its "friend," the Deutsche Bank.

[131] Landau/Tomaszewski, *Wirtschaftsgeschichte*, p. 85.
[132] Janusz Kaliński, "Austrian Banks in Poland up to 1948," in: Rathkolb et al. (eds)., *Bank Austria Creditanstalt*, pp. 259–264.
[133] BA-CA, CA-V, S.P. Akt, Nr. 446, CA to Riehle, Oct. 18, 1939.

In the main, it was because of political considerations, be they from the German authorities, from the Slovaks, or from the Hungarians, or because those ruling the Protectorate stood in their way.

The Deutsche Bank certainly had no intention of acceding to Fischböck's program for Poland. On October 16, he was informed that the Deutsche Bank was prepared to see the CA take over Cracow and its surrounding area but that it reserved for itself the East Upper Silesian industrial area, including Teschen, Bielitz, and Oderberg, which were to be controlled out of Kattowitz. Furthermore, because there was some talk of creating one bank for what was left of Poland, the CA would be expected to bring the Cracow branch into its fold should the regional branch ever be created.[134]

The chief proponent of a regional bank was apparently the trustee for the Schlesische Kredit-Anstalt, Hecht, but his enthusiasm appeared limited to himself because none of the German banks, including the Deutsche Bank, were at all interested in the project at this time. The general view was that it would simply slow down the acquisition of needed capital and make a bad situation worse. Fischböck was more supportive of the project, and he discussed the various contingencies with Abs and Kiehl as well as with the office of the bank commissar in late November. Abs and Kiehl indicated that they wanted to maintain the Deutsche Bank's position in Bielitz and Teschen and opposed the creation of a regional bank. Should the latter be created, however, then they would not oppose a major participation by the CA, but reserved the right to maintain their branches in the event such a bank were created. Fischböck unquestionably wanted a significant role for the CA in a regional bank, but pointed out that his major interest was focused less on Poland than on Moravia. He believed that Moravia would be separated from the Czech-dominated Protectorate of Bohemia and placed under the political domination of Vienna. This would make Mährisch-Ostrau the economic center

for the Olsa area it had been in the days of the Austro-Hungarian empire. In this instance, it would be important for the CA to be present in Teschen and Bielitz and a regional bank would obviously be of interest. Should Moravia not be separated from the Protectorate, however, the CA would be much less interested in a presence in Teschen and Bielitz, and the projected regional bank could be dominated by the Deutsche Bank with CA participation. Given the uncertainty of the political situation, Fischböck thought it best to leave the question open and felt that a friendly understanding of the two banks would be worked out if and when necessary. Under these circumstances, the discussion became increasingly speculative. Ministerial Director Wolf accepted the proposition that a regional bank, about which he was very skeptical, would require an important CA role and would, in his view, require the Deutsche Bank to give up its branches in Bielitz, Teschen, and Oderberg because the area would then have too many banks. At the same time, Kiehl bluntly declared that the Deutsche Bank would not give up its branches if the Dresdner Bank and Commerzbank were allowed to remain in those places. The end effect of all this discussion was that everyone hoped Fischböck would settle for Cracow if Moravia remained in the Protectorate, while no one was particularly enthusiastic about the establishment of a regional bank. Work continued on investigating the status of the various Polish banks that would be integrated into the projected regional bank, primarily as a concession to Fischböck, but the idea hinged on his continued interest.[135]

Hecht's program was to use the Schlesische Kredit-Anstalt, of which he was the trustee, as the basis for the establishment of a regional bank that, in his view, was needed to bring more capital into East Upper Silesia. He anticipated that business would pick up. In his view, there was not enough economic leadership in the area and he felt that the Deutsche Bank director there, Gdynia, was not up to his job

---

[134] DB, P 6503, Bl. 39, telegram, Deutsche Bank to CA, Oct. 16, 1939.

[135] DB, P 24222, Memorandum by Kiehl, Nov. 25, 1939; Kiehl to Wolf, Nov. 25, 1939; memo by Rummel, Dec. 11, 1939; discussion with Wolf, Jan. 30, 1940.

and that the contact with the regional business community was insufficient. The establishment of a regional bank was intended to correct these alleged deficiencies as well as put the Schlesische Kredit-Anstalt back on its feet again. Hecht wanted to move the headquarters of the bank from Bielitz to Kattowitz. He claimed support from local businesspeople and from various Reichsbank branches, and also urged that the regional bank could take over some of the other local Polish banks, especially the Internationale Handelsbank, which was Jewish owned and had a very fine building in Kattowitz that could be used to house the new bank. The banking authorities in Berlin certainly paid attention to Hecht's proposal but also raised reservations, pointing out that the future disposition of Jewish and Polish assets had not yet been decided. One of the attractions of the Hecht plan was that the government would be spared the reproach of favoring the major banks. But, in some contradiction to this, the authorities also felt it important that the Deutsche Bank and some other large banks participate in the new regional bank, and they noted that the CA was particularly logical because of its old connections in the region. Ministerial Director Wolf promised Hecht that he would pursue the matter but that nothing could be done until the condition of the Schlesische Kredit-Anstalt as well as other potential local banks could be assessed.[136]

The Deutsche Bank weighed in heavily against this program. In a memorandum to the Banking Supervisory Office, it pointed out that there were ten banks in the region prior to the outbreak of the war, excluding its branch in Kattowitz. The latter had been the largest bank in the area during the period after 1919, and all efforts to compete with it or reduce its influence failed. Of its ninety-member staff, eighty were Germans or ethnic Germans. The only other banks of any significance were the Schlesische Kredit-Anstalt and the Internationale Handelsbank AG, the latter,

as noted earlier, being largely Jewish. In the view of the Deutsche Bank, the credit needs of the region were being well cared for by its Kattowitz branch, by the newly established branches connected with Kattowitz, and by the various branches set up by the other German banks. The Deutsche Bank Kattowitz branch, having been in the region through the period of Polish rule, was particularly experienced and adept at dealing with the problems at hand, and, as the Deutsche Bank argued, the entire business community was grateful for its services. Business was picking up, the workers were being paid, and the Polish banks were not missed. Indeed, those banks faced the problem that they had few creditors and many debtors, and the latter, being either Polish or Jewish, could not repay their debts because their assets were frozen. In the end, therefore, the Polish banks would have to be liquidated. The German banks, assuming they were allowed to engage in fair competition with one another, would be well enough positioned to take care of the needs of the regional economy and there was therefore no need for a new special regional bank that might have a monopolistic position.[137]

As noted earlier, the authorities in Berlin were inclined to accept this position, but they needed to come to some kind of arrangement with the CA, whose claims could not be totally denied. On January 5, 1940, CA Director Fritscher had a meeting with Ministerial Director Gottschick of the RWM and Wolf of the supervisory board in which the CA once more pressed for branches in the Olsa area. At this point, Wolf put matters very bluntly, pointing out that the CA was obstructing the efforts of the authorities who were seeking to find a rational approach to solving the region's oversupply of banks. The only reason the CA was doing this was to anticipate a possible reorientation of the Moravian region in the direction of Vienna; otherwise the CA really had no interest in the Olsa branches. Effectively, Wolf was telling Fritscher that the CA was making their lives difficult in anticipation of something

136 RGVA Moscow, 1458/15/124, Bl. 28–31, memorandum on meeting of Dec. 12, 1939 in Berlin, dated Dec. 15, 1939.

137 Ibid., Bl. 20–26, Deutsche Bank to Reich Supervisory Agency, Dec. 12, 1939.

that showed no immediate likelihood of happening. At this juncture, Fritscher frankly conceded that Wolf had a point. He also noted that the Deutsche Bank was opposed to the plan to divide the BUB's branches territorially and confessed that the entire question would have to await the end of the war. In a later discussion between Wolf and Fischböck about the regional bank issue, Fischböck too found himself forced to admit that there were already enough banks in the Olsa area and forthrightly stated the real calculation behind his persistence: "If the CA sets aside its wishes, then later on it would have no point of departure at all in its negotiations with the Deutsche Bank."[138] Wolf suggested that they try to get some assurances right away and obviously implied that the time had come to terminate the other demands in the Olsa area.

Fischböck seems to have taken this advice. A few days later, he had a discussion with Director Rösler of the Deutsche Bank in which the latter assured him of the Deutsche Bank's intention to let the CA have a share of the BUB and total control of the new bank to be established in Pressburg/Bratislava.[139] Apparently, there seemed no further point in trying to leverage ambitions of uncertain value in Poland in order to get more concessions from the Deutsche Bank. In this way, the tug-of-war over the CA's position in Poland ended, at least for the time being. On February 5, 1940, Fischböck asked the CA management board to approve the taking over of the branch of the Deutsche Bank in Cracow, and Pfeiffer was assigned as the management board member to deal with it. The RWM agreed at the beginning of March, and on April 19, 1940, the CA assumed direction of the Deutsche Bank branch in Cracow. The branch had 50 million Zl in deposits and 1.5 million Zl in accounts receivable. At the time of its takeover by the CA, it employed thirty officials, of whom seven were holdovers from the Deutsche Bank branch or the Berlin headquarters. The Berliners went back home

shortly thereafter. Robert Huber, the head of the branch Stock-im-Eisenplatz was made director of the Cracow branch, while Gustav Czerny from the Branch Section of the central headquarters in Vienna was appointed deputy director.[140]

Pfeiffer was apparently intent on installing the Cracow branch in attractive and roomy quarters, and he succeeded in lodging it in the new bank building of the Bank Handlowy w. Warszawie S.A.,[141] Alter Markt 31 – subsequently renamed Adolf-Hitler-Platz – which was near the now vacated Deutsche Bank branch at Alter Markt 47. It was a move that greatly annoyed the head of the Bank Supervisory Office for the GG and of the GG Bank of Issue, Fritz Paersch, a Reichsbank director and specialist on banking regulation assigned to serve Governor General Hans Frank in this position.[142] Pfeiffer had apparently run from one agency to another, especially in the Ostmark, seeking approval for occupying the building and finally succeeded in getting a letter from Seyss-Inquart ordering that the CA branch be allowed to move in. At the time, Paersch's office had not yet been established, and the official in charge, Richard Zetzsche, who had never been consulted, apparently simply yielded. Paersch, when he took over, felt unable to act in view of the fact that the bank's customers had already been informed of the change of address. Nevertheless, he did persuade Governor General Frank to issue a formal refusal to the CA to do what it had done already, and when the Dresdner Bank, inspired by the CA's move, tried to take over the offices of the Warschauer Disconto-Bank for its own Kommercialbank, Paersch refused to grant permission. Paersch pointed out to

138 Ibid., Bl. 72, memorandum by Wolf, Jan. 9, 1940 on discussions of Jan. 5, 1940.
139 Ibid., P 6503, Bl. 188–189, Rösler memo for Abs, Jan. 8, 1940.
140 Ibid., Bl. 284, CA to Deutsche Bank, April 20, 1940; BA-CA, CA-V, CA management board meetings, Feb. 5, 1940, March 2, 1940, April 2, 1940, April 10, 1940.
141 In the German documents, this is called the Warschauer Handelsbank. The Polish name will be used here.
142 See Fritz Paersch, "Maßnahmen des Staates hinsichtlich der Beaufsichtigung der Reglementierung des Bankwesens," in: Untersuchungsausschuß für das Bankwesen (ed.), Untersuchungen des Bankwesens 1933, Teil I, Bd. 2.

Director Emil Meyer of the Dresdner Bank that "the financing of the great tasks which the Governor General has in mind for the occupied Polish territories cannot be carried out with the Reich-German banks alone. The Polish banks will also be needed for this. For this reason it is necessary to show regard for their interests too." He was not going to let Pfeiffer's coup serve as a model for others, asking Frank to refuse its formal acceptance in order to reinforce the Bank Handlowy's rightful ownership of the building and recognize that it did not want to give up the property. The CA was thus stuck with having to pay rent and had no guarantee that it could take advantage of the option it had forced on the Polish bank to buy the building. This said, the CA branch certainly did everything possible to take the lead in Cracow banking, acquiring two large domiciles for its directors and furnishing them properly so that the bank could entertain customers and officials "in style." The situation greatly irritated Director Arthur Glathe of the resurrected Kommerzialbank, whose two-room apartment provided no opportunity to compete on the social level, and he asked the Dresdner Bank to approve the acquisition of proper living quarters. Shortly thereafter, the Dresdner Bank provided 2,000 Zl to provide suitable quarters.[143]

At the same time, the CA's ambitions to expand its role in Poland seemed irrepressible. In July, Director Fritscher paid a visit to Paersch about the possibility of setting up another branch in the GG or taking over a Polish bank. Paersch confirmed Fritscher's suspicion that something might soon open up in Warsaw, and that once the auditing of the Polish banks ended in the fall, a decision would be made about allowing a Reich German bank in Warsaw. Because the Crakow branch seemed to be functioning well, Paersch was willing to take the CA interest in Warsaw into account, but he was also prepared to consider its perhaps greater interest in a minority holding in the Allgemeine Polnische Bankverein. He felt that the most promising thing for the CA was a small branch in Warsaw that would work closely with the CA branch.[144] During the period following the establishment of the branch in Cracow, the CA also seems to have made regular efforts to appeal to the authorities in Berlin for permission to set up more branches in East Upper Silesia. This ended up provoking a note from the RWM that declared that it found no need for further branches in the area and was actually trying to reduce the number. In addition, it asked to be spared having to send the CA a formal written refusal to grant its request.[145]

In the fall of 1940, Director Huber of the Cracow branch contacted Paersch's deputy, an official named Laschtowiczka, who had gone to school with Fischböck and had worked at the CA before entering the Polish banking field, to ask about the possibilities of opening new branches in the GG. The CA was by no means alone in making such inquiries because the Dresdner Bank and the other German banks that had not yet established a presence in what was left of Poland had followed suit. Laschtowiczka informed Huber that no decisions were likely until the turn of the year because of the time

[143] For Pfeiffer's report on the building, see ibid., the board of management meeting of April 20, 1940. On Paersch's policies and motives, see a copy of his letter to Emil Meyer of June 3, 1940 to which he appended a letter to Riehle explaining the situation, RGVA Moscow, 1458/15/128, Bl. 93–94. Paersch was especially angry at the former Deutsche Bank director in Cracow, August Neugebauer, who had made a practice of deprecating the Polish banks in an effort to win away their customers. Paersch regarded this as the kind of unfair competitive practices he wished to avoid. Such instances aside, of course, the GG wouldnot be known for its solicitude toward the Poles. Paersch's oversight role in banking was combined with his position as head of the GG's bank of issue. Much can be learned about him and about his policies from Werner Präg/Wolfgang Jacobmeyer, *Das Diensttagebuch des deutschen Generalgouverneurs in Polen 1939–1945* (= Quellen und Darstellungen zur Zeitgeschichte, Vol. 20 (Stuttgart 1975). Hans Frank's achievements in Poland earned him a well-deserved hanging after

his trial in Nuremberg. On Glathe's housing problems, see NARA, T83/155, Anspach to Meyer, Aug. 5, 1940 and Minute by Anspach, Oct. 19, 1940.

[144] BA-CA, CA-TZ, Sekretariat rot, Box 33/CA-BV Filiale Allgemeines, Minute by Fritscher, July 6, 1940.

[145] Ibid., Gottschick to CA Vienna, July 3, 1940.

needed to wind up the business of the Polish banks and make assessments of their status. He believed that German banks would be allowed entry only with the availability of shares in one or more of the Polish banks that had been consolidated, but suggested that it might be useful to take up contact with any Polish bank that seemed interesting.[146]

Another track possibly available to the CA was to pursue the discussions it had launched with the Deutsche Bank about making common cause in the GG if such an opportunity presented itself. The Deutsche Bank certainly seems to have encouraged this interest and expressed a willingness to work with the CA in Poland where this seemed propitious. This was confirmed in early November 1940, when Riehle asked the Deutsche Bank about its plans in the GG and Abs and Kiehl replied that it was hard to say so long as there was no information about what might be possible there. Nevertheless, they wanted to have a branch in any case in the largest economic center in the country, namely, Warsaw. If, however, the RWM wished to establish one or more independent regional banks in the GG, then "we are in agreement with our Viennese friends, the Creditanstalt-Bankverein, to head up such a regional institute as a joint investment."[147]

Although the CA received a copy of this Deutsche Bank reply to the RWM, both banks were also trying to situate themselves in separate positions in Warsaw. Officially, the status of Poland's capital city was a subordinate one, as it "was a special wish of the Führer who wants to have the name Warsaw disappear from the Polish conceptual world."[148] The GG was initially centered in Litzmannstadt/Lodz, which subsequently found itself situated in the annexed areas, and then based in Cracow. From the perspective of the banks, however, Warsaw remained front and center, and on January 24, 1941, the Deutsche Bank made this clear to the CA in no uncertain terms and in a tone rather different from the one it used in the fall of 1940. The CA was informed that the Deutsche Bank "has come to the conclusion that in view of our economic relationships in a place of this size, which has a population of a million and encompasses the chief portion of the industry of the Generalgouvernement, we must be represented, even if the rebuilding of Warsaw and the normalization of economic conditions are in large part yet to be achieved." The Deutsche Bank did not intend to actually undertake the founding of such a branch for another few months because there was a delay indicated by the authorities, but its resolve was shaped by the substantial business interests of the bank in the neighboring eastern provinces, specifically Danzig and Upper Silesia. The Deutsche Bank was specifically motivated to inform the CA of this because it knew of the CA's intention to establish itself in Warsaw and had also learned that the authorities were unlikely to permit both banks to have independent representation in Warsaw. In view of their friendly relationship, an understanding was necessary, and the Deutsche Bank wished the CA to recognize its standpoint and agree to its claim: "Back then, we have left you Cracow after already having set up a promising branch there. But we are convinced that our interests with respect to Warsaw must be viewed as predominant for the reasons that have been stated."[149]

The CA, however, took a very different view of such claims and entitlements. In their reply to the Deutsche Bank on January 30, 1941, Joham and Pfeiffer reported that they had informed Director Gdynia of the Deutsche Bank Kattowitz branch of their intention to petition the authorities to set up a branch in Warsaw right after having taken over the Cracow branch in April 1939, "since we were aware that we would have to care for the territory of the entire Generalgouvernement from the capital city."[150] The decision of the authorities had been held up by the problem of regulating the accounts of the

---

[146] Ibid., Huber to Pfeiffer, Oct. 17, 1939.

[147] Ibid., Abs and Kiehl to Riehle, Nov. 2, 1940.

[148] DB, P 24222, report to the Deutsche Bank, Oct. 7, 1940.

[149] BA-CA, CA-TZ, Sekretariat rot, Box 33/CA-BV Filiale Allgemeines, Abs and Kiehl to CA management board, Jan. 24, 1941.

[150] Ibid., CA to Deutsche Bank, Jan. 30, 1941.

Polish banks, but the ongoing economic inter-connection between Warsaw and the rest of the GG had led the CA Cracow to set up a facility devoted to cultivating and servicing the grow-ing body of Warsaw customers and was indeed offering them "almost all the advantages which an independent branch of our institution could provide." The CA declared itself in agreement with the Deutsche Bank that it was unlikely that the authorities would allow both the CA and the Deutsche Bank to set up branches in Cracow because this would lead to undesirable competition for the same customers and busi-ness. Nonetheless, "so long as the GG forms a political and economic entity and Cracow is the seat of the central authorities it will be expe-dient to have the German credit institutions licensed in Cracow to also maintain the nec-essary branch business in Warsaw."[151] Joham and Pfeiffer concluded this masterpiece of disingen-uousness by suggesting that if Warsaw were to recover fully and be developed further, then the CA and the Deutsche Bank could expand their influence there by jointly assuming a stake in a Polish bank. In the meantime, the facility the CA Cracow had established would serve provision-ally, and both Joham and Pfeiffer looked forward to clarifying the situation in future discussions.

The irritation of the Deutsche Bank at this point was only lightly disguised. While Hitler may have wished to drive Warsaw out of the minds of the Poles, German bankers had no intention of having it driven out of their eco-nomic planning. The Deutsche Bank insisted on having its own branch in Warsaw, adding that "it appears to us neither compatible with our interests nor expedient from your per-spective if business in Warsaw would be con-ducted only by a branch of a bank licensed in Cracow. As you yourself point out, Warsaw is to be viewed still today as the economic cen-ter of the Gouvernement territory, and you must admit that the stream of business from Warsaw is flowing primarily to Danzig and Litzmannstadt/Lodz and that in comparison to these large-scale economic connections, trade relations with Cracow, whose significance we

certainly do not want to underestimate can only take second place."[152] In coming to a "friendly agreement" on these matters, the Deutsche Bank expected the CA to take these views into account. The CA may have conquered Cracow, but the Deutsche Bank intended to rule the banking roost in Warsaw.

It was thus manifest that the CA would have to tone down some of its ambitions in the GG, at least with respect to Warsaw, where the hia-tus was to continue on until the end of the war. Nevertheless, the invasion of the Soviet Union in June 1941 raised new opportunities for the CA in one of those areas where it could also claim to have been active in the past, namely, Galicia and particularly in its capital Lemberg/Lviv, which was eventually incorporated into the GG after some uncertainty as to whether it should become subject to the authority admin-istering the Ukraine. In any case, this was an opportunity that Director Huber immediately pursued. He did not let himself be discour-aged when he learned on June 30 that setting up banking facilities in Lemberg/Lviv was not yet taking place and that civilians were not per-mitted to travel in the occupied area. He was informed that the Kontinentale Gesellschaft für Handel und Industrie in Cracow, which belonged to the Hermann Göring Werke, had been instructed to travel to Lemberg/Lviv and Drohobycz to set up facilities there. He saw no reason why the CA Cracow should not do the same, telling Pfeiffer on July 1 that "I regard it as absolutely essential to prepare the way for the later opening of a branch in Lemberg, that is, to sequester a suitable place now and to secure the later licensing ahead of time."[153] Huber was uncertain whether it was best to have the request for a travel commission come from Vienna or Cracow. He noted that the Reichswerke had justified their request by lay-ing claim to various assets of direct importance to them, and he thought the CA could justify such a journey "in order to look over the local situation and possibly confiscate the building of

151 Ibid.

152 Ibid., Deutsche Bank to CA, Feb. 14, 1941.
153 BA-CA, CA-TZ, Sekretariat rot, Box 39/CA-BV Filiale Kr-Lh, Huber to Pfeiffer, July 1, 1941.

the Polish Lemberg branch of the Allgemeine Bankverein for the Creditanstalt." The Vienna headquarters not only supported this proposal because the CA had previously had an interest in the Allgemeine Bankverein, but also pointed to the fact that the CA had an account receivable from and was involved in the liquidation of the N.V. Nederlandsche Petroleum Maj Photogen, Amsterdam, the owner of mines and wells – a list of these was appended – that were administered by the Naphta AG, whose chief office was in Lemberg/Lviv. The CA wished to have not only a bank building but also a major industrial account in Lemberg/Lviv.[154]

Unfortunately for Huber, Paersch and Laschtowiczka of the Banking Supervisory Office asked that the trip be delayed because they had already turned down such requests from other banks, although they promised to change the policy soon. As was his habit, Huber assured Joham and the managers in Vienna that he intended to pursue every avenue of influence. He had also written to the Allgemeine Bankverein in Lemberg/Lviv to ask for an option on its building and managed to get an assessment of its condition through a contact in Lemberg/Lviv and to ascertain that the key was available! As was its wont, furthermore, the CA additionally drew up a list of its previous holdings and investments in Lemberg/Lviv, which included the branches in Lemberg/Lviv taken over by the Warschauer Disconto-Bank and the Allgemeine Bankverein, various smaller banks, a machine construction company, a brewery, and a variety of petroleum interests. This was submitted to the Banking Supervisory Authority in Cracow to demonstrate how well the CA was installed in Ukraine, Galicia, and Bukovina before 1914 and even before the Russian occupation in 1939. It also had a branch in Czernowitz in northern Bukovina, which it was in the process of liquidating because of foreign exchange problems. By August 1941, when this information was supplied, the decision had been taken to include Lemberg/Lviv in the GG, and the CA formally asked to be allowed to set up a branch because "it is understandable

that under these circumstances we are striving to restore our previous economic position in Lemberg."[155]

When Huber finally was allowed to travel to Lemberg/Lviv in early August, he met with new irritations. The military commander had ensconced himself in the building of the Allgemeine Creditbank and entry into the building was strictly forbidden. Furthermore, a Ukrainian bank had been allowed to take over the building of the Wiener Bankverein, a show of favor to the Ukrainians that outraged Huber.[156] The CA's plan to establish a branch in Lemberg/Lviv was strongly backed by Director Abs of the Deutsche Bank with the supervisory authorities in Berlin, but Paersch held things up by insisting that he had to get his bank of issue established in Lemberg/Lviv first before a private bank could be allowed in. Nevertheless, the CA was positioned to be given priority once private banks were allowed in, and the management board in Vienna was very pleased with Huber and viewed the establishment of the branch in Lemberg/Lviv as something of a settling of scores: "The standing of our bank demands that we get back our former Wiener Bankverein buildings. As is well known, the Polish branches, and thus also the Lemberg branch, were not freely sold by us but rather under the pressure of the Poles. For the same reason, our former majority stake in the Allgemeine Bankverein in Poland was transformed into a minority position."[157] Finally, on November 29, 1941, the CA received its license from the authorities and was able to open its branch in Lemberg/Lviv on December 1 with Arthur Anlauf as its director. Anlauf, who had headed a branch in western Austria, regarded himself as something of an "East Pioneer," and his efforts to promote the business of the Lemberg/Lviv branch and resist attempts by the Vienna headquarters to apply the brakes

[154] Ibid., CA Vienna to CA Cracow, July 7, 1941.

[155] Ibid., CA, signed Pfeiffer and Miksch, to the Banking Supervisory Agency, GG, Aug. 6, 1941, and related correspondence of July 1941.

[156] Ibid., Huber to Pfeiffer, Aug. 11, 1941.

[157] Ibid., CA Vienna to Huber, Aug. 14, 1941.

were to be a source of considerable irritation in Vienna.[158]

The broader problem, however, of how the CA and the Deutsche Bank were going to arrange their engagements in Poland remained open. Director Rudolf Winkelmann of the Danzig branch of the Deutsche Bank met with Huber in December 1941 at the behest of Kiehl and of the man slated to replace him in dealing with the eastern territories, Director Erich Bechtolf. At the meeting, Winkelmann reported that Paersch continued to believe that the German private sector banks should establish themselves as regional banks in the GG. At the same time, the CA's branches were recognized to be valuable because of the long-standing engagement of the CA in these areas. Paersch and Laschtowiczka were concerned, however, that if they allowed the Deutsche Bank to establish itself in the north and the CA in the south, then the Dresdner Bank and Länderbank Wien would ask for similar rights.[159] The problem remained unsolved when Abs met with Pfeiffer and Joham in late January 1942. He subsequently informed Kiehl that he thought an arrangement could be made in which the CA would control Cracow and Lemberg/Lviv while the Deutsche Bank would establish itself in the rest of the GG in close contact with the CA. Most desirable would be the creation of a regional bank in which the CA would be offered a stake.[160]

Paersch did indeed expect the Deutsche Bank to come to terms with the CA concerning Warsaw and avoid the establishment of two banks there. Kiehl met with Joham and Pfeiffer

on February 21, 1942 and proposed that the CA operate its branches in Cracow and Lemberg/Lviv, the Deutsche Bank refrain from establishing itself in Galicia, and the CA disinterest itself in the rest of the GG and especially in Warsaw. The government was apparently planning to let the Deutsche Bank take over the Bank Handlowy and, were this to happen, its Galician branches would be left to the CA. Joham and Pfeiffer, however, wanted 50 percent participation in any regional bank taken over by the Deutsche Bank, arguing that the CA branches would lose business if and when the Deutsche Bank moved into Warsaw. Until this time, German firms had been turning to the CA Cracow in the absence of a German bank in Warsaw. In fact, the Deutsche Bank itself had referred customers to the CA, and Kiehl had to admit that the failure of the Deutsche Bank to establish a branch in Warsaw had enabled the CA Cracow to get more business. This might cease to be the case once the Deutsche Bank was active in Warsaw. Kiehl did not rule out a CA engagement in Warsaw and proposed a 25 percent stake, while Joham suggested a 50 percent stake if the Galician branches of the Bank Handlowy were not given up to the CA. Kiehl went away with the impression that the CA leadership understood the Deutsche Bank position, and would accept a minority stake in Warsaw if they also had CA representation on the administrative council.[161]

It cannot be said that Kiehl's successor Bechtolf pursued the issue of establishing the Deutsche Bank in Warsaw with much vigor or enthusiasm. The situation was indeed quite confusing. Paersch had told the president of the Bank Handlowy administrative council, Stanislaw Wachowiak, that Economics Minister Funk was demanding that the Polish banks be merged with the German ones, and Wachowiak and his colleagues were contemplating resignation. On May 1, however, Bechtolf met privately with Wachowiak and confidentially told him that the Deutsche Bank did not agree with Funk. Like the Bank Handlowy, the Deutsche Bank had a long tradition, and would not in any

158 See BA-CA, CA-V, newspaper report in ibid., and CA management board meeting, Nov. 3, 1941. On Anlauf's performance, see Archivum Akt Nowych w Warszawie (AAN), Rząd, Bestand III, IV, 1290/11–12, Bl. 55, Paersch's minutes of a meeting with Tron, April 15, 1944. See also BA-CA, CA-TZ, Sekretariat rot, Box 11/CA-BV XV, XVI/1–3, Artikel "Eröffnung unserer Filiale in Lemberg," in: Gemeinschaft (Nov./Dec. 1941), pp. 74–76.
159 Ibid., Box 33/CA-BV Filiale Allgemeines, Huber to Pfeiffer, Dec. 10, 1941.
160 DB, B 54, Ulrich to Abs, Aug. 27, 1943.
161 Ibid., memorandum by Kiehl, Feb. 25, 1942.

case attempt a merger for the duration of the war. Instead, the Deutsche Bank would install an "observer" in Warsaw to keep an eye out for Deutsche Bank interests but in no way to take a hostile stance toward the Bank Handlowy.[162] Two weeks later, Bechtolf informed the CA of his trip to Warsaw, which he characterized as a journey intended to examine the situation in Warsaw with an eye toward a possible engagement in Warsaw but not to come to a decision, adding that any decision finally taken would have to be ratified by the authorities in Crakow. He also used the trip to meet with Polish economic circles and get "a picture of the situation and developments from their perspective."[163] Bechtolf told the CA he was aware of its interest in a solution that satisfied both their banks, and he promised to discuss matters with the CA leadership at the beginning of June following a tour he was making of the occupied areas. Not only, however, did the projected meeting not take place, but in mid-June Bechtolf told the CA that it was "not especially pressing," in view of Paersch's opinion that "for political and economic reasons" the preconditions for acting on the role of the German banks in Warsaw were not satisfactory.[164]

While the Deutsche Bank seemed quite content to leave things as they were, the CA was more agitated by the problem, and the recently installed General Director Buzzi told Abs that the Warsaw question should not be neglected lest other banks take the lead. Bechtolf responded to Abs's information in early August by promising the CA that he would consult with Paersch again; if the latter still thought more time was needed, he would then ask permission to send an economic observer to Warsaw. He had already suggested this idea to Paersch in June but was asked to put it off for the time being. At this point, however, Bechtolf felt it important to try again so as to be informed and prepared in the event there was an opportunity to establish a branch in Warsaw, and he proposed sending

Rudolf Stuby, a senior official in the Deutsche Bank branch in Posen. He promised that he would pass on Stuby's information to the CA as well. Buzzi and Joham were quite pleased at this proposal, viewing it as a kind "of visiting card for a later banking branch in Warsaw." While recognizing that the political situation of Warsaw after the war was open, they nevertheless were certain that Warsaw would remain of importance and that such a "precautionary initiatory step"[165] was well advised.

It cannot be said, however, that this did much to increase the tempo. Stuby was allowed to go to Warsaw, but he only went there at the beginning of October, installing himself in the Hotel Bristol. In the meantime, aside from rumors that the GG might be integrated into the Reich, there was no change in the situation with regard to German banking in Warsaw. Paersch still had not indicated when such banks might be allowed to be set up in Warsaw, nor had he indicated whether a German bank or branches would be established.[166] In any case, Stuby was expected to keep the Deutsche Bank and the CA as well as its branches in Cracow and Lemberg/Lviv informed of developments. As Bechtolf had promised the Bank Handlowy back in May, when he first indicated that the Deutsche Bank would appoint an economic observer, Stuby kept his distance from the Polish bank, visiting it only twice during this stay in Warsaw. How is one to interpret the remarkable lassitude in dealing with the Warsaw question? The evidence suggests that Bechtolf had inhibitions – in contrast to Kiehl and the CA leadership – about taking over an old, well-established bank that had had numerous foreign shareholders before the war. There is good reason, therefore, to credit Bechtolf, as does historian Harold James, with considerable courage in his private conversations with Wachowiak.[167] The record also suggests that Bechtolf may have intentionally kept things moving slowly. At the same time,

[162] See James, *Nazi Economic War*, pp. 190–192.

[163] BA-CA, CA-TZ, Sekretariat rot, Box 33/CA-BV Filiale Allgemeines, Bechtolf to CA, May 15, 1942.

[164] Ibid., Bechtolf to CA, June 18, 1942.

[165] Ibid., Bechtolf to CA, Aug. 4, 1942, and Buzzi and Joham to Bechtolf, Aug. 6, 1942.

[166] Ibid., Bechtolf to CA, Oct. 1, 1942.

[167] See James, *Nazi Economic War*, p. 191.

however, one can only assume that Bechtolf and the Deutsche Bank would have acted quickly if competition from the Dresdner Bank made itself felt, and that this was a major concern of both the Deutsche Bank and the CA. But one must also take into account the role of Paersch, who kept on saying that nothing could be done until the Polish bank debts were regulated and the status of the Polish banks cleared, but who was also constantly wrestling with the miserable economic conditions in the GG, the gruesome conditions in the Warsaw Ghetto, of which he was very aware, the poverty and hunger of the Polish population, rising prices and black marketeering, growing political insurgency, and the dangers to the currency issued by the bank with which he was charged. The reality was that there were insufficient economic incentives in this part of the GG to encourage financial institutions to settle down comfortably in Warsaw.[168]

Poland: The Business of the CA Branches

What the future would bring, of course, remained uncertain, but the CA branches in Cracow and Lemberg/Lviv had been established before the defeat at Stalingrad in February 1943 and well before the Normandy invasion of June 1944. It is important to view the business activities of these branches and subsequent developments from the perspective of their expectations in 1942. In doing so, however, it cannot be emphasized strongly enough that the CA had not been following the trail of the Deutsche Bank or the Germans generally in taking over the Deutsche Bank Cracow branch and setting up the Lemberg/Lviv branch. It was not dragged into Poland unwillingly. On the contrary, the CA was extremely aggressive in establishing itself in those places and would have set up more branches had this been possible; indeed, it even tried to take the lead in the GG. These were horrible places, centrally connected with the Holocaust, that is, the mass murder of the Jews, as well as with the expropriation of both Poles and Jews and their forced labor under unspeakable conditions. When the Germans invaded Poland in 1939, there were 60,000 Jews in Cracow. Between May 1940 and March 1941, they were removed from the traditional quarter of Kazimierz to a ghetto in Podgorze in the south of the city. The ghetto was destroyed by the Germans in March 1943, and the inhabitants either shipped to death camps or to the nearby forced labor camp at Plaszow. One might also add that Cracow had an active Jewish resistance movement that conducted organized attacks in the center of the city. Is it even remotely conceivable that the staff of the CA Cracow was unaware of the "cleansing" of Jews in Cracow and of their use as forced laborers, leaving aside the fact that Cracow was the center of the GG from which many of the anti-Semitic actions were launched?

As for Lemberg/Lviv, it presented, if such was possible, an even more deplorable scenario. The Germans' attitude toward the 200,000 Jews found in the city when they arrived in the spring of 1941 is captured in a letter sent to Director Tron, then of the Deutsche Bank, by a nephew serving in the army in January 1942: "One could write volumes about Lemberg, which the Russians completely ruined during their rule. There is really no lack of filth, much less still of Jews, who are here in large numbers. A third of the population (roughly 140,000) is composed of Jews."[169] Lemberg/Lviv was already the scene of ghastly pogroms launched against Jews by Ukrainian nationalists. The Lemberg ghetto, which had been established at the same time as the CA Lemberg/Lviv branch under gruesome circumstances in November 1941, was dissolved in March 1942 when its inhabitants were sent to either death camps or forced labor camps.[170] Here, too, the CA found itself in a region where some of the worst crimes of the Holocaust were committed, and it is unthinkable that those working for the bank had no

---

168 One can learn much about Paersch's problems and the deteriorating conditions from the *Diensttagebuch des Generalgouverneurs*, pp. 354–355, 468.

169 DB,V2/158, Letter to Tron, Jan. 31, 1942.

170 See Thomas Sandkühler, *"Endlösung" in Galizien. Der Judenmord in Ostpolen und die Rettungsinitiativen von Berthold Beitz 1941–1944* (Bonn 1996).

inkling of what was going on. Such things, of course, were not the subject of correspondence, just as they were not the subject of later introspection, and actual evidence of knowledge and engagement is sparse.

Nevertheless, the CA Cracow has the dubious distinction of being the only branch of a major bank, at least up to the point of this writing, to have had a direct involvement with a substantial number of concentration camps for which some records have been found.[171] It was a business that did not last long, specifically from September 1, 1941, to April 1, 1942, and involved the CA Cracow acting as a transmitter of cash transfers from the families of concentration camp inmates to their relations imprisoned in Auschwitz, Buchenwald, Dachau, Flossenbürg, Gross-Rosen, Mauthausen-Gusen, Neuengamme, Neu Sustrum, Oranienburg, Ravensbrück, Stutthof, and Wewelsburg-Hadeborn. Nearly all of the transfer recipients were Poles, but a small number of Jewish inmates were also able to receive cash from their families. None of the available evidence explains why the CA Cracow was given what apparently was an exclusive assignment in this area. It would appear to have come from the Foreign Exchange Office in Cracow because the bank always referred to being empowered to make the transfers by that agency, and the transfers, which were handled in the bank by its Transfer Section, usually were made formally to the commandant of the concentration camp involved but actually went to an account at a local savings bank or an administrative office of the camp. It was possible to transfer up to 100 Zl a month; the bank handled the clearing arrangements involved and charged 4 Zl for its services. In the spring of 1942, the entire arrangement was brought to an abrupt halt, and the families were no longer allowed

to send money to their relatives in the camps. Manifestly, this was business on which the bank made a profit, although it hardly could be called "big business." The bank obviously had to be connected with the SS authorities in charge of such matters, but it would be stretching things to think that it had a "close and trusting" collaboration with the concentration camp administrations or their commandants because so many camps were involved. Furthermore, the little correspondence there was with the camps had a purely formal and bureaucratic character. Finally, the Cracow branch appears to have had a section devoted to concentration camp business that carried out this business more or less mechanically once the bank had printed up the appropriate forms.[172]

The real crux of the matter historically and morally was that this seems to have been just another bank operation for as long as it lasted and that those involved were forced to come face to face with some of the human realities of the camp system. In February 1942, for example, the CA Cracow had sent a list of 785 names to Auschwitz along with a transfer of 50,839 Zl (25,419.50 RM). Sixty-two (12.6 percent) of those listed were sent the maximum 100 Zl by their families. Quite a few transfers were for 96 Zl, which meant that the 4 Zl fee had been deducted by the bank from the maximum. A substantial number, however, were for 20 Zl, and 40 Zl–60 Zl. On March 30, 1942, the Auschwitz concentration camp sent back a list of approximately 600 names of "prisoners who are no longer here – or rather, cannot be identified" and returned 40,211 Zl (20,105 RM), leaving a balance of 10,628 Zl received by those prisoners still at Auschwitz. It cannot be assumed that all these persons were dead. In their original accounting, for example, the camp authorities had "mistakenly written off" Julian Bartolewski, who turned up in the camp after

171 The discovery was made by Bertram Perz and was reported in Marianne Enigl/Stefan Janny, "Das grauenvolle Geheimnis der CA," in: *Profil* 38/30 (Sept. 14, 1998), pp. 52–58. The original documents will be cited here, but they only confirm what Perz found earlier. The relevant documents are in State Archive Krakow (Archiwum Państwowe w Krakowie I Województwa Krakowskiego), BN-I-3–6.

172 There is no further information about the "KZ-Abteilung" mentioned on p. 52 of the *Profil* article cited in note 171. The fact that the bank was permitted to handle the clearing operations involved reflected no special regard for the bank but rather a matter of convenience for the Foreign Exchange Office and for the camp administrations.

all and presumably received his 100 Zl. In any case, the Auschwitz authorities duly returned the money to the CA Cracow, which then dutifully returned the money to the relatives in question, reporting that the intended recipient was no longer in the camp or could not be found. In some cases, however, the family members knew that their family member was deceased and asked that the money be returned. There was similar correspondence with respect to other concentration camps. Buchenwald returned 495.50 RM in May 1942 for nineteen Polish inmates who no longer could be found.[173] There is no record of how managers and employees at the CA Cracow felt about these pathetic efforts to provide some food or make other provisions for concentration camp inmates, let alone what they thought had happened to those who could not be found. Whatever the case, it has been estimated that between 70,000 and 75,000 of the 140,000 to 150,000 Poles sent to Auschwitz died there.[174]

The management of the CA Cracow and Lemberg/Lviv certainly did not dwell on such matters, and the concentration camp business, which ended in the spring of 1942, was, so to speak, a by-product of the region in which the bank was operating. It is important, therefore, to consider its ambitions and expectations, and a great deal can be learned from the presentations of the Cracow and Lemberg/Lviv branches at the "Southeast Conference." The conference was organized by the CA in Vienna in July 1942, just after the Deutsche Bank assumed its majority of the CA and at a time when Abs and Joham were laying out their Southeast European strategy. Both the strategy and the conference will be discussed later in this study, but the contributions of the CA branches in the GG will be given special attention here.

The GG, in the view of the Cracow branch, had turned "the Reich's neighboring country" into a "bridge to the East." Concerning the future tasks of the region, the bank agreed with Walter Emmerich, the head of the Economic Division of the GG, who argued that the agrarian overpopulation of the GG made it a natural source of cheap industrial labor with low living costs for the future. This was why it was important to have a currency and customs border between the GG and Germany. On the one hand, the region could be built up industrially so as to serve the war economy and then the peace economy. On the other hand, it was a natural supplier to East and Southeast Europe because of its favorable geographic location. While the promising trade was being interrupted by the necessity of acting as a thoroughfare for troops, which made the transport of goods difficult, and by the concentration on war production, the trade, especially with Slovakia and Hungary, was nevertheless substantial and was likely to increase under calmer circumstances.[175]

Although a native of Hamburg, where he had served as a syndic and was well known in business circles, Emmerich was no stranger to the Austrians. Bürckel had brought him in as an economic advisor, and he had been a major advocate of the elimination of the Jews from economic life and the creation of a new racialist economic order. This kind of program could be realized on a larger scale in the GG, and it was no accident that Frank had summoned this arrogant economist and "rationalization" fanatic to serve in his administration. Emmerich firmly believed in the consolidation of the small business and commercial sectors and saw the elimination of Jewish small businessmen and merchants as a major precondition for accomplishing these goals. Nor was it an accident that the commercial sector in the GG came to be dominated by Hamburg merchants and wholesalers who celebrated Emmerich at a birthday party as Ali Baba and themselves as the Forty

---

[173] For these materials, see State Archive Krakow, BN-I-3-5.
[174] Franciszek Piper, "Die Rolle des Lagers Auschwitz bei der Verwirklichung der nationalsozialistischen Ausrottungspolitik," in: Ulrich Herbert et al. (eds.), *Die nationalsozialistischen Konzentrationslager. Entwicklung und Struktur*, 2 vols. (Göttingen 1998), vol. 1, pp. 390–414, esp. pp. 396–397.
[175] The CA Cracow contribution to this meeting is to be found in DB, P 11726, the Protocol of the Southeast Conference, July 15–17, 1942.

Thieves.[176] The characterization was quite appropriate because some of these firms took over Jewish wholesale houses along with their capital and inventories. Such wholesalers were established in the forty-plus districts of the GG and then united in an umbrella organization, the Commercial Society of German Merchants in the Generalgouvernement. The leading merchant firms – Heinrich Brand, G.m.b.H., R.T.H. Möller & Co., and, in the chemical field, W. Biesterfeld & Co. – were centered in Hamburg or, as in the case of Heinrich Brand, had an important base there. As will be shown, the CA Cracow did considerable business with such firms.

The Cracow branch also presented an optimistic picture of business possibilities in its area. Despite the various inconveniences connected with controls and regulations by the authorities, as the CA Cracow pointed out, "with respect to the possibilities for activity by German firms in the Generalgouvernement one should note additionally that the assets of the former Polish state, furthermore the enterprises which were in Jewish hands, and those whose further existence were otherwise endangered are administered by the Trusteeship Section of the Governor General's office as well as the Trusteeship Bureaus in Cracow, Warsaw, Lemberg/Lviv, Lublin, and Radom."[177] While the Cracow branch admitted that the GG was in no position to supply all its needs under existing conditions, its rich supply of cheap labor would, in the future, provide a basis for industrialization. At the moment, this excess labor was being sent to the Reich, so that in addition to the prisoners of war already employed there, 830,000 agricultural and industrial workers had been sent to Germany who could transmit such savings as they had back to the GG without difficulty.

The Lemberg/Lviv branch could not present quite so optimistic a picture because the Russians had left considerable devastation

behind them and eliminated all private property. Reprivatization would take time, and it was likely that the GG would administer a substantial portion of agriculture in the region as well as the important timber and oil industries itself. Businessmen wishing to establish themselves would have to start up personally in the area, and there were, according to the bank, many merchants and others applying to set up in the area. The CA branch had been asked to provide lists of businesses that might be available, but the GG was not providing such information, which meant, once again, that interested parties would have to come themselves and contact the relevant official agencies. What all this implied was that it would be very difficult for businessmen to purchase enterprises in this region, but there were opportunities to lease enterprises held in GG trusteeship, especially timber mills, oil wells, and refineries.[178] In order to promote interest and gain customers, the CA produced an "economic overview" of the GG for its customers in August 1942 that detailed the conditions of the regions, identified the relevant authorities, and provided information on every industry.[179]

But whatever fantasies these CA branches entertained in the summer of 1942, in reality doing business in the GG presented numerous hazards and produced increasingly disappointing results. The profitability of the Polish branches helps to explain both the optimism of 1942 and its short-lived character:[180]

Year	Cracow	Lemberg	Total Profit
	Zl	Zl	Zl
1940	409,019.02	–	409,019.02
1941	786,143.20	–52,623.76	733,519.44
1942	1,646,252.12	274,152.84	1,920,404.96
1943	857,694.51	324,270.16	1,181,964.67
Totals	3,699,108.85	545,799.24	4,244,908.09

---

176 Emmerich plays an important role in Götz Aly and Susanne Heim, *Vordenker der Vernichtung. Auschwitz und die deutschen Pläne für eine neue europäische Ordnung* (Hamburg 1991), esp. pp. 222–227, 232–235.

177 DB, P 11726, protocol of the Southeast Conference, July 15–17, 1942.

178 Ibid.

179 AAN Rząd, 1402, "Generalgouvernement. Wirtschaftliche Übersicht," printed manuscript (August 1942).

180 AAN Rząd, 1403, Bl. 27, Bericht der Treuverkehr Deutsche Treuhand Aktiengesellschaft über die Gründungsprüfung der Creditanstalt Aktiengesellschaft Krakau, Jan. 1, 1944.

An important source of this record of instability arose from the fact that a disproportionately large part of the bank's business was connected with the efforts to organize, control, collect, and finance the harvests, most of which were supposed to go to Germany. The peasants were required to deliver the bulk of their production in return for cash payment and premiums in kind, and the punishments for failures to deliver quotas became increasingly draconian. Because the Germans had immediately excluded the Jews from all aspects of agrarian trade, and because there were no adequate Polish firms or replacements available, the GG had set up a Central Agricultural Agency owned and run by the state for gathering, storing, and distributing agricultural products. It was a highly centralized, large, and often unwieldy apparatus that combined a host of functions separated in the Reich's own food supply bureaucracy.[181] The activities of the Central Agricultural Agency were financed by a consortium of private and public banks, whose May 1943 quotas for the upcoming harvest campaign were divided in the following manner. The two most important public banks servicing the GG were former Polish government-owned held in trusteeship by the GG, the Agrarbank with 16 percent and the Landeswirtschaftsbank with 11 percent. The publicly chartered Bank der Deutschen Arbeit had a 6 percent share. The leading private banks were the Kommerzialbank with 14 percent, the Commerzbank with 8 percent, and the CA Cracow with 11 percent.[182] These periodic credits to the Central Agricultural Agency, not being limited to the wheat harvest alone, imposed a considerable strain on the CA Cracow's liquidity. In January 1944, the harvest finance credit amounted to 10 million Zl, but 615,000 Zl were provided for eggs, 1.6 million Zl for conserved meat, 1.8 million Zl for potatoes, and 5.1 million Zl for premium goods

for the peasantry. The total amounted to 19.2 million Zl or about 20 percent of the accounts receivable of the CA Cracow.[183]

Even in the period when there was considerable optimism, in the second half of 1942, there was concern in Vienna and Berlin about the liquidity of the CA Cracow and Lemberg/Lviv due to the peculiarities of the situation in the GG. Walter Tron, who had taken over Pfeiffer's responsibility for supervising the CA branches in Poland, reported on the problems of providing credits in the GG at the CA working committee on September 25, 1942. A substantial portion of the bank credits were being given for financing the harvest, as well as its storage and transportation, and one could not expect these credits to be paid off until the turn of the year. An attempt was being made to relieve the situation by shifting some of the burden to the state-controlled Agrarbank and Landwirtschaftsbank. The question of getting security for the credits was less easy to solve because establishing a claim on the production was often not sufficiently secure. This was because the firms in the old Reich did not always have enough capital to make them sufficiently creditworthy and because Polish law, which still obtained in credit matters, made it difficult for a bank to gain control over the securities put up for credits. Obviously, there were always risks in this business, but one did not want to take losses. The CA working committee also urged Tron to discuss matters further with the authorities in Cracow as well as to contemplate reducing risks and taxes by turning the branches into an independent regional bank.[184]

Tron had also asked Huber to report on these problems to the Deutsche Bank during a visit to Berlin. In reply, Huber painted an unsatisfactory picture. Of Cracow's 100 million Zl in deposits, 40 percent came from the public sector, which was notoriously unstable and had recently withdrawn 30 million Zl virtually

---

[181] See the description by its president, Karl Naumann, "Ziele und Aufgaben der Ernährungs- und Landwirtschaft im Generalgouvernement," in: Joseph Bühler (ed.), *Das Generalgouvernement. Seine Verwaltung und seine Wirtschaft* (Cracow 1943), pp. 113–130, esp. pp. 124–126.

[182] DB, V2/1, memorandum of May 27, 1943.

[183] See BA-CA, CA-TZ, Rechtsabteilung rot, Box 5/ Creditanstalt AG, Cracow, the audit of Jan. 1, 1944.

[184] BA-CA, CA-V, CA working committee meeting, Sept. 25, 1942.

overnight. Nevertheless, the Cracow branch had lent out 80 million Zl. Lemberg/Lviv was in even worse shape because there was a balance of 20 million Zl in credits and in debits, and Cracow had to place 6 million Zl at Lemberg's/Lviv's disposal to relieve the situation. Tron had gone to Paersch to gain permission to transfer 10 million Zl from Germany, but Paersch viewed all transfers to the GG from outside as a danger to the currency. Director Huber was not only upset by the liquidity situation but also by the competition. The Kommerzialbank had made a comeback in 1942 and actually had a larger amount of business than the CA branches. Huber thought the Kommerzialbank especially advantaged by being an affiliate and not a branch of the Dresdner Bank and thus having much more autonomy. Also, the Kommerzialbank corresponded in both German and Polish, thereby giving the impression of being more indigenous. A major reason for Huber's desire to have the Deutsche Bank establish itself in Warsaw, a desire that had been frustrated until now, was his hope that it could join with the CA branches and form an independent regional bank by taking over a Polish bank as well. But the most interesting of those banks, the Bank Handlowy, only had 75 million Zl in new business and capital of 25 million Zl. This was even less than the CA branch in Cracow.[185]

The Cracow banking authorities were quite aware of the CA difficulties and unhappy about them. Apparently, Pfeiffer did not have a very firm hand, and Tron had to listen to considerable criticism when he made his maiden visit to Paersch and his staff on October 12–13. In the view of the Supervisory Office, the CA Cracow had expanded too rapidly, without paying attention to the composition of its assets, and was very hard hit by the withdrawal of large sums of government deposits. As a result, it was operating below the liquidity standards established in the GG, and it was the only one of the major banks to be doing so. Yet another complaint was the lack of coordination between Cracow and Lemberg/Lviv, and the sense that each of the branches was going its own way. Tron promised

to review the credits that had been given, to subordinate Lemberg/Lviv to Cracow, and to remedy the liquidity situation. But when he broached the question of a regional bank, he was left with the comment that the future structuring of the banking situation would have to wait on decisions to be made in Berlin.[186]

Although Tron continued to negotiate with Paersch and the authorities in Cracow to reduce the pressure on the CA branches, the measures taken were insufficient. The relief that might have been provided by reducing seasonal demand for credit was undercut by the GG's decision to promote the storage of agricultural products for 1943 before 1942 had come to an end.[187] To be sure, both Tron and the authorities in Cracow promoted the reduction of accounts receivable by offering participation in some of the larger ones to the Agrarbank and the Landwirtschaftsbank. Furthermore, there was an indirect increase of the discount facilities available by Paersch's bank of issue because the CA deposited 5 million RM at the Reichsbank branch in Vienna as backing for the Cracow bank of issue. Both Tron and the supervisory office in Cracow, however, sharply criticized the failure of the branches in Cracow and Lemberg/Lviv to increase the number of depositors.[188]

Tron made a point of reporting regularly on the situation in occupied Poland, and he noted little change in the liquidity situation of the CA branches as 1943 began. By June, there was some modest shifting of the balance of deposits in favor of private persons and enterprises and away from public monies. The demand for credits, however, had increased substantially, and was expected to increase primarily because of the "harvest procurement action," which was being sped up. Tron repeatedly emphasized that the risks in the GG were "conditioned by the general circumstances," and that it was essential that the branches not only check on those applying

---

[185] DB, B 54, Minute by Abs, Oct. 22, 1942.

[186] AAN Rząd, 1402, Bl. 244, memorandum of the Banking Supervisory Agency, Oct. 20, 1942.

[187] BA-CA, CA-V, report to the CA working committee, Nov. 27, 1942.

[188] DB, V2/1–2, CA Vienna to CA Cracow, Oct. 24, 1942.

for credits to make sure that they had the requisite capital, profitability, and good management,
but also that the branches themselves maintain
the reserves they needed under the circumstances. Likewise, it was essential that the stores
of food and goods put up as security be insured,
especially against robbery. Security was indeed
a problem, especially in Lemberg/Lviv, where a
Ukrainian SS unit, planned to be a half million
men strong, was being recruited.[189]

It was very difficult, however, to lend with
much sense of security to the merchants and
the businessmen who had decided to do business in the GG, or even to the big merchant
houses that had arrived in Emmerich's wake. In
1943, the bank was to give the Cracow branch
of Heinrich Brand a 1.5 million Zl cash credit
for which 1.1 million Zl were put up as security. But the bank was worried about the legal
foundation of this security and attempted to
persuade Leo Brand in Berlin, who owned
80 percent of the capital, to give a guarantee for
the loan. Brand, however, was disinclined to do
so but did agree to leave his share of the profits
in Cracow. It was very hard for the CA to press
the issue. The risks in the GG really demanded
a larger guarantee, but the CA had a "pleasant"
relationship with the firm, and did not want to
do anything to jeopardize the business they did
together.[190] W. Biesterfeld & Co. was an especially important client of the CA branches. At
the beginning of 1944, its Cracow branch had a
1.8 million Zl credit from the CA Cracow, but
there is no evidence that this credit and its security was problematic.[191]

The same could not be said for another
Hamburg firm, G.L. Gaiser, which at the end
of September 1943 had a total of 9 million Zl
in credits from the CA branches, primarily for
goods used as premiums to pay peasants for the
harvest, for example, textiles, cigarettes, vodka,
and other desired consumer items. The CA
Vienna was very unhappy about the engagement and made efforts to limit the credits, get
better security, and see the firm's books. But
the owner, a man named Brettschneider, had
not only failed to provide the paperwork but
also had not paid a visit to the Cracow branch
despite promises to do so. Additionally, he had
used some of the borrowed money to construct
a factory for the processing of fruit and vegetables in Nieledew without consulting with
the bank, and then borrowed another 500,000
Zl from the Agrarbank for yet further investments. However, Tron was also forced to admit
that the Cracow branch considered G.L. Gaiser
to be one of the best-organized and managed
of the "deployment firms" aiding in the harvest
activities. Although Tron talked about forcing
the firm to either heed their wishes or relin-
quish its account, it still had a credit of 2.1 million Zl with Cracow and 1.8 million Zl with
Lemberg/Lviv at the beginning of 1944.[192]

Another North German firm whose activities in the GG produced discomfiture in Vienna
was the Bremen firm of F. Undütsch & Co.,
which owed 3.8 million Zl to the Lemberg/
Lviv branch in July 1943. The CA-Lemberg/
Lviv feared losing the account to the competition if Vienna intervened to reduce the account
and demand better security. The fact was that
F. Undütsch & Co. had no capital in the GG
itself and only inadequate capital back home,
and that however sympathetic Vienna was to
the competition problem "this consideration,
of course, cannot lead to our taking risks for
which we are unable to take responsibility."[193]
Here again, however, Undütsch, which did
"wholesale and retail trade with goods of all
kinds," still had 1.2 million Zl in credits with
the Lemberg/Lviv branch at the beginning of
1944.[194]

---

[189] Ibid., reports from Tron, Jan. 27, 1943 and June
       2, 1943.
[190] DB, V2/2, Minute in Tron papers, Sept. 4, 1943, and
       CA to Deutsche Bank, Sept. 16, 1943.
[191] See BA-CA, CA-TZ, Rechtsabteilung rot, Box 5/
       Creditanstalt AG, Cracow, the audit of the banks as of
       Jan. 1, 1944, made in connection with their forming
       into an autonomous Creditanstalt AG in Cracow,
       subsequently renamed the Creditverein AG.

[192] Ibid., DB, V1/1, and memorandum by Tron, Sept.
       30, 1943.
[193] Ibid., V1/2, CA Vienna to CA Lemberg, July
       8, 1943.
[194] See Abschlussbilanz der Creditanstalt AG, Krakau
       nach dem Stand vom 1. Januar 1944, BA-CA,

In one important instance, the CA Cracow actually lost a major account when it expressed reservations about a change in the nature of the guarantees provided by the Hamburg firm of Kunst & Albers, which had a 2.25 million Zl credit with Lemberg/Lviv and a 500,000 Zl credit from Cracow. The firm was trying to protect itself by changing its organizational arrangements in the GG in light of the political and military situation, and Tron was raising questions for precisely the same reason. Albers, however, apparently expected immediate assent to his wishes from so good a client and took his business to the Landwirtschaftsbank. But the matter caught the attention of Abs because the firm was "an especially valued customer of the Hamburg branch of the Deutsche Bank," and Tron had to explain the situation.[195]

If it was difficult to decide about giving credit to firms with a measure of reputation, it was even more difficult to decide what to do with individuals eager to better their fortunes in the GG. A good illustration is Sepp Marek, a former employee of Philipp Haas & Söhne who had become trustee of the formerly Jewish-owned wholesale textile firm of Salomon Rebhuhn in Cracow. He wanted a credit of 600,000 Zl to supply textiles for the harvest. Tron inquired about Marek with his former employer and was told that Marek "was a very experienced, but not always completely serious person who tended to be a wheeler-dealer."[196] Director Huber, in contrast, had a very high opinion of Marek. The bank had good experience with him, and he was well thought of by the authorities. In the end, Tron approved the credit, although he hoped its size would be reduced.

The CA had entertained hopes that there might be an opportunity for it to act as an intermediary in the sale of trusteeship business, especially to ethnic Germans and later to demobilized German soldiers, but there is no evidence that such expectations were seriously

realized. In July 1942, Huber had told Paersch that he was getting inquiries about loans to purchase GG trusteeship-held enterprises and thought that such loans would be paid off quickly from the profits the new owners would make. A major dilemma, however, was that many of the Jewish and other enterprises taken over were badly indebted and run down, so that their future competitiveness was in doubt. While the evidence is inadequate to judge the extent to which persons were prepared to invest for the long run, such evidence as is available suggests that the majority of those asking for a loan were the trustees of these enterprises, that is, people like Marek.[197]

The GG was well known for corruption and speculation, especially among the trustees placed in the various firms and banks to oversee confiscated and active Polish enterprises and confiscated Jewish enterprises. The GG authorities took a dim view of them. Paersch and others thought that some of the Poles were more reliable and honest than the Germans, who were accused of taking excessive salaries and exploiting their charges.[198] It is no wonder that the banking business there took on this speculative quality. The record shows that Tron and his colleagues sought to reduce engagements, especially in Lemberg/Lviv, as much as they thought possible. As Tron glumly reported at the end of July 1943: "In these circles, we have already pointed repeatedly to the special risks in the credit business in the GG. These risks have increased because of the sharpening of the political conditions in the GG mentioned earlier. On the other hand, despite the advisable restraint, we have not been able to escape the expansion of credits that have recently become necessary primarily as a consequence of the gathering of the harvest, since the majority of the deployment firms belongs to our circle of customers and we cannot very well expose ourselves to the charge, which unfortunately can

---

CA-TZ, Rechtsabteilung rot, Box 5, Audit of the Creditanstalt AG, Cracow.

[195] DB, V2/3, Abs to Tron, Dec. 21, 1943 and Tron to Abs, Dec. 28, 1943.

[196] DB, V2/1, Minute of June 19, 1943.

[197] AAN Rząd, 1402, Bl. 282–285, Banking Supervisory Agency report on visit by Huber, July 27, 1942.

[198] See the *Diensttagebuch des Generalgouverneurs*, pp. 185–186, 222–223.

be raised all too easily, of sabotaging the financing of the harvest."[199] Doing business in the GG was thus filled with moral hazard, and this undoubtedly explains the exceptional concern of Tron and his colleagues for solid guarantees. Indeed, it must have been a relief to deal with the native Austrian Julius Meinl concern, which had extensive credits from the CA Cracow – 5.6 million Zl in January 1944 – but whose account was guaranteed by the Vienna office to a very large extent.[200]

Similarly, a good credit risk like Oscar Schindler, whose finished enamel factory, Deutsche Emailwarenfabrik Oscar Schindler, had a 457,516 Zl credit from the CA Cracow but was also a creditor of the bank, having a personal account of 102,765 Zl. Schindler had established himself in Cracow early in the occupation, leasing a shut-down plant belonging to the Jewish firm "Rekord" and then buying it when it was auctioned off in June 1942. By this time, he was producing almost solely for the army, and his company was declared an armaments plant. By 1943, he had 700 employees, 500 Poles and 200 Jews, and was planning to expand further. His operation was largely self-financing, but he used the CA as his personal bank. In the course of his rapid expansion, he found that the Cracow Labor Office was not meeting his needs and began to take Jewish workers from the SS forced labor camp that was 3 km away. To avoid the time-consuming march back and forth for his workers, he then decided to set up his own little labor camp, with local SS and police administering it. In August 1943, he received a large new army contract, which forced him to expand his landholding and increase the size of his labor force. The plan was to begin production at the expanded plant on March 1, 1944. By that time, he had been approved for a 1.8 million Zl credit from the

Landwirtschaftsbank in addition to his credit with the CA and was employing 1,250 employees, 700 of whom were Jews, on three shifts.[201]

Needless to say, these credits were not being given to Schindler because he was saving Jews, as we now know, but because he was constantly making a good case for receiving more forced labor and successfully fighting off those who wished to kill the Jews rather than work them to death. Certainly the CA branches were not in the business of funding righteous gentiles. While the number of private credits of the Cracow branch had increased greatly by the beginning of 1944, government agencies continued to constitute a substantial portion of the creditor accounts of the CA Cracow, and these were heavily implicated in holding property taken from Jews and Poles and in forced labor. The account holding the profits from the administration of the GG amounted to 5.7 million Zl; the General Direction of the State Monopolies amounted to 6.1 million Zl; the account of the government in Cracow amounted to 7.4 million Zl; the Trusteeship Administration amounted to 6 million Zl. The account of the head of the SS and police in Cracow was 3.5 million Zl. The engagement with government agencies and the SS was proportionately greater in Lemberg/Lviv, where the account of the Trusteeship Office of the Governor of the District of Galicia amounted to 13 million Zl, to which should be added another 7.2 million account for the Trusteeship for Forests and Timber Mills, and another approximately 15 million Zl for district timber mill administrations. The head of the SS and police at the forced labor camp in Lemberg/Lviv had an account of 1.2 million Zl with the CA branch there.[202]

An account of especially sinister origin was the approximately 8 million Zl placed with the CA Cracow by SS Standartenführer Erich Schellin, an SS economic specialist involved in disposing of and depositing the enormous assets and funds seized during the so-called Aktion Reinhard. This operation involved the

---

[199] DB, V2/1, Report of July 28, 1943.

[200] The credits for Cracow and other places are scattered through the working committee meeting reports in BA-CA, CA-V, and see the audit report in BA-CA, CA-TZ, Rechtsabteilung rot, Box 5/ Creditanstalt AG, Cracow.

[201] Ibid., and AAN Rząd, 11/1360, Exposé, March 16, 1944.

[202] BA-CA, CA-TZ, Rechtsabteilung rot, Box 5/ Creditanstalt AG, Cracow, Audit report.

mass deportation of Jews to death camps and forced labor camps that began in the spring of 1942 and was presided over by the former Gauleiter of Vienna and now SS police leader in Lublin, Odilo Globocnik, and in Galicia by SS Gruppenführer Friedrich Katzmann.[203] Much of the money and precious metals were transferred to the Reichsbank by SS Hauptsturmführer Bruno Melmer while the money retained by Schellin was put into accounts at the Kommerzialbank. In keeping with the favoritism shown to Dresdner Bank organizations by the SS, the deposit in the Kommerzialbank was 79 million Zl, but 8 million Zl was held in an account at the CA Cracow. It is very difficult, however, to identify this account from the listing of bank creditors developed as of January 1, 1944. But, as at the Reichsbank, the SS might have used a name to disguise its ownership of the CA account. If this were the case, then the most likely candidate would have been the Association of Bulgarian Gardeners, Cracow, which had an account at that time of 7,445,140 Zl, one of the largest on the list aside from the GG government and trustee organization and of a size that more or less fits the amount deposited by Schellin. In the absence of further evidence, this can only be a guess, but this association certainly must have been something other than what its name suggests.[204]

The extant documentation on the CA Cracow and Lemberg/Lviv is totally uninformative about the vast amount of slave and forced labor used by enterprises that had accounts with these banks. This is not surprising for two reasons. First, the use of such labor was a fact of life and simply assumed, as was evident from the report on Schindler. Second, the question of what kind of labor was used and where was never really open for discussion, any more than was the extermination of a substantial portion of the Jewish labor force in the so-called harvest festival of the summer and fall of 1943, when a large number of the Jewish slave laborers were massacred on Himmler's order. Much of the killing took place around Lemberg/Lviv, but the bank's records reveal absolutely nothing, and the same is true of the much larger Cracow branch, which dealt with firms spread all over the GG.[205]

The Bayerische Versicherungs-Bank in Cracow, for example, had a deposit of 250,000 Zl in the CA Cracow. The fact that it headed a consortium of companies that insured the equipment and buildings at the forced labor camp in Plaszow and that its officials visited the camp on inspection tours was obviously not the business of the bank. At the same time, it is hard to imagine that persons at the bank were unaware of the activity on the account and that persons working at the bank and the insurance company had no contact with one another.[206] What was really important to the bank, of course, was getting good accounts, and not to have to worry from where they received their labor supply. This is well illustrated by the CA Lemberg/Lviv, which at the turn of 1942–1943 was very anxious to get an account with the Karpathen-Öl AG, a company set up to pull together the disparate oil fields in Galicia and turn the area into a "Texas." Here, Tron and Joham were able to use the good services of Hermann Josef Abs, who contacted Karl Blessing of the Continental Öl AG, one of the Karpathen's parent companies, to urge the latter's general director, Karl Grosse, to look favorably on an account with the CA Lemberg/Lviv. The effort was successful, although the CA had to share the business

[203] On the Aktion Reinhard, see Sandkühler, *Endlösung*, chs. 4–5. Also see the excellent article by Ingo Loose, "Die Beteiligung deutscher Kreditinstitute an der Vernichtung der ökonomischen Existenz der Juden in Polen 1939–1945," in: Ludolf Herbst/ Thomas Weihe (eds.), *Die Commerzbank und die Juden 1933–1945* (Munich 2004), pp. 223–271. DB, P 24222, Kiehl to Abs, May 4, 1939.

[204] BA-CA, CA-TZ, Rechtsabteilung rot, Box 5/ Creditanstalt AG, Cracow, Audit report. The Reichsbank used the cover name of "Max Heiliger" for its account. See Walter Naasner, *Neue Machtzentren in der deutschen Kriegswirtschaft 1942–1945* (Boppard am Rhein 1994), p. 406.

[205] See Sandkühler, *"Endlösung,"* ch. 9 and Christopher Browning, *Nazi Policy, Jewish Workers, German Killers* (Cambridge 2000), esp. ch. 3.

[206] On the insuring of Plaszow, see Gerald D. Feldman, *Allianz and the German Insurance Business, 1933–1945* (Cambridge 2001), pp. 405–409.

with the Dresdner Bank, which had done business with the Beskiden-Öl AG, a predecessor company of the Karpathan.[207] What is historically interesting about the Karpathan Öl AG, aside from the economic ambitions involved, was that it was a major employer of forced labor, including a significant number of Jewish forced workers, and that one of its leading directors was Berthold Beitz, who used his position until he was drafted into the army to "stock up" on Jewish workers and, along with his wife and some like-minded colleagues, to do whatever he could to save Jews from being mistreated and taken away to be murdered.[208]

As in the case of Schindler, the CA had nothing to do with the forced labor situation, something that might have interested the bank only if the companies in question failed to find the labor they needed. All of the major industrial enterprises with accounts at the CA banks in the GG employed forced labor, and it is hard to imagine that the officials of the bank in Vienna, Cracow, and Lemberg/Lviv were not aware of this.[209] There can be no way of knowing, however, what exactly bank officials and employees knew or felt, or how they acted without direct evidence, and the uncovering of such evidence is often purely fortuitous. A unique and thus far singular instance that is quite revealing occurred at the opening of the CA branch in Cracow in 1996. At the celebration, the bank invited seventy-five-year-old Krystyna Blicharska, a Pole who had worked at the bank in 1941–1945. Following the celebration, she wrote an article about her experiences for the newspaper of the Industrie- und Handelsbank

in Cracow, *Tesaurus*. Initially, she worked in the section of the bank that handled the accounts of the concentration camp inmates discussed earlier, remembering how they were registered in a card file and some of the larger camps involved. She also remembered being referred to Oscar Schindler in an effort to help Jews of her acquaintance, meeting him, and receiving a promise of help. This suggests that there was a network of people "in the know," and this undoubtedly extended to the camp. Most remarkable, however, was her statement that "Director Czerny from Vienna helped a cell of the Polish resistance greatly by warning it of a planned visit from the Gestapo." There was nothing about Czerny's record that would make one suspect him of such sentiments and extremely dangerous actions. Czerny, who was born in 1902, had been a member of the National Socialist company cell since 1933 and had joined the NSDAP in 1935. He was sent to the Cracow branch when it opened and ended up as director of the Lemberg/Lviv branch before the German evacuation. The only explanation for his behavior in Cracow that one can surmise is that he became morally offended by what was going on around him and decided to act on his changed convictions. Otherwise, he seems to have behaved the way bankers were expected to behave in these circumstances.[210]

They were expected to behave cautiously and, has been shown, there was considerable discomfort with the quality of many of the accounts and the securities that had been offered. This was not only true of some of the merchant houses and other smaller enterprises mentioned earlier, but also of larger industrial works with which the CA in Cracow and Lemberg/Lviv were engaged. As was usually the case, the Reichswerke Hermann Göring played an important role in this area, gaining control of the coal mines in particular. The Reichswerke also gained control over some heavy industrial

---

[207] DB, V2/2, the Karpathan-Öl AG account, see CA Vienna to CA Lemberg, Dec. 12, 1942; Ulrich to Tron, Dec. 15, 1942; CA Lemberg to Bechtolf, Jan. 11, 1943; Ulrich to Tron, Jan. 18, 1943.

[208] For this remarkable story, see Sandkühler, *Endlösung*, pt. III.

[209] As Raul Hilberg points out, the chief exploiters of Jewish labor were the heavy industrial firms in Poland, and a comparison of the list provided by Hilberg and the CA accounts shows that the CA was engaged with the largest of them, as is discussed later in this chapter. See Raul Hilberg, *Vernichtung*, III, p. 564, and BA-CA, CA-TZ, Rechtsabteilung rot, Box 5/Creditanstalt AG, Cracow, audit report.

[210] BA-CA, CA-V, Columbus Project File, CA Cracow to CA Vienna, translation of Krystyna Blicharska, "Ohne freie Wahl," in: *Tesaurus*, transmitted on Jan. 12, 1996, see ÖStA/AdR, BMI, Gauakt Gustav Czerny, Nr. 139.091, Czerny's record.

works owned by former Czech enterprises now under its control. The CA Cracow found itself significantly invested in a number of these enterprises as the member of a consortium headed by the Kommerzialbank Cracow, of which the Commerzbank Cracow and the Bank der Deutschen Arbeit Cracow were also members. One of these was the Ostrowiecer Hochöfen und Werke AG, whose credit with the CA Cracow amounted to 6 million Zl at the beginning of 1944. The Ostrowiecer was originally supposed to have backing from the Dresdner Bank, but the RWM had not allowed the Dresdner Bank's guarantee to be transferred to the GG, so that Paersch's Bank of Issue had to come to the rescue with a 10 million rediscount credit for Ostrowiecer bills in July 1943. At the same time, it was intended as a bridging credit until the Dresdner Bank could transfer its own guarantee funds. What is significant here is that it reflected the banking authority's concern about the liquidity of the banks in the GG and the quality of their accounts receivable.[211]

This was displayed in even more dramatic fashion in the case of the Stalowa Wola, Poland's largest steel works, which was formally taken over by the GG. Göring also had his eye on this enterprise, but it was sequestered by the army in late 1942 and handed over to the management of the Stahlwerke Braunschweig GmbH. By this time, the army was overriding any wishes, both public and private, that it felt interfered with war production. In 1943, the debt of the Stalowa Wola to the CA was 10 million Zl – it owed an equal amount to the Kommerzialbank – which had grown to 12.6 million Zl by the beginning of 1944. What disturbed the CA in both Vienna and Cracow in 1943, however, was that no one was accepting liability for the debt. The Realization Trusteeship for Heavy Industrial Assets in Berlin referred the banks to the Hermann Göring Werke, which in turn argued that its Poldi-Hütte was trying to negotiate a new lease. In the meantime, however,

the army had taken over the works and handed the administration over to the Stahlwerke Braunschweig. It was simply too large a debt for so cloudy a legal situation, and both the CA and the Kommerzialbank were threatening to liquidate the debt if matters were not straightened out. They recognized, of course, that this would be impossible given the importance of the firm to the war effort. Here, too, they were supported by the banking authorities in Cracow and finally, in June 1943, the Realization Trusteeship in Berlin agreed to back the debt of Stawola Wola at the CA up to 12.5 million Zl.[212]

One could not always escape industrial engagements under wartime circumstances, but the CA worried about both its liquidity and its long-term interests in Cracow and Lemberg/Lviv. This was especially evident in its handling of the Flugmotorenwerke Reichshof GmbH, a Polish enterprise placed under trusteeship and then leased to the Daimler Benz AG in Stuttgart. Daimler Benz used the Deutsche Bank as its house bank, and this may have been one of the reasons why the company wished to move its account from the Commerzbank Cracow to the CA branch there in the fall of 1942. It also desired a 4–8 million RM credit. The CA Vienna wrote to Director Rummel of the Deutsche Bank about this prospect, pointing out, on the one hand, that its liquidity would only permit it to grant such a high credit by forming a consortium and, on the other, that it needed to know if Daimler-Benz had any long-term intentions with respect to Reichshof. If all that was involved was a temporary lease with no long-term interests on Daimler Benz's part, then the CA would find it hard to become involved. As it turned out, it did not do so.[213] Yet another illustration of the CA's holding back with credits was instructions it gave in March 1943 to both branches, on the advice of Laschtowiczka of the banking authority in

[211] See the correspondence between the Bank of Issue and the Kommerzialbank of July 29, Oct. 14, Nov. 3, and Nov. 9, 1943, and DB, V2/3, Cracow to Tron, Nov. 11, 1943.

[212] DB, V2/6, V2/2, memorandum by Tron, Jan. 27, 1943 and CA to the Stahlwerke Braunschweig, June 17, 1943, and BA-CA, CA-V, CA working committee meetings, Jan. 27 and March 23, 1943.

[213] DB, V2/2, CA to Rummel, Oct. 23, 1942, and CA Vienna to CA Cracow, Nov. 18, 1942.

Cracow, that the banks exercise great caution in giving credits to construction firms because it was unlikely that the overwhelming majority of construction plans in the GG, especially in the Lemberg/Lviv region, would be realized. The risk in the construction sector was to be calculated as carefully as possible.[214]

Needless to say, these banks were not working for a regime famed for its caution or tolerance, and one could not escape membership in a "patriotic" consortium like the one organized under the leadership of the Kommerzialbank for the Deutsche Umsiedlungs Treuhandgesellschaft mbH, Lublin, which had been created for the purpose of helping ethnic German settlers to establish themselves in the occupied areas. It cannot be said that the CA Cracow and the CA Vienna were especially enthusiastic in March 1943 about the invitation to participate in a third tranche of the credit for 20 million Zl of which the CA Cracow was expected to take 20 percent, that is, 4 million Zl. The CA in Vienna agreed with Huber that the participation was "not agreeable" in view of the liquidity situation in the GG and that they probably would have to make use of the Polish Emission Bank's willingness to provide a guarantee, which would mean that the bank would make no money at all on its loans. Nevertheless, they also agreed with Huber that there was no way out and were willing to go along provided that the other banks took their assigned shares. The actual full credit, which was supposed to be guaranteed by the Reich, had been negotiated between the Dresdner Bank and the Finance Ministry as well as the Reich Commissar for the Strengthening of Germandom, that is, Himmler, who added to the security of the loan by promising a deficiency guarantee. This offer had been made directly to the Dresdner Bank, which also functioned as the responsible party for the loan having been selected to head the consortium. As it turned out, however, Himmler did not keep his promise, and the Dresdner Bank, through the Kommerzialbank, now asked the CA to step in and assume some

responsibility for the guarantee. This, the CA Cracow with strong backing from the Vienna home office, absolutely refused to do, arguing that it was inappropriate to change consortium agreements in midstream and strongly suggesting that because the Dresdner Bank had been selected to lead the consortium, it should also fully enjoy the responsibilities that came with it.[215] The CA had 3,880,888 Zl as a credit for this account at the beginning of 1944. Whether the credits had done much good is difficult to say, but the authorities themselves admitted having done very little to help the ethnic Germans and, by this time, they were burying them thanks to their murder by the Polish resistance. It was a telling commentary on the situation in the GG in 1943 that Tron was contacted by Director Meixner of the Landwirtschaftsbank to ask if there might be a job in Vienna because the Polish resistance movement had just passed a death sentence against him and "experience showed that one can count on being carried out such sentences."[216]

The significance of the security issue can be measured by the reports of CA bankers in 1943–1944. With the coming of summer 1943, there was promise of a good harvest and some success in increasing production through incentives so that it appeared theoretically possible that one could both deliver to Germany and feed the Polish peasants. Nevertheless, even the "Eastern Pioneer" running the Lemberg/Lviv branch, Arthur Anlauf, sent a rather grim report to Tron on the dangers presented by partisans and "criminal bands" in the Galician-Ukrainian region who had been strengthened recently by a few hundred Soviet paratroopers. Indeed, the "bands" had attained a size of 30,000–50,000 troops and had medium-sized artillery at their disposal. There was particularly heavy fighting in the Tarnopol area, and army and police reserves had to be sent from Lemberg/Lviv. It

---

[214] Ibid., CA Vienna to CA Cracow and Lemberg, March 29, 1943.

[215] Ibid., and V2/3, CA Vienna to CA Cracow, March 26, 1943; CA Vienna to Dresdner Bank Berlin, July 8, 1943; CA Vienna to Dresdner Bank Berlin, Dec. 17, 1943.

[216] Ibid., V2/1, memo by Tron, Oct. 8, 1943. On the situation of the ethnic Germans, see *Diensttagebuch des Generalgouverneurs*, pp. 689, 760–761.

was distressing that there were attacks not only on persons but also on entire villages in Galicia, and while Lemberg/Lviv was basically quiet, not a night went by when homes and businesses in the region were not plundered and soldiers shot at. All this was accompanied by the burning and destruction of wheat stores, so that the bringing in of the harvest was itself endangered. For the bank, there was a special problem, namely the fact that its credits to the so-called deployment firms mobilizing the harvest were secured by the stocks of food and other goods connected with the operation and the issue of whether insurance would cover their value.[217]

This insurance issue was especially important and terribly complicated. On the one hand, the government was prepared to compensate losses to "political" bands but not to bands of ordinary "thieves," against whom normal insurance was required and was limited to 20 percent of value. The interesting problem was how to distinguish political "thieves" from nonpolitical "thieves." The diverse first category included "members of the Polish resistance movement or ideological opponents (Communists), or, finally, enemies [acting out of a] personal feeling of hatred (Jews)."[218] Despite the dangers and risks, the demand for credits, even if somewhat diminished, persisted primarily for purposes of hoarding goods that could be gotten as long as the transportation system was functioning reasonably well under summer conditions. Tron argued, however, that a fundamental source of the difficulties encountered both in increasing the number of depositors and in reducing the demand for credit was the tendency of German firms doing business in Poland to transfer as much of their earnings as possible back to the Reich and for Polish enterprises to extract high profits. Tron attributed what was tantamount to a German capital flight from the

Generalgouvernement to the generous clearing regulation of Paersch's office and the consequent laxness of the foreign exchange authorities. As for the Poles, they had to take in high profits in order to procure basic goods on the black market for their employees. The only bright spot was that there had been a substantial increase of deposits from 109 million Zl to 136 million Zl over the year because large firms were now playing the role of creditors instead of debtors at the bank. What really disturbed Tron's colleagues on the CA working committee, however, were the "general conditions" Tron repeatedly described. On July 28, after hearing from Tron once again, the working committee "repeated its previously expressed view, that the transformation of the branches into an independent bank would be desirable because of these risks."[219]

Creating the Creditanstalt AG, Cracow

The program of unifying the branches in Cracow and Lemberg/Lviv into a single regional bank with its headquarters in Cracow and a branch in Lemberg/Lviv that was now launched was obviously inspired by the political situation in the GG, whose true horror, brutality, and inhumanity were veiled by the language employed by Tron and his colleagues in dealing with "general conditions" they described. As has been shown, they were part and parcel of those conditions, but it is important to recognize that they were also functioning as bankers and it obviously made good sense either to get out of a bad neighborhood or to cut one's risks if unable to do so. In this case, it was prudent to establish an independent regional bank whose liability would be limited to its own invested capital. The effort of the CA to create a regional bank out of its two branches in the GG is not to be interpreted as the CA on the march, as it had been in the early years of the war, but rather the CA in retreat. Naturally, it could not be spoken of in this manner. Tron

---

[217] Ibid., Anlauf to Tron, July 16, 1943.

[218] This categorization of the enemy, with its strong suggestion that Jewish resistance was not legitimate, apparently was widespread, and Tron was simply adopting a standard formula. See Thomas Sandkühler, "*Endlösung,*" p. 196. Apparently, it was considered unreasonable for the Jews to hate the Germans who were murdering them.

[219] BA-CA, CA-V, Reports of July 20 and July 28, 1943, and ibid., CA working committee meeting, July 28, 1943. This view had already been expressed in September 1942; see p. 208 of this chapter.

had consulted with Abs about this plan, and Abs supported it. Nevertheless, Tron wanted to make doubly sure that the Deutsche Bank did not view the plan as in any way prejudicing the possibility of a regional bank involving Warsaw and reported to Bechtolf, telling him that Stuby had reported that Paersch did not view the licensing of German banks in Warsaw as "acute," although there were reports that the Bank der Deutschen Arbeit was also interested in the Bank Handlowy. Paersch made clear, however, that no commitments had been made, that the Deutsche Bank group would get a hearing, and that there was no reason to petition for a license or to discuss personnel questions. Tron, however, apparently did have personnel issues on his mind, indicating that he thought Director Fritz Baghorn, who had come from Leipzig and was employed at the HTO in Litzmannstadt, would be a particularly suitable director of the projected bank because he "knows the situation in the East." Like Paersch, however, Bechtolf thought discussion of personnel questions premature.[220]

Indeed, during the final months of 1943, Paersch took the position that the entire question of Warsaw was in no way ripe for discussion while supporting the CA plan for merging its branches in a regional bank and expressing the wish of his office that the Deutsche Bank be part of such a regional bank, should it be expanded to include Warsaw. Rather remarkably, the CA viewed the situation as one in which it could again seek to claim leadership in the event that the Deutsche Bank became involved in a regional bank. On September 13, 1943, it asked that the Deutsche Bank cede leadership to the CA because it had developed a clientele and a wealth of experience and knowledge in managing the two branches, which, along with the historical connection between Vienna and Galicia, made it suitable to assume the lead position. In contrast to the situation in 1940–1941, when the Deutsche Bank sharply rejected such pretensions on the part of the CA, it now treated them rather casually, pointing out

that it was premature to discuss the modalities of their cooperation in Poland until one had a clear view of the political and economic situation. Furthermore, it preferred not to discuss the CA's arguments for a primary role, being convinced, as it noted, not without a tone of irony, "that the friendly solution of this question will be the smallest problem of banking activity in the Generalgouvernement."[221]

The CA now moved ahead with its plan to forge its branches in Cracow and Lemberg/ Lviv into an independent regional bank. The environment surrounding this creation was not without its surreal qualities. This is well illustrated by a report from Huber to Tron of January 15, 1944, telling him of a report he had received of a meeting of the Chief Office for Food Supply and Agriculture in Zakopane, where Hans Frank had reportedly said "that new troop transports go to the front daily, so that he is convinced that no Russian will come into the territory of the Generalgouvernement." Perhaps this was plausible given the fact that the Allied invasion had not yet taken place, although the situation in Italy was hardly cause for rejoicing. Huber went on to claim that "[i]n general the situation is viewed optimistically. The fact that the first transport of women and children left Lemberg is not given any broader significance since this measure is necessary to ease the provisioning and housing situation in Lemberg. There is a rumor at the Lemberg branch that the municipal captain is undertaking preparatory measures for the departure of his section; but according to one version this seems to be a precautionary measure only, while according to another there is the possibility that the civilian administration will be replaced by the military."[222]

The mixture of illusion and delusion also found rather open expression in the discussion of the new regional bank. Not only the CA branches but also the Commerzbank

---

[220] DB, CA Cracow, Nr. 137, memorandum by Bechtolf on discussion with Tron, Aug. 18, 1943.

[221] BA-CA, CA-TZ, Rechtsabteilung rot, Box 5/ Creditanstalt AG, Cracow, CA to Deutsche Bank, Sept. 13, 1943 and Deutsche Bank to CA, Oct. 1, 1943.

[222] Ibid., Huber to Tron, Jan. 15, 1944.

branch in Cracow, and later the Arbeiterbank, were seeking to establish themselves as independent entities, and neither the supervisory authorities in Cracow nor those in Berlin contested the economic logic behind these efforts. Riehle, who had to deal with the issue at the turn of 1943–1944 while trying to function in the badly bombed Reich Economics Ministry in Berlin, thought the arguments made by the CA particularly cogent but, like his colleagues in Cracow, he was concerned "that incorrect conclusions, at least for propaganda purposes, could be drawn" from the creation of independent banks. He wondered if a more propitious time might not be found and if the CA and the Commerzbank should be granted permission at the same time.[223]

The CA, in fact, was anxious to have the new bank formally established on January 1, 1944, and actually began technical preparations for the merger shortly thereafter. Matters did not move that quickly when it came to securing permission from the supervisory agencies in Cracow. Tron visited Cracow in January and had no less than three meetings with Paersch, Laschtowiczka, and another official, Government Councilor Fessler. The supervisory office had already rejected the petition of the Commerzbank to set up an independent bank and told Tron that their decision with respect to the CA petition was largely dependent on whether there would be a significant investment by the Deutsche Bank. They frankly admitted that "optical reasons were playing the decisive role" because "the simple transformation of branches in the GG into an independent bank at just the present time would leave behind the worst possible impression (withdrawal from the GG)."[224] But if the Deutsche Bank were to become a party to the new bank, then an entirely different situation would be created

because it could be seen as reflecting "not a withdrawal from the GG but even a strengthening of the interest of a Reich German bank in the GG." Tron had no doubt that the supervisory agency wanted to find a way to license the new bank and that the "optical issue" was central. Fessler, for example, did not care at all whether the Deutsche Bank was actually represented at the founding of the institution; all he cared about was that the Deutsche Bank's participation appeared in the press. Furthermore, the size of the stake was less important than that the participation be real and not nominal.

Tron, therefore, had every reason to be optimistic about securing approval for the independent bank, and he also asked the supervisory authority to affirm that this would in no way prejudice the possible acquisition of a Polish bank, whether independently by the Deutsche Bank or as an addition to the new bank. This was easily done because the entire question of the Polish banks "today still remains completely open and will be decided by the final fate of the GG." Laschtowiczka was also very accommodating on the question of what name to give the bank, the choices apparently being between "Unionbank AG" and "Creditanstalt AG." The preference was for the latter, but there was some concern about the name should some Polish bank be acquired. Laschtowiczka pointed out that it all depended on the legal and economic status to be given to the Poles. If the "Polish element were eliminated," then the name would not matter at all, but if the Poles were brought in, as Laschtowiczka anticipated, then some appropriate change would have to be made.[225]

This "great project" of a regional bank that would include a Polish bank and would be run by the CA and the Deutsche Bank loomed over the discussions despite the fact that its realization seemed further away than ever. Tron apparently believed in it; he was constantly insisting that the authorities in Cracow assure him that the expansion of the regional bank being created would not prejudice the larger bank they wanted to create. This was even

---

[223] Ibid., Riehle to Paersch, Dec. 27, 1943 and CA to Riehle, Dec. 15, 1943. The CA letter mentions the condition of the RWM but argues that everything had been approved by the Cracow authorities so that no real effort was required in dealing with the CA request.

[224] Ibid., memorandum by Tron, Jan. 28, 1944.

[225] Ibid. Presumably, Laschtowiczka anticipated keeping his name no matter what the circumstances.

relayed to the man Tron wanted to have as the head of the new bank, Fritz Baghorn, a banker who headed up the HTO in Litzmannstadt and whose knowledge of the situation in Poland seemed to qualify him for the position in Cracow. Paersch and his colleagues raised no objections to the appointment of Baghorn, but they were less enthusiastic about Huber, who nevertheless had to be kept on because he had been an established figure who by now embodied the prestige of the CA. Czerny, however, enjoyed considerable repute for his competence, while everyone was ready to see Anlauf depart.[226]

If anything was clear, however, it was that Deutsche Bank participation was required for the regional bank to gain approval. Tron personally wrote to Abs on February 1, laying out the situation and reiterating his position that the projected arrangement would not prejudice future developments with respect to the Bank Handlowy and might even promote them. He emphasized that the strong leadership offered by Baghorn would also be a positive factor. Tron knew that Abs was well aware of the difficult economic situation in the GG and the risks involved, but he believed that the cautious credit policy pursued in Cracow had reduced these considerably. Tron admitted that Lemberg/Lviv was a more serious problem, above all politically, and that he was paying close attention to it.[227] In fact, Tron had required that there be an audit of both banks, which determined that creditors held 204 million Zl at both banks in January 1944, while accounts receivable amounted to 132 million Zl. The banks were now instructed to have extra reserves in the amount of 400,000 Zl for recognizable risks and they were contemplating having a general accounts receivable reserve of 2 percent to 3 percent if it could be tax free. The CA and the Deutsche Bank were thus quite nervous about the Cracow and Lemberg/Lviv branches, but

this of course strengthened the case for turning them into an independent enterprise.[228]

The Deutsche Bank yielded to the entreaties of Tron and the CA, but while it agreed to a 20 percent stake, it also asked that the Deutsche Bank be kept off the supervisory board lest this prejudice the future solution of the Polish bank problem.[229] Abs particularly resisted having a seat on the projected bank's supervisory board, "so that – as soon as the larger solution in the GG (Warsaw) becomes acute – the objection cannot be raised that the Deutsche Bank is already represented in common with the CA in the GG."[230] Despite this, Tron continued to have difficulty getting the Cracow authorities to approve the creation of the bank. They had agreed to the capitalization of the bank at 6 million Zl, and they were initially prepared to see the Deutsche Bank limit its stake to 20 percent. But it was the "optical" situation that Paersch and his colleagues considered as most important, and they viewed the Deutsche Bank's failure to provide sufficient "optics" with great irritation. They took umbrage at the Deutsche Bank's desire to stay off the supervisory board and demanded an explanation, and also asked that it raise its stake to 33 1/3 percent. Tron felt that he could not evade responding, and he wrote directly to Abs asking what he was supposed to say. There was considerable consternation at the Deutsche Bank, where it was also felt that it was demeaning to the CA to have to accept so large a Deutsche Bank participation in what after all was supposed to be a CA bank.[231]

Abs was most unhappy about the situation, which ran counter to both his short-term and his long-term strategy. He telegraphed back to his colleagues in Berlin that "The only possibility to avoid the conditions of 1/3 participation and the supervisory board position that I see is

---

226 Ibid. DB, V2/60, vol. 5, and correspondence between Tron and Baghorn, Dec. 1943–Feb. 1944.

227 DB, CA Cracow, Nr. 137, Abs to Tron, Feb. 1, 1944.

228 BA-CA, CA-V, CA working committee meeting, Feb. 10, 1944.

229 DB, CA Cracow, Nr. 137, CA to Deutsche Bank, Feb. 15, 1944.

230 BA-CA, CA-V, CA working committee meeting, Feb. 10, 1944.

231 DB, CA Cracow, Nr. 137, Tron to Abs, Feb. 22, 1944 and Deutsche Bank telegram to Abs, Feb. 25, 1944.

if the CA in Cracow rejects such an engagement of the Deutsche Bank as going too far. Not an agreeable formula! We cannot prevent the establishment of the bank from our side by refusing to concur. I recommend that Herr Bechtolf insert himself in the negotiations with Tron to be held in Cracow. I see the reason for our holding back only in our desire not to over extend ourselves with respect to the great plan and to keep alive the desire of the Gouvernement authorities to have us there."[232]

At the beginning of March, Tron once again negotiated with Paersch. Tron argued that there was an agreement between Vienna and Berlin that the Deutsche Bank would not be represented on the supervisory board, and he felt that it was not "optically" necessary to give the Deutsche Bank's financial participation further visibility. Paersch did not buy this argument. While he dropped the demand for a one-third stake, he stood fast on the supervisory board membership question, indicating that he did not care who it was that served on the supervisory board nor whether the person assigned to the post remained on the board for any length of time. He once more reiterated his assurance that this would in no way prejudice the situation should a larger bank be created, and was even prepared to state this in writing. If the "larger" solution involving Warsaw was to happen, it would in no way be affected by the supervisory board membership.[233]

At this point, Tron felt that he had accomplished the maximum, especially because Paersch had turned down Arbeiterbank efforts to set up an independent bank after having earlier turned down the Commerzbank. This was realized at the Deutsche Bank as well, whose leaders were happy to see the monetary participation limited to 20 percent and who decided they could not forgo membership on the supervisory board. Rösler explained that "as unappealing as we find this development, since we already have a sufficiently large engagement with the holdings

now in our portfolio, we have been unable, in view of our close relations to the Creditanstalt, to refuse our collaboration and have decided to give our agreement."[234] What is puzzling about the correspondence and maneuvers connected with the Deutsche Bank's position is the extent to which any of those involved believed that there was a future in the GG at this point or were merely acting this way. This is especially true in the case of Abs, who apparently wanted to keep all doors open for the "great project" in Warsaw, and it is remarkable how often this was reiterated. While the supervisory authorities in Cracow and Berlin approved the founding of the Creditverein AG, as it was to be called, in mid-March 1944 with the proviso that the Deutsche Bank take a 20 percent participation and a position on the supervisory board, Paersch hastened to inform the Deutsche Bank in writing that "the intention, basically agreed upon by me and the relevant Reich agencies, to transfer a number of Polish corporate banks into German hands at a suitable time will be pursued further. I will not view the projected capital and supervisory board participation in the newly founded Creditanstalt A.G., Cracow as a renunciation of your wish to be considered in taking over a Polish bank institute."[235]

Considerable thought was given to the composition of the Creditverein AG's supervisory board and management board prior to its formal establishment on May 16, 1944. Tron planned to act as chairman of the supervisory board, and Hermann Kaiser was to represent the Deutsche Bank. It was deemed important, however, to secure the services of leading persons from industry who resided in the GG. Director Rösler of the Deutsche Bank strongly suggested that Tron try to get Otto Berve of the Gräflich Schaffgott'sche Werke in Gleiwitz, a leading coal producer. Berve was settled in the area, had some banking experience, and

---

[232] Ibid., Telephone report by Wuppermann to Berlin on instructions from Abs, Feb. 26, 1944.

[233] Ibid., Report by Bechtolf, March 4, 1944, and ibid., V2/1, memorandum by Tron, March 6, 1944.

[234] DB, CA Cracow, Nr. 137, Rösler to Kimmich, March 15, 1944.

[235] Ibid., Paersch to Deutsche Bank, March 18, 1944. The formal approval by the supervisory authority in Cracow dated March 18, 1944 is to be found in ibid. The approval of the Berlin authorities came on March 30, 1944, ibid.

had been appointed president of the Gau Economic Chamber Kattowitz. Kiehl knew Berve well, and Rösler suggested that Kiehl be asked to recruit Berve, which he did successfully. Problems arose, however, in connection with other candidates from major firms, and one hoped to gain suitable ones in the future. Regarding the management board, Baghorn and Huber were placed in charge in Cracow while Gustav Czerny took over in Lemberg/Lviv.[236]

The political and economic logic of the decision of the GG's banking supervisory authority in allowing the CA and the Deutsche Bank to establish the Creditverein AG was clarified when Director Joseph Schilling of the Commerzbank renewed the effort to create a subsidiary bank in the GG in May 1944. Now, Paersch demonstrated a friendlier attitude and also explained the favor he had shown to the CA. Paersch pointed out that the initial rejection of the Commerzbank's request, which was one of a number of such petitions, was the result of general political considerations because "a piling up of such re-organizations on the basis of such petitions could easily provide cause for misunderstandings. The impression could possibly be created that the German banks are striving to distance themselves from the development in the Generalgouvernement, while the real purpose of the transformations – the more individual treatment and the intensification of business here – would be overlooked. These considerations make it appear appropriate not to decide on the petitions all at once but rather at certain intervals, one after the other on the basis of their urgency." The CA's request to establish a subsidiary bank seemed both important and quite urgent because of its large volume of business and its servicing of the Deutsche Bank and Reichskreditgesellschaft's customers. Furthermore, the Deutsche Bank was putting up a substantial portion of the capital and also took a position on the supervisory board. Under these circumstances, the creation

of a subsidiary bank would not be open to criticism. Paersch hoped Schilling would understand the economic and political logic behind this decision and now expressed a willingness to move forward with the Commerzbank case at the end of May 1944.[237]

Such "optics" notwithstanding, time was running out for the German adventure in Poland, indeed, for the Third Reich altogether. The situation had worsened progressively in 1943–1944, not only because of the Warsaw Ghetto Uprising in April–May 1943 in the wake of the increasing deportation of the Jews to the death camps and the Warsaw Uprising of August–September 1944, but also because of growing resistance by partisans, usually identified by the Germans as "bandits," who robbed banks, sabotaged trains, and assassinated Germans, altogether making life increasingly difficult for the occupiers. Needless to say, it was hard not to be aware of the deteriorating military situation in the East. It was a sign of the times that in July 1944 Standartenführer Schellin removed the 8 million Zl he held at the Creditanstalt, placed it with the Kommerzialbank, and then tried to remove all the money to Germany. For Paersch, it was probably more a matter of principle than of "optics," but he insisted that something be left in the GG, and Schellin thus had to settle for 30 million Zl and leave 49 million Zl in the GG.[238]

The history of the Creditverein AG was primarily that of its dissolution and disappearance, but business went on to the last minute. The CA tried to reduce its losses and secure such protection as was possible under the circumstances. In late April, Tron was able to report that, thanks to the cautious credit policy, accounts receivable in Lemberg/Lviv had been reduced significantly and that half of these were guaranteed by bank guarantees or other guarantees in the Reich while the remainder were liable to

[236] Ibid., Rösler to Tron, April 12, 1944, correspondence between Kiehl and Berve, and report on these appointments, May 24, 1944.

[237] AAN Rząd, 1401, Bl. 110 and 25–26, Commerzbank to Banking Supervisory Agency Cracow, May 16, 1944 and Paersch to Schilling, March 22, 1944.

[238] Diensttagebuch des Deutschen Generalgouverneurs, pp. 652–653, 707, 761–765; James, Nazi Economic War, p. 194; Wixforth, Expansion, pp. 572–573.

claim or suit in the Reich.[239] In June, Tron gave another upbeat report to the effect that accounts receivable stood at 110 million Zl as opposed to 156 million Zl in October and deposits were increasing substantially, so that the credit business could be covered by normal deposits. Abs asked that the working committee of the CA be informed of "larger engagements"[240] of the new bank now that it had been founded. This was somewhat odd in light of the fact that the Lemberg/Lviv branch celebrated the creation of the Creditanstalt AG, Cracow by moving to Cracow, and the Cracow offices moved in January 1945 to Breslau, then to Liegnitz, and then to Vienna. The "major engagement" of the Creditanstalt AG, Cracow seems to have been leaving Poland and cutting its losses in the process. Tron reported in September 1944 that the departure of the Lemberg/Lviv branch from Lemberg/Lviv had entailed no losses other than the writing off of inventories, while Cracow had reduced its accounts receivable to 86 million Zl by the end of June, and the deposits declined from 199 million Zl to 187 million Zl, of which 96 million Zl was in cash. This meant that there had been a considerable break in potential profitability because there was obviously no return on cash holdings.[241] In November 1944, Tron was able to report that accounts receivable now stood at 63 million Zl from a one-time high of 156 million Zl and that no new credits had been given, while deposits stood at 180 million Zl.[242] The CA's role in Poland had manifestly become history – and was to remain history until 1996. As for the German presence, it came to an end at the beginning of 1945, when the offices of the GG and the bank personnel left Cracow. Grotesquely, prior to this departure the CA Cracow and the Kommerzialbank were competing with each other for permission to keep one office in Cracow to conduct what

remained of banking business. The question was determined on the basis of the bank that had the most accounts, and the Kommerzialbank won the competition. Paersch and the supervisory office joined the exodus, Paersch appearing next in history as the head of the Landeszentralbank Hessen in 1961. He thus ended up in a safer venue with a better job.[243]

Yugoslavia – Before the German Invasion

Whereas the CA struggled to reassert itself in Poland during the war, it already had an established position in Yugoslavia that antedated the Anschluss. Historical claims, therefore, played much less of a role, and developments between 1938 and 1945 were decisive in determining the adaptation and transformation of existing arrangements. As has been discussed earlier in this study, the CA had maintained an interest, in fact a majority interest, in the Allgemeiner Jugoslawischer Bankverein, Belgrad–Zagreb[244] (AJB), and in many respects this had been the linchpin of the Southeast strategy pursued by the CA and the Deutsche Bank after the Anschluss. This bank had been founded in 1928 by the Wiener Bankverein, the Banque Belge pour l'Étranger, Brussels (a subsidiary of the Belgian Société Général), the Basler Handelsbank, Basel, and the Böhmische Unionbank, Prague. The Wiener Bankverein was the largest shareholder and brought its already existing Yugoslav branches into the AJB. When the CA took over the Wiener Bankverein in 1934, it also took over its shares in the AJB. Originally capitalized at 100 million dinar, its capital was reduced to 60 million dinar (105,448 RM) in 1934.[245] It

[239] BA-CA, CA-V, CA working committee meeting, April 26–27, 1944.

[240] Ibid., CA working committee meeting, June 13, 1944.

[241] Ibid., CA working committee meeting, Sept. 26, 1944.

[242] Ibid., CA working committee meeting, Nov. 22, 1944.

[243] See on the exodus from Cracow, Breslau, and Liegnitz, the file of the Bank Supervisory Agency, AAN Rząd, Nr. 1319, especially the memorandum of Jan. 21, 1945. For Paersch, see Ernst Klee, *Das Personenlexikon zum Dritten Reich. Wer war was vor und nach 1945* (Frankfurt a.M. 2003), p. 447.

[244] The German term for Zagreb, "Agram," will not be used here except in quotations.

[245] Koliander, *Beteiligung*, pp. 122–123 (Dinar 100 = RM 5.69). See the excellent account of the Allgemeiner Jugoslawischer Bankverein (= AJB) in Vesna Aleksic, "The History of the Allgemeiner Jugoslawischer Bankverein AG in Belgrade in the

had headquarters in Belgrade and Zagreb and branches in Novi Sad and Ljubljana.

At the time of the Anschluss, the CA held 49.7 percent of the AJB's capital, that is, 149,000 of the 299,216 shares; the Société Général held 38.8 percent (116,184 shares); the BUB held 3.9 percent (11,898 shares); and the Basler Handelsbank controlled 5 percent (15,899 shares). The CA gained direct majority control by buying up a few hundred shares through an intermediary in early 1938 and supplemented this stake indirectly through shares held by its friendly shareholders.[246]

Yugoslav businessmen held the majority and the chairmanship of the five-man supervisory board in 1938, which was responsible for approving the bank's business report, but the administrative council, which was responsible for the appointment of the management board and overseeing the administration of the bank, was dominated by foreigners, who comprised half of that body. The presidency had been vacant since the end of 1932, when President Hugo Weinberger resigned because of the banking crisis. The council was therefore chaired by its first vice president, Paul Ramlot of the Société Général. His colleague Robert Gheude was also on the council. The CA was represented by Oscar Pollak of the CA management board and Alfred Schwartz of the Budapest branch of the CA. Otto Freund represented the interests of the BUB, and Emil Müller those of the Basler Handelsbank. Of the six members formally designated as living in Yugoslavia, the most important was a Romanian-born Czech citizen, Edmond Goldschmidt. A dominant figure at the bank, Goldschmidt resided in both Belgrade and Zagreb, and his contract allowed him to reside in Vienna too if he so desired.[247]

Goldschmidt's special position was a product of his very cosmopolitan banking background.

He had been director of the Romanian Commercial Bank in Bucharest, which was affiliated with the Banque de l'Union Parisienne and the Banque Belge pour l'Étranger, and he subsequently became the director of the latter and was responsible for its interests in Central Europe and the Balkans. In 1931, he was made a member of the AJB administrative council to replace the Belgian Georges Theunis, and he was reappointed in 1934 and given a special contract in 1936. In 1932, he had been assigned by the administrative council to a special position as chairman of the management board charged with the oversight and coordination of the work of the long-time managers of the AJB, Mavro Kandel, David Hochner, Fran D. Favale, and Juraj Pajanović. The position of president of the administrative council had been vacant too long at this point, and there was a strong wish to have someone with the time and skills to look after the interests of the major shareholders. The AJB did a great deal of business with Yugoslav timber companies and exporters of meat and grain products, and a special concern of the shareholding banks was that these companies use their services in conducting their business. In 1937, for example, Pollak complained to Goldschmidt that the AJB client Predović AG was using the Länderbank and Mercurbank, not the CA, when doing business in Austria because the CA rates were higher. Goldschmidt subsequently informed the AJB directors to ask Predović to sacrifice the minor advantages involved and deal almost exclusively with the CA in view of the credits it was regularly receiving from the AJB. Goldschmidt's most important contributions to the bank, however, were in gaining important credit accounts and consolidating major accounts receivable. The bank owed many of its successes and high liquidity to his efforts.[248] The attractiveness of the

---

Context of Yugoslav Banking History after 1918," in: Rathkolb et al. (eds.), *Bank Austria Creditanstalt*, pp. 228–233.

[246] Auditor's report on the CA 1938, p. 155 and Business report for 1937 and 10th Shareholders' Meeting, April 30, 1937, Archives of Yugoslavia (= AJ), AJB, 151/2.

[247] Ibid.

[248] See AJ, AJB 151/4/4, the Pro Memoria concerning Goldschmidt of Oct. 26, 1935, the contract with Goldschmidt of Oct. 26, 1936, and the correspondence with Pollack of June 1 and the AJB of June 1937. See also ibid., AJB 151/5/5, Nikolia Berković to Georg Saal, March 23, 1940.

AJB to the CA was probably in no small measure due to Goldschmidt's excellent management.

At the same time, Yugoslavia was of great military and economic interest to the Germans, who wished to exploit its mineral resources: copper, bauxite, chromium, and zinc. The Bor mines were particularly important, although the need for investment in order to make their minerals accessible and transportable was a great problem. The Deutsche Bank was especially attentive to the possibilities opened up by Yugoslavia, especially in view of its close connection with the Metallgesellschaft and the Otavi mining company, and it had been discussing the role it might play in financing such efforts with the Creditanstalt for some time, that is, at least back to 1935. In July 1936, Gustav Schlieper, Abs's predecessor on the supervisory board of the CA, sent a memorandum to President Schacht of the Reichsbank outlining the issues involved in German investment in a Yugoslav bank and the procurement of industrial raw materials from Bulgaria, Greece, and Yugoslavia. This followed on nonbinding discussions between Schlieper and the CA on investment in the AJB. The CA had declared itself ready to propose to its Belgian partners in the AJB that the Deutsche Bank provide additional capital both for the liquidity of the Yugoslav economy and for the reorganization of the AJB in return for a place on the AJB administrative council. The Deutsche Bank wished to open up rediscount possibilities in the chief commercial centers of interest to German industrial and commercial interests – Ljubljana, Zagreb, and Novi Sad – especially because the Yugoslav National Bank was unreliable in this respect. Furthermore, it was willing to work with the Dresdner Bank in this effort. The AJB was especially attractive because it had a trained and experienced staff, but the Deutsche Bank also emphasized the desirability of collaboration with the CA, thus strengthening the Austrian connection as well as its existing ties with the Belgian bank. At the same time, Schlieper made clear at this point that such an arrangement would not offer complete German control of the AJB, but that this was not necessarily desirable because it would involve responsibility for the deposits

in the bank, possible conflict with the Italians, and difficulties with the Yugoslav authorities. Furthermore, the Deutsche Bank was hesitant about investing in the mining business in Yugoslavia unless the Yugoslav government was willing to resume payment of old prewar bonds in which the Deutsche Bank had invested. The CA seems to have been anxious to get a firm commitment from the Deutsche Bank, and Schlieper discussed his memorandum with the RWM at the beginning of 1937. By this time, enthusiasm for any kind of extensive project had waned because of the improvement of German-Italian relations, which forced caution on the Germans and aroused the suspicions of the Yugoslav authorities. Nevertheless, a stake in the AJB remained attractive as a means to increase German influence, strengthen ties with the CA, and acquire an opening to the west through the Belgians. But it was considered a barrier to further progress that a non-Aryan headed the bank, and the support of Franz Neuhausen, who was the Party man at the German consulate in Belgrade, was viewed as being of special importance.[249]

Despite these intentions, the ambitions of both the Deutsche Bank and the Dresdner Bank had been stymied by transfer problems, and nothing was done until the Anschluss revived the issue under much more favorable conditions. On May 16, 1938, the Deutsche Bank again contacted the RWM with a somewhat revised version of Schlieper's earlier memorandum for Schacht and pointed out that the development of the AJB into a "German bank" had been made much easier thanks to the annexation of Austria. It noted that IG Farben was also anxious to create a German bank in Yugoslavia and that contact had been made with the Dresdner Bank as well. While the CA believed that the Belgians would be willing to sell their shares in the AJB, the Yugoslav government appeared anxious that the Belgian

[249] BAB, R 31.01, vol. 15535, Bl. 35–45, 54–55, Schlieper to Kohler, Feb. 11, 1937; Deutsche Bank to Reinhart, Dec. 12, 1936; Schlieper to Schacht, July 15, 1936 and memorandum; discussion with RWM, Jan. 16, 1937.

holding be retained. On one count, however, the CA was totally optimistic, namely that "the elimination of the Jewish leadership would not present any difficulties."[250] The fact that the CA had procured a majority holding and that it hoped to acquire the BUB stake as well, a matter of much less import once the Germans took over Prague, meant that the AJB was already under the control of a German institution.[251] Even so, the most significant aspect of this history is that the CA had been in collusion with the Deutsche Bank regarding the AJB well before the Anschluss and that the Deutsche Bank and the Dresdner Bank worked with the Reichsbank and the RWM to promote the creation of a strong German banking presence in Yugoslavia. The Anschluss now made it possible to achieve this goal in partnership with the CA.

The Anschluss marked the beginning of a succession of personnel changes in the AJB administrative council designed to eliminate its Jewish members, replace them with Aryans, and undermine the position of Goldschmidt and pave the way for his elimination. It is important to note that the Yugoslav banking system required the appointment of a supervisory board that received and approved the business reports of a bank and was composed of Yugoslav nationals, and an administrative council that oversaw the management of the bank and appointed the management board. The administrative council, therefore, was central to the operation of the bank and represented it at the shareholders' meetings. Accordingly, in preparation for the shareholders' meeting of April 30, 1938, Alfred Schwartz resigned his position, and Joham joined the administrative council as second vice-president.[252] Pollack tendered his resignation on June 22, 1938, and the news was announced at the October 24, 1938, meeting of the administrative council. Otto Freund apparently continued formally to represent the BUB until its takeover by Walter Pohle of the

Deutsche Bank, when he resigned from the BUB, was thrown into prison by the Gestapo; he died shortly thereafter, either by his own hand or at the hands of the Gestapo. Still, the most important development at the October 24, 1938, meeting certainly was Ramlot's announcement that the dominant shareholders had agreed to the appointment of Georg Saal to the administrative council. Joham proposed not only that Saal should be appointed to this position but also that he should share the management of the AJB with Goldschmidt in the future and be appointed to the executive committee of the administrative council. In fact, Saal was already at the meeting of October 24 and participated in its deliberations. All the same, none of this was much of a surprise, certainly not to Goldschmidt and probably not to anyone present. Goldschmidt was aware of the decision at the beginning of September because Saal had shown him the courtesy of visiting to personally brief him, and Ramlot had written to him. Consequently, Goldschmidt had instructed Director Hochner that he and his colleagues were to treat Saal right away as a member of the administrative council with a status similar to his own.[253]

The forty-nine-year-old Saal, a Reich German who was trained as a banker and held posts in cooperative and clearing banks, had been heavily engaged earlier in the rather murky efforts by the German Foreign Office and the Mitteleuropäische Wirtschaftstag to organize credits for Germans and National Socialists in Austria and the lands bordering on Austria and also to provide financial help for "illegals" after 1934. He had worked closely in his various banking functions for the Ossa-Vermittlungs- und Handelsgesellschaft, an ostensibly private concern headed by Max Winkler that had been founded in 1926 at the behest of the German Foreign Office for the purpose of promoting German economic penetration of Austria and the areas adjacent

[250] Ibid., Bl. 77–81, Deutsche Bank to RWM, May 16, 1938.

[251] Ibid., Bl. 82, RWM memo of Oct. 19, 1938.

[252] AJ, AJB, 151/2/2, Ramlot to the CA, Joham, Schwartz, and Freund, April 30, 1938.

[253] Ibid., administrative council meeting, Oct. 24, 1938, and Goldschmidt to Hochner, Sept. 4, 1938, ibid., AJB, 151/90/115. On Freund, see James, *Nazi Economic War*, p. 154.

to it. Winkler was an important go-between for the National Socialists in Austria, and the Austrian government, well aware of his activities, deported him to Germany in 1936. In the following period, Saal was active in Belgrade and Berlin on behalf of the German Chamber of Commerce to promote German economic interests in Yugoslavia. Despite his contacts, he did not seem to have had a steady job.[254]

Saal's fortunes certainly looked better after the Anschluss. When Director Heinz Osterwind of the Deutsche Bank tried to arrange a meeting with Fischböck about the Deutsche Bank situation in Vienna, Osterwind immediately suggested that Saal be used. As Pollems reported to Abs: "Herr Osterwind praises the exceptional relations of Herr Saal with the Vienna Party agencies, through which it would be very easy to arrange a meeting with Fischböck. In this connection, Herr Osterwind asks if it would not be opportune to use the services of Herr Saal, who presently is in Vienna and still without any function, to ensure contact with Party agencies by assigning him the task of arranging such contacts and by compensating him for a week or so on a per diem basis."[255] There is no evidence that this advice was followed, but Saal subsequently tried to get a position at the CA,[256] and by the late summer he had been offered the position at the AJB, a post for which he appeared well suited by both his experience and his political credentials.

The Aryanization of the AJB, which would not be completed until the end of 1940, was closely connected to its "Germanization," and the appointment of Saal reflected both processes. This is not to say that Saal was a fire-eater. Pollack, who apparently got to know him through his banking activities in Vienna, seems to have thought him a decent person

and colleague and even sent Saal condolences when his wife died in an accident.[257] As has been shown, Saal also treated Goldschmidt with respect, and while it was clear to all that the AJB could not really have two general directors and that Goldschmidt was going to be forced out as soon as Saal was in place, one of their colleagues on the administrative council, Nikola Berković from Sarajevo, felt comfortable enough with Saal to importune him to back a considerate departure for Goldschmidt, not only because of his many services to the bank and the high regard in which he was held, but also because Goldschmidt was only a few months short of the ten-year period required to acquire Yugoslav citizenship.[258] On March 16, Goldschmidt had been asked in a discussion, probably with Ramlot and Joham, to step down, and he tendered his resignation as a member of the administrative council on May 25, 1939. He was allowed to remain on as a representative of the Belgian shareholders of the AJB and as a consultant until March 31, 1940, when he formally resigned those functions. He moved to Atlantic City, New Jersey, and, in November 1940, he still represented the Zagreb branch of the bank in a legal matter. He also seems to have received at least part of the money owed him by the bank because the Yugoslav foreign exchange restrictions were relaxed in his case.[259]

Given the subsequent fate of Yugoslavia, Goldschmidt certainly was a great deal safer and more secure than he would have been in Belgrade. In the meantime, the Germanization of the bank had made great strides. When Joham joined the AJB administrative council, the ownership of the majority by the CA was far clearer than the ownership of the CA, where the VIAG and Deutsche Bank were in competition. Joham certainly preferred the Deutsche Bank, and he somewhat gingerly called the latter on May 13, 1938, claiming that he had heard rumors that

254 See Karl Stuhlpfarrer and Leopold Steurer, "Die Ossa in Österreich," in: Ludwig Jedlicka/Rudolf Neck (eds.), *Vom Justizpalast zum Heldenplatz. Studien und Dokumentationen 1927–1938* (Vienna 1975), pp. 35–64. See also AJ, AJB, 151/5/5, Saal's correspondence relating to these activities.

255 DB, B 51, Pollems to Abs, May 12, 1938.

256 See AJ, AJB, 151/5/5, letter of Saal, possibly to his wife, of July 28, 1938.

257 AJ, AJB, 151/4/4, Pollack to Hochner, Feb. 11, 1940.

258 Ibid., AJB, 151/5/5, Berković to Saal, March 23, 1940.

259 See ibid., AJB, 151/2/2, Goldschmidt's resignation of May 25, 1939, and AJB, 151/4/4, which also contains his resignation of March 31, 1940 and his correspondence from the United States.

negotiations were taking place in Berlin about Yugoslavia. He also told Director Pohle that the VIAG and the RKG, with which he was being forced to work more closely, "interest themselves extraordinarily for the Yugoslav business." Abs and Pohle were quite suspicious of the CA at this time, and Pohle coolly responded that they would inform the CA if something special happened.[260] By the turn of the year, however, the Deutsche Bank and the VIAG had come to terms about the CA, and the way had been paved for collaboration in an open effort to Germanize the AJB.[261]

An important step in this direction was smoothed by the Deutsche Bank takeover of the BUB following the creation of the Protectorate. On May 15, 1939, Pohle invited Hermann Josef Abs to represent the BUB on the AJB administrative council in place of Freund.[262] Things went somewhat less smoothly, however, when it came to the proposal to appoint Franz Neuhausen, the German general consul in Belgrade, to the presidency of the AJB, which had been vacant since 1932. Neuhausen, a close friend of Göring since the First World War, also bore the ominous title of "Authorized Special Commissioner of the Minister President Field Marshal Göring for Yugoslavia in the Framework of the Four Year Plan."[263]

"Fat Franz," as he was, perhaps affectionately, called in Göring's entourage, was a mining and metals expert. A well-placed National Socialist, he had taken up residence in Belgrade and was charged with looking after German economic interests in Yugoslavia. The opportunities were many because Germany increasingly dominated the Yugoslav economy by buying its imports at well above world prices and dumping them to get foreign exchange. Britain and

France did nothing to counter such German and Italian trade practices. As a consequence, the government of Milan Stojadinović was helpless to resist German domination even in those instances where it sought to do so. Neuhausen was thus a key figure both politically and economically in the realization of German interests, and he was to become the dominant figure in the Serbian economy after the German invasion in 1941.[264]

The idea of appointing Neuhausen to the presidency of the AJB took shape in June–July 1939 and was pushed by Fischböck in the course of a visit to State Secretary Friedrich Landfried of the RWM on June 30. Landfried was playing a key role in the development of German-Yugoslav trade agreements in which Germany was to receive raw materials and metals in return for the sale of various finished products, including surplus, often old and obsolete weapons for the Yugoslav military. As Fischböck explained to Landfried, the appointment of Neuhausen was aimed at servicing the needs of the German economy in Yugoslavia, especially by providing credits for the intended participations of German interests in the context of the Four Year Plan. He pointed out that most banking institutions in Southeast Europe did not have sufficient deposits to provide needed credits and asked that this situation be remedied by allowing the AJB to hold the successive installments that the Yugoslav military paid for German weapons deliveries. As one installment was paid, the AJB would proceed to hold the next one and, in this way, the bank would have a yearly annuity in dinar that would ensure its ability to perform its credit functions. Fischböck assured Landfried that the bank was consolidated and liquid with 60 million dinar in share capital, 250 million dinar in deposits, 60 million dinar in participations, and about 100 million dinar in tangible assets. He admitted, however, that deposits had decreased substantially in the

[260] DB, B 51, Minute by Pohle, May 13, 1938.
[261] See RGVA Moscow, 1458/2/83, Bl. 130, the report by Fritscher at a meeting with Reich Credit Commissar Ernst, Jan. 23, 1939.
[262] DB, B 69, Pohle to Abs, May 15, 1939.
[263] See his letterhead, e.g., in DB, B 69, Neuhausen to Fischböck, July 15, 1939. On his friendship with Göring, see Willi A. Boelcke, *Die deutsche Wirtschaft 1930–1945. Interna des Reichswirtschaftsministeriums* (Düsseldorf 1983), p. 271.

[264] For a good discussion of German economic interests, see Wilhelm Deist et al., *Ursachen und Voraussetzungen des Zweiten Weltkrieges* (Frankfurt a.M. 1995), pp. 401–411and Frank C. Littlefield, *Germany and Yugoslavia, 1933–1941: The German Conquest of Yugoslavia* (New York 1988), chs. 2–3.

fall of 1938 and that a significant loss of Jewish depositors was to be anticipated.[265]

Fischböck had already discussed these issues with Neuhausen and, on July 6, formally asked him if he would accept a position on the administrative council and then an election to its presidency. He admitted that the Belgian shareholders had not yet responded to this idea and also pointed out that he had discussed the question of buying them out with Landfried. This depended on gaining the support of the Finance Ministry for the use of foreign exchange for the purchase, which would also have to rule on the idea of using the armaments loan dinar installments to strengthen the AJB's liquidity. In any case, Fischböck believed Landfried took a positive attitude and hoped that Neuhausen would join in support of these efforts.[266]

Needless to say, the appointment of Neuhausen also had to have the support of Göring, and Fischböck had visited Four Year Plan State Secretary Paul Körner on June 30 to ask him to secure Göring's support. Fischböck discovered, however, that not everyone was quite as sanguine as he was about the consequences of a significant withdrawal of Jewish deposits. While obviously supporting the idea of giving the AJB as German a character as possible, Olscher and Abs were quite concerned that the proposed solution, that is, the appointment of Neuhausen, could lead to a substantial loss of Jewish clientele. Fischböck, while not denying the problem, argued that the bank was sufficiently liquid to withstand such withdrawals and supplied Körner with information provided by Saal on the status of the bank and a list of "Jewish and anti-German customers" likely to leave the bank if it took on an openly and pronounced German character. Göring found Fischböck's arguments persuasive and approved Neuhausen's nomination on July 5.[267]

Fischböck and Göring's entourage also wished to buy out the Belgian shareholders and thereby complete the Germanization of the bank.[268] For the moment, however, the Belgians held a significant block of shares and were not at all happy about the nomination of Neuhausen. On July 7, therefore, Ramlot wrote to Abs on behalf of himself and his colleagues and took the position that an appropriate president of the administrative council would be a Yugoslav businessman and that this would assure "a stable clientele of depositors." He noted that this clientele had always been local. They were unwilling to support the election of either of the two nationalities represented among the large shareholders and were opposed to the appointment of a politician. In their opinion, an appropriate candidate was the former governor of the Yugoslav National Bank, Milan Radosavljević. Abs had met Ramlot in Denmark and then again in Amsterdam, where August Callens was also present, and he did not disguise his sympathy with their position in a letter to Hasslacher on July 11. He pointed out that there was no evidence that the Société Général wished to abandon its interest in the AJB but "rather is inclined and ready to collaborate further, and I believe that it is right to also continue to draw them into collaboration." In Abs's view, such a posture precluded majoritizing them. He urged, therefore, that the question of the presidency of the administrative council be handled with caution and that one should limit oneself to gaining support for Neuhausen's appointment as a member of the administrative council rather than as its head.[269]

Abs's attitude reflected his and his colleagues' preference for working with major European banks, especially one so important and distinguished as the Société Général, and this policy continued, albeit in a very difference context and with different results, after the war started.[270]

[265] DB, B 69, Fischböck and Joham to Landfried, July 6, 1939.

[266] Ibid., Fischböck to Neuhausen, July 6, 1939.

[267] Ibid., memorandum by Fischböck, July 6, 1939; Saal had sent the lists to the CA on June 23; Ministerial Director Marotzke informed Fischböck of Göring's decision on July 5.

[268] Ibid., Hasslacher to Abs, July 7, 1939.

[269] Ibid., Abs to Hasslacher, July 11, 1939.

[270] See Harold James, "The Deutsche Bank 1933–1945," in: Lothar Gall et al., *The Deutsche Bank 1870–1995* (Munich 1995), pp. 332–333; Lothar Gall, *Der Bankier Hermann Josef Abs. Eine Biographie* (Munich 2004), pp. 78, 80–82, 264; Herman van

This was a policy, however, that Abs at this point could advise but not impose on Joham, who was under the thumb of Fischböck, and decisions were taken in Vienna that preempted Abs's efforts. On July 12 Joham wrote confidentially to Ramlot to inform him that the CA intended to officially make a recommendation for the presidency of the administrative council. He pointed out that Fischböck had traveled to Yugoslavia to see if the person in question – Neuhausen is not mentioned by name – would be acceptable in Belgrade and found that the proposal was positively received by the political and economic leadership in Yugoslavia. As Joham gingerly put it, a significant element of the approval arose from the fact "that greater disadvantages for the institution are to be feared from a rejection than would be in the case of the appointment." The CA would therefore place its majority holding behind the person in question. Joham hoped that this would not lead to bad feeling between the CA and the Société Général and, furthermore, that Ramlot "would want to be the voice for the unavoidability of this solution." Joham also informed Ramlot that another CA director would be presented for the administrative council, namely, Ludwig Fritscher.[271]

Under these circumstances, Abs had to back down and write to Ramlot that Neuhausen was being proposed by the CA as well as express the hope that Ramlot and Callens could work with the new president. On July 15, the CA formally informed the Société Général that it was nominating Neuhausen, stressing his importance for German-Yugoslav relations, furthermore, that along with the BUB, which was now in the hands of the Deutsche Bank, there was a majority to push through the election.[272]

Unsurprisingly, Neuhausen was pleased to accept Fischböck's invitation to become president of the administrative council, pointing out that "a German bank is a necessary instrument that I need if I am to care for and lead German economic interests in Yugoslavia in the framework of the Four Year Plan according to the desires and instructions of General Field Marshal Göring." He did hope that the differences with the Belgian group would be carried out in a friendly manner, with respect to both his nomination and the taking over of their shares in the future. He believed that he would be able to use his influence with Göring and Economics Minister Funk to gain support for the purchase of these shares as well as for the use of the dinar installments paid for the Yugoslav armaments loan.[273]

Not everyone at the AJB was quite as overjoyed by Neuhausen's impending appointment and his plans. A Deutsche Bank official visiting Belgrade on July 13 found General Director Saal in a gloomy state of mind.[274] Saal had asked Milan Radosavljević sometime earlier if he would stand for the presidency, and the latter had answered affirmatively. Saal clearly regretted the decision for Neuhausen. He feared that when the news of Neuhausen's appointment got out, it would mean the loss of 40–50 million out of 90 million in deposits, mainly from Jewish-owned accounts. Saal also reported that Neuhausen believed they would receive the foreign exchange needed to buy out the Belgians, but then suggested that the Dresdner Bank should be offered the shares. Saal thought this reflected the influence of Keppler, who was now operating out of Berlin but it certainly must have been as disturbing to the Deutsche Bank official as to Saal. No less troubling to Saal, however, were signs that Neuhausen would push business that violated good banking practice and put a strain on the AJB's resources. In one case, Neuhausen promoted the granting of a 500,000 dinar credit, announcing that he personally would vouch for the borrower. In another instance, he asked if the AJB had given credit to the Yugoslav aluminum factory, and when told that this was the case, Neuhausen

---

der Wee and Monique Verbreyt, *Die Generale Bank 1822–1997. Eine ständige Herausforderung* (Tielt 1997), pp. 254–256.

[271] DB, B 69, Joham to Ramlot, July 12, 1939.

[272] Ibid., Abs to Ramlot (in French), July 14, 1939; CA to Société Général, July 15, 1939.

[273] Ibid., Neuhausen to Fischböck, July 15, 1939.

[274] Ibid., memorandum, July 17, 1939. The signature is unreadable.

announced, "I want this factory."[275] While Saal recognized that Neuhausen's intention was to have the plant placed in the hands of German interests, he was fearful that Neuhausen also intended to use the AJB to acquire industrial enterprises on its own.

Indeed, the Deutsche Bank official was anything but reassured about Neuhausen after meeting with him and having some of Saal's worst suspicions confirmed. Neuhausen told him "that he finally had an instrument in his hand with which he could do something, and that we will see what he is going to make out of the bank."[276] He then went on to suggest something that was anything but promising and demonstrated that he had little understanding of banking. Neuhausen complained that the regulation of the Reichsmark clearing rate was determined by the Yugoslav National Bank alone and argued that the AJB should play a role in its determination. The Deutsche Bank official viewed this as utterly impossible because the amount involved averaged between 10 and 20 million RM, and the AJB did not have the liquid means to acquire significant amounts of Reichsmark receivables of Yugoslav exporters, quite aside from the loss of interest and the exchange rate risks.

The Belgians, of course, were not privy to these intentions, which they most certainly would have deplored, but they did tell the CA that they were "unpleasantly surprised" by the decision to nominate and elect Neuhausen, and they reiterated their position on the need for Yugoslav leadership and nonpolitical appointments. They reminded the CA of how suspicious and mistrustful the Yugoslav public was and pointed out that the bank could not fulfill its mission as a supplier of credit if it lost its depositors. They could not understand how or why the CA should depart from tried and true principles, and while they claimed to have nothing against Neuhausen personally, they would only vote for a nonpolitical and native Yugoslav for the presidency.[277]

At this point, the problem for Ramlot and his colleagues was how to make the best of a bad situation at the impending shareholders' meeting in mid-August while at the same time dealing with these developments and their implications for their position in the AJB. On July 24, Ramlot met with Joham and once again emphasized how astonished the Belgians were to have been presented with a fait accompli despite the fact that they were so large a shareholder. Clearly, "one intended to leave the previous path of loyal collaboration," and the Belgians anticipated an offer for their shares payable in a Western currency. In the meantime, however, they wished to have their rights as a business partner respected. In view of Neuhausen's prestige, they were prepared to vote for his joining the administrative council but would vote only for Radosavljević for the presidency. Joham proposed that the Belgians come to Vienna and meet Neuhausen personally in the hope that personal contact would allay their reservations and possibly even pave the way for Neuhausen's acceptance of their proposal. As for Belgian shares, Ramlot turned down the idea of selling them to the CA because it had given an option to the BUB, which was being confirmed during Ramlot's visit to Prague.[278]

At the beginning of August, however, there was little movement on the Neuhausen question because both Fischböck and Neuhausen himself would not budge on the issue of the presidency. Hasslacher was especially worried that the Belgians would be alienated by this stubbornness and told Olscher: "Avoiding this now lies not only in the interest of the Deutsche Bank, which is befriended with the Belgians, but it is especially necessary for the CA, which itself of course remains dependent on foreign connections – quite aside from the fact that the Belgians have always gladly offered their services also with regard to the western banks."[279]

---

275 Ibid.
276 Ibid.
277 Ibid., Galopin to the CA management board, July 19, 1939.
278 See ibid., report of Joham, July 24, 1939; BUB to Société Générale de Belgique, July 24, 1939, and undated report by Rösler to Abs.
279 Ibid., Hasslacher to Olscher, Aug. 7, 1939. Hasslacher sent a copy to Abs, assuming incorrectly that Abs was directly involved in the negotiations planned for the 12th. See ibid., Abs to Hasslacher, Aug. 9, 1939.

He appealed to Olscher to intervene so that the projected discussions with the Belgians in Vienna scheduled for August 12 would result in a compromise. If Neuhausen would agree to the vice-presidency, perhaps by the inducement of more money, the Belgians might be pacified and there would be calm at the AJB. That might be a way to escape the consequences of what Hasslacher described as a "perhaps too hasty and one-sided action."

Abs, who Hasslacher erroneously thought would be at the August 12 meeting, and who clearly shared Hasslacher's view, was much relieved when he finally got to Vienna on August 14 to learn from Fischböck that the meeting with Ramlot had ended satisfactorily. The Belgians agreed to vote for Neuhausen's appointment to the administrative council but to abstain in the vote on his appointment to the presidency, while Radosavljević would be invited to join the administrative council as vice-president; if he declined, Berkowitz, already a member of the council, would assume the vice-presidency. Abs would also be elected to the Council as representative of the BUB. A decision was taken not to establish an executive committee but rather to "secure the majority influence of the Creditanstalt through the appointments to the management board." As shall be shown, this was not only important for the Germanization but also for the Aryanization of the bank.[280]

As things turned out, however, both the administrative council and the general shareholders' meeting on August 15, 1939, turned out, at least superficially, to be less problematic than anticipated. At the shareholders' meeting, the resignations of Otto Freund, Edmond Goldschmidt, and Milan Marić were formally announced. Ramlot used the occasion to give special praise to Goldschmidt, whose resignation was attributed to the "known reasons."[281] At the same time, Abs, Fritscher, and Neuhausen were nominated to the council and then received

unanimous approval at the general shareholders' meeting that followed the council meeting. Interestingly, the unanimity was justified by the past practice of avoiding even the appearance of one group of stockholders outvoting another by having those nominated voted in unanimously. Furthermore, a vote on the appointment of officers for the administrative council was also avoided. While it was originally intended to have another administrative council meeting following the shareholders' meeting, it turned out that the Yugoslav minister of commerce first had to approve the elections and register the new members. A formal election could not be held under these circumstances, and Ramlot announced that the shareholders had agreed to settle these matters in friendly discussions and that the outcome would be announced once the legal formalities had been fulfilled. It was not until the administrative council meeting on December 2, 1940 that Neuhausen was formally elected president on a motion by Abs while Joham stayed on as vice president.[282]

By that time, important changes had taken place in the ownership of the AJB and in the composition of its personnel. While the actual sale of the 45 percent share held by the Belgian and Swiss banks was not to take place until September 1940, the outbreak of the war in September 1939, the offensive in the West in the spring of 1940, and the occupation of Belgium significantly changed the position of the Société Général in the AJB before it sold its shares. At its July 9, 1940, meeting, therefore, the working committee of the CA decided to "practically exclude the administrative council members sent by the Société Général de Belgique and also to have no further reports on the bank transmitted to them."[283] As Fritscher reported to the RWM shortly thereafter, "Naturally the Belgians are presently completely excluded from any influence on the administration of the Jugoslawische Bankverein. This fact has been

[280] Ibid., memo by Abs, Aug. 14, 1939.
[281] The protocols of both the administrative council and shareholders' meetings of Aug. 15, 1939, are to be found in AJ, AJB, 151/2/2.

[282] Ibid., administrative council meeting of Dec. 2, 1940.
[283] BA-CA, CA-V, working committee meeting of July 9, 1940.

used by us to terminate all Jewish personnel including the Jewish managing directors."[284]

Fritscher himself had taken this matter in hand at the July 12 meeting of the AJB administrative council where he announced "that in view of the decisive German participation in our institution, it appears necessary to carry out the Aryanization of the personnel of our bank," and presented a resolution that by December 31, 1940, the bank would only employ Aryan personnel.[285] One Yugoslav member of the council, Ljubljana lawyer Ivo Benković, explicitly accepted the proposal "in principle." He pointed out that this meant eliminating 40 out of 150 employees, including directors, vice-directors, and section heads, in a very short time and would involve substantial costs. He believed that it would have been better to delay the deadline to the middle of 1941, to strive to encourage voluntary resignations, and to be as liberal as possible in dealing with those who agreed to depart. Apparently, this proposal was seriously debated, but the decision was unanimous for Fritscher's proposal after George Saal warned against delaying matters, especially from the standpoint of the "psychological" effect of such a delay, especially on those affected, and argued that the leadership deficit could be made up for by persons already in the ranks of the bank. It was Saal, however, who was assigned the task of dismissing the Jews at the bank and its branches, among them the long-time director in Belgrade, David Hochner, and the director in Zagreb, Mavro Kandel. He also had to replace as many key persons as possible, and it goes without saying that ethnic Germans and other Aryans applied for the newly opened positions once news of the Aryanization of the bank's personnel was known.[286]

As such job-seeking vultures were descending on the AJB, more weighty ones were scrambling for the shares that would be available once the Belgians and Swiss sold their holdings. To the great irritation of the CA, for example, Dresdner Bank Director Hans Pilder had privately negotiated with the Belgians about purchasing their shares.[287] The CA's own negotiations with the Belgians had proven to be difficult. In January 1940, Joham negotiated with Ramlot in Zagreb about the sale of the shares and, on Fischböck's instructions, offered 5 Swiss francs per share, which was 25 percent of their market value. Ramlot rejected the offer as totally insufficient and demanded 15 Swiss francs per share. An important factor in the situation, however, was that the RWM's ministerial director, Gustav Schlotterer, an SS man and a major figure in economic policy making, was in a position to supply foreign exchange for the purpose of making the purchase at a higher price than Joham had offered. The lack of foreign exchange had been the major stumbling block in getting the Belgians to sell, and it was Schlotterer's willingness to help out that had led the CA to reopen negotiations. Schlotterer thought the Belgians would settle on 10 Swiss francs, but Abs, who was also involved in the matter and knew what Schlotterer was prepared to release in foreign exchange, kept Joham in the dark and urged him not go much above his original offer while suggesting that 10 Swiss francs might be possible. Abs pushed this tactic because Ramlot was not authorized to make a deal, and it was better to have Ramlot report back a lower than a higher price to his colleagues.[288]

Apparently, the CA offered 9 Swiss francs per share, but the negotiations broke down because the Belgians continued to demand 15 Swiss francs and seem to have been emboldened by the competition for the shares from another large German bank, probably the Dresdner. In August, Fritscher told the RWM that the time

[284] DB, B 69, Fritscher to Martini (RWM), Aug. 9, 1940.

[285] AJ, AJB, 151/2/2, administrative council meeting, July 12, 1940.

[286] AJ, AJB, 151/90/115, Saal to Hochner, Aug. 18, 1940. This file also contains lists of those let go and new appointments as well as information on Aryanization costs. For job requests, see AJ, AJB, 151/90/116. See also BA-CA, CA-V, CA board of management meeting, May 14, 1940.

[287] Ibid., CA management board meeting, Dec. 11, 1939.

[288] DB, B 69, memorandum by Abs, Jan. 22, 1940, and BA-CA, CA-V, CA management board meeting, Jan. 9, 1940.

had come to renew the negotiations on the basis of the changed political situation, but he felt it important that the CA get guidelines for the negotiation from the RWM. Also, he felt that something needed to be done to strengthen the bank, whose 60 million dinar capital base and 407 million dinar balance seemed inadequate for the amount of German-Yugoslav business that could be expected. Much more capital was necessary in Fritscher's view, especially because the bank had bases in both Belgrade and Zagreb and, should Yugoslavia fall apart because of Serb-Croat conflict, it would be important that both parts of the bank continue to function smoothly in their respective states. Fritscher thus suggested three possibilities for expansion within Yugoslavia. The first would be to take over the Anglo-Prager Creditbank. This was considered a matter of pressing concern by both the Reich Protector's Office in Prague and Neuhausen, who viewed the bank as a nest of Free Masons who supported the former Czech leader Beneš. With branches in London and New York as well as Southeast Europe, the bank was also thought to favor the Allies. It had a capital of 14 million dinar and a balance of 300 million dinar. A second important option would be to reacquire the shares of the Jugoslawische Union-Bank that the CA had been forced to sell off in the reorganization of 1931. The shares were now in the hands of the Continentale Gesellschaft für Bank- und Industriewerte in Basel (Contvalor). The Union-Bank was somewhat larger than the AJB, having 60 million dinar in capital and a balance of 516 million dinar, and it also had branches in Belgrade and Zagreb. The CA was quite anxious to gain control over the bank and merge it with the AJB because of the Italian interest in it and the Italian desire to expand its interest in Croatia. Finally, the Yugoslav branches of the Živnostenská banka in Prague presented a third possibility for expansion. Fritscher believed that the Živnostenská banka was prepared to give the AJB a majority in these holdings if it could maintain a minority interest.[289]

The first order of business, however, remained the acquisition of the Belgian shares in the AJB. The final negotiations were conducted by Abs and by Director Alfred Kurzmeyer of the Deutsche Bank. A Swiss citizen and former official at the Mendelssohn Bank in Amsterdam, Kurzmeyer joined the Deutsche Bank in 1939 and worked closely with Abs on special assignments until the end of the war. He conducted the last phase of the negotiations with Callens, during which they agreed on the sale of 116,484 shares at the price the Belgians wanted, 15 Swiss francs, or 8 RM, per share. The purchase price of 994,773 RM was to be paid through the German-Belgian clearing arrangements by October 10. In addition, the Belgians asked for and received partial payment in the amount of 660,660 RM for monies held on account at the AJB. They were also to receive partial payment on the AJB's 1938 dividend, which had not been paid out, because the Belgians no longer had any interest in investing money in the bank. The Baseler Handelsbank was to retain its small holding. Ramlot and Gheude agreed to step down from the administrative council immediately so as to avoid the necessity of a vote at the AJB's next shareholders' meeting.[290] The fact that the payment to the Belgians, whose country was occupied, was now governed by a clearing arrangement with Germany meant, of course, that they were being paid in overvalued Reichsmark rather than Swiss francs.

With this agreement in place, the next issue was to allocate the newly acquired shares among the German banks that were interested in acquiring a stake in the AJB and to assign administrative council seats to their representatives. Although the CA had every intention of retaining its majority in the AJB, it was anxious to get the other German banks, especially the Dresdner Bank, to make exclusive use of the AJB for their Yugoslav business and, if possible, to put resources into the AJB. Fischböck had negotiated with Hans Pilder of the Dresdner

---

[289] DB, B 69, Fritscher to Martini, Aug. 9, 1940. On the Union-Bank, see also DB, P 6504, Bl. 59–60a, Joham to Riehle, Sept. 26, 1940.

[290] Ibid., undated memorandum by Kurzmeyer and confirmation by the Société Général, Sept. 17, 1940, and BA-CA, CA-V, report by Abs to the working committee of the CA, Sept. 3, 1940.

Bank about this in the fall, and learned that the Dresdner Bank was not only willing to use the AJB but had the prospect of actually putting some dinar into the AJB if it was successful in receiving monies from the Yugoslav state arising from prewar debts. Fischböck drew up an agreement to be made with the Dresdner Bank, promising it a 25 percent option on the shares it expected to acquire from the Belgians, and binding it to make exclusive use of the AJB in return for the option to purchase these share and to have a seat on the administrative council, but this never seems to have been sent.[291]

Even without a formal agreement, however, it was clear that the Dresdner Bank was going to get a portion of the shares. Abs knew this was unavoidable, but he wished to control the situation so far as possible. As the purchase of the Belgian shares was about to take place in the fall of 1940, he told the CA working committee that the CA must maintain its 51 percent stake in the AJB and that the Deutsche Bank was to receive no fewer shares than the Dresdner Bank in the division of the sale of newly acquired shares. In addition, "it is further agreed that the Dresdner Bank, if its inclusion in the administrative council cannot be avoided, should at any rate get only one seat, whereby, however, it would be well advised to exclude the person of Dr. Pilder."[292] Whether this distaste was because of Pilder's aggressiveness or because of other traits, is difficult to say, but Abs certainly found sharing with the Dresdner Bank hard to swallow.

The Dresdner Bank was not alone in claiming a seat at the table. The BUB and its ambitious director, Walther Pohle, were also laying claim to a place, even challenging the primacy of Vienna. In a letter to Abs, he argued that the industrial sector of Bohemia-Moravia had close connections with Yugoslavia and that industrial interests had to take priority where previously

Vienna had the central role in monetary and trade relations with the southeast. The BUB had to cultivate industrial relations with Yugoslavia, and that made it necessary "to have a firm position in a leading bank."[293] Pohle emphasized that the BUB was in no position to compete in Germany, so that the southeast had to be its logical goal, but there it also faced considerable competition from other banks in the former Czechoslovakia. The BUB had been successful in holding on to its 3.4 percent stake in the AJB despite Société Générale's attempts to purchase it in the past and had given it an option, and the BUB assumed that the Société Générale would have given the BUB a first option on its shares because of their old connection. Instead, it had sold to the CA, but the BUB now expected a suitable portion of the Belgian shares because the BUB had loyally backed the politics of the CA in the AJB, especially the renunciation of a dividend for 1938. The BUB had also invited a CA representative on its supervisory board and had helped give the CA its position in Slovakia. Furthermore, the BUB needed a position commensurate with its business in Yugoslavia and certainly a stronger one than the Reichs-Kredit-Gesellschaft, which was also seeking a stake. Fundamentally, Pohle was asking the Deutsche Bank to support its position over and against the CA, claiming that it was in the interest of the Deutsche Bank to strengthen the BUB.

Abs dismissed Pohle's complaints about the Belgians' failure to give the BUB an option on its shares, pointing out that it was the Deutsche Bank that did the negotiating for the CA. He also reported that the Dresdner Bank would be represented on the AJB supervisory board by Pilder – apparently Abs had no luck in keeping Pilder out – and that the Deutsche Bank would be represented as well. Furthermore, it was necessary to bring the RKG in because of the VIAG's role in the ownership of the CA. Abs did agree, however, to ask the CA to increase and round out the BUB position and subsequently promised to ensure that the BUB

[291] See DB, B 69, Pilder to Fischböck, Sept. 29, 1939; Fischböck to Pilder, Oct. 2, 1939; Pilder to Fischböck, Oct. 5, 1939; Fischböck to Pilder, Oct. 7, 1939, and agreement, but with handwritten notation that it had not be sent.

[292] BA-CA, CA-V, working committee of the CA, Sept. 3, 1940.

[293] DB, B 69, BUB to Abs, Oct. 8, 1940.

continued to have its representation on the administrative council.

By the end of 1940, decisions could be taken on the new members for the administrative council. The new appointees were Pilder, who represented the Dresdner Bank, Guido Schmidt, to represent the Hermann Göring Werke in Berlin, Reichsbank Director Jacobus Soengen, who had been posted to the Yugoslav National Bank in Belgrade, and Dragan Tomljenović of the "Juganil" KG in Belgrade, which belonged to IG Farben. A decision was made to include representatives of major industrial interests as well as Pilder.[294] At this point in time, the CA controlled 88.5 percent of the AJB shares because the shares bought from the Belgians had not yet been sold off. The issue of quotas, however, remained a problem because the RKG was demanding the right to purchase some portion of the Belgian shares. Pilder, however, strongly objected to any diminution of the Dresdner Bank position, and Abs agreed that the Dresdner Bank and the Deutsche Bank did the most business in Yugoslavia and that the RKG was a minor player by comparison. Most importantly, now that the Dresdner Bank had agreed to enter a condominium with the Deutsche Bank in the AJB, it was important to maintain its loyalty. He thus proposed at the end of December that the Dresdner Bank and the Deutsche Bank hold 15 percent of the AJB shares and the RKG get 7.5 percent.[295] At the beginning of 1941, a new complication arose when Eugen Bandel of the Commerzbank entered the picture and asked to be included among the German banks invested in the AJB. Bandel had contacted Pilder and Neuhausen about this request, and Riehle of the RWM made no objections. It worried Abs, however, who felt that there were too many participants in the AJB, which lacked the capital and capacity to service everyone. Another danger was that Pilder believed that all these problems could be solved by the CA renouncing its position as majority shareholder, a proposition Abs totally opposed. Nevertheless, Abs decided to play the honest broker and proposed a new division of the shares formerly held by the Belgians whereby the Deutsche Bank and the Dresdner Bank each would hold 12.5 percent of the total AJB capital, and the Commerzbank and the RKG were to each get 6.25 percent of the share capital. Subsequently, the Deutsche Bank, which had negotiated with the Belgians for the sale of the shares to the CA, also bought them from the CA and sold them on its behalf to the banks and, in the process, made a profit of 104,000 RM for its services.[296]

At the same time, measures were being taken to increase the capitalization of the bank. The most important step was the increase of its share capital from 60 million to 100 million dinars at the shareholders' meeting on December 2. Neuhausen also contributed to improving the bank's liquidity by offering to deposit the 15 million dinars the Reichsbank had put at his disposal through the Yugoslav National Bank; the offer was accepted.[297] Concerning the Jugoslawische Union bank, negotiations were undertaken by Joham in the fall of 1940 with Contvalor, while the issue of the Prager Kreditbank branch in Belgrade was caught between the desires of the AJB to take it over and the wishes of the BUB and the Protectorate authorities. The issue of the Yugoslav branches of the Živnostenská banka in Prague no longer seemed so problematic by the end of the year. In any case, conditions for the AJB were to change radically in 1941.

The CA in the Former Yugoslavia

Although German political and business interests in Yugoslavia were well aware of the kingdom's instability and, as has been shown, took precautionary measures for the event that a separate Croatian entity were created, the friendly relations between Germany and the Yugoslav regime seemed to offer a measure of stability

[294] AJ, AJB, 151/2/2, meeting of Dec. 2, 1940. It is unclear whom Soengen represented.
[295] DB, B 69, Abs to CA, Dec. 10, 1940.
[296] Ibid., memoranda by Abs, Jan. 23, 1941; Bandel to Abs, Jan. 29, 1941; memorandum by Abs, Feb. 10, 1941.
[297] BA-CA, CA-V, CA management board meeting, May 27, 1940.

for the pursuit of German economic interests. All this was changed by the demonstrations and military coup following Yugoslavia's signing of the Tripartite Pact in late March 1941. Hitler thereupon resolved to destroy the Yugoslav state. Belgrade was bombed, and the Germans invaded in early April. None of this was conducive to normal business. As in the cases of Czechoslovakia and Poland, the tearing apart of a nation inevitably created complicated banking problems made all the more difficult by the aspirations of the major banks.

Yugoslavia had already been threatened with dissolution because of the tensions between Serbs and Croats, and the German invasion enabled the creation of a puppet state of Croatia under the murderous anti-Semitic and anti-Serb leadership of the Catholic-fascist Ustasha. Needless to say, the division of the country had implications for the banking situation. The old arrangement had obviously been advantageous for the CA, which had a majority share in the only German bank in the former Yugoslavia. Joham was anxious to maintain this situation under the new circumstances and to prevent the Dresdner Bank from establishing an independent position in Croatia. On May 9, 1941, Joham met in Marburg/Maribor with Riehle and other Berlin officials from the Banking Supervision Office and the RFM to discuss these problems. There appeared to be a consensus that the AJB should be divided into two independent banks because the Croats no longer wished to have a bank in common with the Serbs. A new bank was to be established in Agram/Zagreb that would take over the Agram/Zagreb branch of the AJB, and the AJB was to remain in Belgrade in its existing form with a new name. Hasslacher, Rafelsberger, and Neuhausen, who was now Plenipotentiary for the Economy in Serbia, had laid down guidelines for the new banking arrangements. They agreed that in Croatia, as in Serbia, there would be only one German bank; in both cases, the CA would take the lead position, but other major German banks would be allowed to participate as minority shareholders. The new bank in Croatia would be called the Kroatischer Bankverein AG and have a capital of 1 million

dinar and reserves of about 20 million dinars. The parties involved were inclined to have the composition of the leading shareholders modeled on the Belgrade bank. In short, the banks were to be parallel institutions. Joham took these discussions as a signal to have statutes drawn up for the Croatian bank by a lawyer with the object of creating a new entity that would then take over the AJB's Croatian branch. Under this arrangement, the CA would dominate two banks in the former Yugoslavia. There were, to be sure, other changes. Because of the new territorial arrangements benefiting Hungary, the AJB branch in Neusatz/Ujvidek/Novi-Sad was to be separated from the AJB and given to the CA branch in Budapest, but this was effectively a transfer within the CA group. Less fortunate from the CA's perspective was the Italian takeover of the AJB branch in Laibach/Ljubljana, which was now in Italian-occupied territory, although plans were afoot to reestablish CA interests there. Joham doubted that there would be much basis for expanding the branches of the AJB, except perhaps in Nish/Niš, but he had high hopes for the acquisition of the Prager Creditbank branch in Belgrade, a plan supported by Riehle and Neuhausen as well as the Jugoslawische Unionbank, the Banque Franco-Serbe, and the Jugoslavenska Banka. This would enable the AJB to make up its losses in Croatia. As for the new Kroatischer Bankverein, it would have to build up a branch network in Croatia once the borders were settled. At the same time, the CA anticipated that it would acquire the Kroatische Gewerbebank, whose proprietary institution was the Böhmische Industrialbank, and the Jugoslavenska banka. The Dresdner Bank was out to acquire the latter bank, but Joham was hopeful that the common sentiment in Berlin and Zagreb about there being only one German bank in Croatia "would make the competition efforts by the Dresdner Bank meaningless."[298]

---

[298] BA-CA, CA-V, report by Joham at the CA working committee meeting, May 23, 1941. This report is also to be found in RGVA Moscow, 1458/9/139, Bl. 39–44.

The Dresdner Bank used its influence in Berlin to gain permission to secure its own bank in Croatia, however, while it continued to be represented on the supervisory board of the Belgrade bank, which was renamed the Bankverein AG. This meant, however, that the Dresdner Bank would give up claims to be represented in the Kroatische Bankverein. As a result, 12.5 percent of the new shares were available, and Abs proposed that the BUB get a part or even all of these shares. Nonetheless, the difficulty with this proposal was that the RKG wished to increase its shares in the Kroatische Bankverein over what it held in the Belgrade bank by 6.25 percent, and this would inevitably lead the Commerzbank to ask for parity with the RKG. At the same time, the BUB too, encouraged by Abs, would ask to increase its stake. From Joham's perspective, the most important thing was to maintain the CA majority and to ensure that the Deutsche Bank group – CA, Deutsche Bank, and BUB – held three-quarters of the shares in Agram/Zagreb. (The group held 92.3 percent of the shares in Belgrade.) In the final arrangement, the CA held 55 percent of the shares, the Deutsche Bank 15 percent, and the BUB, RKG, and Commerzbank 10 percent each.[299]

Like Slovakia and Hungary, the new satellite state of Croatia, which was ferociously nationalistic and bigoted, sought to defend its interests in every way possible. Accordingly, Joham explained to Abs on October 27 that the new Bankverein in Agram still had not been formally established because of differences between the German and Croatian governments and because the interest-free loan of 100,000,000 Croatian kuna (5 million RM) transferred by the CA to found the Agram/Zagreb bank had been put in a blocked account by the Croatian State Bank. The Croats seemed to feel that this would have made it the highest

capitalized of all the Croatian banks, although these had raised their capital in the meantime. Then there was the issue of CA claims against the Croatian Bankverein of 47 million kuna denominated in Reichsmark. To cover the exchange rate risk and reduce the debt, the Croatians were asking the CA to raise its capital transfer to 125,000,000 kuna. While the Croats did not contest the fact that the chief shareholders were German, they were also pushing for participation by the Bosnische Landesbank, which would have to take place at the expense of the German shareholders. Finally, the Croats were demanding that two-thirds of the administrative council members be Croat nationals. Joham thought that could be avoided by promising that Croat interests would be respected by a council with more Germans and by appointing Nikola Berković of Sarajevo as president of the Bosnische Landesbank with Joham serving as vice-president.[300]

These matters were finally settled at the end of the year, when the CA petitioned Riehle for support in making a loan of 125,000,000 kuna to the Bankverein für Kroatia AG, Agram and to allow the transfer of 1,820,000 RM to its Reichsmark account at the Bankverein.[301] At the first administrative council meeting on March 30, 1942, four Croat businessmen and one Croat official held half the seats, and the remaining five positions were held by German bankers: Joham, Abs, Bandel (Commerzbank), Pohle, and Rohdewald. Berković became president, and the Landesbank für Bosnien und Herzegowina was made a small shareholder with a 1 million kuna stake. The supervisory board was composed of four Croats and the CA official who had functioned in a similar capacity in Belgrade, Georg Tengler.[302] One of the two previous managers in Agram/Zagreb, Director Favale, departed, and Director Juraj Pajanović stayed on. The CA decided to add someone

[299] RGVA Moscow, 1458/9/138, Bl. 151–152, CA to Deutsche Bank, June 20, 1941; Ulrich to Abs, July 19, 1941; Ulrich to Rösler, Aug. 15, 1941; Ulrich to Pohle, Sept. 19, 1941, DB, B 69 and chart showing German bank participations in the Southeast, Feb. 1942.

[300] DB, P 6504, Bl. 310–312, Joham to Abs, Oct. 27, 1941.

[301] RGVA Moscow, 1458/9/139, Bl. 120–122, CA to Riehle, Dec. 18, 1941.

[302] AJ, AJB 151/3/3, meeting of the administrative council and constituent assembly of the Bankverein, March 30, 1942.

from its own ranks in the person of Wilhelm Rauber of the Bank für Kärnten.[303] At the time of its founding, there were plans afoot for the Bankverein für Kroatia to take over 40 percent of the shares of the Landesbank für Bosnien und Herzegovina, but this was subsequently vetoed by the Croatian government in another demonstration of its independence.[304]

A far more aggravating illustration of Croatian economic nationalism, however, was the Croatian government's treatment of foreign shareholders in the S.H. Gutmann Aktiengesellschaft in Belišće. This enterprise, which had its origins in Vienna and was run by a branch of the Gutmann family, was the largest owner of private forests and the leading wood producer in Croatia. It also produced wood by-products, railroad ties, and barrels; owned stone quarries; and had carp fisheries that provided 500,000 kilograms of carp to Germany. It had built a railroad to carry its production to nearby Esseg and was highly mechanized in its production. Its costs were low, its production high, and most of the original investment came from the Gutmanns. The capital amounted to 40 million dinars, composed of 200,000 shares worth 200 dinar each. No more than 25 percent were in Croatian hands, and the remaining 75 percent were held outside Croatia. The CA already held some shares, but when Croatia was created as an independent state, it proceeded to buy up a majority stake. Fundamentally, the CA viewed the enterprise as primarily foreign owned, not Croatian. Nevertheless, the CA had kept the Croatian authorities and the German embassy in Agram/Zagreb informed and tried to assure Economics Minister Košak that the CA intended to work hand in hand with the Croatian authorities in running the enterprise. Košak viewed the matter differently, seeing Croatian control of S.H. Gutmann as a matter of national interest, and rather blatantly tried to exclude the Germans. He demanded that the shareholders change their shares into named shares denominated in kuna in the limited time before the shareholders' meeting scheduled for August 3. The major item of business was an increase of the capital by 60 million kuna. Shares that had not been converted were considered invalid and their votes could not be cast. At the same time, the government acquired the new shares on its own behalf. As a result, the 86,583 CA shares could not be voted and indeed appeared totally worthless, while the government assumed full control of what was to be renamed the Forstindustrie AG Hasslacher, "representing" the Bankhaus Gebrüder Gutmann, which had two apparently legitimate voting shares, and pathetically and vainly protested both the exclusion of most of the foreign shareholders and the raising of the capital by a Croatian minority of shareholders. Subsequently, the CA and other foreign shareholders protested to the German embassy and to the RWM in Berlin.[305]

The CA had placed too much faith in German Ambassador SA-Obergruppenführer Siegfried Kasche. He took the view that the Croatian government had the law on its side despite the CA's claims that it had fulfilled the requirements. Furthermore, as he telegraphed Berlin, he had informed representatives of the CA that "I do not intend to exercise political pressure on the Croatian Government on behalf of German interested parties, since the nationalization effort, especially with respect to landed properties, forests, etc., which has been carried out by the Croatian Government in connection with Aryanization, represents a justified measure that does not restrict crucial German interests. The silviculturally warranted exploitation of the forests will be secured through the Croatian State."[306] While the

---

[303] BA-CA, CA-V, CA working committee, May 21, 1941.

[304] Ibid., CA working committee meetings of Aug. 12, 1941, and Jan. 9, 1942.

[305] See RGVA Moscow, 1458/9/139, Bl. 72–80, 86–97, CA to Klucki, Aug. 13, 1941; CA to Lange, Aug. 8, 1941; CA protest to the General Assembly of S.H. Gutmann, and meeting of the General Assembly on Aug. 3, 1941.

[306] StA Nürnberg, Nr. 4928, Kasche to the Foreign Office, Aug. 5, 1941. On Kasche, see Ernst Klee, *Das Personenlexikon zum Dritten Reich. Wer war was vor und nach 1945* (Frankfurt a.M. 2003), p. 299. Kasche played a big role in the Croatian Holocaust and was hanged in Zagreb in 1947.

Croatian government did not promise the CA compensation, it did promise to satisfy German wood requirements, and Kasche suggested to the CA that the only way the CA might get some kind of recompense for the "legal situation created by the Croatian Government" would be to come to a negotiated arrangement. That apparently never happened. The evidence suggests, rather, that the Croatian government promised to let the CA take the case to court but created obstacles that made it impossible to do so. Given the performance of the CA in its Aryanizations, the situation was not without some piquancy, and the Croatians were clearly the superior swindlers. Even in August 1944, the Reich Banking Economic Group was complaining to the RWM about various measures taken by the Croatian government to mistreat German shareholders.[307]

It was certainly easier to deal with an occupied people, at least in the short run, and the situation in Belgrade required a great deal less consideration for the local inhabitants. The German invasion created a situation of high liquidity but little business activity and much uncertainty. The AJB, of course, had to be "refounded" under the new circumstances, and this was done at the general meeting of shareholders on February 28, 1942, where the name was changed to Bankverein AG.[308] The composition of the administrative council was left basically unchanged. Georg Saal remained on as general director, but an Austrian official of the CA, Ludwig Sehn, was appointed to work with him. The forty-eight-year-old Sehn was far from happy at finding himself in Belgrade; he had to live apart from his wife in a city and country that had suffered considerable destruction. As he resignedly wrote to a friend, "I see my task above all, as a German in an exposed post, to be unreservedly in the service of my homeland."[309]

The CA seemed to view its participation in the Bankverein in Belgrade in the same way. It chose to book its shares in the bank at half their nominal value, that is, at 5 RM rather than 10 RM for every share worth 200 dinars. This was justified by the fact that the bank had not paid a dividend since 1930, with the exception of 1937, when it paid 4 percent, and in 1938, when its shareholders decided to forgo the 4 percent dividend to increase the bank's resources. Investment in the bank had thus never been lucrative and was now certainly unlikely to be so after the destruction wrought by the war and the depreciation of the dinar to 20:1. Nonetheless, the major shareholders had decided to uphold the prewar decision to raise the capital of the bank from 60 to 100 million dinars – a decision confirmed at the shareholders' meeting on February 28, 1942 – "in order to maintain and promote German economic connections to the southeastern region."[310] Needless to say, this was a reduction of the real value of the investment as well, but it was justified by the bad economic situation and the unsettled status of the debt of the former Yugoslav state.

On the more positive side, the Bankverein could now add to its assets thanks to the insistence of the authorities on a consolidation of the banks in Serbia. Indeed, the Belgrade branch of the Prager Creditbank, a modern banking institution with a good staff, was allowed to continue operations only if it were eventually to merge with the Bankverein. In practical terms, this meant the Bankverein could carry out its plans to take over the Jugoslawische Unionbank, into whose quarters the Bankverein was moving, and the Belgrade branch of the Prager Creditbank, which belonged to the BUB. The earlier plan to take over the Jugoslawenska banka was set aside because the Dresdner Bank was now planning to lay claim to that bank, a step that eventually would lead it to drop out of the Bankverein administrative council and to its participation in the bank. Taking over the Prager Creditbank branch proved a rather complicated affair; the

---

[307] See RGVA Moscow, 1458/9/178, Bl. 15–19, Economic Group Banking to RWM, Aug. 5, 1944, and its complaint concerning the handling of CA legal claims of Feb. 4, 1942.

[308] DB, B 69, general shareholders' meeting of the AJB, Feb. 28, 1942.

[309] AJ, AJB, 151/5/5, Sehn to Firma Schindler & Co., Vienna, July 25, 1942.

[310] DB, B 69, CA note of March 6, 1942, and notice of March 26, 1942.

negotiations in Prague for the assessment of its worth and other problems dragged on through 1942. The merger did not formally take place until June 1943. In March 1943, the Bankverein also took over the Belgrade branch of the Laibach/Ljubljana-based Kreditanstalt für Handel und Industrie. In any case, these acquisitions further increased the size and role of the Bankverein.[311]

The CA had thus established itself as the leading German shareholder in the major banks of Serbia and Croatia, and it also picked up important assets in the former Slovenian territories occupied and then annexed by the Reich. On April 18, 1941, the RWM instructed the CA to set up offices in these areas to pay wages and salaries and to provide operating credits of up to 5 million RM, later reduced to 3.5 million RM as a result of reduced need, that would be guaranteed by the Reich. The CA acted immediately, instructing its branch in Graz to set up offices in Marburg/ Maribor and Cilli/Celje, and also instructing its branch in Klagenfurt to set up an office in Krainburg/Kranj. In mid-May, the head of the civilian administration of Lower Styria authorized the CA to set up branches in Marburg/ Maribor and Cilli/Celje, and his counterpart in Carinthia authorized the establishment of a branch in Krainburg/Kranj and a special branch office in Veldes/Bled. These branches were established by taking over and liquidating local branches of other banks, those of the Laibacher Kreditbank AG in Marburg/Maribor, Cilli/Celje, Pettau/Ptuj, Windischgräz/Slovenj Gradec, and Krainburg/ Kranj; the branch of the Jugoslawische Unionbank in Marburg/Maribor; the branch of the Erste Kroatische Sparkasse in Cilli/Celje; the Genossenschaftliche Wirtschaftsbank AG in Krainburg/Kranj and Veldes/Bled; and the Cillier Creditanstalt AG, Cilli/Celje with its

branch in Marburg/Maribor. The Länderbank Wien was less favored than the CA because the latter had more extensive Balkan interests, but it did receive a branch in Marburg/Maribor, which was composed of the Marburg/Maribor branches of the Erste Kroatische Sparkasse and the Genossenschaftliche Wirtschaftsbank.[312]

Finally, the CA entertained ambitions in Laibach/Ljubljana, which was under the control of the Italians, but these were continually frustrated. Both the Credito Italiano and the Banco die Roma had moved in, and the Bankverein Agram had a branch in Laibach/Ljubljana. Initially, Joham thought it might be a good idea to put an Italian on the Bankverein Agram administrative council in order to increase collaboration. There was also discussion of creating a bank in Trieste in which the Italians and the CA would have a participation of 40 percent each, while the Croats would get 20 percent. This, however, came to naught. Another possible project, proposed by Italian banker and former CA administrative council member Alberto D'Agostino, was to establish a bank in Laibach/Ljubljana, half of which would be owned by the CA and the other half of which would be owned by the Banca Nazionale de Lavoro. Abs urged Joham to follow up this idea, especially if such a bank could extend its range beyond Laibach/Ljubljana. This was another effort by the Deutsche Bank to use the CA as a wedge into an area of Southeast Europe controlled by the Italians, but time would show that the Italian-German relationship did not have much of a future.[313]

---

[311] AJ, AJB, 151/5/5, Joham to Saal, June 12, 1941; ibid., AJ, AJB, 151/3/3, Abs pressed strongly for the conclusion of the negotiations in Prague at the administrative council meeting of May 4, 1942, and their completion was announced in the April 1944 report of the administrative council.

[312] See BA-CA, CA-V, the report by Pfeiffer at the CA working committee meeting of May 23, 1941, and the more detailed account by Ulrike Zimmerl, "Regionalbanken im Nationalsozialismus: Die Instrumentalisierung österreichischer Geldinstitute in den Bundesländern," in Gerald D. Feldman / Oliver Rathkolb / Theodor Venus / Ulrike Zimmerl, *Österreichische Banken und Sparkassen im Nationalsozialismus und in der Nachkriegszeit*, vol. 2 (Munich 2006), pp. 13–258. On the Dresdner Bank, see Chapter 6, pp. 506–507 in this volume.

[313] See DB, P 6504, Joham to Abs, Oct. 27, 1941, and BA-CA, CA-V, CA working committee meeting, June 10, 1942.

The Business of the CA-controlled Banks in the Former Yugoslavia

This is not the place to provide a full account of the business of the banks in Belgrade, Agram/Zagreb, and the annexed areas of Slovenia, but something should be said about banking there between 1941 and 1944.

In the case of the Bankverein Belgrade, the occupation ushered in the bank's involvement in the anti-Semitic measures of the Military Commanders Southeast. As has been shown, the bank had already rid itself of Jewish employees, but now it became a party to the despoliation of the Serbian Jews. On June 21, 1941, the Bankverein, following the instructions of Neuhausen to all Serbian banks, sent a list of its Jewish customers and their assets. At the same time, it cautioned that it was not always aware of which firms and persons were Jewish. The list included accounts small and large, as well as clients' securities holdings and life insurance policies. Among the individuals listed, for example, were the long-time director of the bank, Alfred Hochner, and his wife, Wilhelmina. In April 1942, a further list of Jews with assets in the Jugoslawische Unionbank AG, which had been taken over by the Bankverein, was issued. In July 1942, one-quarter of the deposits with the bank were "Jewish monies." At the same time, the systematic confiscation of Jewish assets by the authorities posed a problem for the Bankverein because it had given credits and lines of credits to Jewish-owned firms that antedated the war. Manifestly, these debts were unpayable under the circumstances, and on May 15, 1942, the Bankverein wrote to the office of the General Plenipotentiary for the Economy in Serbia asking that liens be placed on the seized property of the Jews involved. In this way, one would "avoid damage to pure German capital, which is the owner of our bank." A few days later, the Commissarial Administration of Jewish House and Landed Property, Belgrade assured the Bankverein that it would give priority to the sale of Jewish property against whose owners the bank had claims.[314] It is hard to tell how much the Bankverein received in this manner because it was still asking for money from Jewish property sales in 1943 and, at the end of the year, was allowed to claim 89,409 dinars from the military administration's account bearing the total "Aryanization receipts." In October 1944, however, its claims on the office of the Head of Military Administration amounted to 72.2 million dinars for "Aryanization receipts."[315] The Bankverein did hold mortgages on a substantial number of properties belonging to Jews, but it is unclear from the records whether there were profitable foreclosures. At the same time, the bank did permit its pension fund to purchase an apartment building from the commissar's office for 7,760,000 dinars in May 1943.[316] It is also interesting to note that Georg Saal and his wife acquired a villa in Belgrade from the commissar's office that was formerly Jewish owned.[317] Finally, the bank also acted as an administrator of safety deposit boxes containing Jewish-owned securities, jewels, and other valuables, a service for which it charged fees.[318] Insofar as the contents of the safety deposit boxes at the Bankverein and other banks were not assessed and disposed of prior to late 1944, the chaotic situation led to their being transferred from Belgrade to Vienna, where they were placed at the CA. When the Reichsbank office in Vienna refused to take them under its wing and assess them, the Dorotheum agreed to undertake the task and to auction the contents off. Some of the jewelry and other valuables were sold for

---

[314] AJ, AJB, 151/16/32, Bankverein to General Plenipotentiary for the Economy in Serbia, May 15, 1942, and Commissarial Administration of Jewish House and Property Holders, Belgrade to the Bankverein, May 28, 1942. This file contains substantial material on the bank and anti-Jewish measures.

[315] Ibid., Chief of the Military Administration of the Military Commander Southeast to the Bankverein, Dec. 29, 1943, and AJ, AJB 151/16/132, report on the financial status of the Bankverein, Oct. 4, 1944. DB, P 11726, the report of Saal at the South-East Europe Conference in Vienna on July 15–17, 1942.

[316] AJ, AJB, 151/3/3, administrative council meeting of May 17, 1943.

[317] Ibid., AJ, AJB, 151/5/5, undated statement of the spring of 1942.

[318] Such cases can be found in ibid., AJ, AJB, 151/17, along with cases of jewelry deposits in ibid., AJ, AJB, 151/37.

dollars or Swiss francs. The Dorotheum collected 390,189.80 RM from the auction. The proceeds were placed in the CA account of the Trusteeship Administration of the Military Administration in Serbia.[319]

The major business of the bank was not, of course, these matters but rather the engagement in German industrial and commercial activities that had brought the Germans into Belgrade in the first place. The war and German occupation, however, had significantly affected the composition of this business, as the following table showing the distribution of credits given by the bank shows:

Branch	1942	1941
Banking and Credit Institutes	1.76%	2.49%
Mining and Smelting	45.06%	12.82%
Metal Processing and Trade	3.95%	9.74%
Chemicals	2.16%	3.79%
Textiles, Leather, Clothing, including trade with Raw Materials	3.58%	21.33%
Food Products, Grain, and Agricultural Products	36.23%	31.59%
Woodworking and Forest Products	1.31%	3.04%
Storage and Transport	0.47%	1.98%
Electrical Industry	0.61%	5.14%
Other	4.87%	8.28%[a]

[a] See AJ, AJB, 151/2/2, report of the administrative council, 1943.

Whereas mining and smelting and agricultural credits amounted to 44.41 percent in 1941, they constituted 81.29 percent of the credits in 1942, the increase for the mining and smelting category amounting to 32.24 percent, accounting for the lion's share of the change. Indeed, the accounts of the Serb mining companies – Antimon AG, the Bor copper mines, Jugo-Montan, Jugo-Asbest, and the Trepka mines – amounted to 522 million dinars at the end of 1942. The largest accounts were those of the Bor mines, amounting to 354 million dinars,

and Jugo-Montan, amounting to 111.1 million dinars. As Saal reported, the demands of the mining companies had been so great that the credit needs of wheat and food exporters to the Reich had to wait.[320] Neuhausen strongly supported these credits at a meeting of the administrative council in May 1943, pointing out that the Bor copper mines were in the hands of the Reich. Preussag, the Mansfelder Kupferhütte, and Südostmontan shared in the ownership. The last named company had recently been founded with a capital of 30 million RM. It belonged to the Reich, and was responsible for taking over, controlling, and expanding the mining resources of Yugoslavia. It had taken over Jugo-Montan. There were plans to greatly increase the production of the Bor mines, which Neuhausen declared to be "decisive for the war."[321] Although the Bankverein authorized a credit of 400 million dinars for the Bor mines in 1943, Neuhausen stressed that it was virtually guaranteed by the Reich and that he was instructing the Bankverein to pay 350 million dinars back as soon as possible.[322]

Neuhausen was in no way exaggerating the importance of the Bor mines, which produced 40 percent of the Reich's copper supply. Working conditions for the forced and slave laborers, including several thousand Hungarian Jews, deployed in the expansion of the mines were truly atrocious.[323] Securing labor was indeed a problem for Armaments Minister Speer and the Organisation Todt, which was in charge of much of the work, but there is no record of this having been discussed at the Bankverein in Belgrade. Joham apparently took Neuhausen at his word and reported back to the CA's working committee in early June 1943 that business had expanded at the

[319] See BAB, R 26VI, vol. 463, Gurski of the military administration in Serbia to Gramsch of the Four Year Plan Office, Oct. 12, 1944, and the extremely detailed report by Gurski of March 2, 1945.

[320] See ibid., AJ, AJB, 151/5/5, memorandum by Saal, Dec. 23, 1942.

[321] Ibid., AJ, AJB, 151/2/2, administrative council meeting, May 17, 1943.

[322] Ibid.

[323] Braham, *Politics of Genocide*, II, pp. 343–352. For an excellent discussion of the labor situation at the Bor mines, see Sabine Rutar, "Arbeit und Überleben in Serbien. Das Kupfererzbergwerk Bor im Zweiten Weltkrieg," in: *Geschichte und Gesellschaft* 31 (2005), pp. 101–134.

Bankverein to the tune of 500 million dinars largely because of the mining credits, but that substantial sums were expected to flow back that would become available for the bank's regular business, especially in financing food exports. At the end of October, however, he was far less sanguine, pointing out that the financial situation of the bank was greatly strained because the limited refinancing possibilities made it hard to satisfy the needs of exporters while the Bor mines continued to feed at the credit trough.[324] In mid-December, he wrote to the finance minister and pointed out that the credits to Bor granted by the Bankverein were intended to be operating credits that would be held in bounds and would not affect the operation of the bank. The situation was now such, however, that the bank could not fulfill other tasks important for the war effort: "We must emphasize hereby that all the financial wishes of German businesses arising from the import and export business with Serbia are concentrated at the Bankverein AG Belgrade and that the bank also has to bear the chief burden of financing the harvest, so that the maintenance of the liquidity of the bank requires special attention."[325] In Joham's view, the expansion of Bor could not be financed out of operating credits, which would be a very unhealthy banking policy, but rather out of investment credits. A consortium had been created for this purpose, and the 110 million RM involved were guaranteed by the Reich. Joham felt it essential that the Bankverein limit its operating credit for the Bor mines to 100 million dinars and asked the Reich to guarantee this amount. He seemed to have a good case because a consortium headed by the Deutsche Bank had granted the Bor two ten-year investment credits of 25 million RM in 1943 and then provided another two such credits in 1944, concluding with a 25 million RM credit in September 1944, that is, at a time when the Germans were abandoning the Bor region and moving their equipment home.

These consortia credits were guaranteed by the Reich, and while the CA was supposed to participate at a level of 3 percent, the Deutsche Bank agreed to absorb this holding, probably because it, through the Bankverein, was contributing enough to the cause already. That was certainly Joham's view, and on February 14, 1944, he sent yet another letter to the finance minister that was an almost exact replica of the one he had sent in December and asked for a meeting with the authorities and those in charge of the Bor mines. There is no record of a meeting, but a report on the financial situation of the bank in October 1944 shows that the Bankverein credit remained unsecured.[326]

In Serbia, as in Poland, one of the bank's primary functions was to finance the harvest and food exports and imports was a primary function of the bank, and doing so while servicing the mining industry was one of the enormous challenges it faced. The CA was the chief shareholder in the Vienna-based Südosteuropäische Getreide-Handels-Gesellschaft, and its principal holding in Serbia was the Cereal-Export AG, Pantschowa-Belgrade. The business had been very hard hit by the war in 1941, but it seemed to have recovered quite substantially in 1942. It was not only delivering wheat, oats, fruit, and sunflower seeds to the Reich and Italy, but it also played an important role in supplying foodstuffs to the military forces and to the German-administered mines and forests. Between 1942 and 1943, trade increased by 221.7 percent.[327] By October 1944, however, the financing of this trade had also become a problem. In the case of the Cereal-Export AG, the credit issue was solved by the fact that the CA guaranteed a substantial portion of the credits provided, which could hardly have been

---

[324] BA-CA, CA-V, CA working committee meeting, June 2, 1943, and Oct. 9, 1943.

[325] BA-CA, CA-V, S.P. Akten, Nr. 481, Joham and Buzzi to RFM, Dec. 17, 1943.

[326] DB, B 69, Joham to Pollems, Jan. 14, 1958; Minute by Miksch, Jan. 13, 1958; Joham to Finance Minister, Feb. 14, 1944, and ibid., report on status of the bank, Oct. 4, 1944.

[327] See AJ, AJB, 151/3/3, the 1942 and 1943 reports of the Sudosteuropäische Getreide-Handels-Aktiengesellschaft for the CA management board, and BA-CA, CA-V, the report on this trade by the Bankverein management board of April 1944.

a great consolation, but in this case the Bor mine company once again reared its ugly head because it had received 15 million in credits to buy foodstuffs from the Cereal AG and had initially contested the bills. Even the omnipresent and venerable Julius Meinl AG branch in Belgrade had not secured its 94.2 million dinar credit with goods because the approval from the Vienna head office had come too late![328]

The situation of the Bankverein had been deteriorating significantly since at least the spring of 1944, if not earlier, and the bank had also developed serious personnel problems. A major factor, of course, was the military situation. On April 16–17, the Orthodox Easter, the Allies conducted massive air raids on Belgrade and other Serbian cities. The raids shocked residents of Belgrade, who had apparently thought they would be spared by the Allies after the damage done by the German Stukas in 1941, and led to considerable panic and flight from the city. There was no electricity, and water and food were in short supply. Serious damage halted all economic activity for several days. The bank was open only two hours a day until things settled down.[329] These events, however, revealed major problems in the Bankverein's administration that attracted the attention of the authorities in Belgrade and Berlin. On April 28, CA Director Fritscher received a report from a CA official named Kamm that, in contradiction to the report issued by the Bankverein, most of the Serb banks had opened their doors and begun operations right after the bombing, while the Bankverein, which as a German bank should have set an example, seemed paralyzed. It limited withdrawals to 50,000 dinars and announced that new credits would not be issued. No one was consulted or asked for help and these measures made a terrible impression not only on German authorities and in business circles but also on their Serbian counterparts. To compound the problems, Director Sehn went off to Vienna and left Saal, who seems to have

been ailing and very confused, to his fate. The result was an unbearable situation and a stream of complaints about the bank's performance.[330]

Until this time, the CA management board seems to have held back from doing anything about complaints concerning Saal's increasing inability to function effectively, possibly because Sehn protected him.[331] Now, however, the head of the Military Administration warned that he would intervene. Riehle also insisted that something be done. Joham reported in the first week of May that Saal was being dismissed and ordered back to Vienna, where he continued to be paid to the end of the year. He died in Ybbs on December 24, 1944. Saal was replaced by Director Hans Böhm-Bawerk, the head of the CA Credit Department.[332] Joham was not certain this was sufficient, however, and he also believed that Sehn was not the right man in the right place, a view strengthened by reports on the situation in Belgrade from Pohle of the BUB. Some thought was given to sending Abs's talented personal assistant, Franz Heinrich Ulrich. As Joham described the situation: "I received the impression from the conversation with Herr Pohle that far more will be expected from the Bankverein AG Belgrade than a banker is normally in a position to perform. The manifold financing problems of the German companies that crop up daily and that the Bankverein is often expected to solve, even when the preconditions for bank credits do not exist, require

[330] RGVA, 158/9/140, Bl. 4–5, Kamm to Riehle, April 28, 1944.

[331] See AJ, AJB, 151/7/10, unsigned memorandum, most probably by Sehn on a conversation with Kamm, dated Vienna, April 24, 1944, of a conversation with Kamm in Belgrade on April 21 in which Kamm reported on conversations with Buzzi, Joham, and Fritscher, where he had the impression that they wished to get rid of Saal but were held back from doing so because Sehn protected him. Sehn pleaded comradeship and a desire to maintain it, but Kamm took the view that the bank came before friendship.

[332] See BA-CA, CA-V, S.P. Akten, Nr. 481, the telegram from the Military Administration Southeast to CA, May 3, 1944, and ibid., 6–8, the exchange of telegrams with Riehle at the beginning of May and Riehle to Neuhausen, May 5, 1944. On Saal, see AJ, AJB, 151/99.

[328] DB, B 69, report on status of the bank, Oct. 4, 1944.

[329] See AJ, AJB, 151/3/3, report of the administrative council, July 1944.

a man in this position who has contact with the relevant agencies, and who can advise them objectively without burdening the Bankverein with obligations which it can neither accept nor bear."³³³ It is doubtful whether Abs would seriously have considered sending Ulrich off to Belgrade at this point, and the management remained in the hands of Böhm-Bawerk until the impending end. In the summer, however, the Bankverein also lost the services of Soengen and Neuhausen. The former was placed in charge of all banking matters in Serbia, while a new German bank, the Südbank, was authorized by Berlin. Under these circumstances, Soengen could not remain on the administrative council without confronting a conflict of interest. As for Neuhausen, his presence on the council was based on the assumption that the Bankverein would be the only German bank. In August, however, the Dresdner Bank was allowed to establish itself in Belgrade. It thereupon sold its shares in the Bankverein to the CA, and Pilder left the council. With more than one German bank in Belgrade, Neuhausen now felt he could not stay on the council and also resigned.³³⁴ To the bitter end, however, the most pressing problem remained the reduction of credits, especially to the Bor mines. Abs sought to help by appealing to the Four Year Plan authorities, urging the establishment of a special bank in Serbia to enable the Bor mines to repay the Bankverein. This, however, was in September, when Joham was already instructing the staff in Belgrade to prepare for what was tantamount to an evacuation and to reduce credits as much as possible.³³⁵ Böhm-Bawerk and Sehn left Belgrade in early October 1944, the Bankverein's business placed in the hands of its one Serbian director, Ljubomir Celegin. Efforts to reduce the bank's engagements continued through the fall, but Joham could boast little success or cooperation in dealing with the

various mining companies. The bank, he dolefully reported, was in an embarrassing situation and was a credit risk.³³⁶ In any event, the CA's wartime banking business in Serbia had come to a dismal end.

While the German business in Agram/Zagreb was also coming to an end at this time because of the military and political situation, the circumstances at the Bank für Kroatien, AG were less dramatic. Of course, what distinguished the state of affairs there from that at its counterpart in Belgrade was that the Croatian bank did not have large-scale accounts of the kind plaguing the Bankverein in Belgrade, and its liquidity was reasonably satisfactory. In September 1944, Joham described the liquidity situation as "favorable," and even in November he was able to report considerable deposits and an understandable effort to limit engagements.³³⁷ Croatia, needless to say, was a relatively underdeveloped country with small-scale industry and an agriculture and forestry sector in need of improvement. In order to promote the economic relations between Croatia and Germany, an agreement was made when the bank was created to set up a national economy section at the bank in collaboration with the Südosteuropa-Gesellschaft, the costs of which were to be shared between the society and the bank.³³⁸ Unfortunately, there is little information in the available records of how it functioned, or indeed of the business of the bank, because of the unwillingness of the present Croatian government to make its archives available. It does not, however, appear to have been a very dynamic enterprise and was plagued by the general situation in the country. At a meeting of the various banks in July 1942, Director Rauber reported that political conditions were highly unstable and the government lacked support. The growing unpopularity of the Germans and Italians was bolstering the

---

³³³ DB, B 69, Joham to Abs, May 22, 1944.

³³⁴ AJ, AJB, 151/3/3, Joham to Abs, Aug. 19, 1944, and Abs to Joham, Sept. 1, 1944; ibid., Soengen to Joham, April 12, 1944, and Military Commander Southeast to Sehn, July 31, 1944.

³³⁵ DB, B 69, Joham to Abs, Aug. 30, 1944, and Abs to Joham, Sept. 1, 1944.

³³⁶ BA-CA, CA-V, CA working committee meetings, Sept. 26 and Nov. 22, 1944, and report on the bank of Oct. 24, 1944, and ibid., S.P. Akten, Nr. 481.

³³⁷ Ibid., CA working committee meetings, Oct. 29, 1943, Sept. 26, 1944, Nov. 29, 1944.

³³⁸ See ibid., CA working committee, May 23, 1941.

partisan insurrection. The partisans controlled the local mines, and wood exports to Germany had simply stopped. The situation was inflationary, and the banks found it difficult to locate suitable credit customers or investment possibilities. In November 1942, Joham pointed out that the balance of the bank had not increased much and took this as a sign that it was not playing a very significant role in the agricultural development of Croatia.[339]

The new branches in the annexed areas of Slovenia in Marburg/Maribor, Cilli/Celje, and in Krainburg/Kranj were inevitably caught up in the somewhat confused Party, SS, and ethnic economic policies of the region. There was a substantial amount of business to be done by these branches, especially Marburg, and credits increased by 4 million RM in the third quarter of 1941.[340] Reports rendered at the end of the war provide some sense of the nature of business in Marburg/Maribor and Cilli/Celje. Most of the credits given at the former went to ethnic Germans who had set up business after the annexation. The deposits came from various Party agencies – 2 million RM out of 13 million RM – larger industrial enterprises, and a clientele of ethnic Germans, Austrians, and Reich Germans. Cilli did not have many Party agency deposits and primarily did business with ethnic German enterprises.[341]

Certain accounts were particularly outstanding for either political or military reasons. In June 1941, the branch in Marburg/Maribor provided a Reich-guaranteed credit of 250,000 RM to the head of the Main Office for Administration and Economy, General Trustee for the Production of Building Construction Materials in the Recovered Areas of the Districts of Styria and Carinthia. It then provided another 250,000 RM, and the Krainburg/Kranj branch also gave a 100,000 RM credit. This SS construction materials effort was closely connected

to the SS settlement program and was meant to serve it as well as the resettlement program in the region.[342]

The CA Marburg/Maribor was particularly anxious to gain the business of large industrial firms working for the army, some of which were attracted to the region by the large number of refugees from those areas of Yugoslavia occupied by Hungary and ethnic German settlers. From the very outset, the CA branch faced strong competition from the Länderbank Wien branch and from the highly active Director Karl Klimpel, who had previous experience in the area and good contacts with the locals.[343] The competition became particularly keen with reports in late 1943 of the plan of the Vereinigte Deutsche Metallwerke in Frankfurt to build a large new plant for airplane parts in Marburg. To get a foot in the door, the CA branch had given advances of 100,000–200,000 RM that were promptly reimbursed by the Bank der Deutschen Luftfahrt. When the Länderbank branch offered larger advances, the CA branch responded by offering credits of 1.5–2 million RM. At the same time, the CA branch was giving this money although they did not know much about the actual ownership and status of the new works.[344] It was in fact very difficult to get exact information about the status of the VDM Luftfahrtwerke Steiermark GmbH, and by October 1944, it had secured an operating credit of 5 million RM from a consortium composed of the Luftfahrtbank, which put in 2 million RM, and the CA and Länderbank branches, which each provided 1.5 million. The firm had plans for huge, risky investments, however, and in December was thinking about doubling its call for operating credits. But Director Tron, who had taken a hand in the matter, appeared very

[339] Ibid., CA supervisory board meeting of Nov. 27, 1942, and DB, P 11726, Vienna Southeast Conference, July 15–17, 1942.

[340] See BA-CA, CA-V, the report attached to the CA supervisory board meeting, Nov. 4, 1941.

[341] BA-CA, CA-TZ, Sekretariat grün, Box 16/CA 8, File 12, Report to Joham, Nov. 11, 1950.

[342] BA-CA, CA-V, CA board of management meetings of June 24, Aug. 22, and Nov. 10, 1941. See also Jan Erik Schulte, *Zwangsarbeit und Vernichtung: Das Wirtschaftsimperium der SS. Oswald Pohl und das SS-Wirtschafts-Verwaltungshauptamt 1933–1945* (Paderborn 2001), pp. 244–245.

[343] BA-CA, CA-TZ, Sekretariat rot, Box 40/CA-BV Filiale Li – Md, File 6, Internal minute, July 24, 1941.

[344] See ibid., minute by the CA Vienna, Nov. 11, 1943.

cautious about providing more without further discussion.[345]

There was yet another big project in which the CA Marburg/Maribor sought to gain a foothold, and that was the construction of a big aluminum plant by the Vereinigte Aluminium-Werke AG in Sterntal, near Pettau. The CA was anxious to get the accounts of the projected plant, but the construction firms involved, which actually worked with the Marburg/Maribor branch of the CA, were paid directly through the Berlin office of the VAW, which belonged to the VIAG. Moreover, and more irritatingly, the Länderbank seemed to have established contact with the Sterntal office. This led the CA branch to appeal to both the Vienna headquarters and to Director Heller for support in getting this business. There is no record as to whether this effort was successful.[346]

Whatever the case, there was clearly a tension between the desire to get as much of the business connected with the war effort as possible and the need to make rational business decisions by reducing risk as much as possible. This was particularly evident in Lower Styria. The civilian administration of the region decided in early 1942 to take over the power companies there along with the Traifailer Kohlenbergwerks-Gesellschaft and to set up the Energieversorgung Südsteiermark AG, Marburg with a capital of 5 million RM. The capital needs of the new corporation as well as the costs of paying off previous owners in Switzerland and elsewhere amounted to 15 million RM, and it also needed an immediate operating credit of 6 million RM. The government turned to the CA and the Länderbank for credits. The latter, eager to provide the credits, asked for two-thirds of the business on

the grounds that its own plans to take over the Traifailer company had been frustrated.[347] The Creditanstalt and, in particular, Abs were more cautious because neither the legal ownership of the power companies nor their financial situation was clear because the books had either been destroyed or were in Belgrade and elsewhere. The CA was very insistent, therefore, on a Reich guarantee for any credits given and on working closely with the Länderbank. In July 1942, it still did not have a clear picture and was thinking of asking for a mortgage guarantee for the projected credits.[348] In the end, both the CA and the Länderbank held 60 percent of the investment credits given to the state-owned enterprise and also managed to get a mortgage guarantee. It would appear that the coal and cement works connected with the Energieversorgung Steiermark proved quite profitable and a good investment, at least until the Slovenes came and took it back.[349]

2. THE CA, THE DEUTSCHE BANK, AND THE SOUTHEAST EUROPE PROGRAM

The cooperation between the CA and the Länderbank in many respects reflected the intended role for the Viennese banks in Southeast Europe. They were two members of a small club of banks that also included Schoeller & Co. and E. von Nicolai (formerly Rothschild), and they were expected to take the lead in the business with Southeast Europe. As the Association of Ostmark Banks and Bankers claimed, "the Ostmark banks possess affiliations or even their own branches, thanks to the old status of Vienna, because of its key position and its historical role in the southeast, never fully lost even after the collapse of the Monarchy. Where this was not the case, they have been

---

[345] See the memorandum by Tron of Oct. 12, 1944, and his minutes of Sept. 16, 1944, and Dec. 11, 1944, DB, V2/1. See also, Norbert Schausberger, *Rüstung in Österreich 1938–1945. Eine Studie über die Wechselwirkung von Wirtschaft, Politik und Kriegsführung* (Vienna 1970), pp. 78–79.

[346] See BA-CA, CA-TZ, Sekretariat rot, Box 40/ CA-BV Filiale Li – Md, File 6, CA Marburg to CA Vienna, Oct. 7, 1943; CA Vienna to Heller, Oct. 12, 1943.

[347] See Chapter 6, pp. 505–507, this volume and BA-CA, CA-V, CA working committee memorandum of Feb. 25, and July 15, 1942.

[348] BA-CA, CA-V, CA working committee meeting, Feb. 27, 1942.

[349] See NARA, T83/125, the Dresdner Bank working committee, June 18, 1943 and the report of June 4, 1943.

established in the more recent past."[350] The Ostmark banks were thus assigned the task of having a central place in facilitating the Reich's trade with the region. While the Viennese banks were expected to finance German exports, their branches, affiliates, and other German banks in the southeast had the task of helping to finance imports from the region into Germany. At the same time, this group of banks in the Southeast was also expected to provide long-term credits to increase the business capital of German enterprises in the region because the transfer of capital was so difficult.

Some of this certainly was wishful thinking in anticipation of better times after a German victory. The RWM had set up the Reich Economic Chamber Working Group Vienna-Southeast in 1940 to explore ways Vienna could become more central to the transit trade with the southeast and overcome the dominance of Hamburg and Bremen in the region. The working group, closely connected to the Südosteuropa-Gesellschaft, produced a substantial number of memoranda and concrete proposals. What is clear from these documents is that much remained to be done to strengthen Vienna's position, and wartime problems obviously did not help matters.[351]

The most important decisions were made in Berlin, of course. The CA had established its lobbying office in the Reich capital, and the Reich governor of the Ostmark, Baldur von Schirach, also had a delegate there in the person of Rudolf Kratz. Kratz, who had previously worked in Bürckel's office, was in regular contact with Gau Economic Advisor Rafelsberger and with August Heinrichsbauer, the business manager of the Südosteuropa Gesellschaft, of which von Schirach was president. Kratz, Rafelsberger, and Heinrichsbauer were all anxious to promote a concentration of effort in the Southeast and were particularly hostile to banking competition in the region. Rafelsberger was

especially interested in promoting harmony between the CA and the Länderbank. He and Kratz actually hoped to persuade the authorities in Berlin to create a Südostbank as a supervisory body to monitor the conduct and policies of the Austrian banks, but Riehle turned the proposal down. The latter feared that the local residents in the countries involved would shy away from the German banks for fear that such a supervisory bank would violate bank secrecy and would then turn to their national banks instead. Neither Kratz nor Rafelsberger thought much of this argument, but they were unable to move Riehle and sought instead to try to forge a "gentleman's agreement" among the CA, Länderbank Wien, Bankhaus Schoeller, and Bankhaus E. v. Nicolai. There is no evidence that they were particularly successful in their efforts to have an "educative" effect on the banks, especially because the Länderbank, while willing to cooperate with the CA when it was to their mutual interest, feared being totally supplanted by the much larger and more powerful CA.[352]

As the expansion of the CA had demonstrated, there was good reason for such concern, especially because it was allied with the Deutsche Bank, which played along with and promoted the idea of using Vienna as the base for expansion into Southeast Europe. This was well demonstrated when Franz Hasslache appeared before the general shareholders' meeting of the CA on May 14, 1942, to provide an account of the bank's situation in the context of the great expansion of the war since the shareholders' meeting of April 5, 1941. Despite the many hardships and demands produced by the war in the east, he believed that "we are now confronting once again new great and decisive events from which we ultimately expect that a long period of peaceful labor is finally being safeguarded."[353] Hasslacher recounted

---

[350] BAB, R 63, vol. 83, Bl. 2–3, Association of Ostmark Banks and Bankers to the Southeast Europe Society, Sept. 10, 1942.

[351] These are compiled in an undated collection in BAB, R 7, vol. 3438.

[352] BAB, R 63, vol. 83, Bl. 1, 69–72, 116–117; for the correspondence on this, see Kratz to Heinrichsbauer, June 22 and July 7, 1942; Kratz to Rafelsberger, June 30, 1942; see also Chapter 6, pp. 488–489, in this volume.

[353] BA-CA, CA-TZ, Sekretariat rot, Box 23/CA-BV XX/VII–XII HV 5.4.1941, XX/I–VII HV 4.5.1942, File 3, Speech of Hasslacher on May 4, 1942.

the transformations that had taken place in the former Yugoslavia, and the return of the CA to Lemberg/Lviv. Nevertheless, he made clear that the bank had no intention of expanding further eastward, not only because the banking business was being otherwise regulated there, but also because "we want to devote our forces chiefly to the southeastern region, which lies closer to us." In his view, the task there were less a matter of changing the economic division of labor than of greatly increasing the production of raw materials and boosting the productivity of agriculture. He presented the change in the CA's shareholding through the Deutsche Bank majority in the context of these tasks in the Southeast because the Deutsche Bank was engaged in that region itself. Nevertheless, Hasslacher noted that the CA's independence was guaranteed and that one could anticipate a shifting of many tasks and responsibilities to Vienna to simplify and speed up business with the southeast in collaboration with the Berlin partners of the CA.

The CA would not, in fact, engage in any further expansion through the domination of banks in the southeast. It is interesting to note, however, that it began to reminisce about the past and feel renewed hunger pangs when the Italians changed sides and the Germans occupied the territories of the Austro-Hungarian monarchy taken under the Treaty of St. Germain. Operating on the assumption that there would be a reordering of the banking sector, the CA wrote to Riehle pointing out that it formerly had branches in Trieste, Bozen, Görz, Pola, and Meran. The Trieste branch had been founded in 1861, the others between 1904 and 1910. Marshal Badoglio, the governor of the occupied area in 1919, had closed these branches but the Trieste branch was still in liquidation. The CA thus hoped that its claims would be recognized when the time came to reorganize the banking system.[354] An active if indirect CA interest in Trieste was also maintained through Hasslacher, who was appointed economic advisor to Gauleiter Friedrich Rainer

of Carinthia, the head commissar in Trieste. Hasslacher later claimed he had done his best to promote economically rational and politically civilized behavior in the area, which may well have been the case, and that he sought to keep the existing banks intact while making them independent of their Italian proprietary institutions.[355] There is no evidence that any serious progress was made in reviving the CA branch in Trieste. When Joham visited Trieste in April 1944 and discussed the possibility of setting up a German bank and CA representation there, he was informed that the matter was not considered urgent but that Rainer had instructed that, should a German bank be set up, the CA was to have priority. Another option was CA participation in the Banca Triestina, although Joham learned that the shareholders were not prepared to accept a CA majority in negotiations. Joham and his colleagues on the CA management board then agreed to strive initially for a 50 percent stake in the bank. There is no evidence that any progress was made in this matter which, given the date, is hardly surprising.[356]

If the CA did not gain majority holdings in other banks in Southeast Europe, it did significantly improve its position where the Deutsche Bank played a dominant role, above all in Bulgaria and Rumania. As part of the arrangement whereby the Deutsche Bank took a majority in the CA, the former granted the latter a 30 percent stake in the Deutsche-Bulgarische

---

[354] RGVA Moscow, 1458/2/93, Bl. 182, CA to Riehle, Sept. 13, 1943.

[355] See StmkLA, Vr 734/1946, Hasslacher's postwar testimony of May 17, 1946, Landesgericht für Strafsachen Graz, Franz und Jakob Hasslacher, pp. 91–93. Hasslacher claimed that he turned down an offer from Kaltenbrunner to go as economic advisor to Hungary before the 1944 invasion because he did not want to have anything to do with the "Jewish question" and that he disapproved of the resettlement policies in the areas annexed from Slovenia. His chief task in Trieste was to advise on the big insurance companies headquartered there.

[356] BA-CA, CA-V, CA board of management meeting, April 21, 1944. There is an excellent account of the German and Austrian role and Rainer's policies in Trieste by Gianmarco Bresdola, "The Legitimising Strategies of the Nazi Administration in Northern Italy: Propaganda in the Adriatisches Küstenland," in: Contemporary European History 13/4 (Nov. 2004), pp. 425–452.

Kreditbank, Sofia and the Banca Comerciala Romana, Bucharest. The Deutsche Bank held a majority of the shares of both banks, and these cessions to the CA along with 30 percent of the shares of the BUB in Prague were intended to compensate the CA for the surrender of shares in the Universale Bau-AG to the VIAG. The Deutsche Bank also promised to use its influence to gain the CA a place in the German-Greek friendship pact that it had concluded with the National Bank of Greece in Athens. In this way, the CA would have the Deutsche Bank's support in areas where it did not have a strong presence before. Abs and his colleagues envisioned the arrangement as a genuine partnership, where the Deutsche Bank and the CA would exchange information and experiences on those areas where they played a dominant role in a bank. Each bank would provide the other with advice and information on the business dealings of their various banks, the nostro business; at the same time, and most importantly from the standpoint of the Deutsche Bank, the loro business – the customer business – was to be expanded. It was thus essential that the CA strengthen the role of Vienna in Southeast European commercial business by making strong connections with the firms from the region that already were in Vienna or to get them to set up offices in Vienna. The Deutsche Bank was quite prepared to have the CA win over customers in this way even at its own expense, provided those customers were given terms as good or better than those they received from the Deutsche Bank. The Deutsche Bank would provide personnel and technical assistance, but the initiative had to come from the CA to restore Vienna's traditional position in Southeast Europe. Under existing conditions, a great deal had to be cleared through Berlin, but one could hope and expect greater decentralization when the war was over.[357]

As has been noted earlier in this study, the Viennese Party leadership, Rafelsberger in particular, desired this stress on Vienna. As a member of the CA supervisory board and Gau economic advisor, he would indeed have liked to make the CA dominant in Prague, Bulgaria, and Rumania, an idea that Abs evaded in their discussions. Abs was anxious to fire the CA up, but not to excess. He was very willing to give the CA a seat on the supervisory boards of the Bulgarian and Romanian banks as well as a seat at the table in Greece, but he became quite irritated when Vienna and Berlin newspapers, reporting on the CA's expansion, stated that the CA would have a voice in appointments, greater influence in Greece, and a role in Turkey. Abs complained to Hasslacher and pointed out that this could lead to misunderstandings. This was true. Ambassador Franz von Papen, who worked closely with the Istanbul branch of the Deutsche Bank, had asked Director Hans Weidtman whether the stories were correct and whether the CA would be setting up a branch in Istanbul. Weidtman wrote to Abs, his direct superior, asking that Papen be assured that there would be no change in the character of the Istanbul branch. At the same time, Weidtman wanted to make sure that if the Deutsche Bank plans to take over the Banque de Salonique worked out, the CA would not be given a stake and would reserve the business for the Deutsche Bank. Abs hastened to ask Weidtman to assure von Papen that the independence of the Istanbul branch would be maintained and that the CA was not to take a direct interest in Turkey but that it would have some involvement in Greece.[358]

---

[357] See DB, B 53, the Abs memorandum of April 22, 1942. Much of the thinking behind this position came from a memorandum for Abs by his assistant Franz Ulrich of Feb. 19, 1941. At that time, Ulrich argued that the CA could not be given access to the Deutsche Bank–controlled banks in Bulgaria

and Romania because they had no real relationship with the CA, but the taking over of majority control of the CA obviously changed the situation. See DB, P 24158, Ulrich to Abs, Feb. 19, 1941.

[358] DB, B 53, Minute by Abs on discussion with Hasslacher, May 13, 1942; ibid., DB, P 6505, Bl. 28 and 33, Weidtman to Abs, May 16, 1942 and Abs to Weidtman, June 1, 1942. On the relationship between Abs and Weidtman and his branch, see Jonathan Steinberg, *The Deutsche Bank and Its Gold Transactions during the Second World War* (Munich 1999), pp. 39–59.

Within these confines, however, Abs and his colleagues in Berlin were quite serious about making Vienna as much of a center for business with Southeast Europe as possible, and imparting the Deutsche Bank's own experiences and sharing its access to the government agencies in Berlin with the CA. In fact, Abs proposed the formal establishment of a CA office in Berlin to maintain regular contact with the authorities. Between May 20 and June 5, 1942, a group of six CA section heads led by Alfred Heinisch, who held power of attorney and was charged with the Southeast Secretariat at the CA, went to Berlin to see how the Foreign Relations Section of the Deutsche Bank, which was headed by Abs and his aide Ulrich, functioned. Apparently, they were very impressed by the Berlin operation. Ulrich, however, was not much impressed by the visitors. His report for Abs reflected the Berliners' reservations toward their Viennese "partners": "The most prominent speaker was Herr Heinisch, who also earned this designation because he was talking quite a bit. The gentlemen are all specialists in their particular areas but do not have any universal training in foreign business, for which also they evidently have had little opportunity because a central foreign section where all the threads run together does not exist at the Creditanstalt-Bankverein. Business is taken care of wherever it originates, at the relevant credit section or the account management section. We do not have the impression that any one of the gentlemen especially stands out and would be qualified to build up a foreign organization for the Creditanstalt-Bankverein, to have all the threads come together there, and to exert a fructifying and promotive effect on all the offices involved.... Herr Reiß, who appears to be under consideration for the Berlin office of the Creditanstalt-Bankverein, ... does not leave one with the feeling, even from a purely external impression, that he would be particularly suited to establish useful connections with the Reich agencies, etc."[359]

One worked, of course, with what was available, and it was people like Tron who were sent to Vienna to make up for Austrian deficiencies. Still, rather than sending selected mediocrities to broaden their horizons in Berlin, a more fruitful approach to the sharing of information and experiences probably was the holding of the Southeast Conference in Vienna on July 15–17, 1942. It was hosted by the CA, opened by CA General Director Buzzi, and graced with the presence of Joham and Abs as well as the directors or representatives of the banks in Belgrade, Cracow, Lemberg/Lviv, and Agram/Zagreb as well as the branch in Budapest and the banks in Bulgaria and Romania. The central message of the CA and Deutsche Bank leadership was that sharing information was essential if domestic customers interested in doing business with the Southeast were to be properly informed about those who were buying and selling in the region and also about clearing requirements, exchange regulations, and other special aspects of doing business in the countries involved. Abs was very insistent that they all had to be informed about the multitude of regulations governing trade and punctilious in obeying them. Not doing so would provoke the enmity of the national banks, which could deny refinancing facilities and thus endanger the position of German banks in the countries in question. Also, concessions made to one customer were likely to be demanded by others. The chief thing, however, was providing customers with the latest information because customers who dealt with other banks as well would soon know where they were best served. Similarly, when domestic customers traveled abroad to make their contacts, it was important for the banks to pay close attention to the hotel arrangements so that the banks belonging to

---

359 DB, P 6505, Bl. 45–46, report by Ulrich for Abs, June 4 and June 9, 1942. Heinisch had been a member of the Party cell organization of the CA since

1932 and was promoted to his position in 1939. See ÖStA/AdR, BMI, Gauakt Alfred Heinisch, Nr. 238 797. The other visitors to Berlin were Maximilian Grien, head of the Document Section; Reiß, who was head of the branch at Elterheimplatz and supervisor of a small deposit account department in Hernals; Edlitzberger, who was head of the Foreign Correspondence Section; and Pleban of the Foreign Exchange Section.

the concern in various countries would make immediate contact with the German customers and mediate the appropriate contacts. To win customers and provide them with up-to-date information, it was essential that the banks provide the requisite reports on a regular basis and that these reports be shared with Berlin and Vienna.[360]

The reports given at this meeting did indeed provide a wealth of information on conditions in Poland and Southeast Europe along with great detail on doing business with the controlled economies of the region. Furthermore, the evidence suggests that the injunctions of those who had organized the meeting were followed and that regular and detailed reports were sent in about changes in the economic, political, and regulatory situation in the various countries where the Deutsche Bank and the CA had banks and did business.[361] It is difficult, of course, to tell how effective all these stepped-up activities were. Certainly the Deutsche Bank had infused a considerable amount of energy into the efforts of the CA to play its appointed role in Southeast Europe, but the conditions in those countries, as has been described, were always quite difficult and uncertain.

3. THE EXPANSION OF THE CA CONCERN
IN SOUTHEAST EUROPE AND THE POLISH
TERRITORIES: THE GESELLSCHAFT
FÜR AUSSENHANDEL (GESFA) AND
THE SÜDOSTEUROPA GETREIDEHANDELS
AG (VIGOR)

Without doubt, the Deutsche Bank vigorously pursued its technical assistance program for the CA, investing considerable effort in coordinating activities for the greater good of the Deutsche Bank group, of which the CA was a prominent member. What must not be overlooked, however, is the high degree to which the CA had been acting on its own initiatives in

Southeast Europe all along. The CA's engagement must be measured not simply by its banking activities; above all, its role as a concern with large holdings in a variety of commercial and industrial enterprises must be taken into account.

An important manifestation of the CA's efforts to engage actively and directly in the export-import business in Southeast Europe was the founding of the Gesellschaft für Außenhandel mbH, Wien (Gesfa) on April 3, 1939. As noted earlier, the corporation had been founded when the CA decided to go it alone in its banking business in Slovakia rather than collaborate with the Länderbank and decided to try to meet the challenge presented by the concentration in Berlin by launching a Viennese commercial initiative.[362] The initial capital of the Gesfa was 100,000 RM; 75 percent was provided by the CA, the remainder by Schoeller & Co. The original aim had been to organize a single association of enterprises interested in foreign trade, especially with Southeast Europe, not for the purpose of engaging in such business itself but rather to act as a kind of information clearing house. It was to aid its members in finding favorable financing for their activities, in establishing and maintaining foreign connections, in taking up export initiatives, and in handling the technicalities of exporting. The government authorities dealing with associations, however, did not approve of setting up an association for such purposes, and the CA then decided to create the projected organization in the form of a commercial corporation. In July 1940, the Deutsche Bank and the RKG each invested 12,500 RM in the capital of the Gesfa. In 1940, the Gesfa joined forces with another company involved in trade, the Osteuropäische Handelskompagnie, and planned to ally with the influential Mitteleuropäische Wirtschaftstag. The latter decided not to invest, but Freiherr Tilo von Wilmowsky, the business manager of the Handelskompagnie, joined the supervisory board and invested 25,000 RM in capital.[363]

---

360 The protocol for the Vienna Southeast Conference is to be found in DB, P 11726.
361 A collection of these reports is to be found in DB, P 25005.

362 See pp. 165–166 of this chapter.
363 DB, P 6503, Bl. 255–256, Fischböck to Abs, March 19, 1940, CA management board meetings,

Once established, the Gesfa concluded that it should concentrate its activities abroad and set up outposts in the most important locations in the southeast. The outbreak of the war, however, created difficulties for this project. Capital was difficult to transfer and thus had to be raised in the countries involved, which meant the capital had to be kept very low or borrowed. In the latter case, repayment was to be made from profits. It was also difficult to find suitable personnel to staff the offices abroad. Nevertheless, some progress was made. In 1939–1940, offices were set up in Pressburg and Bucharest ("Sarcomex" S.A.R. Pentru Comertul Exterior). In Sofia, offices were set up for tobacco exports (Handelsaktiengesellschaft "Sofia" in collaboration with a Bulgarian group) and for paper products (DEBU, Deutsche Bulgarische Papierhandels AG, Sofia). There was also an office in Zagreb ("Transmar" Handels AG). In the late fall of 1941, a branch of the Gesfa was established in Drohobycz in Galicia, and there were plans to establish an office in Prague. In January 1941, the capital was raised to 200,000 RM, with the CA and the Bankhaus Schoeller still acting as the chief shareholders.[364]

The Gesfa was not much of a moneymaker. In June 1940, the CA and Schoeller put additional money at its disposal to cover part of its 1939 debt, and in March 1941 they granted it a credit of 50,000 RM. Schoeller apparently lost interest in the investment and sold its 50,000 RM investment in January 1942 to the CA, which became the only shareholder. Director Fritscher of the CA served as chairman of the supervisory board. This was not a position the CA wished to retain, however, and in the summer of 1942 it sought to interest the firms associated with the Südosteuropa Gesellschaft in Vienna with the opportunity to participate in 49 percent of the Gesfa shares and thus gain access to the offices in Southeast Europe and the advantages they offered. The CA also

contemplated selling another 25 percent of the shares to various agencies that dealt with Southeast Europe. Abs strongly supported the projected distribution of the shares while urging that careful watch be kept over the existing investment because of the risks involved.[365]

Judging by the condition of the Gesfa branch in Drohobycz, there was indeed good reason to be wary. Both the Gesfa, in other words the CA, and the CA branch in Lemberg/Lviv had provided substantial funds and credits, but the auditor's report at the end of 1942 was extremely negative. The Gesfa branch had invested in a variety of enterprises, not only involved in trading but also in a warehouse, a department store, a variety of retail businesses, and some small manufacturing enterprises. The consuming public was too small and too poor to purchase the products on offer. Moreover, the branch had trouble finding staff and had to resort to employing fourteen Jews in addition to the seventy-six other employees. The management of both inventory and funds was very unbusinesslike, and the auditors expected no profit in 1943. Here, too, the Gesfa sought investors and purchasers, but the problem appears not simply to have been Galicia but more generally with the Gesfa itself, where the auditor urged a very careful investigation of all its operations.[366]

Despite these negative evaluations, however, the situation seems to have improved in 1943–1944. In January 1943, Fritscher gave an upbeat report, especially about the Bulgarian enterprises in which the Gesfa was involved. It had taken a stake in the Bulgarian firm of Dimiter Boschiloff AG, and they planned to import frozen fruits and vegetables into the Reich. Abs was duly impressed by this "pioneering work," but was, as before, "of the opinion that a suitable partner for this company should be sought which would also be in a position to take over the facilities later on."[367] The Gesfa

May 2, 1939, and March 11, 1940, and BA-CA, CA-V, the lengthy report on the Gesellschaft für Außenhandel of July 15, 1942 for the CA executive committee.

[364] Ibid., the management board meeting, Jan. 13, 1941.

[365] Ibid., CA management board, June 27, 1940, March 31, 1941; executive committee meeting of July 15, 1942 and report.

[366] See DB, P 6516, Bl. 99–103, report sent to Abs on Aug. 25, 1943.

[367] BA-CA, CA-V, CA working committee, Jan. 27, 1943.

apparently aroused in Abs his old prejudice against direct engagement of banks in business operations, a view that continued to be widely held in Berlin.[368] Investors were hard to find, but things seemed to be getting better. In June 1944, Fritscher reported that, despite the bad political situation, the Gesfa as a whole was maintaining its position and covering its costs. The branch in Drohobycz made a profit in 1943 that enabled it to make up for the losses of the previous years, while the subsidiary in Pressburg was receiving lucrative orders from the local authorities. The Gesfa thus appeared to be putting its finances in order. This was of course happening while the Third Reich was moving toward collapse, as evidenced by Fritscher's report of September 1944 that the Gesfa had a temporary surplus of 300,000 RM as a result of government-paid compensation for war damages.[369]

Although the CA created the Gesfa in order to expand its Southeast European business, the heart of the CA's engagement in Southeast Europe as a concern or holding company for business enterprises lay elsewhere, namely, in the Vienna-based Südosteuropäische Getreidehandels AG. Until 1939, it was known as the Internationale Getreide Handels AG. The CA's 70 percent stake in the company was acquired when it took over the Bodencreditanstalt in 1931 following that bank's collapse in 1929. The remaining 30 percent was in the hands of the Alfihado AG, a Swiss company. The chief figure in the company was its president until 1938, Alexander Schindler, a Czech citizen who was a major figure in the international wheat trading business and whose company bore the name of Schindler & Stein. Schindler was Jewish, the shareholders in Alfihado were Jewish, and the grain trade in Austria and much of Southeast Europe was in fact dominated by Jews. Internationale Getreide was a major company in the grain trade, handling as much as 50,000 train carloads of wheat in 1936–1937. It had a particularly impressive

purchasing organization in Romania named Vigor, which was used as the shorthand name for Internationale Getreide and then for the Südosteuropa Getreidehandels AG, and that name will be used in the discussion that follows.

Following the German takeover, the CA proceeded to vigorously Aryanize the leadership of Internationale Getreide, and all the Jews, including Schindler, were removed from the administrative council and the management board. By May 1938, the chief figure on the administrative council was Hans Friedl, who was to remain the CA's chief interlocutor in its dealings with Vigor until 1945, and the chief manager in this phase was Alfred Baron Fromm. The complete Aryanization of the ownership of Internationale Getreide was a matter of great urgency in the spring of 1938 because the Reich Grain Bureau in Berlin, which was charged with the management of the Reich's grain supply, was extremely anxious to use the services of Vigor. It had attempted to set up its own purchasing agency in Romania, but the results were a poor second to those achieved by Vigor. As a consequence, the Reich Grain Bureau immediately contacted the CA after the Anschluss, explained its interest in using the services of Internationale Getreide, but also insisted that the company be 100 percent Aryanized. As a result, the CA was forced to purchase the shares of Alfihado, and Friedl appealed to the authorities in Vienna for permission to do so at what normally would have been a high price. As Friedl diplomatically put the matter, "in view of the fact that we are dealing with foreign shareholders who are abroad, the transaction has to be carried out according to normal business principles." In other words, one could not cheat the Jews abroad the way one cheated them at home. Also, Friedl noted that Schindler was a man of great influence and, because the business was almost entirely in Jewish hands, he could do a great deal of damage. Friedl admitted that Schindler was behaving very "correctly," trying to serve the company even though he had involuntarily given up the presidency. It was important "in the public interest," therefore, to pay what had to be paid, although Friedl also pointed out that the way the payment was arranged would keep the costs

---

[368] See BA-CA, CA-IB, AVA, 01/05-06/1, Nemling to CA, May 2, 1939.

[369] BA-CA, CA-V, reports of the CA working committee, June 13 and Sept. 26, 1944.

and foreign exchange issue relatively low. Friedl had his permission within a week, and subsequently the CA had 100 percent ownership of what was to be renamed the Südosteuropäische Getreidehandels AG.[370]

The final settlement with Schindler was not without its unpleasant aspects, however. There were differences in the calculation of the payment. Schindler threatened to sue, and his account in Czechoslovakia was blocked. Ultimately, the matter was settled out of court. At the same time, Schindler was greatly irritated by less tangible aspects of the CA's behavior. He much resented a claim made by the CA that he had not been forced out of the presidency at the end of April 1938 when he could demonstrate with written evidence that the exact opposite was the case.[371] Undoubtedly, however, he was most offended by charges made by Inspector Josef Wirth, a CA official put on the administrative council together with Friedl, that Schindler had left Vigor in bad shape. Schindler claimed this was not the case at all, having constantly warned that the apparatus built up in Romania was very expensive and could only be paid for by an aggressive effort to do international business. Instead, the new leadership had cancelled old orders and prevented the effort to get more business with the result that costs were not being covered by new business. In his view, the opportunity presented by German business made Vigor potentially even more profitable than before, but the new leadership was not taking advantage of this. In sum, he insisted that "one should not but the blame for mistakes in the present on the former management."[372]

Obviously, Schindler would have run the business differently from his successors and had a different business philosophy of aggressively making up for losses by seeking international business. The CA, however, had not acquired 100 percent ownership of the Internationale Getreide-Handels AG on the basis of careful investigation of its status but rather because it was under severe pressure from the Reich Grain Bureau. Wirth only discovered the actual situation of the company in the summer of 1938, and in the following weeks he claimed that just hearing its name made him feel sick.[373] The company had made a profit in 1936–1937 but suffered substantial losses in the next fiscal year. The balance for 1937–1938 showed a total loss by the Internationale Getreide-Handels AG of 640,978 RM and a loss of 290,000 RM on its operations in Romania, Hungary, and Poland. The lion's share of the loss – 240,000 RM – was in Romania because of the liquidation of the Exportul Cerealelor Braila. After learning of these losses, Wirth simply did not want to deal with the matter for weeks, and he tended to make Schindler the scapegoat. The sources of these losses, as explained by the CA when it drew up the balance in the following year, hardly suggest that the bulk of them could be laid at Schindler's doorstep. A major cause was the firing of the Jews in the company, who accounted for 80 percent of its management and staff, and the settlements with them, "despite certain limitations," were quite expensive. Then, because of the "changed economic and personnel situation" there was a natural period of "slack," in which costs were not covered. Then there were losses from an overlooked debt to an Italian firm and from spoilage of a shipment of corn from Yugoslavia to England. The biggest losses were in Romania. The firm of R. Stein, which had previously handled the purchasing organization, had to be liquidated because of the high costs of lawsuits connected with alleged violations of the Romanian exchange regulations. As it turned out, Stein won the case but had to liquidate because of the high costs. Its successor firm, the Exportul Cerealelor Braila, allegedly had to be liquidated because its reputation had suffered from the various court cases of its predecessor, although the CA report noted that nearly 100 percent of its employees

---

370 BA-CA, CA-V, S.P. Akte, Nr. 488, Friedl to Schumetz (Bürckel's office), May 20, 1938, and other relevant documents. Part of the payment was made in the form of a grain elevator, and Schindler used the cash he received to repay debts owed to the CA.

371 Ibid., Schindler to CA, Sept. 14, 1938.

372 Ibid., Schindler to Wirth, Aug. 27, 1938.

373 BA-CA, CA-IB, Getreide, 20/07, Görnandt to Friedl, Jan. 25, 1941.

were Jewish and "another type of Aryanization appeared excluded." Another problem was that the Romanian National Bank arbitrarily reduced the exchange rate of the Schilling in the clearing arrangement with Austria in 1937, which brought more unexpected losses. Last, business possibilities were very limited because of the political developments so that earnings were reduced. In general, therefore, it would appear that the losses of 1937–1938 had much more to do with political developments and Aryanizations and the peculiarities of doing business in Romania than with what was soon described as "Jewish mismanagement."[374]

At the same time, in contrast to Schindler's marketing approach, the new management was beholden to the Reich Grain Bureau, whose operations were funded by a large banking consortium of which the CA was a member, and whose purpose was to produce a high degree of order and stability in the market. It was no accident that the new director appointed to work with Fromm as head of Vigor on August 1, 1938, Friedrich Görnandt, took the job on the recommendation and urging of the Reich Grain Bureau. He had made his career in the grain trade, and during the First World War he had served in Ukraine as director of the German-Austro-Hungarian Economic Zentral Agency in Kiev.[375] His lengthy correspondence with Friedl suggests a person of considerable dynamism and energy, a staunch believer in the German cause, and a man committed to turning Vigor into a solid, reliable, and successful instrument of the Reich Grain Bureau. He had expected to take over a company that was making a profit, and he was most unhappy to discover that the opposite was the case and to have Wirth disappear and leave him to his own devices. But he was resolved to turn things around, believing that everything depended on "whether or not through the new internal organization, to be created in common with my colleague, and through the expansion of the

Balkan trade, which is being undertaken with the support of the Reich Grain Bureau placing its confidence in me, we will have the material success we are striving for."[376] Görnandt, who worked very well with Fromm, is difficult to characterize, but one has the sense that he was a model of what constituted the entrepreneurial spirit in a controlled economy.

This was well illustrated by the Aryanization of the firm of Jakober & Cie., an important feed grain producer in Vienna. The company's facilities had caught the eye of Director Donner of the Reich Grain Bureau in the summer of 1938, who believed that they needed to be placed into "serious Aryan hands" and would be of great value to Vigor. Initially, there was some competition for the company from the cooperatives, and the Aryanization itself was in the hands of the Property Transfer Bureau. It was subsequently taken over by the Kontrollbank, but there was considerable disagreement over the price to be paid and the "Aryanization fee." The common denominator in the to and fro over the price and the fee was the constant reduction of what the Jakober family was supposed to receive in their blocked account at the CA. The Reich Grain Bureau strongly supported a settlement that would give Vigor the facilities. They reached an agreement in August, but it was not officially confirmed by the Kontrollbank, and there was still no news in November. During this time, Vigor had taken over the Aryan employees to retain their services. Finally, Görnandt had enough. He angrily wrote to Friedl charging that the Kontrollbank was delaying things and failing to realize how pressing the matter was. It was causing an "unheard of harm to the economy of the Ostmark." Farmers were deprived of the fodder they needed. A huge amount of storage space was sitting empty. Provisions for the employees were in jeopardy, and it was impossible for the firm to conduct its transit business

---

[374] See BA-CA, CA-IB, Getreide, 20/09, the draft of the balance, April 26, 1939, and statement on the company, March 31, 1939.

[375] Ibid., report to Friedl, Oct. 16, 1939.

[376] Ibid. These remarks were made in the context of an angry letter claiming that the CA was not giving him sufficient financial reward for his successful labors and pointing out that under the Führer principle, performance was to be rewarded.

to function, which in turn meant the loss of foreign exchange. Görnandt emphasized that the value of Jakober & Cie. lay in its continued operation, that the Kontrollbank had no right to try to get more money given the price regulations in force, and that a higher price would threaten the firm's profitability. He therefore proposed that the Kontrollbank be given three days to come to terms and that he be authorized to personally report these "unbelievable conditions" to Bürckel so that the latter could take energetic measures.[377]

Görnandt had no compunctions about using such muscular tactics even with the CA. This was made abundantly clear in the fall of 1940, when Görnandt got wind of a plan by the Gesfa to set up a company in Bucharest with the name "Sagromex" to trade in grain. He was quite alarmed and pointed out to Friedl in a letter from October 18 that the Südosteuropäische Getreidehandels Gesellschaft had its own company for such purposes, H. Müller, and that this company was highly favored by the Reich Grain Bureau, which believed that Müller had become something of a concept in Romania and wanted to keep things that way. Görnandt denied that he wished to deprive another member of the CA concern the right to engage in whatever business it wished, but he pointed out that Vigor had fought long and hard for its position and continued to do so in the face of jealousy and opposition on the part of firms in Hamburg and Berlin. This competition made use of every mistake or untoward event involving Vigor. It certainly would make use of an effort by another CA-controlled enterprise to enter into the same business as Vigor. It could also be seen as a violation of the market order desired by the Reich Grain Bureau, which had already inquired with him what was going on. As Görnandt bluntly put the matter: "It is therefore a natural foregone conclusion that, in the interest of our enterprise, I energetically use my elbows against every disturbance, no matter from where it comes, as soon as I feel that this

construction, which has been consummated with endless effort, could in some way be unfavorably influenced."[378]

A month later, Görnandt sent Friedl an even more insistent letter stating that complaints were being made by a rival enterprise that the CA firms were seeking to "trustify" the Romanian grain business and that "the Presidium of the Reich Bureau must get the impression that your bank intends to sabotage the planning of grain imports and exports to the German Reich, which has been put under [the bank's] supervision by the Reich Economics Ministry and draw its conclusions from this." Görnandt found it depressing that he had not been consulted and warned that the goals of Vigor could not be represented properly if it lost the confidence of the agencies in Berlin.[379]

Görnandt may have been temperamental, but he was also quite successful. To be sure, his management constituted a major switch of emphasis from international trade in grains to the guided management of the grain supply with the object of securing grain for Germany and organizing its distribution. In contrast to the past, there was no speculation or free pricing but rather the regulations of an ordered market and fixed profit allowances. For 1938–1939, he could report that Vigor had handled 206,000 tons of grain products, a large amount involving imports into the Reich, and a net profit of 6,368 RM despite the need to deal with past losses. Most important had been the building up of Vigor's position in the Balkan states. In Romania, the purchasing agency had been reconstructed and taken over by the firm of H. Müller, Braila. Görnandt had persuaded Heinrich Müller, an apparently successful and highly regarded grain merchant with whom he had served in the efforts to mobilize the Ukrainian food supply in 1918, to take over in Braila. He was much favored by the Reich Grain Bureau, and had been given special assignments. He handled approximately a quarter of German imports from Romania. In Bulgaria, the firm used was the Cereal-Export AG in Sofia, which

---

377 Ibid., Getreide, 20/09, Görnandt to Friedl, Nov. 9, 1938, and memorandum by Fromm on the history of the Aryanization.

378 Ibid., Görnandt to Friedl, Oct. 18, 1940.
379 Ibid., Görnandt to Friedl, Nov. 16, 1940.

was headed by Sergey Kalendjieff, who also ran the Cereal-Export AG in Belgrade. Kalendjieff could also boast the confidence of the Reich agencies and had managed to attain a monopoly position for his firm in Bulgarian exports of wheat to the Reich. As for Yugoslavia, the relatively low export of wheat to Germany was compensated by the sale of fruits, while the future prospects in grains appeared quite promising because of an arrangement concluded between the Reich Grain Bureau and the Yugoslav government under which the Cereal-Export AG could participate in the exports of the Yugoslav state monopoly and thus get a quarter of the trade with Germany. Because of the exchange restrictions, the various branches of Vigor could not operate with their own means to any great extent, but they were able to get credits from the banks in their respective countries that were guaranteed by German banks, while the CA had given an operating credit of 5,530,000 RM, most of it going to guarantee the aforementioned foreign bank credits. Naturally, the CA-owned Allgemeine Jugoslawische Bankverein in Belgrade provided the Cereal-Export AG with credits.[380]

In 1939–1940, Vigor paid a dividend of 5 percent and continued its expansion, dealing in more products and building up its facilities. Jakober & Cie. was transformed into the Ostmärkische Kraftfutterwerk, and the Bömisch-Mährische Exportmalzfabriken AG, Brunn was created out of the liquidated firm of Export-Malzfabriken Schindler & Stein AG.[381] Despite the fact that Vigor was in so many respects the product of Aryanizations, getting rid of the Jews employed at its companies in the Balkans remained a constant preoccupation. Even Heinrich Müller's company in Romania continued to employ Jews in the spring of 1940. Friedl, who normally seems to have accepted Görnandt's reports without comment, felt called upon to write to Vigor about the

problem: "Out of general considerations as well as in view of the special tasks of our organization, it does not seem to me bearable any longer that we still employ Jews in our Romanian branch. I must therefore ask you to exercise the greatest possible influence on Herr Müller that the few Jewish office personnel still employed in Braila be phased out. In particular, it seems to me that the further employment of a Jewish bookkeeper is dangerous and unbearable."[382] It is highly likely that Görnandt paid heed to these instructions, although he was most positive about the measures taken at the beginning of 1941 by the anti-Semitic regime in Romania itself to eliminate the Jews from the grain business and to organize its production and distribution system to fit in with that of Germany.[383] The process, however, never seemed complete. In July 1941, for example, when Vigor became involved in organizing the milling and exporting of oil seed to Germany through one of its companies, "Solagra," it turned out that some of the best mills were still in Jewish hands. Discussions about the acquisition of one of the mills were held with the Reich Fats Agency. The agency "was strongly interested in taking this object out of the hands of the Jews and to give it to a German group predestined for it."[384]

In Bulgaria, the "Jewish question" took an unexpected and very irritating turn for Görnandt when his key man, Kalendjieff, and his wife were accused of being Jews, which they were not. Görnandt saw this as yet another plot by the competition to hurt Vigor, but Kalendjieff actually made a trip to the Reich Grain Bureau in Berlin to reassert that he was an Aryan and apparently did so successfully. Kalendjieff, in fact, even promoted an Aryanization project for Vigor by suggesting that it get into the business of selling sheep and goat skins to Germany. Seventy-five percent of this profitable business was in the hands of Jews when the Bulgarian government, carrying out its own anti-Semitic

[380] Ibid., report on Südosteuropäische Getreide-Handels-Gesellschaft for 1938–1939, Feb. 1940.

[381] BA-CA, CA-V, report presented to supplement the CA working committee meeting of Nov. 4, 1941, dated Jan. 1942.

[382] BA-CA, CA-IB, Getreide, 20/07, Friedl to Südosteuropäische Getreide-Handels AG, May 17, 1940.

[383] Ibid., Getreide, 20/09, Vigor to Friedl, Jan. 3, 1941.

[384] Ibid., Report to Friedl, July 17, 1941.

measures in economic matters, decreed that the Jews were to be prohibited from further activity in this business. Kalendjieff thought that this was an opportunity for Vigor; it could use its egg-purchasing organization, which was based at eighteen important railroad centers, to gain entry into this business. Görnandt decided to support the proposal because he trusted Kalendjieff's judgment and considered this to be a good way to preempt competition from any other group.[385]

There were vaster projects, however, that occupied Görnandt's thoughts. The war against the Soviet Union and the occupation of Ukraine opened up long-range even if not immediate prospects for Vigor, and in 1941 and 1942 Görnandt sent back a series of chilling reports to Friedl. He noted that conditions in Ukraine were for the time being too chaotic to allow for private firm activity, and the German rulers had set up the special Central Trading Corporation East to manage the situation while maintaining the oppressive collective farm system created by the Soviet regime. Central Trading was now being asked by the Reich food agencies and occupation authorities to supply experienced personnel for the management of the grain harvest in Ukraine. Hermann Göring, however, was promising that the grain business would be privatized at the beginning of 1943, and this held out the prospect that those firms supplying such personnel would be given a priority when privatization came, and would also be well rewarded with hardship pay for working "under unspeakably primitive conditions." They were being called upon to demonstrate the spirit of the royal merchants and Hanseatics, who had once gone overseas, but this time they were challenged "to seize upon this unprecedented chance for their future. Here much more is involved, namely, that in our great struggle for existence it is the

utilization and exploitation of the products of Russia's soil for Germany and all of Europe that, after our unrivalled military successes, constitute the main focus of our final goal."[386] Görnandt reported that there was a desperate need for a bank accounting and oversight system to monitor the collection and shipment of foodstuffs collected from Ukrainian peasants. Therefore, banking personnel were also needed, and Görnandt was urged to talk to Friedl about supplying personnel from Vigor and the CA and thus ensure that the Creditanstalt and the traders connected with it be placed "in the vanguard for the future."

This future, as Görnandt told Friedl a few months later, was to be one in which "the mobilization of the Russian grain harvests is intended not only for Germany, whose supply of bread is assured; rather, it is the provisioning of all of Europe from Russian territory that our Führer has in mind, so that the needy peoples – the Italians, Belgians, Scandinavians, Dutch, Spaniards, and Greeks – who must have grains independently of overseas supplies, can get as much as they need." The Ukrainian bread basket was the key to solving the immediate problems of the war. Once it was controlled by the Reich, the German armies would be cared for and the Russian forces would be finished off quickly. Without that food supply, Görnandt argued, "a mass starvation of previously unknown dimensions among the Russian population would be the certain outcome of an extended war." Germany and a German-dominated Europe would enjoy autarky in its food supply and, as Görnandt reported to Friedl, "The great future development of Vigor, as I see it, will without question take place in Russia at the moment when, as is anticipated, a free economy is in place."[387]

Görnandt took the prospect of the reprivatization of the grain trade in the conquered Eastern regions very seriously, and he lobbied to make sure that the firms of the Danubian

[385] On Kalendjieff's "Jewishness," see Kalendjieff to Director Erich Rossa of the Reich Grain Bureau, Oct. 28, 1941, and Görnandt to Friedl, Feb. 14, 1942, and other relevant documents; on the proposal to go into the animal skin business, see Vigor to Friedl, April 25, 1942.

[386] Here Görnandt was reporting on the remarks made at a meeting of the grain importers he attended. See ibid., Görnandt to Friedl, Nov. 10, 1941.

[387] Ibid., Görnandt to Friedl, Feb. 12, 1942.

and Alpine regions had their "place in the sun" along with those of the old Reich. Görnandt was very disappointed at the poor response of the Vienna firms to the summons to send people to the east to work for the food administration there, and the influx of trained people was insufficient to meet the demand. General Director Fleischberger, a Bavarian merchant who directed the Central Trading Corporation East and who knew Görnandt well, complained that many of the people who came to work for him were incompetent, corrupt, and draft dodgers. Fleischberger labored heavily under Göring's demands for grains from the Ukraine, and in September 1942 he asked Görnandt whether he would be willing to take over the Central Grain Office in Kiev. While Görnandt found this kind of responsibility attractive, he reminded Fleischberger of his responsibilities in the southeast and doubted that the CA would let him go on leave to work in the Ukraine. He did point out, however, that he had very specific ideas for Vigor in Russia, and hoped to build up an organization in the Azov-Black Sea area once privatization of the grain trade had taken place: "In this case, he also considered going to Russia himself for half a year, together with his leading colleagues in Bucharest and Sofia, and then, after establishing the organization, to turn it over to the leadership of suitable younger people."[388] Clearly, therefore, Görnandt was more than ready to take the initiative in making the most of the opportunities potentially provided by the National Socialist regime's eastern policy, in which he apparently believed, and there is no evidence that Friedl had the slightest reluctance about encouraging or supporting these plans for Vigor.

At this point, however, Görnandt was very reluctant to return to public service, and while he definitely saw that Vigor's future – and his own ambitions – lay in Russia, he had more than enough to do at the moment with respect to Vigor's pressing problems. Many of them were in fact caused by the Russian adventure. On July 15, 1942, Görnandt reported to Friedl

on the great changes taking place at the Reich Grain Bureau. The number of officials there was being reduced from about 2,900 to 1,400 and nearly all of those released were being sent to Ukraine. This meant that the private merchants and the cooperatives would have to take over many of the tasks previously performed by the bureau, especially storage of products and direct delivery to consumers. Because the firms now would also be preserving the imported goods and transporting them to customers, the work of Vigor's Vienna office would be increased considerably. At the same time, the previous services of the bureau as a negotiator with other governments would cease, and the individual firms would have to take on this task. The bureau would continue to oversee both prices and fulfilment of the provisions entailed by Germany's economic agreements with the countries in question. Finally, the grain trade with Hungary, which previously had been conducted solely by the Reich Grain Bureau, would now be transferred to the private firms. Accordingly, Vigor was to become the leading trading partner of the "Futura" company, which, as Görnandt noted, "promises an interesting and significant boost to our business."[389]

That business, however, was extremely complicated, indeed messy, and depended on a host of economic and political factors as well as the natural ones that were always present when dealing with agricultural products. It is important to realize that the CA's engagement in this business was not limited to Vigor but also extended to other important merchant firms. This is well demonstrated by a memorandum on the subject of September 1943. Among the companies in the grain trade, Vigor certainly got the lion's share of CA credits, having received a 15 million RM credit and acquired another 35 million RM for the harvest of 1943–1944, but substantial credits were also given to M. Friessacher & Söhne, Friedrich Glatz, and Dr. H. & H. Putz. Additionally, the CA had a number of small, less important firms as customers. The three firms

---

[388] Ibid., report on Görnandt's discussion with Fleischberger, Sept. 10, 1942, sent to Friedl.

[389] Ibid., Getreide, 20/07, Görnandt to Friedl, July 15, 1942; see also BA-CA, CA-V, the report to the CA working committee, July 15, 1942.

mentioned earlier took credits not only from the CA but also from the Länderbank and the Bank der deutschen Arbeit and were thus part of consortia arrangements. These firms participated in domestic enterprises in the countries of Southeast Europe that pursued trade in grains and other agricultural products. The financing of these firms was often done by credits from domestic banks affiliated with the CA, the Comro in Bucharest, the Deutsch-Bulgarische Bank in Sofia, and the Bankverein AG in Belgrade. The credits given by these banks were frequently guaranteed by the CA in Vienna. The affiliated banks also gave credits for the grain trade of other companies in no way involved with the CA directly. It is not surprising that the officials at the CA who were associated with Vigor, like Friedl and Ernst Lanz, followed the grain trade very closely with the full extent of the CA's engagement in it in mind.[390]

Nevertheless, the affairs of Vigor were always of paramount concern to the CA, and a report of July 1943 provided a survey of its status and, in particular, the status of its subsidiary companies.[391] As usual, the situation in Romania was central, and here the most important factor was the affairs of the Müller-Cereal-Export SAR, Bucharest-Braila (MCE), which had a capital of 20 million lei, 80 percent formally belonging to Müller and the remainder to various Romanians. Despite the bad grain harvest of 1942, the MCE was able to pay a 6 percent dividend and substantial honoraria thanks to the large business it did in legumes and the oil seed from "Solagra" SAR, in which it unofficially had a 30 percent interest. While the MCE did not engage in speculative purchases because it only bought products for which there was a sales order, the Romanian government introduced a speculative element by failing to authorize exports on time, and a considerable amount in credits had to be taken from the Romanian banks. An excellent grain harvest was expected

for 1943, but the Romanians were striving to have it all sold through their own purchasing agency, Incoop, and to exclude German firms. How much Germany would get depended on the outcome of the negotiations between the two countries, but the likelihood was that in 1943 the MCE would once again earn its profits from legumes and seed oil.

The prospects seemed better in Bulgaria, where the Cereal-Export AG, Sofia was almost entirely owned by Vigor. It had paid a 6 percent dividend in 1942 and sold a variety of products. Its section dealing with grains had a special arrangement with the Reich Grain Bureau, the so-called Special Action Bulgaria, which involved the purchase and distribution of foodstuffs for the Wehrmacht. The other two sections of the Bulgarian operation were devoted to eggs and to sheep and goat skins, and the prospects for all products in 1943 seemed quite good.

The situation in Serbia, which because of the war had been quite grim in the second half of 1941 and early 1942, picked up significantly. There were two companies involved, the Cereal-Export AG, Pantschowa and the Cereal-Frucht AG, Belgrad. The former, as commissioned by the General Plenipotentiary for Serbia, engaged in the export of wheat, corn, and sunflower seeds from the Banat, and had a 50 million dinar credit from the Bankverein Belgrade that was guaranteed by Vigor. Because a very good harvest was anticipated, the credit need was expected to be extraordinarily high, and Vigor worked with the Reich Grain Bureau in Berlin to develop clearing and other arrangements to meet the company's needs. The Cereal-Frucht AG Belgrade was a subsidiary company of the firm in Pantschowa, and appears to have been mainly concerned with supplying provisions to the mining and timber operations in Serbia.

Finally, Vigor's new engagement in Hungary primarily involved the export of oil seed in collaboration with the "Futura" company. The oil seed was paid for by credits from the Hungarian banks given against the presentation of bills of sale. Because of the requisite clearing arrangements, which could take as long as two months,

---

[390] See BA-CA, CA-IB, Getreide, 20/09, the report by Lanz for Friedl, Sept. 1, 1943. Lanz became a deputy director in 1944.

[391] This report, dated July 28, 1943, is to be found in DB, P 6516, Bl. 95–98.

Vigor had to make large payments into the German-Hungarian clearing. The worth of these sales was 30 million RM, and the company thus needed credits amounting to 15 million RM to deal with the business. Also, the Reich Fats Agency was importing oil seed on a special basis and needed a 10 million RM credit from Vigor to do so.

Manifestly, the company's business report tried to present Vigor's situation in as favorable a light as possible. But Berlin also received both the general report and auditor reports on some of Vigor's branches, and here they came under the critical eye of the head of its chief economist, E. W. Schmidt, who fed Abs a series of analyses and comments that Abs found alarming. Abs was quite ready to be alarmed because over the previous two years he had asked regularly for better information and more thorough reports. As he pointed out to Hasslacher on September 3, 1943, the CA now was engaged not only in Southeast Europe but also in the Generalgouvernement; he was convinced that the investments of the CA were quite risky because they were in any and every type of business, they were not organically connected, and they were easy prey for self-serving as well as self-interested accounts by those involved. He considered it extremely important that independent accountants examine the reports critically and determine what the risks actually were.[392]

Schmidt's critical stance on Vigor gave Abs an opportunity to press this position, and he asked Schmidt to produce a long letter to Friedl bearing Abs's signature.[393] He instructed Schmidt to assume that Vigor belonged 100 percent to the CA and to argue, on the basis of the material at hand, "that without a doubt the business must

also entail substantial speculative risks." Abs thought that the letter might conclude by suggesting that a trading establishment belonging to a bank requires much more supervision than an independent customer working with its own capital.

The eleven-page document Abs sent to Friedl on September 8, 1943, was very formidable indeed.[394] It began by pointing out that his detailed discussion and various queries were to be understood in the context of the massive engagement in Vigor and that special attention was required with reference to "debtors whose own capabilities does not correspond to the extent of their business engagements." In his exhaustive remarks, he raised several points: the Müller-Cereal-Export was really losing money, its 6 percent dividend was unjustified, the prices paid were too high, and, finally, there were unexplained inconsistencies in prices paid for the same products. In addition, he suggested that the political risks being run by the MCE in view of the self-serving practices of the Romanian government were underestimated, and he worried about the Romanization policy eventually extending to the MCE. He also questioned claims that the MCE was not running any exchange risk. The structure of the debts to the Romanian banks, Abs warned, was problematic and might lead to big CA losses. He was happier with Vigor's Bulgarian operation from both an economic and a political perspective. He did not think "Bulgarization" was as much a danger as "Romanization," but he did note the dangers of bureaucratic direction and high taxes. He was also concerned about a devaluation of the Lewa and the effect this might have on Vigor assets in Bulgaria. As to Vigor's Serbian operations, Abs expressed great dissatisfaction with the lack of pertinent information and especially criticized the fact that the credits being taken by Pantschowa were twenty times its capital including reserves. He also noted some unanswered question regarding Vigor's functioning in Hungary. In any case, Abs's letter concluded along the lines that

392 DB, P 62, Bl. 306, Abs to Hasslacher, Sept. 3, 1943. It is interesting to note that beginning in 1942, the protocols of the CA working committee include not simply lists of important credits given but also rather full reports on firms in the CA concern to which large credits have been given as well as status reports on enterprises to which very large credits have been given. This may have been a result of Abs's call for better information.

393 Ibid., Bl. 304, Abs to Schmidt, Sept. 3, 1943.

394 For this discussion, see ibid., Bl. 259–269, Abs to Friedl, Sept. 8, 1943.

he had asked Schmidt to develop, leaving the impression that Vigor was something of a mess and in desperate need of an audit. Recalling the situation in August 1938 and the attacks on Schindler, it appears that an "Aryan misadministration" had replaced the alleged "Jewish misadministration" and that Vigor had never been more "speculative"!

Görnandt seems to have been well aware of the attitude toward his enterprise in some circles, and he responded somewhat in the manner Schindler had replied to Abs, by emphasizing the dynamic nature of the grain business. At a meeting of the Vigor supervisory board in February 1942 he reminded everyone "first of all to always realize and never to overlook that fact that in our enterprise one cannot employ the measure of a factory or a similar enterprise which allows a precise and strict overview of the present and future on the basis of firm precalculations, that is, plant capacity, machines and the available raw materials, as well as wages, sales, etc.... The success of our enterprise lies almost exclusively in its trade. Among all branches of the economy, it is possibly the grain trade in particular which, irrespective of all the competence, industriousness, or foresight of a wise business management, and completely apart from its own wishes, must almost daily adapt and subordinate itself again and again to changing circumstances." It was a business, after all, that dealt with living products, subject to weather, soil, and other conditions but also subject to political circumstances in the producing lands, the goodwill of their governments, and their willingness to export.[395]

In short, it was an intrinsically speculative business requiring a dynamic approach, but in contrast to Schindler's argumentation the heart of the speculation from Görnandt's perspective was intimately connected not to the conduct of business in the liberal sense; the connection, rather, was service to the war effort. When Friedl responded to Abs, therefore, after having Lanz, to be sure, send a long list of replies to

the technical questions raised, he stressed the essential points about doing such business in the context of the war and the goals of the regime. He told Abs that the CA and Vigor's leadership were completely aware of the risks and had been so from the very start. They had taken over Vigor at the behest of the Reich agencies, turning what they considered to be a disorderly and run down organization into what Friedl and Görnandt purported it to be, namely, a well-managed, internally stable, and profitable business that had the trust of the authorities. These, Friedl added, "in what is a very flattering manner employ our corporation, usually alone or in a leading position, for special assignments and larger commissions." Vigor, therefore, did its work in the interests of the Reich, but also in its own interests and in those of the Ostmark. While it worked together with other Ostmark grain firms – Friesacher, Glatz, Putz, and so forth – none of them had the capital that Vigor had. Giving up business to them, something Abs seemed to hint at as being desirable, would strain the resources of these firms "and would mean for us only the loss of possibility to make profit but not a reduction of risk."[396] Friedl tried to reassure Abs about the care that was being taken to ensure sound financial and economic practices under the circumstances. Nonetheless, there were always dangers doing business in a foreign country, and the threat to the MCE from the Romanian government policies was simply a commercial and political risk that had to be faced. For if the MCE were closed down, it would have to be liquidated. But it had to be the goal to keep the company operating so as to supply the Reich with the grain it needed.

Whether Abs's doubts were laid to rest by these replies was, in a sense, beside the point once such an answer had been given. He thanked Friedl for clarifying the situation and understood the bases on which Vigor operated. The entire operation depended on the war and its outcome, and the CA had become invested in this cause. If the war ended in victory, Görnandt could expand Vigor and the CA could go into business in the

---

395 BA-CA, CA-IB, Getreide, 20/12, Report by Görnandt to the supervisory board meeting on Feb. 25, 1942.

396 Ibid., Getreide, 20/07, Friedl to Abs, Sept. 16, 1943.

East. If not, everything would collapse. Needless to say, the situation in the Balkans became ever more chaotic in the course of 1944, but Friedl treated the financial dangers somewhat casually, reporting that most of the business was being conducted with Reich guarantees even if actual compensation for war damages might not be paid.[397] As for the ever temperamental Görnandt, who seems to have remained a true believer to the bitter end, his sentiments were well expressed in his 1944 Christmas greetings to Friedl: "Unfortunately, in the last half year we have had to take hard blows. Not only did we have to witness the collapse overnight, so to speak, of all that we have built up, in long years and with love and energy, in the Southeast, but the personal fate of our valued co-workers and friends in Romania and Bulgaria no doubt has strongly affected us also emotionally. After the rain, sunshine comes again. I thus express my strong hope that the new year will bring the desired change for the better. If life should continue to have any meaning at all, then we will not only survive in this great conflict between good and evil but ultimately succeed in the end. I believe this with confidence, likewise also in the revival of Vigor's mission in the Southeast at the right moment."[398]

Del-Ka

Vigor was the most important enterprise controlled by the CA engaged in international trade and was playing a central role in the southeast program, but it is important not to overlook other major enterprises in the CA concern that were also engaged in this expansion into the Southeast. To be sure, Friedl and Görnandt tried to give the impression that the CA had taken over Vigor in order to satisfy the demands of the Reich Grain Bureau, especially in trying to quiet Abs's doubts, but it should be obvious from the discussion that it was Vigor's role as a part of the CA concern that was uppermost in their minds and not the kind of "normal"

banking business they did with other grain merchants. Furthermore, there are other important examples demonstrating the aggressiveness of the CA in trying to build up and consolidate its concern outside Germany and Austria proper. These examples are not only important to illustrate the ambitions of the CA in the Third Reich but also to examine the full extent of its vigorous efforts to promote Aryanization in Southeast and East Central Europe.

An especially important case was that of the Del-Ka shoe concern, which, like Vigor, became a product of and then an instrument for Aryanization abroad under the aegis of the CA. Founded in 1907, Del-Ka was 75 percent in the hands of a Jewish family, the Klausners; the CA held 16 percent of the company. It had ten sales branches in Vienna and six in other parts of Austria, and had contracts with twenty-eight independent sales operations. It owned 100 percent of the Del-Ka Schuhindustrie- und Handels-AG, Budapest and held stakes in the Orzel shoe firm in Cracow and Divota AG in Zagreb (operated by the American Shoe Company). It also owned a holding company in Vaduz, the Continentale Industrie- und Handels-AG. As one might expect, Del-Ka was a prime target for Aryanization.

Because the complicated story of its Aryanization has been recounted elsewhere, the discussion here will concentrate on the political aspects of the Aryanization and on the functioning of the CA as an industrial and commercial concern.[399] The major figure in the family and 50 percent shareholder in Del-Ka, Ludwig Klausner, was arrested March 11 and sent to Dachau soon thereafter. The placing of Jewish family owners in Dachau or other concentration camps, thereby making them hostages for the surrender of their enterprises and assets, became something of a standard procedure in large Aryanizations, and to the extent that the CA was involved, it became a conscious beneficiary of such practices. Coincident with the

---

[397] BA-CA, CA-V, CA working committee meeting, Sept. 26, 1944.

[398] BA-CA, CA-IB, Getreide, 20/09, Görnandt to Friedl, Dec. 21, 1944.

[399] See Felber et al., *Ökonomie der Arisierung*, II, pp. 104–169. The account by Ulrike Felber is based on materials in the BA-CA, CA-IB, gathered by this author and placed at her disposal.

arrest of Klausner, Joseph Starkl, a Party member, a long-time employee of the company, and the head of the large Mariahilferstrasse branch, took over as commissarial administrator of the company. This all happened in the first days of the Anschluss, but Ludwig Klausner had earlier sought to preempt taking over his shares by trying to sell the business to the Magdeburg firm of Tack & Cie., which itself had been Aryanized by the firm of Carl Freudenberg in Weinheim an der Weinstrasse.

The Del-Ka shares were held by Klausner in a depot at the CA, which the CA received permission to open. Starkl intended to use the services of the CA in the Aryanization of Del-Ka. This was necessary because the CA was the house bank of Del-Ka and held its own share in the concern. The CA was well aware of Tack's interest and also knew that other German companies, especially the Stuttgart shoe firm Salamander, were interested in Del-Ka. Starkl, with the knowledge of the CA, sought and received permission from the authorities to go to Dachau and get Klausner to agree to an arrangement with Tack for the operation of Del-Ka. A contract was worked out and submitted for accounting and legal analysis.

The dealings with Tack and Starkl's collaboration with the CA had come in good time to preempt the plans of Salamander, whose lawyer Hermann Weyss had contacted the authorities in late April and asked that Klausner be brought back to Vienna to negotiate with Salamander representatives. He pointed out that the four other members of the Klausner family holding shares in Del-Ka were highly dependent on Ludwig Klausner and were quite at sea without his direction. As far as the CA was concerned, Del-Ka's chief shareholder was now the German Reich. But Del-Ka's Jewish directors having been dismissed, as Weyss's statement made clear, "the remaining Aryan directors are so overburdened with work, hence unavailable, that it would be impossible for them to travel to Dachau, as important as the matter may seem."[400]

The Klausner family members, however, were so anxious to have Ludwig's advice and help that they were prepared to make a 10,000 RM contribution to the National Socialist People's Welfare Organization from what they received for their shares as well as for the costs of guarding Ludwig Klausner, his upkeep, and his trip to and from Dachau. What was at stake, according to Weyss, was the employment of Del-Ka's 400 employees and their families that would be guaranteed if Salamander took over Del-Ka.

Neither the CA nor its ambitions, however, could be dismissed so easily. The bank's leadership saw Del-Ka as important, but it was not the only company in the Austrian shoe industry in which the CA had an interest. In a letter to Minister Hans Fischböck of April 29, 1938, discussing these interests, the CA reported that it had instructed its lawyer to negotiate with Ludwig Klausner and his sister Fanny Hulles, who had an 8.33 percent interest in Del-Ka and was also under arrest, to see if they would sell their shares to the CA for a provisional price of 15 Schilling a share. The CA would act as a trustee to sell the shares to a buyer approved by the authorities. The price finally paid to Klausner and Hulles might be lowered if an examination of the status of the company and the price received justified this. In the meantime, the important thing according to the CA was that Del-Ka and those dependent on it were able to declare the firm Aryan and were not driven into unemployment and financial difficulty. Aside from its shares, the CA was also owed considerable money for the credits it had given.

In addition to Del-Ka, however, the CA had an interest in another firm largely in Jewish hands, the "Aeterna" Schuhfabriks-AG, which along with Del-Ka and Bally was one of the three largest shoe producers in Europe. Moritz Altstadt and his wife, Clara, owned a majority stake of 57.75 percent. The CA held 20.2 percent of the shares. Del-Ka and the leather factory Fr. Vogl in Mattighofen each held 9.5 percent, the latter being Aryan. The rest was owned by various small shareholders, most of whom were Jewish. As in the case of Del-Ka, the Aeterna was under the commissarial direction of a

400   ÖStA/AdR, MfWuA, VVSt, Industrie, Box 341, Zl. 496a, Hermann Weyss to the Police Headquarters, April 30, 1938.

National Socialist willing to work with the CA, Josef Grödl, who was described by the CA as an "apparently very reliable man, who keeps constant contact with us."[401] Here, as in the case of Del-Ka, a solution was sought under which the CA would take over the majority shares as trustee from the owner, Altstadt, in this case, to sell them off to an acceptable Aryan. Altstadt and his wife "were completely aware of the situation" – a phrase often used with respect to the Jews being pressured to sell – and were ready to cooperate. Here again, however, the immediate transfer of the shares into the hands of an Aryan trustee was deemed essential to get business moving again, not only for the sake of the 750 employees of the firm but also because Aeterna's suppliers were suffering, as were the various shoe merchants and stores to which Aeterna delivered.

Finally, the aforementioned considerations led to yet a third Jewish-owned firm that the CA informed Fischböck was of interest to it, namely, the "Hermes"-F. Hulles Schuhverkaufsgesellschaft. It was owned by Ludwig Klausner's sister, Fanny Hulles, and her son, Emil – both of whom had been interned – and employed 249 persons, of whom 135 were Aryan. The company had been very hard hit by the boycott of Jewish businesses. Hermes was a major purchaser of Aeterna products. It was unable to pay its debts either to Aeterna or the CA, and it was likewise unable to pay either its rent or its workers. Friedl thought the best way to solve the problem was for Aeterna to buy Hermes, but to do this Aeterna had to be Aryanized itself.

The politics of Aryanizing the shoe business was convoluted indeed, and it was to become more complicated because of conflicting political and economic interests.

The biggest immediate problem for the CA in the spring of 1938 was that the Party was actively persecuting Jewish shoe companies by posting SA men in front their stores and painting warning against patronizing Jewish

firms on their windows. The CA thus had a direct interest in the Aryanization of the enterprises in which it had stakes and to which it had given credits. Its offer to buy out shares and serve as trustee holder of the shares could not officially be interpreted as an attempt to attain permanent ownership of the enterprises. The model, in fact, was the Gerngross department store, whose shares were also acquired by the CA at this time, and which subsequently were to be sold off while retaining its banking business.[402]

Nevertheless, when it came to selling the shares of Del-Ka to the Magdeburg firm Tack, the CA leadership began to develop serious reservations. One issue, of course, was the sale of Del-Ka to a German rather than an Austrian enterprise. Because of the regulation that Austrian purchasers who met the requirements were to be given priority over those from the old Reich, the representatives of Tack consulted with Hans Kehrl on March 29. Kehrl did indeed declare that any agreement made between Klausner and Tack had to contain a clause that a suitable Austrian purchaser was to receive priority. Robert Glatzl of the CA attended the meeting, and while he did not think that there was an Austrian shoe firm that had the requisite capital to take over Del-Ka, he was very concerned by a remark Kehrl made that, if taken over by Tack, Del-Ka's name needed to be changed. Glatzl strongly opposed this. Aside from the expense of changing all the signs and doors, the name "Del-Ka" had become a household word and was responsible for attracting a great deal of business.[403]

There was another matter of great importance to the CA if Tack were to take over Del-Ka, namely, that it continue to have Del-Ka's business. This was a right it could claim as an important shareholder and creditor of Del-Ka. While the plan to sell the shares to Tack seemed to be moving forward in the spring of 1938, there is evidence that the CA began to seek ways to block it. Here it received

---

[401] BA-CA, CA-IB, Del-Ka,03/07-08, Friedl to Fischböck, April 29, 1938, and CA to O. Eberhardt, May 10, 1938.

[402] See the discussion of the Aryanization of Gerngross AG in Chapter 2, pp. 130–132, of this volume.

[403] Ibid., Glatzl report to Heller, March 30, 1938.

considerable help from Josef Grödl of Aeterna. At a meeting at the CA on May 13, Grödl and Starkl met with Friedl to discuss the ongoing plan to turn the Del-Ka business over to Tack, a plan that seemed to have the approval of Otto Eberhardt, who worked in Wilhelm Keppler's office. Fischböck, however, refrained from giving such support. At the same time, Grödl complained that a sale of the business to Tack would mean that Del-Ka would no longer be sold shoes by its chief suppliers, above all Aeterna, which now had been Aryanized, but also by a number of other Austrian firms that were Aryan in character. This solution would do serious damage to the native Austrian shoe industry and undermine links that had been built up over a long time.[404]

In 1938, the CA was commissioned by the Property to serve as trustee of the shares of the Altstadt family – the arrangements for the transfer were completed in May – and of Ludwig Klausner, who surrendered his claim to the shares in November. The price he received had been revised downward from 10 RM to 4 RM per share. Klausner was released from Dachau and could leave the country. The CA reported to the Property Transfer Bureau, as if to provide assurance that the Jew Klausner did not walk away with any reward for his life's labors, that "the money realized from shares was used by Klausner to pay his various debts, chiefly tax liabilities, before he left the Ostmark."[405]

The CA faced more complications in dealing with the shares held by Fanny Hulles's Hermes. The firm was placed under the administration of Alfred Proksch, who previously handled its advertising and who, along with his brother Hans, was a member of the SS and had been involved in the July 1934 Putsch. In a long and very revealing letter to the VVSt of July 20, 1938, Alfred Proksch claimed that he had tried very hard to find an Aryan purchaser for Hermes who came from the Ostmark but was unsuccessful in getting anyone with

sufficient capital. At the same time, he was aware that the CA had effectively taken over Del-Ka and Aeterna along with Aeterna's retail businesses, "Paga," "Astra," and Parsch. Aeterna was the chief creditor of Hermes, and Proksch knew that Aeterna wanted to bring Hermes into what was becoming a CA shoe corporation. Knowing that "such concern building never lies in the interest of a National Socialist economic policy," Proksch informed his contacts in the VVSt of his apprehensions. He was apparently instructed not to let Hermes fall into the hands of the CA concern, whereupon he informed Aeterna of his intention not to sell to them. Allegedly, the result was that Aeterna first offered Proksch a position in the concern if he would end his resistance and then pushed forward persons as buyers who were really straw men for Aeterna, while the CA created all kinds of financial difficulties for Hermes. In his search for someone with the financial means to take over Hermes, Proksch made the acquaintance of a Rhenish shoe businessman, Anton König, who was not only a Party man, but also an "old fighter" and willing to finance a takeover of Hermes by the Proksch brothers. In order to avoid a conflict of interest in making this proposal, Proksch stepped down as commissarial administrator of Hermes and recommended another Party man and SS member to replace him. At the same time, the CA recommended a member of the Aeterna and Del-Ka administrative councils, Josef Ziegler. As of late July, no commissar had been appointed, and Proksch had not received preliminary approval for the takeover of Hermes on the grounds that the Hermes branches had to be divided and that König was not acceptable because he was a Reich German. Proksch charged that the division of Hermes would make it unviable and was nothing more than an effort by the CA to destroy the company if it could not take it over and then buy out the branches individually because they would bear the burden of the Hermes debts. As for the rejection of König and the Proksch brothers, Alfred was outraged that Party members with such records should be rejected when it was well known that there was an insufficient number of Aryans with

404 BA-CA, CA-IB, Del-Ka, 03/07-08, meeting of May 13, 1938.
405 ÖStA/AdR, MfWuA, VVSt, Industrie, Box 341, Zl. 496a, Bl. 114–115, CA to Dr. Jäger, Aug. 6, 1940.

sufficient capital in the Ostmark to purchase such enterprises.[406]

Subsequently, Ziegler did become commissarial administrator of Hermes, where he raised strong objections to both König and the Proksch brothers. On the one hand, he argued that the delivery arrangements with Aeterna would be replaced by contracts with König. On the other, he repeatedly warned that, "as an old leather expert," he did not think that either brother knew enough about the business to manage it properly. Ziegler had sent Party colleagues to the Proksch brothers to urge them to withdraw and gave repeated warnings to the VVSt.[407] Nevertheless, the Proksch brothers were viewed by Bürckel as ideal Party restitution and compensation cases and, as a result, they were provisionally awarded the right to purchase Hermes in September with the condition that they maintain the contract with Aeterna, close down one of the branches, and agree to financial supervision by Ziegler. The Proksch brothers objected to these terms, and the Hermes case was handed over to the Kontrollbank in October, when an agreement was finally reached. The first two conditions were accepted, and the oversight by Ziegler, tantamount to having the fox guard the chicken coop, was surrendered in return for Hermes's sale of its Del-Ka shares to the Kontrollbank which, in turn, sold them to the CA.

While Alfred Proksch's demonstration of radical National Socialist, anticapitalist sentiments was anything if not self-interested, there is no reason to doubt that he held such views, as did many others in the Party. More importantly, he was absolutely correct about the concern-building ambitions of the CA. This becomes evident from an unsigned and undated proposal that must have been written before the takeover of Hermes by the Proksch brothers in the fall because it argues for the takeover of Hermes by Aeterna. This proposal envisioned the expansion of Aeterna's production and of its holdings in other firms in order to rationalize its operations and increase its market share at home and abroad.[408] Under existing circumstances, Aeterna produced for a great variety of customers and often did so at different times of the year. It had to send salespersons to these customers and also had to cater to different tastes and wishes. At the same time, it needed to have a group of shoe sellers who sold Aeterna products exclusively or were bound by contract to sell a fixed quantity of its products, for example, Hermes, the Pasch firm, Del-Ka, and the Herzl firm in Graz. In this system, Aeterna was able to produce for nine months of the year, while its workers were on part-time during the other months. However, if Aeterna greatly expanded the number of sales outlets with a permanent connection to itself and an obligation to take Aeterna products, it could count on a fixed volume of sales over the entire year and reduce costs. It could eliminate part-time work, provide the workers with greater security and benefits, strengthen the specialization of the skilled workers, reduce material usage and time, raise profitability by increasing the production necessary to ensure constant demand, be more competitive at home and abroad, make full use of plant capacity, and comply with the new social legislation that made it so difficult to let workers and employees go. To accomplish these goals, Aeterna would continue to exist and be allowed to expand its production in such a way as to be employed over the entire year, while it would add Del-Ka, Hermes, Friedrich Pasch, and a substantial number of small and medium-sized enterprises in the provinces to its holdings so as to constitute a new commercial enterprise. Aeterna products would account for 60 percent to 70 percent of what the members of this enterprise would sell. While these various sales units would maintain their independence so as to serve the individual needs of their customers, the leadership at the top would combine responsibility for production and sales. This would make possible a unified, efficient, and cheaper procurement of materials as well as a better distribution of inventory. It would

[406] ÖStA/AdR, Materie-Bürckel, RK, Box 48, Ordner 100, Alfred Proksch to Pg. Ing. Waschke, VVSt, July 20, 1938.

[407] Ibid., testimony of Josef Ziegler, Oct. 3, 1938.

[408] It is to be found in BA-CA, CA-IB, Del-Ka, 03a/04.

also allow for the elimination of traveling sales-men, for better oversight of the financial deal-ings between the concern and its members, and for more efficient calculation of prices.

The proposed arrangement, as the author of this synopsis viewed it, would serve not only the CA's holdings in the shoe business but also other enterprises in the CA concern because the industry produced different types of shoes made of a variety of materials. Particular men-tion was made of the Semperit AG, a rubber producer, and textile enterprises that could act both as suppliers on the production side and as sellers making use of the Aeterna sales organi-zation. Naturally, the CA would also function as a banker to the expanded organization. Finally, it was anticipated that 30 percent of the shoe concern's production would be exported. The new regime in Austria expected the firm to do "pioneering services" in the export area, and in this respect Austria's shoe industry was now in a position to compete with Czechoslovakia and Hungary because, as had been the practice in those countries, it would also receive export rebates. In this way, it would acquire the foreign exchange to buy raw materials not available in the Reich.

One can only guess at the identity of the author of this wide-ranging program, but the style, tone, and ambitions expressed make it reasonable to suspect Josef Ziegler, who was to play a role in the CA shoe concern not dis-similar from that of Görnandt in Vigor. Be that as it may, CA Director Friedl, who dealt with these holdings for the management board, and Robert Glatzl of the Concern Division of the CA found in Ziegler a very valuable man to direct the CA shoe enterprises and look after their interests with the authorities. The thirty-eight-year-old Ziegler actually had rea-sonable qualifications to head a shoe business. He had studied leather working, had manufac-tured and sold Lederhosen, and had also worked at the Supervisory Agency for Leather and the Economic Group for the Leather Industry in Berlin. An ardent National Socialist, he had been a Party member since 1932 and an exile follow-ing the July Putsch; he could thus claim com-pensation and restitution for his alleged services

and sacrifices. He did so by asking to take over Hausschuhfabrik KG Alfred Friedmann Company, a leading producer of house shoes. Friedmann owned 25 percent, Charlotte Posner another 25 percent, and Ludwig Klausner the remaining 50 percent. It was a major supplier of Del-Ka, in which it also held 200 shares. Initially, Ziegler dealt with the VVSt and then with the Kontrollbank, acquiring the com-pany between August and October at a price so low that it caused some distress even in the Kontrollbank. He renamed the firm "Nesta" and placed its management under one of his Party cronies, Harry Teichmüller. Ziegler's funds actually never sufficed to buy the com-pany, but he did so anyway with a credit from Aeterna, where he was a member of the admin-istrative council. The money, in effect, came from the CA, and "Nesta" now was also part of the CA concern.[409]

Ziegler was clearly interested in feather-ing his own nest and was in a good position to do so as head of the Special Group for Shoe Retailing. In this position, he assumed an important role in the attempt to deal with the shoe shortage that arose in the Ostmark after the Anschluss, heading a committee to nego-tiate with the Czech branch of the Bata shoe concern for the production of 1.5 million shoes for the Ostmark beginning in December 1939.[410] Increasingly, however, Ziegler's chief preoccupation was advancing his fortunes in the service of the CA shoe concern. Because of his good connections and knowledge of the field, he attracted the attention of the CA leadership quite early and was invited to join the Aryanized Aeterna administrative council in April 1938 and also to serve on the Del-Ka council. He was clearly very useful in dealing with the Party authorities and official agencies in the leather business. His active role in the CA concern was greatly enhanced on October 24, 1938, when he replaced Josef Starkl as factory leader and effective general director of Del-Ka.

---

409 Felber et al., *Ökonomie der Arisierung*, II, pp. 148–152.
410 BAB, R 10/VI/62, vol. 5, Material on shoe plan-ning. I am grateful to Anne Sudrow for providing this reference and information.

Starkl was accused of "asocial behavior," of not being industriousness, of having badly managed the preparations for the Christmas shopping season, of unsatisfactory wage policies, and of having used the company car exclusively for himself and his wife.[411]

While Aeterna and Del-Ka pursued their business in 1939–1940, adding to their holdings in the shoe sales business in large measure by Aryanizations, it was not until September 1940 that the VVSt finally agreed to treat the CA as the legal owner of rather than the trustee for the shares of Del-Ka and Aeterna. In effect, it accepted these large shoe enterprises as part of the CA concern. The long delay undoubtedly reflected continued hostility in the Party, manifested especially in the resistance to the Aeterna effort to take over the Paga and Pasch retail chains, which the Gauleiter in Salzburg and the Lower Danube thought should be reserved for worthy Party members.[412] It may also have reflected a certain reluctance within the VVSt to face the reality that sufficient capital to produce a "rationalized" shoe business in the Ostmark could only be found in the CA.

Whatever the case, once the CA actually legally owned Aeterna and Del-Ka, one could proceed with the project contained in the 1938 exposé discussed earlier. On December 11, 1940, the supervisory boards of Aeterna and Del-Ka met at the CA.[413] Director Friedl chaired the Aeterna board meeting, which was lengthier and fuller in content than the Del-Ka meeting. This was quite fitting because, as Friedl explained, the two companies would continue to exist but Aeterna would be the "proprietary company." They would form a "joint operating entity" that would serve to reinforce the old reputation of the shoe industry of the Ostmark, to preserve it, and, moreover, to expand it also in the Southeast." The models to be employed in the reorganization were those used in the

Reich by the Tack and Salamander concerns and were based on a close coordination of production and distribution whereby certain levels of production and sales would be guaranteed. Friedl pointed out that this fit in with the planning efforts of the Reich. Del-Ka and the various outlets and distributors would be bound to the proprietary company as a subsidiary. Aeterna and Del-Ka would coordinate their balance sheet accounting, and the CA would sell its shares in Del-Ka to Aeterna, so that the latter would have the shares of what had become its subsidiary. Aeterna was to expand its property holdings and facilities in Atzgersdorf bei Wien by purchasing Del-Ka property and by buying "Jewish property" that was likely to become available in the near future. Nevertheless, the need for additional production facilities was anticipated, and both companies were contemplating the acquisition of shoe factories in the Protectorate that were to be Aryanized, for example, Tip-Top in Prague or Brüder Reichsfeld, Marke Standard in Vesely. To ensure greater coordination and uniformity, Friedl announced that Josef Ziegler was to become chairman of the management boards of both Aeterna and Del-Ka and would give up his supervisory board seat on Aeterna. Josef Grödl was to join the management board Del-Ka management board as a deputy director in addition to his position as an Aeterna director. In the fall of 1941, he fell prey to complaints about his management and lost his position, thus leaving Ziegler as sole master of the house. A number of other personnel decisions were announced, of which perhaps the most important was that Director Fritz Kraus of the Kaufhaus der Wiener, formerly Gerngross, would replace Ziegler on the Aeterna board of supervisors.

By this time, of course, the Third Reich was at war and had already conquered much of Europe outside the Soviet Union. Although the idea of the CA shoe concern engaging in overseas commerce to England and elsewhere had to be shelved for the time being, the CA shoe business was now becoming part of the Southeast program and was actively engaged in that region and Poland. As in Austria, anti-Semitism and

---

411 BA-CA, CA-IB, Del-Ka, 03/04-05, administrative council meeting, Oct. 21, 1938, administrative council to Starkl, Oct. 22, 1938, and Ziegler to Friedl, Oct. 28, 1938.

412 Felber et al., *Ökonomie der Arisierung,* II, pp. 135–140.

413 The protocols are to be found in BA-CA, CA-IB, Del-Ka, 03/04-05.

Aryanization were an integral part of the CA expansion in these areas and, as in the case of Vigor, the two cannot be separated.

Most of the expansion in Southeast and East Central Europe would involve the expansion of Del-Ka's distribution and retail business. The planned expansion of Aeterna's production in the Protectorate, on the other hand, was an exception, not only because of its focus but also because the acquisition would not become an official part of the new concern. Efforts by Aeterna to expand its facilities in Atzgersdorf in 1941 had been turned down by the authorities because of wartime shortages, and Aeterna had no easy time dealing with the authorities in the Protectorate. Glatzl found the negotiations extraordinarily difficult and drawn out. In March 1942, the company was able to buy the Brunner Schuhfabrik "All Right" in Trebitsch, which, at the time, employed 500 workers and produced 3,000 pairs of shoes daily, primarily women's shoes but also wooden shoes and sandals. It also had a facility for repairing military boots. Prior to the German entry into Prague, the business had been owned and run by Anton Klinger, a Jew who went abroad in May 1939 and decided not to return. He and other Jewish investors were accused of mismanagement and misappropriation of funds, a not uncommon practice of adding insult to injury when dispossessing Jews. They had allegedly violated the foreign exchange regulations, hence their assets were declared property of the state. The administrator assigned to the Trebitsch plants was apparently quite successful in promoting the firm's recovery, and it was sold to Aeterna for 950,000 RM, a price that was considered excessive. On the positive side, Glatzl found that the Czech workers – of the 500 workers only 7 were German – to be very willing to work and industrious. The only other important shoe factory in the Protectorate was the Bata factory in Zlin, which employed 2,000 workers and was known to spend a great deal of money on its "beauty of labor" programs. Aeterna therefore decided it too would have to invest in worker welfare and set up an apprentice program as well. Aeterna bought the factory facilities, but the land and building at Trebitsch actually belonged to the Mährische Bank in Brünn, which was a subsidiary of the CA.[414]

Trebitsch flourished under wartime conditions. At the end of June 1943, it employed 823 workers and reached an average production of 3,000 pairs of shoes a day. Its military shoe repair facility was considered a model for the Protectorate, and it had large contracts from the Waffen-SS in Munich.[415] Much of the credit for the success of Trebitsch was attributed to Ziegler. As one subordinate wrote: "With General Director Ziegler taking over the leadership of our plants, much waste and imperfection has been cleared away. His élan, vision, and his skill to place people in the right place and to lead them, in one word, to be father of us all, is a guarantee for a successful and fruitful collaboration, as well as for the attainment of the goal we have set of becoming the greatest shoe factory and distribution organization of the south east. With the takeover of the plant in Trebitsch, still greater tasks have developed for those fortunate enough to be able to collaborate in a responsible position; it was a matter, after all, of blowing German breath into this Jewish factory on Czech soil."[416]

---

[414] On the background and sales, see Brunner Schuhfabrik to Price authorities in Prague, Nov. 16, 1943, and ibid., Del-Ka, 03a/04, Glatzl to Del-Ka board of managers, June 25, 1942 along with sales contract dated March 13, 1942.

[415] Ibid., Del-Ka, 03a/03, report of the management board to the supervisory board, July 19, 1943.

[416] Ibid., Del-Ka, 03/06-08, undated and unsigned retrospective on five years of plant history, probably written in 1943 or 1944. It would be interesting to know the extent to which Trebitsch was involved in the National Socialist programs to research and create shoes out of artificial leather and leather substitutes and in the standardization and rationalization programs promoted by the Reich Leather Agency, with which Ziegler had been involved, and by the Kaiser-Wilhelm-Gesellschaft research in this field. The testing of these shoes was done at Sachsenhausen Concentration Camp, and is a lesser known horror story. See Anne Sudrow, "Vom Leder zum Kunststoff. Werkstoff-Forschung auf der 'Schuhprüfstrecke' im Konzentrationslager Sachsenhausen 1940–1945," in: Helmut Maier (ed.), *Rüstungsforschung im Nationalsozialismus. Organisation, Mobilisierung and Entgrenzung der Technikwissenschaften* (Göttingen 2002), pp.

Ziegler does seem to have been enthusiastic, and he had strong ambitions to take a leading role in both the shoe business and its Nazification. At the same time, he apparently was someone with whom calmer souls could work, as became clear in his relationship with Glatzl, who was the major CA director involved with Del-Ka's expansion. Glatzl certainly had no compunctions about Aryanization but seems to have been totally apolitical otherwise. He joined the Party in 1938, made appropriate donations to it, and was viewed as completely unobjectionable with respect to both political attitude and character. When an effort was made by the Party to find out more about Glatzl, Ziegler stopped the effort dead in its tracks by declaring that Glatzl was "a very reputable person and a Party comrade, who always helps me in the best manner possible."[417] Surveying Del-Ka's involvement in Hungary, Slovakia, and Poland, it is clear that the two men worked hand in hand to promote their goals.

Del-Ka had owned a subsidiary in Budapest since the mid-1920s, and when the CA took over the Klausner shares in the spring of 1938 it acquired the Budapest shares as well. The company had been run by Ludwig Klausner's son, who went to England on business in March and decided not to return home. The administrative council had a Hungarian majority, as required by law; with the Klausners gone, it was composed of three very prominent Hungarians headed by former Hungarian Foreign Minister Gustav Gratz. They had expressed their concern about the situation to Glatzl in mid-May 1938 and suggested they might resign rather than maintain responsibility under such unclear and uncertain circumstances. Glatzl, however, dissuaded Gratz from taking such a step because it would do damage to the company.[418]

By July, a more concrete discussion could be held, and Glatzl met with Gratz again. Glatzl showed particular concern about the Jews in the company, and was undoubtedly relieved to learn that the three Hungarians on the administrative council were all Aryans. He told Gratz that the Klausners would be replaced by himself and Theobold Graf Czernin. Czernin, it should be noted, was in the SS and was the brother of Bürckel's secretary; he was probably appointed because of these connections and his position as a representative of the VVSt. In his conversation with Gratz, Glatzl spoke quite openly about the new Hungarian "Jewish Law" to go into effect on November 1, 1938, which aimed at reducing within five years the number of Jews to 20 percent of those employed in an enterprise, while maintaining the salary paid to them at 20 percent of the salaries paid by the company. Gratz was unable to provide Glatzl with more details about the law but did assure Glatzl that he had long sought to prevent the hiring of any more Jews at Del-Ka because his good friends, the ministers of commerce and finance, had been pressing him to keep Del-Ka as "free of Jews" as possible. Gratz also assured Glatzl they were in agreement that the company's lawyer, a "Jew of especially evil repute in Budapest," should be replaced by a "not too expensive Aryan lawyer." When it came to Professor Salgo, a Polish Jew who did the company's taxes, a decision was made to retain him for the moment because his charges were low and his influence with the Hungarian tax authorities very high. Last, Glatzl, while admitting that Hans Klausner had run the business well, asked that Klausner should no longer be able to draw on the firm for expenses or salary.[419]

Jewish employees and service providers were not, of course, the only problems Glatzl and Gratz had to face in dealing with Del-Ka. Hans Klausner had to be replaced, and Gratz warned that it was best done by a Hungarian because "foreign directors have an especially hard time working in Hungary and constantly have to bear the chicanery of the authorities."

214–249, and "Das 'deutsche Rohstoffwunder' und die Schuhindustrie. Schuhproduktion unter den Bedingungen der nationalsozialistischen Autarkiepolitik," in: *Blätter für Technikgeschichte*, Peter Dornhauser (ed.), 60 (1999), pp. 63–92.

[417] ÖStA/AdR, BMI, Gauakt Robert Glatzl, Nr. 105717, Ziegler to Pg. Kampe, Dec. 18, 1939.

[418] BA-CA, CA-IB, Del-Ka, 03/01, Glatzl report to Friedl, May 19, 1938.

[419] Ibid., Glatzl report on discussion with Gratz, July 1, 1938.

The most serious question concerned the possible sale of the Hungarian Del-Ka to interested native purchasers, but both Glatzl and Gratz ruled this out because payment in pengö could not be transferred to Germany while payment in Reichsmark would not be acceptable to the Hungarian National Bank, which needed the foreign exchange for armaments.

There were indeed multiple headaches connected with the Hungarian Del-Ka. They began with the administrative council. Although the Hungarians on the council allegedly were well-positioned and important persons, only Gratz really did anything useful. Nevertheless, because of his political views Glatzl did not consider him to be a satisfactory long-term chairman. Glatzl himself was very unhappy with his Austrian colleague Czernin, who had both inappropriate ambitions and a bad character. In November 1938 Czernin, having been appointed a member of the Del-Ka administrative council, announced to the CA his interest in acquiring a 51 percent share in Aeterna and Del-Ka. The CA responded by pointing out that there were other candidates, for example, Grödl, Josef Ziegler, and Fritz Kraus, all Party members like Czernin, but that they viewed him as a competent as a businessman who could run the concern in a National Socialist manner. If he had the requisite financial means and the approval of the authorities, they would welcome him as a majority shareholder. In short, the CA put him off politely.[420]

Czernin, however, continued to have dreams of glory, wanting to be personally involved in the purchase of the Hungarian Del-Ka, and in April 1939 he told Glatzl that he had found a Hungarian group willing to join him in purchasing it. Glatzl sarcastically replied that there were plenty of Hungarians around anxious to get the firm on the cheap but that the CA had no intention of "dumping" the business, and that if Czernin thought that he would get an especially low price he should drive the thought from his mind. Czernin, contrary to this advice, continued to hope to buy the shares of the Austrian Del-Ka, which led Glatzl to point out – rather less politely thanks to his colleagues who were there in November 1938 – that this would need the approval of the VVSt and that no one could force the CA to provide the purchaser of the shares with the 1.6 million RM credit Del-Ka was presently enjoying. Glatzl had the impression that Czernin left the conversation "very depressed."[421] Czernin was indeed a very bad credit risk. He had borrowed excess amounts of money from colleagues, including Ziegler, failed to pay a restaurant bill, and tried to collect on dubious bills of exchange. By summer 1939, the CA had quite enough of him, and the VVSt lost interest in him so that he was asked to leave the Del-Ka administrative council in Budapest and the supervisory board in Vienna. He took these decisions with ill grace but was powerless to do anything about them. His successor in Budapest was Josef Ziegler.[422]

By July 1939, the three Hungarian members of the administrative council had also resigned, and one of the key replacements was the director of the CA Budapest, Erwin Bokor. It was only now that the problem of getting a competent director to replace Hans Klausner was solved "since the shoe business in Hungary is irritatingly Jewified, hence it was truly difficult to identify a director who is a Hungarian citizen and also an Aryan."[423] In fact, in order not to place in charge two Jewish women already working for the company, the CA had allowed the management to be in the hands of a totally unsuitable Hungarian, Aladár v. Illek, and was very happy to replace him with Johann Gally. Gally had been recommended by the CA Budapest manager Böhm and was apparently quite competent so that management improved substantially. Much progress was also made in reducing the number of Jews at Del-Ka Budapest. Of the 200 employees in March 1938, 80 percent were Jewish, while in May 1939 the number of Aryans was 134, with 47 Jews remaining, that is, 25 percent were Jewish.

[420] Ibid.,Del-Ka,03/06-08,CA to SS-Untersturmführer Theobald Graf Czernin.

[421] Ibid., Del-Ka, 03/01, report by Glatzl, April 12, 1939.

[422] See ibid., Del-Ka, 03/04-05, Glatzl to Pfeiffer, June 15, 1939, and other relevant correspondence.

[423] Ibid., Friedl and Glatzl to Bokor, May 31 and July 21, 1939.

Further "progress" was reported in August 1940: the number of Aryans in the office had risen to 152 and the number of Jews reduced to 32 (17.39 percent). The Jews, however, accounted for 31.13 percent of the personnel costs, so that the next step was to concentrate on eliminating the more highly paid Jews.[424] What is remarkable about all this is the extent to which the CA directors, who were driving the elimination of the Jews at Del-Ka, devoted so much attention to the question yet were unable to achieve full success at this time because of the dependence on Jewish employees. As Glatzl reported to Friedl in November 1941, "the handling of the Jewish question at Del-Ka was from the very beginning difficult because in Hungary – especially in the provinces – qualified Aryan employees were hard to find. From the standpoint of both income and numbers, Jewish staff members were in the majority in these enterprises. At the end of October, there were still seven Jews in the service of the Hungarian Del-Ka. The management of the firm has received instructions that all Jews are to be dismissed in the course of December."[425] "Success" was achieved at the end of 1941 when Del-Ka Budapest finally no longer employed any Jews.[426]

The business of Del-Ka Budapest seemed to run reasonably well under the circumstances, that is, in view of the shortages of supplies, government regulations, and other problems arising from the war. In 1942, it had five branches in Budapest and fourteen in the provinces. Not only was it well supported from Vienna, but it also received important credits from the CA Budapest, Bokor playing an especially important role in this respect. The Hungarian subsidiary, however, was closely controlled from Vienna, and Friedl and Glatzl insisted that they be invited to all meetings of the directorial board.[427] After the German occupation

of Hungary in March–April 1944, the tone at Del-Ka Budapest was quite upbeat. The Del-Ka Slovak director Josef Seifert, who was in Budapest at the time, reported to Ziegler on April 7 that, on March 19, the SS and security forces took all necessary measures to ensure that leading Jews could not flee while the government ordered the liquidation and/or Aryanization of all Jewish enterprises. Seifert noted that this measure was of special interest to Del-Ka because it opened up the possibility of taking over these businesses. Despite enemy bombings and subsequent evacuations to the countryside, he anticipated good business because shoes were in high demand.[428] By October 1944, however, the situation was desperate despite the fact that the company had 5 million pengö more in sales than it had had in October 1943. This was primarily in Budapest because the company had abandoned six of its best branches. The people there were anxious to get rid of their money and get hold of necessities should they have to flee. Del-Ka Budapest also provided advanced pay for its staff should it need to depart. In the branches occupied by the Russians, there were considerable stores of shoes and stockings, but it was impossible to make contact or get necessary transport. Grotesquely, Del-Ka Budapest also reported that it had experienced a "great day" on October 16 when Horthy's attempt to declare an armistice was preempted by Ferenc Szálasi's seizure of power: "Policy was newly transformed, the Jewish question was ruthlessly brought to its solution, and there was no more putting off of the mobilization of all forces on the side of Germany." To be sure, the Russians continued their approach, but Director Gally and his chief employees were at their posts and intended to remain there unless forcibly taken away, which may well have been the case.[429]

Whereas Del-Ka was already ensconced in Hungary before 1938, Slovakia seemed to offer a genuine opportunity for new expansion in the Southeast. In October 1940, Glatzl went to

[424] Ibid., Del-Ka, 03/01, Report by Strupf, Aug. 10, 1940.
[425] Ibid., Del-Ka, 03/09-10, Glatzl to Friedl, Nov. 14, 1941.
[426] See ibid., Del-Ka, 03a/01, the report of the directors' meeting of Nov. 6, 1941.
[427] Ibid., Del-Ka, 03/09-10, Friedl and Glatzl to Ziegler, March 25, 1942.

[428] Ibid., Seifert to Ziegler, April 7, 1944, and report of April 21, 1944.
[429] Ibid., Report of Del-Ka Budapest, Nov. 6, 1944.

Pressburg/Bratislava for a discussion with Franz Stephan, then director of the Pressburg BUB branch and later director of the Union-Bank, and Eugen Reisinger, head of the Economic Office of the Deutsche Partei. Glatzl inquired about the advisability of setting up one or two Del-Ka branches in Pressburg/Bratislava by taking over Jewish enterprises. In response, they warned him that the Slovak government had finally turned to the Jewish question with some sense of urgency and had set up something like the Property Transfer Bureau. The candidates for the Jewish firms that had been put up for sale lacked money but had good political and government contacts, so that whoever was in charge was inclined to delay a decision. At the same time, the Jewish owners, recognizing the situation, had refrained from refurbishing their inventories. The BUB was in a position to refuse to guarantee the applications of Slovak candidates. However, Stephan and Reisinger cynically proposed that the Del-Ka rent an empty shop, put up the name Del-Ka in big letters and the name of some ethnic German interested in the business in small letters, and temporarily seek a shoe concession. In this way, it would be possible to buy up large stocks of shoes because "the Jews have an interest in freely selling their inventories, not wanting to risk getting worse prices in an Aryanization."[430] In November 1940, Stephan wrote to Glatzl pointing out that some empty stores were available in very frequented streets and urged that Del-Ka set up a branch. Another German shoe dealer had chosen this route, namely, to rent without Aryanizing, but he dealt primarily in luxury shoes and was thus not a competitor to Del-Ka.[431]

If this proposal was not initially pursued, it was because Del-Ka had turned its attention to the Poliky-Popper AG in the Protectorate, which was 30 percent in Jewish ownership, but the German firm of Rieker from Tuttlingen beat them out and prevented a good sales organization in Slovakia from falling into their laps.[432] Nevertheless, they now intended to gain control of a few well-situated businesses, and they did so in mid-1941 to create the basis for the establishment of a subsidiary company in Pressburg/ Bratislava. As Del-Ka later explained, "the time was also rightly chosen because shoe retailing in Slovakia was to an improbable percent in the hands of Jews or their straw men, and we were striving to rent business facilities in a favorable location in the wake of the Aryanization taking place."[433] By early 1942, Del-Ka had successfully applied to the various authorities to create the "Del-Ka Schuhindustrie- und Handels-Aktiengesellschaft, Pressburg." It already had branches in Pressburg/Bratislava, Tyrnau/Trnava, and Sillein/Zilina and was planning to add more. The capital of 1 million Ks was held in trusteeship by the Union-Bank Pressburg and another 1 million Ks was given as a credit by that bank to assist the shoemakers involved because they lacked the money to operate on their own. The CA Vienna acted as guarantor for the 2 million Ks involved. The use of the Union-Bank Pressburg, which belonged to the CA, enabled Del-Ka to get around the difficult transfer problems between the Reich and Slovakia. Josef Seifert was appointed director of Del-Ka Pressburg/Bratislava. He was an ethnic German and had been recommended by both the Deutsche Partei and the Union-Bank. The enterprise was meant to provide work and business for ethnic Germans in Slovakia who were shoemakers or in the shoe business. Del-Ka had already organized them into a working community to procure raw materials, expand their enterprises, and produce quality products. Del-Ka, as a part of the CA concern in Slovakia, was built up on the basis of Aryanization, German ethnic politics, and the help of the CA's subsidiary bank in Slovakia. It is a measure of this cultivation of the ethnic Germans that Glatzl made a point of using

---

[430] Ibid., Glatzl memorandum, Oct. 18, 1940. As Stephan and Reisinger noted, this method had been used by the Haas rug company. See later in this chapter.

[431] Ibid., Del-Ka, 03/04-05, BUB Bratislava to Glatzl, Nov. 5, 1940.

[432] Ibid., Glatzl to Stephan, Feb. 8, 1941.

[433] Ibid., Del-Ka, 03a/1, Del-Ka to RWM, March 14, 1942.

Ziegler, who was a member of the new company's administrative council, to pressure the Union-Bank to provide funds for cost-of-living increases for Del-Ka's employees. Ziegler was particularly keen on the implementation of National Socialist social policies.[434]

In Poland too, as in Hungary and Slovakia, there was considerable consultation and collaboration between Del-Ka and the banks affiliated with the CA. Nevertheless, this took place under difficult circumstances because of the elimination of the Polish state and the partition of Poland, which inevitably affected the condition of Del-Ka interests there. In 1933, Del-Ka owned the largest and most important shoe business in Poland, the Orzel AG, 45 percent of whose shares were in the hands of Del-Ka Vienna, 45 percent in the possession of the Continentale Industrie- und Handels-AG in Vaduz – a holding company belonging to the Klausner family – and 10 percent in the hands of the Jewish General Director Hermann Zins of Del-Ka Cracow. The structure of ownership changed between 1933 and 1939 in order to deal with the problems of doing business in Poland, so that at the time of the German invasion, the bulk of the shares were in the hands of the Vaduz holding company, while a small block continued to remain with Zins. Del-Ka's interest in Orzel took the form of credits, so that Orzel owed Del-Ka a considerable amount of money. But to resurrect Orzel and take it over was not an attractive proposition after the German invasion because its assets were scattered among the three parts into which Poland had been divided. The business in the area annexed by the Russians was obviously lost and was to be found in utterly miserable shape when the Russians were driven out in the spring of 1941. The best Orzel outlets in Kattowitz, Königshütte, and Sosnowicz, that is, in portions of Poland annexed to Germany, were in the hands of the Head Trusteeship Office East. Those remaining were under the control of the Property Transfer Bureau that had been set up in the GG.[435]

If Orzel was as divided as was Poland, its available assets nonetheless remained attractive, as did the prospect of building up Del-Ka's business in former Poland. The three big branches in Kattowitz, Königshütte, and Sosnowicz lay in the populous mining district. The Kattowitz branch had done as much business as the main Vienna branch prior to the war. There were also individual outlets in Bielitz, Tarnowice, Czenstochau, and Lodz. In a survey of the situation by Del-Ka officials in December 1939, they concluded that the branches in Kattowitz, Königshütte, and Sosnowicz were very much worth Aryanizing through Del-Ka, and that the administrators appointed by the Head Trusteeship Office East were capable persons who would be willing to work for Del-Ka. The situation was such, however, that they would have to be supplied from Del-Ka Vienna. As for the GG, the most promising available business was the Schuhaus Steigler, which had formerly belonged to a Jew and was now administered by a Del-Ka employee, Frank Patterer. They thought that the Cracow Property Transfer Bureau would be amenable to such a solution. They also believed that the authorities in Bielitz were likewise inclined to support Del-Ka over and against the competition from Salamander.[436]

But as a report of early July 1940 by Adolph Hauptvogel of the Del-Ka head office in Vienna showed, matters had become rather more complicated than anticipated.[437] The branches in the Kattowitz district and in Cracow were being administered separately, so that Patterer in Cracow had nothing whatever to say about the Orzel branch under the Head Trusteeship Office East and vice versa. In neither place was there any obligation to honor claims coming from the old Reich against Orzel. In Kattowitz, efforts by Del-Ka to lease the outlets were turned down by the Head Trusteeship Office East, which would only agree to contracts allowing for individual trusteeships that could cover their costs and

---

[434] Ibid., Glatzl to Ziegler, Sept. 9, 1942.

[435] See ibid., Del-Ka, 03a/02, Glatzl's remarks on an auditor's report, March 11, 1942, and Del-Ka to RWM, March 25, 1942.

[436] Ibid., Del-Ka, 03/01, reports of Dec. 8, 1939, and of Feb. 29, 1940.

[437] The discussion that follows is based on this report, sent by the CA Cracow to Pfeiffer at the CA Vienna on July 15, 1940, BA-CA, CA-TZ, Box 39/ CA-BV Filiale Kr-Lh, File 17.

a modest compensation for the trustees. Despite efforts to gain support from authorities in the Reich, the authorities in Kattowitz would not allow a leasing that would enable Del-Ka to lay claim to the Orzel debts owed to it.

In Cracow, the authorities were much more sympathetic to Del-Ka and prepared to support a Del-Ka petition to lease branches in the GG, but they would not guarantee success. The official in the GG charged with commercial enterprises, Böheim, was particularly supportive of Del-Ka and viewed Orzel's declaration bankruptcy as an opportunity for Del-Ka to lay claim to the outlets and run them. Initially, business interests in the Reich had been holding back from acquiring assets in the GG because it was believed that the area might be used as compensation for the acquisition of colonies. Now, however, the area was considered to be permanently in the hands of the Reich, and Directors Huber and Cerny of the CA Cracow "see a great future for businesspeople from the Reich who exploit and take advantage of this good, one-time opportunity."[438] The CA branch, therefore, was prepared to support a leasing plan encompassing Warsaw, Tarnow, and Cracow with a 40,000–50,000 Zl credit and with the expectation that Del-Ka make good its claims against Orzel and establish itself permanently in the area once the war was over. At the same time, Del-Ka would also lease the Schuhaus Steigler presently administered by Patterer, which would require another 50,000 Zl. Hauptvogel warned that "experience shows that Aryanization becomes ever more difficult the longer one waits," and there was no certainty that the same administrators would be maintained. The leasing of the Orzel branches and Steigler in the GG had to be viewed as a "one-time opportunity" to acquire these enterprises at relatively little cost and risk. At the same time, he urged that they pursue the effort to lease the Kattowitz branches with the Head Trusteeship Office East in Berlin.

The CA Cracow did its utmost to push Hauptvogel's ideas, writing to Director Eduard Tampe, the head of the CA Mariahilferstrasse

branch in Vienna and a member of the Del-Ka supervisory board, urging that Del-Ka not pass up the opportunity. He noted that the acquisition of administered firms in the GG was not yet possible and that leases were granted only in certain instances, with the result that "since the shoe trade in Cracow before the war was mostly in Jewish hands and was divided among many businesses, the few shoe factories and stores (such as Del-Ka, Bata, Salamander) naturally have great opportunities."[439] They had very high praise for Patterer. Indeed, the demand for shoes and cheap wooden sandals was so great that hundreds of persons were standing before the stores he administered, the police having to limit the number of persons who could enter the stores. In this way, Del-Ka had the opportunity to build up a big business once peace came.

Despite Huber's urgings, however, "special considerations," as Tampe informed him on July 19, led the Del-Ka supervisory board to decide against pursuing the leasing opportunities in Cracow. Huber was puzzled by the decision and continued to think that the Cracow officials would be very supportive.[440] The exact reasons for the decision are hard to determine. Undoubtedly the problem of dealing with authorities in Kattowitz and Berlin, on the one hand, and Cracow, on the other, created uncertainty, and there was concern about having to supply Poland from Vienna. CA Director Friedl was particularly skeptical and wanted to reduce the engagements in Poland, dismiss Patterer, and disengage from Kattowitz, where he felt the costs and effort would be very disproportionate to the returns.[441] Huber kept on pushing because he was convinced that if Del-Ka leased the Orzel facilities in Cracow and demonstrated that a well-managed company was in a position to take over, Del-Ka would attain a monopoly position in the area and the GG would then look with disfavor on other firms from the old Reich coming in.[442] In mid-August 1940,

438 Ibid.

439 Ibid., CA Cracow to Tampe, July 15, 1940.

440 Ibid., Tampe to Huber, July 19, 1940, and Huber to Pfeiffer, July 23, 1940.

441 BA-CA, CA-IB, Del-Ka, 03/04-05, Friedl to Ziegler, May 17, 1940.

442 Ibid., Huber to Adolf Hauptvogel, Aug. 7, 1940.

however, Glatzl reiterated Del-Ka's stance, pointing out that their efforts to take over the branches in Kattowitz, Königshütte, and Sosnowicz had been stymied, probably because of competition from firms from the old Reich, while the attempts to straighten out the question of who owned the Orzel shares in the GG had produced nothing but legal confusion. Glatzl told Huber that all efforts by Del-Ka to establish itself in Kattowitz and the GG were now being terminated because the tasks of Del-Ka in Austria and Hungary were sufficiently great to justify abstention in Poland, and a disappointed Huber seemed to have no choice but to accept this decision.[443]

In the fall of 1940, however, the leadership at Del-Ka had a change of heart. One of the reasons certainly was that it found it had Austrian friends in the GG. In November Patterer reported to Del-Ka directors Ziegler and Adolf Hautpvogel that GG Economic Inspector SS Oberführer Karl Gestöttenbauer, who came from Vienna, was holding open a wholesale shoe business in Lublin for Del-Ka in order to prevent Bata from taking it.[444] Shortly thereafter, Glatzl informed Huber that Del-Ka had been invited to bid for the branches in Kattowitz, Königshütte, and Sosnowicz after all. If this were combined with acquisitions in the GG, then the situation had changed substantially. Even Friedl no longer rigidly opposed going into Poland. There was yet another incentive. Huber had informed Glatzl that the Deutsche Bank had been making inquiries about Ortel's Aryanization situation, and this inquiry could only have been prompted by the Deutsche Bank's customer Tack & Co Cie. In Glatzl's view, if Tack & Co Cie. was interested in something, "then experience shows it cannot be a bad business." Glatzl informed Huber that it was likely that he, Ziegler, and Friedl would come to Cracow to look into the situation. In the meantime, he asked Huber to use his good connections to see if there were other competitors for Orzel or parts of it. One method

to secure it would be for Orzel to go into bankruptcy and for Del-Ka to acquire parts of it. These options reflected the concern that Del-Ka might purchase or lease Orzel facilities in the GG while the trustee authorities in the annexed areas would suddenly offer Orzel to some competitor. Del-Ka wanted all or most of Orzel, and because Orzel was indebted to it from the prewar period, Del-Ka could call in the debts, drive Orzel into bankruptcy, and then take it over. This solution seemed all the more feasible because the exact status of the shares at the Vaduz holding company, the Continentale, were unclear. Klausner sometimes claimed that the shares belonged to the holding company, at other times that they were his personal property. He employed a British straw man in his dealings with the Cracow Property Transfer Office because he feared it would not honor his claims. As Huber reported, Böheim of the Cracow Property Transfer Office had "enough of these Jewish obstructionisms" and was contacting his counterpart at the Head Trusteeship Office East to get Del-Ka to make its claims and drive Orzel into bankruptcy. Whatever the case, Del-Ka now worked closely with Huber and especially with Gestöttenbauer and their Austrian allies in the Cracow trustee office to attain their goals.[445]

Nevertheless, it was not until the end of January 1942 that Glatzl could report firm plans to Huber about setting up a "Del-Ka Ost Schuhindustrie- und Handels-Aktiengesellschaft" with head offices in Cracow. The delay was undoubtedly entailed in part by the war against the Soviet Union and the inclusion of Galicia in these plans but also by the usual bureaucratic procrastination.[446] By summer Hauptvogel was able to provide a report on Del-Ka Ost, which was now "in formation." The sales organization would be

[443] Ibid., Glatzl to Huber, Aug. 16, 1940 and Huber to Glatzl, Aug. 20, 1940.
[444] Ibid., memo by Glatzl, Nov. 14, 1940.

[445] Glatzl to Huber, Dec. 5, 1940, and Dec. 11, 1940; Huber to Glatzl, Dec. 22, 1940 and Glatzl to Huber, Dec. 31, 1940, and ibid., Del-Ka, 03/09-10, Glatzl's report on phone conversations with Huber, Dec. 9–10, 1940. On Gstöttenbauer, see Frank, *Diensttagebuch*, p. 948.
[446] BA-CA, CA-IB, Del-Ka, 03/09-10, Glatzl to Huber, Jan. 30, 1942.

composed of branches from five groups: first, the Orzel branches under the Trusteeship Office in Cracow, which were composed of branches in Cracow itself, Warsaw, and Tarnow; second, branches in the petroleum region of Galicia, Stanislau, Drohobycz, Boryslaw, Stryj, and Kolomea; third, branches in Lemberg/Lviv, one in the city itself and the other in Halicka; fourth, the Steigler firm in Cracow; and last, branches in Przemysl, Tarnopol, Lublin, and Tschenstochau. At the time of the report not all these branches were operative – none of the last four had been set up – and permission to take over or establish branches had not been given in all cases. The plan, however, was to have a sales organization with a network of fifteen outlets. Available inventories of shoes, especially a large former Russian one in Lemberg/Lviv called "Promtorg," were to be used as collateral for some of the takeovers. The new company was to have a capital of 1 million Zl, while 1.7 million Zl was needed for creating the new branches. Del-Ka was not, of course, new to Poland; the brand name had enjoyed and could be expected to enjoy considerable popularity again.[447]

The negotiations with the authorities for the takeover of some of these assets, particularly the Orzel branches in the GG, had not been easy. Glatzl had been warned that the personnel at the GG were changing and that it would be wise to conclude arrangements with them as soon as possible. GG negotiator Seifert had proven quite cool in his discussions in June 1942 concerning the acquisition of Orzel assets because Glatzl and Ziegler were reluctant to pay much for outlets that produced no income, and he was not willing to make any concessions. At the same time, however, Glatzl was very anxious to find a suitable location for the Del-Ka business, namely, in the Adolf-Hitler-Platz of Cracow, and Steigler looked very promising for the purpose of running a profitable outlet. In the end, Seifert agreed to accommodate them on the estimation of Steigler's profit in 1940–1941. One incentive to do so was that the rents were low. Del-Ka also promised that the businesses

thus acquired would employ war veterans, adding a desired social dimension to the arrangement. In Glatzl's view, veterans would not have the money to handle such outlets alone, and it would be better for Del-Ka to employ them. The Orzel shares continued to be a problem for Del-Ka because the authorities in Kattowitz indicated that they would honor the claims of any Aryan purchaser who managed to get hold of them. Seifert also wanted the question of the shares clarified. Glatzl, therefore, decided to make direct inquiries in Vaduz himself to see what the situation actually was. There is no evidence as to what was discovered about the status of these shares and whether anything was done about them. He believed they were not worth anything because they were encumbered by tax debts to the former Polish state, which was why no great effort was made to purchase them.[448] The most pressing matter in the spring and summer of 1942 was to establish Del-Ka Ost, and there was genuine irritation on the part of Huber and Cerny when, once again, Friedl suddenly raised questions about the profitability of the venture. Huber warned that the authorities would lose all patience and he would be considered quite "mad" in Vienna if questions about profitability were raised after three years of negotiation.[449]

Glatzl was convinced that Orzel would rise again in its new guise as Del-Ka Ost, like a phoenix out of the ashes, but everyone was well aware that doing business in Poland was not easy. Quite aside from the conditions in the country, there was a shortage of adequate personnel, and the CA Cracow had periodic cause to complain about slowness in the repayment of its substantial credits and to point out that the security provided by shoe stocks was of limited value if the shoes were sold off to customers.[450] Del-Ka Ost was formally founded in early 1943. It made a modest profit that year, and it expected that

[447] Ibid., Hauptvogel report of July 16, 1942.

[448] See ibid., Del-Ka, 03a/02, Glatzl's remarks on the Orzel audit, March 11, 1942.
[449] Ibid., Del-Ka, 03/09-10, Glatzl to Czerny, June 26, 1942; Huber to Glatzl, June 27, 1941; CA to Bank von Liechtenstein, June 29, 1942.
[450] Ibid., Glatzl to Patterer, Aug. 14, 1942; CA Cracow to Glatzl, Oct. 1 and 9, 1942.

profits would be higher in 1944 because the price commissar had raised the profit margin. While the signs were good in the first part of the year, by fall 1944 Del-Ka Ost was ending its brief existence. Business came to a standstill in East Galicia as the Russians advanced, and on October 30, the decision was made to shut down for the duration of the war in Cracow as well because Cracow was now in the war zone. A further difficulty was that Patterer had been drafted and that Vienna did not want the entire business left in the hands of Poles, however reliable those in question may have been. The only success the enterprise could boast in the final months of 1944 was that it had managed to sell off its shoe inventory.[451]

Indeed, in a few months the people responsible for Del-Ka's expansion were to be in full retreat, and in the future the CA would have to deal with claims from some of the Jewish former owners of Aryanized firms that had been central to Del-Ka's development between 1938 and 1945. As early as May 1945, Director Joham was already gathering information on the previous ownership of Del-Ka.[452] Budapest was in Russian hands. The Germans working for Del-Ka in Pressburg/Bratislava were fleeing the Czechs for their lives, arriving at the border as mere beggars. As Glatzl ruefully commented: "Unfortunately, today this is the fate of hundreds of thousands and millions of poor devils, and all those who have brought so much blood guilt upon themselves have cleared out in a cowardly way. I do not hear anything good from Trebitsch either. The top Nazi, Ziegler, is supposed to be leading a tranquil existence in Upper Austria."[453] Glatzl was having his own difficulties in Vienna, but then again, he was not a "top Nazi," however much he may have collaborated in the cause.

The CA Textile Concern

The engagement of the CA in the textile business antedated 1938 and was already international in character but, as in the case of the shoe business, entry into the Third Reich promoted expansion and affected the way the business was run. It goes without saying that the "Jewish question" was always present in one form or another. The discussion here will be limited to two of the more important engagements in the field involving Vienna-based companies that were involved in Southeast Europe, the Aktiengesellschaft der Teppich- und Möbelstoff-Fabriken, vorm. Philipp Haas & Söhne and the Hanf-Jute- und Textilit-Industrie AG (HITIAG). The discussion that follows will deal primarily with the former concern, and developments at the HITIAG will be used to further illuminate the subjects under discussion. This being the case, the chief characteristics of the HITIAG should be briefly mentioned first. A producer of hemp, jute, and similar textile products, it had factories in Austria and Hungary and interests in Yugoslavia and Bulgaria. The CA held only 34 percent of the shares; 27 percent of the shares were held by Ralli Brothers, an English firm whose shares were subsequently held at the CA as enemy property after the war broke out. The Länderbank held the 10 percent of the shares that had previously belonged to the Guttmann family and the 8 percent block of the Bankhaus Nicolai once owned by the Rothschild Bank. For all intents and purposes, however, it was part of the CA concern. After the Anschluss, its Jewish administrative council members and its Jewish general director, along with other Jews in the company, resigned or were dismissed. The elimination of the Jews at the HITIAG was no easy task because 33 percent of its employees were Jewish, above all those in managerial positions. Although the company reported on June 30, 1938, that officially it employed no more Jews, it asked that six be kept on for between one and six months so that the administration could continue to function effectively.[454] CA

---

[451] On business in 1943–1944, see the report of June 19, 1943, ibid., Del-Ka, 03a/03; ibid., Del-Ka, 03/09-10, report to Glatzl, Dec. 9, 1943, 03/06-08; Del-Ka Vienna to CA Cracow, Oct. 30, 1944, situation report, Nov. 26–Dec. 2, 1944.
[452] See his memo of May 22, 1945, ibid., Del-Ka, 03a/12/01.
[453] Ibid., Del-Ka, 03a/1, Glatzl to Loefen, Aug. 21, 1945.

[454] BA-CA, CA-IB, Hanf-Jute, 06/01, HITIAG to State Commissar for the Private Economy, June 30, 1938.

Director Pfeiffer took over as president of the administrative council, and Oswald Hermsen, a Party member who came from Hamburg, was made chairman of the management board. The surviving records suggest that Hermsen was a very domineering personality who got on poorly with some of his colleagues and who dominated the affairs of the concern.

Despite its name, Jewish ownership of the Aktiengesellschaft der Teppich- und Möbelstoff-Fabriken, vorm. Philipp Haas & Söhne had long been a thing of the past. Interestingly, the name was retained even after 1938, probably because it "sold." It was an old and distinguished firm that dealt in rugs and textile products of many kinds. Founded in 1810, it had been turned into a public corporation in 1885. The Wiener Bankverein had acquired a substantial portion of its stock around the turn of the century, and the CA acquired the shares when the banks merged. In March 1938, the CA held 99.58 percent of the shares. The firm was headquartered in Vienna and had its chief production center in Ebergassing. It had a large sales and distribution network that had grown throughout the Austro-Hungarian monarchy before the war. Although the network had shrunk, Haas continued to retain separate companies bearing its name in Prague and Budapest, and a factory in Sopron, the Soproner-Teppich-und Textilwerke AG, vorm. Philipp Haas & Söhne, Budapest. The shares were divided between the home company and the CA.[455]

When it came to the administrative council of the concern, however, there was a good deal of Aryanizing to do. Five of the seven members, including the president, Franz Rottenberg, were Jewish and were asked to resign. CA Director Hans Friedl replaced Rottenberg. The Jewish general director in Vienna, Karl Roth, and Director Fritz Drexler, who had fled to Prague, were dismissed on March 29, and other Jews working at Ebergassing were let go as well.

The old directors were replaced by Rudolf Nowaczek and Richard Frauenfeld. The latter was an "illegal," brother of a Gauleiter, and a long-time Party member, who had returned from Germany and was hired by Friedl. This did not spare him from attacks by the National Socialist Company Organization in Ebergassing, which accused him of nepotism, spending too much money on company cars for his own use, and various forms of unsocial behavior, prompting his workers to view the state of affairs in the company under his leadership as "the continuation of typical Jewish conditions that were common before the upheaval."[456] Needless to say, the fervent National Socialist Frauenfeld was outraged by these charges and was fed up with Labor Front pressures, but he seems to have won out in the end and worked well with Nowaczek. The case casts interesting light on the personnel difficulties and radical tone that could characterize labor relations in the months after the Anschluss. As a report of November 1938 showed, the problems at Ebergassing led to as much as a 60 percent reduction in production, and it was only in July that the situation began to improve so that it ranged between 25 percent and 80 percent more than the previous year. The situation was undoubtedly helped by the expansion of the work force between March and October, from 385 to 593, and by raising wages by between 10 percent and 14 percent. As for sales, they improved steadily throughout the entire period, helped by rising demand at home and two large contracts from Romania. Exports did suffer somewhat because of shipment difficulties created by the political situation, the U.S. boycott, and uncertainties about government pricing policy. Haas, however, appeared to be in good shape by the end of 1938.[457]

It appears that Nowaczek managed most of the affairs of the concern, especially abroad, while the CA's chief representative was Josef

---

The surviving papers of the HITIAG are to be found in ibid., Hanf-Jute, 06/01-03.

[455] Ibid., Haas,07/14, Response to a U.S. Occupation Authority questionnaire, Jan. 27, 1948.

[456] See ibid., Haas, 07/06, the NSBO complaint to the Gau Administration, Nov. 21, 1938, and Frauenfeld's twenty-one-page missive to Friedl, Dec. 3, 1938.

[457] See ibid., Referat Patzak, 30/02, report of Nov. 18, 1938.

Patzak of the CA's Industry Section. Friedl resigned from the Haas supervisory board in May 1940 because the increase of his duties left him without time to serve.[458] In any case, the CA not only had to pay attention to the Haas enterprise at home, but also to the one in Hungary, and in addition it had to devote attention to the other textile enterprises in the CA concern that were abroad. In every case, the issue of personnel Aryanization was given close attention. In reports of June 12, 1939, to Fischböck he was informed that all Jews in the management of the Sopron factory, which employed 535 workers, had been replaced by Aryans, although mention was made of one manager who was kept on as he was not considered Jewish under Hungarian law. Concerning the other Jewish personnel, the company was following Hungarian laws for Jews, but an effort was being made to speed up the process of getting rid of them. A similar situation existed at the Haas firm in Budapest, which was devoted to sales. One Jew remained in a managerial position. As the report unabashedly explained, "Recently Major Ribenyi has been hired as a director, who for the present will be introduced to his tasks by the previous Jewish director Pollak. Naturally the latter will depart at the appropriate time. Herr Pollak's power of attorney has already been terminated."[459]

These reports also noted matters such as the modernization of production facilities, but the obsessive concern with eliminating Jews from the company's management and dismissing Jews faster than required by the Hungarian law was striking. It is to be found not only with respect to the Haas companies but also in reports on other CA concern textile enterprises in Hungary. Such was the report issued on the Stefan Felmayer & Söhne Blaufärberei und Kattundruckfabriks AG in Stuhlweißenburg/Székesfehérvár, a profitable dyed products and cotton prints producer, completely owned by the CA. Matters were somewhat

more complicated in the case of the Ujpester Tuchfabrik, AG in Budapest, a cloth manufacturer. The CA owned 68 percent of the firm's shares, and the remainder were believed to be in the hands of a Jew, David Goldmann. The shares were in Switzerland, however, and the sale was held up by the arrangement of Goldmann's emigration. The Jews on the supervisory board had been replaced, but the commercial director was a Jew. He was supposed to leave the firm at the end of June 1939, but there was no replacement in sight as that deadline approached; as a report that month noted, "it is very difficult to find Aryan professionals in the textile branch in Hungary, and there are considerable difficulties in getting work permits for foreigners."[460]

"Progress" was steady, but not always fast. In a report on the Jewish situation in the CA textile concern in April 1940,[461] Patzak boasted that there was not a single Jew left in the CA textile firms in the Ostmark, but admitted that problems remained elsewhere. The Jewish commercial director at the Ujpester Tuchfabrik, for example, had still not been replaced. Left unmentioned in this report, but highly significant, was the fact that the Ujpester Tuchfabrik had been taken over by the Soproner Haas AG in October 1940 to form the "Sporoner und Ujpester Tuch- und Teppich-Fabriken AG, Budapest," and that the Gestapo had confiscated the 10.18 percent of the shares presumably belonging to David Goldmann. The merger created one of the largest vertically organized textile enterprises in Hungary. The CA was still seeking to buy these shares, presumably from the Finance Ministry, but all the shares were now in Aryan hands.[462] Felmayer

---

[458] Ibid., Haas, 07/06, Friedl to Hans von Weinczierl, May 8, 1940.

[459] BA-CA, CA-IB, Referat Patzak, 30/02, report to Fischböck, probably by Patzak, June 12, 1939.

[460] Ibid. On Felmayer see the report of Patzak for Friedl, Oct. 14, 1938, and related documents, BA-CA, CA-IB, Felmayer, 37/01-02.

[461] BA-CA, CA-IB, Referat Patzak, 30/02, Report, probably by Patzak, of April 22, 1940.

[462] See the memorandum by Patzak of Jan. 15, 1944, in ibid., Haas, 07/07. Given the fact that the CA had been trying to get the shares since 1940, it was obviously not doing very well. Reports on the Sporoner und Ujpester Tuch- und Teppichfabriken are to be found in ibid., Ujpester Wollwaren AG, 18/02. On the Aryanization of the Goldmann shares, see chapter 2 of this volume, pp. 149–152.

apparently no longer had any Jews, but there was still a Jewish director at Sopron because a replacement had not been located. At Haas in Budapest, there were no more Jews in leading positions, but there were still two employed in branches; they had been given notice, but replacements had yet to be found. The HITIAG was, if anything, even more rigorous in its personnel policies in Hungary than Haas. It not only reported on how many Jews remained and when they were to be dismissed but also on the attitudes of employees. For example, it noted that a plant engineer was "a Hungarian, Catholic, hostile to Jews."[463] The relentlessness of the company in ferreting out Jews can be measured by a report to Director Hermsen that it had been discovered that a member of the administrative council in Budapest was a Jew who had been baptized in 1919, and that his wife was also a baptized Jew. Under such circumstances, "it will be necessary to dismiss the person named from our administration and to coopt another man from Hungary in his place."[464] Presumably, in Hungary such persons could be more easily replaced than those with technical and professional skills, but as has been shown, this was far from easy. It was even more difficult in Yugoslavia, where the CA controlled the Textilwerke Mautner AG in Zagreb. Zagreb had two Jews in its commercial direction, and Yugoslavia could offer few professionals in the field and tended to bar foreigners.

Nonetheless, it was the Haas enterprises that took the lead in the Creditanstalt's Southeast European ambitions in the textile field, and the Haas concern was very much centralized in Vienna. In addition to its Hungarian holdings, Haas also had outlets in Prague; in October 1939 it began activity in Pressburg/Bratislava, finally creating a Philipp Haas & Söhne AG there in May 1940 after some difficulties gaining approval from the Slovak National Bank. As in Hungary, where Haas used the facilities of the CA Budapest, and where Director Bokor served on the administrative councils or supervisory boards of the CA-controlled firms, in Pressburg/Bratislava the Union-Bank helped finance the enterprise and was represented on the administrative council along with Friedl, who served as president, and Rudolf Nowaczek of Haas in Vienna. Because Haas Pressburg/Bratislava had been created in 1939, Jewish employees were not an issue, but the firm had pursued a policy of renting and then taking over former Jewish business places that were liquidated.[465]

Haas also succeeded in expanding into Bulgaria, setting up a branch in Sofia in January 1941 that opened up for business in June 1941 in well-appointed offices on one of the best squares in Sofia. Friedl and Nowaczek served on the administrative council, which had a Bulgarian majority. In 1942, Haas also created a new company in Vienna, the "Allgemeine Ein- und Ausfuhrgesellschaft m.b.H. Wien," to promote its imports and exports. The concern was particularly interested, however, in establishing itself in Bucharest. It had earlier had an important and profitable branch there that had been confiscated by the Romanian government in 1916 and taken over by a Romanian group; Haas received very little compensation. Apparently, the entire business had been very badly run down. Under the more favorable situation of 1940, Haas became interested in reestablishing itself in Romania, especially because it had both a good name and old contacts. The original idea was to have the Haas firm in Prague found a company in Bucharest, an arrangement that appeared convenient and was of little moment financially because all the Haas companies were really owned by the CA and Haas Vienna. The authorities both in Prague and in Romania were agreeable to the somewhat complicated arrangement thus developed, but the Romanians insisted that the RWM in Berlin also approve the proposal.

[463] BA-CA, CA-IB, Hanf-Jute, 06/01, report to Pfeiffer, Aug. 19, 1938.

[464] Ibid., Pfeiffer to Hermsen, July 5, 1938.

[465] On Haas & Söhne in Pressburg, see the report of Aug. 31, 1944, ibid., Haas, 07/07. Del-Ka took Haas as a model in the acquisition of Jewish business premises; see report by Glatzl of Oct. 18, 1940, ibid., Del-Ka, 03a/01.

The RWM, however, turned down the proposal because it did not consider the creation of the company in Bucharest necessary and was also unhappy that Haas had gone to the National Bank in Prague for permission instead of to the RWM. Director Nowaczek and the Haas interests now turned to Hermann Neubacher, a former mayor of Vienna then serving as German ambassador in Bucharest. Neubacher was certain that the RWM would change its mind. It remained opposed, however. That position was considered all the more disastrous result because the Romanians had given their assent. Although Heinrich Müller of Vigor urged the CA to make a new appeal to Berlin, nothing seemed to change the situation. Nowaczek was furious, and his response demonstrated that Haas shared both the Southeast European pretensions and the historical resentments that were so typical of the CA as a whole: "Quite aside from the fact that the Ostmark in particular is being given the task of handling the Southeast economically and that our firm, on the basis of its decades long active connection with the southeast, is in our opinion qualified to collaborate in this task, we would also view this as a kind of compensation for the great injury resulting from the sequestration and liquidation of our enterprise at that time."[466] Were the RWM more agreeable, Nowaczek and his friends would undoubtedly have had even more to resent later on, but this was not the mentality of these businessmen in 1942 or even later.

The HITIAG ran into similar difficulties in Romania, where it hoped to acquire a major jute producer, the "Societa Textila Franco Romana gia Birman et Fiu," 90 percent of whose shares were in Jewish possession. Because of the anti-Semitic legislation in Romania, the owners were anxious to sell. The HITIAG considered the firm an exceptionally promising acquisition that fit in well with its production program. As in the case of Haas, the HITIAG appealed to Ambassador Neubacher, emphasizing that it was a firm from the Ostmark and that the CA was its bank. Once again, however, there

were difficulties with the RWM, which, to be sure, was not opposed to German investment in Romanian enterprises but favored investment in more essential industries such as oil and transportation. At the same time, Hermsen was worried that the firm would fall into Italian or Greek hands, especially because his knowledge of the opportunity came from Italian sources. By June 1941, some nine months after Hermsen had first shown interest in acquiring Birmen & Sons, he had even more to worry about because of recent political developments in German-Romanian relations. Göring had met with state leader General Antonescu in Vienna and demanded complete German access to the Romanian oil and metal industries. As compensation, he agreed that the Romanian regime could "Romanize" the rest of its industry, and a special State Secretariat was established for that purpose. The Romanian regime of course totally frowned upon any further Germanization. Neubacher thus found himself in a situation where Antonescu might approve a Germanization only to have it promptly turned down by the Secretariat, whose position would be then confirmed by Antonescu. Irritating too was the fact that "the Jews are no longer in such a rush to Aryanize, but rather make a pro-forma Romanization for themselves. Aside from this, the Romanian authorities still prefer the Jews over us."[467] While the HITIAG was also trying to use its Romanian lawyers and contacts to engage in a pro forma "Romanization," there is no evidence that it succeeded. It is worth noting that the HITIAG's efforts to take over former Jewish plants in former Polish territories, where Aryanization should have been simpler, were also frustrated. Its attempt to get the Head Trusteeship Office East to agree to the sale of the Lenko AG, a major jute producer in Bielitz, led to unsatisfactory results; the Trusteeship Office would only lease the company for three or four years with an option to buy, while Hermsen felt that only a ten-year lease would make sense given the amount of

---

[466] BA-CA, CA-IB, Haas,07/07, Nowaczek to Patzak, Nov. 21, 1942, and Müller to Lanz, Dec. 10, 1942.

[467] Ibid., Hanf-Jute, 06/01, Hermsen memorandum, June 7, 1941, which also contains the considerable correspondence on the Romanian problem.

improvement and modernization the company needed.[468] In the end, therefore, Hermsen and the HITIAG fell back on their plants in Austria, Hungary, Bulgaria, and Yugoslavia, where they were confronting increasing labor and supply difficulties as the political and military situation deteriorated.

The same, of course, held true of Haas, although CA Director Patzak seemed curiously oblivious to the dangerous situation in Hungary. In a report of June 3, 1944, he positively gloated at the manner in which the Hungarians were finally realizing that they had to give full support to their German allies. As for the Jewish employees, there had been none at the Haas firms for some time, but the one remaining at Soproner and Ujpester and the two remaining at Felmayer had been dismissed. In his assessment of the situation of the CA enterprises, he saw "in general no reason for any great worries for the near future."[469] The factories had recovered after the events of March, production had increased, raw materials had been released by the new regime, and although war production had become paramount, the adjustment was satisfactory. The situation of Haas in Budapest was more difficult because consumer purchases had flagged, "which is above all due to the measures against the Jews. It is clear that a consumer group dropped out which can only gradually be replaced."[470] But Patzak did not view this condition as catastrophic and was hopeful that the efforts to help municipal employees and similar social actions would improve the situation. In general, he considered the situation of the textile industry better in Hungary than in the Reich because it needed to import. There were unlikely to be shutdowns as long as the government measures in favor of civil servants, workers, and farmers promoted production and consumption, and additional substantial military contracts were provided for. Reporting from Hungary later that year, was much more

sober in tone than Patzak, perhaps because the HITIAG plants had been bombed and he was unable to save his inventory from the Russians even with SS help.[471] In contrast to Patzak, Hermsen gave no indication that he expected 1945 to be a good year.

Nineteen forty-five was a good year, but for the Allies and hardly in the sense Patzak thought it would be. The situation from the vantage point of Vienna was rather gloomily.[472] Because textile production of the type engaged in by Haas was not considered essential to the war effort, some of its machinery was dismantled and placed at the disposal of the Wiener-Neustädter Flugzeugwerke. Sales had dropped because of raw materials shortages. When the war was in its last throes, the major offices of Haas in Vienna on Stock im Eisenplatz 6 had been totally destroyed and other offices damaged and plundered. The Vienna firm would recover under the aegis of the CA, but its holdings in the southeast were permanently lost to the new regimes that established themselves there. As for the HITIAG, it was thrown back on its badly damaged plants at home, and Hermsen returned to Hamburg, which could not have been very pleasant either.

Stölzle Glasindustrie AG

The Stölzle Glasindustrie AG is a particularly noteworthy example of the CA's efforts to expand its industrial concern under the post-Anschluss dispensation. An old family-dominated firm going under the name of Stölzle Österreichische Glasindustrie AG The company was based in Vienna and had production centers in Altnagelberg and Köflach. It also owned a brewery in Neu-Nagelberg and had a branch in Budapest. Prior to the downfall of the Hapsburg monarchy, it had plants in Hermanshütte and Erdweis in the Sudetenland, but these were taken over and formed into a Prague-based Czech firm bearing the Stölzle name. The Czech company continued to

[468] See the correspondence between Hermsen and Pfeiffer of March 1940 in ibid.

[469] Ibid., Referat Patzak, 30/02, Patzak report, June 3, 1944.

[470] Ibid.

[471] Ibid., Hanf-Jute,06/02-03, Hermsen report of Oct. 30, 1944.

[472] Ibid., Haas, 07/14, Response to a U.S. Occupation Authority questionnaire, Jan. 27, 1948.

work very closely with its Austrian counterpart. Gottlob Kralik-Mayerswalden was head of both companies for four years, and the plants of the two companies were in close proximity to one another despite the border. Also, the Czech company had a large export business that was handled by the Austrian company. The CA acquired more than 80 percent of the shares of the Austrian Stölzle in a restructuring of the company in 1934, thus effectively making it part of the CA industrial concern. Insurance compensation following the total destruction of the Köflach plant in 1934 enabled reconstruction along modern lines, although production costs in the Austrian glass industry continued to remain high. Nevertheless, the domestic glass industry was protected and Stölzle was successful in exporting its products abroad and was able to pay good dividends between 1935 and 1938. Things did not go as well with the Czech firm, especially after Kralik retired from the leadership of the Austrian company and thereby ended the unified direction that had previously existed. The Czech firm's president, Victor Landesmann, disliked Kralik and was jealous of the Austrian firm's success following the reconstruction.[473]

The events of 1938 were to have important consequences for both companies. Once the Anschluss came, a top priority for the CA was the Aryanization of Stölzle's administrative council. Its president, Franz Rottenberg, was replaced by Hans Friedl as CA representative, while Robert Glatzl replaced the other Jewish CA management board member, Otto Russo, who was to commit suicide. There appears to have been difficulties in getting a formal written resignation from another Jewish council member, Paul Mayer. That was necessary to remove his name from the Stölzle entry in the Commercial Registry. The CA asked the Gestapo for assistance and forwarded the letter of resignation for Mayer to sign, stressing that Mayer "certainly is ready to [sign the letter] right away and without making the slightest

difficulty."[474] Nevertheless, the CA repeated the request on May 10. Whether this was necessary because Mayer was in custody or because he had fled is unclear, but his removal from the council was dated May 26.

The new order was not without its problems for the management and operations of Stölzl. The logical person to head the Austrian concern was a man named Rudolf Müller, but it turned out he was married to a Jewish woman and thus could not be appointed factory leader, although he continued to be employed in a managerial position throughout the war. This problem was ultimately solved by the appointment of another Stölzle director, Anton Schneider, who was then given the task of checking the racial credentials of all the employees of the Stölzle plants.[475] A problem that was far less easily solved concerned Director Mika Schäfler of the Austrian Stölzle. He was a Romanian Jew who had become an Austrian citizen and had received medals for his wartime service. Moreover, everyone – including Glatz – agreed that Schäfler had been doing a splendid job promoting the company's export business. At the time of the Anschluss, he was traveling in the United States and Mexico drumming up business for the company; upon returning to Europe in April, he engaged in negotiations for Stölzle in France and England.[476]

The Anschluss greatly complicated the export situation of Stölzle. The company could no longer refer to "Austria" as the source of its products, and German goods abroad were often boycotted, especially by Jewish firms. Glatzl feared losing the account of the Bourjois Cosmetic firm in Paris and New York. Stölzle continued to dominate the market for perfume bottles, except in England where its products were handled by the International Bottle

---

[473] Ibid., Stölzle, 16/07, Report for the CA working committee meeting of June 16, 1939, and discussion between Glatzl and Kralik, April 25, 1938.

[474] Ibid., Glatzl to Geheime Staatspolizei, April 25 and May 10, 1938. The letters were signed by Heller and Glatzl.

[475] Ibid., Discussion between Glatzl and Kralik, April 25, 1938, and Glatzl to Schneider, Sept. 9, 1938.

[476] Ibid., this discussion is based on Glatzl's memorandum of his discussion with Kralik of April 25, 1938. See also ibid., Stölzle, 16/05-06, Glatzl to Friedl, May 27, 1938.

Company. The I.B.C., however, was owned by an "Ostjude" named Meyer, and this account was viewed as especially endangered. Kralik took the position that Stölzle could increase its sales in Belgium, France, and the Balkans, especially in Greece, Bulgaria, and Turkey, but Glatzl felt that the company desperately needed the services of Schäfler, whom he wanted to bring back to Austria and employ as a consultant because he could not give him a managerial position. Glatzl complained, however, that employees at Stölzle had warned Schäfler that it was unsafe to return to Austria. Although Glatzl viewed these warnings as a reflection of hostility to Schäfler, it is more likely that the warnings not to return were sincerely meant by persons concerned about Schäfler's welfare. In any event, Kralik, who was a German citizen and a Party member, put ideological considerations aside and was anxious to retain Schäfler's services. He negotiated with him in London and was quite prepared to solve the problem by hiring him in Prague, thus enabling him to do business for Stölzle companies both in England and throughout Europe outside the Reich. Schäfler was now without financial resources, so that Kralik and Glatzl could feel confident in cynically calculating that the Meyer family, with whom Schäfler was close, would continue the contracts with Schäfler if only to ensure his livelihood. When Director Rudolf Müller went to Paris in June, he found that he had to give a big discount to Bourjois to keep its business and that both the Bourjois and the Coty companies offered to market their products with Stölzle bottles in places where offense was not taken by their coming from the Reich.[477]

By late October, however, Stölzle appears to have lost all its business in France, in large part because the French glass producer St. Gobain had succeeded in persuading the French government to require that all imported bottles bear the name of the country of origin. The anti-German boycott thus became very effective, and Director Schneider of Stölzle proposed that it might be circumvented if the company manufactured bottles for the French market with Brosse & Cie, which belonged to St. Gobain, which may have been playing a double game in the entire matter. If Stölzle was licensed to produce its bottles through Brosse, they would not have to be designated as coming from Germany, thereby evading the boycott. Nonetheless, Stölzle would have had to send employees to Brosse who were experienced in Stölzle's production methods and would thus impart their knowledge to the French workers. Upon being asked to decide on the matter, Glatzl was extremely negative: "Under no circumstances, in our view, is it is acceptable to send German workers to France to make the employees of the French competition acquainted with our most secret production methods. If, with respect to the designation of the origin of the wares and a certain boycott movement on the part of Jewish customers, it is not possible to cultivate French business, then you will have to forgo this market. Just to get modest licenses for a brief period from French producers, we will not reveal our manufacturing secrets to this country."[478] If Glatzl had been primarily concerned about holding on to markets a few months earlier, he now seemed to think it most important to toe the line politically in looking after Stölzle's interests. He asked Stölzle to check with the Vienna or Berlin authorities about using Jewish personnel abroad so as to determine whether they should be let go immediately or only after suitable Aryan replacements had been found. He recognized that the termination of the arrangement with Schäfler in London would mean the loss of a big English customer, I.B.C., but he now appeared ready to have Stölzle run this risk. Undoubtedly, Glatzl became optimistic in view of the annexation of the Sudetenland and the impending recovery of the old plants there, a development to be discussed shortly. He could not imagine whence the French would get their quality glass now that the Sudetenland had been annexed.

---

[477] Ibid., Müller to Glatzl, June 10, 1938.

[478] BA-CA, CA-IB, Stölzle, 16/07, Glatzl to Schneider, Oct. 26, 1938 in response to Schneider to Glatzl, Oct. 25/26, 1938.

As this description suggests, Glatzl and the CA were directly and quite openly engaged in dealing with the opportunities and problems created by the new regime. Germany's takeover of the Sudetenland and later invasion of the Czech state enabled Stölzle to reunite its Austrian and Czech branches, and the management of its operations was strengthened by hiring an experienced glass industry specialist to serve as general director, Ferdinand Wintersberger, who had excellent connections with the authorities in Berlin. Nonetheless, Glatzl and Wintersberger had to tread warily in dealing with the local Party authorities in Austria. Much to Wintersberger's discomfort, Stölzle had turned over substantial space in its main offices to the Ortsgruppe Schleifmühle, a local party group, right after the Anschluss, and he found himself in a small office that he shared with two secretaries, depriving him of the opportunity even to telephone in peace. Overcrowded conditions also affected all the other employees. Although Stölzle offered the Schleifmühle group alternate facilities in a nearby building, it refused to move because it did not deem the space as well lighted as the rooms in which it was now ensconced. Stölzle then proceeded to seek a more agreeable facility for this group, finally finding one that had been vacated by its former Jewish renters and that it thought suitable. At the same time, Glatzl prevailed on Friedl to intervene in the matter, pointing out that the CA owned 87 percent of Stölzle. Friedl sent CA Company Leader Pfeiffer to negotiate with the leader of the group, Eduard Bernhart, who worked at the Securities Section of the CA. Wintersberger, also a Party member, tried to explain to Bernhart that, being the one primarily responsible for Stölzle as plant leader, he really needed the space. Still, Wintersberger did not feel he could be very forceful, fearing that he might be charged with behaving improperly toward an organ of the Party. Ultimately, Bernhart and his group were prepared to move, but only if Stölzle covered all the expenses and also provided facilities comparable to those Bernhart and his companions had been enjoying, namely, rooms with mahogany-covered ceilings and walls and a variety of other luxurious office features. By the end of 1939, the

difficulties and problems of "properly" housing the Ortsgruppe Schleifmühle group reached a point at which the Stölzle management began seriously considering moving part of its offices elsewhere despite the disruption to operations this would cause.[479] The evidence suggests that it decided not to spend the money needed to move Bernhart, and that Wintersberger would continue to be ill housed, occupying small and ill-furnished rooms. Apparently, he partially solved the problem by traveling a great deal to the Stölzle affiliates. Trying to find a director to assist Wintersberger in Vienna in February 1944, the CA offered such a position to Walther Salvenmoser of Ostmark-Keramik AG, who, however, threatened to resign after only a few days on the job. The primitive working conditions at Stölzle, where he had to share his office, suffered from windy conditions, did not even have a decent desk or conference table, reminded him of the way business was done in Poland.[480] It may well be that it was the Russians who in the end succeeded in dislodging the Ortsgruppe Schleifmühle.

The reluctance of Stölzle to finance the local Party organization in the style to which it was growing accustomed, to the company's great irritation, also reflected concern about the expenses involved and the contradictory behavior of the authorities toward the Austrian glass industry. The Anschluss had ended the protection of the Austrian glass industry, destroying its competitiveness with its German counterpart, and the price commissioner, the RWM, and the Economic Group for the Glass Industry were intent on rationalizing the industry and bringing both its costs and prices into line with those of Germany. Thus, Stölzle was ordered to charge the prices laid down by the glass cartel in Dresden, which put immense pressure on Stölzle to cut costs and to modernize its facilities, especially in Köflach. In this effort, however, Stölzle ran into trouble with the local

---

[479] Ibid., Stölzle, 16/05–06, memorandum by Glatzl, June 30, 1939 and report by Glatzl to Fritscher, Dec. 6, 1939.

[480] Ibid., Stölzle, 16/09, Salvenmoser to Friedl, Feb. 22, 1944.

Labor Front authorities, who complained that working conditions at Köflach "defied every description."[481] But the Labor Front's demands for social and technical improvements were held up by complicated negotiations involving the RWM, the Group for the Glass Industry in Berlin, and the Gau Economic Office in Styria for the consolidation and rationalization of all the glassworks in the Ostmark for the purpose of lowering production costs and bringing it up to standard with the old Reich. As Glatzl pointed out to the Labor Front officials, this program involved considerable reconstruction and reorganization, and there was little point in making the improvements requested until there was an agreement among the various parties involved and the necessary funding measures were in place.[482] The rationalization of labor thus had to take precedence over the "beautification" of labor. Even more troublesome, however, than the problem of satisfying the Labor Front demands was the issue of gaining acceptance for the rationalization plan devised by the Reich Economic Group for Glass, the RWM, and Stölzle from the authorities in the Gau Economic Office in Styria and the office of Reich Commissar Bürckel. The plan was to merge the Stölzle plants with those belonging to the Wilhelm Abel family in Oberdorf; an unprofitable glass company in Voitsberg called "Futurit," which had been in Czech-Jewish hands and seems to have been placed under an administrator from Graz, was to be allowed to be shut down. Much to the surprise of everyone who expected the plan to sail through, both the economic office officials in Stryia and Bürckel's representatives refused to accept the plan, claiming that it was too "liberalistic." They denied permission to shut down Voitsberg and demanded a decisive role for the Styrian authorities in the management and supervision of any new enterprise. Because the companies concerned, Stölzle and Oberdorf, were private Aryan firms, and because no government money was involved, this claim by the local Party authorities to a voice in the affairs of the companies was found to be quite extraordinary and complaints were registered with the RWM.[483] While the proponents of the projected syndicate managed to ward off interference from the authorities in Graz, in part with the help of the governor of Styria, Armin Dadieu, the actual plan seemed much less attractive by early 1939. While Wilhlem Abel had initially agreed to bring the Oberdorf company into the syndicate in return for being placed in charge of the rationalization program, but he became disturbed that the arrangements made did not sufficiently protect his family's interests. At the same time, Stölzle pursued its ambitions in the Sudetenland more actively.[484] The syndicate was thus scotched before it was even launched, and Stölzle attended to its own rationalization efforts. Very substantial sums were spent to bring Köflach up to standard with new machinery and improved production methods. Apparently, the great effort undertaken was not without its critics, and in June 1944, Director Friedl made a point of writing to Dadieu concerning the success of Köflach's modernization and good performance despite wartime problems. He sent him the report of the Köflach management, pointing out that "the attempt is being repeatedly made from time to time to present this undoubtedly finest, most modern, and most productive container glass factory as uneconomic, overindebted, etc., and I do not want to fail to transmit these illuminating materials for your information."[485] By this time, the CA had given Stölzle-Vienna 5.8 million RM in cash credits alone, although it hoped to raise its capital in such a way as to reduce the debt and increase its own already substantial 83 percent holding in the company.[486]

[483] See the lengthy report by C.M. Grisar of the Economic Group Glass Industry to the RWM of Nov. 15, 1938, ibid., Stölzle, 16/02.
[484] See ibid., Wintersberger to Glatzl, Jan. 15, 1939, and ibid., Stölzle, 16/07, Abel to the CA of Jan. 27, 1939. For the syndicate agreement, which is undated, see ibid., Stölzle, 16/08.
[485] Ibid., Stölzle, 16/09, Friedl to Dadieu, June 13, 1944.
[486] Report for the management board, July 14, 1944.

[481] Ibid., Stölzle, 16/07, DAF District Office Voitsberg to Glatzl, Nov. 19, 1938.
[482] Ibid., Glatzl to DAF District Office Voitsberg, Nov. 26, 1938.

The CA's engagement in the affairs of Stölzle, both financial and personal through Glatzl's and Friedl's involvement, was evident in the expansion of the company's interests abroad. This began in the fall of 1938, when the annexation of the Sudetenland provided Stölzle with an opportunity to reacquire the glass factory at Hermannshütte bei Mies and the glass-forming and machine factory at Erdweis near Budweis. The reacquisitions were justified on both historical and economic grounds and had the support of the RWM and the glass industry organizations. The foreign exchange authorities cooperated in the financial arrangements. The negotiations, which took place at the beginning of 1939, were conducted by Friedl with the Böhmische Escompte-Bank (Bebca), the house bank and chief creditor of the Czech Stölzle firm. The Czech Stölzle gave up its production facilities and was reduced to the status of a marketing firm for Stölzle products.[487] Once the Germans entered Prague, the CA and Stölzle sought to liquidate the Czech firm and create a Prague office for the marketing of Stölzle products. That effort was successful but led to ugly altercations with the Bebca. The bank had apparently milked the Czech Stölzle by charging excessive interest rates and failing to fulfill its responsibilities. Glatzl's enthusiasm for Director Kralik vanished when he also discovered the latter's mismanagement of the company. In any case, the events of 1938–1939 restored control from Vienna over both the plants and the marketing operations as they had existed before the First World War.[488]

In contrast to the relative simplicity of the reacquisition of assets in the former Czechoslovakia, the efforts of the CA and Stölzle to acquire new production assets of importance in the region exposed them once again to the vagaries of National Socialist policies. The enterprise of interest was the Glashütten-Werke, vormals J. Schreiber & Neffen, a venerable manufacturer of high-quality glass products with factories in the Sudeten town of Reitendorf and the Slovak town of Lednicke Rovne. The headquarters of Schreiber had always been in Vienna, but it officially relocated to Reitendorf after 1919 at the insistence of the Czech government. The company had a big export business in the so-called boycott countries and elsewhere, and a staff of 1,100 highly skilled workers, many from families that had been in the glass industry for generations. Schreiber was an Aryanization case. Of the 20,000 shares, 8,512 belonged to a Viennese Jew, Ignaz Kreidl, and 4,430 were the property of Frederike Selahettin, a Jewish woman who had been married to a Turkish officer and, after her divorce from him, to an Austrian businessman. She had fled to London, claiming to be a Turkish citizen, which, on account of her first marriage, she was under Turkish law. But because of her origins and her second marriage, the German authorities considered her an Austrian German. The remaining shares were in the hands of an Aryan family, the Schreibers. In June 1938, the Kreidl's shares were confiscated by the Gestapo and declared the property of the Land of Austria, as were the shares of Frederike Selahettin, which were deposited at the CA in the account of the state commissar for the private economy in Vienna. He intended to sell them for the benefit of the Land of Austria at the best possible price. Given the fact that the Schreiber factories were in Czechoslovakia, it was virtually impossible to market the shares until the situation changed. When the Czech lands came under German control, Stölzle took an option to buy 65 percent of the shares, that is, those formerly in Jewish hands, and indicated that it would try to buy up the remainder. The CA promised to provide financial support as the principal shareholder in Stölzle, and it also gave assurance that it would not ask for a Reich-guaranteed credit to fund Schreiber's reorganization or the wage payments and debts owed in Slovakia.[489]

---

[487] Ibid., Stölzle, 16/05-06, report by Glatzl, Jan. 7, 1939.

[488] See the report by Glatzl on the extremely nasty meeting of Oct. 5, 1939, with the leading officials of the Bebca, ibid.

[489] This account is based on the brief of May 11, 1939, by the Berlin lawyer for Stölzle, Willi Hess, as well as the other relevant documents in ibid.

This plan ran into what Stölzle's lawyer called "unanticipated difficulties" when the Gau economic advisor in Reichenbach came to the conclusion that Schreiber was a Jewish firm. The Gauleiter in Troppau thereupon ordered the appointment of a commissarial administrator to take control of Schreiber and to determine its fate. The person in question apparently had ideas of his own and planned to apply for a Reich-guaranteed credit. The leadership of Stölzle and the CA were aghast. First, they could not understand how Schreiber was Jewish when its Jewish-owned shares had been in government hands for almost a year. Second, there was the danger that if the shares were not placed in safe hands rapidly, they would lose value as the Schreiber factories were unable to pay their bills and at risk of losing their workers. This conflict dragged on into the summer of 1939. The one side insisted that the firm was at least 24 percent Jewish because Selahettin's shares had been placed in a Prague bank that was considered Jewish even though the bank had been taken over by an Aryan bank. The other side derided such arguments and complained about the damage being done.[490] It is difficult to discern the real motives behind the authorities in Reichenberg and Troppau, but one detects a desire to keep Stölzle from gaining strength, especially because of its financial backing by the CA. It would also seem that one of the Schreiber family members, Konrad Schreiber, wanted to take charge of the Reitendorf plant and had the ear of the Gau leadership. Owning only 10 percent of the shares in the company, however, he was in no position to take charge financially. Fortunately for the CA, Wintersberger had very good contacts at the RWM and in the glass industry organizations and was able to argue Stölzle's case with increasing success. This did not mean, however, that matters were settled quickly. Indeed, it was not until more than a year later that Stölzle was able to formally

acquire the shares in question and then build up a 75 percent majority.[491] At the same time, a plan was prepared to separate the Lednicke Rovne plants from Schreiber because it was hard to manage plants in the Sudetenland and in Slovakia at the same time and the financing of the modernization and expansion of the Lednicke Rovne operations required complicated special arrangements because of Slovak regulations. In these efforts, Glatzl worked closely with Director Franz Stephan of the Union-Bank in Pressburg/Bratislava.[492]

In its efforts to move into Southeast Europe, the CA viewed Stölzle Glasindustrie, with its long history of export sales and business in many parts of the world, as a particularly promising member of the CA concern. Quite aside from its reacquisitions and acquisitions in the Czech lands, Stölzle had maintained a separate subsidiary in Budapest since 1921, the C. Stölzle's Söhne ungarische Aktiengesellschaft für Glaswaren, which was primarily engaged in marketing operations. The Budapest subsidiary also had large warehouse facilities.[493] Both Wintersberger and the CA were anxious to promote business in Hungary, but as usual there was the "Jewish question" because of Hungary's complicated handling of the problem. Director Friedl of the CA was especially concerned, writing to Wintersberger in May 1940 that "I would like to ask you in particular to devote your attention to the quickest way of continuing and concluding the Aryanization, since, aside from the fact that it is our obligation to also cleanse our foreign enterprises of Jews, it could possibly be held against us if Jews are still employed at one of its concern firms."[494] Friedl asked Wintersberger to handle this

490 See Glatzl's angry and highly critical account of a grotesque meeting of the various parties in Reichenberg on Aug. 18, 1939, ibid., Schreiber, 19/01-02.

491 See the meeting of Aug. 18, 1939 and other related documents in ibid., Referat Glatzl, 47/01-02.

492 Ibid., also see ibid., Stölzle, 16/07, the Glatzl report on the discussion with Stephan, Feb. 15, 1940, and BA-CA, CA-V, the CA management board meeting, Dec. 20, 1941.

493 See BA-CA, CA-IB, Stölzle, 16/18, Stölzle to the Bundesministerium für Vermögenssicherung und Wirtschaftsplanung, June 22, 1948.

494 Ibid., Stölzle, 16/08, Friedl to Wintersberger, May 16, 1940.

problem personally and to make sure that not only the management but also all the employees in Hungary were Aryans, and requested that Wintersberger report back in three months on the results of his efforts. Undoubtedly, he had great "success," and the Hungarian operation proved to be important for Stölzle. In the summer of 1942, Wintersberger asked permission to turn to other banks in Hungary for credits if he was unable to get the increase he had requested from the Hungarian CA; in light of the upturn of glass imports from the Reich and the prospect of greatly increased sales in Hungary, his request was approved.[495]

Although Wintersberger and the CA seemed to have made considerable efforts at expanding their production, marketing, and storage facilities in Eastern and Southeastern Europe, the evidence suggests that they had little or no success. Their efforts are worth noting, however, as an indication of the ambitions they reflected. Probably the most serious effort was made in Bulgaria in the spring of 1942. Wintersberger was interested in setting up facilities in Bulgaria and had broached the idea to Friedl, who then used the services of another CA official, Ernst Lenz. The latter was in contact with the very well-connected head of the Cereal-Export AG in Sofia, Sergey Kalendjieff, who, as mentioned before, dominated the wheat trade with Germany and worked closely with Vigor. The focus of their discussion was the Erste Bulgarische Glasfabrik in the seaside town of Gebedje. The company was Jewish owned, and, under recent Bulgarian legislation, had to be Aryanized, at least to the extent that majority ownership had to be in Aryan hands. A 49 percent minority remained in Jewish hands, and one possibility was for Stölzle to buy this stake and to gain control through Bulgarian front men. Another was to go into partnership with two Bulgarian wholesalers. Klalendjieff was interested in the prospect of building up a Bulgarian glass operation because he was looking for a supplier of glass jars for fruit conserves and bottles for milk. Wintersberger's concern, on the other hand, was to secure effective

control over the Gebedje facilities and to combine German and Bulgarian production with an eye toward gaining control of the market not only in Bulgaria but also in Turkey and Greece as well. Wintersberger was scheduled to go to Bulgaria at the beginning of June 1942, but there is no evidence in the available documents that anything came of his efforts.[496]

Nor does anything seem to have come of inquiries made by Glatzl. Apparently encouraged by the Southeast Europe Conference of July 1942, he explored the possibilities of Stölzle acquiring a glassworks in Greece and also followed up on Deutsche Bank suggestions that a trading company composed of CA concern firms be set up in Turkey in which Stölzle would be a participant.[497] These ideas involved complicated bureaucratic and financial arrangements; other schemes were simply ill-fated because of the military realities. After reading a report on the reorganization program for the Crimea and the importance of the glass industry in view of the large supplies of sand and chalk, Wintersberger came up with the idea of constructing a large glass factory in the Crimea. The idea was welcomed by the German general commissar for the area, to whom it was communicated by Director Buzzi of the CA. The commissar was less interested in creating a glass industry than in securing a supply of jars and bottles for packaging the large quantities of fruit and fish harvested in the Crimea. He suggested that a contract be signed but was eager to have construction completed within a year rather than the two years proposed by Wintersberger. He also noted that discussions could take place only after a civilian administration had replaced the military administration. Wintersberger thought that the time could be shortened if there was something left of the Soviet glass factory in the area and suggested that a new company be established to carry

---

[495] Ibid., Glatzl report of July 4, 1942.

[496] Ibid., Wintersberger to Lanz, April 27, 1942 and Lanz to Wintersberger, May 19, 1942.

[497] See ibid., Glatzl to Wintersberger, July 20, 1942; Glatzl to Arnold Friese, Aug. 17, 1942; and Helmut Lemm to Wintersberger, Sept. 30, 1942, and related correspondence.

on the work.[498] Of course, it would not be too long before the German administration in the Crimea was confronting the problem of preserving itself rather than fruits and fish.

The Crimean glassworks was not the only ambitious and unrealizable project Wintersberger entertained in 1942. Yet another was finding suitable storage and office facilities in Belgrade. Ernst Lanz of the CA pointed out to him that he would have to get permission from Neuhausen, who was in charge of the Serbian economy and, when and if he received it, he would ask CA Director Ludwig Sehn to look around for a suitable location. Lanz made clear, however, that he was not very enthusiastic about the idea, pointing out that "It should not be difficult at present to find a suitable business location for your firm in Belgrade, but it is questionable whether at this time an appropriate market for luxury goods will be found in Belgrade. Moreover, one must keep in mind that, because the possibility of disturbances cannot be ruled out, a luxury glass business is very endangered. For this reason, one does not see any valuable items displayed in all those businesses with such wares."[499]

There is no record of what exactly Glatzl, who had received a copy of this letter, thought of Wintersberger's plans for Belgrade at this point. All the evidence suggests that he and the CA continued to have high hopes for the development of its glass interests. The greatest problem appears to have been the concentration of management in the hands of the ambitious Wintersberger. The appointment of Walther Salvenmoser of Ostmark Keramik to the management board in February 1944 was aimed at solving these managerial problems; the move would also have placed two ambitious Party men at the head of Stölzle. As noted earlier, Salvenmoser was appalled by his working conditions, but he also had greater ambitions and suggested the merger of Ostmark

Keramik with Stölzle. He would then assume general direction of the expanded concern while Wintersberger would concentrate on the glass business. While Wintersberger welcomed Salvenmoser's projected assistance, there is no evidence that either he or Friedl was prepared to go so far to accommodate such ambitions.[500]

Glatzl continued to pay close attention to the situation of Stölzle for the CA. He was unhappy with developments, especially with the beer production at Neu-Nagelberg. On one occasion, he complained that the beer was flat because of poor compression; on another, he found a snail in a bottle.[501] Nevertheless, production was up and the core plants, especially the glassworks in Köflach, had all converted almost entirely to war production. At the same time, the automatization and rationalization programs were highly successful, significantly reducing the number of skilled workers needed and making it possible to employ forced Eastern European workers and prisoners of war. In January 1945, when the authorities were threatening to shut down Köflach, Friedl could argue against this by pointing to the high productivity of the plant and its great importance to the war effort because other glass factories had been shut down.[502]

Whatever Stölzle's contributions to the war effort, it is worth noting in conclusion that the firm seems to have assisted some of the CA's officials in preparing for the coming peace. In a letter of February 10, 1945, Glatzl inquired if Stölzle had a nice glass service for twelve persons available because he needed to purchase a wedding present and if it could put together a collection of glassware for daily use, that is, beer and wine glasses and the like. Assistance of this kind was needed even more by Director Joham, who, after his residence had been bombed, lost his entire set of dishes and glasses. He was hopeful that Stölzle could provide a "Nizza" table

498 See ibid., Wintersberger to Friedl, Aug. 14, 1942, General Commissar for the Crimea to Stölzle, Aug. 20, 1942; Wintersberger to General Commissar for the Crimea, Aug. 29, 1942.

499 Ibid., Lanz to Wintersberger, Nov. 23, 1942.

500 Ibid., Stölzle, 16/08, Salvenmoser to Friedl, Feb. 22, 1944 and related correspondence.

501 Ibid., Glatzl to Wintersberger, Oct. 7, 1940 and March 16, 1943.

502 See the report by Glatzl on Stölzle of July 14, 1944, and Friedl to Gau Economic Advisor Alfred Fleischmann, Jan. 23, 1945, ibid., Stölzle, 16/09.

service set and also procure a coffee and tea service, which it did, and which he locked up in the cellar of one of the CA buildings to ensure its safety.[503] A fitting end to Stölzle's Southeast Europe program!

Leykam-Josefsthal AG für Papier- und Druckindustrie

The dominant position of the CA in the wood and paper industry, as discussed in the previous section in connection with Aryanizations, was most formidably represented by its participation in the Leykam-Josefsthal AG. This was a vertically organized concern engaged in wood processing as well as the production of cellulose and a wide variety of paper products. Its most important plants were in Grantwein, and the company also had factories in Wampersdorf, Pitten, Breitenau, Schwarzenau, and Spittal a.d. Drau. In early 1939, the concern employed 1,543 workers and 197 staff employees. The CA owned 59 percent of the company's stock; the second largest shareholder was the Länderbank Wien with 8.6 percent.[504] After the Anschluss, Erich Heller took over as chairman of the administrative council, and Director Leonard Wolzt served as vice-chairman. Heller took a great interest in the company until he left his position as chairman of the supervisory board of the CA and also retired from Leykam. He was replaced in the spring of 1940 by CA director Hans Friedl, who also paid close attention to Leykam affairs. The dominant figure at Leykam was General Director Walter Schmeil, who seems to have been an energetic and talented manager.

Leykam was significantly affected by the Anschluss. There were no prominent Jewish shareholders, but the company did have Jewish employees. By the fall of 1938, matters were settled with them, but not with the two directors, who asked for settlements of 35,000 and 54,000 Schilling respectively. Heller and Schmeil decided to give them 20,000 RM each, subject to the approval of Rafelsberger, who had been called on to sanction other settlements with Leykam employees. Of far greater moment for Schmeil, however, was the opportunity to take advantage of the plans for the economic development of the Ostmark and to secure support from Hans Kehrl for a large-scale investment program of 4 or 5 million RM to expand cellulose and paper production at Gratwein and to shut down or sell off less promising or already shut-down plants.[505]

In these efforts, Schmeil received some indirect and not exactly pleasant assistance from German Labor Front head Robert Ley, who paid a surprise visit to the Gratwein plants in May 1938 with Gauleiter Jury and other local government and Party officials. Brushing aside the offer by plant managers to show him around, Ley went to view the facilities himself, shook hands with each and every worker he encountered, and "in a very temperamental manner made known the impressions he had received, declaring that the factory was a pigsty. It was a disgrace, an actual crime, to expect of German workers that they work under such conditions."[506] Ley chewed out the managers, who in his view deserved to be arrested, and he severely reprimanded the local authorities for failing to exercise proper control. He demanded that the conditions be corrected forthwith and threatened to return in four weeks to make sure the situation had been remedied.

As might be expected, the Lykam management defended itself against charges of being deliberately negligent and unconcerned about its workers. At the same time, it admitted to the flaws in worker facilities and declared that it was willing to spend hundreds of thousands on improvements, but that this would only be possible because of the improved economic

---

[503] Ibid., Glatzl to Franz Stöger, Feb. 20, 1945; Glatzl to Walter Heinrich, Feb. 23, 1945; Glatzl to Stöger, March 26, 1945.

[504] Peter Melichar is incorrect in stating that the CA owned 100 percent of the shares; see Felber et al., *Ökonomie der Arisierung*, vol. 2, p. 338. For the distribution of shares, see the report of the Reich Economic Assistance Credit Committee of Feb. 8, 1939, BAB, R2/15542, Bl. 220.

[505] BA-CA, CA-IB, Leykam, 10/02, meeting between Heller and Schmeil, Oct. 10, 1938.

[506] Ibid., report by Director Rengelrod, May 15, 1938.

conditions since the Anschluss and the expectation that the economic problems of the industry could at last be effectively dealt with through large-scale investments. Leykam reminded the authorities that Austria had been in an economic crisis since 1930. The paper industry, at one time selling half of its production in Asia and abroad, had lost its markets because of the previous regime's currency policy and the lack of capital investment, which was rendering Austria uncompetitive, especially with Germany. Gratwein had been particularly hard hit by these developments as well as by floods in 1937, and was in truly desperate need of modernization and investment. While acknowledging the validity of Ley's complaints, Leykam declared itself a victim of economic and natural conditions that had been beyond its control. Once again, it called on the authorities, especially Kehrl and Minister Fischböck, to support its appeals for a large-scale investment program as it had been developed by Schmeil.[507]

At the meetings of the Leykam administrative council, Schmeil was able to instrumentalize Ley's visit to Gratwein and the need for modernization to gain support for a program of securing millions in credits. As he reportedly put the matter at the March 28, 1939, meeting: "General Director Dr. Schmeil expressed the problem in clear antitheses: one decides either to let the paper factory die and invest nothing or to carry through the proposed investments. The first decision is impossible for economic and political reasons, hence the second solution take place, since a muddling through, as has been the case before, is no longer permissible in the framework of the Greater German economy. Both economic and political considerations, but also the complete adaptation to the Four Year Plan, the increasing prices of wood along with the reduction of sales prices compel rationalization...."[508]

Leykam was in fact a significant illustration of the problems connected with Austria's economic integration into the Reich. Its industrial plant was insufficiently modern to compete, and the authorities in Berlin understood the need to provide breathing space and money so as to give the Austrians an opportunity to catch up. The pressure, however, was bound to increase because the Austrians were to be subjected to more and more pressure to raise productivity and lower their costs. In the case of Leykam, rising wood prices combined with demands from Berlin to lower prices made adjustment particularly urgent, and Schmeil placed the need to procure modern high-performance machinery front and center. Both he and the CA leadership were convinced that the investments would pay off and that Leykam could be made competitive within reasonable time. Furthermore, the Technical Commission set up by the RWM to determine which companies and plants were eligible for credits had placed Leykam on its list. On April 19, 1939, the Credit Committee of the Economic Aid Program for Austria approved a Reich-guaranteed consortia credit for the company amounting to 3 million RM for the period 1941–1953, and by July 1939 the CA had put up another 2 million RM in long-term credits and 1 million RM in a short-term credit. Manifestly, this constituted a very significant CA commitment to Leykam.[509]

Despite these intentions, the implementation of the investment program was slowed down significantly by the outbreak of the war. The authorities in charge of iron allocation refused to supply Leykam with what was needed, which meant not only a delay in the program at Gratwein but also the loss of the money already disbursed. Schmeil tried to reverse the decision by using an influential member of his supervisory board, Karl Seeliger, a defense economy leader and an influential person in the publishing and paper businesses, to plead Leykam's case

[507] Ibid., letter to the Bezirkshauptmannschaft, Graz, May 28, 1938.

[508] Ibid., Leykam, 10a/04-05, administrative council meeting, March 28, 1939. For the significance Schmeilgave to Ley's appearance at Gratwein, see the meeting of June 17, 1938, ibid.

[509] See BAB, R2/15542, Bl. 220–224 and R2/15552, Bl. 142–145, the Reich Economic Aid credit committee meetings of Feb. 8, 1939, April 13, 1939, and July 19, 1939, and BA-CA, CA-V, CA board of management meetings of July 12 and July 17, 1939.

to Kehrl. But Kehrl replied negatively, pointing out that Leykam's very substantial needs were not sufficiently urgent to be placed in the category of military requirements.[510] Matters had not improved very much a year later, when Friedl reported on a conversation with Kehrl in which Friedl had "given account of the extraordinary difficulties from which in particular the 'Ostmark' paper industry suffers, for example, the rising cost of wood, the rising cost of coal, shortage of workers, transportation difficulties, price stops, allocation contingents, etc. President Kehrl immediately confirmed the correctness of the argumentation, but pointed to the inescapable higher interests that exist during the war and that preclude relief, at least at the present time."[511]

Although Schmeil became increasingly resigned to the situation, he by no means ceased to be an entrepreneur. Indeed, he labored to expand Leykam significantly after the conquest of Poland and concocted a series of measures within the concern to make an important Polish acquisition financially possible. The Polish acquisition was the Kluczewska Fabryka Papieru & Cellulozy in Klicze b/Olkusyk. Klicze lay between Cracow and Kattowitz, but the headquarters of the company was in Warsaw. It was a large, mixed plant that manufactured paper, cellulose, and wood products. Thirty percent of the shares were in Jewish hands, but the entire enterprise had been taken over by the Head Trusteeship Office East (HTO). Many of its facilities were in bad shape and investment would be necessary, but the company was very similar in its productive structure to the Leykam plants at Gratwein. Schmeil and Seeliger had reviewed a variety of potential acquisitions in the former Poland in 1939 before deciding on Klutsche/Kluczewska, and their decision was in important measure motivated by the possibility

of Leykam being appointed by the HTO to administer the company before deciding to lease or purchase it.[512] The success of these negotiations with the HTO was reported in April 1940 in rather self-serving terms: "We have considered it to be our duty to strive for this decisive expansion of our circle of influence and hope, after the war happily coming to an end, to be able to integrate this well-equipped work, which in its size and capacity nearly approaches that of our works at Gratwein. Next to the interests of the Reich, which we care for here as trustees, we hope to serve the interests of our enterprise in equal measure."[513]

The counterpart to this expansion of production to Poland was closing down and selling off unprofitable or insufficiently productive works belonging to Leykam, so that by the fall of 1941 Leykam could count on receiving 2.2 million RM for the plants. At the same time, negotiations for the purchase of Klutsche from the HTO were successfully completed. The purchase price was to be 4.3 million RM, with another 2 million for mobile assets. Leykam was to make an initial payment of 1.5 million RM, and then the rest in three yearly payments of 600,000 RM and four yearly payments of 750,000 RM plus 3 percent interest on the balances. While Leykam, under strong pressure from CA Director Friedl, sought to gain a reduction of purchase costs in the event of forced shut down or incapacity to get needed raw materials, the HTO refused to make such concessions.[514]

At the meeting of the Leykam supervisory board on October 31, 1941, Friedl ultimately approved the plan to buy Klutsche, but not before he subjected the company to a rather critical review. He noted that Gratwein's modernization had by far not achieved all that was desired, largely because of the war, but that much

---

[510] BA-CA, CA-IB, Leykam, 10/03-04, Seeliger to Kehrl, Sept. 23, 1939, and Kehrl to Leykam, Sept. 28, 1939. On Seeliger, see *Wer Leitet? Die Männer der Wirtschaft und der einschlägigen Verwaltung 1941/1942* (Berlin 1942), p. 931.

[511] BA-CA, CA-IB, Leykam, 10a/04-05, Leykam supervisory board meeting, Oct. 31, 1941.

[512] See their undated report of 1939 in ibid., Leykam, 10a/03-04. The name "Klutsche" will be used here because it is the one used in all the documents.

[513] Ibid., Leykam, 10a/04-05, report of the management board to the supervisory board meeting of April 26, 1940.

[514] BA-CA, CA-V, CA board of management meeting, Nov. 4, 1941.

remained to be done. Klutsche was costly, and Friedl urged selling off smaller works belonging to Leykam at Pitten and Olbersdorf. He even urged selling off the plants at Spittal and Wampersdorf, which were still productive but nonetheless dispensable and for which there was a market. While he did not think that Leykam would normally want to sell off the plants at Breitenau, he urged this also so that Klutsche could be paid for more easily. Breitenau, in fact, was to be sold off to Samum, which was of course in the CA concern. Schmeil had been calling for an increase of Leykam's capital, and while Friedl was willing to consider this, he seemed rather insistent that there was a good alternative in going further with the sale of other assets. Friedl also emphasized that the approval of the purchase of Klutsche had been made because solid evidence seemed to favor it. Thus, he was impressed with the fact that Leykam had been administering the company for more than a year and had a chance to operate it firsthand. Additionally, the chairman of the management board of Kontropa (Bunzl & Biach), Otto Fenzl, had made a detailed study of Klutsche and believed that the company could bring a decent return. Last, Friedl was impressed with Leykam's sales organization and believed it could successfully penetrate the Generalgouvernement.

Friedl's measured optimism was, as might be expected, exceeded by Schmeil, who was convinced that the existing Leykam turnover of 15–16 million RM per year would increase to 22–23 million RM with Klutsche in the concern. Seeliger, whose good contacts at the HTO seemed to have played an important role in the success of the negotiations, was not only optimistic about the present but also about the future: "When the war is successfully ended by Germany, and we can only go forth from this conviction, then he [Seeliger] sees very extraordinary chances for Klutsche. The far-reaching reconstruction work, which is being planned for Upper Silesia and about which he [Seeliger] is informed through his close connection with the Gau leadership of Upper Silesia, opens up quite outstanding prospects for Klutsche.... The prospects that are opening up with regard to the

Gouvernement and the more distant East are to be similarly judged."[515]

It was difficult to actually realize some of these prospects as the war went on. Originally, Lykam planned to buy the sales organization of Klutsche in Warsaw, which still operated independently, and to develop it. But the Generalgouvernement opposed this, and Klutsche used the Lykam organization. Schmeil himself, however, had become very cold to the idea. As Director Fiala of the CA reported, "General Director Schmeil then explained that the security situation in Warsaw gets worse from day to day. The partisan attacks are on the increase and paratroopers landed by the Bolsheviks commit many acts of sabotage. The risk connected with taking over the sales corporation of Klutsche is quite large, since the entire storage facility can be destroyed by air attacks. Also, guarding the business of the sales organization of Klutsche would be extraordinarily difficult. Given these considerations, he cannot justify investing approximately a million Zloty at the present time."[516]

All this suggests that Schmeil was losing his optimism by early 1944. Seeliger, however, remained confident even as late as July 1944, and this obviously rested on his sublime unwillingness to think the unthinkable. As he had on past occasions, he noted that Klutsche was functioning well despite the difficult conditions. He was less optimistic about its prospects because of the difficulties in getting wood and because of other problems, but "despite all this, he was convinced that the decision of the supervisory board to buy Klutsche has been shown to be completely correct...."[517]

The mistake, of course, was far bigger than the purchase of Klutsche. The role of the CA, however, not only in approving of the expansion of Leykam in this manner, but also in urging the sale of so many of its assets for this

[515] BA-CA, CA-IB, Leykam, 10a/04-05, Leykam supervisory board meeting, Oct. 31, 1941.
[516] Ibid., Leykam, 10a/03-04, Report by Fiala, Jan. 3, 1944.
[517] Ibid., Leykam, 10a/04-05, Leykam supervisory board meeting, July 7, 1944.

purpose, casts an interesting light on the mentality of Friedl and other CA leaders in making crucial decisions about firms in their industrial concern.

The Automobil-Verkehrs-Anstalt G.m.b.H. (AVA)

If Leykam's expansion was limited to Poland and its other international interests were primarily concerned with securing wood supplies rather than establishing production or sales facilities in Southeast Europe, the Automobil-Verkehrs-Anstalt GmbH (AVA), by contrast, sought to expand from Austria to all of German-occupied Europe as well as to other countries doing business with the Reich. It was a special banking facility devoted to the installment financing of vehicle, radio, and bicycle purchases. Founded in 1931 by the CA, the company was 75 percent owned by the CA and 25 percent owned by the Oberbank. Its practice was to ask for a 25 percent down payment and to then give its customers the opportunity to repay their purchases on a monthly basis for between one and two years. The average time appears to have been ten months. It seems to have been a low-risk business because the AVA worked closely with major insurance companies that reinsured its customer credits. In early 1939, the CA provided 6 million RM in credits to the AVA and was prepared to go up to 8 million RM.[518]

The Anschluss, to be sure, did create some very unpleasant financial risks of a political nature for the AVA because the Gestapo and various Party agencies made a practice of requisitioning Jewish-owned automobiles and were quite indifferent as to whether payments were due on them. In many cases, the autos were not returned because they were declared forfeit to the Reich, and in the rare cases that they were returned, they were in such bad shape as to be unusable. On legal advice, the AVA decided to launch claims against the past owners of the automobiles forfeited to the Reich, so that the Jews involved were not only victims of the

organized auto theft by the regime but also had to pay what was owed on the vehicles. This, however, entailed very substantial legal costs. At the same time, the AVA had a hard time finding out which vehicles were taken by the Gestapo and which were taken by Party agencies. But this did not solve the problem by any means, and both the AVA and the insurance companies, to whom the AVA tried to shift the burden, were fearful that they would end up in court against the Gestapo or Party agencies. In November 1939, they were also worried about the deadline for making civil claims connected with damages during the events of March 1938. Happily for them, however, they only had to report such claims and these were handled administratively. Nonetheless, it was not until 1942 that the 36,377 RM owing from the NSDAP was finally paid.[519]

While the CA, as will be shown, was very anxious to promote the expansion of the AVA, it was anything but happy about competition it might face from the old Reich. When reports circulated that the Verkaufskredit AG in Berlin wanted to set up an office in the Ostmark, CA Director Fritscher made haste to stop the effort in its tracks, pointing out to the VVSt that the AVA and some other companies fully satisfied the need for such credits and did so on more favorable terms. Furthermore, they were unwilling to accept the entry of old Reich competition in this field into the Ostmark until Ostmark firms were allowed to compete in the old Reich.[520]

Meanwhile, the AVA was increasing its business very considerably and it needed new and better offices for its expanded staff. In June 1939, it purchased a building belonging to Leontine Hacker and her children, Alfred, Cornel, and

---

[518] BA-CA, CA-IB, AVA,01/05-06/1, Joham and Fritscher to Deutsche Bank, Feb. 27, 1939.

[519] Ibid., AVA to Glatzl, July 20, 1938; AVA to Anglo-Danubian-Lloyd, July 20, 1938; Müller-Fembeck to AVA, July 18, 1938; Glatzl to Fritscher, Nov. 15, 1939; AVA to CA, April 6, 1943. There is a file of correspondence dealing with these questions and listing the Jewish victims in ÖStA/AdR, Bürckel-Materie, Automobil-Verkehrs-Anstalt Wien, Bl. 1-36.

[520] BA-CA, CA-IB, AVA, 01/05-06/1, Fritscher to Pg. Eduard Bargezi, VVSt, Oct. 6, 1938.

Erwin, for 325,000 RM. This Jewish family had owned the Silberwarenfabrik Moritz Hacker, which it obviously no longer controlled. The building was located at Hanuschgasse 1/Operngasse 2. The CA actively promoted speedy VVSt approval of this Aryanization, which it presented not only as a business requirement for the AVA but also as a means of providing facilities that met the regime's "beauty of labor" standards. In addition, it pointed out that the CA had given large credits to the AVA, which it owned, and that plans were afoot to increase the capital of the AVA.[521]

It is important to note that the CA was heavily engaged in the organized despoliation of the Hacker family. The building was sold on June 3, 1939, and the 275,655 RM actually collected after the deduction of the mortgage found its way into the family's blocked accounts. A substantial portion of the monies available to the family was put up as security for the payment of the Reich Flight Tax, some was to be used to pay the Atonement Tax and other taxes, legal fees, and debts. The balance left after these payments in December 1939 was 43,882.38 RM, which was divided between Leontine and Alfred Hacker. Basically, the Hackers had no direct disposal over these accounts, and it was the CA that released a certain amount of money for living expenses and otherwise paid out medical and other bills. Because Leontine and Alfred Hacker were unable to flee, they were given access to the monies put up to secure their Reich Flight Tax in early 1941. She was subsequently deported to Theresienstadt, and he was deported to the East. Neither survived. Erwin and Cornel Hacker were luckier. The former ended up in Sydney, the latter in Los Angeles. After the war, they and their lawyers corresponded with the CA about the disposition of their accounts and about the issue of compensation from the Austrian government.[522]

The main concern of the CA in this instance was to enrich the AVA and, indirectly, itself. In the course of 1939, it sought to raise the capital of the AVA from 133,333 RM to 500,000 RM and met with a rather frosty reception from the RWM. Initially, the CA lobbyist in Berlin, Robert Nemling, thought he could gain approval for the capital increase from the Reich Commissar for Credit Institutions, but he was informed that such increases were only reported to that office, and that the approval had to come from the RWM, specifically from the office of Privy Councilor Kohler. Kohler, however, was unhappy with the AVA petition, which was not detailed enough. Also, he had the impression that the AVA was an automobile factory rather than a financing enterprise, and he was inclined to turn down the request because the CA had such a large stake in the company. He looked more favorably on CA investment in an enterprise that was engaged in finance as "the strong participation in an industrial enterprise does not really belong to the actual tasks of a bank."[523] Nemling pointed out that this attitude, which was obviously very critical of Austrian banking practice, was quite widespread in Berlin. In this case, however, Nemling felt confident that Kohler would approve if the argument could be made that the increased capital was more in tune with the amount of business done by the AVA and if the CA were to invest its own money rather than turn to the capital market.

The extent of the CA's interest in the expansion of the AVA was clearly demonstrated in the course of 1939. At the management board meeting of May 4, 1939, the CA approved raising its credit to the AVA from 7.5 to 10 million RM, while the Oberbank, which had been given a 25 percent stake in the AVA, raised its credit from 1 to 2 million RM.[524] Nonetheless, probably most telling as well as informative were the efforts made to prolong the furlough and, generally, to prevent the drafting of the

---

521   Ibid., CA to the VVSt, May 9, 1939.
522   The depressing and very extensive documentation is to be found in BA-CA, CA-TZ, Sekretariat grün, Box 1/AVA III–VIII, X, XII–XV.

523   BA-CA, CA-IB, AVA, 01/05-06/1, Nemling to CA, May 2–3, 1939.
524   BA-CA, CA-V, management board meeting, May 4, 1939.

general director of the AVA, Franz E. Demuth, into airforce intelligence. At the end of 1939 Fritsche did his best to prevail upon his close friend Major Walter von Huber to assist in the Demuth case, pointing out that it was a truly exceptional request and outlining the activities and plans of the AVA. At the time, the AVA, which employed eighty-six persons, was financing the purchase of 15,000 cars and trucks, primarily in the Reich and Ostmark. The credit extended in this way amounted to 15 million RM. The AVA also had branches in Munich, Stuttgart, and Reichenberg. The company was particularly involved in providing cars to army agencies, which had sequestered some 3,000 of them. This required complicated arrangements with those who had used the vehicles previously. Additionally, in line with government policy, the company was interested in promoting exports. Planning to set up subsidiary enterprises in Slovakia and Hungary, it was already in the process of establishing branches in Pressburg/Bratislava, Budapest, Agram/Zagreb, and Belgrade. It was helping to smooth the way for automobile deliveries by the Saurerwerke AG and by Graf & Stift, an automobile producer belonging to the CA, to the Slovak railroads and postal services. AVA financing was a precondition for the delivery of fifty Henschel trucks to Hungary. Furthermore, there were plans afoot for the AVA to finance the delivery of buses to major Hungarian customers. In sum, the company was doing vital work for both the war effort and the economy, and its activities could hardly be carried out without the company's key officer. The CA thus requested a permanent deferment for Demuth, a move that already had the support of the Ostmark governor's office as well as of Rafelsberger.[525]

Demuth received another exemption from service. But although he was indispensable in running the AVA, the expansion of the concern was primarily the work of Director Glatzl. Glatzl was particularly interested in establishing the AVA in Pressburg/Bratislava, visiting the

city twice in May 1939, once in the company of Demuth. He took a rather sober view of the situation in Slovakia, which he viewed as a "young state" suffering from inadequate commercial development and poor roads. Clearing arrangements with Germany, although leaving a balance very much in Slovakia's favor, made for only limited prospects for significant imports from the Reich. He was especially distressed by the automobile duties, which were quite low for French imports but very high for German autos. Although autos still could be imported from the Protectorate, the producers there were being integrated into the Four Year Plan and thus in no position to send many vehicles to Slovakia. Even so, Glatzl had high hopes that the situation for such imports from the Reich would improve, and he worked to pave the way for the AVA to set up a branch in Pressburg/Bratislava. In this endeavor, he received considerable help and support from Director Stephan of the Union-Bank, who brought him into contact with the leadership of the Deutsche Partei Party. His major interest here was in reducing the customs duty. Slovakia lacked an automobile credit facility, and Glatzl managed to get the local automobile dealers to agree on using AVA once it was established. At the same time, Stephan promised that his bank would provide financing and would help handle the business. He also noted that the purchase of radios by installment was very popular in Slovakia. The Dutch firm Phillips seemed to have a monopoly position, and Stephan promised to look into the subject.[526]

Indeed, Stephan appears to have been an extraordinarily useful person. The Slovak financial authorities were initially unwilling to license the AVA on the grounds that it was a bank and that the government was eager to reduce, not expand, the number of banks operating in the country. Happily for the AVA, Stephan persuaded the official that the company would restrict itself to installment plans for purchasing automobiles. By early May 1941, the AVA branch was established, the Union-Bank providing capital of

---

[525] BA-CA, CA-V, S.P. Akten, Nr. 451, Fritscher to the Military-District Command, Luftwaffe, Nov. 29, 1939 and to Major Walter von Huber, Dec. 1, 1939.

[526] BA-CA, CA-IB, AVA, 01/05-06/1, Glatzl report of Sept. 17, 1940.

250,000 Ks and 25,000 Ks in reserve funds to be invested in the Slovak Reconstruction Loan, with the undoubted object of pleasing the government.[527] Apparently, however, Stephan did not live up to his promises of providing loans for AVA purposes, and the AVA complained to the CA in October 1944 that it had the "most unpleasant experiences" with the Union-Bank. These had been the basis of the AVA efforts to set up a branch back in 1939–1940, but Stephan refused to supply the credits, a matter made all the more embarrassing for the AVA because the automobile and machine sales firms in Slovakia were branches of Vienna firms with which the company had good business relations. The AVA had spent considerable sums making up forms and dealing with the lawyer that had been recommended, and thought the Union-Bank should pay the 20,000 Ks incurred. If the AVA had not complained before, it was because of the close relationship between the CA and the Union-Bank, but the entire affair was causing the AVA a loss of prestige and a considerable amount of unpleasantness.[528] The outcome of this plea and the development of the AVA's activities in Slovakia is not evident from the record.

The AVA also developed interests in the Protectorate. Here, too, Glatzl took the initiative, writing to Director Pohle of the BUB in July 1940 to inform him of the importance and solidity of the AVA. He indicated that both the Deutsche Bank and the Reichs-Kredit-Gesellschaft had each expressed a willingness to extend the AVA 2.5 million RM in credits after Deutsche Bank Director Gröning had submitted a very favorable report on the company's status. After looking into the matter, Glatzl and Demuth determined that the only enterprises in the Protectorate similar to AVA were Jewish owned, so that very soon there would be a market for the AVA, which was planning to open either a subsidiary company or a branch in Prague. Naturally, it would turn to the BUB for financing.[529]

The BUB in the meantime identified a formerly Jewish-owned company that had been prominent in the business, the "Generalia" Handels-Aktien-Gesellschaft, Prague, and this could be taken over and refinanced by the BUB and the AVA. The BUB also agreed to supply credits to the AVA. Because it was difficult to found new enterprises in the Protectorate at the time, the BUB arranged for the liquidation of "Generalia" as a Jewish enterprise. Meanwhile the AVA would operate under the name of a credit cooperative, the "Meta," with which the BUB had good connections.[530] This seems to have proven a successful and satisfactory arrangement for the AVA.

The situation for the AVA in Hungary was especially complicated. The automobile credit business there was run by a company with the name "Rata." It had been financed by the CA branch in Budapest and the Anglo-Danubian-Lloyd insurance company and was owned and managed by Friedrich Franz Schwarz. It had a high standing and seems to have been very competently run. The Budapest branch credit given to the "Rata" since the summer of 1938 had been urged by CA Director Fritscher as a means of helping out the Anglo-Danubian Lloyd's business with the "Rata." When the CA Vienna asked its Budapest office to supply credits to help in the establishment of an AVA branch in Budapest, the Budapest office replied that it could not afford to fund the AVA without terminating its credits to the "Rata." Also, Bokor and Böhm did not think that the local banks would come through because they were so tied up with government bonds. The fact was, however, that the Hungarian branch itself was quite short of capital and reluctant to give credits to an AVA branch unless the bank could be guaranteed substantial business. Glatzl was not at all happy with this attitude, pointing out that the Rata belonged to a Hungarian Jew, Schwarz, "and in the long run it will not be possible for our Hungarian subsidiary branch to advance credits to the Jew's business." Bokor, however, was uncertain that

527 Ibid., BUB Bratislava to CA, Nov. 26, 1940.
528 Ibid., AVA, 01/03, AVA to CA, Oct. 23, 1944.
529 Ibid., Glatzl to Pohle, July 3, 1940, and July 29, 1940.

530 Ibid., Pohle to Glatzl, July 26, 1940; AVA to CA, Sept. 28, 1940.

the AVA would be licensed in Hungary because it was a German firm and suggested instead that the AVA strive to Aryanize the "Rata."[531]

It is unclear whether Schwarz was an Aryan, as he claimed to be. It is possible that he might have been an Aryan under Hungarian law. Whatever the case, an expert report for the CA of November 27, 1939, gave the company high marks for its management and operations during the three years of its existence. Nevertheless, as the author who penned the report also noted, the "Rata" was in financial trouble because the CA Budapest had cancelled its credits effective December 31, and although the company was expecting financing from Hungarian banks and a Hungarian insurance company, it was running into difficulty. Schwarz seemed ready to sell out to the AVA and either enter into a partnership with it or have it assume the dominant role and even to bow out personally. In the view of the author, the CA had an obligation to expand the relationship with Hungary for economic and political reasons and could well afford to do so. He pointed out that 80 percent of the autos handled by the "Rata" were of German origin, and that it was vital to Germany to have a role in the business in Hungary.[532] The ultimate outcome, however, of the AVA's attempt to establish itself directly or indirectly is unclear. In February 1940, negotiations with the "Rata" were stalemated because Schwarz demanded a price that was deemed unacceptable. At the same time, the CA branch and the Anglo-Danubian appeared ready to fund an AVA branch, which did not seem possible under existing Hungarian legislation, or to undertake the credit business themselves with the silent engagement of the AVA.[533] In any case, the CA in Budapest was obviously more cooperative than the Union-Bank in Pressburg/Bratislava, but it was much easier for the AVA to do business in German-controlled areas, as has been demonstrated in Prague and was being demonstrated in Poland.

The interest in developing AVA business in the Generalgouvernement seems to have found expression only at the turn of 1941–1942. The initiative was taken by Director Huber of the CA's Cracow branch, who had been receiving numerous inquiries about providing installment credits for automobiles and agricultural machinery. CA Vienna, however, had denied the Cracow branch permission to conduct this business even though, as Huber noted, the banks in the old Reich were engaging in it. Huber had asked Glatzl if it would not be possible for the CA to set up a financial enterprise that could engage in the installment business, and Glatzl invited Demuth to join him on a journey to Cracow and Lemberg he was planning to take at the beginning of January 1942. While the CA had previously been cool to doing installment business in the GG, the situation had changed, "especially because the Generalgouvernment is no longer a borderland; also there appear to be quite a few resettlement actions taking place."[534] In addition, CA Director Fritscher was interested in promoting the creation of an AVA branch in Cracow, and Glatzl was quite optimistic about the prospects because he was personally acquainted with SS-Oberführer Gstöttenbauer, the economic inspector for the GG, and felt certain that he would get the support of the authorities. He also thought that the Cracow branch had the requisite money. Both Fritscher and Glatzl calculated that the long-term prospects for big business in the GG were very good because of the AVA's close connections to the Steyr works and the automobile producers and dealers in the Ostmark. Huber himself was not overly optimistic about the immediate prospects for the sale of autos in the GG, but he thought the market for agricultural machinery much better and supported the setting up of an AVA branch in order to beat out any competition.[535]

531 Ibid., AVA, 01/05-06/1, CA Budapest to CA Vienna, May 15, 1939, July 3, 1939; Glatzl report on a meeting with Bokor and Böhm, Aug. 4, 1939.

532 Ibid., Report, signature unrecognizable, Nov. 27, 1939.

533 Ibid., AVA, 01/03, AVA to CA, Feb. 2, 1940.

534 Ibid., AVA, 01/05-06/1, Glatzl to Demuth, Dec. 29, 1941.

535 Ibid., Glatzl to Demuth, and Glatzl to Huber, Jan. 13, 1942; discussion with Huber, Jan. 20, 1942 (all falsely dated as 1941).

The AVA had more extensive plans in the Lemberg area. In early 1942, Glatzl informed the branch director there, Arthur Anlauf, that the AVA planned not only to conduct its usual business but also to find an available woodworking factory for the assembly-line production of furniture, in particular stools and bunk beds for barracks. Demuth and Glatzl believed there would be a huge market for these products in the East, and Lemberg was a particularly desirable location because its transport connections were quite good. Furthermore, the AVA was planning to resettle the workers from a woodworking plant in Prague to the Lemberg region so as to ensure satisfactory production. Because the Galician region was now under the governorship of the old Austrian National Socialist SS Gruppenführer Otto Gustav Wächter, Glatzl was quite optimistic about receiving support from the authorities. Anlauf seemed to have complained about the bank facilities in Lemberg, but Demuth thought them quite adequate given the conditions there and seems to have wanted to set up his AVA branch in the CA branch building. Nevertheless, the AVA plans to go into the furniture business in Lemberg were not to be realized. As Anlauf informed Glatzl, all the furniture factories in Lemberg were already leased, the most import to Nissel & Kämmer, a Hamburg firm that did its business with the CA. The available wood supply was insufficient to justify the creation of another plant, and the only possibility Anlauf could suggest was a company in Ukraine, which fell under the jurisdiction of the Reich commissar for Ukraine.[536]

Planning for the establishment of an AVA branch in the GG continued through 1942. Demuth, who constantly faced the threat of being called up for military service, was reluctant to build up anything too big until after the war. In fact, the AVA had lost a large part of its staff to the draft, and Glatzl was anxious to keep Demuth around as long as possible. Poland actually seemed to offer a good opportunity to do this because another CA concern member,

Del-Ka, was also planning to establish itself in Poland, and Glatzl, Friedl, and Fritscher all thought that Demuth might be used to head both the Polish Del-Ka and the Polish AVA. Glatzl had been informed that the head of the economic division of the GG, Brandl, was in a position to get deferments for economic leaders in the GG. Demuth would thus be freed from military service. An additional advantage was that his salary would be split between Del-Ka and AVA. Demuth was prepared to spend half of every month in Cracow.[537]

For whatever reason, there was no need to implement this draft-dodging plan, and both Del-Ka and the AVA were able to establish their Polish subsidiaries under separate leadership. The AVA was created in the second half of January 1943. Whatever venturesome plans that may have been entertained earlier, the position at this point was to cut risks. Glatzl was firm about granting only credits that were 90 percent reinsured by the Hermes credit guarantee company, which was part of the Allianz insurance concern. The AVA in Cracow not only had the approval of the GG authorities, but was also accepted by the Kommerzialbank, which belonged to the Dresdner Bank, and the Commerzbank branch in Cracow. They agreed to accept another credit institution in Cracow with the understanding that when credits reached a certain level they could participate in the business as well. The long-term advantage of the creation of the Polish AVA, assuming there was going to be any, was that it had established something of a monopoly for itself in the installment credit business. In the short run, the AVA seems to have played an important role in financing the conversion process applied to gas-powered generators in the hauling business.[538]

But the major worry of the AVA in the last two years of the war was to avoid being shut down as part of the rationalization program in the banking business, a subject to be discussed in more detail later in the study. At the beginning of

---

[536] Ibid., Glatzl to Anlauf, Feb. 6, 1942 and Anlauf to Glatzl, Feb. 12, 1942.

[537] Ibid., AVA, 01/03, Glatzl to Fritscher, Feb. 10, 1942, and June 2, 1942.

[538] Ibid., Glatzl to Huber, Jan. 4, 1943 and June 2, 1943; Huber to Glatzl, May 28, 1943.

March 1943, Gau Economic Advisor Rafelsberger and the Ostmark steward of the Reich Group Banking, Hans Stigleitner, sought to close down or significantly reduce the installment credit business as part of the RWM effort to reduce the number of persons employed in the Reich banking business. The AVA claimed to be the largest installment credit business company in the entire Reich, pointing also to its activities in Slovakia, the Protectorate, and the Generalgouvernement. Furthermore, it claimed that all its credits went to armaments plants or to enterprises important for the war effort and that it had reduced its staff very substantially as part of a rationalization of its operations. Rafelsberger and Stigleitner responded by authorizing the AVA to continue operations. At the same time, they called for two other Viennese competitors to cease giving new credits and authorized the AVA to conduct the necessary negotiations with these companies, one belonging to the city insurance company, the other to the Zentralsparkasse. Both these companies were to be allowed to reopen once the war was over. The initial decisions made were designed to favor the AVA but to preserve the Vienna installment credit business in the future. In April 1942, however, the situation suddenly changed. The RWM not only decided that all the installment credit organizations in the old Reich were to continue business on the grounds that they had already completed the rationalization process. It also assured that it would not object if the Gau leadership in Vienna decided to shut down all the Vienna companies. It was not simply a war-conditioned shutdown of some Viennese companies but rather a shutdown that would enable the old Reich companies to take advantage of the situation and service the Ostmark as well.[539]

This, of course, was precisely what the Ostmark companies wished to avoid. Apparently, the AVA succeeded in its efforts to survive and Demuth was spared military service. In 1944, the AVA employed thirty-seven persons including those called up for military service. Its business, which stood at a high point

of 19.5 million RM in 1939 when it acquired the Hacker property, fell to 6.5 RM million in 1940. There was another sharp drop in 1943, when it fell to 4.5 million RM, and in 1944, when it fell to 2.5 million. Manifestly, the AVA was well prepared for the low demand of the postwar years, its foreign expansion, of course, having simply collapsed.[540]

Semperit

A final case study of the CA's expansionary drive in the National Socialist period is provided by the "Semperit" Oesterreichisch-Amerikanische Gummiwerke AG, which was renamed the Semperit Gummiwerke AG in July 1941. Founded in 1869, the company was reorganized in the 1920s through the merger of the major Austrian rubber producers. Its main factories were located in Traiskirchen, Wimpassing, and Stadlau. Prior to the Anschluss, the CA owned 31.0 percent of the shares, the Oesterreichische Industriekredit owned 7 percent, and members of the Reithoffer family, which had previously operated the plants in Wimpassing under the name Menier J.N. Reithofer, owned 15.1 percent. The remainder was scattered in Austrian and foreign hands. After the Anschluss, the VIAG took over the Industriekredit shares but then sold them to the CA on instructions from the Finance Ministry. The CA then made further purchases on the market to acquire a 54.4 percent majority; the Reithoffer group held 22 percent of the capital. The company's chief products were tires and tubes for every type of motor vehicle and bicycle along with rubber footwear and other rubber goods. It was also active in coal mining. In addition to being the most important rubber producer in Austria, it also had branches in Cracow, Budapest, Bucharest, and Yugoslavia. Some of the shares were held through a holding company in Switzerland.[541]

---

[539] Ibid., AVA, 01/05-06/1, AVA to CA, April 12, 1943, and related documents.

[540] See ibid., AVA, 01/03, the business report for 1944, and *Die österreichischen Wirtschaftsunternehmungen im Interessenkreis der Creditanstalt-Bankverein. Eine Festschrift für Generaldirektor Josef Joham* (Vienna 1949), p. 223.

[541] See BAB, R 8135, vol. 9360, the report of the Deutsche Revisions- und Treuhand-AG, Wien, Jan. 31, 1942.

One aspect that makes the Semperit especially notable in comparison to so many other important producers of strategic goods in the CA concern is that the CA not only held on to it and expanded its stake but also warded off unfriendly takeovers by competitors in the old Reich. The most important of these was the Continental AG in Hanover, but the Phoenix Gummiwerke AG in Hamburg-Harburg was also interested in Semperit. The particular vulnerability of Semperit was technical. It could not be integrated into the Reich economy, meet the requirements of the Reich authorities, or successfully compete with Continental or Phoenix if it did not acquire the necessary technical know-how and expand and rationalize its facilities. The technological advantages of the old Reich producers forced the CA leadership to seek an agreement whereby Semperit would acquire technical assistance in its modernization in return for either company's possible participation in the ownership of Semperit. Director Heller initially negotiated with Phoenix in the summer of 1938, and the company was prepared to come to terms if it received half the CA shares for which it would provide equivalent value in its own shares as compensation. The Reithoffer family strongly supported accepting this offer, but Heller, joined by Hasslacher, also negotiated with Continental. Heller was disinclined to engage in an exchange of shares with either of the two companies, but he was prepared to have the CA give up shares in return for large-scale technical assistance. What saved Semperit for the CA, however, was the refusal of the RWM to support giving Continental such influence over Semperit, which would have been tantamount to direct or indirect control, on the grounds that it did not want to sanction an IG-Gummi along the lines of IG Farben. The leadership of Continental thus had to make the best of the situation. It knew the government would force it to share its technology, and it wanted to avoid giving Phoenix any further competitive advantages. It therefore agreed to provide technical know-how and personnel to Semperit in certain limited areas of production. Semperit would compensate Continental by selling its 50 percent stakes in two Yugoslav

rubber producers, and Continental would sell its stake in a company in Cracow. The agreement, signed on April 28, 1939, assured that Semperit would remain Austrian and under CA control. In this case, at least, the policy of preventing old Reich takeovers was successful, in good measure because of the RWM's hostility to creating the kind of monopolistic power in rubber that already existed in the chemical industry.[542]

The RWM found it much easier to issue directives to a less formidable industry. Although Semperit had been saved for Austria and the CA, it was still vulnerable to local Party interests and directives from Berlin. The Party leadership was anxious to promote a major industry and employer, but, at the same time, Berlin was calling for Semprit to shift as much production as possible to artificial rubber (Buna) and to rationalize and modernize its operations. The company thus needed large-scale financing. The CA poured considerable credits into Semperit in 1938–1939. In August 1939, for example, Semperit received cash credits from the CA amounting to 3 million RM payable at the end of 1940, 1 million payable at the end of November 1939, and a Reich-guaranteed credit of 1,720,000 RM. The CA regularly provided such credits until the end of the war.[543] What the company needed above all, however, were investment credits, and here the Semperit and the CA sought to tap into the consortial funds of the Reich Economic Aid program. In September 1938, it applied for a credit of 6,471,000 RM, after initially applying for 2 million RM less in July to expand Buna production and to rationalize its production facilities. The credit committee decided to award 4,648,000 RM for expansion and development at Wimpassing

542 Ibid.; BA-CA, CA-V meetings of the CA executive committee, Sept. 16, Oct. 21, Nov. 25, 1938; Jan. 20 and April 1, 1939; BA-CA, CA-IB, König & Ebhardt, 19/01, Messner to Hasslacher, March 13, 1942. See also Paul Erker, *Competition and Growth: A Contemporary History of the Continental A.G.* (Düsseldorf 1996), pp. 41–42.

543 BA-CA, CA-V, executive committee meeting, Aug. 21, 1939.

and Traiskirchen, and it asked Semperit to hold back on projects at its older facilities. In October 1939, the annexation of the Sudetenland provided Semperit with cause to return with a request for another 4 million RM, this time to develop and expand the plant at Engerau that had belonged to the "Matador" Gummiwerke AG but was now in 100 percent possession of Semperit. As the company explained in its application, the political and government agencies in the Ostmark had repeatedly called for the large-scale development of the Engerau plant to promote the economic development of the entire region. When combined with the plants at Wimpassing and Traiskirchen, it would have a production program meeting the needs of the Four Year Plan and make Semperit competitive with the old Reich producers. Nevertheless, the proposal was temporarily tabled by the credit committee on the grounds that the wartime situation and shortages of raw materials would make it impossible for the new facilities to be used to full capacity. The logical implication of this decision would have been to shut down one of the three plants; instead, Semperit decided to return with a request for a reduced Reich-guaranteed consortia credit of 2.5 million RM on the grounds that shutting down Engerau would lead to unemployment and "would encounter the greatest resistance on the part of all the authorities and political offices." It also argued that it needed to at least reduce costs by acquiring more modern machinery. Whether this really convinced the credit committee is hard to say, but the committee's response to the request concluded by noting that the district governor and Gau economic advisor of the Lower Danube had personally called to support the reduced credit and "stressed its extraordinary urgency and necessity." It is no surprise that this pressure worked and the credit was granted.[544]

There was, indeed, considerable political touchiness about anything that would reduce Semperit's workforce or production, and Hasslacher and Friedl were often engaged in dealing with its leadership problems. After the outbreak of the war, Semperit undertook a considerable workforce reduction in September 1939 that was carried out primarily by Director Hans Karthaus, who had been appointed by the RWM because of his expertise in Buna production and in the rubber production business more generally. The Reich Agency for Rubber in Berlin had mandated such reductions, which involved the release of 2,519 workers by the end of January 1940 and periodic reductions of the workweek. Karthaus had also stopped work on the construction of a shoe factory at Wimpassing in the spring of 1939. Birthelmer was extremely upset, but he could hardly overturn manpower and production decisions made in Berlin. The German Labor Front representatives showed great concern that the dismissed workers be provided with job. Local officials, especially the mayor of Engerau, worried that workers would leave Engerau to look for employment elsewhere. It later turned out that the layoffs were excessive and premature, and in 1942 Karthaus had the misfortune of being charged by a German Labor Front official with an "unsocial attitude" both because of his role in the release of workers and his alleged failure to look after working conditions while his superior, General Director Franz Messner, was abroad. Heller stoutly defended Karthaus, and the more serious charges were dropped. Karthaus demanded and received a hearing before a Court of Honor on April 25, 1942. He was found guilty of failing to act in conformity with Labor Front policies. By this time, however, Karthaus himself had become convinced that he could not usefully continue on at Semperit, and the CA was anxious to cool down the situation, informing Gauleiter Jury and other Party officials that Karthaus had finished his assigned task of modernizing the Semperit plants and that his contract would not be renewed in June 1942.[545] Walter Kastner,

[544] A full record of the Semperit credit applications and their disposition between Sept. 15, 1938 and Dec. 22, 1939 is to be found in BAB, R2/15560, Bl. 17–31.

[545] See BA-CA, CA-IB, Semperit, 14/01, Heller to Karthaus, April 23, 1942; CA to Jury, April 29, 1942; decision of the Court of Honor, April 25, 1942; Hasslacher to Karthaus, May 5, 1942; Karthaus to

formerly of the Kontrollbank, replaced him on the Semperit management board, and was also joined by Hanns Reithoffer.

Despite such difficulties with the leadership of Semperit, and there were to be more serious ones, the CA could be well satisfied with the company's development and its investments, especially because the most important ones were guaranteed by the Reich in a consortium where the CA had a 10 percent share. By 1941, its expansion into occupied and unoccupied Southeast Europe was impressive, and Messner gave a very fulsome report about Semperit's acquisitions and strategy at a supervisory board meeting on February 4, 1941, chaired by Hans Fischböck.[546] Having taken the Engerau factory after the occupation of the Sudetenland, Semperit took over "Matador" in Prague following the creation of the Protectorate and operated it as a commercial enterprise. Messner emphasized that Semperit was very active in making "Matador" an important player in the Protectorate market despite efforts by competitors like Bata to discriminate against it. Also, Semperit had been granted the leadership of the Reich Tire Storage Facility by the German authorities in the Protectorate. Although that brought no immediate profit, it promised to give Semperit control of the tire market there when peace came. Progress was also made in Slovakia, here Semperit was expanding its sales organization and could compete with Bata. Although the Slovak government was eager for the country to have a rubber industry of its own, Semperit was striving to undertake a modest amount of production in addition to selling its products. This included buying up a Jewish property that was being auctioned off for its raincoat production.

Messner claimed that fine progress was also being made in Hungary, where the Semperit branch had been turned into an independent corporation that worked closely with the Hungarian branch of the CA. At the same time, it developed strong ties to the Hungarian authorities. The head of Semperit in Hungary also functioned as a specialist on rubber questions for the Hungarian government and was thereby in a position to act as an intermediary between the Hungarian and the German ministries dealing with issues of trade in rubber goods. The situation in Romania, by contrast, where the company owned the "Semperit" Cauciuc S.A.R. in Bucharest, was somewhat more difficult because of the attitude of the Romanian authorities. Nonetheless, the company still hoped to expand there and looked in particular to the possibility of buying up Jewish-owned shares in a Romanian company. The situation in Poland, where Semperit owned the two companies in Cracow, the Krakauer Gummiwerke AG and the "Semperit" Handelsgesellschaft mbH, was much more satisfactory, especially because the former was now 100 percent in the hands of Semperit. The least satisfactory situation was in Yugoslavia, where Semperit had a plant in Krainburg and worked with Continental in marketing matters. The major difficulty was the political situation. If things remained stable, then Semperit would have to attempt to set up plants in more favorable locations, that is, in Zagreb/Agram or Belgrade/Beograd.

Messner tended to view Semperit's situation from the perspective of the advantages it would gain from its current development once the war was over. He noted approvingly, for example, that at this time its prices were competitive with those of the firms in the old Reich, that the authorities increasingly recognized the importance of the firm, and that its rationalization was working. The obvious problem under existing conditions was that exports were limited and domestic production was increasingly devoted to military purposes. Messner thus couched his arguments in terms of the Reich's plans for expansion, pointing out that Semperit was part of a general reorganization of the Reich rubber industry. Its ability to build up its position, in his view, arose from the variety of items it produced, its emphasis on quality, and its fortunate geographical situation in the Greater German Reich, which

Hasslacher, May 6, 1942, and various related documents and correspondence.

[546] Ibid., Semperit, 14/05, Semperit supervisory board meeting, Feb. 4, 1941.

gave it a certain freedom of action to the south. This meant that the company had to concentrate on the future of the rubber industry in a "European sense." Consequently, Messner believed, Semperit had to strengthen its position in Hungary and also to watch developments in Bulgaria and Romania closely. He was particularly eager to find a way to take over the Ungarische Gummiwarenfabriks AG (UGF) in Budapest, which also had a small factory in Brasov in Romania. The CA had 25 percent of the shares of the UGF and was willing to sell its shares to Semperit in agreement with the leadership of the Hungarian firm. The RWM also supported the idea of a 25 percent Semperit stake in the UGF, and all were agreed that it was necessary to avoid the impression of a German takeover. If a syndicate could be formed, then Germany's prestige in Hungary would be strengthened and Semperit would have no competitor in Southeast Europe. At the same time, Messner also wished to secure partners in the West, which would be possible particularly if the sole right of German representation with the firms of Englebert in Liege and Hutchinson in Paris was achieved. In this way, Semperit, as an Ostmark firm, would stand in second place only to Continental in the Reich and in Europe.

The CA leadership certainly must have appreciated both Messner's extraordinary ambition and his efforts to turn the Southeast program into a reality. In September 1942, with CA General Director Richard Buzzi as chairman and Director Hans Friedl as one of four supervisory board members present, Messner was even more aggressive in pushing forward his plans. He warned against losing valued personnel, and announced that one of the managers implicated in the Karthaus affair would not be fired but rather sent to undertake a new important task as head of the Southeast Central Office in Bucharest. The office was to direct the business of Semperit in Bucharest, Sofia, and Istanbul; look after the business of Semperit in Romania, Bulgaria, Turkey, Greece, and Serbia; and "above all try to paralyze or contain the penetration into the economic interests of Semperit due to the competition of

the Conti[nental]."[547] An especially curious note was struck by his discussion of what to do with half-Jewish employees at the company headquarters. Messner asked that a policy be formulated in view of the "absolutely contradictory statements of the Party – and military agencies – and other economic bodies." They decided on two policies. First, production must in no case be disturbed. Second, attention had to be paid to domestic political developments and the problems of maintaining peaceful relations in the central headquarters. Half-Jews were not to be employed abroad, either permanently or temporarily, and they were not to be given key positions where they would be in a position to judge Semperit's total structure or its productive possibilities. It is hard to know what to make of this, except that the company did employ half-Jews in its central offices, and that it had to tread warily in continuing their employment.

At the same time, Messner certainly appeared very anxious to follow the National Socialist line, both in his discussions of Germany's role in Europe, and in the actual policies of Semperit. He announced a series of appointments of Labor Front activists to company leader positions in consultation with Gauleiter Jury – including that of himself as factory leader in the Vienna headquarters – and made note of how pleased Jury was by the various factory assemblies he had attended at the invitation of Semperit. Indeed, what seems to have won him Messner's devotion above all was the expansion of Semperit, as he noted that capacity had been increased at Traiskirchen and that finances should not stand in the way of a further expansion there. As he bluntly put it, if there was a decrease in production in the West – obviously because of bombing – Semperit would be in a position to claim more resources, be it in the form of additional credits or an increase in its share capital. The supervisory board gave him full support in this position.

[547] Ibid., Semperit, 14/01, meeting of the Semperit supervisory board working committee, Sept. 2, 1942.

The CA certainly was generous with its credits, especially during the last years of the war. In late 1943, it increased the volume of credit to Semprit from 1 million RM to 12 million RM, and it granted a credit line of 18 million in 1944. The funds were not intended for long-term investment; in large part covered by Reich guarantees, the money was to be used so far as conditions allowed. The chief financial need arose from the greatly increased corporation and profits taxes as well as from the demand by suppliers for payment in cash. Semperit also received a 4.5 million RM credit from IG Farben to purchase Buna. As was to be expected, production increasingly concentrated on military needs, and the cash flow from military payments helped reduce operating costs before higher taxation became a major financial burden. Because Semperit had become so important a military producer, it could make use of foreign labor, that is, forced labor, at its Austrian plants. Its labor force of 11,693 in July 1944 was actually larger than its 11,217 person workforce at the end of 1943. The percentage of foreigners employed at Semperit in July 1944 was 44 percent, and they came from seventeen nations. Semperit had become quite "European," although its impressive body of European outlets and plants grew steadily smaller as the Reich retreated into its own borders, and, of course, its Austrian plants were also affected by Allied bombing.[548]

Under the circumstances, Semperit's development in the years 1938–1945 was something of a success story and was a good illustration of the CA's Southeast program at work. In many respects, Messner was one of its most energetic representatives. In this context, however, his fate is quite surprising. On May 23, the Semperit supervisory board was informed that Messner was arrested for a serious violation of the foreign exchange regulations. The members were assured that Semperit itself was not involved or affected. This assurance was repeated at the July 26 meeting. On October 30, 1944, the Semperit management board informed the working committee of the supervisory board that Messner had been sentenced to death by the People's Court for high treason and that his assets and privileges were forfeit. His colleagues responded to this news by deciding that he was to be removed from his position and his contract cancelled, that his pictures were to be removed from wherever they hung, and that the news was to be imparted both at the plants and in the foreign branches by word of mouth. Gauleiter Jury was expected to report on the situation to the supervisory board. On November 28, 1944, Kastner was asked to replace Messner as head of Semperit. A very diffident Kastner tried to decline with the claim that he was not certain that his appointment met with the approval of all who should have approved, but Buzzi assured Kastner that there was a misunderstanding and that not only Buzzi himself, but also Gau Economic Advisor Felix Herle, a member of the supervisory board, and Gauleiter Jury thought he was the only person suitable for the position.[549] Franz Josef Messner was beheaded on January 9, 1945. He had made considerable contributions to the German war effort in his work as Semperit general director, but he was also a member of a small Catholic resistance group and, under the code name "Oysters," had provided the Office of Strategic Services with information on industry and production. Of course, one may think he was opportunistic in everything he did, but this is not very convincing. He was obviously a very complicated person and embodied many important aspects of the Austrian quandary, including the postwar neglect of resistance figures. In this respect, as will be shown, Messner was not alone.

---

548 For most of this information, see the supervisory board meeting of July 26, 1944, ibid., 14/05. See also BA-CA, CA-V, the reports of Jan. 1942, Feb. 27, 1942, Oct. 29, 1943.

549 BA-CA, CA-IB, Semperit, 14/05, Semperit supervisory board meetings of May 23, July 26, Oct. 30, and Nov. 28, 1944.

CHAPTER FOUR

Serving the Regime in Peace and War

As has been shown, the CA retained a high level of initiative once it had recovered from the initial difficulties created by the German takeover of Austria, and it also managed to maintain its character as an industrial holding company despite its heavy losses in the initial stage of German rule. This was true both under the domination of the VIAG and then after the Deutsche Bank took over a majority stake. The CA was not only allowed to pursue its ambitions in Southeast Europe and in Poland, but it also was encouraged to act as a spearhead in advancing its own and the Deutsche Bank's interests as well as German interests more generally. At the same time, however, the CA was also expected to participate in granting credits in collaboration with other leading banks for a variety of projects and enterprises promoted by the regime. As might be imagined, most of those projects pertained to the rearmament and war effort, but some also were linked to the effort to rationalize and modernize the Austrian economy. While pursuing its various activities, the CA also had to cope with the vagaries of the National Socialist regime and measures taken in the later years of the war to rationalize the banking industry because of the manpower shortages. As has been repeatedly demonstrated, the CA was not only a bank but also an industrial holding company and was thus directly involved in making managerial decisions connected with the "real economy" and in dealing with the authorities not only

as a bank but also in this managerial capacity. In attempting to protect its interests, the CA invariably had to balance economic and political considerations in circumstances that became increasingly risky.

1. THE CA AND THE ECONOMIC AID PROGRAM AND CONSORTIAL CREDITS

The engagement of the CA in the Reich Economic Aid program for Austria created by a law of April 8, 1938, illustrates many of these problems. Under this law, the Reich agreed to guarantee credits designed to ease the economic integration of Austria into the Reich, to make the Austrian economy more competitive, and to promote the Four Year Plan. It was largely the brainchild of Hans Kehrl of the RWM. Initially, the amount to be guaranteed was set at 50 million RM, half to be used as "house bank" credits for individual enterprises to be partially guaranteed by the Reich, and the other half to be used for consortial credits to be guaranteed in full by the Reich. The entire operation was based on a bank consortium for each of the 25 million RM in which the Länderbank Wien and the CA shared the leadership and contributed 2.5 million RM each; the Deutsche Bank and the Dresdner Bank also contributed 2.5 million RM each, thus maintaining parity between the major Austrian and German banks. A total of twenty-six banks were members of the consortium, which was managed by the Kontrollbank. The credits were to be granted before April 1, 1940, and were to be paid back at the latest by April 1, 1953. The Reich guarantees, on the other hand, could not be called on before April 1, 1945. In reality, the granting of credits continued into 1941, and the amount the Reich was willing to guarantee was increased to 75 million RM. The management, following the liquidation of the Kontrollbank in 1940, was turned over to the Wiener Giro- und Cassen-Verein, which acted as a depository for securities for the Vienna banks and, like its predecessor, was owned by the leading Vienna banks. The CA and the Länderbank Wien remained the joint leaders of the consortium. The credit applications to the credit committees were vetted by the various Party economic authorities, chambers of commerce, and trade associations as well as by the bank expected to act as house bank for the individual applicant.[1]

As has been noted earlier, some of these credits were given to assist Aryanizers, and the CA had been cautious in its willingness to serve as the house bank for some of the applicants for sound banking reasons. Of far greater moment, however, was the substantial number of applications for the purpose of getting companies back on their feet, maintaining employment, and making enterprises competitive once Austria was integrated into the Reich economy. Here, political and social factors could weigh quite heavily, and economic decision making could become quite complicated. An especially good example that has particular pertinence to the CA as an industrial holding company was the sewing machine producer Rast & Gasser Oesterreichische Nähmaschinen-Fabrikations GmbH. The company had been founded in 1868 and specialized in the manufacture and repair of sewing machines. Its products were

highly regarded both at home and abroad. As was the case with so many manufacturers, it experienced difficulties in 1933–1934. The Rast and Gasser families did not have the capital needed to cover the company's losses, and the company became heavily indebted to the CA. Rast & Gasser transformed itself into an unlimited company in order to avoid liquidation, but it did intend to dissolve the existing firm. At this point, however, an engineer, Kurt Österreicher, applied to the CA for support in reviving the enterprise, which he received, and an Oesterreichische Nähmaschinen-Fabrikations was established that leased the existing land and factories from the Rast und Gasser OHG. The CA owned the new company, which it financed with credits, while the OHG, which also owed large sums to the CA, put up the plants and the properties on which they stood as security for the loans. Production and sales improved, but the company produced no profits between 1934 and 1937.[2]

The Anschluss made the situation much worse. Sales abroad, which had been handled by Jewish merchants, fell significantly. Moreover, the company and its successors could no longer distinguish its products as Austrian in competition with their German counterparts. At the same time, domestic sales decreased in the expectation that German producers would enter the market and sell more cheaply. The CA thus found itself having to grant increasing operating credits in order to keep the company afloat and its approximately 350 workers employed. Consequently, in June 1938, the CA turned to the Ministry for Economics and Labor and asked for assistance to maintain the company or, alternatively, for permission to shut it down. Reich Commissar Bürckel's office took up the matter, authorized expert investigations by the special subgroup for sewing machines of the Economic Group for Machine Construction

[1] See Feldman, "German Banks," in ZfU 50: 1 (2005), pp. 5–16; the extensive documentation in RGVA Moscow, 1458/2/48; see also BA-CA, CA-V, Joham's report at the CA executive committee meeting of May 27, 1938. On the discussion of this arrangement at the Länderbank, see Chapter 5, pp. 456–457, 472–473 of this volume.

[2] This and much of the account to follow is based on BA-CA, CA-IB, Rast & Gasser, 42/03, Heller to Gau Inspector Sepp Nemec, Dec. 21, 1938, and the materials presented to the Reich Economic Aid credit committee in RGVA Moscow, 1458/2/172.

and the Reich Curatorium for Economic Efficiency, and then decided that an attempt should be made to keep the company going. There were a number of motives for this. First, the company was Austria's only sewing machine producer and had a specialized and very skilled workforce, so that it was viewed as important for the economy of the Land of Austria. Second, the skills involved in constructing sewing machines made the company a potential producer of special military equipment as well. Finally, despite the job opportunities opening up, there was a great reluctance to dissolve the stock of skilled workers that had been employed by the company for years. Needless to say, this effort could not be undertaken unless the company was reconstructed and modernized because the opinion that radical measures were necessary was unanimous.

One of these measures, to the constant irritation of old Reich producers and merchants, was to extend the period during which Rast & Gasser would be protected from competition from the old Reich for a year. This was quite effective, but it was not something that could continue forever. At some point, the company would have to face its competition from the old Reich. A second measure, which was much less promising, was the replacement of Kurt Österreicher, who was a Jew, by Josef Rast, who, everyone agreed, was unsuited to run the company and who had in fact mismanaged it before Österreicher came on the scene. Heller and the CA went hunting for a suitable engineer and believed that they had found one in the person of a German, M. Erich Liebers, whom they contracted to take over on January 1, 1939. Rast was extraordinarily hostile to the new appointment, however, so that difficulties could be expected. Finally, experts were called in to develop a reorganization plan for the company. The first plan was drawn up by an engineer named Dransfeld who came from the Special Group for Machine Construction, visited the company in September, found the condition of the production facilities shocking, and thought that the required investments would be so high that it would be most economical to shut Rast & Gasser down and let old

Reich companies produce sewing machines for the Ostmark. When Bürckel disagreed with this recommendation, Dransfeld refused to act as a consultant in the matter any further. The CA then turned to another recommended expert, Hermann Funcke, who provided a report that echoed Dransfeld's judgment but then made some basic recommendations in view of the fact that the authorities wished to keep the company in operation despite its losses. On the basis of these investigations, the CA informed Bürckel's office at the end of 1938 that it could not justify further investment to keep Rast & Gasser afloat but that it would do so if noneconomic reasons appeared most important. It was then prepared to cover some of the company's losses and to apply for a Reich-guaranteed credit. It did not fail to note, however, that the company's situation had deteriorated because of the rising price of iron products and the difficulty of acquiring iron, and that Rast's handling of these matters was incompetent.

It is unclear what moved Liebers to take on the management of the snake pit that was Rast & Gasser, where he not only faced the expected hostility of Rast but also found himself in conflict with some of the workers, who demanded investments in new machinery and pay raises and threatened to engage in "self-help" if they did not get their way. Behind this hostility, as Liebers quickly discovered, lay anxiety over a possible shutdown and resentment against the bank. There was an effort on the part of the workforce to mobilize the German Labor Front and the authorities against the CA. Two of the workers' spokesmen, Goschenhofer and Waldstein, "expressed themselves in the meanest manner about the alleged Jewish machinations of the bank. The bank behaves itself now as it did earlier and one sees nothing of a National Socialist way of handling financial matters. Goschenhofer was ready to show Gauleiter Bürckel and, if necessary, also the Führer the true face of the bank. The bank aims to deprive Herr Rast of his rights, something that the retinue will never allow. Rast was a victim of the terrible interest policy of the bank and the DAF should take care with the help of the district leader that the bank debts with their interest and interest on interest should be eliminated."[3]

Manifestly, Rast and his worker friends were trying to place the blame for the potential closing down of Rast & Gasser on the CA. Whether Bürckel, in his opposition to shutting down the company, was responding to such "social" pressures and considerations is difficult to tell, but he certainly was trying to protect an Austrian asset. It is interesting to note that Hans Kehrl of the RWM echoed Bürckel's views in recommending to the Reich economics minister that a Reich-guaranteed credit be granted, pointing out, in total contradiction to the expert opinions that had been solicited, that "in the case before us we are dealing with a well-established manufacturing enterprise with a specialized production program which is also worth maintaining in view of its suitability for taking over military contracts in the production of precision mechanical parts."[4] The Economic Group for Machine Construction supported this position, conceding that the technical evaluations of the firm had been rather dismal but arguing that modifications here and there and the prospects for economic revival made the survival of the firm feasible if the CA would provide the necessary financial relief. As for the CA, it agreed to provide a Reich-guaranteed credit of 580,000 RM for the period of two to ten years and to suspend interest payments on the old debt for the period of this credit.[5]

All this, however, turned out to be more or less make-believe, and it was quite clear that Rast & Gasser was not to be saved by temporary measures. It is possible that the appointment of Fischböck as chairman of the CA management board may have helped to ease the situation and create a willingness on all sides to accept the inevitable. The obstreperous Rast was bought off at modest cost, and the CA proposed the solution of transferring the machinery and

manpower to the Wertheim company, which was also under its control. Whatever the case, by the fall of 1939 the CA had escaped a serious further investment in Rast & Gasser, the sewing machine business was left to the old Reich firms, and the facilities and manpower of Rast & Gasser were placed at the service of the German war effort via Wertheim. In June 1941, Wertheim was able to report that it had successfully put Rast & Gasser in order and was getting good results as well as making good use of the much-needed workers that it had acquired.[6]

Most of the other Reich Economic Aid engagements of the CA in its function as a house bank were more modest in cost and more prosaic in character. For example, when "Phönixwerk" a producer of fruit and vegetable products, asked for 15,000 RM to invest in machinery, the CA declared itself ready to handle the credit. Owner Johann Lachout was recommended as a Party member, and he put up solid securities for the loan. Although he was one of many producers and his operations were not deemed vital to the industry, his claim that he could expect a substantial increase in business because of the shutting down of Jewish competitors appeared well grounded.[7] Ultimately, he seems to have been favored; he is recorded as having been granted a 226,666 RM consortial credit.[8] There was much less willingness to grant 30,000 RM to the Holzstoff- und Pappenfabrik, Ing. Adolf Fahrner in order to reopen a sawmill. Fahrner could not be recommended as a Party supporter because he was rather apolitical, and he was held responsible for the failure of his enterprise as a result of his excessive optimism. The Linz branch of the CA had done business with him for many years, and he was viewed as a reliable person worthy of support but not for as much as he was asking.[9]

3   BA-CA, CA-IB, Rast & Gasser, 42/03, Liebers to Heller, Feb. 18, 1939.
4   RGVA Moscow, 1458/2/172, Bl. 2–3, Kehrl to RWM, May 22, 1939.
5   Ibid., Bl. 13–15, 25. Credit committee meeting, May 4, 1939, and related documents.
6   See the correspondence in BA-CA, CA-IB, Rast & Gasser, 42/03, also the Wertheim report of June 11, 1941, ibid., Wertheim, 17/05.
7   BAB, R2/15533, Bl. 43–45, 8th credit committee meeting, Aug. 31, 1938.
8   See BA-CA, CA-IB, Kontrollbank, 34/01, the Kontrollbank report of 1940.
9   BAB, R2/15533, Bl. 212–215, 5th credit committee meeting, Aug. 20, 1938.

It is very difficult to draw any straightforward conclusions about the engagement of the CA in the Reich Economic Aid program as a house bank, and the evidence suggests that the program was not terribly effective on the whole. One of the curiosities of the situation was that less than half of the 150 million RM in authorized guarantees had actually been taken by early 1939. This was the subject of some discussion in governmental circles in Austria, and that is quite revealing of the dilemmas and weaknesses of National Socialist economic and financial steering measures. In one memorandum, for example, the author pointed out that it took time for such opportunities to receive sufficient publicity and confidence on the part of potential applicants.[10] There were too many banks involved and none of them seemed to have a real interest in pushing the idea. The Austrians were also not used to getting "objective help" from the state and viewed agents of the rationalization bureaus with suspicion, thus leading to a lack of initiative on the part of the factory owners in seeking financial aid. Another barrier was the application. Completing the application required skill in formulating responses, and applicants were left without proper help in dealing with them. The banks often turned down proposals by applicants immediately. At the same time, the banks themselves were often at a loss to understand the implications of the financial request for the future structure of the enterprises involved. A significant difficulty was the "shyness" of applicants when it came to presenting all the information required, not only business and financial information but also political information. Many who applied were not National Socialists or were politically indifferent. Gau economic advisors were well aware of who had supported the previous regime or opposed the National Socialists. Past debts also weighed heavily on potential applicants, who could expect little relief by taking on new ones. A further problem was shortage of raw materials because the Reich was still using the old

allotments of 1937. Of great importance – and here there seemed to be general agreement – was that the German protection of Austria from competition from the old Reich was inhibiting adjustment and modernization. Although most customs barriers between the Ostmark and the old Reich had been lifted in October 1938, the continuation of so-called territorial protective measures meant that many middle- and small-sized enterprises could afford to make do with old machinery and did not have to adjust to German prices by modernizing and rationalizing. Rast & Gasser was a good example. Once these protective measures were ended, however, the need for investment credits would increase substantially. Finally, the massive process of Aryanization that had taken place in 1938–1939 was creating serious problems for the new owners because they were finding out that they did not have the necessary capital to carry on former Jewish enterprises, could not qualify for normal credits from the banks, and thus could also be expected to apply for guaranteed credits.

What emerges from this rather critical memorandum as well as from a reading of the credit committee's meetings is that the economic development program for Austria devised by Kehrl and his colleagues was internally contradictory and was bound to fail, and that the banks were dragged along more or less willingly because they were allegedly protected by the Reich guarantees and under political pressure. As the memorandum suggests, some of the banks nipped applications in the bud at the initial stage of the process. Most importantly, however, the credits were often designed to cure ills resulting from the Anschluss itself. The goal was to protect the Austrian economy and to provide for a gradual adjustment to German prices. The gradualness of the adjustment, however, prevented the energetic modernization and rationalization that was endlessly discussed but never actually implemented. It is notable, for example, that special credits were given to Austrian firms to help them withstand the price reduction program of the government for iron and paper products. Indeed, numerous credits were given to compensate for National

---

[10] ÖStA/AdR, Bürckel-Materie, Box 11, 2210/0; the memorandum is unsigned and undated but from early 1939.

Socialist economic controls and interference in the free market.

The most problematic cases, as noted earlier, arose in connection with Aryanizations. In numerous instances companies, especially in the areas of textiles and apparel, justified requests for operating credits and credits to expand on the grounds that they had become competitive because of the disappearance of Jewish competitors. Aryanization was seen as an instrument to promote "rationalization" by the regime, but in fact the liquidation of enterprises occurred simply because they were Jewish owned. This could hardly be called an acceptable form of quality control. In many instances it was tantamount to the abandonment of quality control and was simply the elimination of competitors long viewed as unwelcome by their Aryan counterparts. There were often ideological claims that alleged Jewish business methods had been responsible for the previous uncompetitiveness of Aryan firms. Far more consequential, however, were the number of cases in which Jewish-owned enterprises were taken over by persons whose business qualifications and capital were very limited but who had been "old fighters," had been incarcerated when the Party was illegal, had been engaged in terrorist activities, or had a son in the SA or the SS. These were not cases of "wild Aryanizations" that had taken place during the first months of the regime. Rather, they were often individuals out to profit from the disappearance of the Jews who had tried to run the enterprises themselves and had suddenly found themselves without the wherewithal to do so. It is difficult to escape the impression that the economic aid programs, insofar as they involved the use of house banks for smaller credits, constituted a highly politicized and often economically ad hoc form of credit giving that had little to do with the pretensions of rationalizing the sectors of the Austrian economy they were intended to aid.

From an economic point of view, the Reich-guaranteed consortial credits granted under the Reich Economic Aid program for Austria were of far greater consequence. As of December 1940, according to Section B (Trusteeship) of the Kontrollbank, the consortium of twenty-six banks had given slightly more than 47 million RM to twenty-four firms. Of the 47 million RM provided by the banks, the CA and the Deutsche Bank provided 4.1 million RM and 4.2 million RM, respectively. The Länderbank Wien and the Dresdner Bank provided 4.1 million RM and 4.2 million RM, respectively. With the exception of the government-owned Preussische Seehandlung, which contributed 4.5 million RM, no other bank reached the level of the Viennese banks and their German partners.[11]

As a member of the consortium, the CA in some cases provided funds for credits to firms with which it had little or no connection. The largest consortial credits were granted to the Zellwolle Lenzing, which received no less than 20 million RM, and the Zellwolle Lenzing AG, Abteilung Papierfabrik, which received 2 million RM. Lenzing's major bank connection was the Länderbank Wien, but the CA had a share of 1.9 million RM in the Reich-guaranteed credit for this pet project of Kehrl's − 1.7 million RM of this credit was long term until 1950 − which proved a bottomless pit financially.[12] The CA also provided 200,000 RM of the 2 million RM credit granted to the AEG Union Elektrizitäts-Gesellschaft, Wien. The credit given by the consortium to the Viennese branch of the Berlin-based concern because it was under too much financial pressure to support its Vienna operation.[13]

The CA had a great interest in securing credits for Semperit AG, in which it had a 52.88 percent interest. As noted in the previous chapter, there was powerful political support behind giving Semprit credits even when the CA was not sure it could carry out its expansion program because of the wartime situation. Nevertheless, Semperit AG had been granted a total of 4,548,000 RM in Reich-guaranteed consortial credits. By 1942, the CA had given

[11] BA-CA, CA-IB, Kontrollbank, 34/01, 1940 report of the Kontrollbank.
[12] The chief source on the size of these credits is ibid. The CA quote can sometimes be gleaned from the list of debtors developed in June 1942, DB, V2/3.
[13] See BAB, R 8127/15879, Bl. 76−80, the correspondence of the Kontrollbank, Feb. 1939.

Semperit various forms of credit amounting to 5.6 million RM, including 673,000 RM in long-term credits until 1952.[14] Similarly, the CA was an interested party in granting long-term Reich-guaranteed investment credits to Leykam-Josefthal AG für Papier und Druckindustrie because it owned 54.8 percent of the shares. Leykam had been granted a 3 million RM consortial credit in April 1939 with the proviso that the CA agreed to a standstill on the credits it had granted in addition. The CA did not agree to such an unconditional standstill, but it is difficult to tell what was finally decided. On the one hand, the amount on the list of consortial credits at the end of 1940 is placed at 470,000 RM. On the other hand, Leykam is listed in mid-1942 as owing the CA 3.9 million RM, 3.8 million of which was long term until 1950 or 1952. Leykam was having difficulties in carrying through its program because of the iron shortage, so that the credit it had requested may have been reduced. Alternatively, the CA may have given the entire Reich-guaranteed credit initially requested by Leykam on its own account.[15]

Even though the CA only held 12.34 percent of the shares of the large steel producer Schoeller-Bleckmann, 80 percent of the shares being held by the Schoeller-Bleckmann interests at the Schoeller Bank, the CA was part of a syndicate that had been created in 1923 and, along with the Schoeller and Bleckmann shareholders, helped determine the basic policies of the concern. The Schoeller group had four votes, the Bleckmann interests and the CA three each.[16] The CA leadership was anxious to promote the major investment and expansion program launched by the company after the Anschluss that had the goal of expanding its business in the old Reich, increasing its exports, and, most importantly, fulfilling

military contracts. In April 1938 it increased its bridging credit from 666,700 RM to 1,555,500 RM, and it joined with Schoeller in increasing their joint credit of 1 million RM to 2,333,300 RM.[17] In January 1939, the firm asked for a Reich-guaranteed credit of 7 million RM to be funded by the CA and the Schoeller Bank. A decision was taken to grant a guarantee for 5 million RM of the credit. This may have been because of the heavy bank debts of Schoeller and the plan to use these debts to increase the capital of the company. However, the additional 2 million RM was supplied by means of a house bank credit by Schoeller with a one-third participation by the CA.[18] By the end of the year, however, the military was calling for a much greater expansion of Schoeller-Bleckmann and was prepared to provide a combination of interest-free and interest-bearing credits, but it was asking for guarantees from the Schoeller Bank and the CA for a third of the credits. The banks, however, considered this impossible, and in a meeting between Philipp von Schoeller, Erich Heller, and Hans Kehrl on November 29, 1939, Kehrl conceded that the house banks could not afford to undertake the obligation proposed and other solutions had to be found.[19] The financing of Schoeller-Bleckmann became a very complicated matter and was handled by a variety of means during the war because it was an extremely important producer for the war effort. The CA certainly remained a strong supporter of the enterprise, having granted 6.7 million RM in credits by June 1942 and given 400,000 RM as a long-term investment credit until 1951.[20]

The CA was to sell its shares of the Elin AG für elektrische Industrie at the beginning of 1940 to the Continental-Gas-Gesellschaft in Dessau, but it was successful in retaining the

---

[14] See p. 310 in this volume.

[15] See pp. 298–299 in this volume and the sources cited in notes 11 and 12.

[16] See BA-CA, CA-IB, Schoeller, 15/02-03, the post-Anschluss syndicate agreement, dated Sept. 5, 1938, as well as the documentation of the CA involvement with the Schoeller-Bleckmann supervisory board.

[17] BA-CA, CA-V, executive committee meeting of April 29, 1938.

[18] For the credit request, see BAB, R 2/15541, Bl. 195–201, the 18th meeting of the credit committee, Jan. 25, 1939, and BA-CA, CA-V, CA working committee meeting of April 1, 1939.

[19] BA-CA, CA-IB, Schoeller, 15/04-05, memorandum by Heller on meeting of Nov. 29, 1939.

[20] BA-CA, CA-V, report, June 10, 1942.

company's banking business and participated in the 2 million Reich-guaranteed credit given to the company for rationalization purposes. Elin, like Schoeller, was a significant enterprise, and its powerful supervisory board was chaired by Heller of the CA and also included General Director Hans Malzacher of the Alpine Montangesellschaft, General Director Georg Meindl of Steyr-Daimler-Puch, and General Director Heinrich Bleckmann of the Schoeller-Bleckmann Werke. By mid-1942, the CA had given the company 1.3 million RM in credits, including a 171,000 RM long-term credit until 1950.[21]

Another large Reich-guaranteed credit in which the CA had a particular interest was the 3 million RM credit granted to the Rottenmanner Eisenwerke Komm.Ges. Schmid & Co. The company had come into existence in that form in 1937 when Walter Schmid-Schmidsfelden, the president of the Blech- und Eisenwerke Styria AG, and his brother August, the more important of the brothers although only the vice president, moved their operations to Rottenmann and took over the Rottenmanner Eisenwerke AG, vormals Gebrüder Lapp. The latter was heavily indebted to the CA and was part of its concern. It was in danger of closing down because of economic conditions and its unprofitability. The goal of the Schmid-Schmidsfelden family was to take advantage of the water supply, transportation facilities, and the available terrain. The CA seems to have had no qualms about selling its shares, a process completed by late 1938.[22]

By that time, of course, the Anschluss had taken place, and the plans for the development of the Rottenmanner enterprise were now

significantly determined by the new regime's program for the economic development of the Ostmark as well as its intention to develop and use its heavy industry for military purposes. August Schmid-Schmidsfelden was well positioned to take advantage of these opportunities because he was a prominent industrialist and had been a Party member since 1933.[23] Initially, Schmid-Schmidsfelden planned to construct a modern rolling mill for fine steel sheet in Rottenmann but then shifted the project to Linz so that he could coordinate production and share energy resources with the Reichswerke Hermann Göring under construction there. Although work had already begun, the Air Command vetoed the plan, and a new location had to be found. The decision was made for Krems despite the need for more facilities than would have been required in Linz because of Krems's proximity to the projected Oder-Danube Canal. This was a costly project, and although the Rottenmann company had been granted a Reich-guaranteed credit of 3 million RM for Linz, it needed 6.1 million RM as a long-term investment credit and requested this in late 1940. At the same time, it admitted to delays because of the wartime situation. It does not seem that this amount was ever formally granted; the liquidity of the company was expected to improve because its facilities in Rottenmann were being used solely for military production and it was likely that the army would buy them. The money could then be used for Krems. The project was supported by the Economic Group for Iron and Steel on the grounds that a decentralization of iron and steel production in the Ostmark was highly desirable. The CA, Rottenmanner's house bank, however, did come through, providing 3.4 million RM as an advance against the requested credit and also held 910,000 RM on its books as a long-term credit until 1950.[24]

Another large industrial producer that benefited from the house bank function of the

---

21 On the sale of the Elin shares, see p. 62 in this volume and BA-CA, CA-V, the CA working committee meeting of March 5, 1940. For the credit, see BAB, R2/15581, Bl. 148–151, the report of June 16, 1939.

22 For a brief history of the company, see Alexander Stocker, *Austria Haustechnik AG. Eine Firmen Geschichte und Betriebsanalyse mit Schwerpunkt der Jahre 1989–1999*, Diss. (Graz 2000), pp. 15–22. See also BA-CA, CA-IB, Rottenmanner, 42/04, Heller to Schmid-Schmidsfelden, Nov. 30, 1938 and Heller to Hans Malzacher, Dec. 1, 1938.

23 ÖStA/AdR, BMI, Gauakte August von Schmid-Schmidsfelden, Nr. 29.022.

24 BAB, R2/15569, Bl. 30–36, 138, credit committee meeting of Dec. 17, 1940.

CA in connection with the consortial credits was the Leobersdorfer Maschinenfabrik AG, which produced excavators and conveyors. It had launched a major development program in 1939 and was granted a credit of 1,395,000 RM as well as a long-term credit of 105,000 RM until 1953. The CA held the latter and regularly gave a variety of credits to the company.[25] Such credits were certainly welcome to the company. It had a solid reputation and was producing for the war effort, and the CA viewed it as a long-term customer. The CA was happy to have such customers, as was illustrated by its support of the Lohnerwerke GmbH, which produced body parts for automobiles, trolley cars, and trucks. It was owned and run by five brothers. One of them, Max, was involved in the July 1934 putsch and briefly imprisoned. The firm was boycotted and had to close down. It reopened after the Anschluss and soon found itself with a mass of contracts from the railroads, post office, municipal streetcar companies, and automobile firms. At the same time, it began negotiating for military contracts. The firm employed 274 workers at the end of 1938. Finding itself needing to undertake a major investment program, it applied for a credit of 550,000 RM. It then raised the amount requested to 800,000 RM, with 250,000 RM to be used for operating expenses. The credit committee was concerned, however, that the 500,000 RM being asked for was too much given the limited capital possessed by the Lohner family. A more gradual approach was urged, and the CA agreed at the beginning of 1939 to provide 250,000 RM as an 85 percent Reich-guaranteed operating credit, and the question of providing an investment credit was put on ice. In June, the firm again applied for support, this time for a consortial 100 percent guaranteed credit of 350,000 RM. Between the spring of 1938 and the spring of 1939, it had doubled its contracts. Manifestly, as the credit committee openly noted, the firm was benefiting from its political position and could be expected to receive special consideration and more contracts from public agencies in the future. While it did not have the desired amount of capital at its disposal and was forced to pay its debts from current business, one could reasonably expect that it would continue to be able to do so because of the political situation. In this instance, the CA not only acted as the house bank for Lohner but also as the promoter of its further borrowing. In July 1940, the CA representative on the credit committee actually initiated a discussion of a new Lohner request for an additional credit of 75,000 RM to set up a repair shop for the Luftwaffe, for which it had received a 100,000 RM loan from the Luftwaffe. He went on to justify the application by pointing to the lack of capital available to the company in comparison to its indebtedness and was successful in gaining approval for the additional credit, which was 85 percent guaranteed.[26] Ironically, the Lohnerwerke turned out to be all too good a credit risk from the CA's point of view. Not only did it not take the 75,000 RM credit it had been offered but it also paid back its debts in 1943 so that in January 1944 Joham was encouraging a colleague to visit the company and see if it might not be interested in borrowing more money![27] Such were the rewards for participation in the July 1934 putsch!

The Reich Economic Aid for Austria consortium was by no means the only government-promoted aid program with which the CA and the Länderbank Wien were involved. In the fall of 1938, the RWM summoned the banks to set up a new Reich-guaranteed 25 million RM consortium for the reconstruction of the Sudetenland. The CA and the Länderbank were insistent on playing a much smaller role than in Austria for obvious reasons, and they both took a 4 percent stake, that is, up to 1 million RM each. In the spring of 1942, however,

25 I have been unable to find a record of the credit application. Some details are contained in a Deutsche Bank report on the CA working committee meeting of June 10, 1942, DB, P 6505, Bl. 50–53.

26 For the credit discussions of 1938–1939, see BAB, R2/15589, Bl. 2–4, 10–11, 67–71; for the additional credit, see ibid., R2/15566, Bl. 178–179, the 45th credit committee meeting, July 24, 1940.

27 BAB, R 8121/623, minute of discussion with Joham, Jan. 19, 1944.

an additional 20 million RM Sudetenland aid credit was created, the CA again taking a 4 percent, that is, 800,000 RM, stake.[28] Yet another large consortial credit was set up in November 1940 for the annexed areas of Poland, this time for 100 million RM, which was headed by the Reichs-Kredit-Gesellschaft. The consortium had eleven members, three of whom – the RKG, the Deutsche Bank, and the Dresdner Bank – provided 15 million RM each, while the CA and the Länderbank Wien held quotas of 6 million RM apiece. Whether the CA or other banks were very enthusiastic about these patriotic engagements is hard to say, but the terms suggest an effort to spread and limit the risks involved as well as to reduce the drain on liquidity. The banks had a right to offer sub-holdings to friendly banks; the initial consortium was set at a 50 million RM total, and the Reich undertook an obligation to take over credits after five years if requested by the banks.[29] Yet another "patriotic" consortial credit was the 60 million RM Reich-guaranteed resettlement credits for South Tyroleans wishing or needing to resettle in Austria. The CA and the Länderbank jointly headed up the consortium. The CA took a 15 1/3 percent share for individual credits less than 50,000 RM and a 27 percent share for consortial credits more than 50,000 RM. Thirty million RM of the credit fell in the first category, 20 million RM in the second, while the German Resettlement Trust Corporation (DUT) reserved the right to assign the remaining 10 million RM as it felt necessary. The total CA participation was capped at 16,750,00 RM. These monies were subsequently used to resettle Germans from the former territories of Yugoslavia taken over by the Italians in 1941.[30]

Through its branch in Cracow, the CA was also a participant in the large credits for the DUT for resettlement in the Generalgouvernement. By mid-June 1942, the CA had given diverse credits to the DUT adding up to 2,773,000 RM.[31] Here the banks involved were serving the SS and its resettlement policies, but the CA and other banks also provided large credits for German trade relations with its allies. In 1941, for example, in the wake of a German-Romanian credit agreement, the Deutsche Bank headed a 90 million RM credit consortium. The CA took a 5 percent share – as did the Länderbank – which amounted to 4.5 million RM, but the credit for Romanian business given by the CA amounted to 6,772,000 RM, 5,265,000 RM being a long-term credit due in seven years.[32] As was the case with most of the important banks, the CA participated regularly in the very large consortia financing the Reich Agency for Wheat, Fodder and other Agricultural Products. In the fall of 1942, for example, the Deutsche Rentenbank-Kreditanstalt in Berlin launched a 400 million RM credit to finance the transfer and distribution of the wheat harvest for 1942–1943. The CA provided 9 million RM for this credit, which bore 4 percent interest per annum and was supposed to be repaid in three installments between the summer of 1943 and the beginning of 1944.[33] This was, of course, in addition to its financing of Vigor, which the CA owned and which operated in accordance to the instructions of the Reich Agency for Wheat.[34]

There is, of course, nothing surprising about the fact that the CA was deeply embedded in the war economy and a participant in the various government-promoted consortia so far

---

[28] For the discussion led by Ministerial Director Lange in the RWM on Oct. 8, 1938, see NARA, T-38/204, Länderbank to Dresdner Bank, Oct. 10 and Nov. 2, 1938; BA-CA, CA-V, CA executive committee, Nov. 25, 1938; ibid., CA management board meeting, May 11, 1942.

[29] RGVA Moscow, 1458/15/136, Bl. 8–9, RWM memorandum of Nov. 11, 1940.

[30] BA-CA, CA-V, CA management board, Jan. 9, 1940 and CA working committee, March 5, 1940. On the resettlement from former Yugoslav territories,

see ibid., Joham's report of July 17, 1941 to the CA management board.

[31] See pp. 114–115, 189, 215, 247, 301 in this volume and DB, V2/3, list of debtors developed in June 1942.

[32] See ibid., and BA-CA, CA-V, CA management board, Jan. 17, 1941 and CA working committee, March 13, 1941.

[33] Ibid., CA management board meeting, Oct. 26, 1942.

[34] See pp. 256–261 in this volume.

discussed. As the Reich Economic Aid programs demonstrated, these consortia also involved CA credits given in its capacity as the house bank for various applicants and as a member of consortia funding the development of various companies, in which in some cases, Semperit, for example, it had a participatory interest. Nevertheless, if one examines the lists of companies to which it had given credits in mid-1942, it is clear that many of its largest credits were granted to concerns and firms in which it did not have, or no longer had, an ownership interest, and in whose operations it usually had no direct voice by means of supervisory board membership. This is not to say that people like Hasslacher, Joham, Fritscher, and other ranking persons in the CA did not have informal influence through personal and business contacts. Nevertheless, these enterprises took credits from the CA, sometimes as a direct client of the bank and sometimes from the CA operating in a consortium in a "normal" bank-industry connection, that is, not as a part of the CA concern.

2. FINANCING OLD HOLDINGS IN NEW GUISES

Former members of the CA concern loomed large among the list of CA debtors, and the most striking of these was the Steyr-Daimler-Puchwerke AG (SDPAG), which was on the CA books as a debtor to the tune of 18,836,000 RM in mid-1942. It had once belonged to the CA and was probably the largest asset lost in 1938 to the Reichswerke Hermann Göring. The SDPAG was one of a number of former CA concern members incorporated into the Reichswerke: the Steirische Gusstahlwerke AG, the Maschinen- und Waggonbau-Fabriks-AG in Simmering, and the Paukerwerke AG. The CA was eager to continue handling the banking business of the companies whose shares it had sold off – Krupp's Berndorfer Metallwerke, for example, continued to bank with the CA and had outstanding credits in June 1942 amounting to 1.2 million RM – and it was reasonably successful in doing so with the Reichswerke companies. In

May 1939, an agreement was made to provide the Reichswerke a 28 million RM credit to be divided among the four subsidiary companies after the elimination of the old cash credits still on their books. The SDPAG was to get 18 million RM; Steirische Gusstahl, 5 million RM; Simmering, 3.5 million RM; Paukerwerk, 1.5 million RM. Undoubtedly to the irritation of the CA, it had to share the granting of these credits with the Länderbank, which was entitled to a 25 percent share.[35] On the occasion of an SDPAG bond issue in 1940, the Länderbank sought a ratio of two-thirds for the CA and one-third for itself, but the CA held on tenaciously to its advantage.[36]

This is hardly surprising given the vast expansion of the SDPAG that began very soon after its takeover by the Reichswerke. The expansion was part of the Austrian economic recovery program and figured in plans to make Austria central to the Reich's armaments program. Both the army and the air force were interested in using a vastly expanded military production complex in Austria as the gateway to further expansion in Southeastern and Eastern Europe. Plans for a vast increase in ball bearing production developed in 1939 and then carried out in 1940 made the SDPAG a rival of the firms in Schweinfurth. This was accompanied by the building of airplane engine plants in Steyr and Graz, and followed in 1944 by establishing a tank plant, the "Nibelungenwerk," in St. Valentin, which was second only to Krupp. The SDPAG's capital increased from 11 million RM in 1938 to 80 million RM in 1943, and the direct investments of the SDPAG amounted to approximately 328 million RM between 1938 and 1944. Its sales increased from 57 million RM to 456 million RM during this period. Although the SDPAG came under the control of the Luftwaffe-owned Bank der Deutschen Luftfahrt (Aerobank) when the Reichswerke were broken up at the end of 1942, the

---

[35] BA-CA, CA-V, CA management board meeting, May 2, 1939 and CA working committee meeting, May 17, 1939.

[36] Ibid., CA working committee meeting, July 10, 1940.

expansion of the SDPAG went on uninter-
rupted. That was due in large part to the leadership of General Director Georg Meindl, an
able but utterly ruthless and vicious National
Socialist manager. On excellent terms with
Göring and the SS, he turned the SDPAG into
a major center of slave and forced labor.[37]

Under such circumstances, the granting
of generous CA credits to the Reichswerke
was a foregone conclusion. In March 1941,
the CA provided an impressive cash credit to
the SDPAG of 13.5 million RM along with
a guarantee credit of 2,667,000 RM. The
other aforementioned subsidary companies
of the Reichswerke were not forgotten. The
Steirische Gusstahlwerke, for example, received
a 3,750,000 RM cash credit and a 266,750 RM
guarantee credit.[38] The big money, however,
went into investment credits, and here there was
increasing cause for concern. The state-owned
Industriebank had provided a nine-year 18 million RM credit in 1939, and the Aerobank had
given the SDPAG a 24 million RM investment
credit in 1940.

The chief consortium members for the
SDPAG in the Ostmark were the CA and
the Länderbank Wien. The CA had the leading position, claiming a share of business with
SDPAG three times as large as the Länderbank
Wien's share. Although the Länderbank Wien
wanted a larger share, Fischböck, who was the
only banking representative on the SDPAG
supervisory board, was very tenacious about
maintaining the CA's advantage. Because the
Deutsche Bank and the Dresdner Bank each had
a 25 percent share of the SDPAG business, this
meant that, in the rivalry between the Deutsche

and Dresdner Banks, the Deutsche-CA group
was favored over the Dresdner-Länderbank
group. There were those in the SDPAG who
thought that the reverse should have been the
case. In November 1940, a compromise was
reached whereby the CA maintained the lead
with a one-third share while the Länderbank
Wien increased its share to 16 2/3 percent, thus
changing the original ratio from 3:1 to 2:1. The
Deutsche Bank seemed to have supported the
compromise because of the favored position of
its rival with the Reichswerke as a whole.[39]

The CA and Länderbank Wien had together
taken a 10 million RM share of the 24 million
RM Aerobank credit, 7.5 million RM falling to
the CA and 2.5 million RM assigned to the
Länderbank. Eight million RM was supposed to
be repaid in three payments in 1943–1945, and
the remaining 16 million RM was to be transformed into a publicly offered loan repayable
at the end of 1946. If the loan did not succeed,
then the money was to be paid back in four
payments per year starting at the end of 1946. As
the Aerobank informed the two Viennese banks
in July 1942, however, even though the SDPAG
had recently increased its capital by 50 million
RM and had successfully launched a bond issue
in the same amount that was successful with the
public, it was impossible to cover the investment
credit as intended because of new investments
called for by Field Marshall Göring. It is worth
noting that the CA had participated in the marketing of the bond issue with a quota of 23 percent. Nevertheless, as the Aerobank reported,
the investment credits could only begin to be
paid off at the end of 1946, while the Reich
economics minister had agreed to extend his
guarantee to 1949. Apparently, the payments for
1943–1945 were made, and the CA obviously
had to accept the delay of the repayment of
the remainder. In October 1943, however, the
Aerobank reported that the 24 million investment credit was no longer enough because of
the expansion of the airplane engine production
in Steyr and Graz, along with the purchase of
the Nibelungenwerke, so that a capital emission

37 See Bertrand Perz, "Politisches Management
im Wirtschaftskonzern. Georg Meindl und die
Rolle des Staatskonzerns Steyer-Daimler-Puch
bei der Verwirklichung der NS-Wirtschaftsziele
in Österreich," in: Hermann Kaienburg (ed.),
Konzentrationslager und deutsche Wirtschaft 1939–1945
(Opladen 1996), pp. 95–112. On the Aerobank,
see Lutz Budraß, *Flugzeugindustrie und Luftrüstung
in Deutscheland 1918–1945* (Düsseldorf 1998),
pp. 498–503.
38 BA-CA, CA-V, CA management board meeting,
March 20, 1941.

39 DrB, 29575-2001 BE, memorandums by Andre,
June 14, 1940 and Nov. 19, 1940.

of 20 million RM at 150 percent was needed along with a bond issue of 30 million RM.[40]

The CA continued providing operating credits for the concern, especially in connection with the Nibelungenwerke: 10 million RM at the beginning of 1944 to run until the end of the year and another 12.5 million RM at the beginning of 1945 until the end of that year.[41] The Länderbank also participated in providing credits, albeit at a lower level. Certainly those involved must have realized as the war went on that they were dealing with an endless project, although the SDPAG certainly had modern facilities that would be potentially valuable in the postwar period, a point made at the Länderbank in connection with its decision. Nevertheless, even though Richard Buzzi of the CA and Leonard Wolzt of the Länderbank Wien were on the SDPAG supervisory board, they clearly had no say in dealing with Meindl. Indeed, when the Länderbank Wien suggested that they might try to extend the 1945 credit for only half a year or at least ask for a commission for holding the credit available for a full year, the CA was so terrified by Meindl that it warned against even holding a consultation with the Länderbank Wien on the matter lest Meindl get wind of it![42]

The Reichswerke Hermann Göring, in its various incarnations, was continually in need of considerable credit. This was also true of the heavy industrial side of the Austrian Reichswerke, namely, the Alpine Montan mines and the iron and steel works centered in Linz. The Reichswerke had wrested the Alpine away from the Vereinigte Stahlwerke in February 1939, and it was thereafter called the "Alpine Montan Aktiengesellschaft Hermann Göring, Linz." It was the pet project of Paul Pleiger, the cofounder and director of the Reichswerke. Its deputy general director was Hans Malzacher,

an ambitious, talented, and hard-nosed industrialist who replaced Meindl at the Alpine in February 1938. In contrast to Meindl, whom the Vereinigte Stahlwerke regarded as a friend of Göring and a danger to its interests, Malzacher, who had held Austrian and Swiss citizenship but had given up the latter because of criticism within the Party about having an important industrial facility in the hands of a foreigner, was fundamentally apolitical and totally devoted to business. He was opposed to excessive and economically wrongheaded expansion in Linz and would have accepted an offer by Vögler to become head of the Vereinigte Stahlwerke had not Göring blocked him from leaving the Reichswerke in 1940. Ultimately, however, he ran afoul of the empire-building Gauleiter August Eigruber, and Göring permitted him to take leave in October 1941.[43] Malzacher was very highly regarded by the CA. He had served as a consultant for its heavy industrial holdings in 1933–1934, then as central director of the CA-controlled Eisenwarenfabriken Lapp-Finze in 1935–1936, and general director of the Simmering-Graz-Pauker AG in 1936–1938 before becoming general director of the Alpine Montan in February 1938. Hasslacher and Joham told Malzacher that they would back him if he would offer to become chairman of the CA management board. Malzacher turned down the suggestion, feeling himself too much the industrialist to play a role best assigned to a banker.[44]

Malzacher's departure meant the end of economic rationality at the Alpine and of the realization that the company could not radically expand in both the heavy industrial and the weapons sectors of the Reichswerke.

[40] See BAB, R 8121/715, the correspondence of the Bank der Deutschen Luftfahrt dealing with the SDPAG between 1940 and 1943.

[41] BA-CA, CA-V, CA management board meetings, Feb. 1, 1944, Jan. 8, 1945.

[42] DrB, 13790-2000, memorandum by Teichmann and Gruber, Jan. 12, 1945.

[43] See Oliver Rathkolb, "Am Beispiel Paul Pleigers und seiner Manager in Linz – Eliten zwischen Wirtschaftsräumen, NS-Eroberungs- und Rüstungspolitik, Zwangsarbeit und Nachkriegsjustiz," in: Oliver Rathkolb (ed.), NS-Zwangsarbeit: Der Standort Linz der "Reichswerke Hermann Göring AG Berlin" 1938–1945, 2 vols. (Vienna, Cologne, Weimar 2001), vol. 1, pp. 287–320, esp. pp. 292–296.

[44] See Hans Malzacher, Begegnungen auf meinem Lebensweg (Villach 1968), pp. 32–71.

The Alpine had originally received a 15 million RM credit from a consortium composed of the CA, the Länderbank Wien, and E. von Nicolai. This was increased to 25 million RM in November 1941. As in the case of the SDPAG, the CA was the lead bank, assuming 13,750,000 RM of the credit, and the other two banks took shares of 8,250,000 RM and 3,000,000 RM respectively. In mid-1942, the actual amount of CA credit to the Alpine was 7,966,000 RM.[45] The financial operations of the Alpine, however, were anything but stable. The credit in question was increased to 40 million RM, briefly reduced to 25 million RM, and then increased again to 40 million RM. By the end of the war, the Alpine was asking the consortium for 45 million RM. In the meantime, however, it had borrowed 60 million RM from the Reich, interest free. The Alpine expected it would not have to pay the credit back when it became due in 1945 because the finance minister had more or less promised that the credit would be forgiven. A further problem was that the Alpine was losing money because of its obligations to supply large amounts of ore to the Vereinigte Stahlwerke, an obligation the Alpine was counting on being brought to an end. There is no record of what the CA management thought of this, but it undoubtedly shared the concerns of the Länderbank Wien, which felt the Alpine should turn to the government for the 5 million RM credit it was requesting from the banks and that the consortium should be expanded so as to reduce the burden of the 40 million RM in credits already allocated.[46]

The CA also gave large credits to another important former member of its concern, the Pulverfabrik Skodawerke-Wetzler AG that had been taken over by IG Farben in 1938 and turned into the Donau Chemie AG. In June 1942, the CA listed IG Farben as having a 3 million RM credit, which was in fact a credit given for Donau Chemie. There were an additional 1,335,000 RM in credits given to the Donau Chemie sales organization provided by the Kärtnerring branch of the CA in Vienna.[47] Donau Chemie became a small Austrian IG within the larger IG Farben in 1939, encompassing the former Pulverfabrik Skodawerke-Wetzler AG, the Chemische Fabrik Wagemann, Seyback & Co. AG, the Carbidwerk Deutsch-Matrei AG, and the Österreichischer Kunstdünger- und Schwefelsäure und Chemische Fabrik AG, and these were subsequently merged into Donau Chemie in 1941.[48] The Austrian market was too small to absorb the output of this chemical conglomerate, but production for the war effort provided substantial business. Considerable expansion and investment were required to meet that demand. At the same time, some plants had to be shut down and some product lines abandoned because they had become obsolete or redundant. From the perspective of the IG Farben management, Donau Chemie was to serve not only the war effort as much as possible but also the interests of the conglomerate in Southeast Europe: "The Donau Chemie should take care of the interests of the IG in the industrialization in the Southeast particularly in Hungary and partially in Romania, while Dynamit Nobel Pressburg should also deal with Rumania aside from Slovakia, Bulgaria, Serbia, and Croatia."[49] It should be noted that the CA, through the Union Bank in Pressburg/Bratislava, also had interests in Dynamit Nobel, providing large operating credits, and also voted shares at its general shareholders' meetings. The engagement of the CA thus paralleled the interests of IG Farben.[50]

---

[45] BA-CA, CA-V, CA management board meeting, Nov. 10, 1944; DB, V2/3, list of debtors developed in June 1942.

[46] DrB, 13790-2000, report on discussion between Rasche and Teichmann, March 14, 1945.

[47] DB, V2/3, list of debtors, June 1942.

[48] BAB, R 8128/A1384, Bl. 121–124, Gattineau to the Südost-Ausschuss of IG Farben, Jan. 21, 1939.

[49] Ibid., Bl. 191–192, meeting in Donau Chemie, May 16, 1941.

[50] See the administrative council meeting of the Union Bank on Jan. 22, 1941, where Dynamit Nobel received 12,000,000 Ks., the largest amount of any of the big companies listed, and also BA-CA, CA-TZ, Sekretariat rot, Box 7/CA-BV IV, V, Stephan to Miksch, Oct. 13, 1941 concerning its share voting at Dynamit Nobel shareholder meetings.

Nevertheless, the CA had a very special long-term interest in Donau Chemie and was very anxious to get as much of its credit business and that of IG Farben enterprises in Austria as it could. There was considerable irritation at the CA, for example, that it only received a 4 percent share of the consortial loan of 40 million RM floated for the Stickstoffwerk Ostmark AG, Linz, the first tranche of which was issued in 1940 while a second was scheduled for 1943. The Länderbank also got 4 percent, while E. von Nicolai got 2 percent and Schoeller 2 percent only for the 1943 tranche. By contrast, the Deutsche Bank got 27.5 percent, the Dresdner Bank got 20 percent, and the Deutsche Länderbank AG, Berlin got 17 percent. The last-named bank, headed by Karl Pfeiffer, was totally controlled by IG Farben, which used it to handle its basic banking needs. Of the fifteen banks in the consortium, only four were Viennese, and their quotas added up to 10 percent for the 1940 tranche and 12 percent of the 1943 tranche.[51] This distribution of quotas did not bode well for the role of the Austrian banks in the anticipated financing of Donau Chemie's expansion, and at the beginning of 1941 CA Director Rudolf Pfeiffer approached the leadership of Donau Chemie where he expressed astonishment at the low quota of the Austrian banks in the Stickstoffwerk Ostmark consortium and went on to plead that a consortium for Donau Chemie be composed largely, even exclusively, of Austrian banks. While the managers at Donau Chemie pointed out that Pfeiffer was better advised to complain about the Stickstoffwerk Ostmark consortium to the Deutsche Bank, which dominated most IG consortia, they were more sympathetic to the idea of an Ostmark consortium in which the leading place would be shared by the CA and the Länderbank Wien. They were quite critical of the manner in which large banks in the old Reich simply treated a leadership position in a consortium as an entitlement, as was the case with the Deutsche Bank with respect to IG Farben. To be sure, the Länderbank Berlin

would head up such a consortium because of its special relationship to IG Farben, but the Donau Chemie consortium would otherwise be limited to Ostmark banks. It was anticipated that the company would need 25.1 million RM, which was to be raised by increasing its capital and by a consortial loan.[52] Much of the support for this capital increase was to come from within IG Farben itself, particularly from the Kalle AG, but it was thought important that Donau Chemie be regarded as a genuine Ostmark concern and that an Ostmark consortium float a 3 million RM loan.[53]

Financing the expansion of Donau Chemie was particularly difficult because the concern had not been making a sufficient profit and its capital was inadequate. It needed both current account credits, which it received from the Deutsche Länderbank Berlin, and consortial support for longer-term investment. IG Farben bought the land on which the construction was to take place in order to relieve the Donau Chemie of this expense until it could get its new operations going. Pfeiffer, however, aggressively sought both the current account credits given by the Deutsche Länderbank Berlin and the leadership of the consortium and paid a visit to Director Ulrich Kersten of IG Farben in Berlin in May to make these claims, suggesting that he had the support of Karl Pfeffer and the powerful Max Ilgner of the IG management board. This was a good example of Rudolf Pfeiffer's clumsiness, and there was no intention of giving the CA exclusive credit-granting rights or allowing it to take precedence over the Länderbank Berlin. In August, Ilgner decreed that the latter bank was to head any consortium, while the CA and the Länderbank Wien were to act as the chief members of the consortium. Donau Chemie received a 7 million RM bridging credit at the end of 1941, which was then raised to 10 million RM in October 1942. The Länderbank Berlin provided 50 percent of these credits, while the CA and the Länderbank

---

[51] BAB, R 8129/1007, Bl. 5 and 8, undated memorandum of fall 1940 by the Deutsche Länderbank AG.

[52] BAB, R 8128/A1384, Bl. 263–264, 215–216, Bachem to Karl Pfeiffer, Jan. 18, 1941.

[53] Ibid., Bl. 206–209, Kersten memorandum, March 27, 1941.

gave their credits on a 60:40 ratio, with the CA getting the larger quota. The credit was extended in December 1943, and the combined interest and commission was set at 5 percent despite Rudolf Pfeiffer's effort to have the rate set at 5.5 percent. Director Heinrich Gattineau of IG Farben felt that Donau Chemie was suffering too much from the shutting down of some of its previously lucrative operations and had to calculate carefully. He maintained that the lower interest rate, which Karl Pfeiffer was willing to grant, was more appropriate.[54]

This arrangement also reflected the failure of Rudolf Pfeiffer's attempt to reserve the engagement of the Vienna banks with Donau Chemie exclusively for the CA. Director Wolzt of the Länderbank Wien had apparently appealed to Karl Pfeiffer for the inclusion of his bank, and the latter was influential in having the Länderbank included, and he also urged Wolzt to accept the 5 percent already forced on the CA.[55] One has the sense that these investments ultimately failed their purpose because the new facilities at Donau Chemie were heavily damaged from Allied bombing and did not come on line, while the real value of the company lay in its suspended peacetime production so that one could only consider its promise to lie in its postwar activity whenever that could be resumed.[56]

3. FINANCING NEW WARTIME PRODUCERS IN COLLABORATION WITH THE AEROBANK: PICHLER AND SPANIEL

As these examples show, the CA often worked hand in hand with the Länderbank Wien, and

54 Ibid., Bl. 187, 193, 195–199, memorandum by Kersten, May 14, 1941; Karl Pfeiffer to Ilgner, May 15, 1941; Karl Pfeiffer to Kersten, May 15, 1941; memo of Aug. 8, 1941; and BAB, 8129/991, Bl. 1, 37, undated list of credits for Donau Chemie, and minute by Karl Pfeiffer, Dec. 10, 1942.

55 See ibid., Bl. 44–46 and 32–33, Karl Pfeiffer to Wolzt, Feb. 10, 1942, and Wolzt to Pfeiffer, Feb. 27 and March 19, 1942, and the exchange between Karl Pfeiffer and Rudolf Pfeiffer, Oct. 14 and Oct. 20, 1942.

56 BAB, 8129/A1384, Bl. 284, memorandum by Bachem for Ilgner, Jan. 12, 1945.

both banks worked closely with special banks that had sprung up to deal with the banking needs of the war effort, particularly the Aerobank and IG Farben's Länderbank Berlin. In the concluding years of the war, problems of production interruptions due to shortages of material and labor, bombing, and delay of payment necessarily affected credit decisions and, without in any way laying oneself open to charges of defeatism, calculations about the future of credit seekers under peacetime conditions were also allowed to come into play as the case of Donau Chemie demonstrated.

A good illustration of these various features of credit decision making was the case of Maschinfabrik Ing. B. Pichler & Co, originally a rather small enterprise that made machines for cigarette manufacture at its plant in Floridsdorf. It was refounded in May 1941 and converted itself into a producer of airplane machine gun parts with considerable success; in 1942, 95 percent of its production was for the Luftwaffe. Later, it also produced products for U-boats. Its expansion had involved a good deal of Aryanization. It purchased two Aryanized factory buildings, the Maschinenfabrik Mechanische Werkstätte Ing. Lerner, and then a shut-down Vienna factory belonging to A.H. Pollack's Söhne. The machinery of the latter was sold to help pay for the Aryanization. Much of the firm's financing had been handled by the Aerobank with the encouragement and support of the Air Ministry, but the Aerobank was anxious to have a partner in granting credits and invited the CA to join in the financing because Pichler had been a customer of the CA. In January 1944, Director Joham of the CA visited Pichler's headquarters to discuss this with a representative of the Aerobank and with Pichler and a member of his staff. Joham stated that the CA considered Pichler a solid customer and viewed the enterprise favorably, but the CA as a private firm could not simply join the Aerobank in giving credits because that involved investing in an expansion of Pichler at the behest of the Reich. But the Reich itself was no longer giving credits to expand the armaments industry and was also demanding that Pichler pay back the extra profit he had been allowed in charging prices above the established ceilings. The CA considered this repayment demand very detrimental to Pichler's capacity to deal with the requested credits. The Aerobank informed Joham, however, that the Air Ministry would not budge from this position. Joham basically desired more assurances that Pichler would be able to pay the 6 million RM he felt Pichler needed, while Pichler felt that he could manage with 4 million RM. In the end, Joham took a wait-and-see attitude and left the negotiation of a financial plan to the Aerobank and Pichler.[57]

In fact, not only Joham but also the Aerobank was troubled by the gap between Pichler's wishes and the means available to the company, and there was a general feeling that Pichler needed to find a firm interested in helping it to increase its capital. There was also considerable unhappiness with Pichler's investment in a parachute company, the Fallschirmbau Eschner. Eschner's products had still not received Air Ministry approval, and the company was seen as a distraction from Pichler's main focus. Another problem was that although Pichler had valuable contracts, the Air Ministry's slowness in paying its bills created cash flow problems. The CA, therefore, was being invited to take an equal share of the credits for Pichler under circumstances where the Aerobank itself was troubled by the situation. A very detailed report by the industry inspectors of the Aerobank at the end of July 1944 produced a guardedly favorable appraisal. The immediate strength of the company lay in its military contracts. It seemed to have sufficient labor; it employed 752 male and female workers, 458 of whom were from the Reich, 197 of whom were foreigners, and 97 of whom were prisoners of war. The report strongly urged an increase in the company's capital and the elimination of the Eschner investment, and although it supported granting a 3 million RM operating credit, it considered

it essential that the Air Ministry pay its bills quickly and not in two months as was presently the case. Perhaps the most interesting aspect of the report was its discussion "of the extremely important question ... what will the firm produce after the war."[58] The answer was that it could go back to producing cigarette machines because the Lerner firm had large contracts that could not be carried out because it had not been producing such machines. Also, it could go back to producing electric meters for houses and factories because many of them had been destroyed by wartime bombing and there one could expect a great demand. In fact, the Pichler firm would be in a position to produce a variety of appliances and equipment to meet the orders of a projected reconstruction ministry after the war. Ultimately, this evaluation seems to have led to an Aerobank decision to provide a 1 million RM investment credit at the end of October 1944, but it came with a rather jaundiced view of Pichler and his firm: "A rapidly developed enterprise whose growth was conditioned by the war. The people involved became rich quickly without any great accomplishments on their part. To this must be added a certain speculative tendency as evidenced by the participation on the Eschner, Fallschirmbau firm in Vienna."[59]

The CA was much less willing to grant an investment credit, although it did try to create the basis for one by promoting a capital increase through the Thüringer Gas AG, an effort undertaken especially by Director Tron. This fell through, however, and the CA was unprepared to provide the credit and also demanded a termination of the Eschner investment. In fact, the CA even refused to provide operating credits at the end of 1944, after Pichler reported that the Air Ministry had not paid his bills for the previous six weeks and that he was unable to pay his workers. Apparently, the Aerobank continued to provide support, although it was clear that Pichler's production for the war effort would be coming to an end.[60]

57 See DB, V2/1, memorandum by Tron of Nov. 23, 1943, and report of the Aerobank credit division, on a discussion with Pichler, Nov. 22, 1943; BAB, R 8121/591, memorandum on a discussion with Pichler and Joham, Jan. 26, 1944.

58 Ibid., report of July 29, 1944.

59 Ibid., Aerobank credit protocol, Oct. 27, 1944.

60 Ibid., reports by Döring, Oct. 6 and Dec. 7, 1944, and CA to Aerobank, Oct. 16, 1944.

In a not dissimilar case, Aerobank-Creditanstalt's financing of a wartime entrepreneur also led to a very hesitant and even negative position on granting credits as the war came to an end. The enterprise in question was that of Gustav Spaniel, who seems to have found a device to make flak artillery more efficient, thus leading to considerable contracts with the Air Ministry and support from both the Aerobank and the CA for investment and for current account. In March 1943, for example, the CA gave Spaniel a one-year credit of 400,000 RM to carry out a military contract.[61] Nevertheless, there was always considerable concern about the great disproportion between Spaniel's assets and the money he was spending on investment and, as in the case of Pichler, he was being urged to find an investor with sufficient capital to correct the situation. Director Tron of the CA, who handled the case for the bank, was sufficiently alarmed in the course of 1944 to put a stop to the credits and, much to Spaniel's irritation, the Aerobank was not forthcoming with operating credits either. At the beginning of 1945, however, Tron was more favorably impressed with Spaniel's earnings and considered it possible to grant long-term credits if Spaniel found a way to finance them over the long term. The Aerobank remained skeptical and suspicious and was also irritated that the CA received better security for its credits than the Aerobank. In January 1945, Director Struck of the Aerobank expressed his concerns directly to Tron, pointing out that Spaniel was asking for between 300,000 and 500,000 RM in operating credits and, even more disturbingly, that Spaniel had invested 900,000 RM during the previous three years with his own earnings although he had no more than 100,000 RM in capital. Struck considered this irresponsible in view of the absence of any certain basis for financing these investments over the long run. Tron himself had been worried enough to insist that Spaniel reduce its 600,000 RM in credits from the CA, and these had been reduced to 150,000 RM. Struck and the Tron decided to

keep one another informed about the situation. In early February, Spaniel paid off a substantial portion of the CA credit, and this suggested to Tron that its earnings were high and that, after an audit in March, the time might have arrived where one could talk about investment credits again. Spaniel himself, however, had not come to the Aerobank with further requests, and while Spaniel must have benefited from the great need for flak in 1944, the market for flak was certainly reaching its terminus in the winter of 1945.[62]

In contrast to the aforementioned cases where the CA functioned as the house bank of enterprises producing for the war effort but the common engagement with the Aerobank involved considerable reservations and skepticism on the part of both banks, the funding of the Optische Werke C. Reichert did not appear at all problematic. Indeed, it was a source of some competition between the Aerobank and the CA. A family firm founded in 1876 by Carl Reichert, it was known for its production of high-quality microscopes, projectors, cameras, and other equipment deemed important to the war effort. The CA had shown great interest in the company, helped with its restructuring, and provided it with a 760,000 RM long-term credit backed by mortgages that did not have to be fully paid off until the end of 1960.[63] It also provided other credits backed by receipts from its contracts. In late 1941, the firm planned a large expansion of its physical plant, and the Aerobank offered a 1 million RM investment credit. At this point, the CA negotiated with Otto Reichert, who headed the company, and offered to provide the credit at exactly the same conditions as the Aerobank and also to revise the old credit along more favorable lines. Reichert was extremely impressed by the forthcoming attitude of his house bank. As he informed his Berlin representative, "it seems to

---

[61] BA-CA, CA-V, CA management board meeting, March 29, 1943.

[62] BAB, R 8121/542, correspondence between the Aerobank office in Vienna and Berlin, Jan. 6, 12, 26, and Feb. 3, 1945; DB, VI/2, memorandum by Tron, Jan. 5, 1945.

[63] BA-CA, CA-V, CA working committee, May 23, 1941.

us extraordinarily expedient to accept the proposals of the Creditanstalt-Bankverein, since working together with a Vienna bank (realizing the credit payments, making payments, etc.) is significantly easier than with a Berlin agency."[64] Reichert, therefore, decided to turn down the Aerobank credit while thanking that bank for creating a situation in which the CA was influenced to offer the same terms.

The Aerobank leadership viewed all this as somewhat disingenuous and complained to Joham that the CA was trying to cut it out of the business with Reichert. The latter, however, pointed out that there were special problems connected with the Aerobank credit because of the already existing credits and guarantees provided by Reichert to the CA, and that these guarantees would run afoul of those being asked for by the Aerobank. This difference between the two banks resulted in a negotiation between General Director Fritz Rudof of the Aerobank and Joham on December 3, 1941, in which both banks agreed to collaborate in the investment credit and the operating credits for Reichert. In the case of the investment credit, the CA would be offered a 40 percent share, while the Aerobank would accept a 40 percent share in the operating credits. Appropriate adjustments were then made with respect to the guarantees. Manifestly, the CA had to surrender its plan to be the sole creditor of Reichert because one could not simply go against the will of the Aerobank and the powerful Air Ministry behind it, just as Reichert had to accept the inconvenience of having to deal with Berlin. Reichert, however, was a good investment for the banks, which was the obvious reason for their desire to give it credits. Not only was it making good money during the war, but it was to outlast the war and the need to deal with the Berlin Aerobank.[65]

[64] BAB, R 8121/589, Wolfgang Minameyer to Aerobank, quoting a letter from O. Reichert, Nov. 22, 1941.

[65] Ibid., Aerobank memorandum on discussion with Joham, Nov. 25, 1941; CA to Aerobank, Nov. 25, 1941; memorandum on meeting between Joham and Rudof, Dec. 3, 1941; CA to Aerobank, Dec. 10, 1941, and Aerobank to CA, Dec. 19, 1941.

The importance of the Aerobank during the war, however, was unquestionable, and this was amply demonstrated by the case of Martin Miller AG, a producer of forged and steel products whose major plants were in Traismauer on the Lower Danube. The CA owned 89.19 percent of its shares at the time of the Anschluss. It was thus part of the machine and metal products industry section of the CA concern and, in contrast to the companies discussed earlier, the CA was directly involved in its ownership and management. This makes it a fitting point of departure of the discussion that follows on the role of the CA industrial concern in the domestic war economy.

4. MARTIN MILLER AND OTHER MACHINE AND METAL INDUSTRY FIRMS IN THE CA CONCERN

Although it was not able to retain many of its industrial holdings after the Anschluss, the CA was successful in holding on to its control of Martin Miller, but only after major trials and tribulations. These began shortly after the Anschluss. when the CA was approached by the firm of Schmidt & Clemens, which proposed they join forces with the Martin Miller AG and reorganize the latter as a producer for the Luftwaffe. Schmidt & Clemens had been founded in 1879 as a company marketing steel products in Frankfurt am Main and later built a plant for high-grade steel production in Berghausen near Cologne. Its headquarters remained in Frankfurt. It seemed to have excellent contacts with the Air Ministry, and it was also in the process of turning itself into a concern by buying up other companies. The Air Ministry wished to increase the production of adjustable propeller parts manufactured at Berghausen, and the basic idea was for Martin Miller to expand to produce these parts with the assistance and support of Schmidt & Clemens. Whatever reservations the CA leadership may have had about the Schmidt & Clemens proposal, it was rapidly disabused of the notion that it could choose not to work with Schmidt & Clemens when the Air Ministry official in charge declared that if the CA did not agree to cooperate and also give Schmidt &Clemens a stake in Martin Miller, then the Air Ministry would confiscate the shares or forcibly dissolve the company.[66]

By late 1938, the CA agreed to the forced collaboration and to selling half its shares to Schmidt & Clemens. Two Schmidt & Clemens representatives were placed on the supervisory board and its sales director was appointed to the Martin Miller management board. On August 8, 1939, this shotgun marriage was consummated with the signing of a syndicate contract and the sale of half the shares, worth 365,000 RM, to Schmidt & Clemens. In 1940, the capital of the company was increased from 2,250,000 RM to 3 million RM, and there was a further increase to 5 million RM in 1942, so that each of the partners held 2,490,000 RM of the Miller shares. Under the syndicate contract, the CA and Schmidt & Clemens had a first option should either the one or the other wish to dispose of its shares.[67]

Both sides chose to be secretive about their relationship and the ownership of Martin Miller more generally. Glatzl became very exercised in 1941 when the auditing firm used by the company, Treuverkehr Deutsche Treuhand AG, wanted to include information in the Martin Miller business report pertaining to the role of Schmidt & Clemens and to the debts owed to the CA. As Glatzl told the leading director at Martin Miller, Alfons Pfeifer-Schiessl, "we, as an armaments industry, must pursue only one purpose, namely, to publish a management board report that says as little as possible. The situation of the firm, its ties to other concerns, etc. are none of the business of outsiders."[68] He also emphasized that such information would be noted abroad and that wartime secrecy requirements had to be followed.

The actual expansion of Martin Miller began in the fall of 1939, accompanied by the aforementioned capital share increase, investment credits from the Aerobank of 7 million RM, a credit of 1,250,000 RM from the CA, and a government grant of 3.5 million RM.[69] Although the expansion and production were very successful, the relationship between the CA and Schmidt & Clemens was filled with tension. This became especially apparent in October 1940, when the huge overruns on the construction at Traismauer led to a suggestion by Schmidt & Clemens that the Air Ministry be asked to take over the costs along with Martin Miller and then turn the company over to Schmidt & Clemens to administer. Director Friedl of the CA was infuriated by this suggestion, which he viewed as tantamount to throwing the CA out of Martin Miller and undermining its banking business with the company.[70]

There appears to have been good reasons for the CA's suspicions, entertained especially by Director Glatzl, that some members of the Air Ministry and the leadership of Schmidt & Clemens were working together to have all the shares go to Frankfurt. This became especially evident in 1941, when a new expansion program was planned so that Martin Miller could help meet the needs of the Flugmotorenwerke Ostmark GmbH, which was being established at this time. This would require large new credits for Martin Miller, and Glatzl was summoned to a meeting at the Air Ministry in early September with Max von Hellingrath, the right-hand man to the powerful head of the ministry section dealing with firms and industrial financing, Alois Cejka.[71] Hellingrath was joined by another ministry official, Le Suire. Schmidt & Clemens were represented by Director Josef Mazalka, its leading manager who more or less called the tune at the company, and Carl Schmidt. Glatzl suspected that

66 BA-CA, CA-IB, Miller, 11/02, report by Walter Manske, Feb. 26, 1944.

67 Ibid., Miller, 11/10, CA to the Federal Ministry for Assets and Economic Planning (Bundesministerium für Vermögenssicherung und Wirtschaftsplanung), July 4, 1947.

68 Ibid., Miller, 11/02, Glatzl to Alfons Pfeifer-Schiessl, May 14, 1941.

69 Ibid., Miller, 11/07-08, report on Martin Miller AG development programs, Oct. 2, 1944.

70 Ibid., Referat Glatzl, 47/04, memorandum by Friedl, Oct. 31, 1940.

71 On these officials, see Budraß, Flugzeugindustrie, pp. 490–493, 577–578.

Mazalka had instigated the meeting as part of his more general conspiring against the CA. There can be no question that the CA was in bad odor with the officials involved, who took the view that banks had no business owning industrial concerns. Le Suire had repeatedly stated that "it is not the job of banks to participate in industry; concern building was not only frowned upon by the Reich but also by the Party."[72] Hellingrath was rather more blunt about his intentions, who Glatzl reported saying that the Ministry "views the present participation of the Creditanstalt in Martin Miller only with disquiet because it is not a matter for banks to participate in shareholding. The Creditanstalt must come to an agreement with S. & C. about the transfer of our holding of Miller shares to that firm." Glatzl found all this very aggravating because it not only overlooked that Schmidt & Clemens was building up a concern of its own but also that it had become heavily indebted to the Aerobank in doing so and estimated that its debts would be 50 million RM if it also tried to buy the remaining Martin Miller shares. Logically, Schmidt & Clemens should have been overjoyed in having a financially strong partner in the CA, and Glatzl suspected that Mazalka and Schmidt were trying to make their concern totally dependent on the Reich as had been the case with some other manufacturers in the aviation industry.

In addition to these arguments for ending the CA's investment in Martin Miller, Hellingrath tried to argue that there was a conflict between the CA and the Aerobank over the credits being given to Martin Miller. Glatzl was able to parry this claim in large part by pointing out that the CA had on its own surrendered the entire mortgage it held as security for its credit to the Aerobank. This did not fully mollify Hellingrath, however, who insisted that the Aerobank could not be satisfied with the secured investment credit alone. As a member of the Aerobank supervisory board, he had to insist

that the CA also had to allow the Aerobank a suitable portion of the regular banking business of Martin Miller. Ironically, Glatzl found it considerably more pleasant to deal with General Director Rudof of the Aerobank. There were hints of tension between the Aerobank and the Deutsche Bank, which were not helpful to the CA because it was so closely identified with the Deutsche Bank at this point. Nevertheless, Rudof was more sensitive to the situation of the CA than the Air Ministry officials, which Glatzl attributed to the fact that Rudof saw things from the perspective of a "banking man." He expressed gratitude for the CA's willingness to surrender the mortgage it had held as security and offered to join together with the CA in providing investment credits and allow the CA appropriate security in the form of a mortgage for the credit it granted. He also welcomed the CA as a partner in providing operating credits to Martin Miller and suggested an Aerobank stake of 25 percent. Last, he suggested that the Aerobank and Martin Miller conclude a long-term agreement on the financing of Martin Miller and urged that CA Director Friedl come to Berlin to work out such an arrangement.

Rudof was the only ray of hope in what certainly was a terribly gloomy visit to Berlin for Glatzl. Mazalka had become increasingly sinister, threatening to ruin Martin Miller by shifting all the Air Ministry's lucrative business to his company while leaving the bad contracts to Traismauer and thereby force the CA to sell at least some shares so that Schmidt & Clemens had a majority. The Air Ministry was under the illusion that Schmidt & Clemens was doing its best for Martin Miller with regard to technical matters. In reality, it had done next to nothing, and Mazalka showed up for about ten days a month. In short, the Aerobank appeared increasingly as a welcome partner and protector of the CA's interests in Martin Miller. This did not, necessarily mean, however, that the remaining Martin Miller shares in CA hands were inviolate. The Air Ministry insisted that Schmidt & Clemens have a first option on those shares, and Glatzl and Friedl told Rudof that what they wished most was the banking business of Martin

---

[72] For this and the quotations and discussion that follow, see BA-CA, CA-IB, Miller, 11/07-08, the memorandum by Glatzl on the discussion in Berlin, Sept. 8, 1941.

Miller. Rudof assured them in discussions held in September and November 1941 that, whatever the ultimate ownership of the shares, the Aerobank would limit itself to 25 percent of the operating business with Martin Miller and also would make every effort to keep 75 percent of the business with the CA.[73]

At the beginning of December, the CA gave Martin Miller a cash credit of 200,000 RM, which was then combined with the previously granted 3.5 million RM investment credit to form a substantial operating credit. The mortgage backing for what had previously been a 3.5 million RM investment credit was given up, and the Aerobank was invited to take a 25 percent share. Joham was sent to Berlin to negotiate the further collaboration with the Aerobank. Friedl had already agreed that Schmidt & Clemens would also receive a 25 percent quota of the operating credit for Martin Miller. In April 1942, there followed the 3 million RM capital increase divided between the CA and Schmidt & Clemens mentioned earlier.[74] The CA did not participate in an investment credit for this second big expansion of Martin Miller, but the government provided a subsidy of 2 million RM and the Aerobank an investment credit of 4.5 million RM.[75] At the same time, there were growing suspicions that Mazalka was a dubious character in numerous respects, that he had engaged in smuggling goods over the French border and was profiting from the food supplies intended for workers. Also, there were indications that Mazalka had effectively forced the Schmidt brothers to expand operations far more than they intended. Most seriously, however, there was evidence that Mazalka's accounting practices were in violation of price regulations and tax laws.[76]

In 1943, yet a third expansion of Martin Miller was in the offing, while the relationship with Schmidt & Clemens festered to the point that the CA decided to present its complaints to the ministry. On March 27, a meeting was held at the CA in Vienna that included Cejka, Hellengrath, and other officials, Rudof of the Aerobank, and Buzzi and Friedl for the CA. The CA complained that the anticipated assistance to Martin Miller from Schmidt & Clemens had proven "practically meaningless," and that Mazalka had no technical expertise in his role as a member of the management board and was also heartily disliked. Most serious, however, was the CA's charge that Schmidt & Clemens had been collecting 10 percent of the turnover of Martin Miller for alleged services under the agreement of 1938 that it had not performed. Schmidt & Clemens had received 200,000 RM in 1941, 600,000 RM in 1942, and 2 million RM in 1943. Cejka found this serious enough to order an investigation to determine whether the CA was correct in its complaints. Certainly Schmidt & Clemens's cause could not have been helped by the arrest of Mazalka by the criminal police in early March for violations of the wartime economic regulations, an event, it is worth noting, that occurred before the investigation order by Cejka.[77]

The ministerial investigation confirmed the CA's position that the payments made to Schmidt & Clemens were not justified by its performance, whereupon the latter surrendered its shares in Martin Miller to the Air Ministry, which in turn placed them with the Aerobank. Nevertheless, Schmidt & Clemens was given a payment of 775,000 RM for the shares despite the judgment about the 10 percent of Martin Miller's turnover it had been collecting. What caused the most chagrin at the CA, however, was that it had a first option on the transfer of the Schmidt & Clemens shares under the contract, but that the Air Ministry had lodged the shares with the Aerobank as a temporary measure while it sought to

---

[73] BAB, R 8121/630, Aerobank to CA, Feb. 15, 1944.

[74] Ibid., correspondence between the CA and Aerobank for 1942; BA-CA, CA-V, CA management board meeting, Dec. 2, 1941.

[75] BA-CA, CA-IB, Miller, 11/07-08, report on Martin Miller AG development programs, Oct. 2, 1944.

[76] Ibid., Referat Glatzl, 47/04, report by Friedl, Oct. 27, 1942, and Friedl to Heller, Feb. 3, 1943.

[77] BAB, R 8121/630, memo by Rudof, April 2, 1943, and report by Manske, Feb. 26, 1944, BA-CA, CA-IB, 11/02. On March 8, 1943, Gauleiter Jury ordered the removal of Mazalka from his positions pending the outcome of the state prosecutor's investigation of the charges against him, ibid., 47/04.

place the shares with the Vereinigte Deutsche Metallwerke-Luftfahrtwerke AG (VDM). In fact, Cejka not only wanted these shares to go to the VDM but also, under the guise of wartime necessities, to transfer the CA shares in Martin Miller to the VDM as well!

The VDM had been founded by bringing together a number of light metal and copper producers in 1930. It began to prosper after 1933 thanks to military contracts. Production for the Luftwaffe assumed particular importance, and the VDM decided in July 1942 to separate its production in this sector and create a separate company, the VDM-Luftfahrwerke AG. The plan was strongly influenced by the military authorities, and the Aerobank assumed 75 percent of the shares. The Air Ministry ordered the plants in Heddenheim and Hamburg to be moved to central Germany, Silesia, and Metz, and the company established a headquarters in Berlin that called itself the Continentale Metall AG.[78] One should also note that the VDM-Luftfahrt was receiving substantial credits in 1943–1944 from a consortium of the CA, the Länderbank Wien, and the Aerobank for the development of the VDM Luftfahrtwerke Steiermark GmbH in Marburg/Maribor that was to produce airplane parts.

It was one thing for the CA to cooperate in a consortium to support a VDM project sponsored by the Air Ministry, but quite another for it to surrender its stake in Martin Miller and, in addition, to be cheated of the option to recover the shares surrendered to Schmidt & Clemens. Rudof of the Aerobank sought to mollify the CA in February 1944 by reminding it of the discussions he had held in 1941 with Glatzl and Friedl, their fatalistic attitude toward the shares, and their desire to retain 75 percent of the Martin Miller business. In Rudof's view, the decision to transfer shares to the VDM in no way affected this policy, and he reaffirmed this commitment. At the same time, he reminded the CA that he had also sought to provide

the CA with other lucrative business, particularly a role in financing the Flugmotorenwerke Ostmark GmbH, and welcomed further cooperation with the CA.[79]

In fact, the shares did matter to the CA, and the directors at Martin Miller and the CA leadership thought the idea of giving the VDM a role in Martin Miller extremely undesirable from a technical point of view. The two issues were linked. Undermining the case for giving the shares to the VDM on technical grounds could open the way for proposing an alternative that would save Martin Miller for the CA concern. The connection and the alternative to the Air Ministry proposal was made very explicit in a memorandum of Martin Miller manager Walter Manske of February 26, 1944, which recounted the unhappy history of the CA-Schmidt & Clemens relationship and then went on to point out that replacing the latter with the VDM would be to repeat the past mistake.[80] Schmidt & Clemens had been useless to Martin Miller, and the problem would be all the greater with the VDM because the VDM had no experience whatsoever with the processing technology employed at Martin Miller. The notion that the VDM could make use of these products was also false because the Munitions Ministry ring controlling forged products determined allocations, and the VDM at the moment was limited to 12 percent of Martin Miller's production. Manske considered the claim that VDM control of Martin Miller shares would increase productivity to be "laughable" because if anything had increased production it was the disappearance of Mazalka and his colleagues. Manske was also able to play on differences of opinion within the Air Ministry, pointing out that its technical expert, General Engineer Reinhard Bullinger, was totally at odds with Cejka of the Industry Office and considered it "absurd" to think that the VDM could satisfy its need for semi-finished products by controlling the shares of a drop forge work. In Bullinger's view, if Martin Miller needed

78   A brief history of the VDM can be found in the list of holdings of company records held by the Hessisches Wirtschaftsarchiv (http://www .hessischeswirtschaftsarchiv.de).

79   BAB, R 8121/640, Aerobank to CA, Feb. 15, 1944.
80   BA-CA, CA-IB, Miller, 11/02, Manske memorandum of Feb. 26, 1944.

a close connection with another enterprise, then it was with one that produced iron and steel and could satisfy its raw materials needs. Manske had also been supplied with ammunition against the VDM by the Lower Danube Gau administration, which had also consulted experts and similarly came to the conclusion that the VDM offered nothing to Martin Miller from a production standpoint. And this was not all. The head of the Munitions Ministry Ring for Forged Products, Director Gerhardt, stated at a meeting on November 4, 1943, that he would not pay heed to a purely financial transaction such as the transfer of shares to the VDM in determining the allocation of forged products, and he shared the view that Martin Miller needed a connection with a raw materials producer. Nevertheless, Manske pointed out, the VDM, apparently "at the wish of certain circles," was striving with all the means at its disposal to gain control of the majority of the shares of Martin Miller.

In Manske's view, one had to do the right thing technically and have Martin Miller ally with an iron and steel producer. Investigations and discussions had shown that the right choice would be the "Berg & Hütte" concern, which could supply Martin Miller with an additional 6–7,000 tons monthly. Martin Miller and the CA, therefore, intended to ask the Ministry of Munitions, that is, the ministry of Albert Speer, to transfer the shares at the Aerobank back to the CA and to offer "Berg & Hütte" an option on them. At the same time, "Berg & Hütte" would be assigned the task of providing the needed iron and steel for the planned expansion of Martin Miller and would be informed of the processes involved insofar as this was deemed necessary.

The enthusiasm for "Berg & Hütte" was not purely technical and certainly not accidental. The Berg- und Hüttenwerksgesellschaft, which had its headquarters in Teschen, was a holding company active primarily in Silesia, the Sudetenland, the Protectorate. It was headed by Hans Malzacher, an old associate of the CA. Malzacher was more than just a major industrialist at this point, however: he was also one of Speer's "crown princes," serving as Speer's

deputy for the organization of the armaments industry in the Southeast. He was thus also closely associated with the very powerful Walther Schieber, the head of the Armaments Delivery Agency. These personal connections were all the more valuable to the CA because Speer's Munitions Ministry had taken over the planning functions of the Air Ministry in August 1944, and this meant that Martin Miller was no longer subject to Cejka's office in matters of planning but rather to Gerhardt's Ring for Forged Products in the Munitions Ministry. This constellation of personalities and bureaucratic structures opened up the opportunities that the CA was now pursuing.[81]

It is difficult to tell exactly when Director Friedl, who was the chief actor for the CA in 1943–1944, contacted Malzacher about the Martin Miller situation. In November 1940, he telegraphed Malzacher that the Ring for Forged Products had overturned previous Air Ministry plans in connection with the VDM and Martin Miller and that he had contacted the Gau leadership. The question was who was in charge of planning. Gauleiter Jury was taking the position that he would accept VDM participation in Martin Miller if it was under the Air Ministry but would not do so if it was under the Munitions Ministry and needed an association with a heavy industrial firm. Friedl found the situation especially difficult because questions of planning and production policy were normally settled by the chief shareholders, but it was by no means clear in this instance who the chief shareholders were. He asked Malzacher to send him a telegram he could use with the Gau leadership to say that the matters would be cleared up soon and thus hold up any action that might help the VDM. In Friedl's view, the Gau leadership was overlooking what he viewed to be the central question, namely, whether Martin Miller should ally with a raw

81 On the organization of Speer's ministry, see Dietrich Eichholtz, *Geschichte der Deutschen Kriegswirtschaft 1939–1945*, 3 vols. (Berlin 1984–1996), vol. 2, pp. 327–391, vol. 3, chs. I–II, VII, and see also, Militärgeschichtliches Forschungsamt (ed.), *Germany and the Second World War* (Oxford 2003), vol. 5, part 2.

materials producer or a manufacturer. At the same time, Friedl and Glatzl appealed directly to the Munitions Ministry to argue their case and particularly to oppose the VDM idea that Martin Miller become in effect a sole supplier to the VDM because other customers such as the Flugmotorenwerke Ostmark might have to be given priority. In the CA's view, Martin Miller needed a raw materials supplier, and this was the view also taken by Director Gerhardt of the Ring for Forged Products.[82]

These developments at the end of 1943 seemed promising and formed the background for the Manske memorandum of February 26, 1944, but matters remained unsettled and confused in the late winter and early spring. This became evident in a report by Glatzl on a conversation with Director von Gadolla of the Berg & Hütte AG, who reported on a conversation with Malzacher. The latter had told him that the Speer ministry had suddenly come up with a new division of the Martin Miller shares whereby the CA would have 15 percent, the VDM 26 percent, the Krainischen Eisenindustrie Aßling 51 percent, and the remainder would be sold to the public. Both Malzacher and Gadolla were outraged by this totally new and surprising proposal. Malzacher pointed out that Aßling had very high costs, was endangered by partisan attacks, and could supply only 50 tons of steel, not the 1,500 needed for the projected new program. He found this solution totally unacceptable. Aside from the objections stated, he also had an obvious and open interest in Martin Miller himself. Traismauer had developed splendidly, and General Director Pleiger had recently told Malzacher that he was most impressed with the production there as well as its ability to pay off its debts, and he considered it an excellent investment even for the postwar period. Malzacher, who had invested 250,000 RM in a Polish smelting plant, was anxious to find something better and was

prepared to put his money in Traismauer if the CA would welcome him as a partner. He proposed that he suggest to Speer that, should this combination be accepted, he would personally take over the management of Traismauer, take 5 percent of the shares held by the Aerobank on his own account while offering 15 percent to the VDM, and leave the CA with 80 percent. Not surprisingly, Glatzl felt certain that the CA would welcome such an arrangement. Malzacher also urged that Director Manske join forces with Gadolla, who was his chief aide, and that they both go to Gauleiter Jury to persuade him of what needed to be done and that the CA follow up with a visit of its own to Jury. Malzacher's proposal, of course, changed the terms of the discussion. Its most immediate effect was a decision by Schieber, after discussion with Field Marshall Erhard Milch, to appoint Malzacher as chairman of the Martin Miller supervisory board regardless of how the shares were to be divided. Schieber emphasized that it was important to have an iron industry man at the summit of the company who had both technical competence and enjoyed the confidence of everyone involved. Manifestly, this was a clear victory for the heavy industrial solution.[83]

It was not until summer that matters were finally settled, however. In early July, Malzacher telegraphed Friedl that Cejka had proposed that the CA get 74 percent of the shares and the Aerobank 26 percent, and that the CA give Malzacher 5 percent. He believed that Cejka might also desire a supervisory board seat. Malzacher urged the CA to accept this offer. Friedl, of course, was extraordinarily grateful to Malzacher and had no objections whatsoever to working with the Aerobank. He was also quite prepared to see a supervisory board with Malzacher as chairman and himself as deputy chairman serving along with Glatzl to represent the CA, Rudof and Cejka sitting for the Aerobank, and Gau Economic Advisor Waibl representing Gauleiter Jury. Under the agreement finally reached at the end of the

[82] BA-CA, CA-IB, Miller, 11/02, Friedl to Malzacher, Nov. 20 and Dec. 10, 1943; CA and the Ministry for Armaments and War Production, Dec. 10, 1943; Ring for Forged Products to Gau Economic Advisor Waibl, Frankfurt, Dec. 7, 1943.

[83] Ibid., Glatzl memorandum of March 13, 1944, and Schieber to Jury.

month, the Aerobank would hold 26 percent of the shares through the purchase of Schmidt & Clemens shares in its possession, and the remaining shares would be sold back to the CA, which would also buy Martin Miller shares held by the company itself and scattered shares owned by private persons. It would then hold 74 percent of the shares, and Malzacher would purchase a 5 percent share in the company.[84] The Aerobank seems also to have been satisfied with this arrangement, paying 1,300,000 RM for its portion of the Schmidt & Clemens shares, while the CA paid 1,190,000 RM to get back the remainder.[85]

The convoluted history of the ownership of Martin Miller between 1938 and 1945 is a revealing case study of the forces at play in the business history of the Third Reich with the special twist of the problems created by the CA's efforts to maintain its character as an industrial concern. Its success against very substantial reservations in the Air Ministry bureaucracy and against private business interests eager to take over Martin Miller owed everything to the capacity of the CA leadership to wheel and deal in the Byzantine environment of agencies and firms vying for position in the war economy. One should not overlook the fact that through all of this, the CA management board considered Martin Miller a lucrative investment and played a very direct and active role in its affairs. A lengthy and detailed report on Traismauer of October 2, 1944, shows that the investment in the plants and their expansion had produced very satisfactory results, and that Pleiger had been correct in praising its progress just as Malzacher was wise in involving himself in its affairs. Its sales had increased from 3,676,736 RM in 1941 to 12,315,428 RM in 1942 to 16,579,776 RM in 1943. It had twenty-five customers who paid more than 50,000 RM for its products, including Daimler-Benz, Henschel, the Flugmotorenwerk Ostmark, and Junkers. Its

largest customer was the VDM Luftfahrtwerke, providing 6,202,000 RM in receipts in 1943. The VDM had obviously been a very good customer, and it had better claims in this capacity than as a supplier. Similarly, it was not totally out of line for the Air Ministry to have considered the Krainische Eisen, Aßling as a suitable partner in the capacity of a supplier of raw materials because it provided 1,462,000 RM in deliveries to Traismauer in 1943, and was second only to the Silesiastahl in Gleiwitz, which provided 1,547,000 RM in deliveries in 1943. It was, however, disadvantaged by transport problems and partisan warfare. Manifestly, the situation of the firm became more precarious and uncertain in 1944–1945, but it was hardly alone in this respect. An important measure of its increased production was the blue-collar labor force, which increased from 135 in 1939 to 1,474 as of December 1, 1943. Only 783 were native workers; 298 were "Ostarbeiter" and 393 were POWs. In 1944, the number of blue-collar workers stood at 1,704, 1,027 of whom were Germans, 334 of whom were "Ostarbeiter," and 334 of whom were POWs. Separate barracks had to be provided for the different categories of worker. Special kitchen facilities also had to be provided for foreign workers who were not treated equally with the German workers. The firm had very few skilled workers, most of those supplied by the labor offices requiring training.[86]

The CA watched over these workforce questions and had very pronounced views on how they were handled. On October 5, 1944, Glatzl complained to the Martin Miller management board about its plan to replace the entire workforce in the forging plant with concentration camp labor, pointing out that "serious production losses are unavoidable through the change in the workforce and besides this the drop in productivity will necessarily lead to financial setbacks for the enterprise, which is in the

[84]   Ibid., telegram from Malzacher to Friedl, undated; Friedl to Malzacher, July 10, 1944; Friedl to Malzacher, July 28, 1944.

[85]   BAB, R 8121/123, Aerobank to CA, Sept. 2, 1944.

[86]   BA-CA, CA-IB, Miller, 11/07-08, report of Oct. 2, 1944. I have used the 1943 figures provided by Referat Ketterer, which differ somewhat from those in this report and which also provide the figures for 1944, ibid., 27/04.

process of expansion."[87] Unless the authorities were demanding the use of such labor, the CA disapproved of it at Traismauer. Furthermore, Friedl had discussed the issue with Gau Economic Advisor Waibl and Malzacher, and both were of the same opinion as the CA. The CA thus insisted on being informed about this type of decision. There is no reason to think that humane considerations were involved here. In the same communication, the CA also asked the management board not to hire consultants on the basis of one- or two-year contracts that required the company to provide wages to their wives should they be drafted. Here, too, the CA asked that the supervisory board be consulted before such contracts were made. The CA, as a large shareholder, was thus fully cognizant of the labor practices of the firms in its concern and took an active role in determining them where this seemed possible or desirable.

In the case of Martin Miller, the CA fought a successful battle to maintain an important holding. In the case of Teudloff-Vamag Vereinigte Armaturen- und Maschinenfabriken AG, by contrast, the CA battled to recover a position it had been forced to surrender in 1938. Teudloff-Vamag, a manufacturer of valves and fittings, had been reorganized under CA auspices in 1934 and became a part of the CA concern, which owned 85 percent of its stock. By 1938, thanks to the CA support and the work of a talented director, Hans Liebl, Teudloff-Vamag had been transformed into a very modern producer that satisfied nearly all of Austria's domestic needs. As noted in Chapter 1 of this study, the Vereinigte Armaturengesellschaft (VAG), Mannheim, a sales syndicate of the six largest valve and fittings producers in Germany, used its connection with the RWM and, with the support of Bürckel, laid claim to majority control of Teudloff-Vamag. It claimed that firms in the syndicate had already been engaged with an Austrian predecessor company before 1934 and were thus seeking to restore their historical position. They justified their demands by pointing to their RWM contracts and arguing

that Teudloff-Vamag would cease to be competitive once Austria became integrated into the German economy because its prices were 60 percent above German levels, primarily because of high raw materials costs. Additionally, Teudloff-Vamag had been negotiating with the VAG for the license to produce drop coat hydrants, and this added to the leverage that the German syndicate could exercise. The CA was thus forced to join the syndicate and negotiate away its majority, dealing primarily with General Director Fritz Reuther of the most important firm in the syndicate, Bopp & Reuther, GmbH, Mannheim-Waldhof. Under the terms of the agreement, the CA sold off 51 percent of the shares and joined the syndicate for a five-year period ending on June 14, 1943. If the syndicate was then terminated, then another 25 percent of the shares was to be sold to the VAG. Under the 1938 agreement, the CA was to remain the chief supplier of credits to Teudloff-Vamag no matter what the distribution of the shares so that the company retained its "Austrian" character. The capital of the company was increased at the end of 1940 from 1 million to 1.5 million RM, the CA taking 250,000 RM of the new shares. At this point, the CA owned 43.2 percent of the shares, while the VAG owned 53.2 percent, with the remainder in the hands of small shareholders. For reasons to be explained later, the CA had sold an additional 231 shares to the VAG in 1939. After the lapse of the syndicate in June 1943, the total VAG holding amounted to about 78 percent of the shares, while the CA retained 19 percent.[88]

From the very beginning, the leadership of the CA had been extraordinarily unhappy

[87] Ibid., Miller, 11/02, CA to Martin Miller AG management board, Oct. 5, 1944.

[88] See Chapter 1, p. 83. BA-CA, CA-IB, Referat Glatzl, 47/01-02, undated postwar report, ibid., 47/05, reports by Kurt Stadtl for Hans Friedl, Dec. 15, 1941, May 10, 1944; BA-CA, CA-V, CA executive committee meeting, Jan. 20, 1939 and management board meeting, Dec. 4, 1940. The German members of the syndicate were: Bopp & Reuther GmbH, Mannheim; Klein, Schanzlin & Becker AG, Frankenthal (Pfalz); Pörringer & Schindler, Zweibrücken; Breuerwerke GmbH, Frankfurt-Höchst; A.L.G. Dehne, Halle/Saale; Amag-Hilpert AG, Nürnberg.

about what it came to view as the rapacity of the VAG. In the spring of 1939, for example, Reuter asked the CA to sell 300 shares so that Bopp & Reuther could increase its holding to 25 percent, while the other members of the syndicate could increase their holdings proportionately. Heller, however, was only willing to provide enough shares for Bopp & Reuther to get its desired 25 percent and for the others to get a proportionate amount. He would only sell 231 shares. Heller bluntly told Reuther: "As you know, the Creditanstalt-Bankverein has no interest in selling further shares. I only could carry out your wish with the consent of my colleagues because I could claim that the participation of Bopp & Reuther on the enterprise at 25 percent would bring your firm certain advantages. For the Creditanstalt it was undoubtedly a sacrifice to reduce its participation in the capital of Teudloff-Vamag A.G., for the enterprise is flourishing and our obligations to it will practically remain the same whether we have more or fewer shares."[89]

Relations between the CA and the VAG worsened rapidly for both production and financial reasons. The production problem was that Hans Liebl came to the conclusion that the future of Teudloff-Vamag lay in the production of steel products for the oil and chemical industries rather than the cast iron products produced by the VAG companies. There was no oil industry in the old Reich and thus little incentive to produce steel cast valves and fittings, and there were also no patents, so that Liebl could only learn about them from American journals and publications. However, he also acquired considerable direct experience with steel cast production. The one company that had produced for the Galician, Romanian, and Hungarian oil industries was Mannesmann-Trauzl, where Liebl had worked between 1927 and 1933. Hans Leibl's son Rudolf had also worked for Mannesmann-Trauzl before joining Teudloff-Vamag to head its sales department. They were both dead set on having Teudloff-Vamag specialize in the area and

become the leading firm in the entire Reich. Nevertheless, they encountered nothing but frustration in dealing with the VAG concern, which treated the production of steel cast products, in which they had no experience whatever, with great skepticism and refused to lend their support. Only the CA was willing to provide the necessary funding for the new product line. Whatever common interests existed at the time of the syndicate agreement had evaporated by 1941–1942, and CA officials came to view the VAG as a hostile force. They believed that the VAG had only demanded control of Teudloff-Vamag because it wished to eliminate competition, and they thought that it was trying to hold back Teudloff-Vamag's development in order to drive down the value of its shares in preparation for the period after the syndicate contract lapsed in June 1943 so that it could acquire the shares to which it was entitled on the cheap. In the meantime, the CA was bearing the total burden of the credits, which amounted to 2.8 million RM at the end of 1942 and which had been almost totally used up. The company now employed 600 workers, which was four times the number employed in 1938.[90]

By the spring of 1944, the suspicion and bad feeling toward the VAG had grown considerably. In the CA's view, the VAG had first blocked and then slowed down the development of Teudloff-Vamag out of ignorance and also out of venal motives. Reuther and his colleagues had constantly stressed the financial weakness of Teudloff-Vamag, pointing to its relatively limited capital when compared to its large credits, and had even inquired if the CA would not perhaps wish to give up its connection with the company entirely. The goal was certainly to put pressure on the CA to accept a lower price for the shares it had to sell off to the VAG under the agreement. But the CA also suspected that Bopp & Reuther, which had considerable capital of its own, wanted to take over the financing of Teudloff-Vamag or turn it over to another bank. The CA, however, had every reason to be satisfied with the way its credits had been used.

[89] BA-CA, CA-IB, Referat Glatzl, 47/01–02, Heller to Reuther, June 28, 1939.

[90] Ibid., Referat Glatzl, 47/05, report by Carl Stahl for Director Friedl, Dec. 15, 1942.

The company's turnover had increased from 3,225,000 RM in 1938 to 9,485,000 RM in 1943, and profits having also increased substantially. The CA leadership was prepared to both test the terms of the agreement and to press the issue of the price for the 25 percent of the shares to be sold to the VAG. Because no actual date for the sale of the shares had been set, the CA was quite prepared to drag things out and hold out for a fairer arrangement. At the supervisory board meeting of the syndicate on July 15, 1943, Friedl took the position that the shares were worth well over 200 percent of par, but also that the conditions had changed since the agreement had been made and that Teudloff-Vamag no longer belonged to the same category of producer to which it had been assigned at the time of the agreement. Indeed, Friedl now offered to pay 200 percent for the shares in the hands of the VAG! This was not only a turning of the tables on Reuther, but it also placed the onus of dragging things out on the VAG, which had anticipated that the value of the would be much lower than it was. Furthermore, the CA was prepared to accuse the VAG of trying to sabotage the favorable development of the company. The VAG sought to strike back with legal claims and also by making conditions very difficult for Hans and Rudolf Liebl. The former resigned his position in the spring of 1944, and Rudolf threatened to do so, but the CA was set on doing everything possible to stand behind him in recognition that the wartime success of the firm was largely the doing of him and his father. As was usually the case, the labor behind such success was of a somewhat dubious nature. In 1943, Teudloff-Vamag employed 536 workers, of whom 236 were Germans, 195 were foreigners, and 105 were POWs. The battle between the CA and the VAG seems to have remained unsettled even after the war, but the CA and Rudolf Liebl joined forces to found a successor company, the Österreichische Armaturen-Gesellschaft mbH, in 1947.[91]

Unlike the cases of Martin Miller and Teudloff-Vamag, the other CA holdings in the machine and metal industry went basically unchallenged, but all had to convert to some form of war production in order to survive, and the CA necessarily became involved in assisting this process in its own interest. A striking example of this was Hutter & Schrantz, a producer of wire mesh, grids, and woven felt that dated back to the past century. The firm was increasingly engaged in metalworking even though it was also regarded as a textile producer. It prospered even under the difficult economic circumstances of the post-1918 period and, in 1938, boasted seven factories in Austria, two in Czechoslovakia, and one in Hungary. Of these ten factories, only three produced textile products, and the rest were engaged in metalworking. The firm did a considerable amount of export business.[92]

It continued to do so even after the war began but encountered significant difficulties independent of the increasing priority given to war production. As was so often the case with exporters, Hutter & Schrantz had previously employed Jewish sales representatives, and they had to be replaced despite the difficulties involved. In February 1940, the management board decided to fire its Jewish sales agents in Holland, Romania, Hungary, Peru, India, Egypt, and Palestine.[93] An even more serious problem was an order given by the authorities in Berlin in the spring of 1941 that German firms were no longer to service Jewish firms abroad or firms that were considered hostile to Germany. Orders placed by such customers after April 2, 1941, were not to be filled. This produced a host of dilemmas. One major problem, of course, was figuring out whether a customer was Jewish, let alone anti-German. In instances where one did know, as in the case of the important Hungarian market where the field was dominated by Jews, the losses were far greater for an Austrian firm like Hutter & Schrantz than for

---

[91] This account is based on the report of Carl Stahl to Hans Friedl, May 10, 1944, and a note to Friedl of May 11, 1944, ibid. On the post-1945 history, see *Festschrift für Josef Joham*, pp. 39–42.

[92] See *Festschrift für Josef Joham*, pp. 135–143.

[93] BA-CA, CA-IB, Hutter & Schrantz, 09/02, Hutter & Schrantz management board meeting, Feb. 27, 1940.

Reich firms, which did much less business with Hungary. Needless to say, holding up deliveries was damaging to the customers, who were inclined to look elsewhere for their woven felt products. This meant that one could lose such customers even if they turned out not to fall in the prohibited categories or even if they were subsequently Aryanized. At the same time, Hutter & Schrantz was stuck with the ordered material, which was especially burdensome if one were dealing with a customized order that could not be sold elsewhere.[94] The CA, and especially Director Rudolf Pfeiffer, who was assigned to deal with the firm, was informed of these problems, but there is no evidence that it could do anything about them. At the same time, the CA did assist Hutter & Schrantz with its business in Poland, where its branches in the Generalgouvernement were quite helpful in providing contracts.[95]

Director Pfeiffer of the CA was often very directly involved in the management of Hutter & Schrantz. Its superannuated and ailing leadership had been the subject of complaints from the Party.[96] This was no small matter because the company employed 2,000 persons in 1939, and Pfeiffer actually had to function as plant leader intermittently. In October 1941, for example, Pfeiffer attended a meeting of the nine plant stewards and with the new plant leader, Director Heinrich Kral, made a point of assuring everyone that, although he was turning responsibility over to Kral, he would continue to devote as much time and energy to Hutter & Schrantz as his schedule would allow and would visit its plants. While much of the discussion pertained to wages and similar issues, there were serious political questions to be considered as well. The plant steward at the Pinkafeld factory reported that the mood in his plant was good and added for the record that Pinkafeld workers had been strongly supportive of National Socialism even

before 1938.[97] Nevertheless, after the invasion of Russia in June, some underground Communist propaganda showed up, but the perpetrators were found out and arrested by the Gestapo, thus quieting things down. Another plant steward in Vienna also reported on unrest following the beginning of the war in Russia, which he attributed to letters from soldiers at the eastern front.

Hutter & Schrantz's wartime fate depended in large measure on how successful it was in transforming itself into a producer for the war economy. A great deal of effort was therefore, expended in acquiring military contracts and getting certified as an armaments plant. The management board meeting on December 1, 1939, reported "very colossal liquidity as the result of larger receipts for military deliveries and other payments."[98] Representatives of the company met regularly with military authorities to determine how the company could qualify as a military producer, and they seem to have been very successful in their efforts despite the call up of workers from time to time.[99] The dialogue between company representatives and the Armaments Inspectorate was increasingly characterized by an insistence on the part of the latter that peacetime production was of no interest whatever and that production for the war effort would receive full support, while the former sought to argue that it was ready to release workers to the army but that it was inefficient to send away experienced workers.[100]

What saved the day for Hutter & Schrantz in the end was the conviction on the part of the military authorities, strongly encouraged by Ostmark Governor Baldur von Schirach and Gau Economic Advisor Walter Rafelsberger, that the company was ideally suited to produce generators. Pfeiffer was especially enthusiastic and insisted that the managers of Hutter & Schrantz do everything possible to get into the generator-producing business. At a meeting in

94 See ibid., Hutter & Schrantz, 09/03, Hanatschek to Pfeiffer and Eberharter, and memorandum of Nov. 11, 1941.
95 See the correspondence of 1940 in ibid.
96 See ibid., the Gau Economic Advisor to Pfeiffer, April 5, 1939.

97 Ibid., meeting of Oct. 7, 1941.
98 Ibid., Hutter & Schrantz, 09/02, Hutter & Schrantz management board, Dec. 1, 1939.
99 See, for example, the reports of July 19 and Sept. 16, 1940, in ibid.
100 See ibid., report of March 3, 1941.

January 1943, Rafelsberger argued in the strongest possible terms that the Ostmark plants were particularly well suited to produce generators and that Hutter & Schrantz had to dismiss all reservations and objections and persuade its workers that the company's future, not only in war but also in peace, lay in the production of generators, particularly for trucks and other vehicles.[101] Such production was not without its problems. The authorities in Berlin had the habit of changing the types of generators they wanted to order, but the firm seems to have overcome this and other difficulties; in July 1944, the management reported that the financial situation was satisfactory above all because of the money being made on generators. Furthermore, because the firm produced for the army, navy, and air force, it was able to deal with the procurement instabilities that otherwise plagued generator production.[102] There can be no question that Hutter & Schrantz was one of the CA's most promising holdings, even under the dismal conditions of 1944.

Another was the Eisenwarenfabriken Lapp-Finze AG. Headquartered in Kalsdorf bei Graz, this producer of steel wire, screws, locks, fittings, rivets, nuts, and bolts had been founded in 1868. The CA owned 60 percent of the company's stock; the remainder was spread among small shareholders. In addition to its production facilities in Kalsdorf, Lapp-Finze also had a small plant in Lembach-Feistritz near Marburg/Maribor, which had served as the productive facility for its Yugoslav holding in Zagreb, the firm Zeljeso-prometno. Changes in Yugoslav commercial law in 1938 significantly limited the capacity of either Lapp-Finze or the CA to direct the affairs of Zeljeso-prometno, but the Yugoslav holding did prove useful in serving Lapp-Finze's ability to reduce competition in the region. The CA also held the shares of a metalwares plant in Sopron controlled by Lapp-Finze, but here again local national interests limited German control.[103]

Following the Anschluss, Lapp-Finze's chief concerns were to get public contracts and modernize and rationalize its operations so as to be competitive with its old Reich rivals. To secure public contracts, it had to demonstrate its character as an Aryan firm, and the leading director at Lapp-Finze, Hans Hartung, worked hand in hand with Director Heller of the CA in getting the only Jew on the administrative council, Alexander Mamorstein, to step down in March 1938 and in obtaining the approval of the authorities so that Lapp-Finze could get contracts to supply its wares to the Vienna street car company.[104] The chief focus of the firm, however, was on rationalization and increasing production in light of the new circumstances, and it could boast considerable success by the end of 1938. It thereupon launched an investment program to expand its production facilities and enter into military production.[105] Once the war started, Lapp-Finze's increased capacity impressed the military authorities, and it was soon the recipient of important military contracts from both the Luftwaffe and the army.[106]

The destruction of the Yugoslav state in the spring of 1941 opened up important opportunities for Lapp-Finze. It was able to take full control of its plant in Lembach-Feistritz, which was now located on German territory, and provide security for a CA credit of 50,000 RM for Lembach-Feistritz in June 1941. This was increased by 25,000 RM in August.[107] The facilities at Lembach-Feistritz were relatively small, however, and by no means modern. Lapp-Finze could also now seriously contemplate acquiring new manufacturing facilities in the region that complemented its own production and offered additional advantages. The firm in question was the Titan AG, which was located in the

[101] Ibid., supervisory board meetings, Jan. 3 and Feb. 1, 1943.
[102] Ibid., Hutter & Schrantz, 09/05, report of July 17, 1944.

[103] This information is culled from the documentation in BA-CA, CA-IB, Lapp-Finze, 10/01 and Lapp-Finze, 10/10.
[104] Ibid., Lapp-Finze, 10/01, correspondence between Hartung and Heller, March 26–31, 1938.
[105] See ibid., the report to the administrative council, Feb. 28, 1939.
[106] Ibid., Lapp-Finze, 10/09, memorandum, Nov. 8, 1940.
[107] BA-CA, CA-V, CA board of management meetings, June 3 and Aug. 18, 1941.

southern Carinthian town of Stein in the vicinity of Laibach/Ljubljana. What made the company particularly attractive, in addition to the fact that it had been very profitable, was that it produced a line of products that complemented the production program of Lapp-Finze and that it had a foundry, something Lapp-Finze lacked.

It is significant that Director Friedl of the CA played a very active role in promoting the acquisition of Titan for Lapp-Finze. Following the German victory and occupation of the Carinthian territory to be annexed, Titan was placed under the control of the civilian administration and its sale would require its approval. As early as May 1941, Friedl was able to inform Hartung that the shares were owned by three shareholders, none of whom had a majority. One of them, Titan's general director, Nikola Kostrencic, appeared ready to sell and expressed a willingness to contact the other shareholders and arrange a meeting in Vienna toward this end. Friedl was worried, however, that one of the German banks might buy the Jugoslavische Bank AG and then proceed to find other parties with an interest in Titan. It was important, therefore, to win the support of the Gau Economic Office for an acquisition by Lapp-Finze.[108] When Hartung pursued this avenue, however, he soon stumbled on a number of complications. The Gau economic advisor in Klagenfurt, Winkler, informed him that there could be no disposition of Titan until its ownership and status were clarified in Agram/Zagreb. Discussions with members of the Chamber of Commerce in Klagenfurt gave Hartung the feeling that there were forces and persons trying to sabotage Lapp-Finze's efforts and to have Titan acquired by a Carinthian industrialist. He told Friedl that speed was necessary and suggested that the CA's acquisition of the shares would give it an advantage in further efforts to win over Winkler and the authorities. Friedl, however, seems not to have taken any further steps, and in early November a much-alarmed Hartung learned that a number of firms were vying for Titan and urged Friedl to use his connections

to acquire Titan for Lapp-Finze. Friedl, however, refused to intervene directly and suggested that the CA branch in Krainburg be brought into play because it had direct contact with the local authorities. He also noted that if matters dragged out, a point could come when Titan would no longer be of great interest because the urgency created by the wartime situation could evaporate, and Lapp-Finze then could well take care of constructing its own foundry after the war. Friedl did in fact immediately contact the branch in Krainburg and asked it to ascertain where things stood with the authorities and whether it would be possible to get detailed information about Titan, inspect the works, and negotiate with the owners about a transfer to German hands. Nevertheless, Hartung was set on acquiring Titan and thought the foundry would continue to be important after the war. Manifestly, he felt it essential that the CA be more energetic in its approach.[109]

Friedl, however, was really fully behind the effort, and the branch in Krainburg was providing valuable intelligence. He had learned, for example, that Lapp-Finze's application to acquire Titan had never been answered because there were other contenders, most notably the Carinthian chemical industrialist Auer von Welsbach. Also, Lapp-Finze had not applied to the proper agency and was urged to direct its next application to Gau Finance Officer Meinrad Natmessnig. Hartung was advised to make his appeal by describing Lapp-Finze in some detail, stressing that it had been the winner of the Gau Diploma and its other National Socialist accomplishments. He was to stress that Titan was intended both to complement the operations in Kalsdorf and also to continue exporting to Croatia, something that Lapp-Finze had been doing for years anyway. He was also to state that Lapp-Finze had sufficient financial resources for the purchase and the operation of Titan. In short, Hartung was to say that "we are applicants with expertise whose

[108] BA-CA, CA-IB, Lapp-Finze, 10/09, Friedl to Hartung, May 21, 1941.

[109] Ibid., Hartung to Friedl, July 29, 1941; Hartung to Friedl, Nov. 6, 1941; Friedl to Hartung, Nov. 10, 1941; Friedl to the Krainburg branch, Nov. 10, 1941; Hartung to Friedl, Nov. 27, 1941.

point of departure is not profits from the boom but rather genuine constructive work." On this basis, Hartung was to ask to be taken into the competition, be allowed to conduct an inspection of the works, and be supplied with needed information. He was also to emphasize that they had business dealings with the Croatian shareholders and that the shareholders were willing to negotiate. Finally, Hartung was to keep the Krainburg branch and its director, Leopold Faiß, informed and work closely with him.[110]

This approach seems to have worked; only a few days after making the application in this manner, Natmessnig informed Lapp-Finze that it was considered a legitimate applicant for the purchase of Titan. He pointed out that the Gau had actually assumed ownership of Titan in September. As the only agency that could arrange the sale, it was eager to sell Titan and place it in "good hands." Lapp-Finze was invited to send four or five persons to inspect Titan and was also supplied with the requisite financial information. The CA was obviously playing an important and effective role in orchestrating Lapp-Finze's effort with respect to Titan, but it also was directly engaged in assessing Titan's value. Hans Moessmer of the CA Industrial Section had already evaluated Titan on the basis of information available to him and concluded that some of the assessments of its value were excessive, a position shared to some extent by Hartung. It appeared that the purchase price, whatever it was, would have to be supplemented with modernization investments. Hartung was anxious to have the CA represented in any personal inspection of Titan, which Natmessnig did not quite understand. In late December, he asked Faiß why the CA was so interested in Titan, and Faiß had to explain that Lapp-Finze belonged to the CA concern and that the CA was assisting as an intermediary. Natmessnig informed Faiß that the Dresdner Bank was complaining that the CA was trying to sell Titan to foreigners, which was obviously false but also a good illustration of the competitive techniques the Dresdner Bank employed in the recently acquired territories.

Faiß also learned that Auer von Welsbach was showing renewed interest in Titan, and he was by no means alone. Lapp-Finze's achievement by the end of 1941, therefore, was to be in the running for Titan. It owed much to Friedl and Faiß for having come so far, but matters were anything but settled.[111]

The best evidence for this was that Lapp-Finze did not finally take over Titan until the spring of 1943. To be sure, matters seemed settled at the beginning of that year when Friedl reported to the management board that an agreement had been reached with the Croatian shareholders under which Lapp-Finze was to take over Titan including all its physical assets, creditors, and good debts for 1.4 million RM. It was anticipated that Titan would be integrated into Lapp-Finze and run as "Plant II," thereby reducing personnel costs. The CA cash credit for Lapp-Finze was raised by 1.5 million RM to cover this purpose, thus bringing the total to 2 million RM.[112]

The actual takeover of Titan, however, depended on the approval of the Gauleiter of Carinthia, Friedrich Rainer, and it was not until spring that he finally decided to approve the sale to Lapp-Finze. The general inclination was to give Titan to some local Carinthian industrialist, probably Auer von Welsbach, and Lapp-Finze was forced to play the same music provided by the CA's orchestration advice of 1941, only this time more forcefully and loudly. In a memorandum of May 28, 1943, it reiterated all the technical reasons militating for a takeover by Lapp-Finze, especially the fact that it made good sense for Titan to be acquired by a company producing the same products. Once again, Lapp-Finze stressed its National Socialist character and the fact that it had now received three Gau diplomas, so that it was qualified to take over Titan for not only good business reasons but also because of its fine political reputation.

[110] Ibid., Friedl to Hartung, Dec. 1, 1941.

[111] Ibid., Natmessnig to Lapp-Finze, Dec. 8, 1941; Hartung to Friedl, Dec. 16 and 18, 1941; Faiß to Friedl, Dec. 22, 1941; Friedl to Faiß, Dec. 22, 1941; Friedl to Hartung, Dec. 22, 1941.

[112] BA-CA, CA-V, report by Friedl to the CA working committee, Jan. 27, 1943 and CA management board meeting, Jan. 7, 1943.

Lapp-Finze claimed that "it certainly is understandable that the Carinthian Gau would give preference to a Carinthian competitor if he had the same qualifications in a technical, commercial, and financial respect and if thereby not only the continuation of the present operation in Stein but also the expansion and further development appeared guaranteed. It can be stated without immodesty on the part of Lapp-Finze, that a comparison in this respect with the other applicants falls in its favor."[113]

Perhaps Lapp-Finze won out through its arguments, but certainly of great importance was the person chosen to transmit its petition and to put in his own powerful support, namely, Hans Malzacher, a member of the Lapp-Finze supervisory board. Malzacher, of course, had also been general director of Lapp-Finze in 1934–1936 and spoke with experience and with great authority on the armaments industry. He straightforwardly asked Rainer to change his position because he considered it impossible for Titan to be turned over to a Carinthian industrialist when it was so obviously complementary to Lapp-Finze. He also placed special emphasis on the Titan foundry, which would compensate for the foundry at Sopron that had been lost after 1918. At the same time, he stressed that the combination would enable Lapp-Finze to compete successfully with the old Reich firms. He considered the Lapp-Finze acquisition of Titan healthy from an economic point of view and thus hoped that Rainer would get his economic advisor to also see the light. He concluded by asking Rainer to inform him of his decision, a request that strongly suggested there was yet another last word that might be spoken if the right one were not.[114]

This was a stunning illustration of the networks that so often determined business decisions in the Third Reich. This is not to say that the takeover of Titan was not economically rational, and perhaps the most remarkable thing was the number of obstacles that stood in the way of a rational solution, above all the provincial ambitions and considerations that were obviously influencing the decisions of the Carinthian authorities and held things up between the spring of 1941 and the spring of 1943. The CA was obviously very supportive of Lapp-Finze, and the firm was well provided with military contracts thanks to the energetic leadership of Hartung and his close alliance with Friedl and Malzacher. By 1944, of course, things were going badly even for so well situated a firm. The plants in Carinthia were plagued by increasingly violent partisan incursions, and the situation in Kalsdorf, despite its substantial supply of workers, including forced labor, became increasingly desperate because of nearby bombing raids and transportation dislocation. It suffered from shortages of supplies and the military's increasing tendency to reduce or cancel contracts. Nevertheless, the firm had developed considerably in the course of the war and had been favored by the CA with credits and backing, a condition that would continue after 1945.[115]

The CA's role in promoting the wartime adjustments and expansion of other holdings in the metalworking and machine industries was less complicated than Lapp-Finze but nevertheless of great importance. This certainly was true of the Kassen- Aufzugs- und Maschinenbau AG F. Wertheim & Co., an important producer of elevators, safes, cash registers, and steel office equipment. The CA owned almost 100 percent of the company's shares, which it inherited when it took over the Wiener Bankverein. The company had made the mistake of acquiring the Marchegger Maschinenfabrik at the beginning of the economic crisis and was in dire straits.

---

[113] BA-CA, CA-IB, Lapp-Finze, 10/09, Lapp-Finze petition, May 28, 1943.

[114] Ibid., Malzacher to Rainer, May 29, 1943.

[115] See the correspondence in ibid., especially Hartung to Moessmer, Dec. 21, 1944. See also *Festschrift für Josef Joham*, pp. 27–32. In 1944, the Karlsdorf plant employed 479 male and female workers, 100 of whom were foreigners and 19 of whom were POWs; see BA-CA, CA-IB, Referat Ketterer, 27/04. During the war Lapp-Finze employed 820 workers, 89 "Ostarbeiter" largely from the USSR, and British POWs. The rest came from a host of countries. See Stefan Karner, Peter Ruggenthaler, and Barbara Stelzl-Marx (eds.), *NS-Zwangsarbeit in der Rüstungsindustrie. Die Lapp-Finze AG in Kalsdorf bei Graz 1939–1945* (Graz 2004), p. 115.

But it was fortunate to come under the leadership of engineer Ernst Bruno in 1930, who sold off the Marchegger Maschinenfabrik and brought in new managers, who helped to turn things around. Not only was Wertheim thereby saved, but it also developed a very extensive and profitable export business. At the time of the Anschluss it was the leading elevator exporter in the Reich. Bruno seems to have been very effective in turning the Anschluss to his advantage. In May 1938, for example, when the military authorities in Vienna were ordering a large number of safes, he asked the CA to intervene with the authorities on Wertheim's behalf to prevent firms from the old Reich from entering the Vienna market. He pointed to the policy of promoting Austrian reconstruction through Austrian firms, and also to the fact that metal costs in Austria were so high that it could not successfully compete on the international market for safes and that Wertheim would be driven out of the domestic market if it were not favored with the local military contracts.[116] This effort was apparently very successful: Wertheim had what Bruno characterized as "enormous contracts" for safes in 1938–1939, and this was largely responsible for the success of the firm at this time.[117] Furthermore, while the elevator export business had fallen off in 1938–1939, Wertheim could still claim first place in this field and ask for special consideration. When Semperit was planning to order six large elevators for its plants in Wimpassing, Bruno appealed to Director Heller of the CA to intervene on its behalf with Semperit, pointing out that the RWM had instructed that strong exporters be favored as much as possible in the domestic market.[118]

The coming of the war further reduced the export business, and a ban on the production of steel safes and office equipment in the spring of 1940 put an end to most of Wertheim's

lucrative business in this area. This did not prevent Wertheim from expanding and prospering, however. Even before the war, the company's facilities had been found inadequate, and the CA supported both the acquisition of additional land and plants and the construction of a large new plant. The most important acquisition was the firm of Fr. Wiese & Co., which was to be Aryanized. Bruno was anxious to get hold of this company and its assets for two reasons. He wanted to make them available for Wertheim, and he was aware that old Reich competitors were interested in Wiese and intended to prevent the establishment of rival firms in Vienna. The CA supported this plan and, as a result, the Property Transfer Bureau agreed to a sale to Wertheim. After the war, it was to be the subject of a restitution claim launched by the Wiese family against Wertheim.[119] There was apparently no intention to hold on to Wiese or even some of the older and scattered production facilities in the long run, and the chief focus of attention for both Bruno and the CA was the acquisition of an available property and construction of a large new plant at an industrial site on the Wienerbergerstrasse.

The idea of building a large new facility dated as far back as 1908 and had been promoted by the Wiener Bankverein and then the CA. The latter decided to actually finance construction after the Anschluss, seeing this as the only way to compete with the old Reich competition. This decision also served as an occasion for Bruno to push Wertheim into the armaments business. The Weapons Office of the Supreme Command of the Army (OKH) approached Wertheim's Berlin representative in 1938 upon hearing of the construction plan, and it determined that the new factory building would be very suitable for the production of heavy machinery needed for military purposes and that Wertheim could acquire the necessary technical know-how. This was of immense importance once the war started because without the conversion to military production

[116] BA-CA, CA-IB, Wertheim, 17/04, Wertheim to CA, May 5, 1938.

[117] Ibid., Wertheim, 17/05, the development of Wertheim is described in a self-laudatory report by Bruno of June 11, 1941.

[118] Ibid., Wertheim, 17/04, Bruno to Heller, March 8, 1939.

[119] See ibid., Wertheim, 17/08, report for Heller, May 12, 1939, ibid. There is a very ample record of the case.

Wertheim would have been excluded from the supply of steel plate and its skilled workers and technicians would have been shifted to plants producing for the war effort. It would have been thrown back to its traditional role of manufacturing peacetime products but without having either the raw materials or the manpower it required. Thanks to the decision to build the new plant and to enter into military production, Wertheim became a privileged producer for the war effort.[120]

Construction of the new plant began in November 1939. The CA provided a special credit of 1.2 million RM specifically for this purpose in addition to a 1.4 million RM operating credit.[121] It also directly intervened twice with the military authorities in Vienna and Berlin on behalf of Fritz Waage, the architect in change of the construction, to secure him a temporary exemption from military service.[122] Despite such delays, Wertheim was able to fill military orders, and the military authorities were sufficiently satisfied to award the company further orders. Additionally, as has been noted earlier, Wertheim also took over the machinery and labor force of Rast & Gasser and converted it to military production. Bruno anticipated a stabilization of its production in 1942.

It is interesting to note that while Bruno concentrated on military production and was immensely proud of the medals and other forms of recognition bestowed on himself and his workers, he constantly had the firm's export business and peacetime production in mind. Although he admitted in June 1941 that elevator exports were down and largely limited to Romania and Bulgaria and that he faced tough competition from the Italians in Croatia, he still hoped for business in Greece. What he thought most important was that the company prepare for a rapid resumption of elevator and safe production once hostilities ceased. He did not want to see Wertheim overrun by the old Reich competition, declaring that "we have the intention of not giving up our leading role in exports to the Southeast and also to bring, along with Poland, the Sudetenland and Protectorate, and also South Germany into our marketing area."[123] In short, Bruno sought to do everything possible under wartime conditions to ensure Wertheim's competiveness when peace returned.

Wertheim apparently had considerable success in developing a market for its products in the east, setting up branches for its sales organization and technical bureaus in 1941–1942 in Riga, Warsaw, and Lemberg.[124] The CA seemed well satisfied with the results in September 1942. It decided to consolidate and extend its credits, both the 2,908,000 RM allocated for new construction and the 3 million RM cash credit. Wertheim had slightly overdrawn its construction credit because it had received permission to build a new office building, but it had used only half of its operating credit. The CA, therefore, decided to provide a single 4 million RM credit until June 30, 1943.[125] The company also paid reasonable dividends under the circumstances, 5 percent in 1941 and 3 percent in 1942. In 1943, it decided not to pay a dividend and to apply the money to amortization. Despite the cautious balance sheet policy of Wertheim, it had not only made full use of its credits by September 1944 to the tune of 4,278,000 RM but was also requesting an additional 1 million RM to run until July 1945. Wertheim had by this time reached the height of success as a producer for the military. It had very large contracts, but the military was neither giving advances nor paying its bills on time, in part because the military agencies in Berlin with which Wertheim dealt had been bombed. Wertheim was having to pay cash to its suppliers, who were in the same boat.[126]

---

120 Ibid., Wertheim, 17/05, Bruno report of June 11, 1941.
121 BA-CA, CA-V, CA management board meeting, Nov. 25, 1939.
122 Ibid., S.P. Akten 447, CA to Wehr-Ersatz-Inspektion, Sept. 22, 1939; Heller to Major General T. Gautier, Feb. 6, 1940; CA to Capt. Nemling, Feb. 27, 1940.
123 BA-CA, CA-IB, Wertheim, 17/05, Bruno report of June 11, 1941.
124 Ibid., Wertheim, 17/04, Wertheim to CA, Sept. 8, 1942.
125 BA-CA, CA-V, report to the working committee of Sept. 25, 1942.
126 Ibid., report to the working committee and meeting, Sept. 25, 1944; BA-CA, CA-IB, Wertheim, 17/04, Wertheim to CA, Dec. 14, 1944.

The end of the war found Bruno exhausted, sick, and unable to carry on, and it is interesting to note that Heinrich Fiala of the CA's Industry Section made a point of praising Bruno for his efforts on behalf of the firm during the previous fifteen years. When worker representatives, while not denying Bruno's achievements, nevertheless criticized him for having gone so heavily into war production, the answer given, and probably a correct one, was that the alternative would have been to be closed down and to lose Wertheim's workforce. The connection between Wertheim and the CA was also to be maintained in the coming years.[127]

In contrast to Wertheim, which had to undergo considerable adaptation to wartime demands, the Maschinenfabrik Heid's production program needed little alteration. Founded in 1883 and located in Stockerau, the firm had distinguished itself in the production of agricultural machinery, machine tools, high precision lathes, and clutches. The company had suffered in the post-1918 period, like Wertheim, but then underwent fundamental reorganization under a talented and energetic general director, Josef Musil, with the strong support of the CA, which owned between 60 percent and 70 percent of its shares. Musil promoted serial production and accumulated patents and exclusive licenses that gave the company a considerable edge in the market, and he managed the company throughout the war. Heid had worked closely with Wertheim at various times, and it is interesting to note that the CA asked Musil to take over Bruno's position at the end of the war. Heid's products were much needed in the war economy, and it was flooded with contracts. Its capital had to be increased in 1942 from 1 million RM to 1,350,000 RM, at which time the CA's share increased from 60 percent to 72.5 percent. CA credits amounted to 2.8 million RM in July 1942. Military orders were so heavy at this time that Heid had to give up some contracts to firms in France. The company employed 1,000 workers at the end of the war, and while one can assume that some percentage of them were

non-German, the actual composition of the workforce is not known.[128]

Understandably, the CA was interested in making the most of outstanding managers, and it called on Musil in 1938 to take over the management of the Lüster- und Metallwarenfabrik Alois Pragan & Bruder GmbH, a chandelier and lighting fixtures manufacturer. As the owners were Jewish, the shares were acquired in the Aryanization of the firm. Musil bought 49 percent of the shares, the CA held the remaining 51 percent. The company, renamed "Austrolux," was in considerable need of modernization at the time of the purchase. Musil undertook this task and converted to war work after the war started. In the winter of 1944, when the authorities in Berlin undertook a drastic program of shutting down plants that were not the absolutely highest priority, a decision was made to close "Austrolux." Both the CA and Musil fought tenaciously to keep it open on the grounds that it was the only such plant in Austria and that a substantial portion of its workers could not be easily transferred to other plants. They seem to have succeeded. They later had to fight the restitution claims of the former owners by claiming that the sale had been voluntary and made necessary by the poor condition of the company in 1938.[129]

The CA seemed less enthusiastic about retaining C. Schember & Söhne, Brückenwaagen und Maschinenfabriken AG, a manufacturer of large scales for locomotives and railroad cars. The family company, based in Vienna-Atzgersdorf, was founded in 1888 and was incorporated in 1917. At the time of the Anschluss, the chief manager of the firm was a family member, Kornelius Schember.[130] The firm enjoyed a worldwide reputation for its products, which included

---

[127] Ibid., meeting of July 19, 1945; *Festschrift für Josef Joham*, pp. 19–26.

[128] On the company in general, see ibid., pp. 33–38. The information on the company during the war is sparse, and most of this information is culled from the report to the CA working committee of July 15, 1942, BA-CA, CA-V.

[129] For the Aryanization and restitution issues, see BA-CA, CA-IB, Pragan, 41/01-02; on the fight to prevent the wartime shutdown, see ibid., Austrolux, 21/01-02.

[130] *Festschrift für Josef Joham*, pp. 43–45.

machine parts for the construction industry, forged products, and automobile parts, and it also held a number of valuable patents. It had interests in Czechoslovakia and Hungary, and it did a considerable amount of exporting worldwide. In 1924, it entered into an agreement for technical cooperation with W. & T. Avery of Birmingham, the largest manufacturer of scales in Europe. W. & T. Avery was connected to the Soho Trust Co., which acquired 25.4 percent of Schember's shares. The CA was the largest shareholder, having 72.7 percent of the shares in its possession at the time of the Anschluss.

With the takeover of Austria by Germany, Schember was very interested in securing municipal construction and military contracts. Although well qualified technically, it had to go through considerable gyrations to demonstrate its Aryan character in order to meet the racial standards of the military agencies. Needless to say, the four Jews on the board, including Franz Rottenberg and Alexander Marmorstein, were replaced. Directors Heller and Fiala joined as representatives of the CA, along with Heinrich Bleckmann and Walter Trappen, the head of the Tacho-Schnellwaagenfabriken in Duisburg-Grossenbaum and Karlsruhe. Trappen headed a company that did business with Schember as well as with W. & T. Avery; the Soho Trust appointed him as its representative in place of the two Englishmen who had previously served on the administrative council. All four of the new members had to show evidence that they were Aryans, and Schember, who had divorced and remarried, also had to prove that he was in fact divorced from his first wife and that his new wife was an Aryan. Somewhat grotesquely, the members of the Soho Trust, bearing the names Sir James Fortescue Flannery, Baron Charles Edward Martineau, Sir Charles Herbert Smith, Walford Hollier Turner, and Percy Herbert Mills, also had to attest to their Aryan credentials and were apparently successful in doing so.[131]

During the first months after the Anschluss, Schember suffered from the high costs of its raw materials, which hurt its competitiveness, and operated at only 40 percent of capacity. Where it normally employed about 500 workers, it only employed 170 at the beginning of the spring. This began to change rapidly soon afterward thanks to contracts from the military, especially a long-term contract for the production of special machine parts. Kornelius Schember became quite active with expansion plans, and in March he wrote to Fiala proposing that the CA support his application for a long-term Reich-guaranteed credit for the new production and the employing of an additional 250 workers. There is no evidence that the CA did so, although it had provided 250,000 RM in operating credits, to which it added another 50,000 RM in July. When Schember sought larger investment financing for its military production in the spring of 1940, the CA refused outright, insisting that this was the task of the military, and urged Schember to turn to the government-owned Deutsche Industriebank in Berlin. It did so, and the Industriebank gave Schember a five-year 500,000 RM credit with the security of a mortgage on its property. The CA, however, was itself now engaged and provided an operating credit of 700,000 RM for the special production program in February 1941, which raised the CA operating credit at this point to 950,000 RM. The special credit was renewed at the end of 1941 and the end of 1942, in each case for a year. In the fall of 1942, Schember raised its capital from 800,000 RM to 1.2 million RM. Because the Soho Trust Company was now an enemy alien firm, it was not allowed to participate in the purchase of the new shares, so the CA's stake was increased to 81.3 percent and that of the Soho Trust Company was reduced to 17 percent. Schember was also paying a 5 percent dividend.[132]

---

131 See BA-CA, CA-IB, Schember, 15/02, Schember to Fiala, June 16, 1938; Fiala to Heller, Sept. 2, 1938; Fiala to Heller, Sept. 13, 1938; Schember to Heller, Oct. 26, 1938.

132 See the article in the *Völkischer Beobachter* (June 26, 1938); ibid., Schember to Fiala, March 10, 1939, and application; Heller to Schember, April 26, 1940, and May 7, 1940. On the 1939 credits, and the 1941–1943 credits, see BA-CA, CA-V, CA management board meeting, July 12, 1939, Dec. 3, 1941, and Dec. 14, 1942. On the credits of 1940–1941,

Given Schember's increasing wartime success, it is somewhat ironic that the CA had seemed quite anxious to sell off its shares in 1939–1940. In late 1939, the CA was negotiating a possible sale to the Privilegierte österreichisch-ungarischen Staats-Eisenbahn-Gesellschaft. That provoked the Tacho-Schnellwaagenfabrik GmbH to enter with a higher bid, which the CA then accepted. The banking business was to remain with the CA, and the agreement was subject to RWM approval. The deal did not come off, however, because of delays in gaining the agreement of the Foreign Exchange Office in Düsseldorf and the RWM.[133] Nevertheless, the CA appears to have still been interested in selling the Schember shares. In April–May 1940, Director Tron of the Deutsche Bank, at that time the head of the Leipzig branch, corresponded with Director Joham of the CA about selling the shares to Stephan Baron von Thyssen-Bornemisza. The latter apparently actually visited Schember, but he was also interested in putting his money into some Austrian breweries. Nothing came of Tron's effort to mediate a sale of Schember for the "usual" 2 percent commission, however.[134]

Much of the CA's coolness to holding on to Schember was the result of lack of confidence in Kornelius Schember, who had been ill and whose performance since his recovery was lackluster. When Heller left the supervisory board in 1940 to take up his position with the VIAG, he was replaced by Friedl who, after visiting Schember, wrote Heller that "I have gained the impression that there are certainly some bases that would make possible the good employment of the works under conditions of peace and that would perhaps make possible an expansion of the work, since the space situation there appears to have been solved in a very

satisfactory way. The entire enterprise, however, leaves a somewhat neglected impression, which I attribute, aside from many other circumstances, to the lack of a purposeful, industrious plant leader. You yourself have made me aware of the reduced viability of Herr Schember."[135] A major problem in dealing with Schember was that he was lacking in means and could not simply be asked to retire. Director Bruno of Wertheim was called upon in an effort to find someone to assist Schember. But Schember seemed quite resistant to being shunted aside in this manner, telling Friedl in June 1941 that he was in fine shape, that the number of workers had increased from 254 to 462 since 1940 and would reach the 500 mark, and that he had good staff and could certainly use more help but that the biggest problem was giving the employees a well-deserved raise.[136] By this time, Friedl was probably himself convinced that if the leadership was not all he wished for, Schember-Atzgersdorf was still a worthwhile investment. He rejected a possible alternative of investing in the Schember Ungarische Waagenfabriks AG in Budapest. Schember itself only had a 10 percent stake in the company, whose shares were in the hands of Jews. Although there was much talk of finding a way to push the Jews out, some of the manipulative methods proposed for a shareholders' meeting seemed to Friedl totally unethical and ultimately counterproductive. He much preferred that Schember-Atzgersdorf export to Hungary than that Schember in Hungary export to Germany and also felt that such money as they had should go into Atzgersdorf.[137]

The fact that Friedl demonstrated such inhibitions in dealing with Jews, at least in Hungary, is to his credit, even if it also made good business sense. In 1943, Schember paid a 6 percent dividend, and the contract with Kornelius Schember, who had obviously been underestimated, was renewed. The firm employed a total of 451 workers in 1943, 227 German

see Friedl's report to the CA working committee meeting, Feb. 4, 1941, and on the capital increase, see BA-CA, CA-IB, Schember, 15/05, Fiala's report of Oct. 17, 1942.
[133] See BA-CA, CA-V, the CA management board meetings of Dec. 6, 1939 and Dec. 13, 1939; BA-CA, CA-IB, Schember, 15/02, CA to Schember, Feb. 24, 1940.
[134] See the correspondence in ibid., Schember, 15/05.

[135] Ibid., Friedl to Heller, June 11, 1940.
[136] Ibid., Fiala to Bruno, Aug. 23, 1940 and Schember to Friedl, June 13, 1941.
[137] Ibid., memorandum by Friedl, Sept. 21, 1940.

males, 48 females, 53 POWs, and 123 foreign workers. In 1944, the total was 398 workers, 183 German males, 43 females, 49 POWs, and 123 foreign workers. The firm was badly damaged by Allied bombing, but survived the war under Schember's leadership and as a member of the CA concern.[138]

5. THE CA CONCERN'S CONSTRUCTION ENTERPRISES

The CA concern had important holdings in construction companies. The demand for the services of such companies increased dramatically after the Anschluss, because of National Socialist projects for reconstruction in the Ostmark and then because of the war effort. If these companies were kept quite busy, however, they were also burdened with the problem of securing the raw materials and the labor they needed. The Austrian war economy increasingly relied on foreigners, forced laborers, POWs, and concentration camp prisoners, and the construction industry, where work could be extremely arduous, made use of all these groups to fill its labor needs. As has been shown, the CA was informed that firms in its concern were employing foreign labor and POWs, and evidence has been presented that members of the CA Industry Section had precise information about the numbers of such works. Furthermore, the CA not only provided credits to the complex of heavy industrial and weapons firms centered in Linz, many of which were fed with slave labor from Mauthausen and its sub-campus, but it also gave credits to the major military production enterprises that had grown up in Wiener-Neustadt and that employed large numbers of such workers. In February 1944, for example, the Rax-Werk, which was engaged in the rocket program and was a notorious employer of slave labor, asked for a1.5 million RM credit to supplement the 500,000 RM credit it had already received.[139] The CA also

provided credits to construction firms outside its own concern. Wayss& Freitag is a good example. In June 1942, this company received 1,735,000 RM in credits from the CA, having previously received 2 million RM in credits in 1939–1940 as well as some smaller credits in connection with large contracts.[140] It was heavily engaged in construction projects involving forced and slave laborers. In some cases, it set up its own camps at construction sites. Between 1940 and 1942, it employed Viennese Jewish laborers for road construction in Traunstein until they were deported to the East. There is no way of knowing from the existing sources whether the CA leadership was fully aware of this customer's labor practices when it gave it credits, and this remains a problem even in assessing its knowledge in its dealing with the firms in its own concern. Nevertheless, it was hardly in a state of innocence, as shall be demonstrated in considering four of the construction companies in the concern: the Wiener Brückenbau- und Eisenkonstruktions-AG, the Universale Hoch- und Tiefbau AG, Wien, the Steierische Bau-Gesellschaft, Graz, and the Wienerberger Ziegelfabriks- und Baugesellschaft, Wien.

The CA owned about 92 percent of the shares of Wiener Brückenbau, which had a capital of 1.5 million RM. The company produced all sorts of steel structures, especially steel railroad and road bridges, steel structures for smelting and chemical plants, funiculars, electrical cranes, and coaling elevators for locomotives. The company had been on something of an upswing even before the Anschluss, and the coming of the Germans and their major production programs gave it every reason to anticipate a flood of business. The same held true for firms in the Reich; two of the leading ones, the Saarland firm of Seibert Brückenbau and the Dortmund firm of Dortmunder Brückenbau C.H. Jucho, showed great interest in Wiener Brückenbau. As early as April 1938, each of

---

138 On the number of workers, see ibid., Referat Ketterer, 27/04, the undated report by Director Ketterer.

139 BA-CA, CA-V, CA working committee, Feb. 10, 1944.

140 See DB,V2/3, list of CA debtors developed in June 1942; on the 1939 credits, see BA-CA, CA-V, CA working committee, Nov. 17, 1939 and management board meetings of Jan. 5 and March 28, 1940.

these companies had contracts with Göring's Reichswerke for the construction of four blast furnaces, and they were anxious to do more business in Austria. The owner of the former firm, Bernhard Seibert had learned from the Deutsche Bank that the CA might be interested in selling a bridge construction firm and paid a personal visit to the CA and to Director Hans Liebl, who seems also to have been serving Wiener Brückenbau at this time, to inquire about such a purchase. Liebl was particularly worried because Seibert had access to Gauleiter Bürckel; the two knew one another from Bürckel's service in the Saaarland. Director Heller of the CA, however, seemed anxious to retain Wiener Brückenbau for the CA and was quite protective of the company. C.H. Jucho was more interested in working with Wiener Brückenau and proposed a partnership under which Jucho would join in projects that exceeded Wiener Brückenbau's capacity. Jucho held discussions with Heller and Liebl, and they were agreeable to such an arrangement. The record is unclear, however, as to whether it came to anything.[141]

The major problem facing Wiener Brückenbau in the spring of 1938 was expanding its grounds and production facilities. It was trying to purchase land leased from the Dorotheum and was having difficulties coming to an arrangement because the city wished to take over the land. Heller and the CA promoted another solution by proposing that Wiener Brückenbau take over the shares, land, workers, and machinery of the Wiener Eisenbau AG, which was in the possession of the family of Oswald Graf Seilern. This solved Wiener Brückenbau's desperate need for expanded facilities, and in January 1939, the CA provided the necessary credits for the acquisition of Wiener Eisenbau.[142]

The CA seemed quite ready to supply Wiener Brückenbau with as much credit as it needed, easing the way, for example, for a large order of iron poles for the Österreichische Kraftwerke AG in Linz in April 1938, and then assisting with getting the firm contracts in Romania.[143] In November 1940, the CA increased its cash credit to the firm from 2.29 million RM to 3 million RM. The CA not only viewed this positively because of the large contracts the company had received, but also because its plans for rationalizing the use of its new facilities after the war promised long-term success.[144] In June 1942, Wiener Brückenbau was aggressively pursuing opportunities in the Balkan countries, especially Romania and Hungary, and was using CA contacts with Romanian banks toward this end.[145] Certainly Wiener Brückenbau had expansive ambitions in German-controlled Europe. Liebl informed the CA in March 1941 that it was investigating investment in a Romanian foundry, considering participation in the Aryanization of a large enterprise, and consulting with the general commissar for the occupied Netherlands, Hans Fischböck, about steel bridge building and crane construction enterprises that might be available.[146]

The available records do not indicate whether anything came of these ambitions, but they do recount what was for the CA a very satisfying success story. Turnover increased from 5,022,000 RM in 1940 to 7,066,000 RM in 1941. In September 1942, it was estimated that turnover would come to be between 8 and 10 million RM that year; the final figure was 10,594,000 RM. The company was able to reduce its debt from 6,110,000 RM at the end of 1941 to 700,000 RM in 1942. The CA viewed its cash credit of 1.6 million RM more as a stake in the company than as a credit. It paid 5 percent dividends in 1940 and 1941, and

---

[141] On Seibert, see BA-CA, CA-IB, Wiener Brückenbau, 02/02, Liebl to Heller, April 19, 1938; for the Jucho proposal, see Jucho to Wiener Brückenbau, April 12, 1938 along with its draft of an agreement.

[142] BA-CA, CA-V, CA executive committee meeting, Jan. 20, 1939; BA-CA, CA-IB, 02/01, the correspondence of 1938–1939.

[143] For the correspondence, see ibid, Wiener Brückenbau, 02/02.

[144] BA-CA, CA-V, CA executive committee meeting, Nov. 14, 1940; BA-CA, CA-IB, 02/03-04, report of Nov. 8, 1940.

[145] Ibid., memorandum of June 27, 1942 and related correspondence.

[146] Ibid., Liebl to CA, March 25 and 27, 1941.

a 6 percent dividend in 1942. To be sure, debt began to rise again; the company had debt of 1.8 million RM and anticipated it would need another 1 million RM in early 1944. This was attributed, however, to cash flow problems common at this time because the government had ceased to pay any advances against contracts and was paying its bills very slowly.[147]

The surviving records do not provide much information about the Wiener Brückenbau labor force, which totaled 997 men in June 1943, 151 of whom had been drafted into military service. It had contracts that involved participation in the construction of power plants in Schwebeck and Lavamund, the Drau Power Works projects, and it was also involved in the 1943 naval construction program at the Rax Werke in Wiener-Neustadt. There is no way of telling how many, if any, foreign workers, POWs, or slave laborer the Wiener Brückenbau employed.[148]

That is not the case with the Universale Hoch- und Tiefbau AG, Austria's largest and most important construction company. The company's correspondence with the CA provides little information on its labor practices, and there is a dearth of information about its practices at the numerous construction sites where it operated, but the company earned considerable notoriety for using forced labor and concentration camp prisoners. Universale was very much engaged in projects where such labor was used. It was, for example, involved in construction at the Reichswerke, where it, along with the other firms working there, drew labor from the thirteen special barracks set up for "Ostarbeiter." The company was quite active in building power plants that employed foreign workers. At the Tauernkraftwerk Kaprun, it employed 150 foreign workers, which put it in the top nine such companies, and it was also one of the firms participating in the construction of a transformer station at Ernsthofen and a power plant at Ybbs-Persenbeug. Perhaps the worst blot on the company's record came at the beginning of 1943, when it took over the construction of the Loibl tunnel to connect Carinthia with Slovenia, a pet project of Gauleiter Rainer. A special SS sub-camp of the Mauthausen concentration camp was set up to supply labor. The project became particularly infamous for the mistreatment of the slave labor by the SS at the Loibl camp as well as the ghastly working conditions in the tunnel. A final example shows that Universale was also quite active in at least one of the occupied countries, namely Norway, where it cooperated with a number of other firms in constructing a railroad link between Fauske and Narvik. The SS supplied Croatian and Serbian concentration camp inmates for the project.[149]

There is no evidence that anyone at the CA or Universale lost any sleep about these matters. What they did lose sleep about was the perpetuation of their relationship, which had been very much to their mutual profit until the late spring of 1942, when, as part of the Deutsche Bank takeover, the CA sold a 61.27 stake in Universale to the VIAG and retained a 26 percent stake for itself. The VIAG then turned its shares over to the Alpen-Elektrowerke, which it

---

[147] BA-CA, CA-V, reports to the CA executive committee of Sept. 25, 1942 and Feb. 10, 1944.

[148] See Markus Purkhart, "Die Draukraftwerke," in: Oliver Rathkolb/Florian Freund (eds.), *NS-Zwangsarbeit in der Elektrizitätswirtschaft der "Ostmark" 1938–1945. Ennskraftwerke– Kaprun–Draukraftwerke–Ybbs-Persenbeug–Ernsthofen* (Vienna, Cologne, Weimar 2002), p. 226, and Florian Freund/Bertrand Perz, *Das KZ in der Serbenhalle. Zur Kriegsindustrie in Wiener Neustadt* (Vienna 1988), pp. 92–93.

[149] See the interview with Florian Freund, "Zwangsarbeit im 'Dritten Reich'. Ein Überblick. Dimensionen der Zwangsarbeit in Österreich," in: Forum Politische Bildung (ed.), *Wieder gut machen? Enteignung, Zwangsarbeit, Entschädigung, Restitution Sonderband der Informationen zur PolitischenBildung* (Vienna 1999), pp. 46–53; Michael John, "Zwangsarbeit und NS-Industriepolitik am Standort Linz," in: Rathkolb (ed.), *NS Zwangsarbeit*, vol. 1, p. 80; Margit Reiter, "Das Tauernkraftwerk Kaprun," in: Rathkolb/Freund (ed.), *Elektrizitätswirtschaft*, p. 183; Christine Oertel, "Die Umspannwerke Ernsthofen," in: ibid., p. 247; and Christine Oertel, "Das Donaukraftwerk Ybbs-Persenbeug," in: ibid., p. 269; Josef Zausnig, *Der Loibl-Tunnel: Das vergessene KZ an der Südgrenze Österreichs. Eine Spurensicherung* (Drava 1995); Manfred Pohl, *Philipp Holzmann. Geschichte eines Bauunternehmens 1849–1999* (Munich 1999), p. 256.

owned. It was a serious loss for the CA because Universale had performed a variety of important functions for the CA and also had been making a great deal of money. As noted earlier in this study, Universale was originally the Österreichische Realitäten AG, which handled the CA's real estate interests. The construction side of the company was originally the "Universale-Redlich & Berger AG," which had been created in 1916. In November 1939, the company was renamed "Universale" Hoch- und Tiefbau AG. While continuing to have substantial real estate holdings, its chief activities were now in the construction sector where, among a host of other construction projects, it also serviced the construction needs of the various enterprises in the CA concern. The Anschluss certainly made a big difference in its business even before the war started. Its turnover increased from 6.3 million RM in 1937 to 10.2 million RM in 1938 and stood at 25 million RM during the first half of 1939. The number of workers it employed increased from 865 in 1937 to 1,894 in 1938 and stood at 3,959 in 1939. In 1939, it was filling contracts at seventeen building construction sites and twelve sites involving underground construction, including large construction sites engaging between 400 and 600 workers. Among its many building projects in 1938–1939 were the Festspielhaus in Salzburg, the Technical University in Graz, new facilities for the *Völkische Beobachter* in Vienna, power plants, transformers, dams, and workers' housing projects in Linz, Graz, Pinkafeld, and Vienna. It also undertook a number of civil engineering projects in this period, including work on numerous bridges, on the Autobahn, and on other road construction projects.[150]

Obviously, the coming of the war created some difficulties for Universale, above all because of the shortage of skilled workers and engineers due to conscription. But the firm was nonetheless able to continue and to complete large projects for the Nibelungenwerke in St. Valentin and also for CA concern firms such

as Martin Miller in Traismauer and Wertheim & Co. It also completed airfield construction projects in Fliegerhorst Schwechat-Ost. Although it had to slow down its work on Autobahn construction, it did manage to receive more than 300 POWs for this work and was also successfully engaged in projects for the Alpen-Elektrowerke AG in Kaprun. It also worked closely with the Organisation Todt on construction projects in occupied France and Belgium and engaged in the construction of SS barracks. The CA provided large credits for these projects, totaling 4.4 million RM in May 1940. By August, however, the credits had been reduced to 650,000 RM. The rising and falling credits reflected the taking on and completion of contracts, and the CA obviously had every reason for confidence. Indeed, the future looked very bright in 1940; the Universale report concluded that "next year, after the peace, substantial amounts will be given to promote home construction."[151]

The Statthalter in Vienna, Baldur von Schirach, did indeed have a program for the construction of 12,000 apartments in Vienna. The municipal government was to finance the construction of 6,000 apartments. The financing of the remaining 6,000 was to be equally divided between banks, commercial enterprises, and industrial firms. The CA and Universale were of course expected to be participants. The basic idea was to provide housing for the workers employed by large firms in Vienna. Note was taken of the fact that the CA's interest was limited because most of the companies in which it held stakes operated outside Vienna.[152] Such preparations for peace, however, were quite premature in 1941. There was, however, to be plenty of housing repair and construction work for Universale after 1945.[153]

In the meantime, Universale found itself flooded with wartime production, primarily in the Ostmark but also in Upper Silesia, the Generalgouvernement, and France. In the

150 See the lengthy account and financial report for 1938–1939, undated but obviously produced in early 1940, in BA-CA, CA-IB, Universale, 16/01-02.

151 Report attached to the Universale supervisory board meeting of Nov. 21, 1941, ibid.

152 See the memorandum of Jan. 11, 1941 and related documents, ibid.

153 See, *Festschrift für Josef Joham*, pp. 63–70.

Polish lands, for example, Universale built the new seat of General Governor Hans Frank in Cracow, but also a railroad bridge near Rybnik in Upper Silesia, and a tunnel in Strzyzow in the Generalgouvernement. It can well be imagined what kind of labor was used for these projects. The labor situation in the Ostmark certainly led to a drastic change in the labor force. At the end of 1940, Universale employed 4,975 workers, 3,818 Germans, 344 foreigners, and 813 POWs. At the beginning of October 1941, it employed 5,127 workers, of whom 2,816 were Germans, 1,207 foreigners, and 1,104 POWs. Thus, 45 percent of the workforce was foreign, and the employment of these foreigners, aside from their lower productivity, created special difficulties because of language problems.[154]

The CA was greatly interested in the affairs of Universale, which was understandable given that it had given the company a cash credit of 1.5 million RM that was extended until the end of 1942 along with a liability credit of 1,333,300 RM.[155] Fritscher had served as chairman of the supervisory board after Heller left, and Ernst Lanz of the Concern Section of the CA kept an eye on the firm, or at least he tried to do so. The general director of Universale, Heinrich Goldemund, who had been Vienna's director of civil engineering from 1908 to 1920, was seventy-eight years old in 1941. Despite his great distinction, he was not at the height of his powers and not easy to handle. When Lanz went on one of his tours and sought to get technical and financial information on the firm, Goldemund told Lanz not to speak with his staff and not to make frequent visits. Lanz reported that Goldemund had stated that "in general he did not see why the bank suddenly troubles itself with things which basically are not its business and that I should get out of the habit of asking too much, since he does not want me to trouble myself too much with business details.... Goldemund said that he does not like my

coming too often." Because Lanz thought that was his job, he found Goldemund's attitude very perturbing and intended to make more frequent visits. Clearly, Goldemund was no longer up to the job, and Fritscher felt it necessary to contact Fritz Todt to ask for advice about a possible replacement. Goldemund retired in 1943, and his son, Heinrich Goldemund Jr., along with other directors, took charge. The CA no longer had problems with management unfriendliness.[156]

A big problem of an entirely different nature arose in the summer of 1942 after the CA had sold its majority holding in Universale to the VIAG. Glatzl reported to General Director Buzzi of the CA about a meeting at the Martin Miller construction site in Traismauer, where Goldemund and Director Schöll were present to discuss the Speer ministry's decision to have Martin Miller double its capacity as soon as possible. In the course of the discussion, the Universale directors turned their attention to the changed ownership of their company and complained that the VIAG and Alpen-Elektrowerke seemed to be treating Universale as if its exclusive task was to undertake underground civil engineering projects, despite the fact that Universale had always been engaged in building construction as well and that its directors specialized in that field. Now they had come up with a scheme whereby the CA was to use its 26 percent of the shares to create a new corporation that would be solely devoted to building construction and that could serve the CA just as well as the old firm had. Glatzl pointed out to Goldemund that this could badly affect the relations with the VIAG and Alpen-Elektrowerken, and suggested that Goldemund discuss the idea with Heller and Buzzi first. Glatzl's own analysis of the situation was that the Universale directors were fearful of losing their very lucrative business with the CA concern and that the CA might turn to some other firm to handle the construction projects of the various firms within the

---

154 See BA-CA, CA-IB, Universale, 16/01-02, the reports of March 6, June, and Dec. 3, 1941.

155 BA-CA, CA-V, working committee meeting of Nov. 4, 1941.

156 BA-CA, CA-IB, Universale, 16/01-02, Lanz report to the CA management board, Jan. 27, 1941, Fritscher to Todt, March 13, 1941.

concern.[157] There is no evidence that this was to be the case. On the contrary, in June 1944, when Universale had a big construction job for Martin Miller for which it had neither sufficient manpower nor equipment, it was the managers at Martin Miller who negotiated to bring in another construction firm to assist with the project and told Glatzl that they had no binding obligation to make sole use of Universale.[158]

Indeed, the CA stood strongly behind the efforts of Universale to participate in the construction of water power plants in Slovakia, where the CA played up its continued stake in the company and its majority holding in the Union-Bank, Pressburg.[159] The CA also continued to provide credits in 1943–1944, although the sums needed seem to have been reduced, perhaps because the Alpen-Elektrowerke AG was in a position to provide needed financing. Whatever the case, Universale was slated to emerge from the war safely ensconced in the CA concern while the VIAG and its participations disappeared from the scene.

In 1944, the CA gave Universale its 98 percent stake in another construction company, the Steirische Bau-Gesellschaft, Graz. The company had been continuously losing money because of mistakes made in the reorganization of its brick works in St. Peter near Graz in 1938–1939. Bad planning, combined with the labor and raw materials shortages created by the war, led the CA to the conclusion that it was in no position to solve the Steirische Bau-Gesellschaft's problems and was in danger of losing its entire investment. CA director Lanz, who handled the company for the Industry Section, was reasonably confident that the Universale branch in Graz could step in and remedy the Steirische's difficulties both materially and financially. The company was sold for its book value of 342,705 RM, which was half the value of the 685,500 RM in shares held by the CA.[160]

What makes the CA-Steirische relationship of particular historical interest was that the CA received a large amount of information on the company's labor problems, which were substantial. This was especially evident in the spring and summer of 1943, when the company tried to go over to three shifts in order to make up for production losses during the winter and rainy periods. The result was considerable resistance from the workers and little appreciable gains in production, a situation that continued after it reverted to the two-shift system. The firm appealed to the Reich Labor Trustee for Styria and Carinthia, and asked the Labor Front to "enlighten" the workers on the importance of "providing the war economy with that which is necessary for victory."[161] The company also urged that the workers be warned that if they remained unwilling to work and continued to withhold their labor, they would be forced to exchange jobs with workers who were doing their duty at sites that were exposed to bombing or partisan activity. This "clarification" seems to have had little effect, however. Some workers stopped working after five hours and others refused to follow orders. From the standpoint of the company, this was nothing short of sabotage, and the Labor Trustee advised calling in the Gestapo. The latter appeared at ten o'clock at night when the shift changed and put one of the chief offenders in handcuffs for transport to a concentration camp, and the lesser culprits were warned of what would happen if they gave the slightest cause for offense.

The company found the Gestapo intervention "impressive" and believed that it would now have discipline and order. This did not, of course, solve the ongoing problems of an extreme shortage of lathes or air raid alarms that at this time began to increase in frequency.[162]

The workers in 1943 appear to have been primarily Austrians from Styria, Germans, and Hungarians. By 1944, there were relatively few German workers left and some had been replaced

[157] Ibid., Glatzl to Buzzi, July 30, 1942.
[158] Ibid., Miller, 11/02, memorandum by Glatzl, June 8, 1944.
[159] See the correspondence for August 1942, in ibid., Universale, 16/01-02.
[160] BA-CA, CA-V, report to the working committee of Sept. 26, 1944. See also BA-CA, CA-IB, Steirische

Baugesellschaft, 43/01, Lanz to Hermann Riecke, the deputy chairman of the Steirische supervisory board, Sept. 19, 1944.
[161] Ibid., Steirische Bau-Gesellschaft to Reich Trustee, Graz, July 26, 1943.
[162] Ibid., undated report of August 1943.

by "Ostarbeiter," who were also in short supply by then. The Steirische received an allotment of ten such workers in 1944. It then had forty-five foreign workers, and this entailed the expense of setting up separate barracks and maintaining supervisory personnel to watch over them. The CA made some effort to help the Steirische with its labor problems and asked the director of the Wienerberger Ziegelfabriks- und Baugesellschaft, Hermann Leitich, whether he had any suggestions. The CA then informed the Steirische that some of the brick works in Styria had been using Italian workers. As the Steirische reported, however, it would have go to Udine and recruit workers there itself, and it had no contacts there. The company had tried to recruit "usable" Italian workers, but they were very hard to find. Most preferred to work at home, and those who were prepared to work in the Reich were expensive. The Labor Office tried to supply some Bosnian workers, but they were found to be "totally useless for intensive work" and had a strong tendency to walk off the job. When one of them came down with typhus, the company nearly had to close down the camp.[163] All this could only have reinforced the decision of the CA to sell its shares in the Steirische.

Of far greater importance to the CA, however, was the Wienerberger Ziegelfabriks- und Baugesellschaft, Wien. The company was a major producer of bricks and clay products, and the CA held 78 percent of its shares. It not only serviced the Austrian market with building materials before the Anschluss but also engaged in considerable export business. It operated seven plants on its properties in Vienna, which were well equipped with a variety of modern ovens and employed 2,500 workers and 100 white-collar employees and officials in 1935.[164] The Austrian construction industry in general and brick producers more specifically were under pressure from Austria's high production costs when compared to the old Reich from

wage increases, but the industry benefited from the promotion of construction after the Anschluss, which even led to the reopening of small brick-making companies that had been shut down in the previous years. As the labor market became tight by the end of 1938, Bürckel and the authorities began to apply pressure to put unemployed Jews, the number of whom had of course grown in the wake of the Aryanizations, to work in brick making. When the leadership of the Wienerberger was first confronted with this suggestion at the beginning of 1939, it took a completely negative attitude, but labor market pressures soon caused it to succumb and to begin employing some Jewish workers in the spring of 1939, fifty in April and another twenty in the summer. They were, in fact, to continue employing Jewish workers into 1944 and probably 1945.[165]

The Wienerberger regularly complained about the "inferior" quality of the Jewish workers, but the coming of the war rendered it more willing to accept more Jewish workers and even to employ them in more important tasks. It was viewed as the "last way out," especially when requests for foreign workers were not met. In June 1940, 330 of the 2,100 workers at Wienerberger were Jews and 90 were POWs. At the clay products plant, 89 of the 542 workers were Jews: of the 282 workers at the brick plant in Vösendorf, 30 were Jews and 26 were foreigners. In the summer, the total number of Jews increased to 441, with 336 working at the clay products plant and 105 at the brick plant.[166] At the same time, the Wienerberger manager had come to the conclusion that some Jews were less "inferior" than others: "Insofar as the productivity of the Jewish workers is concerned, this is very uneven. In general, one is dealing with persons who are not accustomed to manual labor and whose performance is therefore below average. We have, however, succeeded in putting together Jewish worker parties whose

[163] Ibid., Steirische Bau-Gesellschaft, 43/02, CA to Steirische Bau-Gesellschaft, March 17, 1944; Steirische Bau to CA, March 23, 1944; Steirische Bau to Lanz, March 27, 1944.
[164] *Festschrift für Josef Joham*, pp. 71–78.

[165] Wolf Gruner, *Zwangsarbeit und Verfolgung. Österreichische Juden im NS-Staat 1938–1945* (Innsbruck, Vienna, Munich 2000), pp. 78, 80–81, 85–86, 197–199.
[166] Ibid., p. 97; BA-CA, CA-IB, Wienerberger, 18/01, quarterly report for the first quarter of 1940.

performance is thoroughly satisfactory."[167] Some were even put to work at the ovens, although always with Aryan workers in more responsible positions. The goal was to replace the "inferior Jewish workers" with POWs, but that effort ran into difficulties. To further compound this mean-spiritedness, the company had also asked permission to reduce the hourly wages of underperforming Jewish workers and to diminish the pay of those doing piecework by allowing the pay to fall below what hourly workers received. The company also wanted to eliminate certain payments in kind for Jewish workers (e.g., coal) and to reduce piecework pay by 10 percent because Aryan workers had deductions for certain benefits unavailable to Jewish workers and thought it was wrong to have Jewish workers take home more pay than their Aryan counterparts.

Wienerberger's tale of labor woes developed apace as the war progressed. In 1941, it had received about 250 Italian workers as part of an arrangement between Germany and Italy, but they seemed to be of weak constitution and unused to steady labor, a problem compounded by their disappointment with the food supply. Only 100 remained by the third quarter of the year, but the number of French POWs increased to 200. Thus, 28 percent of the workforce was foreign. A further problem was that Jewish workers were being taken away and the gap was hard to fill.[168]

At the end of 1941, there were still 82 Jews working at the company. The number dropped to 60 in March 1942, then to 24 in September 1942, and 21 in 1943, where it remained until June 1944, when it declined to 14. The largest increase in the workforce came from the arrival of "Ostarbeiter," who accounted for 650 of the 1,476 workers employed in late 1944. Another 126 were other foreign nationals, and 77 were POWs. What is surprising at first sight is that the company employed 609 German nationals even at this late date. Part of the explanation may come from the way the Wienerberger used

its leverage on construction companies and the authorities by insisting that its labor needs be met at least in part, first, through the transfer of construction workers during the winter season to the brick producers so that the bricks could be produced, and second, by threatening not to be able to provide the bricks needed to repair Allied bombing damage.[169]

The CA received the reports of the Wienerberger and was well aware of its labor problems and practices. In 1942, it provided a current account credit of 1.5 million RM, and although not satisfied with the company's profitability, the bank recognized the problems under which the company labored. At the same time, the CA strongly approved of Wienerberger's plans to expand once it was more profitable because it had every expectation that there would be a great demand for its products in the postwar period.[170] These expansionist plans, however, were threatened in two ways. Wienerberger's plans ran afoul of the desire of the Viennese municipal authorities to expand the green areas in Vienna and reduce the number of brick-making plants. There were also plans afoot to create a community construction firm to undertake the task of postwar rebuilding, and it was also expected that the CA and other banks would participate in the financing of that firm. In April 1942, the CA, the Deutsche Bank, the VIAG, and Rafelsberger joined forces to work toward a settlement with Vienna whereby the Wienerberger would surrender such land as the municipality considered vital and build new brick works on previously unused land.[171]

The CA stood firmly behind the Wienerberger in opposing plans to create a publicly chartered construction company, and made clear to the city that it had an obligation to its private clients and would not engage in any discussion about such an enterprise. This

[167] Ibid., management board report to the supervisory board, June 30, 1940.
[168] Ibid., report for the third quarter of 1941.

[169] Ibid., Wienerberger, 18/04-05, pro memoria of April 20, 1943 and, for the figures, other reports of 1941–1944.
[170] BA-CA, CA-V, report to the CA working committee, Feb. 27, 1942.
[171] DB, B 53, discussion between Rafelsberger, Heller, and Olscher, April 15, 1942.

seems to have been done with the support of Rafelsberger, so that here National Socialist ideology took a back seat to promoting private enterprise.[172]

The Wienerberger firm seems to have done a good job in mastering its wartime difficulties as best it could. Production increased substantially in 1943–1944, and it also managed to cover its costs if not make a profit.[173] It suffered badly from bombing in the summer of 1944, but it was to play a significant role in rebuilding once the fighting was over. Its ruthless approach to the labor question during the war is undeniable, and the CA leadership was well aware of its practices. In fairness, however, two matters need to be taken up in this regard. First, it seems quite remarkable that the company retained even a very small number of Jews until the bitter end and one wonders why this was the case. The use of massive numbers of Jewish concentration camp prisoners at Ebensee or other centers of underground war production in 1944–1945 by other companies was, after all, rather different from keeping a small number of Jews (twenty-one and then fourteen) employed in Vienna. Undoubtedly, there must have been some economic justification, but this does not necessarily mean it was the only reason. The documents available to this author provide no answer to this question. Second, there is the behavior of the Wienerberger's general director between 1940 and 1945, Hermann Leitich. He had come from the CA and, not being a Party member until July 1938, he was more or less stuck at his desk with nothing to do because of Pfeiffer's hostility. This seems to have been why he went to the Kontrollbank, where he worked on Aryanization with Kastner. When the bank was dissolved, he went to the Wienerberger. After the war, he and Kastner were charged by the state prosecutor for their role in the Aryanization of the Hotel de France, but the court rejected the charge. What is relevant here, however, is that the Wienerberger

factory council provided a letter of reference for Leitich that not only praised his character and emphasized his innocence of being a regime supporter – standard matter in such documents – and his efforts to keep the company's workers from being drafted but also recounted, on the basis of documents found at the company, that the SS had approached Leitich with an offer to buy the Wienerberger and then to employ political prisoners at the company. Leitich was offered the opportunity to stay at his job and receive Party honors. The correspondence showed that Leitich turned down this offer in a letter to the economic leader of the SS, Oswald Pohl, and that he would rather leave the company and be drafted than accept the offer and have the company turned into a forced labor camp.[174] Certainly, the CA would not have been willing to sell any more of its major assets, and it is reasonable to assume that Leitich's response was in line with CA interests. In the absence of further evidence, it is impossible to assume anything more than that Leitich was committed to maintaining the Wienerberger as a private company and, in the process, as much of his own integrity as possible.

6. COAL, CHEMICALS, AND OIL

The CA concern did not include any coal mining enterprises, but it retained a half interest in the Montana Kohlenhandels-GmbH with its partner in the Aryanization of the company, Adolf Bauer.[175] The retention of the CA interest in the Montana was by no means written in the stars. At a discussion between Director Abs of the Deutsche Bank and the VIAG and Director Heller of the CA on April 4, 1938, Abs had asked about the availability of a large coal distributor that might be available for acquisition by a German corporation, and Heller mentioned the Montana but pointed out that it was still not in Aryan hands and also that the

---

[172] BA-CA, CA-IB, Wienerberger, 18/02, CA to Heller, Nov. 15, 1943.
[173] BA-CA, CA-V, report by Fritscher to the CA working committee, June 13, 1944.
[174] Memorandum by the Wienerberger Factory Council for the court, Jan. 24, 1946, Sondergericht für Strafsachen Wien, Akte Hermann Leitich.
[175] See pp. 38, 153–155 of this volume.

Klöckner concern had already shown interest in acquiring it. Heller went on to say that "such a solution is not desired, however, since the Montana A.G. and thereby its coal business has been able to profit extraordinarily well through its flexibility and would then lose its freedom."[176] Heller then went on to suggest that the Deutsche Erdöl AG might be considered for a participation in the Montana.

From the perspective of the CA, its successful Aryanization of Montana in alliance with Bauer preempted Abs and even Heller from pursuing a course involving an old Reich firm. Bauer, a Party man with excellent connections and a shrewd operator, was undoubtedly instrumental in helping save the Montana for the CA. He subsequently stoutly resisted efforts by the Deutsche Kohlengesellschaft, which did the marketing for the Reichswerke's ever-expanding coal empire, to penetrate the Austrian market with Upper Silesian coal by assuming a share in the Montana. When the Deutsche Kohlengesellschaft representative Herbst argued that the government wanted the banks to get out of all marketing operations, Bauer stood loyally by the CA: "I replied to them that the Creditanstalt-Bankverein has been operating its coal business since 1891 and that it cannot be imposed upon to freely renounce a participation that has become dear to it. To this must be added that, on the other side, the Montana benefits from this participation because it is the supplier of the industrial enterprises belonging to the Creditanstalt concern. And finally what must also be taken into account is that I could not wish for a better and more agreeable partner than the Creditanstalt, to which beyond this I owe a debt of gratitude for putting me in my present position and which has been to the greatest extent helpful to me financially by granting credits."[177] Bauer also appears to have been quite successful in warding off renewed efforts by the Klöckner concern to gain a foothold in Montana, employing

similar arguments that the CA would have to give up its coal marketing operation. This time the issue was marketing coal from the newly acquired mines in the former Yugoslavia, but Bauer pointed out that there was not only hostility toward banks selling coal but also against coal producers entering this field, and that it would be best to retain the existing arrangements whereby Montana and Klöckner worked together in distributing the coal in question.[178]

The CA had every reason to think Bauer a good investment, and as the case of Universale and its construction work for various CA concern members demonstrated, the CA did try to create linkages in its concern. Bauer had exaggerated, however, when claiming that Montana was benefiting from sales to the CA concern. In November 1940, he complained to Fiala that, of fifteen concern firms he listed, only two were getting coal from Montana. He was particularly upset that Semperit, the second largest firm in the Ostmark, bought practically nothing from Montana. Knowing the sensitivities of the managers in charge of buying coal, he proposed that the CA inquire of its concern firms from whom they were buying their coal and how much they were taking. With this information, he could then see what the possibilities were and how to deal with the individual companies. He was convinced that Montana would have something to offer in almost every case, and he also asked the CA to intervene directly with General Director Messmer at Semperit.[179]

There is no information as to how much coal CA firms subsequently purchased from Montana, but a report by Bauer on the period from April 1 to October 31, 1943, indicated a great increase in Montana business. Its turnover grew from 4,625,000 RM in the same period of 1941 to 7,114,000 RM in the period covered by the report. The profit picture was less rosy, having been 9.1 percent in 1941 and standing at 7.29 percent in 1943, while costs as a percentage of turnover were 5.12 percent in 1941 and 5.44 percent in 1943. Bauer attributed the increased costs to the wages of the French

[176] DB, B 51, memo by Pohle on meeting of April 4, 1938.
[177] BA-CA, CA-IB, Montana, 21/01, Bauer to CA, April 25, 1940.
[178] Ibid., Bauer memorandum of May 27, 1941.
[179] Ibid., Bauer to Fiala, Nov. 8, 1940.

POWs employed by Montana and the fact that it had to pay for unworked shifts at various times rather than have the workers drift off to other employment.[180] Although things were obviously much worse in April 1945, he can be found reporting to Director Friedl of the CA on his efforts to ship coal via Salzburg and hoping that the encirclement of Vienna, which he had fled, would be halted at Wiener Neustadt.[181]

In contrast to its coal marketing operations, the future of the CA in the field of chemical production was much more open to question after the Anschluss. Its most valuable asset, the Pulverwerk Skodawerke Wetzler, was lost to IG Farben very soon after the Anschluss, and what was left was the "Akalit" Kunsthornwerke AG, a producer of a plastic-like product made primarily out of casein and used in the production of combs, buttons, furniture ornaments, fashion accessories, and the like. The company had been founded in 1920 by Leopold Pasching, who, with family members, held 70.2 percent of the capital. The CA held 35.9 percent of the capital in 1938. The company was located in Brunn am Gebirge. The Anschluss was anything but favorable to its business. It depended on imports of casein, primarily from southern France. More than three-quarters of its production was exported. Germany was a market but also a large producer itself and thus a serious competitor once trade barriers went down. The period 1938–1939 brought a slowing down of business and financial difficulties for "Akalit."[182]

If the company had simply maintained its old product lines, it would have been killed off by the Anschluss and the coming of the war. Production for the military saved the company. Thanks to the initiative of its leadership, "Akalit" managed to get a substantial contract for producing special containers for the military, and this was followed by military orders for various thermoplastic products requiring use of a spray casting process.[183] The army apparently

paid the costs of the new machinery that was required, although it also insisted on retaining ownership of the machines. Nevertheless, the prospects for the company did not appear bright, and when Glatzl evaluated the situation in March 1940, he came to the conclusion that the CA had to value its holding at zero. Although the CA continued to provide credits and to maintain a moratorium on old debts, the future of the military contracts for "Akalit" was far from clear in 1941.[184]

The big breakthrough for "Akalit" came at the beginning of 1942, when it received a major contract from the firm Karl Freudenberg in Weinheim an der Bergstraße for shoe heels. It used rubber from Semperit, wood, and plastic. By the end of 1944, it was to produce 10 million pairs of heels, primarily for civilian use.[185] In the last years of the war, the company thus had plenty of business but considerable difficulty finding the labor it needed. It initially used German women obligated to do war work, but it found their performance unsatisfactory and switched to Russian POWs at the beginning of 1942. They proved very satisfactory, especially because the management sought to provide them with a decent amount of food. In the fall of 1942, however, they were replaced by Polish workers obligated to work in the Reich, who proved at once less productive and twice as expensive as the Russians. By the beginning of 1944, nearly all the firm's workers were foreigners. The Poles had been supplemented by Ukrainians for part of 1943, but production dropped when the Ukrainians were sent to work on the harvest. At the end of 1944, the company employed 100 workers, 35 "Ostarbeiter," the rest German. This, however, was not a good sign because this meant that the Poles and other foreigners had been taken away for work deemed more important, and the company was worried that it would be shut down unless it procured new important

---

[180] Ibid., Bauer to Fiala, March 30, 1944.

[181] Ibid., Bauer to Friedl, April 2, 1945.

[182] *Festschrift für Josef Joham*, pp. 81–84, and report of Oct. 20, 1939, BA-CA, CA-IB, Akalit 01/02-03.

[183] See ibid., the report on the firm of April 22, 1940.

[184] Ibid., report of March 27, 1940, and March 15, 1941. See also BA-CA, CA-V, the CA management board meeting of May 13, 1941.

[185] BA-CA, CA-IB, Akalit 01/02-03, reports of March 27, 1942, and Feb. 11, 1943.

war contracts. It was suffering heavily from bomb damage, a situation that was becoming steadily worse, as Pasching resignedly reported to Glatzl in late March 1945.[186]

There is a paucity of sources on many of the CA's holdings, but there appears to be no important holding that is more undocumented and obscure than what was called its "petroleum concern." It was a holdover from the days when the CA was still trying to play the role of a multinational investor, and the two leading oil groups among its oil interests, Fanto and Gallia, were among the CA's ten largest debtors in 1931.[187] The form taken by the CA petroleum concern before the Anschluss had been determined by the restructuring of the CA after 1931. Almost all the petroleum interests of the CA had been placed in a holding company, the N.V. Maatschappij voor Beheer van Effecten, Amsterdam (MBE). The CA held slightly more than 58 percent of the shares, and the Société Continentale de Gestion Monaco (Gesco), in which nearly all of the CA's international holdings had been placed, held slightly more than 41 percent. The MBE owned the assets of a number of companies: the Allgemeine Mineralöl-Industrie AG, Hamburg (AMIAG); the F.C. Oil Company, Hamburg; 50 percent of the Baltoil AG, Danzig; the Deutsche Fanto-Mineralöl-Industrie GmbH, Hamburg; the Fanto-Benzin-Import AG, Zurich; the Fanto Petroleum Maatschappij, N.V. Amsterdam; and the "Gallia" Mineralölprodukte Vertriebsgesellschaft AG, Vaduz, Liechtenstein.[188] These firms did not drill for oil but rather were primarily engaged in the storage, marketing, and transport of oil and oil products. The Deutsche Fanto and the AMIAG had a fleet of inland waterway vessels along with a variety of harbor stations used for storage, processing, and loading and unloading purposes. They also had 375 gas stations in 1939, a network of 334 in the former Sudetenland, 36 in Upper Silesia, and 5 in Hamburg. Additionally, they had a fleet of

tank cars, trucks, and vehicles. The Gallia also had a substantial number of tank cars and iron oil containers.[189] At the time of the Anschluss, there was also an Austrian Fanto with headquarters in Vienna and a refinery in Vösendorf, and a Fanto in Prague. The Austrian Fanto, in other words, was a producer as well as a distributor and marketer of petroleum products. The shares of the Czech Fanto were in the hands of a Swiss holding company, the Continentalen Gesellschaft für Bank- und Industriewerke, Basel (Contvalor).

Once the Germans had marched into Austria, the German army's agencies lost no time in making contact with the Austrian oil companies and concluding a delivery contract with them on March 21, 1938. There was a special interest in the Austrian Fanto because of its refinery and other oil-processing facilities. Indeed, already in the fall of 1937, Director Richard Ullner of the "Olex" company, which did business in Germany for the Anglo-Iranian Oil Company, had expressed interest in acquiring the Austrian Fanto. After the Anschluss, he argued even more forcefully that Fanto and "Olex" were a perfect fit. "Olex," which already controlled 11 percent to 12 percent of the German market, would acquire a 13 percent market share in Austria. In other words, there would not be a great disparity between its market share in Germany and the newly acquired Ostmark. Furthermore, "Olex" could offer something that no German oil company could, namely, payment in foreign exchange to Gesco for its share of the Austrian Fanto, as had been demanded by the Gesco president, Michael Terestchenko. "Olex" was in a position to pay in pounds, something a German company could not do under the existing exchange regulations. However, "Olex" was indirectly a foreign company and the Reichswerke Hermann Göring was anxious to get its hands on the Austrian Fanto companies, of which there actually were a total of four. Consequently, the Reichswerke set up a new distribution company, which

[186] Ibid., reports by Glatzl, Feb. 22, 1943, Jan. 31, 1944, Dec. 16, 1944, March 27, 1945.

[187] Stiefel, *Finanzdiplomatie*, p. 99.

[188] BA-CA, CA-V, Treuhand Bericht 1938, pp. 89–90.

[189] See DB, P 6528, Bl. 63–64, the memorandum on the various firms of what was here called the Fanto-Gallia Concern, Jan. 31, 1940.

then joined the Gasoline Association and bought up the Austrian Fanto in the spring of 1938. Apparently, as Director Ludwig R.E. Schmidt reported to Abs of the Deutsche Bank, the Gasoline Association paid a hefty price for the Austrian Fanto because "Olex" and Anglo-Iranian wanted to buy the Czech as well as the Austrian Fanto and was prepared to offer a considerable amount of foreign exchange for the acquisition. The Reichswerke, through the Gasoline Association, came into possession of the refinery and other facilities it had been seeking, at least until the Allied air forces eliminated them in July 1944.[190]

It was no accident that Schmidt not only informed Abs of the purchase of the Austrian Fanto but also thanked him for his good advice because Abs had obviously helped to broker the arrangement. Schmidt had the support of Keppler and Fischböck, and he also benefited from the information at Abs's disposal because of his negotiations with the CA at this time for the so-called friendship agreement, but he did not have Abs's understanding of the complexities of the international oil business. Abs sought to smooth the relations between "Olex" and the Gasoline Association because Ullner had also sought Abs's support, indicating how much "Olex" would like to work with the Deutsche Bank again. The Deutsche Bank had long been involved in the oil business, and Abs showed particular interest in the CA petroleum holdings. In a meeting with Heller on April 4, 1938, Abs pointed out to Heller that various companies in the old Reich were showing interest in Fanto, and Heller promised to inform Abs should he receive any inquiries.[191] Nevertheless, Abs was sensitive to the interests of Joham and Gesco. Terestchenko was prepared to sell off

all the oil interests in the MBE, a position not shared by Joham. As Abs noted, however, selling off CA foreign assets would be politically tricky so soon after the Anschluss, and would make an undesirable impression. Consequently, the CA losses were limited to the Austrian Fanto, and the other petroleum holdings remained with the CA. Joham proved quite tenacious in holding on to Fanto despite Abs's obvious interest in brokering a sale of the entire complex. In January 1939, Abs wrote to Joham saying that he realized that Joham was unwilling to separate the CA from Fanto but asking that he be informed should Joham change his mind. Later in the month, Abs informed Joham that there was a party interested in purchasing Fanto outright or in part, and while Joham agreed to discuss the matter, nothing appears to have come of it. All the evidence suggests that Joham considered Fanto the province of the CA and that it was high on his personal agenda as well and that Abs simply came to accept this and left the Fanto and its affairs to the CA to the very end of the war.[192]

Indeed, the CA's grip on these holdings was strengthened during the war insofar as circumstances allowed. As part of the arrangements with the CA's foreign shareholders after the Anschluss, the entire capital of the Fanto Hamburg was transferred to the CA. In October 1938, the assets of the Fanto in Prague and in the Sudetenland were transferred to the Deutsche Fanto in Hamburg, the price being paid by a cancellation of the debts owed to the CA. Apparently, it proved much harder to gain control of the 75 percent of the Prague shares held by Contvalor in Basel. In early 1941, that holding was increased to 76.2 percent by a capital increase, and Contvalor was very satisfied with its returns on this investment. It thus demanded a very high price in foreign exchange to be paid over three years, and Joham was still negotiating with Contvalor in

190 Wittek-Salzberg, *Die wirtschaftlichen Auswirkungen*, pp. 92–93; DB, P 6528, Bl. 47–54, Ullner to Joham, April 5, 1938; memorandums by Abs, April 14, 1938; Schmidt to Abs, May 17, 1938. For the complicated history of the oil industry, see Rainer Karlsch/Raymond G. Stokes, *Faktor Öl. Die Mineralölwirtschaft in Deutschland 1859–1974* (Munich 2003).

191 DB, B 51, memo by Pohle on a discussion between Abs and Heller, April 6, 1938.

192 DB, P 6528, Bl. 58, Abs to Joham, Jan. 5, 1938; ibid., P 6503, Bl. 199, 207, Abs to Joham, Jan. 20, 1939, and Joham to Abs, Jan. 27, 1939. See ibid., Vo1/2318, a report by Ulrich for Abs, May 31, 1945; ibid., Vo1/4850, a report by Abs to the Allied authorities, Aug. 28, 1946.

March 1941.[193] One of the more bizarre aspects of this quest for actual control of the Prague shares involved the effort to buy up the shares of N.V. Nederlandschen Petroleum-Maatschappij "Photogen," Amsterdam, which held 23.75 percent of the Prague shares. "Photogen" was in liquidation at the beginning of 1941, and some of its shares were in the hands of the Bankhaus Nicolai, the successor to the Viennese Bankhaus Rothschild, but 20 percent of the "Photogen" shares had been in the hands of the House of Rothschild in Paris. It was easy enough to purchase from Nicolai but much more difficult to find the Paris shares because neither the administrators of the bank in Paris nor the German Institute for the Researching of the Jewish Question in Frankfurt am Main, which held some of the Rothschild archives but had not yet organized them, could locate the "Photogen" shares or even information about them. The CA used the good offices of the Deutsche Bank in this effort, which lasted between January 1941 and February 1942, but was unable to find the material it sought. It finally hoped to have the RWM simply declare the shares lost and somehow work out a CA acquisition, again through the good offices of the Deutsche Bank. There is no record in either the CA or Deutsche Bank files of these shares being found or acquired. From a practical standpoint, this did not matter much because the Fanto Prague was being run in German interests anyway, but the desire to gain legal control through stock ownership was typical of the prevalent mentality in the Reich business community and reflected once again Joham's interest in the Fanto holding.[194]

The basic CA strategy for maintaining its Fanto interests, as far as one can determine from the limited documentation, was to support and finance the integration of the Fanto into the military preparations of the Reich and strengthen its own hold on the enterprise in the process. An important opportunity came in April 1939, when Rohdewald of the Reichs-Kredit-Gesellschaft reported on a meeting with the Oil Section of the RWM, where there was discussion of expanding Fanto Hamburg "in a discreet and confidential manner in the interests of the Reich ... as well as the increasing inclusion of Fanto Hamburg in the state managed procurement of crude oil."[195] The RWM wanted to know, however, whether Fanto was up to these tasks, organizationally and in terms of personnel, and whether it was prepared to collaborate in providing the necessary financial means to accomplish the tasks involved. The CA responded affirmatively.[196]

The CA's commitment to engaging Fanto in the RWM effort to acquire supplies of oil for military purposes was reflected in the conclusion of a "friendship contract" between Fanto and the Economic Research Corporation (WIFO) at the end of 1939. This organization had nothing whatever to do with research, economic or otherwise, and had been founded in 1934 as camouflage for a Reich-funded company for the storage of fuels for the army and air force at a time when the prohibitions of the Treaty of Versailles were still in effect. They were no longer in effect by 1938–1939, but the subterfuge was maintained, and the CA became a participant. It is significant that the connection with the WIFO was accompanied by a transfer of the AMIAG from Hamburg to Vienna so that it could take over the business of the Gallia in Vienna.[197] The CA-Fanto connection was no longer being challenged. When, in January 1940, the Hamburg shipping firm of Joh.T. Essberger proposed a consolidation of the Elbe river shipping that would include Fanto, the WIFO urged that the CA support the venture with a promise that the WIFO would protect its interests. Nevertheless, the CA was keen on protecting its own interests and

[193] BA-CA, CA-V, executive committee meeting of Oct. 21, 1938; management board meeting of Feb. 19, 1941, and working committee meeting of March 13, 1941.

[194] For the correspondence of 1941–1942 with the Deutsche Bank and other agencies on this effort, see DB, P 6528, Bl. 132–152.

[195] Ibid., P 6502, Bl. 317, telegram from Rohdewald to Joham, April 5, 1939.

[196] Ibid., P 6528, CA to Rohdewald, April 7, 1939.

[197] On the WIFO, see Karlsch/Stokes, *Faktor Öl*, pp. 180–181. See also BA-CA, CA-V, CA management board, Dec. 6, 1938.

opposed the takeover of the Fanto tanker fleet by Essberger, and Joham apparently succeeded in convincing the RWM that it should remain independent.[198] The CA was indeed prepared to pay a high price in supporting Fanto in Hamburg, which it considered undercapitalized. At the beginning of September, the CA turned the Fanto debts into equity and agreed to raise its capital from 300,000 RM to 3 million RM in order to support its construction program.[199] In August 1941, the Fanto Hamburg further consolidated its hold on the old MBE assets by buying up the shares of the Gallia, Mineralölprodukte-Vertriebs-Gesellschaft AG, Vaduz-Wien.[200]

It would seem that the CA was also successful in protecting itself against what was probably the greatest threat to its autonomy, namely, the Kontiental Öl AG founded in March 1941 by a consortium of banks headed by the Deutsche Bank. The new corporation was to be state dominated but was also to include privately owned international oil holdings, in particular French, Belgian, and Dutch stakes in Balkan oil firms, and to put them in the service of the Reich. It aimed to become a great new world-class international oil concern on the model of Standard Oil or Royal Dutch Shell, and these pretensions expanded considerably after the invasion of the Soviet Union. Abs had played an important role in the founding of Konti Öl, as the company was known, and he seemed well aware of the risky nature of the enterprise, in which government officials and bankers played the major role but in which real experts in the oil business were notably absent. The enterprise has often served as a model of monopolistic National Socialist state-private industrial collaboration, although it is now seen as an illustration of its failure.[201] In any case, the Deutsche Fanto was to be brought into this

net by pressure from the authorities in Berlin to build up its Bulgarian oil engagements. In negotiations at the end of 1941, there was an agreement that the Konti was to get a stake of 50 percent in the Deutsche Fanto in return for building up the Fanto transport fleet. The Konti was to be given a six-month option on purchasing 50 percent of the Fanto shares. But the negotiations, which required the "solution of many preliminary questions that will take some time," seem to have come to naught. The Konti ended up without a stake in the Fanto. It thus appears as another illustration of Joham's skills at stonewalling in matters pertaining to the Fanto.[202] The company, under the leadership of Kurt Winterstein, seems to have done quite well as late as 1944–1945 and asked the Deutsche Bank at the end of the war how to get into contact with the CA to pay off a mortgage that was due. The CA was able to maintain its interest in Fanto after the war and, indeed, to join forces with the Deutsche Bank in doing so in 1958–1959.[203]

7. ENNSER SUGAR

In contrast to the oil business, where the CA was deftly able to sidestep the regime's amateurish effort to organize a resource in which it was woefully deficient, the beet sugar business was filled with pitfalls in which ideological issues and internal Party rivalries and ambitions hampered rational economic decision making. Prior to the collapse of 1918, sugar production in the old regime had been centered in what became Czechoslovakia. The Austrian Republic only had six factories, most of them in Lower Austria and the Burgenland. They were insufficient to meet Austria's needs, and an effort was made

---

[198] Ibid., CA management board, Jan. 24, 1940, and March 27, 1940.

[199] Ibid., CA management board, Aug. 28, 1940 and working committee, Sept. 3, 1940.

[200] Ibid., CA working committee, Aug. 12, 1941.

[201] See Karlsch/Stokes, *Faktor Öl*, pp. 208–211 and Lothar Gall, *Der Bankier Hermann Josef Abs. Eine Biographie* (Munich 2004), pp. 109–111.

[202] BA-CA, CA-V, CA management board meeting, Dec. 5, 1941, and working committee meeting, Jan. 9, 1942. Fanto does not appear on the list of Konti holdings, DB, VI/2375 and VI/24.

[203] See ibid., VI/2318, memorandum by Ulrich for Abs, and the contracts in S. P. Akten, Nr. 1088, 1203, BA-CA, CA-V. I am grateful to Martin Müller for supplying me with information on the Fanto from the DB.

to increase production by setting up a major new factory and refinery at Enns in Upper Austria, which was also located in a major beet-producing area and had favorable transportation connections. The CA played a leading role in this effort, which resulted in the establishment of Oberösterreichische Zuckerfabriks AG in Enns in 1928. At the time of the sugar company's founding, the CA owned 65 percent of the shares, and the Zuckerfabriken A. Popper & Co. in Zborowitz-Kojetein in Czechoslovakia, which was owned by the Redlich family, held 35 percent of the shares. This development owed much to widely recognized and appreciated expert Hans von Redlich, who managed the company until the spring of 1938. The company proved very successful, effectively fighting the insects infesting the beet leaves with spraying actions. Von Redlich played a very important role in this effort. The CA made considerable financial sacrifice but was also rewarded by steadily increasing production.[204]

Jews played an extremely important role in the pre-1938 sugar industry. The Bloch-Bauer Group controlled the Österreichische Zuckerindustrie AG, Bruck/Leitha, and Strakosch Brothers controlled the Hohenauer Zuckerfabrik. The Hirmer Zuckerfabrik and the Siegendorfer Zuckerfabrik Conrad Patzenhofer's Söhne, both located in the Burgenland, belonged to a Jewish family. The Bloch-Bauer, Strakosch, and Patzenhofer families were all Jewish; the Sugar Section of the Länderbank Wien marketed their production. The one significant firm that was not Jewish owned was the Leipnik-Lundenburger Zuckerfabriken-AG, the majority of whose shares belonged to the von Schoeller and von Skene families.[205]

The Aryanization of these companies, insofar as it was required, had a variety of complexities and solutions. The Länderbank Wien played a very active and dishonorable role in selling off Bloch-Bauer's Österreichische Zucker to Reich German Aryanizers.[206] In the case of the Hohenauer, however, a number of projects competed with one another that reflected the interests vying for position in the sugar industry. One of these was promoted by the Reich Food Estate, represented by the head of the peasant cooperatives, Graf Johannes Hardegg, that proposed having the beet root peasant cooperative take over the Hohenauer. Hardegg claimed that the Aryanization was not only urgent, but also that it was necessary to satisfy the goal of the cooperative to have its own sugar manufacturing operations. During the crop season, Hohenauer employed some 1,300 workers and was serviced by 8,500 farmers. There was the danger that they would turn to other crops if their interests were not satisfied. Hardegg therefore proposed that the cooperatives take over not only Hohenau, but also the Zuckerwarenfabrik A. Eggers Sohn and the "Eggochemia," which produced chemical and pharmaceutical products. The Reich Food Estate was, of course, a highly ideological organization, and Hardegg and his allies bitterly noted that most of the Austrian sugar industry had been "either in the hands of large banks or Jews." The fear was that Aryanization would be used to promote capitalist interests at the expense of the farmers. They were especially alarmed by a counterproposal emanating from the Schoeller Group, which called for creating a consortium of Schoeller's Leipnik-Lundenburger Zuckerfabriken, Hirmer and Siegendorfer, Österreichischen Zucker and Oberösterreichischen Zucker, the CA, and the Länderbank Wien to take over and run Hohenauer under Schoeller, with the banks providing the necessary financing. The new company would be capitalized at 6 million RM, 2,650,000 RM of which would be provided by the aforementioned sugar companies. The remainder to be provided by the banks. The CA was to provide 1 million RM, and the Länderbank's share was not to exceed that of the CA. The Schoeller plan infuriated the Food Estate leaders, who saw it as a scheme

---

[204] *Festschrift für Josef Joham*, pp. 193–198.

[205] Felber et al., *Ökonomie der Arisierung*, pt. 2, pp. 816–850. On the role of the Länderbank Wien in the sugar business and its Aryanization, see Chapter 5, pp. 466–469 of this volume.

[206] See Chapter 5, pp. 466–469 of this volume.

to consolidate the existing enterprise with the object of dictating prices to farmers. In their view, productivity should determine the price of sugar beets, and firms that failed to produce satisfactorily, especially the Hirmer firm, should be shut down. They viewed the Schoeller interests as pursuing "the goal of in this way having the sugar-beet price determined by the costs of the weakest factory, a demand that is unacceptable from a National Socialist economic perspective."[207] All this reflected the oddities of "National Socialist economics," which usually supported cartels but sometimes supported individualist competition. In this case, the capitalist interests wanted a tight cartel, and the cooperatives were demanding individualist competition! Under such circumstances, the views of the political leadership, in this case Gau Economic Advisor for the Lower Danube Heinz Birthelmer, and Rafelsberger, were of great importance. Both men strongly opposed the plan to place Hohenau on a cooperative basis. Rafelsberger was especially opposed to turning agriculturalists into industrialists. At the same time, Birthelmer was aware that Schoeller intended to cut the cooperatives out altogether and believed that some of the sugar factories mentioned in the consortium did not really have the money to participate to the extent claimed, so that in the end the banks would have to provide special credits and have even more voice in the running of Hohenau. Birthelmer was most worried, however, that the Schoeller plan might not succeed and that the Food Estate program would then win out, something he wished to avoid in any case.[208] In this, however, he was unsuccessful. The Schoeller solution was not viewed as properly National Socialist,

and a company set up by the cooperatives, the Landwirtschaftliche Zucker AG, was able to use funding from the cooperatives' central clearing to buy Hohenau.[209]

Most important from the perspective of the CA, however, was the Oberösterreichischer Zuckerfabriks-AG in Enns. It presented a considerable variety of "problems" insofar as Aryanization was concerned. First, a substantial block of shares were in non-Aryan hands, and there was considerable Aryanization to do. By the time of the Anschluss, Enns had increased its capital from 6 to 9 million Schilling, and all the shares were tied into a syndicate headed by the CA. The distribution of shares by percent was:

CA	37.2%
CA sub-participants	6.9%
	Total CA = 44.1%
Zborovice-Kojetiner Zuckerfabriken	13.2%
Zborovice-Kojetiner sub-participants	22.7%
	Total Zborvice-Kojetiner = 35.9%
Österreichische Zuckerindustrie	3.4%
Böhmische Escompte-Bank und Credit-Anstalt, (Bebca) Prague	16.6%

According to CA calculations, 59.6 percent of these shares were in Aryan hands, that is, those of the CA and the Bebca and 83 percent in the hands of the CA's sub-participants (5,200 of 6,250 shares). Slightly more than 40 percent of the shares were in non-Aryan hands.[210] Second, there was a substantial number of Jews on the administrative council, either because they owned shares or were involved in the sugar business or both. They included Franz Rottenberg, who served as president for the CA, and also Ferdinand and Leopold Bloch-Bauer, Felix Bunzl, Isidor Pollak of the CA, as well

[207] ÖStA/AdR, MfWuA, VVSt 342c, Industrie, Zl. 612, Bd. 20, Position paper of the Reich Food Estate representatives with respect to their proposal (Feb. 10, 1939) and the Schoeller proposal (Aug. 26, 1938), all of which were submitted to the Kontrollbank. The Schoeller plan was supported by the CA executive committee at its meeting on Oct. 16, 1938, BA-CA, CA-V.

[208] BA-CA, CA-IB, Hirmer, 38/01, supervisory board meeting, Oberösterreichische Zuckerfabriks-AG, Aug. 4, 1938.

[209] Felber et al., Ökonomie der Arisierung, pt. 2, p. 836.

[210] BA-CA, CA-IB, Ennser Zuckerfabrik, 05/02-03, CA to Deutsche Bank, Nov. 17, 1938.

as Felix, Harry, and Hans von Redlich, Hans Friess, and Walther Loebl. Rottenberg, Leopold Bloch-Bauer, Bunzl, Friess, Loebl, Pollak, and Felix and Harry Redlich resigned immediately after March 13. That left Ferdinand Bloch-Bauer and Hans von Redlich on the council, and their continued service reflected yet a third "problem" at Enns, namely that Hans von Redlich played a central role in actual operations. Exactly what special service Bloch-Bauer performed is unclear, aside from his 3.4 percent stake, but quite possibly there was some feeling that he had to be kept on as a player in the beet sugar industry nationally and internationally.[211]

The reasons for retaining Hans von Redlich, however, were quite clear. He not only could boast talent and achievement, but he also enjoyed great popularity. On March 15, the workers and employees sent a representative, Hermann Hochgatter, who worked in the Vienna office of the company and was a Party member, to von Redlich with a message that read: "We ask you, dear Herr Doctor, to continue on as our leader, and we stand completely united behind you. We were always conscious of seeing in you an upright and social-minded person. This resolution was unanimously taken on the occasion of an assembly of all the workers and employees on the basis of your message to voluntarily and happily work for the well being of our laboring people in the National Socialist State we have created." The message was sent in the name of all the workers and employees in their function as members of the National Socialist Factory Cell Organization (NSBO), and was signed by two company officials, Franz Palik and Anton Scheibert.[212]

This was certainly not in the spirit of the feverish anti-Semitic activity that took place in the weeks following the Anschluss, but apparently it was briefly possible to entertain the notion that exceptions might be made, at least temporarily. This seemed to have been

the view of Director Heller of the CA, who had replaced Rottenberg as president of Enns's administrative council. He wrote to the president of the Industrial Association, August Schmid-Schmidsfelden, at the end of March, pointing out that von Redlich had stayed on at the behest of the CA because he had done so much for the company and because he wanted to prevent a "vacuum" in the management of its business. While recognizing that von Redlich's appointment might only be provisional, he nevertheless was careful to emphasize that this decision was strongly supported by the workers and employees as evidenced in their resolution and letter. A particular problem for this arrangement, however, was that the "Transition Committee for Jewish Business" in Linz had appointed Franz Palik as provisional commissar for the company, and Palik had in turn appointed another official of the company to have oversight over the books. Manifestly, this created a confusing situation and could easily lead to conflicts. Heller thus proposed that von Redlich retain his duties with respect to personnel and management but that Palik act in a supervisory capacity in Enns while Hermann Hochgatter act in a similar capacity in Vienna. The implication was that a non-Aryan could not be given a completely free hand, and those who had supported the retention of von Redlich would have supervisory functions and be a check on the situation.[213]

The evidence shows that Schmid-Schmidsfelden made some effort to be accommodating, but the arrangement was clearly unsatisfactory. By April 5, von Redlich decided to resign as leading manager of the company. He knew that he would not be easy to replace, and as a final service he suggested the appointment of Ernst Reissig, a very experienced person who held a leading position with the Ostdeutscher Zuckerfabriken in Klettendorf, Upper Silesia. Heller was grateful to von Redlich both for leaving without having to be asked and for the replacement suggestion. When von Redlich asked if he should also resign his

[211] The lists of the administrative council members are contained in BA-CA, CA-IB, Ennser Zuckerfabrik, 05/02-03.

[212] Ibid., Enns workers to Hans von Redlich, March 15, 1938.

[213] Ibid., Heller to Schmid-Schmidsfelden, March 30, 1938.

seat on the administrative council, Heller said that was not necessary at the moment and also expressed the hope that von Redlich would act as a consultant to help out the new general director. This, however, also proved a fantasy. Rafelsberger's office vetoed the appointment of Reissig for reasons never given, although it may have been because Reissig was not an Austrian. A worried Heller was beginning to fear that the "bonds of discipline and order" were loosening because of lack of leadership in Enns.[214] He now proposed the appointment of Anton Jungbauer, the former general director at Zborovice-Kojetiner. To be sure, Jungbauer had been retired for some years and was over seventy, but he was Aryan, allegedly in good shape, and prepared to take the job for a transitional period. Jungbauer had already agreed to serve on the administrative council.[215] The problem was finally solved by the appointment of Ludwig Güttl, who was in his early fifties, had been in the sugar business for more than twenty years, and had been employed by the Central Association of the Sugar Industry. Güttl had already applied for a position at Enns, and Heller interviewed him and seemed satisfied that he could do the job.[216]

The Aryanization of the administrative council proved far less complicated. Only two Jews remained after March 13, and when it became obvious by April's end that Jews would not be tolerated and the managerial problem was being solved, both von Redlich and Bloch-Bauer resigned. Finding the right Aryans from a business and strategic point of view was, of course, less simple. Jungbauer was one of the new appointments and played the role of a senior statesman on the council, an undoubtedly more relaxing job than running the company. An important appointment from a business and strategic point of view was Karl Nowotny, a director of the Bebca Bank in Prague. He was

a Sudeten German, and during the Reich's absorption of the Czech lands he distinguished himself by his close collaboration with the major German banks, above all the Dresdner Bank.[217] His bank was the chief Aryan shareholder on the council aside from the CA. The CA was represented by Heller and Fiala. Heller was to be replaced by Director Rudolf Pfeiffer of the CA after Heller left the CA in the spring of 1940. Pfeiffer unctuously promised to perform the duties entrusted to him in a "National Socialist spirit."[218] The political appointments, however, were of great importance, the most significant being that of SS Oberführer Franz Langoth, a major political leader in Linz and already a member of the CA administrative council. Langoth replaced Heller as president of the administrative council, and his backing and identification with Enns could obviously be extremely useful. In addition to the appointment of a Gau inspector, Stefan Schachermeyr, three other persons were appointed to represent the agricultural cooperative and peasant interests in the sugar beet industry, all of whom were identified as peasants. The importance of these interests has already been noted.[219]

The Aryanization of the ownership of Ennser moved very slowly. The Redlichs were quite willing to sell the shares held by their Zborovice-Kojetiner Zuckerfabriks AG and began negotiating through their lawyer as early as May 4, 1938. They were willing to sell for the nominal share value even though they thought the shares were actually worth considerably more. However, they wished to be paid in Czech currency in Prague rather than blocked marks.[220] While Heller and his colleagues claimed that the shares were not worth as much as before the Anschluss, the CA was

---

[214] Ibid., note by Fiala for Heller, April 26, 1938.

[215] Ibid., memorandum of meeting of Heller, Redlich, and Fiala, April 5, 1938; Heller to Schmid-Schmidsfelden, April 27, 1938.

[216] Ibid., Ennser Zuckerfabrik, 05/04-05, administrative council meeting, May 6, 1938.

[217] On Nowotny, see Wixforth, *Auftakt zur Ostexpansion*, pp. 48–50 and Kopper, *Zwischen Marktwirtschaft und Dirigismus*, pp. 317–320.

[218] BA-CA, CA-IB, Ennser Zuckerfabrik, 05/07, supervisory board meeting, May 28, 1940.

[219] These appointments were made at the administrative council meeting, May 6, 1938, BA-CA, CA-IB, Ennser Zuckerfabrik, 05/04-05.

[220] Ibid., Ennser Zuckerfabrik, 05/02-03, meeting of May 4, 1938.

nevertheless very anxious to get its hands on the 32,200 shares and was prepared to use the money owed it from another Czech company to pay the Redlichs. In early June, it sought and received permission from the VVSt to solve the problem in this way, but the ultimate decision was with the Foreign Exchange Office. That agency, however, refused to approve the agreement, which made the CA all the more nervous because of rumors that the Länderbank Wien was trying to purchase the shares. The CA then heard rumors that the Bebca had bought the shares, but this was false. The Bebca, however, then offered to buy the Redlich shares and to sell them along with his own shares in Ennser to the CA. The CA continued to complain that the price was too high because Ennser could not be expected to be as profitable as before. The matter dragged on until November 1938, when Director Heller of the CA turned to the Deutsche Bank. He explained the bank's problems with getting the shares and added that the Reich Food Estate was now showing interest in purchasing some of the shares for the cooperatives. That, in Heller's view, would further reduce the value of the shares. He was desperate to acquire them and had the full support of Rafelsberger's office but was blocked by the Foreign Exchange Office. He now proposed that they could take advantage of the negotiations for acquiring the Sudetenland branches of Czech banks to purchase the shares. The CA had promised to sell some of the Jewish-owned shares to the cooperatives at the cost of purchase. The acquired shares could be used for that purpose, and the CA would be happy if the Deutsche Bank wished to acquire other shares for its own use or for sale to its friends. Apparently, Abs was able to intervene with the foreign exchange authorities in Vienna and get an agreement to use funds acquired with the Czech bank branches to make the share purchases. Nevertheless, by the end of January 1939, the CA and the Deutsche Bank still had not gained possession of the 48,100 shares in Czech possession. Nowotny suggested various schemes by which the Bebca might buy the shares for the account of the CA, but this would have the effect of creating a foreign debt for the CA, that

is, for Germany. This was something the Foreign Exchange Office was now willing to contemplate in anticipation of changed currency relations between the Reich and the rump Czech state. Abs, however, remained skeptical.[221]

Most importantly, the pursuit of these shares and, indeed, of all the shares in Czech possession was running into trouble with Hans Kehrl of the Reich Economics Ministry. He had been engaged in the economic despoliation of the Czech lands well before the actual march into Prague in alliance with the Dresdner Bank and in the interests of the Reichswerke Hermann Göring. Heller, who had been pressing the RWM for support, had to tell Abs that Kehrl had spoken out against the acquisition of the shares on the grounds "that the means necessary for this were needed for more important purposes."[222] In a note to the CA on February 6, Kehrl pointed out that the need to purchase the shares in Prague would become less pressing because the Bebca would soon be transferred into German hands. Because the invasion was not to take place until March 20, this was a rather remarkable piece of information to be conveying at this time. At the same time, Kehrl also wanted the CA to explain "why and to what extent the further acquisition of the shares in non-Aryan possession still seems necessary under these circumstances."[223] In its response to Kehrl, the CA explained that 59.6 percent of the Ennser shares were in Aryan hands. The largest portion, 43 percent, belonged to shareholders in the Reich, among them the CA with 37.2 percent, and outside the Reich 16.6 percent were in the hands of the Bebca. But 40.4 percent of the shares were still in non-Aryan hands, and the CA was anxious to get them out of Jewish control because of the substantial minority shareholding rights involved. A third of the non-Aryan shares came from the Zborovice-Kojetiner Zuckerfabriken, and the remaining two-thirds were in the hands

[221] Ibid., Heller to Deutsche Bank, Nov. 17, 1938; CA to Deutsche Bank, Dec. 17, 1938; report by Heller, Jan. 26, 1939; Heller to Langoth, Feb. 23, 1939.
[222] Ibid., Heller to Deutsche Bank, Feb. 7, 1939.
[223] Ibid., Kehrl to CA, Feb. 6, 1939.

of the Jewish Redlich and Friess families as private holdings. The CA, of course, agreed that matters would be simpler if the Bebca were under German control, although the CA still believed that it would be better to have the Bebca's own shares in Ennser transferred to Reich-German possession. This was even more the case since the authorities had mandated that the shares were to be transferred to the farmer cooperatives. At the same time, the CA urged Kehrl to permit continuation of the effort to get the Jewish-owned shares and "not to underestimate the danger lying in the fact that the 35.9 percent share of the capital is not meaningless from the standpoint of corporation law, and that they could sell their shares to other foreigners, who could make better use of their rights."[224]

In the meantime, the German banks and the banks to be Germanized were making use of their powers. Even before the march into Prague, Nowotny was in contact with the CA about the sale of all its shares in anticipation of the exchange rate changes expected to come shortly. Matters were simplified by the occupation of Prague, when Nowotny could work even more openly for German interests as the Dresdner Bank took over the Bebca, and the Deutsche Bank under Director Walther Pohle took over the BUB. In the meantime, the Redlich brothers fled to London, from whence they still showed interest in selling their shares in April 1939, possibly for a low price if the payment was made in sterling.[225] Matters moved apace with respect to the Bebca shares in its own possession, and the Bebca controlled shares in the possession of the Zborovice-Kojetiner Zuckerfabriken, which Pohle now offered to purchase for the BUB and then place at the disposal of the CA. The Bebca planned to treat the shares owned by the Jewish families in London the same way, that is, to sell them to the BUB for the account of the CA, and it was reportedly negotiating with them at the beginning of June 1939. The negotiations were apparently not successful; a report of July 10, 1939, indicates that the BUB had purchased only 27,815 shares from the Bebca. When the war ended, the CA and its sub-participants owned 42.1 percent of the shares, the Cooperative Central Bank and the Peasant Beet Growers' League owned 35.36 percent of the shares, and the Redlich-Friess families continued to hold title to 22.54 percent of the shares in their names. The correspondence between the CA and various authorities suggests that no one knew where the shares in question actually were, but it was believed that they were part of the assets under compulsory administration that included the factory in Brünn.[226]

Whatever the case, the happy days when the CA and Hans von Redlich could work hand in hand in the operation of Ennser were over, and nothing reflected this more than the election in June 1939 of Hans Hauswirth, a St. Florian farmer and official of the Beet Sugar Cooperatives Association, to the vice-chairmanship of the Ennser supervisory board. Hauswirth served as a second vice-chairman along with Heller, while Langoth functioned as chairman but also as a third representative of the CA along with Heller and Fiala. The burgeoning conflict between the CA and the farmers' association interests was thus personalized as well as institutionalized in the two vice-chairmen, and this was to continue when Pfeiffer replaced Heller in the following year. These difficulties arose from the compulsory measures the Reich Food Estate enacted to increase sugar beet production. An incentive system of payments was introduced to encourage farmers to grow more sugar beets. The success of this system was dependent, however, on the ability of sugar refiners to cut their costs sufficiently to pay high prices to farmers. The result was a competition of interests. The refiners, eager to cut their costs and increase sales, did not want famers to increase production, and

---

[224] Ibid., CA to Kehrl, Feb. 7, 1939.
[225] Ibid., memorandum of April 24, 1939.

[226] Ibid., Referat Fiala, 26/05, memorandum by Heller, June 3, 1939, and memorandum by Fiala, July 10, 1939. On the distribution of the shares, see the Fiala memorandum of Sept. 16, 1948. For the problems connected with the whereabouts of the shares, see ibid., Ennser Zuckerfabrik, 05/02-03, CA to Property Office, State Minister for Bohemia and Moravia, Jan. 5, 1944.

the farmers sought to gain maximum payments for their crops even if that meant limiting over-all production and reducing the profitability of the refiners.[227]

In September 1939, Hauswirth and Güttl agreed to establish the "Beet Bureau of the Ennser Zuckerfabriks-Aktiengesellschaft" under their joint leadership. It was meant to act as a working community of the firm and the Upper Austrian Sugar-Beet Cooperative. It was to deal with all issues of common concern. Its list of fourteen topics of interest ranged from pricing policy and the recruitment of workers to pest control and dispute resolution. The two parties were supposed to pursue their particular activities independently, even if the cooperative was to use the facilities of the Ennser plant in return for a flat fee.[228]

Güttl seemed to welcome the establish-ment of what was essentially a parallel agency to his own. He was particularly appreciative of Hauswirth's assistance in procuring Polish POWs for the harvest in 1939. Ennser regularly used 400 or more POWs as harvest labor. In some instances, they engaged in what could be described as "sabotage" and the Gestapo had to be called in, but in general the foreign workers proved reasonably satisfactory. Most importantly, here seemed to be a tacit agreement that if Güttl worked with the bureau, the cooperative would supply the sugar beets the factory needed and would use its resources and contacts to maintain and increase production. In December, Güttl recommended supplying Hauswirth with one or two cars so that he and his aide could survey what was going on in the fields.[229]

Hauswirth became distinctly more aggressive in the spring of 1940. His overriding concern was to increase the price paid to the beet grow-ers and to guarantee them a price that would ensure continued production. At the super-visory board meeting of April 29, 1940, after

lobbying Güttl and Langoth, he argued that Enns should set a price even before the harvest began. This was opposed by Heller, who could not understand how Enns could go it alone and argued that the forces determining the price lay elsewhere. Langoth thought that it was prema-ture to set the price without knowing either how the harvest would turn out or how much the company would need for investments and other costs. In the face of this opposition and after an explicit statement by Langoth that the beet price was the central issue for the com-pany, Hauswirth accepted a delay in setting the price.[230]

At the same time, he was also moving on a different front, and it was no accident that he was doing so at a time when it appeared that Heller's domineering and forceful presence in the supervisory board might be coming to an end. At the end of March, Hauswirth informed Güttl that he planned to call a meeting of the Ennser syndicate to discuss the company's sales office in view of the need for the company to save money "in order to be able to pay the beet farmers a suitable beet price."[231] He could find no reason for the company to maintain a sales organization, that is, the Sugar Section of the CA, in Vienna, especially in view of the strict distribution controls and the sale of most of the Enns production on the Upper Danube. Furthermore, he noted that the contract between the CA and Enns, which according to Hauswirth was to expire on September 30, 1943, provided for earlier cancellation and compensation to the CA for its lost commis-sion in the event that a state sugar monop-oly was established. In Hauswirth's view, state market control already existed and reasonable compensation for the CA could be worked out. In short, Hauswirth now proposed that the tie between Ennser and the CA Sugar Section be dissolved and that the costs involved in using its services be eliminated. As Fiala noted in his report to the CA management board, the commission had already been reduced, so

---

[227] See John Perkins, "Nazi Autarchic Aspirations and the Beet-Sugar Industry, 1933–1939," *European History Quarterly* 20 (1990), pp. 497–518.

[228] BA-CA, CA-IB, Ennser Zuckerfabrik, 05/07, the agreement of Sept. 1939.

[229] Ibid., supervisory board meetings, Oct. 10 and Dec. 11, 1939.

[230] Ibid., supervisory board meeting, April 29, 1940.

[231] Ibid., Ennser Zuckerfabrik, 05/02-03, report by Fiala, March 27, 1940.

that the 182,172 RM paid to the CA in 1939 would be lowered to approximately 157,012 RM. That included all the expense the CA incurred in selling the sugar. Needless to say, the CA was quite worried by this attack on its sugar division. For the moment, however, it found an ally in Director Erich Pfennig of the Cooperative Central Bank of the Ostmark AG, which also held shares in Ennser. Pfennig told Fiala that he did not take Hauswirth all that seriously, but that he would unconditionally oppose discussion of the matter, to say nothing of actual measures to terminate the CA contract. He also had compared the commissions charged for sales by the other sugar factories and found the CA prices fully in line with its counterparts.[232]

The CA had another ally in the Länderbank Wien, whose own sugar division was also threatened by the negative attitude toward bank engagement in these activities. The banks were able to ward off a full assault for the time being, but they were undoubtedly on the defensive. This was especially evident in shutting down the Hirmer Zuckerfabrik AG in August 1941 over the objections of the two banks, which were its chief shareholders. They took the position that the shutdown was shortsighted and that Hirmer had a potential future once the war was over. The Main Association of the Sugar Industry, on the other hand, received an expert report arguing that railroad efficiency required that Hirmer be shut down and that it was much less modern than the Siegendorfer Zuckerfabrik. Although Pfeiffer and Director Warnecke of the Länderbank put up a hard fight to maintain Hirmer, they ultimately gave way to the association, which was prepared to pay a good price for the shares if the factory was closed immediately. The alternative, letting Hirmer remain closed but not liquidated during the coming years, threatened the value of the shares and the interests of the creditors. The political effect of the Hirmer liquidation, however, was to improve the position of the beet farmers by reducing the number of

sugar factories they were supplying and cutting overall production costs in the industry.[233]

The lines of conflict within the Ennser supervisory board became sharper in late 1941 and early 1942. Hauswirth's fundamental goal was to guarantee the farmers a beet payment of 4 RM per 100 kilograms of beets instead of the 3.20 RM they had been paid before. Although everyone agreed that the farmers needed a stronger incentive and were delivering below cost, the question was where to turn. The general line of the organizations in the Ostmark was to appeal to Berlin for a subsidy because the sugar industry could not cover its investments and other costs, sell at controlled prices, and still pay what the farmers desired. Hauswirth certainly agreed with such efforts in Berlin, but he was most concerned that Ennser act in any case, arguing at the end of 1941 that the farmers would cut their production in half and Ennser might just as well go out of business. If the farmers were promised the 4 RM rate for 1942–1943, he maintained, he could guarantee the needed beets. Langoth tended to support Hauswirth's arguments and expressed bewilderment at the agrarian leadership's failure to demand more consideration for the sugar industry. Faced with a consensus in the supervisory board that Ennser should at least consider acting on its own, Pfeiffer somewhat gingerly raised the question of whether it really had "the courage, the strength, and also the inclination" to do so and whether such action might not be prejudicial to the entire industry. He reminded his colleagues that "we are in a steered and planned economy." The CA, as a cofounder of Ennser, had done "pioneering" work in investing with very little reward to promote the company, but this was justified by subsequent returns. He claimed that the CA would consider such self-sacrifice again but doubted that it would lead to the desired results. In general, he believed that "Enns hardly would be in a position to do anything independently; we can certainly make proposals and promote them, but we cannot come to any decisions since we

232 Ibid., memorandum by Fiala, April 1, 1940.

233 See the discussions of Aug. 18, 1941, and related documents in ibid., Hirmer, 38/01.

do not – as already stated – find ourselves in a free economy."[234] A hard-pressed Güttl was torn betwixt and between. On the one hand, he recognized that Ennser might have the wherewithal to pay 4 RM for a couple of years before truly finding itself at the end of its rope, but on the other hand, acting alone would be resented by the other producers and would also hurt Ennser's chances for subsidies should the government be inclined to provide them. While Hauswirth flailed about, now calling for Ennser to act on its own, now declaring that the Gauleiter could simply mandate a 4 RM rate, Pfeiffer and most of the others recognized that all solutions had to be made in the context of the controlled economy and all the problems and traps it created.

It rapidly became clear that Berlin would not even discuss paying the 4 RM rate the Vienna Sugar Association had requested. The Ostmark factories would have to pay 3.20 RM whether they could afford it or not, and the Main Association of the Sugar Industry in Berlin or Vienna would then provide a subsidy to bring the amount up to 3.60 RM or 3.80 RM. At a meeting of the bankers in the Ennser supervisory board with Güttl at the end of January 1942, Güttl admitted the company could not afford to pay more than 3.06 RM while Director Pfennig warned that Ennser had never benefited and could not benefit from acting alone and sharply criticized the fact that Ennser had promised its farmers 3 RM, while the other Ostmark producers had not gone beyond 2.50 RM. Pfennig pointed out that things were actually much worse in the old Reich, where the factories were paying 2.20–2.40 RM and large quantities of beets went unharvested. Even then, the Reich was going to have to pay a subsidy of 50 million RM to enable the factories to pay the beet growers at this low level. What becomes evident from this discussion was that Hauswirth was terrorizing Ennser, and Pfennig decided to be quite explicit about the problem, noting that he had heard Hauswirth was abusing his position to interfere with management, that this was creating an insupportable situation,

and that it was high time Langoth said something about it. Pfeiffer agreed completely with Pfennig with respect to both the payments to the farmers and to Hauswirth.[235]

There is no clear evidence as to whether or not Hauswirth ceased interfering with management, but he most certainly did not tone down his activities. In February, the CA felt impelled to present evidence for the entire period 1932–1942 that it was not charging excessive commissions despite Hauswirth's constant complaints.[236] At a meeting of the supervisory board in July, Hauswirth complained about the excessive number of officials at Ennser when compared with firms in the old Reich and warned that the financial situation would make them have to watch every pfennig in the future, particularly if the government provided no support for beet cultivation. He went on to urge that they fire most of the employees and hire only when seasonal work was required. This seemed to irritate Langoth, who rejected such pessimism and believed the company had a future, that it would be protected by the authorities in the Upper Danube against apparent efforts to take away its beet fields, and that government support for beet payments would continue.[237]

The big battle, however, was to come over the role of the CA in the sale of Ennser Sugar. On September 22, 1942, the Gau economic advisor for the Upper Danube, Oskar Hinterleitner, wrote to Langoth asking him to exclude the CA sales bureau from the distribution of Ennser sugar. He pointed to a series of complaints he had received that the use of the CA office slowed down business, that the Vienna office had no sense of market conditions in the Upper Danube, did not provide the types of sugar requested by customers, lacked real contact with the customers, and thus hurt the work of the Sugar Association. Added to this were the complaints about the high provisions charged. Hinterleitner was convinced

[234] Ibid., supervisory board meeting, Nov. 26, 1941.

[235] Ibid., Ennser Zuckerfabrik, 05/02-03, report by Fiala on meeting of Jan. 23, 1942.

[236] Ibid., report to the CA management board, Feb. 2, 1942.

[237] Ibid., Ennser Zuckerfabrik, 05/07, meeting of July 28, 1942.

that the price of sugar could be reduced if the sales bureau were excluded from its "economically unjustified middleman position." As Hinterleitner made clear, however, his demand had also to be seen in the context of the growing demand for a "rationalization" of the banking industry, to be discussed later in this study, and fit in well with the old hostility toward the banks expanding beyond their financial functions. He concluded by saying that "I above all hold it unsuitable for economic policy considerations that a bank should operate as a middleman for goods, as is the case with the sugar business of the Creditanstalt. The present efforts in the direction of banking concentration do not exhaust themselves only in an elimination of competition in the money market but they must also lead even more to bringing the banks back to their actual tasks."[238]

The CA had been selling sugar through its goods department since 1862 and was thus bound to view its "actual tasks" somewhat differently. The immediate problem was to save the CA's situation at Ennser rather than fight the issues of "principle" that concluded Hinterleitner's missive. Pfeiffer helped his CA colleagues draft a letter to Langoth designed to refute the charges against the Sugar Section and show that Hinterleitner was incorrectly informed. The letter argued that the Sugar Association of the Ostmark had spontaneously expressed satisfaction with the work done by the CA, that the conditions on the sugar market were responsible for the difficulties in satisfying the special demands of customers, that the commissions reported to Hinterleitner were inaccurate, and that commissions had been reduced in the past but could not be reduced further because of the complexities and costs of selling sugar.[239] With this information, it was possible to persuade Hinterleitner that he had been misinformed, especially because the business manager of the Sugar Association, Herzog, backed up the CA figures. The letter also promised that there would be further negotiations on the commissions. In light of these circumstances

Hinterleitner did not press his demand for an immediate severance of the connection between Ennser and the CA. From Langoth's perspective, the central issue was that Ennser had a contract with the CA that ran until September 30, 1943, and any changes in the sales arrangements had to be negotiated rather than decreed because of the legal rights involved. He personally felt, as he made clear at the supervisory board meeting of October 13, 1942, that the banks would eventually get out of marketing goods by force of circumstances, but he did not believe that this issue, along with a host of other needed reforms, could be addressed while the war was going on. The members of the board coming from industry and banking strongly supported the CA operation. Roland Loos, a prominent Linz attorney, praised the CA's expertise and efficiency, and Nowotny not only did the same but also pointed out that people entertained the notion that the members of the Sugar Section were bankers rather than the sugar experts they were, and that ultimately they lowered rather than raised prices. Naturally, Hauswirth did not agree, arguing that Ennser could sell the sugar cheaply and more efficiently on its own, a claim that Pfeiffer contested. Not only did Pfeiffer praise for the CA Sugar Section, but he also defended centering sales activity in Vienna because the Sugar Association was also located there. Langoth agreed with Pfeiffer that those wanting to set up sales in Enns were underestimating what was involved. Most importantly, however, he was not prepared to shunt aside the CA, which had made so many sacrifices for the company, and to violate their contract.[240]

This did not put an end to Hauswirth's needling of the CA. In late November 1942, he made a complaint to the Price Oversight Board that the CA was using its commissions to further its position at Enns and to profit at the expense of the farmers. Hauswirth insisted that the CA's services could be eliminated and money saved by using the services of a regional merchant named Ozelsberger to do the selling.[241] The important

[238] Ibid., Hinterleitner to Langoth, Sept. 22, 1942.
[239] Ibid., CA to Langoth, Sept. 29, 1942.

[240] Ibid., supervisory board meeting, Oct. 13, 1942.
[241] Ibid., Ennser Zuckerfabrik, 05/01, memorandum by Hauswirth, Nov. 28, 1942.

thing, however, was that Hauswirth managed to make enough noise to gain the attention of the Sugar Association. In his charges, he damaged not only the CA but also the Länderbank, which had a similar business. The CA Sugar Section tried to strike back by pointing out that Hauswirth did not know what he was talking about and childishly acting as if selling sugar was nothing more than a matter of telephone conversations. As for Ozelsberger, he had no record whatsoever of serving Enns and was part of a clique that Hauswirth was trying to put into power.[242]

The trouble was that the CA claim as the founder of Ennser meant very little in this rather hostile environment. Langoth had served as a protector, but he had been planning during the second half of 1942 to leave office because of Hitler's decision that members of the Reichstag and high Party officials were not to serve as supervisory board members to liberate them from corrupting influences. Langoth had planned to leave in October. A decree, however, allowed him to stay on until March 1943, when he formally resigned and was given a tearful and flowery laudatio by Pfeiffer. There were good reasons for tears on the part of the CA. In late January, Fiala learned from Güttl that a plot was being hatched by Hauswirth, Rudolf Kirchmayr, and Fritz Feitzlmayer, the trio allegedly representing farmer interests, to push the appointment of a coal dealer named Hammerschmidt to replace Langoth. Hammerschmidt had held official positions in the Enns district but had as his main interest driving out the Montana Kohlenhandels GmbH and servicing Ennser with his own coal.[243]

Given such prospects, there was not much for the CA to look forward to at Enns. When the supervisory board met on March 30, the outgoing Langoth was able to thank the CA for voluntarily surrendering its long-standing contract to sell Ennser sugar, although the Vienna bureau of Enns was to remain in place until after the war, primarily because of the housing

problem. The business of selling sugar was now solely in the hands of the management, and Langoth expressed the hope, perhaps not without irony, that it would function as well as it had in the past. Langoth seemed not to be able to say enough good things about the CA, and Pfeiffer could not say enough good things about Langoth. Needless to say, good things were also said about the man chosen by the Gauleiter to serve as chairman of the supervisory board, farmer leader Fritz Feitzlmayer. Pfeiffer appeared relieved, Hauswirth appeared happy, and because Feitzlmayer had a long association with Enns and promised to follow in the steps of Langoth, the solution seemed as logical as anything else that had taken place since 1938.[244]

The documentation on Ennser for the remaining years of the war is very thin. It shows a reduction in available beet sugar and a reduction in production. The company seems not to have had trouble recruiting labor for the harvest periods. In 1943, it employed 600 POWs; in 1944, it had many fewer POWs at its disposal (34), but it did have 597 foreign male and 21 foreign female workers.[245] In the Festschrift for Josef Joham published after the war, Ennser is presented as a study of neglect and mismanagement that had to be rebuilt almost from scratch. It is one of the few cases in which serious credit is given to a Jewish founder, Hans von Redlich.[246] This hardly exonerates the CA for its behavior toward him and the other Jews driven out of the firm, but the change of ownership did not necessarily mean that the CA could reap advantage from the new situation. The CA's steady loss of ground between 1939 and 1943 is an interesting illustration of how Byzantine doing business in the Third Reich could be in a controlled and politicized industry.

The CA Textile Concern

Important cases of CA's holding in the textile, wood, and paper industries have already been discussed in connection with the CA's expansion

[242] Ibid., memorandum by CA of Feb. 10, 1943.
[243] Ibid., Ennser Zuckerfabrik, 05/02-03, memorandum for Pfeiffer, Jan. 23, 1943.
[244] Ibid., Ennser Zuckerfabrik, 05/07, supervisory board meeting, March 30, 1943.
[245] Figures in ibid., Referat Ketterer, 27/04.
[246] *Festschrift für Josef Joham*, pp. 193, 196–197.

abroad and Aryanization. Nonetheless, certain firms, especially in the textile industry, deserve closer attention for what their history reveals about how the CA operated as an industrial concern between 1938 and 1945. One of those is the Guntramsdorfer Druckfabrik AG, a major producer of colored and printed fabrics that was almost 100 percent owned by the CA after its reorganization during the Depression. The company had an excellent reputation and did a considerable amount of export business. As in other cases, the CA presided over the Aryanization of the company's personnel. Guntramsdorfer's managing administrative council president, David Goldmann, who also served as a director, left Austria on March 11, 1938, with his family and was let go for that reason. The other Jews were put on leave and then let go in short order as well, with the one notable exception of General Director Richard Neumann. His case is very reminiscent of Hans von Redlich's in that the NSBO informed the CA on March 19 that "the entire Aryan workforce of the enterprise declares itself to be fully and completely in agreement with the continuation of business operations by General Director Dr. Richard Neumann...."[247] Because the company was leaderless and Neumann's relations with the employees were extremely good, the CA was quite happy about this, but everyone understood that it would be a temporary arrangement. Indeed, Neumann had been let go by early May. Whatever the sentiments involved, his retention would have led to the appointment of a commissarial administrator and would have hurt business. The company nevertheless kept him on as a consultant until a desperately needed marketing director could be found.[248]

Once these personnel issues were settled, the company did quite well in the years that followed. Naturally, it sought to make itself as competitive as possible with its counterparts in the Reich, and the CA seemed quite willing to support its investment program and to provide

the company with a steady diet of credits. In the first half year of 1940, Guntramsdorfer's indebtedness to the CA rose from 1,440,550 RM to 3,500,000 RM. It largest cost was raw materials. The war brought both benefits and problems. Cutting off imports from France and England boosted the demand for production from the Reich. There was also increasing production for the military. On the other hand, the drafting of workers had led to a reduction of the workforce from 399 to 344. It seems to have remained at this level according to a report of October 1941, and there was upbeat discussion of rebuilding the plant once the war was over. At the same time, securing raw materials was becoming increasingly difficult. By June 1942, the number of workers had dropped to 330, and the difficulties in finding raw materials had increased still further. The company was increasingly seeking work for the military. It had received an SS contract to wash more than 200,000 meters of military blankets, but it was also trying to fit in with the armaments program and rented out both space and its workers to the military. The goal was to hold on to its workforce as far as possible for the future. The CA was fully aware that the profitability of the firm, which was based on access to raw materials and strong export sales, could not last through 1942 and that everything would have to be done to secure military contracts for the firm. While the CA maintained a 4 million RM credit line for the company, only half the credit was actually being used.[249] Nevertheless, despite considerable bomb damage, Guntramsdorfer appears to have made it through the war in good enough shape to resume production as a major CA concern member when it was all over.

That could not be said for Gebrüder Enderlin, Druckfabrik und Mechanische Weberei, a manufacturer of woven goods based in Traun bei Linz. The company, which was more than 99 percent in CA possession, seems to have

247   BA-CA, CA-IB, Guntramsdorfer, 06/04, PG Josef Andreas to the CA, March 19, 1938.

248   Ibid., memorandum for Pfeiffer, May 4, 1938.

249   See the projected program asked for by the company in a letter to the CA of April 21, 1938; ibid., the quarterly reports of July 11, 1940, Oct. 7, 1941, June 10, and Oct. 29, 1942; and BA-CA, CA-V, report to the working committee, Sept. 25, 1942.

been doing fairly well both before and after the Anschluss. As had been the case with Ennser and Guntramsdorfer, it had a Jewish managing director, Franz Prager, whose retention was supported by the NSBO cell in the company, but he was let go when it became clear that no Jews were to be kept on.[250] Enderlin, however, did not have much of a future in any case because it fell victim to the consolidation of the textile industry mandated by Berlin in mid-1942. Although it was highly productive and had also been lauded for its social practices, the firm's petitions to stay open were rejected because, among other reasons, it was an enterprise owned by a large bank and was deemed not to be entitled to the protection given to privately owned enterprises. When it was shut down, the CA-owned Pottendorfer Spinnerei und Felixdorfer Weberei took over its machinery and its shares.[251]

In addition to the Guntramsdorfer firm, the Pottendorfer Spinnerei und Felixdorfer Weberei, the largest enterprise of its kind in the Ostmark, the "Patria" Spinnerei und Wirkwarenfabriken AG, and Wollwaren constituted the most important CA textile firms operating in Austria itself. Pottendorfer und Felixdorfer, in addition to the factories in the towns from which it took its name, also had plants in Rohrbach and Ebensee and had built substantial housing facilities for its workforce. It underwent considerable expansion. "Patria" had its production site in Heidenreichstein and was a major hosiery manufacturer. As for the Vienna-based Wollwaren-Verkaufs AG, whose Aryanization has been discussed earlier in this study, it was an important producer of woolen clothing products by 1938.[252]

The CA's textile concern was one of the bank's consolations in 1938–1939, a time when it was losing some of its prize holdings. The improved economic situation following the Anschluss and consumer demand led to a substantial increase in production and sales, the profits from which were used to modernize plants and try to remain competitive with the old Reich firms that had allegedly enjoyed prosperity for six years. The coming of the war was a hard blow because the textile industry was not viewed as a war industry. It was subject to controls immediately on the outbreak of war, received only limited public contracts, and was forced to reduce production. At Pottendorfer und Felixdorf, which had been operating between 150 percent and 179 percent of capacity, the spinning mills were cut back to working at 50 percent of capacity, and the weaving looms were operating at 75 percent of capacity. The government had imposed a regulation requiring all Reich textile works to operate below capacity. Before the outbreak of war, Pottendorf employed 3,350 people, but its workforce was reduced to 840 once war broke out. The slippage was particularly evident in the wool industry. It had been operating at 35 percent of capacity prior to the Anschluss but was then able to increase production to 80 percent of capacity by September 1939 before losing ground because of the outbreak of the war. It was then able to recover somewhat as the war went well. In fact, while not returning to prewar levels, the textile firms stabilized at an acceptable if not desirable level. Production of women's hosiery at "Patria" was severely reduced. It had an army contract for socks, however, that kept 385 of the 590 workers there busy.[253]

As suggested earlier in this chapter, the Anschluss gave the Pottendorfer und Felixdorfer a reason and an opportunity to expand its operations. With CA support, it launched a substantial investment program. The number of employees increased from 2,528 in 1937 to 3,300 in 1938. The company had already been converting to

---

[250] BA-CA, CA-IB, Enderlin, 04/04-05, statement by factory cell, March 17, 1938, and Josef Patzak to Friedl, June 13, 1938. Prager asked for a speedy payment of the money due him for early separation, which amounted to RM 6,676.67, but agreed to a reduction for immediate payment and received RM 3,000 on June 22, signing away any further claims. See his note to the company, June 22, 1938, ibid.

[251] See ibid., the report of the Enderlin management board for the year 1942 and related documents.

[252] For brief histories of these firms, see *Festschrift für Josef Joham*, pp. 145–161.

[253] BA-CA, CA-IB, Referat Patzak, 30/02, report by Josef Patzak to the Concern Division, undated, but probably late 1939–early 1940.

the use of cellulose in 1937, which, of course, fit in well with the Reich's striving for autarky.[254] While the coming of the war put a dent in the company's expansion, it seems to have held its own well enough, and its social policies and successful management earned it recognition in the wartime performance competition in 1942–1943. Gauleiter Jury personally awarded the firm a bronze medal for its health services in September 1942, and the Ebensee plant received special recognition for wartime performance. This was not without a certain irony because Speer's Munitions Ministry decided in 1943 that textile production had to be reduced and the workers transferred to armaments work. As a consequence, the authorities chose to shut down Ebensee. General Director Friedrich von Rüdlhammer strongly objected, pointing out that the plant had been constructed at considerable expense at the express wish of Gauleiter Jury, although there had been partial shutdowns at the more favorably located plants in Felixdorf and Rohrbach. He played up Ebensee's excellent record in health and sanitation and also noted that much less modern and efficient plants were being kept open. He raised particular objection to the conversion of the plant to armaments production, which could only be done by making its facilities unusable for textile production in the future. In the end, a compromise was struck whereby Ebensee would give up some of its workers for armaments production and provide some storage space for military production, but the plant could continue textile production and was struck from the list of enterprises to be shut down.[255]

The Pottendorfer und Felixdorfer managed to expand somewhat despite the wartime troubles. Not only did it acquire the machinery of Enderlin when that firm was forced to shut down, but it also effectively took over the Littai-Pragwalder Textilwerke AG in Pragwald. The Littai-Pragwalder Textilwerke, founded

in 1923, had been on Yugoslav soil. When the Mautner concern was broken up in 1931, it was one of the CA's holdings in that concern. Its entire capital, which was formally lodged in the Vereenigden Textiel Maatschappijen N.V., Rotterdam, was transferred to the CA with the latter's dissolution after 1938 and was then sold to the Pottendorfer und Felixdorfer, almost 100 percent of which was owned by the CA. Following the German annexations in South Styria and the Kraina in 1941, the plants were located on German soil. At the same time, the company headquarters moved from Laibach/Ljubljana to Marburg/Maribor. The company continued to operate sales offices in Agram/Zagreb and Belgrade, and it did considerable business in the Balkans and Turkey, which supplied its cotton. It was a very prosperous and successful company, thanks to a seven-year investment program, and had 522 employees at the end of April 1943. It suffered some disruptions in the labor force as a result of a wave of political arrests conducted by the authorities in 1942. The company was left to operate as an independent subsidiary of the Pottendorfer AG for the time being, but the plan was eventually to make it a branch of the Pottendorfer or to merge the two companies. Rüdlhammer became chairman of the supervisory board, and Patzak represented the CA, while Emmerich Kieslinger was made the sole director. Patzak made clear to Kieslinger that his appointment was limited to two years, after which the fate of the firm would be decided.[256] Its fate, of course, was to be returned to postwar Yugoslavia, so that Pottendorfer did not benefit much from this rather short-term acquisition. While Pottendorfer & Felixdorfer struggled on with, under the circumstances, relative success during the war, its plants suffered severe bomb damage in 1944–1945, all of which were reported

---

[254] See BA-CA, CA-IB, Pottendorfer, 13/10–11, the report to the company shareholders' meeting, June 27, 1938.

[255] Ibid., Pottendorfer, 13/06-07, meeting with the Gau economic advisor in Linz on Sept. 20, 1943.

[256] Ibid., Littai, 40/01, Patzak report to the CA management board, undated but from 1943. On the arrests, see the report for the supervisory board, July 2, 1943; see also Patzak's somewhat irritable letter to Kieslinger, for whose complaints about his living and working conditions Patzak seemed to have little sympathy, ibid., Littai, 40/02.

in grim detail to Patzak and Fiala of the CA concern division.[257]

The "Patria" Spinnerei und Wirkwarenfabriken AG, and Wollwaren was more fortunate in its location at Heidenreichstein on the Lower Danube, which was off the main path of bombing operations. The original name of the company was Spinnerei und Wirkwarenfabriken M. Honig AG, and the change to "Patria" in 1939 was part of its Aryanization. At the time of the Anschluss, the company was in deep trouble. It had not earned a profit for years and had borrowed money from the companies Philipp Haas & Söhne and Enderlin of the CA concern. As Patzak, who had recently been assigned to watch over the CA textile interests, reported in a letter of March 31, 1938, the CA had originally appointed one of its officials, Karl Roth, to devise a reorganization plan, but Roth had been arrested before the plan, which did not take the Anschluss into account, could be implemented. In Patzak's view, the situation was urgent because the company faced bankruptcy and because 600 employees would be put out on the street in an area already suffering high unemployment. The CA thus had to come to the rescue, but at the same time it requested a reorganization plan before doing so. Patzak, however, thought there was no time to lose. A further complication was that four of the five members of the administrative council, whose president was Franz Rottenberg and two of whose members were Karl Roth and Paul Gerngroß, were Jews.[258]

The combination of monetary infusions from the CA, the Aryanization of the company leadership, and the appointment of Karl Weninger as general director managed to turn things around. Despite the war, Weninger was able to report in June 1940 that the company had a workforce of 712, down from 739 six months earlier, that production had been maintained, and that further investments were

being made. As noted earlier, military orders for socks were particularly important in enabling the company to remain in operation. The company apparently employed POWs from Serbia later in the war. Weninger was not without ambitions of his own, reporting to Patzak in August 1942 that he had learned that the RWM was encouraging old Reich firms to seek out acquisitions in Serbia. This confirmed in his mind that "despite the constant claim that Vienna and the Ostmark have the task of penetrating the Southeast, firms from the old Reich are drawn in for this purpose while Ostmark firms are not at all informed about such possibilities."[259]

The little information about Wollwaren-Verkaufs AG that is available suggests that it also initially benefited from the Anschluss. A report to the CA in late 1938 noted that the number of workers had increased from 58 to 135 and that the number of looms in operation had increased from forty-eight to eighty-eight, with four operating on a double shift. Furthermore, the plant at Günseldorf had improved working conditions and was renovating its worker housing. The future, in fact, seemed very bright.[260] It became less bright as the war went on. Particularly onerous was the fact that, as was the case with other textile firms, the armaments industry quite literally moved in on its facilities. A retraining school for armaments workers was set up at Wollwaren that compelled a rearrangement of the plant and the restriction of actual textile production to a small part of the plant. A metalwares factory moved in later, and Wollwaren was shut down for a period. It finally received permission to operate on a very limited basis but then found itself in the midst of heavy fighting. When the Germans retreated, an SS unit was instructed to blow up the factory, but the management seems to have negotiated with the SS to save the severely damaged plant in the last minute. What is remarkable is how quickly Wollwaren and the other CA

[257] See ibid., the reports of July 8, 1944, and March 27, 1945.

[258] Ibid., Patria, 12/06, report by Patzak, March 31, 1938. Roth seems to have been let go but was deported in 1941 and did not return.

[259] Ibid., Weninger to Patzak, Aug. 20, 1942, and his reports of Aug. 9 and Oct. 11, 1940.

[260] Wollwaren 18/06-07, unsigned and undated report but obviously by Patzak from late 1938.

concern textile companies went back into business after the war and made progress that was less dramatic but certainly more solid than that experienced in 1938–1939.[261]

The CA Wood and Paper Products Enterprises

The same could also be said for the major wood and paper products companies in the CA concern, the Samum Vereinigte Papierindustrie KG, Wien, the Leykam-Josefsthal Actiengesellschaft für Papier- und Druck-Industrie, Wien, and the Mürztaler Holzstoff- und Papier-Fabriks AG, Bruck a.d. Mur. The first two of these companies have already been the subject of discussion in this study, the former in connection with the Aryanization of Schnabl & Co., the latter in connection with its ambitions in Poland. The development of the two companies within Austria, along with Mürztaler, also deserves consideration as an important illustration of the strategies the CA employed in the management of its concern.

Samum turned out to be a better investment than the CA had ever imagined. It had undertaken the Aryanization primarily because of Schnabl's heavy indebtedness to the CA and intended to get its money back by selling the company. As rapidly became clear, however, Samum was a money maker. Its former administrator and then general director, Hermann Aldenhoven, a shrewd and competent businessman and Party member, used his contacts and skills not only to ward off constant efforts by old Reich competitors and the military to shut Samum down but actually managed to expand the business.[262] The CA was quite willing to increase its engagement. In formal terms, Samum had entered into a partnership with Vereinigte Papierindustrie AG, which the CA owned. The CA made an original share investment in this limited partnership of 300,000 RM. Samum produced a host of paper product and also added some new ones that would

be of value in peacetime, a paper-based artificial leather, for example. Its sales increased from 2,240,000 RM in 1938 to 5,400,000 RM in 1940, and stood at 6,969,000 RM by the end of 1941. Exports increased from 262,000 RM in 1938, to 495,000 RM in 1941. Samum used all its profits from 1939–1940 to increase its capital to 1,150,000 RM. In August 1941, the CA put another 850,000 RM into its limited partnership stake. Samum was thus able to increase its capital to 2 million RM by the beginning of 1942. In July 1942, the CA limited partnership stake stood at 1,980,000 RM, and it was increased by 1 million RM to expand Samum's capital once again. The CA also had provided Samum with an operating credit of 1.5 million RM, of which only 460,000 RM had been used by July 1942. In November 1944, the credit was suspended because Samum was actually a creditor of the CA![263]

Samum ended up a substantially larger enterprise than it was in 1938. With the improvement in business in 1939, the company seriously contemplated expanding its Vienna plant. It was particularly interested in increasing its coated paper production, which required a considerable amount of space, but new construction at that time encountered numerous difficulties. A solution was found in the willingness of Leykam-Josefsthal to sell its plant in Breitenau in order to fund a prospective acquisition in Poland. Because Breitenau was a big producer of coated and colored paper, Samum would be the largest producer in the Ostmark. The acquisition seemed particularly important also because Samum had gone into the business of producing coated fabric substitutes. Such products, in the view of the Samum leadership, would "have a great future in the settlement of the eastern territories."[264] The CA funded the purchase in 1941 in the belief that it would solve a number of problems at once and thereby limit the increased engagement of the bank in the paper

---

261 See the interesting report by Fiala of November 1947, ibid., Referat Fiala, 26/04, and *Festschrift für Josef Joham*, p. 160.

262 See pp. 140–142 in this volume.

263 See BA-CA, CA-V, the reports to the working committee of January 1942 and July 15, 1942; the working committee meetings of Aug. 12, 1941, July 15, 1942, Nov. 22, 1944.

264 Ibid., report of January 1942.

industry. Leykam could use the money to help finance its Polish acquisition, and Samum could expand without new construction.

As it turned out, the hopes placed in Breitenau were to be disappointed. The military needed the factories for armaments production, and Aldenhoven was able to trade off turning the Breitenau facilities over to the military in return for continuing operations at Vienna-Heiligenstadt. It is interesting to note that 125 of the 494 workers at Heiligenstadt at the end of 1943 were Jews, 50 men and 75 women. The number of Jews at the end of 1944 stood at 117 (48 men and 69 women), out of a total workforce of 419. Jews outnumbered the foreign workers (89 in 1943, 92 in 1944). The majority of workers were natives (219 in 1943, 210 in 1944). The number of women outnumbered men substantially, which was not untypical of a plant producing cigarette paper. In any case, information is lacking on why the labor force at Samum was so constituted. Ultimately, all work there was stopped in early 1945 by the severe fighting and damage to the plant.[265]

Even if hopes of big sales to German settlers in the East never came close to being realized, there was still a chance Breitenau might someday find a market elsewhere for its coated fabrics substitutes. The fantasies with respect to the Polish plant in Klutsche entertained by General Director Walter Schmeil of Leykam and the CA, on the other hand, proved costly and futile. The gamble on Klutsche was not recognized for what it was until late in the game. Schmeil and the CA continued to invest in the major Austrian plant of Gratwein. A fundamental problem, hardly limited to Leykam, was the wood supply, and Schmeil lobbied the authorities to get more wood at lower prices. This included an appeal to Gauleiter Uiberreither in Graz, apparently with the idea that increased lumbering in Styria was needed. Uiberreither may have had some ecological concerns; he responded that "forest-rich Styria cannot suddenly become a forest-poor

territory."[266] In any case, the quest for wood remained Schmeil's constant preoccupation, and the chief focus was Klutsche as a solution to the company's problems. That was all the more the case because the investment program launched before the war in Austria was badly stalled by the wartime exigencies. With strong backing from the CA, Leykam closed down a number of its smaller and less efficient plants in an effort to rationalize its operations. The profitability of Gratwein seems to have improved in the last years of the war, but Leykam remained a big consumer of credits and at war's end, Klutsche was clearly a total loss. On the positive side, Gratwein suffered little damage.[267]

The attitude of the CA toward the last of its major Austrian wood and paper companies, the Mürztaler Holzstoff- und Papier-Fabriks-AG, Bruck a.d. Mur, was ambiguous. After acquiring a significant block of the company's stock through the Österreichische Industriekredit AG in August 1938, it decided to buy up the remaining large blocks of shares held by the Papierfabrik Frohnleiten Carl Schweizer AG, and the Nettingsdorfer Papierfabriks AG. This gave the CA 90 percent control, and it then sought to buy up the scattered shares that remained, apparently with success. It worked closely in these efforts with the long-time director of the company, Otto Salzer. The company had undergone considerable rationalization prior to 1938 and was an efficient, if not very profitable, producer of cellulose, wood products, and paper for export and domestic use. One of its major projects was the construction of its own generating plant using water power from dams on the Mur and relying on its close relationship with the Bruck Electrical Works, which it had financed.[268]

[265] On the composition of the labor force, see BA-CA, CA-IB, Referat Ketterer, 27/04, Samum to CA, March 2, 1945. See also, *Festschrift für Josef Joham*, p. 182.

[266] BA-CA, CA-IB, Leykam, 10a/04-05, Leykam administrative council, July 27, 1939.

[267] See BA-CA, CA-V, report to the working committee, Feb. 10, 1944; BA-CA, CA-IB, Referat Ketterer, 27/04, report by Fiala, Nov. 1947. See also *Festschrift für Josef Joham*, p. 182.

[268] BA-CA, CA-IB, 11/01, Fiala to Salzer, Aug. 16, 1938 and related documents; BA-CA, CA-V, CA executive committee, Sept. 16, 1938. In general, see *Festschrift für Josef Joham*, pp. 173–178.

By the end of 1940, however, the CA began seriously contemplating shutting down Mürztaler to distribute its financial engagement in the wood and paper industry more efficiently. The bank believed that raw materials costs could be cut by closing the plants and distributing its customers to the other CA-owned firms and that considerable money could be realized from the sale of the real estate and, in particular, the small generating plant the company owned. Hasslacher and Friedl, who were particularly interested in the sale, asked Heller to make discreet inquiries with some of his colleagues in the power industry toward this end, and the CA also tried to interest the Reichsbahn in expanding its railroad facilities by taking over the property available at Mürztaler. At the time, however, the Reichsbahn showed little interest.[269]

The CA was primarily motivated by the belief that it could realize the full value of its shares by shutting down Mürztaler and liquidating the company in the expectation that this would help make the purchase of Klutsche for Leykam easier. It confronted chief stumbling blocks, however, in the opposition from the Economic Group Paper and the German Labor Front in Styria, which claimed that the production was needed and wanted to maintain production in the region. Operations at Mürztaler were more profitable in 1943 because of government subsidies for foreign wood and improved productivity of foreign workers at the plants. By early 1944, however, Speer's ministry had decided that Mürztaler should be shut down, its workers put into armaments work, and the machinery used for military purposes wherever possible. Ironically, Mürztaler's profitability increased just as it was being shut down, and interest in the company was being expressed by both Berlin industrialists and the Reichsbahn in March 1944. A year later, the CA could regain control of a relatively undamaged company that was to function in its paper and wood concern quite effectively in the coming years.[270]

The CA in the Twilight of the Third Reich

By all external indications, the CA was highly successful in its integration into the war economy. The bank's balance sheet increased in 1940 by 19.6 percent to 780,693,854 RM, rose in 1941 by 29.2 percent to 1,009,000,000 RM, then increased by 15.4 percent in 1942 to 1,165,000,000 RM, and advanced yet another 10 percent in 1943 to 1,278,000,000 RM. The full growth in 1943 was obscured by the transfer of the bank's business in Carinthia to the account of the Bank für Kärnten. The CA's business in servicing trade in Southeast and East Europe showed increases ranging from 50 percent to 100 percent over 1942. The "Southeast Program" developed in the summer of 1942, therefore, seemed to be working. One could argue that the bank had reestablished itself in Poland, Hungary, Slovakia, Serbia, and Croatia with banks of its own as well as in Bohemia and Moravia and in Bulgaria in alliance with the Deutsche Bank. Its partnership with the Deutsche Bank had in fact left the CA with a good deal of independence, and the Deutsche Bank no longer challenged but rather supported the CA's remaining industrial holdings in the CA concern. These, as has been shown, were substantial. The CA paid a 6 percent dividend for the years 1940–1943. There was, of course, a darker side that became ever more evident in 1943–1945, leading to a decision to delay establishing a financial statement for 1944. As was the case with all financial and industrial enterprises in the Reich, the CA was heavily invested in various forms of state paper. In 1940, the volume of such holdings increased from 87,700,000 RM to 155,433,537 RM, and by 1943, it stood at 428,400,000 RM. Participation in consortia for major military investments such as the Flugmotorenwerke Ostmark took on a discomforting character and led the CA management board to decide in April 1944 to argue for a widening of the consortium and a

269   BA-CA, CA-IB, Mürztaler, 11/01, Heller to Karl Augustin, March 26, 1941; Salzer to Friedl, March 28, and Oct. 18, 1941.

270   BA-CA, CA-V, working committee meeting, Nov. 4, 1941; report to the working committee, March

23, 1943; report to the working committee, July 28, 1943; BA-CA, CA-IB, Mürztaler, 11/01, report by Friedl, Feb. 10, 1944; reports on the shutting down of Mürztaler and related negotiations, March 1944.

reduction of the CA engagement. Similarly, the effort to join together the branches in Cracow and Lemberg and turn them into an independent bank were also signs of an effort at self-protection as the CA became increasingly aware that victory had become an open question and by no means a certainty.[271]

At the same time, the CA also shared in the struggle of the major banks against the hostility of the National Socialist regime, a struggle made all the more difficult by the pressure to mobilize the economy for the war effort in the last years of the war. In general, the National Socialists of more radical economic persuasion favored savings banks and other publicly chartered local and regional institutions over the large commercial banks with numerous branches and subsidiaries. Nonetheless, the major banks had not only weathered the Banking Investigator of 1933 thanks to the skills and support of President Hjalmar Schacht of the Reichsbank but were also reprivatized in 1936–1937 and then grew as the Reich expanded territorially and as the need for the services of large banks increased once war started. At the same time, however, the major banks lost two of their main supporters with the dismissal of Schacht in 1938 and the transfer of Friedrich Ernst from his position as Reich credit commissar to the Administration of Enemy Assets in 1939. Kurt Lange, a Party man with little sympathy for the banks, became the main person responsible for banking and credit questions at an increasingly dominant and arbitrary RWM. The ministry was empowered to take such measures in the field as it deemed necessary even if they overturned existing laws and contractual provisions. In 1940, plans were afoot in both governmental and Party circles to overhaul the banking system after the war and scale back the role of the major banks. There was something of a consensus among the state and Party agencies that the Reich was "overbanked," and that a "rationalization" was called for that would remedy the situation by shutting down superfluous branches, reducing personnel,

and limiting the influence of the major banks. In January 1941, Lange sharply attacked the banking sector in a speech to the bankers themselves and announced that measures would be taken, emphasizing the importance of placing the banks under National Socialist leadership for the postwar period. At the same time, the RWM officialdom was anxious to avoid a frontal assault, lest the banking organizations use their political connections to challenge the RWM. To make informed decisions, the RWM sought information from the organizations and asked them to propose voluntary measures. Ironically, the greatest resistance came from the savings banks' organization, which did not reply to the ministry's request until five months after the end of September 1941 deadline.[272]

The Economic Group for Private Banking was much more cooperative as well as respectful of the deadline. It felt that voluntary measures were much preferable to government action. Following the summons of the Reich Supervisory Board for the Credit Industry to present proposals, the Economic Group met in Berlin and agreed to solicit proposals from its members. The CA was asked to report on the possibilities of reducing the number of branches and sub-branches in Vienna.[273] The CA and Länderbank Wien were also asked to consider shutting down 10 percent of their branches. In its reply, the CA pointed out that it had been consolidating branches for the previous fifteen years, beginning with the closure of twelve branches of the Anglo-Bank in 1926 and culminating in the closure of

---

[271] See the CA business reports for 1940–1943 in BA-CA, CA-V, ibid.; CA working committee meetings, Feb. 10, and April 26–27, 1944.

[272] See the excellent article by Johannes Bähr, "'Bankenrationalisierung' und Großbankenfrage. Der Konflikt um die Ordnung des deutschen Kreditgewerbes während des Zweiten Weltkrieges," in: Harald Wixforth (ed.), *Finanzinstitutionen in Mitteleuorpawährend des Nationalsozialismus (= Geld und Kapital. Jahrbuch der Gesellschaft für mitteleuropäische Banken- und Sparkassengeschichte. 2000*, Stuttgart 2001), pp. 71–94.

[273] See BA-CA, CA-TZ Sekretariat rot, Box 33/ CA-BV Filiale Allgemeines, File 3, Reich Supervisory Board for Kredit Affairs (Kreditwesen) to Economic Group for Private Banking, June 3, 1941; meeting in Berlin, attended by Pfeiffer, Aug. 16, 1941; Economic Group to CA, Aug. 21, 1941.

thirteen branches when it merged with the Wiener Bankverein in 1934. Indeed, it had closed a total of thirty-five branches during this period, as another ten had been closed belonging to the Bodencredit-Anstalt (9) and the Niederösterreichische Escompte-Gesellschaft (1). While still maintaining thirty-one branches in Vienna, the CA had also taken over the business of the Österreichischen Industrie-Kredit AG and had been planning to set up a branch in its place, but had refrained from doing so because of the war. A plan to consolidate the branches at Kärtnerstrasse and Stock-im-Eisen-Platz had failed because of the inability to find quarters sufficient to meet the needs of the two branches. All this was a bit disingenuous, of course, because the chief source of the CA's virtuous behavior was the flood of bankruptcies of the pre-1938 period.[274]

The CA also took the opportunity to make invidious comparisons with its competition. It pointed out that the Länderbank Wien had not shut down the branches of the banks out of which it was formed in 1938 and thus had thirty-five branches. It had even opened a new branch in Atzgersdorf. The CA also pointed out that six new banks had come into Vienna since the Anschluss, including the Commerzbank, the Bank der Deutschen Arbeit, the Deutsche Bau- und Bodenbank, and the Deutsche Verkehrs-Kredit-Bank. Unsurprisingly, its heaviest fire was directed at the savings banks. The Erste österreichische Spar-Casse had opened ten new branches since 1938, and the Zentralsparkasse der Gemeinde Wien had opened six new branches and for a total of forty-one branches in Greater Vienna. The CA had held nonbinding talks with the Länderbank Wien and other banks about closing branches. Although they, and possibly the Erste Österreichische, were willing to negotiate the consolidation of some branches, the Zentralsparkasse saw no reason to shut down any of its own. Under the circumstances, the CA found it impossible to make concrete proposals in view of how the other banks, especially

the savings banks, had expanded since 1938 and were unwilling to guarantee that they would not expand further.[275]

By the spring of 1942, these stonewalling tactics, which were being pursued throughout the Reich, were no longer acceptable. Speer, Göring, and Hitler's deputy and soon to be secretary, Martin Bormann, all pressed for rationalization in the interest of the war economy. Thus "inspired," the Reich Group Banking decided to close down 10 percent of all branches. In the case of the CA, this meant closing five branches in Vienna. It was anxious to resist plans to shut down more branches, especially in the provinces, where the Gauleiter of the Upper Danube Eigruber proposed closing the CA branch in Linz in deference to the Bank der Deutschen Arbeit.[276]

Fortunately for the CA, it enjoyed considerable support from Ministerial Director Joachim Riehle, who was in charge of the banking desk at the RWM. After meeting with Riehle in Berlin on June 19, 1942, Abs reported that Riehle recognized that the major banks were hard hit by the measures ordered from on high, but that "he personally takes the view that this should not go so far that the branches of a large regional bank, such as the Creditanstalt, should be excessively reduced because this would take away its productive capacity. He points out that such a tendency reigns in the Gaue of the Alpine and Danubian areas and that the Upper Danube Gau has already demanded the dissolution of the branch in Linz. He would only accept this if the Gau entirely surrenders its shares in the Oberbank for the CA."[277] Riehle was much less supportive of the CA's position on the Bank für Kärnten, where there was also a conflict with the Gauleiter, but he was in general well disposed toward the CA. Riehle also mentioned that he would welcome the creation of a CA branch in Berlin, and Abs pointed out that in the agreement between the CA and

[274] Ibid., CA to Economic Group for Private Banking, Oct. 9, 1941.

[275] Ibid.
[276] BA-CA, CA-V, CA working committee meeting, June 10, 1942.
[277] DB, P 6505, Bl. 62, Abs memorandum of June 19, 1942.

the Deutsche Bank, provision was made for the establishment of an independent CA office at the Deutsche Bank that could conduct its own negotiations with the authorities. Riehle declared that such an office could only do its job if it was well led and kept constantly informed by the managers in Vienna, but he obviously approved of direct contact between the CA and the authorities in the Reich capital.

As this conversation indicated, the biggest problems posed by bank rationalization for the CA were in the provinces. This was made especially evident in November 1942, when CA General Director Buzzi and Gau Economic Advisor Rafelsberger took a tour through the Ostmark. They constantly encountered criticisms that the CA had provincial banks and CA branches side by side. In the course of the discussions, Buzzi was happy to report that the basic intention was "to completely maintain the dominant position of the CA" even if this meant having branches take over provincial banks by means of merger. In Styria, for example, the Gau was prepared to have this happen provided it was guaranteed appropriate influence.[278] As has been shown earlier in this study, and in Ulrike Zimmerl's examination of the CA in the regions and provinces, the issue was less one of "bank rationalization" than of the ambitions of the Gauleiter and of regional and provincial officials. The tactics and goals of the CA were neatly summarized by Hasslacher to the CA working committee in January 1943: "President Hasslacher emphasizes the necessity in pursuing the rationalization idea of taking into consideration to a certain extent the conceptions of the various Gauleiter since the solutions can only be carried out in adjustment to local conditions.... President Hasslacher sums up that the foundations of anchoring CA business in the Alpine districts will probably be changed in agreement with the Gau leadership, but that in so doing the material and ideal influence of the bank ought in no way to be diminished."[279]

Whether other CA leaders shared this optimism is hard to say, but one can be certain that Director Tron did not. In a letter to Abs in March 1943, he expressed his fear that the "so-called bank rationalization in the Ostmark ... will be carried out to the largest extent on the back of the CA."[280] What concerned him was not closing banks as a wartime measure but rather the trend toward establishing Gau banks and the potential for permanent danger to the position of the CA. He feared the day would come when the Gauleiter would find the CA majority on such banks burdensome and undesirable, and the CA would lose its position as a regional bank with a network of branches and end up with stakes in banks it could not control. While granting that the coexistence of provincial banks and branches in close proximity could be problematic, he feared the end result would damage the CA's long-range development and its internal management.

These were by no means baseless fears about developments that might arise in the long term. The bank rationalization program became tied up with the much larger effort of the Party to gain control over the banks. The so-called Bormann Committee of Gau Economic Advisors established in the fall of 1942 was intended to be an instrument for assaulting the major banks. The goal was to strip the major banks of their branches and to turn the branches over to regional banks and savings banks.[281] What saved the day here, as in so many other respects, was that the Third Reich had no long run, and that it was possible for the major banks to maneuver in the short run to prevent the worst. The banks countered some of the demands for greater National Socialist influence by putting Party members on their management and supervisory

[278] BA-CA, CA-V, CA working committee meeting of Nov. 27, 1942.

[279] Ibid., CA working committee meeting, Jan. 27, 1943. For the discussion of the various cases, see pp. 90–94 in this volume and Ulrike Zimmerl, *Regionalbanken im Nationalsozialismus. Die*

Instrumentalisierung österreichischer Geldinstitute in den Bundesländern in Gerald D. Feldman/Oliver Rathkolb/Theodor Venus/Ulrike Zimmerl, *Österreichische Banken und Sparkassen im Nationalsozialismus und der Nachkriegszeit* (München 2006), vol. 1.

[280] DB, P 6508, Bl. 128–129, Tron to Abs, March 11, 1943.

[281] Kopper, *Bankenpolitik*, pp. 349–353; Bähr, "Bankenrationalisierung," pp. 80–88.

boards. Rafelsberger, for example, who was to become a member of the Bormann Committee, accepted an invitation to join the CA board of supervisors in the spring of 1942. There is good evidence to suggest that this was a long-term interest because Rafelsberger claimed to have told Hasslacher that he intended to leave politics after the war and had concluded an agreement with him for a position in the private sector.[282] It is reasonable to assume that Rafelsberger helped Buzzi and Hasslacher deal with the challenges presented by the Gauleiter. In any case, by late 1943 not only the plans to change the Reich's banking system but also the closing of banks as part of the wartime bank rationalization were brought to a halt by Allied bombing raids and the chaotic negotiations entailed in trying to shut down branches.[283]

Tron's solicitude for the interests of the CA with respect to "bank rationalization," not to mention his position on the CA management board, illustrates what had clearly become very cordial and supportive relations between the two institutions. One would like to know more about their collaboration. Tron appears to have acted as a go-between. One area of collaboration between the two banks that does deserve special attention, although it was probably not deemed as important at the time as it was to be in the 1990s, is the role of the CA in the Deutsche Bank's gold transactions. This involved the shipment of some five metric tons of gold in bars and coins to and from the Deutsche Bank depository at the CA. A substantial portion of it was sent to the Deutsche Bank Istanbul branch in Turkey. It is safe to assume that all the gold was stolen and had been taken from depositories in occupied countries or from Jews, shortly before or after they were murdered. One of

the oddities of the bulk of the evidence is that, although it comes from the CA records, it was not found in Vienna but rather in the records of the Deutsche Bank branch in Istanbul when it was being liquidated in 1960. They are records of Deutsche Bank gold holdings that passed through the Deutsche Bank depository at the CA in Vienna between 1941 and 1944.[284]

The gold involved was not used to buy chromium, as was originally thought, or indeed anything else needed for the German war effort or for consumption, such as tobacco. Rather, the gold was by and large sold to diplomats, German military personnel in Turkey, and other individuals, and what made it a lucrative business was the high price paid for gold in Turkey because of inflation there. One could make a handsome profit if one sent checks denominated in "free Reichsmark" received as salary or for other reasons from Turkey, where the Turks were turning down such Reichsmark checks, to Switzerland. The Reichsbank office in Zurich cashed in the checks for Swiss francs, which were then used to purchase gold that was sent by air back to Turkey, where it was sold on the free gold market at a handsome profit. This business took on more indirect forms as Swiss and Turkish regulations tightened in the last two years of the war. Transactions at the Deutsche Bank Istanbul were directly credited to the branch's gold giro accounts by the Reichsbank. Whether using Swiss francs or gold giro accounts, the Deutsche Bank and the Dresdner Bank, the two major players in this business, were then in a position to buy gold from the Reichsbank. This gold, usually already smelted into gold bars by Degussa, was then transported, usually via Vienna, to Turkey, where it was sold at a much higher price than possible on the regulated gold market. In this way, the Reichsbank was able to monetize the

---

[282] Rafelsberger's political views are unfathomable; he complained that the National Socialist regime was sliding into fascism, and he was also embittered that Baldur von Schirach did not pay enough attention to his ideas. Whatever the case, there is no reason to doubt his interest in going into business after the war. For these intentions, see his addition to his testimony in Innsbruck on Feb. 2, 1947, Landesgericht für Strafsachen Wien, Vg 6b Vv 2191/48.

[283] See Bähr, "Bankenrationalisierung," pp. 88–91.

[284] See Jonathan Steinberg, *The Deutsche Bank and Its Gold Transactions during the Second World War* (Munich 1999), pp. 13, 79–86, and table 3 (pp. 131–149). In addition to gold, there were also transfers of French francs, Dutch guilders, and diamonds. The last gold shipment was on April 28, 1944, while the last currency shipment was on September 1, 1944.

stolen gold it had received, secure desired foreign exchange in return, and then let the banks sell the gold in Turkey, where it financed salaries as well as various propaganda and espionage activities conducted by Ambassador Franz von Papen and the other Germans there.[285]

Although the CA and the Länderbank Wien served as conduits for the gold transfers to Turkey, the Dresdner Bank tried at least once to prevent the Länderbank Wien from becoming involved in this business.[286] The CA's involvement in the gold business was quite limited in that there is no evidence that it bought or sold gold, or sought to do so, but selected CA employees seem to have played a much more active role than their counterparts at the Länderbank Wien. The limited evidence to be found in the CA archives shows that the Deutsche Bank Istanbul had specifically requested the services of the head of the CA's Post Section, Eduard Herdy, and of one of the CA's foreign exchange dealers, Pleban, to accompany gold shipments to Turkey by plane. The request was made on April 30, 1943, and the CA then requested travel permission for Herdy from the Gau Economic Chamber on May 7, a three-month visa for Herdy from the Turkish consulate in Vienna on May 22, and an extension of the travel permission in Herdy's passport from June 14 to July 10. The most explicit communication was a letter to the Gau Economic Chamber requesting a three-month visa with the right to go and come more than once; it pointed out that Herdy "will on many occasions in the near future have to accompany gold transports from the Reich to Turkey, which will be sent by air from Vienna." The CA pointed out that these shipments were "in the interest of the Reich" and needed to arrive at their destination without problems.[287] In postwar interrogation, Director Kurt Hausmann of the Istanbul branch explained the gold transactions

and also remarked that the practice had been to send the gold by messenger but then a decision was made to use air transport because it was cheaper.[288] This does not explain, however, why Hausmann specifically asked for Herdy and Pleban if only someone was needed to accompany the gold. The impression that more was involved is strengthened by an exchange of letters between Hausmann and Tron in July 1943 found in the Deutsche Bank archives. On July 2, Hausmann wrote thanking Tron and the CA management board for providing Herdy, who "this time again was very useful." Tron replied on July 15 assuring Hausmann that the bank had gladly provided Herdy and would do so again if requested.[289] Unfortunately, there is no further information, but some modest conclusions can be drawn about the CA's involvement. First, the Deutsche Bank branch in Istanbul used the services of CA staff on more than one occasion in these gold transactions, and it is highly likely that Herdy was involved not only in the safe delivery of the gold but also in its disposition. Second, Tron and the CA's management board were aware of the gold transactions and had approved of Herdy's (and Pleban's) services to their colleagues in Berlin and Istanbul. This, of course, does not prove that anyone involved knew the provenance of the gold, but it is hard to imagine that they thought it came from heaven rather than from hell. In any case, the gold transactions were brought to an abrupt halt when Turkey ended all diplomatic and economic relations with Germany on August 2, 1944.

By that time, of course, life was becoming hell for the Reich thanks to the constant aerial bombardment. In February 1944, a report on the bombing of the Deutsche Bank in Berlin was sent to the CA management board to help it prepare for the likelihood that it would meet a similar fate. The report outlined the vulnerabilities of the CA's roof and the kind of damage that was

[285] Ibid., pp. 39–58. See also the counterpart study for the Dresdner Bank by Johannes Bähr, *Der Goldhandel der Dresdner Bank im Zweiten Weltkrieg. Ein Bericht des Hannah-Arendt-Instituts* (Leipzig 1999).

[286] See Chapter 6 in this volume, pp. 522–523.

[287] These documents are to be found in BA-CA, CA-TZ, Sekretariat rot, Box 9/ CA-BV IX–XIII.

[288] See his undated testimony [Oct. 4, 1946], which is an annex to the OMGUS Deutsche Bank investigation of 1946–1947, Exhibit 338, NARA, RG 260, 2/191/15.

[289] DB, V2/60, Hausmann to Tron, July 2, 1943 and Tron to Hausmann, July 15, 1943.

likely to be caused by the different types of bomb. It also strongly urged that typewriters and other equipment be removed to evacuation areas and placed in cellars, that interior windows be replaced with boards because glass was in short supply, that rugs and wood chairs be removed, especially from the ballroom in the Octogon, that elevators be walled up, and that a host of other measures be taken to minimize damage. These measures would, of course, require manpower, and if Ostarbeiter and POWs were not available, then the staff members would have to rely on such skills as they possessed, at the expense of their regular work.[290]

A year later, the bombs were falling in Vienna. Joham wrote to Abs on February 16, 1945, asking how business should be conducted between their banks and branches given the long interruptions in telephone, telegraph, and postal service, and what was to be done if contact with Berlin was cut off by the enemy. Joham reported that, despite much damage in the vicinity, damage at the CA headquarters had thus far been limited to shattered glass. Two branches in Vienna had suffered heavy damage, and the branch in Innsbruck had been destroyed. The Deutsche Bank advised Joham on February 24 on handling business with branches that had been destroyed but refused to comment on what would happen if Berlin was cut off because that was not an imminent threat. In the meantime, the situation in Vienna grew worse. On February 26, the CA telegraphed the Deutsche Bank that four bombs had fallen on the Schottengasse headquarters on February 21. The damage to the front and rear of the building, the main offices, and the Octogon was severe, but no lives had been lost and no one had been wounded. Customers were continuing to be served, and the deposits and valuables stored at the bank were completely intact. This telegram did not reach the Deutsche Bank in Berlin until days after it was sent, and on March 8, Directors Rösler, Abs, and von Halt expressed their regrets over the damage. They were relieved that no one had been injured and expressed their confidence that "with your

energy you will quickly succeed in the unimpeded carrying on of activity in your house."[291]

All this, of course, was whistling in the dark, and although some of the whistling continued on in a very muted way, the economic rationality that had been so important in the adaptation of the CA to the Third Reich now also accompanied its preparations for the regime's demise. The CA management board was now composed of four members: Buzzi, Friedl, Joham, and Tron. Fritscher died in an accident in November 1944. There appeared to be no immediate need to replace him, and his functions and positions were divided among remaining directors.[292] On March 9, a report on the status of the CA was sent to Director Oswald Rösler of the Deutsche Bank. The bank's domestic business in 1944 had been maintained and yielded a high gross profit, thus permitting another 6 percent dividend. The losses experienced by the bank were "war losses," resulting from the bombing of buildings and the loss of foreign holdings in Cracow, Bucharest, Belgrade, Sofia, Budapest, and Agram/Zagreb. All of these losses were candidates for Reich compensation and "therefore perhaps not be recognized as losses for tax purposes." The CA management board, therefore, decided to delay the establishment of the balance sheet for 1944 as long as possible in order to have a clearer view of the effects of the war on its business. In the meantime, it suggested following the model of Wertheim AG in 1943; that firm was financially strengthened by having very high write-offs and by slightly reducing the combined dividend and honoraria received by the supervisory board members, who were to be given a lump sum payment. A decision was also taken to silently liquidate the Gesellschaft für Aussenhandel, "since business abroad is in any case being cut back on its own."[293] It is worth

290 DB, V2/1, report to the management board, Feb. 19, 1944.

291 DB, B 54, Deutsche Bank to CA, March 8, 1945; Joham to Abs, Feb. 16, 1945; Deutsche Bank to Joham, Feb. 24, 1945; telegram CA to Deutsche Bank, Feb. 26, 1945.

292 Ibid., P 6509, Bl. 150, Hasslacher to Rösler, Nov. 30, 1944.

293 Ibid., Bl. 13, report to Rösler (signature illegible), March 9, 1945.

noting that the quest for business and expansion in the southeast had died a slow death. As late as the spring of 1944, Joham was in Trieste to discuss the establishment of a German bank in the city along with a representation of the CA. He was advised that the establishment of such a bank was not pressing at the time but was assured that if such a bank were established, the CA would be favored. This was to be a "war loss" that it was happily spared.[294]

The wartime CA management board met for the last time on March 30, 1945, to discuss emergency measures arising from the chaotic communications situation. A decision was taken to establish a liaison office in Salzburg or Badgastein for purposes of overseeing the CA's branches and holdings, supervising customer business and providing advances to employees and retirees, and fulfilling tasks that the headquarters in Vienna could no longer handle. Finally, "the carrying out, setting up and supervising of the aforementioned emergency measures will be turned over to management board member Dr. Joham."[295]

Apart from his obvious competence, which explains why he was kept on after 1938 despite his ties to the pre-1938 system, Joham was also untainted by Party membership. The other management board members certainly were aware Joham was the only one of them who might be acceptable to the Allies, and there is no reason to think that any of them were so fanatical as to believe that anything but an Allied victory was in the offing. It is most doubtful, however, that they had any idea that Joham had been providing sensitive and secret information to the Allies, above all to Allen Dulles and the U.S. Office of Strategic Services (OSS) in Bern, since at least September 1943.[296] Under the

code name 680, he reported in September 1943 that the Allied raid on Wiener Neustadt was "a complete surprise and considerable damage was done. 300 workers of the Messerschmidt Werke were killed. Several halls were damaged and a number of planes on the ground destroyed. The so-called Rax Werke, which was previously a locomotive factory but which is now making parts for the so-called rocket, was also badly damaged.... There was practically no flak in Wiener-Neustadt. Since the raid a considerable amount of flak which was in Vienna has been transferred to the country. For instance, there were anti-aircraft guns on the roofs of the majority of the banks which were served by members of the staff. The guns have all been taken out to Wiener-Neustadt and to other important places round about Vienna and the members of the bank staffs must go on duty during the night."[297] He went on to discuss troop movements from the Voralberg and Belgium to Italy, changes in the location of fighter production, the Romanian wheat crop and supplies to Germany, and the vain efforts by the AEG to sell its Hungarian interests. He also pointed out that the raid on the rocket plants in Peenemunde were quite successful in destroying aboveground facilities but did not damage the underground installations, which included the power plant. Joham did note, however, that the combined effect of attacks on various parts of the Reich, "especially in Ludwigshafen, have also had a considerable effect on the reduction of the so-called secret weapon." Last, he reported that morale in Vienna and everywhere else was "very bad" and that even "members of the Gestapo are now withdrawing."

Another report, dated September 15, 1943, discussed the size of the turbines being built for rockets at a plant in Frankenthal in the Palatinate. Joham also identified the locations of the plants being used to produce chemical filters for rockets. He informed the OSS that rocket production was still not sufficient to make extensive use of them, but that there was a rumor that they would be fired at Britain in

---

[294] BA-CA, CA-V, CA management board meeting, April 21, 1944.

[295] Ibid., CA management board meeting, March 30, 1945.

[296] He is identified by name in a report to the OSS secretariat of September 16, 1943 as a "director of various companies, including the Austrian Kreditanstalt," NARA, RG 226, Entry 134, Box 171, Folder 1078. I am grateful to Richard Breitman for bringing this to my attention and to Raffaella Luciani for locating some of the materials discussed here.

[297] NARA, RG 226, Entry 190C, Box 10, F160, Report of Sept. 1943. The report was in English.

February 1944. This was identified as the A-4 program, and the chemical work for the project was supervised by Director Otto Ambros of IG Farben at Ludwigshafen. Joham supplied information on a second secret weapon, an enormous cannon being produced at the Bochumer Verein, and identified the size and color of the plant building in which it was being constructed. A similar cannon was being produced at the Oehrenwerke, but it had suffered 20 percent destruction due to bombing.[298]

Another series of reports attributed to Joham were sent in February 1944. He not only reported extensively on airplane, locomotive, and tank production in Austria and elsewhere, and the transfer of industries and production to Bohemia, Silesia, and possibly the old Maginot Line, but he also provided political analysis of the situation in Austria. He noted that the food situation was steadily worsening but that there was little public reaction to the Moscow Declaration of October 30, 1943, that declared Austria to be Hitler's first victim and nullified the Anschluss. Joham reported that anti-German sentiment was very strong and that there was support for Austria becoming part "of a large economic entity composed of perhaps Hungary, Croatia and Czechoslovakia." He said that even socialists held that view. There was, he noted, little public support for monarchism. He made clear that the Gestapo was actively monitoring any signs of open or secret opposition.[299]

How is one to explain this extraordinary performance? There can be no question that Joham proved extremely important and valuable intelligence and that he was risking his neck. If he had begun spying for the OSS only after the Moscow declaration on Austria, one might attribute his actions in large measure to opportunism. But Joham had begun providing intelligence to the Allies well before the declaration. That Joham's activities were dangerous would be demonstrated in January 1945 by the beheading of Franz Messner of Semperit. Regardless, Joham was well aware of the risk he was running with the Gestapo. One did not, of course, have to be a political or military wizard to know that Germany was losing the war, but that was not the same as knowing precisely how the war would end. Hermann Josef Abs, whom Joham resembled in so many ways and with whom he maintained friendly contact until his death in 1959, could also see the handwriting on the wall and had contacts in the German resistance, but he was careful to avoid doing anything heroic. Abs fled to Hamburg in April 1945 and had a glorious career after the war without having demonstrated the kind of courage that Joham had clearly displayed.[300] It is interesting to note, however, that Joham never spoke publicly about his activities after the war, which suggests, as in the case of the failure to celebrate the sacrifice of Franz Messner, how ambivalent postwar Austrians were about resistance to the National Socialist regime. The very fact that Abs had resistance contacts was of some advantage to his reputation in postwar Germany; Joham, by contrast, apparently saw no advantage whatever in letting his actual deeds become known. Joham's postwar silence, however, makes his actions all the more mysterious. In the absence of any statements by Joham himself, one can only try to explain his activities on the basis of circumstantial evidence. Kurt Grimm, a wealthy anti-National Socialist lawyer who had fled in 1938, was presumably an important influence on him. Grimm, who worked closely with Allen Dulles, had close

298 NARA, RG 226, Entry 134, Box 171, Folder 1078, Report of Sept. 15, 1943.

299 NARA, RG 226, Entry 134, Box 170, Folder 1077, reports of Feb. 24–25, 1944. In these reports Joham was responding to, among other things, specific questions communicated to Joham's contact person from the OSS. Lists dated Feb. 24–25 are to be found in ibid., Entry 190c, Box 10, Folder 160. An excerpt from the report of Feb. 24, 1944 is to be found in Neal H. Petersen (ed.), *From Hitler's Doorstep: The Wartime Intelligence Reports of Allen Dulles 1942–1945* (University Park, PA 1996), p. 230, where Joham is identified as a financier but misspelled as "Johan." Joham's reports – in this case the name is misspelled as "Johann" – are also mentioned in Christof

Mauch, *Schattenkrieg gegen Hitler. Das Dritte Reich im Visier der amerikanischen Geheimdienste 1941–1945* (Stuttgart 1999), pp. 177, 370 A. 94.

300 Lothar Gall, *Der Bankier Hermann Josef Abs. Eine Biographie* (Munich 2004), pp. 121–122.

contacts with socialists, Catholics, and liberals, and he was an important contact person for opposition figures inside and outside Austria. He had served as an advisor to Joham before the Anschluss and was to become the "grey eminence" of the CA after the war. Grimm was almost certainly Joham's contact with the OSS, and he may well have helped to persuade Joham that working with the Allies would best serve his political future after the war.[301]

This, however, is hardly a totally satisfactory explanation of Joham's decision to become an Allied spy, and it is necessary to tread on very slippery ground to find one. Joham had never been a National Socialist and never became one, and the German takeover had cost him his position as general director. The Deutsche Bank had protected him and offered both him and the CA refuge in 1938, but it could not save the bank from the loss of major industrial holdings. He continued to believe in the CA's role as an industrial concern and undoubtedly resented the loss of his position and of the bank's assets. He also clearly believed in the CA's mission in Southeast Europe, and it was this part of Third Reich imperialism that enabled him to work hand in hand with Abs. At some point, however, probably in the second half of 1943, Joham must have come to the conclusion that the Third Reich had no future and, perhaps, that whatever future it might have offered him little personally and was potentially threatening to his vision of the CA. There is no evidence that Joham had any moral vision, but he did have a vision for himself and for the CA that seems to have driven him throughout his life, and it is very well possible that the National Socialists also disgusted him. He had, after all, never been one of them even if he was no democrat. The general view among Austrians, he reported, was that the German takeover had brought Austria

nothing but misery, and he certainly shared that view. His claim that many Austrians favored some form of economic union with Austria's neighbors to the south quite possibly reflected his own views, which were rooted in the pre-1914 Central European order. In any case, these attitudes and beliefs may have sufficed to drive him to risk his life as Agent 680.

Joham landed quite comfortably on his feet at the war's end. As in 1938, he was the best Austrian banker around, and this time he also was in somewhat better repute with the new regime. On April 12, 1945, he became president of the Association of Austrian Banks and Bankers once again, and on June 28, 1945, he was made public administrator of the Creditanstalt. On July 25, he was reappointed to the general council of the Austrian National Bank. He had to wait a bit to become general director of the CA again; that happened on February 26, 1948. For all intents and purposes, he became de facto general director when appointed public administrator. Joham presided over the dismissal of Buzzi and Friedl from the management board, with what feelings one does not know. Tron simply disappeared back to Germany and the Deutsche Bank, perhaps happy to have his Austrian experience behind him.[302] During the years of occupation and reconstruction, Joham fought to get compensation for or the return of the CA assets lost to the German occupiers. At the same time, he and his colleagues were also struggling with the demands for restitution and compensation from those who had been despoiled with so much assistance from the CA. At the same time, he played a formidable role in Austria's economic and financial reconstruction. It is fair to say that his career, with all its ambiguities, embodied the interwar and postwar history of the CA and, indeed, of Austria.

[301] See the interesting remarks of Heinrich Treichl, *Fast ein Jahrhundert. Erinnerungen* (Vienna 2003), pp. 295, 299–300. See also, Siegfried Beer, Target Central Europe: American Intelligence Efforts Regarding Nazi and Early Postwar Austria (Working Paper 97-1, Center for Austrian Studies, University of Minnesota 1997), pp. 5–6.

[302] There is a good curriculum vitae for Joham in the CA archive material gathered for the celebration of the CA's 100-year anniversary. On his appointment as public administrator and the dismissals of Buzzi and Friedl, see the materials in BA-CA, CA-TZ, Sekretariat grün, Box 15/CA 5,7, File 7.

PART II

THE LÄNDERBANK WIEN AG IN
THE NATIONAL SOCIALIST PERIOD

CHAPTER FIVE

The Mercurbank, the Länderbank Wien, and the Anschluss, 1933–1939: The Role of the Dresdner Bank

In contrast to the battle for control of the Creditanstalt among various German government and Party agencies following the Anschluss described in Chapter 1, the Dresdner Bank's control of what was to be the Ostmark's second largest bank in the Third Reich, the Länderbank Wien AG, was relatively uncontested and was indeed the outcome of Germanization and Aryanization efforts that began well before the Anschluss. The Länderbank Wien AG, established in July 1938, was primarily the product of the merger of two banks under the aegis of the Dresdner Bank, namely, the Viennese branch and Austrian holdings of the Zentral-Europäische Länderbank (Banque des Pays de l'Europe Centrale=BPEC), on the one hand, and, on the other, the Mercurbank. Formally, the latter took over the former, and the firm that resulted from this merger took the name Länderbank Wien AG. Given the special circumstances of the two banks involved in the transactions, it would be useful to trace their histories prior to 1938.[1]

---

[1] The general account follows that of H. Kreis's undated "Exposé zur Länderbank AG" in National Archives of the United States (= NARA), RG 260, German External Assets Branch, 390/44/20/04, Box 21 and Dieter Ziegler, "Die 'Germanisierung' und 'Arisierung' der Mercurbank während der Ersten Republik Österreich," in: Dieter Ziegler (ed.), *Banken und "Arisierungen" in Mitteleuropa während des Nationalsozialismus (= Geld und Kapital. Jahrbuch der Gesellschaft für mitteleuropäische Banken- und Sparkassengeschichte*, Stuttgart 2001), pp. 15–42. I have also made use of the business reports for both banks.

I. ON THE ROAD TO THE ANSCHLUSS

The Österreichische Länderbank Wien was founded in 1880 and functioned as the bank of the municipality of Vienna. It also had an extended network of branches in the old Austro-Hungarian empire as well as significant branches abroad, notably in Paris and London. These foreign assets were lost in the war, and the Länderbank emerged after the signing of the Treaty of St. Germain with substantial liabilities that became unmanageable as a result of postwar inflation. The problems were solved in January 1920 by a French banking group in collaboration with one of the Länderbank's chief creditors, the Bank of England. The bank was obliged to move to Paris under the name "Zentral-Europäische Länderbank" or "Banque des Pays de l'Europe Centrale" (BPEC) in return for the settlement of old debts and its reorganization and recapitalization.[2] The bank's activities nonetheless remained centered in Vienna and Austria under a special law of October 7, 1921, stipulating that a substantial portion of the bank's assets and the money invested by the French had to be placed in Austria and

---

[2] See Philip L. Cottrell, "Aspects of Western Equity Investment in the Banking Systems of East Central Europe," in: Alice Teichova/Philip L. Cottrell (eds.), *International Business and Central Europe, 1918–1939* (Leicester 1983), pp. 209–355, esp. pp. 316–321. See also, Charlotte Natmeßnig, *Britische Finanzinteressen in Österreich: Die Anglo-Oesterreichische Bank* (Vienna 1998).

that the prior ratio between Austrian creditors and debtors would be maintained as far
as possible. Benefiting from French patronage, the bank maintained its Austrian character
because three-quarters of its assets and liabilities
were located in Vienna and its obligations to its
Parisian ownership were by and large treated
as its own capital. The Paris office's business
tended to be restricted to foreign exchange, discounting, and bond business. The Vienna office
served as a source of funds for investment in
the Austrian economy and also looked after the
bank's interests in Czechoslovakia, where it serviced the Bank für Handel und Industrie (formerly the Länderbank Prag); Poland, where its
banking holding was the Allgemeine Kreditbank
in Warsaw; and Romania, where it controlled
the Romanian Creditbank in Bucharest. It also
acted as the depository for a substantial holding of Trifailer mines in Yugoslavia belonging
to the proprietary bank. The Austrian branch of
the BPEC was viewed both by the BPEC and
by the French government as a financial and
commercial bridge to the successor states of the
Austro-Hungarian empire and to East Europe.
It was intended to serve France's interests
through a policy of *pénétration pacifique*. Exactly
how successfully it functioned in this respect is
hard to say, but the management of the bank's
business was strongly influenced by such considerations, and the concern to maintain its
liquidity had the singular advantage of enabling
it to be the only bank in Austria to weather the
economic crisis at the beginning of the 1930s
without having to undergo restructuring.[3]

The Mercurbank, by contrast, was from
early on something of a German outpost in
Austria. Incorporated in 1887, the Mercurbank
enjoyed the patronage of the Österreichische
Länderbank until 1898. It thereafter entered
the sphere of interest of the German Bank für
Handel und Industrie, the later Darmstädter

und Nationalbank (Danat). It received help from
the New York banking house of Hallgarten &
Co. in 1928, when it raised its capital from 12
to 20 million Schilling. Almost 98 percent of
the Mercurbank's business was done in Austria,
where it functioned as a medium-sized bank
serving primarily medium-sized businesses
in the Vienna area. It also controlled a small
banking operation in Budapest that mainly
handled foreign exchange transactions, the
Wechselstuben AG "Mercur."

In the late 1920s and early 1930s, the
Mercurbank's German connection was anything
but a help. The collapse of the Danat Bank in
July 1931 caused a run on the Mercurbank and
left it in dire straits. The available evidence suggests that the Austrian government was far more
interested in the Mercurbank's salvation than
the German interests banking involved were.
The Dresdner Bank, in which the German government had taken a majority stake during the
banking crisis, took over the Danat Bank and,
along with it, the Mercurbank and its problems.
The Austrian government was interested in saving the Mercurbank and was willing to mobilize money from the savings banks and other
public institutions toward that end, but it was
only prepared to do so if the Germans would
also help save the bank. The Dresdner Bank had
inherited 6.9 million Schilling in claims against
the Mercurbank that would have been lost if the
Mercurbank had been allowed to go under. An
alternative was for the Dresdner Bank to transform the debt into equity at the same time the
share capital of the Mercurbank was reduced
from 20 to 15 million Schilling and to assume
majority ownership of the bank. This involved
some sacrifice because the Mercurbank debt
was denominated in dollars and sterling and
thus entailed a substantial foreign exchange loss.
After investigating the bank's prospects, weigh-
ing potential gains and losses, and, undoubtedly,
taking the political pressures from the Austrian
side into consideration, the Dresdner Bank
decided to join in saving the Mercurbank.[4]

---

[3] For a well-researched and thoughtful history of
the Länderbank Wien in the interwar period, see
the unpublished *Diplomarbeit* of Georg Friedrich
Ransmayr, "Die Zentraleuropäische Länderbank
der Zwischenkriegszeit. Eine Pariser Bank mit
Wiener Blut" (Wirtschaftsuniversität Wien 1993).

[4] NARA, T83/129, see the meetings of the Dresdner
Bank management board, April 4 and April
6, 1932.

In August 1932, the capital of the Mercurbank was fixed at 15 million Schilling, 94.95 percent of which was now in the hands of the Dresdner Bank. There is no evidence of particular enthusiasm for this transaction; the Dresdner Bank appears to have looked upon it mainly as a sacrifice on its part. Indeed, prior to its acquisition of the Mercurbank, the Dresdner Bank seems to have never been much tempted to follow the lead of those who had wished to pave the way for an Anschluss by means of economic penetration. It did not, for instance, follow up on an invitation from the German Foreign Office to try to draw the Austrian middle class and farmers into the German cooperative banking structure following the collapse of the Austrian cooperative banking system in 1926.[5]

If the Dresdner Bank had any expectations, it was that the Mercurbank should make money. It complained in March 1933 that the Mercurbank was not taking advantage of improved conditions and reduced customer withdrawals to do more business in Austria.[6] At the end of the year, the Dresdner Bank seems to have taken the initiative in pushing the Mercurbank to lend between 6 and 8 million Schilling to the Austrian Alpine-Montangesellschaft, the country's most important heavy industrial enterprise, which was under the control of the German Vereinigte Stahlwerke (Vestag). The loan was to be repaid in installments between 1934 and 1936 and to be covered by ore, coke, and metals as well as a Dresdner Bank guarantee. The Vestag agreed to cover the guarantee by purchasing the ore involved and paying the Dresdner Bank even before the ore had been delivered. The complicated arrangement was an important breakthrough for the Mercurbank, which, as noted earlier, normally gave credits to rather small enterprises. The deal is especially interesting on account of who did the negotiating. The two chief negotiators for the banks

were Samuel Ritscher and Gabriel (Gabor) Neumann, both of whom were Jewish. Ritscher had served on the board of the Dresdner Bank in the early 1920s after many years of having worked for Austrian and German banks in the Near East. He had then taken a position in the Reichs Kredit Gesellschaft before returning to the Dresdner Bank as a member of its supervisory board, where he played a major role in the merger with the Danat. After the merger, he moved back to the Dresdner Bank management board and was also a member of the Mercurbank administrative council.[7] Neumann was a Hungarian citizen and served as second vice-president of the Mercurbank administrative council; the first vice-president, also a Jew, was Siegmund Bodenheimer of the Dresdner Bank. Neumann actively involved himself in the bank's business, serving as much as a manager as a director, and took part in negotiating deals such as the one with Vestag. His services seemed to be highly valued; the Dresdner Bank renewed his contract for four years at the end of 1933 on what appears to have been very satisfactory terms for Neumann. Negotiating for the industrial firms were Albert Vögler, the general director of the Vestag, and Anton Apold, the general director of the Alpine. Apold was to "distinguish" himself as supporter of "Greater Germany" and as an anti-Semite. He joined the Party and the SA at the beginning of 1934.[8]

---

[5] See Karl Stuhlpfarrer/Leopold Steurer, "Die Ossa in Österreich," in: Ludwig Jedlicka/Rudolf Neck (eds.), *Vom Justizpalast zum Heldenplatz. Studien und Dokumente* (Vienna 1975), pp. 35–64, esp. p. 46.

[6] NARA, T83/129, Dresdner Bank management board working committee meeting, March 22, 1933.

[7] The Austrians used the term "Verwaltungsrat" or "administrative council" until April 1939, when they changed over to the German term "Aufsichtsrat" or "supervisory board." This is the term used in present-day Austria, in pursuance of the 2nd Decree to the Introduction of Commercial Regulations in the Land of Austria of Aug. 2, 1938 and the introduction of German corporation law. The terminology in this study will follow that of the historical usage of the Austrian corporations.

[8] NARA, T83/128, Dresdner Bank management board working committee meeting, Dec. 18, 1933; the approval of Neumann's contract renewal is to be found in the management board working committee meeting of Dec. 4, 1933, ibid. Neumann received a salary of 40,000 Schilling a year from the Mercurbank, from which 8,000 ATS would be deducted if the bank did not make a profit, and 20,000 RM from the Dresdner Bank as well as 1.5 percent honoraria from the net profit of the

This was obviously not a constellation of individuals the recently installed government in Berlin looked upon with approval, but racial and political criteria apparently did not have the kind of priority they were to attain later. Nevertheless, it soon became evident that at least some in the leadership of the Dresdner Bank were susceptible to ideology and adventure as the personnel of the Dresdner Bank was Aryanized in the wake of the National Socialist seizure of power. Jewish members of the Dresdner Bank's staff were systematically eliminated after January 1933. Their removal was facilitated by the government's majority stake in the bank and the Law for the Restoration of the Civil Service of April 7, 1933.[9] Hardly less important were the steps toward the Nazification of the Dresdner Bank management board. Hitler's economic advisor, the "old fighter" Wilhelm Keppler, took a direct interest in this matter and played an influential role. A minor figure in the chemical industry who had tried, with very limited success, to mobilize the business community for the National Socialist cause before 1933, Keppler exercised considerable influence after Hitler took power. The situation at the Dresdner Bank at the turn of 1933–1934 led to his intervention. The retirement of all the Jewish directors except Samuel Ritscher, who was protected by his war record and the standing he enjoyed in the Reich Economics Ministry (RWM), created a situation in which new directors were needed. As Ritscher lost influence, Carl Goetz, an outstanding banker who had joined the board in 1931, increasingly became the most influential figure on the board, especially after his appointment as chairman of the supervisory board in 1936. It was Goetz who went searching for new management board members in 1933–1934, at which point Keppler took it on himself to suggest Karl Rasche, who had been head of the Westfalen Bank. At this time, Rasche did not openly express his political sympathies. He did not become a member of

the SS until 1938 and of the Party until 1940 as the follow-up to a request by Himmler in July 1937.[10] Nevertheless, Rasche was enthusiastically supported by Keppler and, even more energetically, by Keppler's cousin, Fritz Kranefuß, who was already in the SS and played a major role in mobilizing businessmen for Heinrich Himmler's "Circle of Friends." Goetz was never a Party member, but then Rasche was not one in 1934 either, and Goetz accepted Rasche's appointment to the board. Goetz was a very serious and talented banker; however, he had a distaste for purely political appointments and was intolerant of incompetence. For these reasons, he resisted the self-nomination of the head of the Cooperative Banking Section of the Dresdner Bank, Professor Emil Meyer, another cousin of Keppler's and a founding member of the Keppler Circle. Meyer joined the Party and the SS in 1933 and apparently felt entitled to a place on the board because of his Party membership and connections. Goetz did not think that Meyer was properly qualified, and he yielded to the pressure only after three months of protest. As a counterbalance to this blatantly political appointment, three new members were appointed to the board: Alfred Busch, as a full director, and Hans Pilder and Hugo Zinsser as deputy directors. They, along with two other deputy directors, Alfred Hölling and Gustav Overbeck, were made full directors in 1941. They were experienced businessmen and not Party members. Goetz characterized Busch after the war as an "anti-Nazi," Pilder as an "old democrat but of weak character," and Zinsser as "opportunistic and ambitious, but not National Socialist." Manifestly, however, they were the beneficiaries of the recent Aryanization, and the majority of non-Party members on the board, Goetz included, did not impede continuous collaboration with the regime or the Dresdner Bank gaining the reputation of being the "SS-Bank."[11]

Mercurbank. The latter was expected to make a profit in 1933.

9 Dieter Ziegler, "Die Verdrängung der Juden aus der Dresdner Bank 1933–1938," in: *Vierteljahrshefte für Zeitgeschichte* (= VfZG) 47 (1999), pp. 187–216.

10 See the correspondence in Staatsarchiv Nürnberg (= StA Nürnberg), Nl 4265.

11 Ibid. See also Christopher Kopper, *Zwischen Marktwirtschaft und Dirigismus. Bankenpolitik im "Dritten Reich" 1933–1939* (Bonn 1995), especially pp. 136–139, 283.

These changes were taking place at a time when both German and Austrian National Socialists were showing great interest in the Anschluss question. Austria was not a democracy during this period. It had developed its own peculiar brand of clerical-corporatist fascism under its Christian Social Party chancellor, Engelbert Dollfuß, who served from May 20, 1932, until his assassination in an abortive National Socialist putsch on July 25, 1934. Dollfuß had created his own party movement, the Fatherland Front, into which he integrated the right-wing paramilitary Home Guard (*Heimwehr*) set up after World War I to fight the Communists. Dollfuß had banned the Communist Party and, in 1933, the National Socialist Party; with Italian backing, he sought to suppress the Austrian advocates of an Anschluss with Germany. German efforts to promote an Anschluss became virulent after Hitler's assumption of power, and both German and Austrian National Socialists stepped up their efforts to penetrate Austria politically and economically. They were particularly interested in the potential political use of the Mercurbank, which was the most important of the very few German-controlled banks in Austria. Although much smaller than the Creditanstalt, which after the 1931 crisis had come under the control of the Austrian government, and the French-controlled Länderbank, the Mercurbank was viewed in some Party circles as a potentially valuable asset in promoting German economic penetration. Through it, they hoped to shore up the support for an Anschluss and for Austrian National Socialists in the face of growing Austrian government resistance to German destabilization efforts and to National Socialist agitation against the Austrian regime.

Those hopes notwithstanding, the Dresdner Bank appeared concerned above all about the profitability of the Mercurbank. Despite growing pressure from government and Party officials, it seemed very reluctant to intervene politically in Mercurbank affairs in 1933 and the first half of 1934. Comments from the Foreign Office are indicative of the forces driving the bank in a more German direction as well as the limitations on change imposed by the Austrian government. At the end of May 1934, Ministerial Director Karl Ritter of the Commercial Section of the Foreign Office held a meeting with a certain "Dr. Weber" and a Baron von Wächter, who will be further identified shortly, two of his Foreign Office colleagues, along with Anton Apold, the president of the administrative council of the Mercurbank, Gabriel Naumann, the vice-president, and Samuel Ritscher, a Dresdner Bank director and administrative council member of the Mercurbank.[12] The first item on the agenda was the "personnel policy" of the Mercurbank. Quite remarkably, Ritscher, Neumann, and Apold told Ritter that "for a long time now and even before the political transformation in Germany they had been concerned about a coordination [*Gleichschaltung*] of personnel policy." Fifteen of the sixteen new employees hired since March 31, 1932, were Aryan, and the one non-Aryan had been appointed by the Dresdner Bank for "special reasons." Of the seven newly named directors and managers with power of attorney, six were Aryan and only one non-Aryan, the latter being required for special financial tasks. Three new members had been appointed to the administrative council since March 31, 1932, and all were Aryans and, as will be shown: National Socialists Arthur Hämmerle, Anton Apold, and Otto Kämper.[13]

One of the three members of the management board, Julius Ruben, obviously a Jew, had resigned. Of the two remaining members, Jacques Kahane and Alois Hitschfeld, the former was a Jew. They had hoped to replace Ruben with someone new and to hire a fourth manager despite the fact that the bank was really too small to justify more than a two-person management board. Those trying to change the top leadership of the Mercurbank had refrained from making these appointments, however, because such appointments had to

12 NARA, T120/2891, E455136-140, memorandum of Ritter, June 2, 1934.
13 The document mentions four persons, one with the name Stockinger, but this name does not appear in any of the business reports.

have the approval of the Austrian authorities, and that raised the danger of political complications. Various names were discussed, and the Mercurbank representatives present promised to do more about the personnel problem. What was remarkable about this part of the discussion was that Neumann, to whose continuation in office no one objected at the time, was a Jew, as was Ritscher, and both were apparently willing to engage in this "coordination" of the bank and its manifestly anti-Semitic personnel policy. Second, this policy had obviously been consciously pursued since March 1932, that is, before the National Socialists came to power. A plausible explanation, at least in the case of Neumann and Ritscher, was that they thought it politically and socially wise to limit the number of Jews in the bank and that some measure of German domination had to be endured because a German bank owned the Mercurbank. They may also have calculated that the Austrian government would impose limits on this personnel policy and stand as a barrier to Germanization as well as to Aryanization. The other two issues discussed at this meeting with Ritter were more prosaic, although certainly not innocent. One involved granting more credits to "German-oriented enterprises" in Austria, and here the Mercurbank was to play an important role. The other was to promote trade that would be favorable to German interests.

A good deal more was expected from the Foreign Office and the Mercurbank, and the prodding that came from Austrian and German Party agencies and officials was emphatic. They demanded that more had to be done by the banks to help the Austrian National Socialists and the advocates of Anschluss, who were complaining bitterly about the Mercurbank's inactivity. In May 1934, Theo Habicht, the NSDAP inspector for Austria, went to the Foreign Office in Berlin and presented a note for Ministerial Director Karl Ritter complaining about the inadequate role of the Dresdner Bank and the Deutsche Bank in Austrian banking affairs. The note was written by Rudolf Weydenhammer, the former director of the Deutsche Bank branch in Munich who had

since become the head of the Economic Office of the NSDAP in Austria. He was also one of the organizers of the July 1934 Putsch in which Dollfuß was murdered. The accusations against the Deutsche Bank will be dealt with in the relevant section of this study. The role of the Dresdner Bank was of much greater concern to the proponents of Anschluss because of its control of the Mercurbank, which, they contended, was behaving no differently than it had before 1933. Among other things, Weydenhammer and Habicht were annoyed that the Mercurbank refused to participate in a mobilization of credit for German settlers in Carinthia, another one of those populist schemes that was quite unattractive from a banking point of view but that was supported by the Agrarian Policy Office of the NSDAP. The bank's refusal was construed by Weydenhammer as a lack of support for the "national idea." He was, to be sure, not entirely surprised by such behavior, arguing that "Jewish influence predominates" at the Mercurbank and that its managers were always showing up at Fatherland Front and pro-Dollfuß demonstrations. Weydenhammer did concede that the dependence of Austrian commercial banks on the Austrian National Bank made it difficult for them to run political risks. Nevertheless, he thought that it would be possible to "infiltrate the management" of the Mercurbank, put in more pro-German members, and stop policies aimed at financially supporting the Austrian government. Weydenhammer called on the Foreign Office to ask the Dresdner Bank to clarify the size of its holdings in the Mercurbank, to explain what it had done to influence the personnel policies of the Mercurbank, and to specify how many of the Mercurbank's officials were Aryans.[14] The questions were "loaded," and this was the beginning of a campaign to push the Dresdner Bank to move the Mercurbank in a pro-National Socialist direction. It was well known that 95 percent of the Mercurbank's capital was owned by the Dresdner Bank, and it was also well known that most of the Mercurbank's

---

[14] See *Documents on German Foreign Policy* (= DGFP) *1918–1945*, Series C, Vol. 2 (Washington, DC, 1959), No. 451.

management board was Jewish – there were seven Jews on the administrative council – and that it employed a substantial number of Jews. It was undoubtedly this intervention that inspired the aforementioned meeting between Ritter and the Mercurbank representatives at the end of May and the presence of Weydenhammer in the guise of "Dr. Weber."

The pressure did not let up, however. On June 1, 1934, two representatives of the Austrian National Socialist leadership, probably Habicht and Weydenhammer, showed up at the Dresdner Bank bearing Keppler's calling card and conveying a verbal message for Directors Pilder and Meyer regarding the Mercurbank. They wanted an increase in the bank's capital stock, and they had requests concerning "personnel." They made reference to Anton Apold, the general director of the Alpine Montangesellschaft, who had become president of the administrative council in 1933, and Otto Kämper, who joined the administrative council in March 1934. Otto Kämper was the leading director of the Deutsche Bau- und Bodenbank, which was a subsidiary of the Reichs-Kredit-Gesellschaft and the majority shareholder of the Wiener Baukredit-Bank. Kämper was an advocate of populist banking projects, such as the financing of housing construction, and of the economic penetration of Austria. He was very active in the collaboration between German agencies and Austrian National Socialists to provide financial aid and credit to Nazi refugees fleeing the Austrian authorities.[15] Even more telling, however, was the appointment of Apold as president, which may have been a product of the loan to the Alpine. Previously, there had been two vice-presidents; first vice-president Siegmund Bodenheimer, who had come from the Danat and then represented the Dresdner Bank, and second vice-president Gabriel Neumann. Both were Jews. As noted earlier, Neumann had recently negotiated the loan for the Alpine with Apold and was the chief figure in determining

the Mercurbank's policies. Apold had made the short journey from extreme right-wing paramilitary politics to National Socialism. He joined the Party and the SA in April 1934 and was very successful at raising money for the Party from Austrian industrialists.[16] He was involved in various antigovernment and putschist activities and was about to become involved in more. Manifestly, Keppler and his Austrian National Socialist associates viewed Apold and Kämper as potential allies in doing something about the Jewish domination of the Mercurbank. They also asked that Julius Ruben, a long-time employee of the Mercurbank who had become one of its three full directors, be dropped from the management board. He had, as previously mentioned, already been let go at that point.[17]

The next step was a June 4 meeting at the Foreign Office with representatives of the Austrian NSDAP, the Dresdner Bank, Ministerial Director Ritter, and Councilor of Legation Hermann Hüfer, who had been the recipient of Weydenhammer's May memorandum. The meeting was clearly intended as a follow-up to the Habicht-Weydenhammer visit in May and to give weight to the demands presented to the Dresdner Bank a few days earlier with Keppler's support. The result was an agreement to pursue a policy of cautiously replacing the leading members of the administrative council and management board at the Mercurbank. The details were to be worked out in discussions between the Dresdner Bank and Austrian NSDAP leaders.[18]

These events were taking place at a time when Austro-German relations were relatively stable. The Austrian government was showing interest in bringing German capital into

---

15 For Kämper's work on the credit committee of the Vereinigte Finanzkontore GmbH that provided such credits, see Bundesarchiv Berlin (= BAB), R2, Vol. 1573.

16 Österreichisches Staatsarchiv (= ÖStA/AdR), Bundesministerium des Inneren (= BMI), Gauakt Anton Apold, Nr. 162.242.

17 It is worth noting that the spelling of names in this document is often wrong. Apold, for example, is spelled as "Appold." NARA, RG 260, External Assets Investigations 1945–1949, 390/44/31/01, Box 539, unsigned memo of June 1, 1934.

18 DGFP, Series C, Vol. 2, No. 479, Hüfer Notiz, June 4, 1934.

Austria and was prepared to go along with schemes to mobilize the savings of Austrians with pro-National Socialist sympathies. It was prepared to contemplate personnel changes at the Mercurbank along with a certain amount of personnel sharing between the Mercurbank and the Deutsche Bau- und Bodenbank for such purposes. This was quite evident at a meeting on June 6 attended by Weydenhammer, once again identified as "Dr. Weber"; Baron Otto Gustav von Wächter, a high-ranking official of the Austrian Finance Ministry and also a National Socialist;[19] another leader of the Austrian National Socialists, Dr. Fritz Riegele, who was also Hermann Göring's brother-in-law and representative of the Austrian NSDAP leadership in Berlin; Dr. Viktor Gerold Kaspar, an Austrian National Socialist who chaired the program to aid Austrian National Socialist refugees and worked for various business organizations; and Dresdner Bank director Hans Schippel. The participants contemplated putting "Dr. Weber," that is, Weydenhammer, on the Mercurbank administrative council, along with the personnel director of the Austrian National Bank, Dr. Emil Pallausch, and they discussed creating links to both Austrian government institutions and the Party.[20]

By the end of June, the plan to use the Mercurbank to support National Socialism in Austria had been advanced yet further by a memorandum from Kaspar with "proposals to support the struggle for Austria." There was much criticism in Austrian National Socialist circles that Austro-German trade was in the hands of "Austro-national and Jewish circles," and questions were being raised as to whether this trade should not be terminated. In Kaspar's view, the real problem was that pro-Anschluss economic assets and savings were being spread among a number of banks and that no systematic effort was being made to use the potential economic power of supporters of the National Socialist cause. What was needed, therefore, was a concentration of this economic power so that it could be used to promote German and Anschluss interests, to ensure that Austro-German trade was concentrated in the hands of trustworthy individuals, and to work toward political as well as economic ends. That would require that reliable individuals in the banking system work together to support proponents of Anschluss and provide them with the money they needed to function. Kaspar viewed the Mercurbank as the leading bank in this effort despite its paradoxical situation. It belonged to the Dresdner Bank, which was under the control of the Reich, but it was also the most "Jewified" bank in Austria. It was essential, therefore, that the Mercurbank become the central repository of pro-German assets and that it increase its capital and radius of action so that it could service reliable individuals who traded with the Reich. In Kaspar's view, the success of the National Socialist movement in Austria would depend on the ability to concentrate and utilize the banking system in this manner.[21]

There was some evidence of changes at the higher levels of the bank between the shareholders' meetings of March 1934 and March 1935, although it is hard to tell whether they were a consequence of the aforementioned Aryanization efforts. The decision to drop Ruben from the management board had been made before the meetings discussed earlier. Hans Schippel of the Dresdner Bank replaced

---

[19] Wächter was involved in the July Putsch and apparently lost his job, but was very much back in business after the Anschluss, first as an SS Oberführer charged with purging the bureaucracy and later as an SS Brigadeführer later in charge of Lemberg and then governor of Cracow during the National Socialist occupation. See Maren Seliger, "NS Herrschaft in Wien und Niederösterreich," in: Emmerich Tálos/Ernst Hanisch/Wolfgang Neugebauer/Reinhard Sieder (eds.), NS-Herrschaft in Österreich. Ein Handbuch (Vienna 2000), pp. 237–259, esp. p. 252 and the correspondence between Wächter and Hans Blaschke in ÖStA/AdR, BMI, Gauakt Hans Blaschke, Nr. 91.283.

[20] NARA, RG 260, External Assets Investigations 1945–1949, 390/44/31/01, Box 539, Memorandum, June 6, 1934; See also Stuhlpfarrer/Steurer, Die Ossa in Österreich, p. 56.

[21] NARA, RG 260, External Assets Investigations 1945–1949, 390/44/31/01, Box 539, memorandum, June 30, 1934.

Bodenheimer as a vice president, but Neumann held on to his post and Bodenheimer, Ritscher, and Regierungsrat Fritz Lemberger-Marker, all Jews, remained on the administrative council. Another Jew, Jacques Kahane, dominated the two-man management board. The other full manager was the non-Jew Alois Hitschfeld, who was married to a Jew. It is unclear whether Egon Schwarz, who left the administrative council at this time, was Jewish. The number of non-Jews on the administrative council increased significantly with the appointment of Tilo Baron von Wilmowsky of Krupp, who was head of the German section of the Central European Economic Congress. As will be shown later, Wilmowsky represented particular Krupp interests in Austria, but he was also extremely well connected and appears to have been used by the Foreign Office and other interested parties to try to "improve" the personnel situation at the Mercurbank. In June 1935, he wrote to Carl Clodius of the Foreign Office that plans were afoot to put a third director on the management board, namely Adolf Warnecke, the director of the Bregenz branch. His appointment would be welcomed by Party members at the bank. Even more welcome to the Party members was the news that Arthur Seyß-Inquart, who had been a major Austrian contact with the NSDAP since 1931, was going to be appointed to the administrative council and placed in charge of the Legal Department by special arrangement. Tilo von Wilmowksy believed that these moves would put an end to the criticisms of the bank's personnel situation and the conflicts arising from them. By September 1935, however, neither of these appointments had been made. Warnecke was not to be appointed until the second half of 1936, and Seyß-Inquart was never to serve the Mercurbank.[22]

Nineteen thirty-five was not, in fact, a particularly good year to realize either the personnel program for the Mercurbank or its potential for economic penetration of Austria. The goal of economic penetration depended on decent relations between Austria and Germany,

and relations had taken a very bad turn in July 1934 following an attempted putsch by Austrian National Socialists and the murder of Chancellor Dollfuß. Many of the Austrian National Socialist leaders involved in the economic program were implicated in these events, including Apold, who received a heavy fine.[23] The government crackdown and worsening relations with Germany inevitably had a negative effect on the economic schemes of the pro-National Socialist forces. Apold's position as president of the administrative council became a liability rather than an asset. That was clearly well demonstrated by the fate of the proposal that the Mercurbank open up a major branch in Innsbruck "in order to be of real help to German-minded circles there and to fill a gap created by the numerous bank mergers in Austria." Apparently, even the non-National Socialist members of the Mercurbank leadership were interested in expansion in this manner, and the Mercurbank had applied to the Austrian Finance Ministry for permission to do so, but the request was firmly rejected for the express reason that Apold's chairmanship of the administrative council precluded the Mercurbank's expansion into the provinces. As Pilder of the Dresdner Bank reported to Director Meyer in September 1935, the Mercurbank had to be cautious in pursuing growth given its limited capital. But although still vulnerable, the bank was doing well and expansion could be justified if circumstances permitted. Ironically, it is most likely the barrier to government approval was Apold, not the Jews on the administrative council.[24]

It is by no means easy to detail how the tension between banking and business interests, on the one hand, and political considerations, on the other, played themselves out prior to the Anschluss. The general context is important for understanding developments at the

---

[22] DGFP, Series C, Vol. IV, Editor's Note to No. 164, Tilo von Wilmowsky to Clodius, June 23, 1935.

[23] Apold was fined 349,000 Schilling, but only had to pay 70,000 thanks to the intervention of a government contact. See ÖStA/AdR, BMI, Gauakt Anton Apold, Nr. 162.242.

[24] NARA, RG 260, External Assets Investigations 1945–1949, 390/44/31/01, Box 539, Memorandum, Pilder to Meyer, Sept. 2, 1934.

Mercurbank. After July 1934, German government policy was to hold firmly to every economic position that pro-Reich forces had in Austria, even if that entailed sacrificing economic gain or sound business practices. In late 1936, for example, the German Foreign Office intervened with the Foreign Exchange Office of the RWM on behalf of the Bayerische Hypotheken- und Wechselbank in Munich to reverse a refusal to grant a special request by the bank to credit Reichsmark debts of the Salzburger Kredit- und Wechselbank in Salzburg and the Bank für Kärnten in Klagenfurt against the blocked mark securities accounts of the two Austrian banks. Were this to be allowed, the Bayerische Hypotheken- und Wechselbank would retain its existing holdings in the two Austrian banks, even though they were bringing it financial losses, and would thus adhere to the Reich policy of not surrendering an inch of German interests in Austria. The Foreign Office pointed out that it was urgent for the Foreign Exchange Office to allow this expensive breach of the currency control regulations. It finally did so also because of political considerations. The general director of the Creditanstalt, Josef Joham, had been heard to say that he intended to use the uncertain status of the shares as an opportunity to try, as he had in the past, to drive the Bayerische Hypotheken- und Wechselbank out of the Bank für Kärnten.[25]

The Bayerische Vereinsbank, which had holdings in three Austrian banks – the Hauptbank für Tirol und Vorarlberg-Tiroler Landesbank, Innsbruck; the Bank für Oberösterreich und Salzburg, Linz; and the Steiermärkische Escompte-Bank, Graz – had an easier time getting permission from the Foreign Exchange

Office to circumvent the currency control regulations. It had held these shares since 1920; in 1934, the Foreign Office had asked banks not to surrender such holdings without asking for Foreign Office approval. When the opportunity arose for the Bayerische Vereinsbank to increase its stake in the Steiermärkische Escompte-Bank, Graz, it turned to the Foreign Office. It asked for and received approval for the purchase of the additional shares on the grounds that everything possible should be done to increase German engagement in the Austrian economy.[26]

There are other significant illustrations of this stubborn attention to the maintenance of German interests in Austria and to the watchdog role played by Austrian National Socialists. There was much criticism of IG Farben in early 1937, for example, for selling its majority stake in the small Continental Bank in Vienna to the Julius Meinl AG, which was viewed as legitimist and anti-German. The transaction was seen as propaganda for the view that Germany did not support the Austrian National Socialists sufficiently, and Victor Kaspar strongly warned the German Foreign Office that "the surrender or weakening of the German position in Austria, irrespective of whether and to what extent it has economic significance, must be thoroughly and under all circumstances prevented or categorically forbidden."[27]

This was, in fact, the policy. A revealing illustration of this policy at work was an effort by President Hjalmar Schacht of the Reichsbank in July 1937 to satisfy a request from his counterpart at the Austrian National Bank, Victor Kienböck, in the course of a personal visit. Kienböck asked that the Germans sell their 120,000–130,000 Schilling stake in the Niederösterreichische Handels- und Gewerbebank to Austrian interests. The bank actually belonged to the "Ossa-Vermittlungs- und Handelsgesellschaft,"

[25] See note by Clodius of the Foreign Office to the Reich Bureau for Foreign Exchange Management, Nov. 6, 1936; Clodius to the Bayerische Hypotheken- und Wechselbank, Nov. 6, 1936; Politisches Archiv Auswärtiges Amt, Berlin (= PA Berlin), R 110996 Reich Bureau for Foreign Exchange Management, March 8, 1937. The amount involved was 1.6 million RM and thus quite substantial, and the Foreign Exchange Office demanded that the Bavarian bank contribute 10 percent of the amount to the Gold Discount Bank to the fund for promoting exports.

[26] Ibid., R 110997, Clodius to Bayerische Vereinsbank, Aug. 21, 1937; Bayerische Vereinsbank to Foreign Office, Sept. 3, 1937, and to Reich Bureau for Foreign Exchange Management, Sept. 3, 1937; Kalisch to Reich Bureau, Sept. 22, 1937.

[27] Ibid., R 110996, Kaspar to Clodius, Feb. 6, 1937; von Papen to the Foreign Office, March 6, 1937; Kaspar to Clodius, April 24, 1937.

an ostensibly private concern founded in 1926 at the behest of the German Foreign Office for the purpose of promoting the economic penetration of Austria and the adjoining countries and headed by the former mayor of Graudenz and later head of the infamous Head Trusteeship Office East in occupied Poland, Max Winkler. The Ossa took a somewhat dim view of the usefulness of this little bank because Austrian government controls were so stringent that it could not be employed for penetration purposes so long as Austro-German relations were bad, and it was likely to be a minor asset under even the best of circumstances. Winkler, seems to have had a number of poor business investments on his hands that he was constantly trying to sell before he was finally called in and told that "the Führer and Reich Chancellor and the Reich government are not in agreement with this attitude and want to retain all holdings in Austria."[28] The Foreign Office took a similar position with Schacht. Foreign Minister Constantin von Neurath, State Secretary Ernst Freiherr von Weizsäcker, and Ambassador Franz von Papen all expressed the view that German assets in Austria should not be given up on principle. The mere fact that Kienböck, who was regarded as hostile to German interests and whose mother was a Jew, wanted the shares in Austrian hands seemed reason enough to deny the request. Despite Schacht's embarrassment, economic, financial, and central bank relations had to take second place to the no-surrender policy with respect to German assets in Austria.

Political interests had become primary, not only with a view toward what might occur in Austria but also with respect to the future of the Reich's interests in Southeast Europe and to German autarky policies.[29] Concerning the developments in Austria, whether the Jews with

important positions on the Mercurbank were as single-minded in blocking National Socialist ambitions in Austria as the National Socialists claimed is hard to say, and putting the interests of the bank before those of the Party could be justified on many grounds. The National Socialists in Berlin and Austria saw the bank from a purely instrumental perspective, often as little more than a cash cow for Austrian National Socialists in need. In early June 1935, for example, Viktor Kaspar sent Director Meyer of the Dresdner Bank a letter of introduction for Pg. Rudolf Brandl of the St. Pöltner Kartonfabrik. Brandl wanted a credit of 250,000 Schilling for the company from the Mercurbank. The bank did not find the collateral he offered adequate, however. Brandl then turned to the Party, which turned to Kaspar, who then turned to Meyer with the argument that the requested credit was very much in keeping with the political line and that everything had to be done to keep the "politically close enterprise" in operation. He hoped, therefore, that Meyer would support Brandl and that the Dresdner Bank would promote a favorable decision. Meyer received Brandl within a few days of receiving this letter, and Brandl left Berlin with the sense that his company had Meyer's "friendly protection." In mid-September, when the credit was about to come through, Brandl was able to thank Meyer for his support once again and invite him to visit St. Pölten.[30]

It was one thing to give credit to people like Brandl but quite another to throw more Jews out of the Mercurbank, especially because the Austrian government, acting through commissars appointed to regulate the behavior of enterprises, could be expected to interfere.[31] From the perspective of Keppler and the Austrian National Socialists, the issue of personnel changes at the Mercurbank remained crucial. The Austrian National Socialists were constantly complaining to Keppler about the

[28] PA Berlin, R 110997, draft of letter to Schacht, July 31, 1937, and note for Clodius; also Schacht to von Neurath, July 8, 1937; von Neurath to Weizsäcker, July 7, 1938; telegram Weizsäcker to the Foreign Office, July 8/9, 1937; Dreyse to von Neurath, July 27, 1937; On the Ossa, see Stuhlpfarrer/Steurer, "Die Ossa in Österreich," pp. 35–64.
[29] Norbert Schausberger, *Der Griff nach Österreich. Der Anschluss* (Vienna 1975), pp. 326–328.
[30] NARA, RG 260, External Assets Investigations 1945–1949, 390/44/31/01, Box 539, Kaspar to Meyer, June 5, 1935; Brandl to Meyer, June 8, 1935; Brandl to Meyer, Sept. 17, 1935.
[31] NARA, T83/128, Dresdner Bank, working committee of the management board, Jan. 27, 1936.

situation at the bank, and Keppler responded by putting heat on the Dresdner Bank. In late March 1936, he wrote to Goetz to point out that the bank still had a "Jewish management board" and that he was hearing complaints about Jewish administrative council member Regierungsrat Fritz Lemberger-Marker, who seems to have been playing an important role in internal discussions and decisions, especially in the area of German-Austrian barter deals. Keppler admitted that matters had been made much worse by the Austrian government's removal of Apold from all his positions, but he still demanded that Goetz pay attention to the situation and finally do something to improve the situation. He reminded Goetz that, in the last analysis, the situation at the Mercurbank influenced attitudes toward the Dresdner Bank.[32]

In April 1936, a new set of behind-the-scenes proposals was cooked up at a meeting in Keppler's office attended by Riegele; a Major Jagwitz; Wienecke, as a representative of the Foreign Organization of the NSDAP; and Directors Rasche and Meyer of the Dresdner Bank. The top priority at this point appeared to be the appointment of a reliable Aryan to the management board, and the proposal was made to give the job to the director of the Industry Bureau of the Creditanstalt, Hans Fischböck. If this appointment were to be made, it might be possible to try to get rid of some of the fourteen Jewish managers with power of attorney at the bank. At the same time, a replacement had to be found for Apold, and it was proposed to appoint the general director of the Alpine Montangesellschaft, Georg Meindl, a reliable Party man, as his successor and president of the Administrative Council. The administrative council of the Alpine, however, also presented some difficulties because of the Mercurbank's right to a seat. It seemed essential not to elect a Jew, that is, neither Neumann nor Ritscher. Apparently, Erwin Daub of the Vereinigte Stahlwerke had agreed to accept the position as the representative of the Mercurbank interests,

and the seat was to be held open for him. Some names were mentioned as replacements for the Jewish managers with power of attorney who were to be let go. Those in attendance at the meeting, however, were not at all certain they could accomplish their purposes – the Mercurbank was not represented at all at the meeting for obvious reasons, and neither Goetz, nor Pilder, nor any other non-Party man on the Dresdner Bank board was present – and Meyer was to go to Vienna to see what could be achieved.[33]

He evidently did not achieve much. Fischböck was placed in charge of dealing with the collapse of the Phönix insurance company and would subsequently rise to "higher" functions after the Anschluss. He obviously had no time for the Mercurbank, and in July 1936 the third director position was given to Adolf Warnecke, as had been proposed earlier when Tilo von Wilmowsky had been dealing with the problem. Warnecke's National Socialist sympathies were well known; he had joined the Party in April 1936. A good illustration of the blockage of National Socialist ambitions was the response to a letter to Keppler from the German ambassador to Austria, Franz von Papen, of June 17, 1936. Von Papen had been visited by National Socialist lawyer Erich Führer, who had unsuccessfully defended Otto Planetta, the assassin of Dollfuß, and who had himself been incarcerated for a few months for his role in the July 1934 putsch.[34] Führer had complained frequently about the miserable situation of pro-Reich lawyers in Austria, and Papen and Führer had repeatedly asked that the Mercurbank hire a nationalist lawyer because, as Papen pointed out, "it is certainly not the Reich's wish that now,

---

[32] StA Nürnberg, Nl 3908, Keppler to Goetz, March 20, 1936.

[33] Fischböck is spelled "Fischbach," Riegele is spelled "Riegel," and Apold is spelled "Appold." Fischböck, who was to have an important and detestable career in Austria and Holland, worked for the Creditanstalt between 1928 and 1937. NARA, RG 260, External Assets Investigations 1945–1949, 390/44/31/01, Box 539, memorandum of a discussion in Keppler's office, April 23, 1936.

[34] See Gerhard Jagschitz, "Die Anhaltelager in Österreich," in Jedlicka/Neck, *Vom Justizpalast*, pp. 128–151, esp. p. 137.

as before, a Jewish lawyer represents the interests of this institution, which is in the property of the Reich."[35] Führer suggested that Keppler contact his cousin Meyer about the situation. But when Keppler did so, Meyer replied that he had passed on the proposal but that he did not think the situation could be remedied until the matter of reorganization of the administrative council and its presidency was settled.[36]

The changed political situation in the summer of 1936 and the "improvement" of German-Austrian relations under the July agreement seemed to encourage Keppler to take up Führer's idea once again. Dresdner Bank director Schippel apparently wrote to Director Warnecke about the legal representation question, but the fundamental issue of the administrative council had become dormant.[37] The projected appointment of Meindl to replace Apold also appears to have been put on ice. It seemed to be linked to a large credit for the Alpine, and this appears to have been part of a larger program connected with Tilo von Wilmowsky's schemes for Central Europe. Wilmowsky visited Meindl in September 1936 to discuss these matters, but Wilmowsky deliberately refused to tell Meindl anything about the personnel issue and advised him not to "meddle in such matters." Meindl was advised to turn to Wilmowsky or Director Pilder, both of whom were on the Mercurbank administrative council, if he had questions or problems.[38] Action was indeed soon to be taken, but a report Pilder gave to his colleagues at the Dresdner Bank betrayed considerable nervousness. Pilder said the liquidity of the bank was favorable, but he also noted the centrality of the personnel issue and the problem of having certain leading

figures who were not Aryan step down, pointing out that "the fact should not be disregarded that a large part of the clientele is not Aryan, and this requires especially careful handling but will in the next weeks be conclusively regulated."[39] Despite Wilmowsky's advice, Meindl preferred to turn to the less cautious Meyer for information. Meyer told him that he worked very closely with Keppler and sought to promote Keppler's wishes with his colleagues. As he noted, however, personnel matters interested the political agencies more than economic ones. The major concern at the moment was the elimination of Director Kahane, who had been on the board since 1927, and this apparently had priority over changes in the administrative council. Meyer claimed he had sent someone to Vienna to expedite the matter and to come to a settlement with Kahane.[40]

The person in question was probably Leonhard Wolzt, who had begun to play an important role for the Dresdner Bank in Austria. The concentration on Kahane did not mean that the desired reorganization of the administrative council was neglected. At a council meeting on September 23, 1936, Schippel reported that Lemberger-Merker had personally given him his resignation from the board. In March 1937, three new members, who were obviously not Jewish, were added to the board: Otto Böhler, the director of the important industrial firm of Böhler & Co.; Ludwig Herberth, a prominent Vienna businessman; and Alfred Prinz zu Hohenlohe-Schillingfürst of the Vienna banking firm of Schoeller & Co. The only Jews left were Neumann and Ritscher.[41] Of the three new administrative council members, only Böhler had no ties to the National Socialists. He had been close to Dollfuß and was well connected with the leadership in the existing

[35] NARA, RG 260, External Assets Investigations 1945–1949, 390/44/31/01, Box 539, von Papen to Keppler, June 17, 1936. On Warnecke's politics, see ÖStA/AdR, BMI, Gauakt Adolf Warnecke, Nr. 41.737.

[36] Ibid., Meyer to Keppler, June 24, 1936.

[37] Ibid., Meyer to Veesenmayer, July 14, 1936; Keppler to Meyer, July 18, 1936; Meyer to Keppler, Aug. 3, 1936.

[38] Ibid., Pilder is spelled as "Bilder." See Meindl to Meyer, Sept. 18, 1936.

[39] NARA, T83/128, Dresdner Bank, management board meeting, report by Pilder, Aug. 29, 1936.

[40] NARA, RG 260, External Assets Investigations 1945–1949, 390/44/31/01, Box 539, Meyer to Meindl, Sept. 25, 1936.

[41] ÖStA/AdR, Bundesministerium für Finanzen (= BMF), Allgem. Reihe 1938, Nr. 3527/1938 and Geschäftsbericht 1936, administrative council meeting, Sept. 23, 1936.

government. He was also a Rotarian and was reported to have helped Jews financially after the Anschluss.[42] Herberth had joined the Party in 1932. He was married to a woman who was either a full Jew or a "Mischling of the first degree," however, and had appealed to Hitler for dispensation at the time. He was excluded from the Party in 1939 and remained suspect despite his alleged pre-Anschluss actions to help illegals and to reduce the role of Jews in the commercial field.[43] As for Hohenlohe-Schillingfürst, he joined an SA group in 1937 and was known for helping find jobs for National Socialists before 1938. He had married into the Schoeller banking and industrial family and had an obviously "good name," but he was not politically prominent and may well have been protecting his interests because he did not join the Party until May 1938.[44]

The great success of the Aryanizers of the Mercurbank in 1936, however, was the retirement of Director Kahane, whose ill health may have played a role in his decision to succumb to the pressure to step down from the council. At an administrative council meeting on September 23, 1936, Kahane gave his last report on the condition of the bank, which he proudly declared as crowning the efforts at recovery since 1931, and then announced that he planned to go on vacation and retire in April 1937, thus terminating his thirty-five years of service to the bank. The board voted an advance on his salary, which was increased as a reward for his accomplishments, and a committee was appointed to deal with his pension. But what made the meeting quite extraordinary was a lengthy tribute paid to Kahane by Neumann. He praised Kahane for having saved the bank after the 1931 crisis and for having devoted his life to it, and he noted that Kahane had also won the affection of all who worked with him. He also used the occasion to emphasize Kahane's

devotion to Austria: "Herr Kahane is not an Austrian by birth; Austria is his chosen homeland, but he has become a genuine Austrian through his love for this country, through his services to the Austrian economy. The German language is not his mother tongue, but he was never a man of great words; he has always been a man of work and deeds. One knows that when he departs from this institution, he will feel a great emptiness; but much greater still is the emptiness that will result for this institution from his departure."[45] Manifestly, this was not only a personal homage but also a political statement. Although Kämper and Schippel joined with others in expressing appreciation and gratitude to Kahane, everyone present must certainly have been aware of the role played by Greater German and anti-Semitic sentiments in Kahane's departure.

Even with such dubious "successes," the Aryanization of the bank remained difficult for very concrete economic and political reasons. Indeed, it would eventually take an "order from the Führer" (Füherbefehl) to get the process moving again. The political situation was turning increasingly in Germany's favor, thanks to Hitler's international successes, and there was a growing effort by the Austrian government to come to a modus vivendi with the Third Reich that culminated in the July 1936 agreement. Undoubtedly, this atmosphere of cooperation smoothed the way for the events just described. Furthermore, economic cooperation was very much on the agenda. The Mercurbank, for example, joined an Austrian banking consortium in June 1937 to provide credits for the electrification of the railroads, particularly the stretch from Linz to Salzburg.[46]

Naturally, the new situation gave Keppler and his National Socialist cronies in Austria much to do. On the way back from a visit to Vienna at the beginning of July 1937, Keppler met personally with Hitler to discuss the

[42] See ÖStA/AdR, BMI, Gauakt Otto Böhler, Nr. 38.773, the Gestapo report of July 23, 1942.

[43] See his rather large file, ibid., Gauakt Ludwig Herberth, Nr. 39.934.

[44] Ibid., BMI, Gauakt Alfred Prinz zu Hohenlohe-Schillingfürst, Nr. 1700.

[45] ÖStA/AdR, BMF, Allgem. Reihe 1938, Nr. 3527/1938, administrative council meeting, Sept. 23, 1936.

[46] NARA, T83/118, Dresdner Bank, working committee of the management board, June 9, 1937.

situation, and they agreed on the importance of maintaining and expanding German bases of operation in Austria. In a letter of July 15, he informed Ambassador von Papen that as a result of his conversations on the Obersalzberg he would now push the Aryanization of the Mercurbank. He had the impression that the "known Jew Neumann" and President Kienböck of the National Bank were working "hand in hand" to protect Neumann's position, but Keppler "could see no reason why we should allow ourselves to be so extensively told what to do by Austria in the structuring of the Mercurbank." Keppler asked von Papen to support these efforts.[47] There can be no question that Keppler intended to make the most of his conversation with Hitler about building up the German position to push the Aryanization of the Mercurbank by the Dresdner Bank leadership. Keppler informed Goetz on July 13, "the Führer clearly took the position that we must at all costs hold on to and build up these bases, especially the Mercurbank, and that in this connection it is absolutely essential to finally carry out the 'Aryanization' of the Mercurbank since otherwise the desired goal could not be attained."[48]

Goetz's response throws light on the ambivalent relationship between the Dresdner Bank and the Mercurbank as well as on the differences of opinion within the Dresdner Bank. As might be expected, he emphasized that everyone agreed on the need for Aryanization of the Mercurbank and its importance as a base in Austria. He went on to explain that the Mercurbank had been forced on the Dresdner Bank in 1932 as a result of the takeover of the Danat. This "dreadful construction" had existed before the takeover, he noted; it was therefore necessary "to find a way of alleviating so far as possible the danger lurking in the personnel question and the largely Jewish clientele."[49]

Goetz conceded that quick action was now needed because of the Führer's concern, and he intended to ask Meyer and Rasche to take charge of the matter. In his instructions to Meyer, Goetz appended a report by Pilder on previously undertaken measures, and he also reminded Meyer that the Reichsbank wanted to be kept informed and to participate in any decisions connected with the Mercurbank.[50]

The Dresdner Bank was now confronted by two conflicting imperatives with respect to the Mercurbank, as became clear at a July 21 meeting between four directors of the Dresdner Bank and Keppler's aide and deputy, Edmund Veesenmayer, who was to have a deplorable role in the Holocaust. On this occasion, Meyer and Rasche, the leading National Socialists with SS connections on the management board, were present along with Schippel, who joined the Party in 1937, and Pilder, who was not affiliated with the Party Schippel and Pilder were on the Mercurbank administrative council, the former serving as vice president of the administrative council, and both serving as the Dresdner Bank representatives.

Veesenmayer argued that the political situation made the Aryanization of the bank both "necessary and possible," but Schippel and Pilder expressed reservations from the "liquidity perspective," namely, the losses that might result from withdrawals by Jewish customers. The upshot of the discussion was a plan for rapid Aryanization. Gabriel Neumann, whose contract was coming to an end, was to be forced out by October 1, and the Dresdner Bank was to ensure the liquidity of the Mercurbank. Contact was to be made with the Austrian authorities to prevent them from disturbing the process.[51]

Schippel and Pilder certainly did not have the influence or political clout to reverse this decision, but Leonard Wolzt, who had been successfully involved in the settlement with Kahane (who had died in the meantime), was someone to whom Meyer and Rasche

[47] PA-Berlin, R27508, Keppler to von Papen, July 15, 1937.

[48] NARA, RG 260, External Assets Investigations 1945–1949, 390/44/31/01, Box 539, Keppler to Goetz, July 13, 1937.

[49] Ibid., Goetz to Keppler, July 14, 1937.

[50] Ibid., Goetz to Meyer, July 14, 1937. No copy of the Pilder report is available.

[51] Ibid., memorandum, July 21, 1937.

apparently might listen. Wolzt, born in 1902 in Nürnberg, made his early career at the Dresdner Bank in Berlin and seems to have been a protégé of Pilder's. He had briefly been assigned to the Mercurbank in 1933 but then returned to Berlin only to be reassigned shortly thereafter to act as a contact between the Dresdner Bank and Neumann's office. In 1937, Wolzt moved to Vienna and was appointed a director of the Mercurbank and later became the dominant director of the Länderbank Wien AG. Wolzt's political convictions, assuming he had any, are difficult to fathom. He was reputed to have sought membership in a Free Masons' lodge in 1932 and was fined 3,000 RM by the Gestapo in 1944 for giving 10 RM to a Jewish acquaintance. At the same time, he was reported to have supported the NSDAP before the Anschluss. Although he did not join the Party until 1940, he was known to give generously to Party causes, and there were no political objections to his family life and the way he was raising his children. An evaluation by an official in the Gau Economic Advisory Office of Vienna for the Party in January 1944 was probably on the mark: "Director W. is an outstanding businessman who especially understands how to 'make business deals' and therefore cultivates very active contacts with all economic circles and also seeks them with political personalities. He is extraordinarily ambitious and supported the NSDAP early, that is, before the Anschluss. He is considered especially forthcoming and is cheerfully open to all wishes on the part of Party agencies or personalities. This present attitude, however, is to be judged in terms of his character and his past.... In conclusion, it can be said that because of his ambition W. is to be considered 'reliable' for so long as the war and political events do not seem to indicate the need for another position. Such personalities, however, are not rare in the business world."[52]

Wolzt, therefore, was not one to dismiss the economic dangers of politically motivated actions, and he had indeed been asked to consider what would be required in the event of a run on the bank by its Jewish clientele. Back in October 1936, he had written a memorandum pointing out the difficulties the Mercurbank had faced in dropping Kahane and the importance the renunciation of other Aryanization measures had played in preventing serious consequences for the bank. As he explained in a lengthy and carefully reasoned memorandum of July 28, 1937, the plan to dismiss Neumann was even more dangerous. Everything would depend on whether the bank's Jewish customers withdrew their holdings. If they did, the non-Jewish customers might follow suit, and that, in turn, would influence the banks and savings banks that held accounts to the tune of 32 million Schilling in the Mercurbank. The banks and savings banks had already demonstrated their tendency to respond negatively when the insurer Phönix found itself in crisis a year earlier, and they might feel it their responsibility to the Austrian authorities to withdraw their funds in the event the Mercurbank appeared to be in danger. Austria did have legislation on the books permitting a bank to delay withdrawals from large accounts, but Wolzt thought that the use of that prerogative would undermine confidence. If the Mercurbank sought to borrow on the strength of the best loans in its portfolio and pay out on demand, it would have to depend on the Austrian National Bank. The Austrian National Bank did not come to the rescue of the Mercurbank when the Danat failed in 1931, and the Mercurbank had to declare a bank holiday as a result. It was not clear in 1937 what the Austrian National Bank would do, but there would be no way to save the Mercurbank without it. That would mean a dependency on the National Bank and the Austrian authorities that the Mercurbank had consistently sought to avoid.

---

[52] Gau Economic Advisor to Gau Headquarters Vienna, Jan. 7, 1944 and other relevant materials in ÖStA/AdR, BMI, Gauakt Leonard Wolzt, Nr. 19.730. See also Peter Eigner/Peter Melichar, "Enteignungen und Säuberungen. Die österreichischen Banken im Nationalsozialismus,"

in: Dieter Ziegler (ed.), Banken und "Arisierungen" in Mitteleuropa während des Nationalsozialismus (= Geld und Kapital, vol. 5. Jahrbuch der Gesellschaft für mitteleuroäische Banken und Sparkassengeschichte 2001, Stuttgart 2002), pp. 43–118, esp. pp. 93–94.

What, then, were the options for improving the liquidity of the Mercurbank? One was to increase the number of its depositors and investors from Aryan circles friendly to the bank. The bank would need 20–30 million Schilling in new deposits, and that would take time, certainly more than eight weeks. Much had been done to mobilize Aryan capital, but that would be a slow process, especially in Vienna. Another option would be to reduce the number of credits granted, and Rasche and Mayer had ordered Wolzt to do this but the effects would also take some time to make themselves felt. Furthermore, the cancelling of credits could not be kept secret and would lead to a loss of confidence. Another possibility of ensuring liquidity would be a guarantee from the National Bank and the Austrian authorities that they would provide the necessary liquidity. That, however, was precisely the kind of dependency on the existing political and economic system in Austria that the Dresdner Bank and the Mercurbank had sought to avoid, and indeed had avoided since 1931 despite the efforts of the Austrian National Bank and the Austrian authorities to create such a dependency. Wolzt therefore argued firmly against negotiations with the Austrian authorities. Liquidity was not to be accepted at the price of dependency. At the same time, Wolzt also insisted that the Mercurbank could not afford to remain in a state of competitive passivity. He pointed out that only a few weeks before the Creditanstalt had taken the final steps in its refinancing with the help of the Austrian Treasury and had been relieved of 8 million Schilling in pension obligations in the process. This meant that the bank, assuming conditions remained calm, could actually pay out a dividend in the coming year that would give it a significant competitive advantage. In recent years, the Mercurbank had been able to earn 500,000–600,000 Schilling a year and, while its pension burdens had not been relieved it might be in a position to offer a dividend if its earnings remained at present levels. If it lost clients, however, then its modest gains would turn into losses, and it would show a loss precisely at a time when its competitors were showing a profit and paying a dividend.

Wolzt's reflections led to a conclusion that cast the program of rapid Aryanization in an unfavorable light. He did not feel that the Mercurbank could afford any shocks. What was needed was a long and tough fight to get more Aryan customers. He believed that progress had been made and success was possible, and success would open up the possibility of getting rid of more non-Aryan employees. The alternative, in his view, was self-defeating: "If the deadline of October 1 of this year decided by you is not to be changed and if, as a consequence, negotiations have to be conducted with Austrian state agencies and the National Bank, then I see the great danger for the Mercurbank of either going to ruin or sliding into dependence on the Austrian agencies."[53] What this remarkable document meant in concrete terms was that the Mercurbank had to choose between a good measure of present dependence on the Jews and a potentially longer-term, if not permanent, dependence on the Austrian National Bank and the Austrian government. Given the choice, the former was preferable to the latter!

Nevertheless, at least some thought was given to an appeal to the Austrian National Bank and Kienböck. In early August, Veesenmayer informed Reichsbank officials that he and Keppler were planning to travel to Vienna to see Chancellor Schuschnigg and President Kienböck of the National Bank to gain support for the further Aryanization of the Mercurbank and, most importantly, to agree to the discount of a substantial number of Mercurbank bills in an obvious attempt to improve its liquidity. Keppler hoped to get Hitler's approval for this step, and the Reichsbank had suggested that perhaps Kienböck could be made more agreeable if the sale of German holdings in the Niederösterreichische Handels- und Gewerbebank was used as a bargaining chip. Nothing seems to have come of this idea, however, whether because Hitler did not give his approval or for other reasons.[54]

[53] NARA, RG 260, External Assets Investigations 1945–1949, 390/44/31/01, Box 539, Wolzt to Rasche, Meyer and Busch, July 28, 1937.
[54] See PA-Berlin, R 110997, file note by Wilhelm, Aug. 2, 1937.

The big question that remained, therefore, was whether it would be possible to mobilize German support so that Aryanization could be pursued with impunity. If the Mercurbank wanted to avoid dependence on the Austrian National Bank, the logical place to turn was the Reichsbank. Meyer paid a visit to Vice President Emil Puhl, who was becoming the dominant figure in the Reichsbank at this time, to inform him of the situation. Puhl reiterated the Reichsbank's desire to be kept informed, but when asked whether the Reichsbank could help out, Puhl was emphatic that the foreign exchange situation of the Reich made any help from his quarter impossible. At a meeting between Goetz and another Reichsbank vice president, Friedrich Dreyse, which Puhl had also attended, Dreyse did not disapprove of the plans for the Mercurbank but showed no optimism about their being realized.[55]

The only sign of optimism came from Veesenmayer, who had also discussed the question with Puhl and had sent Meyer a lengthy list of German firms and subsidiaries operating in Austria, strongly urging Meyer to contact them directly and also to work on the home offices and proprietary corporations in Germany to promote opening accounts and credits with the Mercurbank.[56] Veesenmayer and Meyer seem to have made a serious effort to accomplish this goal, contacting the Norddeutsche Lloyd and Hamburg-Amerika Line headquarters about having their Vienna offices shift their accounts to the Mercurbank. They had some success with the Norddeutsche Lloyd; the Hamburg-Amerika office in Vienna, on the other hand, proved extremely reluctant to turn away completely from the Creditanstalt, with which it had had very good relations over the years.[57] The effort to persuade German firms to shift their accounts to the Mercurbank inevitably meant undermining the position

of the Creditanstalt and reflected a considerable ignorance about and indifference to the relationships between Austrian and German banks. In October 1937, Veesenmayer called Director Hans Rummel of the Deutsche Bank and told him that "the Deutsche Bank should do as much of its business via the Mercurbank as possible because this bank, which is in German ownership, should be strengthened."[58] Rummel pointed out that doing so would be difficult because the Deutsche Bank had been closely associated with the Creditanstalt for decades, an admission that may have helped to negatively influence the attitude of Keppler's office toward the Deutsche Bank following the Anschluss.

The inevitable problems involved in trying to persuade companies to move their accounts for purely political reasons were greatly complicated by the bizarre situation and the behavior of the National Socialists in the Mercurbank. These oddities were revealed during a visit to the Dresdner Bank on August 5, 1937, probably to Director Meyer, by August Günther, the head of the League of Germans Abroad in Austria and a director of the German Chamber of Commerce in Vienna. Apparently, Günther had also discussed these problems with Veesenmayer, and he was acting at the behest of the Party's Organization for Germans Abroad. He reported that relations between Wolzt and Warnecke were bad, and the competition and conflicts between the two were making it difficult to develop a common program for the acquisition of new clients and to appoint someone from the Mercurbank to the leadership of the Chamber of Commerce. Wolzt clearly had a special relationship with Dresdner Bank headquarters in Berlin, but Warnecke complained that Wolzt never informed him about anything, a complaint apparently also voiced to Meyer, who had had little contact with Warnecke previously. Günther thought Wolzt the more able of the two men, and he considered Warnecke

55   NARA, RG 260, External Assets Investigations 1945–1949, 390/44/31/01, Box 539, unsigned memorandum, probably from Meyer for Rasche and Busch, July 29, 1937.
56   Ibid., Veesenmayer to Meyer, July 31, 1937.
57   See the relevant correspondence in ibid., especially Hugo Sennewald of the Hamburg-Amerika office

in Vienna to the home office in Hamburg, Oct. 1, 1937.
58   Historisches Archiv der Deutschen Bank (= DB), B 51, as reported by Pohle to Abs, April 13, 1938.

"old and too tired." Wolzt's relations with his colleagues were poor. He collaborated with no one and had developed a reputation for being an intriguer. Kurt Fiedler, the representative of the illegal National Socialist Party organization at the Mercurbank and a manager with power of attorney who was slated to become a director, complained to Günther that he was allowed no influence on personnel policy and that he disagreed profoundly with Wolzt's view that a reduction of the number of Jewish employees would endanger the bank.

Meyer noted that this contradicted claims made by Wolzt during his visits to Berlin that he worked closely with Fiedler and another National Socialist manager with power of attorney, Rudolf Schwarz, and that Fiedler shared his views on the danger of firing Jews. It did confirm, however, Veesenmayer's report that Fiedler had insisted Wolzt did not properly represent his views and Wolzt was responsible for making the non-Jewish employees anxious that they might also lose their jobs if Jews were let go. Günther took the position that caution was required but that it was most unlikely that a large amount of Jewish money would be withdrawn. He was particularly skeptical that the savings banks would withdraw their money because the "savings banks as municipal institutions, and the municipalities themselves in Austria are largely anti-Semitic and to be sure not only the Savings Bank of the City of Vienna." Furthermore, the Austrian government would not respond negatively because "the government as well as – above all – the clerical circles were everywhere trying to push the Jews out of positions, which they then, to be sure, sought to fill with their people." Günther assured Meyer that he was prepared to do everything possible to gain clients for the Mercurbank, and thought that as much as 10 million Schilling in accounts could be acquired if major industrial firms and German firms that had traditionally dealt with the Länderbank Wien and the Creditanstalt were tapped. Günther thus belonged to the "optimistic" school that argued that Jewish clients closing accounts was not as great a danger as was sometimes claimed and that compensation

could be found in the business of German and pro-German enterprises.[59]

An intriguing question that is ultimately impossible to answer is whether the Aryanization program endangered the Mercurbank, as a number of Dresdner Bank officials obviously thought it did. Goetz, for example, was very conscious that "the deposits controlled by the Jewish side amount to about 80 percent."[60] Clearly, Party activists inside and outside Austria were anxious to get rid of Neumann. The no less interesting question is what Neumann himself intended to do. He was, after all, no ordinary administrative council member, and he had played a major role in determining policy at the bank and also bore credit for the bank's recent successes. A capable banker and a shrewd man, he was certainly aware that the National Socialists were trying to force him out. He was not likely to sit by idly under such circumstances, and he eventually decided to force the issue, as is evident in a letter of August 6, 1937 to Pilder. He pointed out that he had already for more than a year sought to make clear, both in writing, primarily to Schippel, but also in repeated discussions, that "it is unbearable for a leadership with a sense of responsibility to allow changes which can have the effect of endangering or even damaging the total interests of an institution." Furthermore, he had sought to make the Dresdner Bank understand that "total interests" meant not only the shareholders but also what one today calls its stakeholders, that is, the depositors and creditors, "whose means – in the Mercurbank the relationship is 5:1 with respect to share capital – are entrusted in the

---

59 Ibid., unsigned memorandum, probably from Meyer, of Aug. 5, 1937. Kurt Fiedler had been a Party member since 1932 and had been assigned the task of looking after Party interests at the Mercurbank. See ÖStA/AdR, BMI, Gauakt Kurt Fiedler, Nr. 207.151. It is certainly unlikely that Rudolf Schwarz, who was reputed to join the Party in Munich as early as 1932, would have been supportive of Wolzt's position. Schwarz was in charge of personnel at the Mercurbank, a position he later held in the Länderbank. See ibid., Gauakt Rudolf Schwarz, Nr. 11.876.

60 NARA, T83/128, management board working committee meeting, Nov. 9, 1937.

bank; it extends to the interests of the entire clientele for whose care the bank is summoned, and it comprehends the interests of the entire body of employees whose existence stands and falls with the Institution."

He noted that the respite since the personnel changes in the management and administrative council of the previous fall had been very short indeed, and that "new combinations" appeared repeatedly. People were showing up who had nothing to do with the bank and were demanding changes motivated by political considerations rather than by the purely economic considerations that had previously guided the bank. He had warned for some time that changes in the board of managers or out of the ordinary changes in personnel would lead him to bring up the matter before the entire administrative council. The recent constant to and fro between Berlin and Vienna by functionaries of the bank for no ascertainable business reason was, in his view, an indication that changes were being planned, and it resulted in creating unrest in the bank and producing "an atmosphere, which I must at the present time describe as dangerously threatening." In light of the fact that he did not feel he could take responsibility for this situation alone, he had decided to call a meeting of the administrative council. Before doing so, however, he hoped to discuss the matter with Pilder in Vienna because he wanted the ensuing discussions to be carried out in a "friendly manner."

Neumann's dignified letter was a far cry from the swamp of intrigue and low-level back-biting described by Günther and others, but it was also appropriately threatening under the circumstances. It certainly produced a good deal of nervousness at the Dresdner Bank. Pilder, in informing his colleagues of the letter and trying to find out what to do next, seemed much relieved at Neumann's desire to settle things in a "friendly manner," and he had politely informed Neumann that he would soon respond.[61] At a meeting of the directors of

the Dresdner Bank on August 24, it was unanimously agreed to try to find a compromise with Neumann. Although his contract would not be renewed, he would be offered the opportunity to remain on the administrative council, to propose business ventures and carry them out with the support of the Mercurbank, and to receive a fee upon leaving the board that would be structured in such a way as to give him an interest in the continued prosperity of the Mercurbank. He would also be assured that he would not be replaced by another administrative council appointee who would play a role similar to the one he had played, namely, as a kind of overseer of the management board and general director of the bank. The bank would follow the model typical of Austrian banks, and the new president of the administrative council would not have the kind of freedom of action Neumann enjoyed.[62] Goetz seems to have been particularly interested in pacifying Neumann, and the Dresdner Bank tried to rally the RWM to its position and to mobilize Ministerial Councilor Koehler to support the Dresdner Bank's compromise proposal.[63]

At the beginning of September, Pilder visited Vienna and negotiated with Neumann. The Dresdner Bank was insistent that the administrative council needed a new president but the person would not be as powerful as Neumann had been and would be chosen from the existing administrative council. One candidate was Arthur Hämmerle, a well-known textile industrialist and National Socialist since May 1933; he had been asked at the end of 1936 but had declined, pleading too many other obligations. Another was Alfred zu Hohenlohe-Schillingfürst, a member of the Schoeller banking family who was known for his pro-Reich views. He had only just joined the administrative council and was thus a second choice. Finally, there was Otto Böhler. He was socially quite prominent but had been the chairman of the Compass Bank, which had

---

[61] NARA, RG 260, External Assets Investigations 1945–1949, 390/44/31/01, Box 539, Pilder to Meyer and Rasche, Aug. 16, 1937 and Pilder to Neumann, Aug. 6, 1937.

[62] Ibid., memorandum by Pilder, Aug. 26, 1937.

[63] NARA, T83/128, Dresdner Bank, management board working committee meeting of Aug. 26, 1937.

filed for bankruptcy a few years earlier, and he was thus unlikely to inspire an atmosphere of optimism. Neumann was especially concerned about Ritscher, who was in Egypt and was ill, but whose experience and services for the Mercurbank would be needed. It was proposed that Ritscher be given an office and a secretary so that he could help out with the Mercurbank. That would be necessary from Neumann's perspective because his own departure would leave a gap and Ritscher would be especially useful in keeping up "the connection to Jewish circles." Significantly, even Rasche and Meyer felt that Ritscher's services would be essential in this connection. Pilder thought that the proposal to use Ritscher was constructive and demonstrated, moreover, Neumann's "thoroughly loyal position." Nevertheless, he remained concerned about the two looming dangers connected with Neumann's departure, namely, the attitude of the Mercurbank's Jewish clientele and the need for Austrian government support in overcoming any crisis.[64] Aryanizing the bank while keeping the "important" Jews on board was indeed a difficult task!

Nothing better illuminates the balancing act the Dresdner Bank was pursuing than the draft of a note to the Reichsbank of September 13, 1937. The Dresdner Bank defended itself against claims that its management board had reservations about the release of Neumann from his position. The Dresdner Bank had done everything possible to make the Mercurbank independent of the Austrian National Bank even though it had taken money from savings banks, the postal savings bank, and other institutions directly or indirectly dependent on the Austrian government. Such funds amounted to 32 million Schilling, or half of external obligations. The Dresdner Bank had also tried its utmost to Aryanize the Mercurbank. The management board was totally non-Jewish, consisting of two Germans and one Austrian who

met that criterion. Six non-Aryan members of the administrative council had left and had been replaced by Aryan businessmen, leaving only Ritscher and Neumann. Of the 348 bank employees, only 18 percent were non-Aryan; the percentage of Jews on the staff had been reduced largely by the hiring of new Aryan employees. That was necessary because the Austrian government would not permit firing bank employees without granting them pensions for life.

The Dresdner Bank as the chief shareholder of the Mercurbank, had thus proven itself willing to Aryanize the bank and had done everything possible to achieve that goal and to take protective measures. This said, however, the dangers could not be overlooked. The forced departure of Kahane in September 1936 was not without its price. The growth in the number of creditors had stagnated; the shortfall came to 8 million Schilling. This clientele was largely from Vienna because the bank had not been allowed to expand, and it was therefore largely non-Aryan. What all this meant was that there was little margin for difficulties and, despite all efforts, a high degree of dependence on the Austrian National Bank for discounting bills and on other government-connected agencies. By the fall of 1937, in short, barring a dramatic political change in Austria, it seemed likely that the Mercurbank was either going to remain dependent on its Jewish clientele or become dependent on the Austrian authorities. Because of the political pressures, the Dresdner Bank could not live with Neumann, but, until Austria became part of the Reich, it could not do without him because his dismissal would almost certainly lead to the loss of the Mercurbank as a base for German interests.[65]

---

[64] NARA, RG 260, External Assets Investigations 1945–1949, 390/44/31/01, Box 539, memorandum on a visit to Vienna, Sept. 6, 1937. On Hämmerle's Party connections, see ÖStA/AdR, BMI, Gauakt Arthur Hämmerle, Nr. 169.418.

[65] NARA, RG 260, External Assets Investigations 1945–1949, 390/44/31/01, Box 539, Draft of a letter to the Reichsbank Directorate, Sept. 13, 1937 and NARA, T83/128, Dresdner Bank management board working committee meetings of Oct. 4, 1937 and Nov. 9, 1937. The auditor report, "Bericht über die Revision bei der Mercurbank, Wien vom 19. Mai 1938," confirms the significant loss of depositors at the end of 1936 due to "known reasons" as well as the dependence on Austrian public institutions.

In the last analysis, those eager to drive Neumann out were perfectly correct in thinking that he had no reason to favor German interests and every reason to counter them. Indeed, the latter appears to have been his intention, and he apparently hoped to accomplish that with the cooperation of the more moderate elements in the Dresdner Bank. In October 1937, Neumann approached Pilder and asked for authorization to negotiate with the Länderbank Paris, that is, the Banque des Pays de l'Europe Central, to explore a possible merger of the Mercurbank and the Länderbank. Neumann's motives, as he explained after the war, were twofold: "1.) I wanted to counter the dominant German influence at the Mercurbank with a French-English influence. 2.) In recognition of the competitive difficulties of a small bank over against the powerful Österreichische Creditanstalt, I wanted to create a new major bank."[66] It is most unlikely that Neumann was open about the first motive, which would hardly have been a selling point in Berlin. The second consideration, however, seemed to have got Pilder thinking. On February 1, 1938, Pilder wrote to Goetz and to his Dresdner Bank colleague, Busch, about ideas that had come up in his talks with Neumann that looked "far into the future but were perhaps worth thinking about." He noted that the Deutsche Bank and the Creditanstalt had a friendly association even if it was the Austrian state that held most of the Creditanstalt's capital. In the event of an Anschluss, it was possible that the Dresdner Bank would turn the offices of the small Mercurbank into branches, but that would not amount to much for the balance of the Dresdner Bank. In the case of the Deutsche Bank, however, it would probably integrate the Creditanstalt into the German banking system by taking over the Austrian government's shares. That would require the Deutsche Bank

to increase its capital by 50 million Reichsmark, which would give it a great advantage in Austria and the Balkan countries both because of its large capital and because the powerful banking organization of the Creditanstalt would come under its sway. In Pilder's view, there were "certain possibilities" to preempt that from happening, assuming the situation was deemed acute and one was prepared to do something about it.[67] By the end of February, Goetz seems to have come to the same conclusion and authorized negotiations. Neumann, who was planning to travel to Paris, London, and the United States at the end of March, told Pilder he would use his stay in Paris to speak with General Director Henry Reuter of the Länderbank about a merger of the two banks.

It is important to remember the context in which these discussions were taking place. The Austrian state still existed; the pressure of German influence was growing; and the Mercurbank was not to lose sight of interests of the Dresdner Bank. Pilder, as it turned out, apparently thought he had more than one string in his bow. Although he and Goetz had approved negotiations on the basis of Neumann's proposal, Pilder was also testing another plan with Geheimrat Clodius of the German Foreign Office, with whom he had already raised the question of "whether it is more interesting for the effectiveness of German influence in Austria to control a banking institution like the Mercurbank completely alone or, by giving up the sole influence over the Mercurbank, to make an attempt to acquire a qualified block of shares in the Creditanstalt."[68] The Dresdner Bank could acquire a strong minority stake in the Creditanstalt by selling its shares in the Mercurbank (22 million Shilling); the Eisenstädter Elektrizitätswerke, which it owned outright (3.6 million Shilling); and its stake in the Veitscher Magnesitwerke (2 million Shilling). To the 27.6 million Shilling resulting

66   Institut für Zeitgeschichte, Wien (= IfZG), Do-10/Nl-5, Material Migsch, Fasz. Nr. 128, letter of Feb. 11, 1948, General Director of the Länderbank to Federal Minister Migsch, with appendix "Memorandum on the Origins of the Fusion of the Länderbank and Mercurbank" by Gabriel Neumann, Nov. 28, 1946.

67   Historisches Archiv der Dresdner Bank (= DrB), Nr. 7836-2000, Pilder to Busch, with a copy to Goetz, Feb. 1, 1938.
68   PA Berlin, R 110997, Pilder to Clodius and memorandum, Feb. 25, 1938.

from those sales, it could also add receivables from the Eisenstädter Elektrizitätswerke that would bring the total to about 30 million Shilling, which the Dresdner Bank could use toward buying a one-third minority holding in the Creditanstalt valued at 35.3 million Shilling. Because the basic equity capital of the Creditanstalt had not been paying a dividend, one could justifiably insist that its shares be sold below par. As Pilder pointed out, what made the Creditanstalt interesting was not its unexceptional balance sheet but rather its industrial holdings and influence on 106 companies of every type, including almost all the most important companies in Austria. The advantage of buying into the Creditanstalt was, therefore, that it would vastly expand German interests in the Austrian economy as a whole, and the Dresdner Bank would maintain its influence over the Mercurbank and the Eisenstadt company through its position in the Creditanstalt. The difficulty, of course, was that the Creditanstalt, the Austrian government, and the foreign shareholders in the Creditanstalt would have to consent to the deal. Also, one would need a guarantee that the shares would come into desirable hands and that the Dresdner Bank would be given the influence it deserved by having such a large minority stake. Although there was ample evidence that the German noose around Austria was tightening at this time, the plan in question was still based on very optimistic assumptions about the possibilities of gaining support from the parties mentioned and it also did not deal with the potential reaction of the Deutsche Bank, which, as Neumann had clearly recognized, had its own stake in the Creditanstalt. Last, the plan involved the repatriation of Austrian economic enterprises, and that was viewed with immense hostility in Berlin. When the *Frankfurter Zeitung* reported the rumor that German-Austrian economic negotiations scheduled for January 1938 might involve the repatriation of the Mercurbank shares to Austria in return for Austrian financial concessions, Veesenmayer complained to Clodius about whether it was proper for a respectable German paper to be reporting such rumors, no matter how cautiously it was

done.[69] In any case, although nothing was to come of Pilder's Creditanstalt plan, which ceased to be realistic after the Anschluss because of the role played by other interests, it is indicative of the continued fluidity of the situation and the jockeying for position in the Austrian economy by various German interests.

At the time this plan was being contemplated, the end of February 1938, Neumann had already agreed not to stand for reelection to the administrative council and to accept the termination of the special contract paying 40,000 Schilling a year for his special services to the bank. He did not have a claim to a pension, but under Austrian law his employment could not be terminated before June 30, 1938, and he was entitled to continuation of his pay for the period March–June 1938. But because Neumann "had performed great services, especially in the reorganization of this institution," the Mercurbank suggested he receive a higher settlement than that prescribed and that he be employed for another three years to deal with the bank's foreign relations. It was proposed that he receive 150,000 Schilling in settlement and compensation. At the beginning of March, the Austrian Ministry of Finance proposed reducing the amount to between 100,000 and 120,000: between 60,000 and 90,000 Schilling was to be paid over three years in consulting fees; a settlement of 30,000–40,000 Schilling; and 10,000 Schilling a month for three months as severance pay.[70]

Although Neumann's contract was not being renewed, it appears that the idea of having him conduct business on the bank's behalf, as discussed in August, took concrete shape in the proposed settlement and his assignment to negotiate in Paris. As the negotiations on the terms of Neumann's departure were under way, the Aryanization of the administrative council was being accelerated. It was decided to appoint Meindl to the vacant council seat. The

69 Ibid., Veesenmayer to Clodius, Jan. 5, 1938 and FZ article of Dec. 30, 1937, "Wiener Mutmaßungen über die Mercurbank-Mehrheit."
70 ÖStA/AdR, BMF, Allgem. Reihe 1938, Nr. 21905/1938, Report of Department 15 concerning the Mercurbank, settlement with Vice President Neumann, March 3, 1938.

appointment was pushed through in February so that Meindl could participate in the meeting of the administrative council on March 10, which turned out to be two days before the Anschluss.[71] Needless to say, the German takeover of Austria changed Neumann's situation and the question of Aryanization substantially. The Mercurbank no longer needed to fear dependence on the Austrian government because soon there would be no independent Austrian government on which to depend. As for the bank's Jewish clientele, they would soon be stripped of their assets. Neumann almost immediately found himself in considerable danger. He was accused of trying to withdraw large sums of money as part of his settlement. There is no indication in the surviving records whether he was successful in doing so. His arrest was prevented, apparently by Pilder, who also requested an official leave of absence for Neumann from the Dresdner Bank. Neumann was thus able to escape and go to Paris via Switzerland two days after the German invasion.[72] The changed political situation was to make the question of a Mercurbank-Länderbank merger more significant than ever. Neumann's idea of a merger remained very much alive, but his intention to use it to counter German influence was rendered moot by the circumstances. Nevertheless, Neumann's services to the Mercurbank and, indeed, the Dresdner Bank, had by no means ended.

2. GERMANIZATION AND ARYANIZATION OF THE LÄNDERBANK AND THE VIENNA BRANCH OF THE ŽIVNOSTENSKÁ BANKA

Neumann found himself in Paris earlier than planned because of his perilous situation. He contacted Reuter around March 20 regarding the sale of the Vienna branch. Neumann certainly could assume that Reuter would be concerned about the situation of the Länderbank following the Anschluss, but Reuter apparently did not tell Neumann the extent of his concern. Reuter had been in Vienna two days before the Anschluss; after the war, he claimed to have been very surprised by the arrival of German troops. Because the Bank of England owned a significant block of his bank's shares, he went to London to speak to the bank's governor, Montagu Norman. Reuter tried to persuade Norman to contact Schacht, a friend of Norman's, and to secure protection for the Länderbank in Vienna. He could hardly have had any illusions about the future of the Länderbank Wien, however, and his later suggestion that he was forced to negotiate its sale just does not ring true unless it was meant to suggest that he was a victim of the Anschluss. On March 21, Reuter informed the administrative council of the new situation resulting from the events in Austria so that the council could understand the reasons for the negotiations in which he had decided to engage.[73] Neumann, in his own account of the negotiations, does not mention being told about the trip to London by Reuter but does recall that Reuter claimed to have been approached by representatives of the Deutsche Bank in Paris with proposals. Reuter did agree, however, to negotiate with representatives of the Dresdner Bank under two conditions: first, the Dresdner Bank was to deal only with him and, second, the negotiations on all basic issues were to take place in Paris exclusively.[74]

---

71 NARA, RG 260, External Assets Investigations 1945–1949, 390/44/31/01, Box 539, memorandum, Feb. 4, 1938.

72 StA Nürnberg, Nl 6175, testimony of Pilder, Dec. 26, 1945; IfZG, Do-10/NI-5, Material Migsch, Fasz. Nr. 128, letter of Feb. 11, 1948, General Director of the Länderbank to Federal Minister Migsch, with appendix "Memorandum on the Origins of the Fusion of the Länderbank and Mercurbank" by Gabriel Neumann, Nov. 28, 1946; NARA, T83/135, Dresdner Bank, management board meeting, March 16, 1938.

73 BNP Paribas, Archives Historiques (= BNP Paribas), Registre des Déliberations, 1939.

74 This account is culled from a variety of sources that are at times slightly contradictory, in large part because Reuter was anxious to make a case that he had agreed to part with the Länderbank under duress. Nevertheless, the post-1945 accounts are sufficiently consistent with one another and with contemporary documents to produce a plausible recounting of events both in general and in detail. The most important postwar accounts are Neumann's letter of Nov. 28, 1946 (see Note 66); Pilder's testimony of Dec. 26, 1945 (see Note 72); Reuter's interview with members of the U.S.

Neumann later claimed that these conditions were set because Reuter had discovered that the acting director of the Länderbank in Vienna, Baron von der Lippe, had already approached other German banks in Vienna. Von der Lippe, who came from the Wiener Bankverein and had been pensioned off rather than given a position at the time of the merger with the Creditanstalt, had been brought into the Länderbank Wien only in 1937. Born in 1875, von der Lippe had developed many contacts since joining the Viennese banking scene in 1904. He spoke five languages and was considered an outstanding banker. A political evaluation of October 1939 described von der Lippe as "the typical bank director, and one cannot speak of him having a political position."[75] Reuter suspected that von der Lippe was angling for a permanent position at the Mercurbank and obviously did not trust him. Pilder later confirmed that was indeed what von der Lippe had wanted. Neumann seems to have forgotten another reason that Pilder mentioned in writing at the time, namely, that Reuter's leading directors in Vienna, aside from von der Lippe, were non-Aryans and had left their posts or were about to leave: Vice-President Emil Freund was

Jewish, as were three of the five directors, all ten of the deputy directors, and twelve of the sixteen managers with power of attorney.[76]

In any event, Neumann visited Reuter on March 30 and informed him that the Dresdner Bank was agreeable to exclusive negotiations in Paris and that Pilder had been authorized to conduct negotiations and would be meeting with him in Paris on April 1. The Dresdner Bank seemed anxious that Reuter negotiate exclusively with it. Reuter, although he agreed to discuss all the issues with Pilder first, was prepared to conduct exclusive talks for only a short period. Indeed, Reuter had to devote considerable effort to keep his people in Vienna in tow. Director Joseph Chappey, the native French director on the Länderbank Wien staff, was in regular contact with him and reported that Rasche wanted to negotiate, whereupon Reuter instructed Chappey to make clear that he was not authorized to negotiate. Chappey also reported that his colleagues in Vienna were by no means happy about the negotiations with the Dresdner Bank, which they viewed as a tough interlocutor likely to make the somber situation in Vienna even worse. They seemed more inclined to encourage negotiations with another apparent suitor of the Länderbank, Merck Finck & Co. in Munich, which they viewed as a more substantial enterprise than the rather small Mercurbank. Baron von der Lippe had apparently also sent out feelers to the Creditanstalt. Although Joham told him that there was little point in trying to approach the Creditanstalt and the Deutsche Bank while negotiations were under way with the Dresdner Bank, von der Lippe claimed that "all doors were open" and that no definite decision had been made. There was evidently great concern at the Vienna bank that the interests of the Länderbank would be sacrificed or disregarded, and Chappey urged that von der Lippe be brought into the negotiations in Paris. Reuter rejected that request, insisting that the talks were Franco-German negotiations and that they would be distorted if the Austrian perspective was joined with the French one. He

Government German External Assets Branch of June 12, 1947, in NARA, RG 260, Box 31/34c. Also very revealing is a memorandum by Pilder for Goetz and Busch of April 3, 1938, in StA Nürnberg, Nl 6422. Finally, there are the documents from the files of the BNP Paribas O.A.V. Archives Historiques, including the "Note concernant les revendications francaises sur la Länderbank," and the "Le Cas de la Länderbank" of Aug. 1947, prepared for the French negotiation delegation as well as documents from the period of the actual negotiations in 1938.

75 ÖStA/AdR, BMI, Gauakt Baron Victor von der Lippe, Nr. 114.464, Gauleitung Vienna to Austro Fiat Flugmotoren Gesellschaft, Oct. 16, 1939, and Political Report on von der Lippe, Oct. 6, 1937. The latter document mistakenly identifies him as a National Socialist, but then gives his Fatherland Front membership No. B464814. He became a member on March 15, 1934. This portion is omitted in the German edition. His children were active in the National Socialist movement. Von der Lippe seems to have adopted a wait-and-see attitude toward the National Socialist regime, as was reported in a letter of the Gaul Personnel Office of July 28, 1941.

76 See the list in the BNP Paribas Archives.

also stressed that the utmost would be done to protect the interests of those employed at the bank.[77]

Like Reuter, Pilder needed the full backing of his colleagues for the negotiations and a green light from the authorities in Berlin and Vienna. He had secured his colleagues' approval and had also received permission from the Banking Section of the RWM, which had informed him verbally that he could negotiate but that payment for the Länderbank in Vienna was not to be made in francs or another foreign currency. He was well aware of the advantages of an arrangement for both sides. On the French side, the Länderbank had proven to be of limited value as an asset and was likely to become even more problematic now that the Germans had taken over Austria. The French had no real incentive to invest in the Länderbank even before the Anschluss because of Austrian foreign exchange regulations, and those barriers would presumably become even more stringent under the Germans. The activities of the Länderbank were certainly being watched, but it also enjoyed a certain amount of protection and some freedom of action because it was a foreign bank. As early as March 19, Otto Christian Fischer of the Reichs-Kredit-Gesellschaft who, as will be shown, was not a disinterested party, had written to Reich Economics Minister Funk pointing out that the Central European Länderbank had its official headquarters in Paris. Its general director Henry Reuter was a Jewish Frenchman, and its administrative council filled with foreigners. There thus appeared to be considerable danger that the bank might shift capital abroad, and Fischer urged that the bank be placed under a Reich commissar with knowledge of both Austrian and international conditions.[78]

The RWM representative in Vienna, Hermann Landwehr, opposed such action, pointing out on March 13/14 that the ministry had decreed limited rights of disposition with respect to securities, foreign currency holdings, and real estate owned by foreigners. Violations of the regulations carried heavy penalties. These decrees were then made fully legal with the introduction of the German Foreign Exchange law on March 24. It was most unlikely that the leadership of the Länderbank would run the risk of violating the law, and the requirement that foreign securities and exchange be offered to the Reichsbank meant that one would soon know exactly what was in the possession of the Länderbank. Landwehr dismissed rumors of a run on the Länderbank because of its foreign ownership as false and reported that recent withdrawals fell within the normal range for Austrian banks. He did not think there was any danger that Baron von der Lippe, the only Aryan director of the bank, would do anything against German interests. The Paris owners did, however, have disposition over assets in Vienna and might undertake something. Nevertheless, Landwehr urged great caution in the appointment of a commissarial trustee for the bank in view of the international prominence of many of the administrative board members and that nothing be done without consulting Director Karl Blessing of the Reichsbank.[79]

RWM officials suspected that Fischer was trying to use his position as head of the Reich Banking Group to influence the situation. He and others were well aware that both the Dresdner Bank and the Deutsche Bank were engaged in negotiations in Vienna and elsewhere. Fischer feared that the other banks would be faced with a fait accompli as a result.[80] The fact was that Landwehr and the Reichsbank devoted special attention to the Länderbank immediately after the Anschluss because of its foreign ownership and found Baron von der Lippe "reliable and having completely good will toward the German foreign exchange offices and the Reichsbank," as demonstrated by his having secured $50,000 at the Länderbank for

[77] Ibid., minutes of March 30/31, 1938, by Reuter.
[78] Rossijskij gosudarstvenyi voennyi Archiv (Russian State Military Archive, formerly Moscow "Special Archive" = RGVA Moscow), 1458/2/104, Bl. 3–4, Fischer to Funk, March 19, 1938.

[79] Ibid., Bl. 7–8, Landwehr to the Reich Commissar of the Berlin Stock Exchange, March 24, 1938.
[80] RGVA Moscow, 1458/2/77, Bl. 19–21, memorandum, probably by Riehle, March 24, 1938.

the Reichsbank. The pending negotiations in Paris with the Dresdner Bank were known to the German authorities, and they were anxious to proceed cautiously in their dealings with the Länderbank.[81] Schacht and the Reichsbank had, in fact, signaled their strong approval for the takeover of the Vienna branch of the BPEC to Keppler and Fischböck, who were anxious to have the Länderbank Wien in "Aryan hands" and were encouraging the Dresdner Bank to support a takeover by the Mercurbank. Schacht had actually spoken to leading shareholders of the BPEC and had urged them to withdraw their leading Jewish employees from Vienna as soon as possible, to replace them with Aryans, and to conclude negotiations for a takeover of the Länderbank Wien as rapidly as possible.[82] The Reichsbank played the role of facilitator in the Dresdner Bank's efforts to take over the Länderbank Wien, and Reichsbank director Blessing often intervened in support of the Dresdner Bank.[83] Even if spared a commissar, however, Reuter and his colleagues in Paris must have been aware that German rule was much more stringent than Austrian and that their assets in Vienna could be subject to blockage. At the same time, there was one aspect of the Austrian legacy that made it difficult for the French to abandon or simply sell the Länderbank, namely, the Austrian special law governing bank employees of August 18, 1932, which made it virtually impossible to discharge them and required the payment of substantial pensions. Neumann's proposal that Reuter negotiate with Pilder and the Dresdner Bank, therefore, certainly had its attractions when it came to dealing with these problems.

Pilder, as has been shown, had been taken with Neumann's idea of a merger of the Mercurbank and Länderbank under the aegis of the Dresdner Bank from the very start. The Länderbank was an old and distinguished bank with a fine reputation. In contrast to the Mercurbank, it had a network of branches throughout Austria and close connections with big industry. Enough resources would be at hand in a merged bank to cover pension obligations.[84] It was obvious that Pilder and Neumann worked well together. In the ensuing negotiations, Neumann had the sense that Pilder was anxious to close a deal for purely business reasons and regarded the negotiations as entirely a business relationship. As he later wrote: "In his words and deeds, Dr. Pilder had repeatedly expressed the idea that the Dresdner Bank even under the National Socialist regime had to make sure that its reputation and credit did not suffer abroad, that fairness had to be maintained in international negotiations, so that the Dresdner Bank could enjoy a good reputation and the confidence of the world later when Nazism no longer existed."[85]

At the moment, however, Nazism was very much in existence. One could engage in business as normal business in Paris, but that was not the case in Vienna and Berlin, where business was anything but normal. The economic arrangements for Austria were being made by Keppler, who had been designated as Hitler's Reich plenipotentiary for Austria. Veesenmayer, as had been the case before, often acted on Keppler's behalf. However, a new figure in policy toward Austria now appeared on the scene in the person of Hans Kehrl, an ambitious and ruthless technocrat who was the head of the textile section of the Four Year Plan in the RWM and had been assigned to assist his compatriot Keppler. Keppler's office now worked closely with Hans Fischböck, who became minister of commerce and then minister of economics and labor following the Anschluss. Fischböck worked hand in hand with SS-Sturmbannführer Walter Rafelsberger, the Gau economic advisor, who looked after economic affairs for the Party and who was to become Austria's chief Aryanizer in his capacity as commissar for the private economy.[86] Furthermore, Göring and his Four Year

[81] Ibid., 1458/2/305, Bl. 14–15, undated report, but probably around March 27 by Köhler.

[82] PA Berlin, R27507, Handakten Keppler, Schacht to Keppler, March 29, 1938, and Keppler to Schacht, April 2, 1938.

[83] DrB, Nr. 5467-2000, memorandum by Busch, May 16, 1938.

[84] Pilder account, op. cit. See footnote 72.

[85] Neumann letter, op. cit. See footnote 72.

[86] For Kehrl, see his extraordinarily unrepentant and, in its own bizarre way, highly informative

Plan were vitally and often directly involved in planning and making arrangements. Göring had played a decisive role in accelerating the events that had led to the Anschluss, and he thus laid claim thereafter to an equally decisive say in the handling of the Austrian economy.[87] As important a bank deal as was being negotiated in Paris could not be made without the approval of the political leadership, and the connections of Rasche and Meyer were of vital importance here.

This was especially so because Keppler, Kehrl, and Fischböck were intent on earning Austrian goodwill by preventing German businessmen from descending on the Austrian economy like "locusts" and "colonizing" Austria.[88] With respect to banks, they wanted to prevent the larger Austrian banks from selling off industrial assets to German interests without permission; that goal, as will be shown, was that thwarted in extremely important cases. Keppler, Kehrl, and Fischböck also wanted to keep the Austrian banks independent of the major German banks. As recounted in Chapter 1, they were able to block the Deutsche Bank's ambitions toward the Creditanstalt in many important respects. Their response to the ambitions of the Dresdner Bank were bound to be somewhat different not only because of their ties with Rasche and Meyer and previous collaboration in trying to strengthen the German character of the Mercurbank, which the Dresdner Bank already owned, but also because they thought it desirable that the Länderbank be removed from French control. Moreover, the Four Year Plan authorities were anxious to rationalize and mobilize the credit system, and such considerations were to play a role.

Karl Rasche, who was discussing Austrian banking affairs with Kehrl, played an important role in laying the groundwork for Pilder's efforts. After mulling over the situation and talking to Fischböck and Veesenmayer, Kehrl sent a letter to Rasche on March 28 outlining his thoughts. It is likely that Rasche had taken advantage of their conversations to do his bit to block the ambitions of the Deutsche Bank; Kehrl began by asserting that the Creditanstalt was to remain an independent bank under all circumstances. Kehrl was willing to see the Mercurbank expand by taking over the Länderbank and also the Austrian Credit Institute for Public Enterprises and Works (Österreichisches Credit-Institut für öffentliche Unternehmungen und Arbeiten). The Credit Institute was 93 percent owned by the Austrian Republic and had a capital of 10.4 million Schilling. Its primary function was apparently mortgage lending, but it also was supposed to provide loans for public enterprises and had been involved in the liquidation of a number of failed banks. Kehrl thought that the current situation in Austria made the coexistence of normal bank credit and mortgage credit in one institution desirable and that the Austrian Credit Institute was likely to play an increasingly important role. Kehrl also suggested that the Mercurbank might take over some of the regional banks owned by the Creditanstalt. However, the Mercurbank would then have to promise not to set up branches in those regions and to remain an independent bank. It was not to merge with the Dresdner Bank in Austria or in the regions where it had branches. The expanded Mercurbank would also have to agree to make government-nominated candidates members of its administrative council. Under those circumstances, the government would support the expansion of the Mercurbank and might even agree to withdraw its insistence that the Dresdner Bank not hold a majority in an expanded Mercurbank.[89]

Kehrl declared these to be nonbinding proposals and asked Rasche to think the matter

memoirs: Hans Kehrl, *Krisenmanager im Dritten Reich. 6 Jahre Frieden – 6 Jahre Krieg. Erinnerungen* (Düsseldorf 1973), esp. pp. 118–132.

[87] See Norbert Schausberger, "Deutsche Wirtschaftsinteressen in Österreich vor und nach dem März 1938," in: Gerald Stourzh/Brigitte Zaar, *Österreich, Deutschland und die Mächte. Internationale und Österreichische Aspekte des "Anschlusses" vom März 1938* (Vienna 1990), pp. 177–213.

[88] Kehrl, *Krisenmanager*, pp. 128–129.

[89] DrB, Nr. 7836-2000, Kehrl to Rasche, March 28, 1938, and description of the Österreichisches Credit-Institut, April 4, 1938.

through and then make formal proposals. The fact that the response and the proposals were sent on March 29 in the names of the Dresdner Bank and the Mercurbank, that is one day after Kehrl's letter, suggests that there was considerable consensus about what was being called Kehrl's plan. Goetz's assent had been necessary, of course. He asked for further information on the Länderbank's non-Aryan business, and he also wanted to know which Austrian regional banks were to come under the Dresdner Bank's sway; he then gave his approval to the basic terms outlined by Kehrl.[90] Kehrl's proposals were thus viewed as "a suitable form to develop the Mercurbank and make it a functional instrument for the provision of credit to the Austrian economy." Kehrl was informed about the pending negotiations in Paris and the willingness of the French to give up their Viennese holdings, but he was also told that those negotiating on behalf of the Dresdner Bank and the Mercurbank wanted a monopoly for themselves and were operating under the assumption that no other German or Austrian bank would be permitted to approach the French while the negotiations were under way. They expressed the willingness of the Mercurbank to take over the Austrian Credit Institute, and they were prepared to consider taking over any and all of the four regional banks in Austria if called upon by the government to do so. The Mercurbank and Dresdner Bank promised not to merge, and the Dresdner Bank pledged it would not set up branches in Austria. However, it reserved the right to take up the matter again if another of the major Berlin banks was allowed to set up a branch in Austria. They were willing to put persons proposed by the government on the administrative council. They insisted that the Dresdner Bank maintain a firm majority of the Mercurbank shares, but it would offer shares on the stock market and to private persons in Austria. They asked Kehrl to assist in clearing

the outcome of the Paris negotiations with the German and Austrian authorities once they were completed.

Thanks to the backing of Kehrl and his government associates, the position of the Dresdner Bank in the Paris negotiations was well protected. As early as March 30, that is, a day before serious negotiations in Paris began, Director Eduard Mosler of the Deutsche Bank reported on the projected merger, pointing out that it was an attractive arrangement for the Mercurbank, which was picking up a bank that was double its size. He also remarked that the creditors of the bank were Christian while those with credits from the bank were Jewish.[91] The Deutsche Bank was obviously warned against making further overtures at this point, which also explains Joham's remark to von der Lippe on March 31 that negotiations between them would be pointless.

But Reuter had been approached by other leading German bankers, including Friedrich Reinhart of the Commerzbank and Otto Christian Fischer of the Reichs-Kredit-Gesellschaft, both of whom had good Party connections. Nevertheless, the Dresdner Bank negotiators were able to tell Reuter at the beginning of April that the Dresdner Bank was the only German bank allowed to negotiate for the Länderbank. In retrospect, Reuter recalled the emphasis they placed on their very good connections with Göring and other top National Socialists and how difficult it would be for a French-owned bank to do business in Vienna under the circumstances.[92] It is hard to imagine, however, that Reuter was not well aware of this fact.

Meeting with Pilder and Neumann on April 1, Reuter understandably intended to make the best of a bad situation, and he raised several important demands. There were a number of internal clearing accounts between Vienna and Paris; the former owed the latter money that Reuter wanted to collect, just as

[90] Ibid., see the telegraphic exchange on this between Pilder and Busch of March 29. The letter to Kehrl of March 29 was sent jointly by the Dresdner Bank (Rasche, Pilder) and the Mercurbank (Hitschfeld, Wolzt).

[91] DB, B 0011, file note by Mosler, March 30, 1938.

[92] See NARA, RG 260, Box 31/34c, Reuter's interview with members of the U.S. Government German External Assets Branch of June 12, 1947.

he wished to collect the undervalued reserves in Vienna that belonged to Paris. A matter of particular significance for Reuter was the question of calculating goodwill into the purchase price. The Länderbank name carried considerable prestige, and the bank had also made a profit in the previous year. He insisted that the bank's three large buildings, two of which were very outmoded and all of which were carried on the balance sheets of the Paris office, be taken over by the Länderbank Wien and be valued according to their use and not the very low present value of "bank palaces" in Vienna. A Jew himself, Reuter was anxious to provide some financial protection for the 260 Jews on the Länderbank's staff of 800. He asked that they be guaranteed pensions or severance pay, and he also asked the same for leading figures at three or four industrial enterprises that were particularly close to the Länderbank. Another point of honor was Reuter's demand that the Viennese Länderbank do its business in Paris exclusively with the Länderbank Paris because it would be most "painful" if it were to do otherwise. The thorniest issue in the negotiations was the actual value of the credits given by the Länderbank. Reuter contested the idea, apparently entertained in the Deutsche Bank and in other banking circles, that most of the receivables of the bank were non-Aryan, and he went through the list branch by branch showing that there were only a few cases in the textile and clothing branches involving substantial credits to non-Aryans. Pilder had to admit that he found the picture to be a healthy one, and both sides agreed to look into the matter further, and that the Dresdner Bank would only be asked to calculate what was real and collectible. The source of the problem was quite clear. As Pilder noted: "In any case, there lies in the apparently very radical tendency in the handling of Jewish business in Vienna a special problem in the business at hand." Jews who were good risks were being transformed into bad risks, and while the buyer obviously would not want them, the situation was most certainly not the fault of the seller. Then, of course, there was the pension question. The dismissal of 260 Jews would add an obligation of 700,000–800,000

Schilling annually. Because no special provisions had been made for pensions, the costs would eat into profits, even if the reduced costs made possible by the consolidation of the two banks might offset some of the pension costs. As for the payment to Paris, Pilder reported that this might be done by using a variety of assets held in Vienna that were really not integral to its Austrian business and could thus be used as payment.[93] Neumann was an active participant in the negotiations. Enjoying the trust of both parties, he sought, by his own account, to play the role of mediator. The reality was, however, that he had been acting on behalf of the German side. Nevertheless, Reuter understood his difficult position, and proposed that Neumann's commission be handled by the BPEC and the Dresdner Bank according to principles of "fair play." He received an honorarium of 150,000 Swiss francs from Reuter for his services. Whether he received money from the Dresdner Bank for his consultancy services is unclear.[94]

Whatever form it took, the payment to the BPEC for the Länderbank would require the permission of the RWM. On April 12, 1938, the Dresdner Bank formally requested permission to carry out the transaction. The estimated price of the Länderbank was put at 16.8 million Schilling. The claims on assets held in Vienna by the Paris bank amounted to some 18.8 million Schilling, including foreign exchange holdings; shares in the Allgemeine Kreditbank in Warsaw and the Sphinx Vereinigte Emaillierwerke und Metallwarenfabrik in Prague; shares in and claims on the Czech Schönprisener Zuckerfabrik; a large number of shares in the Yugoslav Trifailer Kohlenbergwerks-Aktien; and standstill claims on the Hungarian Postal Savings Bank. There were also shares of the Paris bank in Vienna. Reuter was willing to

93   StA Nürnberg, Nl 6422, and account by Reuter, BNP Paribas, Memorandum by Pilder, April 3, 1938, Archives Historiques, April 1, 1938. The two accounts are very similar.

94   IfZG, Do-10/Nl-5, Material Migsch, Fasz. Nr. 114, Wolzt to Landertshammer, Jan. 19, 1948 and Landertshammer to Migsch, Jan. 21, 1948.

credit these holdings against the price of the Länderbank. The Dresdner Bank viewed that proposal as "completely fair" because it would otherwise have to sell the assets itself but would not receive payment in strong currencies on account of the currency controls in the countries in question. For the German economy, using these assets to purchase the Länderbank was more advantageous than trying to monetize them. The Dresdner Bank also made a strong political-military argument for the takeover: "The transfer of the Austrian business of the Central European Länderbank into German hands will be unavoidably necessary. The bank is an important sector in the supplying of credit to the Austrian economy. If this instrument is in French hands, it cannot be employed according to the viewpoint of German economic policy. The continued employment in Austria of leading bank officials who are dependent on France is undesirable from the perspective of secrecy. Additionally, some important industrial firms are dependent on the Länderbank, such as the largest Austrian cement factory, Perlmooser; the biggest Austrian sugar factory, Hirm; and the sizeable iron construction firm Waagner-Biro. The employment of and information available to persons dependent on France would also be unsupportable in these places."[95]

Having secured the approval for further negotiation on the terms outlined, Reuter and Neumann worked out a complex and lengthy contract with the Dresdner Bank under which the entire business of the Länderbank Vienna was to be taken over by the Mercurbank. The basis for the negotiations was the balance sheet of the Länderbank on December 31, 1937, and Paris agreed to vouch for the soundness of only the loans it had made until March 11, 1938. This was apparently intended to protect the Paris office from being liable for the status of Jewish debtors after that date. The Mercurbank was to have eight weeks to contest the propriety and care shown in loans given out prior to March 11. Reuter was successful in getting rid of the Vienna Länderbank buildings, and he also

obligated the Mercurbank to take over existing Länderbank contracts, both individual and collective, with its employees and pension obligations to former employees and their heirs. These obligations were also to cover persons put on leave or pensioned off prematurely. The contract specifically stated that persons dismissed or pensioned off as non-Aryans should receive most favored treatment in the sense that they should not be treated any worse than equivalent functionaries and employees at the Creditanstalt. Moreover, exceptional cases that might be treated differently at the Creditanstalt were not to be used to set a new norm at the Länderbank.

Although in the end no money was supposed to change hands because obligations arising from the sale were cleared against one another in special accounts, the sale and exchange of assets were nevertheless involved, and the terms were quite important. The Mercurbank agreed to purchase the shares in the Austrian National Bank held in Paris for 500,000 Schilling. Insofar as the Länderbank Wien did not have sufficient assets belonging to the Länderbank Paris to cover its obligations to the latter, it was to place its 98,000 shares in the Trifailer mines and 13,000 shares in the Länderbank Paris into an escrow account at the Zurich Kantonalbank for the Länderbank Paris and the Dresdner Bank. The former was to collect dividends and exercise the voting rights in these shares. Once the amounts owing by the Länderbank Wien were determined, the shares would be released by the Dresdner Bank to the BPEC Paris. Provision was also made for the international arbitration of disputed claims.[96]

It did not take long for the news of the planned expansion of the Mercurbank to spread. At the Zentralsparkasse administrative board meeting on April 27, Director Walther Schmidt pointed out that he had decided to add another 3 million RM to the 4,150,000 RM deposited at the Mercurbank in view of its anticipated growth. At the same time, he expressed concern

---

95 DrB, Nr. 5467-2000, Dresdner Bank to Ministerialdirektor Lange, RWM, April 12, 1938.

96 The draft of the agreement discussed here is to be found in NARA, RG 260, German External Assets Branch, 390/44/20/04, Box 20, File 34B.

over the rumors about the Zentraleuropäische Länderbank, where the Zentralsparkasse had 6.2 million RM on deposit.[97] The exact shape the Viennese banking scene would take was thus not entirely clear, and at the end of April a number of outstanding issues remained to be settled. These issues were handled primarily by Neumann on behalf of Reuter, and by Pilder and Busch for the Dresdner Bank. Two of the unresolved issues required government action: the taxes and governmental fees entailed in the transaction, and regulations on the transfer of employees and pensioners from the Länderbank to the Mercurbank. In addition, there were technical issues connected with the calculation of the foreign exchange values used in the clearing account set up for the transaction. There was also the problem of deciding on and compensating for the Czech holdings eventually to be returned to the BPEC Paris.[98]

As these matters were being hammered out in early May, the Dresdner Bank outlined the basic terms of the contract that was being drawn up in Basel to Ministerial Director Landwehr of the RWM in a letter of May 2 and was thereby able to secure permission for completing the negotiations. A draft of the legislation needed to meet Reuter's demands in the negotiations scheduled for May 11 between Reuter, Directors Pilder and Busch of the Dresdner Bank, and Directors Warnecke and Wolzt of the Mercurbank was enclosed with the letter.[99] Under the draft legislation, the Mercurbank was obligated to take over and fulfill the contractual obligations of the BPEC Paris to the employees of its branch in Vienna and those employees were to have no right to make claims against the BPEC. The Mercurbank was to be relieved of a variety of taxes connected with the

transaction as compensation for taking over the personnel obligations of the BPEC Paris, which were viewed as unbearably high. The RWM felt it could concede this tax and fee relief without special legislation.[100]

That did not mean, however, that the arrangement was free and clear of older Austrian regulations that remained in force and that lay within the jurisdiction of Finance Minister Fischböck. On May 11, Director Meyer of the Dresdner Bank wrote to his cousin Wilhelm Keppler to inform him of his plan to go to Vienna to negotiate a special arrangement on the fees to be paid in connection with of the Länderbank and Mercurbank merger and the takeover of the Viennese branch of the Živnostenská Bank, and to ask Keppler's support in dealing with Fischböck. Appended to the letter was the draft of a memorandum to Fischböck that pointed out that taking over the Länderbank's pension obligations for Aryan and non-Aryan employees would make the launching costs for the new bank particularly high, and the taxes on property transfers, capital share increases, and taking over business obligations and loan guarantees would make the financial burdens of the transaction intolerable. Those charges amounted to 3.8 million RM, and that figure did not include other taxes and fees that could not yet be calculated or still needed to be taken into account. If these taxes and fees had to be paid in full, the deal simply could not be concluded. The Dresdner Bank argued that the withdrawal of foreign banks from Austria was in the interests of the Reich, but that those banks could not be persuaded to close down their branches so long as fees and taxes stood in the way. It was in Austria's interest to contribute to the effort to persuade foreign banks to leave the country. The Austrian Law Favoring Concentration of October 19, 1934, provided tax relief for mergers, but it was not applicable in this instance because the planned transaction was not a merger in the legal sense but rather a takeover of Länderbank assets by the Mercurbank. The Dresdner Bank, however, could point to another law, issued on

97 BA-CA, Vorstandsarchiv der Zentralsparkasse der Gemeinde Wien (= Z-V), protocol of the 3rd meeting of the administrative commission of the Central Savings Bank of the Municipality of Vienna, April 27, 1938, Zentralsparkasse Verwaltungskommission, 1938, S. 93.
98 DrB, Nr. 5467-2000, Neumann to Pilder, April 27, 1938 and attached correspondence.
99 For the protocol of this meeting, see BNP Paribas, Archives Historiques.
100 RGVA Moscow, 1458/2/68, RWM to Dresdner Bank, May 9, 1938.

July 28, 1926, that provided fee and tax relief for the transfer of the assets and liabilities of the Viennese branch of the Anglo-Austrian Bank by the Creditanstalt, and it asked that a similar enabling law be issued for the planned takeover of the Länderbank. Meyer also sought the support of Keppler and Fischböck for another, more sinister request. The Länderbank Paris insisted that, with the transfer of assets, the Mercurbank also take over the salary and pension obligations of the Länderbank Wien. The Vienna bank had a substantial number of Jewish employees who probably would not want to enter into contractual relations with the new bank and would turn to Paris to make their claims, which might lead to conflicts between the Paris bank and the Reichsbank over the monetary transfers that would be involved. To prevent that, the Dresdner Bank asked that a special law be issued under which the Mercurbank would be formally responsible for all salary and pension arrangements of the Länderbank Wien. The Dresdner Bank was prepared to make this arrangement, which was obviously quite favorable to the BPEC, only, however, if the BPEC would be willing to have the obligations paid in Reichsmark within Austria. The intent behind this proposal was obviously to avoid raising foreign exchange and currency issues. The difficult question of how those payments in Reichsmark was supposed to be taken out of Germany was left completely open.[101]

The efforts of the Dresdner Bank to secure special arrangements for the Mercurbank to complete the merger were embedded in a more comprehensive project that became explicit in its applications for support to the RWM, the Vienna Finance Ministry, and the governor of Austria on May 16–19, 1938. The takeover of the Länderbank Wien was presented in these documents as the linchpin in the development of a larger enterprise that the Dresdner Bank presented as "an – economically – new banking enterprise that, in its volume of business, its organization, and its capital base, will be so

structured that it will be capable of dealing with the new tasks that now face the Austrian economy, especially within the framework of the Four Year Plan, and that it will face in the future. An important field of activity of the new institution will be foreign business in the Southeast European economic area."[102] The Mercurbank was to change its name and was to increase its capital from 10 to 20 million RM. It was to take over the business not only of the BPEC branch but also of the Viennese branch of the Živnostenská Bank of Prague. When it came into existence, the new bank would already have branches in Baden, Bludenz, Bregenz, Graz, Insbruck, Klosterneuburg, Linz, Salzburg, and Wiener Neustadt, and it would also control leading regional banks, namely, the Bank für Kärnten AG and the Bank für Oberösterreich und Salzburg. It would thus be represented in all the leading locations in Austria. Once again, the Dresdner Bank reiterated the burdens placed on the Mercurbank in undertaking responsibility for the Länderbank's employees and pensioners, both Aryan and non-Aryan, and it renewed its appeal for relief from various taxes, a position that the authorities were apparently already prepared to approve. Special stress was placed on the foreign exchange advantages of the arrangement with the BPEC: the settlement with the Länderbank employees would be concluded in a manner that did not involve a drain on foreign exchange. The Dresdner Bank saw itself presenting a "not unwarranted request, but one that was desirable for national political and general national economic reasons."[103] The plan was to conclude the negotiations by the end of June at the latest.

The expansionist program of the Dresdner Bank-Mercurbank was an obvious effort to make the most of the Anschluss and of the very understandable desire of foreign banks to get out of Austria. The RWM welcomed the takeover of the Vienna branch of the

---

[101] PA Berlin, Handakten Keppler, R27506, Meyer and Keppler, May 11, 1938, and draft of letter to Fischböck, May 10, 1938.

[102] DrB, Nr. 5462-2000, Dresdner Bank to the Reich governor of Austria, May 19, 1938.

[103] Ibid., Dresdner Bank to the RWM, May 16, 1938; ibid. Dresdner Bank to the State Finance Minister, Vienna, May 17, 1938.

Živnostenská banka in Prague as an opportunity to supervise it lending activity. The
deal was all the more welcome because the
Mercurbank was not paying for goodwill and
was not assuming responsibility for the acquired
firm's pensioners.[104] The authorities were less
enthusiastic about the planned takeover of the
regional banks in Carinthia and Salzburg, and
Rasche was unhappy to find out that this part
of the original plan was not treated with the
earlier enthusiasm by the authorities. Rasche,
whose digestive capacities had been massively
enlarged by the Anschluss, had hoped to take
over all four of the Austrian regional banks. By
late April, however, he was willing to settle for
the banks in Carinthia and Salzburg, assuming he could acquire them, and to leave those
in the Tyrol and of Styria to the Creditanstalt.
The Bayerische Hypothekenbank, which had a
majority interest in the Carinthian bank, could
be compensated with the Kreditinstitut für
öffentliche Unternehmungen, which largely
dealt with mortgages. Kehrl had originally envisioned that bank becoming part of the enlarged
Mercurbank, and Rasche was obviously ready
to sacrifice it.[105]

This plan, however, ran into difficulties with
a new presence on the scene, Josef Bürckel,
who had been Gauleiter in the Saar and whom
Hitler thus deemed especially equipped to serve
as Reich commissar for the reunification of
Austria with the German Reich. Bürckel's chief
aide in economic matters, Oberregierungsrat
Kratz, complained to Joachim Riehle, the head
of the Banking Section of the RWM, that there
was much dissatisfaction with the special favor
shown to the Mercurbank, and that this was
unfair to the Creditanstalt, whose Balkan interests were viewed as very important. Keppler was
blamed for this discriminatory policy. Fischböck
now also argued that the Creditanstalt deserved
better treatment. Kehrl cautiously argued

for a sense of proportion in strengthen the
Mercurbank in light of its impending takeover
of the Länderbank Wien. Riehle felt that decisions about branches and regional banks had to
await an evaluation of credit needs in the various regions. By the end of May 1938, the advantages enjoyed by the Dresdner Bank and the
Mercurbank because of Keppler's support were
beginning to reach their limits in Austria, and
the time had come to consolidate the advantages of their quick start.[106]

In the meantime, the basic negotiations with
the BPEC and the Živnostenská banka had
been completed, and the special legislation had
been drafted. The Dresdner Bank could send a
more or less final report to the finance minister in Vienna, Fischböck, on June 2.[107] In this
detailed document, the new bank was portrayed
as an institution that would make a special contribution to the economic needs of Austria connected with the Four Year Plan, and particular
emphasis was placed on the role it would play
in Southeast Europe and in the exploitation
of the contacts and operations of its customers in that region. The bank already had a network of branches in Austria, and it also hoped
to gain influence over the Bank für Kärnten
and the Bank für Oberösterreich und Salzburg
by acquiring shares in those institutions. The
Dresdner Bank promised to provide additional
funds to the new institution to help with the
costs of consolidation. The report set out once
again in detail the agreement with the BPEC,
whereby the Mercurbank would take over all
the business of the Länderbank Wien and various
foreign assets would be transferred to the BPEC.
This deal was different from the arrangement
with the Živnostenská banka; in that transaction,
the Mercurbank declined to take over a number
of credits that it did not deem secure and also
insisted that a number of foreign assets held in
Vienna be transferred back to the Živnostenská
banka headquarters in Prague.

[104] RGVA Moscow, 1458/2/68, RWM draft, June 7,
1938. For the terms of the takeover and the contract
itself, see ÖStA/AdR, BMF, Allgem. Reihe 1938,
Nr. 17.016/1938, Mercurbank to Ministerialrat
Dr. Güttl, June 12, 1938.

[105] DrB, Nr. 7836-2000, memorandum by Rinn, April
22, 1938.

[106] RGVA Moscow, 1458/2/305, Bl. 21–23, memorandum by Riehle, May 20, 1938.

[107] NARA, RG 260, 2/217/9, Dresdner Bank to the
State Finance Minister, June 2, 1938.

The volume of business done by the two banks was, of course, vastly different. The total deposits and credits of the Länderbank Wien was estimated at 312 million RM; that of the Živnostenská banka branch in Vienna was estimated at 37 million RM. The Dresdner Bank could boast that it had placed significant holdings in banks and industrial enterprises held by the Länderbank Wien under German influence: the Eisenstädter Bank für das Burgenland AG, the Hirmer Zuckerfabriks AG, the Vereinigte Lederfabriken Plesch, the Österreichische Baukreditbank, Perlmooser Portland Cementfabrik, and Waagner-Biro Brückenbau. The assets initially designated for transfer to the BPEC were clearly in excess of what was needed, and the Mercurbank found itself retaining shares in some of the BPEC's Czech holding: Lobositzer Zucker, the Sphinx Vereinigte Emaillierwerke und Metallwarenfabriken, and the Schönpriesener Zuckerraffinerie. The currency changeover from Schilling to RM would, however, have meant a substantial loss on these assets. The problem was solved by an exchange of these assets for Tiroler Pfandbriefe (bonds) and Alpine Montan shares with the Kreditanstalt der Deutschen in Prague. The new bank was also to take over the buildings and inventory of the Länderbank Wien and the shares held by the BPEC in the Austrian National Bank. The assets to be transferred to the BPEC were the shares of the Allgemeine Kreditbank in Warsaw, the Trifailer shares, BPEC shares, and French railroad bonds, most of which were to be transferred through the Zürcher Kantonalbank; the RWM had already approved the transfer. The final balancing of the transaction with the BPEC remained uncertain. At the moment, the account stood 1.17 million RM in favor of the BPEC, and the Živnostenská banka owed the Mercurbank some 10.4 million RM. It was agreed that the Živnostenská banka would pay the balance in Czech crowns at the old exchange rate of crowns to Schilling.

Turning to personnel questions, the Dresdner Bank reported that the Mercurbank had 350 employees and that it intended to take over another 510 Aryan employees from the Länderbank and another 72 German employees from the Živnostenská banka. The bank believed that number of employees would suffice for the new bank's operations. As for the 140 non-Aryan employees of the Länderbank Wien, they would be let go with a settlement or pensioned off. The costs of the settlements were about 450,000 RM. The 648 pensioners of the Länderbank Wien would be taken over, but not those of the Živnostenská banka. It was estimated that 740,000 RM would be needed to cover the obligations to the Länderbank Wien's pensioners, and that figure would be increased by an estimated 400,000 RM for the non-Aryan pensioners "if the anticipated regulations in the interest of the Austrian economy do not lead to a reduction." Nevertheless, there was a "positive" side to all this: the elimination of non-Aryan personnel and associated changes would save money. There had also been withdrawals during the previous months, undoubtedly by Jewish clients, but the Dresdner Bank was confident these losses could be offset if the takeover of the Länderbank moved speedily. That, in turn, demanded a reduction of the taxes and fees connected with the increase in capital the takeover required and the special regulations to deal with the personnel questions. Without the reduction of taxes and fees, the merger would not be financially possible. As for the special regulations, the Dresdner Bank pointed out that the personnel arrangements under the contract with the Länderbank Wien were "exclusively in the interest of the German foreign exchange management." It meant that the employees and pensioners of the Länderbank Wien, especially the non-Aryans, could not refuse the transfer of their contracts to the Mercurbank and then make claims against the BPEC that would have to be paid in francs, and thus lead to demands for payment in foreign exchange from the Mercurbank by the BPEC. For a variety of reasons connected with Austrian labor law, the Dresdner Bank asked that the employees of the Živnostenská banka be included in the envisioned regulation. In sum, the Dresdner Bank believed the planned transactions would "make a substantial contribution to the support of the Austrian economy and at the same time serve national-political interests in that they transfer two foreign bank enterprises into German possession." Furthermore, in taking over these banks, the Mercurbank might also prevent the kind of customer disquiet and unemployment that would arise from their liquidation. The transactions could not be completed, however, without the necessary legal measures, and the authorities were asked to act as quickly as possible.

If these decisions were made quickly, it was thanks to Meyer and Rasche. In the months leading up to the Anschluss and immediately after, they had pulled every string possible, and that paid off significantly. One influential National Socialist who had apparently given them important support and advice was Dr. Hans Mann, a lawyer who served as the legal advisor for the Gau of Vienna. Mann was angling for and eventually received a position as a syndic of the new Länderbank Wien AG. Director Meyer of the Dresdner Bank strongly supported his appointment, thus solving the "problem" of finding a National Socialist lawyer for the Mercurbank raised by von Papen in the spring of 1937.[108] The Dresdner Bank's National Socialist connections worked productively on its behalf. On June 4, Rafelsberger informed Kehrl that he approved the Dresdner Bank's acquisition of the Länderbank Wien; opening new branches or consolidating existing ones would, however, require special permission.[109] As Director Otto Herbeck of the Mercurbank's legal staff informed Meyer, much was owed to Veesenmayer, who had pushed Fischböck to make quick decisions. On June 3, Veesenmayer personally called Fischböck's office, saying that it was urgent that the Mercurbank matter be taken up right away because Rafelsberger had already approved the transaction.[110]

Clearly, however, there was also a growing inclination on the part of Austrian National Socialist authorities and the RWM to reign in the Dresdner Bank and the new bank it was creating. At the same time, government and Party officials were giving increasing attention to the interests of the Deutsche Bank and the Creditanstalt. There is also strong evidence that Rasche's ambitions may have extended to the Creditanstalt. In mid-June, Kratz reported that Ministerial Director Gottschick of the RWM had called Rafelsberger's office and "in the name of his ministry pointed out that a further increase of the size of the 'Mercurbank' block was not desired, now that the negotiations with the Länderbank and the Živnostenská banka have come to a conclusion. The RWM was not a participant in this, but it will give its approval after the fact. Beyond that, however, a further attachment of banks to the Mercurbank should not take place. This warning is related, as I [Kratz] have heard, to certain plans of the Mercurbank that move in the direction of detaching certain parts of the Creditanstalt and absorbing them. Similarly, there is supposedly the intention to take over a Hungarian and an Italian bank in Austria."[111]

Although the BPEC and the Dresdner Bank had still to settle certain questions or to agree to set them aside, the point had been reached where the new bank could be established once the administrative council and shareholders have their approval in mid-July. In the competition between France and Germany for an outpost for the penetration of Austria and Southeast Europe, the Germans had won, as they did so often in this period. On July 21, the day of the merger, a company assembly at what was to be named the Länderbank Wien AG celebrated the event, and the directors of the Mercurbank telegraphed their thanks to

[108] See the unctuous correspondence between Mann and Meyer of July 11 and 14, 1938, in ibid. Mann was formally appointed at the personnel committee meeting of the Mercurbank on July 12, 1938, DrB, Nr. 5460-2000.

[109] Ibid., 5467-2000, Rafelsberger to Kehrl, June 4, 1938.

[110] NARA, RG 260, External Assets Investigations 1945–1949, 390/44/31/01, Box 539, Herbeck

to Meyer, June 8, 1938, and ÖStA/AdR, BMF, Allgem. Reihe 1938, Nr. 40.387/1938, message of June 3, 1938.

[111] ÖStA/AdR, Bürckel-Materie, 2165/0, Vol. I, Box 92, Kratz to Regierungs-Vizepräsident Barth, June 14, 1938.

Director Meyer for all he had done to bring the event about. Clearly, politics, not economics, had been the decisive force in bringing the merger about.[112]

The same was true of the negotiations leading to the Mercurbank's acquisition of the Viennese branch of the Zvinovstenska banka. It is important, however, to differentiate between the sensible decisions of bankers like Reuter to cut their losses or potential losses in the face of great political risks and uncertainties, on the one hand, and, on the other, the sale of assets under duress and the complete absence of bargaining power. National Socialist Germany's occupation of Austria created a set of circumstances in which foreign enterprises seriously had to consider whether there was any point in remaining in Austria given the new regime's xenophobic and anti-Semitic policies and its interference in the economy. After 1945, the BPEC and the Živnostenskábanka claimed that their branches in Austria were taken over by force and on unfair terms. Certainly, there were problems with the terms or the way they were carried out, but the notion that the banks were forced out of Vienna is beside the point. They clearly had no incentive to stay. The negotiations between the Dresdner/Mercurbank and the BPEC were initiated even before the Anschluss, and there was every reason to pursue them vigorously after that unhappy event. Similarly, it is rather misleading to argue that the Živnostenská banka sold its Viennese branch under duress, as Eduard Kubu and Gudrun Exner do in their work for the Austrian Historical Commission.[113] For this reason, it is necessary to clarify the takeover of the Živnostenská banka branch on the basis of the surviving documentation.

The Viennese branch of the Živnostenskábanka bank dated back to 1898. It serviced Czech interests in Austria, and it also did considerable business in Switzerland and France and the Balkans. It was a very successful institution that weathered the Depression rather well, and it certainly is true that there would have been no incentive to sell it if the Germans had stayed at home. They did not, however, and those managing the Živnostenská banka in Vienna and in Prague were well aware of the miserable xenophobic and anti-Semitic atmosphere that descended on Austria and of the terror and fear aroused by the Gestapo. As far as direct pressure on the Živnostenská banka branch, the only evidence was provided by the deputy director of the branch, Josef Velek. In a lecture in 1990, he described how a representative of the Mercurbank accompanied by two SA men entered the bank on March 13 and demanded that the business be turned over to them. The director, Hynek Havelka, told them that they were talking about a long-term matter that he was in no position to settle on the spot, and that ended the incident. The only evidence that this occurred, as Kubu and Exner note, was the Velek lecture more than a half century later. Nevertheless, it is not implausible that the incident itself occurred because representatives of the Dresdner Bank and the Deutsche Bank did take over banks in Prague in March 1939 in precisely this way.[114] Czechoslovakia was an independent state in March 1938, however, and the departure of the persons in question in the face of Havelka's dismissive stance is indicative of a very different situation. The only other evidence for duress provided by Kubu and Exner comes from Czech sources, specifically, reports from early April about the tension created by the Anschluss and the withdrawal of deposits from the Vienna branch. This could not have been very surprising, however. They also note

[112] DrB, Nr. 5460-2000, Länderbank Wien to Rasche, July 19, 1938 and NARA, RG 260, External Assets Investigations 1945–1949, 390/44/31/01, Box 539, telegram, management board of the Länderbank to Meyer, July 21, 1938.

[113] Eduard Kubu/Gudrun Exner, *Tschechen und Tschechinnen, Vermögensentzug und Restitution. Nationale Minderheiten im Nationalsozialismus 3.* Veröffentlichungen der Österreichischen Historikerkommission 23/3 (Vienna 2004), pp. 54–85.

[114] See the account of Walter Pohle's takeover of the Böhmische Union Bank for the Deutsche Bank and Reinhold von Lüdinghausen's takeover of the Böhmische Escompte Bank following the occupation of Prague in Harold James, *The Deutsche Bank and the Nazi Economic War against the Jews* (Cambridge 2001), pp. 153–154.

that the first mention of the sale of the Vienna branch was at the management board meeting in Prague on May 18, 1938, where it was reported that negotiations with the Dresdner Bank on the takeover of the Vienna branch by the Mercurbank were taking place, that the matter was to be kept confidential, and that the results would be reported in due course. At a postwar interrogation in Nürnberg, according to Kubu and Exner, the director of the Prague central office, Jan Dvorácek, claimed that the negotiations had begun with a short conversation with General Director Goetz of the Dresdner Bank that came about through a director of the Philips Corporation in Holland, and that the negotiations were supposed to be carried on by Dvorácek and Rasche. In any case, the thrust of Kubu and Exner's account is that at this point, and later, the initiative and pressure came from the Dresdner Bank and not from the Czech bank: "From the complex of circumstances in which the problem developed, it is to be concluded that the proposal, better said, the demand to take over the branch did not come from the Živnostenská banka, but from the other side."[115]

A more careful reading of Dvorácek's interrogation at Nürnberg and materials now available from the files of the Dresdner Bank, present a somewhat different picture. Dvorácek made very clear that the situation in Vienna after the Anschluss led to an obvious conclusion: "We immediately saw the situation for us. Under the National Socialist regime, it was impossible for us to maintain our branch although nobody told us or wrote to us officially that we must close the branch."[116] The fact that two Gestapo men were constantly at the bank checking everyone going in and out certainly reinforced this impression. As Dvorácek noted, the bank's first inclination was to turn to the Länderbank branch in Vienna, only to discover that it too was negotiating to pull out. Dvorácek further noted that the contact with the Dresdner Bank came

about in "a normal commercial way," namely, through a familiar business contact, Brümmer of the Philip's corporation, who did business with the Živnostenská banka. Knowing of the difficulties in Vienna, Brümmer suggested that Dvorácek contact General Director Goetz of the Dresdner Bank. Goetz, who was ill, suggested that Dvorácek come to Berlin. Dvorácek met with Goetz briefly and then met at greater length with Directors Rasche and Busch on April 2. Dvorácek came accompanied by Director Prokop Cipera. They came, as Busch reported in a memorandum on the meeting, "in order to propose to us that we take over the Vienna branch of the Živnostenská banka, which operates three sub-branches in Vienna and which has existed since 1898."[117]

The Czech bankers provided basic information about the branch: its assets, liabilities, and personnel. The branch had 122 employees, only one of whom was Jewish. Most of the others were either Czech or German-Austrian. The Czech bank officials and managers were to return to Prague. The Živnostenská banka was likely to hold on to its holding in the Jugoslavenska banka. The upshot of the meeting was that the Živnostenská banka awaited a decision by the Dresdner Bank as to whether it wished to purchase the branch, in which case negotiations were to be taken up in Vienna during the coming week. On April 4, the Dresdner Bank wrote to Dvorácek that "you made us the offer of having the Mercurbank, with which we are befriended, take over your Vienna branch along with three sub-branches. We thank you for being so obliging in making this offer to our institution and we wish to inform you that, after consideration in a very small circle – we are basically ready to have the Vienna branch along with the three sub-branches taken over by the Mercurbank."[118] Noting that Cipera had been designated to conduct the negotiations for the Prague Bank, the Dresdner Bank suggested that discussions begin the following week in

[115] Kubu/Exner, *Tschechen*, pp. 56–62, quotation on p. 72.

[116] See StA Nürnberg, Nl 11870, interrogation of Jan Dvorácek, Nov. 22, 1946.

[117] DrB, Nr. 5462-2000, memorandum by Busch, April 4, 1938.

[118] DrB, Nr. 7836-2000, Dresdner Bank to Živnostenská banka, April 4, 1938.

Vienna; it was confident that everything could be settled satisfactorily and also suggested a neutral auditing of the branch's accounts.

At this point, the takeover of the Živnostenská banka's Viennese branch became part of the larger Dresdner Bank project of expanding the Mercurbank to create a large bank under its control in Austria. This is the context, together, of course, with the new situation created by National Socialist rule, in which the takeover should be seen. There is nothing terribly mysterious or surprising about the engagement of the German and Austrian authorities in this process, as Kubu and Exner periodically suggest.[119] The Dresdner Bank program could only succeed with the approval of the authorities, and, as has been shown in the case of the Austrian regional banks, not all of Rasche's vaulting ambitions were realized. The bank had to use its political contacts every step of the way because the political agencies involved were constantly looking after their own agendas. It is certainly true that once the Živnostenská banka had made an offer to sell to the Dresdner Bank and the Dresdner Bank had secured the approval of the government, the Živnostenská banka could not easily turn to another bank to get better terms. It is quite plausible, therefore, that Dresdner Bank director Georg Rienecker would tell Cipera at a tough moment in the negotiations that "it makes no sense to break off the negotiations. You cannot do anything else since your branch has been assigned to the Dresdner Bank."[120] As noted earlier, the Dresdner Bank negotiators had also impressed this point on Reuter once the negotiations were under way. Nor could the negotiations have been helped much by the Sudetenland Crisis that began in the spring.

The end result was an agreement reached in late June with the cooperation of the Reich economics minister. Given the difficult currency issues involved, the terms could not be called outrageous. The Mercurbank took over all the assets and liabilities of the Živnostenská

banka branch, except for its credits to the firm of Heinrich Klinger, a textile factory that had a branch in Vienna but was really controlled by the Živnostenská banka in Prague, and the Jugoslavenska Bank in Zagreb. The former credit was worth 4.3 million RM, the latter 3.5 million RM. The Mercurbank also reserved the right to reject other credits found to be unsatisfactory; undoubtedly, it had Jewish clients in mind here. It also took over the building in which the bank was housed, and sixty-five employees, who were named in the final agreement. The date of transfer was June 30, 1938.[121] Would the Živnostenská banka have sold its Vienna branch under normal circumstances and for these terms? Most certainly not, and the same holds true for the BPEC with respect to its Vienna branch. The banks acted in the context of the political and economic risk in which they found themselves, and it is misleading to discuss whether they were acting voluntarily or under duress. The duress involved was political and, as was constantly evident during this period, it could only be solved by war.

Before turning to the founding, staffing, and organizing of what was to become known as the Länderbank Wien AG, it is necessary to consider the negotiations with the BPEC and their conclusion. On the BPEC side, the formal confirmation of the agreement with the Dresdner Bank took place on July 19, 1938, at an extraordinary shareholders' meeting. President André Luquet gave a frank but by no means dissatisfied

---

[119] See Kubu/Exner, *Tschechen*, especially pp. 69–70.
[120] See StA Nürnberg, Nl 11870, interrogation of Jan Dvorácek, Nov. 22, 1946.

[121] The terms were communicated by the Mercurbank to Ministerial Councilor Güttl on June 12, 1938, see ÖStA/AdR, BMF, Allgem. Reihe 1938, Nr. 47016/1938. Kubu/Exner seem to treat this and a number of other documents that they could not find as evidence of the constant government engagement in this matter, see Kubu/Exner, *Tschechen*, p. 70, fn. 181. Because banks were highly regulated in National Socialist Germany, there is nothing particularly exciting about this government engagement. Indeed, far more normal and liberal governments have such regulatory powers in bank takeovers. The carrying out of the agreement with the Živnostenská banka and other relevant documents are to be found in an old Länderbank file at the BA-CA Archive. They are primarily of technical interest.

account of the conditions that had led to the sale of its Vienna holdings. Although recognizing that the Vienna branch was very important to the BPEC's operations in East and Southeast Europe, he insisted that it was obvious from the outset that one could not operate such a branch in Germany with its strict controls on the export of capital: "That would mean for us that one day we could again find our assets in the form of blocked holdings and that the future profits of the Vienna branch would present themselves in the form of blocked marks that would lose 90 percent of their value on the way to our coffers."[122]

There was no choice but "to look the new situation cold-bloodedly in the eye." That was no easy matter, given the effort put into keeping the Länderbank afloat during the crisis by "the old clever French methods of doing business," which he defined as maintaining sufficient capital at hand and rejecting large investments deemed risky despite pressure from the Austrian authorities. When the Anschluss came, the BPEC was also in a position where it could avoid dumping its assets on the market and instead wait until a purchaser came with "interesting and concrete proposals." That requirement was fulfilled by the Dresdner Bank, which had a bank in Austria, knew Austrian conditions, and had a respected position there. Luquet praised Reuter for his skillful handling of the negotiations, and he also noted that the negotiations had been "conducted generously and loyally" on the German side. "We negotiated on a basis which from the outset eliminated every form of compulsion with respect to German bank regulations." The assets were to go to Paris at their full value and no "blocked marks" were involved. The non-Austrian assets were all being transferred, and the BPEC's non-Austrian sphere of influence would thus remain intact. The BPEC would have to forego

future profits from Austrian branch business, but, at the same time, it was relieved of liabilities under special legislation. The slate, so to speak, was wiped clean. This also appeared to be the case with the personnel at the Länderbank Wien. Luquet thanked them profusely for their services and wished them well, pointing out that "we have taken care in the contract with our successors to secure the rights of all our co-workers without exception, and we do not doubt that the new owners will faithfully carry out their obligations."

That was, to say the least, optimistic. Germany's racial politics inevitably played a significant role in determining how the agreement with Reuter would be carried out. There was considerable nastiness from the beginning, and Reuter and his colleagues could not but have been aware of it. On May 5, that is, while the negotiations were under way, Director Hanns Schwarz was arrested in the bank and mistreated during his interrogation. He was released, in very bad condition, only thanks to the intervention of the French consul and the Länderbank director in Paris. Schwarz was taken to Brünn, from whence he left for Paris.[123] It is an open question how many of the Länderbank's Jewish employees suffered similar abuse. It was certainly extremely difficult for them to lay claim to their pension rights despite the agreement with Reuter. On August 1, Reuter called Director Busch of the Dresdner Bank to say that he had heard rumors that the dismissal of Länderbank personnel was not being carried out in accordance with the contractual notice period and that the pension arrangements were being made in a manner "unbearable" for those involved. Reuter reminded Busch that the agreement they had made was international in character and that the Mercurbank had taken over the personnel costs, which, in the end, had been exchanged for some of the payment for goodwill. These obligations could not be changed one-sidedly because of instructions from on high, and if that were to happen, the amount paid for goodwill

122   NARA, RG 260, External Assets Investigations 1945–1949, 390/44/31/01, Box 539, Speech by President André Luquet at the Extraordinary General Shareholders' Meeting, July 18, 1938. A copy is to be found in BNP Paribas, Archives Historiques.

123   Landesarchiv Berlin (= LA Berlin), Bl. 438–461, Wiedergutmachungsakten, Akt Hanns Schwarz.

would have to be increased. Busch responded by saying that when the Mercurbank had taken on the compensation of personnel, the amount to be paid had not been determined except by the insertion of a clause under which "the Länderbank employees would not be treated worse than those of the Creditanstalt."[124]

This did not, of course, preclude them from being treated poorly. Pilder cast an interesting light on the entire matter in a memorandum of August 2 in reaction to Busch's report. The memorandum makes clear that the Jewish pensioners were subject to discriminatory treatment with the full knowledge and collaboration of the Dresdner Bank-Mercurbank leadership. It also shows that Reuter must have been aware of this, thus placing him in a somewhat unflattering light. As Pilder noted, because of the particular rights of bank employees in Austria, special regulations had to be issued by the authorities to deal with the dismissal of non-Aryans. This was done in a decree that required the banks to give notice by July 31 to non-Aryan employees that they would be dismissed by August 31 and that they would receive a settlement that was equivalent to eighteen months' pension as severance pay. The Austrian authorities also ordered that the decree be kept a secret, but Baron von der Lippe apparently told Reuter about it at the end of June. That, as will be shown, was one of the reasons why von der Lippe lost his position on the management board. The legality of the Austrian authorities' measure had been investigated by Herbeck and Mann, discussed in all the relevant bodies within the bank, and were the subject of consultations with Rafelsberger. The end result was that the decree would not be contested and was viewed as perfectly legal, although there was a real question as to whether it was binding on the RWM and other Reich authorities. It certainly violated both the spirit and the letter of the law issued in connection with the contract for the sale of the Vienna branch of the BPEC.

Pilder recommended that Reuter say that the Länderbank Wien AG was the only discussion partner on contractual matters. Pilder's greatest concern was that the Länderbank not create the impression, because of von der Lippe's indiscretion, that it was insufficiently observant of the intentions of the political authorities. Pilder also thought Reuter bore some blame for the situation and made an invidious comparison between Reuter's behavior and that of the Arnhold bank, which had taken responsibility for its Jewish employees after its sale to the Dresdner Bank. "The situation of Herr Reuter is very unpleasant. From the very first day he was reproached by the Jewish employees in Vienna that he did not lodge the obligation of making a settlement with the Jews with Paris but had left it to us. I myself, in the course of the negotiations, drew Reuter's attention to the fact that if he placed upon us the settlement with the Jews according to valid Austrian law, he could not thereby count on the Jews getting that to which they would have had claim before the Anschluss. Herr Reuter simply shrugged away this point. Naturally, now that he is attacked by the Viennese non-Aryans because of this attitude (as is known, Arnhold did things differently), he is naturally zealous with us about protecting the rights of the Jews that he himself did not protect."[125]

That argument was not entirely off the mark. Comparison with the non-Aryan and very important German private banking house of Gebrüder Arnhold, which had recently been taken over by the Dresdner Bank and had taken responsibility for the pensions of its employees, was anything but flattering to Reuter. He had been absolutely insistent in the negotiations on avoiding that the BPEC take on any legal obligation toward the Jewish employees. It was one thing for Luquet to say he believed that the Germans would fulfill their obligations toward the Jews but quite another actually to believe this oneself and for Reuter simply to shrug off the very real danger that existed for his employees.[126] The reality was that when Pilder

124 DrB, Nr. 5460-2000, file note by Busch, Aug. 1, 1938.

125 Ibid., memorandum by Pilder, Aug. 2, 1938.
126 StA Nürnberg, A25, statement by Director Teichmann on the taking over of the Länderbank Wien, May 16, 1947.

indicated to Reuter that the Jews would not be let go or receive their pensions in accordance with existing Austrian laws, Pilder and his colleagues simply assumed that legal measures would be taken by the new regime to support lower payments. The moment the Länderbank began terminating employees and paying them only three times their yearly pension as a settlement, the complaints began to flow to Paris along with demands for the international arbitration provided for in the contract with the Dresdner Bank. The Länderbank did continue to pay out but did so more slowly because it was worried that employees who had emigrated might sue for their entitlement in foreign courts.[127] To be sure, the "dejewification" (*Entjudung*)of the Länderbank was successful. According to Rafelsberger's count, of the 5 directors at the Länderbank at the time of the Anschluss, 3 were Jews and 1 was an Aryan married to a Jew, and 130 of the 420 employees were Jews. At the Mercurbank, 6 of the 17 managers or deputy managers were Jews and 10 of the 26 top functionaries were Jews, and there were another 45 Jewish bank officials. By fall 1938, not a single Jew was left at the bank.[128]

How these Jews were treated given the contractual and legal problems involved is a more complicated matter, especially when it comes to dealing with individual cases. Nevertheless, once their treatment – which Pilder himself had characterized as "crass" – gave way to a more cautious approach following Reuter's complaint, one can trace the broad lines of policy toward them and the manner in which the issues between the Länderbank and General Director Reuter more or less worked themselves out in the last months of 1938 and the beginning of 1939. One way to deal with the former Jewish employees was to take advantage of the so-called Gildemeester plan devised by Dutch pastor Frank van Gheel-Gildemeester.

The plan, which had the support of the National Socialist authorities, was intended to finance the emigration of Jews from Austria. The basic idea was for wealthier Jews to pay for their own emigration as well as for the emigration of poor Jews by surrendering nearly all their assets. In early October, Hans Mann, who was personally engaged in these questions, reported that about 109 former Länderbank employees and their families had asked to take advantage of this program and were willing to support payment of the requisite $1,000 per family head to participate. They would also have to cover their personal obligations and their travel costs. That would require the bank to pay them their pension settlements. Mann hoped that this could be combined with a willingness on the part of the BPEC to provide the requisite $110,000 to the Gildemeester committee. Pilder thought this solution quite possible because under the transaction agreement with the BPEC anything owing to the Länderbank by the BPEC in the final calculation of reciprocal obligations would be paid in Trifailer shares, not in foreign exchange, and there would be no loss of foreign exchange to the Reich if the BPEC contributed to the Gildemeester fund. One of the problems with the Gildemeester plan, however, was the difficulty of finding countries to accept the Jews. Moreover, it was also linked to bizarre colonization schemes, for example, in Abyssinia.[129]

At the October 1938 meetings of the supervisory board and personnel committee where the Gildemeester plan was discussed, the basic issues of settling with the Jewish employees were also batted back and forth. Pilder suggested that the pensions for those not emigrating be regulated

[127] See the revealing memorandum by Leese/Herbeck of Nov. 1, 1938, sent to Lange at the RWM by the Dresdner Bank, RGVA Moscow, 1458/2/68.

[128] RGVA Moscow, 1458/2/101, Bl. 95, Rafelsberger, "Short Report on the Activity of the State Commissariat in the Private Economy Regarding Financial Issues."

[129] DrB, Nr. 5460-2000, meetings of the supervisory board committees, Oct. 4 and Oct. 27, 1938. See Theodor Venus/Alexandra-Eileen Wenck, *Die Entziehung jüdischen Vermögens im Rahmen der Aktion Gildemeester. Eine empirische Studie über Organisation, Form und Wandel von "Arisierung" und jüdischer Auswanderung in Österreich 1938–1941. Nationalsozialistiche Institutionen des Vermögensentzuges 20.* Veröffentlichungen der Österreichischen Historikerkommission, vol. 20/2 (Vienna 2004).

in a manner analogous to the old Reich so that larger pensions, depending on the economic circumstances, could be reduced somewhat, for example, from 10,000 RM to 7,500 RM. To help with emigration, some former Jewish employees were given advances against the monies to be paid to them. Care was taken not to exceed their pension claims, however, and to give the monies in such a way that they could not be construed as the equivalent of pension payments. By late October, there was a general desire to get on with final settlements through negotiations with the Jews in question. The situation had not gotten much better from the standpoint of the Länderbank, however. The RWM was insisting that the employees in question were entitled to their full rights under existing law if an agreement could not be reached, and that only in the case of very high settlements and pensions might a 50 percent reduction be allowable. There was, however, no clear regulation of these matters, and the RWM obviously did not support the special regulations that the Austrian authorities had issued some months earlier.[130]

This lack of support became especially clear in early November when the Dresdner Bank, fearing that it would not come to a final agreement with Reuter in forthcoming negotiations in Paris and desiring to avoid the costs and dangers of leaving the matter to international arbitration, sent an appeal to the RWM for permission to let accounts be settled with the BPEC in blocked marks in the amount of 1.5 million to 2 million RM. As usual, it emphasized the costs of paying off pensions and making settlements with the Jewish employees. It also pointed to the unclear accounting problems that could go one way or another. There were also difficulties with credits extended by the BPEC that the Länderbank thought had not been adequately vetted. This plea by the Dresdner Bank for help with the Länderbank met with a very unsympathetic response. The RWM could see no good reason to let the bank use blocked marks in order to make its situation easier. First of all, it had no direct involvement

in the transaction. Second, the Länderbank had every reason to expect it would be obligated to settle with the Jewish employees. Because there had been no measures taken in the old Reich to reduce pensions, there was no reason whatever to assume that such measures would be taken in Austria: "If it [i.e., the bank] is unexpectedly hard hit by these obligations, it has only itself to blame." The RWM also did not think the differences on the two sides so large as to warrant concern, and it ascribed the bad credits to the collapse of Jewish enterprises following the Anschluss. The Mercurbank had great advantages from the takeover of the Länderbank Wien, and the merger put the new bank in a good competitive position with the Creditanstalt. At the same time, the RWM considered it a "bad start" for the Länderbank to be asking for government help when it had not even balanced its books yet and could not give a clear account of its status.[131]

There was nothing to do but settle, and that is what was done in Paris. The Dresdner Bank apparently stood its ground on the disputed loans: the BPEC agreed to deposit 30,000 pounds sterling. That released the shares held in the escrow account to the benefit of the BPEC. Reuter, however, made very specific and in part successful demands with respect to the Jewish employees. He successfully insisted that payments made for October–November 1938 would be paid at the same levels for December 1938–January 1939, and none of these payments would be counted against settlement sums. Reuter was prepared to consider the obligations to the BPEC fulfilled if the Jewish employees received settlements up to five times of a yearly pension, and if the settlements were calculated in a way that took family and social circumstances into account. Reuter, for his part, refused to provide $100,000 for the emigration of more than 100 employees in the context of the Gildemeester plan because he did not think the plan could be carried out, but he was prepared to provide funding for individuals and

---

[130] Ibid., especially the meeting of Oct. 27, 1938.

[131] RGVA Moscow, 1458/2/68, Bl. 45–57, Dresdner Bank and Länderbank to the RWM, Nov. 1, 1938 and draft response by RWM, Nov. 8, 1938.

even groups independently of the Länderbank. The Länderbank basically accepted Reuter's terms, but, allowing for some exceptions, it set the settlement sums at two and a half to three times yearly pensions. This apparently was also the policy at the Creditanstalt. The spirit in which this was done can be measured by the response of Veesenmayer and Pilder to Warnecke's report on settlements that had already been made. They suggested that the pensions might be cut back on the basis of the Decree on the Exclusion of Jews from German Economic Life of November 12, 1938, which had been issued by Göring in connection with the pogrom of November 9–10.[132]

The discussion of these issues ended on an appropriately sour note at the beginning of 1939. The BPEC issued what appeared to be an ultimatum asking that the Länderbank indicate in eight days whether it was prepared to fulfill its obligations to the former employees, Aryan or not. Pilder suggested that they reply that the bank intended to fulfill its obligations insofar as they were in conformity with the laws of the Reich. Furthermore, "since the Länderbank Paris is always criticizing the settlement sums paid out, the aforementioned bank should be told in reply that we are fundamentally ready to issue a decision of the supervisory board under which the settlements with the non-Aryan employees in general should be terminated. Paris should be asked to take a position on this."[133] The Länderbank apparently suspended payments but then resumed them again when Reuter began taking steps to start arbitration proceedings in Switzerland.[134]

Needless to say, whatever compensation the Jewish employees received was usually stolen from them by the government. It is perhaps useful to end this discussion of the creation of the Länderbank Wien AG, which was from beginning to end influenced by the "Jewish question," with an account of what happened to some of the Jews who had worked for the

Länderbank. One such employee, E. Teller, reported in 1947 on his experiences. He was dismissed on July 29, 1938, after twenty-five years of service. He had a salary of 10,400 Schilling and was entitled to full pay for two and a half years and then a pension of 3,600 Schilling a year. He succeeded in getting 6,500 Schilling in cash with no explanation as to why he received that sum of money, but he received no pension at all. Many of his Jewish colleagues received even less severance pay in the same manner. He decided to emigrate and most of the money was spent on clothes and travel costs, and he was not allowed to take more than 30 RM, that is, $12.50, with him. He managed to get a job in Hong Kong; when he boarded a ship in Trieste to begin his journey, he was notified by the BPEC that he would receive $500 upon his arrival in China. He did receive that amount "although," as he said, "it is my understanding that they did not have to make any payment at all to me." Many of his colleagues also received such payments, varying according to length of service and familial status, but all were paid outside of Germany and Austria. Teller, of course, considered himself "lucky as I never was put into a concentration-camp and escaped death in a gas-chamber in Poland." From that perspective, he was fortunate indeed. He returned to Austria and went back to work for the Länderbank even though he had not, as of 1947, still had not received the money owing to him from his employer.[135]

Less fortunate was the case of Ernst Klaar. He had joined the bank in 1909 and was an outstanding accountant who had much to do with the bank's operations in Czechoslovakia and Hungary. The Anschluss hit him hard in every respect. On arrival at his office, one of his subordinates greeted him with a "Heil Hitler" and informed him that he could no longer take orders from him. On May 9, Klaar received a letter from von der Lippe withdrawing his rights to sign on behalf of the bank and putting him on leave of absence. On

[132] DrB, Nr. 5460-2000, personnel committee meeting, Dec. 2, 1938.

[133] Ibid., personnel committee meeting, Jan. 17, 1939.

[134] Reuter account, see note 76.

[135] NARA, RG 260, German External Assets Branch, 390/44/20/04, Box 21, E. Teller to the U.S.A. C.A., June 13, 1947.

July 31, he was informed of the termination of his employment effective August 31, 1938. He was told to report for a settlement on August 8; he was given 13,000 RM and had to sign a receipt stating that this was done at his own request and that it settled all existing claims against the Länderbank. Klaar's salvation, at least temporarily, was Reuter, who first tried to secure a job for him in Ireland and then managed to find one for him in Paris, thereby enabling him to obtain a work permit. As his son later discovered, Reuter had brought twenty-two former Länderbank Wien employees to Paris, where all survived but Ernst Klaar, who was deported to Auschwitz along with his wife in 1942. Apparently, Reuter not only employed such people through the bank, but he also supplied them with money and other forms of assistance personally and used his contacts with M. Couve de Murville, then a Vichy official and later French prime minister, to help Jews. As these cases show, whatever Reuter's lapses in negotiating the agreement with the Dresdner Bank, he certainly appears to have redeemed himself in his efforts on behalf of the Jewish Länderbank employees in the end.[136]

3. ORGANIZING THE LÄNDERBANK WIEN AG, 1938–1939

One of the more curious aspects of the new bank formally founded on July 21, 1938, was its name. Years before, some Austrians active in Berlin had established a Deutsche Länderbank. That firm had come into the hands of IG Farben, which objected to the use of the name "Länderbank" for the new bank, although it was in fact an old and venerable name that had boasted an imperial charter in the prewar days. Finally, an agreement was reached and the new

bank took the name "Länderbank Wien AG."[137] Far more serious, however, were the host of personnel and organizational decisions that had to be made both prior to and after the official establishment of the bank.

The new bank was composed of three older ones that were very different in character. This was evident from the size of their staffs. Of the approximately 1,060 employees in the new bank, excluding the Jewish employees who had already lost their jobs or were suspended, 65 came from the Živnostenská banka, 400 from the Mercurbank, and 600 from the Zentraleuropäische Länderbank.[138] The Živnostenská banka was only a branch of an important Czech bank; in addition to its main office, the Vienna branch also had three smaller offices in the city. Mercurbank had twelve offices in Vienna and four provincial branches: Bregenz, Bludenz, Klosterneuburg, and Wiener-Neustadt. It also had foreign affiliates, the Wechselstuben AG "Mercur" in Budapest, the Kommerzialbank AG in Cracow, and the Banca Commerciale S.A. in Czernowitz. In preparation for the takeover of the other two banks, its share capital had been raised from 15 to 30 million Schilling, that is from 10 to 20 million RM. Its balance sheet at the end of 1937 was 118 million Schilling.

The former Österreichische Länderbank was a larger and more complicated institution. Its share capital was 100 million French francs in 1937, and its balance at the end of 1937 was 280 million Schilling, making it the

---

[136] See George Clare, *Last Waltz in Vienna: The Rise and Destruction of a Family 1842–1942* (New York 1980), pp. 197, 204–207, 224–225, 240–247. George Clare was the son of Ernst Klaar. See Peter Eigner, "Die Konzentration der Entscheidungsmacht. Die personellen Verflechtungen zwischen den Wiener Großbanken und Industrieaktiengesellschaften, 1895–1940," D.Phil. (Vienna 1997).

[137] DrB, Nr. 5460-2000, Pilder account, see note 76. The formal decision was taken at the supervisory board meeting of the Mercurbank on July 12, 1938. This was formally reported to the Finance Ministry on Oct. 3, 1938, see ÖStA/AdR, BMF, Allgem. Reihe 1938, Nr. 57.943/1938.

[138] See BAB, R 8135, Nr. 352, the report of the Deutsche Revisions- und Treuhand-Aktiengesellschaft, Zweigniederlassung Wien, undated. The description that follows is also based on the newspaper reports in ibid., R 25.01, Nr. 4365, Bl. 116–128, and Peter Melichar, *Neuordnung im Bankwesen. Die NS-Maßnahmen und die Problematik der Restitution*. Veröffentlichungen der Österreichischen Historikerkommission, vol. 11 (Vienna 2004), pp. 38–41.

second largest credit bank in Austria. It had nineteen offices in Vienna and five provincial branches: Innsbruck, Linz, Salzburg, Baden bei Wien, and Graz. Additionally, it had a 26.4 percent stake in an Austrian affiliate, the Eisenstädter Bank für das Burgenland AG. In contrast to the Mercurbank, the Österreichische Länderbank was also directly engaged in commercial activities and had significant industrial holdings, although not on the same scale as the Creditanstalt. Its commercial goods division sold coal and coke from the Upper Silesian, Hungarian, and Austrian coal districts to the Viennese gas works and also to dealers on a commission basis. Its sugar business was even more profitable. It marketed the production of the Hirmer Zuckerfabrik AG as well as that of the Siegendorfer Zuckerfabrik Conrad Patzenhofer's Söhne. Such direct nonbanking engagements notwithstanding, the bank's industrial holdings were modest, even in the case of its largest participations. The bank had a 40 percent stake in the Hirmer company, a 58 percent stake in the Vereinigten Lederfabriken Flesch AG, a 22 percent stake in the Perlmooser Portland Cementfabrik, and a 36.5 percent stake in the Waagner-Biro Brückenbau AG.

Such a modest level of industrial investment was not the only difference between the new Länderbank and the Creditanstalt. The former had a share capital of 20 million RM, the latter of 101 million RM; the Länderbank balance sheet was anticipated to be 300 million RM, that of the Creditanstalt was 695.5 million RM. Both banks were under German control, but whereas the VIAG and Deutsche Bank together owned 76.91 percent of the Creditanstalt shares, the Dresdner Bank owned 98.15 percent of the shares of the Länderbank. The only reason it did not own 100 percent was that this would have made it impossible for the Länderbank to be listed on the Vienna Stock Exchange. The Creditanstalt was a major bank in its own right, and its managers had a good deal more autonomy than their counterparts at the Länderbank, which in the last analysis may be fairly described as a large regional bank serving Dresdner Bank interests in Austria and Southeast Europe. The direct role of the Dresdner Bank in Länderbank

affairs was reflected less in its understandable presence on the supervisory board, where it was represented by Rasche, Pilder, and Schippel, than by the very active participation of Rasche, Pilder, George O. Rienecker, and Hermann Richter in the organization of the new bank. Rienecker, a director of the Munich branch of the Dresdner Bank, had been assigned to look after Dresdner Bank interests at the various Party offices and agencies in Vienna and to help with the founding of the new bank. Hermann Richter, another Dresdner Bank director, was assigned to deal with organizational questions. Rasche was formally appointed to act as delegate of the Dresdner Bank to the management board, although he was not a member of the management board. Pilder regularly acted as Rasche's deputy.

Pilder, for all the businesslike objectivity Neumann attributed to him, was obviously not immune to the spirit of the times, and it was most likely he who composed a "Memorandum on the Situation of the Mercurbank/Länderbank in July 1938 at the Time of the Implementation of the Merger."[139] He bluntly stated that the policy of the Dresdner Bank with regard to the Mercurbank had been led by a goal, namely, "at the moment of the Anschluss and the victory of the National Socialist movement in Austria to be able to provide a strong and efficient banking institution for the economic consolidation of Austria with the old Reich," and "despite unspeakable difficulties on all sides, that goal had been achieved with the soon to be completed consolidation. Nonetheless, the economic situation was still uncertain as a result of the 3:2 currency reform, which made wages and raw materials more expensive, and the "redistribution of property relations through the elimination of the non-Aryan element must inevitably lead to a period of pressure on prices." For this reason, he urged a sober policy and the avoidance of too much credit expansion and the acquisition of majority stakes. It was important to steer a middle course and

---

[139] DrB, Nr. 5458-2000, Denkschrift über die Situation der Mercurbank/Länderbank im Juli 1938 im Moment der Durchführung der Fusion.

maintain liquidity. The concentration had to be on long-term goals rather than short-term successes, and from an organizational perspective Aryanization was an opportunity: "The departure of the active non-Aryans – about 50–60 at the Mercurbank and about 130–140 at the Länderbank, among them almost all the directors and deputy directors – creates room for the necessary consolidation and reduction of the administrative apparatus. The projected regulation of the settlement and pension payments to the non-Aryans (even if it is not as crassly carried out as perhaps planned at the beginning) can in any case make possible the settlement of these portions of the retinue under conditions that are not really oppressive for the bank." Without saying so explicitly, Pilder nevertheless made clear that a price was being paid for the elimination of the Jews when he turned to the question of bank leadership. None of the managers at the Živnostenská banka could be kept on, with the exception of Michael Dyszkant, who became a section head. Those at the Länderbank were either Jews or unacceptable for some reason. The Mercurbank had more to offer, but Pilder had to admit that Warnecke, who became one of the top managers of the new bank, had been appointed primarily because he was not a Jew rather than for his managerial promise. The most promising managers appeared to be Hitschfeld and Wolzt. Pilder did not seem very taken with the suggestions that came from Party offices. Rafelsberger and Fischböck had apparently pushed Director Josef Ritter von Paić of the Kontrollbank for a top position, but he was deemed not to have enough experience. Apparently Party influence did play a role in the appointment of the fourth member of the management board, Karl Wilhelm Lehr, who had headed the Dresdner Bank office in Cairo and whose appointment had been strongly supported by Gauleiter Bürckel. What was needed, although no one said so aloud, was a Neumann, someone competent to watch over the management and to participate in business operations. That had been allowed under the old Austrian banking regulations, but it was flatly turned down by the new authorities in Vienna, both because it

would violate German banking law to mix the functions of the supervisory board and management board and because it would involve interference from Berlin in the system of regional banks being built up in Austria.

Clearly, political interference was playing a serious role. As Pilder put it in his matter-of-fact way: "The general situation in Vienna is, as the experience of the last three months has shown, very uncertain and very changeable. But one thing is certain, that every company leadership in Vienna will have to work with authorities that are very strongly Party-oriented." Pilder had high praise for Munich Dresdner Bank Director Rienecker, who was spoken of in Bürckel's office and elsewhere with "appreciation and sympathy." Recognizing that Rienecker was missed in Munich, Pilder considered his presence in Vienna and assistance to the management board of the new bank of the utmost importance: "Vienna at the moment is the place with the greatest future chances for the Dresdner Bank, but also the one with the greatest difficulties." That seemed all the more necessary because Pilder saw serious competition looming in the shape of the Deutsche Bank. The RWM had made clear that it could not keep the Deutsche Bank and the Commerzbank out of Vienna for much longer, and if the Deutsche Bank were to take over the business of the Industrie-Kredit-Bank, which was then in liquidation, and set up its own branch in Vienna, then it would have an advantage over the new bank the Dresdner Bank was creating.

The arrangements of the banking sector in Vienna were to turn out differently. Pilder's remarks show how intent the Dresdner Bank was to strengthen its competitive position so far as possible in Austria through the new bank. This becomes especially evident from instructions the administrative council gave to the Mercurbank management board on July 9, 1938. The author probably was Pilder, who pointed out that the time was fast approaching when a decision would have to be made about which debtors of the old Länderbank were to be accepted. The new bank would then have to cultivate the customers of the Länderbank and the Živnostenská banka it wished to retain. Significantly, the Dresdner

Bank had sent some of its ablest people to assist the Mercurbank in this process, in particular Director Walter Teichmann, his staff of accountants, and Director Rienecker. Pilder warned the Mercurbank directors against becoming distracted by some of the big Aryanization cases coming to the fore, taking the view that "industry in Austria should organize itself and that the bank directors cannot take over these tasks."[140] The important task facing the new bank was to integrate the three banks and, obviously, to do so in a way that satisfied the political authorities, for without their support success in Austria would be impossible.

This certainly was evident in the appointments to the administrative council of the new bank. By this time, of course, Aryanization had carried the day and had been accompanied by a fair measure of political purging as well. At the level of the administrative council, Apold became chairman and, in addition to the highly political acquisitions of recent years, Meindl and Veesenmayer, the administrative council was now also graced with another Party man in the person of Heinz Birthelmer, the general director of the Eisenstädter Elektrizität-Aktiengesellschaft Überlandwerk. Birthelmer had joined the Party in April 1933; after 1938, he held the positions of governor (Landesstatthalter) and Gau economic advisor for the Lower Danube.[141] Some politically acceptable and influential businessmen were added to the group represented by Otto Böhler, Arthur Hämmerle, Alfred Prinz zu Hohenlohe-Schillingfürst, Otto Kämper, and Freiherr von Wilmowsky. They were Robert Hammer, the president of the Association of Corporate Banks and Banking Personnel; Walter Hiedler, director of the Dairyman's Association; and August Schmid-Schmidsfelden, the vice president of the Rottenmanner Eisenwerke AG, vorm. Brüder Lapp. Hammer had joined the NSDAP as early as 1932, having Party No.

1,205,374 and was the member of the Deutscher Klub. Some thought the club was an instrument of Schuschnigg's anti-National Socialist policies, but, at least in the case of Hammer, it was reputed to have provided safe houses for National Socialist leadership meetings. Hiedler's Party credentials were excellent. He joined the Party in 1930 and had been an organizer and speaker in the Braunau am Inn district as well as a participant in numerous brawls and shootouts. He had spent three months in an internment camp in 1934 and had been punished by the government in more minor ways for repeated offenses. He joined the SS and SD in 1934 and worked closely with Keppler and Veesenmayer. Schmid-Schmidsfelden joined the Party in July 1933 and was extremely active in supporting it during the "illegal" period. Beyond his avid support of the National Socialists, he was known, even in some National Socialist circles, for paying very low wages and being a harsh employer.[142] As already mentioned, the Dresdner Bank was amply represented in the persons of Rasche, Pilder, and Schippel. It was important for the Dresdner Bank's dominant role that all three served on both the personnel and credit committees. The former also included Apold, Birthelmer, Hiedler, and Meindl; the latter also included Apold and Hammer. An important role was intended for the administrative council with respect to credits. Rasche proposed not only that the council have a permanent representative on the credit committee in the person of Hammer but also that an additional member who was knowledgeable in the field be asked to serve as an advisor in credit matters. Expertise, however, could no longer replace political considerations, and the council unanimously accepted a proposal by Birthelmer that in cases where an applicant for credit lived in a district whose administrator was a Party appointee, that this person be consulted before a decision was taken.[143]

[140] DrB, Nr. 5460-2000, letter to the administrative council of the Mercurbank and the management board of the Mercurbank, July 9, 1938.

[141] ÖStA/AdR, BMI, Gauakt Adolf Heinrich Birthelmer, Nr. 351.969.

[142] ÖStA/AdR, BMI, Gauakt Robert Hammer, Nr. 279.749; ibid., Gauakt Walter Hiedler, Nr. 21.740; ibid., Gauakt August von Schmid-Schmidsfelden, Nr. 29.022.

[143] DrB, Nr. 5460-2000, administrative council meeting, July 12, 1938.

The importance of such decisions may be measured by an inquiry of Bürckel's deputy Kratz. On July 20, Kratz wrote to Rasche that he had not heard from him since their last meeting, but had heard that there had been disagreements in the administrative council about appointments and wanted to know what was going on. Rienecker responded on Rasche's behalf a few days later with a list of newly appointed directors and the membership of the personnel and credit committee. He also reported on the decision on how credits were to be handled. Rienecker assured Kratz that the personnel decisions "are absolutely in accordance with what was discussed between you, State Commissar Rafelsberger and us."[144] Indeed, as far back as May, Kratz had expressed Bürckel's concerns about appointments to the Mercurbank board in a conversation with the director of the Frankfurt branch of the Dresdner Bank, with whom he was apparently befriended. He indicated he (Kratz) would be at Rasche's disposal if Rasche wanted to discuss the matter, adding that "I believe that I could in certain cases make the decision easier with one or another suggestion."[145]

There can be no question that the management board of the new bank was appointed after consultations with Kratz and, in particular, with Rafelsberger. Rasche and Rienecker met with Rafelsberger just prior to the personnel committee meeting of the new bank on July 12, 1938. Also present at the meeting was Georg Schumetz, who assisted Rafelsberger in banking matters and who had been serving the National Socialist cause in Austria since 1932. In 1940, Schumetz, who at one point had been thought of as a possible Länderbank director, was to join the Zentralsparkasse der Gemeinde Wien as a director.[146] At the personnel committee

meeting, Rasche mentioned repeatedly that every appointment had been cleared with Rafelsberger.[147] Four persons were appointed to the management board: Hitschfeld, Warnecke, Lehr, and Wolzt. The last two had been recruited from the Dresdner Bank; Wolzt had already been on the board of the Mercurbank before the new bank was created. Hitschfeld was put in charge of securities, foreign exchange, and the commercial goods division. The latter now also included a grain products credits section, which had been set up by the Mercurbank after the Anschluss to collaborate with the Getreide bank in Berlin in facilitating the shipment and marketing of agricultural products. Alois Schindler from the old Länderbank, who was apparently experienced in the commercial goods field, was asked to assist Hitschfeld. Warnecke was placed in charge of general operations and the branches, and he was the designated "company leader" of the bank. Lehr was to act as his deputy and to deal with organizational, personnel, and accounting matters. It was anticipated that he would also take charge of some of the branches and offices of the bank, here again presumably to assist Warnecke. Wolzt, who apparently acted as spokesman of the bank, was given charge of consortial business as well as business in Vienna. Although a full member of the management board, Wolzt, like Lehr, had the title of deputy director, possibly for seniority reasons. Apparently, Wolzt was dissatisfied by this and indicated that he might not want the job. Nevertheless, he took it, and he and Lehr were finally made full directors in April 1939.[148] Regardless of their titles, these four men assumed the basic responsibility for the management of the bank.

Four additional directors were appointed. They and the other top managers would constitute the directorate of the bank. These four

[144] ÖStA/AdR, Bürckel-Materie, 2165/2/1, Box 92, Kratz to Rasche, July 20, 1938, and Rienecker to Kratz, July 25, 1938.

[145] Ibid., 2165/0, Vol. 1, Box 92, Kratz to Günther Ladisch, May 14, 1938.

[146] See DrB, Nr. 5460-2000, personnel committee meeting of July 12, 1938; on the meeting with Rafelsberger/Schumetz see ÖStA/AdR, Bürckel-Materie, 2165/2/1, Box 92, memorandum

by Kratz, July 14, 1938; on Schumetz see ÖStA/AdR, BMI, Gauakt Georg Schumetz, Nr. 124.580.

[147] DrB, Nr. 5460-2000, personnel committee meeting, July 12, 1938, for the discussion and quotations that follow.

[148] DrB, Nr. 5460-2000, administrative council meeting, April 17, 1939.

would attend all management board meetings so they could gain an overview of the bank's affairs. All four had been appointed in consultation with Rafelsberger. They were Kurt Fiedler, who had come from the Mercurbank; Josef Ritter von Paić, who had been employed at the Industrie Creditbank and Kontrollbank and whom Rafelsberger and Fischböck had wanted to appoint to the management board; Alois Schindler of the Länderbank, who was known to have been an active supporter of the National Socialists prior to the Anschluss;[149] and Karl Klimpel of the Mercurbank.

Another set of important appointments were the six department heads. Two of them came from the old Länderbank: Edmund A. Ackermann, who had been stationed in Paris, and Reinald Wallner. The others, Josef Hondl, Franz Pilat, Adolf Reiter, and Rudolf Schwarz, came from the Mercurbank. Ackermann, who had applied for National Socialist Party membership after returning from Paris,[150] was put in charge of organizational management at the bank. Schwarz, who had long-standing National Socialist credentials, was charged with personnel matters. As with Pilder's memorandum, it is impossible to imagine that the new bank was not paying a heavy price for dismissing its Jewish directors. As Director Richter, who served as rapporteur at the meeting, made clear without further explanation, certain specialists could not be replaced from the available personnel in Vienna, and it would be necessary to bring in personnel from the Dresdner Bank as well as develop a program to send Länderbank personnel to the Dresdner Bank in Germany to acquire needed skills. Heinrich Pilgrim was placed in charge of the consortial office; Ludwig Schunck was assigned to deal with stock exchange questions; and Karl Pateck was appointed to deal with foreign exchange questions. It was necessary to call on the personnel resources of the Dresdner Bank, in the

person of Hans Trautner, to find someone to head up the Vienna branch office that had formerly been in the Živnostenská banka.

A special problem was presented by the obligation under the agreement with the BPEC to offer a position to the director of the Warsaw bank, Weisz-Ulock. Rasche informed the personnel committee that Rafelsberger had rejected an appointment for Weisz-Ulock on political grounds because of Wesiz-Ulock's legitimist activities. The committee thereupon decided to let the matter rest and to consider a request from Weisz-Ulock for a position only if he "could exonerate himself successfully with the political agencies." A significant problem, raised by Pilder, was what to do with Baron von der Lippe. Pilder felt it important to keep von der Lippe on for a while to ensure continuity, even though his colleagues, especially Birthelmer, voiced "political reservations." There was agreement in the committee that for the reasons given even the employment of von der Lippe for a limited period in the new bank would not be acceptable. Von der Lippe had committed a serious indiscretion, and this seems to have contributed decisively to the loss of his position on the management board.

The basic personnel issues at the Länderbank were settled by the time of its founding in late July 1938, and Rienecker was able to pay a courtesy visit to Kratz on August 3 to inform him of his intention to return to Munich now that the three banks had been united.[151] Nonetheless, important questions pertaining to the structure and personnel of the bank still had to be addressed. The new bank needed to both rationalize and develop its network of branches and offices throughout Austria. Overlap had to be eliminated, but the Länderbank also had to fill in gaps in its branch network and expand its presence. The process began even before the Länderbank Wien AG was formally created. In Vienna, the branches and offices of the Mercurbank and old Länderbank simply merged. These branches and offices, including those of the Živnostenská

[149] ÖStA/AdR, BMI, Gauakt Alois Schindler, Nr. 155.392.

[150] See ÖStA/AdR, BMI, Gauakt Edmund Ackermann, Nr. 166.013. For unexplained reasons, his application was never acted on.

[151] ÖStA/AdR, Bürckel-Materie, 2165/2/1, Box 92, memorandum by Kratz, Aug. 3, 1938.

banka, were given a more uniform character. In Baden, Graz, Innsbruck, Linz, and Salzburg, where the Mercurbank had not had branches or where branches were in the planning stage, the Mercurbank dissolved the old Länderbank branches, which effectively meant that first the Mercurbank and then the new Länderbank, once formally created, took them over. The Mercurbank had a branch in Wiener Neustadt and two offices in Bludenz and Klosterneuburg. At the end of July, the Länderbank requested permission to transform the offices into independent branches because they were in effect performing the functions of branches anyway and because the change would enable them to deal in foreign exchange. Permission was readily granted by the finance minister's office. The authorities did not look with equal favor, however, on the Länderbank's request of July 23 to set up branches in Klagenfurt, Krems, Leoben, St. Pölten, Steyr, and Wels. The bank's argument was that joining together the three banks had greatly increased the business of the new bank and that it would be further increased by the reconstruction program for Austria. It was essential that the bank be represented in important localities where it was not already present. Tourism had increased significantly in Klagenfurt, and heavy industry and coal and ore mining were expanding greatly in Leoben and Steyr. Gau leader headquarters were being set up in St. Pölten and Krems, and it was claimed they would soon need bank branch offices to service their needs.

This proposal faced considerable hurdles. At the very beginning of August, the Austrian authorities were prepared to approve the creation of branches in Klagenfurt, Krems, and Leoben, but opposed establishing a Länderbank presence in St. Pölten, Steyr, and Wels, which they deemed to have sufficient banking facilities because of the already existing branches of the Creditanstalt and the Bank für Oberösterreich und Salzburg. The approval process did not end here, however, and the matter had to be referred to the relevant Gauleiter and to the Reich banking commissar, Friedrich Ernst. Unfortunately for the Länderbank, the Gauleiter of the styria, Siegfried Uiberreither, thought a branch in

Leoben "completely superfluous," and the finance minister had second thoughts about Klagenfurt. When he finally gave his opinion to the Reich banking commissar, he urged rejection of all the proposed branches with the sole exception of Krems.[152]

This was a measure of how far the privileged position enjoyed by the Dresdner-Mercurbank combination in the period prior to the creation of the Länderbank had shrunk. At the July 12 meeting of the administrative council, Georg Meindl was still urging that the efforts to acquire major Austrian regional banks be continued, although he conceded that Creditanstalt resistance and opposition from within the government made success increasingly unlikely. By January 1939, such hopes, which would have given the Länderbank the advantage of having regional banks with their own branches as well as its own regional branches, an advantage enjoyed by the Creditanstalt, were a thing of the past. There was continuing concern about the long delay in securing permission to open new branches. As Pilder pointed out, 90 percent of the bank's business was in Vienna, and a better balance sheet was necessary. At this point, the bank's leader were hoping at least for permission to open branches in Klagenfurt and offices in Villach, St. Pölten, and Wels, and they pulled all strings possible in Vienna and Berlin.[153]

In Vienna, Director Lehr again requested permission for the bank's plans after having received letters from the Gauleiter indicating that they had no objections to the opening of Länderbank branches. He also sent a copy to Kratz asking that he support the effort and pointing out that the bank already had a large number of new customers eager to have a conveniently located branch. Kratz acted on Lehr's request by passing it on to Ministerial Director Riehle of the RWM. As Riehle informed Kratz, the Länderbank had further scaled back its goals, and Pilder informed the Berlin authorities that

---

152 See the correspondence in ÖStA/AdR, BMF, Allgem. Reihe 1938, Nr. 51.162/1938, 52.660/1938 and 53.053/1938.

153 DrB, Nr. 5460-2000, supervisory board meetings of July 12, 1938 and Jan. 17, 1939.

the bank would settle for St. Pölten and Wels and drop Klagenfurt for the time being.[154] Ultimately, however, Commissar Ernst, after receiving a detailed report from the Viennese Ministry for Economy and Labor, decided that only one branch would be allowed, St. Pölten, where the old Länderbank once had a branch and some customers. Wels, a city of 17,000, had enough banks in his opinion, as did Klagenfurt.[155] Ernst told the bank that he would be willing to consider a renewed request, but on July 20, 1939, he again turned down the establishment of a branch in Wels on the grounds that customers there could well be serviced by the branch in nearby Linz.[156] The Länderbank thus had to settle for one new branch in St. Pölten instead of the seven it originally requested.

It was, however, a beneficiary of the annexation of the Sudetenland in the fall of 1938. In the competition between the Dresdner Bank and Deutsche Bank to divvy up the Czech bank branches in the newly acquired territory, the former proved quite successful. The authorities also wished, however, for the more important Austrian banks to take over branches in close proximity to Austria. The Creditanstalt was especially eager to get hold of the Böhmische Escompte-Bank's branches in Znaim, Ludenburg, and Nikolsburg, and it seemed for a while to have assumed it would succeed. The Länderbank, however, put in a bid for those branches, and its position was made stronger by the fact that the Dresdner Bank was getting the Böhmische Escompte-Bank's branches in the Sudetenland. Open competition between the Creditanstalt and the Länderbank, however, was nipped in the bud when Lower Danubian Gau Economic Advisor Birthelmer intervened and forced the two sides to agree

to a settlement under which the Länderbank got the Böhmische Escompte-Bank's branches in Znaim, Ludenburg, and Nikolsburg, apparently by transfer first to the Dresdner Bank and then to its affiliate, the Länderbank, and the Creditanstalt received the branches of other Czech banks in Znaim and Ludenburg. The Bank for Oberösterreich und Salzburg, which was affiliated with the Creditanstalt, was granted a branch in the Bohemian town of Krumau. The fact that Birthelmer was a member of the Länderbank supervisory board undoubtedly was helpful in making sure that the bank was able to attain some of its goals.[157]

As in Austria, so too in Vienna did the Länderbank experience frustration in its efforts to improve its position. It wanted to shift the location of three of its branches in Vienna from districts where it had other branches nearby to districts where it was not represented. The Ministry for Economics and Labor rejected this request on the grounds that the Creditanstalt and Zentralsparkasse Wien already had branches in the districts in question and the districts did not need the services of yet another bank. In the case of Floridsdorf, where the Länderbank was particularly eager to set up offices, it also encountered the resistance of the Danube Association of Cooperatives, which viewed presence of yet another bank in Floridsdorf as threatening to its own interests there. The Länderbank also had only slight success in its efforts to set up branches in outlying areas of Vienna that were municipalized at this time. In

[154] ÖStA/AdR, Bürckel-Materie, 2165/2/1, Box 92, Lehr to Kratz, Feb. 3, 1939, Lehr to the Ministry for Economics and Labor, Feb. 16, 1939; Riehle to Kratz, Feb. 28, 1939.

[155] RGVA Moscow, 1458/2/68, Bl. 83–85, Ernst to Länderbank Wien, March 14, 1939, and Klucki to Ernst, March 1, 1939.

[156] ÖStA/AdR, BMF, Allgem. Reihe 1939, Nr. 34.913/1939 and correspondence in 33.366/1939; ibid., Ernst to Länderbank, July 20, 1939.

[157] On the carving up of the Sudetenland branches, see Harald Wixforth, *Auftakt zur Ostexpansion. Die Dresdner Bank und die Umgestaltung des Bankwesens im Sudetenland 1938/39* (= Hannah-Arendt-Institut. Berichte und Studien Nr. 31, Dresden 2001), esp. pp. 110–114. See also DrB, Nr. 5460-2000, meetings of the administrative council, Oct. 27, 1938, and April 17, 1939; also DB, P6502, Bl. 119, 142, report from Joham for Abs, Oct. 10, 1938, and Abs to Joham, Oct. 25, 1938. It is interesting to note that the model for the taking over of these branches by the Dresdner/Länderbank was the contract with the Živnostenská banka and that the man used for the negotiations was Michael Dyszkant, who was taken over from the Živnostenská banka. See Kubu/Exner, *Tschechen*, pp. 76–77.

its quest to set up branches in Mödling, Liesing, and Schwechat, it received approval only for Liesing, which was deemed sufficiently industrialized to merit a new branch. In the other cases, the presence of savings banks and cooperative banks as well as of Creditanstalt branches already doing business with the most important local industries seemed good reason to exclude the Länderbank. It had better luck with a petition in the summer of 1939 to take over the Vienna branch of the "Hermes" Ungarische Allgemeine Wechselstube and to turn it into a Länderbank branch to serve foreigners in Vienna. It also took over the Viennese business of the Milanese Societá Italiana di Credito in 1939, which suggests that even Germany's Italian ally found it best to leave Austria. In any case, the new Länderbank had thirty-three branches in Vienna in July 1938 and was able to increase the number to thirty-six by the outbreak of the war.[158] Because the much larger Creditanstalt had twenty-four branches, the Länderbank could hardly consider itself seriously disadvantaged by the government's policy of trying to avoid overbanking. One suspects, however, that the new bank did not enjoy an optimal geographical balance in the location of its Viennese branches.

During the brief prewar period, the Länderbank developed and expanded its limited but significant foreign interests. There was considerable uncertainty about what to do with the "Hermes" Ungarische Allgemeine Wechselstube in Budapest. The integration of the Vienna branch into the Länderbank was a rationalization measure, but the precise role of the Budapest organization was a subject of debate. Needless to say, there was no debate about getting rid of the Jewish leadership, an area in which the Dresdner Bank and the Länderbank leadership was well practiced. On July 18, 1938, Pilder informed the management

of what was still the Mercurbank that it was "high time to also Aryanize the management of the Mercurbank, Budapest and thereby to free the path to building up the institute in Budapest and make it serviceable for our needs." He asked that a director be sent to Budapest to put an Aryan in place of Director Rosenfeld and to negotiate a settlement for this purpose. He made clear that "we now want the problem of Budapest to be taken care of and not shelved once again."[159]

Hitschfeld apparently was the director sent, and negotiations were conducted with Rosenfeld, who was entitled to a year's notice, a pension, and an appropriate settlement as a reward for more than twenty-seven years of service. The Länderbank supervisory board thought these entitlements too generous and authorized negotiations on a total settlement of about 50,000 pengö. Veesenmayer also insisted that Rosenfeld be obligated to serve until May 1939 as a consultant to the bank and also to the "Ocean" Ungarische Konservenfabrik und Handels AG, which the bank owned and which Rosenfeld directed. As usual, replacing Jewish banking personnel was not easy. The board had installed Ferdinand Lintner of the Salzburg branch as provisional director, who was described as a member of Konrad Henlein's Sudetendeutsche Party. The board was considering the appointment of a couple of Hungarian savings bank directors; one was quickly dropped, however, and the second was apparently too old. In any event, the bank's leadership was in Aryan hands.[160]

This did not, however, solve the problem of the bank's future, which was first discussed by the Länderbank supervisory board in early October 1938. Veesenmayer, who had developed a special interest in Hungarian matters, pointed out that the economic relations between the two countries had expanded considerably and both German and Hungarian business circles had expressed interest in building up the Hungarian bank. He thought the initiative had to come

---

[158] On the Viennese branches and the relevant correspondence, see ÖStA/AdR, BMF, Allgem. Reihe 1938/1939, Nr. 52.861/1938, 31.578/1939, 31.219/1939. On the Hungarian and Italian branches, see NARA, T83/136, the Dresdner Bank management board meeting, May 15, 1939.

[159] DrB, Nr. 5460-2000, Pilder to Direktion, Mercurbank, July 18, 1938.
[160] Ibid., personnel committee, Dec. 2, 1938.

from the Dresdner Bank and went so far as to suggest that the Länderbank and Creditanstalt might join together to set up a single bank in Budapest to look after German interests. This was a striking illustration of the indifference of an SS man like Veesenmayer to the particular interests of the bank. Rasche took the position that there was no question of "giving up of our interests in Budapest" and suggested instead that the "Mercur" Budapest might be turned into a branch of the Länderbank and thereby escape the need to raise its share capital. Pilder was less opposed to sharing interests in Hungary, suggesting that the Deutsche Bank might be interested in such an investment and that the matter should be discussed with the Reichsbank and investigated further in Budapest.[161] The issue seemed much less pressing at the end of 1938, however, when Hitschfeld reported that business in Budapest was very quiet because of the cessation of wood exports from Austria to Hungary and stagnation of stock market activity. In response to this situation, it was decided to try to expand the bank's business in Hungary.[162]

Undoubtedly, Hungary was on the back burner at this point because of developments in the Czech lands. The new branches in southern Moravia were obviously promising acquisitions, but most important was the takeover of a majority stake in the Pressburger Handels- und Kreditbank AG in April 1939, which was then renamed the Handels- und Kreditbank AG, Pressburg. The Dresdner Bank and Länderbank interest in Slovakia, which was part of the general German preparations for the economic penetration of what remained of Czechoslovakia, anticipated the march into Prague in March 1939. In January 1939, Veesenmayer informed the Länderbank supervisory board that both German and Czech authorities were prepared to permit the Länderbank to be represented in Pressburg, and the opportunity was particularly favorable because a Slovak group had offered an option, still untaken, on the shares of

the Pressburger Handels- und Kreditbank. The cost would be between 300,000 and 400,000 RM. Pilder then proposed that the Länderbank management board be empowered to establish a position in Pressburg without further consultation with the board of supervisors.[163]

Veesenmayer was in a good position to know. Along with Meyer of the Dresdner Bank, he was working closely with friendly businessmen and banks to take over the Pressburg bank. Among his contacts was Karl Novotny, the Sudeten-German director of the Böhmische Escompte-Bank, which controlled the shares of the Pressburger Handels- und Kreditbank. At a meeting on February 23, 1939, this group orchestrated the takeover, planning a general meeting of the shareholders for March 8 as well as a "solemn company assembly" for noon of the same day. At the meeting, with Novotny presiding, the old leadership on the administrative council resigned. Meyer took over the role of chairman and Veesenmayer, Lehr, and Herbeck were elected to the supervisory board.[164]

Finding qualified personnel continued to be a problem. At the turn of 1938–1939, the Dresdner Bank sent twenty of its younger staff members to help out at the Länderbank. The Länderbank planned to send an equal number of its younger personnel for training at the Dresdner Bank and its branches. This hardly was a solution to the problems at hand, however. A successful effort was made to consolidate the central headquarters of the bank in the recently acquired building at Am Hof 2 in central Vienna and to dissolve a second headquarters in the Herrengasse, the former headquarters of the Živnostenská banka branch. In January 1939, the bank faced a number of problems because of the closing down of the Herrengasse branch, the reassignment of von Paić to the Kontrollbank at the behest of Rafelsberger, the return of Director Teichmann of the Dresdner Bank to Berlin, and the current and projected expansion of the bank. Director

---

161 Ibid., working committee of the management board, Oct. 4, 1938.
162 Ibid., personnel committee, Dec. 2, 1938, and supervisory board meeting of April 17, 1939.

163 Ibid., supervisory board meeting, Jan. 17, 1939.
164 Archive of the National Bank of Slovakia, Bratislava (= NOUB), Deutsche Handels- und Kreditbank AG (DHKA), Box 2, File 11. Meeting of Feb. 23, 1939 and administrative council meeting of March 8, 1939.

Hermann Richter of the Dresdner Bank, who had been assigned to the Länderbank personnel committee, recommended a number of changes of assignment and promotions in January 1939 to deal with these problems. The actual changes are of little interest here, but what is revealing is that while Veesenmayer, Wolzt, Birthelmer, and Rasche all agreed that the redistribution of responsibilities was desirable, they were unwilling to formalize the appointments until they had time to see how the managers in question did in their new positions. When Warnecke suggested that at least Franz Schraudolph, who was being moved from the office dealing with the Viennese branches to handle large credits, be formally named to his new position, Pilder objected and insisted that all the new appointees go through a probationary period. The personnel committee intensely watched over appointments, which is not to say that it was prepared to appoint only Party activists. Schraudolph, for example, was not a Party member and appears to have been apolitical.[165] Nevertheless, when the management board suggested that it be allowed to decide to whom to confer the power of attorney for the bank without consulting the personnel committee, not least because so many bank officials were being drafted for military service, Birthelmer and Vessenmayer insisted that the personnel committee be consulted in every case and be provided with "a description of the professional and political suitability of the persons in question."[166]

Like all business enterprises, the Länderbank found itself confronted with the need to conform to Party and German Labor Front demands in dealing with its staff. Unfortunately, the documentary record provides rather limited information on what working conditions were like as seen from below. There certainly is evidence that the National Socialist shop stewards had considerable power over the employees when it came to political matters. When an official of the bank complained about being fired

by his steward for political reasons, the matter was taken up in the personnel committee. It was decided to consult with the Party, to let the man go if that is what the Party wanted, to take a neutral position, or to keep him if the Party so advised. The Party was also to be asked for a political dossier on the person in question.[167]

The Nazification of labor relations at the bank began on the very day of its founding with a company assembly to celebrate the event. Nevertheless, there were signs of impatience with the progress. At the personnel committee meeting on December 2, Veesenmayer and Birthelmer asked for a report on membership in the Party and its organizations, and they also wanted a report on the bank's social benefits and policies.[168] At this meeting, the committee approved the expenditure of 12,000 RM for sports and cultural activities as well as 6,000 RM to acquire a boathouse at the behest of the steward and company council and as a contribution to the "Strength through Joy" program. In the course of the coming months, the Länderbank developed a more extensive program involving sports, a company band, organized hiking and skiing trips, and similar organized leisure-time events. German Labor Front speakers were also invited to "inform" the bank staff about current issues, and efforts were made to improve working conditions, to give Christmas bonuses, and to improve the pension plan.[169] Despite a substantial increase in business, the number of employees remained at approximately 1,550 prior to the war. About 1,000 worked at the main headquarters in Vienna and in the Viennese branches, the remainder in the branches at home and abroad. The management seemed satisfied with maintaining the staff at a stable level, but the drafting of employees into military service was already having consequences for its daily operations.

[165] ÖStA/AdR, BMI, Gauakt Rudolph Schraudolph, Nr. 224.672.

[166] DrB, Nr. 5460-2000, personnel committee meeting, Jan. 17, 1939.

[167] Ibid., discussion in Vienna, Oct. 27, 1938.

[168] Ibid., meeting, Dec. 2, 1938.

[169] Ibid., business report of the Länderbank Wien AG 1938, personnel committee and administrative council meetings, April 17 and personnel committee, May 19, 1939.

4. THE PREWAR BUSINESS OF
THE LÄNDERBANK

When the Länderbank supervisory board met on January 17, 1939, Director Warnecke was able to give a very favorable report of the bank's business during the first half year of its existence. The balance between the end of September and the end of November 1938 grew from 320 million to 346 million RM, and its liquidity was very favorable despite the "loss of credit accounts resulting from the almost completed liquidation of the Jewish engagement." That loss had been more than made up for by credits to firms in the construction and defense industries. Many of those firms were granted larger credits than their balances warranted on account of the "personal quality" of the applicants, and the fact that they were monitored by the authorities justified a higher level of risk. Similarly, the withdrawals of funds by Jewish clients had presented no serious difficulties. The total sum of deposits had increased by 16 million RM. Indeed, the elimination of the Jews from economic life had proven quite profitable. As Warnecke noted: "Special mention should be made of the fact that the bank has managed to collaborate successfully in bringing a large number of non-Aryan enterprises into Aryan hands and beyond that to repatriate some substantial share holdings from foreign possession back to the Reich."[170]

Lehr reported in much the same terms at a board meeting on May 19. The bank's balance had increased by 14 million RM to 344 million RM. The amount of credits granted had increased by a modest 4 million RM. In the booming economy, high liquidity decreased the demand for credit and also encouraged borrowers to pay off old loans. The limited growth in the bank's business was also explained by the continued reduction of its dealings with Jewish clients and by the termination of foreign exchange barriers between the old Reich and the Ostmark, which meant that proprietary companies in Germany could cover the liquidity needs of their subsidiaries in Austria. Consortial business had by now assumed great importance, but Aryanization remained a significant area of activity. Lehr, "while presenting the most important transactions, described the efforts of the bank to participate in the transfer of non-Aryan enterprises into Aryan possession and, through this intermediatory activity, to secure interesting business connections for the bank."[171]

The role of the banks in the elimination of Jews from Austrian economic life was wide ranging and often quite brutal. This is well exemplified by the activities of the Mercurbank after the Anschluss and the new Länderbank Wien AG following its creation in late July 1938. The extensive persecution of the Jews obviously entailed a loss of Jewish customers, but the bank was often an active participant in and profiteer from their departure. In the case of savings and securities accounts, withdrawals were particularly large following the terrible pogrom of November 9–10, 1938. It resulted in the systematic effort to drive Jews from German economic life, a process already well under way in what had been Austria, and the imposition of a huge fine on Jews that was to be paid in the form of a levy on their assets. Moreover, paying the costs of emigration and the Reich Flight Tax were cause enough for Jews to mobilize their liquid assets. These were often placed in blocked accounts that were soon used to pay taxes or were confiscated for the same purpose. As the Länderbank noted in its report for June 1939 concerning the continued reduction of savings placed with the bank, "it is almost exclusively due to the withdrawals of non-Aryan customers in connection with the levy on the Jews and confiscations."[172] This situation was by no means a total loss for the bank. To put it another way, it was often a one-time gain. When Rasche expressed curiosity as to why Länderbank income from the sale of stocks, bonds, and other paper assets decreased from 768,000 RM in 1939 to 625,000

---

[170] Ibid., administrative council meeting, Jan. 17, 1939.

[171] Ibid., supervisory board meeting, May 19, 1939.
[172] Ibid., explanatory notes to the monthly statement of June 30, 1939.

RM in 1940, while the Dresdner Bank had the opposite experience, Lehr explained that "the year 1939 was another year of great changes in which, beyond a partial increase in commission rates, there were also special opportunities to earn money through the sale of Jewish paper assets. To be sure, these Jewish accounts were thereby dissolved, so that there is no longer a question about a repetition of the business connected with them." Furthermore, the bank had additionally collected some 90,000 RM in fees for its assistance in calculating and transferring the Jewish Assets Tax in 1939. Indeed, as Lehr argued, if one calculated sales of paper assets in 1939 and 1940 without taking into account the special circumstances of 1939, sales were actually somewhat higher in 1940![173]

Just as this illuminating if not exactly edifying bit of correspondence demonstrates the capacity to profit from Jewish misfortune to the bitter end, so too does the evidence show that the elimination of credits to Jewish customers, who were transformed into bad credit risks by the policies of the new regime, received a considerable helping hand from the Länderbank. This was already evident in the acquisition of the Vienna branch of the Živnostenská banka. In that transaction, the Dresdner Bank did not obligate itself, as it did in the acquisition of the Österreichische Länderbank, to take over the debtors. Some twenty accounts totaling 3,025,000 RM were deemed "unsuitable to be taken over." Although it is unclear whether all

those named were Jewish, some of the larger accounts, such as the Viennese textile firm of Hermann Pollack's Söhne (354,000 RM), the Banking house of Josef Stein & Co. (221,000 RM), along with smaller ones can be definitely identified as later Aryanization cases.[174]

The bankers involved were well aware that the refusal to grant a credit or the termination of a credit could be tantamount to forcing a company into bankruptcy. This was certainly the case with the Jewish-owned Obereggendorfer Papierfabrik, from which full credit repayment was demanded in March 1938 on the grounds that the company was unable to meet its obligations. Quite aside from the fact that there was no evidence for this because the company had been servicing its debt, the credit contract stipulated that six months' notice had to be given before calling in the debt. When the case came before the courts after the war, the Länderbank was adjudged to have violated the "rules of honest business conduct" and to have engaged in "the active withdrawal of assets." As one of the former Länderbank directors frankly told the court concerning the attitude after the Anschluss, "the tendency was to call in the debts of the Jewish credit accounts wherever possible and feasible." At the same time, the Länderbank stood ready to profit from the liquidation of the Obereggendorfer Papierfabrik in November 1939. It took over the company's property, buildings, machinery, and equipment on condition that it not be charged an "Aryanization fee" for doing so.[175]

---

[173] Ibid., Lehr to Rasche, April 10, 1941. It is quite ironic that the Länderbank played a major role in locating and evaluating compensation claims in connection with confiscated paper assets under the Compensation Fund Law of 1961. The bank collected fees for these various services and also collected interest on the compensation fund (Abgeltungfond) held at the bank. It does appear, however, that the bank officials charged with these matters were Jews returned from camps and exile. See Helen B. Junz/Oliver Rathkolb/Theodor Venus/ with cooperation from Vitali Bodnar et al., *Das Vermögen der jüdischen Bevölkerung Österreichs: NS-Raub und Restitution nach 1945*. Veröffentlichungen der Österreichischen Historikerkommission, Vol. 9 (Vienna 2004), pp. 126–131.

[174] DrB, Nr. 5467-2000, Verzeichnis der Debitoren, die auf Grund der Vorprüfung als nicht zur Übernahme geeignet sind (list of accounts receivable deemed unsuitable for takeover on the basis of preliminary examination), undated.

[175] Ulrike Felber/Peter Melichar/Markus Priller/Berthold Unfried/Fritz Weber, *Ökonomie der Arisierung. Teil 1: Grundzüge, Akteure und Institutionen*. Veröffentlichungen der Österreichischen Historikerkommission, vol. 10/1 (Vienna 2004) and Felber, et al., *Ökonomie der Arisierung. Teil 2: Wirtschaftssektoren, Branchen, Falldarstellungen*. Veröffentlichungen der Österreichischen Historikerkommission, vol. 10/2 (Vienna 2004), pt. 2, p. 444. On the liquidation, see ÖStA/AdR, Ministerium f. Wirtschaft u. Arbeit (= MfWuA),

As this shows, the expulsion of the Jews from economic life and Aryanization was a multifaceted process and often became an integral part of "normal" business operations. It involved, of course, the elimination of Jewish administrative council members, directors, and employees of firms in which banks were major shareholders. That was often done by political authorities or within such enterprises themselves in the early days of the new regime. The situation of the Länderbank was much less complicated than the Creditanstalt with respect to the Aryanization of its holdings. The one serious case in which it was a major shareholder in a Jewish firm was the Hirmer Zuckerfabrik. Ex-Länderbank director Emil Freund and a number of other Jewish directors of the old bank were eliminated from the administrative council and replaced already in May 1938 by Gau Economic Advisor and Länderbank administrative board member Birthelmer and other Party functionaries.[176]

The Dresdner Bank itself, which was well practiced in Aryanization thanks to its German experiences, had at its disposal a special Consortial Section 5 to deal with them. It lost no time in informing all its branches on March 22, 1938, that because of the annexation of Austria, this office would be exploring "the business opportunities available to us insofar as our engagement in 'Aryanizations,' other reconstructions and similar transactions are concerned." It noted that a decree of March 19 had banned non-Austrian enterprises from acquiring or participating in Austrian firms or setting up branches until October 1 but that the Reich economics minister could issue special dispensations. Indeed, a model for such exceptions had been provided by Wilhelm Keppler's office, which Aryanized the Hirtenberger Patronen- und Waffenfabrik that had belonged to the Austrian "Cannon King," Fritz Mandl, and then Germanized it as well by arranging its takeover by the Wilhelm Gustloff-Stiftung,

known before its Aryanization as the Thuringian Waffenfabrik Simson. The key figure in this process, both in Thuringia and in Austria, was the chairman of the administrative board of the Gustloff-Stiftung, state councilor and Gau economic advisor in Thuringia, Otto Eberhardt, whom Keppler had put on assignment in his office for such purposes as well as for Aryanization more generally. Eberhardt was closely associated with cellulose manufacturer Walther Schieber, who was also the managing director of the Gustloff-Stiftung. Both men were part of the circle surrounding the Thuringian governor and Gauleiter Fritz Sauckel, who was closely connected with Keppler. All of these men were enthusiasts for the kind of state-directed enterprise and economy represented by the Gustloff-Stiftung, which had gained a reputation for reducing unemployment. They had no qualms about taking credits from private bankers, however. The Mercurbank had provided credits for the Hirtenberger takeover and, as was noted by the report of the Dresdner Bank Consortial Section, was now positioned "to conduct future financial transactions of the company, which earlier belonged to the sphere of interest of the Austrian Creditanstalt."[177] By October 1939, the Länderbank had supplied what was now called the Gustloff-Werke Otto-Eberhardt-Patronenfabrik with 5,761,000 RM in credits, a substantial portion of the Dresdner Bank's total engagement of more than 17 million in credits, to the various branches of the Gustloff-Werke.[178] Yet another example of Aryanization serving as a wedge for important business connections is provided by the report of a visit by a representative of the Hermann Göring-Werke in Austria to the Mercurbank on March 16, 1938, informing the bank that the Göring-Werke intended "to buy up certain holdings of non-Aryan firms (wood, textiles, etc.)." Shortly thereafter, the Mercurbank wrote to the headquarters of the Hermann Göring-Werke in

---

Vermögensverkehrsstelle (= VVSt), Box Kommissare u. Treuhänder, Nr. 5583, Länderbank to VVSt, Nov. 3, 1939 and VVSt, memorandum of Nov. 2, 1939.

[176] See Felber et al., Ökonomie der Arisierung, pt. 2, pp. 849–850.

[177] DrB, Nr. 7836-2000, report of April 11, 1938. On what might be called a Thuringian mafia, see Willy A. Schilling, Die Entwicklung des faschistischen Herrschaftssystems in Thüringen 1933–1939 (Berlin 2001), pp. 77, 86, 90, 92, 95.

[178] NARA, T83/122, Ausschussitzung, Oct. 17, 1939.

Berlin asking permission to offer the Viennese branch of the company 350,000 RM in credits for the purchases and for the expansion of the Linz works of the Hermann Göring-Werke.[179]

It was important, therefore, for the Dresdner Bank branches to gather information that might be of use to the central office or to the Mercurbank. The Dresdner Bank used the Mercurbank as a source of intelligence concerning Austrian Jewish firms that were potentially available for purchase or investment by interested parties in the old Reich. There was correspondence concerning the Aryanization of the Reininghaus brewery, the Ankerbrotfabrik, and numerous other Austrian firms and hotels in the process of changing hands.[180] This did not always mean, however, that the Dresdner Bank, the Mercurbank, and later the Länderbank were involved in the transactions or successful in trying to become involved. Interest in the food plants of the Gustav und Wilhelm Loew AG in Angern, for example, was quickly abandoned when Wolzt reported that the two brothers had been arrested and sent to Dachau by the Gestapo and that the Reich Food Estate was showing an interest in the firm, which was in fact bought through the German Cooperatives Clearing Bank. The Mercurbank apparently entertained hopes of playing a leading role in the Aryanization of the Gerngross Department Store and its real estate, but the Creditanstalt was to have the dubious distinction of being the primary bank in this Aryanization.[181] In the case of the Gebrüder Reininghaus, the possibilities for the Länderbank became extremely limited because of its takeover by the son of the NSDAP Party treasurer and internecine conflicts among the economic interests in the Party.[182] The

Länderbank was "luckier" when it came to Austria's largest bread manufacturer, Ankerbro. It had been the company's chief creditor, but the Aryanization of the firm turned into an incredible tale of mismanagement and misadventure because of Party interests and efforts to satisfy retailer interests. In May 1939, the Mercurbank had acquired 139,000 shares in the company from Bettina Mendl, a member of the family that owned the company, with authorization to sell. The nominal value of a share was 30 RM at the time, but the authorities had not given approval to sell the shares. In September 1940, the Gestapo denaturalized Bettina Mendl and laid claim to all her assets, a procedure that disrupted the ongoing Aryanization effort. At the end of the year, the Länderbank was still seeking approval to dispose of the shares and ultimately sold them at 11 RM a share to the bakers' cooperative "IBÄCK," which was the successor of Ankerbrot. It had obviously not been a profitable venture, although certainly a sordid one.[183] The Dresdner Bank also seems to have played a role in the acquisition of and the effective Germanization and Aryanization of paper manufacturer Brigl & Bergmeister AG by the Aschaffenburger Zellstoffwerke Berlin, to which it provided substantial credits. Director Busch of the Dresdner Bank sat on the supervisory board of the Aschaffenburgr Zellstoffwerke, learned of its interest in Brigl & Bergmeister, and provided the information that led to the takeover.[184]

Efforts to act as an intermediary sometimes failed. Between April and June 1938, for example, Director Meyer of the Dresdner Bank conducted a lively correspondence with his colleagues at the Mercurbank about the status of the G&W Heller Schokolade- Zuckerwaren- und Obstkonservenfabrik, Austria's largest and most

[179] DrB, Nr. 7836-2000, Besuch des Herrn Werthmann von den Reichswerken, Notiz, March 30, 1938.

[180] DrB, Nr. 7836-2000, Dresdner Bank to Direktionen, March 22, 1938. This volume is filled with reports and correspondence dealing with a variety of firms and concerns of interest to the Consortial Section.

[181] Ibid., Memoranda, April 28, 1938, and April 11, 1938, and Felber et al., *Ökonomie der Arisierung*, pt. 1, pp. 125–127, pt. 2, pp. 84–92.

[182] DrB, 7836-2000, memoranda of Sept. 1 and 15, 1938, and other relevant reports therein, and Felber et al. *Ökonomie der Arisierung*, pt. 2, pp. 791–792.

[183] See ibid., pp. 767–772. See also the Report of the VVSt to the Reichsstatthalter, Feb. 10, 1940, the report of the Kontrollbank, Jan. 31, 1941, and Länderbank to VVSt, Dec. 19, 1940, in: ÖStA/AdR, MfWuA, VVSt, Industrie A, Box 3429, Vol. II, Nr. 609.

[184] DrB, Nr. 7836-2000, Dresdner Bank to Aschaffenburger Zellstoffwerke, June 23 and 28, 1938, and report on the cellulose industry, May 10, 1938.

important producer of sweets. When Meyer inquired about the status of the firm's projected Aryanization, Wolzt informed him that the Heller brothers were negotiating with the Firma Dr. A. Oetker Nährmittelwerke in Baden bei Wien with the mediation of the Mercurbank. Apparently, they were also negotiating with Österreichische Nestlé, which turned out not to have the requisite funds. Because government policy was to favor Austrian over German firms in such cases, Meyer held back but asked that he be informed if the negotiations failed. They did, and Meyer then informed the Mercurbank that the Nuremberg firm of Haeberlein-Metzger was searching for a plant in Austria and had asked the Nuremberg law firm of Oehl and Wegler, with whom Meyer apparently had close relations, to find a suitable prospect. As it turned out, however, Haeberlein-Metzger and other German firms that expressed an interest in Heller ran into competition from Aryan Austrian companies and individuals eager to get their hands on the Heller firm. Matters were made stickier by the interest of one of Göring's favorites in the enterprise. They also ran afoul of various competing Party and business elements in the case of the A. Eggers Sohn Zuckerwarenfabrik. Because the formal policy was to favor Austrians over Reich Germans for acquisitions, Meyer and the Mercurbank were unable to help the clients of Oehl and Wegler in such cases, although they served as a regular source of information for other business prospects.[185]

An Aryanization that benefited an Austrian National Socialist did not necessarily mean

the end of future chances for firms in the old Reich, as illustrated by the example of the sale of the confectionary firm Kreidl-Heller to SS Standartenführer Fridolin Glaß, an active participant in the July 1934 Putsch. When Meyer learned that Glaß was leaving business to devote himself full time to Party work, he asked Länderbank lawyer Hans Mann to check out whether an offer from the Chemische Fabrik von Heyden, a client of the Dresdner Bank, to take a capital stake might be welcomed by the Austrian company.[186]

There was plenty of business to be done in Austria, and Aryanization offered opportunities that could easily be coupled with others. The A. Hering AG in Nuremberg, for example, was a client of Oehl and Wegler as well as the Dresdner Bank. The former asked Director Meyer to prevail upon Director Wolzt to make contact with potential customers from the Hermann Göring-Werke. Hering also wrote to Wolzt directly to point out that one of the firm's specialties was installing ventilation equipment and air raid shelters and that the purchasers of Aryanized plants were being required to reserve as much as 20 percent of their balances for meeting German Labor Front requirements of this type. The Labor Front hoped, therefore, that the Mercurbank would make these services known to Austrian industry.[187]

The most important contribution of the Länderbank to Aryanization was embedded in the organizational structures put in place by the regime to carry out the "dejewification" (Entjudung) of the Austrian economy along with its putative "rationalization" and integration into the economy of the Greater Reich. Göring had already set the tone shortly after the Anschluss by ordering that Aryanization was to be completed in Austria within four years – a great underestimation of Austrian capacities in this field that was undoubtedly motivated by the reportedly substantial number of Jewish enterprises in Austria and Jews involved in the economy. He insisted that large amounts of money

[185] On the role of Labor Minister Ley and Göring in this case as well as the other rather sordid details, see Felber et al., Ökonomie der Arisierung, pt. 2, pp. 797–804; for the correspondence of the spring of 1938 among Meyer, the Mercurbank, and Oehl and Wegler, see NARA, RG 260, External Assets Investigations 1945–1949, 390/44/31/01, Box 539. The Heller Aryanization was also complicated by the fact that the Aryanization was conducted with an unusual amount of cooperation from the Heller brothers and the people taking over their enterprise, so that they were allowed to emigrate and to conduct foreign business for the company. On the negotiations with Nestlé see DrB, Nr. 7836-200, the note to Pilder, May 27, 1938.

[186] Ibid., Meyer to Mann, June 13, 1939.
[187] Ibid., Hering to Wolzt, July 4, 1938, and Oehl and Wegler to Meyer, Aug. 31, 1938.

would have to be mobilized, especially because many of those involved in taking over Jewish assets would not have the necessary means. Consequently, the Reich Finance Ministry would have to provide guarantees for credits given for such purposes, although he admitted the difficulties involved in assessing the worth of assets and the "personal qualities and business capabilities" of those involved. Direct loans by the Reich were also under consideration, although they carried the same risks and were less desirable because of the drain on Reich resources. Göring argued that the needed monies would in the last analysis have to be mobilized by the private economy. Intentionally, Göring's envisioned Aryanization program was not formally pronounced by Göring himself but rather left to the Reich Ministry of the Interior. The ministry communicated the plan within the government in a letter of April 5, 1938, stressing the importance of private financing with Reich guarantees and emphasizing the need to limit the engagement of non-Austrian firms in the process. Rather, "the way to go in principle is for Austrian banks to provide Austrian firms with credits for 'Aryanizations' for which the Reich is then to take on a guarantee. As the Reich Plenipotentiary for Austria [Wilhelm Keppler] reports, this will not mean any great risk for the Reich, since the Jewish firms will be offered for a cheap price and the improving economic situation will increase the value of these firms."[188]

Actually, the matter had already been discussed and decided on at a meeting chaired by Ministerial Director Kurt Lange of the RWM on April 5, 1938, and it was embedded in a general plan of aid for the Austrian economy that went well beyond the Aryanization problem. In addition to the representatives of various government agencies, a substantial number of bankers were also present: Hermann Josef Abs, Walther Pohle, and Hellmuth Pollems of the Deutsche Bank, Erich Heller of the Creditanstalt, and Pilder, Rasche, and Heinz Ansmann of the Dresdner

Bank and the Mercurbank. Lange made clear that the credit action had to be arranged and announced right away because Göring was eager to have it publicized before the plebiscite on April 10. A new consortium was needed especially for Austrian purposes in addition to that already existing for the Four Year Plan. He was thinking of a 50 million RM credit with a lifespan of twelve and a half to fifteen years. Abs and Pilder agreed, urging, however, that, because Austria did not have enough big banks, the savings banks and other German banks be included. Lange insisted that the banks assume at least a portion of the risk and that the loans be granted only where there was reasonable certainty that the guarantee would not have to be called upon. Pilder thought that the banks could take as much as 30 percent of the risk if they had a voice in giving the credits. Abs pointed out that provision did have to be made for a 100 percent guarantee. There was a general agreement that a 50 million RM credit was to be announced to the press by April 10, although further negotiations were to take place on the distribution of risk.

The only point of disagreement was the question of the leadership of the consortium. Heller claimed it for the Creditanstalt, and Rasche and Pilder claimed it for the Mercurbank. A few days later, Lange was able to report to Kehrl that the Finance Ministry had drawn up the necessary legislation for up to 150 million RM in credit aid to Austria, the amount having been raised from the 100 million RM originally intended. In reality, there was no intention of providing for more than 50 million RM immediately, 25 million RM of which was to finance large consortial credits with a 100 percent guarantee, the other 25 million RM of which was for banks to grant to customers with a 70 percent to 85 percent Reich guarantee. Experience was to show that the guarantee was almost inevitably 85 percent. The leadership of the consortium was to be shared by the Creditanstalt and the Mercurbank, later the Länderbank. The Deutsche Bank and the Dresdner Bank were to determine which Austrian bank would take the lead on a case-by-case basis depending on levels of participation. Other banks, including small Austrian ones, were to participate in the credits

---

188 For the Göring plan, see BAB R2/15612, Bl. 2, 4–5, the note to Ministerial Director Schwandt of the RWM, April 9, 1938, and the note of the interior minister to the RWM, April 5, 1938.

below 100,000 RM. A credit committee was to be set up in Vienna in which the RWM, the RFM, the Reich Plenipotentiary for Austria, the state government, and representatives of the Chamber of Commerce, the banks, and the auditing agencies were to be represented. Kehrl was subsequently slated to serve as chairman of the committee and representative of the RWM. Small credits would be approved on the basis of auditor reports alone; larger ones would have to be considered by the entire committee, and those greater than 100,000 RM would also require approval from Berlin. The duration of credits could range from five to fourteen years, and the Reich guarantee could only be called upon after 1945. Although the banks wished to use the committee for refinancing, the government decided that refinancing would have to be handled directly between the individual banks and the Reichsbank. The leading members of the credit action consortium were to be the Deutsche Bank, the Dresdner Bank, and the Creditanstalt, the first two each taking a 25 percent share and the Creditanstalt taking 20 percent. They were expected to divvy up their portions among other friendly banks.[189]

Money was thus available to smooth the Aryanization process. This is not the place to recount the many peculiarities of Aryanization in Austria. The process itself began with the so-called wild Aryanizations of the first months of Nazi rule, with the installation of commissars and administrators at various Jewish enterprises, a substantial number and perhaps most of whom were of very dubious character and competence. It continued with the struggles between the advocates of *Wiedergutmachung* (compensation) to homegrown National Socialists for their "sacrifices" and "suffering" prior to the Anschluss, especially Rafelsberger and Fischböck, and the more "rational" and business-minded Aryanizers represented at times by Bürckel, who worked closely with

Göring, Keppler, Kehrl, and the officials in the RWM. It was the latter group, especially Göring and Ministerial Director Kurt Lange of the RWM, who set out the basic operational lines of Aryanization in Austria, which they intended to take place more rapidly than in the old Reich. At the outset, Jews were forced to report all their assets exceeding 5,000 RM so as to prevent capital flight and to enable the systematic pursuit of Aryanization. Because, as already noted, there was not enough capital available in Austria to purchase these assets, an agency was to be set up to hold them in trust for future sale. This would be made possible through the organized sale of these assets in a manner that would be smoothed over by bank credits, some of which would have to be guaranteed by the Reich itself.[190] The decree mandating the registration of Jewish assets was issued on April 26, 1938, and was followed by the creation of the Property Transfer Bureau (VVSt) in May 1938. The bureau had the task of using information on Jewish assets to arrange for the transfer of assets, the shutting down of unwanted Jewish enterprises, the administering of profits from Aryanizations, and the granting of exceptions to the ban on German acquisition of such assets in Austria until October 1938.[191]

The goal was to create – both for the new owners and for the state – an orderly, legal, and profitable transfer of Jewish assets that would eliminate the often suspect administrators of Jewish enterprises and thus be of service to the economy. There was evidence that was not happening and that the banks were disturbed by what was going on. The situation was described in some detail in a letter of September 17, 1938, from the director of the Franz Josephs Kai branch of the Länderbank in Vienna, Joseph O. Brake, to Oberregierungsrat Kratz in Bürckel's office.[192] Brake pointed out

189　For the meetings on the credit action and various drafts of guidelines held and drawn up between April 8 and 29, 1938, see RGVA Moscow, 1458/2/77, Bl. 81–83, the protocol of the meeting on April 4, 1938, Berlin April 5, 1938 and BAB, R2/15608, Bl. 12–18, Lange to Kehrl, April 8, 1938.

190　There is a well-balanced and thoughtful discussion of the basic history of Austrian Aryanization in Felber et al., *Ökonomie der Arisierung*, pt. 1, pp. 40–164.

191　Ibid., p. 65.

192　For the discussion and quotations that follow see ÖStA/AdR, Bürckel-Materie, 2165/0, Vol. 1, Box 92, Brake to Katz [sic], Sept. 17, 1938.

that the banks were prepared to make available large sums of money for the Austrian economy, but that this was being made very difficult for them "in most cases." He referred to his own experience as head of the Länderbank branch located in the largest business district of Vienna. The branch had dealt especially with the textile industry, which Brake characterized as "almost exclusively in Jewish hands." The bank had given substantial credits to these enterprises, and not only had many of these credits not been paid back, but the firms had also continued to receive credits because their important export business brought in foreign exchange, which was obviously in the national economic interest. This important economic activity was endangered, however, when commissarial administrators suddenly showed up with no experience in the business whatsoever, excluded the Jewish owners, and thus eliminated people who were counted on by the banks for their expertise. The only way out was "Aryanization through some propertyless non-expert … or a liquidation. In both cases the economy loses an asset and the bank its money." The real task of the administrator, in Brake's view, was either Aryanization by an experienced person with money or, in the case of firms that were not significant, liquidation. Instead, there were numerous cases in which some Party agency, sometimes the Gau economic advisor, appointed administrators with the assignment of Aryanizing or liquidating a firm by a certain time and "chasing away the Jewish owner." This was no service to the economy in Brake's view, especially when the administrator also fired the other Jewish employees, particularly those representing the firm abroad. The end effect was that the Jewish owner, who was forced to emigrate, and the Jewish employees were able to refer foreign customers elsewhere, thus ruining the export business and depriving the Reich of foreign exchange. As a result, "the Jew does his business abroad and here we have the bankruptcy of the Aryanized business." Brake argued that it was difficult to give credits so long as one was dealing with unqualified persons, and that one had to be sure one was dealing with qualified persons even if they were not specialists in the field. Alternatively, if there was a shortage of people with sufficient capital, one should turn to the old Reich where, Brake thought, there were certainly people with money and capacity anxious to establish a position in the Ostmark.

This was very revealing of the mixture of economic rationality and cynicism with which the banks viewed the Aryanization business as well as the utter amorality it reflected. The task of placing Jewish assets in the "right hands" became all the more important after the November 1938 pogrom, when Jews could be legally obligated to place their businesses up for sale. The Property Transfer Bureau continued this work, although by no means to completion, until March 1939, when it was dissolved as part of the general dissolution of the Austrian government. Its tasks in the field of industry and wholesale trade were then attached to Section C of the Kontrollbank, the most important organization with respect to the role of the private banks in Aryanization.

The Austrian Kontrollbank for Industry and Commerce was founded in 1914 and played a minor role as an oversight institution for industrial and commercial organizations and a facilitator in commercial transactions. Prior to the Anschluss, it was owned by the Creditanstalt (65.8%), the Mercurbank (20.2%), and the Rothschild Bank (14.0%). After the Anschluss, the Creditanstalt remained the main stockholder. The shares of the Mercurbank were transferred to the Länderbank Wien AG following its creation, and the Rothschild shares to the Bankhaus E. V. Nicolai. In April 1938, important personnel changes were made for the usual "racial" and political reasons. President Franz Rottenberg of the Creditanstalt and Vice President Victor Bergler of the old Länderbank were replaced. Carl Hinke of the Creditanstalt became president, and Wolzt of the Mercurbank stayed on as vice president; he was soon to resign because of his other duties. Josef Joham of the Creditanstalt was appointed to the administrative council along with Baron Lippe of the old Länderbank, but the latter was to depart once the new bank was founded. Hans Mann, who was the key legal advisor to the Mercurbank and the Länderbank Wien AG, was also appointed to the administrative council and took over Wolzt's functions. At the same time, the managing director of the Kontrollbank, Julius Simelis, was replaced by Hermann Leitich of the Creditanstalt. Leitich had good connections with Director Erich Heller of the Creditanstalt, Reich Governor for Austria Seyß-Inquart, and Fischböck. This was an especially significant appointment because Leitich had been placed on leave to take over this job at the personal behest of Minister Fischböck, who had a very high opinion of Leitich. A specialist in labor law and social policy, he had performed a variety of intelligence-gathering services for the Party during its illegal period.[193]

The National Socialist leadership intended to give the Kontrollbank a much more important role, especially with respect to two programs. It was placed in charge of the aforementioned Reich Economic Aid, a program of credits designed to assist Austrian industry to which was added a special program to aid Austrian restaurants and tourist facilities. Although the government intended to support the granting of at least 50 million RM, the consortium dealing with credits lower than 100,000 RM, that is non-consortial credits, as noted earlier, was for half this amount. This 25 million RM credit consortium had been created following a meeting in Berlin on April 7, 1938, at the offices of Reich Banking Commissar Ernst, attended by Joham of the Creditanstalt, Goetz and Rasche of the Dresdner Bank, and Directors Helmut Pollems and Walter Pohle of the Deutsche Bank. The consortium was to be headed by the Creditanstalt and the Mercurbank, and the firms given credits were to receive them through their existing bank connections, and new firms getting credits were to be divided between the two lead banks. The technical management of the consortium was to rest with the Kontrollbank. The consortium was to have twenty-five members. The Mercurbank, the Creditanstalt, the Deutsche Bank, and the Dresdner Bank were each to provide 2.5 million RM, while the

Österreichische Girovereinigung, eventually along with four regional Austrian banks, was also to provide 2.5 million RM. Manifestly, the lion's share of the business was to be done by the major banks. Because the credits were to be guaranteed by the Reich, the undertaking appeared lucrative even if repayment would only begin in October 1941 and if claims against the guarantee could not be made until April 1, 1945 or as late as 1953 in the case of large credits. Furthermore, the Reichsbank agreed to provide rediscount rights for bills on these credits. The position of the Dresdner Bank was particularly strong because it actually owned the Mercurbank and, later, the Länderbank. Rasche lost no time in instructing the Mercurbank to use its influence at the Kontrollbank to make sure "that the management is carried out to our interest." In October 1938, the consortial credit was doubled to 50 million RM, a measure that was strongly supported by Kehrl of the RWM, who was to pay close attention to the distribution of these credits.[194]

The second important program turned over to the Kontrollbank related to Aryanization. On the advice of the German Economic Auditing and Trusteeship Corporation, the Kontrollbank was given the task of handling the Aryanization of larger enterprises by Bürckel in the summer of 1938, and a special Section C was set up for this purpose. It was intended to produce a more planned approach to the entire question. It did not totally replace the Property Transfer Bureau, which still had quite a bit of unfinished business.[195] It reported to the Property Transfer Bureau advisory council on the settlement of major cases. Fundamentally, it was intended to act as a trustee in the sale of Jewish enterprises at what were deemed acceptable prices to qualified persons and thus in a manner that served the Reich's economic interests. The

[193] ÖStA/AdR, BMI, Gauakt Hermann Leitich, Nr. 85.541, and his personnel file at the BA-CA, Archiv der Creditanstalt Personalabteilung (= CA-PA).

[194] DrB, Nr. 7836-2000, file note by Rasche, April 7, 1938; RGVA Moscow, 1458/2/248, Ernst to the Reich economics minister, April 7, 1938, and Dresdner Bank to Oberregierungsrat Reinbothe (RWM), April 27, 1938; BAB, R2, 15608, Bl. 1–29, RWM-RFM correspondence.

[195] Ibid., Bl. 87–97 and Melichar, *Neuordnung im Bankwesen*, pp. 54–58.

administrative council voted to accept these new tasks at its meeting on August 23, 1938. In addition to confirming the appointment of Leitich, it appointed Rafelsberger's right-hand man in banking matters and a later manager at the Zentralsparkasse, Dr. Georg Schumetz, to assist him. Section C was subsequently placed under the general direction of a lawyer and Finance Ministry official, Walther Kastner, who served as Fischböck's personal delegate.[196]

Kastner was reputed to have taken a "national" position during the period when the Party was banned. He was not a Party member at the time of his appointment, however, and only applied for membership in 1940. Although he began paying dues, he was apparently never actually enrolled as a member. Kastner, like Leitich, was an appointee charged with fulfilling Fischböck's goal of promoting a "rational" and "economic" Aryanization of large enterprises in contrast to the more partisan approach of the Property Transfer Bureau. In his extraordinary memoirs, published in the early 1980s shortly before his eightieth birthday, Kastner, who apparently suffered not a tinge of remorse, reported on the purpose of the Kontrollbank, where he had presided over 102 Aryanizations. It was "to withdraw the sale of large enterprises from the purely Party-oriented Aryanization through the Property Transfer Bureau, that strongly tended to ensure that Party members were favored with enterprises at their liquidation value. The way chosen by the Kontrollbank was based on the principle that, to be sure, the Jewish seller should only receive the liquidation value, since they were denied the further operation of their enterprise, but that the acquirer had to pay the commercial value. The difference between these two valuations, after deduction of the bank expenses, was to be delivered to the Reich. I was assigned the responsibility for this accounting."[197] Apparently, Kastner found this

a fair and just procedure and considered himself an honest man for faithfully adhering to the principles on which Section C was founded. This self-appreciation could only have been reinforced by the fact that he was called upon to give expert testimony – and it was certainly expert – in restitution matters after the war and was even employed as a consultant by persons whose assets had been Aryanized.[198]

Nevertheless, when the decree giving Section C its charge was promulgated in October 1938, there was already some discontent about the way Section C was supposed to function. The exact issues and discussions involved are not completely reconstructable, but the general issues seem clear enough from the available documentation. At a meeting of the leading Länderbank supervisory and managing board directors on October 4, Hans Mann reported on the appointment of Kastner as well as the Kontrollbank discussions, noting that the bank profits from Aryanization were to be used for public purposes. At the same time, he asked to be relieved of his position on the Kontrollbank supervisory board "because he himself has reservations as to whether the Kontrollbank will be up to the task it has assumed because of its limited resources and the other high demands in technical and commercial respects connected with this action."[199] Rasche thought that Kehrl should be consulted first about Mann's request. Veesenmayer believed that the Gauleiter of Vienna, Odilo Globočnik, would insist on Mann's resignation. Globočnik, who was later to distinguish himself as both a common thief and a mass murderer, believed that the projected mode of operation of the Kontrollbank in Aryanizations did not bespeak "National Socialist principles." It was then decided that Mann was to resign and that, in his letter of

---

[196] ÖStA/AdR, BMF, Allgem. Reihe 1938, Nr. 34.205/1938, 44.989/1938, 56.929/1938, 57.435/1938.

[197] Walther Kastner, *Mein Leben kein Traum. Aus dem Leben eines österreichischen Juristen* (Vienna 1982), p.108.

[198] Ibid., pp. 112–118 and Walther Kastner, *Entziehung und Rückstellung*, in: Ulrike Davy et al. (eds.), *Nationalsozialismus und Recht. Rechtssetzung und Rechtswissenschaft in Österreich unter der Herrschaft des Nationalsozialismus* (Vienna 1990), pp. 191–199.

[199] DrB, Nr. 5460-2000, meeting of the working committee of the administrative council of the Länderbank, Oct. 4, 1938.

resignation, he was to explain his position and at the same time "express the willingness of the Länderbank to gladly place its good services at the disposal of the Aryanizations." Indeed, the Länderbank was willing to sell its shares of the Kontrollbank, presumably for the purpose of increasing the Kontrollbank's capital.

As it turned out, Mann stayed on the Kontrollbank supervisory board, perhaps because Rasche, who worked very closely with Kehrl, prevailed upon him to intervene on Mann's behalf. Nevertheless, Globočnik, who was obviously more interested in the well-being of his Party cronies than in sound business management, clearly intended to turn Section C into a personal political instrument and was arguing that Leitich should be removed from his director position and, as Bürckel informed Fischböck, "be replaced by a Party comrade who has the full confidence of the Party." Bürckel, who was well aware that Fischböck had a very high opinion of Leitich's abilities, assured Fischböck that he would not ask Leitich to step down, but at the same time proposed that his own protégé, Josef von Paić, be transferred from the Länderbank to the Creditanstalt, made a director, and, appropriately titled, be put on leave to serve as a codirector with Leitich at the Kontrollbank. Bürckel suggested that Schumetz then be transferred to the Länderbank in place of von Paić, although as noted earlier, he was to end up at the Zentralsparkasse.[200] Underlying these Byzantine maneuvers, as Director Abs of the Deutsche Bank discovered, was a struggle between Fischböck and Bürckel that arose because Fischböck and Leitich had both agreed that "aside from the political qualities of the person taking over non-Aryan enterprises, he must also demonstrate real and professional qualifications. This view was placed too much at the forefront by Dr. Leitich, so that there was considerable outrage in some circles. Bürckel then demanded the dismissal of Dr. Leitich, but finally declared himself agreeable to his retention as a managing director of

the Kontrollbank provided that he be assigned a second manager."[201]

Abs noted that those who knew von Paić thought him at once industrious and of fine character, but obviously these qualities – the second apparently quite compatible with Aryanization in these circles – were not the key issue. Rather, the odd mixture of Party politics and cronyism was the driving force in this matter. Bürckel was anxious to place von Paić in a position where he could subsequently become a director at the Creditanstalt, but the proposition was also viewed by the Creditanstalt leaders as a plot to undermine Joham's position. Bürckel's scheme also ran afoul of the terrible personal relations between von Paić and Director Rudolf Pfeiffer of the Creditanstalt, who would never accept von Paić as a colleague even if von Paić were to be put on leave immediately. In the end, Bürckel and Fischböck came to the "Solomonic" decision of transferring von Paić directly from the Länderbank to the Kontrollbank, promising him Pfeiffer's position on the Creditanstalt managing board in a year or two moving forward with the business of Aryanization on the basis of a compromise between the Bürckel-Globocnik position of paying greater attention to political considerations and the Fischböck-Leitich emphasis on competence. In the end, Leitich did not stay on very long, resigning in mid-June 1939 to assume the apparently more appealing position of general director of the Wienerberger Ziegelwerke AG.

If the banks found themselves caught in the middle of these conflicts, which were in part also conflicts about who was to sit on their managing boards, and obviously tended to favor the choice of competent persons to take over Jewish firms, they nevertheless had no compunction whatsoever about Aryanization per se and were happy to support and optimize the Aryanization program. This was also made evident by their participation in the Wiener Giro- und Cassen-Verein (WGCV),

---

[200] ÖStA/AdR, Bürckel-Materie, 2160/00, Vol. II, Box 73, Bürckel to Fischböck, Oct. 29, 1938.

[201] DB, B 51, minutes of a discussion with Olscher, Neubaur, and Heller on Saturday, Nov. 5, 1938, dated Nov. 7, 1938.

which was assigned the task of Aryanizing the private banking sector just as the Kontrollbank pursued the same goal in the industrial sector. Founded in 1872, the bank originally handled clearing business, freight fees, and the finances of the railways. It lost these functions with the German takeover of Austria, but was provided a substitute source of income in fees for its services as the trustee and administrator of banks owned by Jews. Like the Kontrollbank, the WGCV underwent a total change of supervisory board and management personnel, but the Mercurbank/Länderbank supervisory board and management board were even more prominently represented on the WGCV supervisory board than the Creditanstalt, having Robert Hammer as its president and Alois Schindler as one of its vice presidents, along with Alfred Hohenlohe-Schillingfürst and Leonard Wolzt as members. Wolzt later replaced Schindler as vice-president.

Unfortunately, the records of this bank, which acted as trustee for 60 percent to 70 percent of the Jewish banks that were either liquidated or transferred into Aryan hands, no longer exist. They were confiscated by the U.S. authorities, but all trace of them was lost in 1948, so that an account of the specific role of the Länderbank in this connection is impossible to reconstruct. Nevertheless, Peter Melichar's investigation of bank Aryanizations in Austria provides interesting illustrations of Länderbank engagement. The Länderbank had a trustee account of $13,500 for private banker Samuel Lemberger, whose house bank had been liquidated by the WGCV. The WGCV had less luck with the accounts of banker Georg Anninger, who had placed his firm's accounts in Switzerland, where they were protected from the predatory claims of the WGCV by Swiss courts. Anninger's assets were seized by the Gestapo, however, and placed in a blocked Länderbank account. Similarly, the Länderbank held an account in the amount of 25,346 RM, which constituted the largest amount left over from the liquidation of the banking firm of Walter Friedländer, just as it held what was left of the assets of the Grünwald family after the bank bearing their name was liquidated by the WGCV. Richard

Frankenbusch of the Bankhaus Fa. Kanitz managed to sell this bank to Aryan purchasers in what was apparently a relatively fair arrangement under the circumstances, but the 48,557 RM he received was placed in a blocked account at the Länderbank after he sought safety in the United States, a happier fate than that of the Grünwalds or another banker with a blocked account at the Länderbank, Moriz Lebowitsch, who was deported and murdered. The Länderbank was more actively involved in the affairs of another private Jewish-owned bank, Josef Stein & Co., whose owner of the same name managed to flee to the United States. The WGCV liquidated the bank, but the Länderbank was its chief creditor and, despite the fact that Stein continued to pay nearly all his bank's debts from abroad, the Länderbank remained in possession of the securities deposited in the Länderbank and also held a mortgage on the bank building. It is worth noting that the WGCV received an honorarium of more than 13,000 RM for its "services" and collected large fees in every case it could.[202]

The Länderbank also played a particularly significant role as the place of deposit for funds connected with the emigration of Jews and, subsequently, their deportation and murder. This was because it kept accounts for the Central Agency for Jewish Emigration, which had been established by a Bürckel decree of August 20, 1938, for the purpose of centralizing and accelerating Jewish emigration. It was placed under the de facto leadership of the head of the office for Jewish affairs of the Security Service, Adolf Eichmann, who controlled and used the Jewish community organization for these purposes. The object was obviously to drive Jews out of Austria but also to make them pay for their expulsion and despoil them in the process. The centralization of Jewish accounts ostensibly intended for emigration, which were then placed in an account at the Länderbank, was a significant instrument in this process. The most important of these accounts was no less than 200 pages long. It bore the number 29.803 and the title Special Account for Jewish

---

[202] Melichar, *Neuordnung*, pp. 201–202, 281–282, 287, 309–315, 342–345, 411–412.

Resettlement, and was at Branch 29, Wien IV, Wiedner Hauptstraße 12. This account was composed of two blocked accounts, an "Ordinary Account" and a "Special Jewish Resettlement Account." Exactly why funds were deposited in one of these accounts rather than the other is not entirely clear, although it appears that confiscated bank accounts went into the "special account." Whatever the case, they were repositories for funds taken from Jews or from the sale of Jewish assets. The Länderbank was also used for the transfer of funds from abroad to aid Jews in leaving Germany, and it had a dollar account in the name of the Jewish community for this purpose and another one holding contributions from Jewish agencies abroad for distributions and credits to emigrating Jews. The use of these funds required the permission of Eichmann's office and other government authorities, but they were initially thought of as a useful means to speed up the emigration process by providing monies before Jewish assets could be sold off. Similar purposes were served by another account established in 1938, the "Credit Account for Small Enterprise and Trade – Jewish Community, Vienna." This became a repository for liquidated Jewish businesses, allegedly intended to fund emigration, but often exploited to collect monies for the state in connection with the aftermath of the November pogrom. The number of accounts did not end here, however, because the Länderbank also held the funds derived from the sale of the properties of the Jewish community in Vienna and from the sale of securities, all of which were supposed to be used for the care of the Jews who remained. Because the distribution of these funds was under the control of Eichmann's office, the community found itself constantly wanting for desperately needed resources. For reasons not explicitly stated in the sources seen thus far, the Länderbank was the bank of choice for the holding of these funds, but its record of collaboration with the regime, as that of the Dresdner Bank, may be an important part of the explanation of why this was the case. Needless to say, the bank itself was not responsible for the decisions connected with the disposition of the funds involved,

which, as will be shown in connection with wartime developments, were closely related to the Holocaust. At the same time, those involved in handling these accounts for the bank certainly knew from whence the money came and where it subsequently went, as is patently evident from the hundreds of surviving items of correspondence between the offices of the community and the Länderbank in which the former requested the latter to transfer foreign currency to various shipping lines and other agencies involved in the emigration of Jews in return for the transfer of the Reichsmark they had paid for the foreign exchange into the community's account "D" at the Länderbank.[203]

Furthermore, the Länderbank was not entirely a spectator. It was the owner of the "Eigenhaus Betriebs-GmbH," which managed and sold the Jewish real estate that was used to help fund the emigration project. Although the Länderbank was willing to handle the aforementioned accounts and deal with Jewish real estate, it is significant to note that it turned down an offer to handle the direct business of acting as the go-between in the Gildemeester plan and preferred to leave this business to the rather obscure banking house of Krentschker & Co. The Länderbank apparently feared that Jewish émigrés, once leaving the Reich, would declare that they had signed the requisite document transferring their assets under duress and take the bank to court in countries where legal concepts differed from those of the Third Reich. In short, it was one thing to have the monies involved in the emigration project

[203] The discussion here is based on Gabriele Anderl/Dirk Rupnow, *Die Zentralstelle für jüdische Auswanderung als Beraubungsinstitution. Nationalsozialistische Institutionen des Vermögensentzuges* 1. Veröffentlichungen der Österreichischen Historikerkommission, vol. 20/1 (Vienna, Munich 2004), pp. 20–23, 190–194, 314–320. For the correspondence, see Central Archives for the History of the Jewish People (Yad Vashem), File No. AW 2581. Also of great relevance are the scattered references to the Länderbank in the papers of the head of the community, Joseph Loewenherz, in the Joseph Loewenherz Collection, AR 25055, Box 1, Folders 1.1–1.4, Leo Baeck Institute at the Center for Jewish History, New York.

flow through the bank as "normal" accounts but quite another to act as the actual liquidator of these assets. Whether anyone felt pangs of conscience at the Länderbank, either before or after the funds were transferred to finance the deportation of Jews, is impossible to say, but the chief consideration appeared to be the avoidance of foreign lawsuits and the loss of reputation abroad.[204]

Furthermore, despite the absence of a full archive for both the Länderbank and the Kontrollbank, there is substantial evidence of Länderbank engagement in the Aryanization of Jewish enterprises directly and indirectly in connection with the Kontrollbank. It should now be obvious that however aware they might have been of the dubious character of some of the purchasers of Jewish enterprises, the Dresdner Bank and the Mercurbank, and subsequently the Länderbank, were eager to provide credits and gain customers whenever doing so seemed promising. The point is an important one because wrong questions or assumptions about the process necessarily produce misleading answers. In late 1945, for example, Hans Pilder was interrogated about these matters and was apparently asked if the regime put pressure on the Dresdner Bank and the Länderbank with respect to Aryanization. He replied in the negative and pointed out that the Länderbank tended to view the Aryanizers applying for loans very skeptically because of their lack of experience and insufficient capital. Pilder claimed that the bank gave very few credits because of the risk involved and then only when it could be justified on business grounds. Indeed, the only case he seemed to remember was the Zellwollfabrik Lenzing, and this firm had only received credits after it had already been sold by its former owner, Bunzl & Biach, a large and highly successful international enterprise producer of paper and textiles that had bought Lenzing in 1937 − actually, it had been bought from the Creditanstalt in 1932 − and then sold it in May 1938 through its holding company in Zug to the Thüringische Zellwolle AG. Pilder stressed the fact that credits had not been provided for

the Aryanization itself, that no credits had been given to the purchaser, and that the credits given to Lenzing, which were paid back very slowly or not at all, were provided because the new ownership wanted to expand and was the work of a consortium headed by the Länderbank.[205]

This was, to say the least, a rather limited and misleading explanation of what had gone on. There certainly were instances in which the government put pressure on the banks to grant credits, but the relationship between the regime and the banks was usually not that primitive, however primitive some of the individuals involved. The reality was that Aryanization was a massive transfer of assets, a large-scale process in which the banks were inevitably embedded because their services were essential. The alternative for the banks was to miss out on a great deal of business. The conditions for business opportunity were set by the regime policy, and the banks were not doing business on Mars. Certainly some bankers were more enthusiastic than others, and Pilder was probably not very enthusiastic, which does not mean that he and others did not take advantage of the situation. As has been shown already, the Mercurbank had provided credits to assist the Aryanization of the Hirtenberger Patronen- und Waffenfabrik and the Aryanizations conducted by the Hermann Göring-Werke, and such credits had the function of greasing the wheels for future business. Furthermore, it was and is customary for banks to spread risk by forming consortia in the granting of large credits. Finally, as will be shown shortly, there were cases where the bank refused to become involved in granting Aryanization credits for very good commercial reasons; but there was also a very good commercial reason for giving credits in numerous instances, namely, that a great many of the credits were guaranteed by the Reich under a variety of programs. The banks could often make a Reich guarantee a condition for granting a credit, and in numerous instances they did not have to insist because the guarantee was virtually automatic. In sum,

---

[204] Venus/Wenck, *Aktion Gildemeester*, p. 131.

[205] NARA, RG 260, German External Assets Branch, 390/53/07/03, Box 20, File 34A, Interrogation of Pilder, Dec. 27, 1945.

Aryanization created business opportunities and conditions that simply had to be taken into account in doing business under the National Socialist regime.

The Papierfabrik Lenzing AG mentioned by Pilder is a case in point. As noted earlier, it belonged to the Creditanstalt until 1932, when it was sold to the huge Bunzl & Biach paper trust, which planned to modernize the plant and add a cellulose plant to it so as to make it profitable. Bunzl & Biach was a Jewish firm that founded a holding company of the same name in Zug in 1936 and placed the Lenzing shares there in 1937. This did not save the firm from Aryanization. Lenzing itself was sold only after what might be described as a "semi-wild Aryanization" had taken place. Initially, Lenzing apparently was simply taken over by the Thüringische Zellwolle AG, Schwarza a.d. Saale, which then proceeded to introduce a new technical process for cellulose production without asking the real owners. The Aryanization was the work of the same Thuringian National Socialists who had "created" the Gustloff-Stiftung and transferred the Hirtenberger Patronen- und Waffenfabrik to the Gustloff-Stiftung, namely Otto Eberhardt from Keppler's office and Walther Schieber, who was chairman of the management board and plant leader of the Thüringische Zellwolle AG.[206] In May 1938, Eberhardt announced that Bunzl & Biach was prepared to sell Lenzing to Thüringische Zellwolle. Capitalized at 5 million Schilling, Bunzl & Biach asked for market value, while Eberhardt offered 80 percent but then gave only 60 percent because Bunzl was paid 3,099,520 in Schilling for 4,843,000 Schilling worth of shares, which amounted to 2,066,500 RM, minus an "Aryanization fee" of 250,000 RM.[207]

If it proved impossible to simply steal Lenzing without paying anything, it was because there were some other shareholders but, most importantly, because Lenzing owed the Creditanstalt 5 million RM. It was here that first the Mercurbank and then the Dresdner Bank/Länderbank stepped into the breach to assist with financing the Aryanization and the development of the company along the lines desired by Thüringische Zellwolle, which, like the Gustloff-Stiftung, was a government-controlled corporation. It is important to note that the Dresdner Bank was well aware of the previous unprofitability of Lenzing. Its Economic Section had reported in April 1938 that the company had paid no dividends, its financial situation was strained, it had recorded a slight loss in the previous year, and it was not adequately writing off its plant facilities.[208] Nevertheless, Thüringische Zellstoff considered it an important potential producer for the Four Year Plan, and Hans Kehrl took a personal interest in its fortunes. On May 9, just as soon as Director Goetz of the Dresdner Bank learned that Lenzing had been purchased, he asked that preparations be made to provide Thüringische Zellstoff with a credit, although he then asked the next day that they hold back because Eberhardt had reported to Goetz that Thüringische Zellstoff (Schwarza) was in good financial shape.[209]

The same could not be said for Lenzing, however, which had the aforementioned debt to the Creditanstalt and needed money for investment. On May 24, Goetz announced that he was prepared in principle to pursue a credit for Lenzing, provided that certain conditions were met. Three days later, the Dresdner Bank management agreed to discuss a 5 million RM credit, provided that the Reich guarantee 2 million RM and Thüringische Zellstoff guarantee another 1 million RM. Rasche was sent to Vienna to negotiate on the basis of these terms and learned that Lenzing was going to undertake a substantial increase of its capital from

---

[206] Eberhardt died in an automobile accident in 1939, whereupon Schieber assumed his position as Gau economic advisor and received the title State Councilor. In 1942, he was to become the head of the Armaments Delivery Office in the Ministry for Armaments and War Production.

[207] See Österreichische Landesbank, *Der Kampf um Lenzing. Arisierung – Konkurs – Sanierung Vol.I* (Vienna 1953), pp. 3–5 and Felber et al., *Ökonomie der Arisierung*, pt. 2, p. 314.

[208] DrB, Nr. 7836-2000, Economic Office, the Austrian paper and cellulose industry, April 1, 1938.

[209] NARA, T83/135, Dresdner Bank management board meetings, May 9–10, 1938.

1 to 5 or 6 million RM and that Lenzing would also receive between 6 and 8 million RM from the banking consortium set up to aid Austria. Rasche was thus able to report that Kehrl had confirmed the granting of a Reich guarantee that would be built into the economic aid program for Austria and that a further guarantee could be obtained through a mortgage. Here, as in the case of the Hirtenberger firm, the Mercurbank's gain was the Creditanstalt's loss. Once Lenzing was formally in the hands of Thüringische Zellstoff and the debt to the Creditanstalt worked out, Lenzing would use the Mercurbank, later the Länderbank, as its house bank. By June 21, Lenzing had already received a loan under which 2.5 million RM was guaranteed by the Reich and a mortgage. The Creditanstalt was to receive quarterly payments of 250,000 RM beginning on July 1. The Mercurbank was prepared to help Lenzing in every way and thus also agreed that the mortgage did not have to be formerly registered in order to spare Lenzing the high taxes involved. The second half of the credit, which amounted to 2.5 million and was not guaranteed by the Reich, was divided among the Länderbank, which provided 1 million RM, and the central and Munich branches of the Dresdner Bank, which each provided 750,000 RM.[210]

At the same time, preparations were being made for a large increase in Lenzing's capital. In mid-August, Lenzing asked the Länderbank for preliminary financing in the form of an interim credit of 1 million RM. Such a credit had to be approved by the Dresdner Bank, which assented somewhat reluctantly. It had hoped that Director Schieber would give a guarantee in the name of Schwarza, but Schieber had declined to do so. The interim credit was thus made contingent upon its coverage as soon as the capital increase anticipated for September 4 took place. The Dresdner Bank insisted that Schwarza give strong backing to the capital share increase and procure the money needed to cover the interim credit immediately rather than wait until the anticipated

10 million RM Reich-guaranteed credit came through. The Dresdner Bank and, in particular, the Länderbank, had become major direct lenders as well as leading members of the consortium for Lenzinger's loans, which were intended under the Four Year Plan to enable Lenzing to expand to where it could produce 40,000–50,000 tons of highly bleached cellulose for rayon and other synthetic fibers, to have the technical capacity to use beechwood instead of spruce, and to satisfy the raw materials needs of Schwarza, which controlled 96.86 percent of its capital. This did not mean that the Länderbank had any illusions. When asked by the Property Transfer Bureau in July 1938 about the marketability of Lenzing shares, Wolzt bluntly replied that investors could not expect payment of a dividend until 1941 and that only textile companies interested in a secure supply of cellulose might be interested in going so long without monetary profit. Similarly, the Dresdner Bank noted in July 1939 that the plant, which was asking for a revolving credit of 1 million RM, was producing nothing. The construction program was grandiose, however, and the capitalization, which had already been raised from 1 to 12 million RM, was in the process of being increased to 18 million RM. At the same time, Kehrl was promoting, eventually successfully, a merger of the two Lenzing operations, the Lenzinger Zellstoff- und Papier-Fabrik AG with the Zellwolle Lenzing AG.[211]

This was only the beginning of Lenzing's rising costs, which will be taken up again in connection with the Länderbank's wartime activities, but the point to be made here is that there is no evidence whatever for Pilder's assertions in connection with Lenzing. Credits were provided to finance the Aryanization, that is, the

---

[210] Ibid., meetings of May 24 and 27, June 2 and 21, July 6, and Aug. 11, 1938; DrB, 7836-2000, discussion with President Kehrl, June 7, 1938.

[211] NARA, T83/135, meetings of Aug. 18, 1938; DrB. 7836-2000, Consortial Department, Dresdner Bank to Wolzt, Aug. 19, 1938; Busch to Länderbank, Aug. 24, 1938; credit application, Sept. 15, 1938; Dresdner Bank working committee of the management board, Nov. 11, 1938; NARA, T83/120, memorandum of June 15, 1939; working committee, July 21, 1939; credit application, Oct. 12, 1939; NARA, T83/122, working committee, Dec. 13, 1939. See also ÖStA/AdR, MfWuA, VVSt, Handel, Box 287, Nr. 2856, Wolzt to Kraus, Aug. 2, 1938.

payback to the Creditanstalt, and the Dresdner Bank and the Länderbank provided monies of their own not guaranteed by the Reich. That they sought and received Reich guarantees for monies lent for expansion and worked with a consortium is in no way surprising because this constituted normal practice when such large sums were involved. What was not normal were the circumstances surrounding the loans, namely, the Aryanization of Lenzing, the pressure exerted by Kehrl, Eberhardt, and Schieber, and the program for Lenzing dictated by the Four Year Plan. That said, the Länderbank showed no serious hesitation in taking up the "opportunities" provided in this instance by Aryanization, Germanization, and militarization.

Lenzing never came in the purview of the Kontrollbank, and the enterprises handled by that bank were primarily sold off to interested parties without the bank becoming directly involved. An important exception was Lenzing's former owner, Bunzl & Biach. On June 28, 1938, the concern was placed under an administrator. It became the first acquisition of the Kontrollbank, which acquired 76 percent of its shares and 50 percent of each of its holding companies abroad. If control in this case was "shared," it was because the Kontrollbank was anxious to benefit from the foreign exchange the concern earned. The Bunzl brothers were "persuaded" to agree to the arrangement: two of the four had been sent to Dachau, and one of them was subsequently murdered there. Nevertheless, they were also allowed to keep the proceeds of the "sale," and their Reich Flight Tax was to be paid through company earnings. The basic problem for the Kontrollbank was that no one was in a position to buy the entire concern. Finally, in 1942, the shares of what had now been renamed Kontropa were sold to the banks. The Länderbank and the Creditanstalt took 36 percent each; Schoeller & Co. took 18 percent; and E. von Nicolai took 10 percent. The subsequent very complicated engagement of the Länderbank in this Aryanization is thus part of the bank's wartime history.[212]

Nevertheless, the Länderbank was helpful, or tried to be, to the Kontrollbank in other ways. It was represented on the Kontrollbank supervisory board, had contact with Kastner, and was well informed about what the Kontrollbank was placing on the market. It could thus offer its services to potential buyers. An interesting illustration of this is the Welser Papierfabrik GmbH, which had come into the hands of the Kontrollbank. The Dresdner Bank was aware that Peter Reinhold, formerly a finance minister of the Weimar Republic, was interested in acquiring an Austrian paper factory. On September 10, 1938, the bank sent him information about the Welser Papierfabrik along with a draft sales contract that had been offered to other buyers who turned out not to have the means to purchase the company. The Dresdner Bank was careful to point out that the Reich Flight Tax had been miscalculated and was now 300,000 RM instead of 150,000 RM, so that the price would have to be raised. The Dresdner Bank offered to put Reinhold in contact with the Länderbank, which could then arrange for an on-sight inspection of the facilities and examination of the books. In the end, the Welser Papierfabrik was bought by the Elbmühl AG, another firm closely connected to the Länderbank that handled the transaction.[213]

A very important, indeed rather sensational, instance in which the Länderbank extended its "good offices" in a major Aryanization was that of the Österreichische Zuckerfabrik AG, Bruck/Leitha (ÖZAG). Four Jewish family groups, including the Bloch-Bauer and the Otto Pick families, owned about 90 percent of ÖZAG.[214] Karl and Ferdinand Bloch-Bauer ran

[212] Felber et al., *Ökonomie der Arisierung*, pt. II, pp. 311–335.

[213] DrB, Nr. 7836-2000, Dresdner Bank to Reinhold, Sept. 10, 1938; Felber et al., *Ökonomie der Arisierung*, pt. II, p. 282. It is noteworthy that Reinhold managed to acquire another paper company – he had many such interests in Germany – from the Länderbank, namely, the Papierfabrik Obermühl GmbH, ibid., p. 289.

[214] On April 13, 2005, the heirs of Ferdinand Bloch-Bauer and Otto Pick were awarded 26,450,993.36 Swiss francs by the Claims Resolution Tribunal dealing with claims from the victims of NS persecution against the Swiss banks. The lengthy judgment provides an account based on significant documentary

the concern, and they had been strong support- ers of Schuschnigg. This added to the jeopardy into which the Jewish shareholders of ÖZAG were placed by the Anschluss. They thus acted preemptively and sought to prevent a take- over of ÖZAG by forming a syndicate with the Schweizerische Bankgesellschaft in Zurich representing 89 percent of the shares (71,246 of 80,000 shares). Slightly more than 50 per- cent, 40,195 shares, was held in the name of the Swiss bank and for the benefit of the syn- dicate members at the bank in Zurich, and the remaining Jewish-owned shares were held in other locations. Under the terms of the agree- ment, to which the Swiss bank was a party, none of these shares could be sold without the unanimous consent of all the participants in the syndicate. The obvious purpose of this arrange- ment was to place a legal barrier against any attempt by the National Socialists to get hold of the ÖZAG shares, either piecemeal or through a concerted effort, but it was condemned to failure. Karl and Ferdinand Bloch-Bauer fled Austria before the Germans arrived, as did Otto Pick (who was the father-in-law of Ferdinand's nephew Leopold) and other family members. The new rulers in Vienna proceeded to use two frequently methods to gain possession of the assets of prominent and wealthy Jews. One was to make a physical threat to family members unlucky enough to still be in Austria, in this case, Leopold Bloch-Bauer. He was arrested by the SA on March 13 and thrown into jail for nine days. The second method was to initiate

evidence and may be considered the most reliable source for both the events and the sources. See Case No. CV96-4849, Claim Number: 215866/ MC, http://swissbankclaims.org/documents/doc_ 64_ozag.pdf (March 10, 2005). It is more reliable in both its factual basis and its judgments than the account of Berthold Unfried, in: Felber et al., *Eigentumsänderungen*, pp. 816–831. The discussion here follows the account of the Tribunal but is supplemented by materials from the VVSt in the Austrian State Archives. It is important to bear in mind that the claims of this family are ongo- ing and there is no discussion here of the tremen- dous art theft to which they were subjected. See Sophie Lilly, *Was einmal war. Handbuch der enteigneten Kunstsammlungen Wiens* (Vienna 2003), pp. 821–836.

criminal proceedings on charges of tax evasion and fraud. The authorities invaded the ÖZAG offices within days of the Anschluss, seized the company books, and employed someone to examine them with the object of prosecuting Ferdinand Bloch-Bauer on tax charges. The man chosen for this job was Guido Walcher, a National Socialist job-seeker. Although he hardly had the qualifications to undertake such a difficult audit, Walcher managed by late April to produce a report accusing Bloch-Bauer of tax evasion, fraud, and embezzlement. This led to a criminal indictment on April 27, but no specific sum was mentioned in connection with the charges.

What is significant for the discussion here is that the Mercurbank, and subsequently the Länderbank Wien, worked hand in hand in a very brutal and sinister manner with the authorities in seeking to strip the Bloch-Bauer family, the Pick family, and the other Jewish shareholders in ÖZAG of their assets. Leopold Bloch-Bauer was liberated from his jail cell by officials of the Mercurbank, who then pro- ceeded to conduct numerous "discussions" with him against the background of the threat of renewed arrest and possible deportation to a concentration camp. If Leopold Bloch-Bauer managed to depart for Switzerland on May 31, 1938, it was only because of the heavy price he and Otto Pick paid for his release. In mid-May, Otto Pick received a surprise visit in Zurich from Mercurbank syndic and National Socialist lawyer Hans Mann, who demanded that Pick appoint the Mercurbank as trustee of all his family's assets and of Leopold Bloch-Bauer's assets in Austria; in return, the bank would help to procure Leopold's exit permit and, in the process, guarantee the Reich Flight Tax, obvi- ously from those assets. Pick initially resisted, but when Mann promised on his word of honor that Leopold Bloch-Bauer would be allowed to leave Austria, Pick signed the requisite docu- ments. At the same time, Director Wolzt took advantage of Leopold Bloch-Bauer's continued presence in Vienna to pressure him into promis- ing that, when released, he would help secure a large block of ÖZAG shares for purposes of the Aryanization of ÖZAG with the participation of the bank. After arriving in Switzerland, Leopold Bloch-Bauer seemed to have kept his word; at least Otto Pick offered the Länderbank 10,000 shares at a price of 160 RM. That price, especially in view of the price-depressing activities of the tax authorities, was apparently unacceptable, however, and the offer lapsed. Although this offer was made through the Schweizerische Bankgesellschaft, there is no evidence that this was approved by all members of the syndicate and suggests that the bank was deserting the agreement at a very early date.[215]

The Aryanization of ÖZAG stagnated through the summer, but the appearance of potential purchasers on the scene gave the effort new impetus. Two prospective purchasers contended for the company: Clemens Auer, who owned a large milling concern in Cologne, and the Hamburg firm Martin Brinkmann AG, which produced and sold cigarettes. Auer was a Party man with excellent connections. He originally had his eye on another Austrian company, but it ended up being liquidated. He then surveyed the opportunities in the sugar business. Because the Reich Food Estate was interested in the Hohenauer Zuckerfabrik, he set his sights on ÖZAG. On the advice of General Karl Bodenschatz of Göring's office, he paid a visit to Fischböck when Fischböck was in Berlin on November 23. Apparently, Fischböck was encouraging and advised Auer to negotiate with the Finance Office in Berlin for the 21,000 shares of ÖZAG in its possession.[216] These shares had been the property of the Löw family, another Jewish family charged with tax evasion whose assets had been seized in June. The shares were later turned over to the Property Transfer Bureau and sold to Auer. For the moment, however, Auer and Brinkmann were nothing

more than contenders for ÖZAG, which still awaited Aryanization.

The decisive step in this direction was taken on December 3, 1938, when the Property Transfer Bureau wrote to the Länderbank authorizing the bank to buy up all available shares at home and abroad because the tax evasion charges hovering over the company provided a propitious opportunity to acquire the shares on favorable terms. This was to be done as quickly as possible. Auer and Brinkmann were to be invited to make binding offers for the shares. Because the shares had been owned by Jews, the proceeds of the sale were to be placed in a blocked account at the Property Transfer Bureau. In short, the Länderbank was authorized to act as the agent of the Property Transfer Bureau in the purchase of the shares and their sale for the accounts of designated Aryanizers. As was made manifest in letters to Auer and Brinkmann on December 5, the Property Transfer Bureau was obviously trying to take advantage of the uncertainty created by the tax evasion charges to persuade those holding the shares to sell for a lower price, but they were not willing to wait to find out how the case turned out and were most interested in the "Aryanization and repatriation of the enterprise...without consideration, as to whether and which rates one succeeds in securing a majority of the shares."[217] Brinkmann found the situation too risky and refused to make a binding offer. Auer was willing to "repatriate" the shares at 70–75 RM apiece.

The Schweizerische Bankgesellschaft duly informed the members of the syndicate about the offer transmitted by the Länderbank on December 17, but it did not receive the requisite unanimous approval. A letter of December 22 informed the syndicate members that Director Pilgrim of the Länderbank had indicated that ÖZAG might be nationalized, in which case even the current offer could not be expected to hold. Some members of the syndicate apparently were willing to consider it if a better price was offered; others considered the price nonnegotiable. In the view of the Swiss bank, this situation and the fact that some shareholders could not be

[215] See the affidavits of L.L.G. Bentley (Leopold Bloch-Bauer) of May 31, 1946 and Otto Pick of Dec. 13, 1946 from the reports of Albert Perry, NARA, RG 260-M1928-USACA, German External Assets, Reports on Businesses, Exhibits 14–15. I am grateful to Helen Junz for informing me about these and other relevant documents.

[216] ÖStA/AdR, MfWuA, VVSt, Statistik 7881II (Box 717), Clemens Auer to Rafelsberger, March 14, 1939.

[217] The letters are quoted in ibid.

located made the continuation of the syndicate impossible. The bank proposed that, if no objections were voiced by January 15, 1939, the syndicate be dissolved. In fact, the Schweizerische Bankgesellschaft already sold shares well before that date; on December 30, the Länderbank informed Auer that it had procured 26,480 shares at 75 RM per share as well as an additional 10,567 shares. Finally, the Länderbank had a firm offer of another 3,000 shares from the holdings of the tax authorities, and this would give Auer a majority stake of 40,347 shares. By October 1939, Auer had acquired 78,968 or 98.7 percent of the shares, for 6.5 million RM. The average price per share was 82 RM. Prior to the Anschluss, they had been selling for 300 to 350 Schilling per share. Some of the shares had been acquired through further sales by the Schweizerische Bankgesellschaft, others through seizure and sale, as in the case of the Löw holdings. The shares were certainly worth a great deal more, especially because the Property Transfer Bureau, as demonstrated in the correspondence cited earlier, showed no interest in the outcome of the tax case. After ÖZAG was Aryanized, the case was dropped in November 1939.[218] In the last analysis, the outcome was a result of the perfidy of the Schweizerische Bankgesellschaft and the "services" provided by the Länderbank. It is a measure of Wolzt's character that he could testify at the restitution trial against Auer in May 1947 that the negotiations for the sale of the shares in Switzerland were carried out "in complete freedom and completely free of any kind of pressure." Indeed, he grotesquely concluded that "the Bloch-Bauer group still came out much better than other non-Aryan enterprises, which could not take any money abroad at all."[219]

It is worth noting that neither the Länderbank's success in buying the shares nor

Auer's venturesomeness was universally appreciated. When the tax bill turned out to be much lower than anticipated, Brinkmann tried, unsuccessfully, to reenter the scene as a purchaser. Auer, despite his connections to Göring and other powerful Party officials, was viewed with suspicion as a "capitalist." The Reich Food Estate forced him to sell off two of the sugar companies in which it was interested, and the Länderbank, whose involvement in the sugar business was viewed as inappropriate in some circles, was required to promise to refrain from selling any of Auer's sugar production. Such conditions were among the uncertainties of participating in a gigantic robbery, National Socialist style. What is more shocking is how long it took for the scale of the crime to be fully recognized and for appropriate compensation to be made.[220]

In the case of the Aryanization of the Altmannsdorfer Lederfabrik Schnabel & Comp. in Vienna-Altmannsdorf, the Länderbank and the Dresdner Bank were involved in both finding suitable purchasers and offering them credits for the transaction. The Schnabel Aryanization, the bizarre details of which have been told elsewhere,[221] was initially characterized by a tug-of-war between the Kontrollbank, which wanted a purchaser who was competent and financially solid as well as politically acceptable, and Party ideologues who were eager to prevent capitalistic "concern building" and to reward Party loyalists. The firm had been doing a good export business, and the Länderbank wanted to gain it as a customer. In April 1939, it offered Konrad Vetter, a potential purchaser who had management experience in the leather business and who had the financial backing of the Graz firm of Robert Bieber, a credit of 480,000 RM in the expectation that the company would thereafter do all its banking business with the Länderbank.[222] There is no evidence that the Länderbank had much interest in the

---

[218] Claims Resolution Tribunal, Case nr. CV 96–4849, claims report nr. 215866/MC, pp. 18–20.

[219] Testimony of witness Wolzt in Trial of Auer, Riegel, Wolzt u. Konsorten, Landesgericht für Strafsachen Wien, May 21, 1947. For an account of the history, see Weber et al., *Eigentumsänderungen*, pt. II, pp. 647–659 and Felber et al., *Ökonomie der Arisierung*.

[220] See the correspondence in ÖStA/AdR, MfWuA, VVSt, Statistik, Box 717, Nr. 7881, Vol. II–IV.

[221] See Felber et al., *Ökonomie der Arisierung*, pt. 2, pp. 216–229.

[222] ÖStA/AdR, MfWuA, VVSt, Statistik, Box 727, Nr. 7927, Vol. II., Länderbank Wien to Konrad Vetter, April 28, 1939.

ideological and Party squabbles connected with the sale, but the Länderbank, along with the Creditanstalt and the Anglo-Austrian Bank, did have an interest in the company being sold to a wealthy purchaser like Bieber. Victor and Richard Schnabel had owed the banks 370,000 RM since 1926, and the banks hoped that the Kontrollbank would pay back the debt from the proceeds of the sale.[223] Bieber, however, proved unacceptable as a suspected "concern builder" with purely "capitalist" interests in the company. The Kontrollbank then rejected German candidates because they were not from the Ostmark and did not have sufficient capital. Party agencies got into the act and recommended a Party man named Richard Frey, who apparently had sufficient capita. Frey teamed up with Vetter. Rafelsberger and local Party officials favored this solution, but the Kontrollbank did not. It succeeded in scotching the arrangement through the intervention of the Leather Control Board and came up with new candidates, Friedrich Treusch, a German, and Gustav Grunzy, an "Ostmarker," both with experience in the leather business and excellent political credentials. The Dresdner Bank, in particular its Mannheim and Frankfurt branches, had become involved in trying to find purchasers and had recommended Treusch and Grunzy, without ruling out other candidates who might have sufficient funds. In January, the Frankfurt branch guaranteed Grunzy that the Länderbank Wien would provide a credit to cover the balance required for the purchase. The Treusch-Grunzy combination fell through in the end, however, because they did not have enough capital. Ultimately, the Dresdner Bank in Berlin proposed that an offer be made to a Baltic businessman, Mark Melnikov, who had been forced to give up his leather firm in Riga and had been promised a comparable business in the Reich as part of his "resettlement."[224]

The German Resettlement Trust, which had been set up by Himmler as part of the Reich Commissariat for the Strengthening of Germandom, had been urging that Melnikov and his mother, Herta, receive adequate compensation for what they had lost in Riga, and the Reich Economics Ministry thought that Schnabel & Co. would be satisfactory.[225] The Melnikows received a "resettlement credit" of 750,000 RM in February 1941, which was arranged between the German Resettlement Trust and the Dresdner Bank and paid through the Länderbank Wien. For some unexplained reason, the amount had been increased to 835,000 RM by May 1941.[226] Thus ended a long and complicated Aryanization. This case demonstrates the complex ways the Dresdner Bank and Länderbank served the goals of the Kontrollbank.

The Länderbank provided other credits in connection with Kontrollbank Aryanizations. A good illustration of how the Kontrollbank and Länderbank worked hand in hand for the provision of such credits is the 250,000 RM credit given to Silvio Frassine, Ludwig Slupetzky, and Rudolf Valenta in connection with the Aryanization of the Viennese Firma Brüder Haber, Haus für Wohnkultur und Bekleidung.[227] This transaction is also a remarkable illustration of the complexities, both economic and political, involved in such "business." The Kontrollbank sold the firm to the three buyers for 575,000 RM in April 1939. The buyers were to pay 350,000 RM within four weeks, and then to pay the Habers 100,000 RM within a year and another 125,000 RM in ten installments of 12,500 RM in the course of a year along with 4.5 percent

[225] Ibid., Vol. V, Deutsche Umsiedlungs-Treuhand-Gesellschaft to Kontrollbank, Sept. 27 and Oct. 23, 1940 and Dresdner Bank to Kontrollbank, June 17 and July 13, 1940.
[226] Ibid., Vol. IV, Länderbank Wien to Kontrollbank, Feb. 26, 1941; and ibid., Box 1571, Nr. 365, Melnikow to Länderbank, May 30, 1941.
[227] See Felber et al., Ökonomie der Arisierung, pt. 1, p. 113. For the discussion and quotations that follow, see BAB, R2/15547, Bl. 160–168, the 24th credit committee meeting, April 19, 1939.

[223] Ibid., Vol. V, Creditanstalt to Leitich, Jan. 5, 1939; Länderbank to Kontrollbank, Dec. 22 and 30, 1938.
[224] Ibid., Vol. VII, Dresdner Bank Mannheim to Kontrollbank, Dec. 13, 1939; Dresdner Bank Frankfurt to Kontrollbank, Jan. 6, 1940; Dresdner Bank Berlin to Kontrollbank, May 18, 1940.

interest on both amounts. Principal and interest were to be deposited in a noninterest-bearing account at the Kontrollbank that was to be used for the payment of all taxes and fees owed by the Habers. One can only try to imagine the anguish under which the Habers "negotiated" these terms with the Kontrollbank. The chief concern of the banks, however, was to make the purchase possible, make sure that the purchasers were acceptable, and ensure that the investment would be a good one. Slupetzky was required to pay 100,000 RM from his own means, which he did by mortgaging an apartment house he owned and taking a loan from a relative. The three purchasers applied for an 85 percent Reich-guaranteed loan of 250,000 RM to cover the rest of the 350,000 RM. The Kontrollbank had carefully investigated the firm's business and finances. Brüder Haber did a large business in selling home furnishings and clothing on installment. It had been run in a very orderly manner and was found reasonably profitable. Certain unresolved problems remained, however. The firm employed 5 managers and 114 staff. All the managers were Jewish, as were 80 of the staff members. All the Jews had to be fired and replaced by Aryans. That had been easy enough, but a more fundamental issue was the firm's heavy reliance on installment sales.

The Chamber of Commerce, whose advice on both the persons and the enterprise was always asked in such cases, took umbrage at the installment business done by the firm and pointed out that "the crisis-ridden and unhealthy development of purchasing favorably influenced the existence and expansion of such business at that time. Today the economy finds itself improving, unemployment is receding, purchasing power is beginning to increase. The promotion of installment business does not conform to National Socialist economic thought. The applicants are also aware of this and plan to change over from Jewish business methods, an intention that seems welcome." The prospective new owners also wanted to expand the enterprise, and this raised complaints from two groups in the Commercial League, one representing retailers of home furnishings and music, the other representing retailers of textiles, clothing, and leather. They argued that the planned expansion would result in a "department-store-like-enterprise" and hurt retailers. Mistakenly thinking that the applicants were still asking for a 500,000 RM credit, as they had originally, the retailer organizations also charged that the credit asked for was exorbitant. Obviously, however, they would have preferred to see the entire enterprise shut down in the name of retailer interests.

In the last analysis, however, both ideological and business considerations appeared to favor the granting of the credit. The three applicants left nothing to be desired politically. Slupetzky had joined the NSDAP in 1933 and was very active in Party activities both before and after the Anschluss. Valenta, who had been jailed for his political work and had served at the Party headquarters in Munich before coming home, had been awarded the Party Gold Badge. Frassine had been in the Party since 1934 and had an activist record during the "time of struggle." Slupetzky and Valenta also had other assets and business interests, and they had worked out a good division of labor. Frassine and Slupetzky obviously were intended for the key managerial roles, and Valenta, who had few assets, was to take over advertising and window displays. The Länderbank was thus ready to give the full loan, although it did attach some conditions in addition to the expectation that 85 percent of the loan be Reich guaranteed. It insisted that the 100,000 RM owed by Slupetzky be paid within two days of the credit coming through. It also asked that the new owners secure the right to purchase the building in which the firm was housed, which it was renting from a holding company in Zurich that belonged to the Habers.

Despite the willingness of the Länderbank to make money for the purchase available and the high marks given to the purchasers, the credit committee decided not to approve the loan at its meeting on April 19 because of the "basic political-economic question as to whether a department-store-like-enterprise which, beyond this, primarily carries on installment business should be promoted under the Reich

Economic Aid program."[228] Indeed, it was inclined to turn down the loan but decided to refer the matter to Berlin, which taking a very different view, pointed out that such enterprises were not automatically excluded from support. In addition the applicants were persons of means and had very favorable political evaluations. The credit committee was informed on June 12 that the RWM approved the granting of the loan and the Reich Finance Ministry approved the amount. It also learned that the Creditanstalt had given the applicants an entirely separate loan of 100,000 RM over and beyond the Reich-guaranteed loan. In any case, the 250,000 RM guaranteed credit was approved at the credit committee meeting of June 19, 1939. This demonstrated that lower-middle-class Party ideology had its limits. In fact, the firm of Frassine, Valenta & Co. proved to be an excellent credit risk. In March 1940, it offered to pay back 150,000 RM of the loan immediately and the remainder in monthly payments of 10,000 RM beginning October 1. In return, the RWM agreed to drop the two "ideological" provisions in the credit contract, namely, that Frassine, Valenta & Co. limit itself to doing business in textiles and home furnishings and that it stop offering installment plans. Jewish business practices had thus reappeared under acceptable auspices![229]

Manifestly, the Länderbank knew full well the conditions under which companies with which it was directly involved were sold by the Kontrollbank. This certainly was the case with the acquisition of the Jewish-owned Leopold Wolf & Co., the leading coffin manufacturing firm in Austria, by Fritz Allmann. He applied for a 70,000 RM Reich-guaranteed credit from the Länderbank as well as a 20,000 RM interest-free and direct loan from the government. Allmann had much to recommend him under the circumstances. He had been a member of the Party since 1931 and a member of

the Austrian Legion, a militantly pro-German Free Corps organization. He had been forced to flee Austria because of his activities in a group that devoted itself to terrorist activities, and that had led to the abandonment of his carpentry business. Although entitled to restitution, he decided to forgo that claim and asked instead for an interest-free loan from the Reich and a Reich-guaranteed credit from the Länderbank. The Kontrollbank had sold Leopold Wolf & Co. to Allmann for 96,000 RM; the conditions were that he pay 56,000 RM to cover the former owner's Reich Flight Tax, 30,000 RM immediately and the rest in installments. He was also to pay 22,000 RM owed by the previous owner for the Jewish Wealth Tax. This left 15,000 RM to be paid to the Kontrollbank that was used to pay off the "Aryanization fee" in installments over five years. Allmann asked for 50,000 RM to pay for the Reich Flight and Jewish Wealth taxes required immediately by the Revenue Office and 40,000 RM for investment in the company. He expected the 10,000 RM "Aryanization fee" to be payable in installments over a longer period; that was indeed possible, and he was made five payments of 2,000 RM apiece between October 1938 and November 1942. In granting the credit, which was warmly supported by the authorities, the Länderbank noted that the firm was doing well. The only condition the bank imposed was that if Allmann received his interest-free loan from the Reich, his loan from the Länderbank was to be given priority in repayment. Yet for all his merits, Allmann did not receive all he had asked for. At its meeting on June 6, 1939, the committee decided to give Allmann a 40,000 RM guaranteed credit from the Länderbank, not an interest-free loan. Moreover, the 40,000 RM was to be used exclusively for investment and covering operating costs. A further condition was that the 50,000 RM to be paid for the Reich Flight and Jewish Wealth taxes be suspended for the life of the credit, that is, for one to three years. This apparently was not acceptable to the authorities, and Allmann received an additional 25,000 RM credit on July 5 for partial payment of the Reich Flight Tax and the Jewish Wealth Tax. If the credit committee hoped that

---

[228] BAB, R2/15550, Bl. 97–99, 28th credit committee meeting, June 19, 1939 and protocol of decisions, April 19, 1939.

[229] Ibid., Bl. 251; see also BAB R2/15583, Bl. 13–15, RWM file note of June 3, 1939 and letter to the Vienna office, March 20, 1940.

the authorities would suspend the balance, however, it was wrong. Allmann returned with the news that a suspension was not possible, that between 40 percent and 50 percent had to be paid right away, and that the rest could be paid in monthly payments of 1,000–1,500 RM. Allmann, who had so far received credits amounting to 65,000 RM, now argued that he needed the full amount originally asked, that is, 70,000 RM in a guaranteed credit and a 20,000 RM interest-free loan. He then modified but did not reduce his request by asking 15,000 RM from the Länderbank as a Reich-guaranteed credit and a 10,000 RM interest-free loan from the Reich. The Länderbank responded by offering to give another 10,000 RM credit, bringing its total to 75,000 RM, if the Reich would grant an interest-free loan of 10,000 RM. If the Länderbank was reluctant, it was because it had undertaken an examination of the firm and found that Allmann had, through poor bookkeeping, overestimated its value and also that he was taking too much salary for himself. At the end of 1939, Allmann announced that he would not take advantage of the Reich-guaranteed loan that had been granted because he was able to raise the money elsewhere. He failed, however, to pay the 100 RM fee for the auditor's report and was still delinquent in February 1942.[230]

The Länderbank worried a great deal about the financial strength and general quality of Aryanizers insofar as its own financial interests were involved. This was certainly the case with the takeover of the Guggenbacher Papierfabrik Adolph Ruhmann by Adolf Sandner, who had the backing of leading National Socialists. He had established himself as a businessman of modest means, but he did have a fiancée of considerable wealth. He was viewed by the Property Transfer Bureau and also by the Kontrollbank, which became involved in the matter, as the person most likely to revive the troubled Guggenbacher firm. The Ruhmann brothers were willing to sell, a disposition undoubtedly of importance in getting them released from the Gestapo and making it possible to flee to Jugoslavia, where they planned to sell paper and even agreed to sell paper produced by their old firm after Sandner took over. The Länderbank, however, was by no means satisfied with having the company turned over to Sandner. It was owed 1.3 million RM by the Guggenbacher Papierfabrik and was disturbed to find that Sandner was quite shy about discussing how this debt was to be paid off. In the bank's view, Sandner did not have the necessary capital, and the Länderbank thus declared itself ready to run the company itself until a suitably wealthy purchaser was found. The Kontrollbank and the authorities in Styria, however, were very anxious to get the company back on its feet because the failure to sell the company would mean its liquidation and unemployment for the workers at its ten plants. Sandner had rich contacts other than his fiancée, however. A Hamburg businessman, Wilhelm Krefter, was prepared to put up the funds in late 1938 and to make the transfer possible on terms involving only token payment for the company but the assumption of its obligations. Sandner, who was involved in a number of Aryanizations, neither fulfilled his obligations nor maintained the company intact. Choosing instead to milk the enterprise for cash, he claimed that he was fulfilling obligations to the Ruhmanns, which he was not. He was able to keep his creditors at bay for a while, but his doings finally landed him in jail after the war. The Länderbank had been willing to take over the company so as to get its debts repaid, but in this case it was probably lucky not to have been the responsible party in this Aryanization.[231]

---

[230] See Felber et al., *Ökonomie der Arisierung*, pt. 1, p. 110, and BAB, R2/15549, Bl. 133–136, 27th credit committee meeting, June 1, 1939; BAB, R2/15552, Bl. 355, credit committee meeting, July 5, 1939; BAB, R2/15555, Bl. 51–62, credit committee meeting, Aug. 29, 1939. See also ÖStA/AdR, MfWuA, VVSt, Statistik, Box 573, Nr. 422. See also ÖStA/AdR, Reichsstatthalter Wien (= RSth Wien), Reichswirtschaftshilfe (= Rwh)Kg 1535, the two warning letters to Allmann from the Deutsche Revisions- und Treuhand-AG of Dec. 12, 1939 and Feb. 6, 1942.

[231] See Felber et al., *Ökonomie der Arisierung*, pt. 2, pp. 412–438. For the role of the Länderbank, see ÖStA/AdR, MfWuA, VVSt, Statistik, Box 718, Nr.

The Länderbank seems to have looked with greater favor on Emmerich Plach, who purchased the Schafwollwarenfabrik Ernst Stein & Co., a mechanized weaving mill, from the Kontrollbank in April 1939 for 126,840 RM. The firm had been very profitable and was unquestionably being sold at a price well below its real value. In contrast to the aforementioned cases where much effort was made to extol the political qualities of the purchasers, nothing was said about Plach's politics. Great emphasis was placed on the fact that he had been managing of the factory for the past six years and was highly regarded as a textiles expert. The Chamber of Commerce was particularly anxious to see the company, which had a good export record, in Aryan hands. The fact that Plach was able to bring money of his own into the purchase and to use his personal assets as security spoke strongly in his favor. In fact, the Länderbank appears to have been so eager to see the company in Plach's hands that it advanced him 60,000 RM against a Reich-guaranteed credit of that amount for which he was applying so that he could pay by the Kontrollbank deadline.[232]

It is doubtful that the bank was similarly enthusiastic about the three Aryanizers of Stadlauer Lederindustrie Wigner & Co. An important producer of leather products, especially for the Austrian army, the company was highly regarded. Disider Wigner sought to sell the company to a competent and fair purchaser and used his indirect connections to Austrian National Socialist circles to try to find someone acceptable. Unfortunately for Wigner, the Gau leadership in Vienna backed Leopold Zeller and Leo Konrath. The former boasted of having been so devoted to the National Socialist

cause that it led to the ruin of his father's business. Zeller had been forced to flee to Germany, where he was employed in Dachau. Konrath had joined the Party in 1927 and in 1934 fled to England, where he worked as a manager in a hat factory and served the Party's interests abroad. He had been employed by the Property Transfer Bureau after he returned home. The effect of this pressure was to bump out a qualified contender for Stadlauer Lederindustrie Wigner & Co. who was actually in the shoe business. The Kontrollbank found itself supporting Zeller and Konrath and trying to find an acceptable third party to join with them in acquiring the company. This turned out to be Franz Budischowsky, a Czech citizen from the occupied portion of Poland. He was related to a board member of the Shoe Association and had strong support from the governor of the Lower Danube and Gau Economic Advisor Birthelmer. He was also supported by the Leather Supervisory Agency, which had turned down another candidate proposed by the Kontrollbank. Matters were complicated further by Wigner's flight and the danger that Aryanization might be challenged because Wigner held a Hungarian passport and might sue abroad. The administrator of the company proceeded to sell the company to the Kontrollbank for 90,000 RM, which then sold it to the trio of Budischowsky, Konrath, and Zeller for 160,000 RM. Budischowsky paid 45,000 RM, and the other two borrowed 115,000 RM through the good offices of an official in the Gau Economic Office named Eberhardter. The entire affair irritated Bürckel, who had many other candidates, because he was convinced that they had gotten the company for much too low a price. The trio anticipated that exports and military contracts would enable them to pay back their credits, and in July 1939, they applied to the credit committee and the Länderbank for a 150,000 guaranteed credit, which they planned to use to pay back the 115,000 RM loan and to cover operating costs. The credit application had the full support of the Gau economic advisor, the Chamber of Commerce, and the leather-producing organizations and was agreed to by the Länderbank with the proviso that the trio actually formally reorganize the

7886, Vol. III, Länderbank to VVSt, Oct. 31, 1938, Länderbank to Sandner, Oct. 31, 1938, Länderbank to Kontrollbank, Nov. 15, 1938.

232 Felber et al., *Ökonomie der Arisierung*, pt. I, p. 116. According to Weber, the Kontrollbank bought the company for 83,300 RM and sold it for 146,800 RM. The amount of 126,840 RM comes from the BAB, R2/15551, Bl. 193–198, 356, 29th Credit Committee meeting, July 5, 1939.

company.[233] The entire affair most certainly belied the pretension that the Kontrollbank was conducting Aryanization in the public interest and free of Party pressures, and it also demonstrated that the Länderbank, under political pressure, could not resist giving a credit to individuals whom even Bürckel thought very dubious. As it turned out, Budischowsky, Konrath, and Zeller milked the company of huge sums of money in their own interests.

This is not to say that economic policy was thrown totally to the winds, as some of the cases described might suggest. There was, as Fritz Weber convincingly argues, a built-in tension in the Aryanization process between personal enrichment and economic rationalization. Beyond the common denominator of anti-Semitism, it is not easy to sort out the peculiar combination greed, economic policy, economic rationality, and ideology on which the process rested.[234] This was very evident in the role Aryanization played in some selected but representative cases that did not involve the Kontrollbank directly and that came before the credit committee of the Reich Economic Aid for Austria program in which the Länderbank, often represented by Director Wolzt, participated. The guidelines and priorities were set by Kehrl and the RWM in Berlin, but a host of other considerations inevitably came into play.

The Economics Ministry was eager to reduce the number of small trade and craft businesses and wanted to make sure that Aryanization credits from the Reich Economic Aid program were not given to place such enterprises in non-Jewish hands unless it could be demonstrated that doing so was in the national economic interest. This policy was to be pursued "without regard for the person of the purchaser."[235] Needless to say, this saved the banks

the need to give consideration to such cases, but the Länderbank periodically had to consider cases where the granting of credits would have violated sound banking principles. There also seemed to be a consensus that persons of insufficient means should not be given credits for Aryanizations. A case in point is Hans Amtmann, who had been appointed commissarial manager of the Jewish firm of M.&J. Mandl, and was asking for a 100,000 RM credit to assist in his acquisition of the firm. M.&J. Mandl manufactured and sold menswear and sporting goods. It had an excellent reputation, an international clientele, and outfitted the employees of the Mercurbank and Länderbank. It also had a debt to the Länderbank in excess of the 100,000 RM purchase price, and that was by no means its only debt. Amtmann was in effect asking the Länderbank to give him a credit to pay the bank what it was already owed. The Chamber of Commerce had only good things to say about the firm and strongly supported its continued existence but thought Amtmann lacked the means needed for the undertaking and was asking for too little money. It urged him to find a more affluent partner to help out. The Länderbank absolutely refused to provide a credit.[236]

Another dubious case was Alfred Georg Buck, who had taken over shoe manufacturer Hugo Kominik and asked for a credit of 100,000 RM. Kominik had been arrested by the Gestapo in April 1938 and was to be deported in 1941. The continued existence of the firm, which had been shut down because of the non-delivery of leather from Aryan firms, became the subject of debate between those who argued that it could produce for the military and those who felt that its liquidation would help in reducing overcrowding in the industry. The Property Transfer Bureau decided in favor of Aryanization rather than liquidation and sold the firm to Fritz Giebisch of Vienna and Alfred Georg Buck, who came from Stuttgart, for 12,560 RM and an "Aryanization fee" of 15,600 RM. The purpose of the loan was to purchase raw materials and to hire workers in order to

[233] The account given here follows that of Felber et al., *Ökonomie der Arisierung*, pt. 1, p. 113, pt. 2, pp. 216–241, and BAB, R2/15551, Bl. 333–337, 357, Credit Committee meeting, July 5, 1939, which is confirmed by the credit application.

[234] See Felber et al., *Ökonomie der Arisierung*, pt. 1, pp. 221–226.

[235] BAB, R2/15537, Bl. 373–374, 14th credit committee meeting, Nov. 23, 1938.

[236] Ibid., Bl. 41–44.

start up operations again. The Gau economic advisor strongly supported Buck, who had been in the Party since 1930. The Chamber of Commerce and shoe industry association argued that the firm was superfluous and that Buck did not have sufficient means to merit the loan. The Länderbank sat on the fence, indicating its willingness to grant an 85 percent guaranteed credit but holding back on the size of the credit until there was more information as to how much money the applicant himself was prepared to invest. In August 1939, the firm was renamed Mechanische Schuhwerk Alfred Georg Buck. It ran into difficulties in securing raw materials, which led to shutdowns and to efforts by Buck to postpone the "Aryanization fee" until the end of the war. In any case, the guaranteed credit does not appear to have been granted.[237]

Turning to more successful credit applicants, it is important to note that even when the Länderbank was not financing a direct Aryanization, the entire environment of Aryanization could strongly influence the creditworthiness of an applicant. This was evident in the case of the Johann Philipp firm, a small furrier that requested and received an 8,000 RM credit at the beginning of 1939 to move its workshop into more satisfactory quarters. The firm had done quite well between 1918 and 1929 but then suffered heavily in the depression and went into bankruptcy. Philipp had paid off his Aryan creditors but still had two or three installments to pay to his non-Aryan creditors. However, "payment of these items is of no importance at this time because the creditors have fled." Indeed, not only had the firm's Jewish creditors left, but its Jewish competitors had as well. As the report on Philipp noted, "business picked up in March 1938 through the elimination of the Jewish competition."

The Chamber of Commerce also supported the application and "described the general situation in this branch through the Aryanization or liquidation of numerous Jewish businesses as favorable." Philipp appears to have been a safe investment; he repaid the loan in March 1943.[238]

An Aryanization credit was deemed particularly worthy of support if an export business was involved, as was the case with Philipp Weiss & Söhne, a wholesale firm that sold smoking accessories. The firm was taken over by Erwin Schneider, who applied for a credit of 50,000 RM in April 1939 to pay for its purchase and to start it up again. The firm had suffered a loss in 1938 because of the ban on Jewish traveling salesmen, but Schneider obviously intended to hire new employees. There was also a slight problem with Wilhelm Weiss' wife, Hedwig, an Aryan who had divorced her husband and was thinking of opening up a similar business in Berlin that could provide competition. Nevertheless, the Gau economic advisor pointed out that "it is to be expected that the dejewification [*Entjudung*] by Party Comrade E. Schneider who, having acquired the firm of Philipp Weiss & Söhne, has conducted an expressly export oriented business, can be developed through his expert direction to the benefit of the national economy."[239]

Certain political credentials inevitably tipped the balance in favor of granting a credit, even when the Länderbank sought to limit its engagement so far as was politic. Norbert Wieser was such a case. He had been sentenced to hang for his role in the July 1934 Putsch; he sentence was subsequently commuted to twenty years' imprisonment. Wieser had Aryanized "Belko" Berger Volk & Co. in Vösendorf bei Wien, a producer of fruit juices and liquors for the domestic market. He was asking for 120,000 RM in loans and credits to pay the debts of the former owner to the Creditanstalt, back taxes, and the Reich Flight Tax and Jewish Wealth Tax, but

---

[237] Felber et al., *Ökonomie der Arisierung*, pt. 2, pp. 106, 203–205. The VVSt file on this case contains a moving letter by Hugo Kominik's wife to the Gestapo of June 15, 1938 thanking the Gestapo for admitting her ailing husband to the prison hospital but pleading for his release as an innocent and honest man, ÖStA/AdR, MfWuA, VVSt, Statistik, Box 712, Nr. 7849.

[238] ÖStA/AdR, RSth Wien, Rwh, Kg 1443. The Länderbank reported repayment of the loan to the Reichsstatthalter on March 31, 1943. BAB R2/13546, Bl. 147–149, 23rd credit committee meeting, April 5, 1939.

[239] Ibid., Bl. 204–208, 263.

also to make improvements in the plant. He had originally asked for 220,000 RM but then reduced his request. Wieser had no means of his own, although he indicated that he could call on relatives as a last resort. Nevertheless, the Gau economic advisor argued that the political preconditions for granting Wieser a credit were solid, and the Chamber of Commerce emphasized that Wieser, who had apparently administered the company in 1938, had been very successful in its management and that the production of fruit juices was in the national economic interest. This view was shared by the trade association, which stressed that the firm in question was very modern and well organized. The Länderbank declared itself ready to provide a Reich-guaranteed loan on the assumption that a large interest-free credit would be given by the Reich and that Wieser would not be charged the Aryanization tax. It also demanded that Wieser receive a moratorium on repaying a debt he owed to the Creditanstalt. The Creditanstalt, however, refused to agree on the grounds that it had made an installment agreement with Wieser and could not change it by granting a moratorium. Wieser seems to have withdrawn his credit request and found the needed funds elsewhere. There is no record of his having received the credit or, if he received one, of the conditions under which it was given. In any event, Wieser was described as the owner of the company in 1940 and was even in a position to make an offer to purchase new property.[240]

In dealing with applications for Reich-guaranteed credits connected with Aryanization cases, the Länderbank confronted a range of circumstances, some of which were more encouraging from a creditor's perspective than others. There clearly were cases in which the bank, had it been allowed to set ideology aside, undoubtedly would have felt safer lending money to Jewish business owners than to the

individuals dispossessing them. The bank was by no means prepared to lend money to the more dubious applicants, but on the whole it was to follow the lead of the Gau economic advisor and the Chamber of Commerce. And, of course, it was especially attentive to its own auditors. Business interests and opportunities were the guiding factors in decision making, and this could spur the bank to take the leading role in offering a credit. This is well demonstrated by the case of the Znaimer Konservenfabrik Rosenberger & Wahlster, which had undertaken the Aryanization of the Firma Josef Wertheimer, Znaimer Gurken-Konservenfabrik AG. The Jewish-owned firm, which had been in business in Znaim since 1883, had been bought for 60,000 RM. The purchase price basically covered the debts owed on the firm's property. The new owners were obligated to assume those debts and also to pay a 10,000 RM "Aryanization fee." To do so, they applied for a 240,000 RM credit. The factory was located in a region known for its cucumbers and was viewed as very important from a military point of view because of its substantial storage facilities. Rosenberger and Wahlster had money at their disposal, but not enough to buy the produce the firm needed. One of the partners had retired because of an injury, but the other had considerable experience in the production of fruit conserves, and both were well qualified and had good reputations. Although there was no report from the Gau economic advisor or from the Chamber of Commerce, the case was rushed through successfully at the behest of the Länderbank, which considered the matter urgent. In fact, the Länderbank intervened a month later to urge that a temporary Reich-guaranteed credit of another 100,000 RM be granted because of the transport difficulties created by the war. The Länderbank pointed out that the cucumber harvest was still under way, that a large plum harvest was in the offing, and that a substantial tomato harvest was expected as well. It was in the national economic interest that the produce be processed as soon as possible. The Länderbank was even prepared to add an additional nonguaranteed credit. Quite aside from such "national"

[240] BAB, R2/15545, Bl. 218–222. See also, Deutsche Revisions- und Treuhand-AG to Wieser, March 24, 1939; ÖStA/AdR, RSth Wien, Rwh, Kg 1612, CA to Deutsche Revisions- und Treuhand AG, March 30, 1939, and Deutsche Revisions- und Treuhand-AG to Wieser, Oct. 23, 1939.

considerations, it appears that the Länderbank's enthusiasm reflected the view that the firm was an excellent business opportunity and valuable future client. Given the Reich guarantees for such large sums, the bank's generosity appeared quite affordable. The Länderbank strongly supported additional credit requests in the summer of 1940 and 1942, expressing considerable satisfaction with both the management of the firm and its military and civilian contracts.[241]

The Länderbank demonstrated a somewhat more self-serving attitude in the interesting case of the Franz Schmitt AG, a leather producer in Rehberg bei Krems that requested a 500,000 RM Reich-guaranteed credit in July 1938. This request fell in the category of a large credit and was potentially a candidate for a 100 percent Reich guarantee. The Länderbank argued that the company should be a candidate for a consortial credit because it would be contributing to the Four Year Plan. The firm had been shut down since 1937 because of bad economic conditions and alleged prejudicial treatment on account of the owner's National Socialist sympathies; the requested credit was to help in the firm's reopening. It was a potentially important producer of footwear for military and civilian purposes, and local authorities welcomed the prospect of the reopening of the area's largest factory as a step toward reducing unemployment. The Schmitt family owned 40 percent of the company, the Länderbank owned 40 percent, and a Dutch investor, apparently Jewish, owned 20 percent; the Dutch-owned shares were deposited at the Länderbank. The agency in charge of leather distribution was prepared to authorize a large allocation of leather for the firm, provided that 85 percent of it was used for military contracts and that the foreign and Jewish capital participation was eliminated. Nevertheless, the Finance Ministry voiced strong reservations; the ministry thought the proposed eleven-year duration of the credit was

too long, and it also found "it...hard to understand why the Länderbank does not want to take a part of the risk since as a major shareholder it is strongly interested in the granting of the credit." In the end, Franz Schmitt received the credit, but it was scheduled for repayment in 1944.[242]

Besides helping finance the reopening of industrial firms, the Länderbank agreed to give a 248,000 RM credit to the Spa Commission of Semmering in August 1938, albeit only after receiving an explicit statement from Kehrl that the Reich was willing to give an 85 percent guarantee. The purpose of the credit was for the construction of a cable railway up the Hirschenkogel and of a bobsled run. The matter was urgent because the facilities had to be built during the summer so they could be used in the coming winter. Semmering, whose vital tourist trade had suffered, faced a catastrophe if it did not have a good winter season. Jewish visitors, primarily from Hungary and Czechoslovakia, were no longer coming, but the loss of that clientele could be offset by tourists from those countries and the Balkans, "who will visit Semmering precisely because of the absence of the Jews." Semmering had to be turned into a winter sports center with special attractions, and a campaign was planned to defuse "Jewish counter-propaganda." The credit was seen as an integral part of the effort to increase the attractiveness of Austria as a tourist destination and to attract visitors from Vienna. Initially, Director Hitschfeld demanded a 100 percent Reich guarantee for the credit because of the risk involved and the problematic legal status of the Spa Commission, but ultimately the bank agreed to an 85 percent Reich guarantee on the condition that the four largest hotels guarantee half of the credit as well.[243]

Winter sports in Semmering were to have a future, if not as soon as envisioned, which is more than can be said for a more typical

---

[241] BAB, R2/15553, Bl. 136–139, 31st credit committee meeting, Aug. 1, 1939; BAB, R2/15556, Bl. 96–99, 34th credit committee meeting, Sept. 12, 1939. On the 1940 and 1942 credits, see ÖStA/AdR, RSth Wien, Rwh, Kg 2093.

[242] BAB, R2/15601, Bl. 2–18, 24–25, quote on Bl. 25, BAB, R2/15577, Bl. 2–3, BAB, R2/15542, Bl. 240, RFM memorandum of Aug. 22, 1938 and attendant credit petition and reports of July 1938.

[243] BAB, R2/15611, Bl. 3–12, 3rd credit committee meeting, Aug. 3, 1938, and related correspondence.

investment of the period, a 700,000 RM consortial credit headed by the Länderbank for the Machinenfabrik Andritz AG in Graz. This was also intended to restart a company that had enjoyed considerable success before the Great War but had fallen on hard times under the Republic and had been shut down. Eighty-four percent of the company's capital had been in the hands of the Jewish banking house Gebrüder Gutmann, and it was then sold to a Graz lawyer, Knaffel, who put up 600,000 RM, and his associates, who put up another 400,000. Knaffel and his associates appear to have made a business of Aryanization. The company produced water turbines, pumps, cranes, bridge-building equipment, and similar items. The plant had become run down during the Depression and was in need of modernization and investment, assuming one wanted to reopen it. There seemed to be a consensus in favor of reopening and expanding the plant. The Länderbank apparently shared this view; it gave an advance against the credit in January 1939 in the expectation that the application would be successful. The credit was granted with the very explicit blessing of the RWM despite reservations on the part of the credit committee. Subsequently, Andritz was bought by a smaller firm, the Kämper Motorenwerke GmbH of Berlin, which proved totally incompetent and was facing bankruptcy by the fall of 1940. If the RWM kept it open, it was because of pressure from the Gau leadership, which considered it a matter of prestige. The investment clearly turned out to have been a terrible mistake.[244]

Were it not for the political and military considerations, the Länderbank and the other parties involved would not have thrown caution to the wind in this manner. Certainly more caution was demonstrated in most of the other cases, and a clear preference was shown for firms that were producing for the Four Year Plan and other government-supported projects. The Länderbank not only participated in the 400,000 RM consortial credit for the construction firm of Wayss & Freytag AG, which had once belonged to a Reich-German company of the same name. It also gave the company advances against anticipated consortial credits and added direct credits of its own to fund the numerous contracts Wayss & Freytag received after the Anschluss thanks to the fact that it had earlier been denied contracts because of its reputation as a "Nazi firm." The Reich Finance Ministry was far less enthusiastic because of the company's low liquidity and the 100 percent risk involved, but it felt that it had to support the credit because, after the Anschluss, Wayss & Freytag had large road, bridge, and Autobahn contracts and, given the vastly increased business for construction companies, no other firm could be expected to spring into the breach.[245] There were no such reservations in the case of the construction firm of Pittel & Brausewetter, which had a consortial credit of 2.1 million RM. Pittel & Brausewetter was heavily engaged in Autobahn construction and various projects for Organisation Todt. It could count on a minimum turnover of 7 million RM, and one can well understand the readiness of the Länderbank to serve as the firm's house bank.[246]

The Länderbank Wien initiated much business after its establishment, but it also managed many accounts taken over from the three banks from which it had been created. One of its most valuable accounts, for example, was Julius Meinl AG, which imported and sold coffee, confectionaries, spices, and a host of other food products in Austria and in Europe. It had a balance of 35 million RM in 1939. At the end of March 1938, the company ended its banking relationships with the BPEC Vienna and Kux, Boch & Co. and went over to the Mercurbank, which meant, of course, that it ended up as a client of the Länderbank Wien.[247]

---

[244] The extensive documentation is to be found in BAB, R2/15590, Bl. 10–17, 61–65, 67–68, 92–95, 99–100, 110–116.

[245] BAB, R2/15603, Bl. 69–73, 11th credit committee meeting, Oct. 13, 1938, BAB, R2/15534, Bl. 209–211, and RFM file note, Jan. 3, 1939.

[246] BAB, R2/15598, Bl. 3–15, 165–173, 36th credit committee meeting, Oct. 24, 1939.

[247] NARA, T83/119, 122, credit committee meetings of May 13, 1938 and July 21, 1939.

As one of the Dresdner Bank's eight subsidiaries, the Länderbank needed Dresdner Bank approval for its credits. In May 1939, to reduce the burdens on the management board, the Dresdner Bank set up a committee of three management board members to decide on affiliate credits up to 600,000 RM. Credits in larger amounts were referred to the full management board.[248] The Creditanstalt, by contrast, did not operate under such constraints. But whereas the Creditanstalt was compelled to sell off many of its industrial holdings, the Mercurbank and old Länderbank, which had fewer and smaller holdings, were subject to much less pressure to divest themselves of their industrial investments. The one big exception appears to be the Waagner-Biro Brückenbau AG. German steel companies showed interest in acquiring Waagner-Biro shares very shortly after the Anschluss. In late April, the Saarbrücken firm of B. Seibert contacted Baron von der Lippe, who, however, pointed out that the shares could not be sold until the Länderbank was Germanized, and that there would be more powerful contenders for the shares by then. As soon as the Vereinigte Stahlweke (Vestag) got wind of the plan to take over the old Länderbank, it informed the Dresdner Bank that the company was of great importance to the Four Year Plan in Austria and asked that the Vestag be included in the sale of the shares. Subsequently, it was acquired by Böhler and thus became part of the Dortmunder Union division of the Vestag. The connection was not totally broken, however, and the Länderbank did provide Waagner-Biro with substantial credits.[249]

The coal and coke division of the Länderbank was potentially a problem. There were both ideological and economic objections to banks running their own enterprises. The RWM objected to the bank's marketing of coal as harmful to competition. Mayor Hermann Neubacher of Vienna, however, was happy with the services provided to the city and intended to extend the contract, although he also felt that the bank's coal business should be turned into a corporation of its own rather than remain a division of the bank.[250]

Despite such difficulties, the Länderbank was arguably a beneficiary of the forced sale of Creditanstalt holdings. Although the Creditanstalt usually remained the house bank of the companies in question, it was forced in some cases to give up the exclusive right to offer them credits. The Länderbank received the right to offer 25 percent of the credits given to companies that had become subsidiaries of the Reichswerke Hermann Göring. Accordingly, in April 1939, the Länderbank offered the Steyerwerke 4.5 million RM in operating credits, the Steirische Gußstahlwerke 1.25 million RM, the Simmeringer Waggonfabrik 875,000 RM, and the Grazer Paukerwerke 375,000 RM. It is worth noting that the Dresdner Bank and the Länderbank took certain precautions with respect to these credits, insisting on the right to call them in at any time and that the Reichswerke make sure they were paid back if it decided to sell the subsidiaries in question. Rasche felt it especially important to keep a watchful eye on the Simmeringer Waggonfabrik and the Grazer Paukerwerke so that the credits could be recalled immediately if their situation should become unfavorable.[251]

The most important area of business for the Länderbank was its participation in syndicates, usually in alliance with the Dresdner Bank. Taking part in syndicates to provide credits to or float stock and bond issues for the companies of the Reichswerke Hermann Göring and firms in the electric power business was particularly important to the bank. It provided

---

[248] NARA, T83/136, Dresdner Bank management board meeting, May 2, 1939.

[249] ÖStA/AdR, MfWuA, VVSt, Statistik, Box 673, Nr. 3811, B. Seibert GmbH to Gauleiter Bürckel, April 26, 1938; DrB, Nr. 2160-2000, memorandum, April 28, 1938, and NARA, T83/122, Dresdner Bank credit committee meeting of Oct. 17, 1939. On the credits to Waagner-Biro see NARA, T83/136, Dresdner Bank management board meeting, Aug. 3, 1939.

[250] See NARA, T83/135, the report by Lüer and Pilder to the management board of the Dresdner Bank, Dec. 1, 1938.

[251] NARA, T83/136, Dresdner Bank management board meeting, April 25, 1939.

large credits for the Gauwerke Niederdonau, which had absorbed the Eisenstädter Elektrizitätswerke AG.[252] It was a major participant, with the Dresdner Bank, in the credits for the Wiener Neustädter Flugzeugwerke, Wiener Neustadt.[253] Its chief rival was the Creditanstalt, and the Länderbank pursued a policy of participating in as many of the consortia for government bonds, special Ostmark bonds, and industrial credits as it could. The Dresdner Bank sought to help in such efforts, offering it a 2 percent share in the issue of Reichswerke Hermann-Göring stock in June 1938. The Dresdner Bank also backed the Länderbank's to increase its share in the Alpine-Montan consortial credit from the 85:15 percent ratio in favor of the Creditanstalt to 50 percent; in the end, it received a 37 percent share.[254] The Länderbank counted heavily on the Dresdner Bank for support in enabling it to participate in issuing shares of large German corporations. Neither the Länderbank nor the Creditanstalt were initially included, for example, in a consortium led by the Deutsche Bank and the Dresdner Bank for a Daimler-Benks issue in May 1939. To make sure that the Länderbank was not put at a disadvantage, the Dresdner Bank promised to involve it in launching the issue on the stock market. Similarly, the Länderbank repeatedly requested the Dresdner Bank's support in serving as a corresponding bank for large German corporations.[255]

Last but not least, the Dresdner Bank's connections with the Party and the SS were also of no small importance. That was evident in September 1938, when the Gestapo closed its special account and depot containing securities at the Länderbank and asked that the balance and securities be transferred to the Creditanstalt. This was ordered for the purpose of simplifying the Gestapo's banking. When the Länderbank inquired about the decision, it was confidentially told that the rationalization measure was ordered by SS-Obergruppenführer and head of the Security Police, "Heiderich [sic]," who had ordered the simplification of the accounts four months earlier. When he discovered that the Gestapo was still working with two banks, he insisted that the practice be terminated. The Länderbank immediately sought remedy through the Dresdner Bank: "We know that Herr Rasche has good connections to the staff of SS-Reichsführer Himmler and would be especially grateful that we continue to be engaged as a connection for the Secret State Police, Police Headquarters Vienna in case it should not prove possible to concentrate the account with us."[256] All of this appeared very strange to the Dresdner Bank officials because Reinhard Heydrich was in charge of the Security Service (SD) and had nothing to do with the Gestapo. They asked the bank to look into the matter again, but in the meantime Director Meyer got into contact with Veesenmayer and asked him to talk to Ernst Kaltenbrunner, who was the head of the Gestapo, and see what could be done. At the same time, they also contacted the SD and managed to arrange that the SD, which had been keeping its accounts at the Reichsbank, would now move them to the Länderbank![257] All's well that ends well! Whether this would continue remained to be seen, but it should be clear that, on the eve of the war, the Länderbank Wien AG had become heavily invested in the Third Reich.

[252] DrB, Nr. 5460-2000, Business Report 1938 Appendix 2; NARA, T83/136, Dresdner Bank management board meeting of July 17, 1939.

[253] Ibid., Dresdner Bank management board meeting, Aug. 24, 1939.

[254] NARA, T83/135, Dresdner Bank management board meetings, June 8 and 15, 1938.

[255] DrB, Nr. 5458-2000, Dresdner Bank to Länderbank, May 10, 1939, and Rinn report on German companies the Länderbank hoped to serve for their Austrian business, Oct. 10, 1939, and general correspondence in Sept. and Oct. 1939 on this subject.

[256] NARA, RG 260, External Assets Investigations 1945–1949, 390/44/31/01, Box 539, Gestapo to the Länderbank, Sept. 22, 1938, and Länderbank to the Dresdner Bank, Sept. 26, 1938.

[257] Ibid., memorandum for Rasche, Sept. 27, 1938, and Meyer to Veesenmayer, Sept. 27, 1938.

CHAPTER SIX

The Länderbank in the Second World War

The Länderbank was a creation of the Dresdner Bank, but it was also the second largest bank in Austria with its own pretensions. As has been shown, the Länderbank was a beneficiary of its connection with the Dresdner Bank, which offered a host of business connections and opportunities as well as political contacts and protection. The final decision on important matters rested with the Dresdner Bank, however, and the Länderbank periodically had cause to chafe at its subordinate status. Shortly before the war, the supervisory boards of the two banks had held a joint meeting in Vienna with the object of strengthening their ties. Apold praised the Dresdner Bank for its "vision and self-sacrificing activity" that led to the mergers creating the Länderbank Wien AG, for raising its share capital from 15 million Schilling to 20 million RM, and for the attention it had shown to the welfare of the new bank. After Director Lehr had reported on the bank's business, Carl Goetz expressed his gratitude to the leadership of the Länderbank and gave assurance that the Dresdner Bank stood ever ready to assist in difficult circumstances. He then gave a vivid account of the development of the Dresdner Bank since 1931. The difficulties of that year of crisis, he stressed, belonged to the past, as demonstrated by the growth of

the bank's business and the rationalization of its operations.[1]

The year 1931 seemed very far away indeed. It was not only the Dresdner Bank's business that was growing but also the bank itself. It moved rapaciously in the wake of German conquests to acquire new branches. The Länderbank followed its lead and benefited both directly and indirectly from the Dresdner Bank's acquisitiveness. The Länderbank, as previously noted, picked up three branches of Czech banks in the Sudetenland. Before the invasion of Prague and the establishment of the Protectorate of Bohemia and Moravia, as the German hold on the Sudetenland was being consolidated, plans were laid for the takeover of key Czech banks and industries. It was in this context that the Dresdner Bank sought to establish a position in Slovakia and paved the way for the Länderbank's engagement there, leading eventually to the formal takeover of the Handels- und Kreditbank AG, Pressburg after the German march into Prague. In contrast to the Deutsche Bank, the Dresdner Bank, and the Creditanstalt, the Länderbank did not enter into the banking business in Prague. The Dresdner Bank was extremely successful in the Protectorate, thanks in large part to Rasche's close working relationship with Kehrl, which had also been a key factor in the Dresdner Bank's success in

[1] DrB, Nr. 5460-2000, supervisory board meeting, May 19, 1939.

the Sudetenland. In Prague, it took over the Böhmische Escompte-Bank und Creditanstalt (Bebca), a major bank with a substantial number of branches and very important industrial holdings. It also acquired the Länderbank Prag from the Paris Banque de Pays de l'Europe Centrale, negotiating once again with Reuter. That bank was then merged with the Bebca. The Bebca thus became a key affiliate of the Dresdner Bank with a status similar to that of the Länderbank Wien. This is not to say that the Länderbank did not do important business in the Protectorate in connection with the Dresdner Bank and the Bebca. It was not, however, a banking presence in the Protectorate, as it was in the Sudetenland and Slovakia. Moreover, its role in the Sudetenland was rather minor. In the Sudetenland, as in Austria, Göring was eager to set up a 25 million RM aid program based on Reich-guaranteed credits. Both the Länderbank and the Creditanstalt were willing to join, but they made clear from the outset that they could not participate on the same scale as they did in Austria and limited their quotas to 4 percent each.[2]

The Länderbank also found itself playing a role in Poland or, better said, found its role in Poland revived after the German conquest. The Kommerzialbank Crakow, which had belonged to the Mercurbank, was in liquidation when the German armies arrived. The Länderbank still held its capital, however, and the bank also had a branch in Lemberg. The Dresdner Bank, lacking a bank or branch in Poland, was very eager to take advantage of this situation. Director Meyer lost no time in contacting Max Winkler, Governor-General Hans Frank's economic advisor and, after October 1939, head of the Head Trusteeship Office East, the chief agency

responsible for liquidating Jewish and Polish property.[3] Shortly thereafter, the Dresdner Bank began to increase its direct interest in the Kommerzialbank, taking over 40 percent of its 1.5 million zloty capital at the turn of 1939–1940. Subsequently, the capital was increased to 5 million zloty; the Dresdner Bank held 3.75 million zloty in shares and the Länderbank held 1.99 million zloty in shares. If the Länderbank was no longer the dominant force in the Kommerzialbank, it was nevertheless very active in its affairs, and Director Warnecke was a member of its supervisory board throughout the war.[4] In the Sudetenland, as in the annexed areas in the east, a special economic aid program based on Reich guarantees was organized, this time for 100 million RM and under the leadership of the Reichs-Kredit-Gesellschaft. That bank took a 15 million RM quota, as did both the Deutsche Bank and the Dresdner Bank. The leading Austrian banks also had significant quotas. The Creditanstalt, which ultimately was to prove far more active in Poland than the Länderbank, and the Länderbank each took a quota of 6 million RM.[5]

At the same time, the Länderbank was anxious to increase its business in Austria and looked to the Dresdner Bank for assistance in having the German companies with which it did business use the Länderbank to float their share and bond issues on the Vienna Stock Exchange. In April 1940, the Länderbank approached Rasche to ask that the Dresdner Bank prevail upon the Engelhardt-Brauerei AG to use the services of the Länderbank. The Creditanstalt had recently launched issues for the Heinrich Lanz AG and the Continental Gummiwerke AG, which had

---

2 See the discussion led by Ministerial Director Lange in the RWM on Oct. 8, 1938, NARA, T38/204, Länderbank to Dresdner Bank, Oct. 10 and Nov. 2, 1938. On the Sudetenland and the Protectorate, see Wixforth, *Auftakt zur Ostexpansion.* I have also benefited from his unpublished paper of February 2003,"Die Expansionspolitik der deutschen Banken während des Nationalsozialismus als Problem der Forschung," given at the Wirtschaftshistorische Ausschuss of the Verein für Sozialpolitik.

3 NARA, T83/136, Dresdner Bank management board meeting, Sept. 26, 1939. On September 5, 1939, the Dresdner Bank informed Ministerial Director Riehle about this and also asked to open a branch in Teschen through the Bebca branch in Mährisch-Ostrau and also asked to open an office in Bielitz to service the wool industry there. See RGVA Moscow, 1458/15/137, Bl. 37–38.

4 See NARA, T136, Dresdner Bank management board meeting, Jan. 5, 1940, and ibid., T83/197, Konsortialvertrag of May 6, 1943.

5 RGVA Moscow, 1458/15/136, Bl. 8–9, RWM Vermerk, Nov. 11, 1940.

given the Creditanstalt an advantage in new stock issues, and the Länderbank felt it essential to recover its position. Judging by the business reports of the Länderbank for 1940 and 1941, it was able to do lively business on the exchange.[6] The Dresdner Bank also helped in taking the edge off difficult wartime economic measures that had negative consequences for the Länderbank, such as the shutting down of the Hirmer Zuckerfabrik, one of the Länderbank's most important holdings. With the help of the Dresdner Bank, the Länderbank was able to sell its 40 percent stake at 120 percent plus 400,000 RM to an interested buyer who hoped to reopen the company after the war.[7] Apparently, the Dresdner Bank was also willing to see the Länderbank pick up new holdings, for example, its acquisition of 25 percent to 30 percent of the shares of the Erste Grazer Actien-Brauerei vorm. Franz Schreiner & Söhne (Puntigam) in late 1941.[8]

But before turning to the actual business of the Länderbank in these regions and in Austria, it is important to set the context of its activity and describe its relations with the Dresdner Bank as well as its efforts to cope with the demands and pressures emanating from the Party and regime, especially as the war progressed. While the Dresdner Bank always had the final word in appointments to the Länderbank's supervisory board, the Party also paid close attention to such appointments. Birthelmer, as has been shown, was extraordinarily useful because of his powerful political and economic role, but he apparently fell ill in early 1940 and was forced to give up some of his positions. Some of the directors of the Dresdner Bank, obviously not given to sentimentality in such matters, apparently felt that Birthelmer should also be approached about leaving the Länderbank supervisory board, and Veesenmayer was assigned the task

of discussing the matter with Gauleiter Hugo Jury of the Lower Danube. The latter could not see "the slightest reason" for Birthelmer to leave the supervisory board and expressed the wish that he remain on all the supervisory boards on which he was serving. At the same time, Jury could not simply disregard the fact that there was cause for concern and promised to inform Veesenmayer if the situation changed to the point where Birthelmer should be urged to retire from the board. The problem solved itself when Birthelmer died later in the year.[9]

This incident illustrates the kind of political fuss that could arise over what, under other circumstances, would have been routine matters. There were some issues that took care of themselves, such as the question of who should represent the Länderbank in the German-Hungarian Society. The society had asked for a Länderbank representative, but with the explicit proviso that Director Hitschfeld not be appointed because his marriage to a Jewish woman might create difficulties. Wolzt was suggested instead, and Hitschfeld "showed complete understanding for this and emphasized that the personage question is of subordinate significance insofar as he was concerned, but that in his view it was very important that the bank be represented in the society."[10] Hitschfeld was obviously highly valued despite his marriage to a Jewish woman, and he was indeed regarded as something of a wizard when it came to assessing credit risks.[11] He certainly understood how to do what was expected of him.

It should come as no surprise that those in charge of the bank constantly had to be on their guard lest they run afoul of some Nazi satrap, as was grotesquely the case when Karl Wilhelm Lehr offended Bürckel's replacement as Reich governor in Vienna, Nazi Youth leader Baldur von Schirach. Bürckel had instructed Lehr to deposit 850,000 RM in an account in

[6] DrB, Nr. 5460-2000, Länderbank to Rasche, April 6, 1940, and business reports, ibid.
[7] NARA, T83/137, Dresdner Bank management board meeting, June 18, 1941, and DrB, Nr. 5460-2000, supervisory board meeting of Sept. 23, 1941.
[8] NARA, T83/137, Dresdner Bank management board meeting, Dec. 1, 1941.

[9] DrB, Nr. 5460-2000, Veesenmayer to Apold and Veesenmayer to Jury, April 25, 1940.
[10] NARA, RG 260, External Assets Investigations 1945–1949, 390/44/31/01, Box 539, Aktennotiz, unsigned, April 5, 1940.
[11] See Heinrich Treichl, *Fast ein Jahrhundert. Erinnerungen* (Vienna 2003), p. 124.

von Schirach's name, and von Schirach then instructed Lehr that the account was not to be used without von Schirach's explicit approval. Subsequently, Bürckel instructed Lehr to take 150,000 RM from the money given to von Schirach and deposit this sum in the account of SS-Gruppenführer Kaltenbrunner. Lehr informed von Schirach only after he had transferred the money to Kaltenbrunner. Von Schirach was very sensitive about such violations of procedures he had laid down, and it is likely that Lehr was a victim of the notorious rivalry between Bürckel and von Schirach as well as of the shady dealings of the Viennese National Socialists. Whatever the case, Lehr was in trouble. As Rasche informed Apold, von Schirach "was very embittered over this, views it as an offence of the worst kind, and today takes the position that Herr Lehr cannot possibly remain as a member of the Länderbank management board."[12] Lehr realized that he had made a mistake but had no idea that von Schirach planned to eject him. The extent of von Schirach's irritation became clear only when Director Meyer visited von Schirach in Vienna about a large credit for the leadership of the Hitler Youth and von Schirach told him that he found Lehr "unbearable" in his present managerial position. In Rasche's view, this meant that Lehr had to go: "Because the Länderbank must under all circumstances strive to have a good relationship of trust with the leading State and Party agencies in the Ostmark, we will not be able to avoid fulfilling the demand of the new Gauleiter."[13] Rasche suggested that they send Lehr to fill a position in Lorraine, where his chief supporter Bürckel had been appointed head of the civilian administration and would have no objection to Lehr's reassignment.

Fortuitously, a potential replacement for Lehr appeared on the horizon in the person of Josef Paić, whose work at the Kontrollbank was winding down. Paić was still a candidate for an important position at the Creditanstalt, and the bank's leadership was urging him to prepare

by serving for a number of years on the management board of the Oberbank. He preferred, however, to take up Apold's promise to give him a job at the Länderbank when he returned from the Kontrollbank. Apold shared the view that Paić was very talented and that the confidence of the Creditanstalt leadership boded well for the cooperation between the two banks, but he also thought it important that the forty-four-year-old Paić transcend his background as an Austrian banker and gain the kind of experience he needed to master the "banking situation of the Greater Reich." The reasons for this solicitude for the fortunes of Paić are not far to seek. He had been a Party member since 1932 and was active in the National Socialist cause prior to the Anschluss. He was then put on special assignment by the Party for economic questions and also served as an aide to Rafelsberger before being made a director of the Länderbank. Paić was then transferred to the Kontrollbank, where he served as company leader. Subsequently drafted into the army, he served as a first lieutenant in an air force intelligence unit in the Polish campaign and received an Iron Cross; he was also apparently was on special assignment to the Army Group List. He was released from military service in 1940 because of illness. Paić held the rank of an SS Obersturmführer and was characterized by the company steward of the Länderbank, A. Wurm, as "a man of stature and rich knowledge in the economic field, a through and through National Socialist with leadership qualities who understands how to clarify all problems with which he has to deal from a national standpoint." Manifestly, one did not want to lose such a person, and Apold therefore proposed that the Länderbank match the salary Paić would have received at the Oberbank but then send him on special assignment for the Dresdner Bank before having him return as a member of the Länderbank management board.[14]

Rasche now linked the Lehr affair with the availability of Paić. If Lehr departed, the

[12] DrB, Nr. 5460-2000, Rasche to Apold, Sept. 26, 1940.
[13] Ibid.

[14] WrStLA, Gauakt Josef Paić, Nr. 228082, Apold to Rasche, Sept. 1940. For the characterization of Paić, see ibid., the report of A. Wurm, March 9, 1944.

Länderbank would only have three directors on its management board, and it seemed logical to shorten the intended preparation of Paić for the job and thereby "restore as quickly as possible a good relationship with Gauleiter Baldur von Schirach, for considerations of both principle and business." Because Paić had a "good name in Vienna, he will certainly also satisfy the Gauleiter and the bank will be spared further unpleasantness through this rapid solution." Rasche was strongly seconded by Veesenmayer, who also felt that the Länderbank needed to respond quickly to the situation and replace Lehr with Paić.[15]

As it turned out, Lehr stayed on and Paić was to perform other services for the Länderbank. The Dresdner Bank apparently decided to send a "troubleshooter" to Vienna in the person of Dresdner Bank director Alex Haase-Mühlner. Although he never attained a top leadership position in the Dresdner Bank, Haase-Mühlner nevertheless assumed a prominent role and quadrupled his salary thanks to his close friendship with Fritz Todt and Baldur von Schirach, at whose home he was a regular guest. In 1937, he became a member of the leadership of the Reich Labor Service and, in the next year, a member of the Hitler Youth leadership. Meyer used him, among other things, for contact with von Schirach. Meyer had been negotiating with Baldur von Schirach about a large Dresdner Bank credit designed to provide suitable housing for the Reich Hitler Youth leadership, presumably in anticipation of its getting older, and Haase-Mühlner, who was likely to be one of its beneficiaries, was undoubtedly involved. Haase-Mühlner was sent to Vienna at the end of 1940, in part to smooth things over with Baldur von Schirach and also to improve the management of the bank by serving as deputy company leader and working alongside Warnecke, who did not seem to have matters in hand. Veesenmayer appears to have been involved in the effort and to have been very insistent that the managers at the Länderbank cooperate.[16]

Haase-Mühlner was apparently quite successful in dealing with von Schirach. On January 16, 1941, he was able to report to Meyer that negotiations with von Schirach for a substantial credit had been successful and had been approved by the Länderbank management board and that von Schirach was grateful for both the loan and its terms. An additional item of good news was that Haase-Mühlner seems to have persuaded Gauleiter Jury to open an account at the Länderbank. Manifestly, the relations between the Länderbank and these Party leaders had improved greatly and very much to Meyer's satisfaction. Baldur von Schirach had clearly been mollified and Lehr's job in Vienna had been saved thanks to the Dresdner Bank's intervention and the Länderbank's willingness to provide von Schirach with credit. The 1 million RM credit was earmarked for the purpose of purchasing artworks in the occupied areas. Although little use was made of the credit, it was extended until early 1944. It was then renewed for the purpose of buying goods for the provisioning of the army units for whose welfare von Schirach had special responsibility.[17]

Haase-Mühlner also had his enemies, namely the company steward of the Dresdner Bank in Berlin, who was contacted by his counterpart at the Länderbank in Vienna and received a "devastating" report to the effect that Haase-Mühlner had done service for a "reactionary party" even after Hitler came to power. This was enough for Wurm, who detested the "Berliners," and he immediately swung into action. With Warnecke's agreement, Wurm used the visit of some of the

[15] DrB, Nr. 5460-2000, Rasche to Apold, Sept. 26, 1940 and Veesenmayer to Rasche, Sept. 26, 1940.

[16] This information comes from material gathered on Haase-Mühlner in connection with his denazification to be found in DrB, Bestand 108. Dresdner Bank Betriebsrat Akte, DrB, Nr. 50070–2000. I am grateful to Dieter Ziegler for this information. See also NARA, RG 260, External Assets Investigations 1945–1949, 390/44/31/01, Box 539, Veesenmayer to Rasche, Dec. 9, 1940. For the Dresdner Bank credits, see NARA, T83/124 and 136, the management board meeting of Aug. 8, 1940 and the memorandum of Aug. 1, 1940.

[17] NARA, RG 260, External Assets Investigations 1945–1949, 390/44/31/01, Box 539, Haase-Mühlner to Meyer, Jan. 13, 1941 and Meyer to Haase-Mühlner, Jan. 16, 1941. On the credits and their purpose, see NARA T83/137 and 126, Dresdner Bank management board meetings, Jan. 11, 1941, Feb. 26, 1942, Feb. 24, 1944, and June 6, 1944.

Berlin supervisory board members to demand Haase-Mühlner's dismissal from the Länderbank and threatened to resign if that demand was not met. Haase-Mühlner was sent off to Croatia to work at the Dresdner Bank's branch there. Wurm claimed this earned him the enmity of the people in Berlin, although not of his "comrades."[18]

This was, of course, a political matter, and it was important for greasing the wheels of regular banking activity, which increased in 1940–1941. But although Director Lehr could report considerable growth in the volume of business and the number of accounts at the supervisory board meeting in September 1941, he also noted that the war was taking its toll. Between the end of 1940 and June 1941, the balance had increased 42 percent, but sixty-five employees had been called up for military service since the end of 1940. They were replaced by ninety-three persons, all of them intended as temporary employees for the duration of the war. Almost half of these new hires were young boys and girls fresh out of school, and their training would take time and effort. Lehr and his colleagues also had to weather criticism from Pilder, who pointed out that the conscription of employees had not produced the kind of savings at the Länderbank that the Dresdner Bank had experienced. Lehr defended his bank by pointing out that several factors had limited savings on personnel costs: the introduction of Reich pay scales in the Ostmark, the need to hire personnel because of new business, the taking over of personnel in the southern Moravian branches and from the "Hermes" exchange bureaus and the Societa Italiana, and the fact that the Länderbank did not have the modern equipment at the Dresdner Bank's disposal and thus required more personnel. In general, the Länderbank leadership stressed that the Ostmark was still catching up with the Reich and that "so much has changed at the bank that the past situation can no longer be compared with the present one."[19]

From the standpoint of the Dresdner Bank, however, the Länderbank was not always catching up fast enough. Pilder criticized the way the handling of stock exchange orders deviated from the practice of the Dresdner Bank and expressed his displeasure over the fact that some of the better-off bank employees were taking advantage of their knowledge of upcoming market transactions to buy shares about to increase in value. Here, too, Lehr complained about insufficient personnel to assist Director Schwarz in the stock exchange section of the bank; his colleagues did not think share transactions by employees could be controlled. Matters were made all the more difficult for the Länderbank by wartime pressures to shut down branches, the beginning of a rationalization effort that was to intensify in the coming years. Lehr viewed this with alarm because the business of branches being shut down was likely to go to the branches of other banks that were allowed to stay open.

The competition from the Creditanstalt and its affiliated banks in Austria was clearly what Lehr had in mind, and the inferiority and dependence of the Länderbank when viewed in comparison to the Creditanstalt were quite manifest. A discussion of the Länderbank's balance sheet at the April 1942 meeting of the supervisory board is very revealing of the extent to which the Creditanstalt's advantages served as a reference point. When supervisory board member Hiedler noted that the number of the Länderbank's debtors had failed to reach the level of 1939, while the number of the Creditanstalt's debtors had increased substantially, Lehr pointed out that the Creditanstalt had branches abroad whose balance sheets were included in its own, whereas the balances of Länderbank foreign engagements were not integrated into the Länderbank's overall balance sheet. If the balance of the Kommerzialbank in Cracow were included in the balance sheet of the Länderbank, as the balance of the Creditanstalt's branch in the Generalgouvernement was included in the Creditanstalt's balance sheet, Lehr argued, the total sum of Länderbank credits would have risen 38 percent instead of 12 percent.[20]

[18] WrStLA, Gauakt Josef Paić, Nr. 228082, report of A. Wurm, Feb. 23, 1944.

[19] DrB, Nr. 5460-2000, supervisory board meeting of Sept. 23, 1941.

[20] Ibid., supervisory board meeting of April 21, 1942.

Although hard to document or measure, there was a sense among informed circles that the post-Anschluss arrangement of the banking sector was not necessarily stable or permanent and that Austrian interests might reassert themselves more effectively. The Dresdner Bank was especially sensitive to that danger. At a management board meeting on April 9, 1941, Rasche reported on a discussion with Kehrl about rumors regarding a possible merger of the Länderbank and the Creditanstalt.[21] No indication was given as to the source of such rumors, but the leading Austrian Nazis were known to have some hostility to the old Reich dominance in the Ostmark and to prefer more independence for Austrian institutions. It was important for Rasche, therefore, to step up his collaboration with Austrian Nazi leaders, especially the Gau economic advisor in Vienna, Rafelsberger, and to accommodate his wishes. At the supervisory board meeting on September 23, 1941, Rasche reported on a "pleasant discussion" with Rafelsberger in which the latter expressed "his willingness to intervene more than before for the interests of Länderbank." In the course of the conversation, Rafelsberger also discussed the relationship between the Länderbank and the Creditanstalt and thought "it would be ideal to improve the relationship in many respects, for now both sides often have the feeling of being in the way of one another." Director Wolzt was not happy with this characterization; he pointed out that periods of excellent collaboration alternated with periods of tension, suggesting that this was an inevitable state of affairs. He also reported on recent meetings with Director Joham and that they had found a number of bases for collaboration.[22]

This was the sort of thing Rafelsberger wanted to happen, and his wishes were also very much in mind when Pilder announced the plan of the Dresdner Bank to undertake personnel changes to strengthen the role of the Länderbank in Southeast Europe. A Länderbank

official, Homolka, was being sent as the only director to the recently acquired Kroatische Landesbank, and "this will guarantee that there will be a very close collaboration with the Länderbank." Director Paić, who had expressed a desire to "enrich his experience in the southeast," would also be sent into the region. Because the Romanians were demanding that for every German on the board of a Romanian company three Romanians be appointed, his appointment to the board of the Societatea Bancara Romana in Bucharest was not practicable, but he would nevertheless be sent as a contact man while remaining with the Länderbank. Most importantly, Pilder announced that a plan was in the making to ease the burdens of the Länderbank management board by appointing someone whose sole task would be to handle the bank's foreign engagements. They were thinking of a specific person who would travel considerably but have a good deal of independence and who would serve Vienna and Berlin, especially in the Southeast. Rasche noted, with the concurrence of Apold, "this development is certainly completely in line with the thinking of Gau Economic Advisor Rafelsberger, since he is of the opinion that the Ostmark qualifies above all for establishing German ties with the southeast."[23]

The issue of creating a special office for the Länderbank's foreign interests was settled in April 1942 with the appointment of Franz Gold, the managing director of the Deutschen Handels- und Kreditbank in Pressburg. Gold had spent most of his career prior to 1938 as a bank director in Persia, which had kept him from developing much of a political record at home. There seemed to be a consensus that he had done an outstanding job in Pressburg since his appointment in 1940. The decision was taken to appoint Gold, who did not want to work for the Länderbank in a subordinate status, to the position of a full member of the management board. Pilder thought it a good idea to have a management board member appointed to handle external affairs exclusively because the Creditanstalt had its own branches

21 NARA, T83/137, management board meeting of April 9, 1941.
22 DrB, Nr. 5460-2000, supervisory board meeting of Sept. 23, 1941.

23 Ibid.

in the General government in Poland and in Hungary. This would upgrade the Länderbank's international status, and Pilder also thought that by having positions in both Pressburg and Vienna, Gold would be in a better positions to link those interests. At the Länderbank personnel committee meeting where this was discussed, Pilder found himself strongly seconded by Meindl, "if one can thereby bring about a strengthened independence for the Länderbank in business done in the southeast. In Berlin, one hears repeatedly about an excessive dependence on the Dresdner Bank, and he considers greater independence and freedom of action very important for the future development of the bank because otherwise the Creditanstalt-Bankverein will always have a certain precedence."[24] Not everyone present agreed with this assessment. Hans Mann was of one mind with Meindl, but Wolzt sharply criticized "such insinuations, about which one can only laugh" and insisted that the Länderbank had all the independence it needed. Although it was not surprising that Rasche and Pilder shared Wolzt's view, Meindl went so far as to argue that it would have been better for the Länderbank to be an actual branch of the Dresdner Bank than to appear as one while pretending that it was something else. Despite these tensions, Gold was easily appointed to the position, and there was agreement that the Länderbank would be represented in all the Dresdner Bank's branches in Southeast Europe. The presence of the bank in Pressburg would be further strengthened by the appointment of Paić to the management board of the Deutsche Handels- und Kreditbank in Pressburg. Paić, who had been on assignment for the Dresdner Bank in Bucharest, Odessa, and Berlin, had requested the assignment. He viewed it as a "many-sided, international, and interesting business" that, as he had anticipated, enabled him to learn much and where he was content to stay for some time until his return to the Länderbank would be warranted.

These decisions were confirmed at the next supervisory board meeting. Lehr gave a glowing report of the bank's growing business, and Apold congratulated the management and the staff for exceeding the expectations of the supervisory board. Warnecke thanked the supervisory board for its support and made a special point of saluting the Dresdner Bank for its services. But whether there really was all that much for which to be thankful was another question, as there were significant political problems and issues that were covered up. Lehr's report certainly told a story of growth, for example, but it was not of the kind that bankers would necessarily celebrate. There had been an extremely sharp decline of bills of exchange. They constituted 59 percent of the bill portfolio in 1939, 35 percent in 1940, and 9 percent in 1941. The proportion of such bills constituted 15 percent of the bank's balance sheet in 1939 but not more than 2 percent in 1941. Various types of government bills constituted 68 percent of the bank's bill portfolio at the end of 1941. The portion of government paper in the bank's balance sheet had been 10 percent in 1938, 25 percent in 1939, 33.3 percent in 1939, and approximately 50 percent at the end of 1941. As Lehr noted, "this shows the extent to which the bank has joined in the financing tasks of the Reich."[25] At the same time, banks faced a variety of government measures limiting stock market activities, dividends, and interest rates that reduced bank profits and inhibited the bank from pursuing its interests in a traditional manner.

Such economic and financial "steering" measures affected the banking sector as a whole, but individual banks also had to deal with Party interests and personalities on the micro level. The discussions described earlier about personnel, the Länderbank's role in the southeast, and its relationship to the Dresdner Bank, reflected political maneuverings of great significance for the future of the Länderbank. After the April 21, 1942, meeting of the supervisory board, for example, Rasche had a discussion with Apold about new appointments to

[24] Ibid., personnel committee meeting, April 21, 1942, and, on Gold, ÖStA/AdR, BMI, Gauakt Franz Gold, Nr. 293.403.

[25] DrB, Nr. 5460-2000, supervisory board meeting, April 21, 1942.

that body, and in particular the appointment of persons who would represent the interests of the Gau leadership in Vienna and in the Lower Danube. Rasche had normally left such matters to Veesenmayer, but in this case he had brought it up with Apold because of a conversation with the Gau economic advisor for Vienna, Rafelsberger. Rasche had apparently hoped that the two Gauleiter, Rafelsberger and Jury, could agree on one candidate who would be a businessman, but Rafelsberger did not think that Jury would agree to someone he, Rafelsberger, would want. Rafelsberger thought Hiedler fit the model of a Party man from the business world, while Jury was more interested in having someone appointed from his immediate entourage. It would seem that Rafelsberger also had a great interest in giving the Länderbank a more independent role in Southeastern Europe and in the appointment of Gold; Rasche told Veesenmayer that he had discussed both matters with Rafelsberger. In any event, Gold had been appointed, but the question of new appointments to the supervisory board remained unsettled, and Rasche informed Veesenmayer that Apold was empowered to pursue these questions insofar as Veesenmayer would not do so himself.[26]

During this period, Veesenmayer was pursuing a diplomatic and SS career in Slovakia, Croatia, Serbia, and Hungary, a career that made him a leading figure in the Holocaust. He was directly and actively involved in these personnel matters, and he promised Rasche that he would discuss them with Rafelsberger personally.[27] Veesenmayer had a specific agenda that led him to take these issues up with Rafelsberger. In a letter to Rafelsberger of May 1, he pointed out that, in their last conversation, Rafelsberger had promised him to negotiate with Jury about appointing a Party man to the Länderbank supervisory board who would have Jury's trust. Veesenmayer was sorry to learn that this effort had failed, but he still hoped a way would be found to make such an appointment because he did not think it practicable to replace the late

Birthelmer with two exclusively Party people. Veesenmayer thought that the existing composition of the supervisory board took account of Party interests, "not least by my presence."

Veesenmayer then went on to state his position with respect to the Länderbank. He shared Baldur von Schirach's goal of strengthening Vienna for the purpose of penetrating the Southeast economically and politically, and he was thus pursuing the double goal of increasing the independence of the Länderbank and a progressive redirection toward business in Southeast Europe. Veesenmayer made clear that he was not an unconditional supporter of the connection with the Dresdner Bank: "I am aware of the fact that the present dependence of the Länderbank on the Dresdner Bank is contested. It unquestionably has certain advantages alongside certain disadvantages and flaws. I do not believe that it is practicable to undertake fundamental changes during wartime, and all the more so as the gentlemen from the Dresdner Bank as well as the Länderbank are in agreement about letting the Southeast European engagements flourish through special cultivation."[28] Director Gold, for whom Veesenmayer had extremely high regard, had been appointed to the Länderbank management board for this reason, and the Deutsche Handels- und Kreditbank had assumed great importance for reasons having to do with foreign exchange and with the peculiarities of the Slovak state. Nevertheless, one could anticipate the time when part of the business in Pressburg would be shifted to Vienna.

It was in this context that Veesenmayer tried to win the trust of his Party comrade Rafelsberger and to dissuade him from seeking a position on the Länderbank supervisory board for someone close to him. Rafelsberger already had a seat on the Creditanstalt board of supervisors, and unless he also wanted to serve on the Länderbank board of supervisors, the Länderbank, which already appeared disadvantaged in comparison to the Creditanstalt, would find it discriminatory to have merely

26 DrB, Nr. 5461-2000, Rasche to Veesenmayer, April 27, 1942.

27 Ibid., Rasche to Apold, May 4, 1942.
28 Ibid., Veesenmayer to Rafelsberger, May 1, 1942.

a representative of Rafelsberger elected. Veesenmayer insisted he could be counted on to serve Rafelsberger's purposes: "You know my attachment to the Ostmark and Vienna, also know that I am a specialist and good authority on the Southeast, and because I steadfastly intend to devote myself again entirely to economic policy after the war, I am able to make the claim for myself to guarantee that an appropriate consideration be given in all matters pertaining to the interests of the Party."[29] Veesenmayer thus sought to assure Rafelsberger that the Länderbank wished to work closely with Rafelsberger's Gau Economic Office.

This effort appears to have been successful. On May 12, 1942, Veesenmayer traveled to Vienna to discuss these matters with Rafelsberger and Jury, and he apparently convinced them it was unnecessary that they each have a representative on the Länderbank supervisory board. Rafelsberger felt he could empower Hiedler, in whom he had great confidence, to act on his behalf. Jury seemed to have more qualms about this than Rafelsberger, but he was prepared to have Director Warnecke assigned the task of acting as a special contact person with Jury and, in particular, to the man Jury wanted as his special delegate to the Supervisory Board, Fritz Waibl, whom he had just appointed to lead the Gau Economic Chamber. Rafelsberger and Jury also discussed other potential appointments to the Länderbank supervisory board. They voiced no objection to Erwin Daub of the Vereinigte Stahlwerke, and they concurred in adopting a wait-and-see position with respect to another candidate, General Director Karl Rueff of the Austria Tabakwerke AG, who was in bad standing with Baldur von Schirach. Neither Rafelsberger nor Veesenmayer actually objected to Rueff, and Rafelsberger even had a high opinion of his abilities and thought him a victim of unfair reports to von Schirach, but they also felt it necessary to defer to von Schirach and thought he might change his mind. In the course of the conversation, Veesenmayer learned that Jury, who had been a supporter of the Creditanstalt, was now more inclined toward the Länderbank, apparently because of recent changes leading to the dominance of the Deutsche Bank at the Creditanstalt. Jury would "gladly have viewed the Länderbank as his exclusive instrument," and was thus somewhat disappointed that the bank did not accept the appointment of Fritz Waibl as his personal representative. Waibl was a district economic advisor and president of the Niederdonau Gau Economic Chamber, and he served on numerous supervisory boards, including that of the Creditanstalt. Waibl's appointment, however, would have led to a similar demand by Rafelsberger, and Veesenmayer pointed out to Jury that "it is not acceptable for a bank like the Länderbank to concern itself with Party politics, and that it has to keep itself distant from a basic conflict between two Gaus."[30] Veesenmayer assured Jury that he would personally make every effort to watch that Niederdonau interests were given their due. As Pilder concluded from Veesenmayer's report, "for reasons of expediency, one must keep in mind that Herr Jury is to some extent looking for a new bank friendship and consider the extent to which the Länderbank can place itself at the disposal of Herr Jury with respect to his economic wishes."[31]

When it came to meddling in the affairs of the Länderbank in a programmatic fashion, however, it was Rafelsberger to whom one had to be most attentive, especially because he was very much of one mind with Veesenmayer. In a conversation with Veesenmayer, Rafelsberger seemed quite concerned about the organization and effectiveness of the Länderbank. He urged that it follow the apparently successful model of the Creditanstalt and create an executive committee. Rafelsberger also felt that the Länderbank management board lacked "a leading mind," a judgment in which Veesenmayer

---

[29] Ibid.

[30] There are two accounts of Veesenmayer's discussions with Rafelsberger and Jury, one a memorandum by Pilder recounting what Veesenmayer had told him of May 13, 1942, the other a report from Veesenmayer to Rasche of May 12, 1942. Both are in ibid. This quotation is from the Veesenmayer letter.

[31] Ibid., Pilder memorandum, May 13, 1942.

concurred; voicing his pleasure at the appointment of Gold, he hoped that Gold might turn out to be such a leader. Most importantly, Rafelsberger wished for a larger role for the Länderbank in the banks in Southeast and Eastern Europe where the Dresdner Bank had established itself. As Veesenmayer reported: "He would also like to see that the Länderbank be a shareholder in a much fuller manner in Cracow, Pressburg, Agram, and Budapest, not immediately, but in time, and at the same time that suitable men from the Bank be delegated to a greater extent to the administration of these banks."[32] Veesenmayer sought to impress Rasche with how important it was for the Länderbank to show goodwill and follow through on these proposals.

Manifestly, this was a message to the Dresdner Bank as well, and it came at a time when the major banks confronted growing threats to their interests from both government and Party agencies. The RWM and its banking expert, Ministerial Director Joachim Riehle, were pushing for rationalization of the banking industry to put an end to what the ministry perceived as overcrowding in banking sector and to free up manpower by shutting down branches deemed expendable or superfluous. Party radicals, although they hardly could attack the role of private enterprise because of the war effort, had no inhibitions about attacking the banks and could take advantage of the rationalization program for their own purposes. Hitler's secretary, Martin Bormann, took the lead in the effort to strengthen the role of the Party in economic affairs by upgrading the Gau economic advisors and consolidating the chambers of commerce into Gau economic chambers. "Rationalizing" and transforming the banking system was an important part of his agenda and was to lead to the creation of a "Bormann Committee" of thirteen of the most prominent Gau economic advisors in October 1942. Rafelsberger was one of the members.[33]

The rumblings from the Party were felt earlier, however, and Director Goetz of the Dresdner Bank wrote to Rasche in late July urging that the Central Association of German Banks and Bankers become more active and that Rasche assume the leadership and find more effective management for the organization.[34]

Nothing came of this proposal, but the pressures from the Party, above all from Rafelsberger, intensified substantially in early August 1942 in connection with the never-ending problem of staffing the Länderbank supervisory board. In the last days of July, Pilder informed Goetz that Director Gold had called to urge the appointment of the commercial attaché in Pressburg, Erich Gebert, to the supervisory board. Gebert, a Party member of long standing with radical economic inclinations and an SS man, had served as Gau economic advisor in Salzburg and was also president of the Salzburg Gau Chamber of Commerce. Gold praised Gebert for his services to the bank in Pressburg, noted his positions in Salzburg, and also mentioned that Rafelsberger supported him. Pilder told Goetz that he had drafted a letter concerning the proposal to Apold and wanted Goetz's approval. While Goetz had nothing against Gebert, he was about to go on vacation and could not understand why there was such a rush given the fact that the shareholders' meeting was two months away. He also did not like the procedure. Gold was the newest director on the management board, and there had been no discussion of the issue in the administration of the Dresdner Bank or the Länderbank. In any case, Goetz went on his trip, intending to deal with the matter when he returned.[35]

Bank- und Bankiergewerbes 1932–1945 (Munich 2001), pp. 237–245, and Kopper, *Bankenpolitik*, pp. 349–353; Johannes Bähr, "'Bankenrationalisierung' und Großbankenfrage. Der Konflikt um die Ordnung des Deutschen Kreditgewerbes während des Zweiten Weltkrieges," in: Harald Wixforth (ed.), *Finanzinstitutionen in Mitteleuropa während des Nationalsozialismus.* (= Geld und Kapital. Jahrbuch der Gesellschaft für mitteleuropäische Banken- und Sparkassengeschichte, Stuttgart 2000), pp. 71–94.

[32] Ibid., Veesenmayer to Rasche, May 12, 1942.

[33] See Harold James, *Verbandspolitik im Nationalsozialismus. Von der Interessenvertretung zur Wirtschaftsgruppe: Der Centralverband des Deutschen*

[34] DrB, Nr. 5460-2000, Goetz to Rasche, July 27, 1942.

[35] Ibid., Goetz to Rasche, Aug. 9, 1942. One can learn much about Gebert's role in dealing with

This infuriated Rafelsberger, who was obviously behind the proposal, and he wrote Pilder to this effect. Rafelsberger pointed out that Pilder and Rasche had already indicated they had no objections to Gebert and had promised to contact Apold. Now Goetz was off on vacation, and this would lead to weeks of delay. He found the delay inexcusable and thought Party agencies in Vienna would feel the same way. He considered the choice of Gebert particularly fortunate and hoped he could be drawn into the work of the bank right away. Consequently, he asked that Goetz withdraw his objections immediately, that Gebert be invited as a guest to the next supervisory board meeting, and that Gebert's appointment be approved, if necessary by mail. Rafelsberger's missive to Pilder was mild when compared with Veesenmayer's note to Rasche accompanying a copy of Rafelsberger's letter to Pilder: "I wish to remark also in this regard, that for example the pushing of the election of Herr Rueff could not proceed quickly enough, although here there still remain basic difficulties that do not make it seem advisable to rush the matter unduly. When it concerns a National Socialist, however, then one allows oneself time and delays the matter so obviously that one unfortunately is inclined to suspect there is a systematic effort behind it."[36]

Veesenmayer also called Goetz to express his irritation. Goetz continued to object to the procedure of appointing someone in the manner desired and failed to understand the haste, but he told Rasche that the matter should be settled in whatever way was deemed expedient. Goetz noted that the other managing directors at the Länderbank, Warnecke, Wolzt, and Lehr, had all praised Gebert for the help he had given, but they had also raised another consideration. The appointment of the Gau economic advisor of Salzburg would inevitably provoke questions about claims that

might be made by his counterpart in Styria. Yet another problem had come up as Goetz noted, no doubt rather wearily. While he was in Berlin, Economics Minister Funk had asked him whether Ministerial Director Ludwig Klucki might not be made chairman at the Länderbank. Klucki had served as section head of the Austrian Ministry of Finance charged with oversight of enterprises before going to the RWM in Berlin, and he was now eager to return to Vienna. Goetz first thought Funk was talking about appointing Klucki to the Länderbank supervisory board and pointed out that there was no reason to remove Apold, but then found out that Funk was talking about the management board. This was rather odd because Klucki had some experience in savings banks but none whatsoever in universal banking. Warnecke had told Goetz that Rafelsberger had also indicated that Klucki was looking for a position but had the impression that it was for a much better-paying one. In any case, Goetz felt that these personnel issues required considerable reflection, although neither Rafelsberger nor Veesenmayer gave him the sense that reflection was the order of the day.[37]

Even from a political point of view, there was little to recommend Klucki. He seems to have been a very competent official taken over from the old regime, who supposedly supported the National Socialists prior to 1938. He applied for Party membership only in June 1938, but his application was set aside because of the moratorium on admitting new members. He reapplied again in 1943 and was turned down in 1944 without reason. When nominated in 1940 for the Medal in Remembrance of March 13, 1938, an official in the Vienna Gau office protested that real "illegal fighters" who had suffered arrest, loss of job, and the like had not received the medal and found it hard to understand why a person who had made such modest contributions to the Party should receive it. If Klucki's support came from anywhere, it came from the RWM, where he appears to have been highly regarded.[38]

Aryanization questions in Salzburg from Albert Lichtblau, *"Arisierungen," Beschlagnahmte Vermögen, Rückstellungen und Entschädigungen in Salzburg.* Veröffentlichungen der Österreichischen Historikerkommission, vol. 17/2 (Vienna, Munich 2004).

[36] DrB, Nr. 5461-2000, Rafelsberger to Pilder and Veesenmayer to Rasche, Aug. 4, 1942.

[37] DrB, Nr. 5460-2000, Goetz to Rasche, Aug. 9, 1942.
[38] ÖStA/AdR, BMI, Gauakt Ludwig Klucki, Nr. 102.116.

In the end, neither Gebert nor Klucki ended up on the Länderbank supervisory board, but the politics that lay behind the idea of appointing them by no means disappeared with them. As Rafelsberger had demanded, Gebert was invited to be present as a guest at the supervisory board meeting on September 10, 1942, where it was explicitly announced that he would soon join the board as a member. That did not occur, however, possibly because of the ban Bormann issued in August on high Party officials serving on the management or supervisory boards of banks. The point of the ban was to shelter officials from the alleged ideological and material corruption that such activity on behalf of banks might bring.[39] The case of Klucki proved more complicated and important because Rafelsberger had a very special purpose in pushing this appointment, as he made clear in discussions with Rasche and Veesenmayer about the Party's intentions with respect to the future of the Länderbank. One of these intentions was to get rid of Pilder, to whom Rafelsberger wrote on September 19, 1942, informing him about these discussions and the fact that they had led to decisions about the changes and additions to be made to the Länderbank's supervisory board and management board. He went on to remark that: "I have in these discussions expressed the point that in the future the Party can view as acceptable on the supervisory board of so important an institution only such men who through their previous activity have demonstrated that they are, in the sense of the National Socialist idea, especially active and prepared to go on duty. I have in this connection told Herr Director Rasche that for this reason your remaining on the supervisory board of the Länderbank no longer appears possible."[40]

Rasche had asked Rafelsberger that they meet to present this decision to Pilder personally in Berlin, but Pilder was away when the meeting was to take place. Rafelsberger felt that the matter was urgent and could not be delayed. Rasche had also hoped Rafelsberger would consult with Goetz about Pilder and other personnel plans for the Länderbank that had been discussed at a Vienna meeting of Rafelsberger, Rasche, and Hiedler. Rafelsberger was willing to talk to Goetz, but he made clear that such a conversation could only have an "informative character," "because I see in you [i.e., Rasche] the only Party comrade in the management board of the Dresdner Bank with whom I would like to discuss such things in a binding manner." Rafelsberger assured Rasche that he wanted, "if possible," to deal with these questions in an agreeable manner with all concerned, but "I see the best precondition for this if we as Party comrades settle these things and then also carry them out."[41] Rafelsberger had noted the basic agreement between himself and Rasche, except for some slight reservations by the latter concerning some matters, including Klucki. But Rafelsberger was certain that Rasche had now come around in view of the intention to have Klucki play an important role in the tasks that lay ahead.

Both Goetz and Pilder apparently asked Rafelsberger to consult with the authorities in Berlin again about Pilder's removal from the Länderbank Supervisory Board, and Goetz seemed to have had reservations about Klucki's status as well. One may doubt that Rafelsberger ever had any intention of reconsidering his decision, but on September 30, he wrote to Pilder and Goetz saying that he had consulted with the Party chancellery and also with RWM State Secretary Friedrich Landfried and found no change of mind with respect to Pilder. Insofar as Klucki was concerned, Rafelsberger informed Goetz that Landfried had agreed to an arrangement under which Klucki would become a member of the supervisory board but would then be delegated to the management board "to carry out the intended tasks." This was an arrangement that also conformed to Klucki's wishes. Rafelsberger spelled out his own intentions, which were to have Klucki as a person who could undertake the "changes in

[39] DrB, Nr. 5460-2000, supervisory board meeting, Sept. 10, 1942; and Kopper, *Bankenpolitik*, p. 350.

[40] DrB, Nr. 5460-2000, Rasche to Pilder, Sept. 19, 1942.

[41] Ibid., Rafelsberger to Rasche, Sept. 19, 1942.

the leadership apparatus of the Länderbank" that would lead to "this institute making itself independent" in the sense that he had been discussing with Goetz and others.[42]

Pilder resigned his position at the Länderbank following this final decision, and his position on the presidium of the supervisory board was taken by Meindl. A year later, he was driven out of the Dresdner Bank management board at the repeated demand of Landfried and Party agencies. He retired with a substantial pension in recognition of his long years of service and was also allowed to maintain a substantial number of post on supervisory boards of industrial firms. All the circumstantial evidence suggests that he was protected by Goetz, who appears to have been unhappy about his departure.[43] One may be certain that Wurm, the company steward at the Länderbank, was very happy to see Pilder disappear, as was his counterpart in the Dresdner Bank. Wurm's description was very revealing of what irritated Party stalwarts about Pilder: "Even his external appearance reflects an international character. He is one of those plutocrats and Free Masons whom we want to destroy in the war against England. Every one of his characteristics is cold and calculating and only concerned about personal advantage. Members of the Dresdner Bank retinue are supposed to have pictures showing him at the burial of Rosa Luxemburg."[44]

There can be no question about the fact that Pilder was not a National Socialist and never pretended to be one. Although that did not prevent him from participating in Aryanization transactions and paying lip service to various regime policies, as has been shown, he was responsible for a great deal of the Dresdner Bank's international business and was an internationalist in his orientation. Rasche increasingly replaced him in the Czech lands and Southeast Europe because he was more attuned to German goals there and had close connections with Kehrl, SS leaders, and other persons who had become important for political reasons. There is no evidence, however, that Rasche was eager to remove him from either the Länderbank or the Dresdner Bank, and Rasche seems simply to have accepted the situation as it was. Rasche did report to Goetz that Pilder was not particularly liked by SS leaders in Holland, but that undoubtedly was a matter that had to be noted.[45]

The fact that Rasche asked Rafelsberger to discuss Pilder's removal with Goetz suggests that Rasche may have been rather uncomfortable with the situation. Rafelsberger claimed in postwar interrogations at Nürnberg that Landfried had been mobilized to drive him from the Dresdner Bank by complaints from the business circles in the Southeast and in Berlin that Pilder was not as serious as he should have been and tended to mix his personal finances with his banking activities. It is impossible to determine whether there was anything to these accusations, but Pilder certainly would have retained his positions were it not for Rafelsberger and Landfried. It is equally certain that, for Rafelsberger at least, Pilder's shortcomings from a political and strategic perspective were of great importance. As Rafelsberger noted, "so long as he had the Austrian desk in the supervisory board, he was constantly striving to limit the independence of the Länderbank in its activities in the southeast in favor of the Dresdner Bank. This contradicted the economic policy intention that we – I, as the exponent of the Gau Economic Advisor Office – pursued with the Vienna major banks."[46] In the last analysis, it is quite plausible that Pilder had shown very little enthusiasm for the Vienna orientation of Rafelsberger and

---

[42] Ibid., Rafelsberger to Rasche, Sept. 30, 1942, and Rafelsberger to Pilder, Sept. 30, 1942.

[43] Pilder's resignation from the Länderbank was announced at the supervisory board meeting of Nov. 5, 1942, ibid. For his departure from the Dresdner Bank and the role played by Landfried, see DrB, Nr. 1321–2000, Goetz to Pilder, Nov. 30, 1943. I am grateful to Johannes Bähr for supplying me with these and other materials on Pilder.

[44] WrStLA, Gauakt Josef Paić, Nr. 228082, report of A. Wurm, Feb. 23, 1944.

[45] StA Nürnberg, Nl. 13906, declaration by Pilder at Nürnberg, Jan. 16, 1948.

[46] BAB, 99 US7, Fall XI, Vol. 206, Bl. 160–161, interrogation of Rafelsberger, Oct. 5, 1948.

his allies. Although he was prepared to challenge his colleagues at the Dresdner Bank by supporting a 5 percent dividend instead of the 6 percent dividend in April 1942, that probably had more to do with financial calculation than loyalty to the Länderbank.[47] Far more revealing was his proposal to the RWM of August 1942 on the Dresdner Bank's behalf that it take over the Central European Länderbank in Paris and then use it to operate on behalf of the Dresdner Bank in the eastern territories. The proposal was turned down, but it clearly ran against the Rafelsberger policy of promoting the Länderbank Wien for such purposes.[48]

It is hard to escape the impression that the interventions in personnel matters by Rafelsberger and the RWM were, at least in these instances, amateurish and uninformed. Pilder was a genuine banker, and Klucki was not. Indeed, Klucki himself did not think he was entirely competent in the areas where he was supposed to support Rafelsberger's program. At the end of 1942, Goetz reported to Apold that Klucki found his projected position on the supervisory board interesting but that he did not have a clear view of what his mission was supposed to be. He explained that he wanted nothing to do with personnel changes, because he was an outsider, and that he would have to work his way into the problems of the southeast. Goetz thought that the personnel committee would like some say in the appointment, but he did not want to leave Rafelsberger

with the impression that they were dragging their feet. At the same time, Klucki wanted to wait until the new year to make a decision.[49] In the end, Klucki found other employment, probably more lucrative and less troublesome, and Apold announced to the personnel committee in April 1943 that Klucki would not be working with the Länderbank.[50]

The only dramatic event that took place in personnel matters in 1942–1943 was the removal of Pilder. There was apparently a consensus that Directors Franz Pilat and Josef Paić would be appointed to the management board in due course. Paić's political credentials and qualifications have already been discussed. Pilat's special qualities were less clear, assuming they existed. Born in 1896, he had joined the Mercurbank in 1920 and then transferred to the Länderbank in 1938. He joined the Party in that same year but does not appear to have been active politically. He seems to have been much favored by Wolzt; Wurm thought him "dry," "dependent on Berlin," and lacking in "leadership qualities."[51] But while Pilat was in the army, Paić was needed in Pressburg. As for the supervisory board, Karl Pfeiffer of the Länderbank Berlin, who was also a member of the Dresdner Bank supervisory board, left the Länderbank Board, while Meindl stayed on the Länderbank Board and left the Dresdner Bank supervisory board. There was one new appointment in 1943, Fritz von Engelberg, the chairman of the management board of the Dyckerhoff Portlandzementwerke AG in Mainz. It is highly likely that the Dresdner Bank selected the prominent German businessman for nonpolitical reasons.

Nevertheless, political interference and personnel problems did not entirely go away, and attitudes in Vienna created tensions with the Dresdner Bank. There were some painful incidents where the Dresdner Bank had cause for concern, as in the case of a corrupt head

---

47 NARA, T83/137, Dresdner Bank management board meetings, April 9 and April 18, 1942. It is interesting to note that Pilder was back in the service of the Länderbank in 1949, when he served as the Länderbank's representative in Germany as an employee of the firm of Bass & Herz in Frankfurt am Main. At the end of June 1949, he was asked by the Länderbank, as part of the effort to get back Austrian property in the American Occupation Zone, to negotiate with his old employer for the return of various securities belonging to the Länderbank that were still stored at the Dresdner Bank. See Österreichische Länderbank to the Dresdner Bank, June 30, 1949, Dresdner Bank files. Herr Hopf of the Dresdner Bank Archive kindly placed this document at my disposal.

48 StA Nürnberg, Nl 6216, Summary of document of Aug. 5, 1942.

49 DrB, Nr. 5460-2000, Goetz to Apold, Dec. 4, 1942, and Apold to Goetz, Dec. 9, 1942.

50 Ibid., personnel committee meeting, April 20, 1943.

51 Ibid., for Wurm's views, see WrStLA, Gauakt Josef Paić, Nr. 228082, his report of March 9, 1944.

of a Länderbank subsidiary, but the Dresdner Bank was ultimately satisfied with the way the Länderbank leadership handled the matter. In June 1942, Director Teichmann of the Dresdner Bank alerted Pilder, then still representing the Dresdner Bank at the Länderbank, to the fact that the person in question had covered up four credits amounting to 100,000 RM that resulted in a loss of between 10,000 RM and 30,000 RM. Party agencies then intervened on behalf of the culprit and called for leniency, which Teichmann thought they would not have done if they knew the facts. Under normal circumstances, such a person would be fired, but the directors in Vienna decided instead to demote him. Teichmann agreed with this decision because of the manpower shortage.[52] In another corruption case at the end of 1943 – in this instance, the head of a Länderbank branch who had been fired for repeated speculation – the Dresdner Bank refused to show similar "understanding." After sending the Länderbank an inquiry, which Rasche had deliberately cosigned, Rasche received a reply. The Länderbank maintained that it was under no obligation to report such a case to the Dresdner Bank and that it was rather insulting to receive such an inquiry. It also indicated that it was inclined to treat the matter lightly. Rasche positively exploded over the very idea that a violation of the trust that was the essence of the banking profession did not need to be reported to the chief shareholder, especially this case where Rasche, who had done so much for the Länderbank and sat on its supervisory board, had taken it upon himself to send the inquiry. He insisted that it was not up to the Länderbank to decide what was significant to report; what really mattered was his judgment as a member of the supervisory board and its committees. Rasche felt very "sobered" by the spirit of the Länderbank's response because, "as you know, I have personally exerted myself so that your institution would have a certain special position in the confines of our affiliations. But when I now see that, as has been feared in many quarters, the harmonious collaboration

and sense of working together that we have sought from the outset is not supported but rather that centrifugal forces actually have been effective with such intensity – in the last analysis to the detriment of the Länderbank – then I feel severely disappointed in my efforts, and I will probably be compelled to subject my previous judgement and attitude to an appropriate revision."[53] Rasche sent the letter he had received back to the Länderbank with instructions that it be rewritten before it went into the files and that he also anticipated discussing the matter when he came to Vienna. He pointed out that it would have been better if the Länderbank had not climbed on to its "war horse" in the first place to tell him "as your supervisory board member what to do and what not to do."

This extraordinarily sharp letter is worth consideration not as an illustration of whatever residual tact and ethical standards Rasche might have retained but rather as evidence of the extent to which he had supported a special position for the Länderbank and had, as has been shown, promoted a policy of concession to the demands of Rafelsberger and other Party interests that apparently was not particularly popular among his colleagues. Goetz, Pilder, and Teichmann probably felt that there had been too much pandering to Viennese ambitions. Pilder saw the danger of serious irregularities, and Teichmann made his colleagues at the Dresdner Bank aware in early January 1943 that they were potentially undermining their position in Vienna by yielding to Party leaders and their protégés. He reported a comment made by one of the Dresdner Bank officers who had a conversation with Director Gold: "Herr Gold stays in contact with the Party agencies in Vienna in order to make the Länderbank independent, that is, to separate it from the Dresdner Bank."[54] This did not prevent the signing of a rather fat contract with Gold in May 1943 that gave him a 30,000 RM a year salary, 2 percent of distributed profits or, if no dividend was paid out, a honorarium amounting to 2 percent of

---

[52] DrB, Nr. 5640-2000, Teichmann to Pilder, June 8, 1942.

[53] Ibid., Rasche to the Länderbank board of directors, Dec. 20, 1943.

[54] Ibid., note by Teichmann, Jan. 9, 1943.

the reserves for his services to the Länderbank. He was to receive a separate salary and honorarium for his services in Pressburg of 325,000 kronen (at the clearing rate of 11.628 kronen to the RM) with a 30 RM per diem. He was also entitled to a five-week vacation and a generous pension. The contract was to run until the end of 1945 and to be automatically renewable to March 31, 1947, unless notice of termination was given.[55] In the last analysis, it obviously did not matter whether the Dresdner Bank could trust him.

It was truly impossible for the Länderbank to be free of Party interference in personnel matters, as was evident from the "social reports" on the benefits provided to Länderbank personnel, or in the indoctrination of its staff.[56] Denunciations of officers of the bank could not simply be dismissed. At the March 1944 meeting of what was now called the working committee, which combined, as Rafelsberger had desired the personnel and the credit committees of the supervisory board, Hiedler brought criticisms of bank officers that had gained the attention of Party agencies to the committee's attention. The source of the denunciations was the company steward, A. Wurm, some of whose views on personnel have been discussed earlier. He had written a report on the directors of the Länderbank in late February 1944. One of the victims was Director Ferdinand Lintner, whose "provisional" appointment to head the Wechselstuben AG "Mercur" in Budapest in 1939 had become more or less permanent. Lintner had begun his career in 1920 as head of the Salzburg branch of the Zentraleuropäische Länderbank and, according to Wurm, he had been a supporter of the Fatherland Front, clearing out rapidly after the Anschluss to head up the securities section of the Vienna branch. Wurm claimed that he traveled in monarchist and Jewish circles in Budapest and played the "maître de plaisir" to these "half-breeds." He

did manage, however, to acquire various blocks of shares for Berlin, which earned him the support of the supervisory board members in Berlin, who were planning to make him a director in Vienna. Wurm proudly announced that he had blocked this promotion by going to Warnecke and stating "that this was completely out of the question and impossible because in this way honest and industrious Party comrades would never have the chance to advance." Apparently, however, Lintner was now going to be promoted without, to Wurm's horror, consultation with the company council.[57] The campaign against Lintner seems to have succeeded; he was recalled from Budapest in May 1944 despite protest from the Länderbank management.[58]

Another of Wurm's targets was Michael Dyszkant, who had come from the Živnostenská banka. Among other things, he had headed the "Eigenhaus GmbH" and, in that capacity, had been involved in the Aryanization of Jewish properties. Wurm, who had opposed Dyszkant's appointment from the outset, accused him of having promoted Czech education for the children of employees at the Živnostenská banka and of being a member of a Czech organization. He also charged Dyszkant with being brutal toward those below him and servile to those above, and, most importantly, he claimed that Dyszkant had demanded extra rent from the wife of an officer living in a house Dyszkant owned. Dyszkant denied the charges and pointed out that he had sent his son to a German school. He also had the advantage of having been a Party member since May 1938 and thus certified as politically reliable. Wurm also failed to supply the evidence he claimed he had, and Dyszkant was retained. Wurm was particularly angry that Dyszkant had been promoted to director status without the company council being consulted.[59]

---

[55] Ibid., contract signed on May 19, 1943.

[56] Some of these are in DrB, Nr. 5460-2000 along with lengthy discussions of the pension fund and similar issues. There is insufficient information on life at the Länderbank, in contrast to the Creditanstalt, to justify an effort to recount it here.

[57] WrStLA, Gauakt Josef Paić, Nr. 228082, report by A. Wurm, Feb. 22, 1944.

[58] NARA, T83/138, Dresdner Bank management board meeting, May 7, 1944.

[59] Ibid., and ÖStA/AdR, BMI, Gauakt Michael Dyszkant, Nr. 126.723.

Even the personnel director, Rudolf Schwarz, whose National Socialist credentials dated back to 1933, was the subject of Wurm's ire. Wurm accused him of being mean and unfair to his subordinates and tending to favor people who came from the old Mercurbank, whether they were politically acceptable or not. As a result, "he is also today the most hated person in the entire business." According to Wurm, Warnecke had promised to do something about the situation but still had not brought himself to do so. In fact, it appears that Warnecke had sought to engage in damage control in this case. Schwarz, too, was retained to the end of the war.[60]

Finally, Wurm complained about the head of the legal section of the Länderbank, Robert Fischmeister, who was married to a half-Jew. Fischmeister had the salary of a director and was slated to become one without the company council being consulted. In this case, Wurm blamed the bank's syndic, Hans Mann, for protecting him. Mann could hardly be accused of being anything less than a 100 percent National Socialist, and it is obvious that Wurm's deeper complaint was the failure to consult him and to consult his colleagues on the company council about appointments and promotions. Wurm warned that if something was not done about this situation, he would have to resign and the Party activists at the bank would also step down from their positions.

Manifestly, there was considerable discord in the bank that was the result not only of tension between Party fanatics and persons less engaged but also of frustrated ambitions and jealousies. Another important element was resentment toward Berlin and the Dresdner Bank. In Wurm's view, the old Reich in general and the Dresdner Bank in particular was filled with business leaders who were corrupt or of bad character. Pilder and Haase-Mühlner were good examples of this, and the fact that the latter was arrested and ejected from Croatia for making critical comments about Hitler was

further evidence. Even Rasche, the only banker later to be tried at Nürnberg, was described by Wurm as a "blank slate" who had been under the influence of Pilder. Wurm thus concluded, "in view of such a deplorable state of affairs in the leadership of old Reich enterprises, every thinking person is compelled to ask the question of to what end must healthy enterprises in the Ostmark, which had stood on their own feet over decades come into a relationship of dependency on the old Reich? This lies singly and alone in selfish and exploitative motives, for the more knowledgeable persons are, as in so many other fields so also in banking, unconditionally in the Ostmark. If one has destroyed the good Ostmark organization in banking in order to replace it by an antiquated system, we still do not want also to take over a leadership that is unbearable for us."[61] It is clear that Wurm's understanding of Austrian banking history and organization or, indeed, recent history more generally was rather deficient, but he does provide an illustration of anti-German resentment in the Austrian National Socialist camp as well as of the role played by the Party and denunciations in keeping the management of the bank in line.

Even management board members were not spared. As noted earlier, Director Wolzt had to pay a 3,000 RM fine for having given 10 RM to an acquaintance who was partly Jewish. But no sooner had further charges against him been dropped than the forty-three-year-old Wolzt found himself called up for military service in August 1944. The Länderbank appealed the case on the grounds of Wolzt's important duties, and his service was delayed until November. The Länderbank sought his permanent deferment, however, and was still appealing to the military authorities and the RWM in January 1945 over the strenuous objections of the Gau office.[62] By this time, the anticipated changes at the top level of the Länderbank were taking

[60] WrStLA, Gauakt Josef Paić, Nr. 228082, report by A. Wurm, Feb. 23, 1944; DrB, Nr. 5460-2000, Länderbank working committee meeting, March 20, 1944.

[61] WrStLA, Gauakt Josef Paić, Nr. 228082, report by A. Wurm of Feb. 22, 1944.

[62] ÖStA/AdR, BMI, Gauakt Leonard Wolzt, Nr. 19.730.

place. The question of appointing Paić and Pilat to the management board was still not resolved during the first half of 1944, and the result was some uncertainty and resentment as a result. In April, for example, Director Karl Klimpel, who felt unjustly passed over by the new appointments, told this to Warnecke and Teichmann. In a letter to Teichmann, Kimpel argued that, given his seniority and services, he should receive at least the salary of a member of the management board. Teichmann was much irritated, pointing out that Klimpel was too old to be on the management board and was also overreaching himself professionally. Teichmann was no less upset by Director Franz Schraudolph, who followed up on a casual conversation with Teichmann about his career to press for an appointment in Pressburg. Teichmann was anxious to avoid giving the impression of interfering with the appointments at the Länderbank.[63] These episodes suggested that continued uncertainty would only heighten whatever bad feelings existed about the projected appointments and encourage more jockeying for advantage. For that reason, Rasche wrote to Goetz on July 3, 1944, urging that they settle matters once and for all and that Paić and Pilat be appointed to the management board effective January 1, 1945. The contracts were drawn up shortly afterward.[64] In mid-March 1945, there was renewed discussion, this time between Rasche and Teichmann, about personnel changes at the Länderbank. Paić and Pilat were now in place, but Warnecke was reaching retirement age and could be expected to bow out in the coming year. Hitschfeld had already retired on March 7. The chief burdens would now fall on Paić and Lehr.[65] By this time, however, these decisions were more or less exercises in spitting against the wind, and the leadership of the Länderbank was to come from elsewhere.

2. THE LÄNDERBANK IN GERMAN-CONTROLLED EUROPE

So much for the "success" of Rafelsberger and his allies in changing the personnel of the Länderbank. The question remains, however, as to whether the position of the Länderbank in the war years had been transformed in the direction desired by Rafelsberger and others seeking a greater independence for the Länderbank and, most importantly, a greater role for the bank in Southeast Europe. In formal terms, the Dresdner Bank made considerable concessions toward such demands, although it is difficult to tell how far that was voluntary and how far the result of pressure. In May 1940, for example, the Dresdner Bank changed its practice of limiting current Länderbank credits to 2 million RM and taking over amounts beyond that as sub-participations. The Länderbank was now allowed to grant larger credits with the provision that the percentage of debt owing to the bank on its balance sheet not exceed that of the Dresdner Bank.[66] This did not mean, however, that the Länderbank could be the majority shareholder in banks owned by the Dresdner Bank. The only exception had been when the Länderbank was assigned that role, as was initially the case with the Deutsche Handels- und Kreditbank in Pressburg. As will be shown, the takeover of the Zipser Bank by the Pressburg bank in February 1941 and an accompanying capital increase established the Dresdner Bank as the major shareholder. In contrast to the other Dresdner Bank subsidiaries, Länderbank personnel did play the dominant role in Pressburg. When the Kommerzialbank in Cracow was revived in 1940, the Dresdner Bank became the chief shareholder, and the Dresdner Bank was also the dominant shareholder of the Kroatische Landesbank in Agram (Zagreb). Insofar as share capital was concerned, the only banking acquisition in which the Länderbank was sole owner and leading force was the new branch it acquired by taking over and merging the branches of the Kroatische Sparkasse

---

63 DrB, Nr. 5460-2000, Klimpel to Teichmann, April 27, 1944, Teichmann to Klimpel, June 9, 1944, and Teichmann to Schraudolph, June 9, 1944.

64 DrB, Nr. 5461-2000, Rasche to Goetz, July 3, 1944, and Goetz to Rasche, Nov. 22, 1944.

65 DrB, Nr. 13938-2000, discussion between Rasche and Teichmann, March 14, 1945.

66 NARA, T83/136, Dresdner Bank working committee, May 9, 1940.

and the Genossenschaftliche Wirtschaftsbank in Marburg/Maribor following the German expansion into Slovenia in 1941.

The Länderbank might have played a more significant role in Italy during the German occupation. In January 1944, Director Meyer of the Dresdner Bank was interested in finding banking opportunities in the occupied areas of Italy, and he initially sent Director Haase-Mühlner there in the guise of a representative of the Kroatische Landesbank. He hoped eventually to send Director Gold of the Länderbank to look after Dresdner Bank's interests in Italy. In June, Meyer was still pursuing this matter, stressing the importance of having a connection in Trieste and announcing his intention of sending Gold there and of moving Haase-Mühlner to Laibach/Ljubljana to strengthen the position of the Kroatische Landesbank. These plans apparently did not amount to much, for obvious reasons. The sources nonetheless make clear the Dresdner Bank's interest in employing Gold and the Länderbank to realize its ambitions in occupied Italy.[67]

When it came to playing a very important role in Southeast Europe, which was one of the goals of the aforementioned personnel changes so energetically pursued by Rafelsberger, the Länderbank suffered considerable frustration. That was not entirely the fault of the Dresdner Bank. Both the Länderbank and the Creditanstalt, on whose supervisory board Rafelsberger sat, were unhappy with the state of their efforts to gain the special place for the Vienna banks desired by the National Socialist leadership in Austria. When Veesenmayer asked Director Gold to report on the situation in September 1942, Gold claimed to have created a kind of "experimental laboratory" in Pressburg to test ways to increase Vienna's influence. The real problem in gaining special preference for Vienna, in his view, was the bureaucracy in Berlin and the inability to expedite matters. The Länderbank and the Creditanstalt had joined in a petition to Rafelsberger aimed at mobilizing the authorities to improve things and were contemplating the creation of a limited liability company under government supervision that would be given special rights to speed up the approval process for Ostmark business abroad. Veesenmayer had to confess that the procedures in Berlin were based on centralization and monopolization and were very hard to break through. Rasche chimed in that Kehrl was heading up a committee to support Vienna's efforts to decentralize things. Rasche thought that Vienna had a "certain moral claim to a priority position in the southeast." Hamburg, with its long trading experience, also had such a claim, and its pressure to decentralize could be helpful to Vienna's parallel efforts, although there might also be instances where Hamburg could work at cross purposes to Viennese ambitions. Southeast Europe was not the sole focus of Viennese ambitions, however, and Veesenmayer stressed the importance of Vienna playing a role in business in the east, "because there were pioneering tasks to fulfill" there. Wolzt noted that the east was indeed on the agenda of the banks in Vienna, and that the Länderbank and the Creditanstalt as well as the banking houses of Schoeller and Nicolai were interested. Two Viennese "economic observers" in the persons of Dyszkant of the Länderbank and Erwin Schmidt of the Creditanstalt were being sent to the Crimea at the expense of the banks for this purpose.[68]

[67] NARA, T83/138, Dresdner Bank management board meetings, Jan. 24 and June 6, 1944. Haase-Mühlner seems to have been a rather original character with a charmed life. In February 1943, he attended a social evening in Zagreb where he criticized Hitler for promising victory at Stalingrad and expressed the view that the workers had little interest in supporting the war because they would be the most important class under Bolshevism. This caused something of an uproar among those present and demands that he not be allowed to travel abroad. Meyer, however, seems to have protected him as a talented "Schwätzer," and Haase-Mühlner obviously continued to be used for important assignments abroad. See BAB, 99 US7, Fall XI, Nr. 448, Bl. 41–45, the memorandum of Feb. 17, 1943, and Bohle to Lange, May 3, 1943. I am grateful to Johannes Bähr for alerting me to this information.

[68] DrB, Nr. 5460-2000, supervisory board meeting, Sept. 10, 1942.

Given these grandiose prospects, one can well understand the desire of the Viennese banks to operate with greater independence and to emerge from the shadow of the major Berlin banks. The Creditanstalt was far along in this respect. The pressure from Rafelsberger to improve the status of the Länderbank, probably with the hope of making it independent after the war, led to important measures in 1943. In January, Director Meyer proposed that the Länderbank be given significant minority stakes in its Southeast and East European subsidiaries, 25 percent in the cases of Pressburg and Cracow, and 25 percent of the Kroatische Landesbank, when the Dresdner Bank's stake exceeded 51 percent. The Dresdner Bank was to retain the right to repurchase the shares at the same price, however; likewise, the Länderbank was to have the right to resell the shares at the same price if it wished.[69]

In May 1943, the Dresdner Bank and the Länderbank signed a consortial contract based on that proposal that divided the stakes as shown in the table below:

Deutsche Handels- und Kreditbank AG, Pressburg	Total Capital: Ks. 30,000,000
Dresdner Bank	Ks. 22,500,000
Länderbank	Ks. 7,500,000
Total Consortial Shares	Ks. 30,000,000
Kommerzialbank AG, Krakau	Total Capital: Zl. 5,000,000
Dresdner Bank	Zl. 3,750,000
Länderbank	Zl. 1,199,000
Total Consortial Shares	Zl. 4,949,000
Kroatische Landesbank AG, Agram	Total Capital: Kuna 100,000,000
Dresdner Bank	Kuna 51,000,000
Länderbank	Kuna 3,148,000
Total Consortial Shares	Kuna 54,148,000

Under the contract, the Dresdner Bank was entitled to the chairmanship and two further seats on the Pressburg administrative council, and the Länderbank was to receive the deputy chairmanship and one further seat. The Dresdner

Bank was entitled to the chairmanship of the supervisory board of the Crakow bank, and the Länderbank was to get the deputy chairmanship. The Dresdner Bank's control of the Kroatische Landesbank was based on a syndicate arrangement with the Gewerbebank Prag, which entitled the Dresdner Bank to four seats on its board of directors, of which the Länderbank was to have one. Unsurprisingly, the leadership of the consortium, which was to meet regularly, was to be in the hands of the Dresdner Bank, and although each of the banks could represent its own shares at the shareholders' meeting, their voting was to be in accordance with a decision by the consortium, and preference was to be given to consensual agreement. If a vote was necessary, each share had one vote. The oversight over the banks, as before, would be the responsibility of the Dresdner Bank. Shares of the two consortium members were not to be sold without mutual agreement, and the consortium was to be automatically renewable each year unless one of the parties decided to withdraw.[70]

The Dresdner Bank claimed that it had wanted to give the Länderbank a 25 percent stake in all the Southeast European banks in which it had an interest. That plan foundered, it said, on the need for the approval of government agencies both inside and outside Germany, and on complicated tax problems.[71] It was certainly true that foreign governments, even if they were puppet governments, were looking after their interests in the banking field, and that was one reason why the Länderbank could not acquire a stake in Romanian and certain Hungarian holdings of the Dresdner Bank. The convenience of the consortium arrangement was that it fulfilled the goal of giving the Länderbank a larger role without seriously loosening the basic hold of the Dresdner Bank on its subsidiaries. That intention was reflected in the contract as well as in the statement of intent Goetz presented at the November 14, 1943, Länderbank supervisory board meeting. The Länderbank

[69] NARA, T83/138, Dresdner Bank management board meeting, Jan. 26, 1943.

[70] See NARA, T83/138, for the consortial agreement of May 6, 1943.

[71] DrB, Nr. 5460-2000, Länderbank supervisory board meeting, June 30, 1943.

was to be given a consortial participation in the Dresdner Bank's other bank holdings in the east in which the Dresdner Bank held at least 51 percent of the share capital. The Länderbank could thus anticipate receiving a stake in the Ostbank AG in Posen.[72] There is no evidence that the Länderbank invested in Posen, however, but the Dresdner Bank did indicate its intention to offer the Länderbank stakes in its bank holdings in Belgrade. Regardless of the specifics, the transfer of shares did not have much practical significance because the final contract was drawn up only in early 1944, and the conclusion of the arrangement would have to wait on the approval of the Dresdner Bank shareholders.[73] Obviously, therefore, the Länderbank's engagements in Southeast Europe did not really depend on these share transfers or the operation of the consortium in a formal sense, but rather on day-to-day business activity, whether this was done on its own or in collaboration with its parent bank.

The Wechselstuben AG "Mercur" in Budapest

There were, of course, great advantages to having a common policy in Southeast Europe, and there was no conflict between the Dresdner Bank's and the Länderbank's interests in the region. A major problem, however, was that the Dresdner Bank could not always protect the Länderbank from political pressure even if the pressure ran against the interests of both banks. A good illustration of this problem is provided by the convoluted history of the Wechselstuben AG "Mercur" in Budapest. An important industrial holding of that bank, the "Ocean" Ungarische Konservenfabrik und Handels AG, was taken over by the firm Julius Meinl in May 1940; Meinl's expansion was strongly supported by Länderbank credits.[74] In the course of 1941, the sale of the Hungarian

bank was the subject of negotiations that were undertaken not by the Länderbank, but by the Dresdner Bank. Pilder was in charge of the operation, and he or one of his colleagues called the Länderbank management in November 1941 and asked the Länderbank to agree to sell its holding in the "Mercur." The immediate response of the Länderbank was negative, to which the Dresdner Bank countered that the Länderbank should not make difficulties because the sale had already been agreed upon. When the Länderbank again raised objections, the Dresdner Bank not only became more insistent but also asked that the entire matter be treated as a secret. The Länderbank management board thereupon felt it had to give way because it did not think it could disavow the Dresdner Bank's commitment. The sale of the shares, which continued to be kept secret and was intended to be temporary, was made to the Ethnic German Liaison Office, an SS organization that coordinated and promoted racial and settlement policies in Europe. It wanted to use the bank for its various projects but to camouflage the fact that it controlled the bank.[75]

The sale of the shares and the secrecy connected with it rankled the leadership of the Länderbank. This frustration came to the fore in February–March 1943 when the Dresdner Bank suddenly informed the Länderbank that the sale was to be made public and the shares were to be turned over to a private bank, which was to hold them as the ostensible owner. In earlier discussions at the beginning of 1942, Länderbank officials had apparently warned the Dresdner Bank that they were in violation of Hungarian law, which forbade sales of assets by foreign enterprises to other foreign enterprises without government permission.

[72] Ibid., Länderbank supervisory board meeting, Nov. 16, 1943.

[73] Ibid., Länderbank supervisory board meeting, March 20, 1944.

[74] NARA, T83/136, Dresdner Bank working committee meeting, May 23, 1940.

[75] On the negotiations of the Dresdner Bank, see NARA, T83/128, Dresdner Bank management board meeting, Nov. 6, 1941. On the Ethnic German Liaison Office, see Valids O. Lumans, *Himmler's Auxiliaries. The Volksdeutsche Mittelstelle and the German National Minorities of Europe, 1933–1945* (Chapel Hill 1993). For the details of these transactions, see DrB, Nr. 5461-2000, the lengthy letter of the Länderbank to the Dresdner Bank, March 1, 1943.

This transaction was dangerous for both banks because they had important interests in Hungary and the "Mercur" had certain special privileges. From this perspective, the proposed formalization of the sale in a public manner could only make a bad situation worse. The Länderbank took advantage of the moral and political high ground to vent its resentment about the domination of the Dresdner Bank: "We would like to ask you yet again to refrain from undertaking negotiations and making commitments in matters that have to do with our bank and the managerial work of its management board."[76] The Länderbank argued that if the Dresdner Bank had referred Dr. Riehle to the Länderbank, the problems connected with the sale could have been explained and a way could have been found to retain the ownership of the shares in the Länderbank while satisfying the needs of the Ethnic German Liaison Office. It proposed that either the matter be kept as it was or that the shares be secretly sold back to the Länderbank.

There could be no question that the Länderbank was correct. Both Apold and Rasche were apparently leaning toward returning the "Mercur" shares to the Länderbank.[77] It was probably in connection with tensions over this question that the Finanzkontor, which controlled the shares of the bank for the ethnic Germans, asked in early March 1944 that Director Lintner of the Länderbank be recalled to Vienna by the end of June; the Länderbank protested. Rasche thought that this would be a good time to raise the question of buying back the shares and to offer the ethnic Germans a credit to do their business in Hungary in return for the shares.[78] Director Gold was asked to negotiate. At a Länderbank supervisory board meeting on March 20, 1944, he reported on a meeting in Pressburg with the Ethnic German Liaison Office representatives. They offered to sell 50 percent of the shares back to the Länderbank; the Länderbank would hold a subordinate participation for the time being but would be offered the remainder of the shares a year after the war had ended. Gold intended to negotiate further and to propose that the Länderbank repurchase 100 percent of the shares and then give the Ethnic German Liaison Office the subordinate participation. Goetz and Rasche were quite fed up with the Liaison Office and with the problem, however. Germany had just occupied Hungary, and there seemed to be no further need either to cover up the ownership of "Mercur" or to drag out further what from the start had been intended to be a temporary arrangement to satisfy the Liaison Office. They decided to suspend negotiations and wait to see if, as anticipated, Veesenmayer was appointed ambassador to Hungary. If he was, they could count on him to solve the problem in the manner desired.[79] Veesenmayer did indeed become Reich plenipotentiary in Hungary, where he worked hand in hand with Adolf Eichmann in the deportation and murder of Hungary's Jews. Whether he had time to deal with bank questions before the Germans were thrown out of Hungary is unclear. In early May, Dresdner Bank directors Meyer and Zinsser met with a director of the Finanzkontor and proposed that the matter be settled and the ruse to camouflage the bank's ownership bank be ended.[80] Although the details of the transfer of ownership were worked out, the German embassy in Budapest held up the transfer of the shares back to Germany, and there were further delays so that it was only in late January 1945 that the Finanzkontor finally acted. It did so, however, by requesting that the "Mercur" ask the Hungarian National Bank to authorize

[76] Ibid.

[77] DrB, Nr. 5460-2000, Apold to Rasche, Feb. 15, 1943.

[78] NARA, T83/138, Dresdner Bank management board meeting, May 7, 1944. The share arrangements were covered up by the Länderbank acting as the trustee for the Vereinigte Finanzkontore GmbH, a clearing bank used for such purposes and owned by the Reichsbank, the Dresdner Bank, and the Commerzbank. See NARA, RG 260, 390/44/33/3, Länderbank Wien to the Foreign Exchange Office Berlin, Sept. 23, 1943, and Vereinigte Finanzkontore to the Foreign Exchange Office Berlin, Sept. 27, 1943.

[79] DrB, Nr. 5461-2000, supervisory board meeting, March 20, 1944.

[80] NARA, T83/138, Dresdner Bank management board meeting, May 23, 1944.

the transfer to Germany, a procedure that was bound to lead nowhere.[81] By this time, it obviously did not really matter. The case is nonetheless interesting as an illustration of the peculiar mixture of tension and collaboration between the Dresdner Bank and the Länderbank. It shows, on the one hand, the high-handed manner with which the former could treat the latter's interests and, on the other, the capacity of the two banks to join forces in looking after their mutual interests.

The Trifailer Bergwerks AG and the Länderbank Branch in Marburg (Maribor)

The "Mercur" incident was not the only instance in which the business plans of the two banks were frustrated or at least significantly modified for political reasons. In some cases, adaptation was easier and one type of business could be replaced by another. This is exemplified by the role of the Länderbank in the annexed areas of the Slovenian region of Yugoslavia. The defeat of France afforded the Länderbank an opportunity to acquire more than 20 percent of the Trifailer Bergwerks AG. The company's headquarters were in Laibach/Ljubljana, but its mines, cement works, and power plants were on what had become German territory. The general director of the BPEC, Henry Reuter, had fought hard and successfully to hold on to the bank's stake in the company in the 1938 negotiations between the Dresdner Bank and the BPEC. Once the Germans were in Paris, however, the Länderbank proposed that the shares be bought back for the same price for which they had been sold. A significant portion of the shares were already in German hands but widely dispersed. The Länderbank could achieve a controlling majority by supplementing the BPEC holding with shares purchased from Czech and Yugoslavia. The Dresdner Bank agreed to this course of action at the end of July 1940, and negotiations were held in the

fall, with Pilder playing the leading role for the Germans. One complication to the situation was that the Jewish members of the BPEC administrative board, including Henry Reuter, were in Vichy. Although President Luquet and the other non-Jewish French negotiators were ready to settle because they felt that it was impossible to hold on to the shares, the entire board had to agree and the approval of the Vichy government had to be secured. Reuter apparently consulted the French government almost immediately upon receiving information about the proposed stock sale, reporting back that the Vichy government was prepared to see only half the shares sold to the Germans and wanted the supervisory board seats to be divided between the Germans and the French. Pilder was quite satisfied with this arrangement because it gave the French and Germans 30 percent of the shares and thus effective control, and because he had a very reliable partner in Director Henry Jahan of the Banque de Paris et des Pay-Bas, which had been working with the Dresdner Bank. Negotiations were held at the turn of October–November 1940, and an agreement was reached on the sale of the shares by the BPEC to the Dresdner Bank and the Banque de Paris et des Pay-Bas, and on the creation of a supervisory board with a Yugoslav chairman, three Germans, and three Frenchmen. The French board members who were Jewish were to retire.[82]

Satisfaction with this arrangement did not last long. Pilder soon became eager for the two banks – the Länderbank serving as the proxy for the Dresdner Bank – to try to obtain a majority by buying up shares scattered in France and Yugoslavia. He felt certain that the Italians would show an interest in the Trifailer concern because of its location in Laibach/Ljubljana. The effort to acquire a majority continued, but the future of the company became quite unclear in the spring of 1941. It was in the banks' interest to keep the company as a

[81] Ibid., Dresdner Bank management board meetings, Aug. 29, Oct. 4, Dec. 5, 1944, and Jan. 23, 1945 meetings.

[82] See NARA, T83/207, memorandum of July 31, 1940, signed by Pilder, Rasche, and Schippel; Pilder to Schlotterer, Sept. 18, 1940; result of negotiations of Oct. 31, Nov. 2, 1940.

single entity, but the Reichswerke Hermann Göring was becoming interested in its mines, and the Gauleiter in Styria had his eye on the cement works and power plants. On June 6, the head of the civil administration in Lower Styria decided to sequester all the Trifailer holdings on German soil along with four other companies and turn them into a large energy concern, the Energieversorgung Südsteiermark AG, Marburg.[83] While the negotiations on the creation of this concern were under way, the Länderbank was saddled with the problem of financing the Trifailer coal production with a 1.4 million RM credit. The coal was being stored at the pitheads because of the transportation difficulties at the time, which placed a burden on the otherwise flourishing branch in Marburg/Maribor the Länderbank had opened.[84]

The Energieversorgung Südsteiermark AG decided to pay off the purchasers of the Trifailer shares and sell the coal to the Swiss to cover German debts. Because the new power company would require millions in credits, the only business left for the banks was to provide them; the Energieversorgung Südsteiermark AG approached the Länderbank and the Creditanstalt in early 1942 for financing. The Creditanstalt could not but recognize the prior interest of the Dresdner Bank and the Länderbank, and an arrangement was made under which the Länderbank would provide 13,350,000 RM of a 20 million RM credit, and the Creditanstalt would supply the remaining third. Later, the portion of the credit intended for investment was raised from 10 million RM to 18 million RM; the Dresdner Bank took 40 percent of the credit, the Länderbank 60 percent. The Länderbank in turn gave half its quota to other banks. The Energieversorgung Südsteiermark AG had thus become a huge investment in which the Länderbank was the

major party, and the earlier idea of having the Trifailer become a Länderbank holding had become irrelevant.[85]

Nevertheless, the Länderbank was eager to make the most of its branch in Marburg/Maribor, where it had a strong foothold thanks to the business conducted by Director Klimpel in the area. He and his colleagues were very active in acquiring new customers and trying to take away customers from the Creditanstalt branch.[86] This aggressiveness was reflected in a report, probably by Klimpel, to the Länderbank of May 27, 1941, on the successes of the Marburg branch during its first two weeks of existence. It had been able to open many new accounts that did not come from the predecessor banks and was sufficiently successful to be able to pay the Vienna home office back the start-up costs.[87] In mid-June, he and a colleague traveled through the area to visit firms in the hope of tapping in to potential customers, and he seems to have had considerable success. There was also an opportunity to discuss matters with Veesenmayer, then on a diplomatic mission in the Balkans, who told Klimpel that Berlin had not approved an agreement the authorities in Marburg/Maribor had reached with the Italian high commissioner in Laibach/Ljubljana and the Croat authorities to maintain trade between Lower Styria and Croatia. Berlin's goal was to integrate the newly annexed territories into the Reich as rapidly as possible and to prevent the development of any sense of "sovereignty." Klimpel seemed to think that it would nevertheless take some months before trade with Croatia normalized, and he was pleased by the apparently

[83] For the Decree of June 6, 1941 and the subsequent cashing in of the shares, see ibid.

[84] NARA, T83/128 and T83/137, Dresdner Bank management board meeting, May 26, 1941 and July 4, 1941, and working committee, June 5, 1941. See also DrB, Nr. 5460-2000, Länderbank supervisory board meeting of Sept. 23, 1941.

[85] See the CA working committee meeting of Feb. 27, 1942 and the report on the Energieversorgung Südsteiermark AG, Marburg in Archiv BA-CA, Vorstandsarchiv der Creditanstalt (= CA-V). On the Credits, see NARA, T83/137, Dresdner Bank working committee, March 23, 1942, and June 22, 1942.

[86] See BA-CA, CA-TZ, Sekretariat rot, Filiale Marburg, the Creditanstalt internal report of July 21, 1941.

[87] Slovenian National Archive (= SNA), AS 1268, Fasz. 450, Marburg Branch to Länderbank, May 17, 1941.

more moderate trend in the "resettlement" of Slovenians in the area.[88]

The effort to Germanize the area by removing the Slovenes and bringing in German settlers created problems for the Marburg branch, which was flooded with inquiries from the old Reich and the Ostmark about businesses and factories that might be available. Many of the inquiries came from the Dresdner Bank and the Länderbank. Even before the Marburg branch opened in the spring of 1941, the Länderbank had asked the Graz branch for information on textile plants in southern Styria, southern Carinthia, or the frontier region that were up for sale in connection with Aryanization or for other reasons; once the Marburg branch opened, it repeatedly received such inquiries.[89] The number of Jews in Slovenia was small, about 4,500, but they had assets worth taking. The difficulty, as the Marburg branch pointed out in May, was that all purchases or even holdings in enterprises in the area required the approval of the head of the civilian administration, and those seeking permission had to meet various requirements. Purchases by companies from the old Reich were especially frowned upon.[90] Nevertheless, the Marburg branch was supplying the Länderbank with the names of Jewish and Slovene firms that might be "nationalized," for example, the Erste Marburger Strickwarenfabrik, Novak & Co., and Ornik and Mitrović. There was strong interest in the Erste Marburger Strickwarenfabrik, which had been owned by a Jew who had fled the German invasion, Johann Reichmann. The Marburg branch took the trouble to ask the firm's administrator to supply information on its financial status.[91] Although the Reich Commissariat for the Strengthening of Germandom claimed that factories were not available for anyone but reemigrating Germans and veterans, the Marburg branch advised the home office not to take such restrictions too literally. Nothing could be

gained by simply writing a letter of inquiry, but exceptions might be made if one made personal contact with those in charge.[92]

The Marburg branch sought not only to act as an intermediary for purchases and investments in the region but also to undertake the granting of some large-scale credits on its own. In July 1942, for example, it complained that because of the secrecy involved, it could get no information about a plant that was supposed to be built by the Vereinigte Aluminum AG in collaboration with the Reichswerke Hermann Göring in Sterntal bei Pettau. In the end, it seems to have been successful and to have had an account for the new project.[93] Ultimately, of course, Marburg was a branch, not a subsidiary. It did much local business, and, as might be expected, it handled a substantial number of Party accounts and did business with the agencies of the regime. For example, it acted as the intermediary in transferring a notification to the Waffen-SS and Police in Dachau of a 26,000 RM payment for wood for barracks to the firm of Valentin Stampach & Co. from the Marburg account of the construction office of the Waffen-SS and Police in Mauthausen.[94]

The Deutsche Handels- und Kreditbank AG, Pressburg (Bratislava)

The Marburg branch handled small-scale local business compared to that conducted by the Deutsche Handels- und Kreditbank AG in Pressburg (DHKA), an important subsidiary of the Dresdner Bank and the subsidiary in which the Länderbank was most decisively involved. The role the Länderbank played was heavily political. The bank was supposed not only to give the Reich a powerful economic foothold in Slovakia and to strengthen the puppet regime economically in line with German policies, but it was also supposed to service the

88 Ibid., travel report, June 16, 1941.
89 Ibid., Länderbank to Graz branch, April 19, 1941.
90 Ibid., Länderbank Marburg to Länderbank Vienna, May 14, 1941.
91 Ibid., Länderbank Marburg to Länderbank Vienna, May 17, 1941, May 19, 1941, and June 25, 1941.

92 Ibid., Länderbank Marburg to Länderbank Vienna, Nov. 23, 1941.
93 Ibid., Fasz. 468 and 282, Länderbank Marburg to Länderbank Vienna, July 21, 1942.
94 Ibid., Fasz. 466 and 468, payment confirmation, March 26, 1942, and Länderbank Vienna to Länderbank Marburg.

Germans working in Slovakia and to strengthen the ethnic Germans over and against the other ethnic groups in the country.[95]

This highly instrumental use of the bank was already in evidence when the Länderbank took it over in March/April 1939 on behalf of the Dresdner Bank concern. It was a rather chaotic time for the new leadership to assume its responsibilities. Just prior to the separation of Slovakia from Czechoslovakia, Czech-owned banks had transferred their cash holdings to their proprietary banks in Prague. The German entry into Prague initially complicated cash transfers. For the DHKA, the situation carried at once a threat and a promise. The bank was flooded with requests by companies and firms for advances against accounts in Prague to pay wages and salaries. A dozen firms, including Siemens, Danubius Textil-Werke, Pressburg, Stollwerk, and the Apollo-Mineral-Öl-Raffinerie, made such requests amounting to 1.5 million Ks. weekly. A second category of need for advances against existing accounts was to help Reich German industrial circles buy available companies. The DHKA listed 130,000,000 Ks. in "projects" involving such promising firms as the Kabelfabrik Pressburg, the majority of whose shares were owned by a Moravian bank; the Kronpacher Eisenwerk, Mittelslovakei, purchasable through a Swiss group; and the Slowakische Portland-Zement AG, owned by a Swiss holding company belonging to Baron Ohrenstein, a Jew. The DHKA could only warn against the loss of opportunities if the needed cash was not made available: "If the economic development of Slovakia is not to be hindered, then it is urgently necessary that large amounts of liquid means be placed at the disposal of the Deutsche Handels- und Kreditbank. Only in this way will it be possible to strengthen the economic position of Slovakia from a Reich German as well as from an ethnic German perspective."[96] It was an

opportunity not to be missed: "Because of the circumstance that the Jews, in a panic-like manner, want to leave their positions in Slovakia, there is the possibility of bringing first class, especially healthy, industrial enterprises into the German circle of interests. Here, rapid action is especially important, since it is still possible that other than Reich German capitalist circles will take an interest in Slovakia."[97] The Dutch for example, had made their presence felt. The bank was therefore eager that funds in the Czech banks be released as soon as possible and that the transfer arrangements between the authorities in Prague and the Slovak National Bank be expedited so that important opportunities be realized, such as the plan of IG Farben's Dynamit Nobel AG to transfer 50 million Ks. to Pressburg for investment purposes. Despite the aforementioned difficulties, the first year under German control turned out to be a very successful one for DHKA. Its balance sheet increased by 60 percent from 50.7 to 79.1 million Ks. As the administrative council proudly reported, these numbers did not tell the entire story. After the Aryanization of the bank, there was "a complete restructuring of our clientele."[98] The increased business also led to an augmentation of personnel from thirty-six to seventy-five bank officers and employees. At the same time, plans were afoot not only to expand the DHKA's business but also to expand the bank itself by taking over the Sillein branch of the Bankhaus Frankl & Co., Pressburg, the Zipser Bank AG in Käsmark, and the smaller Csereháter Bank AG in Unter-Metzenseifen.

The Bankhaus Frankl & Co., which had its seat in Pressburg and branches in Sillein, Losonc, and Ungvár, had been a limited liability partnership between the Böhmische Escompte Bank (Bebca) and the Jewish banker Arthur Frankl. The Bebca, which came under Dresdner Bank control in March 1939 and was the owner of the Bankhaus Frankl & Co., had viewed the bank as a subsidiary for its business in Slovakia. Bebca had a contract with Frankl,

---

95 For a useful general account of the financial situation in Slovakia, see Roman Holec, "Das Kredit- und Kreditgenossenschaftswesen in der Slowakei," in: Wixforth (ed.), *Finanzinstitutionen in Mitteleuropa*, pp. 164–179.

96 NOUB, DHKA, Box 45, File 512, memorandum, March 22, 1939.

97 Ibid.

98 Ibid., Box 2, File 4, report of the administrative council, March 8, 1939.

who had managed the bank since 1931, under which he held the title of director and had pension rights. Frankl resigned his position in 1939, but the Bebca insisted on treating its obligations to Frankl in conformity with the rulings of the Reich Protector of Bohemia-Moravia. Frankl thus received a one-time settlement instead of a pension. He was also denied certain other contractual rights connected with the Bebca's termination of the limited liability partnership. When Frankl asked for his state pension from the Slovak government, he was turned down because of his status as a partner in a bank! Frankl planned to challenge the settlement in court, but he does not seem to have pursued the matter beyond engaging a lawyer.[99] In any case, the Bebca now proceeded to liquidate the Bankhaus Frankl & Co. The Losonoc and Ungvár branches, which lay in the territory given to Hungary, went to the Ungarische Allgemeine Creditbank, and the Sillein branch was transferred to the DHKA, which transformed it into a branch office.[100]

The Zipser Bank serviced primarily the Hungarian and German communities in the Carpathian region. In contrast to the DHKA, which was a purely commercial bank, the Zipser had a large portfolio of savings accounts and mortgages. Hungarian accounts apparently outweighed German accounts, but the latter were still very important. Each of the two groups was constantly looking to preserve its own particular advantages, and any move by the Slovak government that seemed to favor one side or the other met with immediate complaint and resistance. At the end of 1939, for example, the Slovak government ordered the merger of the Zipser Bank with the Ludová banca in Rosenberg/Ružomberok. The Deutsche Partei reacted immediately with a petition against the merger, pointing out that the Zipser Bank had 40 million Ks. in German assets and that the merger was prejudicial to the interests of German account holders. The Deutsche Partei, which published a newspaper called the *Karpathen Post*, made its position publicly known and also petitioned the German embassy for redress. It soon received reassurances that the Slovak government had promised to refrain from one-sided measures prejudicial to the ethnic Germans.[101]

The DHKA faced some competition for the Zipser Bank from what was to become the Union-Bank, Pressburg, which was established in October 1940 and jointly owned by the Creditanstalt and the Deutsche Bank-controlled Böhmische Union-Bank in Prague. The Union-Bank was the Böhmische Union-Bank (BUB) branch in Pressburg transformed into an independent bank with a share capital of 45 million Ks. The Creditanstalt certainly intended to establish itself in Slovakia, but it was well behind the Dresdner Bank/Länderbank in doing so. The Creditanstalt had initially considered taking over the Escompte- und volkswirtschaftliche Bank, Pressburg, and then, in April 1939, it had contemplated taking a stake in the Pressburger Handels- und Kreditbank, but the establishment of the DHKA precluded that investment. The Slovak government, in its negotiations with the Germans, especially Ministerial Director Riehle and Commercial Attaché Gebert, was prepared to approve the establishment of two large German banks in Slovakia; the BUB and the Creditanstalt joined forces to found the Union-Bank in the fall of 1939.[102] If Riehle gave his blessing to the new German bank in Slovakia and also managed to get the Slovak authorities to agree to grant the two German banks the same rights and facilities as those enjoyed by Slovak banks, he also made clear that he expected "that absolute harmony should reign between the two German banks in this venue."[103]

Whatever that meant, the reality was that the two banks were in competition for the

99 NARA, T83/141, Bebca to Dresdner Bank, Oct. 15, 1940. This volume contains numerous documents connected with the Bankhaus Frankl liquidation.

100 NOUB, DHKA, Box 71, DHKA to Dresdner Bank, Aug. 10, 1940.

101 Ibid., Karpathen-Post to the DHKA, Dec. 28, 1940.

102 BA-CA, CA-V, CA working committee meetings of April 1, 1939, Nov. 17, 1939, July 9, 1940.

103 BA-CA, CA-TZ, Rechtsabteilung rot, Nr. 9, memorandum by Director Franz Stephan, Dec. 16, 1939.

Zipser Bank. Shortly after its establishment, the Union-Bank engaged in discussions with the Zipser Bank. Despite its late start, the bank had good reason to think it might have some advantages over the DHKA. This was evident from a meeting initiated by the Zipser Bank leadership in December 1939 in connection with its efforts to mobilize German interests against the Slovak Finance Ministry plan to merge the Zipser Bank with the Ludová banca. Both the Hungarians and the Germans were upset by the idea because neither wanted to have to absorb a purely Slovak bank. The Union-Bank representatives used the occasion to propose that they continue discussions about cooperation and even the possible inclusion of the Zipser Bank in the Union-Bank sphere of interest. The Union-Bank representative had the sense that the Zipser Bank leadership found the DHKA "all too German" and "would rather seek a connection with a bank that could also show appropriate consideration for its Hungarian clientele."[104] The Union-Bank's interest in the Zipser Bank increased in early 1940, and representatives of the Deutsche Partei also approached the Union-Bank about taking over the small local Csereháter Bank in Unter-Metzenseifen.[105]

Commercial Attaché Gebert seemed at least willing to consider the Union-Bank as a purchaser of these banks. He invited Director Franz Stephan of the Union-Bank to discuss the matter on February 7 and was assured a few days later that the Union-Bank was prepared to purchase the two banks as well as the small Zipser Kreditbank. But it also wished to acquire all of the branches and not, as Gebert suggested, surrender some of the branches to other purchasers. The Creditanstalt also informed Gebert that it was interested in acquiring holdings of the Legiobank, with which it had a friendship pact. The Legiobank owned most of the shares of the Slovakische Allgemeine Kreditbank, which it had taken over during the rationalization of the banking system in Slovakia. The Creditanstalt

had an option of 50 percent of this Legiobank holding, but the Slovakische Allgemeine Kreditbank, which had branches operating in ethnic German areas, was desperately in need of refinancing. The Creditanstalt now offered to take over the entire Slovakische Allgemeine Kreditbank holding of the Legiobank. The Legiobank, which had been run as a Czech bank, was likely to be cooperative, as evidenced by the fact that it had appointed German personnel for those of its branches which were in German ethnic areas.[106]

Obviously, the new Union-Bank was making a claim on everything that could plausibly come to mind, and the Dresdner Bank could hardly be expected to welcome its competition. Riehle had asked that the Creditanstalt get together with the Dresdner Bank and sort things out, but the harmony Gebert demanded was certainly not the order of the day. As Director Ludwig Fritscher of the Creditanstalt reported to Riehle, Fischböck, at this time serving as chairman of the Creditanstalt supervisory board, had met with Director Meyer of the Dresdner Bank but did not find him inclined to discuss an agreement when it came to Slovakia, although Veesenmayer had given Fischböck the impression that the Dresdner Bank wanted one. It appeared to Fritscher, therefore, that the Dresdner Bank wanted a free hand in Slovakia, but he thought that it would end up negotiating anyway, noting somewhat dismissively that "the Länderbank will hardly be able to take an independent position with respect to this complex of issues."[107]

Negotiations did indeed take place, between Fischböck and Veesenmayer, in early March 1940. They both agreed that the German reputation in Slovakia, now that two German banks were permitted, depended on both banks being sufficiently strong and effective as to earn Slovak respect. It was also essential that the banks have enough branches to cover the ethnic German region but that they avoid competing in every locale. This was especially

104 Ibid., Stephan to Fischböck, Dec. 28, 1939, and Fritscher to Fischböck, Dec. 27, 1939.
105 Ibid., Creditanstalt to BUB, Prague, Feb. 16, 1940.

106 Ibid., memorandum by Stephan, Feb. 7, 1940, two letters from the Creditanstalt to Gebert, Feb. 10, 1940.
107 Ibid., Fritscher to Riehle, Jan. 16, 1940.

important in the Zipser area, where ethnic considerations had to be paramount. Concretely, they decided that the Zipser Bank and the Csereháter Bank would be assigned to the DHKA, that is, the Dresdner Bank/Länderbank group, and the Slovakische Allgemeine Kreditbank, the Bratislaver Allgemeine Bank AG, as well as some smaller institutions, would go to the BUB-CA-Deutsche Bank group. The principle of "first come, first served" was certainly at work in this decision; the DHKA had approached the Zipser Bank first, and the Union-Bank had been involved with the Slovakische Allgemeine Kreditbank. In the view of both men, the political aspect was more important, namely, that the DHKA "from the outset conducted its economic reconstruction work in close consultation with the Deutsche Partei in Pressburg and in the process has held most extensively to certain economic-political guidelines of the Party. The Deutsche Partei, on its side, has to no small degree contributed to the building up of the Deutsche Handels- und Kreditbank as a savings bank, a characteristic which is especially important in the Zips."[108] In this instance, the National Socialist credentials of the Dresdner/Länderbank seemed greater, although Fischböck and Veesenmayer had reservations about the manner in which the discussions had been conducted with the Slovak Finance Ministry and the apparent effort to find an arrangement in which the Zipser Bank would retain its identity. In their view, this could only satisfy the Hungarian interests in the Zipser Bank and prevent it from becoming the German institution they and the Deutsche Partei wanted.

The exact intentions of the DHKA toward the Zipser Bank were often uncertain. As early as March 1939, that is right after the Länderbank takeover, directors of the DHKA were discussing the takeover of the Zipser Bank. Yet it was to be a year and a half before this intention, assuming it was that clear an intention, was realized. A great deal of the problem came from the delaying tactics of the Hungarians running

the Zipser; they were obviously reluctant to give up their bank and would not let auditors review the bank's accounts until ordered to do so after DHKA complaints to the Slovenian Finance Ministry. German commercial attaché Erich Gebert, who worked closely with the DHKA on the question and whom Director Gold later proposed for membership on the Länderbank supervisory board, angrily told Ministerial Councilor Hrnĉar of the Slovak Finance Ministry that the refusal to open the accounts was a "sabotaging" of the banking consolidation plans negotiated between the German and Slovak governments.[109] Such a plan had indeed been worked out in negotiations in which Ministerial Director Riehle of the RWM actually went so far as to give the Zipser Bank a week to show good faith.[110] On August 7, 1940, the Slovak Finance Ministry issued a decree ordering the merger of the Zipser Bank with the DHKA, and a week later it ordered the merger of the Csereháter Bank with the DHKA.

If matters continued to move slowly, it was not only because of the stonewalling of the Hungarians. Director Gold, who conducted most of the negotiations, was reluctant to act too forcefully. Indeed, the bankers behaved in precisely the manner to which Fischböck and Veesenmayer had objected when making their decision to give the Zipser Bank to the DHKA. Gold and the Dresdner Bank leadership agreed to try "not to brutally break the 76 year-old tradition of the Zipser Bank without reason."[111] The structural differences between the DHKA and the Zipser Bank presented problems, and Gold felt it important to keep the existing personnel in place and to see how things went. In short, although a merger was planned, the Zipser Bank was to retain a certain autonomy. By early January 1941, however, Gold's patience was wearing thin and even Hrnĉar agreed the Zipser Bank leadership was deliberately making

---

[108] Ibid., agreement conveyed by Gebert to Stephan, March 5, 1940.

[109] NOUB, DHKA, Box 71, Gebert to Hrnĉar, July 6, 1940.

[110] Ibid., Gebert to Hrnĉar, July 19, 1940, ibid; on the negotiations, see the protocol dated May 31, 1940, ibid.

[111] Ibid., Gold to the Dresdner Bank, Aug. 12, 1940.

the negotiations difficult by demanding an exorbitant share price of 525 Ks.[112] The pressure to come to terms was increased by the intertwining of the Zipser Bank question with the plans for a large capital share increase for the DHKA. In the end, the DHKA found itself making considerable concessions. As Director Meyer of the Dresdner Bank reported to Riehle on February 10, 1941, the negotiations had been long and difficult because the Hungarians had mobilized their organizations and the Germans constantly had to appeal to the Slovak authorities. In the settlement, the shareholders of the Zipser Bank had to be paid in cash at a price of 340 Ks. per share, which strained the resources of the DHKA. The accountants claimed that the DHKA was paying 1.6 million Ks. too much. Furthermore, it was going to be quite difficult to integrate the very different types of banking business conducted by the Zipser Bank with that of the DHKA. If they had nevertheless accepted these terms, it was because of the RWM agreement with the Slovak government on banking concentration. In return, Meyer hoped that the RWM would carry out the planned banking concentration process in Slovakia, that the DHKA would be given consideration should there be a dissolution of Slovak bank branches in the Protectorate, and that, with the exception of the German banks already allowed in Slovakia, that no other German banks would be added to the competition in the small market.[113]

Most revealing with respect to the merger, however, was a letter from Gold to Meyer sent a few days later. Gold apparently felt impelled to lay out more directly what had really been at stake in the entire affair, namely, that it was an "ethnic-political" matter.[114] The ethnic Germans had long found the situation at the Zipser Bank "unbearable" because "those circles who profess Magyar identity" were in an advantageous economic position. They saw the takeover of the Zipser Bank as a shifting of the

balance in their favor. The Hungarians wanted to hold on to their position but, Gold added, it was important to note that "these gentlemen were not Germanophobe, but to the contrary, they are completely in support of the new order in the sense of an economically consolidated geographic area under German economic leadership. They express this very skillfully with the formula, 'our policy is friendly to Germany but directed via Budapest.' In this way, they want to say and proclaim that they do not care about the ethnic German cause in Slovakia."

Gold had a dim view of the entire ethnic-political scene in Slovakia, which he found "grotesquely provincial." There was a great deal of opportunism. He illustrated this with the example of a Zipser Bank customer who had long insisted on having his account in Hungarian until he concluded that it really should be in German. As for the Deutsche Partei, it expected "wonderful things" from the takeover of the Zipser Bank, and Gold had to remind its management that the bank had to be run properly if "we are to fulfill our great political goal." In Gold's view, the managers of the Zipser Bank needed to be won over because they "are especially industrious and experienced, albeit somewhat hard business people."

To be sure, it was important to promote Germandom, but the duty of bankers was conduct business strictly by business principles, and Gold was pleased that Meyer and Vessenmayer had emphasized this point in the negotiations with the Zipser Bank leadership. It had been important to point out to Gebert and Riehle that this merger was problematic from a banking point of view. In response, "Ministerial Director Dr. Riehle as well as Commercial Attaché Dr. Gebert emphasized that what was involved here was more than a mere 'business operation' for the Deutsche Handels- und Kreditbank. The entire merger is only a small piece of the plan for the new ordering of banking in Europe that has been worked out in Berlin. Herr Dr. Riehle went so far as to declare that the task must be carried out, even if at first it means a sacrifice for the concern of the Dresdner Bank; the Dresdner Bank has been and will continue to be richly compensated in other areas." Given Riehle's position, it

---

[112] Ibid., memorandum of Jan. 9, 1941 (wrongly dated 1940).
[113] Ibid., Meyer to Riehle, Feb. 10, 1941.
[114] Ibid., for the discussion and quotations that follow, see Gold to Meyer, Feb. 18, 1941.

mattered little whether the Zipser Bank merger was voluntarily.

Gold, who did not share Meyer's view that the price paid for the shares was excessive, pursued a cautious policy of not making too many changes at the Zipser Bank. He wanted to get rid of burdensome real estate holdings gradually and also to take advantage of what the bank had to offer, namely, its important brewery holding, the Poprader Brauerei, and to make it more profitable. He was also interested in promoting its hotel business because the region was an important vacation region. The contract for the merger of the two banks provided for the retention of the two leading directors, Tibor Wein and Tibor Kéler, as well as all the non-Jewish executives and employees of the bank. It also stipulated that a regional committee be established to advise the DHKA on matters pertaining to the business interests in the area covered by the former Zipser Bank.[115]

The DHKA merger with the Zipser Bank – and, at the same time, the Cserehátér Bank – cost 8,050,000 Ks. and paved the way for the anticipated increase of the share capital of the DHKA by 29,250,000 Ks. from 3,750,000 Ks. to 33,000,000 Ks. The official share capital was 30,000,000 Ks.; 3,000,000 Ks. was put in reserve. The Dresdner Bank used its cash holdings at the DHKA for this purpose and took over 27,250,000 Ks. of the shares and offered shares worth 2 million Ks. on the market. The Dresdner Bank thus replaced the Länderbank as the chief shareholder, although as discussed earlier, the Länderbank's stake was increased in the consortial arrangement of May 1942 to 7,500,000 Ks.[116] The role of Länderbank directors Gold and Paić was very important, and insofar as the Länderbank had a major presence in the occupied areas, it was in Slovakia. Gold certainly was a "strong man" and Paić had boosted his "qualifications" by joining the SS in 1938, advancing to the rank of Obersturmführer

and also by serving as economic advisor to the SS Security Service, Department 3D.[117]

The motivations behind the acquisition of the Zipser Bank demonstrate how far the banking business in Slovakia was colored by political considerations. This was evident at the first meeting – there were to be six in all before the war's end – of the regional committee in the Zipser area on September 21, 1942, which was graced by the presence of Director Meyer as well as its chairman, Director Paić. Meyer pointed out that the idea of such regional committees had been developed by the Dresdner Bank, and he went on to describe the organization of the bank, especially in Southeast Europe, and to talk about the "great tasks" of the banks in financing the war and encouraging savings. Paić chimed in on the role of the banks, "which today are not a purpose in themselves but primarily serve the national economy and have to conduct their business in ways that best serve the needs of the people and state."[118]

It was not a proposition about which the DHKA and the Union-Bank could have much doubt. They were well aware that German ambassador and former Storm Troop leader Manfred von Killinger was looking over their shoulders. In August 1940, for example, he voiced his expectation that German firms in Slovakia would demonstrate a high level of performance. He also expressed his satisfaction that the leading circles in Slovakia considered the two German banks exemplary and that, thanks to their labors, important industrial enterprises in Slovakia had made substantial progress. Nevertheless, he thought that the efforts could be increased, and above all, "this must in the future take place on a basis that reflects National Socialist and German economic principles."[119]

---

[115] Ibid., Merger contract, Feb. 21, 1941.

[116] Ibid., Meyer to Riehle, Feb. 10, 1941; NARA, T83/137, DHKA shareholders' meeting, Dec. 30, 1940; ibid., Box 2, File 11, Dresdner Bank working committee, Feb. 5, 1941.

[117] See NARA, RG 338, 290/56/03/02, Box 108, the U.S. military intelligence report on Paić. In 1951, he was exonerated from being a true member of the SS, the Security Service being compared to "the Gallup Institute of National Socialism." See WStLA, NS-Registrierung, 18. Bez., Josef Paić, Nr. 7390.

[118] NOUB, DHKA, Box 2, File 48, regional committee meeting, Sept. 25, 1942.

[119] BA-CA, CA-TZ, Rechtsabteilung rot, Nr. 9, Killinger to the BUB, Aug. 10, 1940.

To have a "reliable picture" of what could be expected, he asked the banks to provide him with a copy of their balance sheets and also report the interest rates they were charging.

The DHKA served the German war effort in a variety of ways. One of its important functions was the transfer of wages earned by Slovak workers in Germany.[120] The chief activity of the DHKA was the provision of credits to Slovak industry and to German firms in Slovakia to promote the German war effort. The DHKA had attained total control of certain firms, for example, the Bratislaver Mühlen AG, the "Dolina" AG für Land- und Forstwirtschaft, the extremely important Landwirtschaftliche Industrie- und Handels AG (Lihag), the Eisen- und Stahlwerke Prakovce AG, and the Zellulosefabrik AG, Turč Sv. Martin.[121] This by no means meant, however, that it could conduct the business of such firms without complication. The potential for complications in Slovakia was considerable. First, there were the demands of the Slovak government, which had a keen interest in "Slovakization" wherever possible and constantly watched out for Slovak advantage. Second, there was the monetary and trade regulations of both Germany and Slovakia, which were remarkably complicated and restrictive. Then, there were the various local diplomatic and ethnic German officials and organizations, whose capacity for interference has already been discussed. Finally, there were the delicate relations between the two German banks, which competed with one another but also needed one another. Bad as the cause for which these banks labored was, considerable imagination was needed to do so successfully.

The operations connected with and conducted by the Lihag are rich in illustrations of these problems. Founded in 1923, the Lihag was an important trading company that dealt in food and food products as well as in coal. It also engaged in various types of trade, including the so-called compensation trade with Turkey, for example, in which the Turks would receive steel in return for cotton. The company was controlled by the DHKA for all intents and purposes, but its shares were in the hands of the Länderbank (36 percent), Rasche (26 percent), Warnecke (25 percent), and Meyer (15 percent). The reason for this odd arrangement was that the shares could not be transferred to Pressburg because of German exchange regulations. In April 1941, Gold and Gebert contemplated schemes for making the transfer via the Protectorate by using the sale of Slovak assets there, but nothing seems to have come of this idea.[122]

The Lihag and the DHKA worked hand in hand in the compensation trade with Turkey. One of the firms that used their services was the Vereinigte Papier-Industrie-Aktiengesellschaft (VPI). The VPI belonged to the Creditanstalt and should have used the Union-Bank, but the Union-Bank had no experience whatsoever with the complexities of the Turkish compensation trade. The Creditanstalt nevertheless complained about the VPI's use of the DHKA, and the VPI leaders sought the advice of Director Gold as to how to deal with the issue. Gold was facing another problem, namely, that the Slovak authorities were demanding that the trade with Turkey be handled by Slovak firms, which would have undermined his cooperation with the VPI. To deal with these problems, Gold concocted a scheme under which the DHKA would set up an "Orient Office" that would provide free advice on trade with Turkey with the understanding that those who received such counsel would agree to use the DHKA's services in conducting their business. Gold was convinced that Slovak firms and other firms wishing to engage in such business would be totally dependent on this advice because of the complexity of the operations involved. Under such an arrangement, the Slovak government demands would be satisfied and Slovak export

[120] Josef Koliander, *Die Beteiligung und Kreditverflechtung der Deutschen Banken in Südosteuropa*, D. Phil., Hochschule für Welthandel (Wien 1944), p. 163.

[121] BA-CA, CA-TZ, Rechtsabteilung rot, Nr. 9, BUB to Creditanstalt, May 6, 1940.

[122] NARA, T83/147, memorandum on credit request for the Lihag, Nov. 12, 1943, and memorandum on capital transfer, April 19, 1941.

firms could be licensed to do business with Turkey. In the end, however, they would have to go through the DHKA for the reasons mentioned. The Lihag could act as the middleman in this trade, and the VPI could be allowed to set up an office for trade with Turkey in the Lihag, and the Lihag would get 20 percent to 25 percent of the profit on the VPI's business. This would give the DHKA a monopoly in what apparently was a very lucrative business. Gold was able to win Gebert's support for this scheme and also to persuade the Slovak authorities that it was the best solution. The only remaining problem was the Creditanstalt, which might object to the favor shown to the DHKA. Gold expected to overcome this difficulty through the good offices of Gebert, who was asked to win Rafelsberger over to the scheme and to persuade the Creditanstalt to come to terms. Gold was prepared to bring a representative of the VPI into the administrative council of the Lihag and to give the Creditanstalt a stake in the Lihag as well. The DHKA also wished to have a stake in the VPI.[123]

These complicated arrangements illustrate the mixture of competition and cooperation among German banks and firms that characterized the German economic role in Slovakia as well as the great importance of the government and Party officials in backing schemes like that proposed by Gold. The need for official approval could, however, lead to increased control and interference by Party agencies. When the Länderbank asked permission from the foreign exchange authorities to use 1.6 million Ks. of the VPI's 4.8 million Ks. to increase the capital of the Lihag, for instance, the permission came with a number of financial and political conditions. The Länderbank was instructed to put the 3.2 million Ks. into the Slovak-German clearing fund for transfer to Germany but also to provide the Foreign Trade Office of the NSDAP Foreign Organization with a complete list of all the officers of the Lihag, to report any changes in personnel, and to provide a yearly report, in triplicate, on the personnel, listing employees by name, nationality, and race. It is

not insignificant that the Dresdner Bank, upon learning of these requirements, was disturbed enough to ask the Länderbank to find out if there were precedents for such conditions. By 1943, however, the Slovak government was the largest obstacle to the DHKA's efforts to situate its Lihag holding so as to put the least strain on the bank's liquidity. The money for the capital share increase of the Lihag from 600,000 Ks. to 2 million Ks. became available after carrying out the arrangements just described, but the Slovak government blocked the planned transfer of the new shares to the Länderbank, thus leaving the DHKA with the new shares. This was correctly viewed as part of the Slovak program of trying to nationalize as many assets in foreign hands as possible and to block such securities from being sent abroad, but it was all quite frustrating from the standpoint of the DHKA.[124]

The Lihag unquestionably added to the liquidity problems that came to strain the DHKA in 1942–1943, not only because of these shares but also because of its expansive business. In August 1942, Director Richard Anspach of the Dresdner Bank contacted Paić and expressed his concern about the fact that the Lihag had accounts outstanding to the tune of 15 million Ks. (approximately 4.4 million RM). He also discussed the question of whether to give the Union-Bank some portion of the credit made available to the Lihag to use for the VPI's needs. Gold was still working on his scheme for joint investment by the two banks in the Lihag and the VPI, but he was meeting resistance from Director Richard Buzzi of the Creditanstalt, who argued that the business of the Lihag was very much conditioned by the war, whereas that of the VPI would continue to be significant after the end of the war. Paić felt it was a mistake to share any portion of the credit with the Lihag under such circumstances because it would give the impression that Gold's project of mutual investment was nothing more than

---

[123] Ibid., memorandum by Anspach, March 20, 1942.

[124] Ibid., Länderbank to Dresdner Bank, June 2, 1942; Dresdner Bank to Länderbank, June 10, 1942; Anspach to Mayer, July 14, 1943; memoranda of Nov. 12 and 16, 1943.

a scheme to help the Lihag out of its liquidity problems. Indeed, the Dresdner Bank felt the time had come to rein in the Lihag. Although it granted an additional credit of 400,000 Ks. for the procurement of fats, it turned down a request to raise the Lihag's credit line from 12 to 17 million Ks. on the grounds that this stood in "crass misrelationship" to its capital and that it needed to conduct its "certainly very interesting business operations" within the limits of the available credit.[125] In the end, however, a substantial credit increase was given in July 1943. Half the amount was taken over by the Hermes Kredit-Versicherung-Gesellschaft, and there was to be a further increase in the summer of 1944 to finance the Lihag's fruit exports. The DHKA admitted that the credits being requested were quite high but pointed out that the Lihag had done well during the past year and most decisive was the fact that "the products here being exported are of eminent importance for the food economy of the Reich."[126]

Needless to say, the Lihag was only one type of firm that received credits and assistance from the DHKA. The bank also financed a variety of enterprises producing for the war effort, sometimes on its own, often in consortia with the Union-Bank and with important Slovak banks. This was, for example, the case with the "Ruda" Bergbau und Hüttenbetriebe, which had belonged to the largely Rothschild-owned Witkowitzer Bergbau und Eisenhüttengewerkschaft, Mährisch-Ostrau – which had been taken over by the Reichswerke Hermann Göring, with the help of the Dresdner Bank, during Germanization and Aryanization in the Czech lands. The "Ruda" had been "nostrified" by the Slovak government in 1941. The DHKA and Union-Bank entered into a consortium with the Slovenskábanka and the Tatra banca to provide for the "Ruda's" credit needs.[127] Another particularly important account was the Apollo Minieralölraffinerie AG, Pressburg,

which was owned by IG Farben. It received credits from consortia involving the Slovak National Bank, the DHKA, the Union-Bank, and the Tatra banca for investment in its plant as well as for oil purchases from Romania and elsewhere. The DHKA had a particular advantage because the Gasolin AG in Vienna, which supplied oil to the DHKA, did its banking with the Länderbank and thus favored the DHKA. This irritated the Union-Bank, which urged the Creditanstalt to do business with the Gasolin AG. The DHKA nonetheless appears to have maintained its position. That was a mixed blessing, however. The "Apollo" suffered considerable losses of plant and oil in the bombing raids of 1944.[128] Another big and, in this case, exclusive war producer receiving large credits from the DHKA was the TECHNA Industrie-, Handels- und Realitätenunternehmen GmbH, a formerly Czech firm located in Prague that had been taken over by the Viennese "Watt" Glühlampen und Elektrizitäts AG. The parent company used the TECHNA to subcontract the production of electrical products in Slovakia that, after being assembled by the TECHNA, were sent to Vienna for distribution. The contracts involved were quite substantial; one, for example, was for a million potentiometers. A particularly attractive aspect of giving credits to the company was that they were guaranteed by the Länderbank, which did a great deal of business with "Watt," and were thus risk-free for the DHKA.[129]

The DHKA contributed not only to the Axis cause in Slovakia but also to the brutal war against the Jews there. Its cruelty owed much to Veesenmayer, who served as a special envoy at the time of Slovakia's breakaway from the Czech state, and to SS Hauptsturmführer Dieter Wisliceny, who was appointed special advisor on Jewish questions in September 1940 at the request of Ambassador von Killinger. The Slovak government's anti-Jewish policy

[125] Ibid., Anspach memorandum, Aug. 4, 1942, and Dresdner Bank to DHKA, Aug. 12, 1942.

[126] Ibid., memorandum of July 14, 1943, DHKA to Dresdner Bank, Nov. 24, 1943, and July 14, 1944.

[127] There is substantial material on the "Ruda" in NOUB, DHKA, Box 71.

[128] BA-CA, CA-TZ, Rechtsabteilung rot, Nr. 7, Union-Bank to Creditanstalt, Jan. 8, 1941; NARA, T83/148, memorandum for Goetz, March 23, 1944, and memorandum of July 24, 1944.

[129] NARA, T83/146, report on the credit by the DHKA, Nov. 10, 1942.

was initially similar to Italy's. Under German pressure, it began to take a harsher line in September 1941. At that time, Jews were systematically excluded from public life and the professions in Slovakia. The elimination of Jewish-owned businesses had already begun in 1939, however, and at the end of 1940 the Central Economic Office, which was simply an agency for handling the "Jewish Question," was authorized to either liquidate or Aryanize all Jewish firms. By January 1942, 9,950 Jewish enterprises had been liquidated and 2,100 transferred into Aryan hands. The liquidations served to relieve Slovak shop owners and businesspeople from competition, and the takeovers were usually to the benefit of large companies. In September 1941, Jews were also required to report their assets. A quarter of Jewish wealth was invested in land, and the Slovak government moved to confiscate Jewish-owned land as a "social" measure. The systematic despoliation of the Jews was seen by the authorities in Berlin as an opportunity to perform a "courtesy" for their Slovak allies and organize the transfer of Jews out of Slovakia, allegedly to labor in the occupied territories. The deportation of the Slovak Jews was ultimately based on an agreement between Germany and the Slovak regime under which the Germans promised to provide food, housing, and retraining for the Jews and thereby satisfy potential reservations on the part of the Church; in return, the Germans were to receive 500 RM per Jew, that is, 45 million RM. This was 80 percent of what the Slovak government expected to receive from its special asset tax on the Jews, so that in the end the Jews would cover most of the Slovak payment to the Germans for the deportations. The deportations, mainly to Poland and carried out in large part with the Slovak railroad system, began in March 1942. The effort ran into a variety of complications arising from the Church's reservations, pressures to grant exceptions, and some public opposition. Nevertheless, a combination of financial incentives and German pressure, in which Veesenmayer played a particularly important role, led to a high level of "success" by mid-1944. Seventy thousand Slovak Jews were deported, of whom only 5,000 returned.[130]

The role of the DHKA in these measures cannot be described in any great detail because of the lack of sources, but it is possible to say something about the different categories of its involvement. An important source of information is a report by the bank to the Slovak National Bank of July 1, 1942, listing the credits given by the bank and its branches to firms and properties formerly in Jewish possession and indicating the extent to which these credits were recoverable. Of the 3,902,436 Ks. in "normal" credits to Jewish firms, the bank believed that the available assets used to cover them, whether in the form of land or other guarantees, amounted to 3,372,993 Ks., and it anticipated losses amounting to 529,443 Ks. When it came to credits given to firms in the process of being Aryanized or to already Aryanized firms where there might be losses, the bank calculated the total amount at 1,208,476 Ks., of which it believed it could collect 889,542 Ks. It anticipated a loss of 318,934 Ks. on already Aryanized firms. From the available information, one has the sense that the Jews had been good risks. Oskar Kramer, for example, who had been lucky enough to emigrate to Nairobi, had left real estate in Pressburg worth 360,000 Ks. as security on a credit of 263,800 Ks. Another had left landed property worth 520,000 Ks. with a debt of 364,760 Ks. A major consideration of the DHKA in assessing its capacity to collect on credits to Aryanized firms was the uncertainty about the policies of the Slovak authorities. If the Slovak government confiscated the properties, for example, would it pay the outstanding mortgages? In the case of L. Kincs's Söhne, "a thriving and well maintained business," the Central Economic Office had taken over the firm's asset, but refused to assume the debts, which the DHKA protested as "a heavy and unjust damaging of Aryan and German creditor rights."[131]

---

[130] Raul Hilberg, *Die Vernichtung der europäischen Juden*, 3 vols. (Frankfurt a.M. 1997), II, pp. 766–794. See also StA Nürnberg, E1, the statement by Wisliceny made in Bratislava on Oct. 7, 1947. He was executed in 1948.

[131] See the documents in NOUB, DHKA, Box 46.

The DHKA and its branches also administered blocked Jewish savings accounts, which, on August 21, 1941, totaled 2,587,069 Ks. One of the more brutal aspects of the Jewish deportation to take place shortly thereafter was that Jews were expected to cover their own deportation costs by transferring 50 percent of their savings to the so-called Emigration Fund. Another decree by the Slovak government required that 60 percent of the balance was to be transferred to the Central Economic Agency. The Slovak government not only received payment from the Germans for Jews, in other words, but also collected contributions from the Jews to pay for their "emigration." The Slovak government received 1,295,350 Ks. from the DHKA for the first levy on savings, and 777,302 Ks. for the second levy, leaving a total of 522,705 Ks. in the accounts. In short, the Jews were forced to surrender 80 percent of what was in their bank accounts, which was in addition to the aforementioned levy on assets. Insofar as insurance policies were concerned, the DHKA simply surrendered Jewish-owned policies it had on deposit in October 1943 to the Slovak Ministry of Finance. Finally, the bank also diligently reported the Jewish accounts set aside for the administration and upkeep of properties.[132]

With the exception of the credits given to Jewish enterprises or for the Aryanization of Jewish enterprises, the other actions connected with the Holocaust in Slovakia obviously were not profitable ventures for the DHKA. They nonetheless illustrate how such banks were engaged in the process. Similarly, whatever it thought of the economic returns, the bank also helped to finance various Party and ethnic German activities. At the end of 1942, for example, it provided a credit of Ks. 350,000 to an engineer, Aladár Polnisch, at the behest of the People's League for Germandom Abroad and the SS Ethnic German Liaison Office for the purpose of bringing groups of Party members to promote the German cause in the Zipser

region. No security for the loan was put up, the Berlin office assuming "moral liability" for its repayment; the bank charged a normal interest rate.[133] It was not easy, however, to satisfy the Ethnic German Liaison Office, which not only stonewalled the Länderbank efforts to get back the "Mercur" in Hungary but also complained in the summer of 1944 that the DHKA was not working satisfactorily with the ethnic German cooperatives despite the Dresdner Bank's promises that it would do so.[134]

By the fall of 1944, the DHKA had other things to worry about, however. It was still in the business of funding emigration, only now it was for sending its Reich German and ethnic German employees to Germany. The bank, of course, sought compensation from the Reemigration Department of the Foreign Organization of the NSDAP.[135] As everyone well knew, that had not been that office's original purpose. At a meeting on November 8, 1944, Director Anspach of the Dresdner Bank, who was on the Supervisory Board of the DHKA, pointed out that "because of the circumstances in Slovakia, a resettlement of ethnic Germans from the Zipser area into the Sudetengau could take place and in any case one has to be organized for a stream of evacuated persons into the Reich."[136] The basic question was whether the Dresdner Bank could risk paying out on the savings accounts, which amounted to 105 million Ks., to the DHKA so that it could pay those affected. This would take four weeks and seemed very risky; the recommended solution was to borrow the needed money from the Slovak National Bank in RM and provide Ks. as security.

These were desperate measures and certainly not what anyone had anticipated in 1939. Nevertheless, insofar as the Länderbank had a demonstrably direct and significant presence in the occupied territories and in the southeast program, it was with the DHKA in Pressburg.

132 For the savings accounts, see ibid., Box 45, File 513; for the insurance policies, ibid., Box 46, File 519; for the property administration accounts, ibid., Box 45, File 515.

133 NARA, T83/146, credit request of Dec. 21, 1942.
134 NARA, T83/149, memorandum of July 27, 1944.
135 Ibid., DHKA to the Dresdner Bank, Oct. 20, 1944; NOUB, Box 30, File 481, DHKA to the Dresdner Bank, Nov. 29, 1944.
136 DrB, Nr. 1840, meeting, Nov. 8, 1944.

3. THE BUSINESS OF THE LÄNDERBANK IN AUSTRIA

The balance sheet of the Länderbank between the end of 1939 and the end of the third quarter of 1944 displays an impressive growth in the volume of its business. This is evident from the table below showing the RM balance and operating profit on December 31 of the years between 1939 and 1943 and on September 30, 1944:[137]

Year	Total Assets	Operating Profit
1939	341,597,000	5,450,000
1940	402,980,000	5,979,000
1941	540,261,000	5,421,000
1942	626,844,000	6,898,000
1943	743,957,000	8,853,000
1944	949,898,000	9,749,000

This was certainly impressive on paper, but it obviously reflected the overheated war economy and its inherent dangers, especially as Germany headed toward defeat. The bank's stock of treasury bills and noninterest-bearing treasury notes rose from 426.6 million RM in June 1943 to 667 million at the end of September 1944. Holdings in Reich bonds and other government securities remained high, although government bonds were sold off in 1944 to maintain liquidity. Indeed, an important turning point in the quest for liquidity came in the last quarter of 1942, when the military procurement authorities ceased to make advance payments for orders and the demand for credits substantially increased. The increase came to an end in 1944, however, so that much of the 200 million RM increase in the total assets between 1943 and 1944 came on the creditor side, while the debtor accounts diminished from 186 million RM to 123 million RM. The drop in credit demand was not limited to the Länderbank alone and reflected the high liquidity of debtors, government compensation to firms suffering from bombings and other war-related damages,

and other end-of-the-war problems that produced a slowdown in the demand for credits. In the case of the Länderbank, however, the drop in credit demand appears to have been disproportional. At the same time, it should not be thought that the bank was not exposed to large credit demand on the part of some of its biggest clients with very large credit lines, which were obviously more risky as the war was coming to an end. In any case, on the assets side of the ledger, the bank held substantial accounts from various banks, savings banks, government agencies, and the City of Vienna as well as from its big industrial customers, which kept funds on deposit at the bank. The Länderbank seems to have been a good investment for its shareholders – that is, the Dresdner Bank – and paid a 6 percent dividend in 1944.[138]

Varieties of "Jewish Business"

Although the flood of Aryanizations ebbed after 1938–1939, some Jewish wealth continued to serve as an "asset" on the ledger of the bank. This was only briefly the case with respect to Jewish-owned bank accounts that fell under the Eleventh Implementing Decree of the Reich Citizenship Law of November 25, 1941. Under this regulation, the property of all German Jews living abroad was subject to confiscation. The measure was closely tied to the "resettlement" of Jews to concentration camps in the East, where they were usually either murdered immediately or worked to death. It also applied, under somewhat different regulations, to Czech Jews sent to the "elite" camp at Theresienstadt. The law caused no end of difficulties for banks, which were now required to seek out Jewish accounts subject to confiscation rather than have them identified by the revenue offices or the Gestapo. A special problem was to determine whether a Jew living abroad on November 27, 1941, had changed citizenship, in which case, his or her property was not forfeit under the regulation.

[137] Taken from the statistical material in ibid., Nr. 5455-2000 and 13790-2000.

[138] NARA, T83/138, Dresdner Bank management board meeting, May 9, 1944; DrB, Nr. 13790-2000, report on a meeting of Rasche and Teichmann concerning the status of the Länderbank, March 14, 1945.

The peculiarities of this grotesque law led to a huge correspondence between the Economic Group for Private Banking, especially in the Ostmark, and the authorities.[139] Unfortunately, there is little available evidence specific to the Länderbank's handling of the decree, but, like other banks, the Länderbank maintained a bogus fastidiousness in dealing with it. On May 20, 1942, the Länderbank wrote to the Reich Group pointing out that under Austrian commercial law, a bank could not surrender money in a savings account without being presented with the savings account book. In the Austrian view, a savings account book was a "virtual negotiable instrument." The Länderbank had turned down requests from, among others, the Gestapo and the Central Office for Jewish Emigration for such monies except in the cases of some very small accounts. The legal department of the Länderbank, however, was not lacking for a solution and suggested that the courts be called upon to make use of a Decree on the Invalidation of Documents that had been issued on August 31, 1915. Recognizing that this was a bit clumsy, and that it would delay the entire process, the Länderbank asked the Reich Group to see if a way could be found to avoid going to court by getting the government to issue a decree that would simply declare the savings accounts books in question as "amortized." It was undoubtedly a relief for the Länderbank lawyers to learn that the problem had already been solved by the revenue office of Berlin-Brandenburg, to which such assets were turned over, and whose president had agreed to assume legal liability for the confiscation of the Jewish savings accounts without presentation of the account books.[140]

An Aryanizer might also have to jump through numerous bureaucratic hoops because of the peculiarities of the Eleventh Implementing Decree. This was the case with Anton Apold, the supervisory board chairman of the Länderbank. After being forced to give up his positions following his involvement in the July 1934 Putsch, Apold had settled at his estate on the Mondsee, which he developed into a model property. In 1940, he sold the estate to Reich Minister Alfred Rosenberg after the Statthalter in Carinthia assured him the acquisition of a Jewish villa in his hometown of Velden am Wörthersee that belonged to the four brothers and two sisters of the Kern family. A trustee appointed by the Statthalter negotiated for the family, and Apold paid 100,000 RM but was also required to pay back taxes owed by the Kerns, including the Reich Flight Tax, and the mortgage on the property, all of which came to 150,000 RM. The Statthalter approved the agreement immediately, but further negotiations with the foreign exchange and tax authorities were necessary. While these negotiations were taking place, the Eleventh Implementing Decree was issued. Two of the Kern family members were already Hungarian citizens and thus did not fall under the decree, but the status of the remaining four family members was in question. Apold found himself in a very unpleasant situation. Not only had he paid for the house but he had also spent money on repairs for the damages done by SA men during the November pogrom. After having lived in the house for two years, he suddenly could not be certain that he actually had title to it. Apold, of course, had contacts to whom he could turn for help. His lawyers in Graz began working on the case in the spring of 1943, and he also asked Rasche to use his influence. The matter, however, had to go up to the Reich finance minister, who finally approved the sale on the original terms in September 1943.[141] Unhappily for Apold, he still did not have clear title in mid-1944 because one of the sisters, who was supposed to be in Prague, failed to register; her case therefore remained under the jurisdiction of the Vienna Gestapo. The case had thus not been cleared, and Apold's lawyers turned to the

[139] See James, *Verbandspolitik*, pp. 225–234; see also NARA, T83/97, memorandum of a discussion among the Viennese Bankers, Feb. 19, 1942; Economic Group for Private Banking to Pfeiffer, March 2, 1942; Economic Group Private Banking to Pfeiffer, March 21, 1942.

[140] Ibid., Länderbank to Reich Group, May 20, 1942, and Reich Group to Länderbank, May 29, 1942.

[141] See DrB, Nr. 5461-2000, the law firm of Ludikar and Priebisch to Rasche, June 16 and 23, 1943; Rasche to Apold, Sept. 27, 1943; and Hesselbarth to Priebisch, Sept. 27, 1943.

Reich Main Security Office in February 1944. Receiving no answer, they once again turned to Rasche in June asking that he use his contacts to get the necessary documents that would settle the case.[142] The surviving records do not make clear whether the matter was ever settled. Apold died in Velden in 1950, where he probably continued to live in the Kern villa. Because most of the Kern's siblings had gone to Prague and Hungary, it is highly likely that some of them had perished earlier.

As noted earlier in connection with the Gildemeester plan, the Länderbank seems to have drawn some boundaries in its involvement with the despoliation of Jews, especially where legal complications might arise abroad. That did not extend so far as to refuse to hold the accounts of the Central Agency for Jewish Emigration, however, or for the Emigration Fund for Bohemia and Moravia, which were intended for similar purposes. In a statement of June 30, 1943, for example, the bank recorded 9.1 million RM from the former and 6.8 million RM from the latter among its accounts.[143] Emigration, except for a small number of persons, had come to an end in October 1941, so that some monies were used for the care of Jews left behind prior to their deportation or of Jews too frail or sick to be deported. Most of the deportations had taken place by October 1942; nevertheless, a substantial amount of money remained in the accounts at the Länderbank, and the accounts grew into 1943. The money came from a variety of sources. The 5,000 Jews deported to the Ghetto of Lodz between October 15 and November 11, 1941, for example, were required to sign a power of attorney giving the Central Agency for Jewish Emigration the right to deposit their money, and these funds were deposited at the Länderbank in their name.[144] This was regular

practice. The Jewish community was required to pay back the government subsidy it received earlier to speed up the emigration process. Furthermore, the sale of Jewish properties and other assets as well as Jewish community property continued, and the proceeds from these sales were deposited in the Länderbank. The repaid subsidy was paid into a special account for Jewish "resettlement," which was used for the upkeep of the Jews sent to Theresienstadt. At present, there is no way to trace these accounts more precisely than has been done by other scholars, but it is important to note that the head of the Jewish community, Josef Löwenherz, could dispose of the accounts only with the permission of the Gestapo and the Central Agency.

The accounts were nothing short of a repository for the liquidation of Jewish assets. In 1942, the City of Vienna, needing to provide for a school for girls, purchased the former Jewish orphanage, which had subsequently been turned into an old age home, for 155,700 RM. The property was to be turned over "as soon as the evacuation of the old people's home can be carried out during the final solution of the Jewish question in Vienna." The money was placed in what had been appropriately called the "liquidation account" of the Jewish community. Thanks to the work of Anderl and Rupnow of the Austrian Historical Commission, we have a fairly clear picture of the general disposition of the accounts in the Länderbank. The so-called Vienna emigration fund had ceased to have the function for which it was intended, and this account was dissolved on August 16, 1942. At this time it amounted to 982,000 RM in cash, to which must be added funds from property sales still not booked, and a "retraining school" in Sandhof that brought the total value of the account to 1.4 million RM. Because it had been decided that the Jews were to pay for their own incarceration in Theresienstadt, this money was transferred to the account for the Emigration Fund for Bohemia and Moravia at the Länderbank. At the same time, the proceeds from the sale of Jewish properties throughout Austria in 1941–1942 were placed in the aforementioned

[142] StA Nürnberg, Rep. 501, B 192, Priebisch to RSHA Berlin, Feb. 18, 1944, and Priebisch to Rasche, June 29, 1944.

[143] DrB, Nr. 5455-2000, Statement of June 30, 1943.

[144] The Trial of Adolf Eichmann, Session 43, May 17, 1961, http://www.nizkor.org/hweb/people/e/eichmann-adolf/transcripts/Sessions/Session-043-01.html (April 20, 2006).

"liquidation account" of the Jewish community, and a last payment to the account in the amount of 460,000 RM is recorded in January 1942. The value of this emigration fund account amounted to 6,744,990 RM a year later, at which time it was transferred to the Emigration Fund for Bohemia and Moravia. The amount increased to 7,603,000 RM in April 1943. At some undetermined point, a total of 8,314,563 RM was transferred to the Emigration Fund for Bohemia and Moravia at the Böhmische Escompte Bank, which was of course a subsidiary of the Dresdner Bank, and 7,600,000 RM was transferred to the Bankhaus Krentschker & Co. for an account in the name of the Emigration Fund for Bohemia and Moravia.[145] Although the Länderbank had no control over the disposition of these funds, it not only remained involved in holding funds and collecting bank charges derived from the continued despoliation of Austria's Jews but it was also a major conduit for financing the concentration camp of Theresienstadt.

There is no reason to suppose that those running the Länderbank had any compunction about being engaged in this business. If anything, they looked for such opportunities. This is demonstrated by their attitude toward the notorious gold transactions of the Dresdner Bank in 1942–1944.[146] During this period, the Dresdner Bank bought 5.752 tons of gold from the Reichsbank. Most of it had been looted from the central banks of occupied countries, but some had also been taken from the Jewish and other victims of the National Socialist policy of deportation and extermination. In addition, it acquired gold smelted into gold bars by the Degussa firm and shipped under the title "Melmer" after SS officer Bruno Melmer, who had been charged with the disposition of gold taken from Jews and others targeted by the National Socialists. The gold was acquired for

sale in Turkey, where the inflationary conditions increased the demand and price for gold. There was thus a profit to be made, and the Reichsbank sold gold to both the Deutsche Bank and the Dresdner Bank for resale to diplomats and other officials in Turkey seeking to protect themselves against inflation and to live high on the hog. The trade ceased only when Turkey ended its diplomatic relations with the Axis on August 2, 1944.

Both the Deutsche Bank and the Dresdner Bank used their leading Austrian bank connections, the Creditanstalt and the Länderbank respectively, as conduits for the transfer of gold to Turkey. In the case of the Dresdner Bank, the operations were organized by Director Max Schobert of the Foreign Exchange Section in Berlin, and the ultimate destination of the gold was the Dresdner Bank-owned Deutsche Orientbank in Istanbul. The Länderbank had two important functions. First, as noted, it served as a depository for the gold that was to end up in Turkey. Second, it served as the repository for the substantial profit made by the Dresdner Bank and held in the form of gold on account for the Istanbul branch after August 1943. It was deposited in this manner so as to protect the profits from inflation in Turkey and also to secure the gold on Reich territory should Turkey decide to join the Allied side. In contrast to the Creditanstalt, which was afforded an active role in these transactions by the Deutsche Bank, the Dresdner Bank simply used the Länderbank as a depository. The amount held on deposit at the Länderbank reached a high point of 380,693 kg., valued at 2.4 million Swiss francs, in 1944. In October 1944, the 293,693 kg in gold remaining at the Länderbank was transferred to Munich, which was deemed safer than Vienna; the gold ultimately fell into Allied hands. There is a general consensus among historians that those organizing these gold transfers knew that they were dealing in stolen gold, and those working at the Länderbank, with its close ties to the occupied territories in Eastern and Southeastern Europe, certainly were aware of the despoliation of the Jews both at home and abroad. If the Länderbank was not directly involved in the decision making or in gold

[145] See Anderl/Rupnow, *Zentralstelle*, pp. 318–320 and Venus/Wenck, *Gildemeester*, pp. 422–425.
[146] This account is based on Johannes Bähr, *Der Goldhandel der Dresdner Bank im Zweiten Weltkrieg. Ein Bericht des Hannah-Arendt-Instituts* (Dresden, Leipzig 1999), esp. pp. 38–39, 43, 52–55, 70, 96–99, 102–103, 142–144, 184–185, 228–232.

transactions of its own, it was not for lack of trying. In September 1942, the Länderbank asked the Foreign Exchange Section of the Dresdner Bank about the current price of gold in Swiss francs and the Reichsbank conditions for gold purchases. Schobert does not seem to have taken well to this query; he replied that the gold provided by the Reichsbank was "not for domestic persons but only for persons residing abroad, for example our branch in Istanbul and then only for business which lies in the German interest." He also stressed that every gold transaction had to be negotiated with the Reichsbank. The Länderbank responded by claiming that it was "self-understood that our inquiry concerning gold is related to a special transaction in the German interest," and it repeated its request for information about fees and commissions it should charge for the client on whose behalf it was acting. Once again, Schobert emphasized that the business was done for the Istanbul account without charge and that charges could not be calculated for gold transactions. The obvious intention was to discourage the Länderbank from pursuing the matter, and there is no evidence that it subsequently became involved in the gold business except as a repository for the Dresdner Bank and its Istanbul branch.[147]

Financing the Military Machine

The primary way the Länderbank served "German interests" in these years was by helping to finance the industrial war effort. There would be little point in going through the long list of credits supplied to various enterprises. The purpose of the discussion here is to put some of the important aspects of this activity and to identify some of the most important firms and concerns with which the Länderbank was engaged and the special features of their

dealings. The Länderbank often participated in consortia with other banks. In 1944, for example, it was part of a consortium to lend IG Farben 170 million RM; the Dresdner Bank and the Deutsche Bank were each to supply 30 million RM and the Creditanstalt and the Länderbank 5 million RM apiece.[148] As this case demonstrates, the Länderbank sometimes participated in consortial lending sometimes in collaboration with and certainly always with the approval of the Dresdner Bank. Industrial finance also involved the Länderbank in a great deal of consortial business with the Creditanstalt and other banks, including specialized banks like the Bank der Deutschen Luftfahrt (Aerobank), which had been set up to finance the aircraft industry but ended up engaged in a broader range of banking activities. By 1941, it was the third largest bank in Germany after the Deutsche Bank and Dresdner Bank.[149] It floated share issues on the market, provided investment credits from the Reich treasury for large projects, and held a large portfolio of shares of its own.

The Dresdner Bank and the Länderbank provided a full range of credits. They usually offered operating and discount credits to the firms with which they dealt and acted as a repositories of their accounts, but they also joined in providing investment credits for large projects. Some concerns, for example, held the status of both creditors and debtors of the bank at the same time, the extent to which the one position or the other predominated depending on their momentary credit needs. Prior to Stalingrad, the banks seemed to have had little difficulty meeting the credit needs of firms producing for the war effort, but the overhaul of the war economy in the course of 1942 and a government decision to cease providing advances on payments for military contracts beginning in October 1942 caused some anxiety in banking circles about the extent to which credit demands would increase. This was reflected at

---

[147] Ibid., p. 53, Alt-Archiv der Dresdner Bank, Berlin, Handakten Salzwedel, telegraphic exchanges, Dresdner Bank-Länderbank, Sept. 28–29, 1942. This file also contains documents on the gold passing through or stored at the Länderbank. I am grateful to Johannes Bähr for providing me with these materials.

[148] NARA, T83/126, Dresdner Bank credit committee, June 7, 1944.

[149] See Lutz Budraß, *Flugzeugindustrie und Luftrüstung in Deutschland 1918–1945* (Düsseldorf 1998), pp. 362–363, 500–501.

a meeting of the Länderbank supervisory board in September 1942 during which a lively but unfortunately not fully recorded discussion of the problem took place. General Director George Meindl expressed concern that the special banks, especially the Aerobank, would expand their activities to the point where they could offer terms that would make it impossible for the private banks to compete, not only in the investment credit field but also in the provision of current account credits. A bank client might then find it most convenient to deal with the special bank for all its business. Rasche saw the situation somewhat differently. The Dresdner Bank, which had set up its own special office for the aeronautics industry under Director Meyer, was used to doing business with the Aerobank, and Rasche believed it could offer competitive terms. A more serious problem, in his view, was that the Dresdner Bank/Länderbank would find it harder to offer operating credits because of their own engagement in granting long-term credits. His hope was that, in the end, the special banks would leave the granting of operating credits to the private banks. That hope was reinforced by Wolzt, who pointed out that another special bank, the Rüstungskontor, was limiting itself to investment credits. Rasche was confident that the Reich would not fully abandon all prepayments on armaments contracts and noted that firms were for the moment only anticipating the need for credits and not actually taking advantage of them, and that many were still benefiting from old prepayments so that it would take some time for the demand to increase.[150]

As it turned out, neither the Dresdner Bank nor the Länderbank was deprived of the opportunity to provide large credits to industry. If anything, the reverse was the case. The matter came up for discussion at the Dresdner Bank in April 1944. Goetz recognized that the bank had no choice but to give such credits under the circumstances but pointed out that "the Dresdner Bank ought not to have the ambition to give large credits alone," and should have

other banks and subsidiaries become involved through sub-participations. As a general principle, he argued, no credit should exceed 10 percent of the equity of the client, although an exception was justified in the case of the Länderbank, which could participate in large credits up to 5 million RM due to its "special circumstances."[151] The question came up again in September 1944, this time at the initiative of Rasche. He warned that the demand for large credits arising from the growth of armaments orders was straining the resources not only of individual banks but also of consortia. This especially affected the Dresdner Bank because it was more engaged in the aeronautics industry than the Deutsche Bank, the Commerzbank, and the Reichs-Kredit-Gesellschaft. The management board came to the conclusion that "for the obviously necessary satisfaction of the anticipated new calls for credits, one must above all provide for an effective expansion of existing consortia. Greatly increased credit demands of a single enterprise or of an entire sector of the armaments industry require for its security a broadening of the shoulders that have to bear it. To make the expansion of consortia easier, it will be necessary, in the one case or the other, to provide the credit with a Reich guarantee. In that way, it would also be possible for publicly owned banks to participate, and they will undoubtedly greet the new investment opportunities for the large means at their disposal."[152] The enthusiasm for limiting the role of the special banks, which can be read into the discussions of 1942, had clearly evaporated and was being replaced by a desire to spread risk and maintain liquidity so far as possible.

Nevertheless, the Länderbank proved very ambitious in its engagement in financing industrial enterprises, especially in the airplane industry, where the Dresdner Bank played a leading role. It is worth noting that these credits, and the balances of the firms and concerns to which

---

[150] DrB, Nr. 5460, supervisory board meeting, Sept. 10, 1942.

[151] NARA, T83/128, Dresdner Bank management board meeting, April 15, 1944.

[152] Ibid., Dresdner Bank management board meeting, Sept. 11, 1944.

they were given, were treated with the greatest secrecy on government order.[153] The business was obviously important and potentially very lucrative. The Länderbank even went so far as to challenge the Dresdner Bank's position in granting credits to the Ernst Heinkel AG, for which a 150 million RM credit was being organized at the end of 1943. The Dresdner Bank and the Länderbank were to have a 22 percent share together, with the Dresdner Bank providing 18 million RM and the Länderbank providing 15 million RM of the 33 million RM participation. The two banks then planned to farm out 16–17 million RM in sub-participations. Goetz, however, was extremely irritated when the Länderbank's management board accepted a participation almost as large as that of its parent bank, thereby showing that it was "completely lacking in a sense of proportion."[154] The end result was that the Länderbank gave up 10 million RM of its participation to the Dresdner Bank; a quota of 5 million RM for the Länderbank was deemed "very respectable."[155]

The Länderbank was allowed larger shares in financing deals for the aeronautics firms located in the vicinity of Vienna, the number of which was increasing as production was shifted eastward to escape Allied bombing. One such engagement was the financing of the construction of a huge factory by the Firma Leichtmetall Bernhard Berghaus, Rackwitz bei Leipzig to produce airplane parts in Engerau/Petržalka near the Slovak border. Berghaus was an accomplished physicist with more than 1,000 patents to his credit, and he owned a number of other companies, including the Berlin-Lübecker Maschinenfabrik and the Sintermetallwerke Bernhard Berghaus at Mittberghütten near Salzburg. He had worked very closely with the army since 1934 and

had very important connections with leading figures in the National Socialist regime, including Himmler.[156] Research in the field of atomic physics at his experimental laboratory in Lankwitz near Berlin led Berghaus to believe that he had developed a technique to produce aluminum plate that would be as hard as steel on a very large scale. In 1941, he developed grandiose plans to employ no fewer than 2,000 scientists to work on the process and to have all the major banks to invest in the idea. He apparently intended to relocate the Lankwitz facilities and to build new plants near Pressburg/Bratislava, which he viewed favorably because of its transport connections and its water power supply. The program would require vast sums. While Berghaus was negotiating with the government and with banks to float a large Reich-guaranteed loan, a modest step was taken in June 1942 when Hans Kehrl gave the Berghaus process a technical certification in support of building a large plant to employ the new process in Engerau/Petržalka.[157] He seems to have worked closely with the Dresdner Bank on the financial side of the project, and this was why the Länderbank was invited to take two-thirds of the 65 million RM investment credit (43,335,000 RM); the Bank der Deutschen Arbeit took the remaining 21,665,000 RM. The credit had a 100 percent Reich guarantee and was to run for fifteen years at 4.5 percent interest. In order to make refinancing possible and spread the risk, the Länderbank then offered substantial sub-participations, adding up to 35 million RM, to the Erste Österreichische

153 See NARA, T83/138, the comments by Meyer asking for strict enforcement throughout the Dresdner Bank concern at the management board meeting of June 15, 1944.
154 DrB, Nr. 30186–2001.BE, Telegram Goetz to Rinn, Dec. 24, 1943, and related correspondence. I am grateful to Johannes Bähr for bringing this to my attention.
155 Ibid., Rinn to André, Jan. 11, 1944.

156 On Berghaus's depressing career, see Christiane Uhlig/Petra Barthelmess/Mario König/Peter Pfaffenroth/Betinna Zeugin, *Tarnung, Transfer, Transit. Die Schweiz als Drehscheibe verdeckter deutscher Operationen (1939–1952)*. Veröffentlichungen der Unabhängigen Expertenkommission Schweiz – Zweiter Weltkrieg, vol. 9 (Zurich 2001), pp. 203–215. Berghaus fled to Switzerland just before the end of the war, where he was protected from extradition to Germany to face trial by the Allies for the brutal treatment of forced labor at his plants. By 1947, the Americans and the Swiss were competing for his patents and professional services. Fully "denazified," he died in 1966 in Switzerland.
157 BAB, R 8121, Vol. 455, memo of Aug. 11, 1941.

Sparkasse (15 million RM), the Zentralsparkasse der Gemeinde Wien (15 million RM), and the Girozentrale österreichische Sparkassen (5 million RM).[158]

Work began in 1942, but the construction program underwent some significant changes. It was thus likely that additional credits would be requested. By October 1944, enthusiasm for the enterprise had waned considerably after Meyer heard bad reports about the company. Director Zinsser made clear to Wolzt, who represented the Länderbank in dealing with Berghaus, that the Dresdner Bank would not participate in an increase of the credit. Berghaus did indeed ask that the credit be raised from 65 to 84 million RM, and the Länderbank sought to persuade the Aerobank to join the consortium. This effort was not successful, and Zinsser told the Länderbank that it could try to widen the consortium but that the Länderbank was under no circumstances to increase its own participation. The basic problem was doubt about the advisability of introducing the new process on so large a scale in Engerau when it had never been tested in the Reich itself. Kehrl seems to have shared Berghaus's optimism, however, telling an official of the Aerobank that "he very much supports the project and wants to avoid that a new process fail because of the conservative position of the other companies. He [Kehrl] welcomes the activity of Herr Berghaus and supports him now as before."[159] Apparently, some assistance was then provided by the Deutsche Bau- und Bodenbank. The construction of the plant, despite the cost overruns, was completed at the end of 1944, which left little time for it to go into full production. The plant

was subsequently dismantled and blown up by the Russians.

A far more important aeronautics investment was the Wiener-Neustädter Flugzeugwerke GmbH, the majority of whose stock were held by the Aerobank. The Länderbank's involvement with this firm dated back to 1938–1939. In 1939, it took 40 percent of the current account credit and the investment credits granted to this Reich-owned company. At that time, that amounted to 1.2 million RM and 2.18 million RM respectively. The Länderbank's portion of the operating credit had increased to 2 million RM by June 1940.[160] By the spring of 1943, the operating credit of the company had reached a total of 25 million RM, with the Länderbank providing 10 million RM and the Aerobank providing the rest. Shortly thereafter, the amounts were doubled because of the suspension of advance payments on military orders. The operating credits needed thus amounted to 50 million RM, with the Länderbank providing 20 million RM.[161] When the credit demand reached 75 million RM in May 1944, the Länderbank's quota became 30 million RM. The Dresdner Bank took over 20 million RM of that amount and then gave out 10 million RM as sub-participations, especially to the Hermes Insurance company, which provided credit insurance. At this time, negotiations were held with the Air Ministry leading to an agreement that this was the maximum credit that would be held at this level.[162] The Länderbank's enthusiasm for holding the lion's share had apparently waned by this time. The Wiener Neustädter was the largest airplane producer in the Reich, and every third Messerschmidt was built there. But that made the plant a prime target for Allied bombing attacks. By October 1944, the firm's cash flow problems were being solved by Allied air raids.

---

[158] BA-CA, CA-V, Anhang zum Bericht über die Prüfung des vorläufigen Entwurfes des Jahresabschlusses zum 31. Dezember 1945 der Länderbank Wien Aktiengesellschaft, Vol. II Anhang, pp. 35–36, 26c.

[159] Ibid., Vol. 454, minute by Rudolf and letter to Wolzt, Oct. 30, 1944. See also NARA, T83/137–138 Dresdner Bank board of management meetings, March 13, 1942, May 26, 1942, June 4, 1942, June 18, 1942, Aug. 11, 1942, March 11, 1943, Oct. 10, 1944, Dec. 7, 1944, Jan. 16, 1945, and Dresdner Bank management board meeting, Dec. 17, 1942.

[160] NARA, T83/122 and 124, Dresdner Bank supervisory board, Oct. 17, 1939 and June 26, 1940.

[161] NARA, T83/125, memorandum of April 21, 1943, credit committee meeting of May 6, 1943.

[162] DrB, Nr. 5124-2000, memorandum of May 31, 1944, and correspondence between the Länderbank and Dresdner Bank, spring 1944, in ibid., 29750-2001, BE.

Government compensation for damages from air raids not only covered the credits but actually enabled Wiener Neustädter to have 5 million RM on its account at the Länderbank. The credit limits remained in place.[163]

Wiener Neustadt was an important production center for aircraft and the war economy in general. It was also a major point for rocket production at the Rax-Werke GmbH, which belonged to the Kassel-based Henschel & Sohn GmbH. The Henschel company had become active in Austria in 1938 by taking over the Wiener Lokomotivfabrik AG. During the war, it moved into aeronautics, founding the Rax-Werke in May 1942, and became one of the key producers for the rocket program, which made considerable use of concentration camp labor. The Rax-Werke GmbH had its own camp, which employed 1,200 workers in July 1943, before it decided to move production to underground facilities in Ebensee. An especially atrocious new sub-camp of the Mauthausen concentration camp was established there.[164] The Rax-Werke received credits from the Länderbank amounting to 2.5 million RM in 1943–1944.[165]

The Länderbank also participated in financing the Flugmotorenwerke Ostmark GmbH in Vienna, whose basic capital was in the hands of Daimler-Benz AG and the Aerobank. The Air Ministry was heavily invested in this facility, which reached its goal of becoming the largest airplane engine producer in the Reich. The Daimler management was apparently unable to make it operational. The Steyr-Daimler-Puch firm's empire-building general director, Georg Meindl, who will be discussed at length later in this chapter, tried to come to the rescue in 1943. He wanted to take the company over and to integrate it and the other airplane and airplane parts manufacturers in Austria into one gigantic holding company within the Steyr-Daimler-Puch concern. Göring apparently thought this concentration of power excessive, but he nonetheless made Meindl the manager of the Flugmotorenwerke Ostmark. Meindl used his excellent SS connections to have a concentration camp, incarcerating some 2,000 inmates, established in Wiener Neudorf to provide labor.[166] The Länderbank had a stake of 15 percent in the 19.5 million RM investment credit provided the company, along with a 20 percent share, that is 8 million RM, in the 40 million RM operating credit. The Länderbank gave a sub-participation of 3 million RM to the Böhmische Escompte Bank, which made sense as the Flugmotorenwerke Ostmark had branches in Brünn and Prague. The Creditanstalt also provided an 8 million RM credit, the remainder coming from the Aerobank (50 percent) and the Bank der Deutschen Arbeit (10 percent).[167] By early 1945, the Dresdner Bank was worrying about the credits it and the Länderbank had extended to the Wiener Neustädter Flugzeugwerke and the Flugmotorenwerke Ostmark. At a meeting in March 1945, Rasche and Teichmann argued that "it would be desirable to put the moral obligation of the Reich, which arises directly from its indirect ownership of the shares, in a legally binding form by the granting of a Reich guarantee."[168]

To speak of "moral obligation" in the context of what had taken place at these enterprises was nothing short of perverse. A large portion of the Reich's war production after 1942 was carried out with forced and slave labor, and all the important companies producing for the war effort that received credits from the Länderbank

[163] NARA, T83/138, Dresdner Bank management board meeting, Oct. 10, 1944.

[164] See Florian Freund, "Die Entscheidung zum Einsatz von KZ-Häftlingen in der Raketenrüstung," in: Hermann Kaienburg (ed.), *Konzentrationslager und deutsche Wirtschaft 1939–1945* (Opladen 1996), pp. 60–74.

[165] DrB, Nr. 5124-2000, memorandum of Feb. 22, 1944.

[166] Bertrand Perz, "*Politisches Management im Wirtschaftskonzern*. Georg Meindl und die Rolle des Staatskonzerns Steyr-Daimler-Puch bei der Verwirklichung der NS-Wirtschaftsziele in Österreich," in: Hermann Kaienburg (ed.), Konzentrationslager und deutsche Wirtschaft 1939–1945 (Opladen 1996), pp. 107–108.

[167] DrB, Nr. 5124-2000, memorandum, July 15, 1944; NARA, T83/138, Dresdner Bank management board meeting, May 9, 1944.

[168] DrB, Nr. 13790, discussion of March 14, 1945.

used such labor. Because the operations of these firms and the number of workers they employed were treated as state secrets, such information was never included in the credit documents and evaluations. There is no evidence that the Dresdner Bank and Länderbank officials were in any way concerned with labor issues, but they could not have been unaware that their financing went to firms using forced and slave labor, often under extremely brutal conditions. The Länderbank, for example, held an account in the name of Sonderkommando Eichmann: the firms employing Hungarian Jews who had been marched to Austria rather than sent to Auschwitz in the summer of 1944 paid the charges for the prisoners' labor into this account. The payments were complicated because the fees charged varied according to prisoners' age, sex, and performance and provision was also made for health care; managing the account must have been anything but simple.[169]

The Länderbank must have been aware of the employment of forced labor because one of the leading and most active members of its supervisory board was Georg Meindl. He had the dubious distinction of being a "pioneer" in the industrial use of concentration camp labor. The Länderbank was significantly engaged in financing Steyr-Daimler-Puch, the firm where Meindl served as general director. Meindl's appointment to take the place of Paul Goetzl, the Jewish former general director, had been more or less forced on the Creditanstalt, which owned 86 percent of the company's shares before being made to sell out to the Reichswerke Hermann Göring. That happened around the time Meindl joined

the Länderbank's administrative council; he had been a candidate to replace Apold in the years prior to the Anschluss when Apold was in political hot water. Like Apold, Meindl had been on the management board of the Alpine Montangesellschaft, but he was looking for a new job in 1938 after the appointment of Hans Malzacher as general director blocked his way to advancement. One of the reasons the Vereinigte Stahlwerke preferred Malzacher to Meindl was that the latter had close connections with Hermann Göring, with whose sister Meindl had become acquainted in Linz. The Vereinigte Stahlwerke struggled unsuccessfully to hold on to the Alpine until March 1939. In the meantime, Meindl had taken over Steyr-Daimler-Puch. Ruling the company with an iron hand, he began a period of modernization and expansion of the production facilities at Steyr and Graz. Production of weapons and vehicles in Steyr was greatly increased. An immense factory to produce roller bearings was built in Steyr-Münichholz. The "Nibelungenwerk" to manufacture tanks was established in St. Valentin. Factories were set up in Vienna and Graz for the production of bicycles, truck parts, and airplane body and engine parts. After the conquest of Poland, Steyr-Daimler-Puch was put in charge of the two largest rifle manufacturers in Poland. Meindl became the director of a veritable industrial empire in Austria. The number of employees under his control increased from 7,000 in 1938 to 50,000 in 1944. The company's capital grew from 11 million RM in 1938 to 80 million RM in late 1943, and its turnover increased from 57 million RM in 1938 to 456 million RM in 1944. During the same period, direct investment in the concern amounted to approximately 328 million.

Meindl cultivated as many important National Socialist leaders as he could. Besides Göring, he was on excellent terms with Gauleiter August Eigruber of the Upper Danube and Gauleiter Siegfried Uiberreither of Styria, both of whom were given seats on Steyr-Daimler-Puch's supervisory board. Moreover, Meindl, an SS member who was promoted to the rank of *Brigadeführer* (major general) in 1944 for his services in arming

169 Gerhard Milchram, "Die Lager der Ungarischen Juden in Neunkirchen," in: *David. Jüdische Kulturzeitschrift* 47 (Dec. 2000), http://www .david.juden.at/kulturzeitschrift/44–49/lager-47 .htm (April 20, 2006). For the companies employing forced and slave labor, many of which are to be discussed here, see Florian Freund/Bertrand Perz/Mark Spoerer, *Zwangsarbeiter und Zwangsarbeiterinnen auf dem Gebiet der Republik Österreich 1939–1945.* Veröffentlichungen der Österreichischen Historikerkommission, vol. 26/1 (Vienna, Munich 2004), pp. 108–125.

the Waffen-SS, had excellent ties to Himmler, who was responsible for the promotion, as well as to Hans Jüttner, the head of the SS Leadership Main Office. Meindl could also call on the assistance of the head of the SS and police in the Ostmark, Ernst Kaltenbrunner, and the head of the Mauthausen concentration camp complex, Franz Ziereis. Meindl faced the same shortage of skilled labor as other industrial managers in Austria, but his talents as a political manager enabled him to overcome SS reluctance to provide concentration camp labor for private industry. In the spring of 1941, he began to employ concentration camp labor from Mauthausen and succeeded a year later in persuading the SS to create a sub-camp for approximately 2,000 inmates near the plants in Steyr-Münichholz. In 1943, a new camp in Gusen was set up to house workers in the rifle factory there. When Allied air raids endangered the company's factories in late 1943, Meindl and the authorities decided to construct underground facilities, which required an even more massive deployment of concentration camp labor; 15,000 prisoners were deployed in the area of Melk, for instance. Thanks to Meindl's skills as a "political manager" and total indifference to the human cost of his management, Steyr-Daimler-Puch was able to resume production only a short time after the end of the war.[170]

It would be absurd to think that Meindl consulted with the bankers and others who financed his enterprise about his labor policies. He had a reputation for not letting his directors deal autonomously with his supervisory board. There is also no reason whatever to think that the bankers involved disapproved of his practices.

The Länderbank certainly showed great interest in having an important part in the financial transactions involving the Steyr-Daimler-Puch. In early 1942, for example, there were reports that the concern was planning to undertake a substantial increase in its capital from 30 million to 50 million RM. It appeared that the Prussian State Bank (Seehandlung), the house bank of the Reichswerke, was going to take the lead in bringing the new issue to the market and setting its price. The Länderbank wanted to play a more important role, and Wolzt, who thought the exclusion of the Vienna banks harmful to the efforts to market the shares, was able to make an agreement with Director Schilling of the Seehandlung, whereby the task of supervising the listing of the new shares on the Vienna stock exchange would fall to the Länderbank. Wolzt was interested in selling blocks of the shares to his bank's favored customers; Schilling was anxious to prevent any competitor from buying a significant block. They thus struck an agreement that the Länderbank would consult with the Seehandlung before selling any block larger than 10,000 RM, and they also agreed to keep in contact about the market quotation.[171] Wolzt also worked hand in hand with Meindl on a plan to return the capital of the concern to private hands, a project for which Oskar Hinterleitner, the Upper Danube Gau economic advisor, and Gauleiter Eigruber had promised Meindl their support.[172]

The context of these machinations was the ultimately successful initiative to separate the armaments sector of the Reichswerke from its heavy industrial sector, and Meindl seems to have used the situation in an effort to increase his power by suggesting to Himmler that the tobacco czar Philipp Reemtsma might buy the shares and that the SS could prevent this by acquiring 51 percent of the shares. The appeal of such a proposition was that the Waffen-SS would thereby control the production of the weapons it needed Oswald Pohl, the head of

[170] In this account, I follow closely the penetrating discussion by Perz, "Politisches Management," pp. 95–112; see also Richard J. Overy, *War and Economy in the Third Reich* (Oxford 1994), ch. 5 and Florian Freund/Bertrand Perz, "Zwangsarbeit von zivilen Ausländerinnen, Kriegsgefangenen, KZ-Häftlingen und ungarischen Juden in Österreich," in: Tálos et al., *NS-Herrschaft*, pp. 644–695. See also NARA, RG 338, 290/56/03/02, Box 110, the reports on Steyr-Daimler-Puch and Meindl. See more generally, Oliver Rathkolb (ed.), *Zwangsarbeit: Der Standort Linz der Hermann Göring Werke AG Berlin, 1938–1945*, 2 vols. (Vienna 2001).

[171] See NARA, T83/137, Dresdner Bank board of management meetings, Feb. 12, 1942, and April 13, 1942, and DrB, 5461-2000, Wolzt to Rasche, April 16, 1942 and April 23, 1942.

[172] Ibid., Wolzt to Rasche, May 21, 1943.

the Economic Office of the SS, turned the idea down, however, because he did not think this would matter in the SS's competition with the army for weapons. Whatever the case, the proposal bolstered Meindl's standing with the SS and clearly helped him win support in his bid for concentration camp labor.[173] The real purpose behind splitting up the Reichswerke was the need to rationalize the increasingly ungainly Reichswerke by putting the armaments sector under the control of Speer and the private sector. State control was not surrendered, however. The Aerobank received 51 percent of Steyr-Daimler-Puch at the end of 1942. Both the Länderbank and the Creditanstalt had been supplying credits to Steyr-Daimler-Puch all along in addition to holding large accounts for the company, and they were represented on the supervisory board by Leonhard Wolzt and Richard Buzzi, respectively.

The Länderbank not only provided credits to the parent company in Austria but also gave both operating and discount credits for carrying out the military contracts in the Polish factories under Steyr-Daimler-Puch's administration. It also guaranteed credits given by the Kommerzialbank in Cracow.[174] At the beginning of 1945, most of the Polish debt had been paid back and the firm had a credit line of 12.5 million RM with the Länderbank. The Länderbank also participated in the 20 million RM investment credit of the Aerobank in the amount of 2 million RM. It had also provided a credit of 1.5 million RM to the Kromag AG, which was part of the concern. At the beginning of 1945, both the Länderbank and the Creditanstalt were asked to extend these credits for a year. The Länderbank felt quite comfortable in agreeing to this request: Steyr-Daimler-Puch had doubled its sales between 1942 and 1943 and had paid a 4 percent dividend. As the bank noted, "the plants, which have been significantly expanded because of the armaments

contracts during the war should be able to be converted without great difficulties to peacetime production."[175]

There was another reason for the bank's willingness to extend the credits for a year instead of for half a year, as the Dresdner Bank urged. As the Dresdner Bank officials dealing with the Länderbank accounts at the end of the war reported: "The account is subject to strong fluctuations. Debt and credit exchange with one another. The Länderbank does not see any possibility of granting only a six-month instead of a year-long extension as well as of asking for a modest commission for holding the money, as we suggested shortly before, because the mentality of Herr Meindl is such that one can anticipate no understanding on his part. Also, the attempt to come to an agreement with the Creditanstalt on this is viewed as dangerous because it is convinced that Herr Meindl will get wind of it. It will therefore make use of its right to agree to the credit under unchanged conditions for another year."[176] Meindl's days of terrorizing people were coming to an end by this time. Soon he was fleeing the Russians; he was eventually captured by the Americans but then let go. The hunt for him resumed, however, and what was allegedly his charred corpse was found on the site of a burned barn. As one of the most important Austrian industrialists of the Third Reich period, Meindl had a very close and very important relationship with the Länderbank. If he had left something of an industrial legacy, it was a legacy marked by extreme criminality.

The Länderbank's involvement with the Reichswerke Alpine-Montan "Hermann Göring" in Linz, another major center of forced labor, was much more substantial. It was shared with the Creditanstalt, which provided 54.6875 percent of the credit, and the Bankhaus E. v. Nicolai, which had a 12.5 percent quota. The Länderbank's share was 32.8125 percent. It was not a happy experience. The initial credit

173 Perz, "Politisches Management," pp. 105–106.
174 For the Polish credits and other relevant credits, see NARA, T83/124, the working committee meeting, Nov. 28, 1940; NARA, T83/126, the credit committee meeting, June 7, 1944.

175 DrB, Nr. 5124-2000, credit request, Jan. 30, 1945, and relevant documentation.
176 DrB, Nr. 13790-2000, memorandum by Teichmann and Gruber, Jan. 12, 1945.

had been 25 million RM, which was then increased to 40 million RM, restored to 25 million RM, and then increased again to 40 million RM. At the end of the war, the Alpine was asking for a 45 million RM credit, claiming, as did numerous other armaments producers, that transportation problems and delayed payment by government agencies increased the need for credit. The consortial banks had asked to see the balance sheets, and what their auditors found was most discouraging. The Alpine had apparently invested substantial sums in various Reich interests by using Reich interest-free loans, which amounted to 60 million RM by 1945. Investments of this scale would never have been made even under normal circumstances. The calculation at the Alpine, however, was that the government loans would never have to be repaid, as the finance minister more or less promised. The Alpine had also recorded substantial losses: 7.1 million RM in 1942, 3.4 million RM in 1943, and 2.3 million RM as of June 1944. The source of these losses was its contract with the Vereinigte Stahlwerke at the time the Alpine became part of the Reichswerke. The Alpine was to supply ore to the Vereinigte Stahlwerke until 1973 at half the normal price. The Alpine was now counting on a change in the terms of the contract because it feared the arrangement would bankrupt it. Considering the situation in March 1945, Rasche and Teichmann came to the conclusion that the Alpine's request for an additional 5 million RM in credits had to be turned down and that the Alpine should be advised to request the money from Berlin as aid from the Reich. The Vienna banks were trapped, but the Dresdner Bank directors thought that anything beyond the 40 million RM should be considered as advance against assistance from the Reich, and that the consortium should be expanded so that the Länderbank's commitment could be reduced to 8 million RM.[177]

The Alpine was an old client that had become a large burden, but there was also obviously old business in Austria that the Länderbank

wished to maintain and cultivate. It no longer had a significant stake in the steel construction firm Waagner Biro AG, which had been taken over by the Vereinigte Stahlwerke, but it continued to supply it with operating credits and had an obvious interest in its success. In early 1941, Director Lehr had a lengthy correspondence with Director Meyer of the Dresdner Bank with the object of securing orders from the Junkers-Werke, which was heavily financed by the Dresdner Bank, and of helping defend Waagner Biro from Junker's complaints about late deliveries.[178] The Länderbank was also supported by the Dresdner Bank when it went to great lengths to satisfy the Julius Meinl concern, which was one of its major clients. When Julius Meinl decided to offer the Länderbank 20 percent of his 90 percent holding in the concern at 200 percent of its nominal value, the Dresdner Bank managers thought the price excessive but concluded that "a negative attitude would endanger the lucrative connection with the Meinl concern and could result in the transfer of the account to the Creditanstalt and Schöller."[179] The Dresdner Bank could not be as obliging in all cases, of course. In the fall of 1942, for instance, the Länderbank wrote to Meyer in the fall of 1942 asking that its very good customer, the Prince von und zu Liechtenstein, be allowed to recover his estate in Johanneshof bei Lundenburg. It had been confiscated by the Czechs after the First World War, and the prince thought he was entitled to its return as a matter of restitution. Unfortunately for the prince, who had distinguished himself as the leading Aryanizer in the paper industry, the German Settlement Society also wanted the estate for its "settlement" work and would agree to give it up only if the prince provided other suitable property. The Dresdner Bank had been a strong supporter of the Settlement Society and had provided it with credit. Needless to say, settlement work, at least

[177] Ibid., report on discussion between Rasche and Teichmann, March 14, 1945.

[178] See the correspondence of Jan.–April 1943 in NARA, RG 260, External Assets Investigations 1945–1949, 390/44/31/01, Box 539.

[179] NARA, T83/137, Dresdner Bank board of management meetings, Aug. 25 and 27, 1941.

for the time being, had to take priority over a Länderbank client, however important.[180]

Lenzinger Zellwolle- und Papierfabrik under National Socialist Mismanagement

During the war, the Länderbank sought to act as banker to the owners of firms it had helped to Aryanize. This was not always a blessing, as was amply demonstrated by the case of the Lenzinger Zellwolle und Papierfabrik AG, with which the Länderbank had been involved since the Anschluss. As has been shown earlier in this study, Lenzing had a difficult start, but its fortunes took a marked turn for the better in late 1939 when, after months of construction work, it finally began producing something. In March 1940, Reich agencies pushed for a further expansion of the company's facilities that would cost 21 million RM. But only 7 million RM of that sum needed to be financed by a Reich-guaranteed credit, and the rest could be covered by write-offs and anticipated profits in 1940–1941. At this point, the Länderbank was joined by the Bank für Oberösterreich and Salzburg, which belonged to the Creditanstalt, as the chief members of the consortium supporting Lenzing's expansion, each of them providing 1.5 million RM. There was also a large credit from the Dutch government, which was of course under German control.[181] The company had a loss of more than 2 million RM in 1940 and produced a not-exactly-noteworthy profit of 14,340 RM in 1941; the anticipated profits were obviously a miscalculation. When the company asked for an extension of its 2 million RM credit with the Länderbank in early 1941, the Dresdner Bank asked to see its books first. As Wolzt reported, Lenzing was not permitted to provide the requested information because its major backer at the RWM, Hans Kehrl, had concluded "that the numbers

pertaining to the interim development, which is unsatisfactory because of production and sales delays (transport difficulties in the supply of sulphuric acid as well as in the shipping of cellulose), should not be made available until a degree of correction of the financial picture has taken place through the first receipts from the 'compensatory payment for increased plant costs' that can basically be anticipated."[182] Wolzt had another meeting with Kehrl during which the latter gave yet more assurances but no figures. Wolzt could report only that he was unable to supply the information at the moment and that a six-month extension would have to be granted in any case. It was perhaps this sort of thing that Kehrl had in mind when he later entitled his autobiography "Crisis Manager of the Third Reich."

Lenzing turned a profit of 2.1 million RM in 1942, but that was anything but the beginning of an upward trend. Losses resumed in 1943–1944, amounting to up to 8.5 million RM by the end of 1944. This certainly was not because of high labor costs; the firm employed more than 500 concentration camp inmates, mostly women, from one of the Mauthausen sub-camps along with Soviet POWs. The real problems lay in over-expansion, expensive experiments with new production methods, and increasing raw materials shortages that brought production to a standstill in 1944. Director Wolzt of the Länderbank, who served as chairman of the supervisory board, found the situation increasingly untenable. At the beginning of 1945, he tried to mobilize Kehrl who, as noted, had been one of the chief promoters of Lenzing's expansion after its Aryanization, to bring the situation under control, and he voiced his that General Director Schieber would devote himself exclusively to Lenzing and take things in hand.[183] Wolzt rejected Lenzing's request for a

---

[180] NARA, RG 260, External Assets Investigations 1945–1949, 390/44/31/01, Box 539, Länderbank memorandum, Nov. 9, 1942; Länderbank to Meyer, Nov. 12, 1942; Meyer to Länderbank, Nov. 16, 1942.

[181] See NARA, T83/122, Dresdner Bank working committee, Dec. 12, 1939; NARA, T83/123, working committee, March 5, 1940.

[182] DrB, Nr. 30796–2001, BE, Länderbank to Dresdner Bank, April 25, 1941.

[183] For Wolzt's correspondence with the Lenzing management of early 1945, see Der Kampf um Lenzing, vol. I, pp. 5–13. There was also plenty of corruption involved in the Lenzing story. See Roman Sandgruber, Lenzing. Anatomie einer Industriegründung im Dritten Reich (Linz, 2010).

new credit, not least because the district leadership had ordered the plant to be closed but its workers retained. Rasche and Teichmann fully supported Wolzt's decision, and they joined forces with the Creditanstalt to call, as usual, for help from the Reich to deal with the desperate financial situation. It would not be long before Wolzt's successors would be contemplating not only the problem of compensating Bunzl & Biach for the Aryanization of Lenzing but also the possibility of seeking the help of the former owners in putting the company back on its feet![184]

Bunzl & Biach: The Most Challenging Aryanization

Bunzl & Biach was reputed to be the world's largest manufacturer paper products and supplier of pulp products, and it certainly was proving a much better investment for the Länderbank than the mismanaged Lenzing. The firm had been partially Aryanized through a series of contracts and agreements with the Bunzl family in the summer of 1938. This outcome came after three of the Bunzl brothers had been sent to a concentration camp; one of them never returned. The terms of the Aryanization left the family with some of its holdings and the right to manage them from abroad. The Kontrollbank bought 76 percent of the capital of the Vienna firm along with 50 percent of the capital of two holding companies in Zug, Switzerland, the Bunzl-Holding Corporation and the Tafag AG. The Tafag was subsequently liquidated and its assets absorbed into the Bunzl-Holding shortly after the agreement with the Kontrollbank. The Kontrollbank had an option to buy the remaining 24 percent of the Vienna shares and the remaining 50 percent holding company shares before the end of 1945. The purpose of this arrangement was to keep the Bunzl family interested in the concern and allow the family to run the concern's international operations from London. Exports constituted 60 percent of the concern's business,

and the agreement was intended to enable the Germans to benefit from the foreign exchange returns on this substantial export business.[185] The concern was very active in Southeastern Europe and did a large volume of business in Russia before June 1941. It was also engaged in the United States and Latin America. The supervisory board, reflecting the concern's ownership, was composed of Kontrollbank officials: Hans Rizzi, Josef von Paić, Guido Jakoncig, Walther Kastner, and Georg Schumetz. The board of directors, composed of Otto Fenzl, Walther Rohrwasser, and Ferdinand Schmidt, appears to have been highly competent. Schmidt, the leading director, had an outstanding reputation, and the company continued to flourish after its Aryanization, It was particularly successful in Russia in 1939–1940.[186] Bunzl & Biach was not fully Aryanized in 1938; rather, the Aryanization continued with the advance of the German armies, over the objections of the Bunzl family. The Vienna firm took over Bunzl & Biach operations in the former Czechoslovakia and Yugoslavia after the German invasions, but the shares of these holdings remained with Bunzl & Biach Holding in Zug and hence out of German hands. At a meeting of the shareholders in Vienna on July 17, 1941, Bunzl & Biach's name was changed to Kontropa (Kontinentale Rohstoffe und Papier AG), a symbolic but important act of Aryanization. The biggest question connected with the concern in 1940–1942 was who was to take over its shares. The Kontrollbank, which held 10,640,000 RM in shares, formally decided at the end of 1940 to go out of business. Although the liquidation of the bank would not be completed until 1943, the disposal of the shares became a very pressing matter. That was no easy task given the size of the holding, and it was no accident that Bunzl & Biach was the first enterprise taken over by the Kontrollbank and the last to be sold.[187]

---

[185] See DrB, Nr. 30316–2001.BE, the protocol of the agreement, July 27, 1938.

[186] Ibid., memorandum by Kühnen.

[187] Felber et al., *Ökonomie der Arisierung*, pt. 2, pp. 311–336; Gregor Spuhler/Ursina Jud/Peter Melichar/Daniel Wildmann, *"Arisierungen" in Österreich und ihre*

[184] Ibid., pt. II and DrB, Nr. 13790-2000, discussion between Rasche and Teichmann, March 14, 1945.

There was much behind-the-scenes maneuvering in connection with the Bunzl & Biach shares. The Creditanstalt was particularly interested in playing a role in the final disposition of the concern, and the Länderbank and the Dresdner Bank also wanted to be involved. The RWM and, above all, Hans Kehrl had definite views concerning Bunzl & Biach, as did Austrian Party leaders and the Kontrollbank. There seems to have been a general consensus that the concern should be kept intact, and the RWM was insistent that the Kontrollbank not sell the shares to a single large company or concern and that a substantial portion of the shares be made available to the public. That took the Henkel AG, a potential purchaser with the means to buy the shares, out of the running; Henkel considered Bunzl & Biach too diversified and was interested in only some of its holdings. The same held true for Papier & Pappe AG, which would have been willing to buy up Bunzl & Biach's paper industry holdings but not the rest of the concern. Dresdner Bank officials and Director Wolzt of the Länderbank had been in contact with the aforementioned firms, which did business with the Dresdner Bank group, obviously in the hope of playing a role in the acquisition of the shares. Rasche also approached another large paper producer, the Waldhof concern, and explored the possibility that Walter Rau, a margarine producer in Neuss, might be interested.[188]

Quite early in the game, Director Wolzt of the Länderbank took steps to interest a major potential investor in Bunzl & Biach. In January 1940, he contacted Director Heinz Ansmann of the Dresdner Bank, who had mentioned a businessman with 10 million RM to invest, and was then put into contact with Eduard Winter, who had sold his Opel concession in Berlin for a great sum of money and was looking for investment opportunities. Wolzt met Winter in mid-January and brought him together with Kastner of the Kontrollbank to discuss the status of the concern.[189] Although the contact had been made, Winter does not seem to have picked up on the possibility for a number of months.

The senior management of the Dresdner Bank and the Länderbank were worried above all about the ambitions of the Creditanstalt. They suspected, correctly, that the Creditanstalt wanted to acquire all the Bunzl & Biach shares for itself. In June 1940, the Creditanstalt thought it might get the shares of Bunzl & Biach as compensation for surrendering its Danube shipping interests to the Reichswerke, and it considered the acquisition a "valuable addition to the Creditanstalt's present engagement in the paper industry." The Creditanstalt also was prepared to consider the proposal that Walther Kastner of the Kontrollbank be appointed to the management board of the concern.[190] In October, Wolzt heard that the Creditanstalt had offered to take the shares as payment for other claims it had against the Reich.[191] Taking over the shares in that way would fit in well with the Creditanstalt's practice of participating directly in the ownership of companies, but it did not have the approval of Hans Kehrl, who refused to sanction an enlargement of the Creditanstalt on that scale. The most he was prepared to do was to let the Creditanstalt assume the Kontrollbank's function as trustee should a purchaser acceptable to the RWM not be found before the Kontrollbank was liquidated. It was undoubtedly with some relief that the Dresdner Bank learned that the decision to liquidate the Kontrollbank in December 1940 did not require immediate transfer of the shares

Bezüge zur Schweiz Veröffentlichungen der UEK, Vol. 20 (Zurich 2002), pp. 120–126. The most precise and evidence-grounded account is to be found in a report by the Kontrollbank to Oberregierungsrat Ronsiek of Aug. 11, 1941, AdR, ÖStA/AdR, MfWuA, VVSt, Firmenbuchhaltung, Box 336, IND.-288, Vol. 1.

188 DrB, Nr. 30316–2001, BE, André to Rasche, Sept. 26, 1940, and Oct. 7, 1940; memoradum by Homolka on report from Wolzt, Oct. 4, 1940; note by Rinn, Oct. 31, 1940.

189 Ibid., Wolzt to Ansmann, Jan. 9, 1940, and Jan. 16, 1940.

190 Ibid., and DB, P6503, Bl. 308, discussion in Berlin, June 15, 1940.

191 DrB, Nr. 30316–2001, BE, André to Rasche, Oct. 7, 1940.

to another trustee, namely, the Creditanstalt, as had been rumored.[192]

As might be expected, the Länderbank did not want to be left out in the cold. It had a long-standing interest in Bunzl & Biach and had taken over an open and unused credit the old Vienna branch of the Central European Länderbank had provided the concern. The credit had been extended into 1939 because the concern had been very profitable and the Länderbank did not want to lose the connection.[193] The Länderbank was obviously too small to consider competing with the Creditanstalt for the entire block of shares but, as has been shown, Wolzt had drawn the Kontrollbank's attention to Winter. One preliminary problem with Winter, however, was Hans Kehrl's lack of enthusiasm. He let it be known that he would prefer to find a businessman who would not view Bunzl & Biach simply as an investment asset and would be an engaged owner. Moreover, the Dresdner Bank was trying to interest Winter in another expensive project in the summer of 1940 that would not have left him with enough money to purchase the Bunzl & Biach shares. Pilder then proposed Hermann Reemtsma, the cigarette manufacturer, as a potential purchaser and agreed to get in touch with him. Länderbank officials worried that the "neighbors," that is, the Creditanstalt, would gain the initiative if they did not find a solution soon. If Reemtsma was not interested, Wolzt hoped that Rasche would be able to persuade Kehrl to accept the idea of finding a small group of purchasers for the shares.[194] That took time, but by late fall, Kehrl had become more flexible. Director F. André of the Dresdner Bank, who had been dealing with State Secretary Heinrich Bauer of the RWM about Bunzl & Biach, reported in mid-November 1940 that there was a growing consensus that it would be hard to find a single party interested in the shares. Bauer thought that a reasonable solution might be to create a consortium that would take over the entire portfolio and keep the concern together but would also sell some of the shares to the public. Kehrl had told Wolzt that he would accept such a solution and had also become more enthusiastic about Winter's involvement. The RWM was willing to talk to Winter and also to discuss the creation of a consortium with Rasche. Rasche's help and contacts were needed to ward off a renewed threat from the Creditanstalt. Fischböck had been trying to persuade Kehrl to let the Creditanstalt replace the Kontrollbank as the trustee for Bunzl & Biach if the shares were not sold by the end of the year. Wolzt asked Rasche to persuade Kehrl not to give the Creditanstalt that inside track and to use the Wiener Giro- und Cassen-Verein instead.[195]

The stage was set for a Dresdner Bank initiative in early December. Winter declared renewed interest in and a willingness to join in a consortium on a large scale. The Dresdner Bank could thus inform the RWM that there was a basis for a consortium with Winter. Kehrl and Bauer of the RWM were pleased by the possibility of a consortium that would include a substantial investor along with a number of firms and interests, including the Veitscher Magnesitwerke (2 million RM), Solo Zündholz (1 million RM), the Grafl. Schönborn Buchheim'sche Vermögensverwaltung Wien (1 million RM), and the Sagener Tuchfabriken Brüder Hoffmann (1–2 million RM). Some of the members of the management board of the Zellstoff-Waldhof also appeared interested, as did former Finance Minister Peter Reinhold. It soon became clear, however, that Reinhold was interested only in getting hold of a paper production facility and wanted to detach the very profitable Wattens plant from Bunzl & Biach. The RWM would never accept such an amputation of Bunzl & Biach holdings. In any

---

[192] Ibid., memorandum by André, Dec. 17, 1940; ÖStA/ AdR, MfWuA,VVSt, Firmenbuchhaltung, Box 336, IND.-288, Vol. 1, report by the Kontrollbank to Oberregierungsrat Ronsiek of Aug. 11, 1941.

[193] See NARA, T83/122, memorandum of Oct. 25, 1939.

[194] DrB, Nr. 30316–2001, BE, Rotermund to Wolzt, Aug. 12, 1940 and Länderbank to Dresdner Bank supervisory board, Aug. 29, 1940.

[195] DrB, Nr. 30316–2001, BE, André memorandum, Nov. 19, 1940, Wolzt telegram to Rasche, Nov. 11, 1940.

event, the Dresdner Bank and the Länderbank could be expected to take a substantial block of shares and would presumably dominate the consortium with Winter. It thus appeared that the 10.6 million RM needed to buy the shares could be raised in this rather complicated way, and the Kontrollbank began handling all other expressions of interest, including one by the Reichs-Kredit-Gesellschaft, in a rather dilatory manner. What might be called a Dresdner Bank group had apparently been formed that would control the Bunzl & Biach shares.[196]

Once again, Rasche used his contacts with Kehrl for the Dresdner Bank group's advantage. The two men apparently discussed the planned consortium in mid-December. The success of this effort became evident at a meeting on December 17 with Kastner of the Kontrollbank and Director Schmidt of Bunzl & Biach. Kastner and Schmidt accepted the RWM's proposal that the Kontrollbank work with the Dresdner Bank to form a consortium in agreement with the RWM. Winter's stake could now be expected to amount to 4 million RM. They agreed to exclude Reinhold and Reemtsma because it was now clear that their only real interest was to gain control of the Wattens plant, which made cigarette paper. Other companies involved in the tobacco industry, such as the Zigarrenfabrik Blasé AG and Sidel-Dreiturm-Wolf, might be invited to participate. The Zigarrenfabrik Blasé and Sidel-Dreiturm-Wolf both purchased packaging materials from Bunzl & Biach, and their participation in the consortium would help ensure that they remained clients. The Dresdner Bank was well aware, of course, of the political problems in Vienna and thought it would be a good idea to bring in some consortial members from the Ostmark to satisfy the Reichsstatthalter's office. It was important that those involved be politically acceptable. Given the circumstances, Kastner was willing to continue to put off the Reichs-Kredit-Gesellschaft on the grounds that the negotiations were very far advanced.[197]

The National Socialist leadership in Vienna was not given to accepting such faits accomplis, however. At the end of 1940, Rafelsberger got wind of what was going on and wrote to the RWM to express his irritation. According to Rafelsberger. Fischböck and Kehrl had been negotiating about the fate of Bunzl & Biach shares and originally backed the idea of marketing them through the Creditanstalt. This plan was disrupted, however, by a new combination organized by the Dresdner Bank in which Eduard Winter would take 4 million RM in shares, the Veitscher Magnesit-Werke 1 million RM in shares, and the Länderbank and Creditanstalt 2.5 million RM in shares each. Rafelsberger reported that he had contacted the Creditanstalt about this scheme and was informed that the Creditanstalt found it unacceptable and intended to maintain its claim to a substantial participation. It was willing to settle for 60 percent and let the remainder go to some other group. Rafelsberger viewed this as a reasonable position and went on to insist that the relevant Party and government agencies be consulted because the matter was of great importance to Vienna.[198]

From a practical point of view, it was impossible to exclude the Creditanstalt totally, and Rasche had urged Wolzt to invite the Creditanstalt to join in the consortium. But when Wolzt discussed this suggestion at a meeting with Kastner and Paić of the Kontrollbank on December 12, they said they had the impression that the invitation would be pointless. They believed that the Creditanstalt still wanted the entire block of shares to make up for the holdings it had lost since the Anschluss and also wanted to combine some of the paper companies in which it was invested and which were not doing well with those of Bunzl & Biach. Furthermore, Bauer of the RWM was greatly angered when he learned of the Creditanstalt's plans to use Bunzl & Biach in this manner, and he had turned a cold shoulder to the Creditanstalt's participation after learning of them. If the Creditanstalt was to receive

[196] Ibid., report by André, Dec. 6, 1940, and Stiller to André, Dec. 12, 1940.
[197] Ibid., memorandum of André, Dec. 17, 1940.

[198] RGVA Moscow, 1458/2/91, Bl. 165–166, Rafelsberger to RWM, Dec. 23, 1940.

a block of the Bunzl & Biach shares, Bauer had to be persuaded to modify his stance. Wolzt was undoubtedly heartened by the Creditanstalt's problems with Bauer, and he was emboldened to contemplate asking that the Länderbank be given the trusteeship of Bunzl & Biach when the Kontrollbank went into liquidation. He also thought that the price of 120 percent of the shares being asked by the Kontrollbank could be reduced to 115 percent.[199]

The RWM did in fact agree to offer a 26 percent stake to the Creditanstalt. As Rafelsberger noted in his letter, the Creditanstalt found that offer unsatisfactory. It appeared that the Dresdner Bank group had won. On December 20, Kehrl informed Rasche that he approved the projected consortium. The Länderbank and the Creditanstalt were to put in 2.5 million RM apiece; if the RWM so desired, they were to offer some of their shares to other parties approved by the RWM. Winter was to put in 4 million RM, and the remaining 3.6 million was to be provided by parties chosen by the Dresdner Bank; the Veitscher Magnesit AG was to put in no more than 1 million RM. Kehrl also urged that Kastner be made a member of the Bunzl & Biach management board, and that a representative of the RWM be put on the supervisory board.[200]

When Wolzt informed the Creditanstalt that the Dresdner group was glad to take the Creditanstalt into the consortium and that the RWM had set the quotas for the Länderbank and the Creditanstalt, Director Hans Friedl was anything but happy. Wolzt reported that "he does not believe that his institution will be prepared to participate in a consortium whose partners are by and large determined by us."[201] Wolzt had the impression that Friedl's position had softened somewhat by the end of their discussion, but he encountered a much more unyielding attitude when he spoke to the powerful Director Josef Joham. Joham informed Wolzt that the RWM had promised the Creditanstalt

the Bunzl & Biach shares as compensation for the Creditanstalt's forced sale of important industrial holdings to the Reichswerke. Moreover, the Creditanstalt was not only to receive all the Bunzl & Biach shares but was also to be allowed to divest certain Bunzl & Biach holdings as suited its own interests. Wolzt could only reply that he had no knowledge of such an agreement and that the RWM had come to its decision aware of the discussion it had had with the Creditanstalt. Joham assured Wolzt that the Creditanstalt intended to fight the RWM decision and to remind the ministry of the promises made in connection with the Reichswerke.

Rafelsberger's December 23 letter to the RWM was undoubtedly the opening salvo of an effort to bring the Creditanstalt back into the picture and to undermine the Dresdner Bank group's plans. The counteroffensive continued with a weakening of Kehrl's following a conversation in January 1941 between Kehrl and Guido Schmidt, the former Austrian foreign minister, who was now working for the Reichswerke. As Wolzt reported, Kehrl remained committed to the scheme he had worked out with Rasche, but he was open to the idea of having the Creditanstalt acquire portions of Bunzl & Biach. After learning of Kehrl's position, Wolzt spoke to Friedl and Joham, who claimed to have accepted the Dresdner Bank scheme but suggested that each of the Viennese banks take 25 percent of the shares. The Creditanstalt also wanted the right to buy the concern's hat body factory, which would cost between 500,000 and 750,000 RM. Both Kehrl and the management of Bunzl & Biach agreed to this, but the latter was insistent that the Creditanstalt's other major request, the right to buy the plant at Wattens, be turned down.[202]

The Creditanstalt had probably overreached itself with the Wattens proposal, and Kehrl seems to have returned to the Dresdner Bank proposal in support of Winter. On February 11, Wolzt, accompanied by Director Rudolf Pfeiffer of the Creditanstalt, paid a visit to Kehrl in Berlin. He told them, as he had apparently done before, that "he had an especially strong

---

[199] DrB, Nr. 30316–2000, BE, Wolzt to André, Dec. 6, 1940.

[200] Ibid., RWM to Rasche, Dec. 20, 1940.

[201] Ibid., Wolzt to André, Dec. 21, 1940.

[202] Ibid., Wolzt to André, Jan. 11, 1941.

interest in bringing in Herr Winter and that he unreservedly wants to fulfill his wishes to have a majority. The Dresdner Bank was thus looking forward to having the Länderbank hold a large block of the shares and to placing them among its customers."[203] The impression that all was going well for the Dresdner group was reinforced when the Kontrollbank asked for and received RWM approval for the proposed Dresdner Bank consortium to be headed by Winter in March 1941.[204] It appeared, therefore, that the Creditanstalt had received all that it was going to receive and that Rafelsberger was no longer interfering.

It was at this point that matters began to go awry. Wolzt and a representative of the Dresdner Bank visited Winter's accountant Röhrsheim on March 12 and told him that the RWM was prepared to offer Winter a majority stake; the Länderbank, he added, would be happy to organize a pool to increase the importance of their holdings. He thought that the Veitscher Magnesitwerke would also join. If Winter was not ready to take up the majority immediately, he could be given an option to do so later. Röhrsheim agreed that the proposal sounded interesting and promising, but he went on to point out that "a certain listlessness is to be observed in Herr Winter with respect to large business transactions since the end of last year, and he could not tell us whether Herr Winter will come to a positive decision at the moment."[205] This must have come as something of a surprise to Wolzt, who reiterated that Kehrl and the RWM were very anxious to have Winter participate, and he offered to let Röhrsheim examine the concern's books. When Winter returned from Paris, he called a meeting with Wolzt and Röhrsheim and asked for a great deal of information about Bunzl & Biach. He also wanted clarification of the legal situation with respect to the holding company in Switzerland and the legal status of other

holdings. Winter claimed that his other activities and his poor health had kept him from raising these issues earlier, but the delay was beginning to worry Kastner, who was ready to accept a price of 120 percent but did not want to face having to raise it because of further delay. Nevertheless, Winter and his accountant undertook a very careful examination of the financial condition and business prospects of the concern, and the Dresdner Bank became more and more impatient.[206]

Indeed, everyone concerned was becoming impatient. On May 2, the Creditanstalt wrote to the Länderbank asking what was going on. Back in January, all that seemed left to do was to determine the allocation of the shares. Four months had passed since then, and the Creditanstalt did not view an audit by Winter's accountant as a sign of progress. Such an audit was unlikely to change the price and would not affect the division of the shares. The Creditanstalt suggested that Winter was using a delaying tactic in order to consider other possibilities. Whatever the case, the Creditanstalt needed to know how matters stood.[207] The Länderbank tried to assure the Creditanstalt that all was well and that final negotiations were underway. But Wolzt and Kastner were exerting pressure because the remaining holdings of the Kontrollbank had to be turned over to the Property Transfer Bureau and the shares then transferred to the Finance Ministry in Berlin. This would mean dealing with a newly reactivated bureaucratic apparatus in Vienna and an unfamiliar one in Berlin. Wolzt was especially anxious to put an end to the delays because the Länderbank was about to sell off its interest in the Hirmer Zuckerfabrik AG, and that made the acquisition of the Bunzl & Biach shares all the more desirable. As far as Wolzt was concerned, Winter could easily be replaced by a couple of large investors from the Ostmark or the Reich. If Winter turned down the project, Wolzt suggested, the Länderbank and Creditanstalt could simply divide the shares. The Länderbank intended to place the shares

203 Ibid., memorandum by André, Feb. 12, 1941, and Feb. 21, 1941.
204 RGVA Moscow, 1458/2/91, Bl. 165–166, RWM memorandum, March 14, 1941.
205 DrB, Nr. 30316–2001, BE, memorandum by Kühnen, March 12, 1941.

206 For the correspondence and discussions, see the materials in ibid.
207 Ibid., Creditanstalt to Länderbank, May 2, 1941.

with some large clients insofar as it did not wish to hold on to them as a replacement for the Hirmer Zuckerfabrik. He now also feared that the Creditanstalt would deal directly with the RWM in order to protect its interests if there were further delays.[208]

Ironically, when Winter finally made a proposal in June, the Dresdner Bank did not like the terms. He wanted a 51 percent stake, offering the Dresdner Bank/Länderbank a sub-participation amounting to a quarter of his holding with a three-year option to buy the shares back. Winter promised that they would work closely in exercising their majority and that the Dresdner Bank group would get the lion's share of Kontropa's banking business. The Dresdner Bank could not accept this because Winter was sparing himself the risk of a genuine 51 percent stake so that he could wait and see how things went while the Dresdner Bank and the Länderbank would be left with their hands tied. After asking Winter to make a better offer, the Dresdner Bank decided that, should things not work out with Winter, it would be prepared to follow Wolzt's proposal and have the Länderbank and the Creditanstalt each take half the shares and market them to the general public.[209]

In the summer of 1941, Winter proposed a new arrangement that the Länderbank and the Dresdner Bank appeared ready to accept and to submit for approval. At the same time, the Länderbank and the Creditanstalt agreed to divide the shares if Winter's proposal proved unacceptable and then to sell an agreed upon portion to the public.[210] Under Winter's proposal, the 10,640,000 shares, each with a nominal value of 1,000 RM, would be divided as follows:

Winter: 28 percent (2,980 shares) for 2,980,000 RM

Dresdner Bank: 5 percent (532 shares) for 532,000 RM

Länderbank: 21 percent (2,234 shares) for 2,234,000 RM

Creditanstalt: 26 percent (2,766,000 shares) for 2,766,000 RM

German Reich: 20 percent (2,128 shares) for 2,128,000 RM

A very important aspect of Winter's proposal was that it provided him with an option on the Dresdner Bank's shares until December 31, 1944, and an option on the Reich's shares until at least that date and as long as until two years after the conclusion of peace with England. In the meantime, Winter was to have control of the voting rights of the Reich shares for as long as he retained his option on them. If Winter took advantage of the options, he would personally hold a majority of 53 percent; in any event, he would control 48 percent of the voting rights in Kontropa. Manifestly, Winter was protecting himself against risk. The share price, reduced from 120 percent to 115 percent, was lower than that the RWM had wanted some months earlier, but it nevertheless seemed fair because the risk involved had increased. Furthermore, the issue of the options on the remaining 24 percent of the Bunzl shares in Vienna and the 50 percent in Zug, formally scheduled to be exercised no later than the presentation of the 1945 balance sheets, would have to remain unsettled until the end of the war, especially because some of the family members were in England. The Kontrollbank planned to turn these options over to Kontropa as a trustee for the Reich.[211]

The tide turned decisively against Winter's proposal in September 1941. On September 4, Wolzt informed Director Kühnen at the Dresdner Bank that no time was to be lost in coming to a settlement with Winter because, as Kühnen reported, "a new group has been formed that is striving via political agencies to bring down the Winter combination. Wolzt told me that the Creditanstalt is also involved, even if it does not appear to be so from the outside."[212] On September 15, Kastner and Röhrsheim received and discussed a plan

[208] Ibid., Wolzt to Rasche, June 7, 9, and 17, 1941.

[209] NARA, T83/137, Dresdner Bank management board meetings, June 18, 1941 and July 7, 1941.

[210] ÖStA/AdR, MfWuA, VVSt, Firmenbuchhaltung, Box 336, IND.-288, Vol. 1, report by the Kontrollbank to Oberregierungsrat Ronsiek of Aug. 11, 1941.

[211] Ibid.

[212] DrB, Nr. 30316–2001, BE, memorandum by Kühnen, Sept. 4, 1941.

from the RWM for the legal work that would be necessary to implement Winter's proposal.[213] But it was too late. Rafelsberger was informing all concerned at this time that Winter's involvement had been rejected by the Gau leadership and he was thus out of the picture. He also offered the Creditanstalt a 26 percent minority interest, which the bank was prepared to accept. The Schoeller group had also expressed an interest in participating in the consortium.[214]

What had happened? There is evidence President Kastner of the Kontrollbank played a role in blocking Winter's proposal; that evidence comes mainly from Kastner himself, however. According to Kastner's memoirs, he was contacted by an important person in the automobile trade with excellent connections to the Berlin authorities and high Party officials – Winter's name is never mentioned – and visited him twice. On the first occasion, he and the unnamed automobile dealer lunched at the Horcher restaurant, which was frequented by high-ranking officers and generals. The evening was spent at a bordello, where Kastner's host appeared to be on excellent footing with the ladies; Kastner was invited to choose a companion but apparently preferred to listen to them tell of their "moving fate of eternal love and its betrayal." On the second occasion, Kastner was invited to his host's splendid villa on the Wannsee, where he was served fine liquor and swam in the lake. During the visit, Kastner's host had a telephone conversation with a high-ranking functionary in Kastner's presence; they discussed the Bunzl & Biach shares, and "with an indescribable lack of inhibition," the host went on to recommend friendly doctors who specialized in the treatment of venereal diseases. Returning home depressed, Kastner claims he then contacted Baldur von Schirach and persuaded the Statthalter that the sale of the majority holding in "this old Austrian enterprise to a Berlin wheeler and dealer would incur great displeasure in Vienna."[215]

Winter opened an Opel dealership on Unter den Linden, which he transformed into an independent dealership in 1937 and then later sold. He had diverse business interests, including a company bearing his name that controlled an airplane repair firm and a parachute factory. He was also without doubt politically well connected and owned a villa in Schwanenwerder. However, the fifty-year-old Winter was known to be industrious and very competent, and he was a married man. None of these facts meant that he did not lead the life described by Kastner, but this picture did not correspond to his general reputation. He had a reputation for working closely with the Dresdner Bank.[216] As has been shown, however, the first meeting between Winter and Kastner was through the agency of Wolzt, and there was nothing about Winter's dilatory approach to the Bunzl & Biach shares to suggest that he needed to introduce Kastner to the Berlin high life to win him over. Also, it is difficult to understand why Kastner went along with the negotiations for so long and why all the others involved at the Länderbank and the Dresdner Bank were so willing to do business with Winter. Kehrl apparently became a strong supporter of Winter, and despite what Rafelsberger had been saying in September, Kehrl was telling Rasche in November that he still supported Winter. Nevertheless, on November 17, Rafelsberger offered the Länderbank parity with the Creditanstalt, that is 26 percent of the shares, and told Wolzt that Baldur von Schirach had reiterated his veto of Winter. It is impossible to determine the role played by Winter's morals, and Kastner's concern that a fine old company like Bunzl & Biach not fall into the hands of a sharp Berlin businessman really should be taken with a grain of salt. It is more plausible that

---

213 Ibid.
214 BA-CA, CA-V, Creditanstalt working committee meeting, Sept. 17, 1941.
215 Kastner, *Mein Leben*, pp. 113–114.

216 On Winter, see H.C. Graf von Seherr-Thoss, *Die deutsche Automobilindustrie. Eine Dokumentation von 1886 bis 1979*, 2nd ed. (Stuttgart 1979), pp. 180, 311, 424. After the war, the autodealership was a major seller of Volkswagen. For Dresdner Bank credits to the Winter concern, see NARA, T83/127, Dresdner Bank Credit Committee, July 25, 1944. See also BAB, R 8121, Vol. 326, the minutes on Winter by the Aerobank of Oct. 30, 1942.

Kastner got fed up with Winter for delaying so long, a sentiment shared by practically everyone involved, and also that the Viennese Aryanizers and Nazis preferred not to have another Berliner controlling Ostmark assets. It is safe to say that Vienna had won out over Berlin in this instance.[217] In January 1942, Winter had a lengthy conversation with Baldur von Schirach that apparently went very poorly. Although Winter had concerns, namely an important assignment for Göring, he still planned to see Kehrl about Bunzl & Biach because he still had 6 or 7 million RM to invest.[218]

Although other interested parties had appeared on the scene, a textile manufacturer named Foradori and an expert on the paper business named Lindenberg, Rafelsberger thought it would be difficult to bring in other outsiders after turning down Winter. Potential buyers were frightened away by the complexity of the concern and were usually more interested in parts of Bunzl & Biach rather than the whole. Nevertheless, it was not until April 1942 that the details of the reprivatization of the concern were finally settled with the division of the shares of Kontropa among the Viennese banks. Kehrlid set certain conditions. The banks were to sell the shares to the public within three years. He also insisted that a suitable person be chosen to head the supervisory board; and he finally agreed to the appointment of Director Walter Hiedler of the Perlmooser Zementwerke AG, who was also on the Länderbank's supervisory board.

The Länderbank and the Creditanstalt each took 36 percent shares. The remainder initially went to Schoeller & Co., and E. von Nicolai subsequently took a 10 percent share. The Länderbank's share amounted to a 4,256,000 RM investment. It was represented by Director Wolzt on the supervisory board. The Länderbank put 1,450,000 RM worth of shares on the market and decided, with the approval of the Dresdner Bank, to hold on to 2,766,400

shares for at least a year. Leaving aside Winter's alleged character deficits, selling the shares to the banks had two distinct advantages over Winter's proposal. First, the banks did not ask the Reich to retain 2.1 million shares with the requirement that it offer them an option to purchase the shares at favorable terms. Second, the banks offered 800,000 RM instead of 600,000 RM for the Bunzl-Holding shares, thus increasing the return for the Reich by 200,000 RM.[219]

While it is difficult to tell how well the shares did on the market, Kontropa was viewed as a good investment by the banks. It was well managed and technically advanced. The Dresdner Bank and the Länderbank had no hesitations about prolonging its credits in March 1945.[220] The Bunzls would be back, but the effort to dispose of their property stands as a remarkable piece of business history as well as a truly repugnant story.

Preparing for the End

This was by no means the only company of which the Länderbank played a role in

---

[217] StA Nürnberg, Rep. 501, Nl 3908, telegraphic exchange between Wolzt and Rasche, Nov. 18, 1941.

[218] DrB, Nr. 30316–2001.BE, André for Rasche and Pilder, Jan. 30, 1942.

[219] Ibid., Dresdner Bank management board meeting, April 2, 1942. There is much misinformation about the settlement, Kastner suggesting that the Creditanstalt took over the shares and sold them to the public. See Kastner, *Mein Leben*, p. 114. Perhaps this was wishful thinking, and Kastner seems to have expected a job on the board of management of Kontropa, but then went on the board of Semperit instead. The Creditanstalt by no means sold off all of its holding, having 2,296,000 RM in shares at the end of the war. See Melichar in Felber et al., *Ökonomie der Arisierung*, pt. 2, p. 329. As Melichar correctly notes in note 81, Harold James is incorrect in thinking that Bunzl & Biach was Aryanized by Keppler and that the Dresdner Bank consortium beat out the Creditanstalt in seeking the shares. The Aryanization was the work of the Kontrollbank, and the shares were divided evenly. See also BA-CA, CA-V, the working committee of the supervisory board of the Creditanstalt meeting of April 8, 1942. Unfortunately, James, *Nazi Economic War against the Jews*, pp. 234–235, note 34 is almost entirely inaccurate. See ÖStA/AdR, MfWuA, VVSt, Box 1374, for a good summary of the privatization of the concern, the memorandum of April 2, 1942.

[220] See DrB, Nr. 5124-2000, the credit request of March 17, 1945.

Aryanizing and to which it happily provided credit. It was the chief supplier of credits to the firm of Pölzl & Weigensamer vorm. Lourié & Co., a plywood manufacturer Aryanized in 1938. The new owners had limited means prior to acquiring the company, which became an important producer for the Luftwaffe and expanded rapidly. There were grand plans for expansion in Yugoslavia and Russia; by 1944, the firm's importance lay in the fact that it had become the main supplier of plywood because sources in Poland and elsewhere were no longer available. Nonetheless, the Dresdner Bank was pressing the Länderbank to limit its engagement, and, much to the annoyance of the firm's other creditor, the Aerobank, both Director Meyer of the Dresdner Bank and Director Hitschfeld of the Länderbank were insisting that the Länderbank be given priority in the repayment of operating credits.[221]

Another Aryanized concern serviced by the Länderbank until the end of the war was the Brucker Zuckerfabrik Clemens Auer, once part of the Bloch-Bauer concern. In June 1944, Auer, who was convinced that Germany was headed toward defeat, decided to take the firm out of his concern and place it under his personal ownership. Nevertheless, the firm remained a very good credit risk and received a credit of more than 3.5 million RM. As the credit approval noted: "The firm taking the credit came out of the non-Aryan holdings of the Österreichische Zuckerindustrie AG; its plants count among the most modern and productive of the Reich."[222] For the time being at least, Wolzt had no reason to regret his role in the affair.

One of the great difficulties in writing about a man like Wolzt is determining what he actually believed at any given time, assuming that the manifestly cynical Wolzt, had any firm beliefs. The problem is particularly acute in dealing with the final months of the war. The case of Auer shows that at least some businessmen were hedging their bets as best they could while continuing to actively engage in business

and the war effort. The same probably held true for Wolzt, who certainly was exposed to persons skeptical about the German war effort. The Gau authorities were probably correct in viewing Wolzt as someone who would be reliable for as long as he considered it worthwhile and a typically apolitical businessman.[223] He traveled quite a bit and reported not only to Rasche but also to Hans Kehrl, with whom he seemed to have good contact, and to the Reichsbank authorities. In mid-March 1944, Wolzt sent a report to Kehrl about a trip to Zurich, where he had spoken with General Director Peter Vieli of the Schweizerische Kreditanstalt and General Director Karl Türler of the Schweizer Bankverein. He was apparently well acquainted with both Swiss bankers, and they talked with him at some length about a special committee of bankers and economists that was secretly discussing the problems of postwar reconstruction.

As Wolzt frankly reported, most Swiss thought that Germany could not hold out much longer and was going to lose the war. He blamed this attitude on Swiss acceptance of Anglo-American claims of success in their air war against Germany. He had found that the Swiss were open to forceful and reasonable arguments to the contrary, but he also admitted that many German visitors only reinforced Anglo-American reporting with their own pessimism. Wolzt noted that the Swiss were terrified by the Anglo-American blacklisting of firms and individuals who appeared too friendly to the Germans. He was also impressed with how much unused industrial capacity there was in Switzerland, noting that the machine, electro-technical, and metal industries were in better shape because of long-term contracts from the Swiss authorities and from abroad, especially from Germany. There was anxiety that there would be fewer such orders in 1944. What Wolzt found most interesting in his discussions with Vieli and Türler was their confidential account of the work of the reconstruction committee, which hoped to promote the rebuilding of Europe, Germany in particular, once the war ended. This had to be done

221 See BAB, R 8121, Nr. 621, the correspondence.
222 DrB, Nr. 5124-2000, Dresdner Bank memorandum of Nov. 15, 1944.

223 See pp. 409–410 of this volume.

in a way that maintained Swiss neutrality and gave the Allies no cause to intervene, but Vieli believed "that an end to the war is possible that would permit the political order to be maintained, especially in Germany, and that would provide the possibility for the Swiss economic forces to be engaged on a private economic basis."[224] They were thinking of using the large store of gold and foreign exchange held by the Swiss to buy raw materials and using the Swiss banks to finance deliveries of industrial goods to Germany or to undertake the production of finished goods in collaboration with the Germans. The German banks, in turn, would have to be willing to guarantee such business. Wolzt's greatest interest at the moment was not the postwar period, however, but rather the question of whether German raw materials could be used in the manufacture of finished products in Switzerland in the present. While Vieli did not reject this proposition out of hand, he pointed out that the clearing arrangements with Germany did not provide sufficient funds to pay Swiss costs and wages. Wolzt and the Swiss bankers agreed, however, to pursue these questions in future meetings.

It is not possible at present to say whether anything came of these discussions; the time was certainly not favorable to their realization. The Swiss obviously were anxious to maintain their German connections and find a basis for doing business after the war. They clearly had illusions about what would be permitted Germany once peace came. Wolzt, as noted, had his eye on the present and was reporting to Kehrl, who had become chief of the planning office in the Armaments Ministry. Wolzt and Kehrl were obviously most interested in gaining goods and supplies through Switzerland during this phase of the war effort.

Nevertheless, there is no evidence that Wolzt was especially patriotic. He certainly developed a personal interest in the end of the war when he was called up for military service in the summer of 1944. His mobilization was repeatedly postponed by appeals from the Länderbank. He was finally called up on January 15, 1945, but Rasche intended to personally intervene on his behalf.[225] Wolzt obviously was deemed a very important bank director, which he was. Wolzt must not have served long. He survived the war and was found working for the Frankfurter Wirtschaftskontor in 1950.[226]

The Länderbank was confronted with problems of its own survival as the war drew to a close, and various measures had to be taken to save what could be saved and minimize damage. The Dresdner Bank was continually involved in these efforts. They included securing the physical evidence of the Dresdner Bank's ownership of the Länderbank by removing the ownership documents from the Länderbank in Vienna and storing the certificate of ownership in Würzburg and the coupon sheet in Regensburg.[227] The Länderbank was taking measures to remove its more important documents to safe places. Some were stored in Steyrmühl and Bregen, and there were plans to remove others to the Salzburg area, although it was proving very difficult to find suitable storage space. The headquarters at Am Hof, Nr. 2 were badly damaged and there was some thought of operating out of Bregenz The Dresdner Bank thought Bregenz was too far away and preferred the Salzburg area. Dresdner Bank officials also made a concerted effort in early 1945 to go through the Länderbank accounts and get the bank to terminate or reduce its credit lines wherever it was thought advisable.[228] These efforts apparently rested on the assumption that the connection between the two banks would survive the war and be continued.

---

224 DrB, Nr. 5461-2000, Wolzt to Kehrl, March 14, 1944 and report on a trip to Switzerland, March 2–7, 1944.

225 NARA, T83/138, Dresdner Bank management board meeting, Jan. 16, 1945.
226 Verein für Geschichte der Arbeiterbewegung, Nachlass Adolf Schärf, Box 29, 4/206, File 13, S. 265.
227 NARA, T83/138, Dresdner Bank management board meeting, Oct. 10, 1944.
228 Directors Teichmann and Gruber went through all credits of more than 200,000 RM toward this end and reported on their efforts in a memorandum of Jan. 12, 1945. Some of the cases have been discussed earlier. See, DrB, Nr. 13790-2000.

There is evidence, however, that the Länderbank was maintaining a certain independence from the Dresdner Bank and looking after its own interests. The leaders of both banks were aware that the war was lost and that the Anschluss would be dissolved. Historical experiences specific to Austria were taking on renewed relevance. A remarkable discussion among Dresdner Bank officials about the Länderbank on September 28, 1944, demonstrates how much the Länderbank was anticipating impending events and preparing for them. In these deliberations, Austria's experiences with the successor states after the First World War became important once again. It was deemed desirable to avoid potential currency problems by sending the profits from the branches in Znaim and in Marburg/Maribor from Vienna back, respectively, to Prague and to the Reichsbank branch in Marburg. There was some skepticism about sending the money to the Reichsbank branch because it was anticipated that the branch would soon move back to the Reich. Moving the money to the Marburg branch seemed pointless because it would probably be plundered in the anticipated unrest that would follow the German departure. The political future was anticipated not only here but also with respect to Austria. "Undoubtedly, there is the danger that these assets will be forfeited as enemy property in the event of the reestablishment of Czechoslovakia and Yugoslavia; unless one also expects that there will similarly be a reestablished Austria that will not be treated as an enemy German state by the Allies."[229] However events might turn out, if the funds were confiscated, individuals remaining in Znaim and Marburg could try to reclaim what they had lost from the reestablished national states, whereas the claims of those who went back to Germany would be directed to Vienna. This was one of many good reasons for the Länderbank to distance itself as much as possible from its German owner.

CONCLUSION

Germany's defeat created a new situation for the Länderbank. It reopened in July 1945, shortly after Germany's surrender. It was under new management, but not the management that had been planned a few months earlier. Paić, Pilat, and Gold had fled; Lehr was gone too, as were Wolzt and Warnecke. Hitschfeld, who was supposed to retire, stayed on until 1957, and Pilat came back in 1957 and remained until 1960. The new key figure at the bank was Franz Landertshammer, who was to stay on for a decade. He had earlier worked for the Mercurbank but left following the Anschluss. He was recalled by the employees of the bank in 1945, initially to serve as administrator and then as general director before being replaced by Hitschfeld in 1955.

The Länderbank Wien was renamed the Österreichische Länderbank in 1948. The new named hearkened back to the bank's founding in 1880. The postwar history of the bank, insofar as it is relevant to the National Socialist period, has been dealt with by Oliver Rathkolb in his contribution to *Österreichische Banken und Sparkassen im Nationalsozialismus*.[230] Nevertheless, certain points need to be made here about the situation of the bank at the end of the war and the debate on what the Länderbank was between 1938 and 1945. Historical assessment necessarily involves deciding how far to stress continuity and how far to emphasize change. This decision is not without political implications. The postwar Länderbank had a great interest in stressing continuity between the pre-1938 and post-1938 institution, just as Austria had an interest in following the Allied lead and in viewing itself as Hitler's first international victim, thus treating the period 1938–1945 as a rude interruption in its history. This view is reflected in the centenary volume about the

[229] DrB, Nr. 1840–2000, discussion in Berlin, Sept. 28, 1944.

[230] Oliver Rathkolb, "Restitution und Entschädigung bei der Österreichischen Länderbank AG nach 1945," in Gerald D. Feldman/Oliver Rathkolb/Theodor Venus/Ulrike Zimmerl, *Österreichische Banken und Sparkassen im Nationalsozialismus und in der Nachkriegszeit*, vol. 2 (Munich 2006), pp. 491–512.

bank produced in 1980 under the authorship of Alois Piperger. It treats the 1938–1945 period in a very cursory fashion and concentrates on the happier years on either side of this great divide and, above all, on the Austrian character of the bank.[231] A similar position was taken in a memorandum written for the Allies by one of the postwar directors of the bank, H. Kreis. He went so far as to insist that the Länderbank did not retain the slightest vestige of German character because the Reich paper assets it possessed were worthless and, indeed, constituted a debt to the bank on the part of the Dresdner Bank. Thus, Kreis argued, "Bearing the name of this old Austrian firm, the bank, as before, so also during the so-called 'Greater German' era, tried to maintain its character as an Austrian banking institution and concentrated its business, one can truly say without exception, on Austria." He went on to contend: "The fact that, on the one hand, the owner's equity of the bank in German hands has been totally lost and, on the other hand, the bank itself because of its title to the Reich loan issues can lay claim to many times larger amounts against the German Reich, shows that the Länderbank Wien AG does not constitute a German asset in Austria in the sense of the Potsdam Declaration but is rather a creditor of the German Reich."[232] But if the Länderbank spokesmen after the war had to contend that they had always really been an Austrian institution, they also had to challenge French claims and implicit Czech claims that the Zentraleuropäische Länderbank in Paris had been forced to sell its Viennese holdings. Here, they had to join with the Dresdner Bank in insisting that the French bank had no legitimate postwar claims to restitution of its assets because it had not sold under duress.

In assessing the real character of the Länderbank between 1938 and 1945 today, it is essential to get away from the self-serving arguments of yesteryear. The Länderbank was

a truly Austrian bank in the sense that, at the time Piperger's book appeared, it had been Austrian-owned for three-quarters of its history, that is, between 1880 and 1921 and again between 1945 and 1980. Between 1921 and 1938, it was a Franco-English owned bank, and between 1938 and 1945, it was a German-owned bank created by the merger of the German-owned Mercurbank, the Czech-owned branch of the Živnostenskábanka, and the Viennese branch of the Zentraleuropäische Länderbank. Whatever it might have been, it was not "Austrian." In 1938, it became a German-owned bank functioning in an annexed Austria. Obviously, most of its personnel and even management were Austrian, and no less obviously it sought to hold on to and cultivate its Austrian clientele. Subsidiary banks, like branches, were established to service customers and enterprises located in various regions. To seriously claim continuity for this history, however, is to stretch the word to the point of meaninglessness. At the same time, the argument that Henry Reuter negotiated under duress back in 1938 is not supported by the documentary evidence. As the German External Assets Branch of the U.S. occupation forces in Austria concluded in 1947, "no specific duress or force was exercised in connection with this transfer other than that resulting from the fact of the Anschluss itself," and the "Laenderbank Paris (The French) have no reasonably justifiable claim for damages or restitution."[233]

This report also concluded that the Länderbank was a German external asset under the definitions used by the Americans, and it also recognized that the bank's holdings in German securities, loans, and debts were worthless and that the bank had an excess of liabilities amounting to 807,314,000 million Schilling. This hardly meant, however, that the Dresdner Bank could be called on to compensate the Austrians, as was attempted, or that Austrian claims against Germany in this regard made any sense. The

[231] Alois Piperger, *Hundert Jahre Österreichische Länderbank 1880–1980* (Vienna 1980).

[232] NARA, RG 260, 390/44/20/04, Box 21, German External Assets Branch, and RG 226, 190/3/33/2, H. Kreis's undated "Exposé zur Länderbank AG."

[233] NARA, RG 260, 390/54/3313, Box 15, German External Assets Branch to U.S. Member, Austrian Treaty Commission, June 28, 1947, Preliminary Report on the Länderbank Wien AG.

matter was put quite well by a critical commentary on the aforementioned American report by those reviewing it for the U.S. German External Assets Branch: "This division does not concur with the statement that the Laenderbank Wien AG is a 'German external asset under present American definition of such assets.' Under present conditions the Länderbank does not constitute an asset at all; it will only reassume the character of an asset after a thorough reorganization which only the Austrian government is able to plan and execute. As in previous bank reorganizations the Austrian Government, in other words the Austrian people, will have to assume the burden."[234] Similarly, the commentator pointed out that the French bank would hardly be better off if it had retained the bank, given its condition and that it was "futile" to discuss the validity of the agreement. Insofar as the French might make a claim to participation in the bank, it would have to be after the Länderbank was reorganized, with its own money, and then only for the two-thirds it had sold, that is, not the Mercurbank.[235]

The effect of these deliberations was to deflect attention from the real issues connected with the Länderbank Wien that were not considered at the time and were repressed over the years. As has been shown here, there was a discussion about how "Austrian" the Länderbank was or should be, and it was promoted by Rafelsberger, Baldur von Schirach, and other Austrian National Socialists who disliked the domination of the Dresdner Bank and were anxious to increase the importance of Vienna. Wanting to escape the control of the Dresdner Bank did not, however, mean rejecting the Third Reich and all that for which it stood. On the contrary, what it meant in concrete terms for people like Rafelsberger, Meindl, Gold, and Paić was greater engagement and influence in Southeastern Europe and potentially the establishment of the bank as a powerful regional bank that would serve Ostmark interests within the context of the Third Reich. If this goal was not pursued energetically, it was not because the level of Germanization reflected in Dresdner Bank control was found particularly agreeable. Rather, it was because the Dresdner Bank was itself so engaged with the programs and policies of the regime and so well connected with Göring, Kehrl, and Himmler that it was difficult for those leading the Länderbank to develop a keen sense of lost opportunities. The time available was really too short for the Länderbank to pursue a strategy of its own effectively. At the same time, the Dresdner Bank did show special consideration for the Länderbank that could not be overlooked.

There is no evidence whatsoever that any significant Austrian figure in the Länderbank had hesitations or reservations about the policies toward the Jews, financing the war effort, or any of the other practices and policies of the regime. On the contrary, the Länderbank worked closely with the Kontrollbank, had no compunction about opening accounts for Eichmann, and cheerfully financed ruthless Austrian industrialists like Meindl. Indeed, a hallmark of its Nazification over time was the appointment of more Austrians to high positions in the bank. If it was German-owned, the Länderbank was nevertheless an Austrian bank insofar as its personnel and many of its engagements were concerned, and its leadership sought to make the most of the opportunities the regime offered. In the same way, it was a beneficiary in many respects of the Dresdner Bank's power during the war; so too did it benefit from the fact that after the war the attention was concentrated on the crimes of the Dresdner Bank. It is high time, therefore, that the entanglements of the Länderbank Wien AG between 1938 and 1945 receive as much attention as the surviving records allow.

[234] Ibid.

[235] Ibid. The American commentator pointed out that the French should not be allowed to pay with the Schilling they were receiving from occupation costs but rather with the free French francs to be given to the Austrian National Bank. This sheds an interesting light on Americans' views of their French ally at this time.

Bibliography

ARCHIVAL SOURCES

Austria

Archive of the Bank Austria Creditanstalt, Vienna (BA-CA)
Vorstandsarchiv der Creditanstalt (BA-CA, CA-V)

CA Vorstandsprotokolle, 1931, 1935–1936, 1938–1945
CA Verwaltungsrats-/Aufsichtratsprotokolle, 1938–1945
CA Exekutiv-Kommittee-/Arbeitsausschussprotokolle, 1938–1945
S.P. Akten (Spezial-Akten)
Prüfbericht der Treuverkehr, Deutsche Treuhand, AG
Allgemeine Weisungen der Direktion, 1938–1945
Allgemeine Weisungen der Organisationsabteilung, 1938–1945

Industriebeteiligungsarchiv der Creditanstalt (BA-CA, IB)

Aspalt (Ungarische Aspalt AG)
AVA (Automobil-Verkehrs-Anstalt GmbH)
Bunzl & Biach (Bunzl & Biach AG)
Del-Ka (Del-Ka Schuhindustrie- und Handels-Aktiengesellschaft)
Ebreichsdorfer (Ebreichdorfer Filzhutfabrik S. & J. Fraenkel AG)
Enderlin (Gebrüder Enderlin, Druckfabrik und mechanische Weberei AG)
Ennser Zuckerfabrik (Ennser Zuckerfabriks-Aktiengesellschaft)
Feinstahlwerke (Feilstahlwerke Traisen AG vorm. Fischer, Traisen)
Felmayer (Stefan Felmayer & Sönne AG)
Gans (Adolf Gans AG, Österreiches Bettfedernfabriks AG)
Getreide (Südosteuropäische Getreide-Handels AG)
Guntramdorfer (Guntramsdorfer Druckfabrik AG)

Haas (Aktiengesellschaft der Teppich- und Möbelstoff-Fabriken, vormals Philipp Haas & Söhne)
Hanf-Jute (Hanf-, Jute- und Textili-Industrie AG)
Hirmer (Hirmer Zuckerfabrik AG)
Hutter & Schrantz (Hutter & Schrantz AG)
Kontrollbank (Oesterreichische Kontrollbank für Industrie und Handel AG)
Krupp (Berndorfer Metalwarenfabrik Arthur Krupp AG; Fried, Krupp AG)
Lapp-Finze (Eisenwarenfabrik Lapp-Finze AG)
Leykam (Leykam – Josefstha, Aktiengesellschaft für Papier – und Druck-Industrie)
Littai (Littai-Pragwalder Textilwerke AG)
Miller (Martin Miller AG)
Montana (Montana Kohlenhandels-Gesellschaft m.b.h.)
Mürztaler (Mürztaler Holzstoff- und Papier-Fabriks AG)
Pappe- und Holzstoff (Pappen- und Holzstofferzeugungs-Ges.m.b.H.)
Patria (Patria Spinnerei und Wirkewarenfabriken AG)
Pottendorfer (Pottendorfer Spinnerei und Felixdorfer Weberei AG)
Rast & Gasser (Nähmaschinenfabrik Rast & Gasser)
Referat Ketterer
Referat Patzak
Rottenmanner (Rottenmanner Eisenwerke AG)
Samum Schnabl (Samum Vereinigte Papier-Industrie K.G., Jac. Schnabl & Co.)
Schember (C. Schember & Söhne Brückenwaagen- und Maschinenfabriken AG)
Schoeller-Bleckmann (Schoeller-Bleckmann Stahlwerke AG)
Semperit (Semperit Gummiwerke AG, Semperit Österreichische-Amerikanische Gummiewerke AG)

Steierische Baugesellschaft (Steierische Bau-Gesellschaft)

Steyr-Daimler-Puch (Steyr-Daimler-Puch AG)

Stölzle (Stölzle Österreichische Glasindustrie AG, C. Stölzle's Söhne Aktiengesellschaft für Glasfabrikation)

Universale (Universale Hoch- und Tiefbau AG)

Wertheim (Kassen-, Aufzugs-/ und Maschinenbau AG F. Wertheim & Co., Wertheim-Werke AG)

Wiener Brückenbau (Wiener Brückenbau- un dEisenkonstruktions AG, Wiener Eisenbau AG)

Wienerberger (Wienerberger Ziegelfabriks AG)

Wollwaren (Ujpester Wollwaren AG)

Zentralarchiv der Creditanstalt "Technisches Zentrum" (BA-CA, CA-TZ)

Secretariat rot

Rechtsabteilung rot

Secretariat grün

Rechtsabteilung grün

Archiv der Creditanstaltung Personalabteilung

Personalakten

Austrian State Archive, Vienna (Österreichisches Staatsarchiv, ÖStA) ÖStA/Archiv der Republik (AdR)

Reichskommissar für die Wiedervereinigung Österreichs it dem Deutschen Reich (RkfWÖ)

Bürckel Materie

RkfWÖ, Personen

Bundesministerium für Finanzen (BMF)

BMF Allgemine Reihe

BMF, Ministerium für Wirtschaft und Arbeit (MfWuA)

Vermögensverkehrstell (VVst), Handel

BMF, WfWuA, VVst, Liegenschaften (LG)

BMF, WfWuA, VVst, Statistik

BMF, WfWuA, VVst, Rechtsabteilung

BMF, WfWuA, VVst, Vermögensanmeldungen

Bundesministerium für Inneres (BMI)

BMI, Gauakten

Styrian State Archive, Graz (Steiermärkisches Landesarchiv, StmLA)

Landesgericht für Strafsachen Graz, Strafverfahren

Vienna City and State Archive, Vienna (Wiener Stadt- und Landesarchiv, WrStLA)

Gauakt Josef Paić

Germany

Deutsche Bank Archive, Frankfurt (DB)
Deutsche Bank Zentrale Berlin, B Series

B 11 Generalsekretariat, Allgemeines, Dr. Schlitter

B 51 Generalsekretariat, Geheim, Creditanstalt-Bankverein, Handakte Abs

B 52 Generalsekretariat, Geheim, Creditanstalt-Bankverein

B 53 Generalsekretariat, Geheim, Creditanstalt-Bankverein

B 54 Generalsekretariat, reditanstalt-Bankverein Handakte Abs

B 57 Generalsekretariat, Creditanstalt-Bankverein, Personalia, Allgemeines

Deutsche Bank Zentrale Berlin, P Series

P 41 Rheinisch-Westfälischer Beirate der Deutschen Bank, Köln

P 6502 Generalsekeitariat, Geheim, Creditanstalt-Bankverein, Handakte Abs

P 6503 Generalsekeitariat, Geheim, Creditanstalt-Bankverein, Handakte Abs, Allgemeines

P 6504 Generalsekeitariat, Geheim, Creditanstalt-Bankverein, Handakte Abs, Allgemeines

P 6505 Generalsekretariat, Abs, Creditanstalt-Bankverein, Allgemeines

P 6508 Generalsekretariat, Geheim, Creditanstalt-Bankverein, Allgemeines, Handakte Karl R. V. Halt

P 6509 General Sekretariat, Creditanstalt-Bankverein, Allgemeines, Handakte Rösler

P 6516 General Sekretariat, Creditanstalt-Bankverein, Allgemeines, Berichte und Bilanzen, Handakte Abs

P 6528 Deutsche Bank, Sonderfälle

P 24158 DB Generalsekretariat, Akte Hermann J. Abs, Banken in Südosteuropae

P 25005 DB, Filiale Goerlitz, Rundschreiben der DB an Niederlassungen

Vorstandssekretariat, Büro Walter Tron

V 2/1 CA-BV, Dr. Walter Tron, Aktenvermerke/Notizen

V 2/2 CA-BV, Dr. Walter Tron, Korrespondenz

V 2/3 CA-BV, Dr. Walter Tron, Korrespondenz

V 2/5 CA-BV, Dr. Walter Tron

V 2/6 CA-BV, Dr. Walter Tron, Berichte

Dresdner Bank Archive, Frankfurt (DrB)

1840–2000

29575–2001

13790–2000

13938–2000

30316–2001

5124–2000

5455–2000
5460–2000
5461–2000
5462–2000
5467–2000
7836–2000

Federal Archives Berlin (Bundesarchiv Berlin, BAB)
R 2 Reichfinanzministerium
R 26 VI Generalbevollmächtier für die Wirtschaft in Serbien
R 63 Südosteuropa-Gesellschaft
R 3101 Reichwirtschaftsministerium
R 8127 Berliner Handelsgesellschaft (BHG)
R 8128 I.G. Farbenindustrie
R 8135 Deutsche Revisions- und Treuhand AG

Political Archive, Federal Foreign Office,
Berlin (Politisches Archiv Auswärtiges Amt,
Berlin, PA Berlin)
R 27 506 Handakten Keppler, betr. Reichs-beauftragter Österreich: Allg. Korrespondenz, Bodenforschung
R 27 507 Handakten Keppler, betr. Reichsbeauf-tragter Österreich: RM österr. Ministerien, Reidchsleitung, Gauleiting
R 27 509 Handakten Keppler, betr. Reichsbeauftragter Österreich R–Z
R 110 997 AA Abt. W; Akten betr. Bankwesen, Sparkassenwesen, Kreditinsitute und Pfand-leihen (Österreich)

Krupp Historical Archive, Essen (HAK),
Works Archive (WA)
WA 4/2873
WA 4/2874
WA 40/59
WA 40/308
FAH 4 C192

Nuremberg State Archive (Staatsarchiv
Nürnberg, StA Nürnberg)
Nuremberg War Crimes Files
Rep. 501
Rep. 502

Vereinigte Industrieunternehmen AG, Munich (VIAG)
Protokoll des Aussichtsrats (1938)

Hungary

Hungary State Archive, Budapest
Z 162 Creditanstalt-Bankverein, Hungarian branch, accounting records
Z 1560 Creditanstalt-Bankverein, Hungarian branch, secretariat
Z 1561 Creditanstalt-Bankverein, Hungarian branch, general meetings

Poland

Central Archives of Modern Records in
Warsaw, Warsaw (Archivum Akt Nowych w
Warszawie, AAN)
Rzad iii Government of
the Generalgouvernement, Banking
Supervision Office
290/11–12
1319
1401
1402
1403

Archivum Pánstwowe M. Krakowa, I
Województwa Krakowskiego, Krakow
Creditanstalt-Bankverein
BN-I/1 CA-BV

Russia

Russian State Military Archive, Moscow
(Rossijskij gosudarstvenyi oennyi Archiv, RGVA)
1458 Reich Economics Ministry

Serbia

Archives of Yugoslavia, Belgrade
151 Allgemeiner Jugoslawischer Bankverein AG

United States

United States National Archives and Records
Administration, College Park, Maryland (NARA)
RG 226 Records of the Office of Strategic Services
RG 242 T 83 Records of Austrian, Dutch, and German Enterprises
RG 260 Records of U.S. Occupation Headquarters
RG 407 Records of the Adjutant General's Office
Microfilm Collection: BDC-SS Membership Files

John F. Kennedy Presidential Library and
Museum, Boston, Massachusetts
James Warburg Papers

PUBLISHED WORKS

Ahlheim, Hannah. "Die Commerzbank und die Einziehung jüdischen Vermögens," in *Die Commerzbank und die Juden 1933–1945*, ed. Ludolf Herbst and Thomas Weihe. Munich, 2004: 138–172.
Aleksic, Vesna. "The History of the Allgemeiner Jugoslawischer Bankverein AG in Belgrade in the Context of Yugoslav Banking History after 1918," in *Bank Austria Creditanstalt. 150*

Jahre österreichische Bankengeschichte im Zentrum Europas, ed. Oliver Rathkolb, Theodor Venus, and Ulrike Zimmerl. Vienna, 2005: 228–233.

Aly, Götz. *Hitlers Volksstaat. Raub, Rassenkrieg und Nationaler Sozialismus*. Frankfurt am Main, 2005.

Aly, Götz, and Susanne Heim. *Vordenker der Vernichtung. Auschwitz und die deutschen Pläne für eine neue europäische Ordnung*. Hamburg, 1991.

Anderl, Gabriele, and Dirk Rupnow. *Die Zentralstelle für jüdische Auswanderung als Beraubungsinstitution. Nationalsozialistische Institutionen des Vermögensentzuges 1* (Veröffentlichungen der Österreichischen Historikerkommission, vol. 20, no. 1). Vienna, 2004.

Ausch, Karl. *Als die Banken fielen. Zur Soziologie der politischen Korruption*. Vienna, 1968.

Bähr, Johannes. *Der Goldhandel der Dresdner Bank im Zweiten Weltkrieg. Ein Bericht des Hannah-Arendt-Instituts*. Leipzig, 1999.

"'Bankenrationalisierung' und Großbankenfrage. Der Konflikt um die Ordnung des deutschen Kreditgewerbes während des Zweiten Weltkrieges," in *Finanzinstitutionen in Mitteleuorpa während des Nationalsozialismus*, ed. Harald Wixforth (Geld und Kapital. Jahrbuch der Gesellschaft für mitteleuropäische Banken- und Sparkassengeschichte). Stuttgart, 2001: 71–94.

Beer, Siegfried. "Target Central Europe: American Intelligence Efforts Regarding Nazi and Early Postwar Austria," Working Paper 97-1, Center for Austrian Studies, University of Minnesota, 1997.

Boelcke, Willi A. *Die Deutsche Wirtschaft 1930–1945. Interna des Reichswirtschaftsministeriums*. Düsseldorf 1983.

Böhle, "Die Expansion der Volksfürsorge Lebensversicherung in den mitteleuropäischen Raum 1938–1945," in *Finanzinstitutionen in Mitteleuropa während des Nationalsozialismus*, ed. Harald Wixforth (Geld und Kapital. Jahrbuch der Gesellschaft für mitteleuropäische Banken- und Sparkassengeschichte). Stuttgart, 2000: 181–211.

Botz, Gerhard. *Nationalsozialismus in Wien. Machtübernahme und Herrschaftssicherung 1938/39*. Buchloe, 1988.

Braham, Randolph L. *The Politics of Genocide: The Holocaust in Hungary*. 2 vols. New York, 1994.

Bresdola, Gianmarco. "The Legitimising Strategies of the Nazi Administration in Northern Italy: Propaganda in the Adriatisches Küstenland." *Contemporary European History* 13/4 (Nov. 2004): 425–452.

Browning, Christopher. *Nazi Policy, Jewish Workers, German Killers*. Cambridge, 2000.

Budraß, Lutz. *Flugzeugindustrie und Luftrüstung in Deutscheland 1918–1945*. Düsseldorf, 1998.

Clare, George. *Last Waltz in Vienna: The Rise and Destruction of a Family 1842–1942*. New York, 1980.

Cottrell, Philip L. "Aspects of Western Equity Investment in the Banking Systems of East Central Europe," in *International Business and Central Europe, 1918–1939*, ed. Alice Teichova and Philip L. Cottrell. Leicester, 1983: 209–355.

Dean, Martin. *Robbing the Jews: The Confiscation of Jewish Property in the Holocaust, 1933–1945*. New York, 2008.

Deist, Wilhelm, Manfred Messerschmidt, Hans-Erich Volkmann, and Wolfram Wette. *Ursachen und Voraussetzungen des Zweiten Weltkrieges*. Frankfurt am Main, 1995.

Dingell, Jeanne. *Zur Tätigkeit der Haupttreuhandstelle Ost, Treuhandstelle Posen 1939 bis 1945*. Frankfurt am Main, 2003.

Ebner, Monika. "Der Bankenzusammenbruch des Jahres 1931 in Österreich." PhD diss., University of Vienna, 1969.

Eichholtz, Dietrich. *Geschichte der Deutschen Kriegswirtschaft 1939–1945*. 3 vols. Berlin, 1984–1996.

Eigner, Peter. "Die Konzentration der Entscheidungsmacht. Die personellen Verflechtungen zwischen den Wiener Großbanken und Industriegesellschaften, 1895–1940." PhD diss., University of Vienna, 1997.

Eigner, Peter, and Peter Melichar. "Enteignungen und Säuberungen. Die österreichischen Banken im Nationalsozialismus," in *Banken und "Arisierungen" in Mitteleuropa während des Nationalsozialismus*, ed. Dieter Ziegler (Geld und Kapital, vol. 5. Jahrbuch der Gesellschaft für mitteleuropäische Banken- und Sparkassengeschichte). Stuttgart, 2001: 43–117.

Eminger, Stefan, and Karl Haas. "Wirtschaftstreibende und Nationalsozialismus in Österreich. Die Nazifizierung von Handel, Gewerbe und Industrie in den 1930er Jahren," *Zeitgeschichte* 29/4 (2002): 153–176.

Enigl, Marianne, and Stefan Janny, "Das grauenvolle Geheimnis der CA." *Profil* 38, no.30 (Sept. 14, 1998): 52–58.

Erker, Paul. *Competition and Growth: A Contemporary History of the Continental A. G.* Düsseldorf, 1996.

Eybl, Peter. "Die Wirtschafts- und Bankenkrise des Jahres 1931 unter besonderer Berücksichtigung der Sanierung der Credit Anstalt." Master's thesis, University of Linz, 1993.

Federn, Walther. *Der Zusammenbruch der österreichischen Kreditanstalt*. Tübingen, 1932.

Felber, Ulrike, Peter Melichar, Markus Priller, Berthold Unfried, and Fritz Weber. *Ökonomie der Arisierung*, part 1: *Grundzüge, Akteure und Institutionen*, part 2: *Wirtschaftssektoren, Branchen, Falldarstellungen* (Veröffentlichungen der Österreichischen Histrokerkommission, vol. 10, parts 1–2).Vienna, 2004.

Feldman, Gerald D. *Allianz and the German Insurance Business, 1938–1945*. New York, 2001.

"German Banks and National Socialist Efforts to Supply Capital and Support Industrialization in Newly Annexed Territories: The 'Austrian Model,'" *Zeitschrift für Unternehmensgeschichte* 50 (2005): 5–16.

Ferguson, Niall. *The World's Banker: The History of the House of Rothschild*. London, 1998.

Fischer, Holger. "Das ungarisch-deutsche Verhähltnis in der Zwischenkriegszeit: Freiraum-Partnersc haft-Abhängigkeit," in *Germany and Southeastern Europe: Aspects of Relations in the Twentieth Century*, ed. Roland Schönfeld (Südosteuropa-Studien 58). Munich, 1997: 59–70.

Freund, Florian. "Zwangsarbeit im 'Dritten Reich.' Ein Überblick. Dimensionen der Zwangsarbeit in Österreich," in *Wieder gut machen? Enteignung, Zwangsarbeit, Entschädigung, Restitution*, ed. Forum Politische Bildung (Sonderband der Informationen zur Politischen Bildung).Vienna, 1999: 46–53.

"Die Entscheidung zum Einsatz von KZ-Häftlingen in der Raketenrüstung," in *Konzentrationslager und deutsche Wirtschaft 1939–1945*, ed. Hermann Kaienburg. Opladen, 1996: 60–74.

Freund, Florian, and Bertrand Perz. *Das KZ in der Serbenhalle. Zur Kriegsindustrie in Wiener Neustadt*. Vienna, 1988.

"Zwangsarbeit von zivilen Ausländerinnen, Kriegsgefangenen, KZ-Häftlingen und ungarischen Juden in Österreich," in *NS-Herrschaft in Österreich. Ein Handbuch*, ed. Emmerich Tálos, Ernst Hanisch, Wolfgang Neugebauer, and Rainer Sieder.Vienna, 2000: 644–695.

Freund, Florian, Bertrand Perz, and Mark Spoerer. *Zwangsarbeiter und Zwangsarbeiterinnen auf dem Gebiet der Republik Österreich 1939–1945* (Veröffentlichungen der Österreichischen Historikerkommission, vol. 26, no. 1). Vienna, 2004.

Friedländer, Saul. *Nazi Germany and the Jews*, vol. 1, *The Years of Persecution, 1933–1939*. New York, 1997.

Fuchs, Gertraud. "Die Vermögensverkehrsstelle als Arisierungsbehörde," Master's thesis, University of Vienna, 1989.

Gall, Lothar. *Der Bankier Hermann Josef Abs. Eine Biographie*. Munich, 2004.

Geng, Carl H. "Der Zusammenbruch der Kreditanstalt und die Sanierungsmaßnahmen der Bundesregierung." Maters thesis, University of Vienna, 1970.

Gross, Jan Tomasz Gross. *Polish Society under German Occupation: The Generalgouvernement 1939–1944*. Princeton, 1970.

Gruner, Wolf. *Zwangsarbeit und Verfolgung. Österreichische Juden im NS-Staat 1938–1945*. Innsbruck, 2000.

Hayes, Peter. *Industry and Ideology: IG Farben in the Nazi Era*. 2nd ed. Cambridge, 2001.

Hilberg, Raul. *Die Vernichtung der europäischen Juden*, 3 vols. Frankfurt am Main, 1990.

Hilferding, Rudolf. *Das Finanzkapital*, 2 vols. Frankfurt am Main, 1974.

Historikerkommission, ed. *Vermögensentzug während der NS-Zeit sowie Rückstellungen und Entschädigungen seit 1945 in Österreich: Schlussbericht der Historikerkommission der Republik Österreich*. Vienna, 2003.

Holec, Roman. "Das Bank und Kreditgenossenschaftswesen in der Slowakai 1939–1945," in *Finanzinstitutionen in Mitteleuropa während des Nationalsozialismus*, ed. Harald Wixforth (Geld und Kapital. Jahrbuch der Gesellschaft für mitteleuropäische Banken- und Sparkassengeschichte). Stuttgart, 2000: 165–179.

Jagschitz, Gerhard. "Die Anhaltelager in Österreich," in *Vom Justizpalast zum Heldenplatz. Studien und Dokumente*. ed. Ludwig Jedlicka and Rudolf Neck.Vienna, 1975: 128–151.

James, Harold. "The Deutsche Bank 1933–1945," in *The Deutsche Bank 1870–1995*, ed. Lothar Gall, Gerald D. Feldman, Harold James, Carl-Ludwig Holtfrerich, and Hans E. Büschgen. Munich, 1995.

The Deutsche Bank and the Nazi Economic War against the Jews. Cambridge, 2001.

Verbandspolitik im Nationalsozialismus. Von der Interessenvertretung zur Wirtschaftsgruppe. Der Centralverband des Deutschen Bank- und Bankiergewerbes 1932–1945. Munich, 2001.

"Banks and Business Politics in Germany," in *Business and Industry in Nazi Germany*, ed. Francis R. Nicosia, and Jonathan Heuner. New York, 2004.

Jedlicka, Ludwig, and Rudolf Neck, eds. *Vom Justizpalast zum Heldenplatz. Studien und Dokumente*.Vienna, 1975.

Joham, Josef. *Rede von Generaldirektor Dr. Josef Joham zur Hundertjahrfeier der Creditanstalt-Bankverein*. Vienna, 1955.

John, Michael. "Zwangsarbeit und NS-Industriepolitik am Standort Linz," in *NS-Zwangsarbeit: Der Standort Linz der "Reichswerke Hermann Göring AG Berlin" 1938–1945*, ed. Oliver Rathkolb. Vol. 1. Vienna, 2001: 23–146.

Junz, Helen B. Oliver Rathkolb, and Theodor Venus, with Vitali Bodnar, Barbara Holzheu, Sonja Niederacher, Alexander Schröck, Almerie Spannocchi, and Maria Wirth. *Das Vermögen der jüdischen Bevölkerung Österreichs: NS-Raub und Restitution nach 1945* (Veröffentlichungen der Österreichischen Historikerkommission. Vermögensentzug während der NS-Zeit sowie Rückstellung und Entschädigung seit 1945 in Österreich, vol. 9). Vienna, 2004.

Kaliński, Janusz. "Austrian Banks in Poland up to 1948," in *Bank Austria Creditanstalt. 150 Jahre österreichische Bankengeschichte im Zentrum Europas*, ed. Oliver Rathkolb, Theodor Venus, and Ulrike Zimmerl, Vienna, 2005: 259–264.

Karner, Stefan, and Peter Ruggenthaler. *NS-Zwangsarbeit in der Rüstungsindustrie. Die Lapp-Finze AG in Kalsdorf bei Graz 1939–1945*. Graz, 2004.

Kastner, Walther. *Mein Leben kein Traum. Aus dem Leben eines österreichischen Juristen*. Vienna, 1982.

"Entziehung und Rückstellung," in *Nationalsozialismus und Recht. Rechtssetzung und Rechtswissenschaft in Österreich unter der Herrschaft des Nationalsozialismus*, ed. Ulrike Davy, H. Fuchs, H. Hofmeister, J. Martel, and I. Reiter. Vienna. 1990: 191–199.

Kehrl, Hans. *Krisenmanager im Dritten Reich. 6 Jahre Frieden – 6 Jahre Krieg. Erinnerungen*. Düsseldorf, 1973.

Kernbauer, Hans. *Währungspolitik in der Zwischenkriegszeit. Geschichte der Oesterreichischen Nationalbank von 1923 bis 1938*. Vienna, 1991.

Klee, Ernst. *Das Personenlexikon zum Dritten Reich. Wer war was vor und nach 1945*. Frankfurt am Main, 2003.

Koliander, Josef. "Die Beteiligung und Kreditverflechtung der deutschen Banken in Südeuropa." PhD diss., Hochschule für Welthandel, Vienna, 1944.

Kopper, Christopher. *Zwischen Marktwirtschaft und Dirigismus. Bankenpolitik im "Dritten Reich" 1933–1939*. Bonn, 1995.

Kubu, Eduard, and Gudrun Exner. *Tschechen und Tschechinnen, Vermögensentzug und Restitution. Nationale Minderheiten im Nationalsozialismus 3* (Veröffentlichungen der Österreichischen Historikerkommission vol. 23, no. 3). Vienna, 2004.

Lacina, Vlastislav. "Tschechische Banken und ihre Verbindungen zum österreichischen Bankwesen bis 1945," in *Bank Austria Creditanstalt. 150 Jahre Bankengeschichte im Zentrum Europas*, ed. Oliver Rathkolb, Theo Venus, and Ulrike Zimmerl. Vienna, 2005: 239–252.

Lackner, Andreas. "Der Zusammenbruch der Credit-Anstalt 1931. Eine Literaturübersicht." Master's thesis, University of Vienna, 1993.

Landau, Zbigniew. "Polish and Jewish Entrepreneurs during the German Occupation," in *Enterprise in the Period of Fascism in Europe*, ed. Harold James and Jakob Tanner. Aldershot, 2002: 178–188.

Landau, Zbigniew, and Jerzy Tomaszewski. *Wirtschaftsgeschichte Polens im 19. und 20. Jahrhundert*. Berlin, 1986.

Lichtblau, Albert. *"Arisierungen," Beschlagnahmte Vermögen, Rückstellungen und Entschädigungen in Salzburg* (Veröffentlichungen der Österreichischen Historikerkommission, vol. 17, no. 2). Vienna, 2004.

Lillie, Sophie. *Was einmal war. Handbuch der enteigneten Kunstsammlungen Wiens*. Vienna, 2003.

Littlefield, Frank C. *Germany and Yugoslavia, 1933–1941: The German Conquest of Yugoslavia*. New York, 1988.

Loose, Ingo. "Die Beteiligung deutscher Kreditinstitute an der Vernichtung der ökonomischen Existenz der Juden in Polen 1939–1945," in *Die Commerzbank und die Juden 1933–1945*, ed. Ludolf Herbst and Thomas Weihe. Munich, 2004: 223–271.

Ludža, Radomir V. "Die Strukturen der Nationalsozialistischen Herrschaft in Österreich," in *Österreich, Deutschland und die Mächte. Internationale und Österreichische Aspekte des "Anschlusses" vom März 1938*, ed. Gerald Stourz and Birgitta Zaar. Vienna, 1990: 471–492.

Lumans, Valids O. *Himmler's Auxiliaries. The Völksdeutsche Mittelstelle and the German National Minorities of Europe, 1933–1945*. Chapel Hill, 1993.

Lütenau, Stefan August, Alexander Schröck, and Sonja Niederacher. *Zwischen Staat und Wirtschaft. Das Dorotheum im Nationalsozialismus*. Vienna, 2006.

Malzacher, Hans. *Begegnungen auf meinem Lebensweg*. Villach, 1968.

März, Eduard. *Österreichische Bankpolitik in der Zeit der Wende 1913–1923*. Munich, 1981.

März, Eduard, and Fritz Weber. "The Antecedents of the Austrian Financial Crash of 1931," *Zeitschrift für Wirtschafts- und Sozialwissenschaften* 103/5 (1983): 497–519.

Mauch, Christof. *Schattenkrieg gegen Hitler. Das Dritte Reich im Visier der amerikanischen Geheimdienste 1941–1945*. Stuttgart, 1999.

Melichar, Peter. *Die NS-Maßnahmen und die Problematik der Restitution* (Veröffentlichungen der Österreichischen Historikerkommission. Vermögensentzug während der NS-Zeit sowie Rückstellungen und Entschädigungen seit 1945 in Österreich, vol. 11).Vienna, 2004.

Neuordnung im Bankwesen. Die NS-Maßnahmen und die Problematik der Restitution.(Veröffentlichungen der Österreichischen Historikerkommission, vol. 11).Vienna, 2004.

Milchram, Gerhard. "Die Lager der Ungarischen Juden in Neunkirchen," *David. Jüdische Kulturzeitschrift* 47 (Dec. 2000), http://www .david.juden.at/kulturzeitschrift/44–49/ lager-47.htm (April 20, 2006).

Militärgeschichtliches Forschungsamt, ed. *Germany and the Second World War.* 8 volumes to date. Oxford, 1990 to present.

Naasner, Walter. *Neue Machtzentren in der deutschen Kriegswirtschaft 1942–1945.* Boppard am Rhein, 1994.

Natmeßnig, Charlotte. *Britische Finanzinteressen in Österreich: Die Anglo-Oesterreichische Bank.* Vienna, 1998.

Naumann,Karl."Ziele undAufgaben der Ernährungs- und Landwirtschaft im Generalgouvernement," in *Das Generalgouvernement. Seine Verwaltung und seine Wirtschaft,* ed. Joseph Bühler. Cracow, 1943: 113–130.

Oertel, Christine. "Die Umspannwerke Ernsthofen," in *NS-Zwangsarbeit in der Elektrizitätswirtschaft der "Ostmark" 1938–1945. Ennskraftwerke– Kaprun–Draukraftwerke–Ybbs-Persenbeug– Ernsthofen,* ed. Oliver Rathkolb and Florian Freund.Vienna, 2002: 231–252.

"Das Donaukraftwerk Ybbs-Persenbeug," in *NS-Zwangsarbeit in der Elektrizitätswirtschaft der "Ostmark" 1938–1945. Ennskraftwerke– Kaprun–Draukraftwerke–Ybbs-Persenbeug–Ernsthofen,* ed. Oliver Rathkolb and Florian Freund. Vienna, 2002: 252–272.

Österreichische Landerbank. *Der Kampf um Lenzing. Arisierung – Konkurs – Sanierung.*Vienna, 1953–1955.

Overy, Richard J. *War and Economy in the Third Reich.* Oxford, 1994.

Paersch, Fritz. "Maßnahmen des Staates hinsichtlich der Beaufsichtigung der Reglementierung des Bankwesens," in *Untersuchungen des Bankwesens,* part. 1, vol. 2, ed. Untersuchungsausschuß für das Bankwesen. 1933.

Perkins, John. "Nazi Autarchic Aspirations and the Beet-Sugar Industry, 1933–1939," *European History Quarterly* 20 (1990): 497–518.

Perz, Bertrand. "Politisches Management im Wirtschaftskonzern. Georg Meindl und die Rolle des Staatskonzerns Steyer-Daimler-Puch bei derVerwirklichung der NS-Wirtschaftsziele in Österreich," in *Konzentrationslager und deutsche Wirtschaft 1939–1945,* ed. Hermann Kaienburg. Opladen, 1996: 95–112.

Petersen, Neal H., ed. *From Hitler's Doorstep: The Wartime Intelligence Reports of Allen Dulles 1942–1945.* University Park, Pennsylvania, 1996.

Piper, Franciszek. "Die Rolle des Lagers Auschwitz bei der Verwirklichung der nationalsozialistischen Ausrottungspolitik," in *Die nationalsozialistischen Konzentrationslager. Entwicklung und Struktur,* ed. Ulrich Herbert, Karin Orth, and Christoph Dieckmann. 2 vols. Göttingen, 1998: vol. 1, 390–414.

Piperger,Alois. *Hundert Jahre Österreichische Länderbank 1880–1980.*Vienna, 1980.

Pohl, Manfred. *Philipp Holzmann. Geschichte eines Bauunternehmens 1849–1999.* Munich, 1999.

VIAG Aktiengesellschaft 1923–1998. Vom Staatsunternehmen zum internationalen Konzern. Munich, 2001.

Pohl, Manfred. and Angelika Raab-Rebentisch, *Die Deutsche Bank in Stuttgart 1924–1999.* Munich, 1999.

Präg, Werner, and Wolfgang Jacobmeyer, eds. *Das Diensttagebuch des deutschen Generalgouverneurs in Polen 1939–1945* (Quellen und Darstellungen zur Zeitgeschichte 20). Stuttgart, 1975.

Purkhart, Markus. "Die Draukraftwerke," in *NS-Zwangsarbeit in der Elektrizitätswirtschaft der "Ostmark" 1938–1945. Ennskraftwerke– Kaprun–Draukraftwerke– Ybbs-Persenbeug– Ernsthofen,* ed. Oliver Rathkolb and Florian Freund.Vienna, 2002: 199–230.

Ransmayr, Georg Friedrich."Die Zentraleuropäische Länderbank der Zwischenkriegszeit. Eine Pariser Bank mit Wiener Blut." Master's thesis, Wirtschaftsuniversität Wien, 1993.

Rathkolb, Oliver. "Am Beispiel Paul Pleigers und seiner Manager in Linz – Eliten zwischen Wirtschaftsräumen, NS-Eroberungs- und Rüstungspolitik, Zwangsarbeit und Nachkriegsjustiz," in *NS-Zwangsarbeit: Der Standort Linz der "Reichswerke Hermann Göring AG Berlin" 1938–1945,* ed. Oliver Rathkolb. 2 vols. Vienna, 2001: vol. 1, 287–320.

Rathkolb, Oliver, Theodor Venus, and Ulrike Zimmerl, eds. *Bank Austria Creditanstalt. 150 Jahre österreichische Bankengeschichte im Zentrum Europas.*Vienna, 2005.

Reiter, Margit. "Das Tauernkraftwerk Kaprun," in *NS-Zwangsarbeit in der Elektrizitätswirtschaft der "Ostmark" 1938–1945. Ennskraftwerke–Kaprun– Draukraftwerke–Ybbs-Persenbeug– Ernsthofen,* ed.

Oliver Rathkolb and Florian Freund. Vienna, 2002: 127–198.

Riemenschneider, Michael. *Die deutsche Wirtschaftspolitik gegenüber Ungarn 1933–1944. Ein Beitrag zur Interdependenz von Wirtschaft und Politik unter dem Nationalsozialismus.* Frankfurt am Main, 1987.

Röhr, Werner. "Zur Wirtschaftspolitik der deutschen Okkupanten in Polen 1939–1945," in *Krieg und Wirtschaft. (= Studien zur deutschen Wirtschaftsgeschichte 1939–1945*, ed. Dietrich Eichholtz. Berlin, 1999: 221–252.

Roloff, Marita, and Alois Mosser, *Wiener Allianz. Gegründet 1860.* Vienna, 1991.

Rosenkötter, Bernhard. *Treuhandpolitik. Die "Haupttreuhandstelle Ost" und der Raub polnischer Vermögen 1939–1945.* Essen, 2003.

Rutar, Sabine. "Arbeit und Überleben in Serbien. Das Kupfererzbergwerk Bor im Zweiten Weltkrieg." *Geschichte und Gesellschaft* 31 (2005): 101–134.

Rutkowski, Hans. *Der Zusammenbruch der Oesterreichischen Credit-Anstalt für Handel und Gewerbe und ihre Rekonstruktion. Ein Beitrag zur österreichischen Bankenkrise.* Bottrop, 1934.

Safrian, Hans, and Hans Witek. *Und Keiner war Dabei. Dokumente des alltäglichen Antisemitismus in Wien 1938.* Vienna, 1988.

Sandkühler, Thomas. *"Endlösung" in Galizien. Der Judenmord in Ostpolen und die Rettungsinitiativen von Berthold Beitz 1941–1944.* Bonn, 1996.

Schausberger, Norbert. *Rüstung in Österreich 1938–1945. Eine Studie über die Wechselwirkung von Wirtschaft, Politik und Kriegsführung.* Vienna, 1970.

Der Griff nach Österreich. Der Anschluss. Vienna, 1975.

"Deutsche Wirtschaftsinteressen in Österreich vor und nach dem März 1938," in *Österreich, Deutschland und die Mächte. Internationale und Österreichische Aspekte des "Anschlusses" vom März 1938*, ed. Gerald Stourzh and Brigitte Zaar. Vienna, 1990: 177–213.

Schilling, Willy A. *Die Entwicklung des faschistischen Herrschaftssystems in Thüringen 1933–1939.* Berlin, 2001.

Schubert, Aurel. *The Creditanstalt Crisis of 1931.* Cambridge, 1991.

Schulte, Jan Erik. *Zwangsarbeit und Vernichtung: Das Wirtschaftsimperium der SS. Oswald Pohl und das SS-Wirtschafts-Verwaltungshauptamt 1933–1945.* Paderborn, 2001.

Seherr-Thoss, H. C., Graf von. *Die deutsche Automobilindustrie. Eine Dokumentation von 1886 bis 1979.* 2nd ed. Stuttgart, 1979.

Seliger, Maren. "NS Herrschaft in Wien und Niederösterreich," in *NS-Herrschaft in Österreich. Ein Handbuch*, ed. Emmerich Tálos, Ernst

Hanisch, Wolfgang Neugebauer, and Reinhard Sieder. Vienna, 2000.

Smaldone, William. *Rudolf Hilferding: The Tragedy of a German Social Democrat.* Dekalb, 1998.

Spitzmüller, Alexander. *Memoirs of Alexander Spitzmüller Freiherr von Harmersbach (1862–1953).* Carvel de Bussy, ed. New York, 1987.

Spuhler, Gregor, Ursina Jud, Peter Melichar, and Daniel Wildmann, *"Arisierungen" in Österreich und ihre Bezüge zur Schweiz (Veröffentlichungen der Unabhängigen Expertenkommission – Zweiter Weltkrieg vol. 20).* Zurich, 2002.

Steinberg, Jonathan. *The Deutsche Bank and Its Gold Transactions during the Second World War.* Munich, 1999.

Stiefel, Dieter. *Finanzdiplomatie und Weltwirtschaftskrise. Die Krise der Credit-Anstalt für Handel und Gewerbe* (Schriftenreihe des Instituts für bankhistorische Forschung e.V.). Frankfurt am Main, 1989.

Die Österreichischen Lebensversicherungen und die NS-Zeit. Wirtschaftliche Entwicklung. Politischer Einfluß. Jüdische Polizzen. Vienna, 2001.

Stocker, Alexander. "Austria Haustechnik AG. Eine Firmen Geschichte und Betriebsanalyse mit Schwerpunkt der Jahre 1989–1999." PhD diss., University of Graz, 2000.

Stuhlpfarrer, Karl Stuhlpfarrer, and Leopold Steurer. "Die Ossa in Österreich," in *Vom Justizpalast zum Heldenplatz. Studien und Dokumentationen 1927–1938*, ed. Ludwig Jedlicka and Rudolf Neck. Vienna, 1975: 35–64.

Sudrow, Anne. "Das 'deutsche Rohstoffwunder' und die Schuhindustrie. Schuhproduktion unter den Bedingungen der nationalsozialistischen Autarkiepolitik," *Blätter für Technikgeschichte* 60 (1999): 63–92.

"Vom Leder zum Kunststoff. Werkstoff-Forschung auf der 'Schuhprüfstrecke' im Konzentrationslager Sachsenhausen 1940–1945," in *Rüstungsforschung im Nationalsozialismus. Organisation, Mobilisierung und Entgrenzung der Technikwissenschaften*, ed. Helmut Maier. Göttingen, 2002: 214–49.

Tönsmeyer, Tatjana. *Das Dritte Reich und die Slowakei 1939–1945. Politischer Alltag zwischen Kooperation und Eigensinn.* Paderborn, 2003.

Treichl, Heinrich. *Fast ein Jahrhundert. Erinnerungen.* Vienna, 2003.

Uhlig, Christiane, Petra Barthelmess, Mario König, Peter Pfaffenroth, and Betinna Zeugin. *Tarnung, Transfer, Transit. Die Schweiz als Drehscheibe verdeckter deutscher Operationen (1939–1952).* (Veröffentlichungen der Unabhängigen Expertenkommission Schweiz – Zweiter Weltkrieg, vol. 9). Zurich, 2001.

Van der Wee, Herman, and Monique Verbreyt. *Die Generale Bank 1822–1997. Eine ständige Herausforderung.* Tielt, 1997.

Venus Theodor. "Geschichte der Bankhaus Gutmann," unpublished MS.

"Abgebrochene Rückkehr – Der Fall des Bankhauses Gebrüder Gutmann," in *Die Republik und das NS-Erbe*, ed. Verena Pawlowsky and Harald Wendelin, vol. 2. Vienna, 2005.

Venus Theodor, and Alexandra-Eileen Wenck. *Die Entziehung jüdischen Vermögens im Rahmen der Aktion Gildemeester. Eine empirische Studie über Organisation, Form und Wandel von "Arisierung" und jüdischer Auswanderung in Österreich 1938–1941. Nationalsozialistische Institutionen des Vermögensentzuges 20* (Veröffentlichungen der Österreichischen Historikerkommission, vol. 20, no. 2). Vienna, 2004.

Weber, Fritz. "Vor dem großen Krach." Habilitation diss., University of Salzburg, 1991.

Wittek-Saltzberg, Liselotte. "Die wirtschafts-politischen Auswirkungen der Okkupation Österreichs." PhD diss., University of Vienna, 1970.

Wixforth, Harald. "Im Visier deutscher Finanzinteressen. Die Deutsche Agrar- und Industriebank in Prag und ihr Schicksal 1938–1940," in *Finanzinstitutionen in Mitteleuropa während des Nationalsozialismus*, ed. Harald Wixforth (Geld und Kapital. Jahrbuch der Gesellschaft für mitteleuropäische Banken- und Sparkassengeschichte). Stuttgart, 2000: 127–164.

"'Die Wiedererwerbung der Filialen ist als Repatriierung anzusprechen' – Die Expansionsbestrebungen der Österreichischen Creditanstalt-Wiener Bankverein in das Sudetenland 1938/39," *Zeitschrift für Bankgeschichte* 1 (2001): 62–77.

Auftakt zur Ostexpansion. Die Dresdner Bank und die Umgestaltung des Bankwesens im Sudetenland 1938/39 (Hannah-Arendt-Institut. Berichte und Studien, 31). Dresden, 2001.

Die Expansion der Dresdner Bank in Europa, vol. 3 of *Die Dresdner Bank im Dritten Reich*, ed. Klaus-Dietmar Henke. 4 vols. Munich, 2006.

Zausnig, Josef. *Der Loibl-Tunnel: Das vergessene KZ an der Südgrenze Österreichs. Eine Spurensicherung.* Drava, 1995.

Ziegler, Dieter. "Die Verdrängung der Juden aus der Dresdner Bank 1933–1938," *Vierteljahrshefte für Zeitgeschichte* 47 (1999): 187–216.

"Die 'Germanisierung' und 'Arisierung' der Mercurbank während der Ersten Republik Österreich," in *Banken und "Arisierungen" in Mitteleuropa während des Nationalsozialismus*, ed. Dieter Ziegler (Geld und Kapital. Jahrbuch der Gesellschaft für mitteleuropäische Banken- und Sparkassengeschichte). Stuttgart, 2001.

Zweig, Ronald W. *The Gold Train. The Destruction of the Jews and the Second World War's Most Terrible Robbery.* London, 2002.

Index